KT-437-548

ECONOMICS EXPLAINED

REVISED THIRD EDITION

Peter Maunder
Senior Lecturer in Economics,
Loughborough University;
Joint Chief Examiner for A Level, University of London,
School Examinations Board

Danny Myers
Senior Lecturer in Economics,
Faculty of the Built Environment,
University of the West of England, Bristol

Nancy Wall
Co-director Nuffield Economics and Business Project

Roger LeRoy Miller
Professor of Economics, University of Texas, Arlington

WITHDRAWN

EG23757

Published by HarperCollins *Publishers* Limited
77–85 Fulham Palace Road
Hammersmith
London W6 8JB

www.**Collins**Education.com
On-line Support for Schools and Colleges

© HarperCollins *Publishers* Limited, 2000

First edition published in 1987
Second edition published in 1991
Third edition published in 1995

All rights reserved. No part of this publication may be
reproduced, stored in a retrieval system, or transmitted
in any form or by any means, electronic, mechanical,
photocopying, recording or otherwise, without either the
prior permission of the Publisher or a licence permitting
restricted copying in the United Kingdom issued by the
Copyright Licensing Agency Ltd., 90 Tottenham Court
Road, London W1P 0LP.

The authors assert the moral right to be identified as the
authors of this work.

British Library Cataloguing in Publication Data
A catalogue record for this publication
is available from the British Library.

ISBN 0 00 327758 5

Edited by Brigitte Lee
Design and typesetting by Derek Lee
Illustrations by Hardlines Illustration and Design, based on
original artwork by Julia Osorno
Cover design by Blue Pig Design Co. and Patricia Briggs
Project management by Patricia Briggs and Brigitte Lee
Printed and bound by Scotprint, Musselburgh

You might also like to visit:

www.**fire**and**water**.com
The book lover's website

Preface and author acknowledgements

This new edition of *Economics Explained* appears thirteen years after the first adaptation of Miller's highly successful US textbook *Economics Today*. The previous editions were very well received and we have now added several new features, topics and policies to meet the needs of new syllabi. We have also revised those sections where inevitably the passage of time has left the coverage somewhat dated. In particular we have extended the number of student-centred activities, many of which have been tried and tested during our teaching.

We are grateful to Su Spencer and Jacqui Blake for their typing of draft chapters, to Brigitte Lee for her careful editing of the manuscript, Derek Lee for the new text design, Julia Osorno for all original artwork, and Hardlines Illustration and Design for artwork new for this edition. Finally, we are very grateful for the immense efforts of everyone involved at HarperCollins; particularly Helen Evans for research and Patricia Briggs for co-ordinating and managing all the related activity through to publication.

EG 23757

EALING TERTIARY COLLEGE
LEARNING RESOURCE CENTRE - EALING GREEN

Contents

Contents

B Market failure and governments

C Introductory macroeconomics

D Microeconomic theory

E Economic issues and policies

Acknowledgements

The publishers would like to thank the following for permission to reproduce photographs in this book: Cadbury's, p. 414; Camera Press Ltd, p. 513; Gerry Penny-AFP, p. 255; Hulton Getty, pp. 22, 24, 270, 411, 477; Foster and Partners, p. 125; Peter Lofts, p. 397; Mary Evans Picture Library, p. 373; Popperfoto, p. 445.

The publishers also wish to acknowledge the following sources of cartoons: David Austin (*Guardian*), p. 299; Jeremy Banks (*Financial Times*), p. 205; Simon Thompson, p. 375. The logos on p. 306 are reproduced by permission of the Conservative, Labour and Liberal Democrat parties.

The authors and publishers are grateful to the following Examination Boards for permission to reproduce Multiple Choice Questions (MCQs) and Essay Questions (EQs) from past examination papers. AEB, NEAB and JMB questions are reprinted by permission of Assessment and Qualifications Alliance (AQA). OSEB, UODLE and UCLES questions are reprinted by permission of Oxford Cambridge and RSA Examinations (OCR). Edexcel and London Examinations questions are reprinted by permission of Edexcel Foundation. London Examinations is a division of Edexcel Foundation.

The Associated Examining Board
Chapter 1: MCQ 3 (June 86), 7 (June 87). Chapter 4: MCQ 2 (Summer 97), 3 (Summer 98). Chapter 5: MCQ 3 (Summer 96), 7 (Nov 91). Chapter 6: MCQ 1 (Summer 98); EQ 2 (Summer 96). Chapter 7: MCQ 6 (June 86). Chapter 8: EQ 1 (Nov 93). Chapter 9: MCQ 6 (Summer 97). Chapter 10: EQ 4 (June 90). Chapter 11: MCQ 2 (Summer 96), 3 (Summer 97), 6 (Summer 98); EQ 4 (June 93). Chapter 12: MCQ 2 (Summer 98, Paper 1); EQ 5 (June 93), 6 (Nov 91), 7 (Nov 93). Chapter 17: EQ 3 (Nov 93). Chapter 23: MCQ 5 (Summer 96), 6 (Summer 97), 7 (Summer 98). Chapter 24: EQ 7 (Nov 93), 9 (Nov 91), 12 (Summer 96, Paper 3). Chapter 26: MCQ1 (Summer 98), 2 (Summer 97), 3 (Summer 98); EQ 4 (Nov 93). Chapter 27: MCQ 2 (Summer 96, Paper 1). Chapter 28: EQ 3 (Summer 96, Paper 3). Chapter 29: EQ 6 (Summer 96, Paper 3), 8 (June 93).

Edexcel
Chapter 17: MCQ 1 (June 98); EQ 1 (Jan 98, Paper 2), 7 (Jan 97). Chapter 24: EQ 5 (Jan 99, Paper 3). Chapter 25: MCQ 1 (June 98, Paper 1). Chapter 31: MCQ 2 (May 99, Paper 1).

Joint Matriculation Board
Chapter 4: EQ 2 (Special, June 90). Chapter 5: MCQ 8 (June 90), 9 (June 90). Chapter 7: EQ 6 (89). Chapter 8: MCQ 2 (June 83); EQ 5 (June 83). Chapter 11: EQ 5 (AS, June 91), 7 (June 87). Chapter 12: MCQ 1 (AS, Paper I, June 92); EQ 1 (A Economics, Paper II, June 91), 2 (AS Economics, Paper II, June 92), 3 (A Economics, Paper II, June 91), 4 (A Economics, Paper II, June 92). Chapter 14: MCQ 2 (June 92). Chapter 15: EQ 2 (June 87). Chapter 19: MCQ 9 (June 91). Chapter 20: EQ 4 (June 85).

Chapter 21: MCQ 10 (June 93); EQ 1 (June 91), 2 (June 87). Chapter 22: MCQ 5 (June 91). Chapter 24: MCQ 7 (June 92); EQ 6 (June 86), 10 (June 91). Chapter 27: EQ 7 (June 92). Chapter 28: MCQ 5 (June 92); EQ 2 (June 88). Chapter 29: MCQ 3 (June 92). Chapter 31: EQ 7 (June 84), 8 (June 87), 10 (June 91).

London Examinations

Chapter 1: MCQ 4 (Jan 83). Chapter 2: MCQ 1 (June 98), 2 (Jan 98); EQ 1 (June 97), 2 (Jan 95), 3 (Jan 99), 5 (Jun 96). Chapter 3: MCQ 1 (July 95, Specimen Paper), 2 (May 99), 3 (Jan 97), 4 (Jan 97), 5 (Jan 99); EQ 1 (Jan 92). Chapter 5: MCQ 4 (June 96), 5 (Jan 99), 6 (June 98); EQ 1 (June 97), 2 (Jan 98), 3 (June 98), 7 (June 93). Chapter 6: MCQ 5 (Jan 98), 6 (May 99), 7 (Jan 97), 8 (May 99), 9 (May 99); EQ 1 (Jan 93). Chapter 7: MCQ 7 (Jan 85); EQ 2 (Jan 93). Chapter 8: MCQ 3 (June 88); EQ 2 (Jan 85), 3 (Jan 89), 4 (Jan 93), 6 (June 85). Chapter 9: MCQ 1 (June 98), 2 (June 97), 3 (June 97), 7 (June 98), 8 (June 96); EQ 4 (Jan 97), 5 (Jan 99). Chapter 10: MCQ 4 (June 93), 6 (Jan 93); EQ 6 (June 94). Chapter 11: MCQ 5 (June 96); EQ 1 (June 91), 6 (Special 88), 8 (Jan 87), 10 (June 90). Chapter 13: MCQ 5 (Jan 84); EQ 3 (June 91), 4 (Jan 86), 7 (Jan 92), 8 (Jan 90). Chapter 15: EQ 3 (June 94). Chapter 17: MCQ 4 (Jan 86), 7 (June 86); EQ 6 (Jan 92). Chapter 18: MCQ 1 (Jan 93). Chapter 19: MCQ 1 (Jan 86), 2 (June 85), 3 (Jan 88), 4 (June 88), 5 (Jan 89), 7 (June 85), 8 (June 83); EQ 1 (June 84), 2 (June 82). Chapter 20: MCQ 1 (Jan 86), 2 (June 85), 4 (Jan 87), 5 (Jan 87), 6 (June 89), 7 (June 83); EQ 1 (June 84). Chapter 21: MCQ 5 (Jun 89), 7–9 (Jan 89); EQ 3 (June 87). Chapter 22: MCQ 1 (June 89), 2 (Jan 89), 4 (June 89); EQ 4 (June 89), 5 (Jan 89), 6 (June 88), 8 (June 96). Chapter 23: MCQ 1 (June 98), 2 (Jan 99), 3 (May 99), 4 (May 99), 10 (June 97), 11 (June 97), 12 (June 99), 13 (June 99), 14 (Jan 99), 15 (June 98); EQ 3 (June 96), 4 (June 98), 5 (Jan 97), 6 (Jan 95); EQ 7 (June 97). Chapter 24: MCQ 6 (Jan 94); EQ 1 (June 90), 3 (June 90), 4 (June 94). Chapter 25: MCQ 2 (June 86), 3 (June 94); EQ 1 (Jan 94), 3 (89), 5 (Jan 92). Chapter 26: EQ 1 (Special Paper, June 86), 3 (Special Paper, June 91), 5 (Jan 99, Paper 2). Chapter 27: MCQ 3 (June 98), 4 (July 95, Paper 1); EQ 1 (June 97), 2 (June 96), 4 Jan 95). Chapter 28: MCQ 2 (89), 3 (Jan 94), 4 (Jan 99), 6 (Jan 94); EQ 1 (June 98), 5 (Jan 90), 6 (June 98). Chapter 29: MCQ 1 (Jan 98, Paper 1); EQ 1 (Jan 99, Paper 2), 4 (Jan 97, Paper 2), 7 (June 98, Paper 2), 9 (June 98, Paper 2). Chapter 30: MCQ 1 (Jan 2000, Paper 1). Chapter 31: EQ 1 (June 85).

Northern Examinations and Assessment Board

Chapter 10: EQ 7 (June 93). Chapter 15: MCQ 3 (June 93). Chapter 16: MCQ 5 (June 94). Chapter 17: MCQ 3 (June 93); EQ 4 (June 93). Chapter 19: EQ 4 (94). Chapter 24: EQ 11 (AS, June 93). Chapter 25: MCQ 5 (June 93). Chapter 27: EQ 5 (AS, June 93). Chapter 28: MCQ 7 (June 94); EQ 3 (June 94).

Oxford and Cambridge Schools Examination Board

Chapter 6: EQ 4 (June 91). Chapter 7: EQ 8 (June 91). Chapter 10: EQ 1 (June 90). Chapter 13: MCQ 2 (June 93); EQ 1 (June 88), 6 (June 83). Chapter 19: EQ 6 (June 88). Chapter 20: EQ 2 (June 88). Chapter 22: EQ 2 (June 88), 3 (June 87). Chapter 31: EQ 3 (July 82).

University of Cambridge Local Examinations Syndicate

Chapter 2: EQ 4 (June 97, Paper 3), 6 (June 98, Paper 3). Chapter 4: MCQ 1 (Nov 98), EQ 1 (June 97), 3 (Nov 92). Chapter 5: MCQ 1 (Nov 98), 2 (Nov 98); EQ 6 (June 92). Chapter 6: MCQ 2 (June 97), 3 (June 98), 4 (June 97). Chapter 7: EQ 4 (June 85). Chapter 8: EQ 1 (June 92). Chapter 9: MCQ 4 (June 98), 5 (Nov 97); EQ 1 (June 92). Chapter 16: MCQ 3 (Nov 97, Paper 1), 4 (June 98, Paper 1); EQ 4 (Nov 97, Paper 3), 5 (June 97, Paper 3). Chapter 18: MCQ 4 (June 97). Chapter 19: EQ 5 (June 87), 8 (June 98, Paper 3). Chapter 20: EQ 3 (June 85), 5 (June 98, Paper 3). Chapter 21: EQ 4 (June 87). Chapter 22: EQ 1 (Nov 87). Chapter 23: MCQ 8 (Nov 98), 9 (Nov 97); EQ 2 (June 98). Chapter 24: MCQ 3 (98, Paper 1); EQ 2 (June 85). Chapter 25: MCQ 6 (June 97, Paper 1). Chapter 27: EQ 3 (June 98, Paper 3). Chapter 28: MCQ 1 (June 97, Paper 1), 8 (Nov 98, Paper 2). Chapter 29: MCQ 4 (June 98, Paper 1), 5 (Oct 97, Paper 1). Chapter 30: EQ 7 (Nov 97, Paper 3), 8 (June 98, Paper 3). Chapter 31: EQ 5 (Nov 88), 9 (June 97, Paper 3).

University of Oxford Delegacy of Local Examinations

Chapter 5: EQ 4 (June 92), 5 (June 89). Chapter 7: EQ 7 (June 89). Chapter 11: MCQ 1 (June 98), 4 (June 96); EQ 9 (June 90). Chapter 13: EQ 2 (June 89). Chapter 14: EQ 1 (June 86). Chapter 17: EQ 5 (June 88). Chapter 23: EQ 1 (June 95). Chapter 26: EQ 2 (June 88, Paper 1).

Welsh Joint Education Committee

Chapter 18: EQ 3 (June 91). Chapter 19: EQ 5 (June 87). Chapter 21: EQ 5 (June 88). Chapter 22: EQ 7 (June 88).

The following questions are reproduced from:

A. Baker (ed.), *Multiple Choice Questions in Advanced Level Economics*, Cambridge University Press, 1981:

  Chapter 1: MCQ 2. Chapter 7: MCQ 2. Chapter 13: MCQ 6. Chapter 15: MCQ 2.

  Chapter 16: MCQ 1 & 2. Chapter 18: MCQ 2 & 3.

MCQs 1 and 7 in Chapter 7, and MCQs 1 and 3–5 in Chapter 31, are reproduced from:

R. Miller and R. W. Pulsinelli, Student Learning Guide 7 to R. Miller, *Economics Today*, eighth edition, HarperCollins College Publishers (US), 1994.

Every effort has been made to contact copyright holders, but if any have been inadvertently overlooked, the publishers will be pleased to make the necessary arrangements at the first opportunity.

How to use this book

This textbook has been carefully designed around several features to help you understand your economics course. These features are outlined below as a guide to guarantee your effective use of this well-established resource.

First, each chapter has brief summaries every few pages to help you identify and remember the main concepts that have been explained. These are numbered and called **key points**.

These key points are subsequently referred to at the beginning of each chapter, by means of a list headed **Key points to review**. These lists have been compiled to encourage you to refer back to the relevant sections that have been covered and on which we build. Following each list is an associated feature to indicate the **learning outcomes** of each specific chapter. Both features have been included to remind you to scan backwards and forwards through the text to appreciate the integrated nature of economics.

Another important educational feature is the **exercise boxes** that occur in each chapter. These appear in tinted panels and are designed to reinforce specific concepts as they develop. Their inclusion is intended to promote interactive learning, to aid recognition of economics in different contexts, and to avoid a process of rote learning. In many instances, these activities have been specifically written for this edition.

Next, whenever a technical term or phrase is introduced, it is identified in bold type. These and other essential terms are gathered at the back of the book with brief definitions to form a **glossary**. This will help you to come to terms with the subject and its particular language. Some important concepts require detailed definitions in the text. These are identified in colour.

The penultimate feature of each chapter is some **case study** material; case study items have been selected not only to complement the exercises within the chapter, but to examine a broader range of issues as well. The intention is to make connections between interrelated theory and complex reality. The concluding case studies are intellectually more challenging than the exercise boxes. However, they apply what has been learnt and prepare you for any data-type question that may form part of a course exam. In most instances these extracts have been taken from newspapers and academic journals; therefore, it may prove interesting to note the sources.

Each chapter concludes with an **exam preparation** section. These sections contain a range of questions, mostly from past papers of the UK exam boards. The number of multiple choice and essay questions that follow each chapter varies according to the nature of the topic, as examiners have a tendency to explore different topics through different exam strategies. Consequently, some chapters have a dozen multiple choice questions and others half a dozen essays.

Answers to all the multiple choice questions and to some of the exercise questions within the chapters are gathered at the back of the book. The relevant exercise questions are identified with an icon **AV** by the specific item. The open-ended questions do not have easily stated answers, and these are left for tutorial discussion.

Finally, for those who use the Internet, we review and suggest 36 **websites** for you to visit. The commentaries attached to the website reviews help set the scene for each of the five parts comprising the book. The websites form a kind of optional extra to help you gain a deeper understanding of the real-world issues associated with textbook economics.

Most importantly, we believe we have designed a book that, in one way and another, will give you the ideas, interest, skills, support and confidence to succeed in economics.

PART A

MARKETS AND MODELS

■ **www.bized.ac.uk**
Without doubt this is the most appropriate URL to commence our web references. The site is organized at Bristol University to encourage the use of the Internet when studying economics and/or business studies. You will find at least three useful features: an Internet catalogue, with over 1500 links relating to various topic areas; an extensive collection of learning resources constructed by teachers; and a data section, which will enable you to access company reports and various sets of economic statistics.

■ **www.adamsmith.org.uk**
This is a three-tiered site, comprising a policy section, an international section and a biographical section. The latter is probably the most useful at the introductory level, since it incorporates economic theory associated with Adam Smith, whom we introduce in Chapter 2.

■ **csf.Colorado.EDU/psn/marx**
This address enables you to access the Marx/Engels archive. It has been written by a real enthusiast and includes biographies, photographs and bibliographies of all their works, together with links to the associated texts. (In this instance it might be worth noting that viewing a site without the graphics markedly quickens the download time.)

■ **www.dti.gov.uk**
In its own words, 'The purpose of the Department for Trade and Industry is to increase UK competitiveness and scientific excellence, in order to generate higher levels of sustainable growth and productivity in a modern economy'. Consequently, there are menu items relating to business support, Europe, regulatory guidance, competitiveness, exports and investments.

■ **www.guardian.co.uk**
■ **www. independent.co.uk**
■ **www.the-times.co.uk**
■ **www.telegraph.co.uk**
Most newspapers are experimenting with their Internet presence and in subsequent sections we shall reference more media sources. In fact, the Net is a relatively easy way to find up-to-date examples to support your economics coursework. Also, visits to these sites enable you to check on the latest sports results.

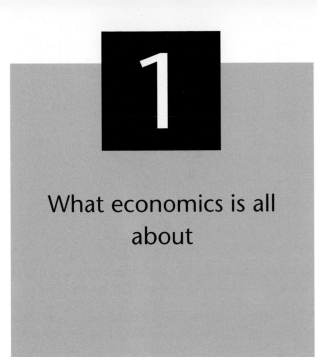

1

What economics is all about

LEARNING OUTCOMES

On completing this chapter you should understand:

- The basic nature, ideas and methodology of economics and some key concepts, such as:

- Scarcity

- Opportunity cost

- Production possibilities curve

- Micro- and macroeconomics

In June 1999 the UN computer announced the birth of the baby that took the world's population past 6 billion. At the very least, each one of these 6 billion people needs food and shelter. Unfortunately, allocating resources in such a way that we can all have what we need and want seems impossible. Even if we all resorted to stealing there would not be enough to satisfy everybody's wants. Consequently, economic problems face you, me, your friends, the nation and the world. These problems are impossible to avoid.

We cannot simply have more and more of everything, because individually and collectively we face a concept called **scarcity**.

Scarcity – a central concept

Scarcity may be envisaged as a two-pronged problem: (1) at any point in time there is a fixed stock of resources; (2) at any point in time there are also millions and millions of wants. Income or wealth are not relevant here.

Note that we are not referring to any *measurable* standard of wants; rather, we are referring to the way people want, need or desire relative to what is available at any moment. If the world were such that everyone could have as much of everything as desired, without sacrifice, then economics would no longer exist as a meaningful intellectual or practical study. But this is not the case. Moreover, we have not just recently moved into the age of scarcity, as many people seem to believe. Scarcity has always been with us and will be with us as long as we cannot get everything we want for free, that is, without charge.

It is important to distinguish scarcity from poverty. Scarcity occurs among poor people and among rich people. It applies to everyone because there will never be enough of everything that people want to go round at zero price or free. And, because there are limits on people's time, even the richest person on earth will still have unfulfilled wants.

Resources (or factors of production) are scarce

The scarcity concept just described stems in part from the existence of finite resources. Resources can be defined as the inputs used in the production of those things that we desire. When resources are productive, they are typically called *factors of production*. Indeed, some economists use the terms resources and factors of production synonymously. The total quantity, or stock, of resources that an economy has determines what that economy can produce. Every economy has, in varying quantities, vast amounts of different resources, or factors of production. Factors of production can be classified in many ways. One common scheme of classification includes natural, human and manufactured resources.

Natural resources = land and mineral deposits

Land with its inherent mineral deposits is the natural resource we think of most often. Some land can grow very large amounts of crops without addition of any fertilizer; other land is incapable of growing anything in its natural state. Today, some economists contend that natural resources are often the least important factors of production in an economy. They believe that what is more important is the transformation of existing natural resources into what is truly usable by humanity, and that that transformation requires the other types of resources: labour and capital. This point becomes understandable if we do not simply think of land as the only natural resource. The resources of the oceans and polar ice-caps are attracting increasing interest. Thus, natural resources include water, climate and vegetation in a global context.

Human resources = labour

In order to produce the things we desire, a human resource must be used. That human resource consists of the productive contributions of **labour** made by individuals who work – for example, coal-miners, ballet dancers and professional soccer players. The contribution of labour to the production process can be increased. Whenever potential labourers undergo schooling and training and whenever actual labourers learn new skills, labour's contribution to productive output will increase. When there is such an improvement to human resources, we say that **human capital** has been improved.

Manufactured resources = capital

When labour is applied to land to grow wheat, for example, something else is used. Usually it is a plough or a tractor. That is, land and labour are combined with manufactured resources in order to produce the things that we desire. These manufactured resources are called **capital**, or more precisely physical capital, and consist of machines, buildings, tools and additions made to natural resources, for example irrigation channels.

Another human resource = entrepreneurship

There is, in effect, a fourth type of input used in production. It is a special type of human resource: entrepreneurial ability, or **entrepreneurship**. Entrepreneurship is associated with the founding of new businesses, or the introduction of new products and new techniques. But it means more than

that: it encompasses taking risks (possibly losing large amounts of wealth on new ventures), inventing new methods of making existing goods, and generally experimenting with any type of new thinking that could lead to a monetary benefit.

Without entrepreneurship, virtually no business organizations could operate. Clearly, entrepreneurship as a human resource is scarce: not everyone is willing to take risks or has the ability to undertake successful business decision-making.

We see the classification of resources in Table 1.1.

Scarce resources produce what are called **economic goods** – the subject of our study throughout this book.

Economic goods

Nearly all goods (and services) fall within the category of economic goods. This is because they are derived from scarce resources and we constantly face decisions about how best to use them. By definition, the desired quantity of an economic good exceeds the amount that is directly available at a zero price.

However, not all goods are economic; *some* are free.

Free goods

There are, of course, a *few* things that nature can provide at a zero price. We call them **free goods**, as opposed to economic goods. Not many are left. Economics textbooks used to call air a free good, but that is really no longer true, because in many of the world's cities pollution makes air unpleasant to breathe. In many mountain areas, clean air is still a free good (once you are there); you can have as much as you want at zero price or free, and so can anybody else who bothers to hike up to where you are. There is no scarcity involved. Who is interested in free goods, then? Certainly not most economists. Perhaps physicists, hydrologists, biologists and chemists are interested in free air and water, but the economist steps in only when the problem of scarcity arises and people become concerned about how to use the scarce resource. We have seen throughout our history that, as population and production increase, many 'free' goods become 'economic' goods, for example land for mining, air for industrial uses, and bottled water for drinking. To the population of native American Indians, tobacco leaves were a free good before the time of Sir Walter Raleigh. The Indians could have all that they wanted. Later, however, tobacco leaves became (and remain) an economic good.

Choice

Scarcity forces us to choose. You have to choose whether to carry on at school or go to work. If you take a job, then you have given up taking unemployment pay. You have to choose between going out or studying. Government policy-makers have to choose between using more resources in the production of military goods or using more resources in the production of, say, educational

---

Table 1.1

Resource classification
We can arbitrarily classify resources or factors of production into natural, human and manufactured resources. We have denoted specific names within those three classifications.

Natural resources	Human resources	Manufactured resources
Land	Labour and entrepreneurship	Physical capital

services. In fact, the concept of choice forms the basis of our formal definition of **economics**:

> Economics is the study of how individuals and societies choose between the alternative uses of scarce resources to satisfy their innumerable wants.

As we see throughout our study of economics, the choices we make affect not only how we live today but how we will live in the future. Moreover, the choices that we can make are constrained not only by scarcity but also by political, legal, traditional and moral forces. In other words, there are numerous non-economic forces that determine and mould our decision-making processes. In this text, however, we shall concentrate on how economic forces affect our choices. We are not denying, though, that the others are important too.

Distinguishing economics from politics?

These days economics is big news. It constitutes a significant percentage of our media coverage. Whenever we pick up a newspaper or turn on the television, we are likely to be bombarded with facts and figures on pollution, unemployment, inflation, privatization, exports, imports and productivity. In fact, most students beginning a course in economics probably assume that they have some understanding of the phenomena involved. The conclusions that the first-year economist reaches, however, may be blurred due to the large amount of political banter that is often associated with the media output on economics.

Politics is sometimes defined as the art of government and, as such, is partly concerned with what choices have to be made, choices that have to be made collectively, for example. Consequently, there are clear lines of demarcation between economics and politics. As Milton Friedman, the winner of a Nobel prize for economics in 1976 and a subsequent adviser to many governments, once remarked: 'In spite of my profound disagreement with the authoritarian political system of Chile, I do not consider it as evil for an economist to render technical advice to the Chilean government any more than I would regard it as evil for a physician to give technical advice to the Chilean government to help end a medical plague.'

1 Look at the first few pages of this book (especially the contents) and identify two aspects of economics that surprise you and two that you expected.
2 Try, in your own words, to distinguish between economics and politics.
3 (a) Select an issue that is currently in the news and write a paragraph, using the concept of scarcity, to describe what is happening.
   (b) Identify some political issues that may cloud the news item you are trying to describe.
4 Compare and contrast the approach of economics and politics to the concept of 'choice'.

KEY POINTS

1.1

- Scarcity exists because we cannot have all that we want from nature without sacrifice.
- We use scarce resources, such as land, labour, capital and entrepreneurship, to produce economic goods.
- Economic goods are those that are desired but are not directly obtainable from nature to the extent demanded or desired.
- Scarcity requires us to choose, and economics is the study of how we make those choices.

Opportunity cost – another central concept

To continue further with our introduction, it is necessary to consider carefully the definition of scarcity: every individual has competing wants but cannot satisfy all of them given limited resources. Therefore, a choice must be made. When the choice is made, some other thing that is also desired has to be forgone. In other words, in a world of scarcity, for every want that is satisfied, some other want, or wants, remain unsatisfied.

Choosing one thing inevitably requires giving up something else. In other words, another possible opportunity has been missed or forgone. To highlight this dilemma economists refer to the concept of **opportunity cost**.

Let us assume that, of all the other things you could have done instead of reading this book, the thing you most wanted to do, but did not do, was watch television. If that is the case, then watching television is the opportunity cost of reading this book.

> Opportunity cost is defined as the highest-valued alternative that had to be sacrificed for the option that was chosen.

Opportunity cost is a powerful concept that allows us to place a value on the resources used to produce something.

Opportunity cost in cyberspace

Those students that use e-mail and the World Wide Web will have noticed that cyberspace is becoming increasingly cluttered with adverts. In fact, it is nigh on impossible to use the Internet without coming across some advertising banner, button, promotion or link. Many of these support the thousands of online stores that already exist, such as Amazon.com and Allgifts.com for books and presents, and

Last Minute.com and Travelscape.com for travel and holidays. Conventional advertising to support offline business is also prevalent, for example Interflora, Prudential, Lindbury wines, Visa, Hewlett Packard, Yellow Pages and British Telecom. In total these advertisers are expected to spend in excess of £60 million on the Web by the year 2002. Consequently, Web pages should be regarded as valuable assets, as potentially many people can visit them every day. The owners of these pages therefore face an opportunity cost for literally every square centimetre on the screen, as they can either use the space to promote their own services and products or sell it as advertising space. For example, the opening page of any search engine, such as AltaVista, HotBot or Yahoo, will be seen by thousands of people every day. If too much of the screen space is filled with ads, users will be inclined to switch to a more dedicated search engine.

5 (a) Describe the opportunity cost experienced by the owner of a search engine such as AltaVista or Yahoo.

  (b) Can you describe a parallel situation faced by the owners of commercial TV?

6 (a) If you used an Internet café to access the Web and purchased a coffee while you were there, would the price of the coffee be part of the opportunity cost of going into town instead of using a computer at home or college? Explain your answer carefully.

  (b) If on your way to the Internet café you got stuck in traffic, would using a mobile phone to make a call reduce or increase the opportunity cost of going into town to access the Net? Explain your decision carefully.

7 At several points in this text there are Web addresses.

  (a) List the opportunity costs involved in choosing a visit to the websites.

  (b) Using the concept of opportunity cost, make an argument for using Web addresses to support your studies.

The trade-offs facing you

Whatever you do, you are trading off one use of a resource for one or more alternative uses. The value of these **trade-offs** is represented by the opportunity cost just discussed. We can examine the opportunity cost of reading this book. Let us assume that you have a maximum of four hours per week to spend studying just two topics – economics and geography (or whatever other subject is relevant to you). The more you study economics, the higher will be your expected grade; the more you study geography, the higher will be your expected grade in that subject. There is a trade-off, then, between spending one more hour reading this book and spending that hour studying geography. This can be more clearly brought out in a graph that shows the trade-off involved.

Graphical analysis

In Figure 1.1, we have put the expected grade in geography on the vertical axis and the expected grade in economics on the horizontal axis. In this simplified world, if you spend all your time on economics, you will get a B in the course, but you will fail geography. On the other hand, if you spend all your time on geography you will get a B in that subject and you will fail economics. The trade-off is a special case: one to one. A one-to-one trade-off means that in this case the opportunity cost of receiving one grade higher in economics (for example, improving from a D to a C) is one grade lower in geography (falling from a D to an E in our example).

Production possibilities curve

Figure 1.1 illustrates the relationship between the possible results that can be produced in each of two activities, depending on how much time you choose to put into each

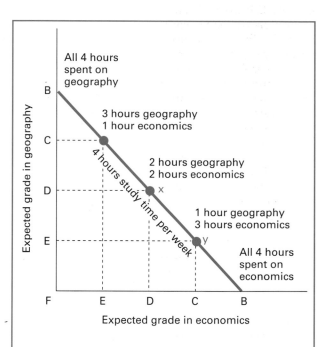

Figure 1.1

Production possibilities curve for grades in geography and economics

We assume that there are only 4 hours total time that can be spent per week on studying. If all 4 hours are spent on economics, a B is received in economics and an F in geography. If all 4 hours are spent on geography, a B is received in that subject and an F in economics. There is a one-to-one trade-off. If the student is at point x, equal time (2 hours a week) is spent on both courses and equal grades of D will be received. If a higher grade in economics is desired, the student may go to point y, where 1 hour is spent on geography and 3 hours on economics, and receive a C in economics but an E in geography.

activity. Economists call this kind of diagram a **production possibilities curve**.*

If you consider that what you are producing is a grade when you study economics and geography, then Figure 1.1 can be related to the production possibilities that you face. The line that goes from B on one axis to the B on the other therefore becomes a production possibilities curve. It is defined as all possible combinations of the maximum amount of any two goods or services that can be produced from a fixed amount of resources. In the example, your time for studying was limited to four hours per week. The two possible outputs were a grade in geography and a grade in economics. The particular production possibilities curve presented in Figure 1.1 is a graphic representation of the opportunity cost of studying one more hour in one subject. It is a *straight-line production possibilities curve*, which is a special case. (The more general case will be discussed next.) If you decide to be at point x in Figure 1.1, then two hours of study time will be spent on geography and two hours will be spent on economics. The expected grade in each course will be a D. If you are more interested in getting a C in economics, then you will go to point y on the production possibilities curve, spending only one hour on geography but three hours on economics. The expected grade in geography will then drop from a D to an E. Note that these trade-offs between expected grades in geography and economics apply when total study time, as well as all other factors that may influence your ability to learn, is kept constant. Quite clearly, if you wished to spend more total time studying, then it would be possible to have higher grades in both economics and geography! However, then we would no longer be on the specific production possibilities curve illustrated in Figure 1.1. We would have to draw a new curve in order to show the greater total study time and a different set of possible trade-offs. Grade As might then be possible!

KEY POINTS

1.2

■ In a world of scarcity, satisfaction of one want necessarily means the non-satisfaction of one or more other possible wants.

■ Any use of a resource involves an opportunity cost because an alternative use, by necessity, is sacrificed.

■ We look only at the highest-valued alternative to determine opportunity cost.

■ The graphic representation of trade-offs that must be made is displayed in a production possibilities curve.

---

* Other terms used for production possibilities curves are production possibilities frontier, production possibilities boundary, production possibility curve and transformation curve. We use the word possibilities rather than possibility to emphasize the multiplicity of combinations of output exemplified in this diagram.

Society's choices

The straight-line production possibilities curve presented in Figure 1.1 can be generalized to demonstrate the related concepts of scarcity, choice and trade-offs facing an entire nation. You may have already heard the phrase 'guns or butter'. Implicit in that phrase is that at any point in time a nation can have either more military goods (guns) or civilian goods (butter). Let us restrict our example to the production of military goods and civilian goods. We assume that these are the only two classes of goods that can be produced in the economy. Table 1.2 shows the hypothetical numerical trade-offs, expressed in terms of units of military goods produced per year. If no civilian goods are produced, all resources will be used in the production of military goods, of which 5000 units will be produced per year. However, if no military goods are produced, all resources will be used to produce 6000 units of civilian goods per year. In between, various combinations are possible. These combinations are plotted as points A, B, C, D, E, F and G in Figure 1.2. If these points are connected with a smooth curve, society's production possibilities curve is obtained,

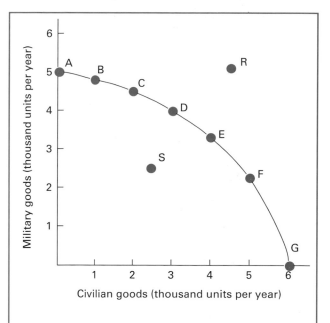

Figure 1.2
Society's trade-off between military goods and civilian goods
The production of military goods is measured in units per year. The production of civilian goods is also measured in units per year. The combinations are given in Table 1.2. Combinations A to G are plotted on the graph. Connecting the points A to G with a smooth line gives society's production possibilities curve for military goods and civilian goods. Point R lies outside the production possibilities curve and is therefore unattainable at the point in time for which the graph is given; point S lies inside the production possibilities curve and therefore represents an inefficient use of available resources.

Table 1.2

Combination	Military goods (units per year)	Civilian goods (units per year)
A	5000	0
B	4800	1000
C	4800	2000
D	4000	3000
E	3300	4000
F	2250	5000
G	0	6000

and it demonstrates the trade-off between the production of military and civilian goods. These trade-offs occur on the production possibilities curve.

Assumptions underlying the production possibilities curve

There are a number of assumptions underlying this particular production possibilities curve. The first relates to the fact that we are referring to the output possible on a *yearly* basis. In other words, we have specified a time period over which the production takes place.

Second, we are assuming that resources are fixed over this time period. To understand fully what is meant by a fixed amount of resources, consider that there are (a) factors that influence labour hours available for work and (b) factors that influence productivity, or the output per unit of input.

Factors influencing labour hours available for work

We must recognize that the number of labour hours will depend on the state of human resources in society. What determines how much labour can be available?

Hours available for work are determined by the following:

1 the size of the population, its age structure, and dependants (children, retired persons)
2 the resulting potential size of the labour force
3 the percentage of available individuals who then choose to work
4 custom and tradition (for example, women working)

Factors influencing productivity

There are a number of factors influencing how productive our society can be. If you recall our discussion of the inputs used in production, then we can list the following:

1 quantity and quality of natural resources
2 quantity and quality of capital
3 health, education, motivation and skill levels of the labour force
4 research and development

We are assuming that at the present time our society is using all its human, natural and manufactured resources to maximum effect *given the state of knowledge* about how

to make military goods and civilian goods. If the state of technology does not change, then our society cannot make more productive use of its resources. Thus we assume when drawing a production possibilities curve that no earth-shaking invention that could significantly reduce the cost of producing either military or civilian goods in our example is possible in the present time period. We are further assuming that the size of the labour force remains the same during this time period, that the health, motivation and skill levels remain the same, and so on. If any one of the factors influencing labour hours or productivity changes, then the production possibilities curve will shift. Any improvement in technology (productivity) will move the entire curve outwards to the right, as in Figure 1.3(a). Any significant reduction in the labour force, all other

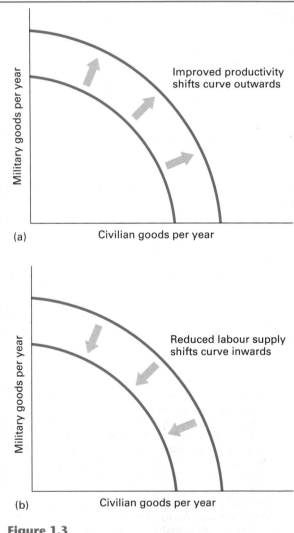

Figure 1.3
Shifting production possibilities curve
In (a) we see that improved productivity will shift the entire production possibilities curve outwards over time. In (b), a reduced amount of labour available to the economy will shift the entire production possibilities curve inwards over time.

things held constant, will shift the entire production possibilities curve inwards to the left, as in Figure 1.3(b).

The third and final assumption that we are making when we draw the production possibilities curve is that efficient use is being made of all available resources. (The concept of efficiency will be examined more closely in Chapter 4.) Society cannot for the moment be more productive with the present quantity and quality of its resources.

Being off the production possibilities curve

Point R lies outside the production possibilities curve in Figure 1.2. Any point outside the curve is impossible to achieve during the present time period. By definition, the possibilities curve relates to a specific unit of time. Additionally, the production possibilities curve is drawn for a given resource base. Under these two constraints, the production possibilities curve therefore indicates, by definition, the maximum quantity of one good available, given some quantity of the other. Point R, lying outside the production possibilities curve, occurs because we live in a world of scarcity. Look at point S in Figure 1.2. It is inside the curve, which means that society's resources are not being fully utilized. This could be due to unemployment.

Sex & drugs & rock'n'roll

By this early point in the course your tutors will have already implied that economics is relevant to most aspects of life. The following exercise will enable you to consider some more examples.

The National Health Service's drugs budget – presently £4.4 billion a year and rising at 9 per cent annually – may be stretched to breaking point by pills that can make you slim, sexy and smart. The Department of Health has held urgent talks on whether Viagra (a new impotence treatment) should be prescribed on the NHS. Xenical, an anti-obesity drug, has also been launched amid claims that, like Viagra, it could cost the NHS hundreds of millions of pounds.

As they prepared to be mobbed by sex-starved fatties, doctors are wondering how they will cope with the demand if drugs which are currently being developed to slow memory loss in those with Alzheimer's disease also prove effective at boosting the brain power of healthy people. Then there is the growing demand for a new and expensive treatment for multiple sclerosis. And the prospect of a range of anti-cancer drugs, now being tested, that may treat the currently untreatable, also at great cost.

The government's decision to exclude Viagra temporarily from the NHS is the first time that a drug with proven benefits to a large number of patients has not been made available. Some studies suggest that one in ten men suffers from impotence. So the British Medical Association (BMA) reckons that providing the blue pills, which cost £4.84 each, to all who could benefit from them might cost £1 billion a year. Pfizer,

the drug's maker, predicts it will turn out much cheaper – perhaps £50 million.

Since more than one in eight Britons is obese, and many more are slightly overweight, Xenical might benefit even more people than Viagra. Consequently, its annual costs are expected to be far higher – around £200 million.

Source: Adapted from *The Economist*, 26 September 1998

8 Use a production possibilities diagram to explain the nature of economic choices in the NHS. (Label one of the axes Viagra and choose an appropriate item for the other.)

9 (a) If the economy grew and generated more tax revenue for the NHS, how would your diagram change, and with what possible results?

   (b) If biotechnology underwent a revolution and tablets generally fell in price by 50 per cent, how would the diagram change, and with what results?

   (c) If more men began to suffer from impotence, how would the diagram change, and with what results?

10 Can you state an equivalent trade-off or choice that has been made by a government department more recently?

11 Use the economic concepts introduced in this chapter to illustrate that rock'n'roll is still an economic good – though its initial popularity began over 50 years ago.

12 Can you identify any aspects of life for which economics has no relevance?

Why the production possibilities curve is bowed outward

In the example in Figure 1.1, the trade-off between a grade in geography and a grade in economics was one to one. The trade-off ratio was fixed. That is, the production possibilities curve was a straight line which, as we pointed out before, is a special case. Figure 1.2 is the more general case, showing a bowed production possibilities curve. The opportunity cost of obtaining more and more units of military goods rises. That is, each additional unit costs society more in forgone alternatives than the previously produced unit. We can see this more clearly in Figure 1.4. Each increment in military output is the same, but look at what we have to give up in civilian goods when we go from the next-to-last unit of military output to the last unit, where the entire economy is producing just military goods. The opportunity cost is very large relative to what an equivalent increase in military goods costs society when we start with none being produced at all. Figure 1.4 illustrates the **law of increasing relative costs**. As society takes more and more resources and applies them to the production of any specific item, the opportunity cost for each additional unit produced increases at an increasing rate.

Why are we faced with the law of increasing relative costs? Why is the production possibilities curve bowed outwards? The answers to these questions are basic, and are related to the fact that some resources are better suited for the production of some things than they are for other things. In other words, many economic resources are not as a rule easily adaptable to alternative uses. Start in a world with a production of no military goods, only civilian goods. At first, we might find some sophisticated engineers working on computerized watering and fertilizing systems, for example, who could easily be transferred to the production of military goods. The job that these people would be doing while producing military goods might be relatively similar to the one they were doing when they were occupied in producing civilian goods. Their productivity might be approximately the same as it was prior to the move.

Eventually, however, when we attempt to transfer manual labourers used to harvesting potatoes to the production of military goods, we will find that their talents will be relatively ill-suited to such tasks. We might have to use fifty manual labourers to obtain the same increment in military goods output that we got when we hired one sophisticated engineer for the first units of military goods. Thus the opportunity cost of an additional unit of military goods will be higher when we use resources that are ill-suited to the task. That cost – of using poorly suited resources – increases as we attempt to produce more and more military goods and fewer and fewer civilian goods.

As a rule of thumb, the more highly specialized resources are, the more bowed society's production possibilities curve will be. At the other extreme, if all resources were equally suitable for all production purposes, then the curves in Figures 1.2, 1.3 and 1.4 would simply have approached a straight line, as in Figure 1.1.

KEY POINTS

1.3

- Trade-offs are represented graphically by a production possibilities curve showing the maximum output combinations obtainable over a one-year period from a given set of resources.

- Points outside the production possibilities curve are unattainable; points inside represent an inefficient use or under-utilization of available resources.

- Since many resources are better suited for certain productive tasks than for others, society's production possibilities curve is bowed outwards, reflecting the law of increasing relative cost.

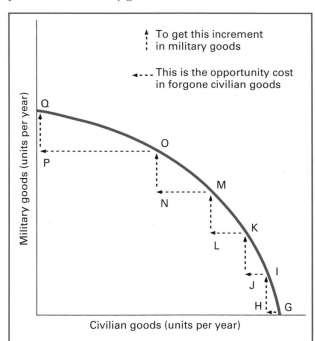

Figure 1.4
The law of increasing costs
Consider equal increments in military goods production, as measured on the vertical axis. Thus, all of the vertical arrows – H–I, J–K, L–M, N–O and P–Q – are of equal length. What is the cost to society of obtaining the first such increment in military goods production? It is a reduction in civilian goods output, G–H. This cost for each additional equal increment in military goods production rises, however. Finally, to get the last increment in military goods production – P–Q – society must give up the entire distance O–P in civilian goods production. The opportunity cost of each additional increase in military goods production rises.

Scarcity revisited

We have emphasized that productive resources are limited. Thus, we must make choices about how we use them. We have to decide how much of which goods we shall produce with our resources. For our purposes here, there will be only two choices: those goods that we consume directly, called **consumer goods** (food, clothes, cars), and those that we consume indirectly, called **capital goods** (machines and equipment). Everyone acts as a consumer in using consumer goods. However, capital goods, such as lathes, factories, machines and engines, are used to make the consumer goods to which we just referred.

Why we make capital goods
Why would we be willing to use productive resources to make things – capital goods – that we cannot consume directly? One of the reasons we use productive resources to make capital goods is that the latter enable us to produce larger quantities of consumer goods or to produce

them more cheaply than we otherwise could. Before fish are produced for the market, fishing-boats and nets are first produced. Now imagine, for example, how expensive it would be to obtain fish for market without using these capital goods. Getting fish with one's hands is not an easy task. The price per fish would be very high if capital were not used.

Forgoing current consumption

Whenever we use productive resources to make capital goods, we are implicitly forgoing current consumption. We are waiting until some time in the future to consume the fruit that will be reaped from the use of capital goods. Indeed, if we were to produce only consumer goods now and no capital goods, then our capacity to produce consumer goods in the future would suffer. Here we see a trade-off situation, one which lends itself to the sort of graphical analysis that we have used already in this chapter.

The trade-off between consumption goods and capital goods

In order to have more consumer goods in the future, we must accept fewer consumer goods today. With the resources that we do not use to produce consumer goods for today, we invest in capital goods that will produce more consumer goods for us later. The trade-off is depicted in Figure 1.5. In (a), you can see this trade-off depicted as a production possibilities curve between capital goods and consumption goods. If we decide to use all our resources to produce goods and services for consumption today, we can produce £2 million worth per year, which is represented as point B. In this extreme case, using all our productive resources for only consumption goods leads to no future growth.

Now assume, however, that we are willing to give up, say, £200 000 worth of consumption today. We will be at point A in Figure 1.5(c). This will allow the economy to grow. We will have more future consumption because we invested in more capital goods today. In Figure 1.5(d) we see two goods represented: food and recreation. The production possibilities curve will move outwards if we collectively decide to restrict consumption each year and invest in capital goods – that is, if we agree to be at point A.

In Figures 1.5(e) and 1.5(f), we show the result of our willingness to forgo quite a bit more current consumption. We move to point C, where we have many fewer consumer goods today, but produce a lot more capital goods. This leads to more future growth in this simple model, and thus the production possibilities curve in Figure 1.5(f) shifts outwards more than it did in 1.5(d). In other words, the more we give up today, the more we can have tomorrow.

KEY POINTS

1.4

■ Consumer goods are used directly by consumers.

■ Capital goods are the means by which consumer goods are produced and are not directly used by consumers.

■ The use of capital requires using productive resources to produce capital goods that in turn will later produce consumer goods.

■ A trade-off is involved between current consumption and capital goods, or alternatively between current consumption and future consumption, because the more we invest in capital goods today, the greater the amount of consumer goods we can produce in the future.

Constructing production possibilities

An economy has a working population of 800 men who can only produce two goods, X and Y. All other resources are specific to the production of only one of the goods. The potential outputs of each good are as follows:

Good X		Good Y	
No. of men	Weekly output	No. of men	Weekly output
100	60	100	25
200	120	200	65
300	190	300	110
400	260	400	160
500	330	500	200
600	380	600	235
700	420	700	260
800	450	800	275

13 Present the data in the form of a production possibilities curve.

14 Comment on the relationship between the change in the number of workers and the change in the weekly output of both good X and good Y.

15 What would be the effects of some of the labour force becoming more efficient at the production of good X while the remainder become more efficient at the production of good Y?

16 Assume that X is an investment good and Y is a consumption good and that, last year, 260 of X and 160 of Y were produced weekly. What would be the consequences if, next year, 330 of X and 110 of Y were produced weekly?

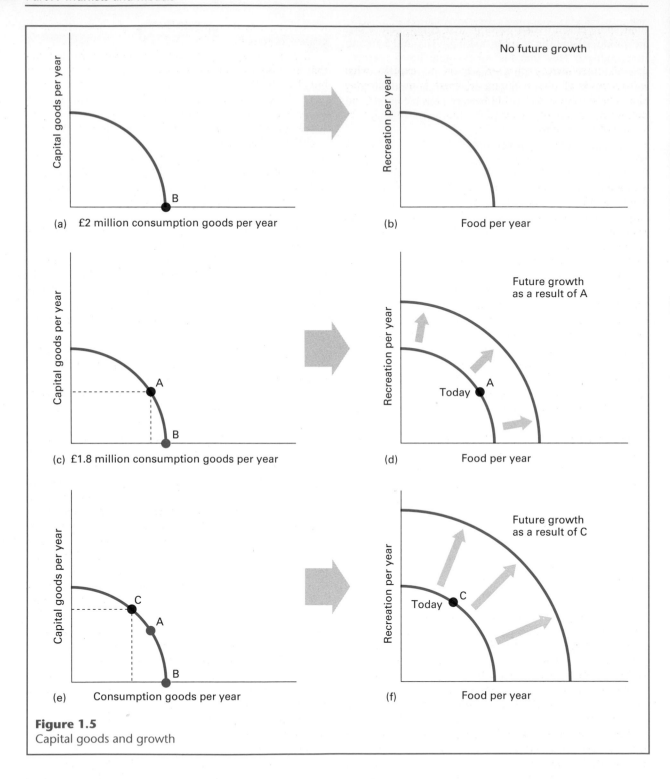

Figure 1.5
Capital goods and growth

The methodology of economics

In this introductory chapter we try to explain what economics is all about. Therefore, apart from identifying the central concepts, we need to consider the methods employed by economists, as these too help to specify the nature of our subject.

Is economics a science?

Economics is a social science that makes use of the same kinds of methods as other sciences, such as biology, physics and chemistry. Like these other sciences, economics uses models or theories. Economic models are simplified representations of the real world that we use to help us to understand, explain and predict economic phenomena in the real world.

For many centuries, most people thought that the world was flat. Using this model, they predicted that if one sailed to the edge of the world one would fall off into space. Columbus, however, applied a new model. His model, or theory, postulated that the world was round. He predicted that one could sail round the world without falling off an edge, because there were no edges. He tested his model, or theory, by sailing and sailing and sailing. He did not fall off any edges, and thereby refuted the flat-earth model empirically.

Economic models, or theories, are no different from those presented in other sciences. They may take on various forms such as verbal statements, numerical tables, graphs and mathematical equations. For the most part, the models presented in this text consist of verbal statements and graphs.

A look at using models

Let us return again to our production possibilities curve concerning you as a student in order to develop our understanding of a model. We looked at the trade-offs concerning your use of scarce time in studying geography and economics. As a model it illustrated the principle of opportunity cost. But you may have thought that various factors were left out of account in this model, so let us now recognize these.

Your performance in either geography or economics was assumed to improve by exactly one grade for every hour of study. There was, it seems, no particular difficulty in using one hour to raise the standard of your assessed performance. Now you may say that you would find more difficulty in improving your performance in economics than in geography: in other words, another two or even three hours would be necessary to move from a C grade to a B grade, and not just one! For some of your fellow students, still more hours than this might be needed, but

for others, less than a full hour might be sufficient to achieve a similar result.

If you reread carefully, you will note that we assumed that not only was the amount of study time held constant but also 'all other factors that may influence your ability to learn'. Thus it was implicitly assumed that it is as effective to study during a hot summer afternoon as during a cold winter evening. Or that it makes no difference whether you are studying alone in your own room or on public transport. What particular book you are reading in the hour of study also makes no difference at all. Now you may well wonder whether, in the light of these and other influences on a student's learning situation, our model is not too simplistic.

What we have just recognized is that there are indeed many factors which would influence a student's performance in a subject. But in our model we are assuming that we are *holding all other things constant*. In our model we are showing the relationship between the amount of time devoted to a subject and the assessed performance resulting from the amount of study. In Figure 1.6 we show this relationship.

Of course, there are other influencing variables, but they are not explicitly shown on any graph that has only two variables, such as study time and grade performance. In other words, the relationships shown on our graphs, by their very nature, cannot explicitly include all of the other relationships that are involved in determining the grades of students. We therefore say that when we draw a graph showing the relationship between two variables, we are holding all other things constant. The graph shown in Figure 1.6 is therefore holding constant, or fixed, the time of year, place of study, student motivation and all other influences on the learning situation. This is sometimes referred to as the *ceteris paribus* assumption, where the words *ceteris paribus* mean 'other things constant'. There is a way to show the effect of changes in 'other things' that are not explicitly depicted in two-dimensional graphs. When some other determining variable changes, it will affect the *position* of the line, or curve, representing the relationship between the two variables on the curve. For example, consider Figure 1.6 showing the relationship between study time and study grade. If the place where one studies affects grade performance and there is a change in study location, that entire line will move somewhere else in the graph when this variable is recognized as a relevant factor in the learning situation.

The important point we are making, therefore, is that an economic model cannot be faulted as unrealistic merely because it does not represent every detail of the real world. Providing the model clarifies and elucidates the central issues being studied then it is worthwhile. The aim is that a model should provide a starting point. That is, a student should be able to proceed from a simple beginning to a fuller understanding of complex phenomena.

The principles we are outlining here are similar to a child playing with a toy pram or gun, as they look and operate something like the real thing but are much smaller

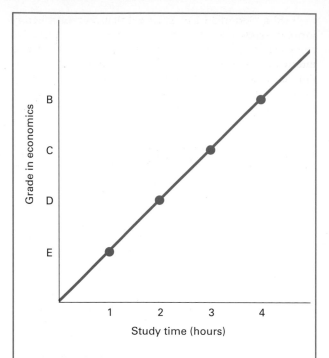

Figure 1.6
The relationship between study time and performance in economics
The grade obtained in economics depends on the amount of time devoted to study of the subject. The relationship is a direct one and assumes that there is no influence on the learning situation other than the amount of time devoted to the study of economics.

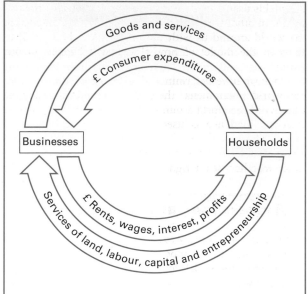

Figure 1.7
The circular flow model: a two-sector economy
In this simplified model there are only households and businesses (or firms). Money is used as the medium of exchange. Households sell the services of land, labour, capital and entrepreneurship that they own to firms. Firms, in turn, pay households rent, wages, interest and profits. Firms also sell goods and services to households for which the firms receive payment in the form of consumer expenditure of money income.

and simpler. Likewise, car designers and engineers might experiment with an idea by simulating a computer model to test performance features before proceeding to the expense of a full-scale prototype.

An example of a commonly used model in economic analysis

Most economists use a model to analyse and explain how income flows around an economy. They begin by ignoring the government sector, the financial institutions sector and the overseas sector. That is, their model represents a simplified, scaled-down economy in which relationships are assumed to exist only between households and businesses.

To make the model effective it is assumed that households sell factors of production to businesses and in return are paid money income in the form of wages, interest, rents and profits. They receive wages for their labour services, interest for the capital services that they provide, rents for the land that they own and profits for their entrepreneurial abilities. (These money incomes are examined in detail later.) This is shown in the bottom loops in Figure 1.7. Firms, on the other hand, sell finished goods and services to households, for which, in exchange, they are paid money. This is shown in the top loop in Figure 1.7.

These assumptions are reasonably realistic. Businesses will only make what they can sell. Production will necessitate buying in land, labour, capital and enterprise, and the monies paid for these factors of production will generate respective income payments.

Already, without building in any of the complications of the real world, we can begin to sense several insights or starting points. Clearly there is a close relationship between the income of a nation, its output and the level of expenditure, and we shall investigate these further in Chapters 13–16. Also, we can see how money enables households to 'vote' for the goods and services desired, and this will be developed further in Chapters 2–4. Finally, the model makes no mention of the role of government, assumes there are no dealings with overseas economies, and omits consideration of the financial institutions and the environment. Each of these aspects, however, is built in by coverage in specific chapters.

How to appraise an economics model

We do not attempt to determine the usefulness of a model or how 'good' it is merely by evaluating how realistic its assumptions are. Rather, we consider that a model is 'good' if it yields usable predictions and implications for the real world. In other words, can we predict what will happen in the world around us with the model? Are there implications in the model of how things will happen in our world?

Once we have determined that the model does predict real-world phenomena, then the scientific approach to analysis of the world around us requires that we consider *evidence*. Evidence is used to test the usefulness of a model. This is why we call economics an empirical science – empirical meaning that real evidence (data) is looked at to see whether we are right.

A closer look at building models

Engineers, architects, weather forecasters, doctors and even children all use models to progress their learning. Economists use models for similar purposes and proceed similarly with mixed results. To use an exceptional, but interesting, example we shall very briefly consider the Phillips machine. Whilst lecturing, during the 1950s, at the London School of Economics, Professor Bill Phillips built a hydraulic machine to depict circular flow. (We have discussed circular flow in Figure 1.7.)

The interesting thing about his model was that it gurgled, gushed, hissed and leaked as coloured water was pumped in and syphoned off. This Heath Robinson type of approach is unusual for our discipline; most economic models are not constructed out of metal, driven by motors and monitored by sensors. Conventional economic models rely on pen and paper and hence are expressed by graphs, in equations or in words. The format of the model, however, is irrelevant, as all models set out to fulfil the same role. They simplify reality in order to make it understandable. They provide a starting point. They enable students to proceed methodologically from simple beginnings to a fuller understanding of complex reality.

17 What academic problems does the Phillips machine present in contrast to traditional economic models?

18 What are the advantages and disadvantages of using a model economy with only two sectors to explain about the circular flow of income?

19 Why is it correct to regard a graph as a model?

20 Construct three separate models to predict the probability that the price of a product (of your choosing) will fall within five years. You only need to identify one determining factor in each model.

21 Make a list of the features (assumptions) that you might include in an economic model to represent a very, very competitive market. (You may like to compare some of your answers with the assumptions of the perfect competition model outlined in Chapter 21.)

Finally, it should be emphasized that no model in any form, in any science, and therefore no economic model, is complete in the sense that it captures every detail and interrelationship that exists. In fact, a model, by definition, is an abstraction from reality. It should capture only the essential relationships that are sufficient to analyse the particular problem in question.

KEY POINTS

1.5

- The phrase *ceteris paribus* is frequently applied in the study of economics and means that all other things have been held constant whilst a relationship between specified variables is being considered.

- Every model, or theory, must be based on a set of assumptions. How realistic these assumptions are is not as important as how effective they make the model or theory.

- The Phillips machine is a large physical structure: taller and heavier than the average man in the street. Most economic models, however, are presented on paper as a graph, equation or statement.

- Models enable generalizations to be made.

Microeconomics versus macroeconomics

Economics is typically divided into two types of analysis: microeconomics and macroeconomics. Consider the definitions of the two terms.

Microeconomics is the study of individual decision-making by both individuals and firms.

Macroeconomics is the study of economy-wide phenomena resulting from group decision-making in entire markets. As such, it deals with the economy as a whole.

The best way to understand the distinction between microeconomics and macroeconomics is to consider some examples. Microeconomic analysis would tackle the effects of changes in the price of petrol relative to other energy sources. It would be involved in the examination of the effects of new taxes on a specific product or industry. If price controls were reinstituted in the United Kingdom, how individual firms and consumers would react to such price controls would be in the realm of microeconomics. The raising of wages by an effective union strike would be analysed using the tools of microeconomics.

In contrast, questions relating to the rate of inflation, the amount of national unemployment, the growth in production in the whole economy and numerous other economy-wide subjects all fall into the realm of macroeconomic analysis. In other words, macroeconomics deals with so-called *aggregates* or totals, such as total output in an economy. It is a study, therefore, of aggregate behaviour rather than individual behaviour.

You should be aware, however, of the blending together of microeconomics and macroeconomics in modern economic theory. Modern economists are increasingly using microeconomic analysis – the study of decision-making by individuals and by firms – as the basis of macroeconomic analysis. They do this because, even though in macroeconomic analysis aggregates are being examined, those aggregates are made up of individuals and firms. Consider an example. Some economists believe that reducing income tax rates will lead to greater total output. Why? Because, using microeconomic analysis, they predict that individuals will respond to lower income tax rates by working longer, taking fewer holidays and taking on second jobs. The task is then to establish whether empirical evidence supports these predictions.

Positive versus normative economics – what is versus what ought to be

Economics is a social science; it uses *positive* analysis. This is a scientific term that relates to the value-free nature of the enquiry; no subjective or 'gut' feelings enter into the analysis. Positive analysis relates to basic statements, such as *if A, then B*. For example, if the price of petrol goes up relative to all other prices, then the amount of it that people will buy will fall. That is a positive economic statement. It is a statement of *what is*. It is not a statement of anyone's value-judgement, or subjective feelings. 'Hard' sciences, such as physics and chemistry, are considered to be virtually value free. After all, how can someone's values enter into a theory of molecular behaviour? But economists face a different problem. They deal with the behaviour of individuals, not molecules. Thus, it is more difficult to stick to what we consider to be value-free or **positive economics** without reference to our feelings.

When our values come into the analysis, we enter the realm of **normative economics**, or normative analysis, which is defined as analysis containing, whether explicitly or implicitly, someone's values. A positive economic statement is: 'If the price of books goes up, people will buy fewer.' If we add to that analysis the statement 'and therefore we should not allow the price to go up', we have entered the realm of normative economics; we have expressed a personal opinion or value-judgement. In fact, any time you see the word 'should', you will know that values are entering into the discussion.

The world of value-judgements is the world in which individuals' preferences are at issue. Each of us has a desire for different things: we have different values. When we express a value-judgement, we are simply saying what we prefer, like or desire. Since individual values are quite diverse, we expect – and indeed observe – people expressing widely varying value-judgements about how the world should or ought to be.

Using positive economics in normative analysis

Even though this economics textbook, along with virtually all others, contains mostly positive economic analyses, such analyses can be used when one passes into the realm of policy-making in which values play a part. Suppose, for example, that you desire to raise the income of employed teenagers. That is a normative judgement (that is, a value-judgement) that you have made and in which you believe. Assume that you are a policy-maker with many options available to you, such as specifying minimum wage levels. Here is where positive analysis can come to your aid.

Suppose that you construct a model of the teenage labour market. Your examination of real-world evidence tells you that in the past raising the minimum wage has not led to higher incomes for employed teenagers.

In fact, you find out that it can even cause increased unemployment among teenagers. Even though your normative goal is to help unemployed teenagers, you may use positive economic analysis to decide that you must seek an alternative policy to raising the minimum wage. Hence, positive economics can be used as the basis for

---

What is the cost of saving lives?

Following the 'dark' days of petrol shortage in 1973, a 55 mph speed limit was introduced in America, since it was widely accepted that fuel consumption increased dramatically as speed increased above 55 mph. During the 1980s, however, new reserves of petroleum were discovered and the shortage problem became less acute.

Nevertheless, a large group of people continued to support the need to maintain the 55 mph speed limit, the argument now being that the lower the speed limit, the fewer the number of fatal accidents on the nation's highways. In fact, American government statisticians estimated that the reduction in speed limits from 65 to 55 mph saved 4500 lives per year.

22 List the opportunity costs of the United Kingdom reducing its speed limit from 70 mph.

23 (a) Place a monetary value on the opportunity costs listed in your answer to 22.
  (b) Explain whether your answer is an example of positive or normative economics.

24 (a) The government could save more lives by adding to the stock of speed surveillance systems used on motorways. Why is this not done?
  (b) Explain whether your answer is an example of positive or normative economics.

deciding on the appropriate policies to carry out one's goals or the goals of the nation.

A warning

It is easy to define positive economics. It is quite another matter to catch all unlabelled normative statements in a textbook like this one, even though an author goes over the manuscript many times before it is printed. Therefore, do not get the impression that a textbook author will be able to keep his or her values out of the book. They will slip through. In fact, the choice itself of which topics to include in an introductory textbook involves normative economics. There is no value-free or objective way to decide which topics to cover in a textbook. The author's 'gut feelings' ultimately make a difference when choices have to be made. From your own personal standpoint, what you might hope to do is be able to recognize *when*

you are engaging in normative as opposed to positive economic analysis. Reading this text should equip you for that task.

KEY POINTS

1.6

- Microeconomics involves the study of *individual* decision-making. Macroeconomics involves the study of *aggregates*. Modern economic theory often involves blending these two branches together.

- Positive economics indicates what *is*, whereas normative economics considers what *ought to be*.

Case Study

Practice Makes Perfect?

Perhaps well-meaning friends or relatives have told you that you should strive for perfection. A common proverb is: 'If something is worth doing, it is worth doing well.' Now what exactly can that mean with respect to your life? Does it mean that every time you undertake *any* task you should continue doing that task until you are certain you have reached your version of perfection, or at least until you are certain you can do no better? I don't think so.

Every one of you is faced with constraints. A major constraint in your life is time. Everyone faces a scarcity of time. Therefore, while you are engaging in the job of doing something to perfection, you are not engaging in any other job (or any other pleasure, for that matter). Otherwise stated, every action on your part involves an opportunity cost. In plain English, the quest for perfection involves use of time and hence is costly to you, as you must give up other valuable alternatives to achieve it.

Let's consider an example. The words you are reading right now are words that we put down on paper. We had to spend time developing an outline for the book, writing down a first draft, correcting that draft in order to write a second draft, then sending the manuscript to one another for criticisms. When the comments came back we each had to go through them and decide which ones were valid and which ones were not. Many of them were incorporated in the third and final draft of the manuscript. Then it went to the publisher, HarperCollins, for editing, page design and layout, printing, binding and distribution. During the production process the proofs were checked for any typographical errors.

Now why did we only do three drafts? Certainly we could have improved on what you are reading by sending the third draft out for review and then rewriting it. Also we checked printed page proofs three times before approving the result. We could have read them four times or five times. Whatever typographical errors are still in this book would probably have been caught. But we didn't write a fourth draft and we didn't read the printed page proofs again. Why not? Because we made a decision that the additional benefits from the additional work would not be worth the additional costs.

How did we calculate the benefits and how did we calculate the cost? With respect to the benefits, we looked at the potential improvement and how much more positively you and your tutors would respond to an additional draft or an additional proofreading. We examined the additional cost, called the **marginal cost**, as the value of the time we would have had to give up to do that extra work. We didn't have an exact number in our heads, but we knew it would take away time from other activities.

So what you are reading is the result of an implicit comparison by us of the costs and benefits of our actions. We wanted the book to be well done, but we know it is not perfect. In *most* situations, whatever *you* do will not be perfect either, because you must incur an opportunity cost to achieve perfection: the value of the time you use in any job.

A general rule of thumb could be as follows: *Undertake any activity up to the point at which the marginal benefit equals the marginal cost.*

This rule applies to studying for exams, polishing your car, looking for a video to rent, working on a report to be handed in next week, or anything. You'll find this same rule in many chapters in *Economics Explained*. For example, in Chapter 24 we shall explain the labour market and see how the decisions, made by employers, to hire or fire are made using this rule. The rule may not lead to perfection, but as a general principle it will enable you to be more efficient.

1 (a) Which of the following are examples of economic good?
  • the preparation of a textbook manuscript for publication
  • the purchase of a textbook
  • a coursework assignment for school or college
  • weeding the garden
  • washing the car
  (b) Which is the clearest example and why?
2 (a) What is the main opportunity cost of your studies?
  (b) Using a production possibilities curve, explain your answer to 2(a).
  (c) Identify two other opportunity costs of studying economics.
  (d) Using the concept of opportunity cost, try to express a monetary value of your studies.

3 (a) In your own words, try to explain what you understand by the marginal cost equals marginal benefit rule.
  (b) Using your own example, explain how this rule relates to the law of increasing relative costs.
  (c) How do you think the marginal cost and marginal benefit rule may be applied to the hiring and firing of labour?
4 How could the marginal cost and marginal benefit rule be used to explain sports stars' continual pursuit of perfection, for example the professional snooker player who practises for the ultimate 147 break?
5 Select an issue that is currently in the news and write a paragraph using economic concepts to explain what is happening.

Exam Preparation

Multiple choice questions

1 A production possibilities diagram does NOT illustrate
  A scarcity
  B monetary exchange
  C opportunity cost
  D attainable and unattainable points

2 The diagram on the right shows the production possibilities available to a closed economy without foreign trade. If the economy produces OK of good X then it forgoes
  A OJ of good Y
  B OA of good Y
  C AJ of good Y
  D KB of good X for OA of good Y
  E KB of good X for AJ of good Y

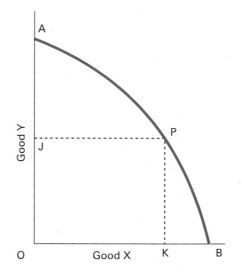

3 In the following diagram, XY represents an economy's production possibilities curve. Which point (**A**, **B**, **C** or **D**) would indicate that the country could increase its standard of living without incurring an opportunity cost?

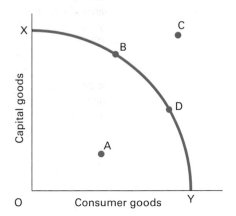

4 The opportunity cost to society of constructing a motorway would be
A the money spent on the road
B the goods and services that could otherwise have been produced had the road not been constructed
C the cost of government borrowing to finance the construction of the road
D the increased taxation needed to pay the cost of the new road
E goods and services that could otherwise have been produced by the labour employed in constructing the road had the road not been constructed

5 A factory produces both cars and trucks. A technological advance makes it possible to produce more cars without increasing the amount of labour or capital used to produce them. There is no technological advance in truck-making. The factory continues to produce both cars and trucks. As a result of the technological advance, the factory can
A produce more cars at a lower opportunity cost, but no more trucks
B produce more cars at a higher opportunity cost, but no more trucks
C produce more cars and trucks, and the opportunity cost of trucks is lower
D produce more cars and trucks, and the opportunity cost of trucks is higher

6 Assume you bought a bicycle for £100 but never use it. A similar bicycle would now cost £120 new, but yours would fetch only £40 second-hand. The present opportunity cost of owning the bicycle is
A £20
B £40
C £60
D £100
E £120

7 A farmer can feed any combination of animals within the following range:

Pigs		Cows
84	and	12
75	and	15

Given the options available to him, what is the opportunity cost to the farmer of rearing one cow?
A 1 pig
B 3 pigs
C 5 pigs
D 7 pigs
E 9 pigs

8 A normative statement in economics
A is one based on facts
B typically contains the words 'what is'
C depends on value-judgements
D is open-ended
E is one based on things that are normal

Essay questions

1 Explain the meaning of opportunity cost and discuss its importance to economists.

2 Describe and draw a production possibilities curve, and discuss the circumstances in which such a curve would change its position and shape.

3 (a) Why is scarcity regarded as the basic economic problem?
  (b) Examine the claim that nothing can ever be truly free.

4 'The format of an economic model is irrelevant.' Explain and discuss.

Economic systems

In this chapter we first look at the definition of an economic system, and then explain the two polar extremes of systems that have existed in the world. We state the three basic questions that all economic systems must answer, and show how in recent years there has been a convergence of the various systems.

Economic systems defined

We characterize an economic system as all the institutional means through which national resources are used to satisfy human wants. By institutions, we mean principally the laws of the nation, but also the habits, ethics and customs of its society. From the outset, you should be aware that all economic systems are artificial in the sense that the institutions in an economy are exactly what human beings have made them.

There are two polar-extreme types of economic system: capitalism and the command economy. Somewhere in between these two extremes is the mixed economy. We outline these in turn.

1 Capitalism is a type of economic system that is typically characterized by limited involvement of government in the economy, coupled with individual ownership of the means of production. In a capitalist system, individuals can pursue their own self-interest without many constraints. The capitalist system is thus one where decisions are decentralized.
2 The command economy is one in which the government controls the factors of production and makes all key decisions about their use and about the distribution of income. Thus, in the command economy, decision-making is a centralized process.
3 The mixed economy, as its name suggests, is one which is a mixture of private decision-making and central organization. Thus, decisions about how resources should be used are made partly by individuals, and partly by the government and other institutions within a public sector.

No matter what the economic system, the fundamental economic problem of scarcity must be solved. Every economic system faces opportunity costs in making decisions.

We consider the different approaches of these types of economic system to solving the problem of scarcity, having first considered in more detail how the character of the institutions varies between the two extreme systems of capitalism and the command economy.

KEY POINTS TO REVIEW

■ Scarcity (1.1, 1.2)   pages 5 & 7

■ Opportunity costs (1.2)   page 7

■ Production possibilities curve (1.2, 1.3)   pages 7 & 10

■ Consumer goods and capital goods (1.4)   page 11

LEARNING OUTCOMES

On completing this chapter you should understand:

■ The meaning of an economic system

■ The differences between a capitalist economy and a command economy

■ Why countries typically have a mixed economy

■ How Eastern European countries have abandoned the command economy

■ The meaning of globalization and its implications

Capitalism: institutions and ideology

Capitalist ideology is based on a set of fundamental assumptions. These assumptions are not, of course, accepted by all, but they must be understood in order to understand what capitalist ideology is all about. The institutions of capitalist ideology are, in many senses, abstract but play an important role in determining the way in which individuals can act in a pure capitalist system.

Our analysis will be limited to a discussion of:

1 the system of private property
2 free enterprise and free choice
3 competition and unrestricted markets
4 self-interest
5 the pricing system in those markets
6 the limited role of government

The system of private property

The ownership of most property under a capitalist system is usually vested in individuals or groups of individuals. The state is thus not the predominant owner of, for example, productive resources that are important forms of property. In the United Kingdom, the government does own certain property, but in general we live with a system of private property.

Private property is controlled and enforced through the legal framework of laws, courts and the police. Under capitalism, the *property rights* of individuals are protected; individuals are usually free to use their private property as they choose, as long as they do not infringe on the legal property rights of others.

Free enterprise and free choice

Another attribute of a capitalist system is **free enterprise**, which is merely an extension of the concept of property rights. Free enterprise exists when private individuals are allowed to obtain resources, to organize those resources and to sell the resulting product in any way they choose. In other words, there are no artificial obstacles or restrictions that a government or other producers can put up to block a business person's choice in the matter of purchasing inputs and selling outputs.

Additionally, all members of the economy are free to choose to do whatever they wish. Workers will be free to enter any line of work for which they are qualified and consumers can buy the desired basket of goods and services that they feel is most appropriate for them. The ultimate voter in the capitalist system is the consumer, who votes with pounds and decides which product 'candidates' will survive; that is, there is **consumer sovereignty** in that the ultimate purchaser of products and services determines what, in fact, is produced.

Competition and unrestricted markets

Competition is rivalry among sellers who wish to attract customers and rivalry among buyers to obtain desired goods. In general, competition exists among buyers and sellers of all resources who wish to obtain the best terms possible when they transact their business.

Competition requires, at a minimum, two things:

(a) a relatively large number of independently acting sellers and buyers, and
(b) the freedom of sellers and buyers to enter or leave a particular industry.

Many participants
The presence of a large number of buyers and sellers means that power is diffuse, that no one buyer or one seller can noticeably influence the price that a particular product fetches in the market-place.

Basically, economic competition – rivalry among buyers and sellers – imposes limits on the self-interest of buyers and sellers. Competition, then, is the regulating force in capitalism.

Easy entry and exit
Another thing that makes competition a regulatory force is the ability of individuals to enter an industry that is profitable. Furthermore, those who feel that they could earn more profits in another industry must have the legal ability to leave the industry they are in now. We say, then, that there are *weak barriers* to entry and exit from industries, so that competition can prevail throughout.

Self-interest and the invisible hand

In 1776 Adam Smith, the author of the *Wealth of Nations*, described a system in which government had a limited role and individuals pursued their own self-interest. Smith reasoned that, in so doing, individuals will be guided as if by an invisible hand to achieve maximum social welfare for the nation. In his own words:

> An individual generally, indeed, neither intends to promote the public interest, nor knows how much he is promoting it ... he intends only his own gain, and he is in this, as in many other cases, led by an invisible hand to promote an end which was no part of his intention. Nor is it always the worse for the society that it was no part of it. By pursuing his own interest he frequently promotes that of the society more effectually than when he really intends to promote it.

> (A. Smith, *Wealth of Nations* (1776), Bk IV, ch. 11, Everyman edn, 1964)

What does self-interest entail? For the entrepreneur it normally means maximizing profits or minimizing losses. For the consumer, it means maximizing the amount of satisfaction possible from spending a given amount of income. From the worker's point of view, it means obtaining the highest level of income possible for a given amount of work. For the owner of a resource, it means obtaining the highest price possible when that resource is sold, or the greatest rent if it is rented.

Capitalism therefore presumes self-interest as the fundamental way that people operate in the system. Self-interest is the guiding light in capitalism.

The pricing system

Capitalism is a **market economy** defined as one in which buyers and sellers express their opinions through how much they are willing to pay for, or how much they demand of, goods and services. A market economy is also called a **price system**. In a price system, or market economy, prices are used to signal the value of individual resources. Prices are the guideposts to which resource owners, entrepreneurs and consumers refer when they make their choices as they attempt to improve their lives. In other words, the **market economic system** is the organizing force in our economy. When we refer to **organization**, we mean the co-ordination of individuals, often doing different things in the further-ance of a common end. This process of co-ordinating economic activity can be considered as being mechanical or machine-like in its mode of working. Hence we can also refer to the market system as using the mechanism of prices to effect changes in resource use. How does the **price mechanism** achieve this?

Resources tend to flow where they yield the highest rate of return, or highest profit. Prices generate the signals for resource movements; they provide information cheaply and quickly and they affect incentives.

The limited role of government

Even in an 'idealized' capitalistic system there is still a role for government, for someone has to define and enforce private property rights. The government protects the rights of individuals and entrepreneurs to keep private property private, and to keep the control of that property vested with the owners. Even Adam Smith, the so-called father of free enterprise, described in detail the role of government in a purely capitalist system. He suggested the need for govern-ment in providing national defence and in eliminating monopolies that would restrict trade. Smith further suggested that the functions of government within a capi-talist system might include issuing money, prescribing standards of weights and measures, raising funds by taxa-tion and assorted other means for public works, and settling disputes judicially. Government is thus essential to the existence of even a purely capitalist system but operates in a restrained way. The words *laissez-faire* referred to in the biography of Adam Smith indicate that the business community should be left alone by government.

Finally – a definition of capitalism

We can now formally define in more detail what we mean by **capitalism**:

> Capitalism is an economic system in which indi-viduals privately own productive resources and possess property rights to use these resources in whatever manner they choose, subject to certain (minimal) legal restrictions.

Of markets and men

Adam Smith (1723–90)

'I have never known much good done by those who affected to trade for the public good,' Adam Smith once remarked. If he put little stock in good intentions, Smith did invest heavily in demonstrating that selfish intentions could lead to public good. In *The Theory of Moral Sentiments* (1759), his first book, Smith tried to show how altruism could come out of self-interest. In his second and more famous book, Smith attempted to reveal how the self-interest of private individuals could be transformed by the sleight of an invisible hand (the unfettered market) into social har-mony and public benefit, producing the wealth of the nation in the best of all possible ways. The result of this effort was *An Inquiry into the Nature of Causes of the Wealth of Nations* (1776), perhaps the most influential econom-ics treatise ever written, one that has set the tone for capitalist ideology for the past three centuries. It is perhaps remarkable that this book, a key refer-ence point on capitalist economics, was written by the same author as *The Theory of Moral Sentiments*.

In addition to Smith's famous 'invisible hand' theme, referred to above, the theme of individual eco-nomic freedom also was quite strong in the *Wealth of Nations*. He believed that any governmental attempt to guide or to regulate the actions of individuals in the economic market-place would end up doing more harm than good. Smith was especially harsh on legally protected monopolies.

Smith's critics of today contend that his model may have fitted the United Kingdom at the time he wrote his treatise, but it does not fit industri-alized Western countries today, when the state plays a major role and large corporations have replaced shopkeep-ers. Nonetheless, for many, the *Wealth of Nations* remains a *laissez-faire* Bible, and Smith remains a cen-tral figure in the development of economic thought.

Notice here that we use the words *productive resources* rather than *capital*. This takes into account not only machines and land but also labour services.

KEY POINTS

2.1

- There is a spectrum of economic systems, with the two extremes being capitalism and the command economy. In between is the mixed economy. These three types of economic system offer differing approaches to solving the scarcity problem.

- An idealized capitalist system works within the institution of private property that is controlled and enforced through the legal framework of laws, courts and police.

- Further, such a system is one of free enterprise, where producers freely choose the resources they use in the products they produce. Consumers have freedom of choice also, as do workers and owners of resources in general.

- Individuals and producers express their desires through the market system, where prices are signals about the relative scarcities of different goods, services and resources.

- The role of government is a limited one.

The command economy: institutions and ideology

Capitalism is not the only theoretical model of an economic system that exists. The polar-extreme alternative to 'pure' capitalism, from a theoretical point of view, is an economic system of a command economy.

The political dimension

Too often the command economy is seen as synonymous with a socialist or communist system. This is quite wrong, as a right-wing dictatorship could also operate a command economy. It is thus misleading to attach a political label to the two contrasting types of economic system. Concern about political control (that is, how democratic a society is) is, strictly speaking, a separate issue from that of economic control. A socialist system could be a democratic society when the key government officials making decisions about the use of resources are elected in genuine elections, that is, where there is a choice of candidates facing electors. A socialist system could also come under

the political control of a dictator just as in a capitalist system. Neither socialism nor communism are theoretically necessary features of a command economy. Nonetheless, it is true that in practice socialism is the main political system under which most command economies are administered. This being so, we now briefly distinguish between **socialism** and **communism**.

Socialism

In a 'pure' socialist system, the state owns the major non-labour productive resources: land and capital goods. Individuals can own consumer goods and consumer durables, but they are not allowed to own factories, machines and other things that are used to produce what society wants. Second, people are induced to produce by wage differentials. However, taxation of large incomes to redistribute income may reduce some of the incentives to produce. Third, the state determines people's wage rates and who should be paid what in government-owned and government-operated factories. Fourth, individuals are allowed to enter only certain areas of activity. They cannot, for example, freely set up their own factories. They cannot become entrepreneurs or capitalists, for the state has this function and controls all enterprises.

Communism

With 'pure' communism all resources, in principle, are owned in common. What, then, about the role of the state? Here we turn to Karl Marx (1818–83), who perhaps more than anyone else in the history of economic thought is responsible for the development of the communist movement.

Marx envisaged the fall of capitalism leading to the rise of socialism and eventually to the world of ideal communism. Marx foresaw a final state where the relations of production and distribution would be: 'From each according to his ability, to each according to his needs.' In fact, in the ideal communist world that Marx predicted would eventually emerge, there would be little or no need for government. Everything would take care of itself, for man's basic human nature would have been changed because the relations of production and distribution would no longer create class conflict and alienation would not occur.

Marxian economics

What was it about the market economy to which Marx objected? Basically he saw a conflict existing between the capitalist class and those they employed as labourers. The capitalists were regarded as exploiting their workers and also possessing considerable market and political power. Marx rejected the notion that the capitalists meekly responded to the wishes of consumers. In their long-term struggle to survive, the capitalists were seen by Marx as trying to cut the costs of production by mechanizing

Ghost of Western economics

Unlike most economists since the time of Adam Smith, Marx saw capitalism as a specific and historically limited form of social organization. The internal dynamics of capitalism, he argued, would eventually create conditions ripe for its overthrow by the working class and the institution of a new form of social organization based on collective ownership.

Marx was a prolific writer, but the culminating work of his career is undoubtedly *Das Kapital*, the first volume of which appeared in 1867. Like Adam Smith and David Ricardo, Marx adhered to the labour theory of value – the theory that the value of commodities ultimately depends on the human labour time expended in their

Karl Marx
(1818–83)

production. The difference between the labour time workers spend producing for a capitalist and the labour time equivalent to the wages they actually receive Marx called surplus value. Here, he argued, was a scientific index of exploitation.

But, Marx argued, it was the workers who would get the last laugh. Capitalists, faced with competition, are continually driven to expand and mechanize production, thus eliminating some labour costs. But since labour is the ultimate source of value, capitalists, in effect, are cutting their own throats. Over the long term, Marx argued, the rate of profit would fall, while at the same time more and more people would be left without jobs. Through a combination of economic crises of increasing severity and the development of class consciousness among workers, capitalism would finally collapse.

---

production, that is, reducing employment. Rising unemployment would eventually provoke the development of class consciousness among workers and the capitalist order would be overthrown.

The Marxian critique of the market economy is, inevitably, the subject of continuing debate. The revolutionary ideology he offered makes him the subject of much study by social scientists. What can we offer here in a brief response to his picture of capitalism as a historically limited form of economic system?

A first comment is that Marx was essentially a critic of capitalism rather than an architect of the ideal communist world that he thought would ultimately emerge. Because of this he is open to criticism concerning how such an economy should actually be organized. In particular, the immense problems facing the central planners in a socialist command economy were played down. The central planners have to make decisions concerning production targets and ensure that the necessary inputs are available in the right place and at the right time to make meeting such targets actually possible. This requires an effective organizational structure or bureaucracy to exist. As regards the labour input, the socialist economy requires some sort of incentive (moral or by way of threat) to exist for people to become fully involved in the economic process. Critics of the socialist economy have thus doubted whether a mixture of patriotic exhortation and brute fear is an effective substitute for the self-interest motivation on which the capitalist system is based.

If we look at the experience of central planning in the Soviet Union, it should give us a picture of how this basically socialist economy performed in its early years.

The growth of the Soviet economy after 1917

Vladimir Lenin and the Bolsheviks came to power in Russia in 1917 soon after the overthrow of the Russian monarchy. Lenin did not immediately get rid of all capitalist institutions in Russia. His New Economic Policy (NEP) allowed small industry and trade to be privately owned. Only heavy industry, transportation, foreign trade and banking remained in government hands. Josef Stalin succeeded Lenin in 1924.

Stalin did not like the inability of central authorities to control the direction of the economy. Stalin felt that there were certain industries that should be treated favourably in order to get the economy growing rapidly. Thus, a course of economic development *in advance* was plotted in **five-year plans**. These plans were called five-year plans because they plotted a course of economic activity for the following five years. Special industries were picked for growth, which was to be 'financed' by obtaining more agricultural produce to feed urban industrial workers. In order to obtain more agricultural products, collectivization was to be the key. Between 1928 and 1932, over 15 million peasant households were formed into over 200 000 collective farms. On the collectives, land and livestock were owned in common – that is, they were not private property.

Agricultural collectivization was not an overwhelming success. Peasants slaughtered and then ate, sold or traded much of their livestock rather than turn it over to the collectives.

Capital goods and growth

In Chapter 1 we showed that there was a trade-off between current consumption and future consumption. If you turn back to Figure 1.5, you will see how we showed, with the use of the production possibilities curve, that the more we invest in capital goods the more likely it is that the economy will grow so as to allow greater consumption by households in the future. The Russian economy after 1928 illustrates this trade-off. There was a marked increase in the proportion of resources devoted to the production of capital goods. Whereas in 1928 investment accounted for about 15 per cent of all output, by 1932 it had doubled. Under the first five-year plan there was a massive development of heavy industry, and the output of the coal, steel and electricity industries increased very rapidly. If you realize that at that time well over 80 per cent of the Russian population lived in rural areas, then you can appreciate the massive emphasis placed on rapid industrialization. The second and third five-year plans continued the emphasis on capital goods, and since, too, the Russian leadership developed an enthusiasm for defence expenditure, there was a reduced share of resources available for production of consumption goods. It was, indeed, machinery and guns rather than butter. The preference for capital equipment and military goods meant that for many Russians a major improvement in the material standard of living was denied them.

KEY POINTS

2.2

- We can simplify the different types of economic systems by looking at them in terms of decentralization. Pure market capitalism would be on one end of the scale, pure command socialism on the other.

- The key attributes of socialism are that (1) the government owns the major productive resources; (2) people are induced to produce by wage differentials, but taxation is often used to redistribute income, thereby reducing some incentive to produce; (3) the rewards for producing are usually set by the state rather than the market; (4) individuals can only enter certain areas of activity and cannot, for example, freely set up their own factories.

- In Russia after 1928 there was less production of goods to satisfy consumer wants. More production went into capital formation.

- Heavy industry grew rapidly. Collectivization of agriculture resulted in lower food production.

Three basic economic questions

In every nation, no matter what the form of government, what the type of economic system, who is running the government or how poor or rich it is, three basic economic questions must be answered. They concern the problem of **resource allocation**, which is simply *how* resources will be allocated. As such, resource allocation answers the three basic economic questions of what, how and for whom goods and services will be produced.

1 *What will be produced?* Literally billions of different things could be produced with society's scarce resources. What mechanism exists that causes some things to be produced and others to remain as individuals' unfulfilled desires?

2 *How will it be produced?* There are many ways to produce a desired item. It is possible to use more labour and less capital, or vice versa. It is possible to use more unskilled labour and fewer units of skilled labour. How, in some way, are decisions to be made as to the particular mix of inputs, the way they should be organized and how they are brought together at a particular place?

3 *For whom will it be produced?* Once a commodity is produced, who should have it? If individuals and businesses purchase commodities with money income, the question then is what mechanism there is to distribute income, which then determines how commodities are distributed throughout the economy.

We now re-examine the capitalist system and the command economy in turn to see how they answer these key questions.

What? How? For whom? In pure capitalism

In pure capitalism, **consumers** ultimately determine what will be produced by their spending – their voting in the market-place, what they are willing to spend their income on. As far as producers are concerned, their motivation as to what goods are produced is determined by the search for profit. Only those goods that can be produced profitably will be produced.

Since resources can substitute for one another in the production process, the pure capitalist economy must decide how to produce a commodity once society votes for it. Producers will be forced (by the discipline of the market-place) to combine resources in the cheapest way for a particular standard of quality. The cheapest way will depend on relative resource prices. Those firms that combine resources in the most efficient manner will earn the highest profits and force losses on their competitors. Competitors will be driven out of business or forced to combine resources in the same way as the profit-makers.

The what and how questions are concerned with production. The for whom question is concerned with the distribution of goods after they are produced. How is the pie divided? In pure capitalism, production and distribution are closely linked because, in the production of goods, incomes are automatically generated. People get paid according to their productivity; that is, a person's income reflects the value that society places on that person's resources. Since income largely determines one's share of the output 'pie' in pure capitalism, what people get out of the economic system is based on what they put into it. Any exception to this situation – for example, the welfare provided to those persons in society such as people with disabilities and the elderly, who are not capable of contributing to the productive process – arises only if that society, through its government, chooses to make it so.

The use of money

In Chapter 1 we showed the **circular flow** model, which gives a simple picture of how a capitalist system works. This model of a monetary economy makes it necessary to explain why we use money. In a capitalist economic system, money is used as a **medium of exchange**. In other words, we have one standard good that everyone knows everyone else is willing to accept in exchange for all other goods and services. Money also serves many other functions that are described in later chapters. If you turn back to Figure 1.7 you will see that, with money being used as a medium of exchange, households sell economic resources to businesses. In return they are paid money income in the form of wages, interest, rents and profits. They receive wages for their labour services, interest for the capital services that they provide, rents for the land that they own and profits for their entrepreneurial abilities. Firms, on the other hand, sell finished goods and services to households, for which, in exchange, they are paid money.

The circular flow diagram does offer us a context within which to understand how the three basic questions are faced up to in the capitalist model.

What goods? Households 'vote' with money for goods and services desired.

How? Competitive forces exert pressures on firms to produce goods and services as efficiently as possible. Competition regulates profits, which are the driving force for firms.

For whom? Goods and services are obtained by those with money available.

Each of these three 'answers' in the pure capitalist model raises many fascinating issues. Is it really true that households possess consumer sovereignty, or are they persuaded to buy goods and services that they do not really want as a result of successful advertising by firms? Does the capitalist model really contain such strong competitive pressures to which firms are responsive? Is the thirst for profits a desirable one? Are those who

invest in the capitalist system concerned only with short-term speculation? Does capitalism allow freedom and create prosperity but lack a basis for community values? How fair is such a system when some households have more money than others? These questions raise some *normative* questions which we cannot ignore.

Limitations in the simple circular flow model of capitalism

Of course, the model of the monetary economy given in Figure 1.7 is an extreme simplification of the workings of capitalism. For example, it has the following shortcomings:

1 Nothing is said about transactions or exchanges that occur within the business sector and within the household sector. The whole production chain between manufacturers of intermediate or component parts is ignored, as is the chain of events that goes from manufacturer to wholesaler to retailer. For example, the model ignores the many steps it takes for a motor car to get to market. It ignores the selling of car tyres and other components to the car assembly firms. The latter sell vehicles to car distributors and retailers before consumers make their decisions on the purchase of a car.

2 The model makes no mention of the economic role of government, which does, of course, tax and spend, as well as regulate. In a purely capitalist world, we would have a self-regulated economy in which the government's role would be minor anyway. In a more complete model of our actual economy, the role of government cannot be ignored.

3 The model assumes that our monetary economy is one that has no dealings with any other economic system. There is no international trade or any other transactions such as tourism. It is a **closed economy**, which is clearly not a picture of a real-life capitalist economic system or **open economy**.

4 Nothing is said about how resources and products come into existence and at what prices they are sold. That is the job of supply and demand analysis and also requires an explanation of our pricing system, which is explained in a later chapter.

5 There is nothing shown in the model relating to what happens to that part of money income of households which is not spent on goods but in fact is saved.

6 The model does not suggest how firms create and expand their production systems so as to be able to offer goods for sale to consumers.

This is a rather formidable list of simplifying assumptions of the model of capitalism. The first assumption means that we are glossing over a great deal of activity that takes place before consumers are involved in paying for goods at the retail level. But once that fact is recognized, this assumption is not a serious flaw in our picture of the working of a market economy. It simply minimizes the multiplicity of markets in the capitalist system. The next assumptions are more substantial for the validity of the capitalist model. We need to explain why there is a widely recognized role for government, and hence, how there is a rationale for a **mixed economy**. We discuss, for example, the role of government in regulating markets in Chapter 9.

We shall also certainly need to develop a picture of how prices are actually determined. This is explained in Chapter 3, and the role of prices is considered in Chapter 4. We need to portray a picture of an open economy, and this begins in Chapter 6. The implications of how the sums available to households are allocated – to consumption expenditures or savings – are analysed in Chapter 15. So in subsequent chapters we shall relax the extremely simplistic model of the capitalist system. But before then we need to show in this chapter how the UK economy exhibits features of a mixed economy. In the case of the UK economy, the three basic economic questions are ones where the answers *do* involve some role for the government. But before we look at the mixed economy we need to consider how the questions concerning the resource allocation problem are answered in a command economy.

KEY POINTS

2.3

■ Any economic system must answer the questions: (1) *what* will be produced? (2) *how* will it be produced? and (3) *for whom* will it be produced?

■ In a capitalist system, supply and demand determine the market prices at which exchanges will take place.

■ Competition is the mechanism that obliges firms to seek efficient ways of production.

■ In a capitalist economy, consumers demand what goods and services they want: those with more money than others can obtain more than those who have limited means of payment.

■ The simple closed economy circular flow model of a market economy does not identify any intermediate economic activity.

■ This model ignores both the role of government and the significance of saving and investment.

What? How? For whom? In a command economy

What goods? In the command economy the decentralized decision-making process is replaced by the collective preferences of the central planners.

How? The central planners decide on not only quantities of output but also appropriate methods of production. They have to co-ordinate all aspects of productive activity through an organized system of resource allocation.

For whom? The forces that determine the relative rewards people get from producing are set by the central planners, not by the market. Thus, market forces are not given full expression to determine wage rates.

Our discussion earlier in this chapter of the growth of the Soviet economy after 1917 showed how economic activity came to be dominated by the state. As regards the first of the three basic economic questions – what goods? – we showed how the central planners favoured the production of capital goods rather than consumer goods. Thus the answer to this question was not that consumers 'voted' in the market-place about what goods they wished to purchase, but rather that they made do with whatever the central planners made available.

We have also indicated something about the second question – how will it be produced? – in a command economy. We showed that to realize their broad objectives the Soviet central planners had to put in place an effective organizational structure. By this we mean that decisions concerning output production targets and the necessary inputs to allow those output targets to be achieved were somehow made in a centralized way. Resources of land, labour and capital had to be made available by the central planners at the right time for the planning process to work. Thus, in contrast to the capitalist system where 'unco-ordinated' competitive pressures are the mechanism whereby resources are combined, in the command economy this co-ordination problem is explicitly undertaken by a few key persons who have to make literally millions of interrelated planning decisions.

The third question – for whom? – raises the issue of how incomes are distributed. Market forces do not fully determine what people earn from productive employment as in a capitalist system, but instead the planning system imposes wage discipline upon state enterprises.

Limitations in the model of the command economy

We showed a little earlier in this chapter how the circular flow model simplifies the basic working of the capitalist system. We were able to point out how some of the limitations in the working of a market economy using money as a medium of exchange gave rise to a role of *some* government intervention. Now, in looking at the polar extreme to a market economy, we need to query whether in a centrally planned economy there is the reverse situation – is there *too much* government intervention? Can the detailed planning process actually work well in practice?

The command economy in reality

By 1990 the Soviet economy was in a state of crisis. Production was falling and the rate of increase in prices was rising. The standard of living for the typical citizen in Russia and elsewhere in Eastern Europe was, in material terms, declining. In short, the planning system was failing to work as intended. Enterprises no longer obeyed the instructions issued by their ministries or their planners. Instead, enterprises began to act autonomously, thus frustrating the planned direction of activity. As a result, enterprises could not confidently expect to receive their planned supplies of raw materials or intermediate products in order to meet their own production targets. Thus the co-ordination of manufacturing activity in Russia collapsed as individual enterprises increasingly negotiated directly with their suppliers.

But apart from these major difficulties of how the planning system came to work not as intended, other problems had become apparent. Despite the early emphasis on capital goods, as we saw earlier, it became evident at least as early as the 1980s that the Soviet economy was suffering from much under-investment. Much of the physical capital was old or even obsolete. It was inappropriate for ensuring plentiful production of domestic goods, let alone for adequately meeting the keener demands of foreign customers in world markets. Furthermore, the quality of what was produced given the capital stock compared poorly with alternatives from countries whose economic systems were characterized by market pressures. In short, consumers in Eastern Europe could not buy domestically produced goods of comparable quality to those available from abroad: what goods were available were in short supply and highly priced.

A further weakness of the command economy is that industrial production was characterized by a deteriorating environment. Air and water pollution in Poland, for example, made concern for the environment in market economies seem almost trivial by comparison. The command economy, with its advantage of state regulation, should have been more able than a market economy to monitor and prohibit environmental pollution caused by manufacturing. However, it did not achieve this.

These were the key factors that explain how the centrally planned economic systems fell into ignominy. Not surprisingly, it came to be perceived that only a market-based allocation system resting on private ownership of resources provided an answer to the basic questions facing the economies of Eastern Europe. Economic prosperity could not be secured by collective motivation but by a system in which market forces played a much greater role in allocating scarce resources. In this way, prices would act much more as signals of how resources should be reallocated.

The dramatic way in which communism *as a political institution* collapsed over a period of about two years between 1989 and 1991 is undoubtedly explained in part by the growing desire for greater political freedom and democracy. It is also true that a major factor for change in Eastern Europe has been the dependence of the latter on the international economy. Financial assistance from Western institutions underpinned the pressure for reform, and what is undeniable is that the command economy was a failing *economic system*.

Our brief review of both the inherent and actual limitations of capitalist and command economies shows that we can expect very few countries in the world to be examples of one or other polar extreme: they are to a greater or lesser extent mixed economies. We must therefore now consider how the private sector and the state relate to each other in some of the real world's mixed economic systems.

Russia – still in a crisis

While government ministers gloat, pessimists see only doom and gloom. Who is right about Russia? Following last August's financial crash, and the appointment of a do-nothing, left-leaning government, it seemed that things could only get worse, and quickly. But three cheers – or even one or two – for Yevgeny Primakov, the prime minister, and his team look decidedly premature. True, to the surprise and in some cases disappointment of outsiders, Russia's economy has not completely imploded, sunk, evaporated or disintegrated. There has been no mass starvation. Advised by its supports to print lots of money, bail out industry, ban the dollar and control prices, the government did nothing. And inaction was – relatively speaking – commendable. Meanwhile the devaluation of the rouble (now worth less than a quarter of its value against the dollar last August), and a higher oil price, have helped some parts of the economy to recover somewhat.

But it is still in dire straits. Real wages and foreign trade have plunged. Northern parts of the country had an exceptionally miserable winter; the electricity went off at times in the far east; food supplies in state-run institutions are dismally low (when a hungry soldier last month robbed a food shop in Vladimir, near Moscow, at gunpoint – stealing $5-worth of food – it hardly rated a mention in the press).

The state's own procurement policies are barely more sophisticated. Bureaucracies, such as the customs and tax services, are ever more shameless in their attempts to squeeze money from those unlucky enough to fall into their clutches. State revenues and spending alike are being siphoned off by corrupt bureaucrats. The foreign-exchange market, once open and liquid, gains a new restriction every second week. This has propped up the rouble, for now, but it has failed to stop capital flight, which is still running at $2 billion a month.

The IMF, still wrangling with Russia, faces agonizing

contortions. It is trying to preserve its credibility as a global financial policeman, even while seeming to act, reluctantly, as a foreign-policy slush fund for those who deem Russia too big and too nuclear to be faced with the consequences of its actions. If the objective were to gain a breathing-space for economic recovery, all this might be regrettable but acceptable. But whereas other troubled economies have used their financial crises as a springboard for greater openness and faster reform, Russia has turned inward and downward. Although Mr Primakov pays lip-service, for example, to the need to attract foreign direct investors, his government has in practice done nothing to help them (treating existing investors fairly, for example, might be a good start). 'There has been no tax reform, no bankruptcy law, no banking reform, no clearing out of corruption, no fundamental change in anything the Russian government does,' notes Martin Taylor, a Russian expert at Baring Asset Management.

Russia has managed to survive largely because – even in the most optimistic era before the crash – so much of its economy was immune to market forces anyway. Mr Taylor estimates that the 'virtual' (i.e., cashless, politicized and corrupt) part of Russia's economy has risen from half of the total before last August to around 70 per cent now. The higher oil price helps too – a $5 rise brings in, at least

in theory, an extra $900 million a month (although how much of that reaches Russia is another question).

But without a functioning financial system, property rights and a more rational tax regime – to name but three much-needed reforms – even Russia's best managers and companies face crippling disadvantages. Russia in 2000 will be one of a miserable clutch of countries where things look less hopeful than they did 100 years ago.

Source: *The Economist*, 24 April 1999

1 What are the indicators of Russia experiencing difficulties in its economic performance?
2 How does the passage explain the ability of Russia 'to survive' despite these difficulties?
3 To what extent do you feel that in order to confront its economic problems, Russia first needs to resolve its political situation?

KEY POINTS

2.4

■ Command economies have come to be failing economic systems. Communism and detailed state intervention have both collapsed as effective alternatives to capitalist economies.

■ Most command economies have recently experienced difficulties in co-ordinating economic activity, resulting in shortages of goods, distorted price relationships, uncompetitive use of resources and deteriorating environments.

The mixed economy: the convergence of two economic systems

Until very recently, it was not difficult to view economic systems as on a scale, with economies exhibiting a dominant strong market capitalism, such as Hong Kong, on the

one hand, through to other economies where economic activity was highly centralized, on the other. Examples of the latter included Albania, Cuba and North Korea. In between were economies with varying degrees of government intervention: the United States and the United Kingdom would be located on such a scaleless spectrum much closer to the pure market capitalist model than the other polar extreme. However, the pace of economic change and transformation has been so rapid in the last decade that any such view of the world is no longer valid. In particular, the dramatic sale of state enterprises has fundamentally altered the relationship between the state and the private sector in many former command economies. Whilst we cannot, for reasons of space, examine all the recent changes in these economic systems, we can show how dynamic is the situation of today's real-world mixed economies. We focus on the United Kingdom, and then consider the countries in transition in Eastern Europe which have been adopting a more capitalist economic system in the last decade.

We shall look briefly at these economies against the background of Table 2.1 showing the proportion of GDP accounted for by government in seventeen of the world's developed countries. The table shows a generally expanding role of the state during the twentieth century in these economies, although there is an apparent slowdown in that expansion during the early part of the 1990s.

Table 2.1

Government spending, percentage of GDP

	1870	1913	1920	1937	1960	1980	1990	1996
Austria	–	–	14.7	15.2	35.7	48.1	48.6	51.7
Belgium	–	–	–	21.8	30.3	58.6	54.8	54.3
Canada	–	–	13.3	18.6	28.6	38.8	46.0	44.7
France	12.6	17.0	27.6	29.0	34.6	46.1	49.8	54.5
Germany	10.0	14.8	25.0	42.4	32.4	47.9	45.1	49.0
Italy	11.9	11.1	22.5	24.5	30.1	41.9	53.2	52.9
Japan	8.8	8.3	14.8	25.4	17.5	32.0	31.7	36.2
Netherlands	9.1	9.0	13.5	19.0	33.7	55.2	54.0	49.9
Norway	3.7	8.3	13.7	–	29.9	37.5	53.8	45.5
Spain	–	8.3	9.3	18.4	18.8	32.2	42.0	43.3
Sweden	5.7	6.3	8.1	10.4	31.0	60.1	59.1	64.7
Switzerland	–	2.7	4.6	6.1	17.2	32.8	33.5	37.6
Britain	9.4	12.7	26.2	30.0	32.2	43.0	39.9	41.9
United States	3.9	1.8	7.0	8.6	27.0	31.8	33.3	33.3
Average	**8.3**	**9.1**	**15.4**	**18.3***	**28.5**	**43.3**	**46.1**	**47.1**
Australia	–	–	–	–	21.2	31.6	34.7	36.6
Ireland	–	–	–	–	28.0	48.9	41.2	37.6
New Zealand	–	–	–	–	26.9	38.1	41.3	47.1
Average	**–**	**–**	**–**	**–**	**25.4**	**39.5**	**39.1**	**40.4**
Total Average	**8.3**	**9.1**	**15.4**	**20.7**	**27.9**	**42.6**	**44.8**	**45.9**

* Average without Germany, Japan and Spain undergoing war or war preparations at this time.

Source: *The Economist*, 20 September 1997

Figure 2.1 depicts the broad trend of an expanding role of the state during the past century in four of the countries shown in Table 2.1.

However, we need to disaggregate the total of government spending in order to see which of the components represents a genuine claim on scarce economic resources. Figure 2.2 breaks down government spending in the same seventeen countries shown in Table 2.1 into four categories:

(i) transfer payments

(ii) government consumption expenditure, which includes what the state spends to hire labour and other inputs to supply various services such as education, health and defence

(iii) interest on the national debt (representing what the government needs to service its past borrowings when its total expenditures exceeded tax and other sources of revenue)

(iv) government spending in capital investment

Figure 2.2 makes plain how categories (i) and (ii) – transfers and consumption expenditures – are the key components of government expenditures. In particular, it is the growth of **transfer payments** which underlines the continuing development of the welfare state in the

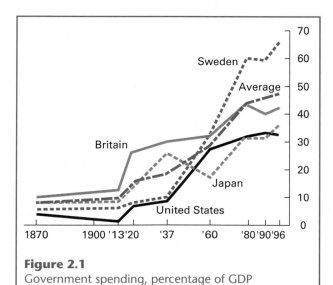

Figure 2.1
Government spending, percentage of GDP

Source: *The Economist*, 20 September 1997

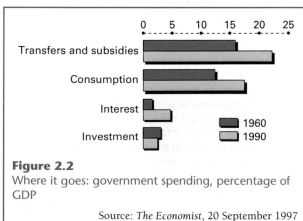

Figure 2.2
Where it goes: government spending, percentage of GDP

Source: *The Economist*, 20 September 1997

Where the jobs are

	1988	1991	1996	1998
Total workforce jobs	26 461	26 685	26 708	27 467
Private sector	20 146	20 837	21 609	22 465
of which government-supported trainees	343	353	181	115
Public sector	6 315	5 848	5 099	5 002
Public non-financial corporations	912	723	1 544	1 539
National Health Service Trusts	124	1 102	1 122	
Other	912	599	442	417
General government	5 403	5 125	3 555	3 463
Central government	2 322	2 178	931	885
HM Forces	316	297	221	210
National Health Service	1 228	1 098	84	77
Other	778	783	626	598
Local government	3 081	2 947	2 624	2 578
Education	1 504	1 416	1 191	1204
Social services	405	414	406	395
Police	194	202	207	207
Construction	125	106	76	59
Other	764	809	744	713
Community Programme	88			

Source: *Economic Trends*, June 1999

4 Which, in 1998, was the largest source of employment for those working in public non-financial corporations – education or the NHS including NHS Trusts? **A✓**

5 What was the fall in the number of employees working in general government between 1988 and 1998 (a) in absolute numbers and (b) as a percentage? **A✓**

6 In which sub-sector of local government was the percentage fall in employment between 1988 and 1998 the greatest? **A✓**

7 In which sub-sector of local government was the level of employment higher in 1998 than in 1988? **A✓**

8 Which sector of public sector employment accounted for about one quarter of all public sector employment in both 1988 and 1998? **A✓**

The private:public mix in three sectors over time (000s)

	Total	Private	Public	Total	Private	Public
Education	1 810	306	1 504	1 886	682	1 204
Health, social work and other services to the public	2 461	828	1 633	2 770	1 176	1 594
Production, construction, transport and utilities	7 698	6 661	1 037	6 849	6 373	476

Source: *Economic Trends*, June 1999

9 What proportion of all those in education were in the public sector in (a) 1988 and (b) 1998? **A✓**

10 What was the percentage increase in the number of private sector jobs in the health, social work and other services sector between 1988 and 1998? **A✓**

11 How would you account for the 54 per cent reduction in the number of public sector jobs within the production, construction, transport and utilities industries between 1988 and 1998? **A✓**

Political views

The balance of the public sector–private sector mixture in the United Kingdom is one that has varied over time because of the differing philosophies of the main political parties towards state intervention. The desirability of less or more public ownership of industry has long been at the heart of the political divide between the Labour and Conservative parties. The Labour Party has generally aspired to an extension of the public sector in the pursuit of socialist ideals. The Conservative Party has broadly opposed any such extension, and indeed has tried to reduce the influence of the state.

Nationalization

The fundamental extension of the public sector in the United Kingdom took place within the space of five years after the end of the Second World War in 1945. Mr Attlee's newly elected Labour government proceeded to take into full public ownership the Bank of England, the coalmines, railways, steel, civil aviation, broadcasting, gas and electricity. Waterways and some road transport also became state owned. The overwhelming reasons for this remarkable interventionist activity were political. The party's commitment to managing the capitalist system and to injecting a socialist philosophy was paramount. Clause Four of the Labour Party's constitution called for 'the public ownership of the means of production, distribution, and exchange'. In practice the party, both in 1945–51 and since, was content to take over what were regarded as 'the commanding heights' of the economy. From the list of new state industries above, it can be seen that these commanding heights included at their core the fuel, power and transport industries. The influence these state-owned industries could have over the remainder of the economy in private hands should be obvious enough. The supporters of **nationalization** in the early 1950s argued that only the co-ordination resulting from unified (geographical) ownership could produce really efficient industries as in the case of the railways. However, it was not too clear whether it was intended that these state-owned industries should be run on a commercial basis: the 'social service' argument was never far in the background. In other words, was the profitability of railways secondary in importance to the availability of rail services, especially in rural areas?

Earlier in this chapter we pointed out that in the capitalist model competition between rival suppliers results in pressures to increase efficiency. But it has long been argued that in some industries, by their very nature, only one supplier can exist. This argument holds that costs per unit of output are lowest when just one single firm supplies, say, electricity, gas or water to all consumers within a locality. For example, if there is more than one supplier of electricity, then duplication in cable systems and generating capacity, the argument runs, results in a waste of scarce economic resources. In these special cases competitive forces are held to be inappropriate as a monopoly

supplier minimizes resource use. We shall examine these arguments closely in Chapter 27, but for the moment we just need to be aware of how the **natural monopoly** argument has been one part of the case for an increase in state intervention in many economies, and not just in the United Kingdom.

In the case of these 'natural monopolies', nationalization was regarded by the Labour government as essential in order to prevent abuse of the consumer. If economic factors pointed to a monopoly situation, then it should be publicly rather than privately owned.

From 1979, the Conservative government transformed the whole debate about state ownership of such industries by its programme of privatization, deregulation and contracting-out. We discuss these issues in Chapter 27, but for the moment we refer to the transfer of assets from the public sector to the private sector. Clearly, a programme of such asset sales can have fundamental implications for the size of the public sector and its importance in the economy. Whilst privatization is not unique to the UK economy, having been adopted by many countries around the world (and by governments of quite different political leanings), it is a phenomenon that has had a crucial impact on the public sector–private sector interface.

The private sector in the United Kingdom

In the previous section it was pointed out that the line drawn between the public and private sectors is one at the centre of political debate. We have also indicated the precise difficulty of defining what constitutes the public sector.

At first sight the private sector element in the mixed economy seems to be free of definitional difficulties. Surely we mean firms owned and controlled by individuals independently of the state? In fact there is a rich variety in the forms of private enterprise in an economy such as the United Kingdom. We have at one end of this spectrum owner-managed businesses, such as corner shops and partnerships. (We formally define types of businesses in the United Kingdom in Chapter 20.) At the other end of the spectrum are giant companies like ICI and Shell, with operations in more than just one country (multinationals). Some giant companies like BP have shares owned by the government, a fact that illustrates the blurred state–private sector divide! There are many distinctive types of institutions, having quite varied objectives and constraints on their operations. These institutions include building societies, insurance companies and the co-operative movement. In their various ways they differ from the imagined nineteenth-century concept of the capitalist enterprise somewhat aloof from the legislative powers of government. Thus today the private sector contains a very mixed group of institutions, and they have been increasingly affected by the predisposition of post-war governments to constrain their behaviour through legislation.

Post-war UK governments have legislated freely on many aspects of industry and trade. They have concerned themselves with the location and physical growth of firms through planning controls and regional policies. Governments have shown increasing concern with the quality and condition of goods and services produced (consumer protection measures). The terms and nature of employment practices – wages and safety aspects – have given rise to much legislation. In short, the varied institutions within the private sector are now much more constrained and answerable than was the case with the nineteenth-century capitalist firm. Some parts of the private sector are very dependent on central and local government buying their goods and services – for example, publishers of school books and firms making electrical-generating equipment. Similarly, government support for research through contracts with companies making technologically advanced goods such as computers and military hardware illustrates how employment in private industry can be sensitive to state patronage.

Modern governments thus affect private enterprise even with small shifts in public expenditure. This shows how truly mixed the character of economic activity in the UK economy now is.

KEY POINTS

2.5

■ Public expenditure by all forms of government in the United States and United Kingdom exaggerates the influence of the state because the total figure includes spending that does not involve any claims on economic resources. Transfer payments from one section of society to another by government should not be included in a list of public expenditure programmes intended to indicate the extent of the state's interference in a pure market economy.

■ In the United Kingdom there has been prolonged debate on the desirability of public ownership or nationalization of the energy and transport sectors of the economy on political and economic grounds. However, the privatization of these sectors in the period 1980–97 has not been reversed by the Labour government since 1997.

■ The problem of natural monopolies – where economic activity tends to be undertaken by a single producer – can be approached by nationalization or public regulatory supervision.

The countries in transition in Eastern Europe

Earlier in this chapter we discussed how the command economies in Eastern Europe abruptly collapsed as effective economic systems. We now consider the challenges and difficulties that these countries faced in adopting the capitalist process of resource allocation. In part the economic difficulties have been over-shadowed by the political stresses accompanying the demise of the communist bloc. The Soviet Union disintegrated in 1991, giving rise to 15 new states. In the same year Yugoslavia also disintegrated and war broke out between Croatia and Bosnia until 1995. In 1993 Czechoslovakia split – peacefully – into two states, the Czech Republic and the Slovak Republic.

However, in terms of the economic aspects of embracing capitalism, these and other countries in Eastern Europe faced formidable challenges. As we indicated at the outset of this chapter, capitalism relies on a system of property rights supported by a legal system capable of protecting an individual's interests. In addition to the establishment of property rights, the introduction of a market-based economy needs to be underpinned by a financial system which can bring about the buying and selling of property and other assets. Legally binding contracts can allow economic agents to engage in economic activity with confidence. Thus a market-based economy assumes that there is an institutional infrastructure encompassing clearly defined rights and obligations within which lots of market participants can pursue individual self-interest in the manner noted by Adam Smith in the *Wealth of Nations*. We noted that the process of privatization in the United Kingdom after 1980 marked a sharp change in direction in the role of the state, even though the preconditions for this process were already in place. It should not be too hard, therefore, to realize how much more significant was the process of selling-off state enterprises in Eastern Europe in the 1990s when neither private firms were clearly established, nor were the legal and financial frameworks in place to help accommodate the proposed enhanced role of such firms in place of the hitherto dominant state-run enterprises. It was no surprise that in these circumstances, together with liberalization of trading links with other countries, Eastern Europe faced an enormous problem of adjustment. The exposure to competition from sources of supply at relatively low world prices meant that much of economic production in Eastern Europe was exposed as being distinctly uncompetitive. All these countries experienced an initial drop in the level of economic activity accompanied by rising prices (explained by the prevalence of shortages of food and other basic consumer goods). Figure 2.5 shows the generally uncomfortable experience of countries in Eastern Europe in making the break from their communist past. However, Table 2.4 also shows some contrasts between these countries.

The first group of twelve countries belonging to the Commonwealth of Independent States (CIS) has experienced a particularly abrupt transition to market forces. These twelve countries share a common political past, all

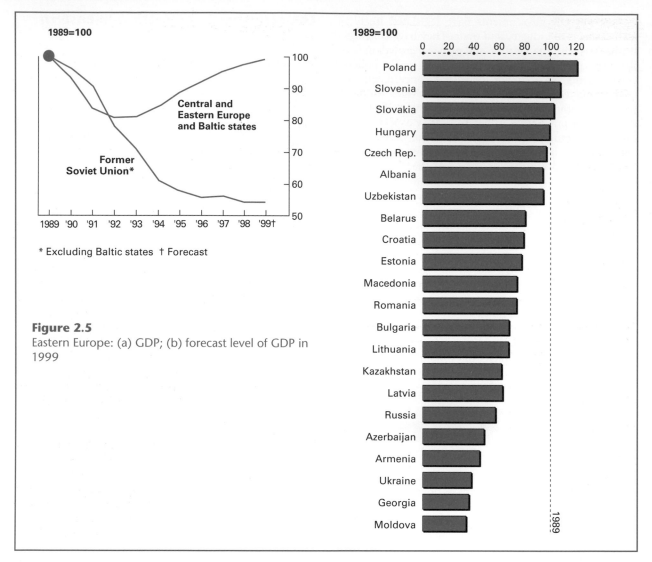

Figure 2.5
Eastern Europe: (a) GDP; (b) forecast level of GDP in 1999

of them being republics of the former USSR after the 1917 October Revolution that brought communism into existence. In all these countries, the centrally planned system left virtually no trace of markets in existence: in short, communism as an ideology was well entrenched. In contrast, the ten states of the so-called CEE – Central and Eastern Europe – had communism imposed upon them later than in the CIS – in the 1940s – and thus had a broadly based market system until the outbreak of the Second World War. Moreover, countries like the three Baltic states (Latvia, Lithuania and Estonia) have a more obvious geographical leaning to Western Europe rather than feeling part of an eastern-inclined deference to a world centred on Moscow. Table 2.4 shows that the CIS countries experienced sharp inflationary pressures in the early 1990s, in part explained by the process of excessive monetary growth arising out of lending to loss-making state enterprises by governments anxious to help avert even high levels of unemployment.

The difficult early process of transition was thus one where newly independent states encountered difficult macroeconomic conditions. Stricter monetary policies had to be introduced to help stabilize the economy. Alongside the process of price and trade liberalization, Eastern European countries restructured their economies by means of privatization. Whereas in the UK former state-owned assets were literally sold off to the highest bidder, in Eastern Europe, and Russia in particular, an ostensibly simpler system was used whereby vouchers were issued free (or nearly free) to the population. This was despite the fact that the ordinary person in Russia had no personal sympathy with this aspect of a property-owning democracy. Given the loss of jobs and steep price increases, it is not surprising that the typical Russian inhabitant can as yet still see little apparent benefit from the demise of communism. It has been indeed a painful, even brutal, adjustment. Any hopes that the influx of Western capital and technology might help transform the situation have been hard to realize. Potential Western sources of help have been discouraged by unwelcome experiences arising from a continuing excessive bureaucracy, corruption and the apparent power of the Mafia.

Table 2.4

Growth rates and inflation in Eastern Europe since 1990 (%)

CIS countries	Average real GNP per capita growth 1990–6 (%)	Annual average inflation rate 1990–6 (%)
Armenia	15.0	896.6
Azerbaijan	–18.7	589.9
Belarus	–8.6	714.9
Georgia	–19.3	2279.3
Kazakhstan	–10.3	604.9
Kyrgyz Republic	–12.7	256.2
Moldova	–16.8	307.7
Russia	–9.2	394.0
Tajikistan	–18.5	394.3
Turkmenistan	–13.1	1074.2
Ukraine	–13.5	800.5
Uzbekistan	–5.6	546.5

CEE countries	Average real GNP per capita growth 1990–6 (%)	Annual average inflation rate 1990–6 (%)
Bulgaria	–1.8	80.3
Czech Republic	0.9	17.7
Estonia	–4.9	116.7
Hungary	–0.6	22.5
Latvia	–10.1	110.6
Lithuania	–6.0	179.3
Poland	3.3	32.4
Romania	0.1	132.7
Slovak Republic	–1.2	14.2
Slovenia	4.4	39.2

Source: 1998 World Bank Atlas

KEY POINTS

2.6

■ Since 1990 the process of transition to a market economy in Eastern Europe has been a painful one. GDP has fallen in most of the newly independent states of the former Soviet Union.

■ The transition has involved these states liberalizing trade and prices and privatizing former state-owned undertakings. There has been a need to introduce a framework of practices and institutions to enable a property-owning democracy to become established.

The global economy

We conclude this review of how economic systems in the late twentieth century have been adjusting the mixture of private enterprise and government direction of economic activity with a brief overview of the so-called **globalization** of the world's industries and markets. As we shall see in later chapters – particularly in Chapters 6 and 30 – this globalization has been driven both by the rapid growth of international trade and capital flows by multinational (or transnational) corporations (MNCs or TNCs). Globalization is a word that has been defined by the European Commission as 'the process by which markets and production in different countries are becoming increasingly interdependent due to the dynamics of trade in goods and services and flows of capital and technology. It is not a new phenomenon but the continuation of developments that have been in train for some considerable time'. The globalization process is indeed not new because, relative to the level of world output, international investment capital flows were at a higher level in the years before the First World War until the early 1990s. What is new about the world's economies in the 1990s has been the rapid process of economic integration of markets. After the Second World War ended, the world was characterized by well over a hundred national markets. Even though MNCs began to re-engage in making overseas capital investments, their foreign subsidiaries were typically operated independently of one another. However, in the last twenty years or so, technological change, together with the cataclysmic political collapse of the communist bloc noted earlier in this chapter and the rapid growth of some developing countries (notably the so-called Asian 'tigers'), have brought about a much closer integration of most of the world's economies. Improvements in transport and communications have made it far easier to sell goods and services around the world. The outcome of what one might call the revolution in electronics is that money and technology enable investors in, say, Hong Kong to buy and sell corporations in the United States. It means that textiles can be made in China and partly in Mauritius and then sold in Brazil.

These examples refer to financial investors and companies. For consumers the process of globalization offers the possibility of a greater choice of goods and services at lower prices. However, as employees, consumers may become threatened by such low-cost imports. (We shall discuss this issue in Chapter 6.) Not surprisingly, therefore, the increase in competitive pressures is a political issue as evidenced by the protests surrounding the November 1999 meeting of the World Trade Organization in Seattle, which duly received much coverage by the world's media. Indeed, in many of the advanced countries globalization is widely perceived as harming the interests of workers, and especially of unskilled workers. Moreover, governments throughout the world protest when MNCs announce the closure or scaling-back of production in particular countries, sometimes only a few years after such plants have been opened with generous government financial assistance. Globalization is, then, a tendentious topic which we cannot pursue further here. For the present, all we seek is to underline the forces of integration of economic systems in the late twentieth century.

Case Study

Globalization – for good or ill?

Governments need to wise up to the information age, not in terms of having the right kind of technology policy or enthusing about the Internet in speeches, but in the more fundamental sense of recognizing that less than full disclosure of information is an economic inefficiency as much as a matter of democracy. This is the deepest lesson of the Asian crisis. There is a great appetite to draw lessons from Asia, to try to avoid repeats. The responses are tending to fall into two camps. One, the backlash camp, has concluded that globalization is a Bad Thing, and needs to be tamed and resisted. It has a lunatic fringe but its more sensible proposals include introducing restrictions on inflows of foreign 'hot money'.

The opposite point of view insists all is for the best in the globalizing world economy, reckons the crisis reflects inadequate liberalization. Its proponents will admit that globalization causes upheavals and problems about the distribution of gains. A new report from the OECD this week, 'Open markets matter', from which the chart is taken, spells out the links between free trade, free investment and economic prosperity. The moral drawn by this camp is that whatever the turmoil caused by the crisis, it is essential to press ahead with more and more deregulation and globalization.

Some more considered assessments of the Asian crisis and its lessons for globalization are starting to filter through. For the backlash camp ignores the huge economic gains that the post-war process of globalization has delivered, while the other camp overlooks the justified political concerns about the costs imposed by the way that process is occurring. A recent paper by Harvard economics professor Dani Rodrik attempts to explain why some developing countries have enjoyed massive gains in per capita living standards while others have not. So, despite the past year's upheavals, Asia has fared well while Latin America has not. He finds the key is not simply the degree of openness to the world economy. Rather, it is how well different countries handle the turbulence that inevitably results from setting sail on the choppy seas of globalization.

'How well' turns out to depend on institutional factors such as the degree of ethnic division within a country, the extent of military repression, the quality of the civil service and so on. These influences – whose measurement is necessarily a bit rough and ready – explain more of the difference in growth than do conventional measures such as exports as a share of GDP. Professor Rodrik concludes: 'The main message that I take from the kind of evidence presented here is that it is not whether you globalize that matters, it is how you globalize. The world market is a

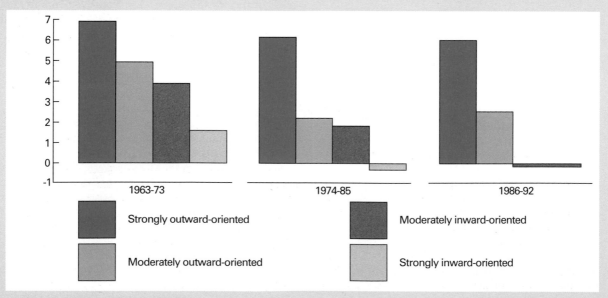

Trade orientation and growth* (%)
* GDP per capita

source of disruption and upheaval as much as it is an opportunity for profit and economic growth.'

   Taking part in globalization therefore demands a programme of institutional reform, which would include – on top of the IMF recipe of low government budget deficits, an anti-inflation strategy and privatization – an improvement in the quality of the government apparatus. It would require increased democratization in place of the typical technocratic approach to economic management in emerging markets. And it would need an improved social safety net so that the damage caused by crises like the present one in Asia does not fall entirely on the very poorest.

Source: *The Independent*, 1 May 1998

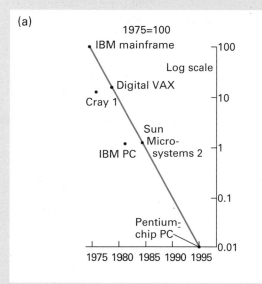

(a) Computers: cost of information processing ($ per instruction per second)

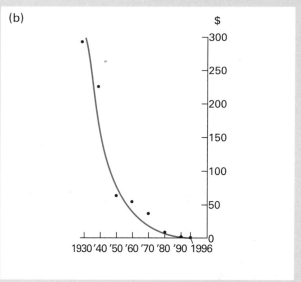

(b) Telephone calls: cost of a three-minute call from New York to London, 1996

Source: *The Economist*, 18 October 1997

1 With reference to the charts, explain how the costs of computing and communication have changed to facilitate globalization.

2 Why is there a debate over the effects of globalization?

3 How would you interpret the relationship between the extent of trade orientation and the rate of economic growth as shown in the first chart?

4 Explain what you think Professor Dani Rodrik means by his conclusions that 'it is not whether you globalize that matters, it is how you globalize'.

5 Explain what is meant by 'improved social safety net' in the passage.

Case Study

The last emperor

'Even when I die', Deng Xiaoping said some years ago, 'they will not call me a great Marxist.' Mr Deng, who never appeared to doubt the Communist Party or his mandate to lead it, was proud to have banished revolutionary notions of class struggle and mass mobilization from a China that had been spiritually shattered and physically impoverished by Mao Zedong's often disastrous rule. 'Not to engage in debates: this was an invention of mine', declared Mr Deng, 'in order to get more

things done.' What was done, however much the accuracy of China's statistics may be in dispute, was a revolution in wealth creation on a scale unparalleled in modern history. Since late 1978, when the Communist Party accepted Mr Deng's insistence that economic growth had to take precedence over class struggle, some 150 million to 200 million people, equivalent to half the population of Western Europe, have worked their way out of absolute poverty.

   When Mr Deng came to power, China wallowed in autarkic stagnation. Today, it attracts more foreign investment than any other developing country. International trade has boomed. Markets, not bureaucracies, set the prices for more than nine-tenths of all finished goods. A private sector has sprung up from nowhere. So, too, has a sector of the economy that falls under the loose heading of 'township and village enterprises' – collectives with a vaguely defined ownership that is neither private nor public. Although the state-owned sector has grown in absolute size, it has shrunk in relative terms. For the first time in four decades, it now accounts for less than half of industrial output.

Yet it took a long time for China to wake. Angus Maddison, an economic historian, estimates in a new paper that between 1820 and 1952, when world economic output rose eightfold, China's product per head actually shrank. Its share of world GDP fell from one-third to one-twentieth. China's income per head fell from the world average to a quarter of it. This historic perspective is important; it is the humiliation of the past that even today drives China's quest for rapid growth.

Since Den Xiaoping set China on the path of liberalization in 1978, its GDP has grown, on average, by 9 per cent a year. Income per head has grown by 6 per cent a year, faster in that period than any other Asian country except South Korea. China's GDP per head has risen from a quarter to half the world average. And its share of world GDP has doubled, to 10 per cent. China, by some measures, is now the world's second-biggest economy after the United States.

What matters, however, is how long this advance can continue. Mr Maddison estimates that even if China's GDP growth slowed to 5.5 per cent a year – a realistic goal given higher rates of growth in Japan, Taiwan and South Korea at comparable stages of their development – China would match America's level of GDP by 2015. Its economy would then account for 17 per cent of the world total, while income per head would match the world average. Since a China more integrated into the world economy would presumably be a country more at ease with itself and with its neighbours, the prospect of such an outcome should be welcomed.

At the third plenum of the 11th Central Committee in late 1978, when Mr Deng's reformists completed their take-over of party policy-making, no mention was made of markets, of economic laws, or even of the peasant economy (which was where the initial reforms, pioneered in Sichuan province, were having their first dramatic effects). Indeed, no law was ever promulgated enshrining the 'household responsibility' system that freed farmers from the Maoist communes and brigades. The new order seemed to take root in a largely improvised way; the government's principal contribution was not to trample down individual enterprise where and when it occurred. Such was to be the typical, often fortuitous, pattern with

many of the big reforms of the Mr Deng era. Only in 1992 did the Communists declare a market economy – albeit a 'socialist market' one – as their formal goal.

One of the fixed pillars of certainty in the shifting structure of Deng's pragmatism was that there need be no connection between economic reform and political reform; or rather, that the dictatorship of the proletariat, through the means of the Communist Party, was the single social reform that modern China had needed. He denied, or at least refused to entertain, the notion that prosperity might encourage other aspirations in China's citizens – greater individual freedom, say, or more accountability of government, or anything, for that matter, that might be considered a necessary ingredient of a civil society. Mr Deng's allegiance to Communist ideology may have been expedient; his allegiance to the party's monopoly on power was absolute.

The frustrations that erupted in 1989, and culminated in the Tiananmen Square massacre, were partly reactive – against economic disadvantage, party privilege and corruption. But they were also an explicit call for new things: freedom, equity and government accountability. None of these problems has been solved. Corruption is worse. The more authoritarian mood in party and government is presumably in part a response to fears that resentment at a self-enriching and self-perpetuating ruling class may again be building.

Sources: Adapted from *The Economist*, 22 February 1997
and 24 October 1998

1 How does the case study illustrate the fact that China has been transformed from an inward-looking country within twenty years into a dynamic, outward-looking market economy?
2 To what extent was this process of transformation pragmatic rather than explicitly programmed in advance?
3 How does the case study indicate the incomplete workings of capitalism in China?
4 Some supporters of capitalism emphasize its relevance in a political context of a democratic system. How would you judge China in respect of the state of political freedom?
5 What evidence might you argue would be relevant for you to be convinced that economic growth has had a tangible impact on living standards for the average family in China?
6 What evidence would you need in order to establish whether China was successfully using its labour resources?
7 What are the implications of continuing rapid economic growth for China's participation in international trade?

Exam Preparation

Multiple choice questions

1 A mixed economy may be defined as one in which resources are

A allocated to meet the needs of both consumers and producers

B used partly for the production of consumer goods and partly for the production of capital goods

C allocated partly by market forces and partly by the state

D used for the production of both goods and services

E allocated by the spending decisions of consumers

2 Using the data in the table, which of the following statements is true for the period shown?

A each country experienced a net outflow of resources

B the net outflow of resources diminished in Hungary

C the former Soviet Union had the lowest standard of living

D taking the transitional economies as a whole, there was a net outflow of resources

E these countries all had Balance of Payments problems

Net transfer of resources to transitional market economies (billion US$)

	1990	**1991**	**1992**
Bulgaria	0.5	0.1	–0.5
Czechoslovakia	0.6	–0.4	–0.2
Hungary	–0.7	–0.8	–0.8
Poland	–3.8	–0.5	–3.0
Romania	1.7	1.3	0.4
Former Soviet Union	–6.4	–3.8	n/a
Total	**–8.1**	**–4.1**	**–4.1**

Essay questions

1 (a) Outline the main features of command economies such as those which used to exist in Eastern Europe before 1989. (20 marks)

(b) What problems caused many of these economies to place greater emphasis on market forces as a means of allocating resources? (40 marks)

(c) How might this greater reliance on market forces have improved the performance of these economies? (40 marks)

2 'During 1992 the rate of inflation in Russia was 1000 per cent, investment declined, unemployment rose and living standards fell. This proves that the experiment with the market system has failed.' To what extent do you agree with this view?

3 (a) Outline the characteristics of a mixed economy. (20 marks)

(b) How do governments try to overcome the problems which would exist in a totally free market economy? (50 marks)

(c) How might such government intervention actually cause a reduction in economic welfare? (30 marks)

4 Consider the view that left to itself the market mechanism is incapable of allocating scarce resources in an efficient manner.

5 (a) Outline the main characteristics of a free market economy. (20 marks)

(b) What are the main advantages of market forces as a means of allocating resources? (30 marks)

(c) Examine the problems which might arise if health care and education were provided solely by market forces. (50 marks)

6 In a number of countries there has been a significant shift from state economic dominance to private enterprise.

(a) Explain the changes which might occur in an economy where this has happened. (10 marks)

(b) How far is this policy equally appropriate for economies at different stages of development? (15 marks)

3

Demand and supply

The cornerstone of economic analysis is the simple demand and supply model. An understanding of what demand is, what supply is, and the relationship between the two is essential for understanding virtually all economics. Demand and supply are two ways of categorizing the influences on the price of goods that you buy. This chapter is an introduction to the study of demand and supply. We look first at demand, then at supply, and then put them together.

Theory of demand

The **theory of demand** can be stated succinctly as follows:

> At higher prices, a lower quantity will be demanded than at lower prices, other things being equal.

Or, looked at another way:

> At lower prices, a higher quantity will be demanded than at higher prices, other things being equal.

The theory of demand, then, tells us that the quantity demanded of any commodity is inversely related to that commodity's price, other things being equal. Thus, the theory of demand states that the price and the quantity demanded move in opposite directions. Price goes up, quantity demanded goes down; price goes down, quantity demanded goes up.

Other things being equal

Notice that, in stating the theory of demand, there is the phrase *other things being equal.** In other words, 'other things are held constant'. Price is not the only thing that affects purchases. There are many others, which we will look at in detail later. One, for example, is income. If, while the price of a good is changing, income is also changing, then we would not know whether the change in the quantity demanded was due to a change in the price or to a change in income. Therefore, we hold income constant, as well as any other factor that might affect the quantity of the product demanded.

Since we are holding all other things equal, or constant, this obviously means that we are holding the prices of all other goods constant when we state the theory of demand. Implicitly, therefore, we are looking at the price change of the good under study relative to all other prices. An understanding of the concept of relative prices is important in the study of economics.

LEARNING OUTCOMES

On completing this chapter you should understand:

■ The theory of demand and the determinants of demand

■ The theory of supply and the determinants of supply

■ The meaning of market-clearing prices and quantities

■ How changes in demand and supply result in changes in market-clearing prices and quantities

---

* This is the **ceteris paribus** assumption, where *ceteris paribus* means other things being equal or held constant.

Relative prices

The **relative price** of any item is its price compared with the price of other goods, or relative to a (weighted) average of all other prices in the economy. The prices that you and I pay in sterling for any good or service at any point in time are called **absolute**, or nominal, prices. Consumer-buying decisions, however, depend on relative, not absolute, prices. Someone may contend that the theory of demand clearly does not hold because, say, the price of CDs went up last year by 5 per cent but the quantity demanded did not go down at all. Assuming that other things in the economy did not change, this indeed may have been a possible refutation of the theory of demand, except for the fact that last year's prices *in general* may have gone up by as much as or more than 5 per cent. It is the price of CDs relative to all other prices that is important for determining the relationship between price and quantity demanded.

Two reasons why we observe the theory of demand

There are two fundamental reasons why the quantity demanded of a good is inversely related to its price, other things being equal.

Substitution effect

Let us assume now that there are several goods, not exactly the same, or perhaps even very different from one another, but all serving basically the same purpose. If the price of one particular good falls, we will most likely substitute in favour of the lower-priced good and against the other similar goods we might have been purchasing. Conversely, if the price of that good rises relative to the price of the other similar goods, we will substitute in favour of them and not buy as much of the higher-priced good. Consider an example. The prices of pizzas, hamburgers and hot dogs are all about the same. Each of us buys a certain amount (or none) of each of these three substitutable fast foods. What if the price of pizzas increases considerably, while the prices of hamburgers and hot dogs do not? What will we do? We will buy more hamburgers and hot dogs and fewer pizzas, since they are relatively more expensive, while hot dogs and hamburgers are now relatively cheaper. In effect, we will be substituting hamburgers and hot dogs for pizzas because of the relatively higher price of pizzas. Thus, you can see how the **substitution effect** affects the quantity demanded of a particular good.

Real income effect

If the price of something that you buy goes up while your money income and other prices stay the same, then your ability to purchase goods in general goes down. That is, your effective purchasing power is reduced even though your money income has stayed the same. If you purchase ten pizzas a week at £1 apiece, your total outlay for pizzas is £10. If the price went up by 50p, you would have to spend £15 in order to purchase ten pizzas. If your money income and the prices of other goods remained the same, it would be impossible for you, at £1.50 a pizza, to purchase ten pizzas a week (as you used to do at the lower price) and still purchase the same quantity of all other goods and services that you were purchasing. You are poorer, and hence it is likely that you will buy less of a number of things, including the good whose price rose. The converse will also be true. When the price of one good that you are purchasing goes down without any other prices changing and without your money income changing, you will feel richer and undoubtedly will purchase a bit more of a number of goods, including the lower-priced good.

In general, the **real income effect** is usually quite small. After all, unless we consider broad categories such as housing or food, a change in the price of one particular item that we purchase will have a relatively small effect on our total purchasing power (given a limited income). Thus, we expect that the substitution effect is usually more important in causing us to purchase more of goods that have become cheaper and less of goods that have become more expensive.

KEY POINTS

3.1

- There is an inverse relationship between the quantity demanded of a good and its price, other things being equal.

- We hold constant other determinants of quantity demanded, such as income.

- The theory of demand holds because when the price of a good goes down (a) we substitute in favour of it and (b) we are now richer and buy more of everything, including the good.

- The substitution effect is the change in quantity demanded resulting from a price change of a good relative to the prices of other goods.

- The real income effect is the change in quantity demanded resulting from a price change that gives the consumer more (or less) real income when money income is unchanged.

The demand schedule

Let us take a hypothetical demand situation to see how the inverse relationship between the price and the quantity demanded looks. What we will do is consider the quantity of wheat demanded per year. Without stating the time dimension, we could not make any sense out of this demand relationship because the numbers would be different if we were talking about the quantity demanded per month or the quantity demanded per decade.

In Table 3.1 we show the price per constant-quality tonne of wheat. The words 'constant quality' take care of the problem of varying qualities of wheat that could be sold every year. By taking an average quality, at an average price of wheat, we recognize differences in the qualities of wheat purchased.

We see in Table 3.1 that, if the price were £10 per tonne, 10 million tonnes would be bought each year; but if the price were £50 per tonne, only 2 million tonnes would be bought each year. This reflects the theory of demand. Table 3.1 is also called a **demand schedule** because it gives a schedule of alternative quantities per year at different possible prices. '

The data in Table 3.1 are shown as a demand curve in Figure 3.1 where the price per constant-quality tonne is plotted on the vertical axis and the quantity measured in constant-quality tonnes per year is plotted on the horizontal axis. All we have to do is take combinations A, B, C, D and E from Table 3.1 and plot the points in Figure 3.1. Now we connect the points and we have a **demand curve**.* It is downward sloping (from left to right) to indicate the inverse relationship between the price of wheat and the quantity demanded per year.

Table 3.1

The demand schedule for wheat
Column 3 shows combinations of price (column 1) and quantity demanded (column 2). These indicate that as the price rises the quantity demanded per year falls.

1 Price per tonne of constant-quality wheat	2 Quantity of wheat demanded (millions of constant-quality tonnes per year)	3 Combination
£50	2	A
£40	4	B
£30	6	C
£20	8	D
£10	10	E

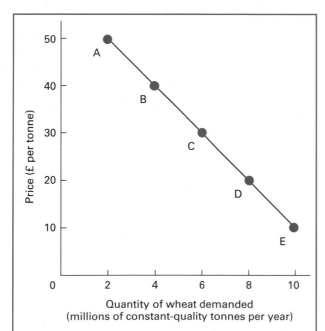

Figure 3.1
The demand curve for wheat
When we connect the combinations given in Table 3.1, we obtain a graphic representation of a demand schedule. It is downward sloping to show the inverse relationship between quantity demanded and price.

Determinants of demand

The demand curve in Figure 3.1 is drawn with other things held constant, that is, with all of the other non-price factors that determine demand held constant. There are many such determinants. The major non-price determinants are (1) income, (2) tastes and preferences, (3) the prices of related goods, (4) changes in expectations of future relative prices and (5) the population (that is, market size). Other non-price determinants of demand are, for example, the season of the year for some goods and the cost of financing the purchase of some very expensive consumer items.

Changes in demand

If one of the above five determinants of demand changes, then the entire demand curve shifts, either to the right or the left. Consider, for example, how we might represent a dramatic increase in the quantity of wheat demanded at all prices because of a medical discovery that, say, bread consumption increased life expectancy! The demand curve would shift outwards, or to the right, to represent an increase in demand. That is, there will now be an increase in the quantity demanded at each and every possible price. We show this in Figure 3.2. The demand curve has shifted from DD to D'D'. Take any price, say £30. Originally, before the great medical discovery, the quantity demanded at £30 was 6 million tonnes per year. Thus, we have witnessed a shift in the demand for wheat. We could use a

---

* Even though we call them curves for the purpose of exposition, we only draw straight lines. In many real-world situations, demand and supply 'curves' will in fact be lines that do curve. In order to connect the points in Figure 3.1 with a smooth line, we assume that, for all prices in between the ones shown, the quantities demanded will be found along that line.

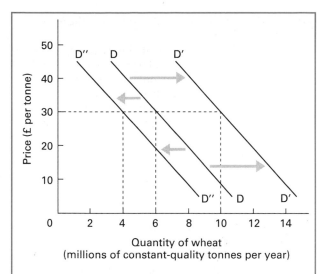

Figure 3.2
A shift in the demand curve
If only the price of wheat changes, we move to a different point (co-ordinate) along a given demand curve. However, if some factor other than price changes, the entire demand curve moves from DD. A medical discovery showing that bread consumption led to a greater life expectancy would mean that at all prices a larger quantity would be demanded than before (shift to D′D′). If a medical discovery indicated shorter life because of bread consumption, the demand curve would shift inwards to D″D″.

similar analysis when discussing a shift inwards, or to the left, of the demand curve for wheat. This might happen, for example, in the case of a medical discovery that bread consumption actually decreased life expectancy. The demand curve would shift to D″D″; quantity demanded would now be less at each and every possible price.

Non-price determinants of demand

We mentioned that there are five major non-price determinants of demand.

Income

For most goods, an increased income will lead to an increase in demand. The phrase 'increase in demand' always refers to a comparison between two different demand curves. Thus, an increase in income for most goods will lead to a rightward shift in the position of the demand curve, from, say, DD to D′D′ in Figure 3.2. You can avoid confusion about shifts in curves by always relating an increase in demand to a rightward shift in the demand curve and a decrease in demand to a leftward shift in the demand curve. Goods for which the demand increases when income increases are called **normal goods**. Most goods are 'normal' in this sense. There are some goods for which demand decreases as income increases. These are called **inferior goods**. Thus demand for black-and-white

television sets has fallen as more people have felt able to buy colour television sets. Margarine used to be another example since at low incomes it was consumed instead of butter. In the case of inferior goods there is a real income effect which is negative. In some exceptional situations this negative real income effect is very marked.

It was Sir Robert Giffen, an economist in the nineteenth century, who pointed out the possibility of some goods (so-called *Giffen goods*) being a rather special kind of inferior good. Giffen claimed that a rise in the price of bread caused such a severe fall in the real income of the very poor that they ate more bread. Consumption of meat and other food which supplemented the diet based on bread was reduced. Bread was still the cheapest food supply but the poor felt unable to spend as much money as before on other foods to augment their diet. The reverse situation also applied. When the price of bread fell, the real income effect permitted a more varied diet again.

It should be noted that the terms normal and inferior are merely part of the economist's terminology; no value-judgements are associated with them.

Tastes and preferences

A change in consumer tastes in favour of a good can shift its demand curve outwards to the right. When skateboards became the rage, the demand curve for them shifted to the right; when the rage died out, the demand curve shifted inwards to the left. Fashion changes can be related to the time of year. Indeed, adverse weather conditions can have a profound impact on consumer spending. June 1998 was the fourth wettest of the twentieth century, with double the average rainfall in England and Wales. Several companies in clothing, garden equipment and food processing issued profit warnings as sales failed to meet expectations. An additional factor depressing the level of consumer spending in the summer of 1998 was the football World Cup. The result of millions of people watching matches on television was that retailers were left with racks of unsold goods.

Unusually wet weather conditions are a good example of seasonal changes in consumer tastes. Sometimes tastes change suddenly for more unexpected reasons. An example here is the dramatic fall in beef consumption in March 1996 when the UK government announced there was a link between BSE and eating beef. Six months later in 1996 there was an outbreak of E. coli 157, a life-threatening food bug, in meat supplied by a butcher in Scotland. A television programme highlighted the poor standard of hygiene in many butchers' shops. It was reported that although none of these problems were found at Dewhurst, a leading chain of butchers' shops, the company found sales dropped 10 per cent almost immediately.

Price of related goods: substitutes and complements

Demand schedules are always drawn with the prices of all other commodities held constant. When we draw the demand curve for butter, we assume that the price of margarine is held constant. When we draw the demand curve for stereo speakers, we assume that the price of stereo amplifiers is held constant. When we refer to related goods we are talking about those goods whose demand is interdependent. In other words, if a change in the price of one good shifts the demand for another good, we say that those two goods are related.

There are two types of related goods: **substitutes** and **complements**. We can define and distinguish between substitutes and complements in terms of how the change in price of one commodity affects the demand for its related commodity.

Consider butter and margarine. Generally, we think of butter and margarine as substitutes. Let us assume that each originally costs £1 per pound. If the price of butter remains the same and the price of margarine falls from, say, £1 per pound to 50p per pound, people will buy more margarine and less butter, and the demand curve for butter will shift inward to the left. If, on the other hand, the price of margarine rises from £1 per pound to £2 per pound, people will buy more butter and less margarine. The demand curve for butter will shift outward to the right. In other words, an increase in the price of margarine leads to an increase in the demand for butter, and an increase in the price of butter leads to an increase in the demand for margarine. Thus, for substitutes, a price change in the substitute will cause a change in the same direction in the demand for the good under study.

With complementary goods, the situation is reversed. Consider compact discs (CDs) and compact disc players. We draw the demand curve for CDs with the price of CD players held constant. If the price per constant-quality unit of CD players decreases from, say, £500 to £200, this will encourage more people to buy more CDs, at any given price, than before. The demand curve for CDs will shift outwards to the right. If the price of CD players, on the other hand, increases from £200 to £500, fewer people will purchase CDs. The demand curve for CDs will shift inwards to the left. In sum, a decrease in the price of CD players leads to an increase in the demand for CDs. Thus, for complements, a price change in a product will cause a change in the opposite direction in the demand for its complement.

Changes in expectations about future relative prices

Expectations about future relative prices play an important role in determining the position of a demand curve because many goods are storable. If suddenly there is an expectation of a rise in the future relative price of X, then we might predict, all other things held constant, that people will buy more now, and the present demand curve will shift from DD to D′D′ in Figure 3.2. If, on the other hand, there is a new expectation of a future decrease in the price of X, then people will buy less now and the present demand curve will shift instead to D″D″ in Figure 3.2.

Note that we are talking about changes in expectations of future relative prices rather than absolute prices. If all prices have been rising at 10 per cent a year, year in and year out for a hundred years, this now fully anticipated price rise has no effect on the position of the demand curve for a particular commodity (if the price is measured in *relative* terms on the vertical axis).* Consider, for example, what would happen to the demand curve for new motor cars if it were known that their price would rise by 10 per cent next year. If it were anticipated that the prices of all other goods would also rise by 10 per cent, then the price of new cars relative to an average of all other prices would not be any different next year from what it is this year. Thus, the demand curve for new cars this year would not increase just because of the anticipated 10 per cent rise in absolute price.

Population

Often, an increase in the population in an economy (holding per capita income constant) shifts the market demand outwards for most products. This is because an increase in population leads to an increase in the number of buyers in the market. Conversely, a reduction in the population will shift most demand curves inwards because of the reduction in the number of buyers in the market. An example of the impact of a change in the number of consumers in a market is the effect of birth rates on the baby-food industry. As birth rates have recently dropped in the United Kingdom, firms producing baby food have started to diversify. They have moved into other fields because of an anticipated shift inwards of the market demand curve for their products.

KEY POINT

3.2

■ Demand curves are drawn with non-price determinants held constant. The major non-price determinants are: (1) income, (2) tastes, (3) prices of related goods, (4) expectations of future relative prices and (5) the population (the number of buyers in the market). If any one of these determinants changes, the demand schedule will shift to the right or to the left.

---

* We assume that *all* prices have been rising, including the value of all the things that you own and the price you are paid for your labour, that is, your income.

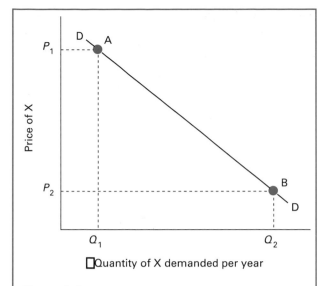

Figure 3.3

Movement along a given demand curve

We show the demand curve DD for a hypothetical good, X. If price is P_1, then the quantity demanded will be Q_1 (point A). If, on the other hand, the price is relatively low, P_2, then the quantity demanded will be relatively high, Q_2 (point B).

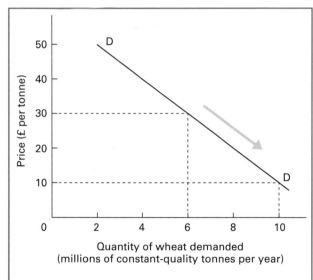

Figure 3.4

A change in quantity demanded

Here we show clearly that a change in price changes the quantity of a good demanded. It is a movement along a given demand schedule. If, in our example, the price of wheat falls from £30 a tonne to £10 a tonne, the quantity demanded will increase from 6 million tonnes per year to 10 million tonnes per year.

Distinguishing between changes in demand and changes in quantity demanded

We have been referring to changes in demand – shifts in the entire demand curve so that the quantity demanded at each and every price changes. The term demand always relates to the entire demand schedule or curve. Demand therefore refers to a schedule of planned rates of purchase. Demand – the demand schedule or curve – depends on many non-price determinants, such as those just discussed.

On the other hand, a change in the quantity demanded can only come about because of a change in price. Look at Figure 3.3. We draw a given demand schedule for any good, say, good X. At a very high price P_1, a small quantity Q_1 will be demanded. This is shown as point A on the demand curve DD. However, at a very low price, say P_2, a very large quantity will be demanded, Q_2. We show this on the demand curve as point B. A change in the quantity demanded occurs when there is a movement to a different point (co-ordinate) along a given demand curve. This movement occurs because the price of the product changes. In Figure 3.4, let us assume that we start off at a price of £30. If the price falls to £10, the quantity demanded will increase from 6 million tonnes per year to 10 million tonnes per year. You can see the arrow moving down the given demand curve DD. In economic analysis, we cannot emphasize too much the following distinction that must constantly be made:

A change in price leads to a change in quantity demanded.

A change in the non-price determinants of demand leads to a change in demand.

KEY POINTS

3.3

■ A change in demand comes about only because of a change in the non-price determinants of demand.

■ A change in the quantity demanded comes about only when there is a change in the price.

■ A change in demand shifts the demand curve and is caused by changes in the non-price determinants of demand; a change in quantity demanded involves a movement along a given demand curve and is caused by a change in price.

Multiplex and megaplex

In the 1930s cinema designers covered Britain in art deco picture palaces. In the last decade many of the old cinemas have been replaced by new multiplexes – which are architecturally less interesting, but have more screens. Now film-going in Britain is about to take another leap, with the rise of the megaplex. Giant cinema complexes are being constructed across the country, as developers gamble that the British appetite for a night out at the movies will keep growing.

UCI is opening a 20-screen complex at Trafford Park in Manchester. It will hold the title as Britain's biggest cinema for less than a year; a 30-screen complex is already under construction in Birmingham by Warner Village Cinemas. Other developments with between 14 and 21 screens are scheduled to open in Glasgow, Bradford, Dartford, Chester, Stockport, Norwich, Portsmouth, Plymouth and Croydon before 2000.

As far as developers are concerned, a complex becomes a megaplex when it has over 14 screens. But is it more than mere size that sets the megaplex apart from the multiplex? The new cinema complexes are meant to provide a new sort of experience.

Will there be enough punters to stare at all these screens? The developers point out that the first wave of multiplexation has coincided with a growth in the movie-going public. Britain's first real multiplex, a ten-screen job, opened in Milton Keynes in 1985. At the time many were predicting the demise of the cinema, in the face of the spread of videos and multi-channel TV. In fact, the opposite has happened. According to *Screen International*, cinema admissions have grown from 74.8 million in 1987 to 140 million last year.

If they are to succeed, the megaplexes will have to deliver another big jump in the cinema-going audience. At the end of 1997 there were 142 multiplex sites in the country, offering 1,222 screens. By the end of next year there will be 188 sites with 1,799 screens, and by 2002 there will be over 2,000 screens in multi-screen cinemas.

Source: *The Economist*, 11 April 1998

1 Is the increase in cinema admissions a movement along the demand curve or a shift in the demand curve?

2 Calculate the percentage increase in the number of cinema screens in 1997 and the expected number in 2002.

3 In the light of your answer above, discuss what factors will be relevant to ensure that cinema admissions continue to grow such that megaplex cinemas can operate profitably.

4 To what extent are both video films and digital television substitutes or complements to cinema films as sources of entertainment?

Supply

Just as there is a relationship between price and quantity demanded, so too there is a relationship between price and quantity supplied. This relationship is called **supply** and involves the following:

> At higher prices, a larger quantity will generally be supplied than at lower prices, all other things held constant.

Or, stated otherwise:

> At lower prices, a smaller quantity will generally be supplied than at higher prices, all other things held constant.

In other words, there is generally a direct relationship between quantity supplied and price. This is the opposite of the relationship we saw for demand. There, price and quantity demanded were inversely related. Here they are directly related. For supply, as the price rises, the quantity supplied rises; as the price falls, the quantity supplied also falls. Producers are normally willing to produce and sell more of their product at a higher price than at a lower price, other things being constant.

Why a direct, or positive, relationship?

There are a number of intuitive reasons why there is normally a direct, or positive, relationship between price and quantity supplied. These involve the incentives for increasing production facing suppliers and the law of increasing costs, discussed in Chapter 1.

Incentives for increasing production

Consider a situation in which nothing else changes except the price per tonne of wheat obtainable in the market-place. If this occurs, farmers will find it more rewarding monetarily than it was before to spend more of their time and resources producing wheat than they used to. They may, for example, switch more of their production from barley production to wheat production because the market price of wheat has risen. The wheat farmer may even find it now profitable to add the use of more labour and machines to the production of wheat because of its higher market price.

The theory of increasing costs

In Chapter 1, we explained why the production possibilities curve is bowed outwards. The explanation basically involved the theory of increasing costs – as society takes more and more resources and applies them to the production of any specific item, the opportunity cost for each additional unit produced increases at an increasing rate. The law of increasing costs exists because resources are generally better suited for some activities than for others; and therefore, when we shift a less well-suited resource to a particular production activity, more and more units of it will have to be used to get the same increase in output as we expand production.

Now apply this analysis to a wheat farmer wishing to increase the quantity of wheat supplied. That farmer will eventually find that each additional output of wheat production will involve higher and higher costs. Hence, the only way that a wheat farmer would be induced to produce more and more wheat would be the lure of the higher market price that wheat could fetch. For example, only if wheat could fetch a higher market price would a farmer be willing to pay overtime rates for workers and the extra costs involved in tilling stony, less desirable land. In a sense, then, it is because of the law of increasing costs that price has to go up in order to create a situation in which the quantity supplied will also go up.*

Supply schedule

Just as we were able to construct a demand schedule, so we can construct a **supply schedule**, which is a table relating prices to the quantity supplied at each price.

---

* Strictly speaking, the theory of increasing costs can be used as an explanation for the generally positive relationship between quantity supplied and price only in the short run, when there is no possibility that improved production techniques resulting from the increased production will actually lower costs.

Table 3.2

The supply schedule for wheat
Combinations of price (column 1) and quantity supplied (column 2) indicate that as the price rises there will be a larger quantity supplied per year.

1 Price per tonne of constant-quality wheat	2 Quantity of wheat supplied (millions of constant-quality tonnes per year)	3 Combination
£10	2	F
£20	4	G
£30	6	H
£40	8	I
£50	10	J

It is a set of planned production rates that depends on the price of the product. In Table 3.2, we show the supply schedule of wheat.

Supply curve

We can convert the supply schedule in Table 3.2 into a **supply curve**, just as we earlier created a demand curve in Figure 3.2. We take the price–quantity combinations from Table 3.2 and plot them in Figure 3.5. We have labelled these combinations F to J. The curve is upward sloping to show the normally direct relationship between price and the quantity supplied. Again, we have to remember that we are talking about quantity supplied per year, measured in constant-quality units.

KEY POINTS

3.4

- There is normally a direct, or positive, relationship between price and quantity of a good supplied, other things being constant.

- Because of the law of increasing costs, suppliers can only be induced to incur higher additional production costs if the market price they receive for their product goes up.

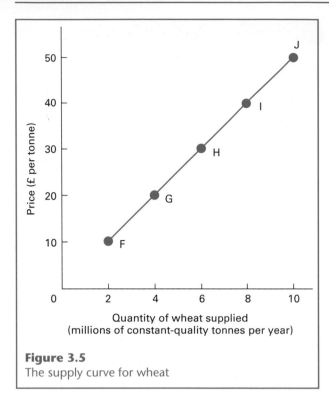

Figure 3.5
The supply curve for wheat

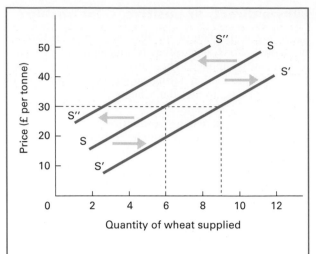

Figure 3.6
A shift in the supply schedule
If only the price changes, we move along a given supply schedule. However, if for example the cost of production of wheat were to fall dramatically, the supply schedule would shift rightwards from SS to S'S' so that at all prices a larger quantity would be forthcoming from suppliers. Conversely, if the cost of production rose, the supply curve would shift leftwards to S"S".

Determinants of supply

When supply curves are drawn, only the price changes, and it is assumed that other things remain constant. The other things assumed constant are (1) prices of resources (inputs) used to produce the product, (2) technology, (3) taxes and subsidies, (4) price expectations of producers and (5) the prices of related goods. These are the major non-price determinants of supply. If any of them changes, there will be a shift in the supply curve.

Shifting supply

A change in the price of the good itself will cause a movement along the supply curve. A change in the non-price determinants, however, will shift the entire curve.

Consider an example. If a new method of fertilizing and planting wheat reduces the cost per tonne of growing wheat by, say, 50 per cent, farmers will supply more wheat at all prices because the cost of doing so has fallen dramatically. Competition among farmers to produce more at each and every price will shift the supply schedule of wheat outwards to the right from SS to S'S', as we see in Figure 3.6. At a price of £30 the quantity supplied was originally 6 million tonnes per year; but now the quantity supplied at £30 a tonne (after the reduction in the costs of production) will be 9 million tonnes per year. This is similar to what has happened to the supply curve of electronic calculators and computers in recent years.

The opposite case will make the point even clearer.

Suppose that a new and totally unknown disease caused a blight on wheat throughout the United Kingdom such that 60 per cent of the UK's total crop is destroyed. Users of wheat products will find a reduced supply. They – in competition with one another – will bid up its price. Ultimately, the users of wheat for wheat-based products will pay greatly increased prices. The supply curve will have shifted inwards to the left to S"S". At each and every price, the quantity of wheat supplied will fall dramatically, due to the crop-destroying disease.

The determinants in detail

The prices of inputs used to produce the product
If one or more input prices fall, the supply curve will shift outwards to the right; that is, more will be supplied at each and every price. The opposite will be true if one or more inputs become more expensive. In other words, when we draw the supply curve of cars, we are holding the price of steel (and other inputs) constant.

Technology
Supply curves are drawn on the assumption of a given technology or 'state of the art'. When the types of production techniques available change, the supply curve will shift. For example, if a better production technique becomes available, the supply curve will shift to the right. A larger quantity will be forthcoming at each and every price because the cost of production will have fallen.

Taxes and subsidies

Certain taxes, such as sales taxes, are effectively an addition to production costs and therefore reduce the supply. Thus, if the supply curve were SS in Figure 3.6, a sales tax increase would shift it to S″S″. A subsidy would do the opposite: it would shift the curve to S′S′. Every producer would get a 'gift' from the government of, say, a few pence for each unit produced.

Price expectations

A change in the expectation of a future relative price of a product can affect a producer's current willingness to supply, just as price expectations affect a consumer's current willingness to purchase. Farmers may withhold from market part of their current wheat crop if they anticipate a higher wheat price in the future. In either example, the current quantity supplied at each and every price will decrease.

The prices of related goods

We saw earlier in our discussion of demand that there are two types of related goods: substitutes and complements. There is a parallel case on the supply side. Some goods are in competitive supply, meaning that one good can be quite easily produced using the same factors of production as an alternative other good. The price relationship between two such goods will therefore have a major influence on the amounts that producers are willing to supply. The relative profitability of the two goods will determine their supply situation.

In the case of related goods or joint products, an expansion of output of one good, for example beef, is necessarily accompanied by a rightward shift in the supply curve of hides (see Figure 3.7). In the case of related goods, an expansion of output of one good gives rise to a parallel expansion in the supply of the related good.

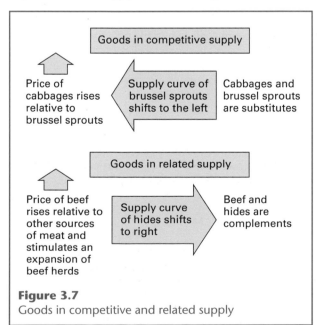

Figure 3.7
Goods in competitive and related supply

KEY POINT

3.5

■ The supply curve is drawn with other things held constant. If non-price determinants of supply change, then the supply curve will shift. The major non-price determinants are (1) input costs, (2) technology, (3) taxes and subsidies, (4) expectations of future relative prices and (5) the prices of related goods.

Change in quantity supplied and change in supply

We cannot overstress the importance of distinguishing between a movement along the supply curve (which occurs only when the price changes) and a shift in the supply curve (which occurs only with changes in other non-price factors). A change in price always brings about a change in quantity supplied. We move to a different co-ordinate on the existing supply curve. This is specifically called a change in quantity supplied.

But a change in technology, for example, will shift the curve such that there is a change in the quantity supplied at each and every price. This is called a change in supply. A rightward (outward) shift represents an increase in supply; a leftward (inward) shift represents a decrease in supply.

> A change in price leads to a change in quantity supplied.

> A change in the non-price determinants of supply leads to a change in supply.

Demand and supply of tea

Serious flooding in east Africa, following hard on the heels of drought last year, has helped push the price of tea to the highest levels seen for about 15 years. The London auction price of tea has almost doubled since January 1997, with buyers chasing what little tea has been available. There is no immediate indication of prices retreating, and one London tea broker yesterday described the increase as 'a bull run unlike anything I've seen for the last 15 years'.

'A medium-quality Kenyan tea was fetching about 105p a kilo this time last year, but now it's up around 180p to 200p,' he said. 'Buyers have been particularly active on behalf of Brooke Bond Foods, part of Unilever; it looks like its latest product, pyramid tea-bags, has been selling particularly well.' These prices are now nudging the 220p peak achieved in the early 1980s, which followed three years of poor harvest.

Tight supplies, following last year's severe drought in Kenya, one of the world's biggest tea producers, and other parts of east Africa, have now been exacerbated by serious flooding. This has washed away many of Kenya's roads, damaged the country's infrastructure generally, and disrupted the flow of exports from the port of Mombasa. Drought diminished Kenya's 1997 crop by 40 million kg, from a typical crop of about 250 million kg. About two-thirds of UK consumption is Kenyan tea.

'Kenya is now back on course for this year but world demand for tea is on the increase and production is not keeping pace,' said one broker. 'India, the biggest producer and consumer, is short of tea, despite record crops last year. A month ago top-quality Indian tea was selling for 160p a kilo; now it's 336p,' he said. Supplies of Indian teas are now also very tight; this year India has had no carry-over of stocks between seasons, and has also been a substantial exporter to Russia.

The outlook, according to several brokers, is for current price levels to continue well into 1998, at least until July, the harvesting peak for India's crops.

Source: *Financial Times*, 28 January 1998

5 Does the rise in the London auction price of tea mean that there has been a movement along the supply curve or a shift in the supply curve?

6 Draw a diagram to show the rise in the price of tea between 1997 and 1998.

7 How does tea illustrate the fact that in commodity markets changes in weather conditions have a major impact on commodity prices?

KEY POINT

3.6

■ If the price changes, we move along a curve – there is a change in quantity demanded and/or supplied. If something else changes, we shift a curve – there is a change in demand and/or supply.

Putting demand and supply together

In the preceding sections on supply and demand, we tried to confine each discussion only to supply or to demand. There is an interaction between the two. In this section, we will discuss how they interact and how that interaction determines the prices that prevail in our economy. Understanding how demand and supply interact is essential to understanding how prices are determined in our economy and other economies where the forces of supply and demand are allowed to work themselves out. Let us first combine the demand and supply schedules, and then we will combine the curves.

The demand and supply schedules combined

Let us place Tables 3.1 (the demand schedule) and 3.2 (the supply schedule) in Table 3.3. Column 1 shows the price; column 2, the quantity supplied per year at any given price; and column 3, the quantity demanded. Column 4 is merely the difference between columns 2 and 3, or the difference between the quantity supplied and the quantity demanded. In column 5, we label the difference as either an excess quantity demanded (shortage) or an excess quantity supplied (surplus). For example, at a price of £10

Table 3.3

Putting demand and supply together (wheat)

We combine Tables 3.1 and 3.2. For the first two prices, we have an excess quantity demanded (a shortage), as expressed in column 5. At the price of £40 or £50, we have an excess quantity supplied (a surplus). However, at a price of £30, there is neither an excess quantity demanded nor an excess quantity supplied. This is the equilibrium, or market-clearing, price.

1 Prices (£)	2 Quantity supplied (tonnes per year)	3 Quantity demanded (tonnes per year)	4 Difference (2) – (3) (tonnes per year)	5 Excess
10	2 million	10 million	– 8 million	Excess quantity demanded
20	4 million	8 million	– 4 million	Excess quantity demanded
30	**6 million**	**6 million**	**0**	**Market-clearing price (equilibrium)**
40	8 million	4 million	4 million	Excess quantity supplied
50	10 million	2 million	8 million	Excess quantity supplied

only 2 million tonnes would be supplied, but the quantity demanded would be 10 million tonnes. The difference would be a negative 8 million tonnes, which we label an excess quantity demanded (shortage). At the other end of the scale, a price of £50 per tonne would elicit a quantity of 10 million tonnes supplied, but the quantity demanded would drop to 2 million tonnes, leaving a difference of (plus) 8 million tonnes, which we call an excess quantity supplied (surplus).

At the price of £30 both the quantity supplied and the quantity demanded per year are 6 million tonnes of wheat. The difference then is zero. There is neither an excess quantity demanded (shortage) nor an excess quantity supplied (surplus). Hence, this price of £30 is very special. This is the **market-clearing price** since it clears the market of all excess supply or excess demand. The market-clearing price is the **equilibrium price**, or the price at which there is no tendency for change. Demanders are able to get all they want at that price; and suppliers are able to sell the amount that they want at that price.

The concept of equilibrium

We have used the term 'equilibrium price'. The concept of equilibrium is important in and of itself because we will frequently be referring to equilibrium situations in different markets and in different parts of the economy. **Equilibrium** in any market is defined as a situation in which the plans of buyers and the plans of sellers exactly mesh, causing the quantity supplied to equal the quantity demanded at the price in the market-place for the good. Equilibrium prevails when opposing forces are in balance. In any market, for a given supply curve and a given demand curve, the intersection gives an equilibrium price. For any given supply and demand, if the price were to drift away from equilibrium – say, because of firms groping about for the 'right' price – forces would come into play to push the price back to equilibrium. Such a situation is one of **stable equilibrium**. An unstable equilibrium is one in which, if there is a movement away from the equilibrium, there are forces that push the price and/or quantity even further away from equilibrium (or at least do not push price and quantity back towards the equilibrium level or rate).

The difference between a stable and an unstable equilibrium can be illustrated by considering two balls, one made of hard rubber and the other of soft putty. If you were to squeeze the rubber ball out of shape it would bounce back to its original form. However, if you were to squeeze the putty out of shape, it would remain out of shape. With respect to the shape of the two balls made out of different materials, the former illustrates a stable equilibrium (in terms of physical form) and the latter an unstable equilibrium.

Now consider a shock to the system. The shock can be presented by either a shift in the supply curve or a shift in the demand curve or a shift in both curves.

Thus, any shock to the system will result in a new set of supply-and-demand relationships and a new equilibrium; forces will come into play to move the system from the old price–quantity equilibrium (which is now a disequilibrium situation) to the new one.

The demand curve and supply curve combined

Perhaps we can understand the concept of an equilibrium or market-clearing price better by looking at the situation graphically. What we want firmly established is the understanding that, in the market, a commodity's price will tend towards its equilibrium, or market-clearing, price. Once that price is reached, the price will remain in effect unless either supply or demand changes.

Let us combine Figures 3.1 and 3.5 in Figure 3.8. The only difference now is that the horizontal axis measures both the quantity supplied and the quantity demanded per year. Everything else is the same. The demand curve is labelled D, the supply curve S. We have labelled the intersection of the supply curve with the demand curve E, for equilibrium. This corresponds to a price of £30 at which both the quantity supplied and the quantity demanded per year are 6 million tonnes. There is neither an excess quantity supplied nor an excess quantity demanded. Point E, the equilibrium point, always occurs at the intersection of

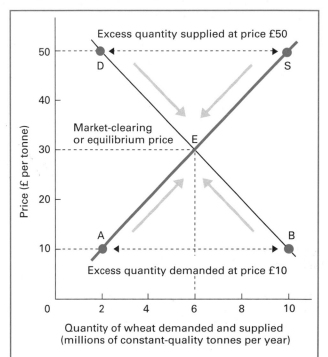

Figure 3.8
Putting demand and supply together
At E there is neither an excess quantity demanded nor an excess quantity supplied. At a price below E, such as £10, an excess of quantity demanded will cause the price to rise. At a price above E, such as £50, an excess of quantity supplied will cause the price to fall.

the supply and demand curves. Now let us see why we said that this particular price is one towards which the market price will automatically tend to gravitate.

Shortages

The demand and supply curves depicted in Figure 3.8 represent a situation of stable equilibrium. In other words, a non-market-clearing, or disequilibrium, price will put into play forces that cause the price to change towards the market-clearing price where equilibrium will again be sustained. Look again at Figure 3.8. Suppose that, instead of being at the market-clearing price of £30 per tonne, for some reason the market price is £10 per tonne. At this price, the quantity demanded exceeds the quantity supplied, the former being 10 million tonnes per year and the latter, 2 million tonnes per year. We have a situation of an excess quantity demanded or a shortage at the price of £10. Demanders of wheat will find that they cannot buy all that they wish at £10 per tonne. But forces will cause the price to rise: demanders will bid up the price and/or suppliers will raise the price and increase output, whether explicitly or implicitly. We will move from points A and B towards point E. The process will stop when the price again reaches £30 per tonne.

Surpluses

What happens if the market price was at £50 per tonne of wheat, rather than at the market-clearing price of £30 per tonne? Clearly, the quantity supplied will exceed the quantity demanded at that price. The result will be an excess quantity supplied at £50 per tonne. This excess quantity supplied is often called a surplus. However, given D and S, there will be forces pushing the price back down towards £30 per tonne: suppliers will attempt to reduce their inventories by cutting prices and reducing output, and/or demanders will offer to purchase more at lower prices. The reason that suppliers will want to reduce inventories is that these will be above their optimal level; that is, there will be an excess over what each farmer believes to be the most profitable stock of wheat. After all, inventories of wheat are costly to hold. However, demanders may find out about such excess inventories of wheat and see the possibility of obtaining increased quantities of wheat at a reduced price. This induces demanders to attempt to obtain wheat at a lower price. If the two forces of supply and demand are unrestricted, they will bring the price back to £30 per tonne.

The point is that any disequilibrium situation automatically brings into action correcting forces that will cause a movement towards equilibrium. The market-clearing price and quantity will be stable as long as demand and supply do not change (that is, as long as the non-price determinants of demand and supply do not change). This is what occurs in a stable-equilibrium situation. And, of course, we are ignoring the possibility of restrictions in the market-place that might prevent the forces of supply and demand from changing price.

KEY POINTS

3.7

- When we combine the demand and supply curves we can find the market-clearing, or equilibrium, relative price at the intersection of those two curves. The equilibrium price is one from which there is no tendency to change and towards which price will gravitate if it is higher or lower.

- At prices above the market-clearing price, there will be an excess quantity supplied, or a surplus.

- At prices below the market-clearing price, there will be an excess quantity demanded, or a shortage.

- Equilibrium in a market exists whenever the separate plans of buyers mesh exactly with the separate plans of sellers, so that quantity demanded equals quantity supplied at the market-clearing price.

- For any stable equilibrium situation, any movement of price away from the market-clearing price will put into play forces that will cause the price to gravitate back towards the market-clearing price.

Price flexibility and adjustment speed

We have used as an illustration for our analysis a market in which prices are quite flexible. There are markets in which this is the correct analysis in reality. There are others, however, where price flexibility may take the form of indirect adjustments such as by way of hidden payments or quality changes. For example, the published price for an airline seat may remain the same throughout the year. None the less, the price per constant-quality unit of airline services differs depending on how crowded the aeroplane is. In a sense, then, you pay a higher price for airline services during the peak holiday periods than during off-peak periods.

One must also consider the fact that markets do not get back into equilibrium immediately. There is an adjustment time. A shock to the economy in the form of a sudden rise in imported prices, a drought, a long strike and so on will not be absorbed overnight. This means that, even in unrestricted market situations where there are no restrictions on changes in price and quantities, temporary excess quantities supplied and excess quantities demanded may appear. Our analysis simply indicates where, ultimately, the market-clearing price will be, given a demand curve and a supply curve. Nowhere in the analysis is there any indication of the speed with which a market will, for example, reach a new equilibrium if there has been a shock. This caveat should be remembered as we examine changes in demand and changes in supply as a result of changes in their non-price determinants.

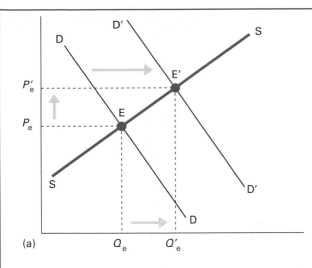

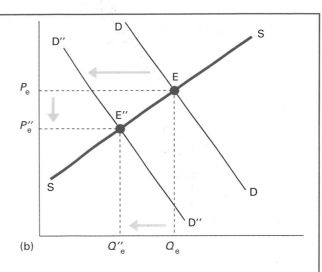

(a) (b)

Figure 3.9
Shifts in demand
In (a), the supply curve is stable at SS. The demand curve shifts out from DD to D'D'. The equilibrium price and quantities rise from P_e, Q_e to P'_e, Q'_e respectively. In (b),

again, the supply curve remains stable at SS. The demand curve, however, shifts inwards to the left showing a decrease in demand from DD to D"D". Both equilibrium price and equilibrium quantity fall.

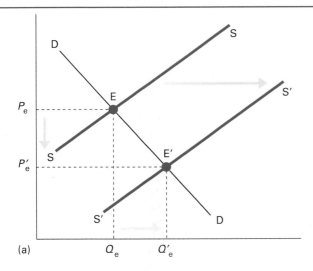

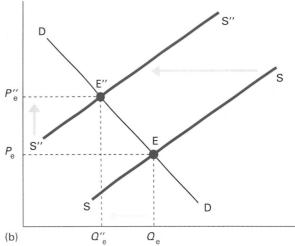

(a) (b)

Figure 3.10
Shifts in supply
In (a) the demand curve now remains stable at DD. A movement outwards to the right of the supply curve from SS to S'S' leads to a fall in the equilibrium price from P_e to P'_e. The equilibrium quantity increases, however, from Q_e to

Q'_e. In (b), the demand curve is stable at DD. A leftward shift of the supply curve from SS to S"S" results in an increase in the market-clearing price from P_e to P'_e. The equilibrium quantity falls from Q_e to Q'_e.

Changes in demand and supply

Now that we have combined both demand and supply on one graph, we can analyse the effects of changes in supply and changes in demand. In Figure 3.9 there are two parts. In (a), the supply curve remains stable but demand

increases from DD to D'D'. Note that the result is both an increase in the market-clearing price from P_e to P'_e and an increase in the equilibrium quantity from Q_e to Q'_e.

In (b) there is a decrease in demand from DD to D"D". This results in a decrease in both the relative price of the good and the equilibrium quantity.

Figures 3.10(a) and 3.10(b) show the effects of a shift

in the supply curve while the demand curve is stable. In (a) the supply curve has shifted rightwards – supply has increased. The relative price of the product falls; the equilibrium quantity increases. In (b) supply has shifted leftwards – there has been a supply decrease. The product's relative price increases; the equilibrium quantity decreases.

Case Study

Precious metals

Compared with gold and silver, platinum and palladium are fairly rational metals. Their prices appear to respond to considerations of supply and demand. However, the markets are thin. And supplies of both metals, but particularly palladium, depend on Russian exports, which are erratic and unpredictable. So price movements can be similarly erratic. Traditionally, platinum has been regarded as the more important of the two metals.

South Africa, for years the main miner of platinum group metals, produced far more platinum than palladium; it had two important uses, in jewellery and autocatalysts; and it cost about four times as much as palladium, which was mainly used for electronics and in dentistry. Today, palladium is elbowing platinum out of the way, thanks mainly to its new popularity as the most effective way of controlling most automobile exhaust fumes. Total demand is running about 50 per cent higher than platinum's in volume terms and its price has almost caught up.

However, some suggest that palladium's success contains the seeds of its own downfall. Russian supplies are now crucial to the demand balance in both metals. South Africa, whose mines produce more platinum than palladium, remains the largest supplier of platinum, providing almost 70 per cent of the total. But the only reason there was a slight surplus in the metal in 1998 was because of an unusually high level of shipments from Russia at the end of the year.

In palladium Russia is the dominant supplier (with almost 70 per cent of the total). This is partly because most of Russia's mines produce more palladium than platinum but also because it has been selling very large quantities from its stockpile. The size of the Russian stockpile is a state secret. Metals marketing group Johnson Matthey (JM) guesses that it does not have much platinum left and will probably reduce exports of this metal in the current year. Hence, it expects a small deficit and a strong price. In palladium it reckons that the Russian stockpile could last for another three to five years. But it also estimates that last year 3 million ounces of Russia's total palladium supplies of 5.8 million ounces came from stockpile sales rather than new mine production.

Prospects for the demand side of the platinum and palladium equations are nearly as uncertain. In platinum jewellery, autocatalysts and 'industrial' are the three main elements, in descending order. And jewellery looks to be in good shape. For, although the most important market, Japan, has been flagging, others, notably China and the US, seem to be deciding that owning platinum is 'cool'.

In the short term JM expects a further fall in autocatalyst usage of platinum. Palladium is increasingly the preferred option for most petrol-driven cars, as hydrocarbon emission standards become more stringent. But diesels use platinum, and so do new 'lean' petrol engines. So the medium term could be brighter. If palladium is pricing itself out of the autocatalyst market, and viable alternative technologies can be found fast enough, the apparent shortage of supplies could come to be yesterday's bogey by the time Russia's stockpile runs out.

It is tempting to call autocatalysts the key to the whole pgm market. Ten years ago they accounted for only 24 per cent of demand for the three main metals, compared with 44 per cent today. Industrial markets for these metals change as fast as the technology they cater to.

Source: *Financial Times*, 14 June 1999

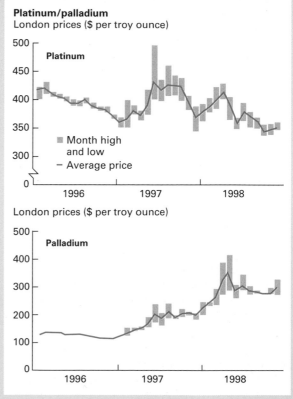

Source: Johnson Matthey/*Financial Times*, 18 May 1999

1 With reference to the charts, did the relative price of palladium compared with the price of platinum rise or fall between 1996 and 1998?
2 Explain what is meant by the comment that the markets for platinum and palladium are 'thin'.
3 The passage states that 'palladium's success contains the seeds of its own downfall'. What do you think the author of the passage meant by this statement?
4 What problems do uncertain availability of supplies and fluctuations in the price of palladium cause for industrial users of this metal?

5 How does the passage highlight the fact that stockpiles are as important as newly mined output in determining the supply–demand balance in the market for metals?
6 Illustrate diagrammatically and briefly explain the likely impact on the price of platinum of (a) increased exports from Russia; (b) a fall in the popularity of platinum as an item of jewellery.
7 How does the passage illustrate the dynamic nature of the market in these two precious metals?

Exam Preparation

Multiple choice questions

1 In drawing a demand curve for personal computers, the assumption of 'other things being equal' means that
A the price of personal computers is held constant
B the supply of personal computers is held constant
C tastes, incomes and price of personal computers are held constant
D all factors that might influence the supply of personal computers are held constant
E all factors that might influence the demand for personal computers, except price, are held constant

2 Which of the following factors will cause the price of strawberries to rise without a shift in the demand curve?
A an increase in the productivity of strawberry pickers
B an increase in real incomes of consumers
C an increase in the wage rates of strawberry pickers
D an increase in the total population consuming strawberries
E an increase in the popularity of strawberries resulting from an increase in the price of raspberries

3 If the demand for a commodity increases but there is no change in the conditions of supply the most likely result will be
A an increase in both price and quantity sold
B a decrease in both price and quantity sold
C a decrease in price and an increase in quantity sold

D an increase in price and a decrease in quantity sold
E a decrease in price, and no change in quantity sold

4 The diagram below shows the demand and supply conditions for coffee where Z is the initial equilibrium point. Other things being equal, which of the points labelled **A** to **E** would indicate the new equilibrium position if coffee producers experienced a rise in the cost of labour used in the production of coffee?

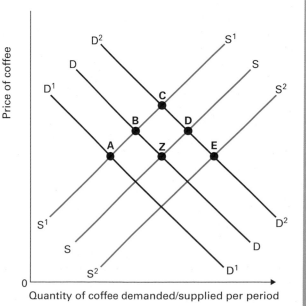

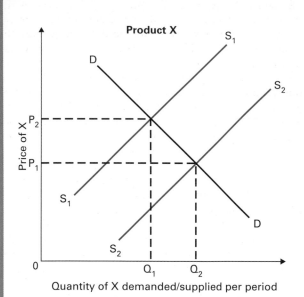

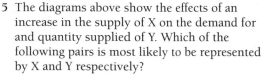

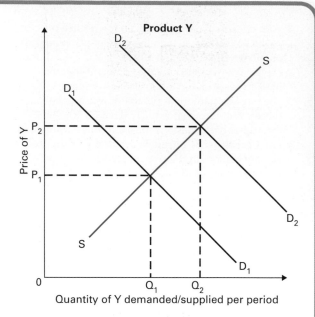

5 The diagrams above show the effects of an increase in the supply of X on the demand for and quantity supplied of Y. Which of the following pairs is most likely to be represented by X and Y respectively?
A potatoes and strawberries
B iron ore and steel
C pork and pigskin
D tea and coffee
E video cassette players and video film cassettes

Essay question

Analyse the determinants of the demand for
(a) holidays in Australia   (30 marks)
(b) heart pacemakers   (30 marks)
(c) robotic welding equipment   (40 marks)

The price system

The model of supply and demand in Chapter 3 was a model of price determination. As such, it gave us the tools of analysis to explain the structure of relative prices within our economy. Now we need to delve into the economic system and look at it as a whole. We would like to answer questions about what determines the kinds of products that are produced and the quantities in which they are produced. In other words, how do we end up using our resources to produce motor cars instead of trains? By what mechanism was paper, ink and glue funnelled into the publishing industry for this very book to be published? To answer these questions we must understand how a price system, or market system, works, in more detail than was offered in Chapter 2. We now define a price or market system as an economic system in which (relative) prices are constantly changing to reflect changes in supply and demand for different commodities. In addition, the prices of these commodities are the signals to everyone within the system about what is relatively expensive and what is relatively cheap. As we shall see, it is the signalling aspect of the price system that provides the information to buyers and sellers about what should be bought and what should be produced. This chapter analyses the way in which the pure market economy works. In Chapter 2 we showed that many Western economies are not examples of this idealized economic system, and so we reconsider the problems that have prompted state intervention in market economies.

LEARNING OUTCOMES

On completing this chapter you should understand:

- The principle of comparative advantage
- Economic efficiency
- How prices are indicators of relative scarcity
- How the price system determines what is to be produced, how goods are produced, and how these goods are distributed
- Reasons why the price system may not always work satisfactorily

Resource allocation

Because we live in a world of scarcity, decisions must be made, whether implicitly or explicitly, about how resources will be allocated. The problem of **resource allocation** is solved by the economic system at work in a nation. As Chapter 2 indicated, resource allocation involves answering the three questions of *what*, *how* and *for whom* goods and services will be produced. Throughout this chapter, we shall show how the price system answers these three basic resource allocation questions.

1   What and how much will be produced? There are literally millions of different things that could be produced with society's scarce resources. Some mechanism must exist that causes some things to be produced and others to remain as either inventors' pipe-dreams or individuals' unfulfilled desires.
2   How will it be produced? There are many ways to produce a desired item, once the decision has been made to produce it. It is possible to use lots of unskilled labour or fewer units of skilled labour. Somehow, some way, a decision must be made as to the particular mix of inputs and the way they should be organized.
3   For whom will it be produced? Once a commodity is produced, who will get it? In other words, what mechanism is there to distribute commodities (and income) once they are produced?

We shall see that in a price system literally millions of individuals are involved in solving these three fundamental questions. The interaction between the individuals within the price system is done without the use of centralized decision-making. Rather, the price system involves *decentralized* decision-making. Each decision in a price system is made by the interaction of the millions of people involved in the decision. In many parts of Western economies much of the decision-making that goes on about what, how and for whom is carried out in markets by voluntary exchange.

Exchange takes place in markets

As a society we have unlimited wants, but we must make choices among the limited alternatives available to us. When you start trading with other individuals, choices arise because you have to pick between alternative **exchanges** that you could make. Individuals in societies have been exchanging goods and services for thousands of years. For example, archaeologists tell us that, during the Ice Age, hunters of mammoths in the Great Russian Steppe were trading for Mediterranean shells.

Voluntary exchange

For the most part, our discussion of exchange will centre on voluntary exchanges between individuals and between nations. By necessity, prior to the undertaking of every voluntary exchange, the act of exchange itself appears to make both parties to the exchange better off. In other words, exchange is mutually beneficial or it would not be entered into. By assumption, if it were not mutually beneficial, individuals and nations would not bother exchanging.

To be sure, involuntary exchanges do occur, and some are quite unpleasant for the losing parties. They occur where coercion is used to alter the behaviour of another person or nation. When individuals are robbed, they suffer an exchange of goods that must be deemed involuntary. We make the assumption that only a very small part of all exchanges are involuntary and hence that such involuntary exchanges will not affect our analysis of the price system.

The **terms of exchange** – the opportunity cost or price we pay for the desired item – are determined by the interaction of the forces underlying demand and supply. This statement, of course, relates only to an unrestricted price system. Many of the terms of exchange – the prices consumers pay – are determined by laws and regulations that are a result of the political process. Additionally, some terms of exchange are determined by custom and by tradition. While custom does not play a significant role in determining prices in developed economies, in traditional societies it has been an important determinant. Customs, regulations and laws are established by individuals acting in some type of collective manner. Thus, in a sense, all terms of exchange are determined ultimately by individuals.

In our economy, the allocation of resources takes place through voluntary exchanges in markets.

Market economics

It is five o'clock in the morning at the Caledonian market in Bermondsey, south-east London. The dealers' torches flash around 300 stalls selling china, picture frames, costume jewellery, dolls, boxes – the detritus from people's houses that finds its way onto the second-hand market. The sellers are British, the buyers foreign. The trade has an old reason for patronizing this desolate spot. Bermondsey, along with three other markets in Britain, is a 'market overt': it has a common-law right established in the thirteenth century, which means that anybody buying stolen goods there before daylight acquires good title.

'That's a nice jug,' your correspondent said, pointing to a coffee jug on the stall of Blanche Wallace, who has been trading at the Bermondsey market for forty-two years. 'That? That's rubbish. Old Joe Lyons used to have them in his coffee houses. I'll get 15 quid for it, mind.'

Second-hand markets, which stretch from car-boot sales to antique fairs, are booming. The supply of goods has grown, as people in need of a few extra pounds collect and sell the things that others do not want.

Two sorts of people work in the serious end of the second-hand economy: scavengers and dealers.

Professional scavengers are known in the trade as 'knockers'. Sometimes they work alone, sometimes in teams which map out a town and leaflet the prosperous-looking areas announcing their arrival. They knock on people's doors asking whether the occupants have any antiques or bits of jewellery they would like to get rid of. The police do not like them, because people get annoyed when they realize they have sold granny's Ming vase for £5.

'Knockers' have been around for centuries. More recent are the scavengers who supply car-boot sales. These events, part of American life for years, came to Britain in the mid–1980s. They started mainly as money-raising charity enterprises, but they have since gone commercial and spread like warm butter.

Organizers charge between £5 and £12 a day ($8–$18) for a stall. Stallholders tend to be unemployed people, or people with a bit of a job, recycling unwanted odds and ends from friends and acquaintances: like nature's scavengers, they turn junk into useful goods. Poor people go looking for things they need; middle-class people wander through them in search of Sunday-morning entertainment and amusing tat; dealers speed round in the hope of a bargain.

Dealers pick the juicy bits from the material the scavengers provide. There are thousands of dealers, part-time and full-time, mostly specializing in something – stuffed animals or Victorian letter-openers with miniature pornographic pictures – but always in a hurry for a succulent bargain.

Dealers dream deals and talk deals. The talk is all of 'hits': buying something cheaper than you can sell it. Legendary hits pervade the conversation – the Portobello dealer, for instance, who recently bought a Bible for £1,600 and sold it for £130,000. Yet the business is not really about making a big profit on one item; it is about quick turnover. The rent for stalls in the Portobello Road demonstrates that good money is made: the most expensive stall is said to cost £290 for a Saturday.

Source: *The Economist*, 30 January 1993

1 How does the second-hand market in china, picture frames and costume jewellery differ from the first-hand (or new) market in these products?

2 In what way does the working of second-hand markets raise the question of fairness in market trading?

3 In the Portobello antiques market, some dealers are from abroad. What difference does this make to the working of a market?

Markets and information

Economists talk about markets a lot. The concept of a market is abstract, for it encompasses the exchange arrangements of both buyers and sellers that underlie the forces of supply and demand. In other words, demand and supply work themselves out in markets. As a general term, the word **market** refers to any arrangement or arrangements that individuals have for exchanging with one another. Economists therefore typically talk about product and factor markets: for example, the sugar and housing markets are examples of the former, and the capital market is one of the latter types of market.

One of the major factors involved in the market is the exchange of information about such things as prices, quantities and qualities. Indeed, markets are collectors of information that reflect the choices of consumers, producers and the owners of resources. All this information is given by one summary statistic: the market price of goods and services. Markets with a price system also involve co-ordination without the help of a central decision-making unit. Market prices are the aids to the co-ordination of the choices of buyers and sellers. Market prices also establish a *signalling system* to indicate when a correct choice has been made – higher profits are made or a commodity is purchased at a 'good' price. In other words, market prices create a penalty–reward system.

Different markets have different degrees of information, and different speeds at which that information is transmitted. The stock market in any Western economy, for example the United Kingdom, has information about the prices and quantities of stocks being bought and sold. This information is transmitted almost instantaneously throughout the country at least, if not the world. Profit-seeking entrepreneurs are constantly looking for ways to make more profits by improving on the information network within markets. That is why every market-maker can now tell you instantly the last price of any stock listed on a major stock exchange.

Why we turn to markets

The reason individuals turn to markets to conduct economic activities or exchanges is that markets reduce the costs of exchanging. These costs are generally called **transactions costs** because they are associated with transacting economic exchange. We can define transactions costs as all of the costs that enable exchanges to take place. Thus, they include the cost of being informed about the qualities of a particular product, its price, its availability, its durability record, its servicing facilities, its degree of safety and so on. Consider, for example, the transactions costs in shopping for a portable microcomputer. Such costs would include phone calls or actual visits to sellers in order to learn about product features and prices. In addition to these costs, we must include the cost of negotiating the sale. The specification and execution of any sales contract is thus included, and ultimately transactions costs must include the cost of enforcing such contracts.

The transactions costs in the most highly organized markets are relatively small. Take, for example, the London Stock Exchange. It is quite easy to obtain immediate information on the price of listed shares, how many have been bought and sold in the last several hours, what the prices were the day before, and so on.

Generally, the less organized the market is, the higher are the transactions costs. No market can completely eliminate transactions costs, but some markets do a better job of reducing them than others do. Historically, as it has become less costly to disseminate information through technological improvements, transactions costs have fallen.

KEY POINTS

4.1

■ Within a price system, supply and demand determine the prices at which exchanges will take place.

■ The price system is also called a market system because exchanges take place in markets where market mechanisms have reduced the costs of buyer–seller exchange.

■ Transactions costs are all costs associated with exchange.

In a price system where there is voluntary exchange, we observe the phenomenon called **specialization**. Specialization involves working at a relatively well-defined, limited endeavour, such as accounting, selling, teaching, writing, making shoes and so on. Most individuals in a price system specialize – they are not jacks of all trades – and they exchange the results of their specialized production activities with others who have also specialized. Just consider a typical UK household that consumes literally thousands of different commodities a year. But the members of that household who work certainly do little if anything to aid the actual production of the commodities used by the household over the year. The fact is that specialization leads to greater productivity, not only for each individual but for each nation. The best way to see the benefits of specialization (and then exchange) is to look at a simple numerical example.

Look at Table 4.1. Here we show total output available for two teams of workers in a small world where they are the only ones around. At first, they do not specialize; rather, each team works 8 hours a day producing both computers and wheat. Team A can produce two computers in 4 hours of work and 2 tonnes of wheat with the additional 4 hours. Team B can produce three computers in its first 4 hours of work, but only 1 tonne of wheat in its second 4 hours. The total amount that the two

teams can, and choose to, produce without specialization is five computers and 3 tonnes of wheat per day.

Now look at what happens when each team specializes. We see in Table 4.1 that after specialization, when team A spends all its time producing wheat, it can harvest 4 tonnes (since it can harvest 2 tonnes in 4 hours). Team B, on the other hand, spending all its workday producing computers, can produce six computers per day (since it can produce three computers in just 4 hours). The total 'world' output has now increased to six computers per day and 4 tonnes of wheat per day. With the same two sets of teams using the same amount of resources, the total output of this economy has increased from five computers per day to six, and from 3 tonnes of wheat per day to 4. Obviously, the two teams would be better off (in a material sense) if they each specialized and then exchanged their products. Team A would exchange wheat for computers, and team B would do the reverse. You should note that our discussion has not dealt with the disadvantage of specialization: monotony and drudgery in one's job. But if we assume that after specialization each individual is indeed doing what he or she could do comparatively better than the others, then we have an appreciation of the concept of comparative advantage.

Comparative advantage

Specialization, as outlined in the example above, rests on a very important fact: different individuals, communities and nations are indeed different, at least when it comes to the skills of each in producing goods and services. In our simple two-team example, if these teams could do both jobs equally well, there would be no reason for specialization, since total output could not have been increased. (Go back to Table 4.1 and make team B equally physically productive in the production of both computers and wheat, producing, say, one computer in 4 hours and 1 tonne of wheat in 4 hours, and then see what happens to our example after specialization.)

In fact, people are not uniformly talented. Even if individuals or nations had the talent to do everything better (for example, by using fewer resources, especially labour hours), they would still want to specialize in the area of their greatest advantage, that is, in their **comparative advantage**. To continue the example, consider the hypothetical dilemma of the managing director of a large company. Suppose that he or she can type better than any of the typists, drive a lorry better than any of the lorry-drivers and wash windows better than any of the window-washers. That just means that the director has an **absolute advantage** in all these endeavours – he or she uses fewer labour hours for each task than anyone else in the company. However, his or her comparative advantage lies in managing the company, not in doing the aforementioned tasks. How is it known that that is where the comparative advantage lies? The answer is quite easy: the managing director is paid the most for being

---

Table 4.1

Before specialization

When team A works on its own without specialization in either activity, it devotes 4 hours a day to computer production and 4 hours a day to wheat production. It produces two computers per day and 2 tonnes of wheat per day. Team B, again not specializing, during the same two 4-hour periods produces three computers but only 1 tonne of wheat. The total output of the two teams will be five computers and 3 tonnes of wheat per day.

Daily work effort

Team A	4 hours	2 computers
	4 hours	2 tonnes of wheat
Team B	4 hours	3 computers
	4 hours	1 tonne of wheat
Total = 5 computers, 3 tonnes of wheat per day		

After specialization

If team A now specializes in the production of wheat, it can harvest 4 tonnes of wheat for every 8 hours of work effort. Team B, now specializing in the production of computers, produces six per day. The benefit of specialization is increased production of one more computer per day and one more tonne of wheat per day than before the teams specialized.

Daily work effort

Team A	8 hours	4 tonnes of wheat
Team B	8 hours	6 computers
Total = 6 computers, 4 tonnes of wheat per day		

a managing director, not for being a typist or a lorry-driver or a window-washer for the company.

Basically, one's comparative advantage is found by choosing that activity that has the lowest opportunity cost. Consider the example given in Table 4.1 before specialization. Team A in 4 hours can produce two computers or 2 tonnes of wheat. That means that the opportunity cost for two computers is 2 tonnes of wheat, so that the opportunity cost for one computer is 1 tonne of wheat. In other words, team A has to give up 1 tonne of wheat in order to produce one computer. What about team B? Since it can produce three computers in 4 hours, or 1 tonne of wheat, its opportunity cost for producing one computer is only 1 divided by 3, or one-third of a tonne of wheat. That is, the opportunity cost of team B for one computer is one-third of a tonne of wheat. Since one's comparative advantage is found by choosing that activity that has the lowest opportunity cost, it is clear that team B should specialize in computer production because it incurs the lowest opportunity cost. Indeed, that is what we show when the teams specialize. Team B spends all 8 hours producing computers.

Although the discussion of specialization and comparative advantage has been couched in terms of labour, it applies equally well to all factors of production.

Division of labour

Within any given firm that includes specialized human and non-human resources, there is a division of labour among those resources. The most famous example comes from one of the earliest and perhaps one of the most famous economists of all time – Adam Smith, who illustrated the benefits of a division of labour with this example:

One man draws out the wire, another straightens it, a third cuts it, a fourth points, a fifth grinds it at the top for receiving the head; to make the head requires two or three distinct operations; to put it on is a peculiar business, to whiten the pins is another; it is even a trade by itself to put them into the paper.

(Adam Smith, *Wealth of Nations* (1776), Bk I, ch. 1, Everyman edn, 1964)

Making pins this way allowed ten workers without very much skill to make almost 48 000 pins 'of a middling size' in a day. One worker, toiling alone, could have made perhaps 20 pins a day; therefore ten workers could have produced 200. Division of labour allowed for an increase in the daily output of the pin factory from 200 to 48 000! (Smith did not attribute all of the gain to the division of labour according to talent, but also to the use of machinery, to the fact that less time was spent shifting from task to task, and so on.)

What we are referring to here involves a division of the resource called labour into different kinds of labour. The different kinds of labour are organized in such a way

as to increase the amount of output possible from the fixed resources available. We can therefore talk about an organized division of labour within a firm leading to increased output.

KEY POINTS

4.2

- With a given set of resources, specialization results in higher output; in other words, there are gains to specialization in terms of higher material well-being.

- Individuals and nations specialize in their comparative advantages in order to reap the gains of specialization.

- Comparative advantages are found by determining which activities have the lowest opportunity cost, or, otherwise stated, which activities yield the highest return for the time and resources used.

- A division of labour occurs when different workers are assigned different tasks. Together, the workers produce a desired product.

Absolute and comparative advantage

Daily work effort

Mrs Jones	4 hours	8 jackets
	4 hours	12 ties
Mr Jones	4 hours	8 jackets
	4 hours	12 ties
Total daily output = 16 jackets, 24 ties		

4 Given the above information, answer the following questions.
(a) Who has an absolute advantage in jacket production?
(b) Who has a comparative advantage in tie production?
(c) Will Mrs and Mr Jones specialize?
(d) If they specialize, what will total output equal?

Daily work effort

Mrs Jones	4 hours	8 jackets
	4 hours	12 ties
Mr Jones	4 hours	4 jackets
	4 hours	12 ties
Total daily output = 12 jackets, 24 ties		

5 Given the above information, answer the following questions.
(a) In what does Mrs Jones have an absolute advantage?
(b) In what does Mr Jones have an absolute advantage?
(c) In what does Mrs Jones have a comparative advantage?
(d) In what does Mr Jones have a comparative advantage?
(e) If they specialize according to their comparative advantages, what will total output equal?

Relative prices

In Chapter 3 we introduced the concept of relative prices. The relative price of a good is defined as the price of that good expressed in terms of how much of other goods must be given up to purchase a unit of the good in question. To establish relative prices, comparison with other prices must be made. Virtually all economic models, like supply and demand, relate individual behaviour to changes in relative, not absolute, prices.

Prices and information

Relative prices are the conveyors of information in the market-place. For the buyers, the relative price of a good indicates what the individual purchaser must give up in order to obtain that good. Suppose that you are told that a loaf of bread will cost you £100 and this you regard as an incredibly high price. But then you are told that you are assumed to be earning £500 per hour. Does that £100 loaf of bread still sound so expensive? Is it any more expensive than, say, a price of £1 for the loaf and a wage rate of £5 per hour? In both cases, you only have to work one-fifth of an hour to pay for the loaf of bread. It is the relative price of the loaf of bread – in this case, relative to the price of your labour – that tells you how expensive it really is (or what your real purchasing power is).

Now consider the relative value of the resources used to produce the bread. Its relative price will, in most cases, indicate the amount of resources given up to produce that good. Hence, when the relative price of a commodity goes up, that bit of information tells the buyer and the seller that the good is now relatively scarcer. Note that neither the producer nor the consumer has to know why that particular commodity has become relatively scarcer. It may not matter to you as a consumer, when allocating your budget, whether the price of petroleum has gone up because of a restriction on imports or because of a new law that requires petrol companies to install more expensive pollution-abatement equipment. The only thing that definitely matters to you is the higher relative price, for that is the basis on which you will make your decision about the

quantity to purchase. The message is transmitted by the higher relative price. Of course, how you respond to the message is impossible to predict on an individual basis, for there are probably an infinite number of ways that a consumer can 'conserve' on a relatively scarcer good.

Changes in relative prices convey information on changing relative scarcity to both buyers and sellers. Of course, buyers respond differently from sellers. Sellers may see a rise in the relative price of a particular good as an opportunity to increase profits, and eventually such information may be translated into a larger amount of resources going to the production of that now relatively higher-priced good. It is in this manner that resources are allocated in a system that allows prices to convey the information about relative scarcities. In a market system prices convey the information to the individuals – both sellers and buyers – in the market-place. There is no need for a central agency to produce information or to allocate resources. This does not mean that problems will not arise and that certain economic activities could not be better handled by other than unrestricted market processes. What it does mean is that spontaneous co-ordination occurs in a decentralized price system and resource allocation requires no outside management. This is what Adam Smith meant by an invisible hand at work.

Relative prices

Assume that in 1995 a pint of beer cost £1 whilst a pint of whisky cost £10. By the year 2000, the respective absolute prices had risen to £2.30 and £18.40.

6 What happened to the relative price of whisky in relation to beer between 1995 and 2000?

Suppose that the average of all other prices rose by 150 per cent over the same 1995–2000 period. That is, in 2000 it cost £250 to buy the same goods and services that would have cost £100 in 1995.

7 What has happened to the relative prices of beer and whisky in comparison with all other consumer goods and services during 1995–2000?

KEY POINT

4.3

■ Individuals respond to changes in relative prices, not absolute prices. Therefore, changes in the general price level – the average of all prices – are not central to the allocative functioning of the price system.

Determining what is to be produced

The decision about what is to be produced depends on the incentives generated within an economic system. Within the price system, the incentive that is foremost is profit: the search for higher profits causes decision-makers to produce a mix of goods whose total effective demand is the greatest relative to the scarce resources available for the production of all goods and services.

Profits

A business person seeks **profits**. We define profits as the difference between the cost of producing something and the price that it fetches in the market-place. (Remember: The only way we are strictly able to define cost is opportunity cost – the value of the resources in their next highest, or best, alternative use.) Another way of looking at profits is as the income generated by buying cheap and selling dear. A business person buys factors of production – land, labour and capital – at a cost that is less than the price obtainable when the finished product is sold. This definition of profit also includes the income received by the buying of anything at a lower price than the price for which it is sold.

We take two examples to see how changes in profitability cause resources to be *re*allocated, and hence determine what is to be produced. In the previous chapters we used the market for wheat to show how demand and supply come together in a free market to determine an equilibrium price. Now let us imagine several farmers who just grow, say, carrots and potatoes. We shall follow through the consequences of a change in one of the determinants of the demand for these goods: a change in consumer tastes.

Suppose that there is suddenly an increased and sustained demand for potatoes because it is believed that eating potatoes – whether boiled, roasted or fried – is good for one's health. This shift in tastes would result in an outward movement in the demand curve for potatoes and their relative price rise in Figure 4.1(b) from P_e to P'_e. If we suppose also that carrot-eating has become less popular, this is translated into an inward shift in the demand curve for carrots. The relative price of carrots falls from P_e to P''_e (Figure 4.1(a)). Assuming now that the cost of inputs into carrot production has not changed, the lower market-clearing price will mean less profit (or maybe even losses) in growing carrots. On the other hand, assuming again that there has been no change in input prices, when the market-clearing price of potatoes goes up, the profits per unit will also rise. The price adjustments and ensuing changes in profitability will lead to resource reallocation. There is a profit incentive for farmers to devote more of their land and labour to growing potatoes. The incentive to minimize losses causes a cutting back on the use of these resources in carrot-growing. Thus the change in consumers' tastes results here in a response by producers to alter their production of carrots and potatoes in favour of the more profitable product – potatoes – since it is in their best interest to do so.

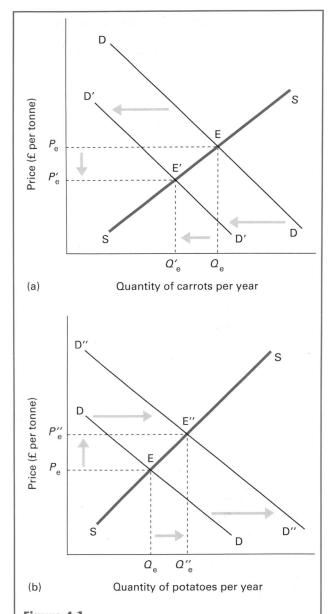

(a) Quantity of carrots per year

(b) Quantity of potatoes per year

Figure 4.1

Shifts in demand cause prices to change

(a) At the original equilibrium, the market-clearing relative price of carrots is P_e. When, because of a shift in tastes, the demand curve shifts leftward from DD to D'D', the relative price of carrots, and hence the profitability of carrot-growing, falls. The new market-clearing price after adjustment would be P'_e with the smaller quantity Q'_e produced. In (b) the demand curve for potatoes has shifted from DD to D"D". The market-clearing price has gone up from P_e to P''_e with the larger quantity Q''_e produced. The profitability of growing potatoes has risen. More resources will flow into potato-growing but fewer will be used in growing carrots.

4.4

■ Within a market economy, businesses seek profits. In their quest for profits, they move resources out of declining industries into expanding industries.

Moving resources between uses

The above examples relate to agriculture but the principle involved – resource reallocation – is generally applicable. The movement of resources in search of higher profits for businesses is simultaneously a movement of resources from lower- to higher-valued uses. When consumers no longer wanted to buy as many carrots, the demand curve shifted inwards to the left (Figure 4.1(a)). Thus, carrots were no longer as valuable from a subjective point of view as they were prior to the shift in demand. Had all the resources remained in carrot-growing they would be generating a lower subjective value to consumers than they could elsewhere in the economy.

Another incentive to shift production would involve the piling up of unsold stocks of carrots. Unsold carrots due to falling orders from vegetable wholesalers and retailers provide information which encourages growers to switch resources to the production of something else.

When some of these resources were moved from carrot- to potato-growing, they were, by necessity, being moved to a use that generated a higher value to consumers. How do we know this? Because the demand curve for potatoes shifted outwards to the right. With a given supply curve, this dictated a higher relative price, which gave an indication that consumers now valued an additional unit of resources in the carrot industry more than in the past.

Note that we have stressed that consumers are the decision-makers that prompt transfers in resources. We will now examine this decision-making process more closely.

Consumer sovereignty

The movement of resources from lower- to higher-valued uses depends crucially on consumer sovereignty. Consumer sovereignty means that the ultimate determiners of how much of what is produced are consumers, not politicians or businesses. In other words, in a world of consumer sovereignty, consumers are the decision-makers. Final production is destined to fulfil their wants and no one else's. In a pure market economy, or price system, each consumer expresses his or her desires (constrained by income) by 'voting' in the market-place with their pounds and pence. When fewer consumers were voting for carrots, this was translated into a shift leftward of the demand curve. When more consumers were expressing their votes for potatoes,

this was shown by a shift rightward of the demand curve for potatoes.

The consumer voting system is not, of course, the same as a majority voting system. No firm has to receive 51 per cent of the available spending votes in order to produce a particular product. There are, for example, speciality car companies like Porsche and Alfa Romeo that receive just a few per cent of the total 'votes' for new cars in the United Kingdom each year. But they continue to exist because there is a sufficient demand to make them profitable. On the other hand, there are many products that are not produced even though they could receive 100 per cent of all of the votes by all of a small group of people who desire those goods. This is because, even with 100 per cent of the votes, there would not be enough buyers for a business person to make a profit on the product. This is also another difference between political voting and money voting. In a market system you do not have to 'vote' for an entire package at one single time. Rather, you 'vote' for different parts – goods and services – of your total consumption package a little at a time. In the political arena you make your decision, at most, once a year, and sometimes only once every five years.

In sum, in a market economy consumers vote with their money, but it is proportional (as opposed to majority-rule) voting. Manufacturers will respond and resources will be allocated proportionally to the way the total population spends its money, or votes with its income.

The market system and efficiency

Consumer sovereignty in a pure price system means that resources will be used as efficiently as possible. The efficient use of resources will occur because business persons in each industry are competing for the money 'votes' of consumers. Consequently, each firm (and hence the economy taken as a whole) will fully utilize its available resources and will generate maximum consumer satisfaction by fulfilling the largest number of consumer desires reflected by money income spent.

There are really two parts to efficiency – **technical efficiency** and **economic efficiency** – both of which are satisfied in a pure market economy or price system.

Technical efficiency

Technical efficiency relates to utilizing production techniques that do not waste inputs. In other words, we can assume that within the market economy businesses will never waste inputs: they will never use 10 units of capital, 10 units of labour and 10 units of land when they could produce the same amount of output with only 8 units of capital, 7 units of labour and 9 units of land. Technical efficiency refers to decisions within a production unit. Managers respond to the prices that are given to them from outside the firm for the resources they must use. Technical efficiency therefore relates to managers responding 'correctly' to the input prices facing them. The more expensive the inputs, the more incentive managers have to economize in the use of them.

Table 4.7

Production costs for 100 units of product X
Technique A or B can be used to produce the same output. B will be used because its total cost is less than that of A.

Inputs	Input unit price	Production technique A (input units)	Cost	Production technique B (input units)	Cost
		A		**B**	
Labour	£10	5	£50	4	£40
Capital	£8	4	£32	5	£40
Total cost of 100 units of product X			£82		£80

Economic efficiency

This concept relates to maximizing the total subjective valuation (sometimes called utility) of our available resources. This means that resources are moved to their highest-valued uses, as evidenced by consumers' willingness to pay for the final products. As we saw above, profits signal resources to move around so that economic efficiency occurs. The forces of demand and supply guide resources to their most efficient uses. In a sense, it is the invisible-hand concept again. Individuals as business persons seeking their own self-interest end up, consciously or unconsciously, generating maximum economic value from their activities.

Economic efficiency refers to relationships outside each firm. That is, economic efficiency refers to market price determination within an economy. Whenever a price system is in operation, market price determination will create the 'proper' signals to market participants so that they will indeed be able to make the correct choices about resource allocation.*

Of course, an economic system can never attain economic efficiency unless within each firm or production unit technical efficiency has already been attained. That is, technical efficiency is implicitly a part of economic efficiency.† Usually, when discussing economic efficiency, economists assume that all profit-maximizing firms are operating technically efficiently.

How can we apply these two efficiency concepts?

1 Technical efficiency means that resources will never be wasted in producing a given output.
2 Economic efficiency means that resources will be directed to their highest-valued uses.

Technical efficiency

Colour television sets will be packed for shops using the minimum amount of cardboard necessary. They will not, for example, be packed in 3-inch-thick cardboard when 3/8 inch will do just as well (and also save on distribution costs because it is lighter).

Economic efficiency

Corrugated cardboard will be used rather than oak or mahogany which have a higher-valued use today for, say, furniture. Furniture-makers will be willing to pay a lot more for that type of wood than will the makers of colour television sets, who need material merely for packaging, not as their principal raw material.

KEY POINTS

4.5

■ If consumers' sovereignty exists, proportional money voting by consumers determines the output mix. Thus, within a pure market economy, resources flow from lower- to higher-valued uses. In the process, the price system attains both technical and economic efficiency.

■ With technological efficiency, inputs are not wasted.

■ With economic efficiency, total subjective valuation of all resources is greatest. Resources are directed to their highest-valued uses.

How will goods be produced?

The second function of an economic system, which was mentioned at the beginning of this chapter, relates to how goods will be produced.

How output will be produced

The question of how output will be produced in a price system relates to the efficient use of scarce resources. Consider the possibility of using only two types of resources: capital and labour. A firm may have the options given in Table 4.2. It can use various combinations of

---

* Even in a pure price system, it is possible for market prices to generate incorrect signals. We look at this problem later.
† Technical efficiency is a necessary but not a sufficient condition for economic efficiency.

labour and capital in order to produce the same amount of output. Two hypothetical combinations are given in that table. The least-cost combination (which is technique B) will in fact be chosen because then profits will be the highest possible. If any other technique were chosen, firms would be sacrificing potential profit.

Moreover, in a price system, competition will in effect force firms to use least-cost production techniques. Any firm that fails to employ the least costly technique will find that other firms can undercut its price. Other firms that choose the least-cost production technique will be able to offer the product at a lower price and still make a profit. The lower price at which they offer the product will induce consumers to shift sales to them from the firm with the higher prices. Inefficient firms will be forced out of business.

All this discussion assumes that technology and resources prices are held constant. But if, say, the cost of capital remained the same and the cost of labour were to decrease considerably in our example in Table 4.2, another production technique such as A might then be less costly. Firms would shift to that production technique in order to obtain the highest profits possible.

Choice of technique

Assume that a business has found that its most profitable output occurs when it produces £172 worth of output of a particular product. It can choose from three possible techniques A, B and C that will produce the desired level of output. We see the amount of inputs that these techniques use along with each input price in the following table.

| Price of input (per unit) | Production techniques | | |
	A (units)	B (units)	C (units)
£10 land	7	4	1
£2 labour	6	7	18
£15 capital	2	6	3
£8 entrepreneurship	1	3	2

8 Which technique will the firm choose and why?
9 What would the firm's maximum profit be?
10 If the price of labour increases to £4 per unit, which technique will be chosen and why? What will happen to profits?

Distribution of total output

The last question that any economic system must solve is distribution – how is total output distributed among competing claimants? The problem of distribution of total output can be separated into two parts, one relating to the distribution of products to consumers and the other relating to the distribution of money income to

individuals. It should not surprise you that the second part of this problem of distribution quickly takes us into the world of normative economics.

Which consumers get what?

In a price system, the distribution of finished products to consumers is based on the consumers' ability and willingness to pay the market price for the products. If the market-clearing price of a bottle of wine is £3.50, those consumers who are able and willing to pay that price will get their wine. Those consumers who are not, will not.

Here we are talking about the rationing function of market-clearing prices in a price system. Rather than have a central political figure decide which consumers will get which goods, those consumers who are willing to pay the market-clearing price obtain the good. That is, relative prices ration the available resources, goods and services at any point in time between those who would like to have the scarce items. If scarcity did not exist, then we would not need any system to ration available resources, goods and services.

Prices are indicators of relative scarcity. The price rations a commodity or service to demanders who are willing to pay an equilibrium price that clears the market. But if demand greatly exceeds supply in a market at the price fixed by an organization that is wholly responsible for supply, for example of tickets for a sporting event, then a secondary so-called *black market* is created. Prices will then be determined by the extent of this excess demand, and middlemen – ticket touts – find it advantageous to trade in this situation.

The determination of money income

In a price system, a consumer's ability to pay for consumer products is based on the size of his or her money income. This, in turn, depends on the quantities, qualities and types of the various human and non-human resources that the individual owns and supplies to the market-place. Additionally, the prices, or payments, for those resources influence total money income. When you are selling your human resources as labour services, your money income is based on the wage rate, or salary, that you can fetch in the labour market. If you own non-human resources – capital and land, for example – the level of interest and rents that you would be paid for your capital and land will clearly influence the size of your money income and thus your ability to buy consumer products.

What are the implications of these observations? Well, if labour services are not paid for at a common wage rate and also not everyone has capital to invest to advantage, then we will soon face normative issues. How fair is such a system when some people have more money than others? The 'for whom' question quickly makes us stray away from the world of positive economics.

A 'perfectly performing' price system may not provide for much equality in income. That is, an efficient price

Own goal?

In the summer of 1998, France was the last country for the final rounds of the World Cup football tournament involving teams from 31 other countries. However, long before the matches were due to take place, the distribution of tickets at the ten venues had become a highly controversial issue. The Comité Français d'organisation provided data in early June 1998 which highlighted the earlier difficulties of football fans trying to obtain tickets by ringing a telephone hotline. It was reported that 20 million calls had been made to the hotline where just 170 000 tickets were available. Controversy centred on the distribution of at least 500 seats for each of the 64 games for the Comité, FIFA (the game's governing body), diplomats, ministers, visiting heads of state and those associated with running the tournament. The Comité sold just over 20 per cent of tickets directly to the French public, and another 14 per cent to the French national football association, football clubs and supporters' organizations. With other tickets allocated to mayoral offices of the relevant cities where the games were due to be played, to local disabled persons and children, it was very apparent that France did not favour giving a high priority to those associated with the game amongst the other 31 countries. National football associations of these other participating countries were given under one quarter of the tickets. The corporate sponsors of the World Cup received just over 13 per cent of the tickets.

The EU Commission had ordered an investigation into these distribution arrangements in February 1998, but the organizers of the tournament rejected moves to allocate more tickets to supporters, especially those in England. The organizers were accused of not advertising the availability of 'Prestige' tickets designed for businesses to impress their clients, who could watch games from hospitality boxes.

In June it was reported that almost 15 000 World Cup tickets had been stolen from the Paris office of an American travel agency, which had been accused of selling fake tickets.

In England problems arose with the Official Receiver being placed in control of one ticket agency that took money for World Cup tickets it did not actually have for sale! Some 20 000 football fans were thought to have lost their money when Great Portland Entertainments was closed down.

On 12 July France won the World Cup beating Brazil 3–0. Whether its distribution of tickets was so clearly a winner seems much less certain.

11 Draw a supply and demand diagram beginning with the attendance capacity of the Stade de France Stadium in Paris of 80 000 spectators as the supply curve. How would you draw this supply curve if it represents a fixed maximum number?

It was reported in the *Daily Telegraph* that those allocated tickets were able to sell these for 20 000 French francs (£2000) each in the foyers of city central hotels in Paris two days before the World Cup Final. Assume that 20 000 French francs is therefore the market-clearing price and that the average official ticket price was 1000 French francs (£100).

12 Now draw a demand curve where the market-clearing equilibrium price is set at 20 000 French francs and where there is a large number of persons willing to pay the average official ticket price of just 1000 French francs.

13 How does your diagram illustrate the fact that demand for tickets for the World Cup was far in excess of the supply available at the average price of 1000 French francs?

14 What would you predict to be the consequences of a shortage of tickets sold at the official prices?

15 The allocation of tickets for the World Cup is a good illustration of how if a market-clearing price is not used on the grounds that this is 'unfair', then the alternatives to it may be just as easily criticized. How does this issue highlight the distinction between positive and normative economics?

16 To what extent would an allocation of tickets that gave a greater proportion to the national associations of the 31 countries visiting France, football clubs and supporters' organizations have helped ease the problems of those wishing to buy tickets?

17 Assume that you were a ticket tout with tickets for one of the games in France in June 1998. If you were asked to justify your role with reference to economics principles, how would you present the case in your defence?

system could still be one in which some people were starving to death. If one of the social goals in a society is to provide more income equality, then something other than the price system must be utilized. Indeed, most Western economies have a taxation system that attempts to reduce the high levels of income of the highest-income-earning individuals; and we also have a system of welfare in which we attempt to transfer some of those revenues collected by taxes to the lowest-earning (or non-earning) members of our society.

Related to the social goal of income equality is the goal of income security. The price system may not guarantee income security to all. A non-market system, using government, may therefore be (and is) an alternative. For example, the provision of government-provided unemployment insurance benefits (paid by taxes) is an attempt to reduce income insecurity among the economy's participants.

This recognition of the shortcomings of a market economy concerning the distribution of goods and services prompts the need for a more general reappraisal of the price system. What perhaps have we too readily assumed in the above analysis?

Evaluating the price system

It is possible to evaluate the price system in terms of what it can and cannot do. When a price system alone cannot satisfy certain social goals, then government or voluntary solutions to problems need to be examined.

What the price system can do

Throughout this chapter we have seen that the price system can communicate information concerning relative scarcity and opportunity costs. And, in a world in which individual preferences are self-determined (rather than programmed), individual preferences can be expressed via the purchase or non-purchase of commodities. The communication-of-information function of the price system, as we have seen, leads to efficiency.

Efficiency
The price system does lead to both technical and economic efficiency. Competition between firms forces them to choose the least-cost production techniques, thus avoiding waste (technical efficiency). In the absence of restraints and imperfections in the system (to be discussed below), maximum economic value is obtained from a given set of resources at any point in time (economic efficiency). In some sense, then, the price system harnesses self-interest in order to provide society with the greatest possible output of desired goods. The price system leads to a movement of resources from lower- to relatively higher-valued uses. Thus, resources will not stay in an industry the demand for whose product has withered away because of a change in consumer tastes.

Individual freedom
Another aspect of the price system which can be listed as something it can do involves maximizing individual, or personal, freedom. Since the co-ordination of social organization through a price system does not require central direction or the use of force by any governmental authority, individual freedom presumably obtains. The price system allows for a type of spontaneous co-ordination that has been described as 'an invisible hand'. The price system permits, as it were, the freedoms of choice and enterprise. Individuals are free to further their self-interest. One of the contemporary champions of the price system has said that

So long as effective freedom of exchange is maintained, the central feature of the market organization of economic activity is that it prevents one person from interfering with another in respect of most of his activities. The consumer is protected from coercion by the seller because of the presence of other sellers with whom he can deal. The seller is protected from coercion by the consumer because of other consumers to whom he can sell. The employee is protected from coercion by the employer because of other employers for whom he can work, and so on. And the market does this impersonally and without centralized authority.

(Milton Friedman, *Capitalism and Freedom*, Chicago: University of Chicago Press, 1962)

Growth
A price system can lead (and historically has led) to economic growth. Remember from Chapter 1 that we defined economic growth as an increase in the productive capacity of a nation over time (a shifting outwards to the right of the production possibilities curve). Since the price system offers a reward-and-penalty signalling system to its participants, there is an incentive to increase productivity because of the reward (profits). No centralized authority must decide which innovations should be utilized to increase productivity; rather, market participants make the decisions, and those who make the correct decisions are rewarded by increased profits. Consequently, one can argue that a price system provides the setting for those who choose correctly. Moreover, because of the penalty of reduced profits, or even losses, resources do not stay in areas where consumer demand no longer exists.

KEY POINTS

4.6

■ Within a price system competition forces producers to seek least-cost techniques of production. Competition is thus the driving-force behind the free-market solution of how goods and services are to be produced.

■ The actual distribution of goods and services is dependent on the ability and willingness of consumers to make payments for these outputs. This ability to pay will be dependent on the size of money incomes. Money incomes are unequal since there is not an even ownership of human and non-human resources.

■ A pricing system can lead to technical and economic efficiency while permitting individual freedom within a dynamic economy. However, a price system may in practice lack strong competitive pressures to promote efficiency.

What the price system cannot do

The 'market' does not always work. That is, there are shortcomings in the way some markets operate that prevent the price system from actually attaining economic efficiency and individual freedom – as well as other social goals. And, of course, every case in which the price system cannot attain a social goal is a case in which non-market alternatives must be considered.

Externalities

If the price system does not register all the costs and benefits associated with the production and/or consumption of commodities, then an externality arises. We define an **externality** as a cost or benefit external to an exchange. In other words, the external benefits or costs accrue to parties other than the immediate seller and buyer in a transaction. An obvious example of an external cost is the pollution of air and water. These are externalities because they result from production and consumption activities in which the parties involved do not take account of such ill effects on others. The point to be made is that, whenever supply and demand do not fully reflect all costs and all benefits of production and consumption, the price system cannot be expected to bring about an efficient allocation of resources. Externalities are an extremely important topic in economics; we treat them in detail in Chapter 10.

Public goods

The price system relates to the tabulation of individual wants only. Many goods and services are not, however, financed by individuals through the market-place. Street lighting and national defence cannot be purchased in small amounts by households and individuals. They can be consumed only on a public, or collective, basis. The price system, then, is considered to be incapable of providing such **public goods** in optimal quantities. In instances like this the market mechanism does not work effectively. These cases are known as examples of **market failure**. (We treat them in more detail in Chapter 10.)

Competition

Implicit in much of the discussion of supply and demand in Chapter 3 and of the price system in this chapter is the notion of competition, where there are many buyers and sellers of products. But even in a price system there may be a lack of competition because of, for example, successful efforts on the part of business persons to restrict competition. Adam Smith realized that

> people of the same trade seldom meet together for fun and merriment, but the conversation ends in a conspiracy against the public, or in some contrivance to raise prices.
>
> (Adam Smith, *Wealth of Nations* (1776), Bk I, ch. 10, Everyman edn, 1964)

Smith's fear of conspiracies and monopolies that would hurt consumers is a fear that is still with us today. For many, this fear has taken on the form of reality, for they believe that there is little competition left in many parts of the UK economy. The price system cannot work to its fullest advantage if there are restraints on trade through monopoly. Whenever the degree of competition declines, the price system becomes less of a perfect mechanism for efficiently allocating resources.

If there is a recognition of the need to ensure a fully competitive market system, then some scope for government intervention is implied. Governments may, for example, wish to restrict the willingness of large firms in particular markets to merge together and dominate them. In Chapter 26 we consider policies in the United Kingdom to make product markets more competitive.

Unequal income distribution

We have already recognized that the market system may operate well in a technical sense, but does so in the context of what some see as an unfair distribution of income and wealth. Government policies to redistribute income and wealth can try to 'correct' this shortcoming of the market mechanism. These policies are discussed in Chapter 28.

Factor immobility

We showed earlier in the chapter how shifts in the demand for potatoes and carrots brought about price adjustments and ensuing changes in profitability for farmers. The end result was that there would be a reallocation of resources, and it was implicitly assumed that this process would take place readily and without difficulty. If we now broaden our horizons we can recognize that in the real world the factors of production will not, in practice, be reallocated as easily as in this theoretical example. Labour cannot readily move from one industry to another since retraining and the relocation of work are likely to be involved.

A second dimension to this problem of the less than perfect mobility of factors of production is the phenomenon of structural change. The dynamics of a real-world economy were noted in Chapter 2. It is not just shifts in demand that prompt the need for resource reallocation but also the process of technological change as represented, for example, by the appearance of microprocessors and robotic equipment. Industries such as steel and motor vehicle manufacturing are undergoing major change in terms of the character of the industrial process. Can a purely market economy handle the reallocation of capital and labour without some government intervention?

Manufacturing in the United Kingdom is exposed to foreign competition both in the home market and in overseas markets, whereas some service industries like plumbing and painting by their very nature face little or no international competition at all. We must recognize that the problem of resource allocation is now more crucial than ever before owing to the rapid pace of technological change and the growing competition in manufactured goods from the newly industrialized countries.

The results of the evaluation

The price system can, it seems, satisfy some social goals, but at the same time it cannot satisfy numerous others. As you might expect, therefore, the actual economic system that exists in the United Kingdom and most developed countries is a combination of the price system and a non-price system. We shall examine some forms of government intervention in markets in Chapter 9.

KEY POINTS

4.7

■ A pricing system cannot easily take care of externalities without non-market intervention. Nor can it provide a sufficient amount of public goods. Where there are such problems in allocating resources, these are instances of market failure.

■ A pricing system may operate in a society where income disparities are so great that government intervention (to achieve the social goal of income equality) is widely accepted as being desirable.

■ A pricing system will not be able to reallocate resources effectively if there is factor immobility.

Case Study

The just price in cigarettes

Supply and demand operate at any time that transactions are made, even when money is not present. When supply and demand interact, prices may change. How can prices be determined if no coin or currency is used in the trading? During the Second World War in prisoner-of-war camps in Germany, barter replaced the kind of exchange described in this chapter, and as time passed, more complex exchange systems developed in the camps. In the article that is quoted in the following paragraphs, you can read about what actually took place. The original article appeared in an economics journal just after the war ended. It remains a classic first-hand description of how markets, money, and supply and demand developed *spontaneously* in the prisoner-of-war camps:

> We reached a transit (prisoner-of-war) camp in Italy about a fortnight after capture and received a quarter of a Red Cross food parcel each week later. At once exchanges, already established, multiplied in volume. Starting with simple direct barter, such as a non-smoker giving a smoker friend his cigarette issue in exchange for a chocolate ration, more complex exchanges soon became an accepted custom. Stories circulated of a padre who started off round the camp with a tin of cheese and five cigarettes, and returned to his bed with a complete parcel in addition to his original cheese and cigarettes; the market was not yet perfect. Within a week or two, as the volume of trade grew, rough scales of exchange values came into existence. Sikhs (followers of an Indian monotheistic religion that rejects idolatry and the caste system of India) who had at first exchanged tinned beef for practically any other foodstuff began to insist on jam and that was worth $1/2$ lb. of margarine plus something else; that a cigarette issue was worth several

chocolates issues, and a tin of diced carrots was worth practically nothing.

> In this camp we did not visit other bungalows very much and prices varied from place to place; hence the germ of truth in the story of the itinerant priest. By the end of a month, when we reached our permanent camp,* there was a lively trade in all commodities and their relative values were well known, and expressed not in terms of one another – one didn't quote bully (canned beef) in terms of sugar – but in terms of cigarettes. The cigarette became the standard of value. In the permanent camp people started by wandering through the bungalows calling their offers – 'cheese for seven' (cigarettes) – and the hours after parcel issue were Bedlam. The inconveniences of this system soon led to its replacement by an exchange and mart notice board in every bungalow, where under the headings 'name', 'room number', 'wanted' (bid) and 'offered' (offer) sales and wants were advertised. When a deal went through, it was crossed off the board. The public and semi-permanent records of transactions led to cigarette prices being well known and thus tending to equality throughout the camp … With this development everyone, including non-smokers, was willing to sell for cigarettes, using them to buy at another time and place. Cigarettes became the normal currency, though, of course, barter was never extinguished.

> The unity of the market and the prevalence of a single price varied directly with the general level of organization and comfort in the camp. A transit camp was always chaotic and uncomfortable: people were overcrowded, no one knew where anyone else was living, and few took the trouble to find out. Organization was

---

* Notice the difference between a transit camp and a permanent camp. A transit camp is where prisoners-of-war were first taken but not where they were permanently going to stay. After they were at the transit camp for some time, it was decided where their permanent 'home' would be in a permanent prisoner-of-war camp.

too slender to include an exchange and mart board, and private advertisements were the most that appeared. Consequently, a transit camp was not one market but many. The price of a tin of salmon is known to have varied by two cigarettes in 20 between one end of a hut and the other. Despite a high level of organization in Italy, the market was (broken up) … in this manner at the first transit camp we reached after our removal to Germany in the autumn of 1943. In this camp – Stalag VIIA at Moosburg in Bavaria – there were up to 50 000 prisoners of all nationalities. French, Russians, Italians and Yugo-Slavs were free to move about within the camp; British and Americans were confined to their compounds, although a few cigarettes given to a sentry would always procure permission for one or two men to visit other compounds. The people who first visited the highly organized French trading centre with its stalls and known prices found coffee extract – relatively cheap among the tea-drinking English – commanding a fancy price in biscuits or cigarettes, and some enterprising people made small fortunes that way. (Incidentally, we found out later that much of the coffee went 'over the wire' and sold for phenomenal prices at black market cafés in Munich: some of the French prisoners were said to have made substantial sums in RMs (Reich marks, the German currency). This was one of the few occasions on which our normally closed economy came into contact with other economic worlds.)

Eventually public opinion grew hostile to these monopoly profits – not everyone could make contact with the French – and trading with them was put on a regulated basis. Each group of beds was given a quota of articles to offer and the transaction was carried out by accredited representatives from the British compound, with monopoly rights. The same method was used for trading with sentries elsewhere, as in this trade secrecy and reasonable prices had a peculiar importance, but as is ever the case with regulated companies, the interloper proved too strong.

The permanent camps in Germany saw the highest level of commercial organization. In addition to the exchange and mart notice boards, a shop was organized as a public utility, controlled by representatives of the Senior British Officer, on a no-profit basis. People left their surplus clothing, toilet requisites and food there until they were sold at a fixed price in cigarettes. Only sales in cigarettes were accepted – there was no barter – and there was no haggling. For food at least there were standard prices: clothing is less homogeneous and the price was decided around a norm by the seller and the shop manager in agreement; shirts would average say 80, ranging from 60 to 120 according to quality and age. Of food, the shop carried small stocks for convenience; the capital was provided by a loan from the bulk store of Red Cross cigarettes and repaid by a small commission taken on the first transactions. Thus the cigarette attained its fullest currency status, and the market was almost completely unified.

Public opinion on the subject of trading was vocal if confused and changeable, and generalizations as to its direction are difficult and dangerous. A tiny minority held that all trading was undesirable as it engendered an unsavoury atmosphere; occasional frauds and sharp practices were cited as proof. Certain forms of trading were more generally condemned; trade with the Germans was criticized by many. Red Cross toilet articles, which were in short supply and only issued in cases of actual need, were excluded from trade by law and opinion working in unshakeable harmony. At one time, when there had been several cases of malnutrition reported among the more devoted smokers, no trade in German rations was permitted, as the victims became an additional burden on the depleted food reserves of the Hospital. But while certain activities were condemned as antisocial, trade itself was practised, and its utility appreciated, by almost everyone in the camp.

More interesting was opinion on middlemen and prices. Taken as a whole, opinion was hostile to the middleman. His function, and his hard work in bringing buyer and seller together, were ignored; profits were not regarded as a reward for labour, but as the result of sharp practices. Despite the fact that his very existence was proof to the contrary, the middleman was held to be redundant in view of the existence of an official shop and the exchange and mart. Appreciation only came his way when he was willing to advance the price of a sugar ration, or to buy goods spot and carry them against a future sale. In these cases the element of risk was obvious to all, and the convenience of the service was felt to merit some reward … Opinion notwithstanding, most people dealt with a middleman, whether consciously or unconsciously, at some time or another.

There was a strong feeling that everything had its 'just price' in cigarettes. While the assessment of the just price, which incidentally varied between camps, was impossible of explanation, this price was nevertheless pretty closely known. It can best be defined as the price usually fetched by an article in good times when cigarettes were plentiful. The 'just price' changed slowly; it was unaffected by short-term variations in supply, and while opinion might be resigned to departures from the 'just price', a strong feeling of resentment persisted. A more satisfactory definition of the 'just price' is impossible. Everyone knew what it was, though no one could explain why it should be so.

Source: R. A. Radford, 'The Economic Organization of a POW Camp', *Economica*, NS, 12 (Nov. 1945), 189–201

1 Why did trade result in 1 tin of jam being worth ½lb of margarine plus something else, while a tin of carrots was worth practically nothing?
2 What was the purpose of the exchange and mart board?
3 How does the passage illustrate the fact that different tastes got reflected in different exchange values?
4 Why were middlemen regarded with suspicion?
5 Were non-smokers better off than smokers?
6 What factors influenced (a) the structure of prices and (b) the general level of prices?

Exam Preparation

Multiple choice questions

1 Which condition defines economic efficiency in production?
   A all factors of production are fully employed
   B all firms are producing at their profit-maximizing levels of output
   C output of any one good cannot be increased without reducing the output of some other good
   D there are no further opportunities for substituting capital for labour

2 The price mechanism helps to allocate resources efficiently because
   A it results in lower rewards being paid to factors of production when the demand for the product they produce increases
   B it will lead to a distribution of output amongst individuals on the basis of greatest need
   C the prices of non-renewable resources will tend to rise as the stock of such resources nears depletion
   D it will always ensure that competition between firms prevents high profits being earned

3 Which one of the following statements that refer to the price mechanism is **not** true?
   A high prices ration out scarce goods in accordance with effective demand of consumers
   B high prices and profits tend to attract resources from less remunerative activities
   C immobility of factors makes the price mechanism less perfect as an allocative device
   D in a private enterprise system the sovereignty of the consumer is absolute

Essay questions

1 Consider the view that, left to itself, the market mechanism is incapable of allocating scarce resources in an efficient manner. (25 marks)

2 What are the economic functions of profit? Is the pursuit of maximum profits by producers in the best interest of society?

3 (a) What do you understand by the term 'economic efficiency'? (10 marks)
   (b) Does the price mechanism allocate scarce resources efficiently? Explain your conclusions. (15 marks)

Demand and supply elasticity

The cornerstone of microeconomic analysis is supply and demand, concepts already discussed in Chapter 3. Microeconomic analysis concerns itself with decision-making by individuals in their capacity as consumers, workers and business persons. Our analysis of microeconomic decision-making involves an examination of how the various decisions made by individuals ultimately determine prices and quantities in the real world.

Remember from Chapter 3 that the fundamental theory of demand is that there is an inverse relationship between prices and quantity demanded, holding other things constant. If the price goes up, less will be consumed or used than before. If the price goes down, more will be consumed or used than before. If you are a decision-maker in a top-management position at, say, British Airways, will knowing the theory of demand help you in any way to decide whether you should change the price of one of your services? The answer is obviously 'no'. You can predict the direction of change in quantity demanded if you raise or lower the price, but you will not be able to tell by how much the quantity demanded will change. In May 1999 Ford announced that it was to give its UK dealers an additional discount of up to £3000 on some Mondeo models on top of the usual dealer margin if the dealers accepted 10 Mondeos or more each month. Clearly, Ford assumed that its dealers would be attracted by this incentive to order more Mondeos. Ford dealers would be likely to offer potential car buyers a keen price for a Mondeo relative to a similar model from another car manufacturer. This example of a lower price for a Mondeo was likely to stimulate car sales sufficiently that total sales revenue was higher than it was prior to the price cut.

In other words, some measure of the responsiveness of consumers to changes in price is necessary in order to estimate the effects of changes in price. Not only management in private firms but decision-makers within government have to have an idea of how responsive people in the real world will be to changes in price. Economists have given a special name to price responsiveness: *price elasticity*. Elasticity is the subject of this chapter.

KEY POINTS TO REVIEW

LEARNING OUTCOMES

On completing this chapter you should understand:

- How to define and measure the price elasticity of demand and supply
- Cross-price elasticity of demand
- Income elasticity of demand

Price elasticity

To begin to understand what 'elasticity' is all about, just keep in mind that it means 'responsiveness'. Here we are concerned with the price elasticity of demand and the price elasticity of supply. We wish to know the extent to which a change in the price of, say, petroleum products will cause the quantity demanded and the quantity supplied to change, other things held constant. We restrict our discussion at first to the demand side.

Price elasticity of demand

We shall formally define the **price elasticity of demand**, which we label e_d, as follows:

$$e_{\mathrm{d}} = \frac{\text{percentage change in quantity demanded}}{\text{percentage change in price}}$$

What will price elasticity of demand tell us? It will tell us the relative amount by which the quantity demanded will change in response to a change in the price of a particular good.

We consider an example where a 10 per cent rise in the price of petrol leads to a reduction in quantity demanded of only 1 per cent. Putting these numbers into the formula, we find that the price elasticity of demand of oil equals the percentage change in quantity demanded divided by the percentage change in price, or

$$e_{\mathrm{d}} = \frac{-1 \text{ per cent}}{+10 \text{ per cent}} = -0.1$$

Notice that this number is pure – that is, dimensionless, a percentage divided by a percentage.*

An elasticity of –0.1 means that a 1 per cent decrease in the price would lead to a mere one-tenth of 1 per cent increase in the quantity demanded. If you were now told that the price elasticity of demand for petrol was, say, –1, then you would know that a 1 per cent increase in the price of petrol would lead to a 1 per cent decrease in the quantity demanded.

Basically, the greater the numerical price elasticity of demand, the greater the demand responsiveness to relative price changes – a small change in price has a great impact on quantity demanded. The smaller the numerical price elasticity of demand, the smaller the demand responsiveness to relative price changes – a large change in price has little effect on quantity demanded.

Price elasticity of demand is always negative

Remember that the theory of demand states that quantity demanded is inversely related to the relative price. Thus, in the preceding example, an increase in the price of petrol led to a decrease in the quantity demanded. Alternatively, we could have used an example of a decrease in the relative price of petrol, in which case the quantity demanded would increase by a certain percentage. The point is that price elasticity of demand will always be negative. By convention, we will ignore the negative sign in our discussion from this point on.

Relative quantities only

Notice that in our elasticity formula we talk about percentage changes in quantity demanded divided by percentage changes in price. We are therefore not interested in the absolute changes, but only in relative amounts. This means that it does not matter if we measure price changes in terms of pence, pounds or hundreds of pounds. It also does not matter whether we measure quantity

changes in, for example, ounces, grams or pounds. The percentage change will be the same.

KEY POINTS

5.1

- Price elasticity is a measure of the responsiveness of the quantity demanded and supplied to a change in price.

- The price elasticity of demand is equal to the percentage change in quantity demanded divided by the percentage change in price.

- The theory of demand states that quantity demanded and price are inversely related. Therefore the price elasticity of demand is always negative, since an increase in price will lead to a decrease in quantity demanded and a decrease in price will lead to an increase in quantity demanded.

- Price elasticity of demand is calculated in terms of relative percentage changes in quantity demanded and in price. Thus, we end up with a unitless, scaleless number.

Calculation of elasticity

In order to calculate the price elasticity of demand, we have to compute percentage changes in quantity demanded and in relative price. To obtain the percentage change in quantity demanded, we can look at

$$\frac{\text{change in quantity demanded}}{\text{original quantity demanded}} \times 100 \text{ per cent}$$

To find the percentage change in price, we can look at

$$\frac{\text{change in price demanded}}{\text{original price demanded}} \times 100 \text{ per cent}$$

There is a slight problem with the computation of percentage changes in this manner. We get a different answer depending on whether we move up the demand curve or down the demand curve.

Consider the hypothetical data presented in Table 5.1 for the quantities of petrol demanded by UK consumers at various prices. For the moment we are just looking at the first four columns.

Columns 1 and 3 of Table 5.1 are simply the quantity demanded and price data for the demand curve represented graphically as Figures 5.1(a) and 5.1(b). Columns 2 and 4 show changes in quantity demanded corresponding to changes in price.

---

* Miles divided by gallons gives a ratio 'miles per gallon'. But when you see a ratio without a dimension, that means that the ratio is comparing two identical dimensions.

Table 5.1

Numerical calculation of price elasticity of demand for petrol

1	2	3	4	5	6	7
Quantity demanded Q (millions of gallons per day)	Change in Q (millions of gallons per day)	Price P per gallon (£)	Change in price P (£)	Average quantities $(Q_1 + Q_2)/2$	Average prices $(P_1 + P_2)/2$	$e_d = \dfrac{\text{change in } Q}{(Q_1 + Q_2)/2} \div \dfrac{\text{change in } P}{(P_1 + P_2)/2}$
0 ⟩1		11 ⟩1		0.5	10.5	$1/0.5 \div 1/10.5 = 21$
1 ⟩1		10 ⟩1		1.5	9.5	$1/1.5 \div 1/9.5 = 6.333$
2 ⟩1		9 ⟩1		2.5	8.5	$1/2.5 \div 1/8.5 = 3.4$
3 ⟩1		8 ⟩1		3.5	7.5	$1/3.5 \div 1/7.5 = 2.143$
4 ⟩1		7 ⟩1		4.5	6.5	$1/4.5 \div 1/6.5 = 1.444$
5 ⟩1		6 ⟩1		5.5	5.5	$1/5.5 \div 1/5.5 = 1$
6 ⟩1		5 ⟩1		6.5	4.5	$1/6.5 \div 1/4.5 = 0.692$
7 ⟩1		4 ⟩1		7.5	3.5	$1/7.5 \div 1/3.5 = 0.467$
8 ⟩1		3 ⟩1		8.5	2.5	$1/8.5 \div 1/2.5 = 0.294$
9 ⟩1		2 ⟩1		9.5	1.5	$1/9.5 \div 1/1.5 = 0.158$

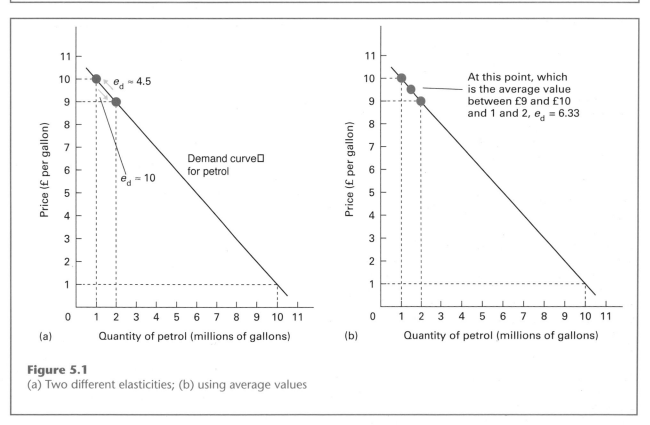

Figure 5.1
(a) Two different elasticities; (b) using average values

We start with a quantity of 1 unit demanded at the price of £10 per unit and move down the demand curve. If we start at a price of £10 with 1 unit demanded, price then falls to £9. Quantity demanded increases to 2. The percentage change in price is

$$\frac{£10 - £9}{£10} \times 100 = \frac{£1}{£10} \times 100 = 10 \text{ per cent}$$

The percentage change in quantity demanded is

$$\frac{2 - 1}{1} \times 100 = \frac{1}{1} \times 100 = 100 \text{ per cent}$$

Thus, price elasticity of demand is equal to

100 per cent ÷ 10 per cent = 10

We now calculate the price elasticity of demand assuming a move up the demand curve. We start at a price of £9 with 2 units demanded. The price goes up to £10 and 1 unit is demanded. The percentage change in price is now equal to

$$\frac{£10 - £9}{£9} \times 100 = \frac{£1}{£9} \times 100 = 11.11 \text{ per cent}$$

The percentage change in quantity demanded is

$$\frac{2 - 1}{2} \times 100 = \frac{1}{2} \times 100 = 50 \text{ per cent}$$

Thus, the price elasticity of demand is now equal to

50 per cent ÷ 11.11 per cent = 4.5

Quite a difference! We show this in Figure 5.1(a).

Using average values

For the same segment of the demand curve, we get different values of price elasticity of demand because the original prices and quantities depend on whether we move up or down the demand curve. The absolute changes in price and quantity are the same size regardless of direction. But the original price is higher when moving down the demand curve than when moving up the demand curve. When moving up the demand curve, the original quantity demanded is greater. Since a percentage change depends on the size of the original value, the percentages we calculate for price elasticity of demand will be affected by choosing a higher price and smaller quantity or a lower price and greater quantity. One way out of this difficulty is to *take the average* of the two prices and the two quantities over the range we are considering and compare the change with the average, instead of comparing it with the price or quantity at the start of the change.

The formula for computing price elasticity of demand then becomes

$$e_\text{d} = \frac{\text{change in quantity}}{\text{sum of quantities}/2} \div \frac{\text{change in price}}{\text{sum of prices}/2}$$

$$\times 100 \text{ per cent}$$

We can rewrite this more simply if we do two things: (1) we can let Q_1 and Q_2 equal the two different quantities demanded before and after the price change, and P_1 and P_2 equal the two different prices; and (2) because we shall be dividing a percentage by a percentage, we simply use the ratio, or the decimal form, of the percentage. Therefore,

$$e_\text{d} = \frac{\text{change in } Q}{(Q_1 + Q_2)/2} \div \frac{\text{change in } P}{(P_1 + P_2)/2}$$

Look again at the example that showed a price elasticity of demand equal to 10 when moving from a £10 price to a £9 price, but gave an elasticity of 4.5 when moving from £9 to £10. We insert our numbers in the average formula just given, so that price elasticity of demand becomes in either case

$$\frac{1}{(1 + 2)/2} \div \frac{1}{(9 + 10)/2} = \frac{1}{3/2} \div \frac{1}{19/2}$$

$$= \frac{2}{3} \div \frac{2}{19}$$

$$= \frac{19}{3} = 6.33$$

We show this in Figure 5.1(b).

Thus, calculating the price elasticity of demand using the mid-point (or average) formula yields $e_\text{d} = 6.33$. This calculation is not affected by the direction of movement along the demand curve; that is, $e_\text{d} = 6.33$ whether we move up or down the demand curve over the range we have been considering.

If we now look again at Table 5.1 we note that columns 5 and 6 give us the average quantities and the average prices. And finally, in the last column, a numerical example of price elasticity of demand is given.

We see that the calculation of elasticity ranges from 21 down to 0.158. What does that mean? Simply that at very high prices for petrol, such as between £10 and £9 a gallon, the response to a 1 per cent decrease in price will be a 21 per cent increase in the quantity demanded. At the other extreme, at relatively low prices for petrol – say, between £2 and £1 per gallon – the elasticity of 0.158 means that a 1 per cent reduction in price will be followed by only 0.158 of a 1 per cent increase in the quantity demanded. Thus, in our example, elasticity falls as price falls.

Different kinds of price elasticity

We have definitions for the varying ranges of price elasticities depending on whether a 1 per cent change in price elicits more or less than a 1 per cent change in the quantity demanded.

a *Price-elastic demand* We say that a good has a price-elastic demand whenever the price elasticity of demand is greater than 1. A 1 per cent change in price causes a response greater than a 1 per cent change in quantity demanded. Candidates for elastic-demand sections of our demand schedule in Table 5.1 are obviously an elasticity of demand of 1.444 and above.

b *Unitary price elasticity of demand* In this situation, a 1 per cent change in price causes a response of exactly 1 per cent change in the quantity demanded.

c *Price-inelastic demand* Here, a 1 per cent change in price causes a response of less than 1 per cent change in quantity demanded. An elasticity of 0.692 and below in the last four rows of Table 5.1 represents a situation of inelastic demand.

Elasticity and total revenues

If you were in charge of the pricing decision for oil for, say, the Organization of Petroleum Exporting Countries (OPEC), how would you know when it was best to raise prices or not to raise prices? The answer depends on the effects of your pricing decision on total revenues, or total receipts, for the oil-producing countries. You might think that the way to increase total receipts is to increase price per unit. But is this always the case? Is it possible that a rise in price per unit could lead to a decrease in total revenues? The answers to these questions depend on the price elasticity of demand.

Let us look at Table 5.2, which is a reproduction in altered form of part of Table 5.1. In column 1, we again show the price of petrol in pounds. Column 2 lists the quantities demanded (we ignore that each value shown is actually in millions, for simplicity). In column 3, we multiply column 1 by column 2 to derive total revenues; and in column 4, we copy the values of elasticity from Table 5.1. Notice what happens to total revenues throughout the schedule. They rise steadily as the price rises from £1 to £5 per unit; then, when the price rises further to £6 per unit, total revenues remain constant at £30. At prices per unit higher than £6, total revenues actually fall as price is increased. So it is not safe to assume that a price increase is always the way to greater revenues. Indeed, if prices are above £6 per unit in this example, total revenues can only be increased by cutting prices – not by raising them.

Table 5.2

The relationship between price elasticity of demand and total revenues
Here we reproduce parts of Table 5.1 in different form. We show the elastic, unit elastic and inelastic sections of the demand schedule according to whether a reduction in price increases total revenues, causes them to remain constant or causes them to decrease, respectively.

1	2	3	4	
Price of petrol (£ per unit)	Units demanded (per time period)	Total revenue $TR = P \times Q$ [(1) × (2)]	$e_d = \dfrac{\text{change in } Q}{(Q_1 + Q_2)/2} \div \dfrac{\text{change in } P}{(P_1 + P_2)/2}$	
11	0	0	21	
10	1	10	6.333	
9	2	18	3.4	
8	3	24	2.143	elastic >1
7	4	28	1.444	
6	5	30	1	unit elastic = 1
5	6	30	0.692	
4	7	28	0.467	
3	8	24	0.294	inelastic <1
2	9	18	0.158	
1	10	10		

Labelling elasticity

The relationship between price and quantity on the demand schedule is given in columns 1 and 2 of Table 5.2. The demand curve DD representing that schedule is drawn in Figure 5.2(b). Figure 5.2(a) shows the total revenue curve representing the data in column 3. Notice first the level of these curves at small quantities. The demand curve is at a maximum height, but total revenue is zero, which makes sense according to this demand schedule – at maximum price no units will be purchased and therefore total revenue will be zero. As price is lowered, we travel down the demand curve, total revenues increase up to a price of £6 per unit, remain constant from £6 to £5 per unit, and then fall for lower unit prices. Corresponding to these three sections, demand is price elastic, unit elastic and price inelastic. Hence we have three relationships between the three types of price elasticity and total revenues.

a *Price-elastic demand*: a negative relationship between small changes in price and changes in total revenues. That is, if the firm lowers price, total revenues will rise when it faces demand that is price elastic. And if the firm raises price, total revenues will fall. Consider an example: if the price of Coca-Cola were raised by 25 per cent, and the price of all other soft drinks remained constant, the quantity demanded of Coca-Cola would probably fall dramatically. That is, the decrease in quantity demanded due to the increase in the price of Coca-Cola would be more than in proportion. Hence, such an increase in the price of

Coca-Cola would lead, in this example, to a reduction in the total revenues of the firms that bottle Coca-Cola.

b *Unit price-elastic demand*: small changes in price do not change total revenues. In other words, when the firm is facing demand that is unitary price elastic, if it increases price, total revenues will not change; if it decreases price, total revenues will not change either.

c *Price-inelastic demand*: a positive relationship between small changes in price and total revenue. In other words, when the firm is facing demand that is price inelastic, if it raises price, total revenues will go up; if it lowers price, total revenues will fall. Consider an example. Imagine that you are managing director of a company which has just invented a cure for the common cold that has been approved by the health authorities for sale to the public. Your company is not sure what price you should charge. It decides on a price of £1 per pill. The firm sells 20 million pills at that price over a year. You feel the price could be raised without too much effect on sales. So next year, you decide to raise the price by 25 per cent. Suppose that the number of pills sold dropped to 18 million per year. The price increase of about 25 per cent has led to approximately a 10 per cent decrease in quantity demanded. However, your total revenues will have risen because of the price increase.

We can see in Figure 5.2(b) the areas in the demand curve that are elastic, unit elastic and inelastic. For prices from £11 per unit to £5 per unit, as price decreases, total revenues rise from zero to £30. Clearly, demand is price elastic. When prices change from £6 to £5, however, total revenues remain constant at £30; demand is unit elastic. Finally, when price falls from £5 to £1, total revenue decreases from £30 to £10; demand is price inelastic. In Figures 5.2(a) and 5.2(b) we have labelled the sections of the demand curve accordingly, and we have also shown how total revenues first rise, remain constant and then fall.

The relationship between the price elasticity of demand and total revenue brings together some important microeconomic concepts. Total revenue, as we have noted, is the product of price per unit and quantity of units sold. The theory of demand states that, along a given demand curve, price and quantity changes will move in opposite directions: one increases as the other decreases. Consequently, what happens to the product of price and quantity depends on which of the opposing changes exerts a greater force on total revenue. But this is just what price elasticity of demand is designed to measure: responsiveness of quantity to a change in price. The relationship between price elasticity of demand and total revenue, TR, is summarized in Figure 5.3.

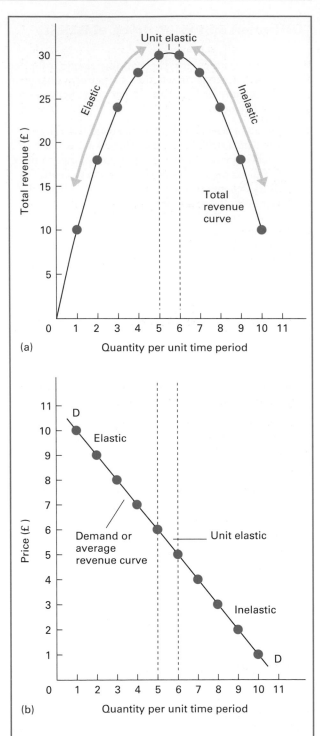

Figure 5.2
The relationship between price elasticity of demand and total revenues
(a) We show graphically what happens to total revenues, and we have labelled the sections elastic, unit elastic and inelastic, which we have also done in the accompanying demand curve in (b).

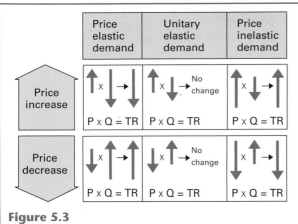

	Price elastic demand	Unitary elastic demand	Price inelastic demand
Price increase	↑ x ↓ → ↓ P x Q = TR	↑ x ↓ → No change P x Q = TR	↑ x ↓ → ↑ P x Q = TR
Price decrease	↓ x → ↑ ↑ P x Q = TR	↓ x ↑ → No change P x Q = TR	↓ x ↑ → ↓ P x Q = TR

Figure 5.3
The relationship between elasticity and total revenues

KEY POINTS

5.2

- Price elasticity of demand is related to total revenues (and total consumer expenditures).

- When demand is elastic, the change in price leads to a change in total revenues (and total consumer expenditures) in the opposite direction to the price change.

- When demand is inelastic, a change in price leads to a change in total revenues (and in consumer expenditures) in the same direction as the price change.

- When demand is unit elastic, a change in price leads to no change in total revenues (or in total consumer expenditures).

Changing price elasticity

We have seen in the example of the demand for petrol that the price elasticity changes as we move along the demand curve. That is, price elasticity is high when price is high and low when price is low. (Look again at columns 3 and 7 in Table 5.1.) As a general rule, along any demand curve that is a straight line, price elasticity declines as we move down that demand curve. Consider the reason why. In our example in Table 5.1, the change in price was always £1 and the change in the absolute quantity demanded was always 1 million gallons per day. Remember that here we are thinking about absolute changes only. What about percentage changes? At the upper end of the demand

curve, a £1 price change is in percentage terms relatively small (£1/[(£9 + £10)/2] = 10.5 per cent), whereas the 1 million change in quantity demanded is a large percentage change of the small quantity demanded (1/[(1 + 2)/2] = 66.7 per cent).

Thus, at the top of the demand curve, the elasticity formula will have a large numerator and a small denominator; therefore, price elasticity is relatively elastic (66.7%/10.5% = 6.33). At the lower end of the curve, the price elasticity formula will have a small numerator and a large denominator; thus, the demand curve is relatively inelastic (10.5%/66.7% = 0.158).

Elasticity and slope

Students often confuse elasticity and slope but they are not the same. We demonstrated that along a linear demand curve (that is, a straight line that has a constant slope, by definition) elasticity continuously falls with price. We must therefore always specify the price range when discussing price elasticity of demand, since most goods have ranges of both elasticity and inelasticity. The only time we can be sure of the elasticity of a straight-line demand curve by looking at it is if it is either perfectly horizontal or perfectly vertical. The horizontal straight-line demand curve has infinite elasticity at every quantity (it has only one price for every quantity). The vertical demand curve has zero elasticity at every price (it has only one quantity demanded at every price). Then we know that it has infinite elasticity or zero elasticity, respectively.

Extreme elasticities

There are two extremes in price elasticities of demand: one is total unresponsiveness, which is called a **perfectly inelastic demand** situation or zero elasticity, and the other is complete responsiveness, which is called an unlimited, infinite or **perfectly elastic demand** situation.

We show perfect inelasticity in Figure 5.4(a). The quantity demanded per year is 8 million units, no matter what the price. Hence, for any percentage price change, the quantity demanded will remain the same, and thus the change in the quantity demanded will be zero. Look at our formula for computing elasticity. If the change in the quantity demanded is zero, then the numerator is also zero, and anything divided into zero results in an answer of zero, too. Hence, there is perfect inelasticity.

At the opposite extreme is the situation depicted in Figure 5.4(b). Here we show that, at the price of 30p, an unlimited quantity will be demanded. At a price that is only slightly above 30p, none will be demanded. In other words, there is complete, or infinite, responsiveness here, and hence we call the demand schedule in Figure 5.4(b) infinitely elastic.

Most estimated demand-schedule elasticities lie between the two extremes. For example, in Table 5.3 we present demand elasticities for selected goods. These

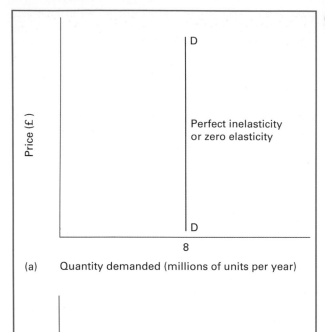

(a) Quantity demanded (millions of units per year)

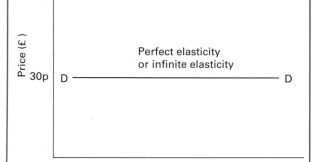

(b) Quantity demanded (millions of units per year)

Figure 5.4
Two extreme price elasticities
(a) Complete price unresponsiveness: price elasticity of demand is zero. (b) At a price of 30p consumers demand an unlimited quantity of the particular good in question. This is a case of infinite price elasticity of demand.

Table 5.3

Price elasticity for selected items

Product	Elasticity	Product	Elasticity
Elastic demands			
Gas	−2.26	Cheese	−1.20
Foreign travel	−1.83	Frozen peas	−1.12
Unit elasticity			
Chemists' goods	−1.00		
Inelastic demands			
Car travel	−0.83	Fruit juices	−0.80
Meat	−0.56	Fresh green vegetables	−0.58
Books and magazines	−0.52	Cakes and pastries	−0.37
Clothing	−0.50	Fresh potatoes	−0.21
Fruit	−0.49	Bread	−0.09
Cigarettes and tobacco	−0.26	Housing	−0.23

Sources: Left-hand column, A.S. Deaton, *Models and Projections of Demand in Post-War Britain*, Chapman and Hall, 1975, pp. 176–80; right-hand column, *Household Food Consumption and Expenditure, 1989*, HMSO, 1990

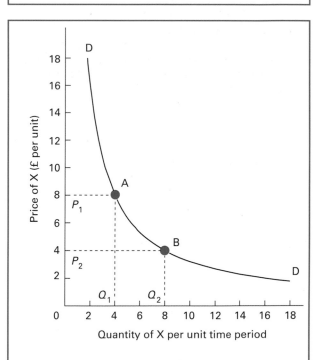

Figure 5.5
Constant price elasticity of demand
If the demand curve is curved in such a way that total revenues (and consumer expenditures) remain constant no matter what the price, then we have a demand curve that is everywhere unit elastic.

elasticities represent average elasticities over given price ranges. Different price ranges would yield different elasticity estimates for these goods.

Constant price elasticity of demand

It is possible to have a demand curve that actually curves in such a way that price elasticity of demand is constant. We give one example in Figure 5.5.

That demand curve, DD, exhibits unitary elasticity at any point. We can tell this by using the total revenues approach. At a price of £8 for this product, four will be purchased and so the total revenue will be £32. At a price of £4, the quantity demanded will be eight, for a total revenue of £32 again. At £2, sixteen will be bought for a total revenue of £32. A reduction in price leads to no change in total revenues; hence, price elasticity of demand is equal to 1. And this is true all along the curve because of its special curved shape. (If we extended DD in Figure 5.5 outwards it would become a very flat line at the extreme ends but, nonetheless, the elasticity at the extreme ends would be just the same as anywhere else on the curve.)

The formula for total revenues is

total revenues = price × quantity

Thus, in Figure 5.5, we measure total revenues by looking at the rectangle formed from the price to the demand curve to the quantity axis. The area of that rectangle is equal to total revenues for the particular quantity under consideration.

Relevance of price elasticity

1 How would you explain the price elasticity of demand for foreign travel of −1.83 in Table 5.3?
2 Given the price elasticity of demand for chemists' goods of −1.00, draw a demand curve. What is the significance of what you have drawn?
3 What does the price elasticity of demand for cheese of −1.20 mean?
4 What is the relevance of this figure for cheese-makers?
5 Do the data in Table 5.3 suggest that snack bars should be wary of increasing the prices of items such as doughnuts and Danish pastries?

KEY POINTS

5.3

■ The price elasticity of demand changes as we move down a straight-line demand curve; it becomes relatively more inelastic.

■ The price elasticity of demand cannot be determined by looking at the slope of a straight-line demand curve. There are two extreme exceptions:

■ when a demand curve is perfectly vertical, it has zero price elasticity of demand; it is completely inelastic;

■ when a demand curve is perfectly horizontal, it has completely elastic demand; its price elasticity of demand is infinite.

The determinants of the price elasticity of demand

We have learned how to calculate the price elasticity of demand. We know that it ranges numerically from zero – completely inelastic – to infinity – completely elastic. What we would like to do now is come up with a list of the determinants of the price elasticity of demand. The price elasticity of demand for a particular commodity at any price depends on

1 the existence and closeness of substitutes;
2 the length of time allowed for adjustment to changes in the price of the commodity.

Existence of substitutes

The closer the substitutes for a particular commodity, the greater will be its price elasticity of demand. At the limit, if there is a perfect substitute, the price elasticity of the commodity will be infinity. Thus, even the slightest increase in the commodity's price will cause an enormous reduction in the quantity demanded; quantity demanded will fall to zero. When we talk about less extreme examples, we can only speak in terms of the number and the closeness of substitutes that are available. Thus, we shall find that the more narrowly we define a good, the closer and greater will be the number of substitutes available. Take an example. If we talk about food and drinks in general, there are not many substitutes. If we talk about tea, there are certainly lots of substitutes, including coffee, milk, soft drinks and so on. Thus, the more narrowly we define the good, the more substitutes there are available and the greater will be the price elasticity of demand. In this example, the price elasticity of demand for all beverages will be numerically much less than it is for, say, PG Tips tea. If the price of PG Tips tea increased by 20 per cent, a lot of people might switch over to another brand of tea such as Typhoo. On the other hand, if the price of all beverages went up on average by 20 per cent, certainly a smaller percentage of beverage consumers would switch over to beverage substitutes, such as food or recreation or whatever else might conceivably be considered a substitute for beverages. The availability of an alternative product for a particular commodity is not the only relevant factor, however, in determining the sensitivity of demand. In the real world consumers do not all react instantaneously to price changes, and so we must recognize the importance of time.

The time for adjustment in rate of purchase

When the price of a commodity changes and that price change persists, more people will learn about it. Further, consumers will be better able to revise their consumption patterns, the longer the time they have to do so. And, in fact, the longer the time they do take, the less costly it will be for them to engage in this revision of consumption patterns. Consider a price decrease. The longer the time that the price decrease persists, the greater will be the number of new uses that consumers will 'discover' for the particular commodity, and the greater will be the number of new users of that particular commodity.

It is possible to make a very strong statement about the relationship between the price elasticity of demand and the time allowed for adjustment: the longer any price change persists, the greater the price elasticity of demand. Otherwise stated, price elasticity of demand is greater in the long run than in the short run.

Let us take an example. Suppose the price of electricity goes up by 50 per cent. How do you adjust in the short run? You can turn the lights off more often, you can stop using the stereo as much as you used to, and so on. Otherwise, it is very difficult to cut back on your consumption of electricity. In the long run, though, you can devise methods to reduce your consumption. If your house has electric central heating you could contemplate switching to gas heating. If you are about to move house, one with gas-fired central heating would have greater attraction than previously. The next time you move house you will have a gas cooker installed. You may even purchase fluorescent bulbs because

they use less electricity. The longer you have to adjust to such a sudden dramatic increase in the price of elasticity, the more ways you will find to cut electricity consumption. We would therefore expect that the short-run demand curve for electricity would be highly inelastic (in the price range around P_1), as demonstrated by D_1D_1 in Figure 5.6. However, the long-run demand curve may exhibit much more elasticity (in the neighbourhood of P_1), as demonstrated by D_3D_3. Indeed, we can think of an entire family of demand curves such as those depicted in the figure. The short-run demand curve is for that period when there is no time for adjustment. As more time is allowed, the demand curve becomes flatter, going first to D_2D_2. Thus, at the price of P_1 elasticity differs for each of these curves. It is greater for the less steep curves (but remember, slope alone does not measure elasticity for the entire curve).

How to define the short and the long run

We have mentioned the short run and we have mentioned the long run. Is the short run one week, two weeks, a month, two months? Is the long run three years, four years, five years? The answer is that there is no one answer! What we mean by the long run is that period of time necessary for consumers to make full adjustment to a given price change, all other things held constant. In the case of the demand for electricity, the long run will be however long it takes consumers to switch over to cheaper sources of heating, to buy houses that are more energy efficient, to purchase manufactured appliances that are more energy efficient, and so on. The long-run price elasticity of demand for electricity therefore relates to a period of at least several years. The short run – by default, as it were – is any period less than the long run.

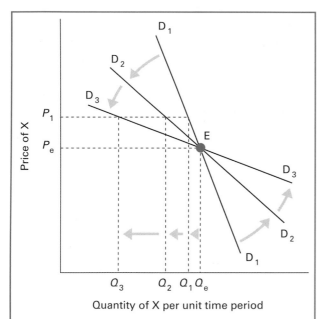

Figure 5.6

Short-run and long-run price elasticity of demand
The longer the time allowed for adjustment the greater the price elasticity of demand. Consider an equilibrium situation in which the market price is P_e and the quantity demanded is Q_e. Then there is a price increase to P_1. In the short run we move from equilibrium quantity demanded Q_e to Q_1. After more time is allowed for adjustment the demand curve rotates at original price P_e to D_2D_2. The quantity demanded falls again now to Q_2. After even more time is allowed for adjustment the demand curve rotates at price P_e to D_3D_3. At the higher price P_1 in the long run the quantity demanded falls all the way to Q_3.

Do cheaper cars create jobs?

In Ruritania, a hypothetical country whose currency is the pound sterling (£), the three firms in the car industry together sold 12 million cars in 1999 at an average price of £5000. However, because the economy is in a depressed state the car industry is not working at full capacity and many car workers are not employed for a full working week.

The car workers' union, Vehicle and General Workers, suggests that each producer reduce his price by £200. This action, the Union argues, would result in another 2 million cars being sold while aggregate profits would be maintained at £4000 million.

6 Calculate the value of the elasticity of demand (correct to 1 decimal place) assumed by the Vehicle and General Workers' Union. Comment on this value. **A✓**

7 A spokesman for the Ruritanian car industry points out that government economists have estimated that the elasticity of demand for cars is, in fact, –0.5. Assuming this estimate is accurate, what would be the impact on the car industry? **A✓**

Cross-price elasticity of demand

In Chapter 3 we discussed the effect of a change in the price of one good on the quantity demanded of a related good. We defined substitutes and complements in terms of whether a reduction in the price of one caused a shift leftward or rightward, respectively, in the demand curve of the other. If the price of butter is held constant, the amount of butter demanded will certainly be influenced by the price of a close substitute like margarine. If the price of CD players is held constant, the quantity of CD players demanded is most likely to be affected by changes in the price of CDs.

What we need to do is come up with a numerical measure of the price responsiveness of demand to the prices of related goods. This is called the **cross-price elasticity of demand**, which is defined as the percentage change in the demand for one good divided by the percentage change in the price of the related good. Hence, the cross-price elasticity of demand is a measure of the responsiveness of one good's quantity demanded to changes in a related good's price.

$$E_{xy} = \frac{\text{change in quantity demanded of good x}}{\text{change in price of good y}}$$

When two goods are *substitutes*, the cross-price elasticity of demand will be positive. For example, when the price of margarine goes up, the quantity demanded of butter will go up, too. A producer of margarine could use a numerical estimate of the cross-price elasticity of demand between butter and margarine. For example, if the price of butter went up by 10 per cent, and the margarine producer knew that the

cross-price elasticity of demand was 1, he or she could estimate that the demand for margarine would also go up by 10 per cent. Plans for increasing margarine production could then be made.

When two related goods are *complements*, the cross-price elasticity of demand will be negative. To use an earlier example, when the price of CDs falls, the quantity demanded of CD players can be expected to rise (Figure 5.7).

KEY POINTS

5.4

- Demand curves can be linear or non-linear. Linear demand curves have constantly changing elasticities as we move along them. Non-linear demand curves may be drawn with constant elasticities of any desired value. We have constructed one that exhibits unit elasticity everywhere on the curve.

- The determinants of price elasticity of demand are (1) the number and closeness of substitutes and (2) the length of time allowed for adjustment to a change in prices.

- Cross-price elasticity of demand is the percentage change in the demand for one good divided by the percentage change in the price of the related good.

- For substitutes the cross-price elasticities are positive whereas for complements the cross-price elasticities are negative.

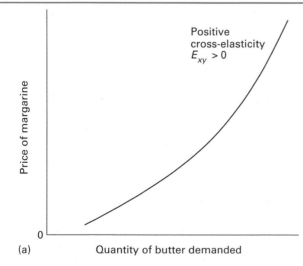

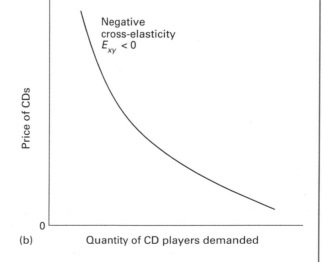

Figure 5.7
Cross-elasticities: (a) substitutes; (b) complements
(a) The cross-elasticity of demand with respect to the price of a substitute. When the price of margarine increases, the quantity of butter demanded also increases.

(b) The cross-elasticity of demand with respect to the price of a complement. When the price of CDs falls, the quantity of CD players demanded increases.

Income elasticity of demand

In Chapter 3, we talked about the determinants of demand. One of those determinants was income. Using the same approach as we did in measuring the sensitivity of demand to changes in price, we can apply our understanding of elasticity to the relationship between changes in income and changes in demand. We measure the responsiveness of quantity demanded to income changes by the **income elasticity of demand**:

e_y = income elasticity of demand

$$= \frac{\text{percentage change in the amount of goods purchased}}{\text{percentage change in income}}$$

Income elasticity of demand refers to a *horizontal shift* in the demand curve in response to changes in income (while price elasticity of demand refers to a movement *along the curve* in response to price changes). Shifts in the demand curve will obviously have major implications for business persons. Those goods whose income elasticity is positive will be ones where markets will grow as consumers have more income to spend. Conversely, goods and services whose income elasticity is negative will be ones that will experience declining markets as consumer incomes increase. Before elaborating on this important matter, let us be clear how to calculate income elasticity of demand.

A simple example will demonstrate how income elasticity of demand can be computed. In Table 5.4, we give the relevant data. The product in question is compact discs. We assume that the price of CDs remains constant relative to other prices. In period 1, six CDs per month are purchased. Income per month is £200. In period 2, monthly income is increased to £300 and the quantity of CDs demanded per month is increased to eight. We can apply the following calculation:

$$\text{income elasticity of demand } e_y = \frac{(8-6)/6}{(300-200)/200}$$

$$= \frac{1/3}{1/2} = 0.667$$

Table 5.4

How income affects the quantity of compact discs demanded

Time period	Quantity of CDs demanded	Income per month
Period 1	6	£200
Period 2	8	£300

Hence, measured income elasticity of demand for CDs for the individual represented in this example is 0.667. Note that this holds only for the move from six CDs to eight CDs purchased per month. In the move for decreased income from £300 to £200 per month and from eight to six CDs per month, the calculation becomes

$$\frac{(8-6)/8}{(200-300)/300} = \frac{2/8}{100/300} = \frac{1/4}{1/3} = 0.75$$

Thus, the measured income elasticity of demand is equal to 0.75.

To get the same income elasticity of demand over the same range of values, regardless of the direction of change (increase or decrease), we can use the same mid-point formula that we used in computing the price elasticity of demand. When doing so, we produce Table 5.4.

This example involves just one product when there is a major increase in one person's income. Now let us consider the economy as a whole and how consumers alter their spending habits as they have more money available to spend. We might reasonably expect to find that spending on some goods and services is very sensitive to quite small changes in income. With yet other goods and services this income elasticity is less marked. We need something to classify the different reactions of consumers.

Different kinds of income elasticity

We have the following definitions for the varying ranges of income elasticities depending on whether a 1 per cent change in income results in more or less than a 1 per cent change in the quantity demanded.

1 *Income-elastic demand* We say that a good or service has an income-elastic demand whenever the income elasticity is greater than 1. A 1 per cent change in income causes a greater than 1 per cent change in quantity demanded. The term luxury goods is sometimes used in cases of income elasticities being above 1, but this is a rather questionable one given that the word 'luxury' has a subjective connotation.

2 *Income-inelastic demand* Here a 1 per cent change in income causes a change of less than 1 per cent in quantity demanded. If the income inelasticity is less than 1 but above zero then this implies that the good or service is not one that is strongly sensitive to changes in consumer incomes. In other words, it is a consumer necessity.

3 *Negative income elasticity* Where the income elasticity is negative then it implies that, in the case of these goods, consumers are prepared to reduce their spending as they get richer. In these situations the relevant goods are inferior goods. In Chapter 3 we suggested that potatoes might be an example of an inferior good.

The importance of income elasticity

As incomes increase and consumers adjust their patterns of spending, there are important repercussions for those engaged in business activity. Table 5.5 shows some real-world estimates of income elasticities in the United Kingdom.

Table 5.5 shows that most foods are normal goods for which expenditure increases as income increases, but at a slower rate. In both time periods – 1985–7 and 1995–7 – the most income-sensitive food groups were cheese, fish, meat and meat products, fruit and vegetables (including potatoes). For these five food groups, a 1 per cent increase in income was associated with an increase in expenditure of between 0.20 per cent and 0.42 per cent in 1985–7, and between 0.18 per cent and 0.32 per cent in 1995–7. Eggs, fats and sugar were the least income-sensitive food groups, for which a 1 per cent increase in income per person was associated with an increase in expenditure of between 0.05 per cent and 0.13 per cent in 1985–7, and between –0.06 per cent and 0.04 per cent in 1995–7. Table 5.5 shows that the estimated income elasticities tend to be lower in 1995–7 than ten years earlier.

If we now consider the implications of these income elasticities for items of food, we can begin to realize the implications for food processors in the UK economy. Let us have in mind the following question: do particular food markets expand or contract as households have more income to spend?

You will note that in none of these ten groups of food-stuffs is the income elasticity as high as 1.0, and in most cases it is closer to zero than 1.0. In one food group it is negative. What does this mean for food processors (and, indeed, farmers)? It means that as households have more income available to spend they devote very little to extra food consumption. As a result, food processors in most of the individual food markets do not experience steadily rising sales of food. Thus, processing firms like United Biscuits cannot expect that the consumption of biscuits in volume terms will show any encouraging growth. So if UK consumers show little or no willingness to munch more biscuits as each year passes by, the only course open to United Biscuits in seeking higher sales is to obtain a bigger share of the static biscuit market. By offering new varieties of biscuit in well-planned marketing campaigns, United Biscuits might then prompt households to switch some of their biscuit-buying to United Biscuits brands. Rival firms would, as a result, face declining sales and lose some of their share of the market.

KEY POINT

5.5

- The sensitivity of the quantity demanded to changes in income is called the income elasticity of demand. For 'luxury' goods the income elasticity is greater than 1; for inferior goods the income elasticity is negative. The degree of income elasticity is a major determinant of how the market for a good or service is growing over time.

Household income and expenditure

We have pointed out that there are different kinds of income elasticity reflecting whether goods are 'luxury' goods, normal goods or inferior goods.

Table 5.6 shows that in 1997 total household expenditure in the UK was just under £500 billion, which represented an increase of 93 per cent in real terms on the 1971 level. (You will recall that in Chapter 2 we defined real terms to mean that the relevant figure has been adjusted for the falling value of money due to rising prices.) Examination of Table 5.6 shows that expenditure increased in all of the categories of household expenditure, with one exception – that of tobacco. Clearly in this latter case, whatever the influence of income on tobacco expenditure, it has been more than offset by health fears such that there has been a fall in the numbers smoking cigarettes. It is also apparent in looking at Table 5.6 that the growth of expenditure on some categories of goods and services has been more rapid than that on others. For example, expenditure by UK householders abroad more than quadrupled between 1971 and 1997. In contrast, expenditure on food grew much less rapidly – by just over a quarter. This illustrates the point made earlier that food as a consumer necessity is not as strongly sensitive to a change in household incomes. What this means is that food as a proportion of household expenditure has decreased from about 17 per cent in 1971 to 11 per cent in 1997, as Figure 5.8 shows.

Table 5.5

Estimated income elasticities of demand

	1985–7	1995–7
Cheese	0.33	0.23
Fish	0.30	0.18
Meat and meat products	0.26	0.23
Fruit	0.42	0.32
Milk and cream	0.14	0.10
Eggs	0.08	0.01
Fats and oils	0.13	0.04
Cereals, including bread	0.17	0.16
Vegetables, including potatoes	0.20	0.24
Sugar and preserves	0.05	–0.06

Source: *National Food Survey*, HMSO, 1998

Table 5.6

Household expenditure in the United Kingdom
Indices 1971 = 100

	Indices at constant 1995 prices						£ billion (current prices) 1997
	1971	1981	1986	1991	1996	1997	
Household goods	100	138	180	227	266	293	86.0
Transport and communication	100	133	175	195	235	247	73.2
Housing	100	121	131	140	149	150	66.5
Food	100	104	109	115	125	127	53.3
Clothing and footwear	100	129	178	200	265	279	31.4
Alcohol	100	127	134	132	131	135	29.4
Fuel and power	100	119	135	146	146	143	28.8
Recreational and cultural activities	100	142	156	182	206	210	24.6
Tobacco	100	89	74	71	59	58	12.4
Other services	100	109	150	200	222	230	94.0
Less expenditure by foreign tourists, etc.	100	152	197	187	254	246	−14.0
Household expenditure abroad	100	193	229	298	380	440	14.9
All household expenditure	100	121	144	166	185	193	500.6

Source: *Social Trends 29*, HMSO, 1999

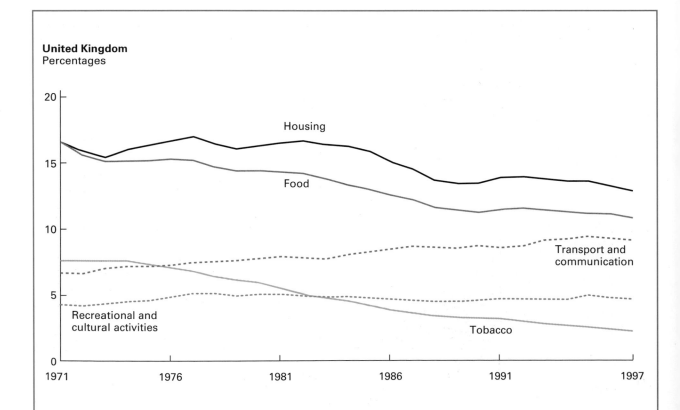

Figure 5.8
Household expenditure on selected items (at constant 1995 prices)

Source: *Social Trends 29*, HMSO, 1999

Different levels of income

Table 5.6 shows the aggregate levels of household spending in the UK in 1997 when individual households had very different levels of income. If we disaggregate the total income of households according to different levels of income, how does the income sensitivity of expenditure vary with the level of income? We can split all UK households into ten groups (or deciles), each accounting for 10 per cent of incomes, as in Figure 5.7. In Group 1 is the 10 per cent of households with the lowest incomes, and in Group 10 is the 10 per cent of households with the highest income. Figure 5.9 shows that spending increases as one moves up from Group 1 to Group 10. But in part these differences in spending arise due to factors other than just the income of the household. The number of persons in the household and their age will also affect levels of spending. Thus in Group 1 the average household size was less (1.3 persons) than in Group 10 (3.1 persons). Also, the average age of the head of householder was a little older in Group 1 than in Group 10. We thus have to be careful not to infer that differences in the income of households explain differences in spending between income groups.

Figure 5.10 shows expenditure on two categories of expenditure – fuel and power, and leisure services. Households in the highest income group – Group 10 – spent just over twice as much on fuel and power as households in the lowest income group. But as a percentage of total expenditure, Figure 5.10 shows that

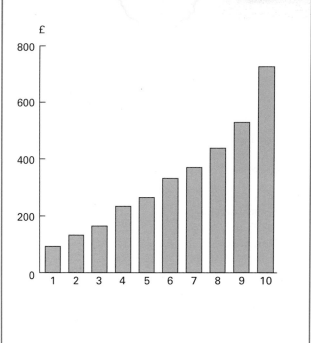

Figure 5.9
Average weekly expenditure by gross income decile group

Source: *Social Trends 29*, HMSO, 1999

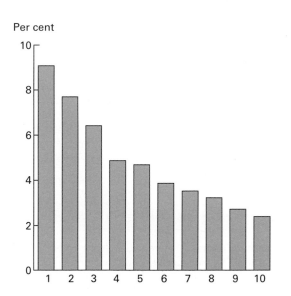

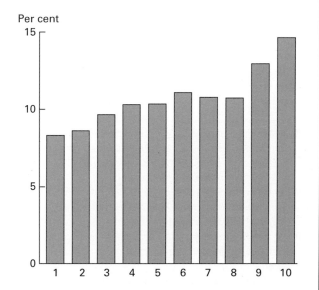

Figure 5.10
(a) Expenditure on fuel and power as a percentage of total expenditure by gross income decile group;

(b) expenditure on leisure services as a percentage of total expenditure by gross income decile group

Source: *Social Trends 29*, HMSO, 1999

Table 5.7

Estimated income elasticities at quintile boundaries

	Lowest 20% of households		Lowest 40% of households		Lowest 60% of households		Lowest 80% of households	
	1985–7	1995–7	1985–7	1995–7	1985–7	1995–7	1985–7	1995–7
Cheese	0.38	0.25	0.34	0.23	0.30	0.18	0.21	0.22
Fish	0.38	0.20	0.39	0.16	0.21	0.17	0.11	0.34
Meat and meat products	0.31	0.21	0.28	0.19	0.17	0.17	0.15	0.22
Fruit	0.44	0.35	0.48	0.33	0.41	0.29	0.32	0.35
Milk and cream	0.26	0.16	0.19	0.06	0.03	−0.02	−0.14	−0.02
Eggs	0.18	0.06	0.15	−0.01	−0.12	−0.19	−0.23	−0.18
Fats and oils	0.26	0.15	0.22	0.02	0.01	−0.07	−0.24	−0.03
Cereals, including bread	0.19	0.15	0.17	0.13	0.06	0.07	0.01	0.19
Vegetables, including potatoes	0.22	0.20	0.18	0.05	0.13	0.15	0.10	0.28
Sugar and preserves	0.21	0.10	0.17	−0.12	−0.16	−0.30	−0.48	−0.33
Miscellaneous food	0.31	0.20	·0.28	0.25	0.16	0.23	0.13	0.40
All food	0.28	0.20	0.25	0.17	0.13	0.13	0.07	0.21

Source: *National Food Survey*, 1997

households in Group 10 spent 2 per cent on fuel and power compared with 9 per cent by households in Group 1. In contrast, in the case of leisure services, not only did Group 10 households spend much more than Group 1 households (13 times more); the proportion of total expenditure accounted for by leisure services was almost twice that of Group 1 households.

The data below present a more disaggregated picture of the influence of income on food spending than we saw in Table 5.5. Table 5.7 shows estimated income elasticities for four household groups divided into the lowest 20 per cent, 40 per cent, 60 per cent and 80 per cent of incomes. (The disaggregation here thus considers the data in one-fifth (quintiles) rather than one-tenths, as in Figures 5.9 and 5.10.)

8 Do the income elasticities generally rise or fall as you compare the lowest 20 per cent of households with the three other household groups in 1985–7? Is this what you would have expected? **A✓**

9 Do the income elasticities generally rise or fall as you compare the data for 1985–7 with that in 1995–7? Is this what you would have expected? **A✓**

10 What is the meaning of the negative signs for items like eggs, sugar and preserves in the highest income group? **A✓**

11 What is the meaning of the estimated income elasticities for fruit? **A✓**

12 The data focus on the influence of income on food spending. How would you expect expenditure also to vary between households regarding other demographic characteristics such as the number of children in the household, whether the household has a freezer, and geographical region in the UK?

Elasticity of supply

The **price elasticity of supply** is defined in a similar way to the price elasticity of demand. Supply elasticities are generally positive; this is because, at higher prices, larger quantities will generally be forthcoming from suppliers. Our definition of the price elasticity of supply, e_s, is the following:

$$e_s = \frac{\text{percentage change in quantity supplied}}{\text{percentage change in price}}$$

We use some hypothetical data to illustrate the price elasticity of supply for petrol. This is done in Table 5.8. Note that the price elasticity of supply remains constant and equal to 1 in this particular example. This is a special feature of any straight-line supply curve that passes through the origin, that is, whose intercept is zero.*

Classifying supply elasticities

Just as with demand, there are different types of supply elasticities. They are similar in definition.

1 If a 1 per cent increase in price elicits a greater than 1 per cent increase in the quantity supplied, we say that, at the particular price in question on the supply schedule, supply is elastic.

---

* If the straight-line supply curve has a vertical intercept then price elasticity is greater than 1 (elastic throughout); if a straight-line supply curve intersects the horizontal axis then its price elasticity of supply is less than 1 (inelastic throughout).

Table 5.8

Numerical calculation of the price elasticity of supply for petrol

1	2	3	4	5	6	7
Quantity supplied Q (millions of gallons per day)	Change in Q (millions of gallons per day)	Price P per gallon (£)	Change in P (£)	Average quantities $(Q_1 + Q_2)/2$	Average prices $(P_1 + P_2)/2$	$e_s = \dfrac{\text{change in } Q}{(Q_1 + Q_2)/2} \div \dfrac{\text{change in } P}{(P_1 + P_2)/2}$
0	2	0.00	1.0	1	0.5	$(2/1) \div (1.0/0.5) = 1$
2	2	1.00	1.0	3	1.5	$(2/3) \div (1.0/1.5) = 1$
4	2	2.00	1.0	5	2.5	$(2/5) \div (1.0/2.5) = 1$
6	2	3.00	1.0	7	3.5	$(2/7) \div (1.0/3.5) = 1$
8	2	4.00	1.0	9	4.5	$(2/9) \div (1.0/4.5) = 1$
10		5.00				

2   If, on the other hand, a 1 per cent increase in price elicits a less than 1 per cent increase in the quantity supplied, we refer to that as an inelastic supply situation.

3   If the percentage change in the quantity supplied is just equal to the percentage change in the price, then we talk about unitary elasticity of supply.

We show in Figure 5.11 two supply schedules, SS and S'S'. Can you tell at a glance, without reading the caption, which one is infinitely elastic and which one is perfectly inelastic?

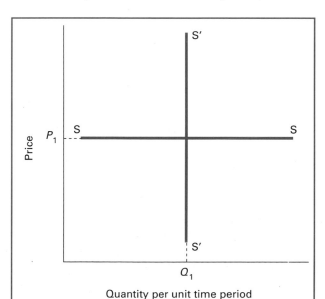

Figure 5.11
The extremes in supply curves
SS is a perfectly elastic supply curve, S'S' is a perfectly inelastic one. In the former case an unlimited quantity will be forthcoming at the price P_1. In the latter, no matter what the price the quantity supplied will be Q_1.

As you might expect, most supply schedules exhibit elasticities that are somewhere in the range zero to infinity.

Price elasticity of supply and length of time for adjustment

We pointed out earlier that, the longer the time allowed for adjustment, the greater the price elasticity of demand. It turns out that the same proposition applies to supply. The longer the time for adjustment, the more price elastic is the supply curve. Consider why this is true.

1   The longer the time allowed for adjustment, the more firms are able to figure out ways to increase production in an industry.

2   The longer the time allowed, the more resources can flow into an industry through expansion of existing firms.

We therefore talk about short- and long-run price elasticities of supply. The short run is defined as the time period during which full adjustment has not yet taken place. Thus, the long run is the time period during which firms have been able to adjust fully to the change in price.

Consider an example: an increase in the price of housing. In the very short run, when there is no time allowed for adjustment, the amount of housing services offered for rent or for sale is relatively inelastic. However, as more time is allowed for adjustment, current owners of the housing stock can find ways to increase the amount of housing services they will offer for rent from given buildings. The owner of a large house can decide, for example, to have two of his or her children move into one room so that a 'new' extra bedroom can be rented out. This can also be done by the owner of a large house who decides to move into an apartment and rent each floor of the house to a family. Thus, the quantity of housing services supplied will increase. We can show a whole set of supply curves similar to the ones we generated for demand. In Figure 5.12, when

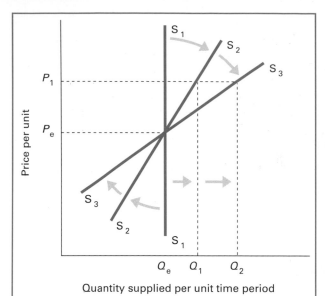

Figure 5.12
Short-run and long-run price elasticity of supply
The longer the time allowed for adjustment the greater the
price elasticity of supply. Consider a given situation in which
the price is P_e and the quantity supplied is Q_e. We assume
that suppliers are unable to do anything in the very short
run even when there is a price increase. Given some time
for adjustment the supply curve will rotate at price P_e to
S_2S_2. Finally the long-run supply curve is shown by S_3S_3. The
quantity supplied again increases to Q_2.

nothing can be done in the short run, the supply curve is
vertical, S_1S_1. As more time is allowed for adjustment, the
supply curve rotates to S_2S_2 and then S_3S_3, becoming more
elastic as it rotates. In Chapter 9 we consider how time lags
can cause considerable fluctuation in the prices of agricultural commodities and foodstuffs. Thus we will develop a
dynamic model of price determination in these markets.

KEY POINTS

5.6

- Price elasticity of supply is given by the percentage
  change in quantity supplied divided by the
  percentage change in price.

- Usually, price elasticities of supply are positive –
  higher prices yield larger quantities supplied.

- Long-run supply curves are more elastic than short-
  run supply curves because the longer the time
  allowed, the more resources can flow into or out of an
  industry when price changes.

Case Study

The potato market

All is not well in the sleepy village of Upwell in Norfolk.
Two brothers, Peter and Robert, are the latest victims of
thieves who operate mainly in Norfolk and Lincolnshire,
the 'Potato Belt' of England. Last week, in the dead of
night, a van drove up, parked outside their warehouse,
loaded up six tons of their produce, and drove off with
the equivalent of £2700 worth of potatoes.

Normally, the humble potato is about as desirable as the
earth it is buried in. But this year it is a prestige product, as
respected as caviar or truffles. This is due more to supply
and demand than its cordon bleu qualities. According to
Robert, crop results in Britain and Europe have been disastrous. 'The whole of northern Europe has been in trouble
with bad weather conditions. Usually Holland sells to us,
but this year it's been the other way round.' The Potato
Marketing Board reports a similar story of scarcity. In recent
years farmers experienced a surplus, so last year they
decided to plant less. In addition, the wet weather during

harvesting last autumn made it difficult to store the
produce. Potatoes are susceptible to soft rot, which can
turn a whole store into a nasty mess.

These thieves, it seems, will stop at nothing. Since
April, Norfolk police have dealt with a spate of midnight
raids in which warehouses were broken into and tons of
potatoes loaded into lorries and driven away. Peter and
Robert grow the Maris Piper variety used by chip (French
fries) shops. 'Everyone who had them asked for more,'
explains Robert. 'They make a wonderful fry.' Chip shop
owners around the country are desperate for them, paying £14 for a 55lb bag rather than the normal £7. Unlike
newer, cheaper crop potatoes, Maris Pipers have that cov-
eted crispy texture after frying and they store well. In the
shops, maincrop potatoes have more than quadrupled in
price, rising from, on average, 6p a pound to an all-time
high of 29p a pound. In such a lucrative niche, it is hardly
surprising that the potato thief will go to such lengths.

Peter and Robert admit that potato farmers in the area
have capitalized on this year's demand. 'But they should

understand,' says Robert, 'that when the farmers do well from potatoes, the whole economy here improves.' Next year there may be less cause for local resentment, since farmers will be planning a larger yield and a lowering of prices. As Robert says: 'that's when the trouble will stop. They'll go back to stealing televisions from shops.'

Source: Adapted from *The Independent*, 27 June 1995

1 What does the extract suggest about (a) the price elasticity of demand for potatoes; and (b) the price elasticity of supply of potatoes?

2 With reference to your answer, explain why the prices of potatoes are subject to considerable fluctuations. Illustrate your answer with a supply and demand diagram.

3 What does the extract suggest about one type of potato being a good substitute for another type?

4 Explain how the demand for potatoes might be affected by an increase in real incomes in the UK.

5 Explain the statement 'when the farmers do well from potatoes, the whole economy here improves'.

Case Study

Britons on the move

The following data show methods of passenger transport in Great Britain during the period 1981–91, together with estimates of the cost of various means of travel.

Distance travelled in Great Britain by mode (billion passenger kilometres)

	1981	1991	1996	1997
Road				
Cars, vans and taxis	394	582	609	619
Bus and coach	49	44	44	43
Bicycle	5	5	4	4
All road	**458**	**638**	**661**	**670**
Rail	34	38	38	41
Air	3	5	6	7
All modes	**495**	**681**	**706**	**717**

Source: *Social Trends 29*, HMSO, 1999

Passenger transport prices in United Kingdom (1981 – 100)

	1981	1986	1991	1996	1998
Motoring costs					
Vehicle tax and insurance	100	146	220	299	335
Maintenance	100	138	195	251	276
Petrol and oil	100	145	156	213	240
Purchase of vehicles	100	116	144	165	174
All motoring expenditure	**100**	**131**	**163**	**205**	**224**
Fares and other travel costs					
Bus and coach fares	100	139	198	261	278
Rail fares	100	137	201	262	278
Other	100	107	137	156	167
All fares and other travel	**100**	**135**	**186**	**229**	**244**
Retail prices index	100	137	185	214	227

Source: *Social Trends 29*, HMSO, 1999

The data show that between 1981 and 1998 the cost of public transport rose by more than the cost of motoring.

1 What was the increased cost of motoring between 1981 and 1998?

2 What was the increased cost of bus and coach fares during this same period?

3 What do the data offer as illustrations of (a) own-price elasticity, (b) cross-price elasticity, in respect of travel?

Between 1981 and 1997 the personal income of households in the United Kingdom rose at an average annual rate of 2.7 per cent. This figure relates to incomes after taxation has been deducted and after price increases have been taken into account.

This is a measure of how much households were better off during this 16-year period.

4 What do these data on income offer as a basis for assessing the changing use of passenger transport between 1981 and 1997 in response to the rise in real incomes?

Exam Preparation

Multiple choice questions

1 Due to a fall in the price of cameras, the demand for film has risen by 20 per cent. The cross-elasticity of demand between cameras and films is −2. Which change in camera prices has brought this about?
   A from $55 to $50
   B from $55 to $45
   C from $50 to $45
   D from $50 to $40

2 A manufacturer progressively reduces the price of his product in an attempt to increase total revenue. The table shows the outcome of this policy.

Price ($)	Total revenue 000's ($)
10	750
9	750
8	750

   What is the price elasticity of demand for the product?
   A perfect inelastic
   B relatively inelastic
   C perfectly elastic
   D unitary elastic

3 If the cross-elasticity of demand for good A with respect to a change in the price of good B is zero, then good A and good B can be assumed to be
   A composite goods
   B substitute goods
   C complementary goods
   D neither substitute nor complementary goods

4 Under which of the following circumstances would an increase in the price of product X result in a fall in the demand for product Y?
   A the demand for Y is income inelastic
   B Y is an inferior good
   C X and Y are complementary goods
   D X and Y are substitutes
   E the demand for Y is price elastic

5 The curve in the diagram shows quantity of goods demanded in relation to income and
   A has a price elasticity of unity throughout its length
   B represents a normal good
   C represents an inferior good
   D represents a good where income elasticity of demand is zero
   E is a 'perverse' demand curve

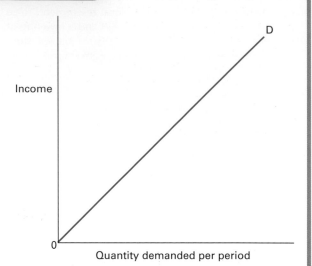

6 When elasticity of demand is equal to unity an increase in price will result in
   A a reduction in the quantity demanded and a decrease in total revenue
   B a reduction in the quantity demanded and an increase in total revenue
   C an increase in the quantity demanded and total revenue remaining the same
   D both the quantity demanded and total revenue remaining the same
   E the quantity demanded falling and total revenue remaining the same

7 The cross-elasticity of demand for perfect substitutes is
   A negative
   B zero
   C unitary
   D infinite

8 Evidence suggests that the cross-elasticity of demand between private and public transport, whilst positive, is very low. It therefore follows that
   A a fall in the demand for private transport would cause a small rise in the demand for public transport
   B a rise in the price of private transport would cause a slight fall in the demand for private transport
   C a fall in the demand for private transport would cause a small rise in the price of public transport
   D a rise in the price of private transport would cause a small rise in the demand for public transport

9 The following revenue situations result from a 1 per cent fall in the price of a commodity. Select the situation describing a commodity having an elasticity of demand equal to unity.
A revenue increases by 2 per cent
B revenue remains constant
C revenue increases by an infinite amount
D revenue falls by 21 per cent

Essay questions

1 (a) Why is demand for Jaguar cars likely to be more price elastic than the demand for electricity? (40 marks)
  (b) Using the concept of income elasticity, explain the significance of an increase in real incomes for the suppliers of:
    (i) private health care
    (ii) bus travel (60 marks)

2 The following data relate to the demand for beef in the UK, as estimated by the Ministry of Agriculture, Fisheries and Food.

Price elasticity of demand	–0.88
Income elasticity of demand	+0.23
Cross-elasticity of demand with respect to bacon and ham	+1.10

  (a) Explain the meaning of these data. (30 marks)
  (b) What is the significance of the data for beef producers? (30 marks)
  (c) Analyse other factors affecting the demand for meat in the UK. (40 marks)

3 A national cinema chain has the following information:
    (i) the income elasticity of demand for visits to the cinema is +2.5
    (ii) the price elasticity of demand for visits to the cinema is –2.3
    (iii) the cross-elasticity of demand for visits to the cinema with respect to the rental payment of pre-recorded video films is +3.8
    (iv) the cross-elasticity of demand for visits to the cinema with respect to the price of popcorn sold in the cinema is –1.0

  (a) Examine the significance of each of these figures for the cinema company. (30 marks)
  (b) What further economic information would the cinema company require in facing a decision to open more cinemas? Justify your answer. (30 marks)

4 Use the concepts of elasticity to analyse the effects on the market for foreign holidays brought about by
  (a) a fall in the price of aviation fuel (5 marks)
  (b) a fall in domestic hotel prices (7 marks)
  (c) an increase in domestic interest rates (8 marks)

5 Consider briefly the main determinants of the demand for a product.

  What factors govern the size and nature of the price and income elasticities of demand in the case of
  (a) an individual's demand for salt?
  (b) consumers' demand for holidays?
  (c) industrial demand for aluminium?

6 (a) Explain price elasticity of demand, income elasticity of demand and cross-elasticity of demand. (12 marks)
  (b) If you had the task of promoting a holiday resort with its various attractions, how far could these concepts help you? (13 marks)

7 (a) Identify the main determinants of the supply of a product. (10 marks)
  (b) Using examples, explain why the price elasticity of supply is likely to change over time. (20 marks)
  (c) Explain, using appropriate diagrams, what factors cause price instability of agricultural commodities. (70 marks)

6

Demand and supply in an open economy: international trade and exchange

So far in this book we have noted differences in the operation and performance of the economic systems of different countries. However, we have not examined the interrelationships between countries in the sense of how international transactions take place. It is the purpose of this chapter to move on from examining markets in a domestic or internal context to analysing international markets.

When we talk about international trade, we refer to the movement of goods and services from one country to another. We must now make reference to the way in which world trade in goods, services and financial assets is financed. How does the United Kingdom pay for its imports? How does the rest of the world pay for exports from the United Kingdom? These are questions that we shall cover in this chapter. We describe several alternative international financial systems. We look at flexible (or floating) exchange rates and fixed exchange rates. Additionally, we examine the measurement and the components of the UK's balance of payments. We shall follow the same approach as earlier in this book. At the outset of our analysis we assume a world where foreign exchange markets are not affected by government intervention. Then we examine the nature of such intervention in international markets.

LEARNING OUTCOMES

On completing this chapter you should understand:

- Floating exchange rates
- Fixed exchange rate systems
- The balance of payments
- The rationale of international trade
- Comparative and absolute advantage
- Arguments against free trade

Floating, or flexible, exchange rates

When you decide to buy foreign products, such as French wine, you have pounds with which to pay the French wine-maker. The French wine-maker, however, cannot pay his or her workers in pounds. The workers are French, they live in France, and they need francs to buy goods and services in that country. There must therefore be some way to exchange pounds for the francs that the wine-maker will accept. That exchange occurs in a **foreign exchange market**, which, in this case, specializes in exchanging francs and pounds. (When you obtain foreign currencies at a bank or an airport currency exchange, you are participating in the foreign exchange market.)

The particular exchange rate that prevails between francs and pounds depends on the interaction of the demand for and supply of francs and pounds. If it costs you 20p to buy 1 franc, that is the **foreign exchange rate** determined by the demand and supply of francs in the foreign exchange market. The French person going to the foreign exchange market would find that he or she needs 5 francs to buy £1. The numbers used here are hypothetical. We shall continue our two-country example in which the only two countries in the world are the United Kingdom and France. Now let us consider what determines the demand and supply of foreign currency in the foreign exchange market.

Our analysis will initially restrict itself to the market in foreign exchange arising from the import and export of goods. In the real world, exchange rates are determined, not only by the demand and supply of currency arising from international trade, but also by flows of capital. We acknowledge this important aspect of foreign exchange markets later in the chapter (see page 101).

The demand and supply of foreign currency

You wish to buy some Bordeaux wine. To do so, you must get French francs. You go to the foreign exchange market. Your desire to buy the French wine therefore provides a supply of pounds sterling to the foreign exchange market. In other words, your demand for French francs is equivalent to your supply of pounds in the foreign exchange market.

> Every transaction concerning the importation of foreign goods constitutes a supply of pounds and a demand for some foreign currency and vice versa

for export transactions. In this case, it constitutes a demand for French francs.

In our example, we shall assume that only two goods are being traded: French wine and Shetland lamb's-wool sweaters. Thus, the UK demand for French wine creates a supply of pounds and a demand for francs in the foreign exchange market. Similarly, the French demand for Shetland sweaters creates a supply of francs and a demand for pounds in the foreign exchange market. In a **freely floating** (or **flexible**) **exchange rate** situation, the supply and demand of pounds and francs in the foreign exchange market will determine the equilibrium foreign exchange rate. The equilibrium exchange rate will tell us how many francs a pound can be exchanged for – that is, the sterling price of francs – or how many pounds (or fractions of a pound) a franc can be exchanged for – that is, the franc price of pounds.

The Big Mac around the world

The Economist first compared the price of a McDonald's Big Mac in a number of countries in 1986. It regarded the long-established Big Mac as the perfect universal commodity now produced locally in sixty-six countries. If the prices of a Big Mac in several countries in local currencies were expressed in dollars using the exchange rate, then it would be possible to see whether exchange rates do equalize the prices of an identical commodity such as the Big Mac.

Big Mac prices

	in local currency	in dollars	30 March 1999 exchange rate of $ to local currency
United States	$2.43	2.43	–
Great Britain	£1.90	3.07	0.62
Spain	375 pesetas	2.43	155.0
Switzerland	SFr5.90	3.97	1.48
Taiwan	NT$70.00	2.11	33.20
France	Ffr8.50	2.87	6.10
Mexico	19.9 pesos	2.09	9.54
Russia	33.5 roubles	1.35	24.7
Australia	A$2.65	1.66	1.59
China	9.90 yuan	1.20	8.28

Source: *The Economist*, 3 April 1999, p. 90

1 In terms of dollars, in which of the above ten countries is the price of the Big Mac (a) the lowest and (b) the highest? **A▽**

2 Why might *The Economist* have regarded the Big Mac a suitable item with which to compare international prices? **A▽**

It is evident that a dollar does not buy the same amount in each of these ten countries. The question arises as to whether the exchange rate between the dollar and the currency of each of the countries shown above moves in the long run to equalize prices of an identical product such as a Big Mac. Some economists think this is the case. We try to establish any evidence of currencies being wrongly valued.

3 Divide the price of a Big Mac in each of the local currencies shown above by the average price in the United States ($2.43). This will yield a new column of data (column 4) which will indicate how, using the US price of a Big Mac as an 'exchange rate', hamburgers will cost the same as in the United States. **A▽**

4 Now work out the difference, as a percentage, between your calculations in column 4 and the exchange rates shown in column 3.

5 In which country was the actual exchange rate on 30 March 1999 and the 'Big Mac exchange rate' almost identical? **A▽**

6 Which country's currency is suggested by your calculations in (4) above as being
(a) the most undervalued against the dollar, and
(b) the most overvalued against the dollar? **A▽**

7 Differences in the prices of hamburgers could exist in the real world for a number of reasons. Suggest one reason relating to (a) supply and (b) demand which could lead to apparent deviations from equilibrium exchange rate values. (Hint: Think about beef.) **A▽**

8 Turn to page 101, where we indicate how exchange rates can move in the light of capital flows. What factor could have an influence on exchange rate values on a given date as shown in the table above? **A▽**

The equilibrium foreign exchange rate

In order to determine the equilibrium foreign exchange rate, we have to find out what determines the demand and supply of foreign exchange. We shall ignore for the moment any speculative aspect of buying foreign exchange; that is, we assume that there are no individuals who wish to buy francs because they think the price will go up in the future.

The idea of an exchange rate is no different from the idea of paying a certain price for something you want to buy. If you like to buy coffee, you know you have to pay, say, 65p a cup. If the price went up to £1, you would probably buy fewer cups. If the price went down to 35p, you might buy more. In other words, the demand curve for cups of coffee, expressed in terms of pounds, slopes downwards following the theory of demand. The demand curve for francs slopes downwards also, and we shall see why.

The demand schedule for francs

Assume that it costs you 20p to purchase 1 franc; that is the exchange rate between pounds and francs. If tomorrow you had to pay 25p for the same franc, then the exchange rate would have changed. Looking at such an increase with respect to the franc, we would say that there has been an **appreciation** in the value of the franc in the foreign exchange market. But this increase in the value of the franc means that there has been a **depreciation** in the value of the pound in the foreign exchange market. Previously, the pound could buy 5 francs; tomorrow the pound will be able to buy only 4 francs at a price of 25p per franc. In any event, if the sterling price of francs is higher, you will probably demand fewer francs. Why? The answer lies in the reason why you demand francs in the first place.

You need francs in order to buy French wine. Your demand curve for French wine, we assume, follows the theory of demand and is therefore downward sloping. If it costs you more pounds in order to buy the same quantity of French wine, presumably you will not buy the same quantity; your quantity demanded will be less. We say that your demand for French francs is derived from your demand for French wine. In Table 6.1(a) we show the hypothetical demand schedule for French wine in the United Kingdom by a representative wine-drinker. In Figure 6.1(a) we show the UK demand curve for French wine in terms of pounds.

Let us assume that the price per litre of French wine in France is 20 francs. Given that price, we can find the number of francs required to purchase one, two, three and four bottles of French wine. That information is given in Table 6.1(b). One bottle requires 20 francs, four bottles require 80 francs. Now we have a sufficient amount of information to determine the derived demand curve for French francs. If 1 franc costs 20p, a bottle of wine would cost £4 (20 francs per bottle divided by 5 francs per pound is £4 per bottle). At £4 per bottle, we see from Table 6.1(a) that our representative wine-drinker would demand four bottles. From Table 6.1(b), we see that 80 francs would be demanded to buy the four bottles of wine. We show this quantity demanded in Table 6.1(c). In Figure 6.1(b), we draw the derived demand curve for francs. Now consider what happens if the price of francs goes up to 30p. A bottle of French wine costing 20 francs in France would now cost £6 in the United Kingdom. From Table 6.1(a) we see that, at £6 per bottle, three bottles will be imported into the United Kingdom by our representative wine-drinker. From Table 6.1(b), we see that three bottles would require 60 francs to be purchased; thus, in Table 6.1(c) and Figure 6.1(b), we see that at a price of 1 franc per 30p the quantity demanded will be 60 francs. We do this all the way up to a price of 50p per franc. At that price, a bottle of French wine costing 20 francs in France would cost £10 in the United Kingdom, and our representative wine-drinker would import only one bottle.

Table 6.1

Deriving the demand for French francs

(a) Demand schedule for French wine in the United Kingdom. In (b), we show the number of francs required to purchase one, two, three and four bottles of wine if the price per bottle of wine in France is 20 francs. We can then find the quantity of francs needed to pay for the various quantities demanded, and in (c) we see the derived demand for francs in the United Kingdom.

(a) Demand schedule for French wine in the United Kingdom per week

Price per bottle	Quantity demanded
£10	1 bottle
£8	2 bottles
£6	3 bottles
£4	4 bottles

(b)

Quantity demanded	Francs required to purchase quantity demanded (at *P* = 20 francs per bottle)
1 bottle	20
2 bottles	40
3 bottles	60
4 bottles	80

(c) Derived demand schedule for francs in the United Kingdom with which to pay for imports of wine

Price of 1 franc	Quantity of francs demanded per week
50p	20
40p	40
30p	60
20p	80

Derived demand is downward sloping

As the price of francs falls, the quantity demanded will rise. The only difference here from the demand analysis in Chapter 3 is that the demand for francs is derived from the demand for a final product, French wine in our example.

The supply of French francs

The supply of French francs is a derived supply in the sense that it is derived from a French person's demand for Shetland sweaters. We could go through an example similar to the one above to come up with a supply schedule of French francs in France. It is upward sloping. Obviously, the French need pounds in order to purchase the sweaters.

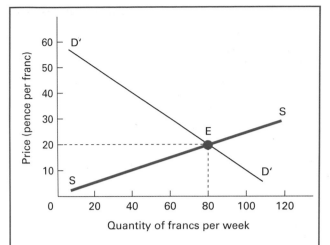

Figure 6.2
The equilibrium exchange rate for two individuals
The derived demand curve for French francs is taken from Figure 6.1(b). The derived supply curve SS results from the representative French purchaser of sweaters who supplies francs to the foreign exchange market when demanding pounds in order to buy sweaters. The equilibrium exchange rate is 20p for 1 franc and the equilibrium quantity of francs in the foreign exchange market will be 80 per week.

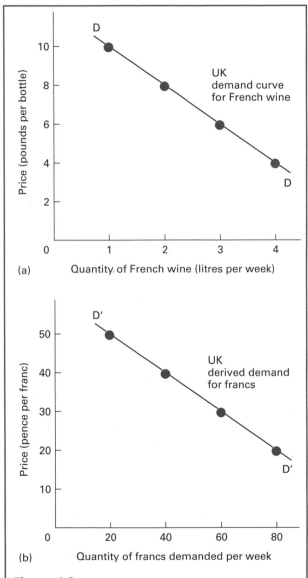

(a)

(b)

Figure 6.1
Deriving the demand for French francs
The resultant demand curve D'D' shown in (b) is the derived demand for francs in the United Kingdom.

If we offer more pounds for the same amount of francs, the sterling price of francs will go up. In principle, the French would be willing to supply more francs when the sterling price of francs goes up, because they can then buy more sweaters with the same quantity of francs; that is, the franc is worth more in exchange for UK goods than when the sterling price for francs was lower. Let us take an example. A sweater in the United Kingdom costs £10. If the exchange rate is 25p for 1 franc, the French have to come up with 40 francs (= £10 at 25p per franc) to buy a sweater. If, on the other hand, the exchange rate goes up to 50p for 1 franc, the French must come up with only 20 francs (= £10 at 50p per franc) to buy a sweater. At a lower price (in francs) of sweaters, they will demand a larger quantity. In other words, as the price of French francs goes up in terms of pounds, the quantity of sweaters demanded will go up, and hence the quantity of French francs supplied will go up. Therefore the supply schedule of foreign currency (francs) will be upward sloping.

We draw an upward-sloping schedule in Figure 6.2. In our hypothetical example, assuming that there is only one wine-drinker in the United Kingdom and one demander of sweaters in France, the equilibrium exchange rate will be set at 20p per franc, or 5 francs to £1. Let us now look at the overall demand and supply of French francs. We take all demanders of French wine and all demanders of sweaters and put their demands and supplies of francs together into one diagram. Thus, we are showing an overall version of the demand and supply of French francs. The horizontal axis in Figure 6.3 represents a quantity of foreign exchange – the number of francs per year. The vertical axis represents the exchange rate – the price of foreign currency (francs) expressed in pounds (per franc). Thus, at the foreign currency price of 25p per franc, you know that it will cost you 25p to buy 1 franc. At the foreign currency price of 20p per franc, you know that it will cost you 20p to buy 1 franc. The equilibrium is again established at 20p for 1 franc. This equilibrium is not established because the British like to buy francs or because the French like to buy sterling. Rather, the equilibrium exchange rate depends upon how many sweaters the French want and how much French wine the British want (given their respective incomes, tastes, and the relative price of wine and sweaters). (Remember, however, our assumption that we have excluded from consideration the relevance of flows of capital in determining the exchange rate.)

A shift in demand

Assume that a successful advertising campaign by British wine-importers has caused the British demand (schedule) for French wine to double. We now demand twice as much wine at all prices. Our demand schedule for French wine has shifted out and to the right.

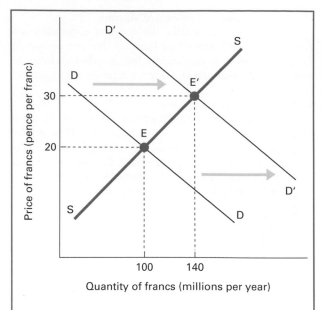

Figure 6.4
A shift in the demand schedule
The demand schedule for French wine shifts to the right, causing the derived demand schedule for francs to shift to the right also. We have assumed that the French supply schedule of francs has remained stable – that is, their taste for sweaters has remained constant. The new exchange rate will be higher than the old one. It will now cost 30p to buy 1 franc. The higher price of francs will be translated into a higher sterling price for French wine and a lower French franc price of sweaters.

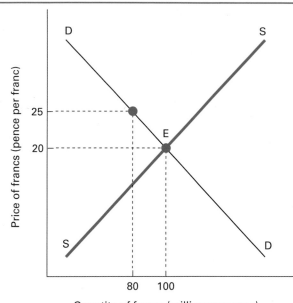

Figure 6.3
The derived demand and supply of French francs
The supply curve of French francs results from the French demand for sweaters. The demand curve, DD, slopes downwards, and the supply curve, SS, slopes upwards. The foreign exchange price, or the sterling price of francs, in millions, is represented on the horizontal axis. If the foreign exchange rate is 25p – that is, if it takes 25p to buy 1 franc – then the British will demand 80 million francs. The equilibrium exchange rate is 20p. At this point, 100 million French francs are both demanded and supplied each year.

The increased demand for French wine can be translated into an increased demand for francs. Our thirst for bottles of Bordeaux wine means that we shall supply more pounds to the foreign exchange market while demanding more French francs to pay for the wine. Figure 6.4 presents a new demand schedule, D'D', for French francs; this demand schedule is to the right and outward from the original demand schedule. If the French do not change their desire for sweaters, the supply schedule of French francs will remain stable. A new equilibrium will be established at a higher exchange rate. In our particular example, the equilibrium is established at an exchange rate of 30p. It now takes 30p to buy 1 franc, whereas it took 20p before. This is translated as an increase in the price of French wine to UK drinkers and as a decrease in the price of sweaters to the French.

A shift in supply

In this last example, we assumed that the British taste for wine had shifted. Since the demand for French francs is a derived demand by the British for French wine, that caused a shift in the demand curve for francs. Now let us assume that the supply curve of French francs shifts outwards to the right. This may occur for many reasons, the most probable one being a relative rise in the French

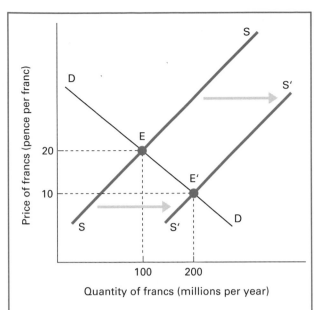

Figure 6.5
A shift in the supply of French francs
There has been a shift in the supply curve of French francs. The new equilibrium will occur at E'. Ten pence, rather than 20p, will now buy 1 franc. After the exchange rate adjustment, the amount of francs demanded and supplied will be 200 million per year.

KEY POINTS

6.1

- The foreign exchange rate is the rate at which a unit of one country's currency can be exchanged for another's.

- The demand for foreign exchange is a derived demand: it is derived from the demand for foreign goods and services (and in the real world also for financial assets).

- The supply of foreign exchange is derived from foreigners' demands for our goods and services.

- In general, the demand curve of foreign exchange slopes downwards and the supply curve of foreign exchange slopes upwards. The equilibrium foreign exchange rate occurs at the intersection of the demand and supply curves.

- A shift in the demand for foreign goods will result in a shift in the demand for foreign exchange. The equilibrium foreign exchange rate will change.

- A shift in the supply of foreign currency will cause a change in the equilibrium exchange rate.

price level. For example, if the price of all French-made clothes went up 100 per cent in francs, Shetland sweaters would become relatively cheaper. That would mean that French people would want to buy more sweaters. But remember that, when they want to buy more sweaters, they supply more francs to the foreign exchange market. Thus, we see in Figure 6.5 that the supply curve of French francs moves from SS to S'S'. In the absence of restrictions – that is, in a system of floating exchange rates – the new equilibrium exchange rate will be 1 franc equals 10p, or £1 equals 10 francs. The quantity of francs demanded and supplied will increase from 100 million per year to 200 million per year. We say, then, that in a free (or floating) international exchange rate system, shifts in the demand and supply of foreign currencies will cause changes in the equilibrium foreign exchange rates. Those rates will remain in effect until supply and/or demand shift once again.

Capital flows

Our analysis of how the exchange rate between Britain and France is determined has been wholly based on an interchange of goods between the two countries. But, as was noted at the beginning of the chapter, this international exchange in goods provides only one part of the demand for foreign currencies. There is a demand, not only for French wine but also for francs, by those UK residents who travel to France for their holiday. They need francs in order to buy food (and wine!) when in France. A further demand for francs arises when, say, a UK firm wishes to acquire a firm in France, or if a UK resident wishes to buy a holiday flat in, for example, Cannes. In these cases we are referring to transactions in financial assets. Those involved in making decisions whether to invest abroad will be sensitive to the actual and expected situation in foreign exchange rates. The *timing* of an investment abroad may be affected by a view on how the foreign exchange rate is expected to change in the future. Investors will be concerned about interest rates and expectations about how prices in particular countries will change. (We discuss these issues later in Chapter 29.) For now we need simply to recognize that many capital transactions are sensitive to market opinions about the future value of sterling against other currencies and differences in international interest rates. Thus, once we recognize the relevance of expected changes in exchange rates, we come to realize that speculation is one aspect in the market for foreign currencies. In short, we should expect transactions in foreign currencies for their own sake.

Dealings in the foreign exchange market reflect the willingness of individuals, firms and financial institutions to shift funds for financial gain. Thus our initial assumption that foreign exchange markets merely serve to satisfy the needs of trade in goods is now seen to be a very limited one.

The equilibrium exchange rate

Based on the following information, draw supply and demand curves for sterling to illustrate the working of the foreign exchange market.

Price of £ ($)	Demand for £ (per annum)	Supply of £ (per annum)
2.00	35 500	39 250
1.90	36 000	39 000
1.80	36 500	38 750
1.70	37 000	38 500
1.60	37 500	38 250
1.50	38 000	38 000
1.40	38 500	37 750
1.30	39 000	37 500
1.20	39 500	37 250
1.10	40 000	37 000
1.00	40 500	36 750

(Hint: Draw the price axis from £1 = $1.00 to £1 = $2.00 and the quantity axis from £34 000 million to £41 000 million.)

9 What is the equilibrium exchange rate?

10 What would the equilibrium exchange rate be if
 (a) the government cuts overseas defence spending by £500 million?
 (b) Saudi Arabia decides to hold an extra £1000 million in sterling balances?
 (c) American airlines buy ten new British-built aircraft, worth £100 million each?
 (d) there is rapid growth in consumer spending in the UK which causes firms to spend an extra £500 million on stocks of imported raw materials?

The fixed exchange rate system

We have just described the workings of a freely floating, or flexible, exchange rate system in international finance. Now we consider a situation in which central banks intervene in order to prevent foreign exchange rates from changing. This is a system of **fixed exchange rates**. As with most systems where a price of a particular good or

service is fixed, the only way that it can remain so is for the government to intervene.

Let us take our two-country example again. Suppose that the price of sweaters has increased along with everything made in the United Kingdom. The French now will buy fewer sweaters than before. They supply fewer francs to the foreign exchange market and demand fewer pounds at the fixed exchange rate. But UK wine-drinkers continue to demand French wines. In fact, they will demand more, because at the fixed exchange rate the relative price of French wines has fallen. So the United Kingdom will now supply more pounds in the foreign exchange market and demand more francs. As in Figure 6.6, the demand curve for francs will shift to D′D′. In the absence of any intervention by central banks, the exchange rate will change. The price of French francs in terms of pounds will go from 20p per franc to 25p. That is, the value of a pound in terms of francs will go down. The pound will suffer a *depreciation* in its value relative to the franc, and the franc will experience an *appreciation* in its value in terms of the pound. But the UK government is committed to maintaining a fixed price of pounds in the foreign exchange market. When the French take their excess pounds and put them onto the foreign exchange markets, the UK central bank will be forced to go into the foreign exchange market and buy up those excess pounds. The Bank of England has to have foreign currency (or gold) to buy up the excess pounds. That is, it has to have a reserve of francs or gold in its coffers to buy the pounds that the French want to sell. It must supply 25 million francs per year to keep the exchange rate fixed, as seen in Figure 6.6.

The only way for the United Kingdom and other countries to support the price of the pound is to buy up excess pounds with foreign reserves – in this case, with French francs. But the United Kingdom might eventually run out of francs. It would no longer be able to stabilize the price of the pound, and a **currency crisis** would ensue. A currency crisis occurs when a country can no longer support the price of its currency in foreign exchange markets. Many such crises have occurred in the past several decades when countries have attempted to maintain a fixed exchange rate that was in disequilibrium. We shall consider this matter in a later chapter. For the moment we mention that the world's major trading nations operated a fixed exchange rate system under the auspices of the **International Monetary Fund** (IMF), which was set up to manage the world's monetary system in 1945. We therefore need to understand how the IMF was supposed to operate. Briefly, the role of the IMF was to help member countries experiencing balance-of-payments difficulties by lending from its gold and currency holdings. These holdings arose out of the subscriptions of the members set by reference to a formula that took into account a country's importance in the world economy. After 1945, members of the IMF established fixed exchange rates for their currencies in terms of dollars and were obliged to maintain the values of their currencies in foreign exchange markets within a

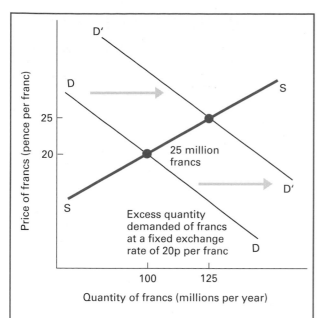

Figure 6.6
Supporting the value of the pound in the foreign exchange market
We assume that prices remain constant in France but rise in the United Kingdom, so French goods become relatively cheaper. The demand schedule for French goods shifts to the right, as does the derived demand schedule for French francs, from DD to D'D'. Without exchange rate controls, the exchange rate would rise to 25p – it would then cost 25p instead of 20p to buy a franc. If the UK government, however, is committed to supporting the price of the pound, it will maintain the price of a pound at 5 francs – at 20p per franc. But at that exchange rate there is an excess quantity demanded of francs at the fixed exchange rate of 25 million per year. The UK government must step in and supply 25 million francs from its reserves annually in order to support the pound in the foreign exchange market.

1 per cent band of their declared par values. In 1970 the IMF created a new reserve asset, **Special Drawing Rights**, which countries could use to settle international payments.

Devaluation

One alternative to a currency crisis or to continuing to try to support a fixed exchange rate is to devalue unilaterally. **Devaluation** is the same thing as depreciation except that it occurs under a fixed exchange rate regime. A particular country unilaterally lowers the price of its currency in foreign exchange markets. The opposite of devaluation is **revaluation**. This occurs when, under a fixed exchange rate regime, there is pressure on a country's currency to rise in value in foreign exchange markets. Unilaterally, that country can declare that the value of its currency in foreign exchange markets is higher than it has been in the

past. Revaluation is the same thing as appreciation except that it occurs under a fixed exchange rate regime.

In 1973 most of the world's major nations adopted floating exchange rates. However, central banks were still prepared to intervene in foreign exchange rates in order to counter sudden shifts in the demand for or supply of currency. Thus an intermediate system of **managed floating** was introduced. This system allows a 'pure' floating system to be modified by occasional central bank intervention in order to smooth out sharp short-run changes in exchange rates while allowing market forces to determine the prices of currencies over the long term.

KEY POINTS

6.2

- Fixed exchange rates are a system where countries determine that their exchange rates should not alter and central banks support the declared rates by intervening in foreign exchange markets.

- Currency crises occur when a country can no longer support the price of its currency and, under a fixed exchange rate system, is obliged to devalue, that is, lower the price of its currency in foreign exchange markets. When a country declares that the value of its currency is now higher than it has been, it has adopted a policy of revaluation, the opposite of devaluation.

- Depreciation is the same as devaluation except that it occurs when exchange rates are floating.

Dollars and deutschmarks

In 1979 the exchange rate mechanism (ERM) was set up to link the currencies of those members of the European Community (now the European Union (EU)) who wished to join. The aim was to limit the extent to which individual currencies could change against those of other members. The United Kingdom did not join the ERM until October 1990 and did so at a central rate against the deutschmark of £1 = DM2.65. The ERM system was put under strain following the unification of East and West Germany, which led to inflationary pressures and prompted the Bundesbank to resort to higher interest rates to contain this problem. These events are discussed later in Chapter 29, but for the United Kingdom the upshot was that the stance of the Bundesbank caused selling pressures to affect several European currencies, and on 16 September 1992 sterling's membership of the ERM was suspended.

Sterling, dollars and deutschmarks

The table shows the market exchange rate on the last working day in each year, 1973–98.

	US dollars per £	Deutschmarks per £
1973	2.32	6.27
1974	2.34	5.65
1975	2.02	5.29
1976	1.70	4.01
1977	1.91	4.01
1978	2.04	3.71
1979	2.22	3.84
1980	2.39	4.69
1981	1.91	4.28
1982	1.61	3.85
1983	1.45	3.95
1984	1.15	3.65
1985	1.44	3.52
1986	1.48	2.85
1987	1.88	2.96
1988	1.80	3.20
1989	1.61	2.72
1990	1.92	2.88
1991	1.86	2.84
1992	1.51	2.45
1993	1.47	2.56
1994	1.56	2.42
1995	1.55	2.21
1996	1.71	2.63
1997	1.64	2.95
1998	1.66	2.77

Source: *The Pink Book* (UK Balance of Payments), 1998, p. 80, Table 9.1

11 In how many years did the value of sterling appreciate during the year against
   (a) the dollar
   (b) the deutschmark? **A**

12 Assume you are an annual visitor from the United States to England during this whole period. Would the changing market value of the pound sterling against the dollar make you contented or discontented in what you get for your dollar? **A**

13 Assume now you are a regular visitor to the Munich Beer Festival. Would the trend in the exchange rate for the pound against the deutschmark make this annual trip an increasingly expensive or reduced cost experience? **A**

14 Between 1973 and 1998, which was the greater percentage fall in the two exchange rates – the pound sterling against the dollar or the pound sterling against the deutschmark? **A**

15 Questions 12 and 13 consider the relevance of exchange rates to you as a person. How do you expect exporters of manufactured goods in the UK to view the movement of the pound sterling in terms of the dollar and the deutschmark since 1993? **A**

Return to the Caledonian market

The Portobello traders did a survey of their customers and found that 38 per cent were foreign dealers. For the dealers, 16 September 1992, so-called Black Wednesday, when the pound collapsed, was a day to celebrate. The foreigners came back. 'You noticed it from one Saturday to the next,' says Stuart Pardoe, of The Good Fairy Arcade in the Portobello market. The foreign clientele has slowly been changing. The Japanese have dropped away, the French and Germans are not as eager, though the Italians are still strong. The new arrivals of the 1990s are Spanish and Portuguese, with tastes less discriminating than those of dealers from more mature markets.

Source: *The Economist*, 30 January 1993, p. 28

16 What is implied in this extract about the relevance of price in the second-hand market?
17 Explain why the UK's withdrawal from the ERM on so-called Black Wednesday in September 1992 could affect this market.

The balance of trade and the balance of payments

We have talked about a flexible exchange rate system and a fixed exchange rate system. With either system, countries are concerned with their balance of payments. The **balance of payments** is a general term used to reflect a summary of all economic transactions between two nations, usually for a period of one year. In a flexible exchange rate system, the balance of payments is always in balance because of automatic adjustments in exchange rates. But since we do not have a truly freely floating exchange rate system the balance of payments is an important topic in international finance.

Current account transactions

Until 1997 the balance of payments transactions of the UK were grouped into three categories: current account transactions, capital account transactions and official financing transactions. Within the current account transactions there was a distinction between trade in visible or merchandise goods and trade in invisibles or services. In 1998 the balance of payments transactions were redefined to bring the UK into line with the terminology of other members of the IMF. Under the new presentation the balance of payments consists of four accounts, namely:

the current account
the capital account
the financial account
the International Investment Position

We now consider these four new sub-groups of the balance of payments in turn.

The current account
This account itself consists of four types of transactions.

(1) Trade in goods
Imports of, say, motor cars from Japan are recorded as debits in the trade in goods account, whereas exports of motor vehicles manufactured in the UK are recorded as credits. Table 6.2 shows that in 1998 credits less debits meant that there was a deficit of over £20 billion.

(2) Trade in services
The UK has had a surplus on trade in services in each year since 1966, and Table 6.2 shows the surplus in 1998 was £12 billion. The trade in services account includes eleven groupings of services such as transportation, travel and financial services. Passenger tickets for travel on UK aircraft which are sold abroad constitute a credit item in the services account. If UK citizens purchase airline tickets from foreign airlines then these constitute a debit item.

(3) Income
This wholly new account consists of the earnings of UK nationals arising from employment abroad as well as investment income on overseas assets. As you might anticipate, it is the second of these earnings in the form of profits, dividends and interest receipts which is the greater part of the income account. The income account was in net surplus of over £15 billion in 1998.

(4) Current transfers
Current transfers are composed of central government transfers and transfers made or received by private individuals. Central government transfers include transactions with international organizations, bilateral aid (see Chapter 30), social security and military grants, but transfers with EU institutions constitute the largest single component of current transfers. Since 1988 such transfers with the EU have consistently shared a deficit. In the case of private transfers, one element here is the remittance of earnings to and from abroad. Here too there is a net deficit in the case of private transfers, as with central government transfers.

Table 6.2

(a) Current account of the UK balance of payments, 1998 (£ million)

	Credits	Debits	Balance
Goods			
Food, beverages, tobacco	10 231	16 258	–6 027
Basic materials	2 512	5 622	–3 110
Oil and other fuels	7 531	4 895	2 636
Semi-manufactures	43 385	45 161	–1 776
Finished manufactures	98 576	111 144	–12 568
Other goods	1 897	1 817	80
Total goods	*164 132*	*184 897*	*–20 765*
Services			
Transportation	11 505	13 649	–2 144
Travel	14 503	20 126	–5 623
Financial services	6 318	171	6 147
Other services			
Total services	*60 070*	*47 817*	*12 253*
Employment from abroad	777	701	76
Income from investments	110 588	95 490	15 098
Total income	*111 365*	*96 191*	*15 174*
Current transfers			
Central government	6 467	6 585	–118
Private transfers	9 129	15 537	–6 408
Total current transfers	*15 596*	*22 122*	*–6 526*
TOTALS	351 163	351 027	136

(b) Capital account

Credits	Debits	Balance
1 269	848	421

(c) Financial account

	Credits	Debits	Balance
Direct investment abroad (net debits)		64 077	
Portfolio investment abroad		34 380	
Other investments abroad		15 872	
		114 329	
Direct investment in the UK	40 792		
Portfolio investment in the UK	20 206		
Other investments in the UK	44 306		
	105 304		–9 025
Total of current, capital and financial accounts	437 736		466 204
Net errors and omissions	8 468		

In the real world difficulties in identifying certain transactions result in ignorance of the precise sums crossing the foreign exchange markets. The element of unrecorded transactions is termed the errors and omissions. It is simply the difference between the overall current balance and the net transactions in UK assets and liabilities. The balance of payments must, by definition, always balance!

The current account balance

This term is a summary statistic that takes into account the four types of transactions just identified. In 1998 the balance was just in net surplus. This outcome was the result of the credits on trade in services and income just exceeding the combined debits on trade in goods and current transfers.

The capital account

The newly defined capital account is in fact in monetary terms of minor consequence relative to the UK balance of payments as a whole. The transactions recorded here involve transfers of ownership of fixed assets and also migrants transfers. Funds brought into the UK by new immigrants are recorded as capital account credits, whilst any funds sent by UK residents who are emigrating to other countries are debits in the capital account.

The financial account

In addition to buying and selling goods and services in the world market, it is also possible to buy and sell financial assets. There is really no difference in terms of the foreign exchange market. If, on the one hand, some people decide to buy shares in French companies, the demand for French financial assets will create a derived demand for francs and a supply of pounds. On the other hand, if the French decide they want to buy ICI shares, that demand will result in a derived demand for pounds and a supply of francs.

Financial account transactions thus comprise investment activity by private individuals, banks, companies and publicly owned undertakings. One would expect that the wide range of persons engaged in this investment activity would vary in their motives. For some the intention is profit-seeking over the long term, while for others funds may be quickly moved in the light of changing conditions. Our earlier analysis of exchange rates excluded the possibility of transactions in financial assets. If we recognize the reality of such activity then participants in capital transactions may alter their behaviour in the light of anticipated movements of the exchange rate.

We have noted that the UK enjoys a net surplus on investment income from overseas assets within the current account. The financial account records the actual flows of investments from which such earnings are derived. Thus the financial account broadly corresponds to the previously named capital account, being a record of transactions in UK assets and liabilities. Thus if UK institutions acquire foreign securities, this is recorded in the financial account as portfolio investment abroad as a debit item. Conversely, if a foreign firm acquires a UK company, this transaction is recorded as portfolio investment into the UK and is therefore a credit item.

The International Investment Position (IIP)

This new term represents the net financial worth of the UK. It represents a balance sheet or stock position of the UK's external assets and liabilities in contrast to the flows of foreign transactions as shown in the financial account. Mention is made here of the IIP merely to complete the relationship between the annual flows and the valuation of the stock of financial assets.

KEY POINTS

6.3

- The balance of payments reflects the value of all transactions in international trade, including the trade in goods, services, earnings on financial assets and transfers.

- The current account balance includes trade in both goods and services and also earnings on investments abroad less payments on investments in the United Kingdom owned by foreigners, plus net government and net private transfers.

- The financial account includes investment flows by private individuals and the public sector. It records the transactions in financial assets, the earnings on which feature in the current account.

Examining the balance of payments

Turn back to Table 6.2 and consider the balance of trade in goods.

18 Which is the largest item of the six categories of trade in goods which was in net surplus in 1998? How do you account for this situation?

19 Which of the items identified in Table 6.2 concerning trade in services is the only one in net surplus in 1998?

Table 6.2(a) shows the investment income on earnings on external assets of the United Kingdom as interest, profits and dividends, and the corresponding payments to overseas residents.

20 Was the United Kingdom in net credit or net debit on these earnings in 1998?

Table 6.2(a) shows transfers both by government and private persons.

21 Was the United Kingdom in net credit or debit in total transfers in 1998? The data below show further details of transfers.

1998	£ million
Net debit relating to European Union institutions	5189
UK financial aid to the United Nations and other world organizations	514
UK financial aid to specific countries	834

22 What do the above figures show about whether the United Kingdom is a net contributor or net recipient of finances as a member of the European Union?

23 Why did the United Kingdom pay financial aid to the United Nations and specific countries but not receive such credits?

The rationale of international trade

We have now examined the ways in which trade in goods, services and financial assets is financed with particular reference to the United Kingdom. We began with the simple example of the interchange of French wine and Shetland lamb's-wool sweaters. Having considered how the foreign exchange market exists for the buying and selling of currencies to make such an interchange possible, we should now examine what is the rationale of such trade between two countries. We need to consider questions such as what are the gains from such trade? What are the costs involved? As consumers we appear to gain when we

can purchase foreign products at lower prices than goods made by domestic manufacturers. But what if foreign suppliers put UK firms out of business and so put some of the UK's labour force out of work? Are the gains from international trade worth the costs?

Putting trade in its place

Trade among nations must somehow benefit the people of each nation by more than it costs them. World trade volume, measured in terms of exports, is shown in Figure 6.7. World trade has grown faster than the rate of increase in world output over many of the post-war years, as Figure 6.7 shows. Clearly, the world's trading nations showed an enthusiasm to participate in international exchange.

Before we examine both the disadvantages of international exchange and its advantages, we should note that the industrial countries account for over 70 per cent of merchandise trade (Figure 6.8(a)). The developing countries, particularly those in Africa and Latin America, account for a small part of international exchange in goods. International trade is of more significance to some countries than others. Figure 6.8(a) shows the top twenty countries in merchandise exports in 1998, while Figure 6.8(b) shows the leading twenty countries in commercial services in 1998.

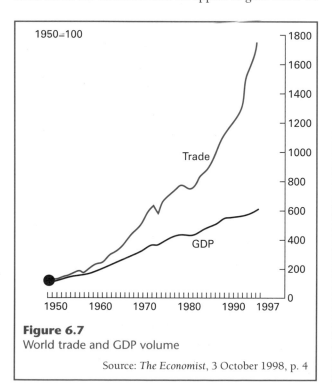

Figure 6.7
World trade and GDP volume

Source: *The Economist*, 3 October 1998, p. 4

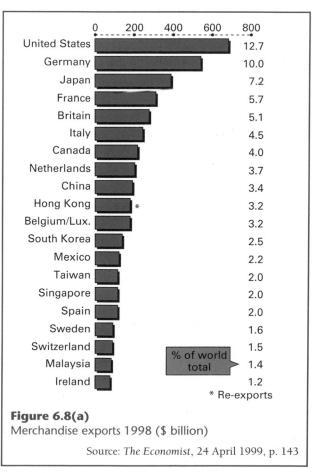

Figure 6.8(a)
Merchandise exports 1998 ($ billion)

Source: *The Economist*, 24 April 1999, p. 143

Although the United States is the largest exporter of goods, trade accounts for a small proportion of the US economy measured by gross domestic product. Exports from several countries in East Asia are a high proportion of gross domestic product. One measurement of the importance of trade is to calculate the sum of exports and imports as a share of GDP. On this measure Figure 6.8(c) shows that in East Asia, Malaysia and Singapore are easily the world's most involved countries in international exchange.

The United States is the Western country that would suffer the least if we imagine the unlikely event of international trade ceasing to take place. In contrast, the United Kingdom is a much more open economy, that is, one heavily dependent on relationships with other countries.

The pattern of the UK's trade with other countries has, historically, been an exchange of exported manufactured goods and services for imported raw materials and foodstuffs. Since joining the then European Community in 1973, the United Kingdom has strengthened its trading links with Europe at the expense of the Commonwealth. The European Union accounts for over half of UK exports and is the source of half of UK imports. How did this trade pattern become established? The answer lies in the principle of comparative advantage that we explored in Chapter 4. We now re-examine that principle in an open economy context.

Comparative and absolute advantage

The reason there are gains from trade lies in one of the most fundamental principles of economics: a nation gains by doing what it can do best relative to other nations. The United Kingdom benefits by specializing in only those endeavours in which it has a **comparative advantage**.

The concept of comparative advantage was first explained by the economist David Ricardo nearly two hundred years ago, and his own example cannot be bettered. Table 6.3 shows the number of man-hours per unit required to produce cloth and wine in a two-country world comprising England and Portugal. It is evident that Portugal has a superior position to England in the production of both cloth and wine. Portugal has an **absolute advantage** over England in both commodities.

Why? The cost of producing cloth in Portugal is 90 per cent of the cost in England. In the case of wine

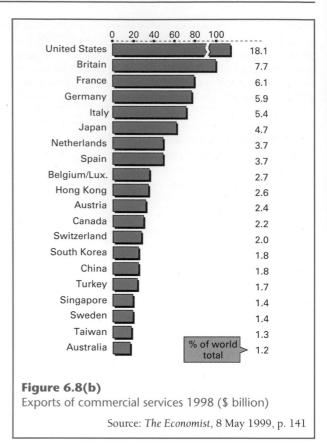

Figure 6.8(b)
Exports of commercial services 1998 ($ billion)

Source: *The Economist*, 8 May 1999, p. 141

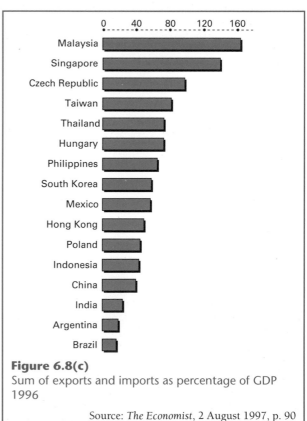

Figure 6.8(c)
Sum of exports and imports as percentage of GDP 1996

Source: *The Economist*, 2 August 1997, p. 90

Table 6.3		

Ricardo's model of comparative cost advantage (man-hours per unit of output)

	Cloth	Wine
Portugal	90	80
England	100	120

Portugal can produce wine at two-thirds of the cost in England. But of the two commodities, clearly it is in wine that Portugal has the greater or comparative advantage over England. But does this mean Portugal gains nothing from trade with England? This at first sight seems to be the case. What Ricardo showed was that England could specialize in cloth production and trade cloth exports for wine imports from Portugal to the benefit of both countries. How is this possible?

In England labour costs per unit are higher than in Portugal for both cloth and wine, but its comparative cost disadvantage is least in the case of cloth. The cost ratios are respectively 10:9 and 12:8. Thus it costs England about 1.1 times as much to manufacture cloth and 1.5 times as much to produce wine as in Portugal.

Ricardo showed that if the two countries exchanged a unit of English cloth for a unit of Portuguese wine both countries gained. England gains by 20 man-hours on each unit of cloth exchanged for wine since it costs 100 man-hours to manufacture cloth but another 20 man-hours to produce wine. How does Portugal gain? Trading a unit of wine costing 80 man-hours for a unit of cloth that would domestically require 90 man-hours means it gains a saving of 10 man-hours. So although it is able to make the cloth at a lower cost than England, Portugal would still gain by specializing in the production of wine. Its comparative advantage is greater in wine than cloth.

Ricardo's model is, of course, a simple one. It assumes there are no transport costs incurred in shipping cloth and wine between England and Portugal. But it indicates that trade could be advantageous at a certain rate of international exchange. Ricardo's model was later modified to explain how the nature of the rate of exchange was actually determined.

Comparative advantage and opportunity cost

An alternative approach to the concept of comparative advantage is to relate it to another concept that we met in the very first chapter of this book. There we noted that comparative advantage emphasizes the fact that cost means opportunities that must be forgone. If the United Kingdom decides to produce military goods it forgoes part of its opportunity to produce civilian goods because the resources used in producing guns and tanks cannot be used simultaneously to produce butter. We drew a production possibilities curve reflecting a society's choice between guns and butter. We can now draw on the concept of a production possibilities curve to show the gains from trade.

Figure 6.9 shows the limiting situations for production possibilities for the United Kingdom and the United States in the case of wheat and cloth. From these data we can draw the two straight-line production possibilities curves.

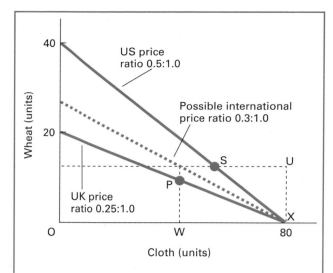

Figure 6.9

	Wheat	Cloth		Wheat	Cloth
UK	20	0	or	0	80
USA	40	0	or	0	80

P, pre-trade production and consumption; OX, cloth production (total specialization) if trade takes place at the given international price ratio; UX, wheat imports; SU, cloth exports.

In the absence of trade the two domestic price ratios are as follows:

UK   1 unit of wheat exchanges for 4 units of cloth
        (or 1/4 unit wheat for 1 unit cloth)
USA   1 unit of wheat exchanges for 2 units of cloth
        (or 1/2 unit wheat for 1 unit cloth)

If the United Kingdom, which has no superior or absolute advantage in either wheat or cloth compared with the United States, could trade cloth on more favourable terms than 1/4 unit of wheat, it would gain. An international exchange of, say, 0.3 units of wheat for one unit of cloth would be advantageous to the United Kingdom. The broken line in Figure 6.9 shows this ratio.

If the United Kingdom now produces, say, OX units of cloth (rather than OW, when no trade takes place), it can purchase UX units of wheat from the United States. The United Kingdom in this case is now totally specializing in cloth and importing all its requirements of wheat. Imports of wheat of UX units equal its cloth exports of SU. International exchange has enabled the United Kingdom to move outside the range of possibilities that were present before trade took place. Point S is beyond point P, which was the situation before trade.

Figure 6.10 shows the price ratios before trade in the United Kingdom and United States. For international exchange to be beneficial, the rate of exchange must lie between the two domestic opportunity cost ratios. The

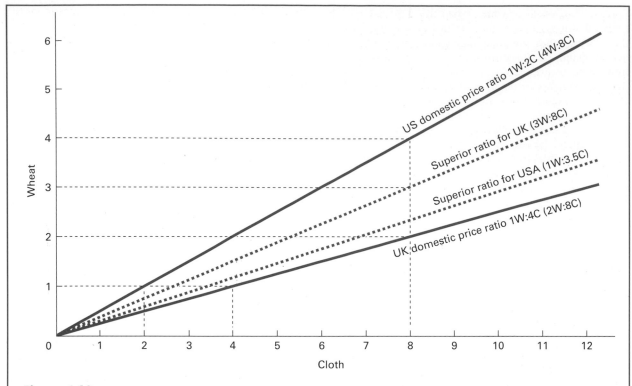

Figure 6.10
Price ratios: can the United Kingdom and the United States do a deal?
The solid lines indicate the pre-trade price ratios in the United Kingdom and the United States. The two dotted lines indicate price relationships between wheat and cloth that would make trade between the two countries worthwhile.

United Kingdom would gain from trade if it could trade 8 units of cloth for 3 units of wheat. This would be better than the domestic price ratio of 8 units of cloth exchanging for 2 units of wheat. Likewise, the United States would gain from an international exchange such as 3.5 units of cloth for 1 unit of wheat. As long as the United Kingdom and United States can agree on a basis of exchange, both countries can gain.

Of course, as in Ricardo's model, we have assumed away the matter of transport costs. For some items these might be so high compared with the cost of the good itself that international exchange is not worthwhile. We have also implicitly assumed that imported goods do not face any increase in price due to the imposition of a tax or tariff. But nonetheless we have shown how, in a simple example of two countries and two products, differences in opportunity cost ratios provide the basis for countries to trade because they specialize in those commodities in which they have a comparative advantage.

You will note that we have referred to how transport costs eliminate some of the potential for international exchange. The following exercise examines how such costs have altered over time.

You may now be wondering why comparative costs

Explaining comparative costs

In his book *A Primer on International Trade*, Jan Pen included the minutes of a typical interview with a student asked to explain the meaning of comparative costs. The dialogue revealed the difficulty encountered by the student in conveying his grasp of the concept.

Pen: Could you explain the groundwork of international trade?

Student (industrious, not too bright):
   Yes. It depends on comparative costs.

Pen: Good. What do you mean by comparative costs?

Student: Well, they are costs. Costs of production, that is. The costs you have to incur when you produce a commodity.

Pen: Yes, but what do you mean by 'comparative'?

Student: I mean that you have to compare them. Compare the costs. That is what makes commerce tick. Then you see which costs are higher and which are lower, and there you are.

Pen: I'm afraid that I don't quite see where we are. Suppose two countries, the United States and Holland, both make cars and bicycles. Now if you want to know the comparative costs of a car in Holland, what exactly do you compare?

Student: I would compare the cost of that Dutch car with the cost of a car in the United States.

Pen   *(sighs)*:
          Suppose the American car is cheaper. Would you import cheaper cars?

Student: Of course.

Pen: Suppose that the Americans also make their bicycles more efficiently than we do. Would you import the bicycles too?

Student   *(sensing that something is going wrong)*:
          No, I wouldn't.

Pen: Why not?

Student: Dutch bicycles are better than American ones.

Pen   *(now sighs very deeply)*:
          Are you sure that they are better? And don't you think that we have lost sight of comparative costs?

24 In your own words, define what you understand by the term comparative costs.

25 If you were the student in this interview, what would you have offered in answer to Jan Pen as the relevant ratios?

should differ between countries. The basic reason for the existence of comparative advantage – whether among individuals, companies, cities, counties, states, countries or continents – lies in the fact that opportunity costs vary. It costs less for different parties to engage in different types of economic activity. Opportunity costs for different countries vary just as they vary for different individuals. Let us consider some of the reasons why opportunity costs and hence comparative advantages differ between nations.

Differing resource mixes

We know that different nations have different resource bases. Australia has much land relative to its population, whereas Japan has little land relative to its population. All other things being equal, one would expect countries with relatively more land to specialize in products that use more land. One expects Australia, for example, to engage in extensive sheep-raising but not Japan, because the opportunity cost of raising sheep in Japan is much higher. Since land in Japan is relatively scarce, its use carries a higher opportunity cost.

There are also differences in climates. We do not expect countries with cold, dry climates to grow bananas. Our earlier examples illustrate the natural resource and climatic differences between countries. Portugal's comparative advantage in wine is not surprising given its easier ability to grow grapes compared with the situation in England, both at the time Ricardo was trying to explain his

It's a small world

The figure shows three measures of changes in transport and communication costs since 1930. The data are in index form with 1930 = 100 measured in 1990 dollars.

26 To what extent has the cost of sending cargo by sea changed between 1930 and 1990?

27 Has the cost of passenger transport become relatively cheap compared with freight transport during this period?

28 In what way could one say that the cost of a three-minute telephone call has changed dramatically since 1930?

29 What relevance do the data have to the expansion of world trade and financial markets?

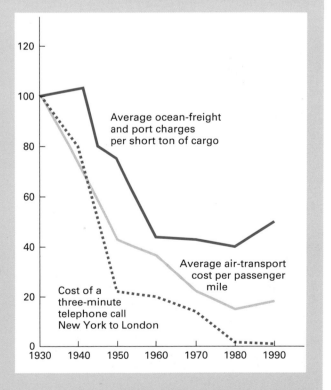

Source: *The Economist*, 20 July 1991, p. 129

theory of comparative advantage and today. Our approach to explaining trade by reference to opportunity cost assumed that the United States was relatively better suited to growing wheat than to manufacturing cloth compared with the United Kingdom.

A third reason why costs differ is quite simply because some countries have superior knowledge of the techniques of manufacturing goods. You will note that we have moved away from primary commodities like wheat and wool and now have man-made products such as synthetic fibres and electronics in mind. Some developing countries, for example, cannot effectively compete with countries in Western Europe in the manufacture of clothes made of polyester and computers since as yet they lack the technology. Remember, back in Chapter 1 we recognized how improved technology can over time help push out the production possibilities curve.

Other factors explaining comparative costs

You will note that the above reasons explaining why comparative costs can differ between countries are quite simply the inherent characteristics of a nation's factor endowment. They are supply-based aspects: Australia is a wool-producing nation since it is relatively well endowed with land, a factor of production that is essential for extensive sheep-farming. But demand conditions can also help explain why countries differ in comparative advantage. Some manufactured goods such as motor cars and household electrical goods are traded between developed countries. The United Kingdom imports cars from France, Germany and Japan – Renaults, Mercedes and Toyotas – and also sells Rover cars to these countries (the Montego and Maestro). Clearly there are differences in the design, specification and performance of all these motor vehicles. Note that we do not have one nation just specializing in motor cars. This is because such consumer goods are not viewed by consumers as being homogeneous (like wheat and wine as in our earlier examples). Consumers throughout the world like different types of modern consumer goods so that it is not the case that one industry is based in one country. Within an industry countries specialize in different types of goods: this trade is known as 'intra-industry trade'.

The terms of trade

Our earlier example of trade between the United Kingdom and United States in wheat and cloth assumed that an international exchange rate between the two commodities would be established such that both countries gained from being open economies. In the real world the terms on which a country exchanges its exports for imports are, of course, measured in monetary terms – as prices. These prices alter for two reasons. First, there may be a change in the ratio of costs of production (and thus internal prices)

in the two countries. A second reason why the prices of one country's products may change relative to those of the other country is a change in the international exchange rate itself. A measure of the influence of both these factors is the **terms of trade**. It expresses the relationship between the average price of, say, the UK's exports and our imports of goods. The average prices are determined as a weighted average, that is, the relative importance of the various items that are traded is duly recognized. If expressed as an index with a base-year value of 100, then a rising index for the United Kingdom would indicate that we have increased export prices on average faster than import prices. The terms of trade are said to have improved. A declining index would indicate that import prices have increased faster than export prices and thus the terms of trade have worsened. These two words to describe the terms of trade – improve and worsen – are more ambiguous than they seem. The UK's terms of trade could be improving, but its competitive position is threatened if producers of manufactured goods in other countries offer more attractive prices in foreign markets. The terms of trade ignore the volume dimension. This picture of whether a country is relatively gaining from trade makes us realize that trade may not benefit every country equally. What are the disadvantages of international exchange?

Trade-weighted exchange rates

The terms of trade compare prices of imports and exports. Exchange rates are the price of foreign currency in terms of domestic currency. But how do we get a measure of the overall value of, say, sterling on the currency markets? We need an index of all bilateral exchange rates, but how do we treat these? The solution is to weight each according to the pattern of trade, that is, in the case of the United Kingdom, allow the influence of the bilateral rates to be greatest in the case of those countries which are the UK's major trading partners.

Figure 6.11 shows that between 1997 and 1998 the UK's trade-weighted exchange rate appreciated sharply. Would this have been favourable or unfavourable to exporters of UK manufactured goods?

Advantageous trade will always exist

From before the beginning of recorded history there have been examples of trade among individuals. Since these acts of exchange have usually been voluntary, we must assume that individuals generally benefit from the trade. Individual tastes and resources vary tremendously. As a consequence, there are sufficient numbers of different opportunity costs in the world for exchange to take place constantly.

As individual entities, nations have different collective tastes and different collective resource endowments. We would therefore expect that there will always be potential gains to be made from trading among nations. Furthermore, the more trade there is, the more specialization there can be. Specialization in turn leads to

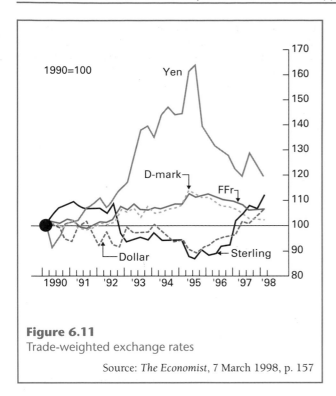

Figure 6.11
Trade-weighted exchange rates

Source: *The Economist*, 7 March 1998, p. 157

KEY POINTS

6.4

■ Countries can be better off materially if they specialize in their comparative advantage.

■ It is important to distinguish between absolute and comparative advantage; the former refers to the ability to produce a unit of output with fewer physical units of input; the latter refers to producing what has the lowest opportunity cost for a nation.

■ Different nations will always have different comparative advantages because of differing opportunity costs due to different resource endowments, technical knowledge and different tastes.

■ The relationship between average export prices and average import prices is the terms of trade.

■ The trade-weighted exchange rate is an index of the average of a country's bilateral rates, weighted by the pattern of its trade with other currencies.

■ Foreign trade can adversely affect certain groups in each country because of increased competition from abroad.

increased output and – if we measure well-being by output levels – to increased happiness. (Admittedly, we are using the term well-being very loosely here.) Self-sufficiency on the part of individuals undeniably means that they forgo opportunities to consume the extra output that becomes available if they are not self-sufficient. Likewise, self-sufficiency on the part of a nation will lower its consumption possibilities and therefore will lower the well-being of its inhabitants. Imagine life in your immediate locality if it was forced to become self-sufficient!

Costs of trade

Trade does not come without cost. If one country has a comparative advantage in producing agricultural crops, other countries may not be able to succeed as sources of agricultural production. Farm-workers in the latter countries that are less efficient at agricultural production will suffer decreases in their incomes until they find other occupations or move to where alternative jobs are.

As tastes, supplies of natural resources, prices and so on change throughout the world, different countries may find their areas of comparative advantage changing. One example of this is in the production of steel. South Korea has become increasingly competitive in steel products, and steel-makers in Western Europe are losing sales to imports. They are feeling the pinch from South Korea's ability to produce steel products at lower cost. The same competitive threat from Japan is to be found in the case of many other consumer goods exported to countries in Western Europe.

Arguments against free trade

There are numerous arguments against free trade, but many on closer inspection turn out to be incomplete. They mainly point out the costs of trade; they do not consider the benefits or the possible alternatives for reducing costs while still reaping benefits.

Infant industry argument

A nation may feel that, if a particular industry were allowed to develop domestically, it could eventually become efficient enough to compete effectively in the world market. Therefore, if some restrictions were placed on imports, native producers would be given the time needed to develop their efficiency to the point where they would be able to compete in the domestic market without any restrictions on imports. In terms of the concept of the supply curve, we would expect that, if the protected industry truly does experience technological break-throughs toward greater efficiency in the future, then the supply curve will shift outwards to the right so that the domestic industry can produce larger quantities at each and every price. This infant industry argument has some merit in the short run and was used to shelter several UK industries in 1918 under the Safeguarding of Industries

Act. The year is significant since the Act was a policy response to the UK's experience during the First World War. When hostilities began in 1914 the United Kingdom was dependent on German supplies in several key industrial sectors. Our dependence on a country which became a foreign enemy had highlighted the need for certain industries to be protected, at least in the short term. This strand of the infant industry argument is very close to the case for protection on grounds of national security, which we discuss next. However, in principle the infant industry case could be applied to industries not of strategic significance in a wartime economy. The general application of the infant industry case can easily be criticized. Often the protective import-restricting arrangements remain even after the infant has grown up. If other countries can still produce more cheaply, the people who benefit from this type of situation are obviously the owners of the firms (and specialized factors of production) in the industry that is still being protected from world competition. The people who lose out are the consumers, who must pay a price higher than the world price for the product in question. In any event, it is very difficult to know beforehand which industries will eventually survive. In other words, we cannot predict very well the specific 'infant' industries that should be protected. Note that when we talk about which industry should be protected, we are in the realm of normative economics. We are stating a value-judgement that comes from our hearts.

National security

It is often argued that we should not rely on foreign sources for many of our products because in time of war these sources might well be cut off and we would have developed few, if any, substitute sources. Such an argument was part of the case for the post-war expansion of UK agriculture. The Second World War had shown the dependence of UK consumers on foreign suppliers who were thousands of miles away. The uncertain passage of ships from the southern hemisphere across the North Atlantic due to the threat from German U-boats appeared to emphasize the case for the more certain presence of home-grown foodstuffs. On the face of it, the argument looked appealing. But as we shall see in Chapter 9, post-war agricultural policy had an impact on the use of resources by limiting the market for food imports. In so far as sales of food to the United Kingdom were restricted, there was a reduced capacity of countries like New Zealand to import items like manufactured goods. Increased UK food production certainly reduced food imports. But the overall impact on the balance of payments was not just on the flow of imported butter and lamb, but also on the sales of motor cars and electrical equipment to overseas buyers.

Protecting a way of life

Free world trade may destroy certain industries in a particular economy as comparative advantages change throughout the world. A society may wish to protect a certain group of individuals who are threatened by international competition because they believe that their particular way of life should be maintained.

Of course, there are always alternative ways to protect particular livelihoods and individual groups. For example, if a country wished to protect watchmakers, rather than restricting foreign trade it could simply give a subsidy directly to watchmakers. This would not raise the price of watches for consumers, but it would serve as a protection of a particular way of life.

Stability

Many people argue that foreign trade should be restricted because it introduces an element of instability into our economic system. They point out that the vagaries of foreign trade add to the ups and downs in our own employment level. However, if we follow this argument to its logical conclusion, we would restrict trade within a country itself. After all, vagaries of trade in particular areas of the United Kingdom sometimes promote employment in other areas. Things are sorted out over time, but workers suffer during the adjustment period. As regards the international sphere, however, people somehow change their position. They feel that adjusting to the vagaries of international trade costs more than adjusting to the vagaries of domestic trade. Perhaps people believe that foreign trade really does not benefit us that much, and thus they argue against it, claiming that the stability of aggregate economic activity is at stake. We should note one difference between the domestic and international situations, however, that lends some truth to this argument. Labour is more mobile within a country than between countries. Immigration laws prevent workers from moving to countries where they can earn the most income. There are also many differences in language and customs that prevent workers from freely moving from country to country. Therefore the adjustment costs to a changing international situation may in fact be higher than the adjustment costs to a changing domestic situation.

Protecting jobs

Perhaps the most frequently used argument against free trade is that unrestrained competition from other countries will eliminate jobs at home because other countries have lower-cost labour than we do. This is indeed a compelling argument, particularly for politicians from areas that might be threatened by foreign competition. For example, a Member of Parliament from an area with textile or shoe factories would certainly be upset about the possibility of constituents losing their jobs because of competition from lower-priced cotton shirt manufacturers in Hong Kong or shoe manufacturers in Brazil and Italy. Again, limitations on imports may help employees in such industries, but at the expense of consumers. And as we have also recognized, attempts at protecting jobs by imposing tariffs, quotas and other restrictions on international trade lead to retaliation by our trading partners. In other words, they start imposing similar restrictions on trade with the United Kingdom. We may end up saving less productive employment at the expense of more productive employment.

Countering foreign subsidies and dumping

Another strong argument against unrestricted foreign trade has to do with countering other nations' subsidies to their own producers and dumping. When a foreign government subsidizes its producers, our competing producers claim that they cannot compete fairly with these subsidized foreigners. To the extent that such subsidies fluctuate, one can argue that unrestricted free trade will seriously disrupt domestic producers. After all, they will not know when foreign governments are going to subsidize their own producers and when they are not. Our competing industries, then, will be expanding and contracting too frequently.

Occasionally, the phenomenon called 'dumping' takes place and is used as an argument against unrestricted trade. Dumping occurs when a producer sells its products abroad at a price below its cost of production. Although accusations of dumping against foreign producers are often heard, they typically only occur when the foreign nation is in the throes of a serious recession. The foreign producer does not want to slow down its production at home because it anticipates an end to the recession and it does not want to bear large costs of financing. Therefore, it dumps its product abroad at prices below its costs. This does, in fact, disrupt foreign trade.

In the past two decades many countries have resorted to a variety of restrictions on world trade. While some restrictions such as complex customs procedures and bureaucratic delays frustrate international exchange, some have more impact. For example, limits on the number of Japanese cars imported into the United Kingdom have a clear impact on the level of international exchange. Such restraints on trade form a reversal of the post-war commitment by the world's trading nations to dismantle tariffs and trade restrictions. Since 1945 members of the General Agreement on Tariffs and Trade (GATT), now called the World Trade Organization (WTO), have agreed to rounds of tariff cuts and helped stimulate the growth in world trade that we noted in Figure 6.7. Some fear that the growing number of these trade restrictions prompted by the world recession could multiply and threaten the whole basis of international exchange. In 1999 the media gave much coverage of the trade dispute between the United States and the European Union concerning bananas. This dispute centred on the EU's importation rules on bananas, which favoured suppliers in former British and French colonies in the Caribbean, Africa and the Pacific as against bananas grown in Central America. At first sight the apparent interest of the United States in pursuing a

dispute for six years seemed odd given that hardly any bananas are grown in the USA. But the USA was sufficiently keen to support the interests of American-based banana distributors as evidenced by its willingness to impose import tariffs on a wide range of European goods. The dispute was eventually resolved but it highlighted the difficulties of the WTO in enforcing international trade rules. Some observers perceive a growing trend in both the USA and EU in the extent to which firms have sought to apply duties on 'cheap' imports that are judged as being 'dumped'. The growth in the number of so-called 'anti-dumping' cases is thus one indicator of the extent to which the 132 members of the WTO remain committed to the belief in freedom to buy and sell across the world.

Does the increase in these *non-tariff barriers* to international trade mean that the future of international trade is in jeopardy? Fears in this respect have been partly allayed by the successful outcome of the so-called Uruguay Round in December 1993. We discuss these matters later in Chapter 29.

KEY POINTS

6.5

- The infant industry argument against free trade contends that new industries should be allowed protection against world competition so that they can become technically efficient in the long run.

- The national security argument against free trade contends that we should not rely on foreign sources for crucial materials needed during time of war.

- Unrestricted foreign trade may allow foreign governments to subsidize exports or foreign producers to engage in dumping – selling products in other countries below their cost of production. To the extent that foreign export subsidies and dumping create more instability in domestic production, they may impair our well-being.

Case Study

The appeal of holidays abroad

Tour operators are reporting a bumper year as holiday-makers flock to make the most of the soaring value of the pound abroad. But while summer bookings for foreign climes are up by 22 per cent on last year, the domestic market is bracing itself for a lean summer with European and Asian visitors finding the cost of accommodation and eating out alarmingly high.

Easter week is expected to create a record, with 1.7 million people due to leave Britain. The most popular spring destinations, such as the Canary Islands, will attract 25 per cent more British holidaymakers than 1997. Increased economic confidence and delayed spending of building society windfalls are seen as contributory factors, but the main reason for such growth is widening popular awareness of sterling's enhanced buying power. According to Thomas Cook, the increase in bookings for France, Italy and Spain almost exactly matches the 13 per cent appreciation in the pound's value in those countries compared with a year ago. Demand for the Greek islands was already rising sharply before the recent devaluation of the drachma, and they are expected to be a favourite choice for those booking late. Meanwhile, demand for trips to America, which is the sixth most popular choice for British holidaymakers, has edged up only one per cent, reflecting the much smaller gain sterling has made against the dollar. Rachel Shirbon, a Thomas Cook manager, said: 'Sterling was pretty strong last year, but what we are finding now is that the perception of its strength is more widespread. This means that people are booking extra holidays or short trips to what they know are good-value destinations.'

The market for weekend breaks in Europe has shown the greatest increase of all, with business in the first three months of this year up 35 per cent on 1997. For travellers to France, the summer outlook is particularly encouraging. Because most choose a self-drive and self-catering holiday, their local spending accounts for more than half the holiday cost and so the currency gains are greater. Jane Williams, marketing manager for Cresta, said demand for villas and gîtes was 30 per cent higher than a year ago. In some areas, this partly reflected reductions, or at least freezes, in sterling rental rates.

The magnitude of the currency change had been further demonstrated (with the help of the budget) by the price of petrol in France falling below that in Britain for the first time in years. Restaurants had also become much cheaper, with the bill for a four-course meal for two with wine coming to £18. But for visitors to Britain, the pound's level is less welcome. Citizens of West European countries make up two-thirds of the tourist market, and their numbers failed to grow last year for the first time since 1991.

The British Tourist Authority predicts that the figures will be flat again this year, with spending per head likely to go down. Visits from Asian countries in recession are set to fall substantially, though they will be more than offset by high-spending Americans. To counter the spread of an image of Britain as a high-cost destination, the BTA is producing half a million copies of a 'Good Value Britain' leaflet.

Source: *Daily Telegraph*, 1 April 1998

1 Explain how the market for holidays abroad by British tourists is likely to be affected by a change in the level of the pound sterling relative to other European currencies.
2 Explain how an upward movement of the pound sterling affects demand for holidays in the UK.
3 How does the extract suggest that the demand for holidays abroad is likely to be more price elastic in the long run than in the short run?
4 It is estimated that tourism is now the world's biggest single industry and that receipts from international tourism have expanded at an average annual growth of over 8 per cent between 1980 and

The rise and rise of the holiday £

	April 1996 (value of £1)	April 1997 1997–8	April 1998	% increase
French franc	7.43	8.92	10.08	13.0
Italian lira	2374	2647	2982	8.9
Spanish peseta	183	224	254	13.4
Greek drachma	356	420	516	22.9
Turkish lira	102 436	196 832	388 949	97.6
US dollar	1.49	1.58	1.64	3.8
Indonesian rupiah	3175	3400	12 649	272.0
Thai baht	35.4	38.8	58.6	51.0

1990. What does this imply about the income elasticity of demand for international travel?

5 Assume that you are appointed as an adviser to the government minister responsible for tourism in the UK. The minister seeks to expand the number of visitors coming to the UK, which is currently the fifth most popular tourist destination in the world. Write a short paper advising the minister of three policies that could be pursued to achieve this objective.

6 Having written the briefing paper for the minister, assume she now asks you to explain why you have not recommended some policies on the grounds that governments have little influence on the number of tourists to the UK. On what aspects of tourism might you have doubts as to the efficacy of government intervention to boost tourism?

Exam Preparation

Multiple choice questions

1 Which one of the following would appear as a credit item in the UK balance of payments current account?
   A the purchase by a German company of a UK car manufacturer
   B money sent by UK residents to their relatives abroad
   C expenditure on local services by British troops stationed abroad
   D the expenditure of American tourists in Britain

2 Which of the following represents an invisible export in the UK balance of payments?
   A payment of dividends to Japanese shareholders of Nissan (UK)
   B spending by Japanese tourists in London on hotel accommodation
   C the purchase of an overseas company by a British firm
   D UK government foreign aid to developing countries

3 Who would benefit from an appreciation of the £ sterling against the US dollar?
   A a British pop group paid in US$s for a North American concert tour
   B a UK unit trust investor with large holdings of North American equities
   C British holidaymakers visiting Florida
   D US students studying in the UK

4 Country X has a comparative advantage in producing wheat and country Y in producing cars. However, the countries choose not to specialize and trade. What is the valid reason for this behaviour?
   A the exchange rate lies within the countries' opportunity cost ratios
   B there is immobility of factors of production between the countries
   C trade is based on absolute rather than comparative advantage
   D transport costs are high relative to the opportunity cost differences between the countries

5 There will be a favourable movement in a country's terms of trade when
   A the value of its exports rises more than that of its imports
   B its import prices rise less than its export prices
   C its export prices fall more than its import prices
   D the external value of its currency has fallen
   E tariffs on imported commodities are increased

6 A country's terms of trade will improve, other things being equal, if
   A the country's currency appreciates
   B the average price of imports rises and the average price of exports falls
   C the average price of exports falls more rapidly than the average price of imports
   D the total value of imports rises less rapidly than the total value of exports
   E import duties are lowered

7 Which of the following items would appear as a credit item on the visible trade account of the UK balance of payments?
   A the purchase of wine from a French vineyard by a British wine merchant
   B the purchase of Scotch whisky by a German supermarket chain
   C the purchase of shares in a British oil extraction company by a Norwegian firm
   D a British supermarket chain purchasing oil extracted in the North Sea
   E a group of Americans purchasing tickets in New York to fly Concorde to London

8 Other things being equal, which of the following would be most likely to decrease the price of the £ sterling in terms of the US dollar?
   A interest rates in the UK rise
   B the UK imposes tariffs on US goods
   C the UK rate of inflation exceeds that in the USA
   D the number of US tourists visiting the UK increases
   E there is an increase in the carriage of US goods by UK shipping

9 The diagram shows the demand for and supply of US dollars. The initial point of equilibrium is X. What would be the new point of equilibrium immediately following increased British investment in the USA?

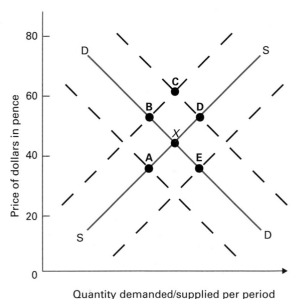

Quantity demanded/supplied per period

Essay questions

1 (a) Examine the benefits that countries can derive from international trade. (60 marks)
  (b) If there are such benefits from free trade, why is the GATT (General Agreement on Tariffs and Trade) necessary to prevent countries erecting barriers to trade? (40 marks)

2 (a) Explain how changes in the external value of the pound (the exchange rate) affect the volume and value of United Kingdom exports. (12 marks)
  (b) Discuss other factors which influence the sales of United Kingdom products in overseas markets. (13 marks)

On completing PART B
you should find the
following websites
useful and interesting.

■ **www.statsbase.gov.uk/gtos2.dbguide.htm**
In this part of the book we introduce the role of governments. Much of this area involves understanding and using statistics that relate to the whole economy. There are many opportunities to retrieve such data freely from the Internet. This site is a good starting point since it provides a web version of the *Guide to Official Statistics*. By viewing the contents page, you can access information and data concerning Chapters 7–12, and more. Specifically: population; education; labour market; health and social care; income and living standards; crime and justice; housing; environment; transport; social statistics; the economy; agriculture, fisheries, food and forestry; production and manufacturing; distribution and other services; and public services.

■ **www.hm-treasury.gov.uk/**
This was one of the first government websites, and it is still one of the best. The site opens with opportunities to search – information on budgets, the economy, including forecasts and the latest indicators, the euro – and there is a comprehensive index, which lists approximately 100 subjects alphabetically.

■ **www.bbc.co.uk**
The BBC homepage provides a gateway to more than 200 individual sites relating to BBC television and radio programmes and other services. Many of these are relevant to your study of economics; for example, check the latest news headlines and/or the World Service. Alternatively, this is a good site to visit if you want to improve your 'Net knowhow', as the 'webwise' button leads you to approximately 1000 pages of help and plainly worded advice on using the Net. But then again, you may just want to know what's on the telly.

■ **www.foe.co.uk**
For a different perspective, it is often interesting to look at information presented by non-government organizations, for example the Friends of the Earth site. It has useful sections called 'Factory watch', 'Millennium round: Game over' and 'Real food'. The first section enables you to find out what is being emitted by firms in your area, and the other two provide an interesting set of opinions on the

World Trade Organization and genetically modified foods. These themes are alluded to in Chapters 9 and 10.

■ **www.ends.co.uk**
ENDS (Environment Data Service) provides a daily news service for European environmental affairs. The homepage allows you to sample the organization's authoritative monthly report and to make links with other environmental resources on the web. The information can be used in conjunction with all the chapter themes in this section – visit and see why it's claimed to be the best environmental website.

■ **www.detr.co.uk**
The DETR, comprising the departments of the environment, transport and the regions, is now the main government department responsible for environmental matters generally. Indeed, as we see in Chapter 10, transport is a significant section that impacts on the environment. The department's homepage provides access to information pertaining to: the role of the government in environmental protection; welfare issues associated with housing; planning and regeneration; and, obviously, details relating to the department's responsibilities for transport, local government and the regions. Students researching coursework for economics, geography or environmental science may find the last three sites particularly useful.

■ **www.jrf.org.uk**
The Joseph Rowntree Foundation is the UK's largest independent social research charity. It supports a wide range of research relating to social policy – in particular, issues concerning housing and unemployment. The website allows you to order reports and print press releases etc. It could also help with your project.

The role of government in the mixed economy

The pricing system answers three basic questions of resource allocation: *What* goods will be produced? *How* will they be produced? And *for whom* will they be produced? The forces of supply and demand acting through the pricing system (that is, the market) affect the bulk of decisions that answer these three questions. But we do not live in a free-market world. In addition to market forces, there are many other forces at work that affect the allocation of resources. One of the most important of these non-market forces is government. Indeed, it is difficult to imagine a world without government. Living without government would mean living without legislation. There would not be any taxes, and without any form of revenue there would also be no motorways, public libraries, law enforcement, colleges or universities, nor any unemployment benefit, state training enterprises or medical services. Hence in reality government is a major part of our economy. In order to understand economics, therefore, an understanding of the nature of the functions of government is required. Of particular importance are the economic functions relating to efficiency and equity and how these are paid for.

LEARNING OUTCOMES

On completing this chapter you should understand:

- Various government functions relating to efficiency

- Various government functions relating to equity

- Public choice theory

- Taxation

Functions relating to efficiency

All UK governments, regardless of political colour, are concerned with maximizing output from a nation's resources. In fact, economists and politicians assume that the electorate always prefer more to less from a given set of resources. Consequently there are various institutional and legislative arrangements in place to limit anti-competitive practices, and these are dealt with specifically in Chapter 27. There are, however, many other government functions that arise in order to overcome the inefficiencies of the competitive market system. Formally all such market inefficiencies are termed **market failure**. Indeed, any situation in which the unrestrained market system causes too few or too many resources to be allocated to a specific economic activity could be stated as an example. Consequently, it would be rather arduous to list all the specific instances of market failure that exist – but by the end of this chapter we shall have dealt with six of the main examples. In this first section, relating to the goal of efficiency, we shall deal with three of the major areas in which the market is recognized to fail. These are:

1. market economies tend to experience business fluctuations;
2. the market system cannot deal effectively with the spill-over (third-party) effects of many economic activities, and therefore alternative systems of allocation need to be considered;
3. market forces cannot provide public goods.

Striving to secure economic stability

In the last hundred years the economy has averaged approximately a 1.5 per cent annual increase in economic activity. Unfortunately, however, this long-term trend has not been achieved at a steady rate, since there have been periodic fluctuations above and below the general upward trend. These fluctuations are related to activity in the broader economy. For instance, at times the overall business climate is buoyant: few workers are unemployed, productivity is increasing and not many firms are going bust. At other times, however, business is not so good: there are many unemployed workers, cutbacks in production are occurring and a significant number of firms are in receivership. These ups and downs in economy-wide activity used to be called 'business cycles', but that term no longer seems appropriate because *cycles* implies predetermined or automatic recurrence, and nowadays we do not experience automatic recurrent cycles. The contractions and expansions of an economy in the twenty-first century vary greatly in length and are best referred to as **business fluctuations**. Inevitably, such fluctuations affect all markets, and consequently governments are concerned with minimizing the effects.

Business fluctuations

As suggested above, during most years the UK economy is growing – output, income and employment are increasing. In other words, the trend in business and general economic activity is upward. But there are fluctuations around what we might call the 'growth-path' line. We have terms for the periods when business activity temporarily pulls us below our upward growth path, and others for periods when business activity moves with, or in excess of, our normal growth path. We call the former a **recession** unless it is extremely severe, in which case it is called a **depression**, and the latter an **expansion** or **boom**. The precise terminology depends upon the severity of the economic conditions being described. For instance, a small change in the direction of the economy over any three-month period (that is, a quarter of a year) would simply be regarded as a 'blip' or 'fluke'; for the trend to be identifiable it must be more continuous. Hence, a downturn would need to persist for at least two successive quarters before it could officially be termed a recession; traditionally it would be recognized by two quarterly periods of negative growth of the real gross domestic product (as illustrated and discussed in 'Progression or recession'). If the recession continues for a number of years, its severity may be recorded by the term depression; in fact, the length of the recession at the beginning of the 1990s was sufficient for some economists to relabel it as a depression. However, the term depression should technically be reserved for extraordinarily long downturns such as those experienced throughout Europe and America during much of the 1930s.

Progression or recession

Economic activity can progress, regress or remain static. The direction of the movement is measured accurately by monitoring changes in the gross domestic product (GDP), which records the total output of an entire economy. The figures show the change in GDP each quarter, compared with the corresponding three-month period of the previous year. The years have been selected to portray trends during a decade.

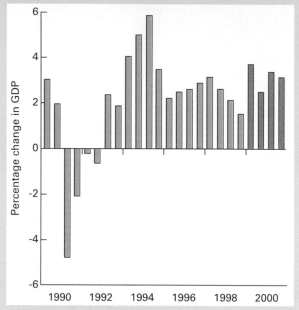

Notes:
a The changes in GDP shown above are adjusted to remove the effects of inflation between 1990 and 2000.
b Q1 = Jan–Mar, Q2 = Apr–Jun, Q3 = Jul–Sep, Q4 = Oct–Dec

Source: *UK Economic Accounts: A Quarterly Supplement to Economic Trends* and *Lloyds TSB forecasts*

1 (a) When did the UK enter into a recession during the 1990s?
(b) When did the recession officially end?
2 State two economic characteristics apart from GDP changes that would enable one to identify a recession.
3 How accurate was the forecast by the Lloyds bank?
4 (a) Is the economy at present going through a phase of expansion, boom, recession or depression?
(b) What forthcoming events may cause it to change course?

It may help if you think of the business cycle in terms of a growing child. The child is on a long-term growth trend with regard to body weight and height. There are, however, temporary fluctuations. The child can become

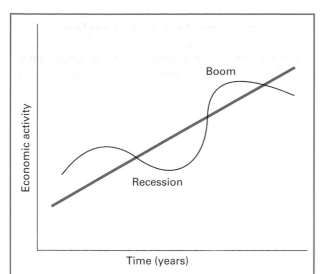

Figure 7.1
Typical business fluctuations
The coloured line depicts the long-term 'growth path' around which economic activity fluctuates – moving in some consistent pattern from boom to recession and back again.

picture. This is particularly true at the turning points of the cycle, when some statistical series will be pointing upwards and others downwards. Hence policy recommendations differ, as do interpretations of how the economy works, and this will become increasingly evident as your study of economics proceeds through the various parts of this text.

KEY POINTS

7.1

■ Government functions relating to efficiency are largely designed to overcome recognized problems of market failure.

■ Business fluctuations above and below a steady upward growth path are typical of modern economies.

■ The ups and downs in economic activity are called booms and recessions. To distinguish them from blips, the contraction or expansion of activity needs to be continuous for at least six months.

■ The fluctuations experienced by an economy lead governments throughout the world to attempt various stabilization policies.

sick or can experience malnutrition and deviate from the long-term trend towards maturity. This would be the equivalent of a recession in the economy. When the child experiences growth spurts, this would be equivalent to an expansion in the economy.

In Figure 7.1 we portray the typical course of business fluctuations. When business cycles were first identified in 1860, it was suggested that it took eight to eleven years to progress through a complete cycle from one boom to another. Since then, however, other economists have challenged this time measurement, with various cycles being identified ranging from three to fifty years.

In other words, there are many explanations for business fluctuations, of which the following is only one. A boom situation leads to 'overheating'; this is characterized by shortages of labour and stock and a consequent rise in prices. This can lead to a recession characterized by falling output, rising unemployment, rising stock levels and stabilizing prices. Commercial properties become vacant and cheaper to rent or buy. Eventually this generates opportunities for a new upswing, which takes advantage of the various cheap unemployed resources.

The typical business fluctuation is not, however, left to its own devices – governments intervene. It does not matter which political party they belong to or which nation they govern, the objective of maintaining a level of economic stability is important. The business communities on which they depend need stability in order to plan confidently and prosper. Unfortunately, though, this objective is easier to state than execute. Both government and academic economists are faced with a number of pieces of information, which rarely form a consistent

Correcting externalities

We now come to the second item on our list of market failures, which represents a major imperfection of the price system. According to the accepted criteria identified by the economist Pareto at the turn of the twentieth century, economic efficiency should describe a situation in which nobody can be made better off without making somebody else worse off. Consequently, in the pure market system, competition would only generate economic efficiency when individuals are faced with the true opportunity cost of their actions. In some circumstances, the price that someone actually pays for a resource, good or service is higher or lower than the opportunity cost that society as a whole pays for that same resource, good or service. In short, it is quite possible that decisions made by one firm or one consumer will affect others to their benefit or detriment.

Consider a hypothetical world where there is no government regulation against pollution. You are living in a town that so far has clean air. A steel mill moves into town. It produces steel for which it has paid for the inputs – land, labour, capital and entrepreneurship. The price it charges for the steel reflects, in this example, only the costs that the steel mill incurred. In the course of production, however, the mill gets one input – clean air – free, by simply taking it. This is indeed taking a liberty, because in the making of steel the furnaces emit smoke. The steel mill does not have to pay the cost of cleaning up the smoke; rather, it is the people in the community who pay that cost in the form of dirtier clothes, dirtier cars and houses, and perhaps even more respiratory illnesses. There has been a spill-over effect, or an **externality**. Actually, there has been an *external cost*. Some of the costs associated with the production of the steel have spilled over to **third parties**, that is, parties other than the buyer and the seller of the steel. A spill-over such as air pollution is called a *negative externality* because there are costs that you and your neighbours pay – dirtier clothes and cars plus respiratory problems. In other words, the neighbours' costs are external to the market transaction between the steel mill and the buyers of steel.

Environmental damage often results from negative externalities. Consequently, a more comprehensive coverage of external costs is provided in Chapter 10 on environmental issues. Within those pages we say something about government attempts to measure and correct external costs.

Before leaving the topic here, however, we should acknowledge that not all externalities are negative. In some instances the production of one good will spill benefits over to third parties. In these instances it is relatively easy to encourage the market to produce efficiently. The government can take responsibility for financing the good or service in question via subsidies to private firms to ensure that they are rewarded for production of a good or service that, if left to market forces, would be under-allocated. An even simpler process is for the government actually to take responsibility for the production of the good or service itself. The next section on public goods will confirm the appeal of this approach. Indeed, if markets are to work efficiently the government production solution is inevitable in certain situations, and these will be reviewed next.

Providing public goods

The third area that we identified in our introductory list as a market failure related to the provision of public goods. In reviewing these government-provided goods and services we shall, to a certain extent, revise themes that have already been raised under the heading of externalities. The benefits that people get from these particular goods depend not on how much they individually have, but on how much other people have – which is part of the rationale for governments providing them.

In order to explain the precise nature of public goods, it is appropriate to begin at the other end of the spectrum and clarify our understanding of **private goods**. Indeed, so far in this text it is these so-called private goods that we have generally discussed, for example petrol, wheat, hamburgers, chips, wine and manufactured commodities. These private goods are distinguished by two basic principles; one can be termed the **principle of rivalry**. This means that if you use a private good, I cannot use it. And conversely, if I use a private good, you cannot use it. For example, when I use the services of a mechanic, he cannot be working at the same time on your car. We compete for the mechanic's services, we are rivals for this resource. Mechanics' services are therefore priced according to our levels of demand and the available supply of their time; the price system enables the mechanic to divide his attention between customers. The other principle that characterizes a private good is the **principle of exclusion**. This simply implies that once a good is provided it is possible to prevent others enjoying the benefits unless they pay. In short, anyone who does not pay for the good or service is excluded. For example, if a road bridge is set up with a toll-gate, then the communications link that the particular bridge offers is available only to those who pay. All others are excluded by the price mechanism.

There is an entire class of goods that are not private goods. These are called **public goods**. In the case of *pure* public goods, both the principles of exclusion and rivalry cannot be applied. They are non-excludable and non-rivalrous in their characteristics. Sometimes a distinction is made between *pure* public goods, which have both of these characteristics, and *quasi-* (near- or impure) public goods, which do not. The major feature of quasi-public goods is that they are jointly consumed. As the name implies, joint consumption means that when one person consumes a good it does not reduce the amount available to others. Hence it is difficult to apply a discriminatory price system. National defence, street-lighting and overseas representation are standard textbook examples of public goods.

Characteristics of public goods

We can therefore list several distinguishing characteristics of public goods that set them apart from all other goods.

1 Public goods are usually indivisible. You cannot buy or sell £5 worth of our ability to annihilate the world with bombs. Public goods cannot be produced or sold very easily in small units.

2 Public goods can be used by increasing numbers of people at no additional cost. For example, once a lighthouse has been built, the first and last ship to pass do so at no extra cost to the lighthouse-keeper; the opportunity cost of an extra ship benefiting from the signal is zero.

3 Additional users of public goods do not deprive others of any of the services of the good. For example, if you use the beams from the lighthouse, other ships do not become excluded from its illumination.

4 It is very difficult to charge people for a public good on the basis of how much they use. For instance, it is nearly impossible to determine how much any person uses or values national defence. It cannot be bought and sold in the market-place, as no one can be denied the benefits even if they choose not to pay.

Free riders

This last point leads us to the **free-rider problem**. It is a problem because it involves a situation in which some individuals believe that others will take on the burden of paying for public goods such as national defence. Alternatively, 'free riders' will argue that they receive no value from such government services as national defence or overseas representation, and therefore really should not pay for it. Consider a hypothetical example: citizens will be taxed directly in proportion to how much they tell an interviewer that they value national defence for the following year. Some people will probably tell interviewers that they are unwilling to pay for national defence because they do not want any of it – it is of no value to them. Many of them would end up being free riders, especially when they assume that others will pay for the desired public good anyway. We all want to be free riders when we believe that someone else will provide the commodity in question.

Look at the problem as it is represented in Table 7.1. Here we show the different possible outcomes depending on whether you decide to pay your share of the annual national defence budget and whether others decide to pay. If everyone else pays and you pay also, the total amount of money spent on national defence would be £20 000 000 100 per year. If you do not pay, the total amount for national defence will fall only by £100 to £20 000 000 000 per year. The difference does not seem to be very much and, expressed as a percentage of the total defence budget, it is very small indeed. There are two other possibilities. If no one else pays and you pay, national defence spending will be only £100 per year, and then if you do not pay and no one else pays either, there will be no money spent on national defence that year.

What is a probable choice that you might make in such a situation? If you pay, either others will or they will not. If they do not, your £100 is not going to matter much; if they do, your £100 will still not matter much. Why not take a free ride? That's exactly what the free-rider problem is all about. Public goods, therefore, may be provided in too small amounts if left to the private sector.

A bridge too far?

Construction of the first new bridge over the Thames in London for more than a hundred years was launched as part of the capital's preparations for the millennium. The pedestrian-only, £16 million steel suspension bridge will run from the steps of St Paul's, linking the cathedral with the new Tate Gallery of Modern Art and the open-air Globe Theatre.

The last crossing to be built was Tower Bridge, which opened in 1894. There have, however, been two replacement bridges since then: Waterloo in 1942, the old one having been dismantled in the 1930s, and London Bridge, which was built in 1967 while the old one was dismantled and sold to an American to be re-erected in Arizona.

Designed by the architect Sir Norman Foster in partnership with the sculptor Sir Anthony Caro and the engineering company Ove Arup, the bridge will feature sculptures, an aluminium deck and stainless steel balustrades. About 4 million pedestrians a year are expected to cross the 4-metre-wide bridge. Sir Norman said: 'The bridge will be lit at night to form a blade of light across the Thames. Pedestrians will have a gentle

Table 7.1

Scoreboard for national defence
The free rider is the one who will gladly let everyone else pay the bill. If you do not pay your share of national defence but everyone else does, there will still be £20 billion per year available for the country's defence.

	If you pay	If you do not pay
And if everybody else pays	£20 000 000 100/year	£20 000 000 000/year
And if no one else pays	£100/year	£0.00/year

promenade walk across, offering them spectacular views. The bridge will improve accessibility for residents, business workers, tourists and visitors, and help to alleviate congestion.'

The bridge has been supported by the Millennium Commission, which has raised the £16 million. Among donors were the Hongkong and Shanghai Bank and the Corporation of London.

Source: Adapted from *The Guardian*, 29 April 1999

5 (a) Explain fully whether the pedestrian bridge described is an example of a 'pure' or 'quasi-' public service, or neither.
  (b) If the same bridge were designed to be lined with shops and takeaway bars, would it change your answer to (a)?
  (c) What are the economic arguments against the bridge as described?
6 Cars are excluded from the new bridge. Discuss if this is an example of the principle of exclusion.
7 We are told in the extract that the bridge will feature sculptures. Is sculpture generally regarded as a public good or a private good, and is street sculpture any different?
8 (a) If a toll-gate system were introduced on this bridge, what may be a fair toll price and how could this be marketed?
  (b) Would a toll-gate system exclude free riders from crossing the Thames?
  (c) Using economic arguments, make a case for or against a toll-system.

Many products and services in our economy are public goods, for example the fire services, the maintenance of law and order, and overseas representation. There is a very strong case for having the government finance them. In fact, even Adam Smith, the prime exponent of free-market forces, recognized that the government must provide them, and in most countries today this is the case.

KEY POINTS

7.2

■ Two further market failures that lead to inefficiency and create government functions are externalities and public goods.

■ Negative externalities, or negative spill-overs, lead to an over-allocation of resources to a specific economic activity. Positive externalities, or positive spill-overs, result in an under-allocation of resources to a specific economic activity.

■ The provision of public goods contributes to a nation's standard of living, as they accommodate positive externalities.

■ Public goods are jointly consumed. The principles of exclusion and rivalry do not apply as they do with private goods.

■ Public goods have the following characteristics: (1) they are indivisible; (2) once they are produced, there is no opportunity cost of additional consumers using them; (3) your use of a public good does not deprive others of its simultaneous use; and (4) there is difficulty in charging consumers on the basis of use.

Functions relating to equity

Equity does not, in its economic sense, simply mean 'equality'. In our context equity relates to 'fairness' and 'social justice', and one accepted role of government is to create a fairer society now and in the future. Hence, from an economist's point of view, government functions relating to equity are to do with selecting goods and services that have special merits and should not be left to market-force allocation, and with deciding how income should be redistributed between the haves and the have-nots.

To highlight the importance of these decisions, it is worthwhile considering the distribution of income *before* any government intervention via taxes and **benefits in kind** (such as state-provided education and health care) have taken place. A traditional way to discuss the measurement of actual money income distribution is via the Lorenz curve.

The Lorenz curve

We can represent the distribution of money income graphically with what is called the **Lorenz curve**, named after US-born statistician Max Otto Lorenz, who proposed it in 1905. The Lorenz curve shows what proportion of total

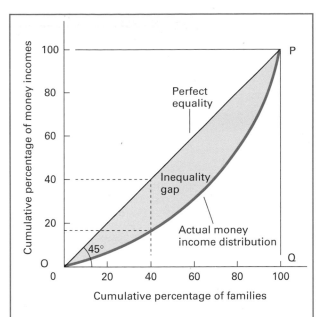

Figure 7.2

The Lorenz curve

The horizontal axis measures the cumulative percentage of families from 0 to 100 per cent. The vertical axis measures the cumulative percentage of money income from 0 to 100. A straight line at a 45° angle cuts the box in half and represents a line of perfect income equality, in which 40 per cent of the families get 40 per cent of the money income, 80 per cent get 80 per cent and so on. The Lorenz curve, showing actual money income distribution, is not a straight line but rather a curved line as shown. The difference between perfect money income equality and the Lorenz curve is the inequality gap.

level of inequality. For instance, from 1949 to 1979 the curve became less bowed; that is, moved towards the 45° line, suggesting a lessening of inequality; since 1980, the curve has moved further from the 45° line, indicating a rise in income inequality. The problem with comparing Lorenz curves by eye is the general, imprecise nature of the calculation. This problem is overcome by using Gini coefficients.

The Gini coefficient

One measure of the degree of income inequality is the **Gini coefficient of inequality**, devised by the Italian statistician Corrado Gini (1884–1965). A diagram showing a Lorenz curve, such as the one in Figure 7.2, can also demonstrate the concept of the Gini coefficient. We compare the area between the straight 45° line and the Lorenz curve of actual income distribution with the entire area under the diagonal – that is, with the triangle that represents half of the box in Figure 7.2 and is labelled OPQ. In other words:

$$\text{Gini coefficient of inequality} = \frac{\text{area between diagonal line and Lorenz curve of money income distribution}}{\text{triangular area under diagonal line}}$$

What does this mean? It means that the Gini coefficient will range from 0 to 1. If we had perfect equality, the Gini coefficient would obviously be 0 because there would be no area between the diagonal line, or curve of absolute equality, and the curve of actual distribution of income. The greater that area becomes, however, the greater becomes the Gini coefficient and hence the measure of inequality. A Gini coefficient of 1 would therefore represent complete inequality. (Even if the coefficient is expressed as a percentage, or index, the same rules apply: 0 simply means that all households have the same income; 100 means that one household has all the income.) In other words, the greater the income inequality associated with a nation, the higher the number of its Gini coefficient. (Finally, it should be remembered that ordinarily Gini coefficients reflect income before taxes and do not include benefits in kind.)

European comparisons of income inequality

As we just described, one way to measure income inequality is by using the Gini coefficient. In the following table we present comparisons of the Gini coefficient for three nations from 1980 to 1994.

When calculated, the Gini coefficient does not include non-money income or income that has been earned unofficially. Moreover, it does not take account of age as a determining factor in income differences.

money income is accounted for by different proportions of the nation's families. Look at Figure 7.2. On the horizontal axis we measure the *cumulative* percentage of families, lowest-income families first. Starting at the left corner, there are zero families; at the right corner, we have 100 per cent of families; and in the middle, we have 50 per cent of families. The vertical axis represents the cumulative percentage of money income. The 45° line represents perfect equality; 40 per cent of the families obtain 40 per cent of total income, 60 per cent of the families obtain 60 per cent of total income, and so on. Of course, in no real-world situation is there such perfect equality of income; no Lorenz curve would be a straight line. Rather, it would be some curved line, like the one labelled 'actual money income distribution' in Figure 7.2. For example, the bottom 40 per cent of families in the United Kingdom received about 18 per cent of total gross money income in 1997/8 (i.e., the position before tax). The difference between perfect money income equality and the Lorenz curve is the inequality gap.

The Lorenz curve is therefore useful for showing the change in income distribution over time, since the further the curve drops below the 45° line, the greater will be the

Comparisons of the Gini coefficient

Nation	Gini coefficient 1980	Gini coefficient 1990	Gini coefficient 1994
United Kingdom	0.327	0.333	0.345
Spain	0.397	0.381	0.340
France	0.417	0.399	0.290

Source: United Nations 1991 and Eurostat 1998

9 (a) Which of the nations listed in the table had most equality in 1994?
  (b) Which of the nations listed in the table had most inequality in 1994?
10 Which nation has improved income equality the most during the years shown?
11 What government policies would help a nation to achieve income equality?
12 Discuss the relevance of two of the factors that affect equality but that the Gini coefficient does not consider.
13 Why is income unequally distributed in all nations?

gross income and/or benefits (including pensions, etc.) *minus* taxation *plus* related government expenditure. It is the government aspects of this equation that will be examined in the remaining parts of this chapter.

KEY POINTS

7.3

- Most governments promote equity, in so far as they are concerned with the distribution of income and providing goods of merit.

- The Lorenz curve graphically represents the distribution of income. The more it is bowed, the greater the inequality of income that exists.

- The degree of income inequality can be measured by the Gini coefficient; Gini coefficients can range from 0 to 1.

- Final income = gross income and/or benefits – taxation + related government expenditure.

Income distribution in the UK

To consider income distribution in more detail in the United Kingdom we need to recognize that people receive income from two basic sources, either as rewards for selling factors of production (Chapters 12, 24 and 25 examine income distribution) or as transfers from the state in the form of benefits (as cash or benefits in kind). The percentages in Table 7.2 show how the actual incomes, before deductions, were acquired in 1997. The total represented £769 billion.

The final distribution, however, is influenced by the manner in which the government taxes this income and the patterns of expenditure that it makes on goods and services. Hence, in terms of a formula: final income *equals*

Table 7.2

UK household incomes 1997

Source of income	Percentage of total in 1997
Wages and salaries	56
Income from self-employment	11
Rent, dividends, interest	10
Social benefits and pensions	21
Government grants and transfers from charities	1

Source: *Social Trends*, HMSO, 1999

Merit goods (and demerit goods)

What constitutes a **merit good** is defined by the political process according to what the government deems to be socially desirable. Once this decision has been taken, those goods that are selected are made available free, or almost free, to all citizens, by the government either subsidizing the production or, more commonly, actually organizing the output itself. Some examples of merit goods in the United Kingdom are museums, ballet and the arts, health services, education and library provision. Note that there is nothing inherent in any of these particular goods that makes them different from private goods. They *can be supplied through the market* and in some countries they actually are (for example, medical care in America).

It is clearly a political decision, therefore, as to what constitutes a merit good, but in general terms they serve two objectives. First, they facilitate a redistribution of real income; as merit goods are largely financed out of progressive taxation, the result is that the poorer citizens get access to a standard of service that they could not otherwise afford. Second, by making these goods readily available to all citizens at well below the market-clearing price, society can take advantage of positive externalities as individuals become better educated and healthier, and ultimately a higher standard of living for the country as a whole can be achieved.

Demerit goods are the opposite of merit goods. They are goods that, through the political process, are deemed socially undesirable. Heroin, morphine and LSD are just some examples of so-called demerit goods. The way the government exercises its role in the area of demerit goods is by taxing, regulating or prohibiting their manufacture, sale and use. Partly, the age restrictions imposed on juveniles purchasing alcohol and tobacco are justified by governments on the basis that these are demerit goods. (Note that there is a subtle difference between making under-age drinking illegal – a demerit good argument – and making drunken driving illegal. The latter law is based on arguments for regulating a negative externality due to its third-party effects.)

Providing a legal system

The courts and the police may not at first seem like economic functions of government (although judges and police personnel must be paid). Their activities nonetheless have important consequences on economic activities in any country. All of us enter into contracts constantly, whether they be oral or written, expressed or implied. When we believe that we have been wronged, we seek redress of our grievances within our legal institutions. Moreover, consider the legal system that is necessary for the smooth functioning of our system. Our system has defined quite explicitly the legal status of businesses, the rights of private ownership and a method for the enforcement of contracts. All relationships among consumers and businesses are governed by the legal rules of the game. We might consider the government in its judicial function, then, as the referee when there are disputes in the economic arena.

Much of our legal system is involved with defining and protecting *property rights*. **Property rights** are the rights of an owner to use and to exchange his or her property. One might say that property rights are really the rules of our economic game. When property rights are well defined, owners of property have an incentive to use that property efficiently. Any mistakes in their decision about the use of property have negative consequences that the owners suffer. Furthermore, when property rights are well defined, the owners of property have an incentive to maintain that property so that if those owners ever desire to sell it, it will fetch a better price.

Establishing and maintaining property rights in certain sections is problematic and leads to an increasing role for governments. This is particularly the case with environmental and intellectual property. We review problems relating to environmental property rights in Chapter 10, and briefly consider intellectual property in the next section.

Intellectual property rights identify the ownership and control of what is called 'non-tangible intellectual output'. Two main examples exist: patents, which protect ideas, and copyright, which protects creativity. Without these two systems of property rights, creative work would have far less value and an immense range of output would occur. Whether this means there is a greater role for the government to play is the topic of the next exercise.

The creative industries

The creative industries could make Britain a world leader once again. The twenty-first century is certainly set to see leisure and entertainment play a more productive part than old-fashioned industries. The sectors concerned in this new force are identified in the chart below. They already account for over £50 billion of economic activity per year, and more than 1 million jobs, and it is widely thought that this 'is where the growth is'. To take just one example, more Britons already work in computer services than ever worked down coal mines.

The creative industries 1998

Sector	Turnover in £ million
Advertising	4,300
Architecture	1,500
Art and antiques sales	2,500
Computer games	890
Crafts	400
Design	13,200
Designer fashion	600
Film	2,000
Music	3,400
Performing arts	830
Publishing	17,500
Software	7,800
Television and radio	5,700

Source: Department of Culture, Media and Sport

14 (a) The creative industries are comprised of many goods and services. State ten examples and categorize them as: public good, merit good or private good.
   (b) List economic arguments for two of the private goods to benefit from government funds.

15 Intellectual property is particularly hard to police. Consequently, much of the British talent will be lost to free-riding pirates. List some of the implications of this statement.

16 According to *The Economist* in December 1998, the support of sympathetic governments will enable the creative industries to make a vital and growing contribution to the prosperity of the twenty-first century. What kind of support do you think they had in mind?

17 Can rock groups and digital interactive shopping channels really replace steel mills and textile factories as the foundation of a nation's wealth?

In Britain it is claimed that we have developed a 'caring society' that looks after each of us from 'the cradle to the coffin'. Some people may well feel that the government has become less caring than it used to be, since general government expenditure has fallen as a proportion of total spending. Nevertheless, more than half of government spending still funds various merit goods, the regulation of demerit goods and the provision of a legal system. (In 1997, general government expenditure totalled £331 billion.)

Redistribution of income

The price (market) system will allocate nothing to those who cannot pay. Left to market forces, owners of factors of production who are paid for their services will have significantly better life chances than their retired, unemployed, disabled or underprivileged counterparts. Consequently, all post-war governments – although with differing levels of commitment – are concerned with the redistribution of income.

In general, the required redistribution uses three systems: the *system of taxation*, especially progressive income tax, which involves taxing high-income earners progressively more than the lower paid (see the closing section of this chapter for more details); the *provision of merit goods* as discussed above, which makes essential services freely available to all; and **transfer payments**.

Transfer payments are those payments made to individuals for which no services are concurrently rendered. The main transfer payments in our system are social security, old-age pensions and various grants. With these cash benefits, recipients are able to buy goods and services of their choice within the market – hence there is a redistribution of funds from the public sector to the private sector.

Some of these income-redistribution schemes are specifically means-tested to ensure that only the poor benefit. Others, however, are available to all as a basic human right, regardless of financial position. In most cases the former selective payments take the form of cash benefits, whilst the latter universal provisions (often provided as merit goods) are known as 'benefits in kind'.

Analysis of disposable income

Official measures of income distribution are presented annually in the government publication *Social Trends*. Several of the related tables are presented according to quintile distribution. Quintile groups involve dividing the population into five groups (as in five simultaneous births – quins). This type of grouping is reflected on the horizontal axis of the Lorenz curve.

From the perspective of income distribution, the starting point of the official analysis is original income, which represents cash income of households before any kind of benefits or taxes are paid. The next stage sees cash benefits being added to original income to arrive at gross income. The third stage, the focus of this exercise, is disposable income. This means that income taxes, national insurance contributions and council taxes have been deducted. In other words, disposable income represents the funds that one is left to spend after the official central and local government deductions.

Percentage shares of disposable household income (United Kingdom)

Year	Quintile groups of households				
	Bottom fifth	Next fifth	Middle fifth	Next fifth	Top fifth
1977	10	14	18	23	36
1997	8	12	16	23	42

Note: Due to rounding the figures may not add exactly to 100.

Source: *Social Trends*, HMSO, 1980 and 1999

18 Briefly describe changes in the distribution of disposable income that occurred between 1977 and 1997.

19 Discuss two policies that are available to a government wishing to reduce inequalities in disposable income.

20 Which government activities affect the standard of living but are not shown in disposable-income figures?

Clearly, the government within a mixed economy has a considerable role to play. Its importance arises as a result of the acknowledgement that the market economy, left to its own devices, fails in several respects. The results of vast numbers of market exchanges, which are freely made in isolation from one another, often end up being nonsensical for society as a whole. Hence the government intervenes.

An important point, however, is that government intervention does not simply remedy market failure – it is more complicated than that. Consider just one instance: without social security benefits the unemployed would starve and be homeless; yet a society with a good benefit system is often accused of destroying the incentive to find work, as well as creating an administratively costly system.

KEY POINTS

7.4

■ All governments want to be considered 'fair'. Consequently, they concern themselves with questions relating to income distribution, the provision of certain goods and services, and the requirements of a legal system.

■ The goods and services that are decided upon as 'good' for society are known as merit goods; those that are deemed 'bad' are known as demerit goods.

■ The provision of merit goods contributes to a nation's standard of living, as they accommodate positive externalities. In the United Kingdom a substantial part of government spending involves the provision of these goods.

■ When it is collectively decided that something is a demerit good, the government regulates or prohibits the use of that good.

■ The government provides a legal system in which the rights of ownership and contract are set out; this is an important prerequisite for economic progress.

■ Income redistribution is achieved through three systems: taxation, transfer payments (cash benefits) and merit goods (benefits in kind).

Public choice theory

The public sector clearly has a vast influence on a mixed economy. In the UK, for instance, it employs about 20 per cent of the workforce. Yet the model used in traditional economics only applies to the behaviour of the private sector – firms and households. We shall attempt to bridge this gap by looking at a modern paradigm: the **theory of public choice**. It has been given this name because it involves hypotheses about how choices are made in the public sector, as opposed to the private sector.

The starting point within this theory is that governments consist of individuals. No government actually thinks and acts; rather, government actions are the result of decision-making by individuals in their roles as elected representatives, appointed officials and salaried bureaucrats. Therefore, to understand how government works, we must examine the incentives for the people in government, as well as those who would like to be in government, and special-interest lobbyists attempting to get government to do something. At issue is the analysis of **collective decision-making**. Collective decision-making involves the actions of voters, political parties,

special-interest groups, and many other groups and individuals.

At the basis of public choice theory is the assumption that individuals will act within the political process to maximize their *individual* (not collective) well-being. In that sense the theory is similar to our analysis of the market economy, in which we also assume that individuals are motivated by self-interest.

To understand public choice theory, it is necessary to point out other similarities between the private sector and the public, or government, sector; then we shall look at the differences.

Similarities in market and public sector theory

In addition to the similar assumption of self-interest being the motivating force in both sectors, there are other similarities.

Scarcity At any given moment, the amount of resources is fixed. This means that, for the private and public sectors combined, there is a scarcity constraint. Everything that is spent by all levels of government, plus everything that is spent by the private sector, must add up to the total income available at any point in time. Hence every government action has an opportunity cost, just as in the market sector.

Competition Although we typically think of competition as a private market phenomenon, it is also present in collective action. Given the scarcity constraint, bureaucrats, appointed officials and elected representatives will always be in competition for available government funds. Furthermore, the individuals within any government agency or institution will act as individuals do in the private sector: they will try to obtain higher wages, better working conditions and higher job-level classifications. They will compete and act in their own, not society's, interest.

Differences between market and public sector theory

There are more dissimilarities between the market sector and the public sector than there are similarities.

Government goods at zero price The majority of goods that governments produce are furnished to the ultimate consumers without direct money charge. **Government**, or **political**, **goods** can be either private goods or public goods, as defined in this chapter. In any event, the fact that they are furnished to the ultimate consumer free of charge does *not* mean that the cost to society of those goods is zero. It only means that the price *charged* is zero. The full opportunity cost to society is the value of the resources used in the production of goods produced and provided by the government.

For example, none of us pays directly for each unit of consumption of defence or police protection. Rather, we pay for all these things indirectly through the taxes that support our government. There is no longer a one-to-one relationship between the consumption of a government good, or politically provided good, and the payment for that good. Consumers who pay taxes collectively pay for every government or politically provided good, but the individual consumer may not be able to see the relationship between the taxes that he or she pays and the consumption of a government-provided good. Indeed, most taxpayers will find that their tax bill is the same whether or not they consume, or even like, government-provided goods.

Use of force All governments are able to engage in the legal use of force in their regulation of economic affairs. For example, governments can exercise the use of *expropriation*, which means that if you refuse to pay your taxes the Inland Revenue may seize your assets. In fact, you have no choice in the matter of paying taxes to governments. Collectively, we decide the total size of government through the political process, but individually we cannot determine how much service we purchase just for ourselves during any one year.

Incentive structure Individuals working in government often face a different system of rewards and punishments than those in the private sector. For example, the costs and benefits of being efficient or inefficient differ when one goes from the private to public sector. They face different institutional arrangements and experience different incentives.

Voting versus spending In the private market sector, a money voting system is in effect. This money voting system is not equivalent to the voting system in the public sector. The main distinction between political votes and money votes is that political outcomes may differ from economic outcomes. Remember that economic efficiency is a situation in which, given the prevailing distribution of income, consumers get the economic goods they want. There is no corresponding situation using political voting. We can never assume that a political voting process will lead to the same decisions that a money voting process will lead to in the market-place. This is because a voter is not usually asked to decide on a single issue (although this happens); rather, a voter is asked to choose among candidates who represent a large number of issues. Indeed, when you vote for a Member of Parliament you are voting for a person who must make thousands of decisions during his or her time in the House of Commons.

A closing note on government failure

Public choice theory emphasizes the vulnerability of those in government. The electorate expects them continually to make correct decisions on difficult questions – yet politicians are only human and may fail occasionally. Indeed, knowing what is genuinely in the 'public's interest' is recognizably a difficult concept. To get a consensus of opinion on a topical economic issue amongst your classmates would be difficult. Similarly, Members of Parliament, with their developed political values, established support groups and, often, constraints of time and information, will understandably find it hard always to reach the right majority decision.

Consequently, we arrive at an ironic juncture. So far throughout this chapter we have justified a role for government intervention on the basis of market failure, and we now close the section by suggesting the possibility of **government failure**. It would be a foolhardy cynic, however, who resolved this problem by claiming a situation of total failure.

KEY POINTS

7.5

■ The theory of public choice analyses how collective decision-making is carried out in the public sector.

■ The market sector and the public sector have the following similarities: (1) both sectors face scarcity and (2) both feature competition.

■ The difference between market and collective decision-making involves the following: (1) many government goods are provided at zero price (there is no user charge system); (2) collective action may involve the use of force; (3) the incentives are different and (4) political voting is not the same thing as money voting.

Taxation

Related to the government provision of goods and services is **taxation** – since taxation may be defined as

the main source of income from which governments finance their spending

Theoretically, therefore, cutbacks in public expenditure in the United Kingdom could ultimately lead to cutbacks in taxation. From the market-mechanism point of view, such reductions would be good, as taxes also distort market forces. This is because taxes are imposed on land, labour, capital and interest (that is, all factor payments) as well as most goods and services (that is, product payments).

Categories of taxation

In the United Kingdom it is traditional to envisage two forms of taxation: direct and indirect. **Direct taxation** is largely the tax of one's income, that is, the tax one is billed for directly and liable to pay as a named individual. **Indirect taxation** by contrast is largely tax on spending, that is, the tax that one may not be aware of, since it is the seller of the good or service who is liable and therefore it has an indirect nature.

Examples of direct taxes

All forms of income on which tax is liable fall into this category. The most obvious and most significant example is income tax. This is usually paid, via the employer, through a scheme known as PAYE – which is short for Pay As You Earn. There are, however, various other forms of income and consequently various other examples, the main ones being:

1 **corporation tax**, which is paid by firms on their profits;
2 **capital gains tax**, which is paid by individuals who profit by selling a capital asset at a higher price than they originally paid;
3 **inheritance tax**, which was formerly called 'death duties' and should therefore be self-explanatory;
4 **petroleum revenue tax**, which is paid by firms operating in the North Sea as an extra burden for them – a kind of payment for the benefits they gain from extracting UK natural assets.

Examples of indirect tax

Most taxes on spending are indirect since it is the seller of the good who is ultimately liable for the tax bill. The most obvious, and most significant, example is **value-added tax (VAT)**, which is at present charged on most goods and services sold in the United Kingdom at a rate of 17.5 per cent (although some essential goods and services are zero-rated).

Other examples of indirect tax include the various duties obtained from specific products, for example:

● **oil duties**, which are paid on petrol, diesel and other hydrocarbon oils;
● **tobacco tax**, which is paid on cigarettes, cigars and pipe tobacco;
● **excise duties on alcohol**, which is paid on wines, spirits and beers.

Each of these specific taxes is charged per unit (for example, per pint, per gallon, per packet of twenty, per litre, or whatever) and it is not entirely clear who carries the tax burden. The seller of the products will usually strive to pass on the tax incidence to the purchaser by raising the price accordingly.

Other types of tax

It may be worth recognizing that other forms of taxation also exist, which are not always collected by the central government. For example, council taxes are the responsibility of the local authorities to assess and collect. Similarly, water rates, airport taxes, and motor-vehicle and TV licences are not the direct responsibility of central government but are administered by appointed public authorities acting on their behalf as revenue collectors. Finally, National Insurance contributions (NIC) paid by employers and employees should also be recognized as a tax, especially as both payments affect the demand and

supply of labour. Between 1980 and 1998, the total tax burden remained reasonably similar, as although reductions in basic income tax were achieved these were offset by increases elsewhere in the general taxation system.

Types of taxation system

All of the taxes mentioned above can fit into one of three types of taxation system: proportional, progressive or regressive.

Proportional taxation

A system of **proportional taxation** means that, as an individual's income goes up, so does the tax in exactly the *same proportion*. Taxpayers at all income levels end up paying the same percentage of their income in taxes. In other words, if the proportional tax rate were 20 per cent, an individual with an income of £10 000 would pay £2000 in taxes while an individual making £100 000 would pay £20 000, the identical 20 per cent rate being levied on both.

Progressive taxation

Under **progressive taxation**, as a person's income increases, the percentage of income paid in taxes increases; or, to express it formally, the *marginal tax rate* is greater than the *average tax rate*. To understand this we need to examine these terms. The **marginal tax rate** is expressed as

$$\text{marginal tax rate} = \frac{\text{change in taxes due}}{\text{change in taxable income}}$$

It is important to understand that the marginal tax rate applies only to the income in the highest **tax bracket** reached, where a tax bracket is defined as

a specified level of taxable income to which a specific and unique marginal tax rate is applied

The word marginal, therefore, merely refers to the last increment. It is referred to in the tinted panel 'UK rates of income tax 1979 and 2000' as the rate of tax that relates to a band of taxable income.

We should compare the marginal tax rate with the **average tax rate**, which is defined as

$$\text{average tax rate} = \frac{\text{total tax due}}{\text{total taxable income}}$$

The difference between the marginal and the average tax rate can be seen in Table 7.3. In this example of a progressive tax system, the first £100 in income is taxed at 10 per cent, the next £100 at 20 per cent and the third £100 at 30 per cent.

UK rates of income tax 1979 and 2000

Rates of income tax in two different financial years in the United Kingdom

	1979–1980			1999–2000	
	Band of taxable income	Rate (%)		Band of taxable income	Rate (%)
Lower	1–750	25		1–1500	10
Basic	751–10 000	30		1501–28 000	23
Higher	10 001–12 000	40		Over 28 000	40
	12 001–15 000	45			
	15 001–20 000	50			
	20 001–25 000	55			
	Over 25 000	60			

21 Using economic terms, describe the main changes in income tax between 1979 and 1999.

22 In 1999–2000 every taxpayer had a tax-free allowance of £4335. For a person with a gross income of £30 000, what was
  (a) the average rate of tax?
  (b) the marginal rate of tax?

23 Compare the tax structure existing in 1979–80 with that in 1999–2000 in terms of
  (a) the distribution of income.
  (b) obtaining the highest level of tax revenue.
  (c) efficiency.

Table 7.3

Progressive tax system
The percentage of tax taken out of each additional pound earned goes up, that is, the marginal tax rate increases progressively with income. Therefore, the average tax rate is less than the marginal tax rate in a progressive tax system, whereas in a proportional tax system the marginal tax rate is constant and always the same as the average tax rate.

Income	Marginal rate	Tax	Average rate
£100	10%	£10	$\frac{£10}{£100} = 10\%$
£200	20%	£10 + £20 = £30	$\frac{£30}{£200} = 15\%$
£300	30%	£10 + £20 + £30 = £60	$\frac{£60}{£300} = 20\%$

Regressive taxation

With **regressive taxation**, a smaller percentage of income is taken in taxes as income increases. The marginal rate is *below* the average rate. The following is an example of regressive taxation. Assume that the more income a family earns, the lower the percentage of its income that is spent on food purchases. Now assume further that the government obtains *all* of its revenues from a 20 per cent sales tax on food purchases. Since food purchases constitute a larger proportion of total expenditure for poor people than

for rich people, the percentage of total income that would be paid in food taxes under such a system would fall as income rose. It would be a regressive system.

The relative importance of these various taxes and how they will affect the incentives to work and the economy generally will be dealt with in Chapter 29.

KEY POINTS

7.6

- Taxes are mainly levied by central government and enable it to finance a large part of its spending.

- The two main forms of tax are direct and indirect. The former are taxes on income (of which there are many forms) and the latter are taxes on spending.

- We can identify other forms of tax which are not necessarily administered or collected by the central government, for example council taxes.

- We can classify tax systems into proportional, progressive and regressive depending on whether the marginal tax rate is the same as, greater than or less than the average tax rate as income rises.

- Marginal tax rates are those applied to marginal tax brackets, defined as the spread of income over which the tax rate is constant.

Public sector spending

The table below reflects many of the themes that we have discussed in this chapter. The concluding questions will highlight that an analysis of public spending provides a reasonable insight into a government's general philosophy of its role within the economy: its priorities and policies.

The figures shown are based on the Comprehensive Spending Review carried out between May 1997 and July 1998. This introduced a new approach to public expenditure, as departmental plans for three years replaced the annual rounds of bids for funds. It was hoped that this would provide a more stable foundation for managing public services.

The final line, **total managed expenditure**, represents the overall public sector spending from both capital and current allocations. It is the grand total that was previously called general government expenditure; and it still represents around 40 per cent of the total domestic expenditure. This figure, however, cannot be cast in stone, as there must be a correlation between the level of economic activity and public expenditure. For example, as unemployment increases the proportion paid out in social security accelerates as more people sign on for benefits. The government can set the level of expenditure for administering social security and even the criteria for different benefits, but the actual cash outlay will depend upon the number of eligible claimants. In economic terms, a significant amount of the social security payments are categorized as demand determined.

Consequently, public spending plans such as those displayed in the table will always contain elements that will vary from year to year. Total managed expenditure, therefore, is broken down into two components: those that can be firmly set for each department and those that will vary each year due to changes in the economic cycle. Accordingly, these components are referred to as **departmental expenditure limits** and **annually managed expenditure**. The latter is scrutinized as part of each year's budget process, whilst specific department expenditure limits are only subject to review if inflation differs from the forecast trend.

The size of the amounts involved highlights the significance of the role that government still plays within the economy. The range of goods and services is still quite significant and the government boasts that it presently spends around £6000 for every man, woman and child in the UK.

1 (a) Define public spending and give some examples of how it benefits you.

(b) Define private sector spending and give some examples.

(c) Which public services seem set to change in emphasis during the years 1998–2002, and what does this suggest about the government's policy?

2 Define merit goods and give examples of their importance from the public spending figures.

(a) Define annually managed expenditure.

(b) Could any of the four elements used to exemplify annually managed expenditure be classified as public goods?

Examples of public expenditure allocation 1998–2002				£ million
	1998–99	1999–2000	2000–1	2001–2
Departmental expenditure limits	**169,200**	**179,200**	**190,000**	**200,000**
of which:				
Department of Health	37,200	40,200	43,100	46,000
DETR: local government and regional policy	32,800	34,300	35,500	37,000
DETR: environment and transport	9,500	9,700	10,600	12,000
Ministry of Defence	22,200	22,300	22,800	23,000
Department for Education and Employment	14,200	15,500	17,300	18,600
Home Office and Legal Departments	9,500	10,500	10,600	10,700
Culture, Media and Sport	900	1,000	1,000	1,000
Annually managed expenditure	**163,800**	**174,500**	**183,000**	**192,800**
of which:				
Social security benefits	94,000	98,900	100,600	105,900
Central government gross debt interest	29,500	28,300	28,400	28,000
Locally financed expenditure	15,800	16,900	18,100	19,400
Accounting and other adjustments	7,800	9,900	13,900	15,100
Total managed expenditure	**333,000**	**353,700**	**373,000**	**393,000**

Source: HM Treasury

(c) Estimate the percentage of general government expenditure that may be influenced by the economic cycle.

3 Assuming that inflation does not exceed 2.5 per cent per annum and that there are no serious fluctuations of the economic cycle, is public sector spending expected to increase, decrease or stay the same?

4 Describe the main ways that revenue is raised to pay for public expenditure. Try to give up-to-date examples.

5 Discuss whether the concept of equity or the concept of efficiency seems to dominate the government plans revealed in the table.

Exam Preparation

Multiple choice questions

1 Which of the following statements concerning externalities is true?
   A If a positive externality exists for good A, A will be overproduced by a price system.
   B If externalities exist, then resources will be allocated efficiently.
   C Efficiency may be improved if the government taxes goods for which a positive externality exists.
   D The output of goods for which a positive externality exists is too low, from society's point of view.

2 Public goods, such as street-lighting, are not supplied through the ordinary market mechanism because
   A the initial capital cost would be prohibitive
   B some households would not be able to afford to make their full contribution towards the cost
   C the benefits would not be confined to the buyers but would automatically be available to non-buyers
   D the provision of public goods is essential and therefore cannot be left to private initiative
   E monopolies would earn excess profits

3 Which of the following characterizes collective, but not market, decision-making?
   A the legal use of force
   B a positive price is charged to users
   C the intensity of wants is easily revealed
   D a proportional rule

4 The income derived from visitors to a historic property is insufficient to meet the cost of upkeep. Which one of the following justifies contributions by the state towards the maintenance of the property?

   A there is no market in historic properties
   B the supply of historic properties is completely inelastic
   C historic properties do not fall into the category of 'public good'
   D the social benefits from maintaining historic properties exceed the cost of upkeep
   E the social costs of maintaining historic properties exceed the private costs

5 Market failure exists if
   A Mr Smith cannot purchase watermelons in his town
   B buyers and sellers must pay the true opportunity costs of their actions
   C third parties are injured and are not compensated
   D the government must provide merit goods

6 Which of the following forms of taxation is most regressive?
   A a progressive income tax
   B a proportional income tax
   C motor-vehicle tax
   D tobacco tax

7 Which of the following taxes is most likely to affect the supply of labour?
   A income tax
   B a tax on corporate profits
   C death duties
   D an increase in employers' National Insurance contributions

8 The term 'marginal rate of tax' is applied to
   A the proportion of income which is paid in tax
   B the amount of tax payable after allowances have been deducted
   C the rate of tax paid on unearned income
   D tax paid out of an increment to income
   E the rate of tax which gives the highest yield

Essay questions

1 (a) Distinguish between public goods and merit goods.
   (b) Discuss the economic arguments for and against public provision of education or police protection.

2 (a) Distinguish between a 'public good', a 'merit good' and a 'private good'.   (30 marks)
   (b) Using defence and education as examples, examine the economic arguments used to justify the provision of public goods and merit goods.   (70 marks)

3 Assess the economic arguments that the production of feature films in the United Kingdom should be subsidized by government.

4 'Left to itself the market mechanism is incapable of allocating scarce resources in an efficient manner.' Discuss.

5 'Progressive income tax promotes equality and penalizes initiative and enterprise.' Discuss.

6 Why do economies have a public sector? Discuss how and why the size and composition of the public sector in Britain have changed in recent years.

7 In what senses could the market system 'fail'? To what extent could your arguments be used to justify the production and distribution of goods and services by the public sector?

8 What have been the main trends in the composition of public expenditure over the last decade? Should the continuing growth of public expenditure be a source of concern?

Economic objectives and economic indicators

At the close of this chapter we shall discuss economic forecasting. However, before we can forecast the future, we need to be certain that we can interpret the present. This necessitates some understanding of economic statistics: their nature and construction. As discussed in the previous chapter, fluctuations in economic activity are characteristic of any economy. These fluctuations are monitored by changes in **economic indicators**, such as prices, employment, money supply, stocks, return on capital, savings, interest rates, balance of payments, output, exchange rates, etc. These indicators are measured and presented in many ways, and this can cause much confusion.

Since economic indicators are produced at regular intervals and form an important backdrop against which the economy is judged, it is important to establish the processes through which they are gathered. Yet many of the variables that are scrutinized are difficult to define and measure. In this chapter the arbitrary nature of the main statistics will become apparent, as we attempt to conceptualize the main economic goals.

LEARNING OUTCOMES

On completing this chapter you should understand:

- Economic objectives
- Unemployment
- How official measurements are defined
- Types of unemployment
- Inflation
- Types and causes of inflation
- Measuring inflation
- Price indices
- Economic forecasting

Economic objectives

All governments, regardless of political persuasion, seek to achieve common economic goals. These goals can technically be referred to as macroeconomic objectives, and it is generally recognized that five main ones dominate.

Stable prices

Stable prices are crucial for business confidence, facilitating existing contracts and enabling the exchange rate system to function smoothly, whereas persistently rising prices cause problems within most sectors of an economy.

If prices are continually rising entrepreneurs are hesitant to enter into contracts as they cannot work out the long-run results of their investments. This is often compounded further by the problems of changing exchange rates and interest rates that often accompany inflation. It is easiest to work within a stable economic environment. Indeed, economists often discuss **menu costs** as the associated effects of inflation on business. These costs consist of aspects such as vending machine alterations, the costs of printing revised price lists, the time spent renegotiating, and so on.

Similarly, inflation affects those who are not economically active. If price changes are not monitored, pensioners, students and those reliant on state benefits suffer, since their fixed incomes need to be revised to be kept in line with price increases. As a result, many aspects of economic activity are now index linked to allow for inflation. For example, savings, business contracts and pensions can all be adjusted in the light of inflation. All that is needed is a reliable price index.

Consequently, since 1947, governments have monitored price increases via the **retail price index** (RPI). For

Table 8.1

Macroeconomic indicators for the United Kingdom 1990–8
The data displayed are taken from various government sources, and as always in these instances the notes are important for proper comprehension. Two other points that need to be emphasized are that the figures are subject to revision and that they are calculated in different ways in other nations.

	1990	1991	1992	1993	1994	1995	1996	1997	1998
Inflation[a]	7.7	9.0	4.1	1.7	2.4	3.5	2.4	3.1	3.4
Unemployment[b]	1.66	2.29	2.78	2.91	2.62	2.31	2.10	1.6	1.3
Economic growth[c]	0.6	-2.3	-0.5	2.0	3.9	2.6	2.3	1.6	2.5
Balance of payments[d]	-15.5	-7.7	-10	-11	-1.5	-3.7	-0.6	6.1	0.1

[a] Retail prices (percentage increase on previous year).
[b] Total unemployment (annual average, in millions).
[c] Annual percentage increase in 'real' GDP.
[d] Current account (total for whole year, £billion).

example, the statistics for the period 1990–8 are presented in Table 8.1. Further discussion of the definition of inflation and the various ways in which it can be measured occurs in the latter half of this chapter.

Full employment

To have a large amount of unemployed labour represents wasted resources. Unemployment clearly has many costs in terms of human suffering, loss of dignity and loss of output. Consequently, all governments are concerned with recording the number of workers without a job. The precise way this is executed changes from time to time. At present 'official' unemployment in the United Kingdom is calculated according to the number registering for unemployment benefit. These claimants are then expressed either as a percentage of the total workforce of 28 million or as an absolute number. In Table 8.1 it is easy to see that percentage unemployment was over 10 per cent in 1993. Further discussion relating to the definition and measurement of this phenomenon follows in the next main section of this chapter.

Sustained economic growth

A long-term objective of all governments is to achieve steady increases in productive capacity. Consequently, economic growth is measured by the *rate of change* of output. In the United Kingdom a commonly used measure of economic output is GDP: **gross** (total) **domestic** (home) **product** (output). To portray accurately the rate of change of actual output, we must correct GDP for changes in prices. When this is done, we get what is called real GDP. Hence, a more formal measure of economic growth may be defined as the rate of change in real GDP over time. As the notes to Table 8.1 highlight, the growth data have been corrected accordingly. It is therefore a clear indicator of boom or recession. The earlier years in the chart clearly represent the recession experienced at the beginning of the 1990s with negative growth rates. A fuller coverage of GDP and how it is calculated is given in Chapter 13, while

the meaning of the concept of economic growth is not fully covered until the final chapter.

External balance

All international transactions are recorded in a country's balance of payments statistics; the official table of figures has already been discussed and presented in Chapter 6. The ideal situation represents a position where over a number of years one nation spends and invests abroad no more than other nations spend or invest in it.

Obviously, economic transactions with other nations can occur on many levels, and for accounting purposes these transactions are often grouped into three categories, namely current account, capital account and official financing. Of these three, the most widely quoted is the current account transactions. This involves all transactions relating to the exchange of visible goods (such as manufactured items), the exchange of invisibles (such as services) and investment earnings (such as profits from abroad). Clearly, therefore, in any one year, one nation's balance of payments deficit is another nation's balance of payments surplus – ultimately, however, in the long run debts must be paid. The data in Table 8.1 show a worrying trend, but the figures need to be considered in a broader historical context. It also needs to be recognized that these specific figures are notoriously difficult to record accurately. (In fact, all the statistics shown in Table 8.1 are subject to subsequent amendments – but the balance of payments amendments are by far the biggest.)

Maintenance of the environment

During the last thirty years policy-makers have become increasingly concerned about the environment. As explained in the previous chapter, this is because markets on their own do not deal effectively with the third-party (spill-over) effects of many economic activities, and therefore governments frequently intervene to influence resource allocation. In fact, environmental issues are at the heart of many new political developments and tax regimes that are presently occurring throughout the world.

To date, there is no agreed way of monitoring the performance of this objective and hence there is no environmental indicator in Table 8.1. We discuss the problems of integrating environmental issues with the broader economy in Chapter 10, and consider some ideas for monitoring performance in Chapter 13.

Priorities: a historical perspective

The order of priority that these objectives are given depends on the government in office. But all governments, in all nations, ultimately desire these same objectives in their quest for economic stability.

This notion – that the government should undertake actions to manage the economy – is, in historical terms, a relatively new idea. In Winston Churchill's budget speech of 1929, he said: 'It is the orthodox Treasury dogma that, whatever the social and political advantages, … no permanent additional employment can … be created by state borrowing and public expenditure'. Since then, however, economic advisers have been appointed by the government to measure and analyse economic trends and to suggest policy for their manipulation.

The turning point for governments being responsible for economic objectives occurred after the Second World War. For example, the White Paper on Employment published in May 1944 stated that the government accepted 'as one of their primary aims and responsibilities the maintenance of a high and stable level of employment after the war'.

Since this statement of intent in 1944, employment policy has been an important criterion for all governments. During the 1980s, it dropped from the number one spot to allow a more concentrated effort on curbing inflation. For example, the Chancellor of the Exchequer in 1998 stated that: 'Price stability is a precondition for … high and stable levels of growth and employment'. During the twenty-first century, however, we may even see inflation and employment take second and third place to allow maintenance of the environment to become the prioritized objective.

KEY POINTS

8.1

- Various economic indicators can be analysed. But first of all their meaning and process of measurement must be understood.

- To achieve economic stability, five macroeconomic objectives are pursued, as follows: (1) full employment, (2) stable prices, (3) equilibrium on the balance of payments, (4) steady growth and (5) maintenance of the environment.

- The macroeconomic objectives change in their order of priority according to the government in office.

The concepts being introduced in this chapter are important to anyone who wants to be sufficiently literate in economics to understand the business and political news content of journalism. There follows a typical extract from a daily newspaper, and it should begin to make some sense …

Making sense of press commentary on the economy

When the Labour government took office in May 1997, there was an overwhelming consensus that it had inherited a 'strong economy'. GDP growth was accelerating, unemployment was declining sharply, and underlying price inflation was stable at a low level. There were no signs of significant deterioration in the balance of payments, and the government finances were improving rapidly each month.

The outgoing Conservatives attributed all this to the success of their structural economic reforms in the previous 18 years (1979–1997), and even on the Labour side there was an admission that the short-term cyclical position of the economy was satisfactory. In fact, this was the reverse of the truth. Actually, Labour inherited an economy that was poised to experience a sharp deterioration.

Source: Adapted from *The Independent*, 20 July 1998

1 (a) State the approximate percentage of GDP growth in 1997.
  (b) State the approximate percentage of unemployment in 1997.
  (c) State the approximate percentage of inflation in 1997.
2 Are the rates of inflation and unemployment higher or lower during the present year? State some up-to-date figures to show the extent of change since 1997.
3 State the direction of movement of any three economic indicators during a 'strong economy'.
4 State the direction of movement of any three economic indicators during a 'sharp deterioration'.
5 In your opinion, which of the statistics referred to will contain the biggest margin of error?
6 What is the number one economic objective of the government at present? Explain your answer.

To fully appreciate the meaning of these terms we need to study the definitions and understand the methods of measurement. Indeed, slight changes in any one definition – changes which might be quite reasonable – can actually change the magnitude of other variables, for example recession, productivity, exchange rates, business confidence and growth. Of the various economic indicators, changes in unemployment and inflation are important, since they have broad effects on many of the other variables. We shall therefore take a detailed look at these two economic indicators; the others are dealt with elsewhere in the text as suggested in the section on economic objectives.

Unemployment

One of the major consequences of fluctuating business activity is the ensuing unemployment, particularly of workers, but also of other factors of production (non-human resources). Unemployment has many costs – in human suffering, in loss of dignity, in loss of output and savings – the list goes on and on. That is why policy-makers in our economy closely watch the official unemployment figures published by the government each month. Unemployment is considered to be a social evil that must be kept at an 'acceptable' level. We can see from Figure 8.1 that the rate of unemployment in the United Kingdom averaged around 2 per cent of the working population for most of the 1960s, and was never above 3 per cent until the mid-1970s. Since then, however, the general trend has been upwards. Admittedly, booms and slumps have masked this trend, but it continues to be an economic and social problem of some concern. Remember that even the 4.7 per cent unemployment rate plotted for 1998 represents approximately 1.5 million people (which is twice as many as were unemployed during the 1960s and 1970s).

The rate of unemployment is measured by dividing the total number of persons defined as unemployed by the total number of persons defined as being within the workforce. Determining who is truly unemployed and who is effectively in the labour force is no easy task.

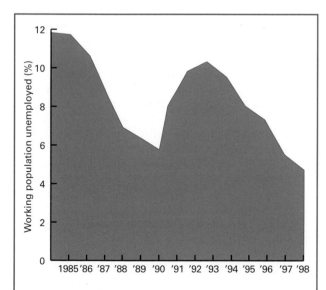

Figure 8.1

The UK unemployment record since 1960

Note: The figures plotted are annual averages.

Source: *Department of Employment Gazette* (*Labour Market Trends* from January 1996)

How official measurements are defined

The **workforce** (working population) is at present defined by the Department for Education and Employment as

> persons over 16 who work for pay or gain or register themselves as 'available' for such work and meanwhile claim benefit

In less formal terms, therefore, the workforce includes the following five groups:

1 employees in employment;
2 employers and the self-employed;
3 those registered as unemployed and claiming benefit;
4 members of Her Majesty's Forces;
5 those involved in government training schemes.

Obviously this is not the same as all those of working age – which would include those involved in full-time education, those in early retirement, housewives, and those who are seeking work but have not registered for unemployment benefit. In numerical terms for 1998, the following figures collated from *Labour Market Trends* may help clarify matters a little further:

Total population aged 16 and over	46 056 000
minus those not involved in workforce	17 343 000
equals total economically active	28 713 000
minus unemployed (ILO definition)	1 766 000
equals workforce in employment	26 947 000

Registered unemployment

There are two official measures of unemployment regularly published in the UK. The most frequently referred to is **claimant unemployment**, which is based on a monthly total of those claiming benefit. This is very easy to collect since it is based on a computer count of all those officially registered as willing and able to work but presently claiming job seekers' allowance. This official measure is recognizably suspect: it excludes all those who are not eligible for benefits; it *officially excludes* all men aged over 60, who since April 1983 no longer have to sign on to claim benefit; and it also excludes those who register as desiring work at commercial agencies but not with the official offices because, owing to marriage or similar circumstances, they are not eligible for benefit. It includes some fraudulent claimers of benefit such as those who work as well as 'sign on'.

The alternative is the standardized unemployment measure, which is based on a quarterly survey of 61 000 households (i.e., approximately 120 000 people aged 16+). The survey defines unemployment as: those without jobs who say they have actively sought work in the last four weeks or are waiting to take up appointment within the next fortnight. Although this is not so easy to calculate and is subject to some sampling error, it has the advantage of being used internationally. In other words, most countries back up their registrant count with a survey-based measure of unemployment. This enables international comparisons, since they all use the same definition and similar sample size.

An agency of the United Nations, the International Labour Organization (ILO), has administered this standardized measure since 1984 and it is displayed in various government publications. This measure is referred to as the **ILO unemployment rate** and it usually indicates a larger number of unemployed.

Consequently, many claim that the 'true' level of unemployment is higher than the official claimant figure. In textbook terms the official unemployment statistics contain a certain amount of **hidden unemployment** incorporating the many categories who are falsely excluded, plus those on the other side who are wrongly included, for example those who claim job seekers' allowance but have no real desire to work.

Measuring unemployment sensitively

Apart from the problem of hidden unemployment, which by its very nature makes reliable statistics of those truly wanting work most difficult to ascertain, there is also the problematic question of who is actually unemployed. The pool of unemployed labour is not a stagnant lake of humans crying for work. The monthly unemployment statistics are a snapshot of those registered claimants who are unemployed when the count occurs (on the second Thursday of each month). This group will obviously change its character, as there are constantly large numbers of people joining and leaving the official books each month. Those joining the pool are referred to as the **inflow** and those leaving it are referred to as the **outflow**. If the inflow and outflow are equal, the unemployment rate stays the same. If the number leaving jobs and flowing into the reservoir of the unemployed exceeds new appointments, the unemployment rate rises.

The important point is that the unemployed are a **stock** of individuals who do not have a job but are actively looking for one. The number of people departing jobs, whether voluntarily or involuntarily, is a **flow**, as is the number of people finding jobs. Picturing a funnel, as illustrated in Figure 8.2, is a good way of remembering and understanding how these stocks and flows work. The figures highlight that unemployment throughout 1997 was on a slow downward trend, as in most months the total outflow was greater than the inflow.

The corollary of this relates to how long people have to wait before leaving the unemployment pool. In formal terms, the duration of unemployment is now longer. For example, in 1955 when unemployment was down to 1.1 per cent of the working population, the average period of each case of unemployment was three and a half weeks. In 1998/9 the average period of unemployment was far longer – in fact, over 40 per cent had been unemployed for six months or more (see Table 8.2).

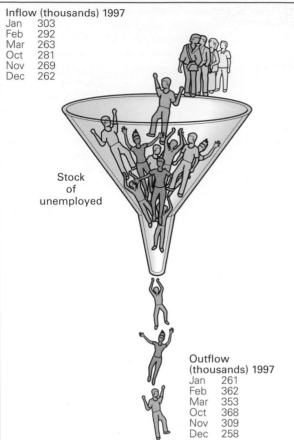

Inflow (thousands) 1997

Jan	303
Feb	292
Mar	263
Oct	281
Nov	269
Dec	262

Stock of unemployed

Outflow (thousands) 1997

Jan	261
Feb	362
Mar	353
Oct	368
Nov	309
Dec	258

Figure 8.2

Visualizing stocks and flows

Unemployment at any point in time is some number that represents a stock, such as the amount of water held in a funnel. People who lose their job constitute a new inflow. Those who find a job can be thought of as the water that flows out.

Source: *Labour Market Trends* (monthly flow figures)

However, the idea of *average* unemployment duration no longer makes much sense, as some groups in our economy are far more vulnerable than others. For example, the old (over 50) endure longer unemployment periods than their younger equivalents.

Similarly, one's gender, occupation, regional location, social class and even marital status affect one's chances of unemployment. Indeed, a white, male, London-based managerial-type owner-occupier, with two children, is statistically less likely to experience unemployment than a coloured youth who is unskilled and lives in Teesside. To a large extent this is due to the way that the labour market operates, which we shall explore in Chapters 12 and 24.

Table 8.2

UK unemployment by duration (thousands)

Duration of claims

	Up to 13 weeks	Over 13 and up to 26 weeks	Over 26 and up to 52 weeks	Over 52 and up to 104 weeks	Over 104 weeks	All
All						
1998 January	565.3	268.5	247.0	163.4	235.0	1479.3
April	499.6	264.1	255.4	160.2	210.6	1389.9
July	500.0	246.2	252.3	170.6	199.2	1368.3
October	479.7	224.5	229.8	168.3	184.1	1286.4
1999 January	558.4	252.7	231.0	171.6	172.8	1386.4

Source: *Labour Market Trends*, Table C.12

Lies, damned lies and statistics

Clearly, statistics are social products that are constructed with certain purposes in mind. For example, claimant-based unemployment statistics exclude all those who are *not* eligible for benefits. Consequently, whenever a government changes the eligibility conditions, the number of claimants also changes. Hence, the official UK claimant number of unemployed was reduced by about 100 000 in the autumn of 1988, when government rules excluded anyone under 18 from unemployment benefit.

In other words, changes in the number of claimants affect official unemployment figures, regardless of the number actually experiencing unemployment. This is particularly relevant to the UK readership, where the government has made thirty such changes to eligibility conditions in less than twenty years since 1979. All but one of these changes had the effect of reducing the official recorded unemployment figure.

Official measures therefore can be construed in such a way as to distort the truth. Consequently, Disraeli's remark about lies and statistics has been echoed several times since he made it two centuries ago, and it has recently been reworked to make the point even more bluntly – now we have 'Liars, damned liars and those who use statistics'. So beware!

7 (a) How is unemployment officially defined in the country in which you are studying?

(b) Identify any two of the changes that were made to the unemployment definition in the UK since 1979.

8 ILO unemployment rates are regularly published in *Labour Market Trends*. In the March 1999 issue, the following countries were showing rates around 4 per cent: the United States, Portugal, Japan, Denmark and Austria.
(a) What do ILO rates of unemployment mean?
(b) Which of the five countries would have had the largest number of unemployed?

9 Study the following table showing unemployment in the UK.

Year	Claimant unemployment rate	ILO unemployment rate
1995	8	8.6
1996	7.3	8.2
1997	5.5	7.1
1998	4.7	6.1

Source: *Labour Market Trends*

Account for the faster rate of decline in unemployment according to the claimant measure.

10 Why are unemployment figures important and, in your opinion, which are the most important set of figures?

Finally, in undertaking a sensitive interpretation of unemployment statistics, it is also necessary to recognize what adjustments have been made to the portrait presented. **Seasonally adjusted** is the most common, and this means that the figures incorporate an adjustment to allow for those seasonal quirks that regularly cause unemployment to be particularly high or low during certain months.

Similar adjustments are made for

1 school-leavers (that is, young persons seeking their first job);
2 adult students (who have registered for vacation work and/or benefit);
3 temporarily stopped (that is, those workers who have been laid off due to bad weather or someone else's strike, and are claiming benefit until they can return to work).

These three groups are excluded as it is felt that they do not form part of the long-term unemployed.

KEY POINTS

8.2

■ Unemployment rates in the United Kingdom during the post-war period have risen from a low of 1 to 2 per cent in the 1960s to levels above 10 per cent in the early 1990s.

■ The working population in official terms includes: (1) employees in employment, (2) employers and the self-employed, (3) HM Forces, (4) those on government training schemes and (5) unemployed persons claiming benefit. The first four of these groups make up the employed workforce.

■ There are two official measures of unemployment: claimant unemployment and ILO unemployment. The former relates to those in receipt of benefits. The latter is based on a survey.

■ When the outflow from the unemployment books decreases, the duration of unemployment increases, and vice versa.

■ The unemployment statistics contain certain problems, and some of these are catered for by the concept of hidden employment.

■ All unemployment statistics should be analysed carefully, noting if possible source, adjustments, age categories, etc.

Types of unemployment

Unemployment can be categorized into four basic types: frictional, cyclical, seasonal and structural.

Frictional unemployment

Of the 28 million people in the workforce, more than 4 million persons will have reported themselves unemployed at one time or another during each year. What we call **frictional unemployment** is this continuous flow of individuals from job to job, in and out of employment. It used to be called **transitional unemployment**, which, as the name suggests, involves people merely moving or changing from one job to another. The modern phrase places the emphasis on 'time taken' to change as a result of certain frictions in the labour market. Indeed, there will always be some frictional unemployment as resources need time to be redirected within the market. To eliminate frictional unemployment completely, we would have to prevent workers from leaving their present jobs until they had already lined up other jobs at which they would start working immediately, and we would have to guarantee first-time job seekers a job *before* they started looking. A complete elimination of frictional unemployment would probably reduce the rate of growth of our economy. One important source of advances in productivity is the movement of workers from sectors of the economy where labour productivity and wages are low to sectors where productivity and wages are high. The search for better job offers is the process by which workers discover areas where their productivity is highest, that is, where they can make the most income. Frictional unemployment can therefore be reduced by the provision of better information services, but it can never be eliminated altogether.

Cyclical unemployment

Cyclical unemployment is related to the business cycle. In fact, cyclical unemployment is defined as unemployment associated with changes in business conditions – primarily recessions and depressions. The way to lessen cyclical unemployment would be to reduce the intensity, duration and frequency of ups and downs of business activity. Economic policy-makers attempt, through their policies, to reduce cyclical unemployment by keeping business activity on an even keel, and these policies will be discussed in Part C and Part E of the book.

Seasonal unemployment

Seasonal unemployment is just that. It comes and goes with seasons of the year in which the demand for particular jobs rises and falls. For example, construction workers often can only work during the warmer months. They are seasonally unemployed during the winter. Resort workers usually can only get jobs in resorts during the summer season. They, too, become seasonally unemployed during the winter; the opposite is true for ski-resort workers. There is little we can do to reduce seasonal unemployment.

Structural unemployment

Presumably, there have been structural changes in our economy that have caused some workers to become permanently unemployed, or at least unemployed for very long periods of time, because they cannot find jobs that use their particular skills. Structurally unemployed persons are usually those who simply cannot find any job they can do. **Structural unemployment** has often been associated with **technological unemployment**, that is, unemployment resulting from the increased use of labour-saving machines.

Unlike cyclical unemployment, structural unemployment is not caused by the business cycle, although the business cycle may affect it. And unlike frictional unemployment, structural unemployment is not related to the movement of workers from low-paid to high-paid jobs. Rather, structural unemployment results when the consuming public no longer wants to buy an individual's services in that location. Instead of going through retraining, individuals persist in their search for employment with 'obsolete' skills in a market with limited demand. Some of these people eventually will go into new industries. In most urban settings this is precisely what happens. However, in some settings this does not happen. Often people refuse to move. They wait for times to improve. The result is a permanent depression in some geographic areas due to labour immobility. (Mobility of labour is dealt with in Chapter 12. Immobility of labour is dealt with in Chapter 26.)

In fact, in some instances structural unemployment is very closely related to **regional unemployment**, too. When an industry concentrated in one area declines as a result of changes in the pattern of demand, the whole area becomes full of workers with nothing to do. To illustrate this you simply need to look at a chart showing regional distributions, and you will notice that unemployment tends to be consistently above the national average in the northern and western areas, especially where the local economy had previously been based on one industry which has now undergone decline (for example, coal-mining or shipbuilding). To the other extreme, the south-east, south-west and East Midlands normally experience fewer unemployment problems than the national average suggests. We shall return to this regional theme in Chapter 27.

Unemployment: finding the right type

11 From the list below, classify each of the unemployed individuals as representing either frictional (F), structural (S) or cyclical (C) unemployment.

(a) James Smith is a car worker from Sunderland who has been laid off because of the recent sharp decline in GDP.

(b) Digs McDuff, from Derbyshire, finds he can no longer get work in the coal mines because of new automated mining techniques.

(c) Priscilla Primm is unable to locate work after finishing her high school education and entering the labour force.

(d) Leroy Cosign, an aerospace engineer, finds himself unemployed because of large cutbacks in defence spending. Since our space programme is also very limited, Leroy has not been able to locate alternative work for the past two months.

(e) Oscar Hammerhead, a skilled carpenter, has found himself out of work because of the housing slump brought on by high interest rates and the recession.

(f) Alice Weatherby quits her job as a salesperson out of frustration stemming from lack of promotion. She begins to look for a management position in a similar work setting.

(g) Patricia Matren returns to the labour force after having a child and is unable to locate suitable work.

(h) Flaps Peterson, an airline pilot, suddenly finds himself laid off because of the dramatic decline in the demand for air transportation caused by the recent recession.

From unemployment types to policy

By categorizing unemployment in the ways above, possible solutions to the various problems become easier to discern. It is clear that the most serious forms of unemployment are those due to declines in demand – namely, cyclical or structural unemployment. In the post-war period advances in economic theory and policy have helped to moderate these problems in many ways, which are discussed in forthcoming chapters.

Similarly, the recognition that frictional and seasonal unemployment exists alters the government's perception of what level of full employment to expect. For example, no government policy would ever aim at 100 per cent of the workforce being employed. This theme will be developed in the next section.

Defining full employment

As already stated, full employment does not mean that everybody is employed. It is obvious that in any dynamic economy some unemployment is unavoidable. The question is, what level of unemployment is unavoidable and at what level does employment become a problem?

According to Lord Beveridge's influential work *Full Employment in a Free Society* (published 1944), an unemployment rate of 3 per cent would be compatible with the aims of full employment. His figure allows 1 per cent for frictional unemployment, 1 per cent for seasonal unemployment and 1 per cent for overseas factors. His inclusion of overseas factors is interesting as many economists ignore the interdependence of one economy's trends with another.

Furthermore, Beveridge's target was effectively adhered to during the post-war period in the United Kingdom until 1971. However, other formulae of what constitutes full employment are also possible. For example, during the same period of time as we were adhering to Beveridge's criterion, the United States employed a different formula. For them post-war full employment represented 96 per cent employment. Their 4 per cent unemployment was to account for frictional unemployment and the various forms of structural unemployment. Yet they, too, have been way off target since 1970.

This raises the question: what does full employment in the twenty-first century represent? Clearly, the variables have changed. Technology has improved, more people have entered into the search for work, unemployment benefits have increased, part-time and flexible working have become more commonplace, and so on. Consequently, neither Britain nor the United States have come anywhere near their previous full-employment targets in the last decade. The 'correct' level needs to be redefined, but economists are hesitant to do so.

Nowadays economists place more emphasis on the concept of a **natural rate of unemployment**. This is a constantly moving rate which relates the preferable level of unemployment to that which is compatible with constant prices. It is based on the principle that every market, including the labour market, has an equilibrium rate. This concept will be discussed in more detail in Chapter 27. Meanwhile, inflation and related ideas need to be introduced.

KEY POINTS

8.3

■ There are many types of unemployment, including frictional, cyclical, seasonal, structural, technological and regional.

■ Frictional unemployment occurs because workers do not have all the information necessary about vacancies, and employers do not know about all of the workers qualified to fill those vacancies. Consequently, 'job search' time must be allowed for when people wish to change jobs.

■ Structural unemployment occurs when the demand for a commodity permanently decreases so that workers in an industry are permanently barred from the job they are used to doing.

■ The level of frictional, seasonal and/or structural unemployment can be used to arrive at an (arbitrary) definition of full employment.

■ The various types of unemployment need to be identified in order to consider policy options.

Inflation

The persistent increase in most prices in the United Kingdom has affected all of us, since inflation is an established post-war phenomenon. In fact, in a Bank of England review of inflation over a 300-year period from 1694 to 1994, it was stated that prices have risen more quickly in the last fifty years than in any period since 1694. Whereas the index of prices merely tripled between 1694 and 1947, it has risen twentyfold since (i.e., by more than 2000 per cent). This means that the 1p of forty years ago is equivalent to about £1 today. To take advantage of a bizarre calculation carried out by the Bank of England (in the same review), if the current size of the £50 note were increased to represent the purchasing power of £50 in 1694, it would need to measure 4 feet by 3 feet, necessitating cash machines the width of double doors and vans instead of wallets. This unusual geometric exercise puts into focus the associated decline of purchasing power as prices rise.

In the remainder of this chapter, we shall examine what inflation is and how it is measured. (How it affects the broader economy will be studied in Chapter 27.)

A definition of inflation

We define **inflation** as a sustained upward movement in the average level of prices. The opposite of inflation is **deflation**, defined as a persistent downward movement in the average level of prices. Notice that these definitions depend on the *average* level of prices, not one-offs. This means that even during a period of inflation, some prices can be falling if other prices are rising at a faster rate. The price of computers and computer-related equipment has dropped dramatically since the 1960s, even though there has been general inflation.

The Office for National Statistics makes monthly official measurements of inflation. They use a technique that involves buying the same 'basket' of goods and services each month, thereby enabling them to assess the purchasing power of money. In recent years, to physically buy the goods (which they do not do – they merely get 'price quotations') would have required more and more money, as inflation was a marked problem up until the mid-1990s. For a historical portrait of inflation rates over the last forty-five years see Table 8.3.

Table 8.3

Inflation rates in the United Kingdom 1953–98

Years	Average annual increase in prices (%)
1953–69	3.3
1970–5	12.0
1976–9	13.5
1980–5	9.7
1986–9	4.8
1990–5	4.7
1996–8	2.9

Do we now need to worry about deflation?

Just when you thought everything was getting better – the inflation rate has been relatively low for a decade – a sudden spate of articles is telling you to be worried. Why? Because there is the prospect of the opposite of inflation – *deflation*. The British government has recently been hearing reports that inflation is running below its target level of 2.5 per cent. But will it ever see negative figures?

The last time deflation occurred in the UK was during the great depression, when prices fell consistently from 1920 to 1935.

A current example of deflation can be found in Japan. Its price level fell every year from 1994 to 1999. Its economy was in a depressed state during that time period. The conclusion, of course, is that recessions and depressions can accompany deflation.

Remember that deflation is defined as a consistent decline in the average of all prices. In the United Kingdom prices, on average, have been rising continually since 1945, but at a decreasing rate. This is called disinflation, not deflation, so do we have a problem or not?!

12 Distinguish between inflation, disinflation and deflation.

13 Identify the main economic characteristics of a depression.

14 (a) What is the present rate of inflation?
　　(b) Does this rate represent an advantage or disadvantage to the economy?

15 How could you protect yourself against the effects of deflation?

Types and causes of inflation

As inflation was a significant problem through the 1960s, 1970s and 1980s, many different explanations for it developed. Here we shall generalize that inflation occurs either because an increase in total demand pulls up prices ('demand-pull' inflation) or because an increase in the cost of production pushes up the prices of final products ('cost-push' inflation).

Demand-pull inflation

When total demand in the economy is rising while the available output of goods is limited, **demand-pull inflation** occurs. Goods and services may be in 'short' supply either because the capacity of the economy is being fully utilized or because the economy cannot grow fast enough to meet the increasing level of demand. As a result of

either, the general level of prices rises. This type of inflation is often experienced as an economy approaches and reaches its full-employment level.

Consider the following possibility: total demand rises and the economy gets closer and closer to full capacity output; in fact some firms (but not all) may well reach full capacity. Any further increases in demand, especially if experienced by the firms that have reached full capacity, will cause them to raise prices. Moreover, if these firms supply intermediate goods to other firms, then the increased price of these intermediate goods means that the cost of production rises for the firms using the intermediate goods. Thus, increases in demand tend to pull up prices, and hence the term demand-pull inflation.

Cost-push inflation

The **cost-push inflation** theory of price increases has emerged as a popular theory. It attempts to explain why prices rise when the economy is nowhere near full employment. Cost-push inflation apparently explains 'creeping' inflation and the inflation that Britain experienced during the 1973–5 recession. There are essentially three explanations of cost-push inflation: union power, big business power, and higher raw materials prices.

Union power, or the 'wage–price spiral'

Many people used to feel that unions were responsible for inflation. Their reasoning was as follows. A union would decide to demand a wage rise that was not matched by increases in productivity. Since the unions were so powerful, employers gave in to their demands for higher wages. When the employers paid these higher wages, their costs were higher. To maintain their usual profit margin, the business people raised their prices. This type of cost-push inflation could occur even if there was no excess demand for goods, and even when the economy was operating below capacity at under full employment.

The union-power argument depends on the unions having a stronghold over their particular labour markets. In terms of evaluating the argument, statistics on days lost in industrial disputes and on trade union membership were referred to. As Table 8.4 suggests, both these variables have shown downward trends since 1979, and so has inflation. Interestingly, this was exactly the opposite of the 1970s experience.

Big business power, or the 'price–wage spiral'

The other variant of the cost-push theory is that inflation is caused when the monopoly power of big business pushes up prices. Powerful corporations are presumably able to raise their prices whenever they want to increase their profits. Each time the corporations raise prices to increase their profits, the cost of living goes up. Workers demand higher wages to make up for the loss in the standard of living, thereby giving the corporations an excuse to raise prices again, and so a vicious price–wage cycle is established.

Table 8.4

Trade union power 1977–97
The figures in the right-hand column represent millions of working days lost due to industrial disputes in the year concerned. The other figures show the total number of union members at the end of each year. These increased by approximately 3 per cent a year during the 1970s and peaked in 1979. However, they declined markedly throughout the 1980s and 1990s.

Year	Number of union members	Working days lost (millions)
1977	12 846 000	10
1979	13 289 000	29
1985	10 821 000	6
1990	9 947 000	2
1995	7 275 000	0.40
1997	7 117 000	0.20

Source: *Labour Market Trends*

Raw materials cost-push inflation

Since the beginning in 1973 of higher and higher prices for all forms of energy, a relatively new type of cost-push inflation has been suggested. It is raw materials cost-push inflation, because the cost of raw materials seems to keep rising all the time. Coal is more expensive, so is petroleum, so is natural gas, and so are many other basic inputs into the production process.

Few economists would deny the impact of the OPEC oil prices in the early 1970s, which contributed to the inflationary surges experienced by most oil-importing countries in the mid-1970s. In fact, it is possible to distinguish an international pattern to inflation in most developed capitalist countries. Figure 8.3 compares more recent rates of inflation for the United Kingdom with those of its trading partners. It appears that a degree of contagion in inflation continues to exist between countries.

Summary

Whether it be union power, big business power or higher prices for raw materials, the resultant increased cost of

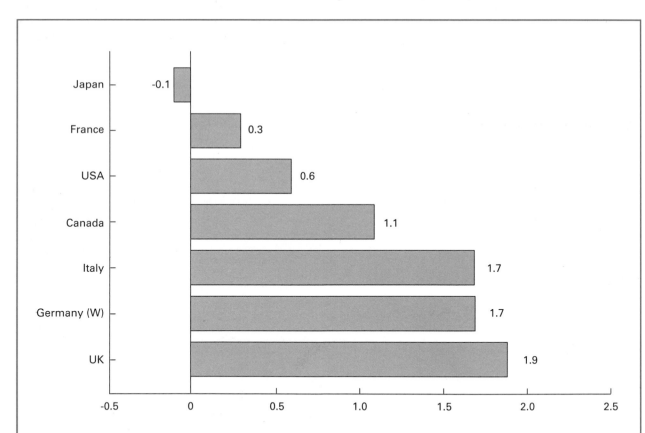

Figure 8.3

Average annual inflation rate for the UK and other major countries during 1998
From this graph it is clear that inflation has reduced in many countries. In fact, Japan shows a negative rate, and this has been the case from 1994 onwards. There is some debate that the low-rate inflation will lead other countries to experience negative rates too.

Source: *Business Monitor*, January 1999

production pushes prices up; *hence the term cost-push inflation.* This suggests that one may control inflation by means of price and income policies. However, judging by the attempts experienced during the 1960s and 1970s, such measures provide only a temporary restraint on price rises. The control of inflation will be returned to in Chapters 17 and 27.

KEY POINTS

8.4

■ Inflation represents a persistent increase in prices. This has been the UK experience in the post-war period. It was a major problem in the 1970s.

■ Demand-pull inflation occurs when the total demand for goods and services rises faster than the rate of growth of supply.

■ Cost-push inflation is due to one or more of the following: (1) union power, (2) big business power and/or (3) raw materials price increases.

Measuring inflation

If inflation is defined as a sustained rise in the general price level, how do we come up with a measure of the rate of inflation? This is indeed a thorny problem for government statisticians. It is easy to determine how much the price of an individual commodity has risen: if last year a light bulb cost 50p and this year it costs 75p, there has been a 50 per cent rise in the price of that light

bulb over a one-year period. We can express the change in the individual light-bulb price in one of several ways: (1) the price has gone up 25p; (2) the price is one-and-a-half (1.5) times as high; (3) the price has risen by 50 per cent; (4) by using an index number.

Index numbers

An index number of the price rise just discussed is simply the second choice multiplied by 100, that is, the index number is 150. All we need to do now is select a base year to compare prices.

Computing a price index

Of course, the problem becomes more complicated when we are dealing with a large number of goods, some of whose prices have gone up faster than others and some of whose prices may even have fallen. What we have to do is pick a representative selection, a so-called 'basket' of goods and services, and compare the cost of that 'basket' of goods and services over time. When we do this, we obtain a **price index**, which is defined as the cost of our representative basket of goods today, expressed as a percentage of the cost of the same basket of goods in some starting year, known as the **base year**.

$$\text{price index} = \frac{\text{cost today of 'basket'}}{\text{cost of 'basket' in base year}} \times 100$$

In the base year the price index will always be 100, because the year in the numerator and in the denominator of the above fraction is the same; therefore, the fraction equals 1, and when we multiply it by 100, we get 100. A simple numerical example of a price index calculation is given in Table 8.5. In this example there are only two goods in the basket: corn and microcomputers. The quantities in the basket remain the same between the base year 1985 and the current year 2000. Only the prices change.

Table 8.5

Calculating a price index for a basket containing two goods only

In this simplified example, there are only two goods: corn and microcomputers. The base-year quantities and prices are given in columns 2 and 3. The cost of the 1985 basket is calculated in column 4 and totals £1400. The 2000 prices are given in column 5. The price of the basket in 2000 is calculated in the last column and is £1700. The price index of 2000 compared with 1985 ends up as 121.43.

1	2	3	4	5	6
Commodity	**1985 basket quantity**	**1985 price per unit (£)**	**Cost of basket in 1985 (£)**	**2000 price per unit (£)**	**Cost of basket at 2000 prices (£)**
Corn	100 bushels	4.00	400.00	8.00	800.00
Microcomputers	2	500.00	1000.00	450.00	900.00
Totals			1400.00		1700.00

$$\text{price index} = \frac{\text{cost of basket in 2000}}{\text{cost of basket in base year 1985}} = \frac{1700.00}{1400.00} \times 100 = £121.43$$

Statistical weights

So far in this section on measuring inflation we have discussed three goods: light bulbs, corn and microcomputers. Obviously price rises in corn will affect the general public more than the price rises in light bulbs and microcomputers. To some extent this was catered for in our simple example by having a larger quantity of corn.

In official measurements, however, each item that is measured is allocated a 'statistical weight' according to its importance for the average family – this is ultimately determined by the percentage of average income that is spent on each good. Therefore, the statistical weight for food will be far higher than that for cigarettes, as changes in food prices affect everybody, whereas cigarette prices only affect smokers.

Price indices

The plural of index is indices, and a significant number of price indices are commonly referenced in the United Kingdom. We shall discuss the five official ones that are most commonly referred to, namely the **retail price index**, the **GDP deflator**, the **tax and price index**, the **producer price index** and the **harmonized indices of consumer prices**.

The retail price index

The most often quoted of all price indices is the retail price index (RPI). The technique used to compile it is basically the same as that outlined above, but of course far more prices are monitored. In fact, the Office for National Statistics is responsible for monitoring the price of approximately 600 goods and services each month. The relevant price quotations are gathered from variously sized retail outlets in 146 areas in the UK. In this way approximately 130 000 price quotes are gathered each month. For example, on 19 January 1999, 536 prices were collected for a pint of draught beer. The average used for the RPI was £1.73 per pint. The price quotations, however, had ranged from under £1.50 to over £2.00.

Once each item has been averaged out for the country as a whole, its relative importance is then accounted for by the average price changes for each group of goods multiplied by the statistical weights. The index is then published in percentage form displaying its monthly change. Some representative figures have already been presented in Table 8.3.

Those 600 items that are chosen for measurement and the statistical weights allocated are meant to represent the *average* household, that is, the household in which the main breadwinner is neither a pensioner nor a millionaire. Indeed, the RPI does not attempt to measure the cost of living of the top 4 per cent in the income scale or those households which rely for the majority of their income on state pensions and benefits (that is, about 15 per cent of the population). In fact, separate price indices are calculated for pensioners.

The collection of this price information is clearly a formidable exercise. Inevitably, new products may be excluded for a year or two, but most purchases relevant to the *average* household are listed. It is not surprising that the cost of carefully constructing the RPI each year has been estimated to exceed £3 million.

RPIX

The features that we have discussed under the heading 'The retail price index' produce what is commonly referred to as the **headline rate**. The headline rate of inflation indicates the change in price of all the selected goods and services. An important aspect that distorts this figure, especially when comparing inflation rates with those of other countries, is home ownership, as mortgage interest payments form a significant weighted part of the headline rate. Hence another measure referred to in the press is **RPIX**, that is, the retail price index *excluding* mortgage interest payments (also abbreviated as RPI excl. MIPs). This figure shows the underlying trend to price changes without the complications of house finance, which differs so much from nation to nation and from one interest rate regime to another. Indeed, RPIX has become the government's official target inflation measure and since 1998 the monetary policy committee of the Bank of England has been instructed to make sure that the annual increase in RPIX does not exceed 2.5 per cent.

RPIY

It should be apparent that no single index will adequately measure all aspects of the inflation process or meet the needs of all users. For example, if indirect taxes such as VAT increase, retail prices also increase. The Bank of England were particularly concerned about such developments, as their monitoring role of inflation had increased. In order to track movements in 'core' prices they published RPIY figures from 1993. Specifically, as well as excluding mortgage interest payments, RPIY excludes value-added tax, excise duties, council tax, insurance tax and airport tax. It is now published monthly alongside the RPI.

The ins and outs of the RPI

Each spring the retail price index basket of goods is reviewed. Items are brought in or dropped out according to changes in patterns of expenditure. In the 1950s, statisticians added ice-cream, Tupperware and televisions. In the 1960s they brought in fish fingers, crisps, jeans and motor scooters. In the 1970s, mortgage payments, yoghurt, wine, cassette recorders and home perms were added to the index. And the following decade saw the inclusion of muesli, strawberry jam, trainers, condoms, multivitamins and unleaded petrol.

16 Which of the following items do you think would have been added to or dropped from the RPI since the 1990s?

boat trip on the Norfolk broads	alcopops
leggings	Internet subscriptions
peaches	disposable nappies
kippers	men's vests
spark plugs	Porsche
stockings	pork sausages
aerobic classes	avocado pears

This question is intended to help you recognize the breadth and care that goes into compiling the RPI. Those interested in the precise details of the basket, however, should see *Labour Market Trends*, Table H.13, or ONS,

The tax and price index

Official comments on these various price indices stress that *price changes only* are being measured. This is because income tax payments and National Insurance contributions are not included. The RPI therefore cannot be regarded as synonymous with a cost-of-living index. In an attempt to overcome this problem, the tax and price index (TPI) was introduced in August 1979.

This attempts to measure the changes in income before tax that Mr Average would need to maintain his purchasing power. For example, the tax and price index stood at 150 in 1998, which meant that Mr Average would need a 50 per cent increase in gross income compared with his base year income in 1987 to maintain his standard of living. To undertake this calculation, changes in the RPI are combined with changes in direct tax (including National Insurance contributions). Obviously, changes in tax rates have no effect on people who do not pay tax, such as pensioners. Additionally, those with high taxable incomes are also excluded from the calculations. This index is meant to measure changes experienced by the average household.

The TPI was launched as a more comprehensive index than the RPI. Yet many regard the introduction of this index as a purely political tool, as the Conservative government that was in office when it was introduced were committed to switching from direct to indirect taxation. This inevitably played havoc with the RPI, which measures prices inclusive of any indirect taxes. The intention was to switch people's focus to the more favourable TPI, which would highlight the reduced direct tax burden and the increase in real income. Nevertheless, the RPI remains as the measure that most commentators refer to every month. A possible explanation for this preference is that the idea of an 'average income earner' is less relevant than the idea of an 'average shopping basket' that everyone spends on.

The producer price index

As described above, the RPI attempts to measure the prices of goods and services bought by the average household in the UK. In contrast, the producer price index (PPI) estimates the prices of goods produced by manufacturers in the UK, for sale in the UK market. It is commonly quoted as relating to 'factory-gate' prices, as it uses price quotations of goods at the manufactured stage, excluding VAT and transport.

The PPI is calculated using around 9000 price quotes supplied by 3700 contributors. The data collection and weighting process is presently under review and in future 7000 manufacturers will contribute the 9000 price quotes. This will make the sample representative of more manufacturing units.

Often journalists and economists – as well as government officials – will make note of changes in the PPI because it represents the prices of manufactured retail goods at an earlier stage of production. In other words, movements in this index are seen as a signal that retail inflation is going to increase or decrease in the forthcoming months.

A point to remember, to avoid confusion, is that the PPI and RPI are made up of very different items. The measurements of price changes are from different perspectives. To consolidate this point, you may find the multiple choice question number 6 on page 158 interesting to attempt.

Glossary of inflation indices

17 The indices that we have dealt with so far are specific to the UK. Other countries will have their equivalents, but none will use an identical basket of goods or the same procedures. To rehearse the different types of inflation referred to in UK government publications, complete the following statements:

RPIX Inflation measured by the retail price index *excluding* _____ .

RPIY Inflation measured by the retail price index *excluding* _____ .

TPI Inflation measured by the retail price index *combined with* _____ .

PPI Inflation measured by _____ of _____ .

RPI Inflation measured by _____ .

The GDP deflator

This index attempts to show changes in the level of prices of *all* goods and services produced in an economy. Consequently, it is the most general indicator of inflation that a nation can use since it incorporates *all* their domestic prices – not just consumer good prices, but also the prices of investment goods, goods and services consumed by the government, and items made for export. In short, it measures the changes in the prices of *everything* produced in an economy. The GDP deflator is measured as the ratio of the value of total domestic output at current prices divided by the same quantity of output valued at the constant prices of a selected base year. We shall return to this process in Chapter 13.

The EU countries' harmonized indices of consumer prices

The harmonized indices of consumer prices (HICP) have been in use since 1996. They enable comparisons of consumer price inflation to be made across the fifteen member states of the European Union. In fact, since January 1999 this set of indices has become the official target measure of inflation for the European Monetary Union. Existing price indices, such as the RPI in the United Kingdom, cannot be used for HICP purposes because of differences in construction and coverage.

The aim is to 'harmonize' the approach of all member states. Consequently, some inclusions are made that some national indices do not reference, whilst others are excluded, notably: housing costs, insurance, health and education. Another significant difference is that the HICP is based on the average household expenditure of the whole population. In short, it includes the expenditure of high-income and pensioner households.

The accuracy of price indices

There is continuous debate about how accurate price indices really are. Do we ever get an accurate view of the 'rate' of inflation? We cannot answer that question completely, but we can point out the potential limitations.

Firstly, you must remember that all indices are based on a specific 'basket' of goods and/or services, and even if they represent identical goods or services, methods can differ. For example, the three main agencies monitoring house prices during 1997 gave a very muddled impression of house price inflation during that period of time. The Halifax house price index rose by 5.8 per cent, the Nationwide index rose by 13.1 per cent and the DETR house price index rose by 7.9 per cent. The possible reasons for this divergence relate to differences in samples (such as property size), methodologies (such as price recording at different points in the transfer process), and the weight given to transactions for each region.

Secondly, there is improper accounting for changes in quality. At the same nominal price a good is actually cheaper if its quality has been improved. Conversely, at the same nominal price a good is actually more expensive if its quality has fallen. To take a specific example, a VCR may cost £250 and the next year it may cost the same. But what if in the second year it is sold with a universal remote control unit that can also operate other electronic equipment? Clearly the price per constant-quality unit of that VCR has fallen. It is difficult for government statisticians to take quality changes into account. Economists working

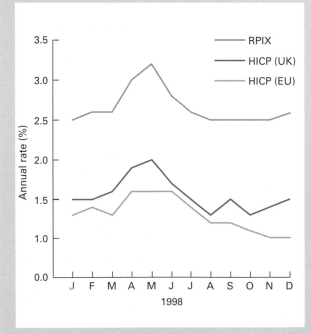

RPIX and HICP inflation rates

Annual rate (%) — 1998

Legend: RPIX, HICP (UK), HICP (EU)

Source: *Labour Market Trends*, March 1999

The chart shows how the inflation rate for the HICP compared with the RPIX. The equivalent annual average figures for the related indices were as follows: European Union 1.3 per cent, HICP (UK) 1.5 per cent and RPIX 2.6 per cent.

18 What do the abbreviations HICP and RPIX stand for? Explain briefly what each is used for.

19 Why is the HICP estimate for the UK normally lower than RPIX?
  (a) Across the European Union, there are fifteen sets of HICP produced each month (one for each member state). Would you expect these figures to be lower or higher than their national equivalents?
  (b) Would you expect HICP rates across Europe to differ?
  (c) Find some up-to-date HICP figures to qualify the answer above.

20 Media reports during 1999 suggest that groceries and cars are consistently more expensive in the UK than Europe (up to 40 per cent dearer in some cases). Would these price distortions affect the UK's HICP position within the European Union?

at the Bank of England acknowledged this dilemma when reviewing inflation during the Bank's long history; given that this was done during its 300th anniversary, one can begin to imagine the problems that can occur over time.

Thirdly, it is also difficult for government statisticians to take into account immediately the introduction of new products, such as personal home computers, cellular phones, DVD players and other consumer products that may not have been widely marketed when the original basket of goods was surveyed. The RPI, at least, is revised annually. The revision is based on information arising from the family expenditure survey, in which 7000 households in the United Kingdom are asked to record their daily spending over two weeks and to give details of bigger purchases over a longer period. Other indices, however, are reviewed less frequently.

Finally, therefore, it may be worth highlighting that all government statistics, including measures of inflation, are best referred to as 'estimates'.

Measuring inflation: an international problem

The following extract is taken from an American textbook to illustrate that problems of estimating changes in the cost of living are not unique to the UK.

The Consumer Price Index has been inaccurate because it ignores many changes in quality, increased discount shopping at club warehouses, and other developments in the consumer market. The statisticians responsible for computing the CPI each month know this. As a result, they have made changes in the index. Without much fanfare, America has modified the way it calculates the CPI. It altered its sampling procedure for food and non-food items, and it made its treatment of rent, hospital prices, and generic drugs more accurate. After those adjustments, government-estimated inflation rates dropped by 0.2 to 0.3 percent. Further calculation changes in 1998 and 1999 will reduce estimated inflation by another 0.75 percent.

Source: Leroy Miller, *Economics Today*, 13th edn, Longman Wesley, p. 152

21 (a) What is the UK equivalent of the United States' CPI?
(b) Do you think the two indices are comparable?
22 (a) The index in the United States is inaccurate because it ignores changes in quality, discount shopping and other developments. Discuss each of these and illustrate with specific UK examples.
(b) Would each of these three omissions also apply to the RPI?
23 Explain how the UK has reduced inflation by massaging statistics since 1990.
24 New products reduce the cost of maintaining a given standard of living. Discuss.

KEY POINTS

8.5

■ Once we pick a 'basket' of goods, we can construct a price index which compares the cost of that basket today with the cost of the same basket in a base year.

■ The retail price index (RPI) forms the basis of many of the indices used in the United Kingdom. The producer price index (PPI) has a different focus. The former monitors changes of prices in the high-street shops, and the latter measures changes in the weighted average of the prices of manufactured goods sold by producers, often through warehouses.

■ Two other indices that can be used to estimate changes in prices and the cost of living are the GDP deflator and the harmonized indices of consumer prices.

■ All price indices suffer from certain inaccuracies. For example, they have a hard time taking into account quality changes, and the 'baskets' may not always be entirely representative of the purchases actually made.

Economic forecasting

Statistical indicators, such as those for unemployment and inflation, contribute to the making of important economic forecasts for the economy as a whole. For this purpose various economic models exist. The emphasis that is given to each variable and the range that is used vary from institution to institution. Understandably, the interpretation of economic events is a complex process and there are over forty recognized forecasters predicting the UK economy. The following exercise is based upon a monthly summary of these forecasts, which is published regularly by the Treasury.

Forecasts for the UK economy

A comparison of independent forecasts, January 1999

	Independent forecasts for 1999		
	Average	Lowest	Highest
GDP growth (per cent)	0.6	−0.5	2.1
Inflation rate (Q4: per cent)			
– RPI	1.5	0.5	3.1
– RPIX	2.2	1.1	3.1
Unemployment (Q4, millions)	1.58	1.20	1.82
Current account (£ billion)	−5.5	−15.0	0.5

	Independent forecasts for 2000		
	Average	Lowest	Highest
GDP growth (per cent)	1.8	0.2	2.6
Inflation rate (Q4: per cent)			
– RPI	2.1	1.2	3.3
– RPIX	2.2	1.2	2.9
Unemployment (Q4, millions)	1.77	1.30	2.77
Current account (£ billion)	–6.6	–17.0	2.5

Source: *Economic Trends*, February 1999

25 (a) Identify and define one economic objective within the forecast.

(b) Discuss the reliability of statistics relating to this economic objective.

(c) What is the permissible margin (+/–) that would be acceptable within the forecast range for this statistic?

26 (a) What were the actual figures for 1999 and 2000?

(b) Were they within the forecast boundaries?

27 Major forecast errors occur when either the national or international environment develops in an unexpected way from the forecasters' model. Take one of these causes of forecasting error and explain it fully. If appropriate, use it to account for the outcome in 1999 or 2000.

Understandably, these model-based forecasts are often wrong, for several reasons. Firstly, it is difficult to predict accurately the behaviour of millions of consumers and businesses to the last detail. Secondly, forecasts may change course owing to sudden changes of events, as examples from any decade can illustrate. The Asian economic crisis during the late 1990s had a major impact on trading nations across the globe. The increase in consumer expenditure following windfall gains due to the conversion of building societies to publicly quoted companies has confused many forecasts relating to the UK in the 1980s and 1990s. And the chaos caused by ethnic cleansing in the Balkans during 1999 will generate its shock waves into the next millennium. Forecasts may also be limited by false assumptions about policy and problems relating to time lags, since it often takes years for a specific policy instrument to work fully through an economic system. And finally, as detailed above, government statistics are themselves incomplete indicators of economic activity and are often revised after publication, as mistakes are uncovered in their collation. So, at times, even the existing data represent pale reflections of activity in the real economy.

The important point, however, is the message conveyed by the forecast; the trend does not have to be 100 per cent accurate. Indeed, there is a difficulty as forecasting models are no different from any other economic model in that they attempt to simplify reality. In the case of the economy this is a complex reality, and hence only the key variables are measured and monitored. However, within an economy there are very many variables to choose from. For our purposes these can be categorized into two main types: **exogenous variables**, which are *external* to the economy in so far as they are determined by world events and policy (such as oil prices and tax rates); and **endogenous variables**, which are dependent on what goes on within an economy (such as employment and inflation). There are more than 120 of the former, and hundreds of the latter. Consequently, the larger traditional models of the macroeconomy contained upwards of 1000 relationships.

In Figure 8.4 we present, for comparison, a dated Treasury model. This has survived all four editions of *Economics Explained*. For us, the attraction of this flowchart is that it is more immediate and accessible than the pages and pages of detailed equations that accompany the computer input of today's model, and it helps to clarify the distinction between endogenous and exogenous variables.

Obviously, any Treasury model is continually revised and the conscientious student may like to reflect (before reading further) on the variables that would need to be added to a more contemporary equivalent.

The older models placed an emphasis on the output side of the economy and little importance was given to price determination. In fact, in Figure 8.4 elements relating to money, credit, monetary policy, retail sales and the environment are clearly missing.

Modern models are far smaller, drawing on a wider range of approaches. For example, a five-equation model (determining real output, money, prices, exchange rates and interest rates) was used by the Bank of England to analyse the inflationary consequences of the exchange rate depreciation of early 1995. Extensions of this model would nowadays rarely exceed twenty core equations.

Cyclical indicators

Another set of indicators associated with forecasting are cyclical indicators. These statistics indicate where we are, where we've been and, most importantly, where we seem to be going. They have evolved, since the 1960s, throughout Europe, to enable governments to predict changes that happen in an economy. These predictions are based on a composite set of statistics that are regarded as running ahead of the general trend. This is because things do not happen simultaneously. Some indicators point in an upward direction, while others still portray a downward trend, especially at the turning point of a business cycle (that is, the peaks and troughs).

The main series of statistics that are assumed to precede the general trend of the economy by changing six to twelve months ahead of the main cycle are referred to as **leading indicators**. This group is broken down into two sub-groups: a longer leading index (which looks for turning points around a year ahead) and a shorter leading index (which indicates turning points around six months ahead). Examples of leading indicators are: housing starts,

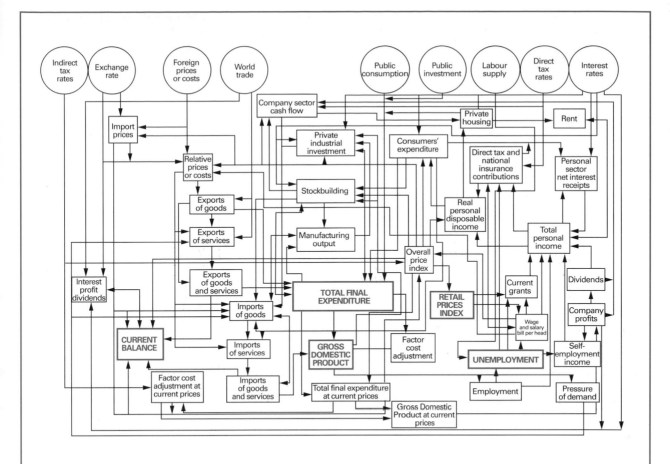

Figure 8.4
Flowchart of a Treasury model
The direction of the arrows between the boxes represents the Treasury's interpretation of the direction of causation between variables. Those variables at the top of the diagram, in circles, are the exogenous variables, and those shown in boxes are the endogenous variables. The coloured framed boxes highlight the main target variables.

Source: *Treasury, Macroeconomic Model Technical Manual*, HMSO, 1978

new car sales, business optimism and the amount of consumer credit. **Lagging indicators**, by contrast, alter in retrospect, that is, usually about one year after the event; hence they confirm what we already know and in forecasting terms are not so important. Examples of lagging indicators include unemployment, investment in plant and machinery, levels of stock and orders for engineering output. Those statistics that are thought to trace the actual cycle are called **coincident indicators**, and obvious examples include money supply and GDP figures.

Do cranes tell the whole story?

On arriving in a foreign city you can get a rough idea of the state of the local economy simply by counting the cranes on the skyline. In fact, the cynic would remark that if you can see more than twelve cranes from your office window you are probably witnessing the start of the next recession.

28 Would crane-counting represent an example of a leading or lagging indicator? Explain your answer carefully.

29 What other visual signs are there that an economy is moving into or out of a recession?

30 Give an example of what may disturb the predictive quality of a leading indicator.

31 Cyclical indicators merely confirm what is already known. Discuss.

We appreciate that there is still a lot of theory and economics for you to understand before you can feel fully confident about forecasting. Indeed, the environment, employment, inflation and growth all need to be dealt with in more depth. This happens in subsequent chapters, specifically Chapters 10, 12, 13, 24, 27 and 31.

KEY POINTS

8.6

- The Treasury model used for forecasting and policy evaluation is based on a computer program. In the past it has contained upwards of 1000 economic variables.

- Economic forecasting is an unreliable science owing to unforeseen events, revised statistics and time lags.

- Associated with forecasting are cyclical indicators; of particular significance in this series are leading indicators that change six to twelve months ahead of the main economic cycle.

Case Study

A guide to official sources of statistics

At several points in this chapter we have stated the latest figures available. In a text of this size, these figures are often out of date before the book even goes to print. It is important, therefore, that you have the confidence to research data for yourself.

To assist you there follows a very brief guide to statistical sources, and some questions to prompt you into action. Those studying at a British university should have access to all of the following publications. Those who are dependent on a school or local library may not be so fortunate. Nevertheless, there is no excuse for not finding the data as the statistics in these various sources duplicate.

Most of the key sources are published by the Office for National Statistics – commonly referred to as ONS. This is a government department, responsible to the Chancellor of the Exchequer. It was formed by the amalgamation of the Central Statistical Office (CSO) and the Office of Population Censuses and Surveys (OPCS) in April 1996. At the same time, a *Guide to Official Statistics* was published. This is a comprehensive reference that signposts where to look for the different indicators. It is an excellent starting point to locate any data or sources not referred to below. It is updated from time to time and most reference libraries will have a copy.

UK National Accounts (formerly known as **National Income and Expenditure**). This publication is normally referred to simply by the colour of its cover as the **Blue Book**. It is published annually in the autumn by the ONS, and is considered to be a most important

source of data for the UK macroeconomy, since it provides a comprehensive breakdown of GDP, over a number of years. As with all ONS publications, recent editions have become more user friendly. For example, they now contain useful notes explaining how to interpret the accounts, a subject index and a glossary of terms.

Economic Trends is published monthly by the ONS. Most of the data are quarterly, extending back over, perhaps, five years. It covers a range of areas including output, prices, employment and international trade. Feature articles explaining statistics are also regularly included. The **Economic Trends Annual Supplement** is particularly useful for obtaining longer series of data, some going back to 1945.

Monthly Digest of Statistics. As the name implies, this is an amalgam of statistics published monthly. It covers a wide range of topics, including economic, social and demographic. In relation to this chapter it presents data on prices, the balance of payments and employment.

Labour Market Trends (formerly known as the **Employment Gazette**). A monthly publication covering labour market issues and offering detailed information on wage rates, productivity, hours worked and so on for various sectors of the economy. It also includes articles about the labour market and information relating to the retail price index in the UK and abroad.

Financial Statistics. Monthly publication of the ONS relating to financial indices such as interest rates, exchange rates and the money supply. Editions since 1997 also show data relating to inflation.

Bank of England Inflation Report. This is produced quarterly alongside the Bank's *Quarterly Bulletin*. The inflation report serves a dual purpose. Firstly, it provides a comprehensive review of various specialized indices and commentary on their forecasts. Secondly, it is the official publication responsible for making the minutes of the monetary policy committee available to the public.

(OECD) Main Economic Indicators. This is a monthly publication of the Organization for Economic Co-operation and Development. This organization comprises twenty-nine member states, including Australia, Europe, United States, Canada and Scandinavia. The publication is designed to provide statistics on recent economic developments. It is divided into two main parts: indicators by subject (including all those discussed in this chapter) and by country. Hence it is useful for comparative purposes. In fact, since March 1997 it has become the best source of cyclical indicators, as a table of composite leading indicators is a regular feature, and it compares the position of twenty-two member states.

Company Reports. These have to be published annually by every public limited company (PLC) and incorporate a detailed set of accounts. Consequently, in these publications the statistical information is specific to one company. Again, most academic libraries will stock a broad range.

1 Newspapers also publish regular summaries of the main macroeconomic series.
(a) Name the data comprising such a series.
(b) Do you think that the data published in the newspapers would be any more or less reliable than the data published by the ONS?

2 (a) Find three up-to-date rates of inflation for the UK.
(b) Explain why there are many different measures of inflation.

3 (a) Using the table below, describe and explain the relationship between house prices and inflation for the years 1986 to 1996.

Year	UK average house prices (£)	Retail price inflation
1986	39 800	3.4
1987	46 400	4.1
1988	58 200	4.9
1989	70 400	7.8
1990	69 500	9.5
1991	68 600	5.9
1992	66 000	3.7
1993	64 300	1.6
1994	66 300	2.4
1995	66 700	3.5
1996	69 100	2.4

Source: *Housing Finance*, published quarterly by Council of Mortgage Lenders

(b) Compare and contrast the reliability of the data shown in the table.
(c) Would a low level of inflation be an advantage or disadvantage to those buying their own houses with a mortgage?

4 (a) Find two estimates of unemployment that record the current UK position.
(b) Explain why these two rates differ.
(c) Which would you regard as the more objective of the two measures?

5 Selecting the appropriate data, discuss the relationship between the national level of inflation or unemployment and the annual accounts of a specific company of your choice.

6 The government recently suggested that in order to assess town-centre performance, local authorities should regularly collect information on a range of indicators. Environmental quality was one of these indicators. Suggest and explain how a local authority could monitor changes to the environmental quality of its town centre.

7 During the 1990s the Royal Statistical Society called for an independent national statistical service to monitor the objectivity, integrity and scope of official figures. Explain the arguments in favour of such a proposal.

8 This chapter has encouraged you to develop a feel for data and to appreciate how they can be used to tell a story and form the basis of a forecast. You should appreciate, therefore, that when the Bank of England increase interest rates by 1 per cent they expect GDP to fall after a year by 0.2 per cent to 0.35 per cent and inflation to reduce by 0.2 per cent to 0.4 per cent after a two-year time lag. Attempt to describe, with the use of appropriate statistics, how you see the economy developing over the next two years.

Exam Preparation

Multiple choice questions

1 Which group would not be included in the official workforce?
   A school-leavers on a Youth Training Scheme
   B people who are overseas in the British army
   C those claiming unemployment benefit
   D married women who register themselves as available for temporary work with a commercial agency
   E the self-employed

2 Which one of the following policies is most likely to reduce the level of structural unemployment?
   A reducing the level of interest rates
   B lowering unemployment benefits
   C increasing the level of consumer expenditure
   D increasing research and development grants for technology
   E increasing labour mobility

3 Main weights in the retail price index for country X, 1987:

Food	250
Transport and vehicles	136
Housing	119
Clothing and footwear	87
Alcoholic drink	65

   It can be deduced from the above table that, on average,
   A people were eating more by volume than they were drinking
   B family expenditure on food was rising faster than expenditure on any other category
   C people placed less value on housing than on transport
   D the cost of housing must have been subsidized more than the cost of transport
   E families spent a smaller proportion of their income on alcoholic drink than on clothing and footwear

4 A fall in the index of retail prices suggests that:
   A the standard of living has fallen
   B the price of sterling has fallen against other currencies
   C the purchasing power of money has risen
   D imported raw materials have become cheaper

5 The tax and price index will rise at a faster rate than the retail price index if there is an increase in:

   A consumer prices in shops
   B duties paid on petrol and alcohol
   C value-added tax
   D income tax
   E all of the above

6 Price indices are constructed on the basis of different baskets. The following summaries of PPI and RPI only overlap at one point: select the letter that represents the overlap.

Category	RPI	PPI
Fresh fruit and vegetables	A	A
UK manufactured consumer goods	B	B
Capital goods (machine tools etc.)	C	C
Intermediate goods (parts etc.)	D	D
Services bought by households	E	E

Essay questions

1 (a) Why is it difficult to agree on what constitutes full employment?   (10 marks)
  (b) Discuss the view that imperfections in the labour market are the main cause of unemployment in the United Kingdom.
    (15 marks)

2 Discuss the economic argument that government should curb the power of trade unions.

3 Is it meaningful to identify different causes of inflation?

4 (a) Explain how the rate of increase in retail prices in the United Kingdom is measured.
    (30 marks)
  (b) Why are there conflicting views as to whether the recorded rate of retail price increases provides an accurate picture of inflation in the United Kingdom?
    (30 marks)
  (c) Explain why the rate of increase in the retail price index would be of much less concern if the United Kingdom were a closed economy.   (40 marks)

5 What are the main characteristics and causes of unemployment in the United Kingdom at present? What are the costs of unemployment to the economy?

6 'The costs incurred from the current level of unemployment in the United Kingdom are unacceptably high.' Discuss.

9

Government intervention in markets

The pricing system answers three basic questions of resource allocation: *What* goods will be produced? *How* will they be produced? And *for whom* will they be produced? The forces of supply and demand acting through the pricing system (that is, the market) affect the bulk of decisions that answer these three questions. But as Chapter 2 pointed out, developed countries like the United Kingdom and the United States are not purely private market economies. In addition to market forces, there are many other forces at work that affect the allocation of resources. One of the most important of these non-market forces is government. In this chapter we shall look at the impact on markets of various forms of government intervention and in doing so draw on the concepts of demand and supply elasticity explained in Chapter 5. Our aim is to show some applications of supply and demand analysis. We first draw on the concepts in the previous chapters to show why agriculture in developed economies is not left to unregulated market forces. Using our theory of free market pricing we can explain why, in the absence of government intervention, the operation of forces on the demand and supply side results in both a low-income and an unstable income situation for the farming community.

In the second part of this chapter we show how the concepts of price elasticity of demand and of supply are helpful in understanding the repercussions of taxes imposed by government. Of course governments need tax revenues in order to help finance a wide range of expenditure programmes. The rationale of government spending takes us back into the macro-field that was the subject of the first chapter in Part B.

The final part of this chapter considers the impact of government policies which control the prices that would operate in a free market. We consider specific policies which fix a maximum price level and appraise the impact in the market for rented accommodation. We briefly preview the problems facing governments attempting general restraints on upward price movements. But first we consider how the free market operates in the agricultural sector. Having considered in turn the demand for and supply of food, we see why governments are so willing to regulate agricultural markets. The labour market provides us with an illustration of another form of government intervention with the price mechanism. We study the effect of minimum wage legislation.

LEARNING OUTCOMES

On completing this chapter you should understand:

- Why governments intervene in agricultural markets

- Policy options to help farmers

- The impact of indirect taxes

Agriculture: demand and supply

The demand side

The root cause of the problem facing the farming community is the fact that there is a limit to how much food people can eat! Adam Smith recognized this in the *Wealth of Nations*:

The rich man consumes no more food than his poor neighbour. In quality it may be very different, and to select and prepare it may require more labour and art; but in quantity it is very nearly the same. But compare the spacious palace and great wardrobe of the one with the hovel and few rags of the other, and you will be sensible that the difference between their clothing, lodging and household furniture is almost as great in quantity as it is in the quality. The desire for food is limited in every man by the narrow capacity of the human stomach; but the desire for the convenience and ornaments of building, dress, equipage and household furniture, seems to have no limit or certain boundary.

(A. Smith, *Wealth of Nations* (1776), Bk I, ch. 11, Everyman edn, 1964, pp. 149–50)

Even if people who are rich can 'afford' to buy huge quantities, they do not do so. We therefore expect that, as households get richer, the percentage of their budget spent on food will fall. This occurs because the income elasticity of demand for food is less than 1. We have previously defined income elasticity of demand as follows:

$$\text{income elasticity} = \frac{\text{percentage change in amount of good purchased}}{\text{percentage change in income}}$$

If the income elasticity of demand for agricultural products is less than 1, for every 1 per cent increase in income there will be an increase of less than 1 per cent in quantity demanded, other things being constant. We saw in Table 5.5 in Chapter 5 that the income elasticity of demand for several foodstuffs in the United Kingdom is now well below 1. Income elasticity is quite low for the richer nations in the world. In fact, the richer the nation, the lower the income elasticity of demand for agricultural products. All nations seem to exhibit income elasticities for food products that are less than 1. Therefore, we predict that agriculture will be of declining importance in all nations as each becomes richer.

Table 9.1 shows the consumption volume for some items of food in Great Britain. It shows that on a per capita basis consumption of most categories of food products was lower in 1997 than in 1987. Examination of Table 9.1 indicates that there are some exceptions to this pattern of falling consumption, for example semi-skimmed milk, reduced-fat spreads and bananas, which seem likely to be explained by changing views as to what constitutes a healthy diet. Nonetheless, the impact of rising incomes on food consumption habits seems clear enough. The income variable underlines Adam Smith's point about the 'narrow

Table 9.1

Estimated household food consumption by all households in Great Britain (grammes per person per week)

	1987	1988	1989	1990	1991	1992	1993	1994	1995	1996	1997
Liquid wholemilk (ml)	1635	1513	1377	1232	1104	995	898	870	812	776	712
Semi-skimmed (ml)	274	350	432	516	579	752	814	863	899	935	978
Cheese	116	117	115	113	117	114	109	106	108	111	109
Butter	61	57	50	46	44	41	40	39	36	39	38
Margarine	113	108	98	91	89	79	70	43	41	36	26
Low- and reduced-fat spreads	31	38	46	45	47	51	52	74	72	79	77
Eggs (number)	2.88	2.67	2.29	2.20	2.25	2.08	1.92	1.86	1.85	1.87	1.78
Sugar	212	196	183	171	167	156	151	144	136	144	128
Beef and veal	192	180	171	149	152	141	133	131	121	101	110
Mutton and lamb	75	78	85	83	86	71	66	54	54	66	56
Pork	90	94	89	84	82	72	80	77	71	73	75
Other cooked and canned meals	70	74	70	62	60	68	60	63	63	62	52
Fish, fresh and processed (including shellfish)	74	74	74	69	65	67	71	71	68	72	70
Potatoes (excl. processed)	1071	1033	1009	996	959	901	875	812	803	805	745
Apples	200	204	206	201	190	187	179	180	183	175	179
Bananas	91	101	113	125	129	144	151	162	176	185	195
All other fresh fruit	209	200	204	198	216	216	224	238	247	263	276
Fruit juices (ml)	204	211	214	202	250	222	236	240	244	258	277
Flour	111	103	93	91	81	81	82	62	57	70	54
Bread	868	859	834	797	752	755	757	758	756	752	746
Cakes and pastries	75	73	69	70	79	76	79	85	85	87	93
Biscuits	151	149	149	149	147	148	142	138	135	150	138
Tea	48	47	46	43	42	39	36	38	39	38	36
Instant coffee	15	15	14	14	15	14	13	13	12	13	11
Canned soups	79	79	77	68	69	70	66	68	64	72	70

Source: *Annual Abstract of Statistics*, 1999

Table 9.2

Percentage of the labour force in agriculture, selected countries

Country	1960	1980	1990
UK	4	3	2
Netherlands	11	6	5
Denmark	18	7	6
France	22	8	5
Ireland	36	19	14
Portugal	44	26	18
Greece	56	31	23

Source: *World Development Reports*

Table 9.3

Agriculture in the EU

Country	As a share of employment (%)	As a share of GDP
UK	2.1	1.0
Belgium	2.7	1.3
Sweden	3.0	0.4
Germany	3.3	0.8
Netherlands	3.7	2.9
Luxembourg	3.7	0.9
Denmark	4.4	2.6
France	4.9	2.0
Austria	7.3	1.1
Italy	7.5	2.7
Finland	7.7	1.1
Spain	9.3	3.0
Ireland	11.1	4.8
Portugal	11.5	2.0
Greece	20.4	7.3

Source: *Financial Times*, 17 March 1998

capacity of the human stomach'. As real incomes rise, consumers prefer to spend their money on foreign holidays, colour televisions and motor cars. The higher income elasticity values for these products compared with those for items of food indicates how society is registering its market preferences. Unhappily for farmers, the slow rate of population growth in the United Kingdom does not offset the disappointing growth in demand due to rising incomes: an increase in sheer numbers (of mouths to feed) does not counteract the basically sluggish market situation resulting from the income determinant. In 1984 the resident population of the UK was 56.5 million. It reached 57 million in 1987, but it was another five years before the UK population exceeded 58 million. It took another five years for the resident population to reach 59 million.

The income inelasticity of demand for food means that society does not want the same number of farmers to continue in production: if numbers do remain constant, their incomes relative to other groups in society must fall. Table 9.2 shows the declining proportion of employment in agriculture since 1960 in seven European countries, and Table 9.3 shows how in each country agricultural output is now a small proportion of gross domestic product.

The supply side

On the supply side technical progress – 'making two blades of grass grow where one grew before' – exacerbates the problems facing the farming community in developed economies. The agricultural sector has exhibited throughout history an impressive record of rising crop yields and improved productivity in livestock production due to improvements in animal husbandry. Table 9.4 shows farming's recent record of improved productivity.

Table 9.4 shows both total production and yields of cereal crops in the United Kingdom in the period 1992–7.

Table 9.4

Cereals production in the UK 1992–7 (thousand tonnes)

Crop	1992	1993	1994	1995	1996	1997
Wheat	14 090	12 890	13 310	14 310	16 100	15 020
Barley	7360	6040	5950	6830	7780	7820
Total cereals (including oats, rye and mixed corn)	22 060	19 490	19 950	21 860	24 580	23 530
Yields (tonnes per hectare)						
Wheat	6.82	7.33	7.35	7.70	8.15	7.38
Barley	5.67	5.19	5.37	5.73	6.14	5.76

Source: Ministry of Agriculture, Fisheries and Food, based on a sample of over 3000 cereal holdings

A cereal story

1 What was the percentage increase in wheat yield between 1992 and 1996? **A✓**

2 What could explain the lack of a consistent increase in wheat yield in each year after 1992? **A✓**

3 Would you expect a year-to-year change in wheat yield to correspond to the change in wheat production? **A✓**

4 Draw a supply and demand diagram illustrating the data in Table 9.4.

The problem of farm prices

Let us now bring together both of our observations concerning the demand for and the supply of food. If the demand curve shifts horizontally only slowly over time while the supply curve shifts very perceptibly to the right due to technical progress, we must surely conclude that there will be downward pressure on prices if there is an unregulated market in the pricing of agriculture. Falling prices for farm output should be the market signal for resources to move out of agriculture. But if resources do not flow out of farming, then the working of the price mechanism is to that extent flawed. If the process of resource reallocation as explained in Chapter 6 does not take place, then there may be grounds for governments to help some farmers who are receiving incomes below those in the non-farm sector of the economy.

You will note that we have just referred to the size of some farmers' incomes. We have seen that the interaction of supply and demand has the effect of depressing farm prices. Now of course for individual farmers their income is the product of output multiplied by prices received per unit. Those farmers who produce little agricultural output will of course have lower incomes than those farmers whose sheer volume of production gives them much larger incomes. This simple point – that some farmers produce little output whereas other farmers are very large and account for a significant proportion of total output – in fact is the nub of 'the farm problem' in developed economies like the United Kingdom and United States. Some farmers whose production is relatively small may never be able to generate enough receipts from the sale of output to be economically viable. In short, the low income problem is not so much because of depressed farm prices but because of the small size of farming operations. Before examining what aid government might offer farmers, let us examine another aspect of farm incomes, that is, their instability.

KEY POINTS

9.1

- The income elasticity of demand is the percentage change in amount of good purchased divided by the percentage change in income. Food products consistently have an income elasticity of demand that is very much below 1. Therefore, as income goes up, the percentage of total consumer expenditures going to food falls.

- Agriculture in developed economies has shown remarkable technological progress.

- The sluggish growth in demand for food in developed economies together with the increased productivity of agriculture means that in a free market there is downward pressure on farm prices and incomes.

- Some farmers receive low incomes simply because they produce very little output.

Unstable prices and incomes

The pressure on prices in unregulated agriculture is only part of the pricing problems facing farmers, however. Farmers in an unregulated market also suffer from unstable prices. Year-to-year fluctuations in weather and livestock production result in price instability – unless there is government intervention. Once more, simple demand and supply theory can be used to show the effect on price of, for example, a bumper harvest or a poor crop harvest. Note that we are using the concept of elasticity again here – this time concerning price and not income elasticity of demand.

Low price elasticity of demand

Not only is the income elasticity of demand for agricultural products low; so too is the price elasticity – agricultural products are relatively price inelastic. Whereas the low income elasticity was important for explaining the long-run downward trend in the farm sector, the low price elasticity of demand is important for understanding the high variability of farmers' incomes in the short run.

Let us consider the change in price that results from an increase in supply due to abnormally good weather conditions. In Figure 9.1 we show the supply schedule shifting from SS to S'S'. It has shifted out to the right, indicating a large increase in production. Notice that the supply schedule here is fairly vertical, indicating that the *price elasticity of supply* in the short-run period under consideration is also quite small (at E). After all, once farmers have planted and cultivated their crops, they can supply no

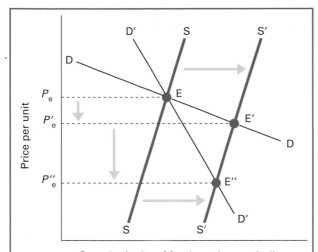

Figure 9.1
Consequences of a relatively inelastic demand
The original supply curve is SS – relatively inelastic supply in the short run at the current price. If the demand curve facing farmers is DD, a shift in the supply curve from SS to S'S' due to good weather will lower the equilibrium price from P_e to $P_e{}'$. But if the demand curve is instead D'D', when the supply curve shifts to S'S', the new equilibrium price falls to $P_e{}''$.

for the latest year available, was indeed very low. Turn back to page 82 to see Table 5.3.

Figure 9.1 shows a rightward shift in the supply curve from SS to S'S'. An example of such a shift was the glut of potatoes in 1992 in Great Britain that led to growers receiving very low prices. An example of a leftward shift in the supply curve would be the impact of frost damage on coffee in Brazil. In June 1994 reports of frost damage at a critical stage in the growth of coffee bushes was sufficient to prompt a rapid rise in the world coffee price. Note that this price change did not arise from the actual shortfall in the coffee harvest but from a predicted shortfall. The frost was believed to have cut the potential for the harvest by at least 20 per cent, implying a loss of between 5 and 10 per cent of world consumption. In September 1994 a tropical storm passing through the Caribbean devastated the banana crop in the Windward Islands, resulting in a loss in export earnings of millions of dollars for Dominica, Grenada, St Lucia and St Vincent. In 1998 hundreds of farmers in Oklahoma went out of business as record high temperatures and a lack of rain had a devastating effect on the output of peanuts and cotton. The lack of grass meant cattle had to be sold at a price half that expected.

The effect on farmers' incomes

So far we have only demonstrated that, for any given shift in the supply curve, the more price inelastic the demand for food products is, the greater will be the resultant change in the market-clearing price. Thus, when there is a bumper crop, the relatively price-inelastic demand for food results in a relatively substantial drop in the market-clearing price for food products.

What, though, happens to farmers' incomes? Well, you have to go back to our discussion of the relationship between changes in price and changes in total revenues and consumer expenditures. This was discussed in Chapter 5. There we showed that any firm facing an inelastic demand would suffer a decrease in total revenues if it lowered price. This analysis holds for the total income in farming. Because farmers are facing a price-inelastic demand for food (that is, as a group they are undoubtedly operating in the inelastic portion of the market demand for food), a reduction in price – for example, from P_e *to* $P_e{}''$ in Figure 9.1 – will result in a reduction in total farm income.

The cobweb

Agriculture differs from manufacturing industry owing to the biological character of its form of production. Because of this the problem of price instability as just outlined is not an irregular phenomenon of this sector of the economy. Indeed, we shall see that price fluctuations can take the form of fairly regular cycles over time. We need only specify three conditions for such cyclical movements in farm output, and hence prices.

more and no less – unless, of course, they decide to store or destroy the crops.

What if the demand schedule is in addition relatively elastic, such as DD (at E)? The new equilibrium price in this case will be set at the intersection of the new supply curve S'S' and the demand curve DD, or at point E'. The old equilibrium price was established at point E, or at a price P_e. The new price $P_e{}'$ obviously lies below the old price.

What if the demand curve is relatively *less* elastic, such as D'D' (at E)? The new equilibrium price will then be established at E'', and the new equilibrium price will be $P_e{}''$, which is even lower than $P_e{}'$. We therefore see that, when there is a given shift rightwards in the supply curve, the more price inelastic the demand for agricultural products, the greater the decline in the market price. Conversely, for any shift leftwards in the supply curve of agricultural products, the greater the price inelasticity of demand, the greater the rise in the market price of agricultural products. For example, if there is a drought, we expect prices to rise rather substantially due to the relative inelasticity of demand for food. Thus, we see that the relative price inelasticity of demand for agricultural products has also been one of the reasons that prices, and therefore farm incomes, have fluctuated more in agriculture than they have in other industries from year to year.

In Chapter 5 we saw that the price elasticity of demand for certain foodstuffs in the United Kingdom, calculated

Assumption 1 There is a time lag before an intended expansion in production actually is available for sale in the market.

Assumption 2 The decision by producers to change their output is essentially taken on the basis of the current market price. Thus supplies in year 2 are dependent on prices actually received in year 1 rather than on what is expected to be received in year 2.

Assumption 3 Producers are many and they each take decisions to adjust their scale of production in isolation from each other.

The result of these three conditions is that if supplies happen to be scarce in one time period the high level of the market-clearing price will prompt producers to begin a major expansion of production. This rise in production will in due course depress market prices, which sets off a major contraction in the scale of production. Let us show how this is explained. In Figure 9.2 the fixed amount available in the short run means that the market-clearing price is P_1. The supply curve indicates that at price P_1 farmers would like to produce Q_2. But they cannot do so until the next harvest (assumption 1). Suppose farmers plan to adjust output to the current market price and try to produce Q_2 (assumption 2). If each farmer's micro-decision overlooks the consequences for total industry output – the macro-situation – then assumption 3 is fulfilled. If indeed output Q_2 is actually harvested, the

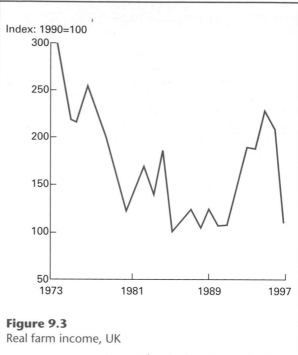

Figure 9.3
Real farm income, UK

Source: *The Guardian*, 9 December 1997

market-clearing price will then be P_2. Now the fulfilment of our assumptions will result in a contraction in production and higher prices. Note that in this example market prices move above and below the equilibrium level P and are not stable. Depending on the nature of the supply and demand curves, this instability of prices could be greater or less than is shown in Figure 9.2. Of course, if farmers do learn from experience they could vary their behaviour, resulting in less dramatic cobweb price and output fluctuations. But while historical experience may modify 'explosive' cobweb-type fluctuations, we can still conclude that agricultural products are characterized by price instability.

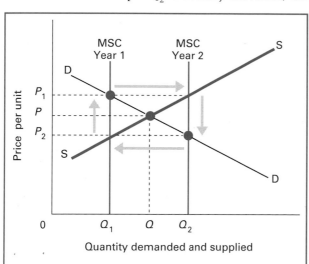

Figure 9.2
How agricultural prices can fluctuate
If there is a poor wheat harvest and no supplies are available from any other source the fixed amount available – Q_2 – means a market, or short-run supply curve, effectively exists (MSC, market supply curve). At price P_1, farmers would like to produce Q_2 but they cannot until the next harvest. If farmers try to produce Q_2 and all of Q_2 is harvested (note the assumption) then the price will be P_2. The price could oscillate around the equilibrium level P but never actually be at that level. A pattern can be drawn which looks like a spider's web – hence the cobweb.

UK farm income

5 How might the fluctuations in real farm income shown in Figure 9.3 be explained?

6 What does the movement of real farm income between 1973 and 1997 imply about the livelihood of farmers in 1997 compared with (a) 1973 and (b) 1990?

KEY POINTS

9.2

- For any shift in the supply schedule, a firm facing a relatively inelastic demand curve will experience a larger fluctuation in the price of the product. It is argued that, since the demand for food is relatively price inelastic, the prices farmers receive for their products fluctuate more than in other sectors of the economy when there are shifts in supply.

- Farmers operate in an environment rather different from other sectors of the economy. When there are many geographically separate decision-making units quite independent of each other and time lags exist before planned changes in output are realized, market-clearing prices will be unstable.

Policy options to help farmers

If farmers suffer from such major fluctuations in prices and hence incomes, what can be done about the problem? Is it a problem anyway?

Many economists would agree that price instability in an unregulated agricultural sector results in a poor working mechanism to effect resource reallocation. Where cobweb-type swings in production occur there is either an excessive expansion of production or an excessive reduction in production. Greater price 'stability' would avoid unnecessary changes in production and perhaps give farmers greater confidence about the future. We can recognize at once, however, that measures which aim at giving farmers greater price stability should not be confused with other policies that are explicitly intended to raise the incomes of farmers above free-market levels. In fact, the two issues tend to be difficult to separate from each other completely. We can show this by examining the **buffer stock** approach to meeting the problem of price instability.

Buffer stocks

Price fluctuations might be minimized if an organization exists that buys in supplies in times of plentiful harvests and sells these when harvests are poor. Its purchases and sales could help to smooth out the course of market prices. In Figure 9.4, we show how such a buffer stock scheme might work.

If the buffer stock aims at maintaining the target price of P_3, then it would buy up supplies that would otherwise result in lower market-clearing prices. In Figure 9.4, buying $R - Q$ would avoid the fall in the market equilibrium price to P_1. If, however, supplies were scarce, then in

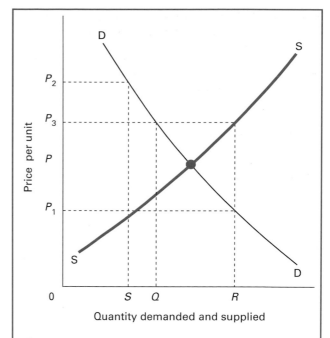

Figure 9.4

The operation of a buffer stock

The aim is to maintain the price of P_3. If the harvest is plentiful, buying $R - Q$ could ensure a market price of P_3 rather than P_1. If the crop is poor, selling $Q - S$ would reduce the market price to P_3 from P_2.

the absence of intervention the market price would be P_2. By selling $Q - S$ output at a price of P_3, then the buffer stock organization would help to make the market price conform to its target price.

Such a scheme is assumed just to eliminate price fluctuations arising from variations in supply. If the target price is set at a level which corresponds to what the average free-market price would have been for several time periods, then it should find that its purchases and sales balance out. It is neither a net gainer of stocks, that is, needs more storage capacity, nor short of funds to purchase stocks when there is a bumper harvest. Clearly, those commodities that cannot be stored over time are immediately ruled out of consideration for any buffer stock scheme. But even where this problem of perishability does not exist, such a scheme assumes that the target price is set at the appropriate level. If the target price turns out to have been set too high, that is, above the actual average free-market price, the buffer stock managers will find more activity in purchasing than selling. They will in fact need more physical space to store such production that has been bought in for stockpiling. The managers of a buffer stock scheme would also of course be facing the need for more financial resources. In order to keep prices stable by buying up excess supplies, they might well need almost unlimited funds to carry on with the task! Perhaps you can therefore appreciate why buffer stocks, while simple in concept, involve tricky problems concerning their financing. Should farmers be left to finance the buffer stock, or should their customers also be involved?

A buffer stock scheme may stabilize prices somewhat, but does not solve the fluctuating income problem. Remember, income is price multiplied by quantity sold. Variations in production will thus result in similar variations in income if the buffer stock is 'successful' in keeping its target price unchanged. How, then, can the unstable income problem be tackled? Here we can again deploy the concept of elasticity, this time unitary price elasticity. You should recall from Chapter 5 that when price elasticity is unitary, total revenue is unchanged when there is a change in prices. In Figure 9.5, the rectangular hyperbola DD–DD_1, where price elasticity is constant and equal to 1, shows how stability of farmers' incomes could in theory be achieved. If production was Q the market price has to be P_1 in order that the aim of fixed total income is fulfilled. At market price P_1 demand is Q_1 so the buffer stock buys in quantity $Q - Q_1$ over and above this market demand.

If production is Q_2 due to a poor crop, stability of income requires a price of P_3 to exist. Given the demand curve at market price P_3 the buffer stock needs to sell $Q_3 - Q_2$ from previously stored output.

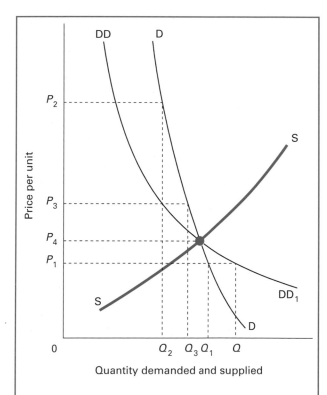

Figure 9.5
Price and income stability
Demand curve DD–DD_1 shows unitary price elasticity of demand. If supplies are plentiful, that is, Q, the required market price for income stability is P_1 and $Q - Q_1$ needs to be purchased by the buffer stock. With a poor crop, that is, Q_2, the buffer stock can release some of its stocks $Q_3 - Q_2$ at the required selling price P_2. What relevance has price P_4?

Corn in Egypt

And Pharaoh said unto Joseph I have dreamed a dream and there is none that can interpret it ... I saw in my dream seven ears came up in one stalk, full and good. And, behold, seven ears, withered, thin, and blasted with the east wind spring up after them. And the thin ears devoured the seven good ears ... And Joseph said unto Pharaoh, God hath shewed Pharaoh what he is about to do ... The seven good ears are seven years.

Behold there come seven years of great plenty throughout all the land of Egypt. And there shall arise after them seven years of famine ... and Joseph went out from the presence of Pharaoh and went throughout all the land of Egypt. And in the seven plenteous years the earth brought forth by handfuls. And he gathered up all the food of the seven years, which were in the land of Egypt, and laid up the food in the cities: the food of the field, which was round about every city, laid he up in the same. And Joseph gathered corn as the sand of the sea, very much, until he left numbering: for it was without number.

Source: *Genesis* 41: 29–49

7 What great advantage did Joseph have in operating the simplest form of buffer stock?
8 What is the contrast between the policy followed by Joseph in Egypt and a present-day buffer stock scheme that makes operation of the latter much more complex?

KEY POINT

9.3

■ In theory the problem of price instability facing farmers can be solved by a buffer stock buying in supplies when harvests are plentiful and selling its stocks when harvests are poor. In practice buffer stocks neither operate with ease nor solve the basic problem facing farmers, which is variable income.

Price supports

So far we have used simple supply and demand analysis to illustrate the problem of price instability facing farmers. Let us now turn to use our understanding of price determination to show the implications of government intervention.

During the 1930s the farm sector in the United States suffered falling prices and incomes. The US government created the Federal Farm Board to begin price stabilization operations for poor farmers. The Farm Board was supposed to use the money to support the price of farm products so that farmers' incomes would not fall so much. Essentially, it bought crops to keep their prices from falling. Then, when the Great Depression got into full swing, a system of **price supports** came into being. There have been some forms of price support for wheat, feed grains, cotton, tobacco, rice, peanuts, soybeans, dairy products and sugar. A type of price-support system was also introduced into the United Kingdom after 1945 and remained at the heart of British agricultural policy until entry into the then European Economic Community (EEC) (now the European Union, EU). So let us now graphically analyse the effect of a price-support system.

A price-support system is precisely what the name implies. Somehow the government stabilizes or fixes the price of an agricultural product so that it cannot fall below a certain level. Look at the supply and demand curves in Figure 9.6, showing the market demand and market supply of wheat. Competitive forces would yield an equilibrium price of P_e and an equilibrium quantity of Q_e per unit time period. If the government sets the support price at P_e or below, obviously there will be no change, because the farmers can sell all they want at the market-clearing price P_e.

Thus to achieve any help for farmers the government will set the support price above P_e – say, at P_s. At P_s the

quantity demanded is only Q_d, but the quantity supplied is Q_s. That is, at the higher price, there is a smaller quantity demanded but a larger quantity supplied. The difference is the *excess quantity* supplied – a '*surplus*'. Producers respond to higher market prices by producing more. That is why we show the supply schedule as upward sloping. At the higher prices, farmers are able to incur higher production costs and still make a profit. They will keep producing up to the point where the support price cuts the supply curve. The government guarantees to purchase everything the wheat-farmers want to sell at the price P_s. The government is therefore pledged to acquire the quantity of wheat represented by the distance between Q_s and Q_d in Figure 9.6.

The price-support system just described gives farmers the benefit of a guaranteed price and there is now not much significance in the market equilibrium – P_e in Figure 9.7. But suppose the government wishes to allow market forces to operate more fully while still committing itself to assisting farmers. The guaranteed or target price system is one such answer. In the case of the United Kingdom, a **guaranteed price**-support system began after the Second World War and was at the heart of agricultural policy until British entry into the then EEC. In 1973 the US government introduced a **target price** system, which incorporates the same principles as the former UK policy. Let us explain how the guaranteed price system operates, again with reference to a diagram.

Guaranteed prices differ from price supports in that the government guarantees that each farmer (who qualifies for inclusion in the system) will receive at least the guaranteed price. If the guaranteed price for wheat, for example, is £50 per tonne, and the market-clearing price is £40 per tonne, farmers may become eligible for so-called **deficiency payments** that will equal the difference between the guaranteed price of £50 and the market-clearing price of £40 multiplied by the total number of tonnes that the farmer has sold on the open market. A deficiency payment is simply another way to describe a direct subsidy paid to the farmer so the terms 'guarantee price', 'deficiency payment' and 'subsidy' are just what they seem to be. The government promised to make up the difference between the market-clearing price and the price which it deemed was appropriate that farmers should receive for their output.

Figure 9.7 shows the working of guaranteed prices in graphic format. We have already analysed market price and the support price in Figure 9.6, where we showed that, when the support price was greater than the market price, there would be an excess quantity supplied ('surplus') at the support price.

The concept of a guaranteed price is slightly different because it involves no direct purchase by government and thus no storage of the crop by government. In Figure 9.7, we show the market demand as DD and market supply as SS. At price P_T the quantity supplied will be equal to Q_T. At that quantity, however, consumers will only purchase it at P_c. Therefore the subsidy to each farmer is equal to the vertical difference between P_T and P_c multiplied by the number of units that the farmer sells. We have

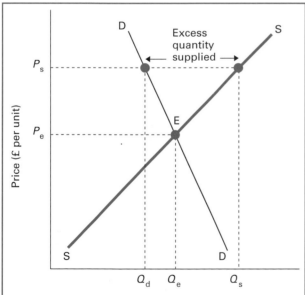

Figure 9.6
Price supports
The domestic market demand and supply curves are given by DD and SS. The equilibrium price is P_e and the equilibrium quantity Q_e. If the government sets a support price at P_s, the quantity demanded is Q_d and the quantity supplied is Q_s. The difference is the excess quantity supplied, or surplus, which the government must somehow take care of.

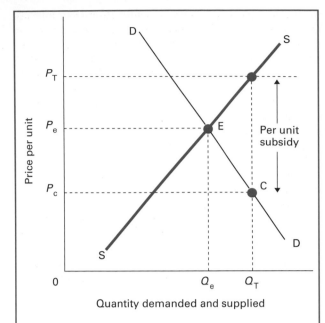

Figure 9.7
Guaranteed prices
We show the market demand curve DD and the market supply curve SS. The market equilibrium price is P_e and the equilibrium quantity is Q_e. The government, however, sets the target price P_T above the market equilibrium price. The total market quantity produced will be Q_T. But the market-clearing price is P_c. This means that the government must pay the vertical difference between P_c and P_T. This is the 'per unit subsidy'.

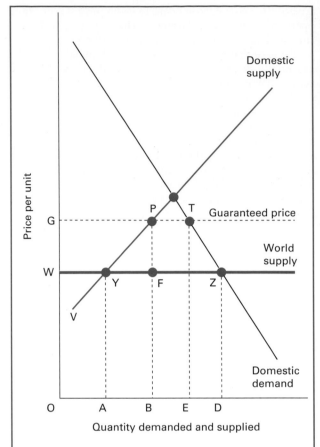

Figure 9.8
The impact of deficiency payments in an open economy
If we assume that New Zealand could supply butter at a price of OW (the world price) then British farmers will supply OA at this price. Imports of butter are AD. The supply curve for both the United Kingdom and imports is thus VYZ. However, the effect of the guaranteed price OG stimulates home production and the UK share of the butter market increases from OA to OB. Imports are now BD. The supply curve for both the United Kingdom and imports is thus VYPTZ. Can you work out what the area OGPB means?

labelled it 'per unit subsidy'. Guaranteed prices therefore lead to a greater use of resources, greater output and greater consumption than in an unrestricted market. With this understanding of the effects of a guarantee system at work we need to pose the question of who pays for the intervention. The funds required to pay farmers these subsidies obviously had to come from somewhere: using taxpayers' money meant that taxpayers were assisting consumers. In so far as rich people paid more in tax than poorer people, the farm-support system in the United Kingdom was viewed by many as being socially acceptable. It was regarded as fair and enabled consumers to enjoy lower prices for food than would otherwise have been the case.

How did the price-support system affect Britain's overseas supplies of foodstuffs? We can now modify our diagram to show the effect of guaranteed prices on imports of food.

If we assume that overseas suppliers of, say, butter are willing to supply an unlimited quantity of food to the British market at a particular price, then the supply curve will be perfectly elastic. If, for example, New Zealand was able to offer Great Britain butter at prices below those at which British farmers could compete, then the market price would be determined by the imported product.

Figure 9.8 shows that at the market price of OW imports of butter from New Zealand amount to AD and home-produced supplies to OA. The effect of the deficiency payment system is to raise the proportion of total supplies accounted for by home-produced supplies and diminish that of imports. The quantity of butter from New Zealand is now BD rather than AD. Thus the price-support system did not shut off supplies from abroad and deny British consumers the benefit of cheap food from countries who for geographical and climatic reasons were able to produce food at low cost. However, the result of the price guarantees was to increase the degree of self-sufficiency of British food supplies.

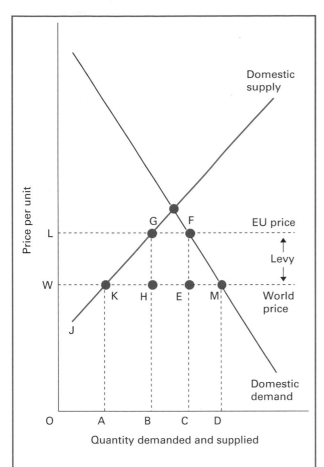

Figure 9.9

The impact of levies in an open economy

If we assume that New Zealand could supply butter at a price of OW (the world price) then British farmers will supply OA at this price. Imports of butter thus dominate the UK market, being AD. The supply curve for both the United Kingdom and imports is thus JKM. However, the effect of imposing a levy WL stimulates home production and the UK share of the butter market increases from OA to OB. Imports are now BC. The new supply curve for both the United Kingdom and imports is JKGF. Can you work out what the area GFEH means?

The European system

On its entry into the then EEC, the United Kingdom began to move the basis of its agricultural support system over to an **import levy** system. Under this method of agricultural support the prices of imported foodstuffs are raised by levies to bring them into line with target prices. Figure 9.9 is a simple illustration of this system, indicating how this policy results in consumers of food supporting farmers directly through high market prices. The levies on imported food are paid into a common farm fund known as FEOGA (the initials of its French title), which is partly used to subsidize the disposal of excess stocks. In so far as the EU's target prices have generally been well above world

prices, the cost of this method of agricultural support has been considerable. For some commodities the output of the EU's farmers has vastly exceeded consumption at the targeted price – hence the infamous butter 'mountains' and wine 'lakes'. The costly storage and subsequent disposal of these stockpiles has, not surprisingly, been a controversial issue. Should excess butter supplies be offered at a substantial discount on world prices to the Russians? Why should low-cost suppliers like New Zealand who are non-members of the EU find their trade unfairly disrupted by the disposal of such stocks?

Not surprisingly, the cost of agricultural support programmes in the EU has been the subject of much critical comment. Agriculture and fisheries have accounted for well over half of the budget of the EU. In 1993 the percentage was nearly three-fifths of the budget, having been two-thirds in 1986. So the Common Agricultural Policy (CAP) has involved a burden for the members of the EU. But as we shall see later, it is not only governments who are affected by supporting farmers: taxpayers and consumers finance subsidies for farmers.

In 1992 the EU extended a recent approach, which involved paying farmers to take part of their cropland out of production – the set-aside policy. In 1994 an area approximately equal to the size of Surrey was out of production. Farmers are paid a sum for the area set aside and also receive direct income payments for each acre planted with cereal crops. However, the latter payment is a compensation for the reduction of guaranteed prices, which are being rapidly lowered to world market levels. The Ministry of Agriculture estimated that in June 1994 the set-aside scheme involved 634 000 hectares in England.

While the set-aside approach tries to tackle the continuing problem of grain surpluses, critics point to the basic problem that the CAP does not work well in terms of supporting small farmers. But this is not surprising because most financial aid for farmers is tied to production. The EU has estimated that about 20 per cent of farms produce about 80 per cent of agricultural output. Farmers who produce on a large scale derive a similar proportion of the financial support for farmers.

If the English countryside is not wanted for growing food, then country conservation may be desirable for its own sake. Critics of agricultural policy argue that a policy for country conservation has not yet been carefully developed. It is argued that subsidies for farmers have encouraged intensive farming methods, which have led to the disappearance of hedgerows, pockets of marshland and coppices, which in turn has reduced both the number and variety of bird and animal life in the countryside. Critics find it hard to discern a clear rationale for the way in which different types of farm qualify for government help. Figure 9.10 shows how government subsidy accounts for a varied proportion of farm income.

Figure 9.10
How different UK farmers are subsidized

Sheep farm, Cumbria

60%

Stowgill Farm, a 480-hectare holding just outside the Yorkshire Dales National Park, is devoted entirely to hill sheep production. The farm is designated as being in a 'Less Favoured Area' and as 'Severely Disadvantaged'. Subsidies contribute about 60 per cent of the farm's total income. This is paid as Sheep Annual Premium and Hill Livestock Compensatory Allowance.

Arable farm, Cambridgeshire

6%

Lynford House Farm, covering 504 hectares near Ely, is entirely arable. Subsidies contribute about 6 per cent of the farm's total income. This is derived from the Arable Area Aid, paid on the wheat crops, and associated set-aside payments.

Fruit Farm, Kent

6.8%

The Four Wents is a 62-hectare hop and fruit farm in the Weald of Kent. 6.8 per cent of the farm's hop income comes from EU aid for hop-growers.

Organic farm, Somerset

5–7%

Aviaries Farm is an organic dairy and arable farm near Shepton Montague. Subsidies and grants contribute between 5 per cent and 7 per cent of the farm's total income, mainly as Arable Area Aid for cereal crops.

Mixed farm, West Midlands

25%

Penilan Farm is a 440-acre mixed arable, suckler cow and sheep farm near the English–Welsh border. It is in what the EU calls a 'Less Favoured Area'. Subsidies and grants contribute about 25 per cent of the farm's total income. They include Arable Area Aid, paid for cereal crops; Sheep Annual Premium Payments (SAPPs); and Hill Livestock Compensatory Allowance (HLCA).

Livestock farm, Wales

37%

Merthyr Farm, a 126-hectare farm in the Snowdonia National Park, has sheep and suckler cows. Subsidies and grants contribute about 37 per cent of its income. It is in a Less Favoured Area, reflecting the harsh environment and lower stocking rates facing hill-farmers.

Source: *The Guardian*, 9 December 1997

9 In the light of the information above, what is the average farm subsidy in the UK? How meaningful is the figure that you have calculated?

10 Would you expect other members of the EU to derive greater benefit from the CAP than the UK?

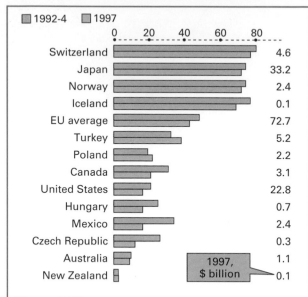

Figure 9.11
Farm subsidies
Producer-subsidy equivalents as a percentage of value of production

Source: *The Economist*, 8 August 1998, p. 97

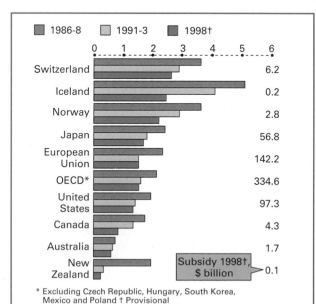

Figure 9.12
Support to agriculture as a percentage of GDP

Source: *The Economist*, 5 June 1999, p. 139

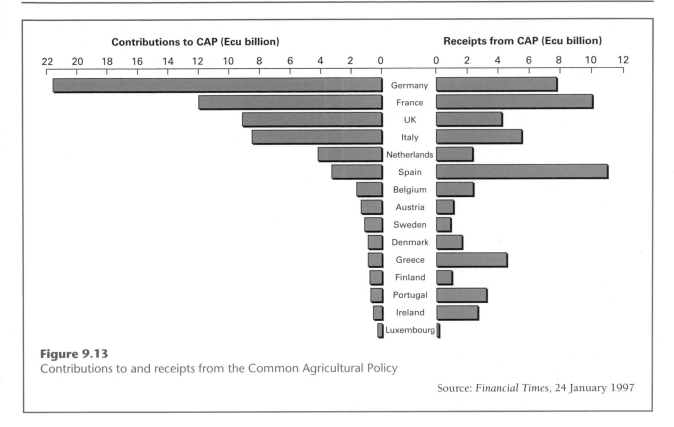

Figure 9.13
Contributions to and receipts from the Common Agricultural Policy

Source: *Financial Times*, 24 January 1997

We have focused attention on the United Kingdom and the EU, but it is important to recognize that farmers in all developed economies are supported through a variety of policies, including price-support programmes, direct payments and cheap loans. The Organization for Economic Co-operation and Development (OECD) calls all such measures for main crops 'producer-subsidy equivalents' (PSE) and has calculated their size. For the OECD as a whole the PSE was $151 billion in 1997, which amounted to 34 per cent of farmers' total income. Although the PSE for the EU was by far the biggest in dollar terms, as a proportion of its agricultural production it was lower than in some other countries. Figure 9.11 shows how the EU compares in terms of PSE with other developed economies. Figure 9.12 shows the extent of government support for agriculture as measured as a proportion of GDP. Figure 9.13 shows how members of the EU make contributions to, and receive payments from, the CAP.

Farmers, taxpayers and consumers

11 With regard to Figure 9.11, what proportion of the value of agricultural production in Canada in 1997 did its farmers obtain other than from government support?

12 Has the cost of agricultural support policies as measured by producer-subsidy equivalents continued to increase in all countries?

13 What is noticeable about the cost of agricultural support in the two countries from the southern hemisphere?

14 With reference to Figure 9.12, has the extent of agricultural support in all OECD countries been rising or falling within the time period shown?

15 In which European country does agricultural support account for the highest proportion of GDP?

16 Figure 9.12 shows that the country with the highest level of agricultural support in 1998 was the United States. How do you account for the fact that as a proportion of GDP, this level of agricultural support was below the OECD average?

17 With reference to Figure 9.13, which countries are net beneficiaries of the CAP?

18 Would you expect countries such as Cyprus, Poland and Hungary as prospective new members of the EU to be net beneficiaries of the CAP?

KEY POINTS

9.4

- Governments in developed economies have tried several methods to resolve the problem of low and unstable farm incomes in a free market.

- Price supports can give farmers a stable price but leave a problem for the government to dispose of surplus stocks at the supported price.

- Guaranteed prices ensure that each farmer will receive the price determined by the government and thus qualify for a subsidy or deficiency payment in excess of the newly determined market price.

- A guaranteed price system has an impact on the use of resources as well as on the levels of domestically produced output, domestic consumption and share of the market accounted for by imports.

- A farm-support system can be based on making food imports more expensive by imposing levies or taxes. This system means that consumers bear the burden of the policy rather than taxpayers.

The agricultural problem in a wider context

Our brief review of farm-support programmes in the real world has illustrated how powerfully the theory of supply and demand can give us insights into present-day political issues. We can see why unregulated markets in the agricultural sector of the economy can work ineffectively. But government intervention, while trying to solve these free-market weaknesses, itself brings further problems. In short, we can appreciate that the interests of the farming community have posed a significant political issue for governments. The farming lobby can have a political influence out of proportion to actual numbers. About 80 per cent of people in France live in towns, but they regard themselves as a predominantly agricultural nation, having grown up in the countryside. Thus trade liberalization in the GATT talks during 1993 found the government in France facing a strong farm lobby. But our case study of the operation of the market system has done more than just point to the implications of government intervention in the agricultural sector. We have moved the focus of our attention away from just one closed economy isolated from all others. Our analysis of the deficiency payments system and import levies pointed to the impact on countries other than the United Kingdom. Modern economies are open economies, that is, they are interdependent. Consumers in different countries demand goods and services from sources other than domestic suppliers. As we saw above in the case of

agriculture, government intervention has implications for the extent of international trade and exchange. We must therefore note the important point that government intervention in a domestic market can have an international dimension. Thus paying UK farmers more than they would receive given the existing world price means there is a world resource allocation impact to be considered. We must look at the whole picture and not just the immediate and local part.

A second point to note about the agricultural sector is that it raises the important matter of how government intervention in markets is to be financed. We referred both to subsidies and levies on imports. The latter are, in effect, taxes on goods. Under the pre–1973 system the United Kingdom used tax revenues to subsidize domestic production. Where did these revenues come from? Under the current system the United Kingdom along with its EU partners raises tax revenue by charging importers of food at the point of entry into the EU. What we now need to do is examine in more detail how governments impose taxes on goods and services. Such taxes are known as indirect taxes. We shall aim to do this with the demand and supply model at the heart of the analysis.

Indirect taxes

Taxes imposed by governments on goods and services are so-called indirect taxes because they are in some form eventually paid by consumers. Such indirect taxes contrast with a tax on one's income or wealth (direct taxes), which is paid directly by the taxpayer to the government. An employer deducts tax from weekly or monthly wages before the employee receives his or her pay packet. The amount of tax deducted depends on the taxpayer's individual circumstances, as we saw in Chapter 7. There is no option concerning non-payment of income tax. However, an item on sale in a supermarket which is subject to tax does not vary in price according to the personal circumstances of the potential purchaser of the good. If someone does not buy the good, they pay no tax. Even if someone does purchase the good that is taxed, that consumer may not be paying all the tax per unit imposed on the good. How can this be?

The supply side

When government imposes a tax on a good or service the effect is to shift the supply schedule upwards and to the left. This is because it is the responsibility of a supplier to collect an indirect tax when goods are manufactured or sold and to pay over the tax to the government. In Figure 9.14 we assume that a good not previously subject to tax now has a tax of $P_3 - P_1$ per unit imposed. This shifts the supply schedule upwards and leftwards by an equal amount throughout the length of the original supply curve.

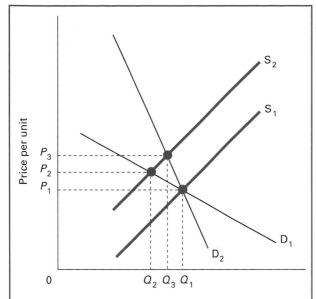

Figure 9.14
The impact of indirect taxes
Demand schedule D_1 shows that quantity demanded is more price sensitive than for D_2. If the pre-tax price for both goods is P_1, the price, post-tax, is P_2 in the case of D_1 but P_3 in the case of D_2.

The demand side

The tax paid by the supplier to the government can be recovered from the consumer by adding the tax onto the price charged. The effect of the tax upon the price and quantity demanded of the good will depend on the price elasticity of demand for that good. Figure 9.14 shows two demand schedules with quite different sensitivities of demand to the prices charged. What difference do the two demand curves make to the situation?

The effect of the indirect tax

The imposition of the tax results in the supply schedule moving from S_1 to S_2. In the case of the demand schedule D_1 the market price now rises from P_1 to P_2 and quantity demanded falls from Q_1 to Q_2. But if the demand curve D_2 is now considered we note the price rises from P_1 to P_3, which is much greater. The fall in the quantity demanded is less – from Q_1 to Q_3 – than in the case of demand schedule D_1. Why is this? It is simply because D_1 indicates that consumers are more sensitive in their willingness to buy quantities of the good as the price is altered. In the case of D_2 the price elasticity of demand is, broadly speaking, lower, reflecting a relatively greater insensitivity of consumers to upward movements in prices charged.

Let us set out the conclusion from this analysis. A government that wishes to raise tax revenue should impose indirect taxes on those goods, the consumption of which is relatively insensitive to a tax-based increase in price. If demand for a good is highly price elastic when the tax is imposed, then the tax revenue obtained is less than where demand is less price elastic.

Our conclusion may not seem too surprising. Thus cigarettes may seem to you to be a more obvious item to tax than, say, works of art. But a moment's reflection should make you realize that low price elasticity of demand for the commodity is not the only relevant aspect in selecting suitable bases for indirect taxes. Consumption of a good has to be sufficiently large for a tax to raise much revenue. Some foodstuffs, as we saw in Chapter 5, have a low price elasticity of demand, but taxing, say, butter and cheese may not be acceptable to a government. The price of basic necessities such as food has long been of political importance and thus governments have seen a more promising base for an indirect tax in the 'optional necessities' of tobacco and alcohol. Thus for many years the price charged for cigarettes, beer, wines and spirits includes a large element of tax. These commodities need not be purchased, although few citizens are total abstainers! Leaving aside the moral question of a government's revenues being at least partially dependent on the addiction of citizens to smoking and drinking, the choice of tobacco and alcoholic drinks as suitable bases for an indirect tax is quite understandable. But do smokers pay all the tax per unit that is imposed? This takes us to the matter of **tax incidence**.

Tax incidence

The term 'tax incidence' refers to who bears the burden of a tax. Does it fall wholly on the consumer, or does the supplier pay part of a tax?

Figure 9.15 shows the demand for two goods which have differing sensitivities of quantity demanded to prices charged. If a tax of the same rate per unit is now imposed on both goods, what happens? In the case of good T, the market price is now P_2 rather than P_1. The tax per unit is BD, of which the consumer pays BC. In the case of good W, the rise in the market price is from P_3 to P_4. Here the consumer pays GH of the same tax per unit GI. Clearly, in the case of good T the consumer pays only a small part of the tax burden. The supplier has to bear most of the tax burden since demand is relatively price elastic. In the case of good W the reverse happens: the supplier bears just the amount HI of the tax burden. The supplier is the more able to pass on the tax burden since demand for W is less sensitive than is the case with good T. The supplier of good W faces less of a difficulty in trading since his or her profit margin in selling good W is that much less squeezed. Both suppliers, however, bear some burden and face the issue of whether they can somehow reduce the costs of selling these goods.

What would happen if the demand curve was perfectly inelastic rather than either of the two situations in Figure 9.15? Here you should satisfy yourself that the full impact of a flat-rate (or specific) indirect tax falls wholly on the consumer.

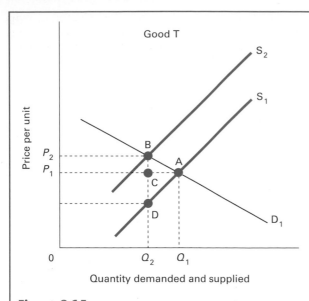 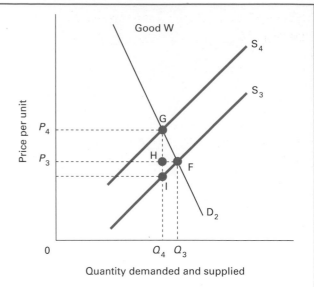

Figure 9.15
The incidence of indirect taxes

Good T			Good W	
Pre-tax price	P_1		Pre-tax price	P_3
Tax per unit	BD (= GI)		Tax per unit	GI
Post-tax price	P_2		Post-tax price	P_4
Consumer's burden	BC		Consumer's burden	GH
Supplier's burden	CD		Supplier's burden	HI

Whose tax burden?

Suppose that the pre-tax price in Figure 9.15 is £13 and Q_2 is 20 units. The specific tax is £10 per unit. The post-tax price now rises to £17 (P_2 in Figure 9.15).

19 What is the tax burden facing consumers per unit? **A✓**

20 How much is the total tax revenue contributed by both consumers and producers? **A✓**

21 What is the tax burden facing producers per unit? **A✓**

22 What is the proportion of total tax revenue contributed by producers? **A✓**

An *ad valorem* tax

Our example of an indirect tax was a flat-rate tax such that the post-tax supply curve shifted to the left throughout its length by the same amount. If the tax varies according to the value of the item as charged by suppliers the tax is called an *ad valorem* tax. Thus a 10 per cent *ad valorem* tax would result in a higher tax being payable on an item sold at £10 compared with an item sold at £5. The effect of an *ad valorem* tax is to make the post-tax supply curve diverge from the pre-tax supply curve as we move from left to right. This divergence is explained of course by the direct relationship of the tax with the prices that producers seek to obtain for their goods. Our earlier example of a flat-rate tax

is the simplest form of indirect tax, but in the real world *ad valorem* taxes are exemplified by value-added tax (VAT), which is charged on many goods and services at a rate of 17.5 per cent. Can you think of reasons why governments might favour a tax on such a sliding-scale basis?

Let us now summarize the matter of the relative burden of an indirect tax: where demand for a good is relatively price sensitive the burden of an indirect tax will be shared between the consumer and the producer. Only in the case of a totally price-inelastic demand schedule would the whole tax burden be borne by the consumer.

KEY POINTS

9.5

- The degree of price elasticity of demand at and around the given market price will be relevant to a government seeking to raise revenue by imposing an indirect tax.

- The nature of the demand and supply schedules will affect how the incidence of an indirect tax is borne between consumers and suppliers.

- Indirect taxes can be at a flat rate per unit or the tax per unit can increase in proportion to the price charged (an *ad valorem* tax).

Market prices and government controls

In the final part of this chapter we move on from consideration of the impact and incidence of indirect taxes to another form of government intervention with free-market prices. Whereas the imposition of such taxes is of a long-standing and continuing nature, our next examination of government intervention is essentially of a type both more limited in scope and short term in its duration. We shall analyse the economic effects of governments applying statutory controls over prices. Price controls can be in the form of specific fixed maximum prices, fixed minimum prices or general controls over prices and/or price increases. We consider each of these policies against a background that intervention is deemed necessary because the existing free-market price (or prices) is (are) for one or more reasons not appropriate.

Specific fixed maximum prices

If the government fixes a maximum price in a given market below the existing market equilibrium price, then that newly established price will have profound implications for the operation of that market. Why? Let us look again at the supply and demand dimensions with reference to Figure 9.16. In the United Kingdom and in several other countries, rents that can be charged for property rented from landlords are subject to controls. The rationale for a maximum price to be charged is that it is necessary to keep

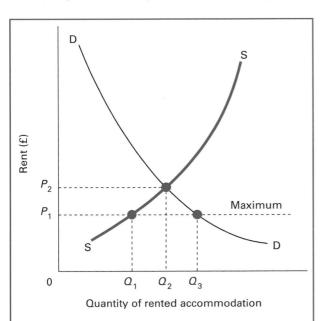

Figure 9.16
The market for private rented accommodation
The free market equilibrium price is P_2. A maximum price for rented property of P_1 means that demand is Q_3 but supply available is only Q_1.

the cost of housing as low as possible. Control of rents charged by landlords is usually one interference with the housing market; tax benefits for owner-occupiers paying for their houses with long-term loans or mortgages is yet another illustration of the social and political concern of governments with housing. Our concern here is not to query the motivation to influence the prices people have to pay for occupying either the houses they own or the property in which they are temporarily residing. But we can point out as an exercise in positive economics that Rent Acts and other policies which permit rent reductions have significant repercussions on both sides of the housing market – landlords and tenants.

In Figure 9.16 the demand for rented accommodation at the maximum rent that can be charged – price P_1 – is Q_3. But at this price – below an equilibrium price P_2 – landlords only supply Q_1 and the distance between Q_1 and Q_3 is unsatisfied demand at the rent P_1. Those unable to obtain privately owned property can only try to buy a house or seek accommodation within the public sector. Landlords who are not prepared to make rented housing available at the controlled price may sell their property, leave it empty or use it for purposes other than temporary accommodation. Whatever response, the upshot is that the supply side contracts and thus a maximum rent policy really only benefits those fortunate enough to find and live in rented accommodation. Our analysis thus points to maximum rent policies discouraging the supply of rented private housing. In the United Kingdom we find that this proposition has been borne out. Since the 1967 Rent Act the percentage of the total stock of dwellings accounted for by rented private accommodation has fallen sharply. Whereas in 1967 the figure was 24 per cent, it has since then fallen steadily to less than 8 per cent by 1990.

Of course, maximum prices only have effects such as in Figure 9.16 if they are set below the equilibrium market price. If set at or above the equilibrium price, then a maximum price will be of no consequence. You should convince yourself why this must be so: consider what the equilibrium price means.

General price controls

Our consideration of interventions in the markets for housing illustrates how governments have a concern to modify the operation of certain free-market prices. But governments also have a general concern about the pace at which all prices move upward. This concern is not new. In 1800 BC the ruler of Babylonia decreed that anyone caught violating his wage and price freeze would be drowned. In AD 301 the Roman Emperor Diocletian fixed the maximum price of beef, grain, eggs and clothing and prescribed the death penalty for violators.

Moving to more recent times, we should note that during the Second World War many countries imposed **price controls** on a wide range of goods and services. Such controls gave rise to the problem of their enforcement and thus control of **black markets**. We can analyse the effect of

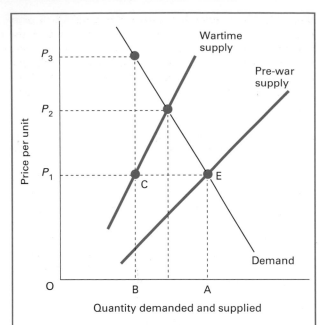

Figure 9.17
Black market and rationing
The market-clearing price is P_1 in peacetime and P_2 in a wartime economy. Price control at the level P_1 means the black market price is P_3. At the controlled price CE is the excess demand. Rationing distributes the available supplies OB when demand at the controlled price is OA.

a black market by reference to the supply and demand diagram in Figure 9.17.

Assume that Figure 9.17 represented the market in, say, sugar in 1938. On the outbreak of war the UK government took over the allocation of the now scarcer raw materials, with the result that sugar producers in the United Kingdom (in common with many other manufacturers) were unable to produce as freely as in 1938. The supply curve then shifted to the left, with the result that, left to market forces, the price would rise from P_1 to P_2. The market mechanism rations the scarcer commodity, but at a price. If the government prescribes a maximum price of, say, P_1, then a black market in sugar can develop. The price in the illegal black market will be bid up to P_3 because that is the price at which all available supplies can be sold. The distance CE represents the shortage at the controlled 'white market' price. If, as seems likely for social reasons, the government is unable to accept the working of the price mechanism in distributing available supplies, what can it do? If it rejects a 'first come, first served' method by which the scarce supplies are distributed, then some rationing system is necessary. What this means is that households are allocated coupons on a regular basis by which they are entitled to claim at least some sugar per week or per month. The quantities may be less than those for which many are prepared to pay. But at least the rationing system meets the objection that because

there is not an equal distribution of incomes, the free working of the price system is unjust in its operation. How else can it be ensured that pensioners and those on low incomes obtain some sugar and other basic foodstuffs?

Price controls thus tend to require the introduction of rationing systems. In a normal peacetime market economy neither is necessary. But that does not mean that the issue of food and other prices is not still politically important.

As we saw in Chapter 8, the rate of movement of prices in general has been the key aspect of government economic policies. But the concern is not new since nearly all post-war UK governments have resorted to policies to control the rate of price inflation. By inflation we mean a sustained and persistent rise in prices. Sometimes governments have used statutory or formal means to moderate the pace of inflation. At other times the policies used have been informal and relied on voluntary co-operation rather than legal sanctions to achieve results. Sometimes the emphasis is on controlling the rate of increase in wages in the belief that wage costs are the key element in determining prices. Yet other policies have been almost solely concerned with limiting price rises irrespective of any justification. The proper place to appraise general policies affecting the whole or greater part of the economic system is within the macro section of this book and hence is deferred until Part E. But from a micro perspective we can emphasize the need to examine the supply and demand aspects of a rise in price, whether it be of one good or many goods. As we have seen, there is upward pressure on the price level if the demand schedule moves to the right and/or the supply schedule shifts to the left. Artificial limits on prices prevent market forces from working themselves out. A kettle of boiling water cannot be controlled by fixing down the lid if there is a force due to heat at work, whether the heat is produced by gas or electricity. At some point the build-up of pressure will force the lid off and have possibly serious effects. The market system adjusts to supply and demand pressures and there are dangers if the government pursues a policy of allowing only uniform rates of increase in wages and prices. Why is this? If prices cannot move according to the circumstances of particular markets, then the resource allocation function of prices cannot operate properly. If relative prices get out of line, then inappropriate signals are being conveyed. For example, if the government has a statutory policy which permits only a flat-rate increase in wages, then those who receive lower wages than the average for all workers are relatively better off. This effect may be viewed as socially desirable but, by definition, there will be a narrowing of the wage differentials between the wages for different occupations. Firms who seek people in skilled jobs cannot pay them more in order to attract them. If there is a shortage, none is indicated by the wage signal in the labour market. The same difficulty arises with a statutory prices policy. In practice, governments recognize that such policies need to be flexible and allow for special circumstances. They have learned that everyone claims to be a special case requiring relaxation from the general adherence to the norm! How many exceptions can there be before no policy is left in force?

Minimum wage rates

In contrast to maximum prices, governments may fix a price which they deem is necessary because the free-market price is 'too low'. Again, setting a minimum price above what would be the free-market price has important effects and our example is taken from the labour market. In the United Kingdom a debate has arisen between those who support minimum wage rates and those critical of them. The latter argue that employment would be greater if wage rates were lower than at the regulated levels. Opponents argue that such state controls are a safety-net to prevent exploitation of workers by private employers. Let us see how we can understand the nature of the debate.

If you look at Figure 9.18 you can see that in an unrestricted labour market there will be an equilibrium wage rate at which equal quantities of labour are demanded and supplied. What if a legal **minimum wage rate** were set above the equilibrium wage rate? Who benefits and who loses from the imposition of a minimum wage rate above W_e? If a minimum wage W_m, which is higher than W_e, is imposed, the quantity demanded for labour is reduced to Q_D. Some of these workers may now be unemployed, but others may be employed at a lower wage elsewhere in the non-controlled sectors of the economy.

The analysis suggests that minimum wage legislation benefits some but not others, but this is not the end of the matter. We revisit this topic later in Chapter 12.

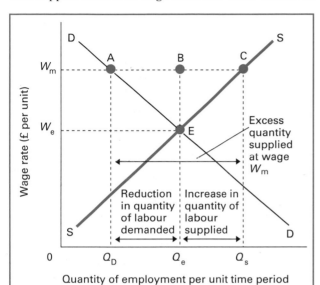

Figure 9.18
The effect of minimum wages
The market-clearing wage rate is W_e. The market-clearing quantity of employment is Q_e and is determined by the intersection of supply and demand at point E. A minimum wage equal to W_m is established. The quantity of labour demanded is reduced to Q_D; the reduction of employment from Q_e to Q_D is equal to the distance between B and A. That distance is smaller than the excess quantity of labour supplied at wage rate W_m. The distance between B and C is the increase in the quantity of labour supplied that results from the higher minimum wage rate.

KEY POINTS

9.6

- Governments tend to modify the operation of equilibrium prices for social and political reasons. Specific maximum price and minimum price controls have effects arising from the mismatch of supply and demand.

- A maximum price fixed below the equilibrium level results in a shortage of supply relative to quantity demanded.

- General price controls raise the possibility that relative prices are distorted and the signalling function of the price mechanism does not work effectively.

- A minimum price above the equilibrium results in surplus of supply relative to quantity demanded.

Case Study

Can we let agriculture die?

A remote hillside farm might seem about as far away as you can get from a global financial crisis. These days, however, even hill farms are not immune from storms on the currency markets.

Richard Nixon, a 60-year-old Scottish farmer, had hoped for another five years tending his flock of 890 blackface sheep at Snar Farm. In 1996, the flock, which straggles across 2500 acres of heather-clad hillside, yielded a profit of about £14 000. In 1997 he made £6500 and this year, he reckons, he will be lucky to make £3500. At the end of next month, he will give up the tenancy he has had for 30 years. Mr Nixon knows exactly what has caused lamb prices to fall: the strength of the pound has made British lamb expensive on world markets, and lost him markets in France. The collapse of the rouble has also hammered fleece and lamb-skin exports destined for Russia.

Although different factors have affected different products, it is the same dismal story for virtually everything else that British farmers produce. Beef-farming has been knocked sideways by the BSE panic. Pig-farmers, encouraged to expand by two years of good prices, have been clobbered as exports of pork and bacon to East Asia and Russia have slumped. Cereal farmers have been hit by a wet summer.

Tales of woe abound. Welsh sheep-farmers face prices as low as 50p for their lambs. A farmer in Somerset has shot some of his sheep, claiming this is cheaper than taking them for slaughter. These are, however, extreme cases. Mr Nixon's experience is more common: whereas last year his lambs fetched between £29 and £36, this year the average is about £17. And, despite the slump, hill-farmers attending this autumn's auctions are still willing to pay around £5000 for a ram (one star stud has fetched £41 000) to breed next year's lambs.

Swings in the market for their produce are the lot of farmers everywhere. But British farmers have been having a relatively good time of it of late. In 1980, Britain was a net importer of beef, lamb and pork; by 1995 it was a net exporter of these foods. After pleas from the National Farmers' Union, the government is considering emergency help for the poorest farmers. But reluctantly. Farmers already get £2.9 billion in direct subsidy and price support through the European common agricultural policy. In any other industry, such a subsidy (about £1 a week for each British citizen) would provoke huge controversy.

Look at farming as just another industry, and it is simply facing the same painful restructuring as, say, microelectronics. There are job losses, some, such as Mr Nixon's, brought about by early retirement. And there is the creation of larger, more efficient units. An economist at the TSB Bank Scotland says that although gains in technology have cut the number of farm-workers, the number of farmers has stayed roughly the same over the past 10 years.

New uses are also being found for land. More working farmers are selling up, cashing in on land prices which are still high because of demand for land by rich city-dwellers. Many of these are either looking to do a bit of hobby farming on fewer than 100 acres, or want to live in a big country house, and use farming tax exemptions to shelter their wealth from inheritance taxes.

For those who want to stay on the land, diversifying into other lines of business – such as holiday homes in remoter areas or golf ranges and courses closer to cities – is the best option. Another hope, though it is not popular with some farmers, is that reform of the common agricultural policy will pay farmers simply for being environmental custodians of their land.

None of this, however, impresses Mr Nixon. He already receives £7000 a year in subsidy to keep sheep off some of bits of his land, deemed to be environmentally sensitive. He has tried a sideline selling mineral supplements for animal feed, and his wife runs a catering business. But their farm is simply too far off the beaten track for tourism to work. Getting out is his only option, and to judge by the abandoned steadings and overgrown furrows further up the valley, it is a decision which has been taken by many others before him.

Source: *The Economist*, 17 October 1998, p. 40

1 Identify the factors which adversely affected Scottish sheep-farmers such as Mr Nixon in the late 1990s.
2 By how much in percentage terms had Mr Nixon's income fallen between 1996 and 1998?
3 What is the level of farm support of £2.9 billion in the UK if expressed as a sum per British citizen per week?
4 Why are some farmers better placed than others to reduce their dependence on farming?
5 Examine the arguments for and against subsidizing hill-farmers like Mr Nixon.

Exam Preparation

Multiple choice questions

1 Primary product prices will fluctuate most when
A the demand and supply curves are both price elastic
B the demand and supply curves are both price inelastic
C the demand and supply curves are both unit elastic
D the demand curve is price elastic and the supply curve is price inelastic
E the demand curve is price inelastic and the supply curve is price elastic

2 Given normal demand and supply curves and other things remaining equal, if a subsidy per unit on bread is withdrawn the result can be shown diagrammatically by
A the supply curve shifting to the left
B the supply curve shifting to the right
C an increase in the gradient of the supply curve
D the demand curve shifting to the left
E the demand curve shifting to the right

3 'Following a freeze in April, America's wheat harvest is expected to be lower than last year's poor crop. Canada has also been hit by bad weather, and some farmers have switched to growing barley…'
(Source: *The Economist*, 3 June 1995).

Assuming no change in the conditions of demand, the likely effect of the above on the price of wheat is
A a small increase in the price due to high elasticity of supply for wheat
B a large fall in the price due to high price elasticities of demand and supply
C a large rise in the price due to low price elasticities of demand and supply
D a large rise in the price due to excess supply
E a large fall in the price due to low price elasticities of demand and supply

4 The table shows the demand and supply schedules for a good before and after the imposition of a tax.

Price ($)	Quantity demanded	Quantity supplied before tax	Quantity supplied after tax
20	340	440	380
19	340	430	340
18	340	410	290
17	340	380	230
16	340	340	160
15	340	290	80
14	340	230	0

What was the amount of the tax?
A $1
B $2
C $3
D $4

5 The diagram shows the demand and supply curves of a commodity. One supply curve applies before the removal of a specific tax on the commodity, and the other after the removal of the tax.

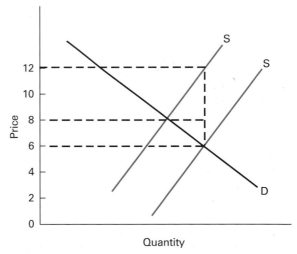

What was the tax per unit of output and what is the price after the abolition of the tax?

	Tax per unit ($)	Price after the abolition of the tax ($)
A	6	6
B	6	8
C	4	6
D	4	4

6 In the diagram the introduction of an expenditure tax has shifted the supply curve from S_1 to S_2.

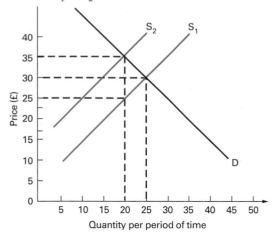

What is the change in suppliers' total net revenue as a result of the tax?
A £100
B £125
C £200
D £250

7 In the diagram OP represents the price which a government wishes to impose on a product.

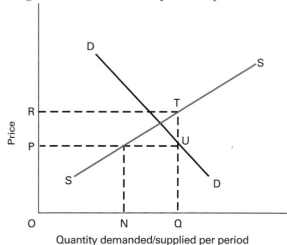

Which of the following would prevent the market price from rising above OP?
A The imposition of rationing to limit consumption to OQ
B A tax on the product of PR per unit
C The granting of a subsidy, represented by OPUQ, to the producers
D The buying of quantity NQ on the market
E The granting of a subsidy, represented by PRTU, to the producers

8 Economic theory predicts that controls which establish rents for housing which are below the equilibrium price
A will improve the quality of rented property supplied to customers
B are an effective method of dealing with excess demand for rented property
C will increase the inflation rate
D will increase the revenue of property owners
E will reduce the quantity supplied of rented property

Essay questions

1 (a) Explain why the European Union needs a policy for agriculture.   (10 marks)
   (b) Discuss the economic reasons why reform of the Common Agricultural Policy (CAP) has been advocated.   (15 marks)

2 (a) What are the problems of agriculture as an economic activity in the European Union?   (10 marks)
   (b) Explain and evaluate the Common Agricultural Policy as an attempt to deal with these problems.   (15 marks)

3 (a) Under the European Union 'Set-Aside' programme, farmers are paid *not* to grow food. What justification could be offered for this policy?   (40 marks)
   (b) Examine the likely economic effects of a decision by the EU to abandon the Common Agricultural Policy.   (60 marks)

4 'Government intervention in the agricultural sector is now being subjected to increasing criticism.'
   (a) What justification has been offered for government intervention in agriculture?   (30 marks)
   (b) Examine the impact of *one* form of intervention.   (30 marks)
   (c) Analyse the economic effects of a gradual withdrawal of support for farmers in the European Union.   (40 marks)

10

Environmental issues

Maintenance of the environment has become an important economic objective for all major political parties at home and abroad. This is because the environmental lobby carries many votes. Indeed, government and public surveys suggest that the electorate are concerned about global warming, traffic congestion, destruction of tropical rainforests, pollution of the air and water, toxic waste, and so on. Yet to date there is still a lack of action and genuine green taxation.

If you have read the previous chapters in this book, the divide between environmental attitude and environmental action is not so surprising. We have indicated that neither a command economy nor a market economy can be relied upon to allocate all resources efficiently. In fact, many examples of government and market failure relate to the environment. Consequently, as you will see, several decisions in favour of the environment involve a trade-off against regulations, taxes or laws as attempts are made to plug the gaps through which the environmental problems flow.

KEY POINTS TO REVIEW

- Opportunity cost (1.2)   page 7
- Shifts in demand (3.2)   page 46
- Shifts in supply (3.5)   page 51
- Market forces (3.7)   page 54
- Market failure (4.7)   page 72
- Externalities (7.2)   page 126
- Macroeconomic objectives (8.1)   page 140

LEARNING OUTCOMES

On completing this chapter you should understand:

- The distinction between private costs and social costs
- Externalities, and their monetary valuation
- Cost–benefit analysis
- Common property
- Transport economics
- Recycling and precycling
- Environmental and ecological economics
- Sustainable development

The environment: beginning and end

Resources
↓
Production
↓
Consumption
↓
Waste

1 Think of examples of how the environment provides resources at the beginning of a product's life cycle.
2 Think of examples of how the environment is used as a waste sink at the end of a product's life cycle.
3 Illustrate the life cycle of two products (from the cradle to the grave), making it clear how they begin and end with the environment.

Private costs versus social costs

When economists think about the environment they often consider costs, and these fall into three categories. First, there are the costs of an individual's actions which are known and paid for directly. For example, when a business has to pay wages to workers, it knows exactly what its labour costs are. When it has to buy resources to commence production it knows quite well what these will cost. Similarly, if an individual has to pay for car repairs, or shoe repairs, or for a concert ticket, he or she knows exactly what the cost will be. These costs are what we term **private costs**. Private costs are those borne solely by the individuals who incur them. They are *internal* in the sense that the firm or household must explicitly take account of them.

Second, there are those costs that are external in so far as the costs of the actions are borne by people other than those who commit them. For example, consider the situations in which a business dumps the waste products from its production process into a nearby river, or in which an individual litters a public park or beach. Obviously, a cost is involved in these actions. When the firm pollutes the water, people downstream suffer the consequences. They may not want to swim in or drink the polluted water. They may also be unable to catch as many fish as before because of the pollution. In the case of littering, the people who come along after our litter has cluttered the park or the beach are the ones who bear the costs. The cost of these actions is borne by people other than those who commit the actions. The creator of the cost is not the sole bearer. The costs are not internalized by the individual or firm; they are *external*.

When we add the *external* costs to the *internal*, or private, costs we get our final, total, category – **social costs**. Pollution problems – indeed, all problems pertaining to the environment – may be viewed as situations in which social costs exceed private costs. Because some economic participants do not pay the full social costs of their actions but only the smaller private costs, their actions are 'socially unacceptable'. In such situations in which there is a divergence between social and private costs, we therefore see 'too much' steel production, automobile driving and beach littering, to pick only a few of the many examples that exist.

KEY POINTS

10.1

■ Internal (private) costs + external costs = total (social) costs.

■ Internal (private) benefits + external benefits = total (social) benefits.

Environmental cost: a private or social bill?

Why is the air in cities so polluted from car exhaust fumes? When drivers step into their cars, they bear only the private costs of driving. That is, they must pay for the petrol, maintenance, depreciation and insurance on their cars. However, they cause an additional cost – that of air pollution – which they are not forced to take into account when they make the decision to drive.

Air pollution is a cost because it causes harm to individuals, for example burning eyes, respiratory ailments,

and dirtier clothes, cars and buildings. The air pollution created by exhausts is a cost that, as yet, specific drivers do not bear *directly*. The social cost of driving includes all the private costs plus at least the costs of air pollution, which society bears. Decisions made only on the basis of private cost lead to too much driving or, alternatively, to too little money spent on the reduction of pollution for a given amount of driving.

Consider the example of lights in hotel rooms. Paying guests know that they will not pay any more on any single occasion if they leave their lights on in the hotel room. Of course, the more frequently all guests leave their lights on, the higher will be the cost of running the hotel and the higher will be the average room charge. But for the individual guest at any one point in time, there is no direct cost to being 'wasteful' with energy used for lights. In essence, lights in a hotel are a free good in the eyes of each hotel guest. We predict, therefore, that people will leave lights on more often in hotel rooms than they will in their own homes. We can look at another example and consider clean air as the scarce resource offered to car drivers free of charge. The same analysis will hold – they will use more of it than they would if they had to directly pay the full social costs.

Environmental files from Eastern and Western Europe

As described in Chapter 2, from approximately the end of the Second World War until the beginning of the 1990s, the countries in Eastern Europe were to a large extent governed by the politico-economic systems of socialism and communism. In those systems, few individual policy-makers had an incentive to keep the environment clean. Although most property was owned by the state, bureaucrats were rewarded for output, not for preserving the environment. The end result was decades of ecological damage. Consider the conditions in the following countries. Then contrast them to the position of Great Britain in the mid-1990s.

Bulgaria
- Farmland soils destroyed by metallic pollution
- Black Sea polluted by oil and sewage

Former Czechoslovakia
- 50 per cent of the forests damaged or dying
- Over half of the rivers heavily polluted
- Almost half of sewage untreated

Former East Germany
- In many areas a majority of children suffer from respiratory diseases
- Groundwater polluted by open uranium waste dumps
- City air pollution forty times higher than in former West Germany

Hungary
- 50 per cent of the population breathe air with pollution levels exceeding maximum safety limits
- Arsenic contaminates drinking water in the southern half of the country

Poland
- Almost all rivers polluted
- In some areas 40 per cent of children suffer pollution-related illnesses

Romania
- Black Sea ports poisoned by toxic waste
- Heart disease and infant mortality high because of high pollution levels

Britain
- Every year factories discharge over 100 000 tonnes of dangerous chemicals (such as benzene and vinyl chloride) into the air, sea and land
- Research has shown an increase in lung cancers near polluting factories and an increased incidence of cancer in children born near industrial locations

4 Which type of cost do most of these ecological disasters represent?

5 Identify which problems may have been reduced if private ownership had existed.

6 Are external costs more likely to exist in capitalist or communist systems?

7 How may these countries achieve to clean up their acts?

8 Is there necessarily a trade-off between pollution clean-up and increased amounts of economic activity?

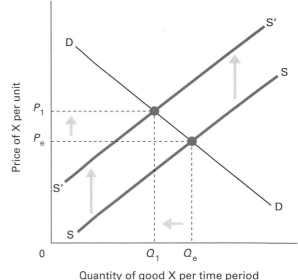

Figure 10.1
Reckoning with full social costs
Here we show the demand for good X as DD. The supply curve SS represents the sum of the costs to the firm for producing that good. If the external costs were included and added to the private costs then we would have social costs. The supply curve would shift upward in a parallel manner to S'S'. In the uncorrected situation the equilibrium price would be P_e and the equilibrium quantity would be Q_e. In the corrected situation the equilibrium price would rise to P_1 and the equilibrium quantity would fall to Q_1.

Externalities

When a private cost differs from a social cost it is a problem of *externality* – because individual decision-makers are not internalizing *all* the costs. Rather, some of these costs remain external to the decision-making process. Remember that the full cost of using a scarce resource is borne one way or another by others who live in the society. That is, society must pay the full opportunity cost of any activity that uses scarce resources. The individual decision-maker is the firm or the customer, and external costs and benefits will not enter into that individual's or firm's decision-making processes.

It will help to view the problem as it is presented in Figure 10.1. Here we have the market demand curve DD for product X and the supply curve SS for product X. As usual, the supply curve includes only internal, or private, costs. The intersection of the demand and supply curves as drawn will be at price P_e and quantity Q_e. However, we shall assume that the production of good X involves externalities that the private business firms did not take into account. These externalities could be air pollution, water pollution, destruction of scenery or anything of that nature.

We know that the social costs of producing X exceed the private costs. We show this by drawing supply curve S'S'. It is above the original supply curve SS because it includes the externalities, or the full social costs of producing the product. Now the 'correct' market equilibrium price is P_1, and the equilibrium quantity Q_1. The inclusion of external costs in the decision-making process leads to a higher-priced product and a decline in quantity produced. We can therefore say that, in an unrestricted situation where social costs are not being fully borne by the creators of these costs, the quantity produced is 'excessive' and the price is too low because it does not reflect all costs.

External benefits also exist

Not all externalities represent a cost. Using a classic example, even people who do not receive inoculations against polio, smallpox, whooping cough and diphtheria benefit from everyone else being inoculated, for epidemics will not break out. A similar example, which has gained government support, applies to the reduction of sexually transmitted diseases, providing sexually active people use condoms. In each case there are third-party benefits that are external to the individual who decides to be inoculated or use a condom. We may refer to the existence of such benefits as a positive externality.

External benefits cause less of a problem than external costs. Indeed, they are given less coverage in this chapter since they do not cause environmental problems. Conceptually, however, they should not prove too difficult to comprehend, as the following questions highlight.

9 What can the government do when the production of one good spills benefits over to third parties?

10 Construct a supply and demand diagram for any product. Show the equilibrium price and quantity. Assuming that the good generates external benefits, modify the diagram to allow for them. Show the new equilibrium price and quantity. How does the revised situation compare with the original, which excluded externalities?

11 When there are external benefits and the market is left to its own devices, are resources over- or under-allocated to the production of that good or service?

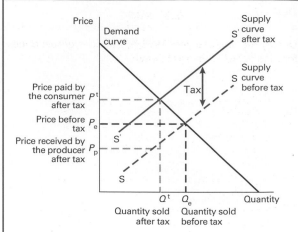

Figure 10.2

The economic effect of a pollution tax
Here we show the demand and supply of a good before and after an environmental tax. The supply curve SS represents the sum of the costs to the firm producing the good, without any consideration of its environmental costs. If a tax is introduced the total costs increase and the supply curve shifts upwards, by the amount of the tax, to S'S'. In the uncorrected situation, where pollution was being taken for granted, the equilibrium price would be P_e and the equilibrium quantity would be Q_e. After the tax is introduced the equilibrium price would rise to P_t and the quantity sold would fall to Q_t.

Internalizing external costs

We can see here an easy theoretical option for reducing the amount of pollution and environmental degradation. Somehow the signals in the economy must be changed so that decision-makers will take into account all the costs of their actions. For example, in the case of car pollution we might want to devise some method whereby motorists are taxed according to the amount of pollution they cause. To a large extent the cheaper tax introduced in 1987 on users of lead-free petrol follows this theory, as the amount of road fuel duty is assumed to be in proportion to the amount of pollutants emitted. Hence there is a price incentive to reduce the number of journeys and/or switch to more fuel-efficient vehicles. By 1997, most petrol sold was unleaded (the market share was approximately a 60:40 split in its favour).

Economic incentives, or **market-based instruments** as they are technically called, are increasingly referred to in government policy documents. The idea is to create charges or tax-type systems that encourage producers and consumers to internalize the costs of their economic actions. Essentially, what is involved is that polluters have to pay for their implicit claim on environmental services.

Hence there is a financial incentive for firms to find ways to reduce pollution.

The polluter pays principle

Facing a charge or tax, firms will be induced (1) to install pollution-abatement equipment or otherwise change production techniques so as to reduce the amount of pollution; (2) to reduce pollution-causing activity; or (3) simply to pay the price to pollute. The relative costs and benefits of each option for each polluter will determine which one or which combination will be chosen. Allowing the choice is the efficient way to decide who pollutes and who does not. In principle, each polluter is given the incentive to meet the full social cost of their actions and adjust production accordingly.

Theoretically, the quantity of environmental pollution should reduce and the price paid increase. This is explained in the diagram in Figure 10.2.

The pollution tax causes the supply curve SS to rise to S'S'. The effect of the tax is to increase the price of the good. As a result, the quantity consumed tends to decrease, the cost being higher for the purchaser. But the price received by the producer is lower than it was before, as the tax is paid to the government. The environmental cost is then shared between the producer and the consumer of the good. Their relative contributions depend on the slope of the supply and demand curves. The more competition there is on the market, the less the consumer will pay.

Car fuel

During the financial year 1998/9, the rates of fuel duties for road vehicles were as follows:

Leaded petrol	49.26 pence per litre
Unleaded petrol	43.99 pence per litre
Super-unleaded petrol	48.76 pence per litre
Diesel (DERV)	44.99 pence per litre
Low-sulphur diesel	42.99 pence per litre
Road fuel gases	21.13 pence per litre

12 Do you think these taxes encourage the use of less harmful fuels?

13 As well as these duties, purchasers of road fuel also pay VAT at the standard rate of 17.5 per cent. Explain how this can be regarded as economically justifiable.

14 What incentives would encourage the use of public transport?

15 Some vehicles are allowed to use 'red diesel', which attracts a much lower duty rate when used off-road. They include agricultural machines, mowing machines, snow-clearing vehicles, gritting vehicles and road construction vehicles. How can this preferential rate be argued as environmentally acceptable?

Is a uniform tax appropriate?

It may not be appropriate to levy a *uniform* tax according to physical quantity of pollution. After all, we are talking about social costs. Such costs are not necessarily the same everywhere in the United Kingdom for the same action.

Essentially, we must establish the amount of the *economic* damages rather than the amount of the physical pollution. A polluting electrical plant in London will cause much more damage than the same plant in a remote rural area. There are already innumerable demands on the air in London, so the pollution from smokestacks will not be cleansed away naturally. Millions of people will breathe the polluted air and thereby incur the costs of sore throats, sickness, emphysema and even early death. Buildings will become dirtier more quickly because of the pollution, as will cars and clothes. A given quantity of pollution will cause more harm in concentrated urban environments than it will in less dense rural environments. If we were to establish some form of taxation to align private costs with social costs and to force people to internalize externalities, we would somehow have to come up with a measure of *economic* costs instead of *physical* quantities. But the tax, in any event, would fall on the private sector and hopefully the burden would be paid for by the polluting firm. Therefore, because the economic cost for the same physical quantity of pollution would be different in different locations according to population density, the natural formation of mountains and rivers and so forth, so-called

optimal taxes on pollution would vary from location to location. (Nonetheless, a uniform tax might make sense when administrative costs, particularly the cost of ascertaining the actual economic costs, are relatively high.)

A particular dilemma, therefore, is how much the government should charge for a 'permissible' amount of pollution. To shed light on this question, economists employ a similar technique to that shown in Figures 10.1 and 10.2. But they analyse small (marginal) changes in the costs and benefits. We develop this approach in the next chapter when discussing welfare issues and will revisit it in an environmental context in Chapter 31.

Meanwhile, it is worth acknowledging that whilst green taxes and similar economic instruments dominate recent government literature relating to the environment, in practice government regulations and controls still dominate the scene.

Environmental taxes in the UK

UK environmental taxes fall into three broad categories:

Energy products
- hydrocarbon duties on transport fuels
- duties on fuel oil and gas oil used for non-transport
- fossil fuel levy (earmarked)

Road vehicles
- vehicle excise duty
- former car tax

Waste
- landfill tax

In 1997 the total revenue received by the government from these taxes was about £26 million. This represented nearly 10 per cent of the total government revenue.

Source: *Economic Trends*, October 1998

16 Give a specific example of a hydrocarbon duty and, using a supply and demand diagram, explain how it works.

17 Vehicle excise duty is paid annually. The following rates were effective from January 1999:

Vehicle type	Standard rate (£)
Car, light good vehicles	150
Motorcycles	15 to 60
Bus	160 to 480
Goods vehicles	160 to 5170

How can vehicle excise duty be defined as a green (environmental) tax and how could it be made greener?

18 What environmental taxes have evolved since 1999?

19 Is it possible that these environmental taxes have other purposes?

KEY POINTS

10.2

- Private costs are those explicit costs that are borne directly by consumers and producers when they engage in any resource-using activity.

- Social costs include private costs plus any other costs that are external to the decision-maker. For example, the social cost of driving includes all the private costs plus any pollution and congestion caused.

- When private costs differ from social costs, externalities exist, because individual decision-makers are not internalizing all the costs that society is bearing.

- When social costs exceed private costs, environmental problems may ensue, such as excessive pollution of air and water. These are problems of externalities.

- One way to make private costs equal social costs is to internalize the externality by imposing a tax or government regulation.

- The taxes imposed should be set equal to the economic damage, or externalities, caused by the pollution-creating activity.

Calculating the value of an externality

To overcome some of the failings of resource allocation created by the market mechanism, economists increasingly attempt to place a monetary value on externalities. This can be achieved through various methods. Three of the most commonly employed approaches are contingent valuation, the travel cost technique and hedonic pricing. Each of these is briefly outlined below.

The **contingent valuation method** relies on survey material in which people are asked, via a questionnaire or interview, to express the value they attach to a specific environmental asset. For example, a sample of respondents may be asked to indicate how much they would be willing to pay to preserve a tropical rainforest. The **travel cost technique** identifies environmental values in terms of the money spent getting to recreational facilities, such as a wildlife reserve, forest or canal. The relevant costs could include fares, petrol and travelling time. Finally, the **hedonic pricing method** attempts to identify a market value for unmarketed environmental services. This is done by analysing the bundle of characteristics that make up a product in order to attach a specific value to the environmental element. This process has been described as establishing a 'surrogate market' and can be easily exemplified

via the property market, where two properties may have identical characteristics except for their location. Hence the price that people are willing to pay for close proximity to a river, woodland, beautiful view or conservation area may be identified.

The underlying principle employed throughout these valuation exercises is **opportunity cost**. For example, when undertaking research into the siting of London's third airport, the monetary value attributed to noise pollution was quantified on the basis of how much it would cost in double or treble glazing to return the houses to their previous level of peace and quiet.

Consequently, identifying the monetary value relating to a specific externality can prove to be very subjective. To take just one example, economists around the world have attempted to identify the value of a statistical life. The values identified enable government transport departments to evaluate proposed infrastructure projects more effectively by encouraging them to consider a dimension that traditional investment appraisal would overlook, namely the value of lives lost or saved due to accidents. The important point arising for our present purposes is that no government seems able to agree on the monetary price that should be allocated. Indeed, official figures used in the early 1990s suggest that an English person's life was worth three times as much as a French person's! This ridiculous suggestion was largely due to different methods of calculation.

Throughout the 1980s government economists employed at the Department of Transport based their value of life on estimates relating to the lost (forgone) contributions to the economy; the stream of lost career earnings. In other words, the opportunity cost of the average victim involved in an accident. Or, as some economists have called it, the 'human capital' approach. In 1988 this meant in monetary terms a death was valued at £608 500. Ten years later, the value had increased to approximately £800 000. The more recent value, however, is based on an individual's willingness to pay to reduce risks and improve safety. In international terms, these values are still quite low. According to a survey of twelve European and Scandinavian countries, the average value for a statistical life is around £1.75 million.

In turn, these figures will greatly affect decisions about road investment. This has been well documented by several government committees, who in their time have examined various road appraisal projects and demonstrated how the estimated net benefits to society are very different according to the monetary value imputed for life.

Is nature beyond price?

Clearly, ascribing monetary figures to any externality is an inexact process, and the figures arrived at are no more than value-judgements. It is often argued, however, that it is better to have a rough estimate than to completely ignore externalities. In fact, it is this kind of thinking that forms the basis of the precautionary principle that most governments follow. In terms of externalities, this means taking care today to avoid possible problems tomorrow. As a consequence, during the last thirty years or so several hundred negative externalities have been allocated a price. The range of assets subsequently being brought into the financial frame stretch from global to local issues, from atmospheric pollution to the loss of a site of special scientific interest. Indeed, Table 10.1 lists several esoteric examples, showing costs that have been estimated for the loss of wildlife and habitat in four countries. (Note that the figures are expressed per person per year, hence some adjustments are necessary to express costs that occur over a number of years in present value terms. See Table 10.1.)

20 Why is the grizzly bear seen to be more valuable than a sea otter?

21 Explain how an economist may use these figures in an appraisal.

22 When would people be asked to put a value on wildlife or habitat?

23 Can you suggest how any of these estimate values may have been calculated?

24 Suggest how a monetary value could be estimated for an environmental asset that you benefit from in your locality.

25 Why do public sector agencies use these valuations more than their private sector equivalents?

Cost–benefit analysis

This method of resource allocation includes externalities as part of its process. Consequently, it manages to reach the parts that most methods of resource allocation leave behind. In these analyses the external costs and benefits are considered alongside the internal (private) costs and benefits. Thus the *total* social costs and benefits are measured. Obviously, for this technique to work all issues need to be expressed in a common denominator for a 'total price' to be arrived at. The 'total (social) price' should attempt to incorporate *all* internal and external costs and benefits. Hence what may not seem viable in conventional financial accounting terms may appear viable in the broader cost–benefit appraisal.

Clearly, such appraisals are easier in theory than practice. There are the problems of valuation to contend with (as outlined above), and there are further problems in selecting the externalities. Inevitably, the selection of what is relevant and what is not will rely upon normative decisions based on value-judgements. For example, when identifying the indirect costs of the Victoria underground line in London the economists conducting the cost–benefit study did not include anything about vandalism or rape; but then the appraisal was carried out by two professional males during 1961 and 1962, a time of 'peace and love'.

Nevertheless, various cost–benefit analysis studies have been attempted, such as the building of motorways, the

Table 10.1

Valuations for selected species and habitats (expressed in 1990 £ per annum per person)

Species		(£ 1990)
Norway:	brown bear, wolf and wolverine	7.90
USA:	bald eagle	6.44
	emerald shiner	2.34
	grizzly bear	9.62
	bighorn sheep	4.47
	whooping crane	0.62
	blue whale	4.83
	bottlenose dolphin	3.64
	California sea otter	4.21
	northern elephant seal	4.21
Habitat		
USA:	Grand Canyon (visibility)	14.04
	Colorado wilderness	4.83–11.02
Australia:	Nadgee Nature Reserve, NSW	14.61
	Kakadu Conservation Zone NT[1]	20.80 (minor damage)
		48.36 (major damage)
UK:	nature reserves[2]	20.80
Norway:	conservation of rivers against hydroelectric development	30.68–55.64

[1] Two scenarios of mining development damage were given to respondents.
[2] Survey based on expert opinion only.

Source: Adapted from D. Pearce (ed.), *Blueprint 4*, Earthscan, 1995, p. 45

Channel tunnel and the relocation of Covent Garden. In most of these studies, a recurring aspect has been the measurement of time saved expressed in monetary terms. The pricing of an indirect benefit (such as time saved) is as difficult as the pricing of an indirect cost because market forces fail to determine prices for use in the cost–benefit study. In fact, a way to distinguish between direct (internal) and indirect (external) is that the former will always have a definite monetary value. Consequently, when appraising new road schemes the government usually chooses not to express the following in monetary terms: traffic noise, visual obstruction, community severance, pedestrian and cyclist impact, disruption during construction and climate change, the excuse being that these costs are 'uncertain and difficult to pin down'.

Cost–benefit analysis, therefore, does not provide clear-cut answers to government policy questions. As outlined above, various dubious estimates are involved, which inevitably lead to concern about the reliability of the process. Hence cost–benefit analysis can offer no more than a framework for government departments to build upon when considering their various options. Indeed, it should be recognized that the technique is merely a method of *identifying* externalities; it does not automatically control them.

Discounting

Another difficulty associated with the pricing of externalities and cost–benefit analysis generally is that governments have to assess the cost of investment today necessary to secure a stream of benefits over a number of years in the future. This problem is no different from that of the private entrepreneur who needs to decide about a capital investment today to secure a stream of profits in the future. A process used to assist with such decisions is known as **discounting**. This involves calculating the *present value* of money that will arise from some future cashflow.

The main reason for such a calculation is that any capital outlay has an opportunity cost: this may be the cost of borrowing or the returns to an alternative investment. For illustration purposes, let us take the cost of borrowing angle. To start with, you must recognize that interest rates are used to link the present with the future. After all, if you have to pay £110 at the end of the year when you borrow £100, the 10 per cent interest charged gives you a measure of the cost of borrowing. Hence, the present value (the value today) of £110 to be received in one year is £100 if the market rate of interest is 10 per cent.

The important point is that £1 in the pocket today will be worth more than £1 in the future because, if you had the £1 today, you could be putting it to work to earn interest. From this it follows that £1 receivable in the future has to be discounted to find what it is worth today. For instance, at a 10 per cent rate of interest, £1 receivable in three years is worth about £0.75 today. This is the same as saying that £0.75 is the sum which will grow to £1 in three years, at 10 per cent a year compound interest. You do not have to work these figures out for yourself, since there are plenty of programmes available for computers, pocket calculators and compound interest tables such as Table 10.2.

So £0.75 is the present value of £1 receivable in three years at a 10 per cent rate of interest. In the same way, you can calculate the present value of a whole series of expenditures (or receipts) involved in investment (see the caption for Table 10.2). In terms of cost–benefit analysis you can compare the present value of the costs with the present value of the benefits. The problem with this technique is that the present value of any sum of money is dependent on correctly judging two factors: the time and the interest rate. The further into the future the sum is calculated or the higher the interest rate used, the less the present value of the sum. To take an extreme example, the cost of a nuclear accident that may take place 500 years from now and impose an economic cost of £10 billion on future generations will be reduced to a present value of 25 pence assuming a discount rate of 5 per cent. This creates yet another problem for those struggling with cost–benefit analysis, since interest rates change at irregular intervals and time horizons shift as projects develop (and public investment schemes are notoriously long term).

Table 10.2

Present values of a future pound (sterling)

| Year | Compounded annual interest rate | | | | |
	3%	5%	8%	10%	20%
1	0.971	0.952	0.926	0.909	0.833
2	0.943	0.907	0.857	0.826	0.694
3	0.915	0.864	0.794	0.751	0.578
4	0.889	0.823	0.735	0.683	0.482
5	0.863	0.784	0.681	0.620	0.402
6	0.838	0.746	0.630	0.564	0.335
7	0.813	0.711	0.583	0.513	0.279
8	0.789	0.677	0.540	0.466	0.233
9	0.766	0.645	0.500	0.424	0.194
10	0.744	0.614	0.463	0.385	0.162
15	0.642	0.481	0.315	0.239	0.0649
20	0.554	0.377	0.215	0.148	0.0261
25	0.478	0.295	0.146	0.0923	0.0105
30	0.412	0.231	0.0994	0.0573	0.00421
40	0.307	0.142	0.0460	0.0221	0.000680
50	0.228	0.087	0.0213	0.00852	0.000109

Calculating a net social price

The government is considering a motorway project which is assumed to have a life of thirty years. It is proposed that users of the motorway will have to pay a toll. The benefits, costs and externalities arising from four possible routes are outlined in the table below (all the figures have been discounted, to express them in present value monetary terms).

	Route A (£ m)	Route B (£ m)	Route C (£ m)	Route D (£ m)
Private benefits	125	130	100	140
Private costs	100	110	120	130
Positive externalities	50	55	55	60
Negative externalities	70	50	40	50

26 Give one example for each of the four accounting categories, and identify which category relates to the 'polluter pays principle'.

27 Which of the routes would maximize profit in narrow commercial terms?

28 Which of the routes would maximize economic welfare?

29 Discounting is used to convert the future costs and benefits of a project to current prices. What difficulties do you foresee in trying to evaluate a motorway project over a thirty-year period?

KEY POINTS

10.3

- Attempts to place monetary value on externalities are problematic. But three basic methods exist, namely: contingent valuation, travel cost and hedonic pricing.

- Cost–benefit analysis involves identifying monetary values for all the internal and external costs and benefits of a project, allowing a total (social) price to be arrived at.

- The problems with cost–benefit analysis are (1) what to include as 'relevant' externalities, (2) how to quantify the externalities in monetary terms and (3) how to effectively 'discount' the criteria to judge the value in today's terms.

- Cost–benefit analysis is used by government departments in investment appraisal of public sector projects.

Common property

Most of the problems relating to externalities (and associated cost–benefit analysis) can only be effectively resolved if property rights can be defined and enforced. For instance, in most cases you do not have **private property rights** to the air surrounding you, nor does anyone else. Air is a **common property** resource, and therein lies the crux of many envi-

ronmental problems. When no one owns a particular resource, people do not have any incentive (conscience aside) to consider their particular misuse of that resource. If one person decides not to pollute the air, there normally will be no significant effect on the total level of pollution. If one person decides not to pollute the ocean, there will still be approximately the same amount of ocean pollution – provided, of course, that the individual was previously responsible for only a small part of the total amount of ocean pollution.

Basically, we have pollution where we have poorly defined private property rights. Hence we do not have a visual pollution problem in people's attics. That is their own property, which they can choose to keep as they want – given their preferences for cleanliness weighed against the costs of keeping the attic neat and tidy.

Where private property rights exist, individuals have legal recourse to any damages sustained through the misuse of their property. When private property rights are well defined, the use of property – that is, the use of resources – will generally involve contracting with the owners of those resources. If you own land, you might contract with another person who wants to use your land for raising cows. The contract would most probably be written in the form of a lease agreement.

Voluntary agreements and transaction costs

Is it possible for externalities to be internalized via voluntary agreement? Take a simple example. You live in a house with a picturesque view of a lake. The family living below you plants a tree. The tree grows so tall that it eventually starts to cut off your view. In most cities, no one has property rights to views; therefore, you cannot usually go to court to obtain relief. You do have the option of contracting with your neighbour, however.

Voluntary agreements: contracting
You have the option of paying your neighbours (contracting) to cut down the tree. You could start out with an offer of a small amount and keep going up until your neighbours agree or until you reach your limit. Your limit will equal the value you place on having an unobstructed view of the lake. Your neighbours will be willing if the payment is at least equal to the reduction in their intrinsic property value due to a stunted tree. Your offering the payment makes your neighbours aware of the social costs of their actions. The social cost here is equal to the care of the tree plus the cost suffered by you from an impeded view of the lake.

In essence, then, your offering your neighbours money indicates to them that there is an opportunity cost to their actions. If they do not comply, they forfeit the money that you are offering them. The point here is that opportunity cost always exists with whoever has property rights. Therefore, we would expect under some circumstances that voluntary contracting will occur to internalize externalities. The question is, when will voluntary agreements occur?

Transaction costs

A major condition for the outcome just outlined is that the **transaction costs** – all costs associated with making and enforcing agreements – must be low relative to the expected benefits of reaching an agreement. If we expand our example to a much larger one such as air pollution, the transaction costs of numerous homeowners trying to reach agreements with the individuals and companies that create the pollution are relatively high. Consequently, we do not expect voluntary contracting to be an effective way to internalize the externality of air pollution. In other words, the property rights approach is not usually possible where many people are involved and transaction costs are heavy.

The ideas of Professor R. Coase

The analysis we have just dealt with follows the lines of the Coase theorem. Professor Ronald Coase's famous 1960 journal paper, 'The problem of social cost', demonstrated that negative externalities do not require government intervention in situations where property rights are well defined and transaction costs are relatively low.

For example, if a farmer wishes to burn straw he will cause pollution. The farmer will take the air for granted and use it as a waste sink. If society, however, were able to put a value on the cost of this pollution, the farmer may be forced to revise his action. For instance, if the farmer happened to cause fire damage to a neighbour's field or house, he would have to pay some compensation to the owner of the property.

The problem that this example illustrates is that the atmosphere is usually regarded as common property. Hence, if a straw-burning farmer can pollute the air with no financial implications, he will. If, however, air could be organized in such a way that it belonged to an individual or organization, the farmer could be charged for making use of it. The essential point is that negotiations between parties become a possibility. The pollution may then stop or be reduced.

Creating a market for an externality is therefore a solution, since it enables polluters to buy rights to pollute and victims to charge to the level that they feel justifies their suffering.

30 Think of some examples of common property.
31 What are transaction costs?
32 Think of an instance in which a market for a negative externality would be plausible.
33 Think of an example in which a market for a negative externality would prove very difficult to operate.
34 How could a congestion tax imposed on vehicles coming into a busy urban area be regarded as a Coasian-type solution to air and noise pollution?

Changing property rights

In considering the problem of property rights it would be correct to assume that initially in a society many property rights are not defined. Ultimately, this situation often leads to allocation problems. For example, if some environmental capital is available at zero price a more than proportionate amount will be demanded, and hence there is a risk of it being over-used. Output will be inefficient if it involves a mix of priced and unpriced inputs. To overcome these issues, something must be done to determine property rights.

Property rights may be assigned to government; bureaucrats can then maintain and preserve the resource, charge for its use or implement some other rationing device. What we have seen with common property such as air and water is that governments have attempted to take over the control of these resources so that they are not wasted or destroyed. A **command and control**-type strategy such as this is easy to understand. To enforce, however, involves government costs, such as inspection, legal action and general policing costs. Selecting an appropriate government regulatory scheme is therefore easier said than done.

To overcome these problems of central regulations, systems are being devised whereby more and more resources are being squeezed into the market framework. This often involves assigning property rights to individuals who then assert control. Hence, the incentive lies with private individuals to act in a beneficial way for their own financial gain. Indeed, whenever property rights can be harnessed in some way to the market, this is seen as preferable to government regulations.

The market for pollution rights

An interesting example of market-based rights is developing through a strategy known as **tradeable permits**. The central premise involved is not much different from a command and control approach, whereby a polluter is granted a permit to emit a certain amount of waste. The distinguishing and important feature with a tradeable permit, however, is that the polluters can buy and sell permits from one another. Consequently, the total amount of pollution will be set, but its distribution will be influenced by market forces. Those who find it expensive to reduce pollution will want to buy more permits, whilst those who find it easy to reduce pollution will be in a position to sell their permits. Examples of these permits are few and far between, but there are some prototypes in America, Canada and Australia.

Tradeable permits are also used by the fishing industries of New Zealand, Australia and the United States – not to regulate pollution but to control, through assigned property rights, the possibility of over-fishing. Each fisherman in the territory concerned is issued with a permit to catch a given quota of fish. The permits are then tradeable, even to the extent that the government may choose to buy back some of the permits in an attempt to conserve the stocks of fish.

The American market for hot air

The first publicly disclosed deal involving the sale and purchase of tradeable permits occurred in the United States between two electric utilities hundreds of miles apart. Specifically, Wisconsin Power and Light found that it would emit fewer pollutants than allowed under the Clean Air Act of 1990. In May 1992, it therefore sold to the Tennessee Valley Authority (TVA) the rights to 10 000 tonnes of sulphur dioxide emissions. It also sold to Pittsburgh's Duquesne Light the right to emit 25 tonnes of sulphur dioxide. The price of the TVA deal was not disclosed, but the *New York Times* estimated that $2.5 million to $3 million changed hands. Less than a year later, the formal process of selling pollution rights, often called 'smog futures', took place on the Chicago Board of Trade on 30 March 1993. A total of 150 010 air pollution allowances granted by the Environmental Protection Agency were auctioned off. The government obtained about $21 million from successful bidders. The right to emit 1 tonne of sulphur dioxide sold for between $122 and $450. Included among the successful bidders were, obviously, electric utilities, but also public interest groups, brokerage firms and private investors.

35 How can American environmental pressure groups reduce the amount of pollution emitted by electric utilities?
36 What objections could be raised against tradeable permits to reduce pollution?
37 (a) Which environmental problems may be solved in the United Kingdom by introducing a tradeable permit system?
  (b) What operational issues would need to be resolved for the system to work?
38 Briefly describe one other method, besides the creation of a market in tradeable permits, by which sulphur dioxide pollution might be limited.

KEY POINTS

10.4

■ A common property resource is one that no one owns – or, otherwise stated, that everyone owns.

■ Common property exists when property rights are indefinite or non-existent.

■ When no property rights exist, pollution occurs because no one individual or firm has a sufficient economic incentive to care for the common property in question.

■ Private costs will not equal social costs when common property is at issue, unless only a few individuals are involved and they are able to contract among themselves.

■ Alternatives to pollution-causing resource use exist.

■ Pollution can be monitored more effectively when private property rights are identifiable.

■ Trading permits encourage people to treat the environment and resource stock as if it were their own.

■ Market-based incentives are preferable to command and control regimes.

Transport economics

As suggested by some of the exercises and examples above, transport and environmental issues are increasingly considered as linked concepts. In fact, since 1997 the UK government has merged the interests of two previously separate departments and formed the Department of the Environment, Transport and the Regions (DETR). In other words, the government has acknowledged that environmental problems are closely associated with transport. Not only are there a number of pollutants arising from motorized transport, there are also the injuries arising from accidents. In fact, a Royal Commission on Pollution estimated the environmental costs of transport to be between £11 billion and £21 billion. Table 10.3 gives some idea of how these totals were arrived at.

Table 10.3

The estimated environmental costs of the transport system, 1994–5 (£ billion)

	Lower end of range	Upper end of range
Air pollution	2.4	6.0
Climate change	1.8 (4.6)	3.6 (12.9)
Noise and vibration	1.2	5.4
Accidents	5.5 (5.4)	5.5 (5.4)
Total quantified environmental costs	10.9 (10.0)	20.5 (18.3)

Note: The figures in brackets refer to the costs attributable to road transport.
Source: Royal Commission on Environmental Pollution, 1994

It is interesting to note that monetary values were not expressed for losses of land, visual intrusion, disruption to habitats, severance of communities or traffic congestion. Therefore, both sets of figures are probably underestimated. Four years later, similar calculations suggested that the environmental costs relating to transport were nearer £50 billion.

What environmental economists recommend is some form of **integrated transport policy**, which commits a greater investment in public transport and subsidizes the use of more environmentally friendly modes of transport, raising the necessary revenue through market-based instruments aimed at motorists. A White Paper along these lines was launched in 1998, representing the first transport policy for twenty-one years. The environmental pressure group Friends of the Earth reviewed it in the following way.

Bike to the future

The year is 2019. Robin has just cycled off to school; Jane leaves the house to take the bus into the office. Art settles down in front of the computer to check the morning's electronic mail. The car stays firmly in the garage, as it has done for days.

Will life ever be like this? It might be, if the proposals set out in the government's White Paper on an integrated transport policy come to fruition. Deputy Prime Minister John Prescott, who launched the paper in July 1998, would like to see superbuses replace cars on the streets and wants to make motorists pay to drive in city centres. The government is cutting back spending on new roads and increasing spending on buses. They want life to be made easier and safer for pedestrians and cyclists. And by 'integrating transport with land use planning', the government intends 'to plan out car dependence'.

It is 21 years forward to our fantasy eco-transport scenario of 2019 – ample time, perhaps. Except that we have (almost) been here before – 21 years ago, with the last such White Paper, produced by the last Labour government in 1977. It promised more money for bus service. It vowed to trim the road-building budget. It even held out the prospect of charging motorists for driving in city centres. It said that more 'attention should be given to the needs of pedestrians and cyclists'. And it promised the radical new policy of changing land use planning 'to decrease our absolute dependence on transport' – one of Friends of the Earth's key demands.

Instead, the past 21 years have brought very different changes to the UK's transport system. In 1977 there were 14 million cars on the road. Now there are 22 million of them. The 1977 White Paper failed to change the way we travel. So why should the 1998 equivalent fare any better?

Source: Friends of the Earth, *Earth Matters*, Winter 1998

39 Identify three examples of environmental cost relating to transport.
40 When do consumers normally express an interest in transport costs? Answer stating examples.
41 What changes have you noticed in transport since 1998, and what economic concepts or policies caused the change?

To make a fair representation of transport economics, it should be acknowledged that it involves more than just environmental issues. Transport economists are concerned with the allocation of resources to move goods and people, which sees them using a whole range of concepts from microeconomics. During the last fifteen years the emphasis has shifted away from public sector-controlled natural monopolies towards freer markets. Indeed, the processes of deregulation and privatization have significantly affected most modes of transport; notably air traffic, buses, road provision and trains. Consequently, transport economics is a growing specialism, with its own dedicated texts and journals. We shall consider it further at the close of this chapter.

KEY POINTS

10.5

- Transport economics is concerned with two main issues: the environment and providing an efficient and competitive transport system.

- In 1998 a new integrated transport policy was launched.

Recycling and precycling

The benefits of recycling seem straightforward. Fewer natural resources are used; for example, every tonne of recycled paper is estimated to save seventeen trees and 3 cubic yards of landfill space. Consequently, an important part of environmental policy during the 1990s involved saving scarce resources via **recycling**. In fact, many local authorities have organized their own recycling programmes. These are visibly evidenced by the container banks of recycling facilities that are lodged in the car parks of many large supermarkets.

Recycling, however, also has many costs. To take an indirect example: used paper has ink on it that has to be removed during the recycling process, and the resultant sludge has to be disposed of; it is estimated that 100 tonnes of bleached (de-inked) fibre will generate approximately 40 tonnes of sludge. More directly, there is the cost of using resources. For instance, the labour cost involved in the recycling process may be more than the saving in scarce resources not used. In other words, 'net' resource use may sometimes be greater with recycling than without it. Hence, even the saving of landfill space might be inefficient, since throwing waste directly into a landfill site may be less costly.

One solution to the recycling cost dilemma is to tackle the problem from the other end and **precycle**. This involves making products in such a way that they are not over-packaged or can be refilled. Detergent companies, for example, have found it advantageous for themselves, the consumer and the environment to package and sell more concentrated forms of detergent. The packages are smaller, the use of resources in packaging is less, and waste requiring disposal is less than with older formulations of detergent. Concentrated juices also represent a form of precycling. In short, any approach to packaging products in a more concentrated and less wasteful form can be considered precycling and may help the environment.

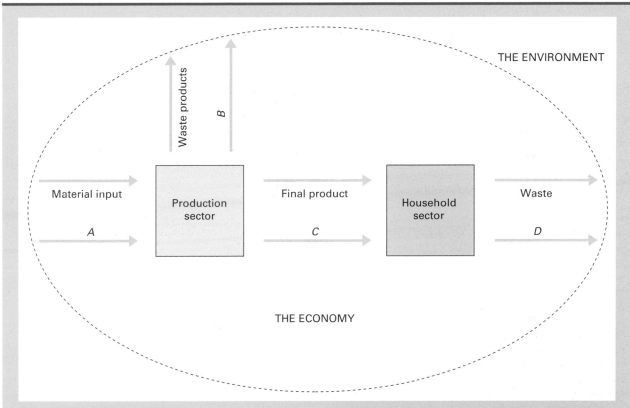

The materials balance model
The materials balances for each sector are as follows: the production sector $A = B + C$; the household sector $C = D$; the whole economy $A = B + D$.

The materials balance model

Economists like to create models, to simplify the reality that they seek to explain. Mainstream economists, however, have tended to ignore the economy–environment interactions. Specialized environmental economists have overcome the problem by devising the materials balance model, which, since the 1960s, has become a standard reference for students being introduced to green economics. And since those hippy days of flower-power many more have taken an interest in studying ecological issues.

The emphasis of this model focuses on the energy used and wasted by economic activity. The first law of thermodynamics provides a starting point. This law explains the 'physics' of economic activity, since it states that we cannot destroy matter, we can only change it. Therefore, all that is extracted from the environment must be returned to it in some form. This material balance aspect is shown in the figure and it clearly highlights that waste (pollution) is an inevitable problem that presents itself at many junctures in the economic system.

In this model the environment is portrayed as having a similar relationship to the economy as does a mother to an unborn child, in so far as it provides sustenance and carries away wastes (of course, the processes involved often take far longer than nine months to complete).

> Alternatively, the environment can be viewed as a large protective shell surrounding the traditionally recognized economic system. Unfortunately, this environmental shell is often treated as a 'free good' and hence beyond the realms of traditional economics.
>
> **42** How does economic activity impact on the environment?

43 State two or three functions that the environment provides to the economy.

44 (a) How may precycling help resolve some of the environmental problems suggested by the materials balance model?

   (b) To what extent would recycling help?

45 Define in your own words what the materials balance model is trying to convey.

Sustainable development

At the United Nations (UN) Conference on Environment and Development held in Rio de Janeiro in 1992, leaders and representatives from over 150 states adopted a declaration committing them to make future development sustainable. In other words, at the beginning of the 1990s there was a broad consensus of world opinion that current economic activity would have deleterious effects on future generations unless careful monitoring occurred. This consensus continues into the millennium. In 1997 the Rio conference members met again in New York to confirm their commitment and a further meeting is scheduled for 2002. In short, a commonly accepted principle is that economic development should not make people better off today at the expense of tomorrow.

Sustainable development in reality

Foresters and fishermen have long been concerned with sustainable yields, since it is in their professional interest to avoid logging trees and catching fish at a rate faster than they can be replaced. Given that there is fairly good knowledge relating to the growth of fish and trees, it is quite feasible to plan for sustainability with renewable resources. Obviously, failure to make such plans would result in the disappearance of the resource in question, perhaps for some period while stocks are given a chance to regrow, or perhaps permanently if that chance is not given. Arguably, extinction may not matter much if there is some other resource to which one can turn. Trees can always be grown somewhere else. Sometimes there are alternative fish stocks to be exploited; often there are not.

The extension from fish and trees to whole economies is fairly straightforward. If there is a concern for the well-being of future generations, it seems logical to ensure that the economy is itself sustainable. Hence, attention needs to be paid to the output of the economy and the underlying resource base that gives rise to that output.

Source: Adapted from D. Pearce (ed.), *Blueprint 3*, Earthscan, 1993

46 What does it mean for an economy to be developed in a sustainable manner?

47 The entire disappearance of some species and habitats represents the failure to manage the sustainable development of an economy. Give some examples of extinction and explain why they have occurred.

48 Given that economies do not rely solely on renewable resources, how can any economy achieve sustainable development?

49 Explain how it is possible to increase economic activity and to use up fewer resources.

The most widely quoted definition of **sustainable development** comes from an earlier UN initiative held in 1987 and chaired by the Norwegian Prime Minister Gro Harlem Bruntland. The Bruntland report stated that

> sustainable development is development that meets the needs of the present without compromising the ability of future generations to meet their own needs

National strategies to achieve sustainability are now being developed worldwide and, broadly speaking, there are two approaches: the **constant capital approach** and the **natural capital approach**. The constant capital approach strives to maintain a country's total capital stock by ensuring that decreases in natural resources are substituted by increases in human-made assets. This approach is of interest to mainstream economists, who believe that the market mechanism can provide the necessary incentive to encourage technological solutions to resource problems; it is sometimes referred to as the 'technocentric approach'. In contrast, the natural capital approach strives to preserve the stock of natural resources. This approach is of greater interest to environmental and ecological economists, who regard the maintenance of environmental capital to be of major importance as they believe that it is not possible to substitute one type of capital with another; it is sometimes referred to as the 'ecocentric approach'. Both these approaches are difficult to support by policy, but at least governments are striving to devise systems that account for the welfare of both present and future generations.

Ecological economics

Ecological economics goes further by portraying the economy as a subsystem dependent on a finite ecosystem. The ecosystem provides resources and assimilates wastes. To highlight the dilemmas this may present, it is common for two models to be presented: the empty world and the full world (as shown below).

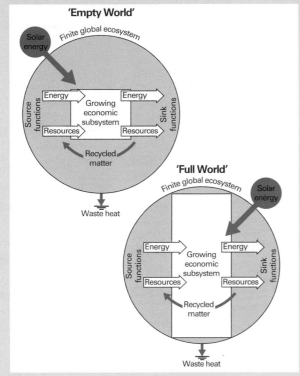

The upper diagram illustrates the past, when the economic subsystem was small relative to the size of the ecosystem. It is referred to as an 'empty world' to depict a time empty of people and their human-made capital, but full of natural capital. The lower diagram represents a situation nearer to today, where the economic subsystem is very large relative to the ecosystem. Accordingly, this is referred to as the 'full world' to highlight that unless qualitative changes occur, the ecosystem is going to be pushed beyond its limits. We have already begun to get signs that this point is imminent, for example global warming, ozone depletion, soil erosion, biodiversity loss, population explosions and resource depletion. These problems highlight the need to consider a sustainable development.

Source: Based on R. Costanza et al., *An Introduction to Ecological Economics*, CRC Press, 1997, ch. 1

50 It could be argued that the output begins and ends with the environment. Explain and discuss.
51 Mainstream economists see technology as instrumental in avoiding global problems. Give examples of future developments and explain how the price system will encourage their development.
52 'The real problems of the planet lie on the waste side of the equation!' Explain and discuss whether technology can improve the carrying capacity of the planet, and how such developments may or may not occur.
53 Describe two government policies to resolve the problem of sustainable development and discuss the viability of each.

KEY POINTS

10.6

- Recycling involves reusing paper, glass and other materials rather than putting them into solid waste dumps. Recycling does have a cost both in the resources used for recycling and in the pollution created during recycling, such as the sludge from de-inking paper for reuse.

- Precycling involves paying attention to long-term resource implications by starting at the packaging stage of a product's life cycle.

- The materials balance model focuses on the energy used and wasted by economic activity.

- Sustainable development is achieved if today's increases in economic activity do not impinge upon the hopes and aspirations of future generations.

Case Study

Ten policy recommendations for a sustainable transport system

In order to confront road users with the environmental costs of their activities and to get them to change their behaviour, the following policies are recommended:

1 Fuel prices should be based on the environmental damage each fuel causes; and price differentials should reflect the environmental advantages of one fuel over another.
2 More research into the cumulative impact of fuel emissions, especially in urban areas.
3 Car taxes need to be differentiated to reflect the emission characteristics of the vehicle.
4 Some means must be found of catching those who do not maintain their vehicle properly and cause excess pollution.
5 Air pollution monitors to be placed in main streets, so that citizens can see the quality of the air that they breathe.
6 Free and open access to the city centres' urban central road network must cease.
7 To make heavy goods vehicles (HGVs) pay for the damage they cause to roads by designing/introducing a tax related to the weight of the vehicle and the number of axles it possesses.
8 To charge road users on the basis of their mileage a fee representing the additional costs they impose on others.
9 Speed restrictions need to be reviewed in an attempt to balance the advantages from time savings with lower numbers of accidents and fuel savings.

10 To use a higher value for life, which should move road investment away from relieving congestion and saving time to reducing accidents.

Source: Adapted from Maddison et al., *Blueprint 5: The True Costs of Road Transport*, Earthscan, 1996

1 Which is the recurring concept that unites the ten points?
2 What do you see as a common problem relating to at least six of the ten points?
3 Many of the recommendations involve an adaptation of the existing fiscal system rather than command and control policies relating to vehicle manufacture and use. Do you think this is a strength or weakness of the recommendation? (Explain your answer stating examples wherever possible.)
4 Make an economic argument to subsidize public transport.
5 How may technological advancement help to resolve problems relating to sustainable transport?
6 Have any of these recommendations influenced recent government policy?
7 Vehicles account for about one-fifth of the UK's carbon emissions. How may some other sections of the economy be brought into the solution for a sustainable future?
8 Previous transport policy has resulted in too much pollution, too much noise, too much congestion, too many accidents, too many roads and too little investment in public transport. To what extent could technological advancement be seen as the cause or solution of some of these environmental problems?

Case Study

A cowboy versus spaceman economy

Professor Kenneth Boulding's influential conference paper (published in 1966) still represents a landmark in environmental economics, since it highlighted in a colourful and delightful way that the traditional view of earth as abundant and limitless was false. Boulding drew attention to the changing nature of the earth's balance by employing the analogy of a cowboy and spaceman economy. In his words:

The closed earth of the future requires economic principles, which are somewhat different from those of the open earth of the past. For the sake of picturesqueness, I am tempted to call the open economy the 'cowboy economy', the cowboy being symbolic of the illimitable plains and also associated with reckless, exploitative, romantic, and violent behaviour, which is characteristic of open societies. The closed economy of the future might similarly be called the 'spaceman' economy, in which the earth has become a single spaceship, without unlimited reservoirs of anything, either for extraction or for pollution, and in which, therefore, man must find his place in a cyclical ecological system which is capable of continuous reproduction of material form even though it cannot escape having inputs of energy …

In the cowboy economy, consumption is regarded as a good thing and production likewise; and the success of the economy is measured by the amount of the throughput from the 'factors of production', a part of which, at any rate, is extracted from the reservoirs of raw materials and noneconomic objects, and another part of which is output into the reservoirs of pollution. If there are infinite reservoirs from which material can be obtained and into which effluvia can be deposited, then the throughput is at least a plausible measure of the success of the economy. The gross national product is a rough measure of this total throughput. It should be possible, however, to distinguish that part of the GNP which is derived from exhaustible and that which is derived from reproducible resources, as well as that part of consumption which represents effluvia and that which represents input into the productive system again …

By contrast, in the spaceman economy, throughput is by no means a desideratum, and is indeed to be regarded as something to be minimized rather than maximized. The essential measure of the success of the economy is not production and consumption at all, but the nature, extent, quality, and complexity of the total capital stock, including in this the state of the human bodies and minds included in the system. In the spaceman economy, what we are primarily concerned with is stock maintenance, and any technological change which results in the maintenance of a given total stock with a lessened throughput (that is, less production and consumption) is clearly a gain …

Source: K.E. Boulding, 'The economics of the coming spaceship earth', in H. Jarrett (ed.), *Environmental Quality in a Growing Economy*, Johns Hopkins University Press, 1966, pp. 9–10

1 Describe two environment–economy interactions.
2 Define in your own words a 'cowboy economy'.
3 Define in your own words a 'spaceman economy'.
4 How may the environmental problems which Boulding's cowboy economy introduces be eliminated or contained by government policy?
5 Discuss the main problems of incorporating environmental factors into the total throughput (GNP).
6 Choose either the sustainable development concept or the materials balance model to explain Boulding's concerns about the 'spaceman economy'.
7 Discuss whether the continual increase in production and consumption of goods is environmentally feasible.
8 Discuss the advantages and disadvantages of using market-based instruments to control the environmental problems that arise from economic activity.

Exam Preparation

Multiple choice questions

1 If a firm's private costs of production are not equal to the social costs of its production, the government could increase economic welfare by
   A taxing the firm if its social costs exceed its private costs
   B taxing the firm if its social costs are less than its private costs
   C subsidizing the firm if its social costs exceed its private costs
   D taxing other firms if social costs are less than private costs in the firm in question
   E subsidizing other firms if social costs are less than private costs in the firm in question

2 Cost–benefit analysis is used to
   A equate social costs and social benefits
   B make producers pay for the external costs of a project
   C measure the net social benefit of a project
   D ensure that society pays for the net social benefits it receives
   E minimize social costs

3 When the social costs exceed the private costs, economists state that there is
   A a positive externality
   B an underproduction of output
   C a negative externality
   D social appreciation of resources

4 With a negative externality
   A all costs are not internalized
   B there is insufficient production
   C price is too low
   D there is insufficient economic profit

5 The efficient way to decide who pollutes and who does not is to
   A establish standards on pollution control and employ an inspectorate to force everyone to meet the standards
   B ban certain polluting activities, such as steel production
   C devise a system in which everybody faces the full social costs of their actions and allow them to decide how to respond
   D impose a tax on all industrial plants in the country

6 In general, pollution exists where
   A people are unconcerned about the hazards associated with pollution
   B there are poorly defined private property rights
   C there are poorly defined common property rights
   D profit-making activity is taken to an extreme

7 One difficulty in using voluntary transactions to internalize externalities is that
   A people are motivated by self-interest and are often unwilling to engage in a transaction that might make another person better off
   B the government usually will not enforce contracts of this type
   C transaction costs of coming to an agreement can be very large when numerous people are involved
   D people usually do not understand what the real opportunity costs are that they face

8 If marketable permits for pollution were traded, an environmental group could buy some, which would
   A drive the price of permits up, but this would discourage firms from polluting less
   B drive the price of permits up and encourage firms to pollute less
   C be counterproductive since the optimal amount of permits had already been decided upon
   D lessen government revenues from the permits, harming other areas of pollution abatement

Essay questions

1 'As with all externalities, the proper way to treat them is to make those who cause environmental damage pay for it.' Discuss.

2 (a) Using examples, distinguish between the meaning of private costs and social costs. (8 marks)
   (b) Discuss the importance of this distinction for a government considering whether or not to introduce road pricing. (17 marks)

3 In what sense can river pollution and traffic congestion be viewed as economic problems? Can economics make any contribution to the solution of these problems?

4 (a) Explain why the emission of pollution by a firm into the atmosphere or into a river may be economically inefficient. (13 marks)
   (b) Evaluate two ways of reducing any economic inefficiency caused by pollution. (12 marks)

5 Discuss the economic advantages and disadvantages of the various government options for controlling sulphur dioxide pollution.

6 (a) Explain what is meant by an externality. (30 marks)
   (b) Examine the impact of introducing any two of the following:
       (i) pollution taxes
       (ii) legal maximum controls on pollution emissions
       (iii) tradeable pollution licence permits (70 marks)

7 Is air pollution through the emissions of exhaust gases from vehicle engines an economic problem? Outline the arguments for and against the use of taxes or subsidies as a means of reducing the amount of atmospheric pollution in the United Kingdom.

11

Welfare issues

LEARNING OUTCOMES

On completing this chapter you should understand:

- How the market for health care in the UK rations
  access for treatment

- The problem of paying for health care by private
  insurance

- The market for education in the UK

- The concepts of marginal private benefits and
  marginal social benefits

- The market for housing in the UK

In Chapter 7 we introduced the concept of market failure and then discussed problems relating to the working of agricultural markets in Chapter 9. In the previous chapter we considered market failure in relation to the environment. Agriculture and the environment are two examples where the state has intervened to influence how supply and demand determine market outcomes. In this chapter we consider three other areas of the economy which in many developed countries are not left to market forces, namely health care, education and housing.

In each of these cases state intervention is not essential. These are not **public goods**. We stated in Chapter 7 that national defence spending is a standard example of a public good. It is not feasible to buy and sell defence in a market-place. Therefore the provision by governments of a measure of protection against the threat of external attack from other countries is not a contentious political issue. We noted in Chapter 7 that while health care can be supplied through the market, as it is in the United States, for many years in the United Kingdom it has been seen as socially desirable for the government both to provide health care and to subsidize its production. Together with the various forms of benefits concerned to relieve poverty which constitute social security, government spending on health and education forms part of what in the United Kingdom is referred to as the **welfare state**. By this term we mean there is some measure of collective provision of these services so as to ensure that poorer citizens get access to a standard of service that they may not otherwise be able to afford within a privately organized market. In Chapter 7 we referred to **merit goods** as the provision of goods or services that have been selected via the political process as being socially desirable. In this chapter we consider in turn the markets for health, education and housing and the reasons for government intervention in each of them. We consider how state provision has operated and the recent introduction of market mechanisms in the United Kingdom aimed to improve the quality of the services provided.

The market for health care

Until the National Health Service (NHS) was founded in 1948, health care was essentially a service that could be purchased by consumers in a market-place supplied by individual doctors. Thus the market for health care was little different from the market for food, clothing or furniture. Consumers requiring medical advice and attention could buy a quantity of health care from their local doctor as seemed appropriate according to their needs and, not least, their capacity to pay. The main problem with such a market is thus readily apparent. Although medical attention may be urgently needed, it may be delayed owing to a person's inability to pay for the services of the doctor. Thus the level of income of a person who is unwell is the determinant of whether health care is provided.

The NHS was founded on the principle of access for all, with the need for medical attention being the basis for treatment rather than the capacity of a person to pay for that treatment. The state took up responsibility in 1948 for providing and financing health care for any resident except for a small minority who wished to continue to purchase health care as private patients. Thus in effect most doctors, like nurses and ancillary staff, became government-paid employees. Hospitals were now government owned and operated, and were available to all as referred by their doctor, or general practitioner (GP), as he or she was called. At the outset it was intended that health care was free of charge to patients at the point of consumption. Thus the cost of meeting such provision was to be met by tax revenue and government borrowing together with social security contributions.

The founders of the NHS seemed to believe that the need for health care was both finite and quantifiable. Given an initial appropriate provision of resources, it was hoped that the burden on the state of ending the financial worries of those who became ill would in due course diminish. In practice since 1948 expenditure on health care has been far from finite. No developed country is able to spend as much on those of its citizens who are sick as would be necessary to take full advantage of improving health-care technology. Thus it has not been possible in the past half-century to eliminate unmet health needs. Indeed, much discussion of health care during this whole period has been characterized by references to 'a crisis in the NHS'. The rationing of scarce resources has been the reality, thus providing endless tension between those seeking treatment on the one hand, and the medical and ancillary professions within the NHS on the other. There has been much parliamentary and political debate caused by this inability to meet the aims, of those who founded the NHS, of ensuring that sufficient resources were provided to meet all genuine cases of need for health care.

Figure 11.1 illustrates the problem that emerged with the provision of health care by the NHS. In the figure the demand for health care, D_1, is downward sloping, but the supply of health-care resources is shown as a vertical straight line SQ_s. It is shown like this to highlight that at any given moment of time the supply of health care is fixed. It reflects the amount of resources made available by the government in the light of its philosophy and other competing claims on tax revenue. If the NHS supplies health care at a zero price, then the quantity demanded Q_d exceeds Q_s by the distance $Q_d - Q_s$. Unless the government is able to provide additional resources of the amount $Q_d - Q_s$, then this quantity of health care is not available to those who seek it. It represents a number of patients unable to receive treatment. Were the market to be allowed to clear at the market-clearing price P, then the situation of an excess demand at the zero price (because health care is free of charge) would not exist. For those unable to receive medical treatment because of the excess demand, their only option, other than paying for private provision, is to wait the time necessary until state provision becomes available. They join

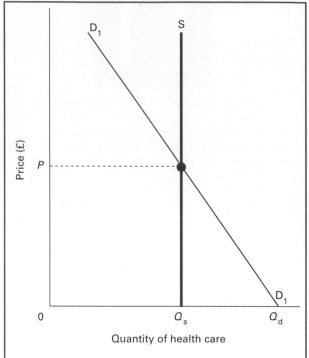

Figure 11.1
The provision of health care by the National Health Service

a **waiting list** and hope that in the fullness of time, which may be a year or more, it is their turn to receive treatment. There is, of course, the possibility that the lives of some of those awaiting treatment are meanwhile at risk. Their need for an operation in hospital is recognized but cannot be met. What Figure 11.1 shows is a situation of scarce health-care resources being rationed by **queuing** rather than by price.

How has this situation come about? Why has the NHS continually faced this 'crisis' of a shortage of resources to meet a demand for treatment unchecked by a need to pay?

Reasons for the pressure on successive governments to find adequate financing of the NHS are not hard to find. A powerful factor that has stimulated demand for health care since the NHS was founded is that of an ageing population. The number of older people is rising, particularly the number aged 75 or more. As one would predict, the need for health care is much higher for those of pensionable age than for those of working age simply because one is more likely to be ill as one gets older. So demographic change has had the effect of adding to the potential number of those demanding health care. On the supply side, technical advance has led to treatment being possible for illnesses for which at one time there was no effective treatment. Hip-replacement operations are now commonplace, but were rare only thirty years ago. New surgical methods spurred by miniaturization of medical instruments – so-called keyhole surgery – and advances in anaesthetics have helped to make greater use of hospital beds.

Waiting around

Health economists and officials argue that the length of a waiting list is not a good guide to anything. A waiting list may include people who are dead, people who have already had their operations elsewhere, and people who no longer need operations. Doctors compile their waiting lists in different ways. Some will not put any patients on their list when they think it is too long already; others will. Some put patients on a list long before the operation is needed; others wait. And many doctors claim to know surgeons who boost their waiting lists to get more private patients, or to strengthen their claims for more NHS resources.

Source: Adapted from *The Economist*, 7 June 1986

1 Is it the number of people on waiting lists that matters, or the length of time people have to wait for treatment?

2 What would be a better indicator of the pressing need for health-care attention than sheer numbers of people awaiting treatment?

3 Does it follow that if the NHS had extra resources from the government there would be a decrease in the number of those on waiting lists?

4 What alternatives could lead to more operations taking place?

These advances in medical technology add to what it is now possible to cure and hence extend the range of what can be offered as the supply of health care. Awareness of this enhanced supply potential has led to an increase in demand for treatment now known to be available. Thus *supply has affected demand*. In addition to these two factors, successive governments have had to face the fact that the NHS is a labour-intensive sector. The number employed within the NHS makes it the largest single employer in the United Kingdom. Table 11.1 shows that there were over 1 million employed in 1998. The cost of financing the NHS rises faster than the rate of price inflation for goods and services generally. Thus despite expenditure of about £61 billion in 1999–2000, equivalent to 7 per cent of public expenditure, the NHS has not been able to meet all the current demands for treatment placed on it. We thus need to consider whether the form and financing of health-care provision in the United Kingdom could be improved by using an alternative system such as is found in many other countries.

Paying for health care by insurance

In countries other than the United Kingdom, health-care provision is dominated by private or public insurance schemes. The principle of insurance seems at first sight to

Table 11.1

Manpower in the National Health Service

	1991	1998
NHS Trusts	124 000	1 122 000
NHS	1 098 000	77 000

Source: *Economic Trends*, June 1999

Note: As from April 1991 NHS Trust hospitals were classified as one of the public non-financial corporations, i.e., part of the public sector but not within the definition of the central government.

Manpower in Great Britain	1997
Medical staff	64 316
Dental staff	3 078
Nursing and midwifery staff	353 933*
Administrative and clerical staff	177 957
Ambulance staff	16 424

* This total excludes agency nurses

Source: *1998 Annual Abstract of Statistics*

be a very feasible way whereby the liability to pay for treatment can be met as and when one becomes ill. The prospect of a large bill for a hospital operation is daunting should one suddenly require such treatment. There is no certainty of the need to go into hospital, but if one does have to do so the costs involved may be enormous. The payment of an insurance premium on a regular basis appears to meet the problem of an unpredictable frequency of need for medical attention at a more modest cost than paying for treatment as required. However, on closer inspection, there are a number of problems with medical insurance. These problems involving the information required by insurance companies lead to an outcome which does not make the operation of an insurance-funded health-care system efficient in an economic sense. What are these information problems?

It has been argued that five conditions must be met if private insurance is to be efficient.* The likelihood of, say, breaking one's leg must

1 be less than 100 per cent;
2 be known or estimable;
3 involve no *adverse selection*; that is, I must not be able to conceal from the insurance company that I am a high-risk applicant;
4 involve no *moral hazard*; I should not, without the insurance company's knowledge and *at no cost to myself*, be able to affect the likelihood of breaking a leg;
5 not enable me without the insurance company's knowledge to affect the amount, and hence the cost to the insurance company, of the treatment I receive (the failure of this condition causes what is known as the *third-party payment problem*).

---

* Nicholas Barr, 'Funding the National Health Service', *Economics*, Spring 1989, p. 5.

If one or more of these conditions is not satisfied, then the provision of health care will not be universal. Thus if I suffer from a chronic or pre-existing illness, the likelihood of needing treatment is almost certain: condition 1 above is not met. If I am an elderly person I am much more likely to require medical care than if I were younger. An insurance company would be likely to offer insurance cover only on payment of a very high premium. Moreover, elderly people have an incentive to conceal potential medical problems to reduce their already relatively unattractive situation as a client for an insurance company: thus condition 3 above is also not met. If a woman becomes pregnant she may need hospital treatment for any illness associated with her pregnancy: this situation means that condition 4 above is also not met. The violations of the conditions listed mean that an insurance-funded health-care system will risk gaps in coverage. The old, the poor and the chronically sick are unlikely to be able to secure insurance in a purely private system. But we have not yet referred to condition 5 above. The **third-party payment problem** is as serious a weakness of the insurance system as those we have already identified. If I have cover for treatment under an insurance system then I have no incentive to minimize access to treatment. Likewise, those giving me treatment will know that, directly or indirectly, they will be paid by the insurance company. The doctor, like me as a patient, will act as though health care were free. The doctor has no incentive to keep the provision of health care under keen scrutiny if all or most of the costs involved are to be met by a third party – the insurance company. The outcome is that condition 5 above is not met so that there is an excessive consumption of medical care.* Recent experience suggests that the third-party payment problem is the underlying reason for the escalating cost of health care in the United States.

Our discussion of an insurance system indicates that in terms of efficiency and equity a privately funded insurance system cannot be expected to work well. We can now also draw on the discussion of externalities in Chapter 7 to lead us to the conclusion that a **market failure** situation exists in the market for health care.

Externalities revisited

In Chapter 7 we recognized a third party in market transactions concerning the steel industry. We showed how producers of steel and buyers of steel could act as though the quality of the environment was of no consequence to the local inhabitants when a steel mill is built in a particular location. In this case we had a negative spill-over. We also recognized the possibility of other cases where the production of a good or service, if left to market forces, would be under-allocated. Where external benefits are present as with a merit good like health, the government

can intervene in order to increase the level of output to that recognizing the benefits arising to society as a whole.

In Figure 11.2 we show the **marginal private benefit** (MPB) in respect of health care for an individual we call James. The MPB curve – actually a straight line – is downward sloping, reflecting the principle that the greater the scale of provision of health care as a merit good, the smaller is the marginal benefit perceived by James. Once an amount of health care Q_1 is provided, James perceives no additional benefit. Thus the MPB curve shows with each unit of health-care provision the change in the benefit as perceived and valued by an individual – in this case, James.

Marginal social cost (MSC) is the cost of providing one more unit of health-care output. It is upward sloping, reflecting rising opportunity costs. These two curves taken together lead to a quantity Q_J of health care where the perceived marginal private benefit from health care equals the marginal cost of its provision at a price P_J. For James this is the amount of health care he should buy. However, if James is now seen as part of a society which also can place a valuation on the benefits of health care, then we need to reflect the **marginal social benefits** of health care. In Figure 11.2 we now add the marginal social benefit (MSB) of health care in addition to the individual valuation of health care by James. Society gains from health care as valued by James. External benefits arise if James is healthy: if James is inoculated against a contagious disease he benefits others who,

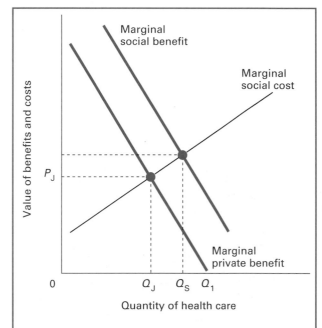

Figure 11.2
Private and social benefits from health
For James the quantity of health care he should buy, Q_J, is where his perceived marginal private benefit (MPB) from health care equals the marginal cost of its provision (MSC). For society as a whole the optimum amount is Q_S where marginal social benefit (MSB) equals MSC.

---

* A parallel example is where you take a damaged car to a garage and seek a quote for the cost of repair. The garage will ask whether it is the subject of an insurance claim or to be paid for privately.

whilst they may not be inoculated themselves, are now less at risk from an epidemic breaking out.

Figure 11.2 shows that for society as a whole rather than James the optimum amount of health care is now Q_S where MSC equals MSB – the marginal social costs are the same as the marginal social benefits. The quantity of health care as far as James is concerned, Q_J, is not an efficient outcome as far as society is concerned. At this level of provision the marginal social benefits exceed marginal social costs: the provision of one more unit of health care results in more benefits than it costs.

Health care: the need for information

In Chapter 3 we implicitly assumed that a consumer will be rational and buy the quantity of a good for which the benefit derived from the last unit consumed equals the price paid for that unit. (We shall explicitly consider this rational behaviour later in Chapter 19.) This assumption supports the proposition that an individual is the best judge of his or her own welfare, but only if we make the further assumption that as a consumer we have perfect information about the goods or services available in a market. However, in the market for health care, consumers do not have a supply of relevant information to be able to act rationally. A doctor or consultant knows much more than a patient about the technical issues of health care. As a result, a consumer of health care is very much in the hands of the doctor or consultant – indeed, literally so in many situations! It is presumed that the expert knows what is best for the patient. This is thus hardly the 'consumer is sovereign' world that we described as relevant in a market economy back in Chapter 2.

Health care provides an example of where there is **asymmetrical information** – the two parties to a transaction do not have equal sharing of information. In the market for

Table 11.2		
Health expenditure as a percentage of GDP in 1980		
	Public expenditure	**Total expenditure**
United States	3.9	9.1
Germany	7.0	8.8
France	6.0	7.6
Canada	5.5	7.3
Sweden	8.7	9.4
Netherlands	5.9	7.9
Australia	4.6	7.3
Denmark	7.7	8.7
Italy	5.6	7.0
Japan	4.5	6.4
Ireland	7.1	8.7
United Kingdom	5.0	5.6

Source: OECD

health care, producers – the doctors and consultants – in practice take both the supply *and* demand decisions. Does this mean that the producers may be stimulated to raise demand if they gain financially thereby? Or do they have an inducement in reverse – to minimize the calls on their time even though in the interest of patients they should offer more treatment? The relatively powerless position of those seeking health care means that we must view the asymmetric information situation as a further reason for regarding health-care provision as characterized by market failure. It is therefore no surprise to find that government intervention has been characteristic of all developed economies since 1950. In most of Western Europe, public insurance schemes have reinforced the coverage available by private medical insurance.

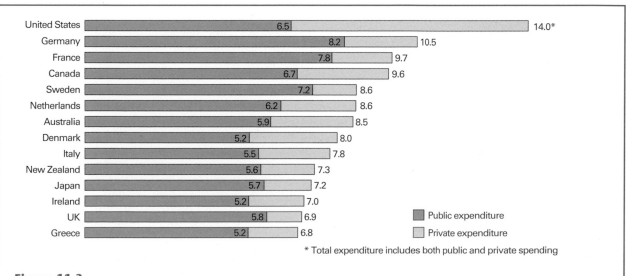

Figure 11.3
Health spending in OECD countries as a percentage of GDP, 1996

Source: *Financial Times*, 2 July 1998

The cost of health

5 How do the data in Table 11.2 illustrate the fact that in 1980 in most developed economies, governments were the predominant funding source for health care? **A✓**

6 Figure 11.3 shows public and private health expenditures in 1996. Do these data suggest whether health spending is generally income inelastic or elastic? **A✓**

7 Spending on health care denotes all the activity to help people make a recovery from ill health. What criteria would you need to determine whether a given level of health expenditure was well spent? **A✓**

8 The data in both Table 11.2 and Figure 11.3 are just at the national level. With reference to the United States, why might it be incorrect to infer that a vast majority of American citizens had no concerns over access to health care? **A✓**

The changing management of the National Health Service

Despite the growth of private medical insurance in the United Kingdom, the bulk of health care is still provided by government. The character of that provision has been changing as a result of reforms arising from the 1990 National Health Service and Community Care Act (the 1990 Act). Before outlining the provision of this Act, we need to understand the background against which it was deemed desirable to alter the organization of the NHS.

In 1989 the Conservative government published *Working for Patients*, a White Paper that proposed 'the most far-reaching reform of the National Health Service in its forty-year history'. The White Paper identified several undesirable aspects of health care that warranted a change in policy.

● Patients had limited freedom in choosing a general practitioner (GP) or in deciding where they could receive treatment once referred by their GP.

● This situation gave little incentive to a GP to offer the best possible service to a patient or little incentive to local hospitals to contain costs more effectively than other hospitals because neither faced a truly competitive situation.

● Hospitals appeared to vary considerably in the cost of delivering health care.

● GPs varied greatly in their willingness to prescribe drugs or refer patients to hospital.

● In referring patients to local hospitals, GPs did nothing to level out imbalances of supply and demand between different regions; thus patients could obtain more rapid treatment in some parts of the United Kingdom than others, even for the same operation.

● There was no incentive payment system for those employed in hospitals to vary the provision and quality of health care.

● There was no incentive for GPs to encourage *preventive medicine* rather than offer treatment for someone already ill.

● GPs could not use the resources available in the private sector, despite long waiting lists for NHS patients.

You will note the frequency with which attention is drawn in this list of shortcomings to the poor incentives in the health-care market. What the 1990 Act did was to try to strengthen such incentives in a reshaped structure of the NHS.

The introduction of the internal market

To bring about a sharper interplay between GPs and hospitals, the 1990 Act identified the former as 'purchasers' of health care and the latter as self-governing providers of health care. GPs, as purchasers, and hospital trusts would each move to a situation of much greater financial autonomy than hitherto. GPs would purchase treatment on behalf of patients through budgets. The providers of health treatment would earn revenues as a result of supplying in competition with one another. Hence within an overall budget determined by the Department of Health, an internal market would be generated between two competing sets of market participants, the GPs and hospitals. GPs were now seen as potentially more in competition with one another. They would now also have incentives to encourage preventive medicine. Hospital trusts would find an incentive to contain costs in order to compete more effectively in seeking custom from GPs. Since the 1990 Act also permitted GPs to purchase treatment throughout the United Kingdom, it was hoped that variations in the use of hospital capacity, for example usage of beds, would be reduced. Hospitals with spare capacity would find it worthwhile for their facilities to be more fully used. Moreover, since private hospitals could now seek custom from GPs, there was a prospect of new additional capacity being made available by either existing firms or new entrants to the health-care market.

The desirability of an internal market and its effects predictably became the subject of keen political debate. Critics saw the 1990 Act as involving an unnecessary increase in hospital managers to administer the sale of treatment in the new competitive environment. Those who supported the creation of the internal market viewed this as the only credible way in which ever-lengthening hospital waiting lists could be reduced. Hospitals would now have to ensure they were efficient users of scarce capacity as represented by operating theatres and would thus help to ease the pain of those who have waited months, if not years, for treatment prescribed long ago.

By 1995 it seemed that the creation of GP fundholders had indeed been a significant one. These GPs had generally been able to get their patients quicker access to hospital than non-GP fundholders. They had generally proved to be effective sources of pressures for faster and better service from hospitals. However, with less than half of the population covered, a two-tier system had developed with the patients of non-fundholding GPs being adversely affected.

'I'm putting you on the waiting list
for a hospital trolley'

On its return to power, the Labour government proposed to abolish the internal market that had resulted in such a system. In practice the new administration retained the basis of a market for health despite claims to the contrary. The 1997 White Paper proposed to maintain the split between buyers of health treatment (i.e. GPs) and suppliers (for example, hospitals), and uphold the ability of buyers to choose where to select their source of custom. The White Paper did not therefore in reality abolish fundholding, but extended its logic by grouping GPs into 481 'primary care groups', each with a fixed budget capable of buying a variety of health treatment. The White Paper proposed league tables of the performance of hospitals in meeting demands placed upon them. Given that it was also proposed to create a Commission for Health Improvement, critics were not slow to see that the new Labour government was willing to adopt earlier measures of Conservative administrations. Was this not a replica of the measures put in place by the Conservatives in the area of education in respect of both school league tables and the creation of an Office for Standards in Education (OFSTED) (see page 208 later in this chapter)? However, an early pledge by the Labour Party during the 1997 general election to cut waiting lists by 100 000 proved to be much more controversial. In February 1998 Mr Frank Dobson, the new Health Secretary, had to face the embarrassment of announcing that the length of waiting lists had actually risen by 100 000 since the May 1997 general election. To disarm his critics, Mr Dobson announced that the government would devote a further £2 billion to the NHS to reduce the record level of 1.26 million persons waiting for access to an NHS bed at the end of December 1997.

In July 1998 the Labour government celebrated 50 years of the NHS. During this half-century opinion polls have consistently shown the general enthusiasm of the British population for Aneurin Bevan's policy of free care for all. The NHS had survived as almost the only lasting achievement of the Attlee government throughout the privatization policy of the Thatcher government. Nonetheless, the survival of the NHS has not been without its own pain. Proof of this is not hard to find. Health authorities have continually found budgets under pressure. In August 1998, the West Hertfordshire Health Authority admitted it was operating a ban on a number of specific drugs and surgical procedures. Its treatment policy listed thirty-two operations and treatments it would not provide except in extreme circumstances. The Health Authority acknowledged it was rationing treatment. In a statement it declared that 'rationing of some kind has always been part of the NHS … Waiting lists are a form of rationing. The difference is that the process is now much more open and transparent.'

Mr Dobson as Health Secretary found himself caught up in further controversy in announcing in January 1999 that GPs could not freely prescribe the anti-impotence drug Viagra. This decision was made on the grounds that the NHS could not bear the costs of free prescription. Critics argued that this represented a new principle when GPs could only prescribe Viagra to patients if they were prepared to pay. By May 1999, Mr Dobson bowed to pressure from GPs to allow Viagra to be prescribed for a less restricted range of medical conditions than originally announced. Mr Dobson's decision was expected to cost the NHS over £15 million per year. Pfizer, the manufacturer of Viagra, had estimated that unrestricted prescription of the drug would have cost the NHS £50 million per year. Mr Dobson's decision highlighted the problem he faced as Health Secretary: 'We have completed a public consultation to help us find a sensible balance between treating men with the distressing condition of impotence and protecting the resources of the NHS to deal with other patients, for example, those with cancer, heart disease and mental health problems.'

Mr Dobson's decision came at a time when many were suffering from influenza, resulting in a severe shortage of hospital beds just when the NHS was experiencing an acute shortage of nursing staff. The media made much of patients reported to be waiting on hospital trolleys in corridors for several hours.

Preventive medicine

In 1992 the Department of Health launched *The Health of the Nation* strategy aimed at securing improvements in life expectancy and quality of life. This new strategy can be seen as one of emphasizing prevention – promoting better standards of health – rather than supplying health care to those who become ill. Arguably, since the NHS was founded in 1948, there has been an undue bias in using resources devoted to health care for the diagnosis and treatment of illness as an indirect way of improving the physical and mental health of the nation rather than achieving this end by direct preventive means. However, we should recognize that such a strategy raises some normative issues. How far should a government use taxes to reduce the temptation to smoke or drink? How far should the government advise citizens on matters of diet? Should it advise the public to take more exercise? Do HIV infection and AIDS justify sexual health as an objective of government policy? If so, how should government try to reduce the incidence of sexually transmitted diseases and the number of conceptions among, say, 16-year-olds?

Health care: an overview

Throughout Western Europe, governments in recent years have faced a growing problem of financing the burden of welfare spending. A theme apparent in policies to tackle this problem is both the role of competition and the use of price incentives. These two related concepts aim to curb costs and enhance efficiency of health-care provision. However, the recourse to market systems such as the internal market model in the United Kingdom will not solve the phenomenon we recognized at the outset of this chapter – the inexorable long-term growth in demand for health care based on technical changes and rising expectations of longer life expectancy. Even in the United States, where spending on health care as a proportion of GNP exceeds that in any other country, there is much dissatisfaction with the delivery of health care and the inequality in its provision. Indeed, there is little evidence to suggest that the average person's state of health in the United States is significantly enhanced by the higher level of health spending compared with elsewhere.

KEY POINTS

11.1

- The supply of health care when provided and financed by the state at a zero price results in those requiring treatment joining a waiting list.

- Advances in medical technology mean that the supply of and demand for health care are interdependent.

- Paying for health care by insurance is not likely to be efficient in part because of the third-party payment problem.

- Health care is a market where externalities exist and those needing treatment face the problem of a lack of information on which to take decisions.

- The attempt to introduce more competition and enhance incentives in the NHS as part of the internal market is a policy that has been much debated. Critics doubt whether its aims either should or could actually be realized.

The market for education

We saw earlier in this chapter that in the United Kingdom the state provided a measure of universal coverage of health care as recently as 1948. In the case of education, the dating of government provision was somewhat earlier. In 1870 the Elementary Education Act had aimed to ensure national provision of the education of children. It widened the scope of what was hitherto available on a commercial basis from private schools, and also that provided free of charge by both churches and charitable institutions. Subsequent legislation helped to ensure that provision of schooling for children up to the age of 10 became both compulsory and free of charge. It was not until the 1944 Education Act that this primary school provision was extended to those aged 15 or 16 as secondary education. For those staying on in school beyond 16 years, schooling was optional but still free of charge. We do not discuss detailed issues concerning types of school, nor many of the details concerning the implementation of the National Curriculum within the past decade. Our concern is a more general one – to discuss the rationale for state intervention in education in the broadest sense, with the United Kingdom uppermost in mind for illustrating the nature and implications of state involvement.

Human capital

Almost on the first page of this book we recognized the role of **human capital** as one of the key resources available in any economic system. Labour is neither a natural resource like land nor a 'manufactured' resource nor inanimate like a tractor or lathe. Since Professor Gary Becker coined the term thirty years ago to describe his book on the economics of education and training, human capital has come to describe aptly the relevance of skills in a country's labour force given the concern to achieve economic growth. In the discussion that follows, we shall focus on state provision of education, and then later briefly consider training together with the role of UK governments with respect to those who leave school and are in employment.

Consumption and investment

Education is both a consumption good and an investment good. The acquisition of knowledge by reading a book – even this one! – can give pleasure and benefits to an individual equivalent to consuming an ice-cream or seeing a film at the cinema. But education can also help advance one in a chosen career if appropriate success is made in certain key examinations. If a financial gain is thereby achieved, then the time spent in the educational process can be seen as an *investment*. By investing in yourself you hope that your enhanced skills add to your potential earning power in the labour market; your qualifications should help you to compete that much better against those less well qualified for a particular job. As far as an employer is concerned, your educational qualification is a means of *filtering* where there is keen competition for a post. We consider the working of the labour market in more detail in Chapter 24. In the meantime, we consider why it is considered desirable for the state to compel children to attend schools until the age of 16.

The provision of compulsory education

If private benefits, both of a consumption kind and also as an investment, accrue to an individual, why should this mean that the state has to intervene in the market for education? It is clear that in this market privately owned suppliers of schooling can exist. The long-established independent schools like Harrow, Eton and Rugby have operated by charging fees for those attending them. But such schools cater for a minority of those aged up to 16 years in the United Kingdom at the present time. For many, attendance at such fee-paying institutions is not a feasible option because parental income is inadequate. Even though some scholarships are available to allow children either a free or concessionary place based on their academic ability, these are few in number. The inability to pay school fees by parents means that private provision serves only a minority of the market. Hence the uneven distribution of income and wealth in the United Kingdom is one basis for the state to intervene in the market for education. This intervention has in practice taken the form of actual educational provision – state schools – rather than the alternative of providing subsidies to existing institutions and regulating their operation. The point we are making here is a crucial one: state intervention may be deemed desirable but it does not necessarily have to involve state-owned and run schools staffed by teachers paid by the state. Rather than offer parents local state-owned schools for their children, there is technically an alternative: to give parents what has been called an *education voucher* to entitle their child to schooling at any school of their choice. The voucher would have a value that represented a contribution to the financial costs of operating the school, which would be paid by the government on presentation of the voucher. This proposal, if implemented, would have a significant impact on the financing and also the running of an *established* state system of schools as in the United Kingdom, and so is a contentious issue. However, we present this alternative here to show that the state does technically have an alternative to undertaking the actual building of schools, equipping them with laboratories, desks, books and other relevant materials, and also hiring staff. In reality, this is what constitutes state sector provision in the United Kingdom, and indeed in most other countries in Western Europe.

Marginal private benefits and marginal social benefits

Earlier in this chapter we considered private and social benefits of health and the marginal social cost as a basis for state intervention. We now examine this in respect of education. In Figure 11.4 we assume an economy with two people, Susan and Vijay. The marginal benefit from education as valued by Susan is shown as MPB_S and that for Vijay as MPB_V. To obtain the marginal social benefit for both persons, we add the two private valuations *vertically*, and hence obtain MPB_{S+V}. MPB_{S+V} intersects MPB_V at quantity W. At output W MPB_S is zero: we have only MPB_V to show at this level of output of education.

To consider how education produces a *social* benefit as well as private benefit for individuals in society, let us now assume a society of, say, a dozen educated individuals. In Figure 11.5 (overleaf) we show MBS as the marginal benefit to society as a whole of the consumption of education by individuals. This shows the *external benefits* that arise in a situation of an educated society. We now add MBS to the MPB for the twelve people in our society and the marginal cost of the supply of education. This is also shown in Figure 11.5. If MSC is the private and social marginal costs of education, an individual would choose to buy Q_1 quantity of education.

This is not the optimum quantity since at this level of consuming education the price paid is still below the marginal benefit to society from that level of consumption.

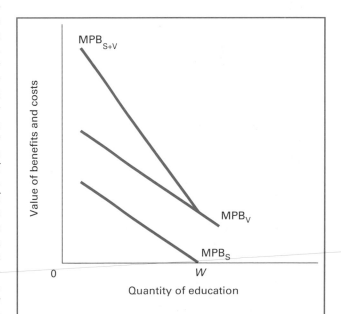

Figure 11.4

Marginal private benefits: the summation of two individuals' willingness to pay

The marginal private benefit schedule in a society of two persons is found by adding the two private marginal benefit schedules vertically.

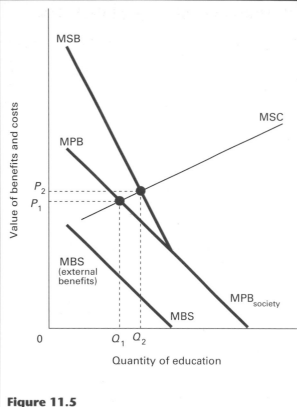

Figure 11.5
Marginal private and external benefits
The MBS schedule is the marginal external benefits to society. When added vertically to the marginal private benefit schedule we derive the marginal social benefit schedule.

The optimum quantity of education for an individual to buy is Q_2. Because of the positive externalities that arise from an educated society, individuals do not purchase the optimum amount of education. If the state subsidizes the provision of education, then in the consumption of education marginal social benefits can equal the costs.* This subsidy, sufficient to allow an individual to buy the amount of education that society would wish, can be made available in one of two ways. You will recall that we said earlier that state intervention could be either state provision or state finance. So the state can either set up its own schools and other educational institutions, or provide finance to privately owned educational establishments such that the quantity of education Q_2 is made available at a price of P_2.

Because in the United Kingdom the chosen course was the first of these two options, it was much easier for the government to bring about a major change in educational policy in 1988. By means of the 1988 Education Reform Act, responsibility for what children learn in state schools

---

* In practice determining social benefits is not easy. However, we are making the point that the benefits to society are not identical to the sum of the benefits derived by individuals. We are nonetheless silent on how individuals pay something to ensure the provision of Q_2.

was taken away from local education authorities and passed to the Department of Education and Science. Thus educational policy became more centralized, as is typically the case in many other countries in Western Europe. A second measure was the delegation of responsibility for management to schools, so that funding now depended on the number of pupils on school rolls. The 1988 Act gave parents the right to vote in a ballot to decide whether their school should apply to the Secretary of State for Education to enjoy self-governing (grant-maintained) status. In November 1992 information was published for the first time for every area of England comparing the examination results of local secondary schools. The government saw these 'league tables' as helping parents to make more informed choices about their children's education. In November 1993 these tables contained more information and now included all independent schools and all colleges in the new sector of further education. Each school must publish a prospectus or brochure every year describing its achievements and what it has to offer. This brochure must include examination results for the school compared with other local schools and national average results. It must also give rates of unauthorized absence. Apart from statistics, the prospectus should give the aims and values of the school, showing its approach to teaching. The governors of each school must also prepare an annual report to be sent to all parents for discussion at the annual parents' meeting. Parents are also entitled to receive a written report on their child's progress at least once a year. A new independent organization, the Office for Standards in Education (OFSTED), was set up to monitor standards in schools; it is required to inspect all state schools at least once every four years. After an inspection the inspectors, who have to be approved by OFSTED, must publish a summary report setting out the strengths and weaknesses of a school.

Critics of the UK's educational system feel that such changes have not adequately addressed the need for more investment in human capital, particularly for those who are not of the highest academic ability.

Elective education

We have discussed why the state intervenes to compel children to attend school until they are 16 years old. When a student can opt to continue in higher education or take a job, how does this decision illustrate the case of 'investment in oneself'? In Figure 11.6 we show the earnings profile of two persons, Jane and Kerry, both 16 years old, who take different decisions: Jane decides to go to a sixth-form college and then hopes to go on to university, while Kerry takes a job on leaving school. For Jane there are assumed to be no earnings until she is 21. While there may in reality be some modest earnings from casual employment, these are ignored. The earnings profile until the age of retirement at 63 years reflects the assumption that Jane will earn more than Kerry when they are both aged 21. Jane *forgoes* the earnings enjoyed by Kerry when she starts work at 16. This sum is equivalent to the area OABC. If the extended period of five years' education until the age of 21 also involves costs to Jane, then the area OCGH is also relevant in an analysis of the worthwhileness of working for examinations at 18 years followed by a degree. If, however, the area represented by the enhanced earnings accruing to Jane compared with Kerry – BDEF – outweighs these two areas of forgone earnings and costs incurred, then the decision to stay on in education is indeed worthwhile. In both the United Kingdom and elsewhere, the evidence available is that staying on in education does indeed generate benefits for an individual like Jane. In doing so it can be used to justify the case for individuals helping to pay for their further education. If people like Jane can have access to student loans, they can help fund the cost of their education provided by the state while still leaving a worthwhile return to themselves, despite the cost of repaying loans on entering the job market. Figure 11.7 (overleaf) shows a recent calculation of this investment. In 1991 the UK government introduced a student loans scheme. Students could borrow £1150 per year paid back over five years after graduation in monthly payments that rise in line with inflation. This scheme is not available to mature students aged 55 years or more. The scheme appeared to offer economies for the government in supporting those in higher education.

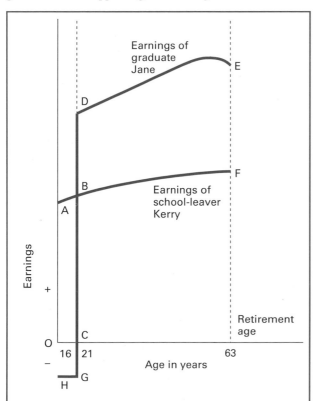

Figure 11.6

Investment in elective education

A student at university who forgoes earnings in comparison with someone who leaves school at 16 may none the less find a degree a worthwhile investment.

Human capital: a global view

The figure shows data collected by the World Bank on the social return to investment in education in low-income, middle-income and the developed economies of members of the Organization for Economic Co-operation and Development.

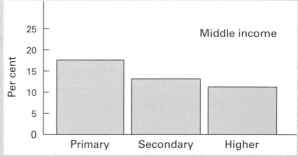

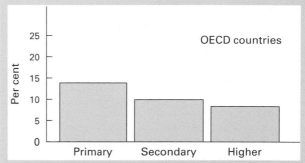

Social returns to investment in education, by countries' income per head (per cent)

Source: *The Economist*, 26 March 1994

9 Why would you expect the social return on investment in low-income countries to be higher in primary education than in higher education?

10 Why might one expect the social return to education to fall as the level of income rises?

11 It has been argued that the returns to educating women are higher than those to educating men. How might you explain this?

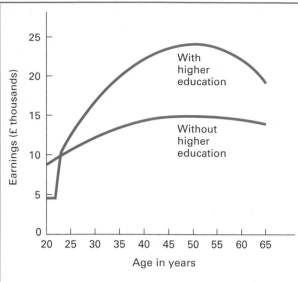

Figure 11.7
The benefits of education
Post-tax annual earnings adjusted for inflation for women
with medium earnings

Source: *Independent on Sunday*, 14 August 1994

KEY POINTS

11.2

■ The supply of education in the United Kingdom and
many developed countries is mainly provided by the
government through the actual provision of state
schools rather than through subsidies to existing
institutions.

■ Government intervention in the education market
recognizes the relevance of positive externalities –
external benefits – that arise if the state extends what
individuals would perceive as the private benefits of
education.

■ Education is both a consumption good and an
investment good.

■ The introduction of student loans to help cover the
cost of higher education is an explicit recognition of
the benefit of education as an investment good.

The market for housing

At the end of Chapter 9 we showed that government intervention in the United Kingdom in regulating rents paid by
tenants to landlords had discouraged the supply of private
rented housing. The housing market is no longer one
where the majority of households live in accommodation
rented from private landlords, as was the case eighty years
ago. But rent controls have not been the only form of state
intervention in the housing market, and thus we need to
consider what other forms of intervention have occurred
to affect the market.

Housing: private and public sector provision

There is no single housing market in the United
Kingdom but several markets, which differ according to
the significance of private and public sector activity. We
can identify four different markets, of which by far the
largest is the owner-occupied market. Figure 11.8 shows
that owner-occupied dwellings now account for about 70
per cent of the housing stock in the United Kingdom.
The second largest section of the total housing market is
the public rented sector. This comprises the housing
stock made available by local authorities (councils) to
meet the housing needs of low-income families. Figure
11.8 makes clear that during the period between 1981
and 1990, the relative importance of council houses and
flats has fallen as a result of policies encouraging council
tenants to purchase their rented property. The third
largest section of the total housing market is the private
rented sector. This is the sector that was the subject of
rent controls between 1915 and the late 1980s; these
were discussed in Chapter 9. Thus in the private rented
sector the market mechanism has for many years been
distorted by government intervention. Nonetheless,
what the private rented market and the owner-occupied
market have in common is a market-based system of
resource allocation where those demanding housing can
transact with those able to supply various types of
accommodation. In contrast, the public rented sector
constitutes the provision of property by local authorities
as though housing were a merit good like health and
education, considered earlier in this chapter. As with any
merit good, if state provision is made available at a price
below market levels, then it is being subsidized by the
taxpayer. We consider later in the chapter how the
financing of public sector housing has become a point of
concern.

The final sector of the housing market – housing
associations – is a relatively new one, as a glance at Figure
11.8 makes clear. Housing associations represent a mix
between the private sector and the public sector. Private
sector finance and government funding together help to
ensure the provision of subsidized accommodation for

those tenants paying rents to housing associations. Figure 11.8 shows that since 1980 housing associations have emerged as a new but still very small supplier of accommodation. Housing associations do in fact have a long history as non-profit-making voluntary bodies, but recent legislation has augmented their role in providing housing for the elderly and people with disabilities. Indeed, housing associations have emerged to play a significant role in meeting demand for rented accommodation in the inner cities, often through rehabilitation of older housing stock rather than new building. The housing associations are now being looked to by the government to help make greater use of those empty private dwellings owned by private landlords who feel deterred by rent controls from making this accommodation available.

We turn now to consider in more detail the impact of intervention in the owner-occupied sector and then in the publicly rented sector.

Owner occupation

In the last thirty years the most important form of housing in the United Kingdom has been owner-occupied housing. This is a dwelling inhabited by those who finance it by means of a long-term loan (a mortgage) from a bank or building society. At any point in time some owner-occupiers will have actually paid for their house or flat, having completed paying back the loans. Others may have been able from their earned income or gifts from those no longer alive to buy a house outright without recourse to a loan. Owner-occupiers have been encouraged for many years to buy dwellings rather than rent them by government policy. The rationale for this stance by the government – the belief in a property-owning democracy – is not peculiar to the United Kingdom. Owner occupation is the major form of housing in several other countries, as Figure 11.9 (overleaf) shows. In eight of the nine countries more than half the housing stock is owner-occupied. Owner occupation is seen in many countries as inherently desirable and not a politically contentious matter.

In the United Kingdom the encouragement of owner occupation took the form of tax relief on mortgage interest. The effect of tax relief is to lighten the burden of tax for those repaying their loans to a bank or building society. The total sum involved for the UK government has been very large – as high as £7.7 billion in 1990–1, but lower than this in recent years owing to falling interest rates charged on mortgages. The continuing strong growth in demand for owner occupation was encouraged in the late 1980s by government policies to *deregulate* financial markets, which made it easier for people to borrow larger mortgages. (We discuss this later

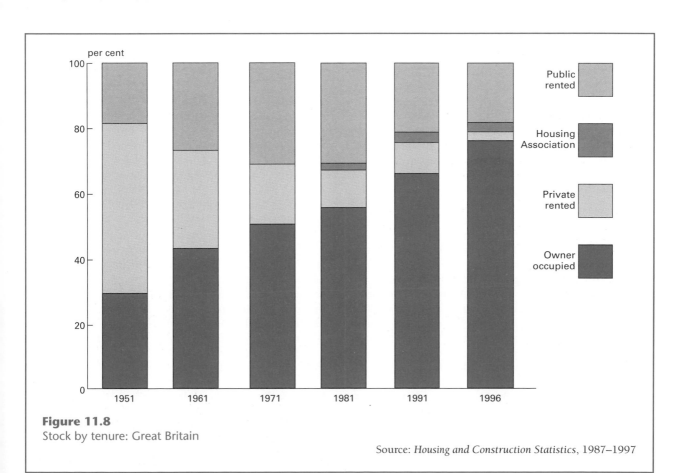

Figure 11.8
Stock by tenure: Great Britain

Source: *Housing and Construction Statistics*, 1987–1997

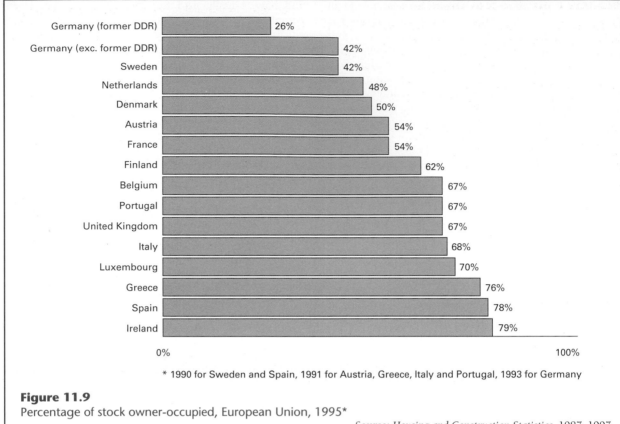

Germany (former DDR)	26%
Germany (exc. former DDR)	42%
Sweden	42%
Netherlands	48%
Denmark	50%
Austria	54%
France	54%
Finland	62%
Belgium	67%
Portugal	67%
United Kingdom	67%
Italy	68%
Luxembourg	70%
Greece	76%
Spain	78%
Ireland	79%

0%   100%

* 1990 for Sweden and Spain, 1991 for Austria, Greece, Italy and Portugal, 1993 for Germany

Figure 11.9
Percentage of stock owner-occupied, European Union, 1995*

Source: *Housing and Construction Statistics*, 1987–1997

in Chapter 28.) Together with low mortgage rates, this enabled many householders to borrow ever-larger sums either to effect house improvements or to move to more expensive housing. In the Spring 1988 Budget, the then Chancellor of the Exchequer, Nigel Lawson, announced that as from 1 August 1988 two or more separate mortgagors could no longer benefit from the shared purchase of a single property. This gave advance notice of the withdrawal of one element of subsidized owner occupation. The result was predictable: a pronounced surge in house prices in the summer of that year. The boom in house prices between 1985 and 1989 varied across different parts of the United Kingdom but was particularly rapid in East Anglia and the southeast of England. However, in 1989 the boom ended and rises in house prices slowed; they actually fell in 1992. The recession in the UK economy reflected in higher interest rates and rising unemployment led to householders losing their former keen interest in the housing market. Indeed, those who had lost their job or whose business had gone bankrupt were now finding difficulty in repaying their mortgage loans. This led to a growing number of house repossessions by the banks and building societies from clients whose financial situations had changed dramatically within a few years. Some owner-occupiers found themselves with dwellings worth less than their outstanding

loan – they faced a situation known as a **negative equity** situation. The government was sufficiently concerned by the slump in house prices that it introduced measures aimed at stimulating the housing market.

In the March 1999 Budget, Gordon Brown announced that MIRAS would be withdrawn from April 2000. This decision had been widely expected and there was general agreement that MIRAS was a distortion in the housing market.

Whilst council tenants were attracted to buy their homes after 1979, some of those who lost their jobs and failed to find subsequent employment have found that home ownership brings the problem of costly necessary repairs. In 1994 the National Housing Forum reported that one in thirteen homes is officially unfit for human habitation and that the owner-occupier proportion is now rising. A total of 1.8 million homes failed to meet all nine basic structural or hygiene standards laid down by the government. The Forum estimated that at least £7 billion of public money needs to be spent to make such homes fit for habitation. However, recent cuts in government funding for rehabilitation of housing mean that there is no obvious strategy to maintain the quality of the privately owned housing stock in the light of the growth in home ownership.

Publicly rented accommodation

As far as housing available from local authorities is concerned, government policy has had the effect of reducing the size of this stock to about one-fifth of the total housing stock, as Figure 11.8 shows. The sale of council houses was a main theme of the Thatcher government after 1979. By 1990 two-thirds of all households owned their homes outright or on a mortgage. Local authorities were also obliged to raise rents much closer to market levels than hitherto. Moreover, these suppliers of accommodation for rent found that borrowing funds from the capital market to expand their housing stock was now severely regulated.

Local authorities are obliged by law to provide accommodation for those declaring themselves to be homeless. Those who meet the relevant criteria (including pregnancy, children in the household or old age) may need to be housed by local authorities in private sector dwellings if no other housing is available. As in the case of the NHS, local authorities have for many years been obliged to ration demand for their housing by recourse to a *waiting list*. Prospective users of local authority housing have to take their place in a queue. Given the poor state of maintenance of some of the public sector housing stock, the long list of names of those seeking accommodation from local authorities and the apparent growing number of the homeless are sad reflections of how the housing market in the United Kingdom is not actually working.

Until 1989 local authorities, broadly speaking, were free to determine their own rents with the support of both subsidies from central government and sums raised from owner-occupiers in the form of rates. However, under the Local Government and Housing Act 1989, the Secretary of State assumed the power to determine annual increases in rents for all local authorities. These increases were to be decided by reference to each local authority's council housing stock relative to that in the country as a whole. However, the existing levels of rents in each local authority were taken as given. At the same time the Act changed the form of subsidy received both by councils and by council tenants.

The government attempted to focus housing benefit more closely on tenants on low incomes. However, since 1989 the cost of housing benefit has risen sharply and now exceeds the sum incurred by the government in mortgage tax relief as income support for those who are owner-occupiers. About two-thirds of all council tenants receive some housing benefit.

What about the homeless?

In the market-place consumers express preferences by paying a 'price'. They do this in order to gain a *private* benefit. In other words, the reward is *direct*. The satisfaction is somehow *internal*, in so far as the investor or consumer reaps a reward in return for their payment. Such personal rewards are all well and good for those who have an income, but what about those who cannot express themselves in the market-place – those without money?

In October 1999 the UK government promised the homeless a moment in the sun of political priorities. A target was set to reduce the number 'sleeping rough' by two-thirds by 2002. Hilary Armstrong, the government minister responsible for housing, said 'it is one of the government's key objectives and £145 million has been set aside over 3 years'.

12 How do most people in the twenty-first century manage to pay the market price for housing in the UK?
13 State two ways that the government subsidized the housing market during the twentieth century.
14 How would you recommend that the £145 million be spent to help the homeless?
15 'Shelter is a basic need that the government should subsidize for everybody.' Explain the economic arguments for and against this proposition.

KEY POINTS

11.3

- The most important sector of the housing market in the United Kingdom is the owner-occupier sector.

- Owner-occupied housing was encouraged by tax relief on mortgage loans.

- Public sector provision through council housing has become less significant due to the encouragement given to tenants to buy their rented accommodation, but is still the second most commonly found type of housing in the UK.

- Rents for public sector housing have risen much closer to market-clearing levels in recent years, but the burden of housing benefits falling on the state has risen sharply.

Welfare and consumer surplus

In Chapter 9 we discussed the impact of indirect taxes imposed by governments, having previously in Chapter 3 examined the process of market-clearing. We can now extend our analysis of the impact of government intervention by examining more closely the nature of market equilibrium. Figure 11.10(a) shows two areas of surplus created at the market-clearing price of OP. The upper part – area *A* – shows the surplus accruing to consumers, this being the benefit from consumption less than what consumers have to pay for it. This area arises because every unit of the good sold at the market price of OP could have been sold at a higher price. All units apart from the marginal unit sold at price OP have been obtained by consumers as a surplus because they are worth more than the price actually paid. The area *B* represents producers' surplus. As in the case of consumers, but this time supplied rather than purchased, the last unit supplied costs producers OP. But supplies were available at a price lower than OP. Thus area *B* represents the unit-by-unit surpluses producers gain in that they are paid more than they would have been willing to receive.

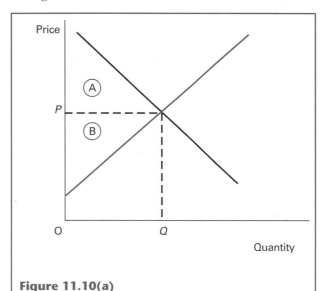

Figure 11.10(a)

Source: *The Economist*, 20 September 1997

In Figure 11.10(b) we show the impact of a tax. As a result of the tax, consumers now pay a higher price and producers receive less revenue than before. Inevitably, this means that both the areas of **consumer surplus** and **producer surplus** are less than before.

In Figure 11.10(c) we show the supply and demand curves for a drug which is available to NHS patients at a charge of OS. Assume now that the government decides to provide the drug free of charge to all who wish to use it as treatment for a particular illness. It is apparent that the original area of consumer surplus of STU will now rise by the area RSU. Thus the new total area of consumer surplus is RTU.

We will return to discuss consumer surplus in Chapters 19 and 26 but provide several multiple choice questions on this concept in the Exam Preparation section below.

KEY POINTS

11.4

- Consumer surplus measures the surplus accruing to consumers for all units bought, which is measured in the area above the price paid below the demand curve.

- Producer surplus measures the surplus accruing to producers for all units supplied, which is measured in the area above the supply curve at the market price.

- The areas of consumer surplus and producer surplus will change in the light of government intervention, for example, imposing or reducing taxes and/or subsidies.

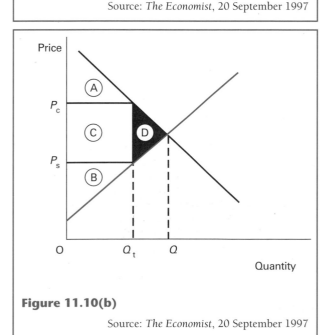

Figure 11.10(b)

Source: *The Economist*, 20 September 1997

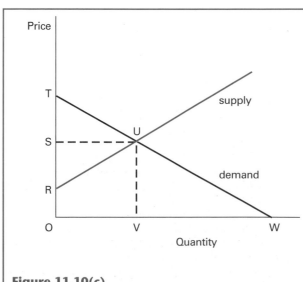

Figure 11.10(c)

Source: *The Economist*, 20 September 1997

Case Study

Fifty years old: in sickness and in health

Some time in the autumn of 1997, though it was hardly noticed at the time, a political milestone was reached: the number of people waiting for hospital treatment rose above the number claiming unemployment benefit – for the first time since mass joblessness became the nation's dominant political issue in the mid-1970s. This week, Frank Dobson, the health secretary, came under attack as new figures showed that, far from falling by 100 000 since the May 1997 election, as promised in Labour's manifesto, the waiting list in England had risen by 140 000, to a record 1.3 million. Mr Dobson said he was embarrassed by the figures. Having harped on about waiting lists during their years in opposition, and having made them one of the main issues in last year's election campaign, ministers know that they will be in hot water if they do not get the queues down soon, and keep them down. Imagine the next election campaign: the Tories revive their classic 1979 'Labour isn't working' posters – only instead of a long line of jobless, this time they feature a queue of patients.

For all Mr Dobson's determination to fix the problem with a mixture of taskforces, threats and money, the omens do not look good. Throughout the 50-year history of the National Health Service, more money has been pumped in, yet the queues have got longer. Despite repeated efforts to cut waiting lists, they have never fallen for more than five successive quarters. But if the government is stuck with a public-relations problem, it will have only itself to blame. For waiting lists are, in fact, a pretty crude indicator of how well the NHS is serving the public. The previous Conservative government tried to point out that factors such as the amount of time spent waiting, and whether the most urgent cases were being treated swiftly, were far more important.

Public-opinion surveys have shown that a queue is regarded as the least-worst way to deal with non-urgent cases given the finite resources of a publicly funded health service. Research by Richard Hamblin and others at the King's Fund, a medical charity, has found that, despite the lengthening queue, the average wait has remained at 13–14 weeks since the 1960s. Despite this, Mr Dobson and Co. insisted from the opposition benches, and still do in government, that the length of the queue matters.

Given the great leaps in medical science since the NHS was created in 1948, the ageing population and the public's rising expectations of an active, pain-free life, it is hardly surprising that waiting lists continue to grow. Hip replacements, now a common operation, have been available only for about twenty years. Transplants and new cancer treatments mean that many who in the 1940s would have died young and left a good-looking corpse now live long enough for their bodies to wear out. The queue for eye surgery has risen by 140 per cent in the past ten years, mainly because there are more elderly people needing cataracts removed. Huge numbers of people with injuries and arthritis now have exploratory 'keyhole' operations using high-tech instruments, to see if they would benefit from more extensive surgery. Such patients thus join the waiting list twice.

These trends are set to continue, so hospital queues may still rise even if, as was rumoured this week, the government plans to mark the NHS's fiftieth birthday in July by announcing a £6 billion ($9.7 billion) increase, phased over three years, in its £44 billion annual budget. Past efforts to cut hospital queues have been based on the false assumption that they are a simple backlog, and that increasing the rate of treatments will eventually clear the backlog. What in fact happens is that the numbers of patients sent for their first hospital appointment by their general practitioners, and the proportion of these put on to the waiting list for operations by hospital consultants, are both affected by the size of the waiting list itself. If the NHS gets more money to do operations, the queues go down briefly; consultants find they have less reason to discourage patients from opting for surgery, and put more on their lists; GPs react to the improved chance of surgery by sending more patients to hospital. Hey presto, the queues lengthen again.

Despite the lessons of history, Mr Dobson is optimistic that he can cut hospital queues by targeting any extra money that comes his way better than his predecessors

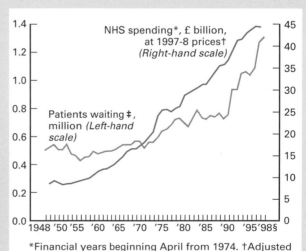

*Financial years beginning April from 1974. †Adjusted by GDP deflator. ‡England. §March.

Impatient in-patients

Sources: Department of Health; Office of Health Economics

did. For instance, the £300 million he got last October was used to tackle 'bed-blocking' by elderly patients stuck in hospital because nothing had been done to help them cope with living at home. This seemed to avert a widely expected winter crisis in the NHS.

Though waiting lists have their merits as a form of rationing, the other obvious method is to restrict the availability of some treatments on the NHS, or withdraw them entirely. Some health-care experts argue that many minor operations such as tonsil removal are of dubious worth and should be stopped. While the waiting-list task-forces are looking at such matters, ministers doubt that they will lead to big savings. In other cases, from the removal of non-painful varicose veins to infertility treat-ments, it could be argued that they do not involve heal-ing the sick and therefore the NHS should not cover them. Again, the taskforces are looking into this – but removing whole areas of treatment from the NHS would be very controversial.

The alternative to such hard-and-fast exclusions is a system of priority points for operations, as was recently introduced in New Zealand. Patients get points for the urgency of their surgery, how badly their ailment is affect-ing their lives, and how long they have waited. Another idea is a formal system of booking operations on fixed dates. People might not feel so bad about waiting for treatment if they had a definite date for admission, and knew they were not being queue-jumped by less urgent cases. Such measures, now under consideration, might build public confidence in the NHS. If so, it would be eas-ier for ministers to quietly drop the pretence that the length of the queue itself is the main indicator of how well the NHS is doing in their hands.

Source: *The Economist*, 23 May 1998

1 How does the chart support the comment that 'the omens do not look good' in relation to the length of waiting lists?
2 How does the passage illustrate the problem of rising demands on the NHS since 1948?
3 Explain why it is held that numbers put on the waiting list are themselves affected by the size of the waiting list itself.
4 Why is the restriction of some treatments on the NHS a contentious policy?
5 What is the merit of a system of priority points for operations?
6 In 1996–7 many health authorities explicitly excluded access to treatment for sex-change operations, reversal of vasectomy, tattoo removal or cosmetic varicose veins. What are the arguments for and against such a policy?
7 To what extent can state health provision be supplemented or replaced by the private sector?
8 NHS patients now have to pay a small proportion of the cost of dental treatment. What are the possible consequences of introducing charges to see a GP?
9 Cancer survival statistics published in April 1999 prompted one of the report's authors to comment as follows:

'Cancer survival is not a lottery. Lotteries are fair. A lottery ticket buys you the same chance of winning whether you are rich or poor and whether you live in Leeds or London. But if you have cancer and you are poor, you have been dealt an unfair hand.'

How would you account for the fact that cancer survival depends in part on income?

Exam Preparation

Multiple choice questions

1 Two policies to reduce the use of illegal drugs are being considered by the government. Policy One involves a health education campaign in schools and on television pointing out the risks of drug usage. Policy Two involves allocating a significant increase in funding to the police to seek out and charge drug dealers which, if successful, will reduce the supply of drugs available.

Which of the following is the most likely result of the two policies?

	Price of drugs		Quantity of drugs traded	
	Policy One	Policy Two	Policy One	Policy Two
A	increase	fall	fall	increase
B	increase	increase	increase	fall
C	fall	fall	increase	increase
D	fall	increase	fall	fall

2 A drug which cures an infectious disease is supplied in a free market. The production of the drug pollutes the atmosphere and imposes additional cleaning costs on neighbouring firms. The diagram shows the costs and benefits of production.

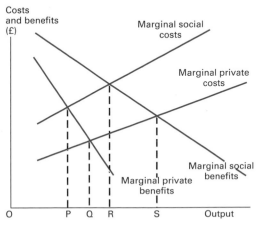

The optimal output of the drug for society would be
A OP
B OQ
C OR
D OS

3 The diagram represents the market for a new vaccine where there are positive externalities in consumption.

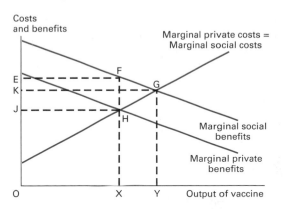

The government is considering subsidizing the production of the vaccine so that output and sales increase from OX units to OY units. The net gain in social welfare is represented by the area
A FGH
B EFGK
C KGHJ
D EFGHJ

4 The diagram below relates to education, which is a merit good. MSB is the marginal social benefit and MSC is the marginal social cost, which is assumed to be equal to the marginal private cost. In a free market the price of education would be P_1 and the quantity demanded and supplied would be Q_1.

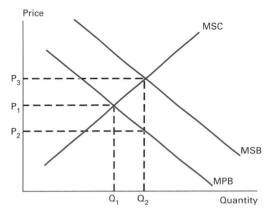

If the government aims to take account of social benefits and costs, which policy should it follow for education?
A make education free of charge to the user

B raise standards so that more education is demanded

C subsidize education so as to stop under-consumption

D do nothing as the market is at a position of equilibrium

5 In the diagram DD and S_1S_1 represent the original demand and supply schedules for car parking. The local authority that owns the car park charges the equilibrium price. If the authority increases the number of car parking spaces from OS_1 to OS_2 the increase in consumer surplus will be equal to the area

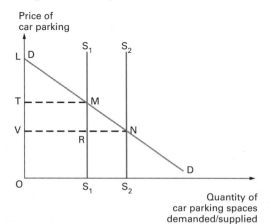

Price of car parking

A MRVT

B MNR

C MNVT

D LNV

E LMRV

6 The diagram represents the market for milk. Producers of milk receive a subsidy, as indicated on the diagram.

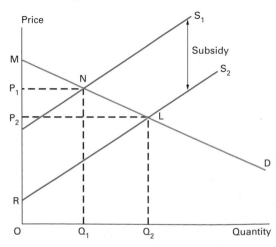

The removal of the subsidy will reduce the consumer surplus by

A P_2P_1NL

B MNP_1

C P_2LR

D P_2ML

Essay questions

1 (a) Define what is meant by
   (i) a merit good
   (ii) externalities
   (b) Discuss the relevance of these concepts to the subject of health care.

2 (a) Explain how the price mechanism assists in the allocation of resources. (12 marks)
   (b) Discuss the case for and against doctors (GPs) charging patients for their services. (13 marks)

3 Explain the difference between a consumption good and an investment good. From the standpoints of both the individual and the economy, is education a consumption or an investment good?

4 Why should the government subsidize the provision of education? How could market forces be encouraged within a state-financed education system like that in the United Kingdom?

5 Explain the difference between consumption and investment. Discuss in which category you would place housing and education.

6 How do (a) rent controls and (b) tax relief on mortgages affect the market for housing?

7 Outline the case for and against
   (a) public sector provision of housing and
   (b) other forms of intervention in the housing market.

8 To what extent do supply and demand determine the provision of housing, health care and teachers?

12

Employment, unemployment and income distribution

LEARNING OUTCOMES

On completing this chapter you should understand:

■ Recent changes in employment and unemployment

■ How structural change affects jobs

■ The impact of new technologies

■ Long-term unemployment

■ Pay differentials

■ Discrimination

■ The minimum wage

■ Policies to increase employment

We are now in a position to examine the causes of unemployment in some detail. But it would be a mistake to look at unemployment without also looking at some important features of the labour market as a whole. We need to examine patterns of employment and the way the labour market works, for it is different in nature from the market for goods and services that we studied in Chapter 3.

Obviously, we can look to the labour market for explanations of the way in which incomes vary from one household to another. Inequality can be due to wage differentials and also to differences in the way wealth is distributed. The latter is greatly influenced by inheritance. But income distribution is mainly determined by what people can earn, and in particular by their vulnerability to unemployment. Some members of society are much more likely to become unemployed than others, and if they do lose their jobs, their income will usually fall very sharply.

A very important cause of unemployment is the structural change that occurs when resources are reallocated to reflect changing patterns of demand.

There is a good deal of international discussion about the best ways of dealing with unemployment. The chapter concludes with a look at some policies that have been used.

The working population, employment and unemployment

The size of the labour force as a whole depends on the number of people available for work. This number in turn depends on the number of people in full-time education, the retirement age, the participation of women in the labour force and, not least, the population of working age. Quite sharp changes in this occur over time. For example, the loss of many young men during the First World War and the relatively low birth rate subsequently meant that fewer people retired during the 1980s than before and after.

Table 12.1 shows how unemployment has risen, and also how employment has grown. (Figure 8.1 showed how unemployment changed during the early 1990s.) The increased participation of women in the labour market has been an important trend. Table 12.2 indicates the significance of this.

It is a fallacy that a rising working population in itself causes unemployment. A growing economy is actually stimulated by the presence of more people available for work. Evidence of this can be seen in both the present and the past. A growing working population has been accompanied by low unemployment in the United Kingdom in the 1950s and 1960s, in Hong Kong for many years until the Far East financial crisis of 1997–8, and recently in the UK. However, if there is only slow growth in output, a growing working population may not be absorbed quickly enough, and the adjustment process can take some time.

Table 12.1

Distribution of the workforce (millions)

	1980	1986	1992	1995	1998
Workforce	26.8	27.9	28.5	28.4	28.7
Unemployed*	1.3	3.1	2.7	2.3	1.4
Workforce in employment	25.3	24.6	25.7	26.0	27.0
Self-employed	2.0	2.6	3.2	3.6	3.5
Employment in manufacturing	6.9	5.2	4.1	4.0	4.1
Work-related training programmes	0.0	0.2	0.3	0.2	0.1

* Claimant count: for definition see Chapter 8, page 141.

Source: ONS, *Annual Abstract of Statistics, 1994 and 1999*

Table 12.2

Female participation in the labour force (thousands)

	1974	1980	1986	1992	1998
Males	16 068	16 247	16 414	16 187	15 997
Females	9 589	10 511	11 435	12 395	12 716

Source: ONS, *Annual Abstract of Statistics, 1994 and 1999*

Most unemployment has its roots in either cyclical changes in the macroeconomy or structural changes – the way the composition of final output changes over time. Cyclical changes reflect the fluctuations in output that occur as part of the business or trade cycle. Structural changes reflect a shifting pattern of demand for different kinds of labour.

Unemployment in recession

In a recession, there is a tendency for incomes to fall and demand for goods and services generally to fall. Firms cut output because they cannot sell it all, and lay off employees because they have nothing for them to do. So this kind of unemployment may be known as cyclical unemployment, or as **demand deficiency unemployment**. Periodic recessions, in which the economy at best stagnates and may actually decline, seem to be a feature of market economies. Although governments can devise policies to reduce the impact of recessions, the United Kingdom has experienced two major recessions in the early 1980s and early 1990s, both more severe and lasting than any other since the Second World War. This was mainly because of the government's fear of inflation.

It is fairly easy to see how recessions affect unemployment: Figure 8.1 shows two sharp increases in 1980–4 and in 1990–3. However, when we come to analyse current events, we usually find that the picture is less clear. The reason for this is that there are **time lags**. Employers do not like making people redundant. They will put it off until they

are sure that the downturn in demand is likely to last. They will try to keep people on in the hope of improved demand. Similarly, when demand improves, they will want to be sure that it is going to be a lasting increase before they commit themselves to higher labour costs.

Generally speaking, we find that the level of unemployment follows the level of output, with a time lag of between one year and eighteen months. It is difficult to be precise about this because the statistical techniques for measuring output quickly are themselves rather imprecise. Time often reveals that output was higher or lower than the statisticians thought and the figures have to be adjusted later. Disentangling the recent trends can therefore be a little tricky. Politicians are apt to read into the figures what they would like to see.

Recovery from the early 1990s recession

	Real output (1990 = 100)	Unemployment (%)*
1990	100	5.9
1991	97.9	8.1
1992	97.4	9.7
1993	99.6	10.3
1994	104.0	9.3
1995	106.9	8.1
1996	109.5	7.3
1997	113.2	5.5
1998	115.9	4.7

* Claimant unemployment (definition page 141).

Source: *National Institute Economic Review, 1997 and 1999*

1 How long was the time lag between the initial recovery of output and the first fall in unemployment?
2 Growth slowed in 1998 while unemployment continued to fall. How can this be explained?

Our conclusion must be that, although the statistics are not easy to interpret, at least with hindsight it is not too difficult to spot the unemployment that is caused by the trade cycle. We shall analyse demand deficiency unemployment more fully in subsequent chapters.

KEY POINTS

12.1

- The size of the workforce depends on a range of social factors, including the age at which people start and finish working and the participation of women.

- Jobs have been created in the United Kingdom, but not always fast enough to employ all the people made redundant and new entrants to the labour force.

- Some unemployment has been caused by insufficient aggregate demand.

Structural unemployment

Underlying the cyclical fluctuations in the economy is a long-run trend. At the beginning of the 1970s unemployment was roughly 600 000. Since then there has been a permanent increase in the level of unemployment. In late 1988 at the height of the late-1980s boom, that is, when unemployment was at its lowest in the United Kingdom since 1980, the figure was 1 661 000, or 5.9 per cent.

Since the growth of output had been running at an average of 3 per cent per annum in the preceding years, few people would argue that residual unemployment was caused by lack of demand. Instead, we must look to structural change as the main explanation for much of the remaining unemployment.

During 1996 and 1997 unemployment again fell to historically low levels as growth in the economy soaked up more labour. It seems likely that improved strategies for matching unemployed people to jobs available helped as well. Better training and more support for job seekers are possible explanations.

See Chapter 8 for further detail on structural unemployment.

Demand and structural change

Why does structural change occur? What is involved? In Chapter 2 we looked at three basic economic questions. What is produced? How is it produced? And for whom is it produced? These three questions can focus our thinking about what happens to employment and to incomes as economies develop.

Over time, what gets produced changes. There are a number of reasons for this. First, the things we, as consumers, want change, for many reasons. In Chapter 3 we found that demand changes when incomes change, when tastes or fashions change, or when the price of a substitute or a complement changes. Consumer sovereignty means that the wishes of consumers are transmitted to producers through the profit mechanism. Falling demand means falling profits (or losses), which give entrepreneurs an incentive to move resources out of their existing lines of production and into new, more profitable lines. So some businesses shrink, or *exit* from the market altogether, while others, those which are producing the things people want most, grow. This idea of exit from the market-place is crucial to the efficient working of the market economy: it is the process by which resources are freed to move into production for which demand is growing.

There is one major cause of structural change that was captured in the above analysis but needs explaining further. In Chapter 6, we learned how comparative advantage makes trade possible and, over time, leads to growth in the standard of living for many people. Comparative advantage does not stand still, however. As countries grow and develop they acquire advantages they did not previously have. Hong Kong in the 1950s possessed a comparative advantage in the production of cheap plastic toys and textiles. As industry developed there its advantage shifted towards clothing and footwear, then towards light manufacturing of any kind, and finally into financial services. Meantime, other countries with low wage costs such as Malaysia, Thailand and, most recently, China and Vietnam have been able to develop strong manufacturing sectors as their advantage in that area grew. (Take a look at your nearest telephone; the chances are it was made in China.) As low-wage economies develop industrially, they become big customers for imports from countries with a comparative advantage in high-technology products such as aircraft and scientific instruments, or in services such as design and education.

Financial problems in the Far East threatened to reduce growth considerably in the period 1997–9. However, many of the countries concerned recovered at least partially and the overall process of structural change continued.

This process has immense potential to increase incomes worldwide. Demand for highly priced domestic products declines as cheaper imported substitutes become available. But a major assumption underlying the theory of comparative advantage is that resources are mobile. They can move from one use to another. In fact, capital is quite mobile. But labour suffers from both **occupational** and **geographical immobilities** which make it difficult for people to change jobs. Structural change leads to structural unemployment when people cannot acquire the skills that are in demand or move to where the jobs are.

Supply and structural change

Not all the causes of structural change originate on the demand side. Some come from changes in the supply of goods and services. When there is technological change, innovations in either the product or the process by which it is created lead to the product being better value for money. Sometimes we get completely new products (electric light bulbs, TVs, fax machines, North Sea gas, Nintendo, soya protein ...). These new products may drive old ones off the market altogether, or more often just reduce demand (for example, candles are still in demand but only for romantic dinners and the like). More often still, productivity (output per person employed) rises and the products become cheaper, and so are affordable for many more people. A mass market develops so that jobs are created as sales rise.

Alternatively, demand for the product may not grow much. People may benefit from the lower prices brought about by technical improvements in production and increased productivity generally, but spend the money saved on other things. Washing machines are a lot cheaper than they were twenty years ago, but have you bought more of

them? In such cases the product will now be produced by much more **capital-intensive** and less **labour-intensive** methods. Far fewer people will be needed to produce them. Only limited market growth can be expected. Many people have been made redundant in similar situations. The fall in the number of people employed in manufacturing shown in Table 12.1 has occurred as capital has been substituted for labour. This is often because of technical change, but it is just as likely to be because capital-intensive production has simply become cheaper.

Investment in new technology makes people more productive. It makes it possible to pay higher wages. It raises the standard of living. But just as when change originates on the demand side, if people who are made redundant are not geographically or occupationally mobile (or both), they are liable to become structurally unemployed. Change itself does not cause unemployment, provided that people can do other jobs. But there are many kinds of problems which make mobility between jobs difficult.

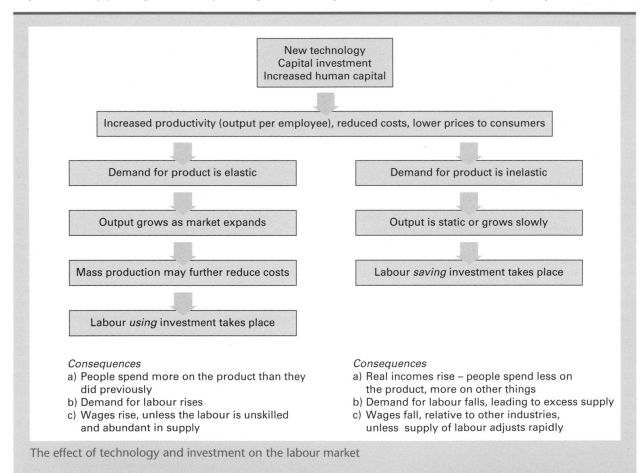

The effect of technology and investment on the labour market

The effect of technology and investment on the labour market

Increasing capital investment, use of better technology and investment in human capital are processes that go hand in hand. They all increase labour productivity and,

together, they are the source of long-run economic growth. All three can be seen to lead to increasing wages and a higher standard of living.

But there are other factors which make the connections complex. For example, in agriculture there has been an enormous amount of capital-spending on machines, and much technical progress in seeds, fertilizers and production methods. What has happened to employment? Many jobs have been lost, and agricultural work is still very poorly paid compared with the rest of the economy.

In order to understand this, we must allow for the nature of the demand for the product and of the supply of labour. The demand for food products grows slowly, if at all. Food has a low income elasticity of demand – most people in the United Kingdom already eat more than enough; higher incomes mean only modest increases in demand for some more expensive foods. So improved technology in agriculture leads to the substitution of capital for labour rather than to expansion of production. The labour needs of the industry then diminish; at any given wage there will be an excess supply of labour. Agricultural workers are widely separated geographically and therefore have a weak union structure. They live on the job and are geographically rather immobile. So inevitably their wages have remained low in spite of massive increases in productivity. Farm workers have moved into other occupations but not fast enough to create conditions of scarcity for themselves.

The diagram shows how different the effects of investment, technical progress and education may be. If demand for the product is static or slow-growing, then employers' labour needs will be progressively reduced and wages will probably stay low. If, on the other hand, the fall in costs and prices leads to a growing market, then the industry may expand rapidly and create new jobs. This is what happens whenever a new product is created, using modern technology to mass produce and develop a large market. Televisions, calculators and VCRs all followed this path. In the initial period of expansion, the wages paid to attract labour to the new line of production may be above average. In the long run, the wages paid will depend partly on whether the skills needed are still scarce.

3 In which of the categories shown in the diagram do the following products belong: soap, computers, refrigerators, cat food, fax machines? **A⃟**

4 Draw a supply and demand diagram showing the effect upon wage rates of falling demand for labour. **A⃟**

5 Will people be able to move easily from the industries where jobs are decreasing? **A⃟**

6 In what areas of the economy is it most likely that jobs can be created? **A⃟**

The effects of structural change

The demand for labour is *derived* from the demand for the product. This means that structural change is a major source of **income differentials**. Firms in growing industries will pay more to attract the labour they need. So pay in the electrical and electronics industries is usually higher than it is in the textile trade. Electronics firms are often located in places with relatively low unemployment (for example, the Thames Valley) and may have difficulty in recruiting all the labour they need. They will have to pay well to attract and to keep people with scarce skills. A textile firm in the north-west of England which has been laying off its employees will pay less well. Some of them may be without work years after they were made redundant. Their skills are abundant in relation to the demand for them, and the possibilities of wage rises may be very limited.

The effect of structural change on the pattern of employment can be observed in the data on employment in different industries over time, shown in Table 12.3. Many of the changes shown here have been mirrored in other countries. However, the shift in employment from manufacturing to services has been especially marked in the United States. Figure 12.1 shows how the share of manufacturing diminished. In the UK, employment in manufacturing in 1996 was down to 27.6 per cent of the total.

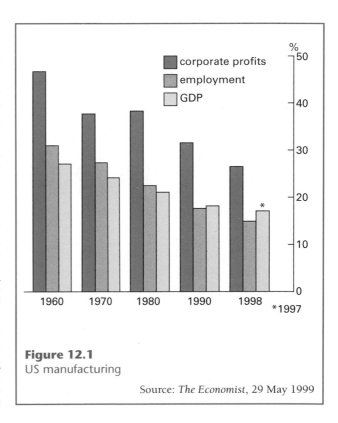

Figure 12.1
US manufacturing

Source: *The Economist*, 29 May 1999

Table 12.3

Employees in employment, UK (thousands)

	1979	1986	1992	1995	1998
All industries and services	23 158	21 387	21 848	22 028	23 237
Manufacturing	7258	5227	4498	4021	4076
Services	13556	14 297	15 758	16 658	17 664
Energy and water	722	545	402	237	222
Chemicals	n.a.	331	309	255	241
Engineering and vehicles*	3380	2372	2000	1245	1303
Textiles	395	249	181	186	184
Construction	1253	989	911	838	1003
Retail distribution	2174	2097	2343	2240	2450
Hotels and catering	950	1042	1227	1262	1316
Banking/insurance	n.a.	n.a.	970	998	1064
Education	1647	1650	1895	1864	1896
Research and development	113	112	90	87	99
Medical and health	1229	1359	1605	1580	1570

* There is a break in this series at 1993.

Source: ONS, *Annual Abstract of Statistics*, 1999

KEY POINTS

12.2

- Substantial unemployment has been created as a result of structural change and the immobilities of labour.

- Structural change may occur because of changes in demand or changes in supply.

- Income differentials may widen when structural change reduces demand for some skills and increases demand for others.

Long-term unemployment

Some people who have been made redundant do not have skills that are in demand in growing industries. Consequently, they have had difficulty in finding new jobs. They have become the long-term unemployed. A distressing result of this story is that being out of work for a long time causes them to lose their skills and work habits. The longer they remain unemployed, the less likely they are to find work again. Even though employers are recruiting, they may prefer to take people who are in work or people who have been unemployed just for a short period. Effectively, the long-term unemployed eventually drop out of the labour force.

Later in this chapter we shall look at some of the ways in which long-term unemployment can be tackled by governments.

Labour market flexibility

When structural change is taking place, labour must move from jobs in declining industries into the jobs created in growing industries. It follows that structural change will proceed more smoothly if labour markets are flexible. This means that they adapt to change, and that people respond to the economic signals created by wage differentials.

A flexible labour market is characterized by several features. Mobility of labour is the most obvious. People need to be adaptable, capable of learning new skills. Training and retraining opportunities must be available. It must be possible for employers to hire people with the skills they need reasonably easily. This, in turn, implies that the labour force has good basic educational foundations.

Perhaps equally important, employers must be able to *reduce* the number of people they employ easily. Herein lies a problem. Many people believe that employees should have some job security. Insecurity is unpleasant. It gives people very little sense of commitment to the job. It can cause real suffering when the effects of unemployment may be to reduce drastically a family's standard of living. For this reason many countries have employment protection laws. They require employers to offer contracts to employees and to make redundancy payments if the job is abolished.

Unfortunately, employment protection can make employers less willing to take on more employees in the first place. One response has been for employers to take on more people without contracts, for short periods of time. Many of these are women or are working part time. This trend can be seen in Table 12.4.

This may explain why female unemployment in the United Kingdom has always been lower than male unemployment. Women are able and willing to adapt to

Table 12.4

Full, part-time and temporary employment (millions)

Year	1989	1992	1995	1998
Males				
Full-time	14.3	13.3	13.2	13.6
Part-time	0.8	1.0	1.2	1.3
Temporary	0.4	0.5	0.7	0.7
Females				
Full-time	6.5	6.4	6.4	6.6
Part-time	4.9	5.0	5.2	5.4
Temporary	0.8	0.7	0.8	0.9

Source: ONS, *Annual Abstract of Statistics*, 1999

However, many Americans are concerned that the jobs that have been created tend to be very poorly paid. There is considerable inequality in the US income distribution.

Other European Union member countries tend to have more employment protection legislation than does the United Kingdom. However, this is now changing. First, after the 1997 general election, the new Labour government decided that the UK should sign up to the Social Chapter of the Maastricht Treaty. This provides for uniform employment protection across the whole single market. Employees can sue for unfair dismissal after one year in the job, rather than, as previously, two. This does give them greater protection.

Second, many EU countries are now finding that companies are avoiding job-protection regulations by hiring more people on part-time and temporary contracts. In France, 86 per cent of newly hired people are now on short-term contracts. This makes quite a break with the past. Figures 12.3 and 12.4 show comparisons of unemployment rates and total employment.

Some people have argued that trade unions create labour market rigidities. To the extent that they are able to raise wages above their free-market equilibrium level and to negotiate binding contracts, they may discourage employment. However, trade unions have rather less power than they used to have, in all countries. It is possible that this is one reason why the UK labour market has become more flexible.

Another factor involves unemployment benefits. It is

employers' requirements, especially if they are not supporting dependants. Figure 12.2 shows the details.

Labour market rigidities

International comparisons have given politicians much cause for thought, worldwide. In the United States, labour markets are clearly more flexible than they are in Europe. There is less employment protection, and unemployment benefits last for only a short time. The incentive to work is therefore greater. Unemployment is lower than in Europe and more jobs have been created.

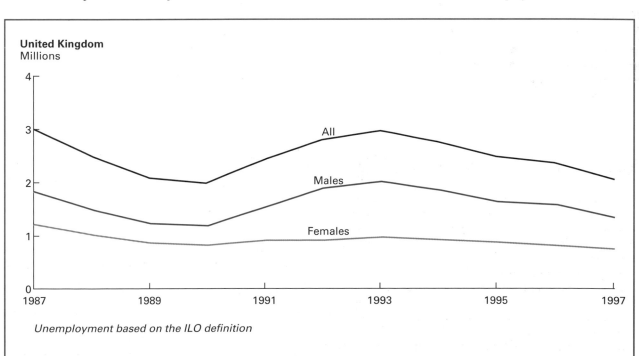

Figure 12.2
Unemployment by gender

Unemployment based on the ILO definition

Source: ONS, *Social Trends 28*, 1998

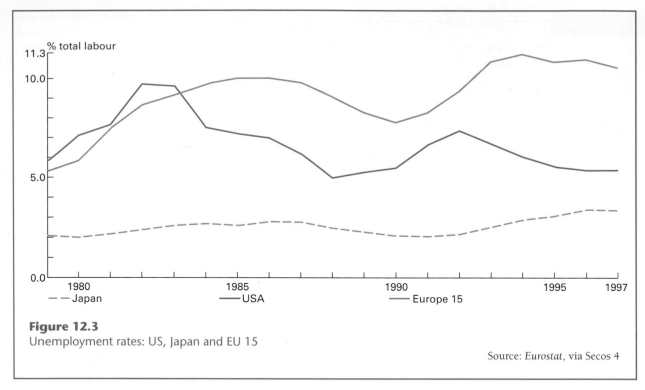

Figure 12.3
Unemployment rates: US, Japan and EU 15

Source: *Eurostat*, via Secos 4

often said that generous unemployment benefits reduce the incentive to work. This is especially likely if people are taxed at low rates of pay: there may be a **poverty trap**. In recent years many governments have made it harder to qualify for unemployment benefits.

In the UK people have had to show that they really are available for work before unemployment benefits are paid. Research findings are unclear on this point, but falling unemployment rates in the period 1997–8 could have something to do with the change. Meantime, it is clear that there are still people whose potential pay is so low that it does not cover the extra costs of working, such as travel, clothing and childcare.

One important consequence of increasing flexibility in the labour market is likely to be a wider distribution of income, that is, greater inequality. First, in order for people to have an incentive to move from a declining to a growing industry, it may be necessary for wage differentials to widen. Jobs in declining industries may continue, but at very low rates of pay. People who live in areas where declining industries have been important employers are unlikely to be able to move house. They may be trapped with a choice between very low wages or benefits.

Second, if governments reduce the real value of benefits, the standard of living of people who are genuinely unable to find work will fall relative to that of those in work. The effect of increasing labour market flexibility should be kept in mind when reading the next section on inequality.

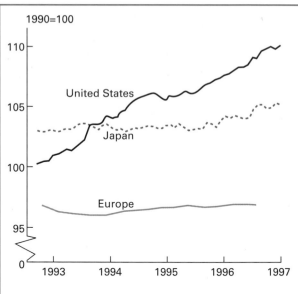

Figure 12.4
Total employment, US, Japan and Europe

Source: OECD, 1997

KEY POINTS

12.3

- If structural change is to proceed smoothly and efficiently, labour markets need to be flexible.

- Labour markets are thought to be becoming more flexible in the United Kingdom, partly because of increasing part-time work.

- There may be further changes in employment protection legislation in the European Union.

- Employment could be protected more, or less: if less, then employers will find it easier to take on and shed labour.

Table 12.5

Gross domestic product and real earnings in recession (1990 = 100)

	1990	1991	1992	1993
GDP	100	97.6	97.2	98.9
Earnings	100	108.2	115.3	120.5
RPI	100	105.9	109.8	111.5

Source: *National Institute Economic Review*, March 1994

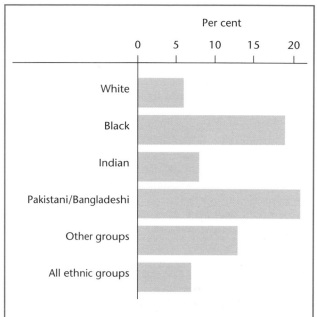

Figure 12.5
Unemployment by ethnic origin, Great Britain (%)

Source: ONS, *Social Trends*, 1999

Inequality

There are many reasons for inequalities in the income distribution we observe in the economy. In this section we shall look first at the effect of unemployment, and then at the reasons why productivity varies between individuals.

One major reason why some families have higher incomes than others is that some people are very much more vulnerable to unemployment than others. A spell of unemployment is apt to reduce current income substantially. But people who suffer long-term unemployment also suffer a process known as de-skilling. The longer they remain unemployed, the rustier their skills and work habits become and the less likely they are to find work. If they are successful in finding a job, it is highly likely to be less well paid than their last employment. So the income-reducing effects of unemployment can be very long lasting. As the number of unskilled jobs has decreased in the economy, people without skills have become very vulnerable to unemployment.

During both the last two serious recessions (1981–2 and 1990–1), real earnings rose almost continuously. The brunt of the fall in gross domestic product was borne by those who were unemployed at some time. Table 12.5 shows the details for the period 1990–3. Comparison with the retail price index shows how, on average, money earnings outpaced inflation, so generating continuously improving standards of living for those in work. In this way, recessions have caused income distribution to widen, making those who experienced unemployment considerably worse off relative to the employed population.

Unemployment does not affect all groups in society equally. Figure 12.5 shows that unemployment is very much higher for racial minorities than it is for whites. However, as we have already seen, women tend to experience less unemployment than men.

Above and beyond the effects of unemployment, incomes vary because people vary immensely in their level of productivity. This in turn has a major influence on earning power.

Innate abilities and attributes
These factors are obviously the easiest to explain and the hardest to acquire if you do not possess them. Innate abilities and attributes can be very strong, if not overwhelming, determinants of a person's potential productivity. Strength, good looks, co-ordination, mental alertness and so on are all facets of non-acquired **human capital** and thus have some bearing on one's ability to earn income.

Education and training
Education is usually placed under the heading of 'investment in human capital', a topic we shall discuss in more

detail later. For the moment, suffice it to say that education improves one's productivity by increasing the human capital one has available for use in the labour market. Education usually allows an individual to be more versatile in the things he or she can do. On-the-job training can be as important as basic education in increasing productivity.

Experience

Additional experience in particular tasks is another way to increase one's productivity. Experience can be linked to the well-known *learning curve* that occurs when the same task is done over and over. Take an example of a person going to work on an assembly line at Ford Motor Company. At first, he or she is able to screw on only three bolts every two minutes. Then the worker becomes more adept and can screw on four bolts in the same time as well as insert a rubber guard on the bumper. After a few more weeks, even another task can be added. Hence, we would expect experience to lead to higher rates of productivity. And we would expect people with more experience to be paid more than those with less experience. More experience, however, does not guarantee a higher wage rate. The *demand* for one's services must also exist. Spending a long time to become a first-rate archer in modern society would probably add very little to the income of the person who becomes an archer. As another example, a more experienced pianist in a society uninterested in music may earn the same as an inexperienced pianist, for they both may earn virtually nothing at all since there is little demand for their talents. Experience only has value if the output is demanded by society.

Capital investment

The more capital people have to work with, the higher will be their productivity. A better machine will enable its operator to increase productivity. In the long run, increases in real wages are generated by this process.

The age–earnings cycle

Within every class of income earners, there seem to be regular cycles of earning behaviour. Most people earn more when they are middle-aged than when they are younger or older. This is called the **age–earnings cycle**. Every occupation has its own age–earnings cycle, and every individual will probably experience some variation from the average.

When individuals start working at a young age, they typically have no work-related experience. Their ability to produce is lower than that of more experienced workers. That is, their productivity is lower. As they become older, they attain more training and more experience. Their productivity rises, and they are therefore paid more. Moreover, they start to work longer hours, in general. At the age of 45 or 50, the productivity of individual workers usually peaks. So, too, does the number of hours per week that are worked. After this peak in the age–earnings cycle, the detrimental effects of ageing usually outweigh any increases in training or experience.

Trade unions

Sometimes employers pay good wages because of market forces. Trade unions may then appear to be quite successful, while in fact making relatively little difference. There are some circumstances, however, in which unions can be successful in raising wages, irrespective of market forces. Where large numbers of employees work on one site, it is easy for unions to recruit and communicate with their members. It will be easy to organize industrial action and this will give the union extra muscle. Similarly, if the production process is highly integrated, so that a large number of people contribute in varied and specialized ways, strike action by a very few people can disrupt production. However, this sort of union power is much reduced by the threat of unemployment, and in the UK has been further reduced by legal restraints.

Inelastic demand for the product

When wage costs are rising, the firm can pass the cost on to the consumer in the form of higher prices for the product. If demand is inelastic, then consumers will continue to buy the product despite the higher price. If, on the other hand, demand is elastic, people will switch to a cheaper substitute or do without the product altogether. So the firm cannot raise prices without facing a substantial drop in demand, and will therefore try to avoid paying higher wages.

Restricted supply of labour

There are various reasons why the supply of labour may be inelastic. Whenever labour is scarce in relation to the demand for it, wages will tend to rise. Supply may be kept scarce by shortages of training facilities (reflecting occupational immobility) or by entry restrictions (as with barristers, reflecting some monopoly power) or by individuals' unique qualities.

When particular skills are in scarce supply, there are said to be **supply constraints**.

Poverty and wealth

During the 1980s and early 1990s, poverty was generally on the increase, despite rising real incomes generally. We have already observed that increasing inequality is a likely consequence of structural change. The way in which falling incomes nationally have mainly affected people who lost their jobs added a further twist. When it is remembered that the people most likely to lose their jobs are the unskilled, it is clear that there is a group within society which is vulnerable on a number of fronts.

Evidence of increasing inequality

The UK has again become a more unequal society after a period in the early 1990s when the gap between the rich and the poor narrowed marginally.

The figures, covering the period 1995 to 1997, show the proportion of the population living on less than half average income rose slightly. This small upturn follows a fall in the early 1990s. The 1980s saw the proportion living on half average income or below rise from 10 per cent in 1979 to 25 per cent by 1991.

While average real incomes before housing costs rose by 40 per cent between 1979 and 1997, those for the top 10 ten per cent rose by 58 per cent. The bottom 10 per cent of the population saw only a 14 per cent increase. The disparity is even greater when housing costs are taken into account.

The figures also suggest that the government's New Deal welfare-to-work scheme must make inroads among lone parents, the sick and the disabled if the incomes of those at the bottom are to be pushed up without big benefit increases.

Source: Adapted from the *Financial Times*,
16 October 1998

7 How can the big differences in income growth over the twenty-year-period be explained?

8 Which are the groups most likely to be on very low incomes, and why?

Wealth and income are not the same

So far we have looked at income distribution primarily as a matter of differentials in earnings, the return to labour. Individuals also receive a return for the ownership of land. This is rent. Individuals receive income as a return to the ownership of capital: this is interest. And, finally, entrepreneurs receive economic profits as a return to entrepreneurial ability, again a form of human wealth. Income is a *flow* received year in and year out. It is the flow received from wealth, which is a *stock* of both human and non-human capital.

Therefore, the discussion of the distribution of income is not the same thing as a discussion of the distribution of wealth. A complete concept of wealth would include tangible objects, such as buildings, machinery, land, cars and houses – non-human wealth – as well as people who have skills, knowledge, initiative, talents and so on – human wealth. The total of *human* and non-human wealth gives us our nation's capital stock. (Note that the terms *wealth* and capital are often used *only* with reference to non-human wealth.) The capital stock refers to anything that can generate utility to individuals in the future. A fresh ripe tomato is not part of our capital stock. It has to be eaten before it turns rotten, and after it is eaten it can no longer generate satisfaction.

Stocks and flows – a digression

The wealth that you have is a stock. (Note here that we are not talking just about shares in a company.) Lots of other things are stocks, too, such as a building that you might own. Stocks are defined independently of time, although they are assessed at a point in time. A car dealer can have a stock of cars that may be worth £50 000. A timber company may have five acres of trees worth £10 000; this is a stock of trees.

On the other hand, the income you make is a flow. Remember, a flow is a stream of things through time. It is a certain number of things per time period. You receive so many pounds per month or so many pounds per year. The number of cars that a car dealer sells per week is a flow; the number of cars he has is a stock. Flows, in other words, are defined as occurring over a given period of time; stocks are defined at a point in time.

If you want to add to your stock of wealth or capital, you must save. That is, you must not consume part of your income. The act of saving is a flow that makes your stock of wealth larger. You should not confuse the act of saving with how much you have in savings. 'Savings' is a stock concept akin to wealth, as we have defined it.

People build up their wealth positions by saving. Savings can be held as cash (not such a good idea if there is inflation) or put into stocks, bonds, businesses, precious metals or consumer durable goods. The purchase of a house, for example, adds to one's accumulated savings, or wealth.

What determines differences in wealth

Each of us either *inherits* a certain amount of wealth, or otherwise has some of our parents' generation's wealth transferred to us in some form. Some people, for example, inherit a home or large estate consisting of stocks and bonds, cash, diamonds and other assets. Some people inherit a small amount – perhaps just a parental contribution to a university grant. And it may be a negative amount – if, for example, we have to support our parents in their old age or pay their debts when they die.

Not surprisingly, wealth is distributed unevenly. In 1994, in the United Kingdom, the most wealthy 5 per cent of the population held 38 per cent of the total wealth, and the most wealthy 10 per cent, 51 per cent of the total. The least wealthy 50 per cent held 7 per cent.

Do the rich get richer 'automatically'? A favourite saying is that the 'rich get richer and the poor get poorer'. This is not a very accurate or well-thought-out statement. In fact, the classical economists such as Thomas Malthus, David Ricardo, Adam Smith and Karl Marx were satisfied that this simple theory was an explanation not only of wealth distribution but also of income distribution. They believed that wealth 'bred' more wealth, and therefore, once one's endowment was established, so was one's income. After all, income – as we pointed out before – is simply the 'return' to wealth. In particular, rent is the return to land and interest is the return to ownership of capital. Clearly, people who own more land and more capital will receive more rent and more interest than those who own no land or no capital. The children of wealthy parents, in other words, are far more likely – all other things being equal – to have an increase in their stock of wealth and hence higher incomes than are the children of poor parents.

This simple classical theory is outmoded in any modern democratic society, according to many economists. Wealth, as we pointed out before, includes non-tangible assets, such as people's skills, knowledge, initiative and talents. The stock of society's human wealth is important in determining income differences. From this point of view, entrepreneurs receive profits as a return to their endowment of entrepreneurial ability, workers receive wage and salary income from their endowment of ability to work.

KEY POINTS

12.4

■ Unemployment leads to falling real income for anyone affected by it.

■ Incomes also depend on many factors such as (1) innate abilities and attributes, (2) education, (3) experience and training and (4) capital invested per employee.

■ Most people follow an age–earnings cycle in which they earn relatively small incomes when they first start working, increase their incomes until about age 50, then slowly experience a decrease in their real incomes.

■ Trade unions may be able to influence wages.

■ Wealth is unevenly distributed and leads to further inequalities in incomes.

■ Wealth is not the same thing as income. Wealth is a stock.

■ Stocks must be distinguished from flows; flows are measured over time. You have a flow of saving, which might be so many pounds per month that you put into your savings account.

Discrimination

It is possible – and, indeed, quite obvious to most – that discrimination affects the distribution of income. Certain groups in our society do not receive wage rates comparable with those received by other groups, even when we correct for productivity. Some argue that all of these differences are due to discrimination against, for example, non-whites and women. We cannot simply accept *all* differences in income as due to discrimination, though. What we need to do is

discover why differences in income across groups exist, and then determine whether explanations other than discrimination in the labour market can explain at least some of those differences in incomes. That part of income differences across groups that is not explained is what we can rightfully call the result of discrimination.

Which people have the high-paying jobs?

White males, on average, occupy jobs in the highest-paying occupations more than non-white males and all females. As for the lowest-paying jobs, they are dominated by females, white and non-white, and by non-white males. Clearly, the distribution of groups across occupations is one of the major reasons why there are income differentials among whites and non-whites, and males and females.

Some argue that this uneven distribution of jobs among groups is the result of past and current discrimination in the job market. In any society where white males dominate management positions, if there is racial and sexual prejudice, then white males will tend to hire white males, rather than non-white males or females.

The theory

Economic theory predicts that discrimination cannot persist because it will be driven out by competition. Employers who do not discriminate will face lower costs than those who do. This is because the non-discriminators will be able to hire women employees or people from racial minorities who will be prepared to work for lower wages than will white males. They will then be able to charge lower prices than can the discriminating businesses, with their higher wage costs. The latter will then be driven out of business.

Unfortunately, this analysis does not appear to be borne out by the evidence. Table 12.6 shows data on male and female earnings. (It is easier to obtain evidence on male–female wage differentials than on racial differentials, so this section will use the former. However, the analysis applies equally to racial discrimination and to sexual discrimination.)

Using simple supply and demand analysis, Figure 12.6 shows that, if there is discrimination, the demand for

---

Table 12.6

Gross hourly earnings of full-time adult employees (1998)

	Lowest decile	Median	Highest decile
All men	£4.88	£8.57	£17.75
All women	£4.22	£7.10	£14.16

Source: ONS, *Annual Abstract*, 1999

females will be less than the demand for males. Hence wages will also be lower. A more sophisticated approach uses crowding theory. This sees the labour market as being split into two parts. As female participation increases, men protect their jobs by devising strategies to exclude women from the higher-paid opportunities in what is called market A, which consists of those jobs in which women are typically not employed to any great extent. Women then crowd into market B, thus increasing the supply of labour to less well-paid jobs and depressing wages in market B further. This is shown in Figure 12.7.

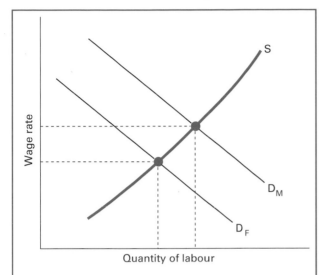

Figure 12.6
Discriminating demand for labour
If employers discriminate, this means that their demand for white males will be higher than their demand for females or people from minority groups. A lower wage rate will be needed to clear the market for the latter.

In this situation, the labour market is to a large extent segregated. Part of it, market A, exhibits widespread discrimination. In the other part, market B, women are not discriminated against and are therefore heavily represented. But the very fact of the large supply of female labour depresses wages.

In fact, it can still make sense for women to persevere in seeking employment in market A. Although they may be discriminated against, their earnings are still likely to be higher than they would have been in market B. Thus a woman who succeeds in becoming a consultant surgeon, in a field in which there appears to be some discrimination, may end up considerably better off than if she becomes a biology teacher, even though in that job she is less likely to be discriminated against.

Labour market discrimination and the household

The effects of discrimination in the labour market spread into the household and family life. Many women will say something like 'we have to put my partner's career first because he earns more than I do and we need the money'. There appears to be a 'glass ceiling': women do well up to a certain point in their careers, but have great difficulty in gaining promotion to the best managerial jobs.

Apart from a sex-change operation, what is the best option for women? Men are often able to earn what may be called a discriminatory premium. That is, by working in an area where discrimination exists they may be able to earn more than is strictly justified by their output. Men in this position will usually share their earnings with a partner; in this way, women get to share the discriminatory premium.

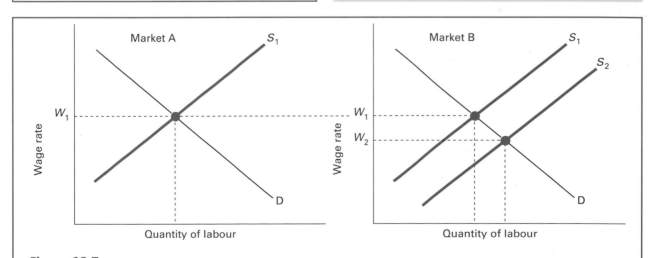

Figure 12.7
The crowding out theory
Market A consists of jobs in which few women succeed. The wage rate W_1 is relatively high. In market B, where the supply of labour S_2 is swelled by women who cannot easily find jobs in market A, wages are lower, W_2.

Within the household, men and women make decisions about how much to work on the basis of their respective comparative advantages. Many men have an absolute advantage in employment, because of their higher pay. This means that, even if a man is actually better at housework than his partner, she will still have a comparative advantage in housework because the opportunity cost of her time, in terms of what she could be earning, is lower.

The outcome is that rational households will decide to supply as much as possible of the man's time on the labour market, and the woman will do much of the housework. In terms of its effect on the distribution of income, this might not matter too much if all women had partners, but for a variety of reasons many do not. Further, it means that women are often in a weaker bargaining position within the relationship when economic choices are being made.

Source: Adapted from Sanne Udsen, *Perspectives on Gender and the Labour Market*, Copenhagen: Economic Council of the Labour Movement

9 What effect does discrimination in the labour market have on the distribution of income?

10 What is the best strategy for a woman who wishes to maximize her standard of living?

11 Why do you think discrimination persists, despite the existence of equal opportunities legislation?

KEY POINTS

12.5

■ Labour market discrimination continues to exist in many, though not all, occupations.

■ To some extent the labour market is segregated into sectors in which discrimination occurs and sectors in which women have worked traditionally, where discrimination is less likely.

Poverty and redistribution in the United Kingdom

Table 12.7 shows how earnings are distributed in the United Kingdom. Earnings consist of wages and salaries and exclude all 'unearned income', that is, income from profits, interest and rent. Neither does wealth in any form appear here. Average earnings are given for each fifth, or quintile, of the population, from the poorest to the richest fifth.

Also shown are the taxes and benefits which redistribute income. Taken together with earnings, these give figures for disposable income – the average amounts which families in each quintile have to spend. Three-fifths of the families surveyed have below-average disposable incomes. Most of the poorest fifth have no economically active family member: they are retired, unemployed or disabled, or caring for the young or the sick. On average, the richest fifth have two economically active family members.

Over the years, benefits have mostly been revised in line with inflation. This preserves their purchasing power. But in the meantime, for people in work, earnings have risen consistently faster than inflation. So their standard of living has gone up. People dependent on benefits have become relatively worse off.

As far as earnings are concerned, a fair amount of redistribution takes place. Because wealth has never been redistributed very effectively or systematically (despite death duties), the distribution of total income (that is, both earned and unearned income) is much more uneven.

Most benefits are means tested. This provides a way of concentrating help on those most in need. However, the sharp decrease in benefits when income rises effectively creates a high marginal tax rate. This can be a disincentive for people who want to stop relying on benefits and find work. If the work is poorly paid, they will find themselves in the poverty trap.

Chapter 7 includes further detail on income distribution together with coverage of the Lorenz curve.

Can minimum wages help?

In 1999 for the first time, the UK introduced a minimum wage of £3.60 per hour. The rate for 18–21-year-olds was set at £3. At the time it was planned, detailed studies of the likely effect predicted that around 2 million people, mainly women, would benefit. The expected increase in the national wage bill was about 0.6 per cent. The Low Pay Commission said 'most businesses, even in low-paying sectors, will be able to accommodate the minimum although some, particularly smaller firms in labour-intensive service sectors, may have to make adjustments'.

The Commission expected that homeworkers, ethnic minorities, lone parents and young people were the ones most likely to see their earnings rise. Figure 12.8 shows the estimated effects. It was also expected that there would be differences in the way regions were affected. Relatively few people working in London and the south-east would benefit. More would benefit in other regions, depending on locally determined rates of pay.

The argument against a minimum wage has always been that it would reduce job creation. The theory is shown in Chapter 9 (see Figure 9.18). Raising the cost of labour could make employers more careful about taking people on, reducing the quantity of labour demanded.

Table 12.7

Redistribution of income through taxes and benefits, 1995–6, United Kingdom (£ per year)

	Quintile groups of households					All households
	Bottom fifth	Next fifth	Middle fifth	Next fifth	Top fifth	
Average per household						
Wages and salaries	1390	4050	10 390	17 610	29 810	12 650
Benefits in kind	30	30	100	290	890	270
Self-employment income	370	570	1250	1670	5050	1780
Occupational pensions	290	950	1310	1790	2410	1350
Investment income	200	340	580	830	2640	920
Other income	150	160	170	250	460	240
Total original income	1430	6090	13 790	22 450	41 260	17 200
plus **benefits in cash**	4910	4660	3360	2130	1200	3250
Gross income *less* taxes	7340	10 750	17 150	24 580	42 450	20 450
Disposable income *less* indirect taxes	6210	9230	14 020	19 400	31 980	16 170
Post-tax income	4280	6890	10 730	15 310	26 890	12 820
plus **benefits in kind**						
Education	1810	1300	1420	1070	830	1290
NHS	1890	1830	1730	1520	1330	1660
Housing subsidy	90	80	40	20	10	50
Travel subsidies	50	70	60	60	140	70
School meals	100	30	10	–	–	30
Final income	8230	10 200	13 990	17 980	29 200	15 920

Source: ONS, *Social Trends*

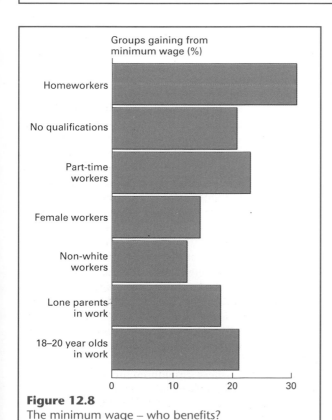

Figure 12.8
The minimum wage – who benefits?
Source: *Labour Force Survey*, Autumn 1997

However, early evidence on the impact of the minimum wage suggests that it will not greatly affect employment, except possibly in hotels and catering. Even there, there are figures to show that the burger joints continued to recruit after the introduction of the minimum wage, just as they had before.

Some commentators have argued that minimum wages do not reduce employment, despite the predictions of economic theory. In practice, the employers who keep wages as low as possible find that they have difficulty in keeping good employees. They have high turnover rates and longer periods of being short-staffed. Minimum wages reduce turnover, giving people time to acquire skills. They also give employers an incentive to train staff and make them more reliable and productive in order to get value for the wages paid. This in turn enhances the employability of the person concerned.

One possibility is that the minimum wage will increase the differential between benefits and wages. It may increase the incentive to work.

Employment policy

Governments can take steps to increase demand in the economy as a whole, and when they do, the effect is likely to be helpful in reducing unemployment. They can increase people's spending power by cutting taxes or reducing interest rates so that people can borrow more cheaply, or they can increase government spending. However, the Conservative governments that were in power from 1979 to 1997 were usually anxious to avoid inflation and so restricted spending in the economy, rather than encouraging it to grow. The Labour government since 1997 seems unlikely to change that policy. The idea of spending to reduce unemployment and increase growth is now widely discredited as likely to lead only to short-term gains, at the expense of accelerating inflation.

Policies directed at unemployment have therefore been focused upon the need to improve labour mobility. Efforts have been made to improve the flow of information about job opportunities. Help has been made available to the long-term unemployed to overcome difficulties they may have in making applications and coping with interviews.

There are serious problems of geographical mobility in the United Kingdom, caused by the nature of the housing market. The right to council housing is acquired by residence in a particular locality. It is not transferable: someone living in a council flat in Glasgow has no rights to council housing in the south-east, even though jobs may be available there. Similarly, owner-occupiers in areas where house prices are low cannot move into areas where they are high unless they have access to the extra money needed. The earnings differentials between low- and high-price areas have to be very large indeed in order to make it possible to move, let alone desirable.

Governments have done very little to remedy problems of geographical immobility. Their efforts have been concentrated upon creating training opportunities.

Training policy

Training policies in the United Kingdom have been steadily strengthened as unemployment has worsened. However, their effectiveness is still questioned. They are carried out by the Department for Education and Employment.

The objectives are identified as:

- to encourage employers to develop the skills and experience of their employees of all ages;
- to provide and encourage appropriate training for young people when they have full-time education;
- to help the long-term unemployed acquire the skills and experience that will help them find regular employment;
- to help the education system become more relevant to working life and more responsive to changing demands and opportunities in the labour market;
- to ensure that the distinctive needs of the self-employed and small firms for training, counselling and other support are met.

The Department for Education and Employment tries to co-ordinate the activities of employers, the education service, training providers and trade unions in an effort to overcome skill shortages and reduce unemployment. The introduction of modern apprenticeships is supposed to have helped to overcome identifiable skill shortages while giving opportunities to young people. The development of a system of vocational education through National Vocational Qualifications (NVQs) has been directed at standardizing recognized qualifications and creating a unified structure which promotes lifetime learning.

Locally, the Training and Enterprise Councils (TECs) are responsible for co-ordinating training needs by fostering communication between employers and further-education providers. Their role is under review, but it seems likely that they or similar bodies will continue to be important in their own areas.

While the existing measures are probably significant steps in the right direction, it is clear that much still remains to be done in improving the availability of skills training to all.

Why training policy developed

Not only is labour geographically immobile, but it is also said to be **occupationally immobile**. That is, people find it difficult to transfer from one job area to another. Yet this is necessary in a dynamic economy. Many government White Papers of the past have highlighted how the UK's problems of unemployment during the 1970s coexisted alongside large numbers of job vacancies. This seemingly odd situation was largely due to the unemployed having the wrong skills and partly due to their lacking information. It was these problems of mismatch between vacancies and unemployed labour that largely provided the impetus for improvements in training.

Since then there has been a slight shift in emphasis. If an economy is to be dynamic in a single European market it must meet the training standards of its competitors and be enthusiastic about overcoming skill shortages. As a result, economic commentators have become increasingly conscious of foreign attitudes to training and more aware of the relationships between training and productivity. It is clear that upgrading skills can have a big impact on productivity (output per person employed). Also, lower-skilled workforces require more supervisory labour in the form of quality control and general management.

There has been a trend in many businesses towards multi-skilling. This means that each employee is capable of carrying out a range of tasks, rather than just one. This makes the workforce more flexible and better able to respond to problems as they arise in production. This has given firms an incentive to provide regular training opportunities. This type of situation occurs often in manufacturing, where employees are likely anyway to need to learn new technologies.

The New Deal

A key policy for the Labour government that came to power in 1997 was the New Deal. This was part of a move towards welfare-to-work, an approach characterized by an active effort to get people into work rather than simply paying benefits indefinitely. Initially in 1998 it applied to 18–24-year-olds who had been unemployed for at least six months. Later it was extended to include some older people.

The New Deal includes many of the previously existing policies. Altogether in 1997 there were forty-two different schemes, which were hard to understand and complex to administer. But it has added a number of strong new provisions. Perhaps the most important is the 'Gateway'. This lasts for four months and consists of intensive advice on job-hunting, and help with applications, training and education. At the end of this period, young people are offered one of the following:

1   a job with a private sector employer who will receive £60 per week subsidy for six months;
2   full-time education or training;
3   six months of work in the voluntary sector, with one day a week of education and training;
4   six months' work with a community project that meets government targets for energy conservation;
5   help in setting up their own businesses.

Options 2 to 4 all allow the person to continue receiving benefits. But young people who refuse to participate in the New Deal lose up to 40 per cent of their benefits, so there are strong stick-and-carrot elements in the scheme. So far, the evidence suggests that young people are being drawn back into the labour market by these means.

The initial budget for the New Deal was set at £3.2 billion. Many employers were recruited to the scheme in order to provide the necessary jobs. The danger with such policies is that the jobs created can be temporary, can fail to provide any enhancement of skills or work habits, and can be generally perceived as 'make-work', temporary expedients. Ensuring that the scheme actually gives real help to the long-term unemployed is expensive. So is the provision of the necessary subsidies. It follows that a good scheme will need to be generously funded. But that means that it must be cost effective. The government needs to be sure that it does not help just those who were likely to have found work anyway.

Is the New Deal working?

Working out whether the New Deal is having a positive impact is virtually impossible, since there is no way of knowing what would have happened without it. Unemployment amongst those eligible for the scheme has been falling quite fast since it was introduced, while it has been edging up for those that do not qualify.

Table 12.8 suggests that the scheme is helping. As of January 1999, 44 000 18–24-year-olds had left the New Deal for unsubsidized jobs. The snag is that this total includes people who would have got a job anyway, people who were already working and claiming benefits fraudulently, and people for whom the New Deal really did produce the desired work.

There have been a number of criticisms of the New Deal's monitoring systems. In time these will lead to improved tracking of what happens to individuals.

12 How has the New Deal affected long-term youth unemployment so far?

13 Find out what has happened since this was written. How successful is the New Deal now?

14 What other measures might be required in the long run?

Watch this space. It is certain that there will be many studies of the effectiveness of the New Deal, and the scheme itself may well be modified in due course. These developments will be extensively reported in the press. Furthermore, the New Deal was introduced at a time when unemployment was falling anyway. A key question involves what happens to the scheme if job losses accelerate and potential employers become much harder to find.

Table 12.8

Where they go to after the New Deal
Government figures for 18–24-year-olds

	Off the claimant count
Unsubsidized jobs	43 760
Other benefits	13 480
Other known, including holiday	9 870
Unknown	33 940
Employer option	9 820
Education/training	21 780
Voluntary sector	6 620
Environmental taskforce	5 910
Total	145 130

Sources: DfEE, ONS

KEY POINTS

12.6

- Earnings undergo some redistribution through the tax and benefit system of the United Kingdom.

- The Department for Education and Employment administers training policies.

- The main aims of training policy are concerned with helping the school-leaver and the long-term unemployed by providing training, assisting the education system to become more responsive to the needs of the labour market, and supporting the self-employed and their small firms.

- Training policies are basically geared towards overcoming mismatch problems between unemployed labour and job vacancies. The aim is to reduce skill shortages and make labour more mobile.

- Training policy is difficult to evaluate and further evidence is awaited.

Case Study

Post-industrial paradoxes

'If work were so great', said Mark Twain, 'the rich would have hogged it long ago.' They have, Mr Twain, they have. The result is that some have work and money but too little time, while others have all the time but no work and no money. We have made work into a god and then made it difficult for many to worship.

Time creates a new growth area. Personal services for the busy save time; education, travel and recreation for the affluent busy, to spend time; equipment and materials for those who want to spend time to save money. These new growth areas will be best served, not by large corporations but by small independents providing a personal and local delivery linked into bigger combinations.

This provides the first clue to how we can hope to find ways through the paradoxes of modern life. We must all, individuals, organizations and governments, learn to take a more flexible approach. People must learn to manage their own lives, performing different tasks for different employers but also working for themselves and thus designing personal 'portfolios' of work. Only one-third of British workers now work the 'normal' nine-to-five day. The proportion will grow smaller. I can see a situation in which it will no longer be possible to draw a hard distinction between full- and part-time work, when 'retirement' will become a purely technical term, and when 'overtime' as a concept will seem as outmoded as 'servant' does today.

This is why investment in education, training and intelligence, for adults as well as young people, is so important to the future of Britain and other industrial societies. In the new world, where we no longer have the security of full-time, life-long jobs or careers, we shall need our wits. Our society will have to become a permanent learning culture. The governments of the past aspired to create property-owning democracies. They should continue to do so, but they need to redefine property. Our future security will lie not in physical property but in our intelligence and our education.

Source: Charles Handy, *The Empty Raincoat*, Hutchinson, 1994, as reported in *The Independent on Sunday*, 20 February 1994

1 What aspects of increasing flexibility in the labour market are already observable?
2 What are the implications of Charles Handy's view for
  (a) someone who is unemployed,
  (b) someone who is deciding whether to continue with education and
  (c) government policy?

Case Study

Women solicitors 'exploited'

Women solicitors are being discriminated against by an unfair pay scale within their profession which rewards male colleagues with much higher salaries.

The President of the Law Society said that 'shameful figures', revealed in a survey released yesterday, meant that firms were 'exploiting' their female staff. The figures, from a survey based on 579 sample firms in England and Wales, show that on the lower rungs, at the level of assistant or associate solicitor, women earned an average of £21 000 compared to men's £24 000. Up the scale, women partners earned £36 000 a year compared to men's £51 000.

Source: *The Times*, 12 October 1996

Boasts of racial equality often conceal bias

Companies that boast about treating ethnic minorities fairly are more likely to discriminate against them, research reveals today. Research from Cardiff University Business School involved sending requests from two purported MBA students, Mr Evans and Mr Patel, for information about job opportunities. Letters were sent to 100 companies. Both candidates had equivalent qualifications.

Of 24 companies with ethnic minority statements in their annual reports, nearly half either ignored the letter from Mr Patel or sent him a more unfavourable response than Mr Evans'.

The Commission for Racial Equality said that the research suggested many companies treated equal opportunities statements like 'designer labels'. 'When we peel away the labels we find that there is little commitment or action that leads to equal treatment', said the Commission's chairman, Sir Herman Ousley. A similar study in 1992 found widespread evidence of systematic discrimination.

Source: *The Guardian*, 22 July 1998

1 What other evidence of discrimination in the labour market do you know of?
2 What disadvantages might businesses that discriminate be likely to encounter?

Exam Preparation

Multiple choice questions

1 The introduction of equal pay legislation in a country increases the pay of female workers. What would be the most likely effect of this increase?
 A a reduction in female participation in the labour force
 B a reduction in the rate of female unemployment
 C a reduction in the wages of male workers
 D an expansion in the supply of female workers
 E substitution of female workers for male workers

2 Following the introduction of a national minimum wage, the level of employment in a country increased. Which one of the following could account for this result?

 A There were unemployed resources and the national minimum wage increased the level of aggregate demand in the economy.
 B There were unemployed resources and the national minimum wage reduced the international trading competitiveness of the country's industries.
 C The government adjusted the way that unemployment figures are measured by reclassifying benefit claimants aged over 55 as 'early retired' rather than 'unemployed'.
 D The demand for labour and the supply of labour were both completely price-inelastic.

Essay questions

1 Why might unemployment rates differ among countries in the developed world? To what extent is an increase in aggregate demand likely to solve the problem of unemployment?

2 What factors contribute to the immobility of labour in the United Kingdom? How effective have government policies been in improving the mobility of labour?

3 Outline the factors which determine the structure of wages in the economy. Explain whether or not there are any economic reasons why, despite equal pay legislation, on average women are paid less than men in Britain.

4 Outline briefly the causes of differences in the wage rates paid to workers of different age, sex, race and skill in different industries and occupations. Discuss the likely effects of the national minimum wage in the United Kingdom.

5 (a) Explain why there are inequalities in the present distribution of income and wealth in the United Kingdom.
  (b) Assess whether the government should introduce policies which are designed to make the distribution of income more equal.

6 (a) Distinguish between income and wealth.
  (b) Discuss the possible economic effects of policies aimed at significantly reducing inequalities in income and wealth.

7 (a) Why is it difficult to agree what constitutes full employment?
  (b) Discuss the view that imperfections in the labour market are the main cause of unemployment in the United Kingdom.

PART

C

INTRODUCTORY MACROECONOMICS

■ **www.ons.gov.uk**

The Office for National Statistics is the government agency responsible for compiling, analysing and disseminating many of the United Kingdom's economic and social statistics. Consequently, the site address had to appear at some point in our listings.

A reason for choosing Section C is that the homepage offers a direct link to StatBase, which provides blue (and pink) book data on line. Another of the links takes you to a 'UK in figures' option, which gives access to a broad range of data showing an up-to-date statistical portrait of how we live in the national economy today.

■ **www.kings.cam.ac.uk/library/archives/ collections/keynes.htm**

John Maynard Keynes (1883–1946) has had a lasting influence on economics. We introduce his theories in Chapters 15, 16 and 17. He has often been described as an economist of genius, and there are many sites constructed by aficionados reviewing his academic and social life (for example **www.bized.ac.uk**, the first site referred to in Part A). The specific URL listed here gives a good indication of the breadth of Keynes's work as well as the extent of his output and influence. The homepage links with an index to the archives held at King's College, Cambridge University. The index is arranged under the following headings: general subjects (containing Keynes's main publications); articles, speeches and broadcasts; editorials and societies; business interests (Keynes made a small fortune speculating on the Stock Exchange); educational interests; and personal papers. The actual archive is physically held in 156 boxes at King's College, Cambridge, which is where Keynes lectured in economics.

■ **www.niesr.ac.uk**

The National Institute of Economic and Social Research (NIESR) was established in 1938, and has had a website since 1996. From 1959 onwards, one of its primary functions has been to forecast the economy. Given the organization's long history, it is understandable that the computer model on which its forecasts are based can be described in very general terms as falling within the Keynesian tradition. As you can see described on the website: 'short-term fluctuations in output are primarily determined by changes in the components of **aggregate demand**. But, in the longer term [and their forecasts presently scan 30 years into the future], output is underpinned by **supply-side** influences'. These concepts are developed within Part C and you will notice that some of our data are drawn from this institute. Indeed, the *National Institute's Economic Review* is published quarterly, and the contents page and summaries of articles can be viewed via this site. Students in higher education may also find the URL useful to access details of current research programmes and associated publications.

■ **www.bankofengland.co.uk**

In Chapter 18 we introduce our coverage of money and financial institutions and subsequently, in Chapter 27, we will review monetary policy in more detail. For both of these topics the Bank of England site is a useful reference point. The homepage has a comprehensive index and its own search engine, so you should easily find the latest announcements; up-to-date monetary and financial statistics; and summaries of the Bank's most recent quarterly *Bulletin* and *Inflation Report* – both of which can also be downloaded in full (in PDF format). Finally, the *City Handbook* is worth a look since it provides a description of the UK's role as a financial centre, including references to more than 150 organizations. This handbook is only available to surfers on the Internet – there is no official published equivalent.

■ **www.economicsuk.com**

This is the website of David Smith, economics editor of the *Sunday Times*. The layout offers a comprehensive insight into many aspects of the UK economy. To follow just three possibilities offered at the homepage, you can read Smith's recent articles, including his 'Look at the week ahead'; you can find summaries of new research that is being published by the Royal Economic Society; or you can participate in a discussion forum by exchanging ideas and questions on economic topics. Whatever you choose, there is always plenty of up-to-date material on hand to complement the theory that we present in the forthcoming section.

13

National income accounting

We now begin a section on the national economy, and, as the subsequent chapter titles suggest, this is to do with aggregates, or totals. In this specific chapter we shall be concerned with the study of total output, total expenditure and total income. In the next couple of chapters we shall deal with the closely related topic of aggregate demand and aggregate supply.

Obviously, policy-makers within governments need to know just how much economic activity is taking place. Consequently, a way of estimating the level of economic activity occurring during a specific time period is necessary. This process is known as national income accounting and it takes place on an annual basis. So that comparisons can be made, the statistics are presented according to internationally agreed conventions. The 1998 UK figures that form a main focus of this chapter have been extracted from the *United Kingdom National Accounts* published in September 1999.

Before we delve into the peculiarities of national accounting systems, however, we need first to establish some general concepts that apply to all nations. You have already been introduced to the basic idea that bringing together various factors of production produces goods and services. The total output (production) of a nation arises from millions of firms (owned by the public or private sector). The total expenditure on these goods and services emanates from millions of households (both at home and abroad). We need to understand the relationship between these millions of firms and households to appreciate how a country arrives at a certain level of total income.

LEARNING OUTCOMES

On completing this chapter you should understand:

■ Economic activity

■ Gross domestic product and its measurement

■ The uses of national accounts

■ The limitations of national accounting systems

Understanding economic activity

It is the flow of goods and services from businesses to consumers and the subsequent payments from consumers to businesses that constitute what we are striving to measure. We have already seen economic activity portrayed in a simplistic manner in Chapter 1, Figure 1.7, and for convenience a modified version is presented in Figure 13.1.

In the simple economy shown in Figure 13.1, there are only businesses and households. It is assumed that households receive their income by selling the use of whatever factors of production they own, that businesses sell their entire output immediately to households, and that households spend their entire income on consumer products. These assumptions are reasonably realistic. Businesses will only make what they can sell. Production will involve buying in land, labour, capital and enterprise, and these factor (of production) services will generate their respective income payments: rent, wages, interest and profit.

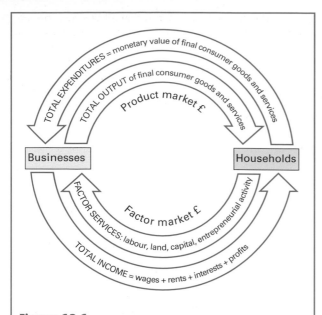

Figure 13.1
The flow of income, product and expenditure
In this model households sell factors of production that they own to businesses in return for monetary rewards. Businesses then sell to households goods and services for which they receive payment.

1 Identify the monetary flows in the factor market. **A✓**
2 Identify the real flows in the factor market. **A✓**
3 Define the factor market. **A✓**
4 Identify the monetary flows in the product market. **A✓**
5 Identify the real flows in the product market. **A✓**
6 Define the product market. **A✓**
7 (a) Identify a voucher or coupon scheme presently on offer.
  (b) Explain how the scheme outlined in (a) may measure the flow within one specific sector of an economy.
8 Explain how the euro may fit with Edward de Bono's thinking.
9 According to Edgar Cahn, a civil rights lawyer, market economies do not value the real work of society, which he described as caring, loving and being a good citizen. Discuss ways of rewarding good citizenship.

Sectoral flows

An important concept to grasp at this point is that money flows in one direction and resources, goods or services flow in the other direction. That is, there are 'monetary flows' and 'real flows'. For example, in the product market – designated by the upper loops in Figure 13.1 – households feed their money to businesses in return for actual goods and services (that is, products). In short, households expect something in return for their money. Similarly, households do not provide their factor services for free; they expect payment, as illustrated by the lower loops in Figure 13.1.

Building on this concept, Edward de Bono, a philosopher who initially made a name for himself with books on lateral thinking, considered the idea of refining 'monetary flows' and 'real flows' to aid the government in selecting areas in need of economic management. He suggested, in 1994, inventing something called 'target currencies' with companies like IBM creating their own economies by issuing their own currency.

Presumably this idea would work, since prototype examples already exist, for example Club Mediterranean issue a village currency to tourists taking their holidays, Tesco, Safeway and Sainsbury's issue loyalty points, and a whole range of businesses deal in air miles.

It is important that profits are acknowledged as a cost of production. You might be under the impression that profits are not part of the cost of producing goods and services; but profits are indeed a part of this cost because entrepreneurs must be rewarded for providing their services, or they will not provide them. Their reward, if any, is profit. The reward – that is, the profit – is included in the cost of the factors of production. If there were no expectation of profit, entrepreneurs would not incur the risks associated with the organization of production and investment. That is why we consider profits a cost of doing business.

From this introductory analysis you should sense that there is a close relationship between a nation's income, output and expenditure. Question 9 in the activity box above highlights that this is complicated by the things you do for love. It should, however, be possible to recognize that the amount of economic activity in an economy can be estimated in three ways:

1 by adding up the value of all the goods and services produced (in a given period of time);
2 by adding up the value of all the income received (during that time period);
3 by adding up the value of all the spending that occurred (during that period of time).

In each case, the result obtained should be identical as

total income ≡ total production ≡ total expenditure

These symmetrical identities are examined in more detail later in the chapter.

KEY POINTS

13.1

■ It is the flow of goods and services from businesses to households and the related payments that constitute economic activity.

■ The simple circular flow model highlights (a) that households sell factor services to businesses that pay for those factor services, the receipt of these payments generating total income; (b) that businesses sell goods and services to households that pay for them, the total output being thus absorbed by total expenditure.

■ Total income must always equal total output which must always equal total expenditure.

■ Economic activity can therefore be measured in three different ways.

Equilibrium in an economy

In Chapter 3 we talked about the concept of equilibrium as a situation where supply and demand are equal. The equilibrium price, or market-clearing price, occurred at the intersection of the demand curve and the supply curve. The special feature about equilibrium is that there is no tendency for price or quantity to change once supply and demand are in equilibrium. Remember that, when the actual price is greater than the equilibrium price, market forces push the price back down towards equilibrium. Unsold 'surpluses' are offered for sale by producers and retailers, for example, at lower prices. Producers will also reduce output. Remember also that, when the price is below the equilibrium price, there is an excess quantity demanded at that price. Forces are set in motion that cause the price to go up. More-than-willing demanders bid up the price. Producers respond by increasing the quantity supplied.

Thus, the important thing to remember from equilibrium analysis is that when we are not in equilibrium forces will work to re-establish equilibrium. The same is true whether we are analysing equilibrium for a single product market or equilibrium for the entire economy. If the total demand for all goods and services is not equal to the total supply of all goods and services, market forces will operate so as to bring total demand and total supply back into equilibrium. In the process, total income and total output may either rise or fall. Indeed, much of this part of the text is designed to analyse the forces behind the rise and fall of total income, total output and total expenditure.

Equilibrium is a concept that pervades all economic analysis. We have actually assumed that equilibrium prevails within the circular flow model represented in Figure 13.1. By requiring that all household earnings be spent in the product market and that all business production can be offered for immediate sale, there can be no discrepancy between the total demand and the total supply of goods and services. Thus, the basic circular flow model in Figure 13.1 accurately represents the total demand for goods and services and that total demand and total supply are automatically in equilibrium. Provided we never alter this model it will continue to function at the same level forever. Such an economy can be classed as being in **neutral equilibrium**. Neutral equilibrium means there are no pressures for change – the established set of flows will simply persist forever.

Leakages and injections

Every economy in reality, however, experiences leakages (withdrawals) via sectors that we have not yet considered. These sectors include financial institutions, the government and overseas. Simultaneously, there are injections of funds into the economy through the same sectors. For example, imports constitute a leakage from our economy because in effect households are spending their money overseas, whereas export earnings represent an injection into the economy as foreign money flows in from abroad and boosts employment of the domestic factors of production. Similarly, savings can be formally regarded as a leakage from the circular flow, since by definition savings represent income generated by output that is not passed on directly in spending. It is likely, however, that most savings will pass through a financial institution and hence back into the system in the form of investment. Investment can be regarded as an injection since it is an addition to the circular flow which does not relate to present consumer spending. The relationships between leakages and injections are considered further in the following practical exercise.

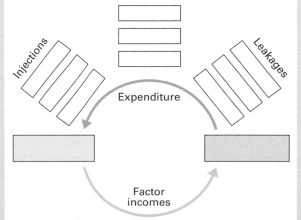

Leakages and injections

A model of income flows

There are three main leakages from a household's expenditure, namely savings, imports and tax. To counterbalance these there are three injections, namely investments, exports and government spending.

10 Locate the monetary flows representing leakages and injections in the appropriate boxes in the figure. **A✓**
11 Locate in the appropriate boxes the following five sectors: households, business, overseas, government and financial institutions. **A✓**
12 Consider one mechanism that may work towards creating an equilibrium between a leakage and its related injection.

Within each sector, *if* the various flows of injection and leakage were equal then the flow of income around the circuit would remain constant. Only when the leakages are perfectly counterbalanced by the injections could the economy be said to be in equilibrium. For example, say we have three leakages from expenditures (savings, imports and tax) with the values 5 + 2 + 3 and three injections (investment, exports and government spending) with the values 2 + 2 + 6. The economy would still be in equilibrium because the total value of the injections (10) equals the total value of the leakages (10). However, the various decisions affecting the leakages and injections of funds are carried out by different groups of individuals with different motivations. Therefore it is unlikely that year after year leakages and injections will remain the same.

However, due to the income–output–expenditure relationship the economy will adjust to new equilibrium levels. For example, if leakages exceed injections, expenditure will be less than factor incomes. Consequently, firms will not receive sufficient revenue to cover their output costs. Stocks will accumulate and firms will cut back output and income until they equal expenditure again. A new level of equilibrium will have been established.

It is the character of the imbalances between leakages and injections that prompts changes in output from year to year. These changes lead to different amounts of income circulating within the economy – which represent different levels of economic activity. (All economies will tend towards an equilibrium but the equilibrium point is not necessarily the point of full employment.) Measuring the annual economic activity is the topic of the next main section.

Measuring the economy's performance

Someone who works around the house preparing meals, doing minor repairs or washing the dishes does not normally get paid. Of course, if the homemaker becomes ill or is injured and the same work has to be purchased from others, the price tag can get pretty high. Nevertheless, when government statisticians count up their estimate of annual national economic activity, they ignore unremunerated work in the home as they find it very difficult to allocate a monetary value to these services. Feminists think this is wrong and are urging governments to place a value on 'unwaged work'.

13 What else will be unrecorded in the official estimate of national economic activity? **A✓**
14 What will happen to the official national accounts if a number of women marry their butlers? **A✓**
15 What will happen to the official national accounts if a large amount of cocaine is smuggled into the country? **A✓**
16 Explain why a rise in car exports will increase the amount of national income. **A✓**

Conclusion

All income is generated by selling factor services. Owners of labour gain wages, the providers of land receive rent, the persons providing capital receive interest, and the entrepreneurs taking the risks gain any profits. These factors of production when combined provide output, the cost of which is identical to the payment for factor services. In fact, it may help if the prices of final goods and services are regarded as bundles of incomes that have been paid out during the course of their production.

Another way of looking at the value of output is from the angle of expenditure. Indeed, you must recognize that all output is sold, even if only to the business's warehouse. Expenditure therefore absorbs the final goods and services in the form of either consumer goods or capital goods and sets the cycle off again. The outcome is that total expenditure ≡ total income ≡ total output. These general identities form the framework of the main aggregates of the UK national accounts, which we shall now examine in more detail.

13.2

- All economies tend towards an equilibrium.

- Imports, savings and tax represent forms of leakage from a nation's economic activities.

- Exports, investment and government spending represent forms of injections into a nation's economic activities.

- The sizes of the injections set against the leakages are important determinants of the annual level of economic activity.

- The equilibrium point is not necessarily a point of full employment.

- For economic activity to be officially recorded there must be an official monetary flow in return for a good or service.

- Total expenditure ≡ total income ≡ total output. These are national accounting identities.

Gross domestic product

An understanding of the United Kingdom national accounting system should begin with a brief discussion of **gross domestic product** (GDP). GDP is regarded as an important measure of any economy. In simple terms, it can be regarded as a nation's annual turnover. In formal terms, we can define GDP as the total market value of all goods and services produced within an economy during a year. In other words, we are attempting to aggregate all the economic activity that has taken place inside the UK domestic territory during the last year.

We are referring here to a **flow** of production. A nation produces at a certain rate, just as you receive income at a certain rate. Your income flow might be at a rate of £5000 per year or £50 000 per year. Suppose you are told that someone earns £500. Would you consider this a good salary? There is no way you can answer that question unless you know whether the person is earning £500 per month or per week or per day. Thus, you have to specify a time period for all flows – income received is a flow. You must contrast this with, for example, your total accumulated savings, which are a **stock** measured at a point in time, not across time. Implicit in just about everything we deal with in this chapter is a time period – usually a year.

What production is included

As we noted, GDP measures the annual value of all economic activity taking place in the UK. These activities range from agriculture and production through to services, and often the output of one business or institution involves many stages. Hence, within the national accounts the emphasis is on value added.

To clarify this point, in Table 13.1 we present the difference between the total value of all sales and value added in the production of a doughnut. You should quickly realize that the sum of the values added is equal to the sale price to the final consumer. It is the 15p that is used to measure GDP, not the 32p. If we used the 32p, we would be **double-counting**, for we would include the total value of all of the intermediate sales that took place prior to the doughnut being sold to its final consumer. Such double-counting would grossly exaggerate GDP if it were done for all of the goods and services sold.

Table 13.1

Sales value and value added in pence per doughnut at each stage of production

Stage 1 A farmer purchases a penny's worth of fertilizer and seed that are used as factors of production in growing wheat.

Stage 2 The farmer grows the wheat, harvests it and sells it to the miller for 2p. Thus, we see that the farmer has added 1p worth of value. That 1p represents income paid in the form of rent, wages, interest and profit by the farmer.

Stage 3 The flour miller purchases the wheat for 2p, and adds 2p to the value added; that is, there is 2p for him as income to be paid as rent, wages, interest and profit. He sells the ground wheat flour to a doughnut-baking company.

Stage 4 The doughnut-baking company buys the flour for 4p and adds 6p as the value added. It then sells the doughnut to the final retailer.

Stage 5 The doughnut retailer sells fresh hot doughnuts at 15p apiece, thus creating additional value of 5p.

We see that the total value of sales resulting from the production of one doughnut was 32p, but the total value added was 15p, which is exactly equal to the retail price. The total value added is equal to the sum of all income payments, including payments in the form of rent, wages, interest and profit.

1 Stage of production	2 Value of sales (p)	3 Value added (p)
Stage 1 Fertilizer and seed	1	1
Stage 2 Growing wheat	2	1
Stage 3 Flour milling	4	2
Stage 4 Doughnut baking	10	6
Stage 5 Doughnut retailing	15	5
Total value of all sales	32	
Total value added		15

Can you calculate the value added?

Suppose you own a small ice-cream factory that has sales, expenses and profits as shown below:

Total sales	£25 000
Labour costs	£9000
Interest on loans	£800
Rent	£3200
Raw materials	£7000
Tools and equipment	£1000
Profits	£4000

17 What is the value added to GDP of the productive activities of your firm?

Excluding non-productive transactions

In economic accounts, not only is it important to assure that GDP measurements are on a value-added basis, but they must also relate to productive transactions only. Examples of activities that are not productive in an economic sense include eating, drinking, sleeping and taking exercise, as it is impossible for one person to pay another to do these things for them. In contrast, activities such as washing, preparing meals, cleaning and looking after children can be provided by others and, more importantly, paid for. For the transaction to be recorded in the national accounts, it must go through the books and a payment needs to exchange hands. Very largely, therefore, productive transactions involve some final purchases of newly produced goods or services, whereas daily economic activity also involves numerous non-productive transactions. These non-productive transactions are typified by transfers of money (or the ownership of used goods). Technically, these are referred to as transfer payments – and we shall illustrate them with four typical examples.

Transfer payments

1 *Buying and selling shares*
When you purchase shares on the Stock Exchange in a public limited company, for example ICI or Marks & Spencer, someone else must sell them to you. In essence, there is merely a transfer of ownership rights – you pay to obtain a share certificate. Someone else, via the Stock Exchange, received your payment and gave up the share certificate. No productive activity is generated and consequently the bulk of the monies involved in this transaction is not included in our measurements of GDP (only the brokerage fees for the productive *services* involved in deed transfers etc. need to be counted).

2 *Government transfer payments*
We have already referred to transfer payments as payments for which no productive services are concurrently

provided in exchange. The most obvious government transfer payments are social security payments, old-age pensions, student grants and interest payments on the National Debt. The recipients make no contribution to current production in return for such transfer payments (although they may have made contributions in the past in order to receive them).

3 *Private transfer payments*
Are you receiving money from your parents in order to live at school? Has a wealthy relative ever given you a gift of money? If so, you have been the recipient of a private transfer payment. This is merely a transfer of funds from one individual to another. As such, it does not constitute productive activity and is not included in GDP.

4 *The transfer of used goods*
If I sell you my two-year-old car, there is no current production involved. Rather, I transfer to you the ownership of a car that was produced several years ago; in exchange, you transfer to me, say, £3000. The original purchase price of the car was included in the GDP in the year I purchased it. To include it again when I sell it to you would be counting the value twice.

However, if the car was bought from a second-hand car dealer, the mark-up between the price at which he bought it and the selling price would be included. The profit represents the salesman's income and is a return for a service. This final example brings us back to the central issue – GDP calculations must incorporate payments for productive services. The car salesman will be very willing to tell you how he has improved the car before putting it out for display on his forecourt – in a way, one may sense that his work has added value and is therefore part of new annual output.

KEY POINTS

13.3

- GDP is the total money value of final goods and services produced in an economy during a one-year period.

- GDP also represents the flow of production over a one-year period.

- In order to avoid double-counting, we look at value added.

- In measuring GDP we must exclude transfer payments; these are merely transfers of monies which do not correspond to any type of productive economic activity.

Measuring gross domestic product: three methods

GDP has been defined as the total market value of all goods and services produced within an economy during a year. Consequently, the Office for National Statistics can use one of three methods to measure its size. They can:

1 add up the *flow of expenditures* made on all goods and services during each year – this is known as the **expenditure approach**;
2 add up the *flow of income* received in the same year by everybody involved in the production of these goods and services – this is known as the **income approach**;
3 add up the specific value of the *flows of output* arising from each sector of the economy – this is known as the **output approach**.

On the very first page of the UK national accounts all three methods of measurement are summarized as main aggregates. By analysing these statistics and the detailed breakdown that follows, we gain an insight into the UK economy and its size, especially as the information given refers to the last eighteen years. Furthermore, since we share a common set of accounting conventions with nations worldwide, we can also make international comparisons.

Despite the fact that very few people study the 300-page accounts from cover to cover, the role of the national accounts is more than just a generator of GDP figures; it is a central reference for those who wish to gain a better feel for the economy and its measurement. To enable you to begin to understand this source of statistics, we shall examine in detail the main categories comprising the expenditure approach. The accounting terminology that we shall describe in the process is shared with our European partners.

Measuring gross domestic product with the expenditure approach

As its title suggests, the expenditure approach measures total expenditure on goods and services produced in the domestic economy. To avoid double-counting, it is important wherever possible to classify expenditures as final because the goods are then no longer part of the economic flow. The Office for National Statistics acquires statistical information from a wide range of industrial and household surveys, import and export documentation, and government accounting data. This enables them to produce annually tables of national expenditure. An example based on the general components is laid out in Table 13.2. The relevant categorizations and terminology are clarified in the following section, where each numbered item in Table 13.2 is explained.

(1) Consumers' expenditure

This is synonymous with household expenditure and covers general retail spending. Traditionally, it could be considered under three headings: **durable consumer goods**, **non-durable consumer goods** and **services**. Durable goods are *arbitrarily* defined as items that last more than a year; these include cars, televisions, furniture and household appliances. Non-durable goods are all the rest, such as food, fuel and clothes. Services are just what the name suggests: insurance, bank charges, funeral expenses and rents.

You should be aware of the fact that there are some goods and services that do not pass through the market-place. For example, food grown on the family allotment or garden certainly represents consumption, but it does not show up in the usual way because it does not pass through an organized market. The £545 billion spending therefore represents only recorded consumer spending; there will be some transactions that do not go through any official books.

(2) Government expenditures

In addition to personal consumption expenditures, there are local and central government purchases of goods and services. (These are grouped under the formal heading of *government final consumption expenditure*.) It is evident from the figures that the government sector is an important spender in our economy, and this is not at all surprising when one remembers that in Britain it provides many of our services, for example health, education, parks, libraries, police, defence and overseas representation. In the most recent national accounts, a distinction is made between expenditures benefiting the individual and those benefiting the collective. Because many of these services are provided free or below cost, they are valued in the national accounts at their cost of provision.

(3) Investment expenditures

Gross capital formation is not the name of a northern dance team but is the official term for investment expenditure. In very general terms, it represents monies spent by business on equipment.

In the national accounts, gross capital formation is made up of three components:

Gross fixed capital formation
changes in inventories, and
acquisitions less disposals of valuables

Table 13.2

Gross domestic product by the expenditure approach (at current market prices)

		1998 (£ million)
(1)	Consumption expenditure	545 124
(2)	Government final consumption expenditure	153 564
(3)	Gross capital formation	151 823
(4)	Export of goods and services	224 202
(4)	*less* imports of goods and services	–232 714
(5)	Statistical discrepancy	1 726
(6)	Gross domestic product at market prices	843 725

Source: *United Kingdom National Accounts, 1999*

As already pointed out, investment in economics does not relate to simple *transfers* of asset ownership among individuals. Thus, if you buy a stock or a bond, that is not investment from the economic point of view; you have simply traded money and received in exchange a piece of paper entitling you to something. Such transfers are not investment, and this is why accountants prefer the term inventories to refer to stocks.

For an economist, investment means expenditure on future productive capacity. In fact, the official demarcation for *fixed capital* only categorizes assets that can be used repeatedly in the production process for more than one year. In short, it relates to newly produced goods that will remain operative over a number of years. The bulk of investment expenditure, therefore, is made up of fixed assets such as industrial buildings, domestic dwellings, plant and machinery. Intangible assets such as computer software, artistic originals and mineral exploration are also included.

Apart from these items of fixed investment there is also investment in working capital. Indeed, it is important to remember that for accounting purposes businesses need to keep a record of unsold finished goods, materials that are to be used during production and work-in-progress. Supplies and stocks are part of the planning process. Consequently, we can identify another category of investment expenditure, namely *changes in inventories*. One would expect inventories to continually increase in a dynamic economy. However, in 1990, 1991 and 1992, the UK actually experienced negative values for this category as stocks and supplies were run down during the recession. To some extent the changes that occur to inventories are an indicator of demand for a nation's products.

Finally, there are assets that are not designed for production or consumption that are acquired and held primarily as a store of value, for example precious stones, antiques and art objects. The purchases and sales of such valuables are also recorded as investment expenditure. This may not seem to complement our definition of investment, but the way it is recorded does reinforce the definition of GDP. Only the items bought and sold during the year are accounted. The appreciation in value over time associated with objects of art is not recorded (here or anywhere at present). Finally, it may be worth noting that valuables represent only 0.06 per cent of total recorded expenditure. This contrasts with fixed assets, which account for 17.5 per cent of total expenditure.

(4) Overseas expenditures
To get an accurate representation of gross domestic product, we must remember to include the foreign sector. That is, we must add to our total domestic expenditure what foreigners spend on our goods and services when they purchase export items. To get a clear idea of the value of the external balance emanating from this overseas trade we must also remember to subtract the value of imports (as these represent another country's GDP).

net exports ≡ total exports − total imports

In numerical terms, for 1998 this would involve subtracting 232 714 from 224 202 (as indicated by (4) in Table 13.2). Once this calculation has been accounted we have more or less arrived at a figure for gross domestic product at current market prices.

(5) The statistical discrepancy
This is an adjustment made to the figures to reconcile the imbalance that occurs between the different methods of GDP calculation. Hence this item will make more sense when another method has been considered. It will be dealt with more fully on page 250 at the end of the next section.

(6) Gross domestic product at market prices
This amount (£844 billion) is one of the key aggregates estimated through the national accounting process. Each year the figure arrived at is widely referred to since it provides a summary of the UK's economic activity and welfare. Movements of this aggregate imply success or failure of the government's economic policies.

Consequently, the GDP at market prices is frequently referred to and it may be useful to remember what it represents. The following equation uses the standard notation adopted by economists to summarize this approach:

$$GDP = C + G + I + X - M$$

where C = consumer expenditure, G = government expenditure, I = investment (or gross capital formation), X = exports and M = imports.

Analysing the UK economy from the perspective of expenditure

Expenditure on the gross domestic product (figures rounded to the nearest £ billion)

	Consumers' expenditure	General government expenditure		Gross fixed capital formation	Changes in inventory	Exports of goods and services	Imports of goods and services
		Central government	Local authorities				
1996	485	90	56	125	2	220	224
1997	517	91	57	134	4	229	229

Source: *United Kingdom National Accounts, 1999*

18 Define, give examples and identify the trends of:
   (a) general government expenditure;
   (b) gross fixed capital formation;
   (c) net exports.
19 Calculate for 1996 and 1997 gross domestic product at market prices.

Has economic activity increased between 1996 and 1998?
20 What problems would inflation cause in comparing these figures?
21 Describe the economic climate that the figures suggest existed in one sector of the economy from 1996 to 1998.

KEY POINTS

13.4

- In the United Kingdom we use three methods for measuring GDP, namely the expenditure approach, the income approach and the output approach.

- The expenditure approach to measuring GDP requires that we add up consumers' expenditure (C), government expenditures (G), investment expenditures (I) and export expenditures (X) minus any import expenditures (M). In general terms, therefore, GDP = $C + G + I + X - M$.

- Included in consumer expenditures are consumer durables, consumer non-durables and services.

- We include government goods and services at their cost, since we do not usually have market prices to value them.

- Gross investment excludes transfer of asset ownership. In very general terms, it includes additions to the productive capacity of a nation, plus repairs and replacements of existing capital goods, and any change in business stocks.

- Overseas expenditures must be incorporated into GDP. Foreigners buying exports are spending on our nation's produce and therefore these monies must be added as they represent domestic economic activity. Conversely, imports must be subtracted.

Measuring gross domestic product with the income approach

By acquiring statistical information from the Inland Revenue (who collate and organize tax returns), the Office for National Statistics is able to produce annually tables estimating gross domestic product. As the name suggests, the income approach adds up all income earned by residents in the production of goods and services. Unfortunately, the figures are expressed in terms that make little immediate sense. For example: *gross operating surplus* and *mixed income* stand for measures of profit (excluding gains made on fixed assets or inventories which do not represent output) and *compensation of employees* means wages and salaries. Finally, you need to remember (from page 246) that certain transfer incomes are not included. For example, payments such as unemployment benefit or state pensions do not represent additions to current economic activity. Payments lost in tax, however, do need to be added and the income table includes all taxes on production.

It is interesting to note that, as anticipated, the final figure for GDP is identical with that on the expenditure table. This is because, in the course of producing the things they sell, firms incur costs which, when totalled, are identical to the sale price of their products. These costs are rewards (payments) to the factors of production, namely (1) wages, (2) profit, (3) rent and (4) interest.

The figures presented in the national accounts published since 1998 include a small amount to allow for income that is not declared to the Inland Revenue. This has become necessary since it is apparent that spending exceeds recorded activity. Conceptually, all economic activity should be accounted and European-wide experience suggests some consideration needs to be taken of 'concealed' or 'illegal' production.

An income approach calculation

22 From the following hypothetical information calculate the gross domestic product at market prices.

	£ million
Compensation of employees	9000
Taxes on production	2000
Government pensions	1500
Unemployment pay and other social benefits	1000
Gross operating surplus	3000

Measuring gross domestic product with the output approach

The various values for this calculation are derived from censuses of production, and statistics on the different forms of income. These enable the Office for National Statistics to produce annually a table showing the composition of final output in terms of the related income generated. This table is broken down into various industrial sectors to show the proportional contributions made within the UK economy.

Obviously, the final figures will be identical to those appearing in the income and expenditure tables. This is because output is only made possible by generating rewards (income) to the factors of production involved. Correspondingly, all output is assumed to be sold (even if it is only in the form of inventories).

What is involved, therefore, is an adding-up of all the contributions to domestic output made by each economic unit in the country (after allowing for stock appreciation). It is important to remember, however, that the emphasis must be on the **value added** by each producing unit, otherwise some output may be counted twice. To avoid such double-counting, the value of 'intermediate' products (that is, the value of products bought in for the production process) must be subtracted from the value of the final product. This concept has already been illustrated in Table 13.1.

Alternatively, it is possible to concentrate solely on the value of final goods and services, as is done largely in the (public) service sector, where all the input costs are totalled to measure the final value of the output. For example, education, health and social work are estimated according to what it costs in total to provide these services in terms of staff wages and maintenance, etc.

The next exercise involves a brief examination of the output approach. However, before you can fully comprehend the figures, we need to clarify the full meaning of market prices.

What price is used to value economic activity?

So far the 'market price' has represented the main reference for the valuation of transactions in the accounts. The final stage, however, in understanding the three methods is to distinguish between market price and basic price figures. The latter remove the distortions caused by taxes on expenditure and subsidies. Taxes on expenditure (for example VAT) merely increase the price of goods and services, while subsidies (for example the rent on certain properties) reduce market prices. Businesses are actually acting on behalf of the government when they collect VAT or claim a subsidy. Therefore, movements in expenditure taxes or subsidies move market prices for the purchasers, but the amount received by producers (other things remaining constant) will remain unaltered. In other words, the rewards to the actual factors of production remain the same when governments move their rates of expenditure tax and/or subsidies. As the aim is to measure real economic activity, that is, assess the productivity of our resources, it makes more sense to measure GDP at basic prices, and this has been adopted as common practice in national income accounting throughout Europe. The following formula should help to clarify this development:

gross value added at basic prices $=$ GDP at market prices minus taxes on expenditure plus subsidies

Consequently, there are a number of different prices used to value inputs and outputs. Those who view historical data may also see a reference to factor prices. These are similar to basic prices but involve subtracting even more taxes. Those who view up-to-date accounts will also see reference to constant prices, and these will be explained towards the close of this chapter.

An output approach calculation

23 The following 1998 data have been extracted from the *United Kingdom National Accounts* published in 1999. Calculate the gross domestic product at market prices for 1998.

	£ billion
Gross value added at basic prices	747.5
Taxes on products	103.5
Subsidies	7.0

The statistical discrepancy

It may not surprise you that, given the thousands of figures involved and the various estimates that have to be made, the final GDP figure arising from each method is slightly different. As noted, the figures are built up from different data sets for each method and although in theory the totals should be identical, in reality they are not. Consequently, an increasing prominence is given to an average figure arising from the three calculations. The difference between each independent calculation and the average figure gives a statistical discrepancy. The statistical discrepancy therefore acts as an adjustment that enables us to refer to one specific figure for GDP and not several possibilities.

13.5

- To derive GDP using the income approach, we add up all the incomes earned by residents in the production of goods and services.

- The statistical discrepancy figure is a balancing item, accounting for the data limitations. It may be formally defined as the GDP (average estimate) less the independent estimates made via expenditure or income methods.

- The output of some service industries is measured in terms of the value of their final cost.

- To avoid double-counting, we must not look at the total sales from each sector but at what has been added in value terms to those component products bought in (see Table 13.1, for example).

- Basic prices remove the market price distortions of indirect taxes and subsidies.

Moving from gross domestic product to gross national income

We have seen that GDP figures measure the total spending, income and/or output made from home-based resources, and therefore exports are included (see the discussion of item (4) on page 248). In contrast, gross national figures measure the total economic activity generated by our nation's resources both at home and abroad. Consequently, these figures provide a total of the incomes received by the country's residents. Up until 1998 these figures were referred to as gross national product (GNP); however, the new term is gross national income (GNI). This may sound complex, but in national accounting terms the only calculation involved is to add to our tables

Table 13.3

Moving from gross domestic product (income) to gross national income in 1988

	(£ million)
Gross domestic product at market prices	**843 725**
Net compensation of employees	76
Net property and entrepreneurial income	15 098
less taxes on production paid to the rest of the world	–3 437
plus subsidies received from the rest of the world	
Gross national income at market prices	**855 462**

Source: *United Kingdom National Accounts, 1999*

a net figure for employment income and property income from abroad – a summary of the 1998 figures is shown in Table 13.3.

Thus we have identified another important definition:

GNI = GDP + net property and employment income from abroad

Some formulae in short-hand

In the following four questions, fill in the items that are missing to complete the formulae. Although this is a seemingly simple exercise, the different definitions are important and this should help you to focus on the distinguishing features.

24 GDP (at market prices) = C + I + G + _____   A✓

25 GDP at basic prices = _____   A✓

26 GNI = GDP + _____   A✓

Moving from gross national income to net national product

We have used the terms gross national income and gross domestic product without really indicating what gross means. The dictionary defines it as 'without deductions', as opposed to 'net'. 'Deductions for what?' you might ask. Deductions for something we call depreciation. In the course of a year, machines and structures wear out, become outdated or are 'used up'. For example, machines need repairs, or replacement, even if firms are only going to continue production at the same rate. In short, fixed capital depreciates. An estimate of this can be subtracted from gross national income to arrive at a figure called net national income (NNI). This moves us towards another definition:

NNI = GNI – depreciation (capital consumption)

Another way of interpreting depreciation can be as that portion of the current year's gross income that is used to replace any physical capital consumed in the process of production. Indeed, another term for depreciation is capital consumption. Consequently, gross investment can be expressed in the following way:

$$\frac{\text{gross}}{\text{investment}} = \frac{\text{replacement}}{\text{investment}} + \frac{\text{expansion}}{\text{investment}}$$

This is a useful formula as it highlights that if we are attempting to measure a country's progress (development), technically we should ignore replacement investment. In practice, however, it is often impossible to separate replacement investment from new investment. Thus it is very difficult to obtain reliable estimates of the consumption of fixed capital.

Consequently, gross figures are more widely used as measures of economic activity. It could be argued, however, that a 'net' figure would be more indicative of a nation's progress and growth.

What is national income?

Regardless of the complexity of accounting systems, the final line of the national accounts may not be reliable. For example, it is clear that capital consumption does not represent an easily identifiable set of transactions, and as a result it is always estimated. In the following table, the figures for depreciation have been extracted from the official accounts and the subsequent questions should get you to reflect on their value.

UK national and domestic product: main aggregates (values at current prices £ million)

	GDP at market prices	GNI at market prices	Fixed capital consumption
1996	754 601	758 824	–83 969
1997	803 889	812 461	–85 834
1998	843 725	855 462	–88 771

Source: *United Kingdom National Accounts, 1999*, Table 1.1

27 For the years 1996, 1997 and 1998 calculate: **A✓**
(a) net domestic product at current market prices;
(b) net domestic income at current market prices.
28 In percentage terms, does the capital consumption figure vary much from year to year?
29 Account for the difference between GDP and GNI.
30 When economists refer to national income, do you think they should refer to GNI, GDP, NNI or NDP? Fully explain your answer.

KEY POINT

13.6

■ By adding property and employment income from abroad into our accounts we can move from a GDP figure (which measures economic activity arising from domestic, home-based resources) to a GNI figure, which measures economic activity from the broader perspective of all national resources, both at home and abroad.

■ Capital consumption (depreciation) represents an estimated figure to allow for the nation's fixed capital that has been 'used up' during the production process.

■ GNI – capital consumption = NNI.

Uses of national accounts

As implied at earlier junctures in this chapter, these accounts have four main uses.

Measuring economic growth
As these figures are a measure of economic activity, the annual national accounts can be compared with previous years and an impression is thereby gained about changes in the standard of living. Indeed, economic growth rates are worked out from these accounts using the following type of formula:

$$\frac{\text{GDP of year to be measured (e.g. 1997)} - \text{GDP of previous year (e.g. 1996)}}{\text{GDP of previous year (e.g. 1996)}} \times 100$$

To eliminate problems caused by inflation it is advisable to use constant price figures when making growth calculations.

Calculating some growth rates

UK gross domestic product at market prices (values at 1995 prices in £ million)

1990	658 480	**1994**	693 177
1991	648 639	**1995**	712 548
1992	648 975	**1996**	730 767
1993	664 018	**1997**	756 430

Source: *United Kingdom National Accounts, 1999*

31 Calculate the biggest percentage increase in economic activity from one year to the next over the eight-year period shown in the table. **A✓**
32 (a) Calculate the percentage of negative growth that occurred in 1991. **A✓**
(b) Describe in your own words what the negative figure for growth in 1991 implies about the UK economy. How long did it take to recover?

Comparing countries
Apart from comparisons across time, these national accounts also offer opportunities to make comparisons between countries in terms of development, affluence, policies and so on. In fact, contributions to international agencies such as the International Monetary Fund, Red Cross, World Bank and the European Union are often assessed as a percentage of a country's GDP.

Analysing government policy
As suggested in the opening lines of this chapter, the statistical tables derived from national income accounts provide an important analytical tool for those economists

who are involved in recommending and evaluating policies on behalf of government.

Forecasting of economic climate

Similarly, business people, research students, trade union representatives and journalists involved in interpreting economic trends will find the statistical breakdowns provided in the various tables most useful for their forecasts and work in general. For example, GDP output estimates are announced quarterly during the year and are regarded as a good short-term indicator of economic prospects. The average GDP figures, however, are recognized as more reliable for forecasting over longer time periods.

KEY POINT

13.7

■ National income accounts can be seen to have two general uses: (1) to make comparisons (between countries and across time) and (2) for planning and evaluation (by government, business people and related parties).

Limitations of national accounts

We have completed our description of the different ways that the national accounts are compiled, the various totals that can be arrived at and the main uses of these statistical presentations. What we have not yet touched on, though, is how reliable these figures are. Inevitably there are some limitations, and we shall deal with these next.

Once this is complete you will recognize how to interpret national account statistics and be in a position to answer questions relating to how sufficient national income accounting is. This is a common theme of academic debate and often the central issue in exam questions.

Taking account of inflation

If a videotape costs £5 this year, ten tapes will have a market value of £50. If next year they cost £10 each, the same ten tapes will have a market value of £100. There may have been no increase in the total quantity of tapes produced and sold, but the market value will have doubled. Apply this to every single good and service produced and sold in the United Kingdom and you realize that national accounts measured in 'current' prices may not be a very useful indication of economic activity. After all, we are really interested in variations in the real output of the economy. What we have to do is correct figures for

changes in general prices from year to year. This is done by converting all money values to a common base year via a price index (at present the government's base year is 1995). Consequently, two sets of figures are produced each year: money GDP and real GDP.

Money GDP is formally expressed in **current prices** or **nominal prices**, and these represent the measurements of economic activity in current 'face value' terms. **Real gross domestic product**, by contrast, represents the same measurement but expressed in terms of a specific base year; the figures are formally referred to as a constant price estimate. The technique of employing constant price measurements makes comparisons across time far more meaningful. For example, consider the following figures:

UK gross domestic product 1988 prices £466 520 million
UK gross domestic product 1998 prices £843 725 million

These figures suggest that in ten years the United Kingdom had become nearly 100 per cent richer. However, we now account for inflation in this ten-year period and express both figures again in constant price terms, as follows:

1988 UK GDP 1995 prices £640 587 million
1998 UK GDP 1995 prices £773 380 million

We can see that in real terms our economic activity had increased from 1988 to 1998 by approximately 20 per cent.

As suggested, the conversion from nominal to real terms is achieved via a price index, for example the retail price index (introduced in Chapter 7). A base year such as 1995 is selected, and so the price index of that year must equal 100. Hence, in 1995, nominal GDP was £712 548 million and so, too, was real GDP, expressed in 1995 values. By 1998, however, inflation had increased by approximately 9.1 per cent, so the price index would have risen from 100 to 109.1. To correct 1998 money GDP for inflation, we divide the price index 109.1 into the nominal GDP figure of £843 725 million and then multiply by 100. The result is £773 350 million, which is 1998 GDP expressed in terms of the purchasing power of 1995. In other words, the value has been adjusted downwards to account for inflation. Such a procedure is known as **deflating**.

Consequently, for the purposes of study, real (deflated) values are more indicative of long-term economic performance than the nominal equivalents. So even if the above calculations confuse you, try to observe trends in prices already adjusted to a base year whenever possible. In the national accounts the figures are often stated in constant prices; you just need to read the table headings carefully.

As the GDP measures *all* economic activity the *retail* price index, which only measures changes in consumer goods and services, is too narrow to deflate GDP perfectly. Consequently, for national account purposes figures are actually deflated using a broader-based price index, which includes the prices of goods and services used in the government investment and export sectors. This broader index is called the **GDP deflator**.

Per capita gross domestic product

Even by looking at changes in real national income one still may be subject to deception, especially if changes in population size have been significant. For example, if 'real' GDP over a ten-year period went up 100 per cent, you might immediately jump to the conclusion that the material well-being of the economy had increased by that amount. But what if, during the same period, population increased by 200 per cent? Then what would you say? Certainly, the amount of GDP per person, that is, **per capita** GDP, would have fallen, even though real GDP had risen. What we must do, therefore, is try to be precise by accounting for price changes and population size changes.

A significant economic variable is real GDP (RGDP) per head. More conveniently, national income per head may at times suffice. These can be calculated quite simply by the following formulae:

$$\frac{RGDP}{\text{total population}} = RGDP \text{ per head}$$

With this formula in mind one can look at population growth in the Third World and begin to sense why many of the people are starving, even though their gross domestic product may increase marginally each year. A further complication arises when income distribution is added to the picture.

Black economy

Another complication that the last exercise brings to mind is that some student incomes will be of the 'unofficial' variety, for example 'casual' jobs over the summer, bar work, helping in the corner shop, painting and decorating, etc. Many of these jobs are sometimes organized on a 'cash-in-hand' basis, so that the employer can avoid certain legislation and/or the employee avoids paying tax. This type of unofficial economic activity is seen as constituting an 'informal', 'underground', 'hidden' or 'shadow' economy and is referred to by economists as the **black economy**. For national accounting purposes, it is defined as 'legal economic activity within the production boundary which takes the form of tax evasion, tax avoidance, or production by clandestine units'.

When unemployment or taxation increases it is assumed that the black economy expands relative to the 'official' economy. Consequently, the discrepancy between official recorded expenditure and declared incomes is one for investigation, especially by the Inland Revenue, who are concerned about the volume of tax evasion. Sir William Pile, a former chairman of the Inland Revenue, estimated that 7.5 per cent of GDP in 1979 escaped official detection. Twenty years later in 1999, estimates of the black economy are even larger, around 10 per cent of GDP; in other words, the black economy could be worth approximately £80 billion.

If this was taxed at the same rate as the rest of the economy it would bring in around £20 billion. Ironically, therefore, 'underground' or 'cash' activities create a further tax burden for those operating within the official economy.

Calculating your part in national income

To consolidate your grasp of the numbers involved and the areas actually measured, you can do no better than actually look at the *United Kingdom National Accounts* (also referred to informally as the *Blue Book*). These are published annually by the Office for National Statistics each September and your local reference library should have a copy.

For those who cannot see it at the library, extracts from the publication have been stated in the previous pages and, if necessary, these will suffice for the following completion exercises, and related questions.

In 199_ the United Kingdom as a whole produced a total income of _____.

In the United Kingdom we have a population of approximately 60 million; therefore GDP per head is roughly _____.

33 Did you earn above or below the average?
34 How would your income be recorded as part of the total? (Answer fully, including an explanation of why it is not recorded, if this is the case.)

Economia sommersa

Every country has the problem of estimating unrecorded activity. In Italy the 'submerged economy', as it is called, has been estimated and included in official accounts since 1987. The effect of this inclusion was dramatic, since it sent Italy's GDP soaring past Britain's. This is not surprising since the Italians estimated that irregular activity (i.e., the non-criminal part of the submerged economy) accounted for 16 per cent of their total production. The United Kingdom is due to begin a similar exercise, as it intends to estimate an inclusion for both legal and illegal activities which it senses are not recorded. The figure, however, is not expected to reach double figures.

35 The Office for National Statistics refers to unrecorded economic activity comprising two types of production, 'legal' and 'illegal'. Give examples of each category and explain which one would represent the black economy.
36 In which industries would black market activities be more apparent?
37 Which type of economy (or country) would have the biggest informal economy?

38 What are the most recent figures you have found about the black economy?

39 Briefly explain how it may be possible to gauge the size of the informal economy.

40 Do you think the informal economy will increase or decrease in the future?

Difficulties comparing countries' accounts

As the last section suggests, a country's national income figures largely reflect what is recorded. In different countries official interpretations of what is eligible for recording changes according to circumstances. For example, the attempts to prohibit alcohol in the United States in the 1920s led to a large illegal bootlegging industry. This replaced a former legitimate industry, and national income figures were affected accordingly. Similarly, 'prostitutes' in those countries where they are state organized will provide an economically measurable service, whereas in other countries this will not be the case.

Not only do laws affect the figures, but so does accounting convention. For example, in the United States government statisticians add to their GNP figures an estimated amount for those foods which farmers have grown and their families have eaten, that is, those foods which inevitably do not pass through a market-place. In contrast, self-sufficiency in the Third World represents a major form of existence, and yet these self-consumed products normally remain unrecorded for official purposes.

These problems are further compounded when there is the need to express world national income figures in a common currency, as this brings in problems of exchange rates. The dollar and sterling values, which are normally used for international comparisons, alter daily against other currencies. Therefore converted figures from the currency of measurement to the common currency are often suspect.

Difficulties measuring welfare

We have presented in this chapter several measures of economic activity, and obviously each measure has a different purpose. This raises the question, however, whether any of them effectively measure well-being.

Few economists regard national accounts as a perfect measure of welfare, since they clearly glorify the materialistic society in which we live. GDP numbers cannot capture our true overall well-being as a nation. For instance, economic activity also produces external costs, such as pollution, noise and accidents. These are not officially measured within national accounts, but they do affect welfare. Similarly, leisure, happiness and health cannot be measured simply in terms of income, output or expenditure. Monetary values do not encompass everything that we care about. Indeed, some things are beyond price.

A rescuer inspects birds killed by pollution after the wreck of the oil tanker *Braer*

What is included in the national accounts?

The wreck of the oil tanker *Braer* in the Shetland Isles in 1993 and of the supertanker *Exxon Valdez* during March 1989 both highlight how economic growth is calculated. The clean-up operations were counted as increasing economic activity, but the environmental costs were not taken into account. Similarly, neither personal work on allotments nor housework count towards the UK gross domestic product, but producing farm surpluses and employing a cleaner does.

41 Why do certain economic activities go unrecorded?

42 Explain how monetary value could be attributed to one of the environmental areas not at present recorded.

43 What are the arguments for and against recording environmental costs as part of national accounting procedures?

44 Name four categories that are included in the national accounts of most nations.

Consequently, new measures of welfare are being developed (especially in the United States), and our case study will explore some of these new concepts. The questions following will help you to investigate further this difficult issue of national accounting and what it actually measures.

KEY POINTS

13.8

■ National accounts are best expressed each year in a common value. At present money GDP is converted into real GDP by expressing all values in 1995 prices.

■ Ideally, changes in population size should be considered to arrive at a per capita figure.

■ Studies of the 'black economy' estimate the amount of 'unrecorded' or 'unofficial' economic activities that go on. These reduce the size of a country's official national income.

■ What is officially recorded as economic activity will differ from country to country.

■ There are critics who contend that national income accounting is not a sufficient measure of welfare. This issue is raised in the next case study.

Case Study

Can GDP stand for green domestic product?

If a government wants to evaluate the effects of pollution on the environment, or to quantify the depletion of natural resources, conventional GDP measurements are no help. To quote Robert Repetoo, an environmental economist based at the World Resources Institute in Washington, DC, 'a country can exhaust its mineral resources, cut down its forests, erode its soils, pollute its aquifers, and hunt its wildlife and fisheries to extinction, but its GDP would not be affected'.

Robert Repetoo has done a significant amount of pioneering work to achieve a greener GDP. For example, his study of Indonesia in 1989 concluded that annual GDP growth corrected for natural depreciation in timber, petroleum and soil resources was 3 per cent lower than the conventionally calculated figure. Similarly, he recalculated GDP figures for Costa Rica to highlight that after accounting for resource depletion the GDP figures could actually be negative. Repetoo argues that such statistics are important because they educate developing countries and show them that their natural wealth is not limitless. He wants the United Nations to take into account the depletion of natural resources when calculating each nation's GDP.

Working along similar lines, Robert Costanza has produced even more controversial results. A paper of his (supported by twelve colleagues) published in *Nature* in

May 1997 estimated that aggregate gross world product was approximately $18 trillion per year, whilst the economic value of 17 ecosystem services was estimated to be in the region of $33 trillion per year.

In very general terms, the kind of formula these environmental economists are suggesting to define green GDP reads as follows:

$$EDP = GDP - D_n - D_e$$

where
EDP = environmentally adjusted domestic product
GDP = gross domestic product
D_n = depreciation of natural capital
D_e = defensive expenditures

In other words, at the very least we need to deduct from GDP amounts to allow for the depreciation of natural capital and defensive expenditures (the monies spent on cleaning up and preventing environmental damage). The problem, of course, is how to place a monetary value on these aspects of nature.

In November 1998, the British government attempted to solve the problem differently. They produced a mix of statistics showing trends in economic, environmental and social criteria. This so-called 'quality of life barometer' monitored a broad range of concerns alongside GDP, such as road traffic growth, air and water quality, wildlife populations, years of healthy life, educational qualifications, and so on. Hence it was different in so far as the metric used for each indicator varied. No attempts were made to express all criteria in a common currency.

1 In your own words, state what gross world product in its standard format would actually measure.
2 Does anything appear on the debit side of national accounts at present?
3 Robert Repetoo and Robert Costanza suggest that we amend our national account recording processes. Itemize what you think should be subtracted from national accounts to arrive at an effective measure for annual progress.
4 Do you think that ecosystem services are more important than economic goods and services?
5 Other economists, such as Professors Tobin and Nordhaus, argue that there is also a need to add activities that are not traditionally included in GDP figures. List the kind of activities that you think they may have in mind.

6 (a) Suggest other indicators that may be used as measures of welfare.
   (b) What problems occur when integrating these into official accounts?
7 When the UK 'quality of life barometer' was launched, the government stated that it wanted the headline indicators to become just as useful and familiar as economic indicators.
   (a) Have you seen these reported in the media?
   (b) What image was portrayed?
   (c) Could you name eight of the thirteen indicators?
8 (a) Try to design your own measure of welfare (in environmental, social and material terms) by completing the pluses and minuses of the following table:
   gross domestic product + ... – ... = welfare
   (b) Discuss the main advantages and disadvantages of using this measure in practice.

Exam Preparation

Multiple choice questions

1 Why are the GNI (gross national income) figures of a nation not considered to be accurate indicators of the welfare of its people?
   A The GNI figures do not allow for environmental depreciation.
   B Welfare includes non-marketable goods and services enjoyed by the community.
   C GNI figures do not include social security benefits.
   D Payments for social workers and doctors are made out of taxpayers' money.

2 The table below shows some data for an economy. What is the equilibrium level of national income?
   A £500 million
   B £600 million
   C £700 million
   D £800 million
   E £900 million

3 The rate of growth of the British economy can best be seen from comparison of
   A per capita gross national product at constant prices
   B total volume of production
   C the terms of trade position
   D quality of life indicators

Investment (£ million)	Exports (£ million)	Government expenditure (£ million)	Savings (£ million)	Imports (£ million)	Taxation (£ million)	Income (£ million)
200	100	50	100	50	50	500
200	100	50	125	62.5	62.5	600
200	100	50	150	75	75	700
200	100	50	175	87.5	87.5	800
200	100	50	200	100	100	900

4 The following figures are extracted from the national accounts of country X for a particular year:

	£ million
Consumers' expenditure	65
Fixed capital formation	20
Net addition to stocks during year	5
Government expenditure	10
Exports of goods and services	10
Imports of goods and services	10
Property income received from abroad	6
Property income paid abroad	4
Taxes on expenditure	6
Subsidies	1
Capital consumption	5

What is the value of country X's net national income (at basic prices)?
A £90 million
B £95 million
C £105 million
D £100 million

5 Which of the following would not give the value of the UK's gross national income?
A gross domestic product + net property income from abroad
B gross national product
C net national income + depreciation
D gross national expenditure – exports
E total factor incomes earned by UK residents

6 A director becomes redundant as a result of a company merger. His salary in employment was £10 000 per annum. He is entitled to a redundancy payment of £5000 (£4000 as a lump sum and £1000 as 10 per cent of his salary). His wife takes up employment at a wage of £1000 per annum and his daughter increases the contribution to the family housekeeping by £500 from her earnings. The net reduction in the contribution of the family to the measured national income in the first year of the father's redundancy is
A £5000
B £6500
C £7500
D £8500
E £9000

7 Which of the following would be correctly regarded as a withdrawal from the circular flow of real national income?
A a rise in consumption
B a surplus on the balance of visible trade
C a rise in public investment
D a rise in private investment
E a deficit on the balance of visible trade

8 Which of the following sets a limit to the real output of an economy in the long run?
A the supply of money
B the supply of factors of production
C the size of the government sector
D the volume of international trade
E the level of effective demand

Essay questions

1 What insights can be gained into the performance of an economy from studying its national income statistics?

2 Explain the words 'gross', 'national' and 'income' in the term 'gross national income'. Should GNI exclude activities not bought and sold in markets, such as housework and state provision of education?

3 (a) How would you compare the standard of living in the United Kingdom with that in Russia and in Ethiopia? (40 marks)
(b) What problems would you face in this task? (60 marks)

4 In 1981 the gross national income of the United Kingdom was estimated to be £250 billion. By 1996 it had risen to £759 billion. To what extent does this increase indicate an improvement in the standard of living?

5 'National income accounting tells us where we think we have been, around six months after we were there: it cannot show us where we are now, nor can it tell us where we are about to go.' Discuss.

6 How adequate a measure of social and material welfare are the UK national accounts?

7 Assume that the United Kingdom has decided to make a significant reduction in the size of its defence budget. Analyse the likely economic consequences of such a decision.

8 (a) As an economist, how would you attempt to assess how living standards have altered since 1945? (40 marks)
(b) What problems do you foresee in making this assessment? (60 marks)

9 'Conventional national accounts apply depreciation to man-made capital; no such concept is used for society's consumption of natural resources.' Explain and discuss.

14

Aggregate supply and aggregate demand

LEARNING OUTCOMES

On completing this chapter you should understand:

- The aggregate demand curve
- The aggregate supply curve
- Putting aggregate demand and aggregate supply together
- Short-run versus long-run aggregate supply curves
- Supply-side economics

In Chapter 3, a model of price determination using supply and demand analysis was given, but the prices that we were referring to were individual commodity prices relative to all other prices. Concern over prices at the economy-wide level is much more general, for it is a concern about why there have been continuous increases in the price level, or why there has been inflation. In Chapter 8, we found out that the UK rate of inflation has varied dramatically over time. We also found out that we have had varying periods of growing prosperity and recession, with accompanying periods of expanding employment and then unemployment.

Why was it, for example, that in 1991 the rate of inflation was 5.9 per cent and the rate of growth was negative (output declined by 2.1 per cent), while in 1997 inflation was 3.1 per cent and output grew by 3.4 per cent? We have to construct a model in our attempt to explain these variations. We shall use the tools of supply and demand but with a major change: instead of looking at the price of *one* commodity, we shall look at the price level (an index of general prices) and how it relates to aggregate demand and aggregate supply. The definition of the price level and how we measure changes in the price level have been described in Chapter 8. The definition of **aggregate demand** is the sum total of all *planned* expenditures in the economy. In Chapter 13, we already discussed total planned expenditures on a theoretical level in an economy that had no government and no foreign sector. In that situation, aggregate demand was equal to planned consumption expenditures by households plus planned investment expenditures by firms. **Aggregate supply** is defined as the sum total of *planned* production in the economy. Again, going back to our simplified economy in Chapter 13, total planned production consisted of consumer goods for households and investment goods for businesses.

Given the above definitions, we can now proceed to construct an aggregate demand curve and then an aggregate supply curve.

The aggregate demand curve

The **aggregate demand curve**, AD, gives the total of all goods and services demanded at various price levels. Otherwise stated, the aggregate demand curve gives the relationship between the total amount of income, or real national output that will be purchased, and the price level. Remember from Chapter 13 that *real* national income consists of the output of final goods and services in the economy – it is everything that is produced for final use, either by firms or by households. Look at Figure 14.1. Real national income is measured on the horizontal axis and price level on the vertical axis. At a price level P_1, aggregate demand will be Y_1. At a price level P_2, aggregate demand will decrease to Y_2. The higher the price level, the lower will be the total real output demanded by the economy, and vice versa.

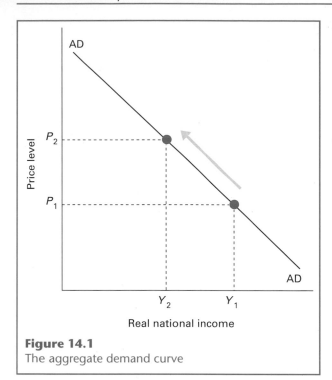

Figure 14.1
The aggregate demand curve

Why the aggregate demand curve slopes down

We cannot explain the downward-sloping demand curve for all commodities in the same way as we explain the downward-sloping demand curve for individual commodities. After all, a change in the price level changes the price of all goods and services, on average. It is important to remember that demand and supply analysis *in the aggregate* is different from microeconomic analysis, despite some parallels. Because the aggregate demand curve expresses the relationship between spending and prices in general, we must look more deeply at the impact of changing prices on spending to see why they are inversely related. The reasons include the following:

1 interest rate effects
2 wealth effects
3 substitution of foreign-produced goods

Interest rate effects

One result of inflation is a rise in nominal interest rates because inflationary premia are added to all interest rates. (This is to compensate for the loss of some of the real value of the loan.) But a rise in interest rates will reduce the quantity demanded of interest-rate-sensitive goods. These goods are those that may be financed by borrowing, such as cars, homes and new factories. Thus the link is as follows:

> price level up → interest rates up → quantity demanded of interest-rate-sensitive goods down → total real income (production) falls

Wealth effects

An increase in the price level reduces the purchasing power of cash balances (that is, notes and coin, and bank and building society deposits). In essence, then, those individuals who hold part of their wealth in cash balances will find a reduction in the purchasing power of their wealth. Actually, every part of a person's wealth that is denominated in money terms only, such as government bonds with fixed interest rates, will suffer a reduction in real value when the price level increases. After all, if you own a £100 bond and the price level doubles, when you cash in that bond the £100 will buy only half as many goods and services at the higher price level.

Consequently, whenever there is a rise in the price level, the real value of all assets denominated in money terms falls. Individuals will therefore tend to spend less. Planned purchases (real national income) will fall.

Substitution of foreign goods

Any increase in the price level in the United Kingdom will make domestically produced goods relatively more expensive compared with foreign-produced goods (assuming a stable exchange rate). This means that an increase in the UK price level will cause planned purchases of domestically produced goods to fall and planned purchases of foreign-produced goods (imports) to rise because they are more competitive. It also means that foreigners will no longer want to purchase as much of UK production (that is, exports) as before. In sum, the demand for UK domestic real output (production) will fall when the UK price level rises.

The aggregate supply curve

The aggregate supply curve represents the relationship between real income, or output, and the price level. It would be nice to say simply that the aggregate supply curve slopes up because, the higher the price level, the more producers are willing to produce – because producers have a greater incentive and they can cover any additional costs incurred in the increased output. But remember, just as with our discussion of the aggregate demand curve, we are talking about changes in the price level – the index of the weighted average of all prices. Every price is allowed to vary. In order to understand the true nature of the aggregate supply curve, we have to examine three situations:

1 large amounts of unused capacity and significant unemployment
2 full capacity
3 an intermediate range between the two

Unused capacity and significant unemployment

When the economy has many factories operating at less than capacity, numerous individuals unemployed and a general under-utilization of the productive capabilities of the nation, it is possible to increase output without there being any pressure on prices. In such a setting, producers can increase supply at will without having to pay higher prices for factors of production. If they need more labour, they can hire someone who was previously unemployed. They need not pay higher wages to attract people. They can put them to work with some previously idle capital equipment. In other words, per-unit costs of output will remain the same, no matter what the volume of output is, as long as significant amounts of unemployment and unused capacity remain. In these circumstances, we would expect the aggregate supply curve to be a horizontal line at the current price level. Consider a current price level of P_1, as given on the vertical axis of Figure 14.2. The horizontal line labelled 'excess capacity' represents that part of the aggregate supply curve, AS–AS, that exists when there is no pressure on prices with any increase in output. Within this range, supply is perfectly elastic.

No excess capacity

Now consider the other extreme situation where there is absolutely no excess capacity. In other words, the economy is at full employment. It is impossible, by definition, for any additional output to be produced. What will the shape of the aggregate supply curve look like now? Obviously, it has to be a vertical line, as shown at output rate Y_2 in Figure 14.2. It is a vertical line because there is only one thing that can happen in such a situation – the price level can rise, but no further increases in output are physically possible. Supply can be said to be perfectly inelastic.

The vertical portion of the aggregate supply curve in Figure 14.2 is also a representation of aggregate supply in the long run. That is, in the long run, when all prices are flexible, the potential level of real national income (total output) is independent of the price level. Rather, it depends only on the supply of resources and the economy's technology. As technology advances and the stock of capital increases, more can be produced and so the vertical line showing full capacity output will shift gradually to the right.

Intermediate range

When there is some excess capacity in some parts of the economy but no excess capacity in other parts of the economy, then, as production is increased, the price of some goods and services will be pushed up (but not the price of all goods and services).

This is the beginning of demand-pull inflation. So-called bottlenecks or **supply constraints** may develop. As firms try to increase output they may experience shortages of certain inputs, most frequently certain kinds of skilled labour. When this happens, firms can try to attract more of the scarce input by paying a higher price for it. They compete with each other for a limited supply of people with scarce skills, thus driving wage rates up. This raises their costs of production, and they then react by raising their prices whenever they can.

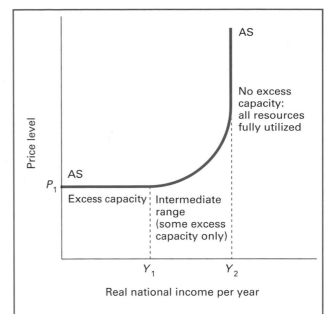

Figure 14.2

The three ranges on the aggregate supply curve

The aggregate supply curve, AS–AS, is a horizontal line up to quantity of real national income Y_1, because there is excess capacity. Output level Y_1–Y_2 is where some sectors experience excess capacity but others do not. The general price level will therefore rise as output increases from Y_1 to Y_2. This is called the intermediate range, where there is some excess capacity. At Y_2 there is no excess capacity – the economy is at full capacity output, employing all of its resources and using its technology to its fullest.

The intermediate range of the aggregate supply curve is, in essence, based on this bottleneck explanation. As the aggregate supply curve starts to slope up, it will become steeper and steeper as full capacity output is approached because, as this happens, more and more supply constraints appear. As they appear certain prices increase. Also in this situation sellers can put prices up anyway without losing customers. Since the price level is a weighted average of all prices, if some prices stay constant and some go up the price level will rise too. This means that if we start at the end of the excess capacity rate of output, Y_1 in Figure 14.2, and increase production, the price level will rise along with real national income. In this range, there is a positive relationship between real national income and the price level. As supply constraints become more numerous, supply becomes less and less elastic. Successive increases in spending lead to smaller and smaller increases in output or real income.

Applying aggregate demand and aggregate supply

Aggregate demand and aggregate supply interact, creating an equilibrium output and price level, which will determine the level of employment and so the level of unemployment.

The data below show how output, unemployment and the price level behaved in the UK.

Year	GDP (1990 = 100)	Unemployment (%)	Inflation (% change)
1988	97.3	8.1	4.9
1989	99.4	6.3	7.8
1990	100	5.8	9.5
1991	97.9	8.1	5.9
1992	97.4	9.8	3.7
1993	99.6	10.4	1.6
1994	104.0	9.4	2.5
1995	106.9	8.3	3.4
1996	109.5	7.5	2.5
1997	112.9	5.7	3.1
1998	115.5	4.7	3.5
1999 est	117.7	4.2	1.4

Source: *National Institute Economic Review,*
1994 and 1999

1 When was GDP growing fastest? **A**✓
2 What was happening to unemployment then? **A**✓
3 How was inflation affected? **A**✓
4 Can there be supply constraints at the same time that significant unemployment exists? **A**✓
5 When was there spare capacity in the economy? **A**✓

Putting aggregate demand and aggregate supply together

Equilibrium occurs at the intersection of the aggregate demand curve (AD–AD) and the aggregate supply curve (AS–AS), at price level P_1 and real national income Y_1. At that price and real national income, aggregate demand and aggregate supply are in equilibrium, as shown in Figure 14.3.

Explaining inflation

In Chapter 8 there was a discussion of demand-pull inflation. Using shifts in the aggregate demand curve and the aggregate supply curve shown in Figure 14.4, we can explain the phenomenon of demand inflation. Start out at price level P_0. Assume that the aggregate demand curve is AD_1–AD_1. An increase in the aggregate demand curve to AD_2–AD_2 will not alter the price level. There will be no inflation. However, as given in Figure 14.4, at any point

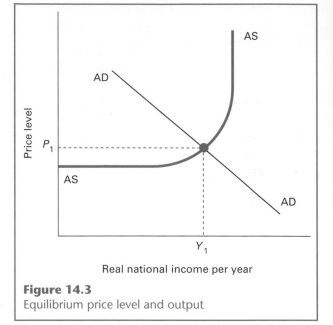

Figure 14.3
Equilibrium price level and output

past a real national income of Y_1 per year, there will be some sectors experiencing full employment or no excess capacity. Therefore an increase in demand from AD_2–AD_2 to AD_3–AD_3 will cause the price level to increase from P_0 to P_1, and any further increase will cause an even higher price level as firms compete for increasingly scarce resources with which to raise output. If the demand curve shifts to AD_4–AD_4, the price level will rise to P_2. Indeed, no output rate greater than Y_2 per year is physically possible. This means that any increase in demand after that output rate will simply result in a higher price level (inflation). In general we refer to output Y_2 as full capacity output.

Demand inflation can be defined as any increase (rightward shift) in the aggregate demand curve after output rate Y_1.

Explaining the Great Depression

The Depression of the 1930s affected business everywhere, but probably most dramatically in the United States. From 1929 to 1933, real GNP fell by 29.4 per cent. Unemployment had reached 25 per cent of the civilian labour force. Prices fell by 23.6 per cent during that same period.

Aggregate supply and aggregate demand analysis can help us to understand what happened during the Great Depression. Look at Figure 14.5. Here we show an aggregate supply curve, AS–AS, with the three ranges discussed above. Assume that during the period 1929–33 nothing happens to shift the aggregate supply curve. In 1929, aggregate demand is AD_1–AD_1. For a variety of reasons – falling international demand for goods produced in the United States, less desired investment by firms, less desired consumption by households, and other reasons – the aggregate demand curve decreases (shifts inwards to

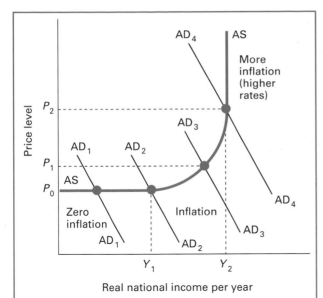

Figure 14.4
Demand-pull inflation
If the aggregate demand curve intersects the aggregate supply curve prior to output rate Y_1, then any increase in demand will not lead to a rise in the price level. Thus, a shift from AD_1–AD_1 to AD_2–AD_2 leaves the price level unaltered at P_0. A shift from AD_2–AD_2 to AD_3–AD_3, however, will cause the price level to increase to P_1. After output rate Y_2, any increase in demand will simply result in a higher price level since, by definition, at full capacity output no more output is physically possible.

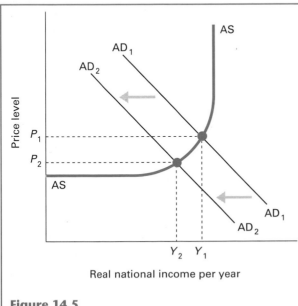

Figure 14.5
Explaining the Great Depression

the left) to AD_2–AD_2. In 1929, the price level was P_1 and the real national income per year was Y_1. By 1933, the price level had fallen to P_2 and the real national income per year had fallen to Y_2.

KEY POINTS

14.1

- Aggregate demand is the sum of all planned expenditures for both consumption and investment purposes, by both the private and the public sector.

- The aggregate supply curve shows the relationship between the price level and total output.

- As long as there is excess capacity, output can be increased. As more and more sectors of the economy reach full capacity, increasing output brings successively larger price increases.

- At full capacity, increasing aggregate demand fails to stimulate increasing output and leads only to rising prices.

Short-run versus long-run aggregate supply curves

In our discussion of the aggregate supply curve, we mentioned that the vertical portion is really equivalent to the long-run aggregate supply curve, since it indicates maximum potential output possible with given resources and given technology.

It would logically follow, then, that the horizontal and positively sloped section of the aggregate supply curves, as given in Figures 14.2, 14.3, 14.4 and 14.5, should properly be labelled short-run aggregate supply curves. In other words, it is only in the short run that an increase in total output in the economy is possible simply because aggregate demand has increased. If we are concerned primarily with the horizontal and positively sloped sections of the full aggregate supply curve, we can label our aggregate supply curves as short run, or SRAS. This will avoid any confusion with questions relating to economic growth, which properly apply only to the long-run vertical supply curve and our ability to shift it outwards over time through saving and investment as well as more efficient use of our resources.

Using diagrams

6 Between 1990 and 1996, productivity in UK manufacturing grew by 18 per cent. Draw a diagram showing how this would affect the long-run aggregate supply curve.

7 Draw an AS–AD diagram to show the situation in 1997. Use the data in the case study on page 262.

8 Draw an AS–AD diagram to illustrate the macroeconomic situation at the present time. Explain the basis of your thinking.

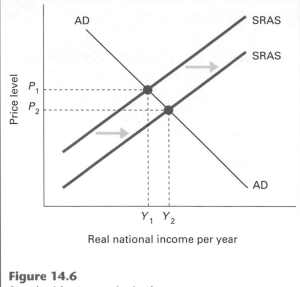

Figure 14.6
Supply-side economics in theory

Supply-side economics

The two examples we have already given to demonstrate the use of aggregate supply and aggregate demand related to shifts in the aggregate demand schedule. Those shifts are often called aggregate demand shocks. We can now look at an example in which there is an attempted shift in the short-run aggregate supply curve. This is sometimes called an aggregate supply shock. The example we wish to discuss concerns the government policy referred to as supply-side economics. Supply-side economics involves creating incentives to increase output. This would improve efficiency and increase real income. The short-run aggregate supply curve would shift to the right and there could be a reduction in the rate of inflation. Supply would expand to meet demand.

Look at Figure 14.6. The aggregate demand curve is AD–AD. The aggregate supply curve is labelled SRAS. The equilibrium price level is P_1, and the equilibrium real national income per year is Y_1. The short-run aggregate supply curve moves outwards so that the equilibrium price level falls to P_2 (that is, the rate of inflation is lower, in a dynamic setting), and the equilibrium level of real national income increases to Y_2 per year.

KEY POINTS

14.2

- Only in the short run can output be increased simply because aggregate demand has increased.

- In the long run, the growth of output depends on the level of investment and the state of technology.

- If people can be induced to work harder or more efficiently, or if investment rises or technology improves, the aggregate supply curve will shift to the right.

Supply constraints, rising costs and inflation

Vacancies One way of estimating the likely extent of supply constraints at any given time is to look at figures for vacancies. Only a proportion of vacancies that occur are notified to employment offices. But when there is a sharp increase in the number of vacancies, it does indicate that employers are having difficulty in recruiting the kind of labour they require.

Consider the increase in vacancies in 1988. The data suggest that at that time, the economy was at point A in the diagram. As demand continued to increase and employers sought to increase output, they were faced with a shortage of suitable labour. It became harder to fill vacancies. Employers offered higher wages, costs rose and so did the price level. (See page 262 for the inflation data.)

When vacancies are rising sharply, it is clear that there are widespread skill shortages: supply constraints are becoming a problem.

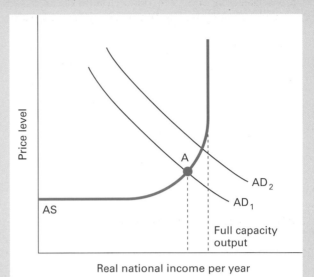

Vacancies notified to unemployment offices (thousands)

Year	Vacancies
1987	235
1988	249
1989	220
1990	174
1991	118
1992	117
1993	128
1994	158
1995	183
1996	228
1997	290

Source: *National Institute Economic Review*, 1996 and 1999

Capacity utilization in manufacturing
Percentage of firms answering yes to the question 'Is your present level of output below full capacity?'

1992	69
1993	65
1994	55
1995	46
1996	51
1997	50

Source: CBI, *Industrial Trends Survey*

Spare capacity After the early-1990s recession, the economic recovery put much idle plant in the manufacturing sector back to work. The Confederation of British Industries' *Industrial Trends Survey*, below, shows that by 1997 many fewer UK firms were reporting spare capacity. When the manufacturing sector is booming, typically, only about 35 per cent of firms have spare capacity.

The trade cycle Looking at the data on page 262, we can begin to answer the question posed at the beginning of this chapter. Why was inflation high, and growth negative, in 1991? In 1988, the economy was booming. Inflation accelerated. It was falling, but still quite high, in 1991. Meantime, the government had raised interest rates to discourage both consumers and firms from spending. Excess aggregate demand was cut back sharply, but the consequence was a fall in output and a rise in unemployment – namely, a recession. By 1997, inflation was under much better control, even though output had recovered and was growing fast. We will return to policy issues in much more detail in Chapter 27, and will deal there with the rather complex situation that developed after 1997.

1 Aggregate demand may change with government policy. How would increasing aggregate demand affect the economy?
2 Draw AD–AS diagrams to show what was happening in 1992 and 1996. Explain what was happening during the four intervening years.
3 How would you expect unemployment to be affected by the changes you have described?
4 Why were vacancies falling in 1991?
5 What has happened to capacity utilization and to vacancies since the above data were collected? What do the figures imply?

Exam Preparation

Multiple choice questions

1 If aggregate demand has risen output will not increase if
   A productivity is rising
   B there are some supply constraints
   C the aggregate supply curve is vertical
   D there is under-utilized capital in the economy

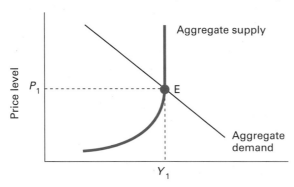

Real national income per year

2 If the economy depicted in the above aggregate demand and supply diagram is initially in equilibrium at point E, an increase in the level of government expenditure will lead to an increase in
   A the level of real national income
   B the level of employment
   C the price level
   D the level of aggregate supply

3 Inflation will decelerate if
   A aggregate demand is constant and input costs rise
   B aggregate demand stays constant and productivity increases
   C aggregate supply falls
   D aggregate supply is constant

Essay questions

1 'Inflation is due to excess demand.' Discuss.

2 Explain how aggregate supply can be increased
   (a) in the short run and
   (b) in the long run.

3 Distinguish between a movement along the aggregate supply curve and a shift of the curve to the right.

4 Is an increase in government expenditure likely to raise prices and wages rather than output and employment even in the presence of substantial unemployment and excess capacity?

5 (a) What determines the level of aggregate supply in an economy?
   (b) Will an increase in gross investment affect aggregate demand or aggregate supply?

15

Aggregate demand: consumption, savings and investment

LEARNING OUTCOMES

On completing this chapter you should understand:

- The basis of Keynesian economics
- The difference between a stock and a flow
- How income, consumption and saving are related
- The non-income determinants of consumption
- Permanent-income hypothesis
- Determinants of the level of saving
- Determinants of investment

In Chapter 14, aggregate demand was defined as the sum total of all planned expenditures over a period of a year. We found that the aggregate demand curve was downward sloping – there is an inverse relationship between the price level and aggregate demand. In order to find the equilibrium price level and the equilibrium level of real national income per year, it was also necessary to use the aggregate supply curve. But supposing we are dealing only with that portion of the aggregate supply curve that is a horizontal line? If there are large amounts of unused productive capacity and unemployment, an increase in aggregate demand will not raise prices and a decrease in aggregate demand will not cause firms to reduce prices. In such a situation, the equilibrium level of real (that is, corrected for inflation) national income per year is completely *demand determined*. Thus, in order to construct a model of income determination, we need only to understand the determinants of aggregate demand. In this chapter, we shall examine what determines the rate of planned consumption expenditures and what determines the rate of planned investment expenditures.

Keynesian economics

John Maynard Keynes, who wrote *The General Theory of Employment, Interest, and Money*, suggested that many prices, and especially the price of labour (wages), are sticky downwards. Therefore, even in situations of excess capacity and large amounts of unemployment, we do not necessarily observe the price level falling. Rather, what we observe is continuing unemployment and a reduction in the equilibrium level of real national income per year.

Keynes argued that, to some extent, the lengthy duration of the Great Depression could be explained by the sticky-downward nature of prices and wages. Thus, a general economy-wide equilibrium can occur, and last for a long time, with excess capacity and high levels of unemployment. Keynes and his followers argued that capitalism was not necessarily a self-regulating system, sustaining eternal prosperity and full employment. Keynes, at the time, was attacking the so-called classical view of the world, which argued that markets would all clear. Prices and wages would adjust; as wages fell, more people would be employed and full employment would never be far away.

Some simplifying assumptions

We have already assumed that prices will not rise when output rises, so for the time being we need not concern ourselves with inflation. We shall be seeing the economy in real terms. In order to simplify the income-determination model that follows, a number of other assumptions are made.

1   There is no government, that is, no taxes and no government expenditure.
2   Firms distribute all of their profits to shareholders.

Mechanic of the market

John Maynard Keynes (1883–1946)

'The ideas of economists and political philosophers ... are more powerful than is commonly understood ... Practical men, who believe themselves to be quite exempt from any intellectual influences, are usually the slaves of some defunct economist. Madmen in authority, who hear voices in the air, are distilling their frenzy from some academic scribbler of a few years back.' The most important 'defunct economist' of the twentieth century is the man who penned these words – John Maynard Keynes. Over the twenty-five years following the end of the First World War, Keynes transformed the way in which economics was viewed as a discipline and as an aspect of government policy.

During the 1920s, Keynes studied European finance and wrote *The Treatise on Money* (1930), efforts on which he would later build as British representative to the 1944 Bretton Woods conference on international monetary policy. At the same time, Keynes amassed a considerable sum by speculating on the stock market,

handling his transactions by telephone before getting out of bed each morning.

It was in 1936, in the midst of the Great Depression, with millions throughout Europe and the United States unemployed, that Keynes's masterwork, *The General Theory of Employment, Interest, and Money*, appeared. The market is not a self-regulating mechanism, Keynes argued. To bring the economy quickly out of depression and end high unemployment, some way of stimulating investment and capital expansion is needed; only by maintaining 'effective demand' – a desire for goods and services among people who have the money income to pay for them – can recessions be warded off. The natural entity to stimulate aggregate demand, Keynes asserted, is the government using a combination of deficit spending and regulation of tax rates and money supply.

Just as Keynes predicted, his theories – those of an academic scribbler – were not really utilized by government policy-makers for many years after the publication of his *magnum opus*. But Keynesian economics, as it is called, became a dominant force in government policy-making in the United Kingdom and elsewhere during and after the 1950s. Though challenged later, it still has considerable explanatory power.

3 There is no depreciation (capital consumption allowance) so that gross private domestic investment equals net investment.
4 The economy is closed, that is, there is no foreign trade.

Given all of these simplifying assumptions, real disposable income will be equal to real national income.

Definitions and relationships

There are literally only two things you can do with a pound's worth of income. You can consume it or you can save it. If you consume it, it is gone for good. However, if you save the entire pound you will be able to consume it (and perhaps more if it earns interest) at some future time. That is the distinction between **consumption** and **saving**. Consumption is the act of using income for the purchase of consumer goods. **Consumer goods** are those that are purchased by households for immediate satisfaction.

Consumption goods are such things as films, food, clothing and the like. By definition, whatever you do not consume you save and can consume sometime in the future.

The difference between stocks and flows

It is important to distinguish between saving and savings. Saving is an action that occurs at a particular rate such as £5 a week. This rate is called a flow. It is expressed per unit of time, usually a year. Implicitly, then, when we talk about saving we talk about a flow or rate of saving. Savings, on the other hand, is a stock concept measured at a certain point or instant in time. Your current savings are the result of past saving. You may presently have savings of £1000 that are the result of four years' saving at a rate of £250 a year. Consumption, being related to saving, is also a flow concept. You consume from income at a certain rate per week, per month or per year.

Relating income to saving and consumption

The relationship of saving, consumption and disposable income is therefore

consumption + saving ≡ disposable income

This is called an 'accounting identity'. It has to hold true at every moment in time. From it we can derive the definition of saving:

saving ≡ disposable income − consumption

Investment

Investment is also a flow concept. Investment is defined as expenditures by firms on new machines and buildings – **capital goods** – that are expected to yield a future stream of income. This we have already called *fixed investment.** Additionally, we include in our definition *changes* in stocks. When some of current output is not sold, stocks increase. Similarly, if demand exceeds current production, firms will run down stocks to meet the demand. To the extent that stocks are run down, investment will be lower.

KEY POINTS

15.1

■ If we assume that prices will not rise as output increases, the equilibrium level of real national income is demand determined. (The economy is on the horizontal section of the aggregate supply curve.)

■ Saving is a flow concept, something that occurs over time. Savings, on the other hand, are a stock. They are the accumulation due to past saving.

■ Saving equals disposable income minus consumption.

■ Investment is a flow concept also. It includes expenditures on new machines, buildings and equipment, new houses and changes in the level of stocks.

Income, consumption and saving

The major determinant of planned real consumption expenditures is clearly expressed in Keynes's 1936 book.

---

* Fixed investment should also include expenditures by households on *new* houses. For simplicity, we shall ignore this aspect of investment in this chapter, as it is undertaken by households and not firms.

According to Keynes's *General Theory*, when we look at consumption we find that:

> the fundamental psychological law, upon which we are entitled to depend with great confidence both *a priori* from our knowledge of human nature and from the detailed facts of experience, is that men are disposed, as a rule and on the average, to increase their consumption as their income increases, but not by as much as the increase in their income.

A relationship is suggested here between the planned consumption expenditures of households and their current income. This relationship is called the **consumption function**. It shows how much all households plan to consume per year with each level of real disposable income per year. The first three columns of Table 15.1 show a consumption function for a hypothetical group of households.

We see from the table that, as real disposable income goes up, planned consumption rises also, but by a smaller amount, as Keynes suggested. Planned saving also increases with disposable income. Notice, however, that below an income of 5000 units the planned saving is actually negative. The more income drops below that level, the more people dissave, either by going into debt or by drawing on past savings.

We can see the relationship between *C*, *S* and *Y* in Figure 15.1.

Graphing the numbers

In Figure 15.2 the vertical axis measures the level of planned consumption per year, and the horizontal axis measures the level of real disposable income per year. In Figure 15.3 the horizontal axis is again real disposable income per year, but now the vertical axis is planned saving per year. All of these are on a pounds per year basis, which emphasizes the point that we are measuring flows, not stocks.

As you can see, we have used the income–consumption and income–saving combinations in Table 15.1. Figure 15.2 shows the consumption function and Figure 15.3 the saving function. The saving function is the complement of the consumption function because consumption plus saving always equals disposable income. What is not consumed is, by definition, saved. The difference between actual disposable income and the planned level of consumption per year must be the planned level of saving per year.

Figure 15.2 shows the consumption function intersecting the 45° line. Along the 45° line, expenditure is exactly equal to income, so at point F, where the consumption function intersects the 45° line, real disposable income equals planned consumption. Point F is sometimes labelled the breakeven income point because there is neither positive nor negative saving. This can be seen in Figure 15.3 as well. The planned annual rate of saving at a real disposable income level of 5000 units is indeed zero.

Table 15.1

Hypothetical real consumption and saving schedules
At levels of disposable income below 5000 units, planned saving is negative. In column 4, we see the average propensity to consume, which is merely planned consumption divided by disposable income. Column 5 lists average propensity to save, which is planned saving divided by disposable income. Column 6 is the marginal propensity to consume, which shows the proportion of additional income that will be consumed, ΔC (the change in consumption) over ΔY (the change in income). And finally, column 7 shows the portion of additional income that will be saved, or the marginal propensity to save.

Combination	1 Real disposable income Y_d (units per year)	2 Planned real consumption C (units per year)	3 Planned real saving $S = Y_d - C$ ((1) – (2)) (units per year)	4 Average propensity to consume APC = C/Y_d ((2) ÷ (1))	5 Average propensity to save APS = S/Y_d ((3) ÷ (1))	6 Change in consumption MPC = $\Delta C/\Delta Y_d$	7 Change in saving MPS = $\Delta S/\Delta Y_d$
A	0/year	1000/year	–1000/year	–	–	–	–
B	1000	1800	–800	1.80	–0.8	0.8	0.2
C	2000	2600	–600	1.30	–0.3	0.8	0.2
D	3000	3400	–400	1.133	–0.133	0.8	0.2
E	4000	4200	–400	1.05	–0.05	0.8	0.2
F	5000	5000	0	1.00	0.00	0.8	0.2
G	6000	5800	200	0.967	0.033	0.8	0.2
H	7000	6600	400	0.943	0.057	0.8	0.2
I	8000	7400	600	0.925	0.075	0.8	0.2
J	9000	8200	800	0.911	0.089	0.8	0.2
K	10000	9000	1000	0.9	0.1	0.8	0.2

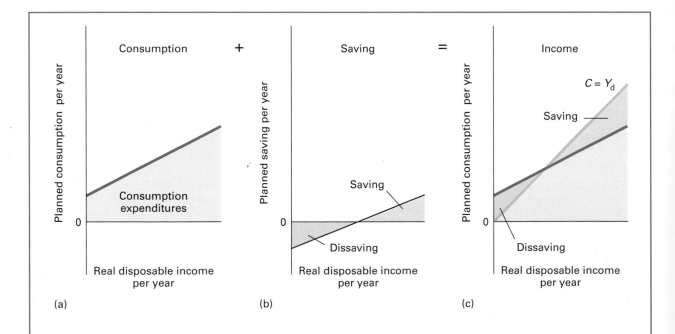

Figure 15.1

The relationship between *C*, *S* and *Y*
Here we show graphically that $C + S = Y$. The consumption schedule is drawn in (a) and the saving schedule is drawn in (b). When we add the two schedules together we get (c). Consumption plus saving must equal income.

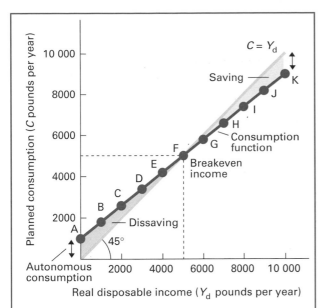

Figure 15.2
The consumption function
If we plot the combinations of real disposable income and planned consumption from columns 1 and 2 in Table 15.1 we get the consumption function. Every point on the 45° line bisecting this diagram is equidistant from the horizontal and the vertical axes. Where the consumption function crosses the 45° line, we know that consumption equals real disposable income and there is zero saving.

Income and consumption data, £ billion, 1990 prices

Year	GDP	Consumption
1950	176.6	122.6
1960	230.0	156.7
1970	307.7	197.9
1980	368.2	247.2
1990	478.9	347.5
1998	552.2	458.6

Source: *Economic Trends*

1 Calculate the percentage of GDP which was consumed in each of the years given.

2 What do these data tell us about the relationship between income and consumption?

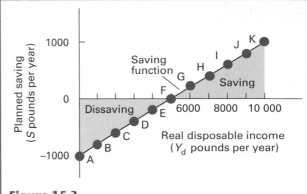

Figure 15.3
The saving function
If we plot the relationship between column 1, real disposable income, and column 3, planned saving, from Table 15.1, we arrive at the savings function shown in this diagram.

Dissaving and autonomous consumption

To the left of point *F* in Figures 15.2 and 15.3 this hypothetical family engages in dissaving. The amount of saving or dissaving in Figure 15.2 can be found by measuring the vertical distance between the 45° line and the consumption function. This simply tells us that if real disposable income temporarily falls below 5000 units, consumption will not be cut back by the full amount of the reduction. People will instead go into debt or consume past saving in some way to compensate for the loss.

Now look at the point on the diagram where real disposable income is zero but planned consumption per year is 1000 units. This amount of planned consumption, which does not depend at all on actual disposable income, is called **autonomous consumption**. In other words, the autonomous consumption of 1000 units is *independent* of the level of disposable income. (We are assuming here that real disposable income does not equal zero year in, year out.) It seems reasonable to assume that some spending continues in order to preserve life.

There are, of course, many possible types of autonomous expenditures. We generally take investment to be autonomous – existing independently of the model.

In contrast to autonomous spending, which is independent, there is also **induced** spending. This is defined as spending which depends directly upon the level of income. Apart from their autonomous elements, saving and consumption are both induced. As incomes rise, both saving and consumption will rise too.

Average propensity to consume and to save

Columns 4 and 5 of Table 15.1 show the **average propensity to consume** (APC) and the **average propensity to save** (APS). They are defined as follows:

$$APC \equiv \frac{consumption}{real \ disposable \ income}$$

$$APS \equiv \frac{saving}{real \ disposable \ income}$$

Notice that the average propensity to consume decreases as real income increases. This decrease simply means that the fraction of the family's real disposable income going to saving rises as income rises. The same fact can be found in column 5. The average propensity to save, which at first is negative, finally hits zero at an income level of 5000 and then becomes positive. In this example, it reaches a maximum value of 0.1 at income level 10 000. This means that the household saves 10 per cent of a £10 000 income.

Marginal propensity to consume and to save

Now we go to the last two columns in Table 15.1. These are labelled **marginal propensity to consume** (MPC) and **marginal propensity to save** (MPS). We have already used the term marginal. It means 'small change in'. The marginal propensity to consume, then, is defined as

$$MPC \equiv \frac{change \ in \ planned \ consumption}{change \ in \ real \ disposable \ income} \equiv \frac{\Delta C}{\Delta Y}$$

The marginal propensity to save is defined similarly:

$$MPS \equiv \frac{change \ in \ planned \ saving}{change \ in \ real \ disposable \ income} \equiv \frac{\Delta S}{\Delta Y}$$

What do the MPC and the MPS tell us? They tell us the percentage of an increase or decrease in income which will go to consumption and saving. The emphasis here is on the word *change*. The marginal propensity to consume indicates how you will change your planned rate of consumption if there is a change in your disposable income. If your marginal propensity to consume is 0.8, that does not mean that you consume 80 per cent of *all* disposable income. The percentage of your disposable income that you consume is given by the average propensity to consume, or APC, which is not, at most income levels, equal to 0.8. An MPC of 0.8 means that you will consume 80 per cent of any increase in your disposable income. In general, we assume that the marginal propensity to consume is between zero and one. In other words, we assume that individuals increase their planned consumption by more than zero and less than 100 per cent of any increase in real disposable income that they receive.

Using the average propensity to consume and the marginal propensity to consume

3 Complete the following table:

Disposable income (£)	Consumption (£)	Saving (£)
500	510	_____
600	600	_____
700	690	_____
800	780	_____
900	870	_____
1000	960	_____

(a) Plot the consumption and saving schedules on graph paper.
(b) Determine the MPC and the MPS.
(c) Determine the APC and the APS for each level of income.

4 Consider the following table, and then answer the questions below it.

Annual consumption (£)	Annual income (£)
5	0
80	100
155	200

(a) What is the APC at the annual income level £100? At £200?
(b) What happens to the APC as annual income rises?
(c) What is the MPC as annual income goes from £0 to £100? From £100 to £200?
(d) What happens to the MPC as income rises?
(e) What number is the APC approaching?
(f) What is the equation for the consumption function in this table?

5 Consider the following table, and then answer the questions below it.

Annual consumption (£)	Annual income (£)
0	0
80	100
160	200

(a) What is the APC at annual income £100? At £200?
(b) What happens to the APC as annual income rises?
(c) What is the MPC as income rises from £0 to £100? From £100 to £200?
(d) What happens to the MPC as income rises?
(e) What is the equation for the consumption function in this table?
(f) In what way has consumption changed in this question compared with the situation in question 4?

Some relationships

By definition, consumption plus saving must equal income. Thus, both your disposable income and the change in disposable income are either consumed or saved. The measures together must total 1, or 100 per cent. This allows us to make the following statements:

1 APC + APS = 100 per cent of total income
and
2 MPC + MPS = 100 per cent of the change in income

In other words, the average propensities as well as the marginal propensities to consume and save must total 1, or 100 per cent.

We can also show some of the key relationships in the theory of income and employment in graphical terms. These are set out in Figure 15.4, which shows how to measure geometrically the average and marginal propensities to consume and to save. As can be seen in (b) and (c), the marginal propensity to consume is equal to the slope of the consumption function, and the marginal propensity to save is equal to the slope of the saving function.

KEY POINTS

15.2

- The consumption function shows the relationship between planned rates of consumption and real disposable income per year. The saving function is the complement of the consumption function, since saving plus consumption must equal real disposable income.

- The average propensity to consume is equal to consumption divided by real disposable income.

- The average propensity to save is equal to saving divided by real disposable income.

- The marginal propensity to consume is equal to the change in planned consumption divided by the change in real disposable income.

- The marginal propensity to save is equal to the change in planned saving divided by the change in real disposable income.

- APC + APS = 1, MPC + MPS = 1.

- Any change in real disposable income will cause the planned rate of consumption to change; this is represented by a movement along the consumption function.

- Any change in a non-income determinant of consumption will shift the consumption function.

The non-income determinants of consumption

So far, the only determinant of spending in our theory of consumption has been income. There are, of course, other determinants of real consumption. They include the following: (1) wealth, (2) expectations, (3) interest rates and the ease with which credit can be obtained, and (4) the distribution of income.

Wealth

Other things being equal, the position of the consumption function will depend partly on the real wealth that individuals have. Wealth includes all the cars, houses, stereos and shares that a household possesses. We predict that, when the real wealth of households increases, the consumption function will shift upwards, and when it decreases the converse will hold. Inflation can affect real wealth and therefore the position of the consumption function.

Inflation can erode the value of money-denominated assets (all other things being held constant), causing the consumption function to fall.

Changes in asset prices affect real wealth, irrespective of the rate of inflation. If house prices rise much faster than the general rate of inflation, people feel richer. They may be able to remortgage their homes for a larger sum, which will give them increased spending power. The consumption function will then shift upwards.

Expectations

Particularly in the short run, expectations can influence the position of the consumption function. If households anticipate better times ahead (higher income) than currently, the consumption function may shift upwards. If they are pessimistic, it may shift downwards.

The interest rate and credit availability

An increase in the interest rate typically leads to a reduction in interest-sensitive purchases such as cars and houses. Most of these are financed by borrowing. Therefore, the higher the rate of interest, the more expensive it becomes to buy a car or a house. Other things being equal, an increase in the rate of interest will lead to a decrease in planned consumption expenditures at every level of real disposable income.

The distribution of income

Income distribution becomes more unequal when some groups of the population become wealthier while others become poorer. A more equal distribution of income may result from redistributive tax and benefit systems, which tax high incomes heavily in order to pay benefits to those

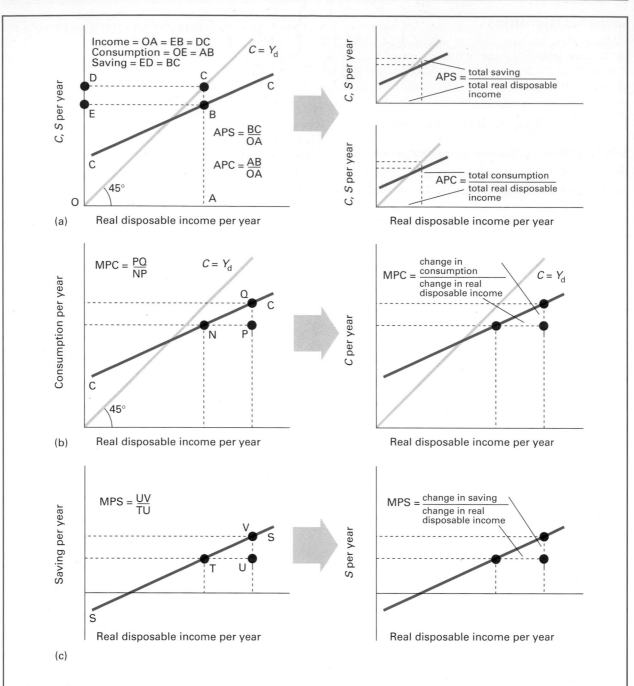

Figure 15.4

Marginal and average relationships

In (a) we show the relationship between the APC and the APS. Start off in part (a) with income level equal to OA. This is equal to the horizontal distances EB and DC. Consumption at all incomes is given by the consumption function CC. Thus, consumption at income OA is equal to the vertical distance AB. We can now find the APC. It is merely consumption divided by income, or AB/OA. To find the APS, we look at the difference between income and consumption. This is shown as the vertical distance CB, which is also equal to the vertical distance DE. In any event,

the APS is equal to saving divided by income or CB/OA. The MPC is shown in (b). It is defined as the change in consumption associated with a change in income. We show that, with a change in income of NP, consumption will increase by PQ. Thus, the marginal propensity to consume is PQ/NP. The MPS is defined as the change in saving due to a change in income. In (c), the change in income is the horizontal distance TU; the change in saving is the vertical distance UV. Thus, MPS is equal to UV/TU.

on low incomes. The rich will tend to have a lower marginal propensity to consume than the poor. Some of the income taken from the rich might have been saved. Practically all the income transferred to the poor will be spent on consumption. So, other things being equal, a more equal distribution of income will shift the consumption function upwards.

Distinguishing between a movement and a shift

In Chapter 3 we made a clear distinction between a *movement along* a supply or demand curve and a *shift in* either of those curves. The same distinction applies when considering the consumption or saving function. Since the saving function is the complement of the consumption function, let us simply talk in terms of movements along, or shifts in, the consumption function.

In Figure 15.5 we show the effect on consumption of a rise in real disposable income of, for example, 2500 units per year, starting from the breakeven income at 5000 units per year. We move upward along the consumption function, now labelled C, from point A to point B. Planned consumption per year will increase by the marginal propensity to consume (0.8) multiplied by the increase in real disposable income, or 0.8 × 2500 units = 2000 units; that is, planned consumption will rise from 5000 units to 7000 units per year. The same analysis holds for a decrease in disposable income. These represent movements along a given consumption function, C.

How do we represent a decrease in autonomous consumption? In Figure 15.5 the autonomous part of planned consumption is 1000 units. If we wish to represent a decrease in the autonomous component of planned consumption, we must shift the entire consumption function downwards by the amount of this decrease. For example, a 500-unit decrease in the autonomous component of consumption will shift the consumption function C down to C′. The breakeven point moves from point A, 5000 units, to point F, 2500 units. If the autonomous component of consumption shifts upward, the consumption function will shift from C to C″. Another way of looking at this is to realize that an increase in the consumption function means that, at *all* real disposable income levels, more will be consumed than before, and vice versa.

Shifts in the entire consumption function are similar to shifts in the demand and supply curves studied in Chapter 3. With a typical supply–demand relationship, a change in the price of the product brings about a movement along given demand and supply curves. Any change in a non-price determinant of demand or supply causes the curves to shift. Similarly, a change in real disposable income will cause us to move along a given consumption function. Any change in the non-income determinants of consumption will cause a shift in the entire consumption function. That is what we were discussing when we referred to changes in the autonomous part of planned consumption.

The changes result from changes other than those in the level of disposable income.

Is the marginal propensity to consume constant?

So far we have assumed that the MPC is constant, which means that the consumption function will be a straight line. Is this reasonable? In practice, it is highly likely that the MPC will fall if income rises. Growth in the standard of living will generally cause people to save a larger proportion of increased income and consume a smaller proportion. A fall in the MPC as income rises would lead to the consumption function levelling off (rising less steeply) as income rises.

When the MPC is constant, so that the consumption function is linear, it can be stated in the form $C = a + bY$, where a is the autonomous element in consumption and b is the MPC (and the gradient of the consumption function).

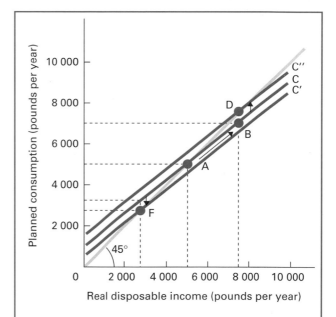

Figure 15.5
Distinguishing between movements along and shifts in the consumption function
Starting at the breakeven real disposable income at point A on line C, if real disposable income increases by 2500 units per year, there will be a movement from point A to point B along that consumption function. Planned consumption will go up by the marginal propensity to consume multiplied by the increase in real disposable income, that is, by 2000 units. Planned consumption will rise from 5000 units to 7000 units. On the other hand, if there were a decrease of 500 units per year in autonomous consumption, the entire consumption function would shift from C to C′. If there were an increase of 500 units per year in the autonomous component, the consumption function would shift from C to C″.

A consumer boom

During the years 1986–8, consumption grew rapidly. There were several reasons for this. Real incomes were rising. Interest rates were relatively low. Saving ratios were also relatively low.

There was more to it, as well. House prices had been rising faster than inflation. People found that they could remortgage their houses and use the extra loans to finance consumer spending.

6 Was the situation described above one of a movement along the consumption function, or a shift?

7 Draw a diagram showing what happened to the consumption function.

trends depends on being able to predict consumption. Recent experience has underlined the difficulties. Changes in savings have brought these to the surface.

KEY POINTS

15.3

■ The non-income determinants of consumption are wealth, expectations, interest rates and the distribution of income.

■ Any change in these non-income determinants will shift the consumption function up or down.

Permanent-income hypothesis

There is another, rather different view of the consumption function. Basically, the **permanent-income hypothesis** holds that consumption does not depend on *current* disposable income but on some measure of expected, or permanent, income. The planning period may be anywhere from two to five years, or even longer, depending upon people's expectations. According to this theory, consumption will not drop drastically even if, for some reason, people's income falls below what they think their permanent income is. Conversely, consumption will not increase very much even if people's income suddenly jumps above the level they consider to be permanent. The permanent-income hypothesis suggests that the level of consumption will stay fairly stable over time. (It is part of the theory underlying those views concerning inflation which stress the importance of money.)

A slightly different view of consumption has been set out in the life-cycle hypothesis. This shows how income varies, for most people, over the years of their lifetime. In the early stages of their careers, most people have comparatively low earning power. They borrow heavily, to set up house and acquire assets of all kinds. In middle age they will earn more, pay off debts and save for old age, when once again they will have smaller incomes. Thus their consumption pattern reflects their long-run expectations of income. Short-run fluctuations in income will affect their spending less than their assessments of their lifetime spending power.

This hypothesis also implies that consumption in the aggregate will be relatively stable over time. Most people's consumption patterns will change little in response to short-lived increases or decreases in income.

The relationship between income and consumption is still subject to a good deal of uncertainty. It matters very greatly too: consumption is the biggest single component of total expenditure. Accurate forecasting of economic

Determinants of the level of saving

Since saving is inversely related to consumption, everything which influences consumption will similarly influence saving – but in the opposite direction.

In particular, people consider interest rates, inflation rates and expectations about the future when taking decisions about saving. Low rates of interest give a poor return on savings held in the form of financial assets such as bank accounts, and may reduce the level of saving. Inflation, however, leads to a reduction in the value of an individual's stock of savings. A bank or building society account is denominated in money terms, so inflation reduces its purchasing power. If people want to keep their savings at a particular level of purchasing power (for example one year's income), inflation will make them want to save more for a while in order to rebuild the real value of their stock of savings. In general, both interest rates and inflation have been found to be important in determining the level of saving in the United Kingdom in the past decade.

Expectations would seem to be important in affecting savings decisions. However, the threat of increasing unemployment has not in practice caused increased saving in the United Kingdom. The world's thriftiest people are the Japanese, who save roughly a third of their incomes. The threat of unemployment in Japan is comparatively low. Cultural factors, and habit, probably play a major part in determining the level of saving.

Determinants of investment

Investment was defined on page 247 as expenditure on new plant and capital equipment, and changes in stocks. Investment levels can be quite volatile. Figure 15.6 shows the level of gross fixed investment as a percentage of GDP. This includes all investment in buildings and plant and machinery.

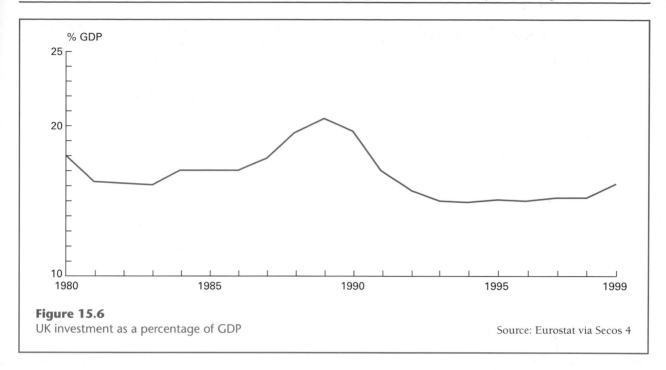

Figure 15.6
UK investment as a percentage of GDP

Source: Eurostat via Secos 4

If we compare investment expenditures historically with consumption and saving expenditures, we find that the latter are relatively less variable over time than the former. Investment decisions are based on highly variable, subjective estimates of how the economic future looks. We just discussed the role of expectations in determining the position of the consumption function. Expectations play an even greater role in determining the position of the investment function. This could account for much of the instability of investment over time. Given this chronic instability, it is more difficult to derive a satisfactory theory of planned investment expenditures. Nonetheless, we shall attempt to construct an investment function.

The planned investment function

Consider that at any time there is a range of investment opportunities that firms can identify. These investment opportunities have rates of return ranging from zero to very high, with the number (or value) of all such projects inversely related to the rate of return. That is, there are certainly fewer investment opportunities with high rates of return than there are investment opportunities with low rates of return. Since each project is profitable only if its rate of return exceeds the opportunity cost of the investment – the rate of interest – it follows that, as the interest rate falls, planned investment spending increases, and vice versa.* There will be an increasing number of projects which yield

a rate of return sufficient to cover interest charges, as interest rates fall. In other words, a fall in interest rates leads to a movement down the investment function.

A hypothetical investment schedule is given in Figure 15.7. If the rate of interest is 13 per cent, then the quantity of planned investment will be £225 million per year.

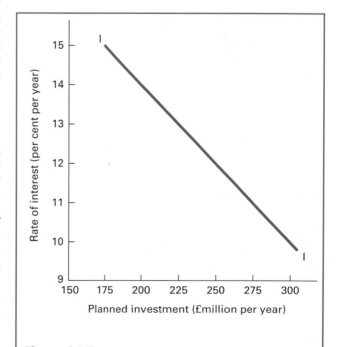

Figure 15.7
Planned investment
If we plot the interest rate against planned investment, we obtain the investment function II. It is negatively sloped.

---

* Even if firms use retained profit (corporate savings) to finance an investment, the higher the market rate of interest the greater the opportunity cost of using those retained profits, which could have been earning interest, at no risk, in the bank. Thus, it does not matter in our analysis whether the firm must seek financing from external sources or can obtain such financing by using retained profit.

Notice, by the way, that planned investment is also given on a per year basis, showing that it represents a flow, not a stock. (The stock counterpart of investment is the accumulated stock of capital in the economy.)

The rate of return on investments is sometimes called the marginal efficiency of capital (MEC), or the marginal product of capital. Keynes recognized that, although interest rates and investment would be related, their relationship (that is, the marginal efficiency of capital or the investment function) could be unstable.

Other determinants of investment

We saw that the consumption function could be related to the level of real disposable income. We also saw that there were other determinants that would shift the schedule up or down. The same analysis can be applied to planned investment. The rate of interest and the rate of planned investment are related. At the same time, there are many other determinants of planned investment. Increased demand in the economy would increase the rate of return. At any given interest rate more investment would take place and the MEC schedule would shift to the right. Other major influences on investment are expectations, the cost of capital equipment, innovation and technology, and the tax treatment of investment expenditure.

Expectations

Firms estimate the future demand for their products in order to assess the likely future profitability of their investments. If higher future sales are expected, then more machines and bigger plants will be planned for the future. More investment will be undertaken.

Each investment undertaken will yield an income stream in the future, which is the profit from the project. This will be total revenue less total cost. Estimating revenue means deciding the likely level of sales, at the price which the market will bear. Estimating total cost requires knowledge of the costs of all necessary inputs, and of any technological problems which are likely to arise. The resulting estimate of likely profit for each year of the life of the investment can then be discounted (that is, reduced by an amount corresponding to market rates of interest) in order to find its present value. If the present value of the total future income stream, yielded by the investment, is greater than the cost of the capital to be invested, then the project looks profitable enough to be viable. (Chapter 10 explained discounting in more detail.)

Of course there are risks involved in any investment project. One of these is the risk that unforeseen events, such as inflation, may cause costs and revenues to be less favourable than the firm's estimates suggested they might be. Technical problems may raise costs unexpectedly. Fashions may change the level of demand. The riskier the project, the greater the likelihood of profit must be before the firm goes ahead with the investment.

When firms have rosy expectations, and a high level of confidence about the prospects for their sector of the economy, the investment function will shift outwards to the right; at each interest rate, more will be invested than before. If they expect the future to be grim, the investment schedule will move inwards, to the left, reflecting less desired investment at each and every interest rate.

Consider the possibility that expectations have improved dramatically. What will this do to the investment schedule? In Figure 15.8 we see that the investment schedule will shift outwards from II to I'I'. The quantity of planned investment expenditures will increase at each and every rate of interest. The rate of return on capital invested is expected to increase so that, at any given interest rate, more investment will take place.

The opposite will occur if expectations take a turn downwards. The planned investment schedule will shift leftwards to I"I". The planned rate of investment expenditures will fall at each and every rate of interest. Chapter 16 looks in more detail at the effect of changing demand on investment.

Cost of new capital goods

If the cost of new plant and equipment suddenly increased (relative to the price at which output could be sold), firms' investment plans may change. In fact, we would expect the investment function to shift leftwards. The opposite would occur if there were an abrupt, unanticipated fall in the relative cost of capital goods. Investment goods become relatively cheaper, even if the price remains the same, if labour costs rise. Labour-saving investment may then increase.

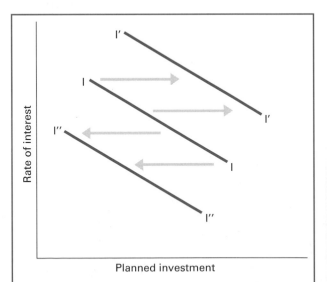

Figure 15.8

Shifts in the planned investment schedule
We start off with a given investment function II. If expectations of future profits have improved dramatically, the investment schedule will shift to I'I'. If expectations change for the worse, the investment schedule will shift to I"I".

Innovation and technology

Both improvements in current productive technology and innovations could generally be expected to shift the investment function to the right, since both would stimulate a demand for additional capital goods. In other words, we would see an increase in the demand for capital goods at any given interest rate.

Taxes on profits

Firms estimate rates of return on investments on the basis of expected after-tax profits. If there is an increase in tax rates on profits, other things being equal, we expect a shift in the planned investment function leftwards. If there is a decrease in tax rates, we expect a shift rightwards.

In the United Kingdom, taxes have generally been designed to encourage firms to plough back profits into the business. For any given rate of interest, investment is likely to be higher if expenditure on capital reduces the tax due.

KEY POINTS

15.4

■ Saving depends primarily on the rate of interest, the rate of inflation, and sometimes, expectations about future economic well-being.

■ Investment is related, though not always closely, to interest rates.

■ Investment is significantly affected by profits or by expectations about future profitability; by the cost (supply price) of capital; by the cost of investment relative to that of labour; and by changes in technology and profits tax.

Case Study

Tracing the links

The table shows the data for the variables discussed in this chapter. A number of events are clearly visible in the figures. In 1988, the Chancellor of the Exchequer observed the accelerating rate of inflation and raised interest rates in order to try to prevent aggregate demand from rising faster than output could expand to meet it. (Keep in mind the case study at the end of Chapter 14, which described the supply constraints that developed during 1987 and 1988.) This process continued during 1989.

By 1990 the economy was growing much more slowly. Inflation was still rising, but more slowly. With a two-year time lag, the real economy had begun to respond to the deflationary policies. The following year

saw the economy deep into recession, with a sharp fall in output and inflation decelerating. Interest rates were cut in an attempt to prevent further falls in output and employment.

The turnaround came early in 1992. Output began to rise again and continued to do so. But there was plenty of spare capacity in the economy and interest rates were kept down until 1997. Then fears of inflation made the Bank of England put interest rates up somewhat.

Saving has fluctuated markedly over the period. One possible factor in this might be the general level of confidence.

The interest rates given below are nominal: they are the Bank of England's base rate, which represents the general level of rates actually charged to borrowers (most

Consumption, saving and investment, £billion, 1995 prices

Year	Income (GDP at mkt prices)	Consumption	Investment	Saving ratio (%)	Interest rate (%)	Inflation (%)
1988	638.8	410.7	117.1	6.2	10.1	4.9
1989	654.5	424.9	123.3	6.9	13.8	7.8
1990	658.5	427.4	119.2	8.2	14.8	9.5
1991	648.6	420.0	109.0	10.1	11.7	5.9
1992	649.0	421.8	108.3	11.8	9.6	3.7
1993	664.0	434.0	109.1	11.2	6.0	1.6
1994	693.2	446.6	113.2	9.6	5.5	2.5
1995	712.5	454.2	116.3	10.5	6.7	3.4
1996	730.8	470.6	121.9	9.7	6.0	2.4
1997	756.1	490.6	130.3	9.8	6.6	3.1
1998	772.3	502.5	141.5	7.2	7.2	3.0

Source: *National Institute Economic Review*, 1996 and 1999

of whom will actually pay much more). In order to decide what real interest rates are, we have to subtract the rate of inflation from the nominal interest rate. This is the rate paid after allowance has been made for the effect of inflation on the value of the loan.

1 Compare the way in which investment fluctuates with the changes in consumption. Which is more volatile? **AV**

2 Examine the percentage changes in income and consumption for the years 1991 and 1992. Did consumption fall in direct proportion to income? Can you give reasons for the changes in consumption? **AV**

3 In general, how important is income in determining the level of consumption? **AV**

4 Have interest rates exerted an influence on the level of investment? What other important factors appear to have affected investment? **AV**

5 Can you detect in the data reasons why the saving ratio has fluctuated? **AV**

6 What has happened to these variables in subsequent years? What reasons can you give for the changes you observe?

Exam Preparation

Multiple choice questions

1 The following data shows income and consumption in an economy:

Income (£m)	Consumption (£m)
400	360
440	392
480	424
520	456
560	488

The marginal propensity to consume in this economy will be
A 0.70
B 0.80
C 0.85
D 0.90
E 0.95

2 If the marginal propensity to consume is rising as income rises, then
A marginal propensity to save is rising
B marginal propensity to save is constant
C average propensity to consume is rising
D average propensity to consume is constant
E average propensity to save is rising

3 A movement in the marginal efficiency of capital schedule from MEC_1 to MEC_2 can be caused by
A an increase in the interest rate
B an increase in the price of capital
C a reduction in corporation tax
D a reduction in national income

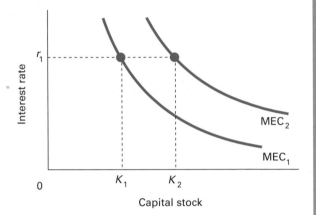

Essay questions

1 What factors determine the level of investment in an economy? Why has the rate of investment generally been lower in the United Kingdom than in most other industrialized countries?

2 Explain the difference between consumption and investment. Discuss in which category you would place housing and education.

3 Explain the factors that could determine

either the level of investment in the motor car industry in the United Kingdom by both domestic and foreign firms;

or the aggregate level of investment in a country of your choice.

16

Income and employment determination: a simple model

LEARNING OUTCOMES

On completing this chapter you should understand:

- How the equilibrium level of real national income is determined
- How leakages and injections can be used to analyse national income
- The multiplier
- Expansionary and output gaps
- The acceleration principle
- The interaction between the accelerator and the multiplier

Why is the equilibrium level of real national income what it is? We can answer this question using a Keynesian model of income determination, subject to simplifying assumptions. The most important assumption is that the short-run aggregate supply curve is horizontal at the existing price level. The implication of this is that the equilibrium level of real national income is demand determined. We do not have to worry about either supply constraints or changes in the price level, at least not initially.

The circular flow can only be in equilibrium when total planned expenditures are equal to total national output. Also, in equilibrium, planned saving must equal planned investment. Whenever this is not the case, there will be unplanned changes in stocks. The unplanned changes will cause either a contraction or an expansion of the circular flow. We can now determine when the circular flow will be in equilibrium. We need to determine when aggregate (total) planned expenditure equals planned production. Since, for the moment, we are ignoring government expenditures as well as the foreign sector (net exports), our analysis involves only planned consumption expenditures and planned investment expenditures.

Determining the equilibrium level of real national income

We are interested in determining the equilibrium level of real national income. But when we examined the consumption function in the last chapter, it related planned consumption expenditures to the level of real income per year.

The 45° line

Along the 45° line, planned expenditures equal real national income per year. In Figure 16.1, at the point where the consumption function intersects the 45° line, planned consumption expenditures will be exactly equal to real national income per year.

Adding the investment function

We add now the other component of private aggregate demand: investment spending I. We simplify our model by considering all planned investment to be autonomous, that is, independent of income. Firms plan to invest a given, constant amount and will do so no matter what the level of income. How do we add this amount of investment to our consumption function? We simply add a line above the C line in Figure 16.1 that is higher by the vertical distance equal to the amount of autonomous investment. This distance is shown by the arrow connecting the consumption function C to the expenditure function, $C + I$.

If we ignore government expenditures and net exports (the foreign sector), the $C + I$ line represents total planned expenditures for the economy at different levels of real national income per year.

KEY POINTS

16.1

- The 45° line shows where planned expenditures will be exactly equal to real national income per year.

- For simplicity, we assume that investment is autonomous and therefore constant and unrelated to the level of real national income.

- When we add autonomous investment, *I*, to the consumption function, we obtain the *C + I* curve, which represents total planned expenditures for the economy, assuming no government expenditures and no foreign sector.

A numerical example

We continue to assume that a Keynesian short-run horizontal aggregate supply curve exists, that there is no government or foreign sector, that investment is autonomous and that planned consumption expenditures are determined by the level of real national income.

Assume that the consumption function has an autonomous component equal to £33 billion per year, and that the marginal propensity to consume, out of real national income, is 0.8, or four-fifths.

Using this consumption function gives us the values for consumption in column 2 of Table 16.1, and also the values of savings in column 3.

Planned investment in column 4 is assumed to be autonomous at a level of £15 billion per year no matter what the level of national income. Column 5 is the sum of planned consumption and planned investment. In Figure 16.2 the horizontal axis measures real national income and the vertical axis measures consumption and investment expenditure. The consumption figures in column 2 are used to plot the consumption function *C*.

Equilibrium will occur when total planned expenditures equal total output. In Figure 16.2 total planned expenditures are given by the *C + I* line, which is also equivalent to aggregate demand. Total planned expenditures will equal total output, or real national income, where the *C + I* line intersects the 45° line at E, because points along that line are equidistant from both axes. At point E, there is no tendency for the equilibrium level of real national income to change. Thus at £240 billion per year, we have the equilibrium level of real national income.

What about employment?

What will be the level of employment associated with the equilibrium level of income? This figure depends on the number of employees required to produce £240 billions' worth of output annually. It may or may not be the number of people wanting work. Given a fixed amount of

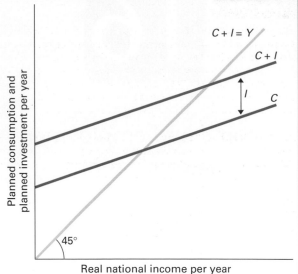

Figure 16.1
Combining consumption and investment
This graph is simply the consumption function with autonomous investment *I* added. The result is the consumption plus investment line, *C + I*, which relates planned expenditures to different levels of real national income, under the assumption that there is no government or foreign sector.

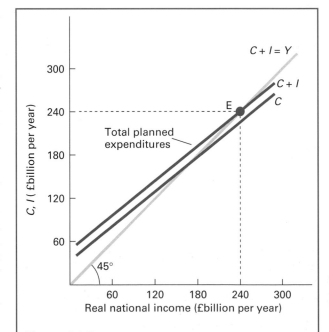

Figure 16.2
The equilibrium level of real national income
The equilibrium level of real national income will be established at that level of real national income per year where total planned expenditures, as evidenced by the *C + I* line, intersect the 45° line.

Table 16.1

The determination of equilibrium real national income

Given that prices are constant and the short-run aggregate supply schedule is horizontal at the current price level, the equilibrium level of real national income is demand determined only. Consequently, whenever total planned expenditures – planned consumption plus planned investment – equal real national income, equilibrium will occur. In our hypothetical example, equilibrium occurs at £240 billion per year, where planned expenditures equal real national income, planned saving equals planned investment, and there are no unplanned changes in stocks.

1 Real national income (£billion)	2 Planned consumption (£billion)	3 Planned saving (£billion)	4 Planned investment (£billion)	5 Total planned expenditures (2) + (4)	6 Unplanned stock changes (£billion)	7 Direction of change in real national income
150	153	–3	15	168	–18	Increase
180	177	3	15	192	–12	Increase
210	201	9	15	216	–6	Increase
240	225	15	15	240	0	No change (equilibrium)
270	249	21	15	264	6	Decrease
300	273	27	15	288	12	Decrease
330	297	33	15	312	18	Decrease

capital and a steady state of technology – reasonable assumptions in the short run, as it takes time to increase capital and improve technology – we can predict that an increase in output will be associated with a higher level of employment, and vice versa.

What happens when there is disequilibrium?

What happens if total planned expenditures exceed real national income (total planned production), or vice versa?

Total planned expenditures exceed real national income

If we start with a real national income at £180 billion, in Figure 16.2, we see that at this real national income level annual planned consumption will be £177 billion. Adding planned investment of £15 billion, we get total planned expenditures of £192 billion, which exceeds real national income by £12 billion. The planned investment of firms exceeds the planned saving of households. In other words, goods and services are being bought at a faster rate than they are being produced. The result of this is seen in column 6 of Table 16.1. Stocks are being run down at the rate of £12 billion a year, exactly the rate by which total planned expenditures exceed real national income (planned production). As a result, firms will seek to expand their production; they will take on more labour. This will create an increase in real national income and employment. Real national income will rise toward its equilibrium level.

Total planned expenditures are less than real national income

Now take the opposite situation. Real national income is at the £300 billion level. At that level of real national income, planned consumption is £273 billion and planned investment is still £15 billion. Total planned expenditures, $C + I$, now equal £288 billion, which is less than the real national income (planned production) of £300 billion. In other words, the rate at which households plan to save exceeds the rate at which firms plan to invest. This means that firms will find their sales less than they had expected. Stocks will accumulate, as we see in column 6, at the rate of £12 billion per year. This unplanned accumulation of stocks causes firms to cut back on their production and therefore to lay off employees. The result will be a drop in employment toward the equilibrium level, £240 billion.

KEY POINTS

16.2

- The equilibrium level of real national income is at the intersection of the total planned expenditure line with the 45° line. At that level of real national income, planned consumption plus planned investment will equal real national income.

- When total planned expenditures exceed real national income, there will be unplanned decreases in stocks; the size of the circular flow of income will increase and the economy will expand.

- Whenever planned expenditures are less than real national income, there will be unplanned increases in stocks; the size of the circular flow will shrink – a lower equilibrium level of real national income will prevail.

- If we know the relationship between real national income and the required labour force, then we can determine the level of employment consistent with any given equilibrium level of real national income.

Consumption, investment and unemployment during recession

To see how falling demand may affect employment, we can consider the events of the last major recession in 1990–2.

Before looking at the data, it is important to remember the distinction between structural and demand-deficiency unemployment. At any time there are people who are unemployed not because of insufficient demand generally, but because structural changes have reduced demand for their services in particular. An increase in low-cost imports may be the cause (as in the case of footwear); equally, employers may be substituting capital for labour (for example, through increased use of computers in firms' accounts departments), or consumers may simply have drifted away from the product (as with coal, as central heating became affordable). If the people made redundant are occupationally or geographically immobile, they may remain subject to structural unemployment for some time.

We can get a rough idea of how much unemployment is structural from the figure for 1999, when unemployment was at its lowest for some time. In that year unemployment stood at 6 per cent of the labour force.

The data below show how falling demand for consumer and investment goods affected unemployment in the years following 1990. Usually there is a time lag between changes in output and changes in unemployment. Unemployment began to fall again in the second quarter of 1993, and fell steadily through the rest of the 1990s.

Aggregate demand can be stable and in equilibrium but at a low level which leaves many people unemployed. This is what Keynes observed in the 1930s.

Consumption, investment and unemployment, £ billion, 1990 prices

Year	Consumption	Investment	Unemployment (%)
1988	334.6	104.7	8.1
1989	345.4	110.5	6.3
1990	347.5	106.8	5.9
1991	340.0	96.3	8.1
1992	339.9	94.7	9.9
1993	348.3	95.5	10.4
1994	356.9	99.4	9.3
1995	364.0	99.3	8.3

Source: *National Institute Economic Review*, 1994

1 How long was the time lag between the first fall in investment and the first rise in unemployment? **A✓**

2 What was the percentage fall in consumption and investment combined in 1990, 1991 and 1992? **A✓**

3 How long did it take after demand for consumer and investment goods started to rise again for unemployment to start falling? **A✓**

4 Evaluate the significance of the level of aggregate demand in the determination of unemployment. **A✓**

5 Has there been another major recession since the one described above?

Another approach: leakages and injections

We can look at the determination of the equilibrium level of real national income using leakages and injections.

In Chapter 13, we defined **leakages** as withdrawals of potential planned expenditures from the income–expenditures stream. Leakages are saving, purchases of goods from other countries (imports) and taxes. Whenever there is a leakage, consumption necessarily falls. Leakages tend to reduce the equilibrium level of national income, unless, of course, leakages are offset by injections.

Injections are additions of potential planned expenditures to the income–expenditures stream. They add spending to the flow. Injections are investment, government spending and foreign purchases of UK goods (exports). Injections tend to increase the equilibrium level of real national income, and they offset leakages.

To simplify, we must continue to assume that there is one leakage – saving – and one injection – investment. Chapter 17 introduces the other leakages and injections.

Attaining equilibrium

When planned leakages equal planned injections, total planned expenditures will equal real national income. Equilibrium will occur because the total planned amount of non-consumption (leakages) equals the total planned amount of injections.

Graphical analysis

In our model so far in this chapter, investment has been autonomous, that is, fixed at some level and not a function of aggregate income. In Figure 16.3 we show real national income per year on the horizontal axis, and saving and investment per year on the vertical axis. The equilibrium level of real national output is determined at point E, the intersection of II and SS.

The bath-water theorem

One can visualize a bath with a specified level of water already in it. The drain is open; this is clearly a leakage. Unless there is an injection, the level of the water will fall.

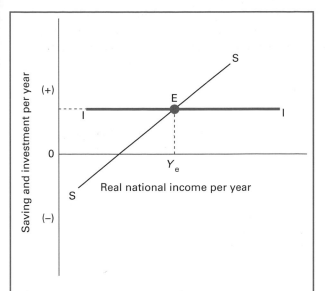

Figure 16.3
Leakages–injections approach to equilibrium
On the horizontal axis we measure real national income per
year. On the vertical axis we measure saving and investment
per year. Saving constitutes a leakage. Investment
constitutes an injection. Leakages equal injections at point E,
yielding an equilibrium level of real national income per
year of Y_e.

The injection will be water from the tap. The leakage
represents saving, the injection represents investment, and
the level of the bath-water represents national output
(which is exactly equal to real national income).

Using the leakages–injections approach

The leakages–injections approach can show us the reasons
why the equilibrium level of real national income may be
different from levels of real national income that policy-
makers might consider acceptable. Leakages in our
simplified example are represented by desired rates of
saving. Injections, on the other hand, are represented by
desired rates of investment. Desired (or planned) saving
and desired (or planned) investment are carried out by
different parts of society and for different reasons.
Basically, households save in order to provide for emergencies, retirement and so on. Firms, on the other hand,
invest in order to increase plant and equipment, as well as
to build up stocks. Since savers and investors are often
different groups of people acting for different reasons, we
have no assurance that desired saving will equal desired
investment at a national output and income level that
results in an acceptable rate of employment. Suppose, for
example, that we start off in equilibrium, where planned
investment equals planned saving. Planned investment
might then rise. But since investment decisions are
frequently made by individuals different from those
making saving decisions, there is no guarantee that

planned saving will also rise by an equivalent amount. As
another example, suppose that after starting out initially
in an equilibrium where planned investment equals
planned saving, savers, for whatever reason, increase their
planned saving. Firms cannot be expected automatically
to increase planned investment by an equal amount.
Indeed, the resulting loss of demand for consumer goods
may make their prospects quite gloomy.

In 1992 investment was low because of the recession,
while savings were comparatively high (as shown in the
case study at the end of Chapter 15). There was a net
leakage from the circular flow. During the period 1993–7,
investment rose steadily. This helped output to grow at an
average rate of about 3 per cent.

Saving and investment: planned versus actual

Figure 16.4 shows planned investment as a horizontal line
at £15 billion per year. Investment is constant and does
not depend on the level of income.

Planned saving is represented by SS. It is taken directly
from Table 16.1, which shows planned saving in column 3
and real national income in column 1. The planned saving
schedule is the complement of the planned consumption
schedule, represented by the C line in Figure 16.2.

Why does equilibrium have to occur at the intersection
of the planned saving and planned investment schedules?
If we are at E in Figure 16.4, planned saving equals
planned investment. There is no tendency for firms to
alter the rate of production or level of employment,
because they are neither increasing nor decreasing their
stocks in an unplanned way.

However, if output is at £270 billion, planned investment is £15 billion as usual but planned saving is £21
billion. This means that consumers will purchase less of
total output than firms had anticipated. There will be an
unplanned increase in stocks of £6 billion, bringing actual
investment into line with actual saving. But this rate of
output cannot continue for long. Firms will respond to
this unplanned increase in stocks by cutting back production and employment, and we shall move towards a lower
level of real national income.

On the other hand, if the real national income is £210
billion per year, planned investment continues annually at
£15 billion; but at that output rate, planned saving is only
£9 billion. This means that households and firms are
purchasing more of the real national income than firms
had expected. They must run down stocks below the
planned level by £6 billion, bringing actual investment
into equality with actual saving. This situation cannot last
forever, either. In their attempt to increase stocks to the
desired previous level, firms will increase output and
employment, and real national income will rise towards its
equilibrium value of £240 billion. Figure 16.4 demonstrates the necessary equality between actual saving and
actual investment. Stocks adjust so that saving and investment, after the fact, are *always* equal.

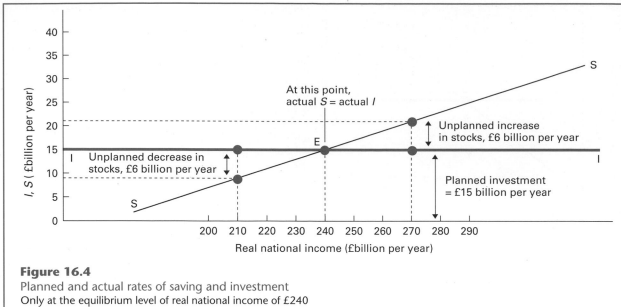

Figure 16.4

Planned and actual rates of saving and investment

Only at the equilibrium level of real national income of £240 billion per year will planned saving equal actual saving, planned investment equal actual investment, and therefore planned saving equal planned investment.

Every time the saving rate planned by households differs from the investment rate planned by firms, there will be an expansion or contraction in the circular flow in the form of unplanned changes in stocks. Real national income and employment will change until there are no unplanned stock changes, that is, until we have attained the equilibrium level of real national income.

KEY POINTS

16.3

■ The equilibrium level of real national income can be found where leakages equal injections, or where planned saving equals planned investment.

■ Whenever planned saving exceeds planned investment, there will be an unplanned increase in stocks. Incomes will fall – the economy will contract.

■ Whenever planned saving is less than planned investment, there will be an unplanned decrease in stocks. Incomes will rise – the economy will expand.

The multiplier

The actual level of real national income is not in fact very stable. We have had long-run growth along with the ups and downs of the trade cycle. We shall try now to explain *why* the equilibrium level of real national income fluctuates and *how* it fluctuates.

In our simplified model a change in autonomous investment will clearly change the equilibrium level of real national output. Figure 16.5 shows the determination of the equilibrium level of real national income per year using the two approaches previously given. In (a) we find that with schedule $C + I_1$ the equilibrium level of real national income will be Y_1, shown on the horizontal axis. Given the consumption function implicit in (a), we have its complement, the saving function, shown as SS in (b). Given a level of investment I_1, the equilibrium level of real national income per year is again Y_1. In (b), we use the leakages–injections approach. Note that the total planned expenditures in (a) consist of two parts – consumption and investment. Initially, investment is at I_1.

Consider an increase in autonomous investment from I_1 to I_2. This shifts the aggregate expenditure or demand schedule to $C + I_2$. The equilibrium level of real national income increases to Y_2 in (a). In (b), the intersection of SS with the new autonomous investment line I_2 is also at that equilibrium of Y_2.

Consider now a decrease in autonomous investment from I_2 to I_3. The aggregate expenditure line will shift downwards in (a) to $C + I_3$. The equilibrium level of real

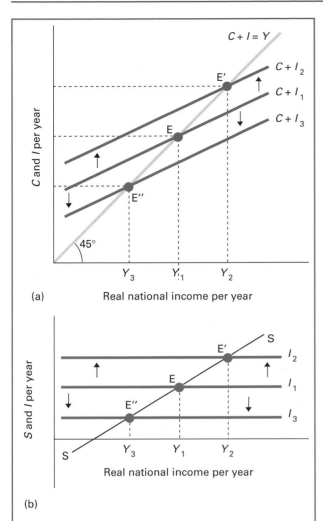

Figure 16.5
Changes in equilibrium real national income
In (a) the $C + I_1$ curve intersects the 45° line at point E.
Therefore the equilibrium level of real national income is Y_1.
This is also shown in (b). Leakages are shown by the saving
schedule SS; injections are shown by the autonomous
investment function I_1. At point E, the equilibrium level of
real national income per year is Y_1. A shift upwards in the
investment schedule to I_2 produces a new equilibrium level
of real national income per year, Y_2. A decrease in the
investment schedule to I_3 produces a new equilibrium level
of real national income per year, Y_3. Notice that the change
in the equilibrium level of real national income per year is
greater than the change in autonomous investment.

national income will fall to Y_3. Part (b) also shows the
equilibrium level of real national income of Y_3.

In sum, then, any change in autonomous investment
will shift the aggregate expenditure line and thereby
change the equilibrium level of real national income. This
same analysis will hold for any change in autonomous
spending, such as consumption.

Shifts in aggregate expenditure

Total planned expenditures depend, certainly, on more
than just real national income. For example, we talked
about desired consumption expenditures also being a
function of wealth, expectations and so on. We talked
about planned investment expenditures also being a function of other variables, such as firms' expectations of
future profitability.

None of these determinants, however, is given in our
current diagrams, just as income, population, the price of
related goods and expectations were not given on the
supply and demand curves we developed in Chapter 3.
Hence, if there is a change in any of these other non-
income determinants of total planned expenditure, the
changes will cause a shift in the $C + I$ curve similar to the
shifts that we just demonstrated graphically in Figure
16.5. Basically, then, changes in total planned expenditures that arise from reasons other than changes in real
national income are represented by shifts in the $C + I$
curve.

KEY POINT

16.4

■ A shift in autonomous consumption or investment will
cause the aggregate expenditure line to shift also. A
new equilibrium level of real national income will then
result.

The multiplier effect of changes in autonomous spending

In Figure 16.5, the change in investment that caused the
$C + I_1$ curve to shift up and down is relatively small
compared with the resulting change in the equilibrium
level of national income and output. It turns out that the
change in the equilibrium level of real national income
will always be larger than the change in autonomous
investment. In Figure 16.6 an increase in investment of £5
billion shifts the $C + I$ line upwards. The new equilibrium
level of income has increased by much more than the
initial increase in investment, in fact by five times that
amount.

This is the **multiplier** effect of changes in autonomous
spending. The multiplier is the number by which a change
in autonomous investment or autonomous consumption
is multiplied to get the change in the equilibrium level of
real national income. In other words, any increases in
autonomous investment will cause a larger increase in real
national income.

To get an idea of how a larger increase in income results
from a given increase in investment, we can follow the

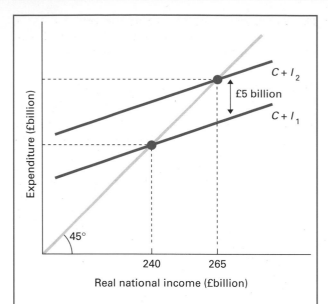

Figure 16.6
The multiplier effect
Investment, and total expenditure, rise by £5 billion. As a result real national income increases by £25 billion.

we know how households will allocate their increased income: consumption will rise by £4 billion and savings by £1 billion.

This addition to consumption adds further to aggregate demand. This time, firms producing consumer goods find sales rising and stocks falling. They will increase output, take on more labour, pay more in wages and earn more profit. Again incomes have risen and a further increase in consumption will occur. If we continue to calculate the increase in induced expenditure occurring as a result of this expansion in the economy, the general extent of the total increase in income becomes apparent. Table 16.2 gives the figures involved.

The multiplier formula

It is possible to find the full extent of the multiplier effect by extending Table 16.2 through many more rounds. In each successive round, aggregate expenditure increases by the previous increase in income multiplied by the marginal propensity to consume, 0.8. See if you can work out the effect of three more rounds of the circular flow. You will find that the sum of all the successive increases in income will be five times the initial increase in investment, if the marginal propensity to consume (MPC) is 0.8 and the marginal propensity to save (MPS) is 0.2.

Alternatively, we can find the formula for the multiplier by comparing the original equilibrium position with the new equilibrium position, after the full multiplier effect has worked its way through the economy. First we define the multiplier:

> the multiplier is the amount by which we would multiply an initial change in expenditure to find the ultimate change in income.

Stated another way, it is the ratio of the change in income to the change in expenditure which brought it about.

progress of the increased injection around the circular flow of money. If investment rises by £5 billion, some firms are buying more plant and machinery. In doing so they increase demand for other firms' products. These other firms will need to increase their output of investment goods and, to do so, will take on more labour. The new employees (assuming they were previously unemployed) will now have wages, profits will have increased, and total income will have risen by the £5 billion spent. If we assume, as before, a marginal propensity to consume of four-fifths and a marginal propensity to spend of one-fifth,

Table 16.2

The multiplier effect of a £5 billion per year increase in *I* – the multiplier process
We trace the effects of a £5 billion increase in investment spending on the equilibrium level of real national income. If we assume a marginal propensity to consume of 0.8, such an increase will eventually lead to a £25 billion increase in the equilibrium level of real national income. Notice that income increases with each successive round but by slightly less than before.

Round	Increase in real national income (£million/year)	Increase in planned consumption (£million/year)	Increase in planned saving (£million/year)
1 (£5 bn/year increase in *I*)	5000	4000	1000
2	4000	3200	800
3	3200	2560	640
4	2560	2048	512
5	2048	1638	410
.	.	.	.
.	.	.	.
.	.	.	.
All later rounds	8192	6554	1638
Totals (C + *I'*)	25000	20000	5000

We can call this change in expenditure ΔI: the Greek letter Δ means 'a change in'. Similarly, we call the change in income ΔY. The multiplier is therefore

$\Delta Y / \Delta I$

ΔY is the difference between the initial equilibrium level of income and the ultimate equilibrium level of income, once the multiplier has fully worked through the system.

What do we know about the equilibrium level of income? We know that planned injections and planned leakages will be equal. It follows that the size of the *increase* in planned injections must be equal to the amount by which planned leakages have increased when the new equilibrium has been reached. Stated symbolically:

$\Delta Y \times \text{MPS} = \Delta I$

$\Delta Y \times \text{MPS}$ is equal to the increase in savings, because the increase in savings is determined by the MPS and the increase in income.

We can now rearrange the equation to arrive at the multiplier. Dividing both sides by the MPS, we get

$$\Delta Y = \frac{\Delta I}{\text{MPS}}$$

And dividing both sides by ΔI,

$$\frac{\Delta Y}{\Delta I} = \frac{1}{\text{MPS}}$$

An alternative way of stating this uses the fact that, in a closed economy with no government,

$\text{MPC} + \text{MPS} = 1$

or

$\text{MPS} = 1 - \text{MPC}$

Then the multiplier can be written

$$\frac{\Delta Y}{\Delta I} = \frac{1}{1 - \text{MPC}}$$

The greater the MPS, and the lower the MPC, the lower the multiplier will be. The common sense of this is that, with a high marginal propensity to save, more of any given increase in expenditure leaks away in savings and therefore does not add to consumption demand. Equally, the lower the MPS, the more any given increase in expenditure adds to consumption and therefore to demand.

If we calculate the multiplier using data on the MPC, we can use it to predict how much a given change in expenditure will affect income.

multiplier $\times$ change in expenditure
= change in equilibrium level of real national
   income

The multiplier, as we mentioned, works for both an increase and a decrease in expenditure. If there has been a decrease, we speak of a downward multiplier effect.

The significance of the multiplier

As we just stated, the larger the marginal propensity to consume, the larger the multiplier. If the marginal propensity to consume is 1/2, the multiplier is 2. In this case a £1 billion decrease in (autonomous) investment will elicit a £2 billion decrease in the equilibrium level of real national income per year. On the other hand, if the marginal propensity to consume is 9/10, the multiplier will be 10. That same £1 billion decrease in planned investment expenditures with a multiplier of 10 will lead to a £10 billion decrease in the equilibrium level of real national income per year.

KEY POINTS

16.5

■ Any change in autonomous expenditure causes a multiplier effect on the equilibrium level of real national income per year.

■ The multiplier is equal to the reciprocal of the marginal propensity to save.

■ The smaller the marginal propensity to save, the greater is the multiplier. Otherwise stated, the greater the marginal propensity to consume, the larger is the multiplier.

Equilibrium output and the multiplier

6 On the following page, you are given some information for a hypothetical economy. Assume that the marginal propensity to consume is constant at all levels of income. Further assume that investment is autonomous.
  (a) Draw a graph of the consumption function. Then add the investment function, giving you C + I.
  (b) Under the first diagram, draw a second diagram showing the saving and investment curves. Does the C + I curve intersect the 45° line in the upper diagram at the same level of real national income as where saving equals investment in the lower diagram? (If not, redraw your diagrams.)
  (c) What is the numerical value of the multiplier?
  (d) What will happen to income if autonomous investment increases by £100?

(e) What will the equilibrium level of real national income be if autonomous consumption increases by £100? ✒️

Real national income (£)	Consumption expenditures (£)	Saving (£)	Investment (£)
1000	1100	___	100
2000	2000	___	___
3000	___	___	___
4000	___	___	___
5000	___	___	___
6000	___	___	___
APC	APS	MPC	MPS
___	___	___	___
___	___	___	___
___	___	___	___
___	___	___	___
___	___	___	___

7 Assume a closed, private economy.
  (a) What is the multiplier if the MPC = 1/2? If the MPC = 3/4? If the MPC = 9/10? If the MPC = 1?
  (b) What happens to the multiplier as the MPC rises?
  (c) In what range does the multiplier fall? ✒️

8 Consider a closed, private economy, in which
  (a) $C = £30 + (3/4)Y$
  (b) $I = £25$
  What will the equilibrium level of real national income Y be equal to in this economy? (Hint: In equilibrium, real national income must equal total planned expenditures, or $Y = C + I$.) ✒️

9 Using the model in question 8:
  (a) What is the multiplier?
  (b) What will the new equilibrium level of real national income be if investment increases by £5? ✒️

10 Using the model in question 8, calculate the new equilibrium level of real national income if the consumption function becomes $C = £35 + (3/4)Y$ (the consumption function shifts upwards by £5). ✒️

The paradox of thrift

The paradox of thrift refers to the outcome of an increase in the saving function. Figure 16.7 shows a shift upwards in the saving function. At any given income, a larger proportion of income will be saved, because people have decided to behave more thriftily. Any of the reasons given earlier for why consumption or savings might change could account for this.

With the initial increase in savings, planned leakages exceed planned injections. Consumption must fall; aggregate expenditure will be less than current output and firms will find that stocks are rising. They will cut production and after a time reduce employment too. So incomes will fall. But of course a fall in income means that saving will gradually fall back again – hence the paradox.

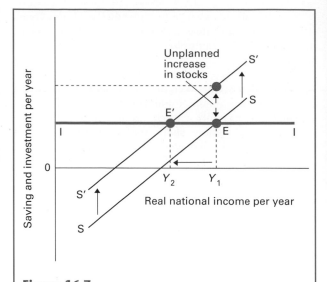

Figure 16.7
The paradox of thrift
With the new savings function S'S', there is a new, lower, equilibrium level of income, Y_2. Here planned saving is again equal to planned investment.

So long as planned saving exceeds planned investment, income will continue to fall because there is a leakage from the circular flow which is not balanced by injections. Incomes will cease falling once the new lower level of saving is again equal to planned investment at Y_2.

The outcome is that an intention to save more, in macroeconomic terms, leads to falling income and employment, and therefore ultimately to falling saving. The high level of saving in the UK in 1991 and 1992 depressed consumer demand with this result. More recently, high rates of saving in Japan during the Asian financial crisis had the same effect.

Is increased thriftiness always 'bad'?

This argument seems to indicate that increased thriftiness on the part of individuals may end up being bad for the nation. The equilibrium level of real national income per year falls, as does the amount of saving. Whether this is bad or not depends on the general level of employment. If people are saving more because unemployment is rising and they are fearful for the future, then increased saving is bad in that it will reduce real income. But supposing unemployment is low. That which is saved is not consumed. More saving means that resources can be reallocated away from consumption and devoted to investment in new plant and equipment. Investment adds to the future productive capacity of the nation. As we shall see in Chapter 31, more investment typically leads to a higher rate of economic growth. The prime example has been Japan. From the 1960s to the early 1990s, Japan saved and invested at a rate nearly double that of the United Kingdom. Its growth rates were correspondingly impressive.

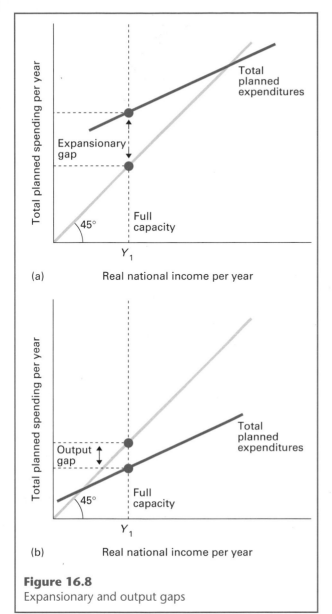

Figure 16.8
Expansionary and output gaps

means that there will be pressure on the price level and that we shall have to abandon our assumption of a fixed price level. The implication is that the economy is on the upward-sloping part of the aggregate supply curve. This corresponds neatly to the UK situation in 1988–9.

It is also possible for the equilibrium level of real national income per year to be less than the full capacity level. When this occurs, we talk in terms of an **output gap**. We show an output gap in Figure 16.8(b). There the intersection of the total planned expenditures curve with the 45° line is at a level of real national income that is below the full capacity level. As we shall see in the next chapter, various government policies can be used to fill the output gap.

Aggregate supply, aggregate demand, inflation and unemployment

11 Draw an AS–AD diagram which illustrates the situation in Figure 16.8(a). Now do the same for Figure 16.8(b).

12 Explain why inflation develops when aggregate demand is high, and why unemployment develops when aggregate demand is low.

The determination of output and prices

For the moment, let us assume that we are no longer in the horizontal portion of the aggregate supply curve but in the upward-sloping portion. How would an increase in aggregate demand affect the price level and real national income (total output)?

The total expenditure curve (which we have labelled $C + I$) relates total planned spending to real income, holding all other things constant. Consider Figure 16.9 (on the next page). Initially, total planned spending (expenditures) rise from $(C + I)_1$ to $(C + I)_2$. The equilibrium level of real national income rises from Y_1 to Y_2.

Now look what happens on the aggregate supply–aggregate demand curves in 16.9(b). Aggregate supply in the short run is given as SRAS – it is upward sloping rather than horizontal. If we start out in equilibrium with aggregate demand as AD_1, then the price level is P_1. But the increase in total planned expenditures also causes the aggregate demand curve to shift to AD_2. This will cause the price level to increase from P_1 to P_2.

Thus an increase in total desired expenditures (aggregate demand) has had a price effect and an output effect. Output went up from Y_1 to Y_2, and prices went up from P_1 to P_2.

What we can say for any increase in aggregate demand is the following: the closer we are to full capacity output, the more there will be an offsetting effect due to an

Expansionary and output gaps

Expansionary and output gaps are sometimes termed inflationary and deflationary gaps. It is possible that the equilibrium level of real national income per year is greater than potential output, perhaps because all the resources needed are fully employed. In Figure 16.8(a) we see that this has occurred. Full capacity output is given as Y_1 per year, but the intersection of the total planned expenditures curve with the 45° line is at a greater level of real national income per year. There therefore exists, at the full-employment level of real national income, an **expansionary gap**. An expansionary gap exists whenever the equilibrium level of real national income exceeds the full capacity level of output. Clearly, an expansionary gap

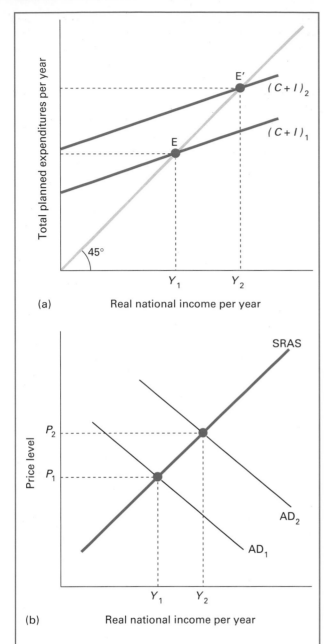

Figure 16.9

The output and price effects of an increase in aggregate demand

Assume that total desired spending is $(C + I)_1$. Assume further that short-run aggregate supply is given by SRAS and aggregate demand is given by AD_1. To begin with, the equilibrium level of real national income is Y_1 in both parts (a) and (b). The equilibrium price level is P_1. An increase in total desired expenditures to $(C + I)_2$ would give an equilibrium level of real national income of Y_2. But the increase in aggregate demand shifts the aggregate demand curve to AD_2 in (b). The equilibrium price level increases to P_2.

increase in prices and therefore less of an output effect. The greater the amount of unemployment (the flatter the short-run aggregate supply curve), the less will be the offsetting price effect and the greater will be the output effect.

KEY POINTS

16.6

■ The paradox of thrift shows how an increase in the saving function produces contraction in the economy and therefore a fall in the level of savings.

■ An expansionary (or inflationary) gap exists when planned expenditure exceeds full capacity output.

■ An output (or deflationary) gap exists when planned expenditure is less than full capacity output, that is, there are unemployed resources in the economy.

■ The closer the economy is to full capacity the more likely it is that increased expenditure leads to accelerating inflation rather than rising output.

The acceleration principle

It was obvious during the nineteenth century that investment fluctuated more than output as a whole. While expenditure on food, for example, is continuous, expenditure on investment can be postponed or brought forward according to circumstance. As sales rise, firms want to increase output. To do so they need a larger capital stock. This is known as the *acceleration principle*, or the accelerator:

> The level of planned investment varies with *changes in the level* of output itself. Otherwise stated, the level of planned investment is related to the *rate of change* of output or sales.

If the capital stock – the value of the machines, equipment and buildings – is related to the sales of a company, then we relate the *change* in sales to the change in capital. But the change in the capital stock – additions to or subtractions from the total amount of equipment, machines, buildings – is what we have called investment. Therefore the change in sales is related to the *level* of investment.

Supposing a firm has £10 million worth of capital. Each year it spends £1 million maintaining that stock of capital. But if sales rise by 10 per cent, it will need to increase investment by £1 million, making investment £2 million in all. So a 10 per cent rise in output has required a 100 per cent rise in investment.

There is an important distinction here between investment which increases the capital stock (net investment) and replacement investment, which simply maintains the existing capital stock. The two together, net investment and replacement investment, constitute gross investment. Replacement investment corresponds to depreciation, or the extent to which capital wears out over a given time period.

If, however, output falls by 10 per cent, the firm will not need to replace the 10 per cent of its capital which wears out each year. It can meet demand with the remaining 90 per cent of productive capacity. In that case investment will have fallen by 100 per cent. Again we see that investment has altered by much *more* than the change in output – hence the term accelerator.

If net output grows by a constant percentage, then the level of investment will be constant also. But if it grows faster than before (or more slowly), then investment will increase (or decrease).

The interaction between the accelerator and the multiplier

Investment is a key determinant of the equilibrium level of national income in the model that we have been using in Part B. If the rate of planned investment follows the acceleration principle, this could explain to some extent the rather dramatic swings in business activity that we have experienced from time to time. This sequence of changes in output is generally known as the **trade cycle** or the **business cycle**. After all, any change in investment, according to our theory, leads to a multiplier effect in which there is a multiple change in the equilibrium level of income and employment.

The accelerator and multiplier interact, affecting business as follows. We assume that the economy is moving towards full employment, national income is rising, and sales are expanding at an *increasing* rate. Because of the acceleration principle, this growth – meaning expected increases in sales – results in a relatively high level of planned investment. Furthermore, because of the multiplier, this relatively high level of planned investment provokes even greater increases in the equilibrium level of national income. Thus, the accelerator and the multiplier tend to reinforce each other, resulting in a strong upward movement in national income.

Eventually, however, the economy nears some level of full capacity. That is, since we have only a certain amount of labour, land and other factors of production, it is impossible to continue increasing national income at the rapid rate that was experienced during the expansion phase of the business cycle. At some point, supply constraints must become a problem and growth of all the components of the economy has to slow down. Sales will not increase forever at the same fast rate; they will begin to increase at a slower rate. This slowdown in the growth of sales means that the rate of growth of planned investment is going to turn down abruptly. However, because of the multiplier effect, the decrease in planned investment will lead to a magnified, or multiplied, decrease in the equilibrium level of income. The reduction in the rate of growth of national income will mean a further reduction in the rate of sales growth, leading to a further reduction in gross investment, and so on. Eventually, the economy will experience a recession and the cycle will start again.

At some point, the capital stock of firms, that is, their actual stock of machinery, buildings and manufacturing equipment, gets into line with their reduced sales rates. When this happens, the stage is set for another upturn, another recovery, and the interaction again of the accelerator and the multiplier.

An alternative view

You will note that the multiplier–accelerator theory of the business cycle is one in which business cycles are self-starting and self-terminating. Each phase of the business cycle automatically leads into the next.

In recent years the evidence for the existence of the accelerator effect has proved to be rather scanty. This has caused economists to look for other determining factors for the level of investment, and also to consider other explanations for the persistence of the trade cycle.

The capital stock adjustment model states that investment is related to the *expected* level of output and the *existing* capital stock. Thus firms will invest more when they expect to have to increase output but less if they already have surplus productive capacity. In practice, therefore, investment will be likely to increase when the economy is nearing full capacity output and to decrease when there is spare capacity. This is a modified accelerator theory which seems to explain changes in investment more satisfactorily.

The real business cycle view

The traditional trade cycle theory outlined above sees cyclical fluctuations as occurring with some degree of regularity and therefore being predictable. The real business cycle theory holds that fluctuations in national income are due to a combination of random supply-side shocks.

The initial impetus for the development of this theory came from the two oil price increases in the 1970s, which both created highly recessionary tendencies in most economies. They shifted the aggregate supply curve upwards and to the left, increased the general level of prices and thus reduced purchasing power, so that in real terms aggregate demand and output both fell.

Other shocks which may be important from this point of view include changes in technology and natural disasters.

The different viewpoints on the trade cycle are complex and we shall return to them in the closing chapters of the book. In the meantime, we should be aware that shocks on both the demand and the supply side of the economy can be important in explaining national income fluctuations, and the theories outlined so far can all contribute to an understanding of this very pervasive phenomenon.

KEY POINTS

16.7

- Increasing output may require investment in extra plant and machinery to create the necessary productive capacity.

- The accelerator shows how investment is linked to the rate of change of output.

- Investment will fluctuate more sharply than output.

- The accelerator and multiplier together can help to explain cyclical changes in output and employment.

Case Study

A regional multiplier effect

In the eighteenth and nineteenth centuries Liverpool prospered. Its docks provided a major worldwide transport link and, as trade in general and the North American economies in particular developed, so the shipping business grew. Both passenger and merchant shipping used its extensive facilities.

From the late 1950s problems developed. Business was lost as most passengers and some freight switched to the air. Further business was lost as the focus of UK trade shifted gradually towards Europe and away from the United States and the ex-colonies. The convenient ports for Europe were on the east coast and the Channel. Yet more business was lost because the ports that were gaining business were able to provide more modern facilities. This all added up to a sharp fall in demand for Liverpool's main product.

Coinciding with the lack of demand for port facilities was the effect upon employment of installing modern port equipment. The shift to use of containers in sea transport and mechanical methods of freight handling made the docks capital instead of labour intensive. Many thousands of dock labouring jobs disappeared.

The steady fall in demand for Merseyside's traditional product meant a loss of income in the region. It meant that investment was low: there were few profitable

opportunities around. Falling incomes for individuals meant less spending power and less demand for consumer goods of many kinds. Retailing, construction and leisure businesses, among many others, experienced a fall in demand, leading them to contract too.

There was a downward local multiplier at work. Liverpool became generally depressed. The initial fall in demand for the port services meant that demand fell generally and many different kinds of business faced extremely difficult conditions over a very long period of time. By 1994, the region's income was so far below the average that it qualified for extra European Union Regional Fund spending.

As the UK economy becomes more closely integrated with the EU economy as a whole, the tendency for incomes to grow more slowly in peripheral regions is increasing. Despite the problems associated with moving, people are leaving Liverpool and other regions with problems and moving towards the south-east of England, where jobs are easier to find.

	Population change,%, 1981–96	Unemployment, %, 1997
Liverpool	–9.5	12.7
UK	+4.1	5.5

Source: ONS, *District Trends*, via Secos

1 Trace the practical effects of falling demand for port facilities on
   (a) the docks themselves,
   (b) a local warehousing business adjacent to the docks,
   (c) a furniture shop in central Liverpool and
   (d) a local supermarket.
   If you were in the area, what evidence of the problems would you be able to observe for yourself?

2 What options are open to people who lose their jobs as a result of a downward local multiplier? What difficulties do these options entail?

3 Can the multiplier process be arrested? How?
4 What effect will the sequence of events in Liverpool have had on the rest of the UK economy?
5 To what extent has Liverpool's problem been replicated in other parts of the United Kingdom?
6 What are the implications for the standard of living in different regions?
7 Using recent data, describe a similar situation in another region or more recently. Explain the likely local impact of the changes.

Exam Preparation

Multiple choice questions

For questions 1 and 2 refer to this diagram.

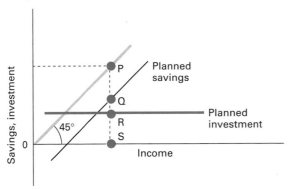

1 Which distance represents unplanned increase in stocks?
   A PQ
   B PR
   C PS
   D QR
   E RS

2 Which distance indicates consumption expenditure?
   A PQ
   B PR
   C PS
   D QR
   E QS

3 The diagram below shows a consumption function for a closed economy with no government.

What can be deduced from the diagram?
A At income levels below OY, saving is negative.
B At income levels below OY, there is an inflationary gap.
C The equilibrium level of income is OY.
D The marginal propensity to consume increases as income increases.

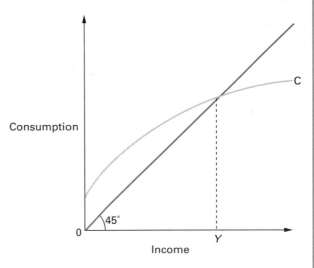

4 In the diagram, S^1 is an economy's initial saving function.

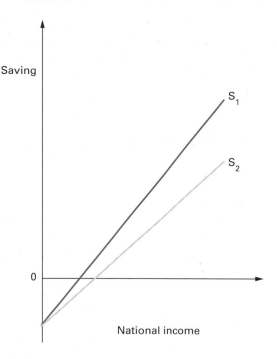

If the saving function shifts to S^2, what effect will this have on the marginal propensity to consume and on the multiplier?

	marginal propensity to consume	multiplier
A	decreases	decreases
B	decreases	increases
C	increases	decreases
D	increases	increases

5 An inflationary gap is the extent to which, at the full-employment level of national income,
  A price increases exceed wage increases
  B national income exceeds national output
  C planned saving exceeds planned investment
  D aggregate demand exceeds aggregate supply

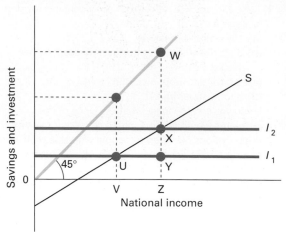

6 The diagram shows the equilibrium level of national income at two different levels of investment, I_1 and I_2. Which of the following ratios gives the value of the marginal propensity to save?
  A UX/VZ
  B VZ/XY
  C WX/XZ
  D XY/VZ
  E XY/YZ

Essay questions

1 Examine the effects of a rise in consumers' expenditure upon national income, investment and savings.

2 Explain why it is important for a government to take account of the multiplier and the accelerator in determining its economic policy.

3 (a) What might cause the level of savings in an economy to change?
  (b) Explain the likely outcome of an increase in the saving ratio, showing the effect.

4 Investment and output are linked. Discuss the extent to which changes in investment cause changes in output and changes in output cause changes in investment.

5 (a) Discuss what determines the level of investment.
  (b) Why is investment important in determining a country's well-being?

6 (a) Explain the impact on the economy of the multiplier and the accelerator.
  (b) Show how a change in either the multiplier or the accelerator might affect macroeconomic policy making.

17

Income and employment determination: government and trade

So far we have left government and trade out of our model of real national income determination. The tools learned already still apply when making the basic model more realistic. In this chapter, we consider how changes in government spending and taxation will alter the equilibrium level of real national income. We shall then explore the relationship between inflation and unemployment, which is a major factor in government decisions about taxation and expenditure. Finally, we examine the effects of foreign trade.

Adding government spending and taxes

We now include government spending in our macroeconomic model, but we assume that the level of government purchases is determined by political processes outside the economic system under study. In other words, we consider G to be autonomous, just as in the last chapter we considered I, for simplicity, to be autonomous.

Figure 17.1(a) shows the new aggregate expenditure function, $C + I + G$. Equilibrium income Y occurs where planned expenditure and real income and output are equal, that is, at the intersection with the 45° line.

Alternatively, we can find the equilibrium level of real national income by using the leakages–injections approach. Remember that, for equilibrium to occur, leakages must equal injections. In this present analysis, we have an additional injection into the system, autonomous government spending. Therefore, in Figure 17.1(b) overleaf, we show a new injections line that is investment plus government spending, or $I + G$. Since investment and government spending are both autonomous, or given, the $I + G$ line is horizontal. Within the model we are using, we have treated saving as induced, depending directly on the level of income. Similarly, taxes constitute a leakage and are dependent on income. They are a leakage because they reduce the level of disposable income, and therefore the level of personal consumption. They very obviously depend on income. Both direct taxes (taxes levied on income itself, such as income and profits tax) and indirect or expenditure taxes (such as VAT and excise duties) rise with income. So we have a new leakage function, the $S + T$ line in 17.1(b). The equilibrium level of income is that which generates a level of savings and tax revenue which is equal to planned investment and government expenditure.

It should be noted that the level of taxes set by the government will influence saving. An increase in taxes will generally lead to both a fall in consumption and a fall in saving. In order to pay the higher taxes, people will save somewhat less. So a given increase in tax rates will lead to a somewhat smaller increase in leakages.

LEARNING OUTCOMES

On completing this chapter you should understand:

■ The impact of government spending and taxes

■ Discretionary fiscal policies

■ The idea of automatic or built-in stabilizers

■ The Budget and fiscal policy

■ The effect of exports and imports on the economy

■ How the multiplier works in an open economy

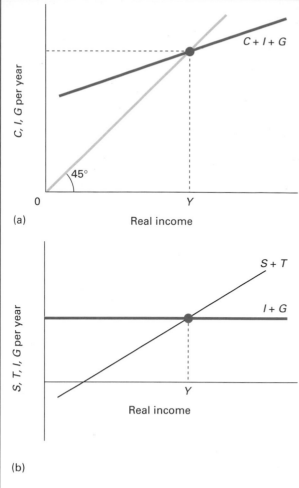

Figure 17.1
Equilibrium income with a government
Aggregate expenditure is *C + I + G*. Equilibrium income is *Y*, the level at which expenditure is exactly equal to income and output. Part (b) shows the injections–leakages approach, with equilibrium occurring where planned *I + G = S + T*.

The multiplier with a government

Our original derivation of the multiplier was based on there being one leakage only, saving. With another leakage, taxes, the story changes. The more of any given increase in expenditure which leaks away as either saving or taxes, the smaller is the multiplier.

We can of course use the original alternative formula for the multiplier, $1/(1 - \text{MPC})$. But this only raises the question, what is the MPC when there is the further leakage of taxes?

When households decide how much to spend on consumer goods, they examine not gross income (before tax) but disposable income (income after tax). Disposable income Y_d can be defined as national income less taxes:

$$Y_d = Y - T$$

Taxes will be levied at particular rates. If the **marginal rate of taxation** (MRT) and the average rate are both equal to 0.2, then

$$Y_d = Y - 0.2Y = 0.8Y$$

If we assume that the average and marginal propensities to consume out of disposable income are 0.9, then

$$C = 0.9Y_d = 0.9 \times 0.8Y = 0.72Y$$

Thus if the MRT is 0.2 and the MPC out of disposable income is 0.9, the MPC out of national income is 0.72. The multiplier is then 3.6.

KEY POINTS

17.1

- Government spending is politically determined and is therefore autonomous, that is, determined outside the model.

- Taxes, though the rates are set by governments, depend directly on incomes, that is, they are induced.

- In equilibrium planned injections equal planned leakages, so *G + I = S + T*.

- In using the multiplier it must be remembered that its level is determined by all leakages.

Keynesian fiscal policy

Keynes observed the 1930s Depression and put forward strong policy recommendations. Whereas governments at that time were intent on policies of austerity, Keynes argued that increased government spending would stimulate the economy, bringing growth and reduced unemployment. His approach was to manage aggregate demand by adjusting taxes and spending in order to create sufficient demand to provide the much-needed jobs.

After the Second World War these ideas became the conventional wisdom. From the end of the war until 1974 there was not a single year in which output fell. Until 1970, inflation was very seldom higher than 5 per cent, and averaged 3.3 per cent for the period 1953–69; unemployment was generally in the range of 1.5 per cent to 2.5 per cent and was never higher than 2.6 per cent. So it must be concluded that in certain circumstances demand-management policies can reduce cyclical fluctuations in the economy. They can provide an economic framework which is conducive to steady growth.

However, it is important to remember that these policies work with a time lag. It can be one to two years before the effects of extra spending on unemployment are visible.

1 Trace the effect of an increase in government spending on pensions, on aggregate demand, output, incomes and employment.
2 What effect will the multiplier have on the macroeconomic impact of increased government spending?
3 What would happen if the government increased spending or cut taxes when the economy was near to full capacity output? Use diagrams to explain your answer.

'This reckless expenditure in chalk will have to cease.'

Discretionary fiscal policies

Governments can choose to vary spending or taxes, or both, in order to expand or contract aggregate expenditure.

Filling the output gap

Figure 17.2 shows an economy in which, initially, expenditure is insufficient to buy all of potential output. Real income Y_1 can be produced by fewer people than are actually seeking work. There is some cyclical, or demand-deficiency, unemployment.

If expenditure can be increased then real income and output can expand and employers will take on more labour. (The implication of there being unemployed resources is that the economy is on the horizontal section of the aggregate supply curve. Aggregate supply can expand to meet any increase in aggregate demand.)

In Figure 17.2, the increased expenditure is shown as arising from increased government expenditure. Aggregate expenditure rises from $C + I + G_1$ to $C + I + G_2$. The resulting level of real national income is Y_2. This corresponds to the level of income at which planned $I + G_2$

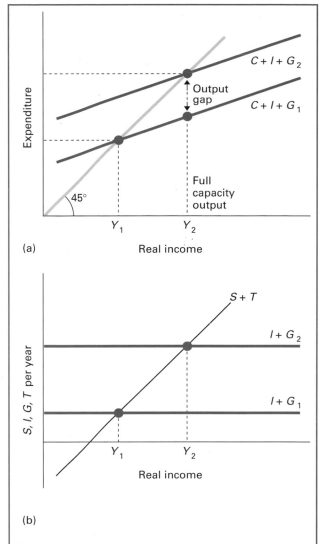

(a)

(b)

Figure 17.2
Reducing unemployment with fiscal policy
At real income Y_1 there is substantial demand-deficiency unemployment. Increasing government expenditure from G_1 to G_2 adds to aggregate demand, causing firms to try to expand output and take on labour. The new equilibrium real income Y_2 is achieved when aggregate expenditure, $C + I + G_2$, is exactly equal to real income and output, and when $I + G_2$ (injections) are equal to $S + T$ (leakages).

is equal to $S + T$ in 17.2(b). An alternative possibility would have been to reduce taxes. This would increase disposable income and therefore consumption. Both increasing spending and decreasing taxes serve to increase the level of the government's deficit so that injections increase in relation to leakages. Or a package of measures would be possible, perhaps including monetary policies. All are discussed in more detail in Part E.

It should be noticed that the eventual increase in income and output is much larger than the initial increase in government spending. This is precisely what we would expect, with the multiplier at work. It means that it is important for the government to be able to predict the multiplier effect of its change in spending. Otherwise it might overdo its expansionary policy, and income could increase by more than the output gap and create the reverse problem.

It is important to remember that increasing aggregate demand can only help to reduce unemployment which has been caused by demand deficiency. If the cause of the unemployment is structural, the unemployed people will not have the skills required by the employers who are expanding. Or they may have the skills but be geographically distant from the jobs being created. Microeconomic policies to reduce immobilities will be needed if a permanent solution to the problem is to be found. This situation too will be examined further in Part E.

Reducing the expansionary gap

Figure 17.3 shows an economy in which, initially, aggregate demand or expenditure exceeds output or aggregate supply. This excess demand arises because the economy is incapable of producing real income Y_1 – there simply are not enough suitable resources available to do the job. The most that can be produced – the maximum potential, or full capacity output, of the economy – is Y_2. Supply constraints are preventing the economy from expanding and, unless expenditure is reduced, prices will rise, probably at an accelerating rate. (The economy is on the upward-sloping section of the aggregate supply curve.) This is sometimes known as *overheating*.

Figure 17.3 shows the effects of increasing taxes to reduce expenditure. The reduced disposable income causes consumption to fall, as shown in 17.3(a). Figure 17.3(b) shows the increase in taxes. This reduces the government's deficit, increasing leakages relative to injections. The reduced expenditure should remove the excess demand and the upward pressure on prices. An alternative would have been to reduce government spending, or some policy combination. Note again that, because of the downward multiplier effect, the eventual decrease in expenditure will be greater than the initial change in spending. In this case the importance of accurate forecasting is even greater. The government needs to have good estimates of the extent to which a tax increase affects the level of consumption. It must know the marginal propensity to consume out of disposable income.

Taxes, spending and the marginal propensity to consume

The effect of government spending will depend upon the marginal propensity to consume of the people who receive the proceeds. For example, if the government decides to raise pensions, it is reasonable to suppose that pensioners have a high marginal propensity to consume and will therefore spend almost all the extra income they are given. Similarly, the effect of a change in taxes depends on the

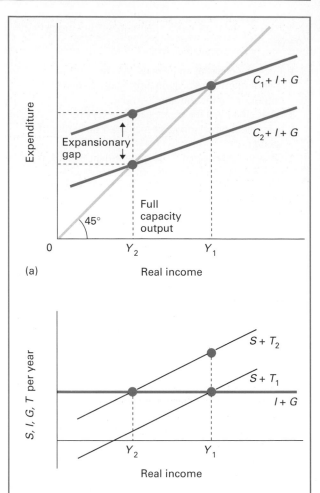

Figure 17.3
Reducing inflationary pressure with fiscal policy
At Y_1, planned expenditures exceed full capacity output. Prices will rise due to aggregate excess demand. To reduce expenditure, taxes can be raised from T_1 to T_2. Disposable income is thus reduced and consumption falls from C_1 to C_2. There is a downward multiplier effect as expenditure falls and equilibrium real income falls from Y_1 to Y_2.

marginal propensity to consume of the people who experience the tax cuts. Cutting taxes on higher incomes will lead to some increase in consumption but also to an increase in saving. So not all of the tax cut will actually be spent. Cutting taxes on lower incomes may have little effect on saving because the people concerned will probably have a high marginal propensity to consume.

Deficits and surpluses

We earlier discussed the possibility of the government increasing expenditures, but we did not discuss how such expenditures would be financed. If we assume no increase in taxes, and if the budget is initially balanced, we can conclude that when the government spends more it ends up with a deficit. If the government is already running a deficit, it will have an even larger one. Fiscal policies have therefore been associated with **deficit spending** on the part of the government. Fiscal policy advocates point out that an increase in the deficit stimulates the economy, whereas a decrease in the deficit has the opposite effect. The government can also run a **surplus**. That is, it can take in more revenues than it spends. An increase in the government's budget surplus would have a depressing effect on the economy, just as a decrease in government expenditures would, or an increase in taxes. The existence of, or an increase in, the government budget surplus presumably reduces total aggregate demand and thereby depresses economic activity.

(d) If government expenditure and the tax rate remain unchanged, what is the government budget deficit or surplus at the equilibrium level of national income following the decrease in private investment?

(e) Suppose the government wishes to achieve a return to the original national income of £10 000 million via increasing after-tax disposable incomes by means of non-taxable cash benefits paid to households. If the consumption function is unchanged, by how much must government expenditure on cash benefits increase? **A✓**

The effects of fiscal policy

4 Redraw Figure 17.2 showing the effect of reduced taxes on real national income. **A✓**

5 Redraw Figure 17.3 showing the effect of reducing government expenditure on real national income. **A✓**

6 Study the data below, and then answer questions (a)–(e) which follow.

The following are data for a hypothetical closed economy which initially is in short-run macroeconomic equilibrium.

(i) The consumption function is given by the equation
$$C = 100 + 0.8Y_D$$
where C denotes consumption in million pounds and Y_D denotes disposable after-tax income in million pounds.

(ii) All government revenue is raised by a 25 per cent proportional income tax. Hence
$$Y_D = 0.75Y$$
where Y denotes national income in million pounds.

(iii) Private investment spending is equal to £1400 million.

(iv) Government expenditure on goods and services is equal to £2500 million.

(v) National income $Y = £10\,000$ million.

(a) What are the initial values of consumption, savings and government tax revenue?

(b) What is the relationship between the average propensity to consume and the marginal propensity to consume in this economy? How does the average propensity to consume vary as disposable income increases?

(c) Suppose that private investment spending subsequently decreases to £1000 million. Other things being equal, what is the change in national income that is predicted by the Keynesian income–expenditure model?

Automatic or built-in stabilizers

In contrast to discretionary fiscal policy, automatic stabilizers need no new legislation in order to make them effective. The system of taxes and benefits works to counteract cyclical changes in the level of expenditure automatically.

Progressive income taxes

As taxable income rises so does the marginal tax rate – to a maximum of 40 per cent. Thus, income tax is progressive: the higher the income, the larger the proportion of it which is paid in tax. Or we can say that, as taxable income decreases, the marginal tax rate goes down. Think about this for the entire economy. Initially, personal income taxes may yield the government, say, £50 billion per year. Now suppose that, for whatever reason, business activity suddenly starts to slow down. When this happens, workers are not allowed to put in as much overtime as before. Some workers are laid off, and some must change to jobs that pay less. What happens to taxes when wages and salaries go down? Taxes are still paid but at a lower rate than before, since tax rates are progressive. Some people who had been paying marginal rates of 40 per cent will now pay only the standard rate of 22 per cent. As a result of these decreased taxes, disposable income – the amount remaining after taxes – does not fall by the same percentage as before-tax income. The individual, in other words, does not feel the pinch of recession as much as we might think if we ignored the progressive nature of our tax schedule. The *average* tax rate falls when less is earned.

Conversely, when the economy suddenly comes into a boom period, people's incomes tend to rise. They can work more overtime and can change to higher-paying jobs. However, their *disposable* income does not go up as rapidly as their total income, because their average tax rates are rising at the same time. The government takes a larger proportion of income in tax, as incomes rise. In this way, the progressive income tax system tends to stabilize any abrupt changes in economic activity. Tax revenue rises as the economy booms and falls as activity diminishes.

During the 1980s, reduced marginal tax rates lessened the progressiveness of the UK tax system. The top rate of income tax was cut in several stages from 60 per cent to 40 per cent, and the standard rate from 30 per cent to 25 per cent. By April 2000, the standard rate of tax stood at 22 per cent. However, this does not alter the fact that tax revenue falls, or grows more slowly, during recession and vice versa during a boom.

Unemployment benefits

Unemployment benefits work like the progressive income tax: they stabilize aggregate demand. When business activity drops, most laid-off workers automatically become eligible for unemployment benefits. Their disposable income therefore remains positive, although less than when they were working. During boom periods, there is less unemployment, and consequently fewer unemployment payments are made to the labour force. Less purchasing power is being added to the economy. So government expenditure automatically offsets fluctuations in income.

The stabilizing impact

Progressive taxes and the benefit system reduce the impact of changes in demand on disposable income, consumption and the equilibrium level of national income. We presented a model in which disposable income – *take-home pay* – is the main determinant of how much people desire to spend. Hence, if disposable income is not allowed to fall as much as it would otherwise during a recession, the downturn will be moderated. On the other hand, if disposable income is not allowed to rise as rapidly as it would otherwise during a boom, the boom will not get out of hand, causing prices to rise, among other things. The government automatically swings into deficit when there is a recession, and back towards surplus when the economy booms. Figure 17.4 shows this graphically. In recent years, governments have tried to balance the budget over the course of the trade cycle. They can still allow the deficit to rise during recession in order to reduce its impact.

The Budget and fiscal policy

Fiscal policy in the United Kingdom is set out in the Budget each spring. The Chancellor of the Exchequer surveys the economy and forecasts are published. The actual changes in tax rates and expenditure plans are explained. Underlying both, there is the policy of the government of the day, which determines what, if any, changes will be made to discretionary policies.

If policy is expansionary the government's deficit (that is, expenditure minus tax revenue) will increase. This means that the **Public Sector Net Cash Requirement**

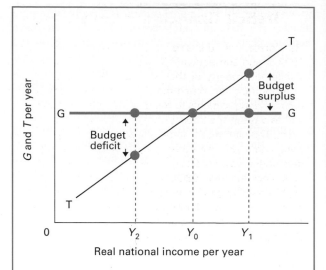

Figure 17.4
Automatic stabilizers
When real national income increases from Y_0 to Y_1, taxes will exceed government expenditures as shown by the vertical distance between GG and the tax line, TT. This government budget surplus, which occurs *automatically* during expansion, could assist in offsetting possible inflationary pressures. Alternatively, when real national income falls from Y_0 to Y_2, the resultant automatic budget deficit could help offset or alleviate the recession.

(PSNCR)* will rise: more borrowing must take place, for the year in hand. Also, the **National Debt** will rise; this is the sum total of all outstanding government debt, past and present. However, an expansionary policy may cause real income to rise, so that tax revenues then rise. This will reduce the deficit somewhat.

If, on the other hand, policy is contractionary, taxes will be raised or maintained. Government spending will be cut. The government's deficit will fall and a surplus may develop. This surplus, or **Public Sector Debt Repayment (PSDR)** may be used to reduce the National Debt. This is what happened in the years 1987–9, although government policy was less contractionary than it appeared to be because the surplus was partly created by the proceeds of privatization.

In recent years it has become politically difficult to raise income tax rates in the UK. Governments have promised at election time not to increase taxes and, for the most part, have delivered on their promises. However, from time to time other taxes have been raised. Changes in government expenditure can still be used to influence the level of demand.

These issues will be taken up again in Chapter 28.

---

* Before 1999, this was known as the Public Sector Borrowing Requirement (PSBR).

Deficit financing in recession

The increase in the size of the PSNCR expected for 1992–3 and subsequently largely reflects the automatic stabilizing property of the tax and benefit system. In a recession (and for some time afterwards) tax receipts are reduced and payments to the unemployed are increased, and as a result the impact on demand is to some extent offset. This 'automatic' stabilization does not require foresight, and it will be automatically reversed when recovery gets under way. Especially in view of the severity of the cycle since the mid-1980s, the existence of this degree of built-in stability is to be welcomed. On this occasion it has been enhanced by allowing public spending on a range of programmes to rise more strongly than was intended a year ago. This came about for a variety of reasons not all connected with the recession, but its effect on activity was appropriate and timely.

Source: *National Institute Economic Review*, 1, 1992

PSNCR

1986	1987	1988	1989	1990	1991	1992	1993	1994
3.1	–1.7	–12.4	–9.8	–2.5	9.0	29.7	43.2	36

Note: A negative PSNCR means there was a debt repayment.

Source: *National Institute Economic Review*, 3, 1994

7 What phase of the trade cycle was the UK economy in early in 1992?

8 How did the built-in stabilizing effect of taxes and benefits help the economy at that time?

9 What was the resulting effect on the PSNCR?

10 Define PSDR and explain why certain years had this experience.

11 (a) What phase of the trade cycle is the economy in right now?

(b) Has government policy led to a change in the PSNCR?

Is there a trade-off between inflation and unemployment?

We have already seen that, when the economy approaches full capacity, supply constraints develop and inflation starts to accelerate. At such a time, unemployment will be relatively low. These are the conditions we have come to associate with a boom. The reverse occurs in recession: unemployment rises, and it becomes harder to negotiate pay increases as fears of job losses mount. This led economists to look for evidence of a trade-off between inflation and unemployment.

This trade-off can be important when governments try to devise appropriate expenditure and tax policies. Supply constraints and accelerating inflation can be avoided if the government can reduce aggregate demand soon enough to have an effect at the right moment. Aggregate demand can be reduced either by raising taxes or increasing expenditure. Similarly, if unemployment is high, it may be possible to reduce that part of it which is caused by insufficient demand in the economy. The government can increase aggregate demand by reducing taxes or increasing expenditure. So an understanding of the relationship between inflation and unemployment can be crucial in determining the success or otherwise of government policy.

The Phillips curve in theory and reality

Some economists have argued that there is a constant *trade-off* between the rate of employment and the rate of inflation. Their argument is that, in order to obtain less unemployment, we have to suffer greater rates of inflation. Or, conversely, in order to reduce the rate of inflation, we have to accept more unemployment. This trade-off has been labelled the **Phillips curve**, named after the late Professor A. W. Phillips, who discovered that in the United Kingdom wages had historically risen rapidly when the unemployment rate was low and had risen more slowly when the unemployment rate was high. His empirical evidence was for the years 1861–1957.

Although Phillips's original analysis published in 1958 was in terms of *wage rate increases* and the unemployment rate, economists have contended that the relationship also holds between *price increases* and the unemployment rate. Indeed, there does seem to be a close relationship between wage rate changes and the retail price index.

Figure 17.5 shows a hypothetical Phillips curve. On this curve, if we are at an unemployment rate of 6 per cent, for example, and want to reduce the unemployment rate to 4 per cent, we have to accept an increase in the rate of inflation of 2 percentage points. If only the world were so simple! If it were, policy-makers could simply set a trade-off menu. Each year they could vote on whether they wanted to have less or more unemployment with concomitantly more or less inflation. Indeed, that is the way many policy-makers talked during the late 1960s and the mid-1970s.

When we look for evidence of a Phillips curve since then, the results are mixed. Look at Table 17.1: there are some sequences of years when the trade-off seems very clear, but there are others where it is less clear-cut. Some economists have said that inflation is dead but others disagree. We shall try to unravel this a little further in Part E.

Table 17.1

Inflation and unemployment in the United Kingdom

	Inflation	Unemployment
1985	6.0	10.9
1986	3.4	11.2
1987	4.1	10.0
1988	4.9	8.1
1989	7.8	6.3
1990	9.5	5.9
1991	5.9	8.1
1992	3.7	9.9
1993	1.6	10.4
1994	2.6	9.4
1995	3.4	8.1
1996	2.4	7.3
1997	3.1	5.5
1998	3.5	4.7
1999	1.5	4.3

Sources: *National Institute Economic Review*, 2, 1988; 3, 1994; 4, 1999

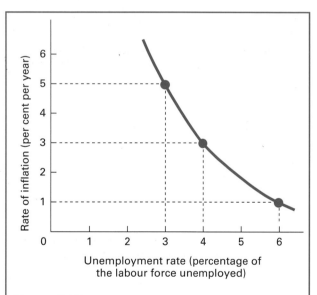

Figure 17.5

A hypothetical Phillips curve

The Phillips curve shows the relationship between the unemployment rate and the rate of inflation. If we want a 3 per cent unemployment rate, we presumably have to live with 5 per cent annual inflation. If we do not want to live with 5 per cent inflation but insist on only 3 per cent, we will have to 'buy it' with more unemployment, since a 3 per cent rate of inflation is associated with a 4 per cent rate of unemployment.

KEY POINTS

17.2

■ Fiscal policy can be used to regulate the level of expenditure in the economy.

■ Demand-deficiency unemployment can be reduced by increasing government spending or reducing taxes.

■ Inflationary pressures can be reduced by increasing taxes or reducing government spending.

■ Built-in stabilizers automatically moderate changes in disposable income resulting from changes in overall business activity.

■ The annual deficit, expenditure minus tax revenue, is known as the PSNCR.

■ If tax revenue is greater than expenditure, there will be a surplus, or PSDR.

■ The Phillips curve refers to the tendency of inflation and unemployment to be inversely related.

Adding exports and imports

We can use the same approaches used so far to incorporate exports and imports. Imports are a leakage from the circular flow, since they constitute spending on goods and services produced overseas. They are treated as induced expenditure, that is, as directly dependent on the level of income. The relationship between the level of imports and income is defined by the propensity to import. The **marginal propensity to import** is that proportion of an increase in income which is spent on imports. Since imports move closely with the level of income in the United Kingdom, this clearly makes sense.

Exports, on the other hand, are treated as autonomous. Rather like investment, they are in fact determined by a wide range of influences which are outside the scope of the basic model. The level of aggregate demand in foreign countries with which the United Kingdom trades extensively, the exchange rate and non-price competitiveness (factors such as design, reliability and after-sales service) all affect the level of demand for UK exports.

As always, the equilibrium condition is that planned injections be equal to planned leakages.

$$S + T + M = I + G + X$$

It is not necessary that any one, or all, pairs of injections and leakages be equal – only that total injections equal total leakages – for equilibrium to occur. The economy could be in overall equilibrium with a government deficit

(*G* exceeding *T*) balanced by a private sector surplus (*S* exceeding *I*), with perhaps also a balance-of-trade surplus (*X* exceeding *M*). Or both government and trade may be in deficit, with the private sector surplus balancing both deficits. Both these situations, and many other such combinations, are consistent with overall equilibrium. (This does not mean that a balance-of-trade deficit could be ignored indefinitely.)

Figure 17.6 shows the effect of an increase in imports. Just as when any other change occurs in injections or leakages, the fall in expenditure brings about a fall in income which is larger than the initial increase in imports, because of the downward multiplier effect.

With foreign trade the expenditure function includes the net balance of exports and imports, *X* − *M*, or net exports. This will be negative if imports exceed exports, creating a net leakage. Figure 17.6(a) shows how, in equilibrium, planned expenditure from all sources must be equal to planned output, that is, the expenditure function must intersect the 45° line. A rise in imports reduces expenditure, leading income to fall from Y_1 to Y_2.

$$\text{total expenditure} = C + I + G + (X - M)$$

The multiplier in an open economy

Our original formula for the multiplier

$$\frac{1}{\text{MPS}}$$

was based on there being a single leakage, savings. With an open economy with a government this can be amended to

$$\frac{1}{\text{MPS} + \text{MRT} + \text{MPM}}$$

where MRT is the marginal rate of taxation and MPM is the **marginal propensity to import**. (Care must be taken that these marginal rates of leakage are all expressed as a proportion of national income, as a whole, when using this formula.)

Clearly with three leakages, the multiplier will be smaller than we have tended to suggest before. An economy which has a large public sector and is very open, in that a substantial proportion of output is traded, will have a relatively small multiplier. This clearly applies to the United Kingdom. The effect of increasing expenditure on imports and the balance of trade can often be a major factor in considering future policy. Roughly 30 per cent of UK output is exported. Imports take a similar proportion of expenditure. The balance, net exports, tends to be a relatively small part of total demand.

Rising imports will tend to reduce employment in domestic firms, and rising exports to increase it. If a rising level of export demand is to be satisfied there must

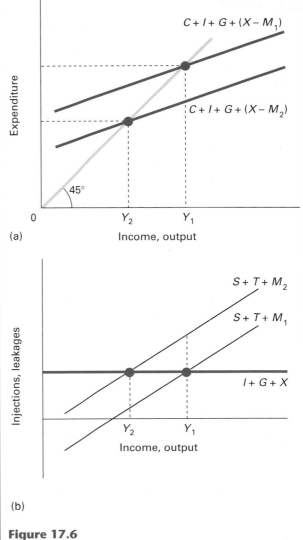

(a)

(b)

Figure 17.6
The effect of rising imports
As imports rise, leakages increase, expenditure on domestic output falls, and there is a downward multiplier effect on income.

be suitable unemployed resources available to expand output. If there are not, rising demand will lead to rising prices rather than increased output. This is likely to reduce foreign demand for domestically produced goods anyway, as price rises erode competitiveness.

The trade cycle in an open economy

In practice, we need to be able to analyse the trade cycle in the context of an open economy. Usually many countries will be experiencing the phases of the cycle together. Those which have important trading links will be affected by what is happening in each other's economies. For example, if the German economy is depressed, some exporters in the United Kingdom who usually are able to sell their products in Germany will find that sales are decreasing. Exports will fall and the UK economy will face reduced injections, and thus a lower level of activity generally. There will be a downward multiplier effect as the recession spreads from one country to another.

Equally, producers who are finding the domestic market slow if the economy moves into recession will be encouraged to seek export markets more energetically. So, provided some economies are *not* experiencing a similar recession, exports will tend to rise when aggregate demand is growing slowly or falling. Meantime, because imports are a rising function of income, low levels of income will generate a low level of imports. The likelihood is that when incomes are low there will be a **trade surplus**.

If, on the other hand, high levels of expenditure lead to excess demand and supply constraints, it is inevitable that both firms and households find themselves unable to purchase all the goods and services they want from domestic producers. Obviously they will turn to imports to fill the gap.

So an economy which is expanding rapidly will typically find that imports increase as full capacity is approached and it gets harder to meet rising demand from domestic resources. At the same time, exporters have little incentive because they can sell easily on the domestic market. With exports down and imports up there will be a deterioration of the trade balance, which will continue for as long as the economy is overheating, and a **trade deficit** is likely to develop. If it becomes large the government may need to take action to reduce it. The necessary policies are described in Chapter 29.

In general we can always look at changes in government expenditure, taxation, exports and imports in the light of their overall effect on injections and leakages, and so on the level of activity in the economy.

The effect of an exchange rate change

If for any reason the exchange rate changes there will be an effect on exports and imports. A lower exchange rate will make exports cheaper and imports dearer. Exports will rise (after a time lag) and imports will fall similarly. This will have a stimulating effect on the economy because injections are rising and leakages falling. The outcome will depend upon whether there are under-utilized resources in the economy, or whether the increased output leads to supply constraints. This will be looked at in more detail in Chapter 29.

KEY POINTS

17.3

- Imports are induced, that is, they depend directly on the level of income. They are a leakage from the circular flow.

- Exports are autonomous, being determined by a wide range of factors. They are an injection into the circular flow.

- In an open economy with a government, equilibrium requires that all planned injections equal planned leakages, $I + G + X = S + T + M$.

- The multiplier depends on the marginal rate of leakage.

- The trade cycle in any one country is considerably affected by the level of activity in its trading partners' economies, and imports and exports are affected by whether the economy is growing or in recession.

Case Study

We promise to cut taxes!

'For enterprise to flourish, the state must get out of the way of the wealth creators. We are the only party that can cut taxes because we are the only party which is serious about controlling public spending.'

Conservative Party Manifesto for the general election, May 1997

'There will be no return to the penal tax rates that existed under both Labour and Conservative governments in the 1970s. To encourage work and reward effort, we are pledged not to raise the basic or top rates of income tax throughout the next Parliament. Our long-term objective is a lower starting rate of income tax.'

Labour Party Manifesto for the general election, May 1997

'We will keep the "golden rule" of public finance, total borrowing should not exceed total investment.'

Liberal Democrat Manifesto for the general election, May 1997

1 List the fiscal policies which can be used to influence (or manage) the level of aggregate demand.
2 What problems are likely to arise with fiscal policies?
3 Why are there likely to be time lags (a) between identification of the economic problem and the implementation of policies; and (b) between

implementation of policy and the resulting effect of the policy on the economy?
4 There are subtle differences between the three approaches outlined above. Explain these differences and say whether the policies have changed in recent years.

Case Study

Are the Asian Tigers still roaring?

Countries which have been able to expand their exports fast have often enjoyed rapid growth. The so-called Asian Tigers (South Korea, Taiwan, Hong Kong and Singapore) provide examples. As they industrialized they developed a strong comparative advantage in certain kinds of manufactured goods. They had sufficiently well-trained workforces to provide skilled labour, but at wage rates below those of the developed countries.

As exports grew, employment in manufacturing expanded and incomes grew. The very substantial – and continuous – injections into the economy brought growth. High levels of investment ensured that supply constraints did not become a problem. The investment was financed partly by domestic savings and partly by foreign capital, coming in particular from Japan. All four countries achieved average growth rates in the range 6–9 per cent.

Until 1997, that is. Then the Asian financial crisis created a phenomenal upheaval. It began in Thailand and South Korea, where the banks had made many large loans to companies that were in difficulties. Confidence in the banking systems collapsed, some businesses failed, foreign capital moved out and exchange rates dropped through the floor. Imports became unaffordable, incomes fell and unemployment rose. The growth process went

into reverse. The contagion spread to Japan, Indonesia and many other countries.

The International Monetary Fund came to the rescue with loans, with conditions attached. These included high interest rates and contractionary fiscal policies. Frightened consumers cut back spending and by 1998, most Asian economies were contracting seriously.

Yet by late 1999, the problem was almost gone. Most governments had decided to abandon strict fiscal policies and try to stimulate their economies with extra public spending. The US was booming and increased its imports as a result. This helped Asian exporters. You can see from the graphs that the tigers were perhaps not back to normal, but greatly strengthened.

1 Explain the theoretical connection between trade and economic growth.
2 In what ways did falling exchange rates destabilise the countries concerned?
3 (a) What would you expect the long-term effects of growth to be on incomes in the tiger countries?
   (b) What would then be the effect on imports?
4 How would you expect the Asian financial crisis to affect UK firms?
5 What has happened to the Asian tigers since 1999?

GDP, % change on a year earlier

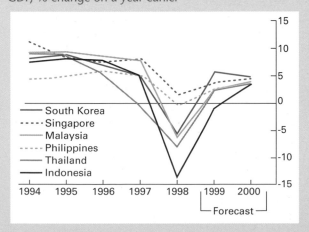

General government budget balances, % of GDP

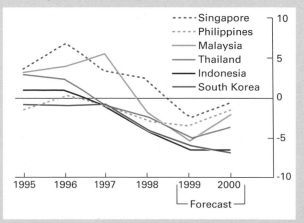

Source: *The Economist*, 21 August 1999

Exam Preparation

Multiple choice questions

1 A reflationary fiscal policy could include
   A a decrease in interest rates
   B an increase in indirect taxes
   C a decrease in government expenditure on capital goods
   D an increase in government expenditure on transfer payments
   E a decrease in personal tax allowances

2 If an economy moves into recession and central government has already planned a budget deficit, tax revenues will
   A rise, thus lowering the budget deficit
   B remain unchanged
   C fall, thus lowering the budget deficit
   D fall, thus increasing the budget deficit

3 If an open economy with government activity is in equilibrium and imports are greater than exports, which of the following must be true?
   A savings are greater than investment
   B investment plus government spending is greater than savings plus taxation
   C taxation is greater than government spending
   D investment plus government spending is less than savings plus taxation
   E government spending is greater than taxation

4 A tax will have a built-in stabilizing effect if
   A tax rates automatically increase in line with inflation
   B yield increases at a faster rate than income
   C yield varies inversely with national income levels
   D yield remains constant as levels of national income change

5 There has been a change in the distribution of income such that higher disposable incomes have been reduced while lower disposable incomes have increased. The most likely effect of this is that
   A consumption and saving remain the same
   B there is an increase in the average propensity to consume
   C the marginal propensity to save increases
   D the marginal propensity to consume decreases

Essay questions

1 In the November 1996 Budget, the UK government announced it planned to limit general government expenditure to just under £315 billion for the next financial year.
   (a) Explain why a government might wish to prevent a large increase in government expenditure.
   (b) Examine the likely economic effects of limiting the growth of government expenditure.

2 (a) Given the assumption of a closed economy, explain carefully the working of the multiplier.
   (b) How is the working of the multiplier affected if the economy engages in foreign trade?

3 (a) Why does the level of economic activity fluctuate?
   (b) Discuss the policies a government might adopt in order to minimize these fluctuations.

4 Briefly outline the determinants of the level of economic activity in an economy such as the United Kingdom. Is it possible for the government to do anything to avoid economic fluctuations or to reduce their effects?

5 Use multiplier analysis to examine the impact on employment and the balance of payments of (a) an increase in private investment, (b) an increase in the marginal propensity to consume and (c) a devaluation of the exchange rate.

6 (a) Examine the factors which influence the size of the national income multiplier.
   (b) Distinguish between the different multiplier effects of
      (i) an increase in social security payments
      (ii) a cut in the top rate of income tax

7 Analyse the likely impact of (a) a decrease in income tax rates and (b) increases in interest rates on aggregate demand and aggregate supply.

18

Money and financial institutions

If someone were to ask you 'How much money do you make?', you might answer in terms of so many pounds per week or per year. In this context, the term *money* really means income or the ability to purchase goods and services – in fact, the term is most generally used to mean income. But in this sense it is being used incorrectly. Counterfeiters 'make money'; as we shall see in this chapter, the banking system also 'makes money'. What you make is income. In this chapter and throughout the rest of the text, we shall use the term money to mean anything which we use as a medium (means) of exchange. You use your cheque-book as a medium of exchange. The money in your bank can be regarded as a medium of exchange. Therefore money is more than just the notes and coin that you have in your wallet or purse, and the official money supply includes more than just **currency** – paper notes and coin.

In this chapter, we shall examine the functions of money, the different types of money that are in existence and the financial system generally. You will find that there have been very extensive changes in the UK monetary system in recent years, and the present system is in many ways vastly different from the past. Take care when reading textbooks: they can go out of date very quickly.

LEARNING OUTCOMES

On completing this chapter you should understand:

- The nature of money
- How money supply is defined and measured
- The British banking structure
- The central bank
- How banks work
- The money supply

The nature of money

There are four traditional functions of money. The one that most people are familiar with and the one that we referred to above is as a *medium of exchange*. However, money also serves as a *unit of account*, a *store of purchasing power* and a *standard of deferred payment*.

When we say that money serves as a medium of exchange, what we mean is that sellers will accept it as a means of payment in market transactions. Without some generally accepted medium of exchange, we would have to resort to barter. In fact, before money was used, transactions took place by means of barter. *Barter* is simply a direct exchange of goods or services. Economic historians often suggest that the switch from barter to the use of money allowed for more rapid economic growth of the Western world, since increased specialization was then possible. It was extremely costly to make all exchanges by barter. Imagine the difficulty you would have today if you had to exchange your labour directly for the fruits of someone else's labour. Imagine the many exchanges that would have to take place for you to get from a position where you owned, for example, twenty-five pairs of shoes to a position where you owned only two pairs but now also had bread, meat, a pair of jeans and so on. The use of money facilitates exchange. Indeed, the existence of money means that individuals no longer have to hold a diverse collection of goods for exchange. Hence, more specialization can occur.

Money as a medium of exchange

As a **medium of exchange**, money allows individuals to specialize in any area in which they have a comparative advantage and to receive money payment for the fruits of their labour. Money can then be exchanged for the fruits of other people's labour. The usefulness of money as a medium of exchange causes more specialization. Moreover, we see that money is more important the larger the amount of trade. Thus, money would not be as important in a society of self-sufficient family units as it is in modern commercial economies.

Money as a unit of account

A **unit of account** is a way of placing a specific value on economic goods and services. Thus, as a unit of account, the monetary unit is used to measure the value of goods and services relative to other goods and services. It is the common denominator, or measure. It thus enables individuals to compare, easily, the relative value of goods and services. Governments use money prices to measure national income each year. A firm uses money prices to calculate profits and losses; and a typical household budgets its regular expenses daily using money prices as its unit of account.

Another way of describing money as a unit of account is to say that it is a *standard of value* that allows economic transactors to compare the relative worth of various goods and services. In short, it acts as an economic yardstick.

Money as a store of value

To see how money is a **store of value**, consider the following simple example. A fisherman comes into port after several days of fishing. At the going price of fish that day, he has £1000s' worth of fish. Fish are not a good store of value because, if the fisherman keeps them too long, they will rot. If he attempts to exchange them with other tradespeople, some of the fish may rot before he can exchange the entire catch for the goods and services that he desires. However, if the fisherman sells the entire catch for money, he can store the value of his catch in the money that he receives. (Of course, he can freeze the fish, but that is costly.)

Inflation reduces the value of money. If it is quite high, it will make money a rather poor store of value. Over time, people get used to this and look for ways of protecting themselves from inflation. They may buy houses, or equities (shares), or paintings, and hold less money. These kinds of property will appreciate: their prices will rise with inflation, though there is some risk that their prices may fall too.

Money as a standard of deferred payment

The fourth function of the monetary unit is as a **standard of deferred payment**. In less technical terms this simply means that money can be used as a means of entering into agreements regarding *future* payments. This function therefore involves money simultaneously as a medium of exchange and as a unit of account. For example, debts are typically stated in terms of a unit of account and are paid with a monetary medium of exchange. The negotiation of future payments is an essential feature of any complex society. Workers negotiate a salary for payment on completion of a job; landlords negotiate a rent that will be paid at regular intervals in the future; shareholders expect to receive a portion of their firm's profits each year, and so on.

It is interesting to note that not all countries will use their own national monetary unit to specify future payments. Often the dollar is used as the unit of account as it is more acceptable as an international medium of exchange.

Liquidity

Money is an asset – something of value – that accounts for part of one's wealth. Wealth in the form of money can be exchanged later for some other asset. Although it is not the only form of wealth that can be exchanged for goods and services, it is the one which is most widely accepted. This attribute of money is called **liquidity**. We say that an asset is liquid when it can easily be acquired or disposed of without high costs and with relative certainty as to its value. Notes and coin are by definition the most liquid asset there is. Just compare them, for example, with a share listed on the Stock Exchange. To buy or sell that share you must pay a percentage commission to the broker. Moreover, there is a distinct possibility that you will get less for the share than you originally paid for it. This is not the case with notes and coin, which can easily be converted into other asset forms. Property forms an even less liquid asset than shares. It can take some time to sell a house and convert the asset into money, and again, the value is uncertain.

However, when we hold notes and coin, we pay a price for this advantage of liquidity. That price is the interest yield that could have been obtained had the asset been held in another form, for example in the form of a savings account. In other words, the cost of holding money (its opportunity cost) is measured by the alternative interest yield obtainable by holding some other asset. Notes and coin are therefore merely one of a whole range of assets which can represent a person's wealth. Of all the assets, however, they are certainly the most liquid.

Why money has value

Today in the United Kingdom all of us accept coins, notes and cheques in exchange for items sold, including our labour services. The question remains why we are willing to accept for payment some bits of paper or metal that have no *intrinsic* value. The reason is that we have a **fiduciary monetary system**. This means that the value of our currency rests upon the public's confidence that money can be exchanged for goods and services. *Fiduciary* comes from the Latin *fiducia*, which means trust or confidence. In other words, in our fiduciary monetary system, money, whether in the form of currency or cheques, is not convertible into a fixed quantity of gold, silver or some other commodity. The various banknotes are just pieces of official paper that cost a fraction of their face value to produce. Similarly, coins have a value stamped on them that is normally greater than the market value of the metal in them. Regardless, currency and bank cheques are money because of their acceptability and predictability of value.

Acceptability

Bank accounts and currency are money because they are accepted in exchange for goods and services. They are accepted because people have confidence that they can later be exchanged for other goods and services. This confidence is based on the knowledge that such exchanges have occurred in the past without problems. Even during a period of relatively rapid inflation, we would still be inclined to accept money in exchange for goods and services. Why? Because it is so useful. Barter is a very costly, time-consuming alternative.

Predictability of value

For money to have a predictable value, the relationship between the quantity of money supplied and the quantity of money demanded must not change frequently, abruptly, or in great magnitude. In this sense, the value of money is like the economic value of anything else. Supply and demand determine what it 'sells' for. What is the selling price of a pound coin? It is what one has to give up in order to 'purchase' a pound. What do you have to give up? You must give up the goods and services that you could have instead. In other words, in order to own a one-pound coin, you give up the *purchasing power* inherent in that pound. That purchasing power might be equal to a magazine or a large chocolate bar. The purchasing power of the pound (that is, its value) therefore varies inversely with the price level. Thus, the more rapid the rate of increase of a price index, such as the retail price index, the more rapid is the decrease in the value, or purchasing power, of a pound. Yet money still retains its usefulness even if its value – its purchasing power – is declining year in and year out. In other words, money is still useful and accepted even during periods of inflation. Why? Because it still retains the characteristic of predictability of value. If you believe that the inflation rate is going to be around 10 per cent next year, you know that any pound you receive a year from now will have a purchasing power equal to 10 per cent less than that same pound this year. Thus, you will not refuse to use money or accept it in exchange simply because you know that its value will decline by the rate of inflation next year.

KEY POINTS

18.1

- Money is defined by its functions, which are (1) as a medium of exchange, (2) as a unit of account or standard of value, (3) as a store of value and (4) as a standard of deferred payment.

- Since notes and coin are widely accepted in exchange for goods and services, currency is a highly liquid asset. It can be disposed of without high transactions costs and with relative certainty as to its value.

- Monetary systems are fiduciary: our money is not convertible into a fixed quantity of a commodity such as gold or silver.

- Money is accepted in exchange for goods and services because people have confidence that money can later be exchanged for other goods and services.

- The purchasing power, or value, of money will fall if there is a rise in the price level.

Defining and measuring the money supply

Money is important. Changes in the total **money supply** and changes in the rate at which it is growing affect important economic variables such as the rate of inflation, interest rates and employment. Although there is widespread agreement among economists that money is important, they have never agreed on how to define and how to measure money. The measures of money used by central banks vary considerably from country to country. In the United Kingdom today there are just two versions of money supply published on a regular basis. These measures do not move in line with one another as they measure different things.

- M0, **narrow money**, includes notes and coin and banks' balances deposited with the Bank of England.
- M4, **broad money**, includes M0 and all sterling wholesale and retail deposits with monetary financial institutions (i.e. banks and other organizations which the Bank of England allows to take customers' deposits).

Over the years, there have been considerable changes in the way the money supply is measured. These reflect changes in the structure of the financial system and changes in economists' and politicians' thinking about the relationships between money and the real economy.

The components of M4

M0 can provide useful information. In mid-1999 it stood at £29 billion. However, it is M4 which is the main measure of money available to spend in the UK. M4 measures money in a fuller sense, not only as a medium of exchange but also as a store of value. Consequently, it includes M0, plus varying kinds of interest-earning asset, that can be converted into money within a short time period. In mid-1999 M4 stood at £800 billion. The component parts of M4 are:

1 notes and coin
2 banks' operational balances at the Bank of England
3 sight deposits
4 retail deposits
5 wholesale deposits
6 time deposits

1 Notes and coin

Notes and coin are the most liquid component of any money supply. They can be spent immediately and are always acceptable.

2 Operational balances at the Bank of England

The other component of M0 consists of the banks' operational balances held at the Bank of England – commonly referred to as the bankers' balances. All banks hold deposits (balances) at the Bank of England for the purposes of settling debts between themselves.

3 Sight deposits

Sight deposits in banks are those which can be withdrawn without notice. They are commonly referred to as current accounts which people can draw on by writing out a cheque. About two-thirds of all sight deposits now pay a rate of interest. Interest-bearing sight deposits are bank accounts which offer normal cheque facilities, immediate access and some interest.

4 Retail deposits

This is a general name for all bank accounts which can be readily used for transactions purposes. Broadly, these are all bank deposits of less than £50 000 and any building society deposits which are withdrawable within one month. These accounts can be regarded as 'active balances' which reflect patterns of consumer spending.

5 Wholesale deposits

These are deposits over £50 000. They are less likely to be spent immediately than are retail deposits. They reflect depositors' needs for a store of value as well as for money to cover transactions.

Certificates of deposit (CDs) provide higher rates of interest but have a fixed maturity date (though they can be sold). They are a useful type of deposit for large sums of money and are widely held by firms.

6 Time deposits

Time deposits represent all those bank accounts which require a period of notice before withdrawal. These may take several forms, and for our purposes it is best to think of them as bank deposit accounts and some building society accounts. Broadly speaking, the longer the period of notice before withdrawal, the better the interest rate is likely to be. These deposits are a major component of M4.

Foreign currency bank deposits

Foreign currency is not regarded as part of the UK money supply. But some residents of the United Kingdom do hold bank deposits in currencies other than sterling. These foreign currency deposits represent potential stores of value, especially if speculators are hoping to make gains from fluctuating exchange rates. And they represent a medium of exchange for overseas expenditure. Money balances such as these, held in countries other than those of their origin, are known as **Eurocurrency**.

Many large business borrowers now turn to the Eurocurrency markets for major loans. They will shop around for the currency in which they can get the lowest rate of interest with an acceptable exchange rate risk. So these money balances can be an important source of funds for investment. It is important to be aware of the existence of foreign currency deposits as a source of spending power.

What do the figures mean?

Measures of money are always hard to interpret. Changes in the figures mean different things depending on the circumstances. The Bank of England has made a number of changes in the way money is measured, over the years. In particular, it now treats bank and building society deposits in the same way. Increasingly, building societies and banks have been competing for business. Building society accounts can be used in the same way as current bank accounts, and many banks offer mortgages. It makes sense to treat them in the same way in the monetary data.

Money measures

Percentage growth of M4

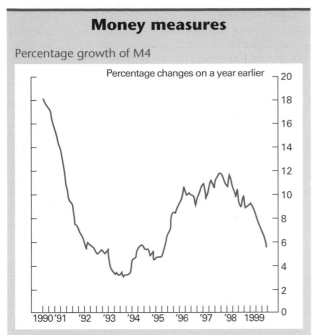

Source: Bank of England, Inflation Reports, November 1998, August 1999

1 Define M4, and describe its growth pattern from 1990 onwards.

2 If an increase in M4 means that bank lending has increased, what consequences may increasing M4 have for the economy as a whole?

KEY POINTS

18.2

■ There are two basic approaches to measuring money supply – the narrow measure and the broader measure. The former gives us M0 and the latter M4.

■ There is no one correct definition of money. The stock of money is made up of notes and coin and a range of different types of deposit held in different kinds of monetary institutions.

Financial markets

In recent years it has become clear that financial markets are vital to the development of all market economies. Most people want to save, for possible hard times ahead or for old age, or sometimes just for a large purchase like a house or car. Most businesses need to borrow, to finance investment in promising lines of production. If all the savers simply kept their savings under the mattress, there would be no funds available for investment. Broadly, this is what happens in the least developed economies where many people are working in agriculture and large numbers are still illiterate. It helps to explain why many countries have great difficulty in improving standards of living.

Small savers cannot afford to take risks with their savings. They need to be sure that the money is safe and will not be lost by the person who borrows it. Firms need to borrow large amounts and do not want to be bothered with a lot of small-scale loans. It is easy to see that there is an important role for banks here. They can take deposits from large numbers of savers and lend the money to firms which have potentially profitable investment projects. The banks take the risks on behalf of the savers. They become experienced in evaluating different kinds of risks.

The institutions which take deposits and pass the money on to borrowers include a wide range of **financial intermediaries**. These are the organizations which, literally, mediate between savers and borrowers. They include banks, building societies, insurance companies, pension funds, and unit and investment trusts. Some of these organizations are very specialized in one particular kind of business – this applies to insurance companies. Other organizations have merged with or bought out specialists outside their own field, or have simply expanded into other markets. You can see this quite clearly when you become aware that your bank is actually a financial conglomerate: it has many different divisions, some of which are not about banking at all. Banks own investment advisers, mortgage specialists and estate agents. They are no longer just banks.

With financial intermediaries no longer falling neatly into one particular group, it is helpful to think first about the different markets in which they operate. There are distinct, separate markets for different types of business. Together, they make up what we loosely term the capital markets or the financial markets. The main ones are described below.

The short-term money market

This is the market for funds lent overnight or for a very short period. Banks lend money in this market – generally known as **money at call**. This means that the lender can recall the loan at any time. Also, a good deal of lending is done by selling bills. A bill is simply a piece of paper which promises repayment in three months' time. **Bank bills** can be used by companies wanting to raise short-term finance; for a fee, they are guaranteed by the bank. **Treasury bills** are used by the government to meet its need for short-term finance. The buyer of any kind of bill (the lender) pays less for it than the maturity value; the difference is the return received, and is equivalent to a rate of interest. All funds on the short-term money market are very liquid – that means that they can be turned into cash in a very short time and with a very small risk of loss.

The bond market

When loans are required for longer periods, bonds may be used. These are loans for a fixed period which can be up to ten or twenty years, at a fixed rate of interest. Again, bonds may be issued by companies (corporate bonds) or by the government (Treasury bonds). The advantage for the buyers of bonds is that if they want to get their money back before the maturity date of the bond, they can sell it. Bonds thus provide a flexible way of lending. The interest rate will usually be higher than that on bank deposits, but there is much less risk than there is with buying shares (equities).

The inter-bank market

Banks frequently find themselves either with a surplus of funds or with a deficit which needs to be covered. Each day they will have to make fresh arrangements to cover their needs. They lend to each other on a very short-term basis in order to use their surpluses as profitably as possible.

The Stock Exchange

Owners of equities and some kinds of bonds who want to sell them can do so on the Stock Exchange. This means that their capital is not permanently tied up: they can realize the value if they want to. Of course, they may not be able to get the price they want for their shares. Shareholders have to accept that if the company does not perform well, then the share price will probably fall.

The British banking system

As we have already seen, the banking system consists of quite a wide range of different types of financial intermediaries. The terminology that is used to describe them is often confusing. As new institutions and systems evolve, new names are given to different parts of the system. However, the old names do not go out of use immediately. If you find terminology in textbooks that you never come across in the *Financial Times* or *The Economist*, you will know what has happened. Here are some of the main categories of institutions.

The retail banks

A retail bank is a privately owned profit-seeking institution. Examples include Barclays, Lloyds and HSBC. Forceful competition from former building societies such as the Abbey National (which became a bank) and from other banks like the Bank of Scotland has challenged their position. Mergers and takeovers, such as that of Natwest by Royal Bank of Scotland, have brought other changes.

Apart from accepting funds from their customers and using them to make profits, the retail banks have other common features. They all have extensive branch networks and are major participants in the clearing system (this involves the daily settling of debts between banks that are generated by customers' transactions). In addition to all the payments made by cheque, further billions are transferred by electronic methods such as direct debit, standing order, credit cards or electronic funds transfer.

The retail banks take deposits and lend to borrowers who wish to spend on consumer or investment goods. They act as intermediaries, spreading risks by lending for a wide range of purposes. Increasingly, they have become involved in mortgage business, which used to be the preserve of the building societies. The range of services they offer has been steadily increasing.

The wholesale banks

The wholesale banks specialize in deposits over £50 000, although the distinction between wholesale and retail banks is becoming blurred as banks generally try to expand beyond their traditional markets. There are two important groups within the wholesale category, however:

- **The merchant banks** The merchant banks specialize in the affairs of large commercial and industrial companies. Indeed, one of their specialisms is issuing new shares. Thus they are sometimes called *issuing houses*. So, merchant banks are very much banks for entrepreneurs, as they organize and administer large-scale loans on behalf of companies. Interestingly, they frequently do not provide the funds themselves. Their specialism is largely service through their knowledge of the relevant markets. Merchant banks are small in size compared with the retail banks. The financial services they offer include advising and organizing take-overs and mergers. This provides some of their most profitable business.

- **The foreign banks** The number of foreign banks in the United Kingdom is large: at present there are roughly 500. The majority of these are located in London, as one of their purposes is to administer the financial aspects of trade between the United Kingdom, their home country and any other country where their interests are represented. They are primarily concerned with international banking activities. London is very much a centre for such activity and these banks hold large stocks of foreign currency deposits. In fact, between 80 and 90 per cent of the liabilities of these foreign banks (based in London) are held in foreign currency. They act as a link between those who have foreign currency deposits and those who want to borrow them. To some extent these foreign currency funds may simply be demanded for speculative purposes on the foreign exchange market, but they are also a major source of capital for investment.

Other financial intermediaries

Although the retail banks ultimately act as a link between millions of lenders and borrowers, they still have to compete with other financial intermediaries to attract their deposits. These other financial intermediaries have their own specialized functions. But recently many of them have diversified. They compete with one another in particular types of financial business. Examples of such intermediaries include **building societies**, **finance houses** and the **National Savings Bank**. Each of their specialized areas of interest is detailed below.

Building societies

Traditionally, building societies took their deposits from millions of small savers and lent to house-buyers for periods of twenty-five or thirty years. As financial intermediaries, they specialized in long-term lending. However, they now offer banking services: cheque accounts, cash machines and a wide range of services that were traditionally the preserve of the banks. They are competing strongly with the banks, just as the banks have been competing for mortgage business. Both sides have diversified. Many experts now think that, as far as their effect on the economy is concerned, banks and building societies are practically indistinguishable.

Building societies have for some years been losing market share. However, this is in large part due to the fact that most of the bigger building societies have turned themselves into banks. It may be that this process will continue.

Finance houses

Finance houses are responsible for financing hire-purchase agreements for periods of two to three years. People usually access the funds through the retailer from whom they are buying the product. In other words, the retailer is often the agent for the finance house. However, finance houses can be approached directly by firms, which can lease equipment from them.

Most finance houses are now subsidiaries of the banks, having at some stage been taken over by them. In any case, they gain their funds largely from the financial and banking sector. These funds are then lent out to those involved in hire-purchase agreements at quite high rates of interest, which reflect the risky nature of this type of lending.

The National Savings Bank

The National Savings Bank is government run and processed through the Post Office. Roughly one-tenth of all savings are at present handled through this bank. Ordinary accounts, investment accounts, savings certificates and premium bonds are all offered to entice depositors. These deposits are then lent to the government, for which they provide a cheap source of finance.

KEY POINTS

18.3

■ The financial network involves many financial intermediaries competing for funds, which can then be lent out, in order to make a profit.

■ UK financial intermediaries include retail banks, merchant banks and foreign banks, building societies, the National Savings Bank and finance houses.

■ In recent years financial intermediaries have become increasingly diversified.

The central bank

At the head of the entire monetary sector there is the **central bank**. All countries have a central bank, in many cases owned and operated by the government. The Bank of England is one of the oldest central banks; it originated in 1694 when a number of businessmen grouped together to form a bank to raise a loan for the government. This bank–government relationship continued to develop and in 1844 the Bank was given the power to control the note issue. In 1946 it was nationalized, making it ultimately responsible to the Treasury and government for the monetary sector and the money supply. It is possible that at some time in the future it will again become independent of the government.

In 1997 the role of the Bank of England was changed dramatically by the new Labour government. There were two major aspects to the changes.

● The Bank of England was given responsibility for monetary policy, given a target inflation rate and made independent of the government in this respect.
● The Financial Services Authority was created to supervise banks and all other aspects of the financial system.

At some time in the future the UK could join the **eurozone**. By becoming a part of the European Monetary Union, it would surrender many of its functions to the European Central Bank. It would cease to be responsible for exchange rate policy and for monetary policy, becoming primarily concerned with domestic banking issues.

Functions of the Bank of England

Here we shall set out the most important functions that the Bank[*] carries out.

***

[*] Whenever 'Bank' is spelt with a capital B it refers to the Bank of England.

Control of the note issue

The Bank of England is responsible for issuing new banknotes and withdrawing old ones. It is the only note-issuing bank in England and Wales, and ultimately it could print as many notes as it liked. This is because today's currency is not backed by gold but by government securities (that is, it is entirely fiduciary). The amount of notes in circulation at any one time is therefore largely dependent on public demand. The Bank is more concerned with money supply as a whole than its specific note component.

The bankers' bank

All banks hold operational accounts at the Bank of England. In short, the Bank of England is the banker for the whole financial community.

Of these accounts, the most important are those belonging to the clearing banks who make settlements amongst themselves after each day's clearing by drawing on their Bank of England accounts.

Finally, the Bank of England may lend money to the banks if they become short of cash. In this context the Bank of England is described as the *lender of last resort*. It is crucially important that the depositors have confidence in their bank's ability to meet its obligations. In order to be sure that they can do this, the banks will turn for a loan to the Bank of England. Normally this is just one way of making sure that the system functions smoothly. In times of crisis, if it is quite certain that an individual bank is in difficulty because it has been badly managed, the Bank of England may allow the bank to fail rather than keep on lending.

The government's bank

As we are all aware, the government collects large sums of money through taxation. The government also spends and distributes equally large sums. Consequently, the government, like any other commercial concern, needs a bank. It has several accounts at the Bank of England. Furthermore, when these accounts run low it is also the Bank that arranges and finances any borrowing. The Bank of England administers the National Debt, making sure that holders of Treasury bonds receive their interest payments and that Treasury bills are paid on maturity. (Bonds are long-term loans to the government, generally for ten to twenty years.)

Control of foreign exchange affairs

As agent for the government the Bank of England supervises the nation's foreign currency reserves. According to the exchange rate policies of the day, the Bank will use these reserves to buy and sell currency on the foreign exchange market. This is done through the aptly named **exchange equalization account**. For many years the United Kingdom has had a managed exchange rate. Although strong market forces can lead to changes in the exchange rate, the Bank of England normally has a target range. It keeps the exchange rate within this range. If the exchange rate starts to fall below it, the Bank uses its reserves of foreign exchange to buy sterling, thus defending its value. Also, it uses the reserves to smooth out day-to-day fluctuations.

Control of monetary policy

The Bank of England has always been responsible for implementing monetary policy, but until 1997 the decisions about policy changes were always made after the Chancellor of the Exchequer had discussed the situation with the Governor of the Bank of England. It was understood that the Treasury would always be in ultimate control of monetary policy.

Since 1997, policy decisions have been made by the Monetary Policy Committee (MPC) of the Bank of England. This consists of the four most senior officials of the Bank and four respected experts in the field who are independent of the Bank and the government of the day. An important part of the Bank's overall responsibility concerns the research and expertise which is needed to ensure that the monthly decisions of the MPC are appropriate to the economic situation. The objective of this important change was to take policy decisions out of the political arena and to ensure that counter-inflation policy was carried out in a firm and efficient way. The way monetary policy works will be explored in more detail in Chapter 27.

KEY POINTS

18.4

- The UK central bank is the Bank of England, set up in 1694, and formally nationalized in 1946.

- The main functions of the Bank of England are (1) to control the issue of notes, (2) to be a bank for the financial community, (3) to be the government's bank, (4) to control foreign exchange affairs and (5) to decide upon and implement monetary policy.

How banks work

The money supply, as given in the definition of M4, was defined earlier in the chapter broadly as notes and coin, and all bank deposits. We now look at how the Bank of England and the banks together determine the stock of money in the banking system at any one time.

A fractional reserve banking system

Predecessors of modern-day banks were goldsmiths and moneylenders. These individuals had the strongest vaults. Other people who had gold (and other valuables) but no means of protection began to ask goldsmiths and moneylenders to store their gold and valuables for safe-keeping. The goldsmiths and moneylenders charged a fee for this safe-keeping service. It turned out that only a fraction of the total amount of gold and other valuables left with these guardians was ever withdrawn over any time period. That is, only a small fraction of clients would ask for their deposits at any one time. Thus, to meet the requests of those clients, the vault-owners needed to keep only a relatively small fraction of the total deposits 'on reserve'.

Now, if you were a vault-owner and knew that only a certain percentage of deposits would be requested in any one time period, you could lend the remainder out at interest and make additional income, besides the fee for the use of your vault. This is how banks grew up as part of a **fractional reserve banking system**. In other words, in such a system, reserves on hand to meet net withdrawal demands by depositors are some fraction less than 100 per cent of total deposits. Nowadays, reserves are not kept in the form of gold but in the form of deposits with the Bank of England and other very liquid assets.

The banks' balance sheet

Banks use double-entry accounting. Liabilities show the deposits: they are liabilities in the sense that the bank is liable to have to make good requests for withdrawals from them. Assets show the variety of ways in which banks hold the funds deposited with them. Some are much more liquid than others: cash is perfectly liquid, while loans and overdrafts are quite illiquid because the borrowers would not be able to pay them back immediately on being asked. The assets and liabilities always balance: all liabilities are covered by an asset. Table 18.1 shows combined assets and liabilities of UK banks.

Table 18.1

Summary balance sheets for all banks in the UK
£ billions, end December 1998

Liabilities
Sterling deposits	970.4
Foreign currency deposits	1081.7
CDs	262.4
Other liabilities	274.3
Total liabilities	2588.7

Assets
Sterling short-term loans	346.1
Sterling advances	727.0
Foreign currency short-term loans	1003.6
Bills	31.3
Investments	340.1
Other assets	140.5
Total assets	2588.7

Source: British Bankers' Association, *Banking Business*

Reserves

Banks must maintain a percentage of their customer deposits as **reserves**. Take a hypothetical example. If the required level of reserves, the **reserve asset ratio**, is 20 per cent and the bank has £1 billion in customer deposits, then it must hold at least £200 million as reserves. It can hold these reserves in the form of notes and coin, balances with the Bank of England and a range of liquid assets, which can easily be turned into cash if required. These include money lent at call on the short-term money market, Treasury bills (short-term loans to the government) and bank bills (short-term loans to firms). If a bank has reserves in excess of £200 million, then it will wish to make more loans (or advances) to customers. If it does not, then it is forgoing interest which could be earned on loans backed by the reserves in excess of £200 million. If, on the other hand, the bank's reserves fall below the £200 million mark, it will have to call in some of its loans. This reduces deposits to the point where the level of reserves is again 20 per cent of total deposits.

Liquidity versus profitability

There is an inverse relationship between liquidity and profitability: the greater the liquidity, the lower the interest rate; the greater the profitability, the lower the liquidity. Advances to customers are the most profitable form of business, but the loans are not liquid because in general they will take time to be paid off.

So banks must carefully balance their need for adequate levels of reserve assets against their desire to earn profits by maximizing advances to customers. If they make too many advances, they may find themselves with insufficient liquid funds to meet their obligations when customers withdraw deposits.

Assets and liabilities

3 Arrange the following items on the proper side of the member bank's balance sheet, that is, under Liabilities or Assets. In the case of the assets, say how liquid each is and explain why.
(a) demand deposits
(b) notes and coin
(c) time deposits
(d) balances with the Bank of England
(e) advances to customers
(f) holdings of government bonds
(g) bank buildings and fixtures
(h) borrowings from other banks

The banks and the Bank of England

Over time there has been a growing demand for bank loans. We observe large increases in banks' supply of money. How does this credit expansion occur?

We have already seen that making loans is profitable for banks. If customers want loans, and their banks consider them to be reasonably good risks, loans will generally be made available. But supposing the banks are short of reserve assets? In order to meet their obligations after the new loans have been made, they may require extra cash.

Their first reaction could be to withdraw their money at call on the money market. Alternatively, an individual bank may be able to borrow on the inter-bank market. (Banks with a temporary surplus of cash will lend to banks which are short of cash.) Another possibility is to sell some bills. These are very liquid assets which can readily be sold for cash.

A bank that is expanding its lending activity may be able to meet its obligations in these ways for some time. But supposing all the banks are seeking to expand their lending activities? If they all withdraw loans from the money market, they will all be left with insufficient cash.

When this happens the banks turn to the Bank of England. The Bank will buy bills from them for cash. This 'relieves the shortage', as the saying is in the City. It ensures that there is always sufficient liquidity in the monetary system. The banks will always be able to meet their obligations.

Why should the Bank of England do this? There are two reasons. One is its role as 'lender of last resort'. If a bank *cannot* meet its obligations, then there would be a rapid and disastrous loss of confidence in the bank. Its customers would all rush to withdraw their deposits at once. The bank would fail, and many of its customers would go bankrupt. The economic consequences of a bank failure would be serious: bankruptcies would entail unemployment and loss of income for large numbers of people. So the Bank of England maintains sufficient liquidity to ensure that banking business continues. There is a second reason why the Bank of England will lend to the banks. If it did not, then the shortage of cash would force up interest rates. Now sometimes this is exactly what the Bank of England wants. If there is a need for a tighter monetary policy, higher interest rates will reduce the demand for loans and, ultimately, the level of spending in the economy. But mostly the objective is to keep interest rates fairly stable. Sharp rises in interest rates are very unpopular, with people with mortgages, people borrowing to buy consumer durables, or firms wanting to invest. So although the Bank of England *could* control the growth of bank lending (and so the money supply) by refusing to lend to the banks, it generally restricts itself to raising interest rates and carries on lending. It relies upon higher interest rates to reduce the *demand* for loans.

What actually happens when the banks borrow from the Bank of England? The banks borrow by *selling* Treasury and bank bills to the Bank of England, which pays for the bills with a cheque drawn on itself. This is done by means of a repo, which is short for a sale and repurchase agreement. This states that the banks will buy the bills back from the Bank in about two weeks' time. When, over time, the Bank of England increases its lending in this way, the cash base of the monetary system increases. The overall effect is that the Bank of England pumps extra liquidity into the banking system by itself creating credit.

If the Monetary Policy Committee decides to *raise* interest rates generally, it will continue to lend to the banks, but at the new, higher repo rate decided by the committee. The banks will then pass on the higher rate to their customers so that all loans cost more.

The cash base of the monetary system has already been defined as M0, or notes and coin plus banks' operational balances with the Bank of England. The result of the Bank of England's lending to the banks is a payment for a bank or a Treasury bill. The previous holder of this bill now has cash and will deposit it in a bank account. The bank will place the cash in its account with the Bank of England.

M0 has increased by the amount of the Bank of England's credit creation. In other words, the cash base of the banking system, sometimes known as the **monetary base**, has increased. The monetary base is the foundation on which bank lending rests; it includes the banks' most liquid reserve assets.

KEY POINTS

18.5

- ■ We have a fractional reserve banking system in which banks hold a percentage of deposits as reserves.

- ■ The liquidity of banks' assets, and their profitability, are inversely related.

- ■ When a bank's holdings of reserves increase, that bank can expand its lending.

- ■ The Bank of England can increase the level of banks' reserves (the cash base of the monetary system) by buying bills from the banks.

- ■ As banks' reserves increase they can expand their lending by a multiple of the initial increase in reserve assets. Thus the money stock increases correspondingly.

The money multiplier

We have already seen that banks need hold only a small proportion of their total assets in the form of cash (notes and coin, and balances with the Bank of England). Consider what happens if they acquire increased deposits of cash by the means just described. Supposing they receive an extra £1 million. They might decide to keep 5 per cent of it in reserve against future withdrawals. They can then make a loan of £950 000. The borrower will spend the money on, say, machines. If the manufacturer of the machines deposits the money in the same bank, it will then have the original reserve, £50 000, and the new deposit of £950 000. If it keeps 5 per cent of the new deposit, £47 500, and makes a further loan of £902 500, further credit will have been created, and the process can go on for some time and many more loans.

Now it is true that, when a loan is spent, the seller of the goods involved could put the money in another bank. But if the cash base is expanding for all the banks, they will all be lending more too. So the resulting increases in deposits will accumulate in all of them.

We can now make a generalization about the extent to which total deposits will increase when the banking system's reserves of cash are increased. If we assume that all banks lend as much as they are able, then the expansion of credit resulting from a given increase in the cash base will be a multiple that increases. We call this multiple the **money multiplier**. The following equation applies:

$$\text{maximum money multiplier} = \frac{1}{\text{cash ratio}}$$

The above approach gives the theory of credit creation, which can help us to understand how lending activity may increase. In practice, however, it seems that banks may commit themselves to making a quantity of loans which they judge to be profitable, and then make sure that they have sufficient liquid reserves to back up their lending. In other words, the process may work in reverse.

Maintaining confidence

In practice there is no single cash ratio applicable to all banks. Instead banks must observe **capital adequacy requirements**. They must keep some proportion of their assets in the form of liquid reserves. The proportions, or ratios, required vary according to the type of lending involved. Riskier kinds of business require a high level of reserve assets to back them.

Maintaining confidence is crucial to the efficient functioning of the banking system. As we have seen, if people lose confidence in a bank they will all want to withdraw their deposits. Since banks operate on a fractional reserve system they could not satisfy all their customers' demands at once, and the bank would crash. The Bank of England maintains confidence by providing liquidity in the form of loans to the banking system when funds are short (the lender of last resort function).

A particular problem arises when everyone believes that the central bank will always rescue a bank which has insufficient funds to meet its obligations. That bank will have no incentive to manage itself effectively. This is called moral hazard because it can lead to banking systems being inefficient.

The Financial Services Authority

Until 1997, the Bank of England was responsible for supervising the banks to ensure that they observed the capital adequacy requirements and made loans in a prudent way. It vetted all banks' accounts at least every three months and met with senior management regularly. Each institution was judged individually and the system was regarded as flexible and efficient.

Then Barings (a merchant bank) collapsed. The immediate cause was a series of very imprudent and fraudulent deals in the Far East markets. It was clearly shown that the bank had been badly managed. This raised a question as to whether the Bank had supervised it properly. Its supervisory department did not come well out of this episode. In addition, there had been other instances of supervision failure. With so much evidence of incompetence, the Bank of England allowed Barings to fail. It was eventually bought for £1 by the Dutch bank, Ing. Many depositors lost money. The shareholders lost everything.

As part of the major changes of 1997, the government set up the Financial Services Authority (FSA) and made it responsible for the supervision of the entire financial system. It works in collaboration with the Treasury and the Bank of England. The expectation is that the FSA will considerably tighten the effectiveness of regular supervision. Its remit includes the vetting of financial advisers and fund managers to ensure that they do not mislead the public. Watch this space: within the next few years it should become clear how well the FSA has succeeded. If supervision works well, moral hazard can be avoided.

To the extent that it can create workable rules which protect depositors from bad financial management, supervision can greatly increase confidence in the banking and financial system, thus making it more efficient and effective in recycling funds for investment in profitable ways.

Supervision does not mean protecting banks: if they are to work efficiently, they must have the incentive of knowing that the Bank of England will not bail them out if they behave imprudently. This is why collaboration between the FSA and the Bank of England is important.

KEY POINTS

18.6

- The maximum money multiplier is the reciprocal of the reserve asset ratio.
- Capital adequacy requirements should ensure that banks do not overlend.
- Monetary policy limits credit creation.
- The Financial Services Authority is responsible for supervising the banks and other financial intermediaries.

The Monetary Policy Committee

Mervyn King, a deputy governor of the Bank of England, has said that the Bank's Monetary Policy Committee (MPC), of which he is a member, does not intend to surprise financial markets when setting Britain's interest rates. Pundits in City banks (and on newspapers, for that matter) ought to do as the MPC does: watch the economic news from month to month, and judge how it affects the MPC's ability to hit its target inflation rate, excluding mortgage-interest payments, of 2.5 per cent.

Perhaps Mr King's message is getting through at last. When interest rates went up in September, most commentators were caught on the hop. When rates rose by a further quarter point, to 5.5 per cent, on 4 November, few were surprised. In a poll of City economists earlier this week, a big majority had forecast an increase. Economists also had no trouble predicting that eurozone rates would rise.

What made an increase in British rates so predictable? The likely reasons would seem to be unexpectedly strong growth, a tight labour market and a hot housing market.

The economy, which grew by 0.9 per cent in the third quarter, is at or above its sustainable trend and looks set to carry on that way. Although some labour market statistics suggest that wage pressures are muted, others indicate that, as unemployment continues to fall, the scarcity of workers, especially those with skills, is pushing average earnings up faster than some on the MPC would like. And September's rate increase has done little to dampen the housing market. According to Halifax, a bank, house prices rose by 2.8 per cent in October alone, the most in one month since 1988. Lately there has been evidence that homeowners have been beginning to borrow against the increased value of their properties – a practice known as equity withdrawal, last seen in the late 1980s and early 1990s. Fear that this will feed already buoyant consumer spending may have helped push rates up.

Although the rate rise was expected, it would be a surprise if all the MPC had voted for it. Two of its members, DeAnne Julius and Sushil Wadhwani, are known to think that Britain's ability to grow without inflation has increased in recent years – or at any rate that it is worth holding interest rates down to test the theory. Others are less optimistic, and ascribe much of Britain's good inflation performance to the strength of sterling: downward price pressures on imported goods have offset and disguised inflationary pressures at home. Mr Wadhwani also thinks it best to assume that sterling will stay at its current heights, implying that imported inflation will continue to

be kept in check. That is an argument against a rate increase. Again, his colleagues are not so sure. They expect sterling to weaken: to offset the effects of this weakening on inflation rates, policy will have to be tighter.

Bank of England's repo rate

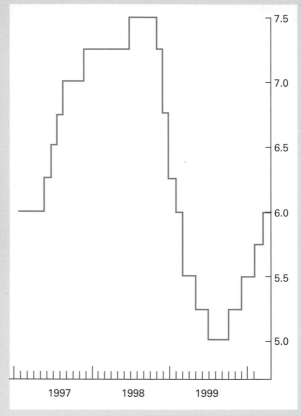

Source: *The Economist*, 6 November 1999

1 In your own words, describe the role of the MPC.
2 Why were interest rates more likely to rise than fall in late 1999?
3 Why were the MPC unlikely to agree entirely on the best policy?
4 Since this article was written, what has happened to inflation? Has it accelerated at any time? If so, what were the reasons?
5 What has happened to interest rates since this article was written?
6 In what ways have monetary policies changed since 1999?

Exam Preparation

Multiple choice questions

1 Which of the following is the least liquid of the assets of a clearing bank?
   A bank bills
   B balances at the Bank of England
   C cash in tills
   D advances to customers
   E money at call

2 Which one of the following is not a function of money?
   A unit of account
   B source of credit
   C store of value
   D medium of exchange
   E standard for deferred payments

3 If all banks observe a 20 per cent reserve asset ratio, by how much can the banking system increase deposits in response to a new deposit of £100?
   A £100
   B £200
   C £400
   D £500
   E £2000

4 Which of the following is a liability to a retail bank?
   A bankers' deposits
   B deposits
   C money at call
   D overdrafts

5 What type of activity is likely to be the most profitable for a bank?
   A making loans and overdrafts to customers
   B buying more Treasury bills
   C buying more bank bills
   D buying shares in other companies

Essay questions

1 What factors determine the levels of advances made by retail banks?

2 To what extent has the Bank of England been successful in controlling inflation?

3 (a) Identify the main types of financial intermediary to be found in the United Kingdom, and explain how they facilitate flows of funds between lenders and borrowers.
   (b) Discuss the argument that financial intermediation can affect a country's rate of economic growth.

4 Why do all advanced economies have a central bank (such as the Bank of England)?

PART D

MICROECONOMIC THEORY

On completing PART D
you should find the
following websites
useful and interesting.

- **www.carol.co.uk**
- **www.ft.com**

Carol is the acronym for Company Annual Reports On Line. As you will see stated in Table 20.1, public limited companies must make their annual reports available to the public. This site offers such an opportunity for companies worldwide. An interesting development at this site is the annual reports designed specifically for the Internet.

Company reports can also be requested by phoning the *Financial Times*. **www.ft.com** provides the same opportunity online. This newspaper's site was upgraded in February 2000 and offers unrestricted access not only to every story in the current edition, but also to its vast archive. The site provides its own business search engine and the stated aim is to be the leading Internet resource for business people everywhere. It is certainly useful for students of economics, especially as it is updated daily. It is also hyperlinked from other sites – such as Barclays Bank, listed below.

- **www.dis.strath.ac.uk/business**

This is another site offering a type of business index. Although it does not have the razzmatazz of many Internet sites, it is a good source of UK sites that contain business information. It is maintained by the Department of Information Science based at the University of Strathclyde in Glasgow.

- **www.barclays.co**

Most big companies (including the banks) operate a website. Our reason for quoting this specific site is that Barclays Bank has provided an excellent service for students. The bottom line is that it is seeking new customers, and the Internet provides a good showcase; so it has filled the window with video-enhanced images. To sample just a snippet: on arriving at the homepage, select 'campus recruitment' and then 'links' – you'll be surprised at the opportunities on offer. CNN, ITN, the *FT*, *The Times*, the Press Association, Reuters, *The Economist* and more are all hyperlinked to enable you to find up-to-date news, which could well accelerate completion of a coursework assignment.

- **www.journals.uchicago.edu/jcr/home.html**

The *Journal of Consumer Research* is one of many academic journals that uses the Internet to promote sales. However, the site is not simply about subscribing. Contents pages and article abstracts are available online. As you can imagine from the journal title, much of the research it publishes relates to microeconomic theory. Try it and see what's happening at the sharp end.

- **www.cbi.org.uk**
- **www.tuc.org.uk**

The demand and supply of labour and their related factor rewards are introduced within a theoretical framework towards the close of Part D. A principal purpose of the exercises and case studies incorporated in this text is to highlight those theoretical positions that need to be applied, and contrasting perspectives can be gleaned by visiting these two sites. The CBI is the UK's leading employers' organization and the TUC represents employees who are members of a union. By exploring and comparing the issues dealt with by these two distinct organizations, the labour market can be analysed in theory and practice.

19

Consumer choice

When we first discussed the theory of demand in Chapter 3, we gave several reasons why the quantity demanded went up when the price of something went down. We pointed out that, as the price of a good falls, individuals would substitute some of that good for other things. Additionally, when the price of one good in a consumer's budget goes down with all other prices remaining the same, that person's buying power will actually be greater. A person not only *feels* better off, he or she *is* better off. With a constant money income, when the price of one good falls, the person clearly has more real spending or purchasing power.

The theory of demand is important, and so too is its derivation, because it allows us to arrange the relevant variables, such as price, income and taste, in such a way as to understand the real world better and even perhaps generate predictions about it.

How do we *derive* the theory of demand? We examine two explanations: first, the traditional **utility analysis** and second, the more comprehensive **indifference curve analysis**. Utility theory appears conceptually attractive on the grounds of its simplicity, but it soon turns out to be rather wanting. Hence we resort to indifference curves as a more rigorous derivation of downward-sloping demand curves.

LEARNING OUTCOMES

On completing this chapter you should understand:

- Utility theory and the related concept of diminishing marginal utility
- The theory that lies behind deriving the demand curve
- Indifference curve analysis and the indifference map
- Budget constraint
- Normal and inferior goods

Utility theory

When you buy something, you buy it because of the satisfaction you expect to receive from having and using it. For just about everything that you like to have, the more you have of it, the higher the level of satisfaction you receive. Another term that can be used for satisfaction is **utility**. This property is common to all goods that are desired. The concept of utility is, however, purely subjective. There is no way that you or I can measure the amount of utility that a consumer might be able to obtain from a particular good, for utility does not mean 'useful' or 'utilitarian' or 'practical'. For this reason there can be no accurate scientific assessment of the utility that someone might receive by consuming, say, a Mars bar or a packet of crisps relative to the utility that another person might receive from that same good. Nevertheless, we can infer whether a person receives more utility from consuming one good versus another by that person's behaviour. For example, if an individual buys more coffee than tea (when both tea and coffee are priced equally), we are able to say that the individual receives more utility from consuming coffee than from consuming tea.

The utility that individuals receive from consuming a good depends on their tastes and preferences. These tastes and preferences are assumed to be given and stable for a given individual. An individual's tastes determine how much utility that individual derives from consuming a good, and this in turn determines how that individual allocates their income. In other words, people spend a greater proportion of their income on goods they like. But we cannot explain why tastes are different between individuals. For example, we cannot explain why some people like yoghurt while others do not.

We can analyse in terms of utility the way consumers decide what to buy, just as physicists have analysed some of their problems in terms of what they call force. No physicist has ever seen a unit of force, and no economist has ever seen a unit of utility. In both cases, however, these concepts have proved useful for academic analysis.

Utility and utils

Economists once believed that utility could be measured. They therefore first developed utility theory in terms of units of measurable utility, to which they applied the term **util**. For the moment, we will also assume that we can measure satisfaction using this representative unit called the *util*. Our assumption will allow us to quantify the way we examine consumer behaviour. Thus the first chocolate bar that you eat might yield you 4 utils of satisfaction; the first bag of crisps, 6 utils; and so on. Today no one really believes that we can actually measure utils, but the ideas forthcoming from such analysis will prove useful in our understanding of the way in which consumers choose among alternatives.

Total and marginal utility

Consider the satisfaction, or utility, that you might receive each time that you hire and watch a video-cassette on your home video. There are many video-cassettes to choose from each year and we might reasonably assume that each of them is of the same quality. Suppose you normally hire one video per week. You could, of course, hire two, three or four per week. Presumably each time you hire another video-cassette per week you will get additional satisfaction, or utility. The question, though, that we must ask is, given that you are already hiring one per week, will the next one give you the same amount of additional utility? That additional or incremental utility is called **marginal utility**, where *marginal* is another term for incremental or additional. Understanding the concept of marginal is important in economics, because we make decisions at the margin. This means that, at a particular point, we compare additional benefits with additional costs.

The way to understand the concept of marginal utility is to consider the specific example presented in Table 19.1. Here we show the total and marginal utility of watching video-cassettes each week. The marginal utility is seen to be the difference between the total utility derived from a specific quantity of video-cassettes, say Q, and the total utility derived from one more, $Q + 1$. In our example, when a person has already watched two video-cassettes in one week and then watches another, total utility increases from 16 utils to 19. Therefore, the marginal utility (of watching one more video after having watched two already) is equal to 3 utils.

Table 19.1

Total and marginal utility of watching video-cassettes

If we were able to assign specific numbers to the utility derived from watching video-cassettes each week, we could then obtain a marginal utility schedule that would probably be similar in pattern to the one below. In column 1 is the quantity of video-cassettes watched per week; in column 2, the total utility from each quantity; and in column 3, the marginal utility, which is defined as the change in total utility due to a change of one unit of watching video-cassettes per week.

1 Quantity of video-cassettes (watched per week)	2 Total utility (utils per week)	3 Marginal utility (utils per week)
0	0	
		10
1	10	
		6
2	16	
		3
3	19	
		1
4	20	
		0
5	20	
		−2
6	18	

Graphic analysis

We can transfer the information in Table 19.1 onto a graph, which we do in Figure 19.1. Total utility, which is represented in column 2 of Table 19.1, is transferred in blocks (represented by broken outlines) to Figure 19.1(a).

Total utility continues to rise until four video-cassettes are watched per week. This measure of utility remains at 20 utils through the fifth video-cassette, and at the sixth video-cassette per week falls to 18 utils, because we assume that, at *some* quantity consumed per unit time period, dislike sets in. If we connect the tops of the total utility blocks by a smooth line, we arrive at a representation of the total utility curve associated with watching video-cassettes during a one-week period. This is shown in Figure 19.2(a). Notice that the total utility curve first rises, reaches a peak, and then falls.

Marginal utility

If you look carefully at Figures 19.1(a) and 19.1(b), the notion of marginal utility becomes very clear. In economics, the term *marginal* always refers to a change in the total. The marginal utility, for example, of watching three video-cassettes a week as opposed to two video-cassettes a week is the incremental change in total utility and is equal to 3 utils per day. Marginal utility is represented by the shaded portion of the blocks in Figure 19.1(a).

We can transfer these shaded portions to Figure 19.1(b) and produce a graphic representation of marginal utility. When we connect the tops of these marginal utility rectangles in Figure 19.2(b) we come up with a smoothly sloping marginal utility curve. Notice that that curve hits zero if more than four video-cassettes are watched per week. At zero marginal utility, the consumer has watched

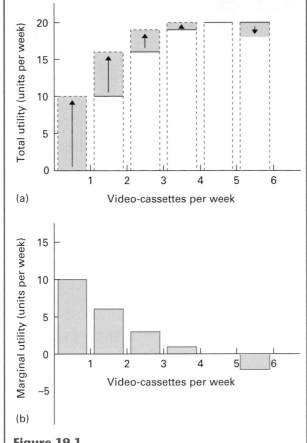

Figure 19.1
Total and marginal utility in discrete units
In (a), the broken outline indicates a total utility for each
rate of viewing of video-cassettes per week. The shaded
portion of each box indicates a marginal utility for each
video-cassette watched per week. When we transfer the
shaded boxes to (b), we have a diagram representing
marginal utility.

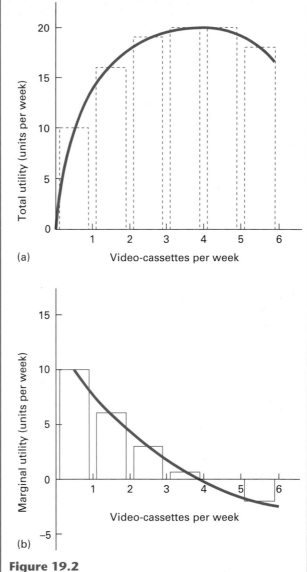

Figure 19.2
Total and marginal utility
If we take the total utility units from column 2 in Table 19.1,
we obtain rectangles like those presented in Figure 19.1(a).
If we connect the tops of the rectangles with a smooth line,
we produce a total utility curve that peaks somewhere
between four and five video-cassettes per week and then
slowly declines (part (a)). Marginal utility is represented by
the increment in total utility, shown as the shaded blocks in
Figure 19.1(b). When these blocks are connected by a
smooth line, we obtain the marginal utility curve (part (b)).

all the videos that he or she wants to and does not want to
watch any more. The last video-cassette watched at zero
marginal utility gives the consumer no additional satisfaction, or utility.

When marginal utility becomes negative, as it does in
this example after more than four video-cassettes per week
are watched, it means that the consumer is fed up with
watching video-cassettes and would require some form of
compensation to watch any more. When marginal utility is
negative, the additional unit consumed actually lowers
total utility by becoming a 'nuisance'.

KEY POINTS

19.1

- Utility is defined as want-satisfying power; it is a property common to all desired goods and services.

- We artificially try to measure units of utility in utils.

- It is important to distinguish between total utility and marginal utility. Total utility is the total satisfaction derived from the consumption of a given quantity of a good. Marginal utility is the change in total utility due to a one-unit change in the consumption of the good.

Diminishing marginal utility

Notice that in Figure 19.2(b) marginal utility is continuously declining. This property of marginal utility has been named **diminishing marginal utility**. There is no way that we can prove diminishing marginal utility; nonetheless, economists for years have believed strongly in the assertion of diminishing marginal utility. Diminishing marginal utility has even been called a 'law'. This supposed law concerns a psychological, or subjective, utility that you receive as you consume more and more of a particular good. Stated formally, the law is

As an individual consumes more of the same good per unit of time, utility increases (up to a point at least). However, the extra utility added by an extra (marginal) unit of that good does not increase at a constant rate. Rather, as successive new units of the good in question are consumed, after some point that total utility will grow at a slower and slower rate. Otherwise stated, as the amount of a good consumed per unit of time increases, the marginal utility of the good tends to decrease.

Calculating marginal utility

Quantity of X consumed	Total utility (utils)
0	0
1	20
2	50
3	70
4	80

1 What is the marginal utility of consuming the first unit of X?

2 What is the marginal utility of consuming the fourth unit of X?

3 When does marginal utility start to diminish?

4 Using your own example, describe the law of diminishing marginal utility. (If possible, make it an explanation of some retail practice.)

Optimizing consumption choices

Every consumer has a limited income. Choices must be made. When a consumer has made all their choices about what to buy and in what quantities, and the total level of satisfaction, or utility, from that set of choices is as great as it can be, we say that the consumer has optimized consumption choices. When the consumer has attained an optimum consumption basket of goods and services, we say that he or she has reached **consumer optimum**.

Consider a simple example that involves two goods. The consumer has a choice between spending income on the rental of video-cassettes and spending income on the purchase of food. Suppose that the last pound spent on food yielded 3 utils of utility, but the last pound spent on video-cassette rentals yielded 10 utils of utility. Would this consumer not increase total utility if some pounds were taken away from food consumption and allocated to video-tape rentals? The answer is 'yes'. Given diminishing marginal utility, more money spent on renting videos will reduce marginal utility per last pound spent, whereas fewer pounds spent on food consumption will increase marginal utility per last pound spent. The optimum – where total utility is maximized – might occur when the satisfaction per last pound spent on both food and renting videos per week is, say, 5 utils. Thus the amount of goods consumed depends on the prices of the goods and the income of consumers.

A little algebra

The idea of consumer optimum can be well expressed in algebraic terms by examining the ratio of marginal utilities and prices of individual products. As already outlined, the consumer optimum idea is based on the principle that a consumer maximizes personal satisfaction when money income is allocated in such a way that the last pound spent on good X, good Y, good Z etc. yields equal amounts of marginal utility. In the following formula, marginal utility (MU) from good X is indicated by MU of good X. For good Y, it is MU of good Y, and so on. The algebraic formulation of the consumer optimum principle therefore becomes:

$$\frac{\text{MU of good X}}{\text{price of X}} = \frac{\text{MU of good Y}}{\text{price of Y}} = \dots = \frac{\text{MU of good Z}}{\text{price of Z}}$$

where X, Y, …, Z indicate the different goods and services that the consumer might purchase.

We know, then, that the proportion of MU of X over the price of X must equal the proportion of MU of any other good or service over its price. You must recognize that the application of this principle is not an explicit or conscious act on the part of consumers. Rather, we are describing a model of consumer optimum.

Making the right decision: getting value for money?

Suppose that a rational man has £10 to spend on a pub lunch. Beer costs him £2 per pint and sandwiches are £1 each. His utility from consumption is as follows:

Beer Pints	Total utility
1	30
2	55
3	75
4	90
5	100

Sandwiches No.	Total utility
1	13
2	25
3	36
4	46
5	55
6	63
7	70
8	76
9	81
10	85

5 How should this person use his money to obtain the highest possible level of welfare? **A√**

6 What would happen to this consumer optimum position if the price of beer increased to £3 per pint? **A√**

7 Why is the principle of consumer optimum purely theoretical?

Source: Adapted from S. Charles and A. Webb, *The Economic Approach to Social Policy*, Wheatsheaf, 1986

We can apply the theory of consumer optimum to the way in which people use their time. Every individual must make a choice among all possible uses of time. For example, the marginal utility received from the last minute used to study economics should not be radically different from the marginal utility received from the last minute used to study geography (assuming, of course, that you are maximizing grades while faced with a time constraint). If these marginal utilities are greatly out of line, then obviously you should change the time-mix.

Remember here that we are not assuming that you receive utility from spending time studying either economics or geography (although this is a possibility). Rather, it is the outcome of the time spent studying – higher grades and perhaps a better job in the future – that generates the utility.

How a price change affects the consumer optimum

Consumption decisions are summarized in the theory of demand, which, you will recall from Chapter 3, states that the amount purchased is inversely related to price. We can now see why by using the theory of diminishing utility.

Decisions to purchase are made such that marginal utility of the last unit purchased and consumed is just equal to the price that had to be paid, that is, the opportunity cost for that last unit. No consumer, when optimizing, will buy ten units of a good per unit time period when the subjective valuation placed on the tenth unit is less than the price of the tenth unit.

If we start out with the consumer optimum and then observe a price decrease, we can predict that consumers will respond to the price decrease by consuming more. Why? Because, before the price change, the marginal utility of the last unit was about equal to the price paid for the last unit. Now, with a lower price, it is possible to consume more than before. If the theory of diminishing marginal utility holds, the purchase and consumption of additional units will cause marginal utility to fall. Eventually, it will fall to equate marginal utility with the price of the final unit consumed. The limit to this increase in consumption is given by the theory of diminishing marginal utility. At some point, the marginal utility of an additional unit would be less than what the person would have to give up (the price) of that additional unit.

Look at a hypothetical demand curve for video-cassette rentals per week for a typical consumer (Figure 19.3). At a price of £5 per video-cassette rental, the marginal utility of the last video-cassette rented per week is MU_1. At a price of £4 per video-cassette rental per week, the marginal utility is represented by MU_2. Because of the theory of diminishing marginal utility, MU_2 must be less than MU_1. What has happened is that, at a lower price, the number of video-cassette rentals per week increased from two to three; marginal utility must have fallen. At a higher consumption rate, marginal utility falls to meet the lower price for video-cassette rental per week.

The substitution effect

What is happening all along, as the price of, say, video-cassette recorder rental falls, is that consumers are substituting the now relatively cheaper video-cassette rentals for other goods and services, such as restaurant meals, live concerts and the like. We call this the **substitution effect** of a change in price of a good, because it occurs when consumers substitute in favour of relatively cheaper goods away from relatively more expensive ones.

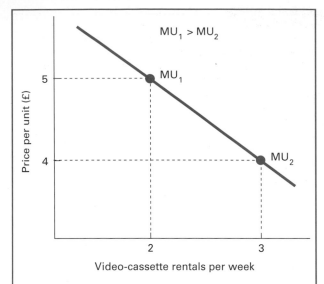

Figure 19.3
Changing video-cassette rental prices and marginal utility

The rate of video-cassette rentals per week will increase as long as the marginal utility per last video-cassette rental per week exceeds the cost of that rental. Therefore, a reduction in price from £5 to £4 per video-cassette rental will allow consumers to increase consumption until marginal utility falls from MU_1 to MU_2 (because of the theory of diminishing marginal utility).

The income effect

There is another reason why a reduction in price would cause an increase in the quantity demanded (or an increase in price would cause a reduction in the quantity demanded). It has to do with the ability of individuals to purchase more or less goods and services when there is a price change in one of the goods and services now being consumed. A fall in the price of any one item being purchased during, say, a week increases the purchasing power of any given amount of money income. A fall in the price of any good being consumed results in an increase in real income – the amount of goods and services that one is able to purchase. Given this increase in real income, most individuals will tend to buy more of most goods and services that they are now consuming. This increase in quantity demanded due to a price reduction, which increases real income, is called the **income effect** of a change in price. (Usually the substitution effect is more important than the income effect, except for price changes of goods that constitute a fairly large part of a person's total budget.)

The demand curve revisited

Linking together the theory of diminishing utility and the theory of equal marginal utilities per pound gives us a negative relationship between the quantity demanded of a good or service and its price. As the relative price of video-cassette rental goes up, for example, the quantity demanded will fall; and as the relative price of video-cassette rental goes down, the quantity demanded will rise. Figure 19.3 shows this demand curve. As the relative price of video-cassette rental falls, the consumer can maximize total utility only by purchasing more of them, and vice versa. In other words, the relationship between price and quantity desired is simply a downward-sloping demand curve. Note, though, that this downward-sloping demand curve (the theory of demand) is derived under the assumption of constant tastes and incomes. You must remember that we are keeping these important determining variables constant when we simply look at the relationship between price and quantity demanded.

Why diamonds are more expensive than water

Even though water is essential to life and diamonds are not, water is cheap and diamonds are dear. The economist Adam Smith in 1776 called this the 'diamond–water paradox'. The paradox is easily understood when we make the distinction between total utility and marginal utility. The total utility of water greatly exceeds the total utility derived from diamonds. What determines the price, though, is what happens at the margin. We have relatively few diamonds, so the marginal utility of the last

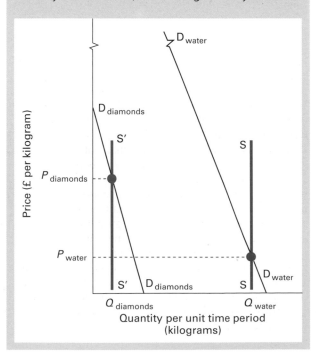

diamond consumed is high. The opposite is true for water. Total utility does not determine what people are willing to pay for a particular commodity; marginal utility does. Look at the situation graphically. We show the demand curve for diamonds, labelled $D_{diamonds}$. The demand curve for water is labelled D_{water}. We plot quantity in terms of kilograms per unit time period on the horizontal axis. On the vertical axis we plot price in pounds per kilogram. We use kilograms as our common unit of measurement for water and diamonds. We could just as well have used gallons or litres.

Notice that we have drawn the demand curve for water with a break in it to illustrate that the demand for water is many, many times the demand for diamonds. We draw the supply curve of water as S at a quantity Q_{water}. The supply curve for diamonds is given as S' at quantity $Q_{diamonds}$. At the intersection of the supply curve of water with the demand curve of water, the price per kilogram is P_{water}. The intersection of the supply curve of diamonds with the demand curve of diamonds is at $P_{diamonds}$. Notice that $P_{diamonds}$ exceeds P_{water}. Diamonds sell at a higher price than water.

8 Would the analysis presented apply to other 'necessities' such as food?

9 Why is the marginal utility of diamonds so high?

10 In hot summers the supply of water in the United Kingdom becomes a matter of concern. Does this affect the utility of water?

Deriving the market demand curve

The demand curve we have been talking about is one that relates directly to an individual. But what about a *market* demand curve, that is, the demand curve that represents the entire market for a particular good or service? How can we derive a market demand curve from the individual ones we have analysed?

Actually, deriving a market demand curve from individual demand curves is not difficult. What we have to do is add together all the individual demands horizontally (assuming that each individual's decisions are made independently of others'). We know that not all people are alike. We know, for example, that even at very low prices certain individuals will demand no video-cassette rental whatsoever. So, to derive a demand curve for the entire market, we must add up each individual's demand. This is what we do in Table 19.2 and Figure 19.4. The figure shows that the individual demand curves are fitted together to obtain the market demand curve for video-cassette rental by what we call *horizontal addition*. Notice that the good's demand is expressed in quantity per time period. We include a time period in the demand analysis because we are talking about a flow through time of a demand for a specific good.

Table 19.2

Video-cassette rentals demanded per week
Individuals A, B and C present us with the various quantities of video-cassette rentals they intend to rent at various relative prices: £2, £3 and £4. When we add quantities demanded by these individuals, we get the total or market quantity demanded at each of these various prices.

	£2	£3	£4
Individual A's quantity demanded	4	3	2
Individual B's quantity demanded	2	1	0
Individual C's quantity demanded	1	0	0
Market quantity demanded	7	4	2

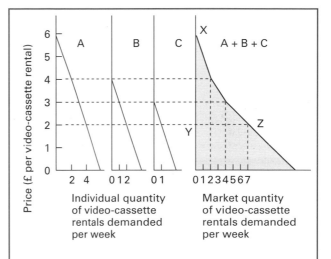

Figure 19.4

Deriving the market demand curve
Individual A's demand curve is shown first, then individual B's and individual C's. By adding these three demand curves horizontally, we obtain the market demand curve represented by the bold line on the right-hand side.

Consumer surplus

Table 19.2 and its graphic presentation in Figure 19.4 provide us with the basis of an understanding of the concept of consumer surplus. We have shown the market demand for a society of three individuals. Suppose now that the rental charge for video-cassette hire is £2. At that price the quantity demanded is seven per week. We note from Table 19.2 that individual A would have been prepared to pay £4 for video hire. Presumably he considered that he would have received at least £4 of utility from viewing a video. Individual B was prepared to pay £3 for video hire and again we can presume that this reflects the utility obtained from watching a particular film. Individual C is not prepared to pay more than £2 for the rental of a video. What significance is there if the latter price is indeed what all three members of our imaginary society actually have to pay for video rental? If the charge made to all three individuals is the same

(£2), then individuals A and B could be said to have received extra utility for which they have not had to pay. It is only individual C who actually equated her utility with the price. Thus in terms of Figure 19.4 the whole of the area above the horizontal line marking the price charged (£2) and below the demand curve is the measure of 'surplus' utility obtained by individuals A and B but not paid for. This area is called **consumer surplus** (it is denoted by the triangle XYZ). The term is of relevance to us when we come to consider whether all consumers pay a common price. Indeed, it might be possible for a producer to charge some individuals more than others – in other words, to discriminate between them and thus transfer some of this consumer's surplus to himself. We examine this possibility in Chapter 22.

Utility analysis – a summary

The analysis of consumer demand using utility theory may appear abstract. That, of course, must be true every time we attempt to hypothesize anything about people's behaviour. But utility theory was developed for a very specific reason. It allowed economists to understand the importance of the factors that influence demand and the quantity demanded.

The theory of consumer choice is a theory that helps economists predict how consumers will react to changes in price, income and so on. The goal of this analysis, as well as of any other in this text, is to allow us to predict what will happen when an important determining variable changes. Because we have used an example concerning consumer choice about video-cassette rentals, this does not mean that the analysis stops there. It can be extended to any good or service.

KEY POINTS

19.2

- The theory of diminishing marginal utility tells us that the extra utility added by the marginal unit of a good consumed falls.

- The consumer maximizes total utility by equating the marginal utility of the last pound (or penny) spent on one good with the marginal utility per last pound (or penny) spent on all other goods. He or she is then in consumer equilibrium.

- In order to remain in consumer equilibrium, a price decrease requires an increase in consumption; a price increase requires a decrease in consumption.

- Assuming that we can measure utility, and further assuming that the theory of diminishing marginal utility holds, the demand curve must slope down – quantity demanded and price are inversely related.

Indifference curve analysis

While the theory of diminishing marginal utility can be fairly well accepted on intuitive grounds, if we want more elegant theorizing we can translate our discussion into graphic analysis with what are called 'indifference curves' and 'the budget constraint'. Here we discuss these terms and their relationship, and demonstrate consumer equilibrium in geometric form.

On being indifferent

What does it mean to be indifferent? It usually means that you do not care one way or the other about something: you are equally disposed to either of two alternatives. With this interpretation in mind, we turn to two choices, video-cassette rentals and restaurant meals. In Table 19.3, we show several combinations of video-cassette rentals and restaurant meals per week that our representative consumer considers to be equally satisfactory. That is, for each combination A, B, C and D, this consumer will have exactly the same level of total utility.

This simple numerical example happens to concern video-cassette rentals and restaurant meals per week, but this example is used to illustrate general features of indifference curves and related analytical tools that are necessary for deriving the demand curve. Obviously, we could have used any other two commodities. Just remember that we are using a specific example to illustrate a *general* analysis.

We plot these combinations graphically in Figure 19.5, with restaurant meals per week on the horizontal axis and video-cassette rentals per week on the vertical axis. These are our consumer's indifference combinations – the consumer finds each combination as acceptable as the others. Each one carries the same level of total utility. When we connect these combinations with a smooth curve, we obtain what is called an indifference curve. Along the indifference curve, every combination of the two goods in the equation yields exactly the same level of total utility. Every point along the indifference curve is

Table 19.3

Combinations that yield equal levels of satisfaction
The combinations A, B, C and D represent varying combinations of video-cassette rentals and restaurant meals per week that give an equal level of satisfaction to this consumer. In other words, the consumer is indifferent about these four combinations.

Combination	Video-cassette rentals per week	Restaurant meals per week
A	1	7
B	2	4
C	3	2
D	4	1

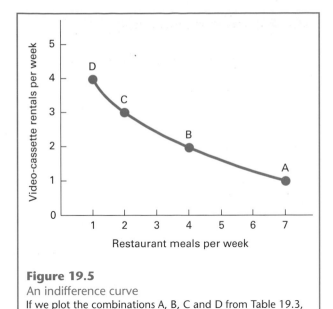

Figure 19.5
An indifference curve
If we plot the combinations A, B, C and D from Table 19.3, we obtain the curve ABCD, which is called an indifference curve.

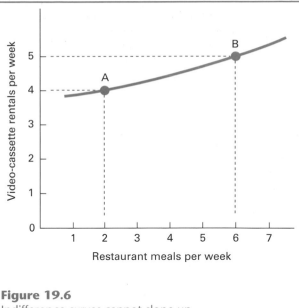

Figure 19.6
Indifference curves cannot slope up
Point B represents a consumption with more video-cassette rentals per week and more restaurant meals per week than point A. B is always preferred to A. Therefore A and B cannot be on the same indifference curve, which is positively sloped, because an indifference curve shows equally preferred combinations of the two goods.

equally desirable to the consumer; for example, four video-cassette rentals per week and one restaurant meal per week will give our representative consumer exactly the same total satisfaction as, say, two video-cassette rentals per week and four restaurant meals per week.

Properties of indifference curves

Indifference curves have special properties relating to their slope and shape.

Indifference curves usually slope down

The indifference curve that we showed in Figure 19.5 sloped down. That is, it had a negative slope. Consider Figure 19.6. Here we show two points, A and B. Point A represents four video-cassette rentals per week and two restaurant meals per week. Point B represents five video-cassette rentals per week and six restaurant meals per week. Clearly, B is always preferred to A, because B represents more of everything. If B is always preferred to A, then it is impossible for points A and B to be on the same indifference curve, because the definition of the indifference curve is a set of combinations of two goods that are equally preferred.

Indifference curves are rarely straight lines

The indifference curve that we have drawn in Figure 19.5 is curved. Why did we not draw a straight line as we have usually done for a demand curve? To find out why we do not draw straight-line indifference curves, consider the implications. We show such a straight-line indifference curve in Figure 19.7. Start at point A. The consumer has no restaurant meals and five video-cassette rentals per week. Now the consumer wishes to go to point B. He or she is

willing to give up only one video-cassette rental in order to get one restaurant meal. Now let us assume that the consumer is at point C. That consumer is consuming one video-cassette rental and four restaurant meals per week. If the consumer wants to go to point D, he or she is again willing to give up one video-cassette rental in order to get one more restaurant meal per week. In other words, no matter how many video-cassettes the consumer rents, he or she is willing to give up one video-cassette rental in order to get one restaurant meal per week. That does not seem to be plausible. According to the theory of diminishing marginal utility, the more of something that a consumer has, the lower will be its marginal utility. Thus, does it not make sense to hypothesize that the more video-cassettes the consumer rents per week, the less he or she will value an additional video-cassette rental? Presumably, when the consumer has five video-cassette rentals and no restaurant meals per week, he or she should be willing to give up more than one video-cassette rental in order to get one restaurant meal. Therefore, once we accept diminishing marginal utility of video-cassette rental consumption, a straight-line indifference curve as shown in Figure 19.7 no longer seems possible. Diminishing marginal utility implies curved indifference curves like that shown in Figure 19.5. In mathematical jargon, an indifference curve is convex with respect to the origin. The reason for this is the theory of diminishing marginal utility. As the individual consumes more of a particular item, the marginal utility of consuming one additional unit of that item falls, or, conversely, as the person

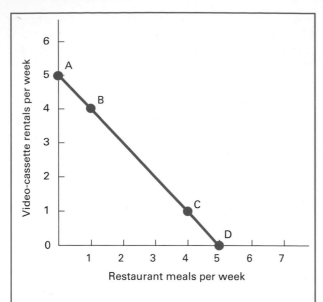

Figure 19.7

The implications of a straight-line indifference curve
If the indifference curve is a straight line, the consumer will be willing to give up the same number of video-cassette rentals (one for one in this simple example) to get one more restaurant meal per week, whether the consumer has no restaurant meals or a lot of restaurant meals per week. For example, the consumer at point A has five video-cassette rentals and no restaurant meals per week. He or she is willing to give up one more video-cassette rental in order to get one more restaurant meal per week. At point C, for example, the consumer has only one video-cassette rental and four restaurant meals per week. Because of the straight-line indifference curve, this consumer is willing to give up the last video-cassette rental in order to get one more restaurant meal per week, even though he or she already has four.

consumes less of it, that good will have a higher marginal utility.

We can measure the marginal utility of something by the quantity of a substitute good that would leave the consumer indifferent. Let us look at this in Table 19.3. Starting with combination A, the consumer has one video-cassette rental but seven restaurant meals per week. To remain indifferent, the consumer would be willing to give up three restaurant meals to obtain one more video-cassette rental (as shown in

combination B). However, to go from combination C to combination D, notice that the consumer would be willing to give up only one restaurant meal for an additional video-cassette rental per week. In other words, the quantity of the substitute considered acceptable changes as the relative scarcity of the original item changes.

Diminishing marginal utility exists throughout this set of choices and consequently the indifference curve in Figure 19.5 will be 'bowed in' (convex when viewed from below). If it were a straight line, marginal utility would not be diminishing but constant; if it were 'bowed out' (concave when viewed from below), marginal utility would be increasing.

The marginal rate of substitution

Above we discussed marginal utility in terms of the marginal rate of substitution between restaurant meals and video-cassette rentals per week. More formally, we can define the consumer's marginal rate of substitution as follows:

> Marginal rate of substitution is the change in the quantity of one good that just offsets a one-unit change in the consumption of another good, such that total well-being remains constant.

We can see numerically what happens to the marginal rate of substitution in our example if we rearrange Table 19.3 into Table 19.4. Here we show restaurant meals in the second column and video-cassette rentals in the third. Now we ask the question: what change in the consumption of restaurant meals per week will just compensate for a one-unit change in the consumption of video-cassette rentals per week and leave the consumer's total utility constant? The movement from A to B reduces restaurant meal consumption by three. Here the marginal rate of substitution of restaurant meals for video-cassette rentals is 1 to 3. If we do this for the rest of the table, we find that, as video-cassette rental consumption increases, the marginal rate of substitution goes from 1 to 3 to 1 to 1. The marginal rate of substitution of restaurant meals for video-cassette rentals per week rises, in other words, as the consumer obtains more video-cassette rentals.

In geometric language, the slope of the consumer's indifference curve (actually, the 'negative of the slope') measures the consumer's marginal rate of substitution. Notice that this marginal rate of substitution is purely

Table 19.4			
Calculating the marginal rate of substitution			
Combination	**Restaurant meals per week**	**Video-cassette rentals per week**	**Marginal rate of substitution of restaurant meals for video-cassette rentals**
A	7	1	
B	4	2	1/3
C	2	3	1/2
D	1	4	1/1

subjective or psychological. We are not talking about financial capabilities, merely about a consumer's particular set of preferences.

The indifference map

Let us now consider the possibility of having both more video-cassette rentals *and* more restaurant meals per week. When we do this, we can no longer stay on the same indifference curve that we drew in Figure 19.5. That indifference curve was drawn for equally satisfying combinations of video-cassette rentals and restaurant meals per week. If the individual now has the possibility of attaining *more of both*, a new indifference curve will have to be drawn above and to the right of the one shown in Figure 19.5. Alternatively, if the individual is faced with the possibility of having *less of both* video-cassette rentals and restaurant meals per week, an indifference curve would have to be drawn *below* and to the left of the existing one in Figure 19.5. Thus, we can map out an entire set of indifference curves corresponding to these different possibilities. What we come up with is an indifference map.

Figure 19.8 shows several possible indifference curves. Indifference curves that are higher than others necessarily imply that more of both goods in question can be consumed. Looked at another way, if one goes from, say, indifference curve I_1 to I_2, it is possible to consume the

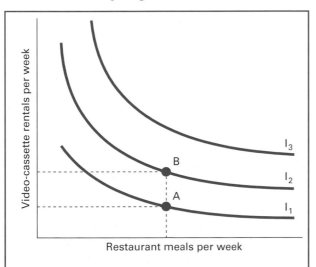

Figure 19.8
A set of indifference curves
An infinite number of indifference curves can be drawn. We show three possible ones. You should realize that a higher indifference curve represents the possibility of higher rates of consumption of both goods. Hence, a higher indifference curve is preferred to a lower one because 'more' is preferred to 'less'. Look at points A and B. Point B represents more video-cassette rentals than point A; therefore indifference curve I_2 has to be a preferred one, since the number of restaurant meals per week is the same at points A and B.

same number of restaurant meals but be able to rent more video-cassettes per week. This is shown as a movement from point A to point B in Figure 19.8. We could do it the other way. When we move from a lower to a higher indifference curve, it is possible to rent the same number of video-cassettes and to consume more restaurant meals per week. Thus, the higher a consumer finds himself or herself on the indifference curve map, the greater that consumer's total well-being – assuming, of course, that the consumer does not become satiated.

The budget constraint

Our problem here is to find out how to maximize consumer satisfaction. In order to do this, we must consult not only our *preferences* – given by indifference curves – but also our *opportunities* – given by our available income, called our **budget constraint**. We might want more of everything, but for any given budget constraint we have to make choices or trade-offs among possible goods. Everyone has a budget constraint; that is, everyone is faced with a limited consumption potential. How do we show this graphically? We must find the prices of the goods in question and determine the *maximum* consumption of each allowed by our consumer's budget. For example, let us assume that video-cassettes rent for £5 each and restaurant meals cost £10. Let us also assume that our representative consumer has a total budget of £30. What is the maximum number of video-cassettes the consumer can rent? Obviously, six. And the maximum number of restaurant meals per week he or she can consume? Three. So we now have, in Figure 19.9, two points on our budget line, which is sometimes called the 'consumption possibilities curve'. The first point is at b on the vertical axis; the second at b′ on the horizontal axis. The line is straight because the prices do not change.

Any combination along line bb′ is possible; and, in fact, any combination in the shaded area is possible. We shall assume, however, that the individual consumer completely uses up his or her available budget, and we shall consider only those points along bb¢ as possible.

The slope of the budget constraint

The budget constraint is a line that slopes downwards from left to right. The slope of that line has a special meaning. To see this, look carefully at the budget line in Figure 19.9. The fall in Y is minus two video-cassette rentals per week (a drop from four to two) for a run in X of one restaurant meal per week (an increase from one to two); and therefore the slope of the budget constraint is –2/1, or –2. This slope represents the rate of exchange between video-cassette rentals and restaurant meals: it is the realistic rate of exchange, given their prices.

Now we are ready to determine how the consumer achieves his or her optimum consumption rate.

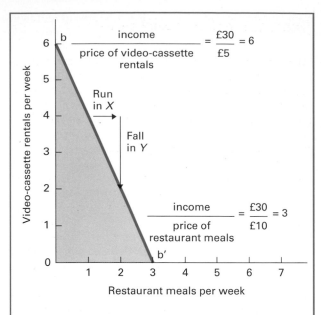

Figure 19.9
The budget constraint
The line bb′ represents this individual's budget constraint. Assuming that video-cassette rentals cost £5 each and restaurant meals cost £10 each and that the individual has a budget of £30, a maximum of six video-cassette rentals or three restaurant meals can be bought. These two extreme points are connected to form the budget constraint. All combinations within the shaded area are feasible.

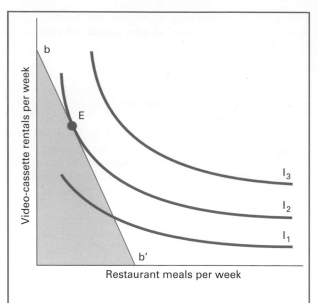

Figure 19.10
Consumer optimum
A consumer reaches an optimum when he or she ends up on the highest indifference curve possible, given a limited budget. This occurs at the tangency between an indifference curve and the budget constraint. In this diagram the tangency is at E.

Consumer optimum revisited

Consumers, of course, will attempt to attain the highest level of total utility possible, given their budget constraint. How can this be shown graphically? We draw a set of indifference curves similar to those in Figure 19.8 and we bring in reality – the budget constraint bb′. Both are drawn in Figure 19.10. Now, since a higher level of total satisfaction is represented by a higher indifference curve, we know that the consumer will strive to be on the highest indifference curve possible. However, the consumer cannot get to indifference curve I_3 because his or her budget will be exhausted before any combination of video-cassette rentals and restaurant meals represented on indifference curve I_3 is attained. This consumer can maximize total utility, subject to the budget constraint, only by being at point E on indifference curve I_2, because here the consumer's income is just being exhausted. Mathematically, point E is called the tangency point of the curve I_2 to the straight line bb′.

Consumer equilibrium is achieved when the marginal rate of substitution (which is subjective) is just equal to the feasible, or realistic, rate of exchange between video-cassette rentals and restaurant meals. This realistic rate is the ratio of the two prices of the goods involved. It is represented by the absolute value of the slope of the budget constraint. At point E, the point of tangency

between indifference curve I_2 and budget constraint bb′, the rate at which the consumer wishes to substitute video-cassette rentals for restaurant meals (the numerical value of the slope of the indifference curve) is just equal to the rate at which the consumer can substitute video-cassette rentals for restaurant meals (the slope of the budget line).

Effects of changes in income

A change in income will shift the budget constraint bb′ in Figure 19.10. Consider only increases in income and no changes in price. The budget constraint will shift outwards. Each new budget line will be parallel to the original one because we are not allowing a change in the relative prices of video-cassette rentals and restaurant meals. We would now like to find out how an individual consumer responds to successive increases in income when nominal and relative prices remain constant. We do this in Figure 19.11. We start out with an income that is represented by a budget line bb′. Consumer optimum is at point E, where the consumer attains his or her highest indifference curve I, given the budget constraint bb′. Now we let money income increase. This is shown by a shift outwards in the budget line to cc′. The consumer attains a new optimum at point E′. That is where a higher indifference curve, II, is reached. Again, the consumer's income is increased so that the new budget line facing him or her is dd′. The new optimum now moves to E″. This is where the indifference curve III is reached. If we connect the three consumer optimum points E, E′ and E″,

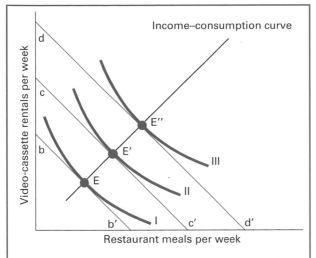

Figure 19.11
The income–consumption curve
We start off with income sufficient to yield budget constraint bb'. The highest attainable indifference curve is I, which is just tangent to bb' at E. Next we increase income. The budget line moves outwards to cc', which is parallel to bb'. The new highest indifference curve is II, which is just tangent to cc' at E'. Finally, we increase income again, which is represented by a shift in the budget line to dd'. The new tangency point of the highest indifference curve, III, with dd' is at point E". When we connect these three points, we obtain the income–consumption curve.

we have what is called an income–consumption curve. The income–consumption curve shows the optimum consumption points that would occur if income for that consumer were increased continuously, holding the prices of video-cassette rentals and restaurant meals constant.

Who cares about the weekly budget?

Assume that you are consuming only meals of pasta and visits to the gym for exercise. Each serving of pasta costs £2, and each visit to the gym costs £4. Given your food and exercise budget, you consume fifteen servings of pasta and five visits to the gym each week. One day the price of pasta falls to £1.50 per serving and the price of gym visits increases to £5. Now you buy twenty servings of pasta and four gym visits per week.

11 Draw the old and new budget constraints, and show the two equilibrium bundles of pasta servings and visits to the gym.
12 What is your weekly budget for food and exercise?

Normal and inferior goods

We have shown in Figure 19.11 that, as income increases, the consumer purchases more of both video-cassette rentals and restaurant meals. This may not necessarily be the case. As income increases, the consumer could purchase more restaurant meals and rent fewer video-cassettes or purchase fewer restaurant meals and rent more video-cassettes. We show these possibilities in Figure 19.12.

In Figure 19.12(a) we show that, as income increases, the consumption of video-cassette rentals increases but the consumption of restaurant meals decreases. In this situation, we call video-cassette rentals a normal good and restaurant meals an inferior good. The definition of a **normal good** is one for which quantity demanded increases as income increases. The definition of an **inferior good** is one for which quantity demanded decreases as income increases. In Figure 19.12(b) we show the opposite situation. As income increases, fewer video-cassettes are rented and more restaurant meals are consumed. Thus, video-cassette rentals become an inferior good and restaurant meals become a normal good.

Price–consumption line

In Figure 19.13 we hold money income and the price of video-cassette rentals constant while we change the price of restaurant meals. Specifically, we keep lowering the price. As we keep lowering the price of restaurant meals, the quantity of meals that could be purchased if all income were spent on restaurant meals clearly increases; thus, the extreme points for the budget constraint keep moving outwards to the right as the price of restaurant meals falls. In other words, the budget line rotates outwards from bb' to bb".

Thus each time the price of restaurant meals falls, a new budget line is formed. There has to be a new optimum point. We find it by locating on each new budget line the highest attainable indifference curve. This is shown at points E, E' and E". We see that, as price decreases for restaurant meals, the consumer purchases more and more restaurant meals per week. We call the line connecting points E, E' and E" the price–consumption curve. It connects the tangency points of the budget constraints and indifference curves, thus showing the amounts of two goods that a consumer will buy when his or her income and the price of one commodity are held constant while the price of the remaining good changes.

Deriving the demand curve

We are now in a position to derive the demand curve by using indifference curve analysis. In Figure 19.14(a) we show what happens when the price of restaurant meals decreases, holding the price of video-cassette rentals

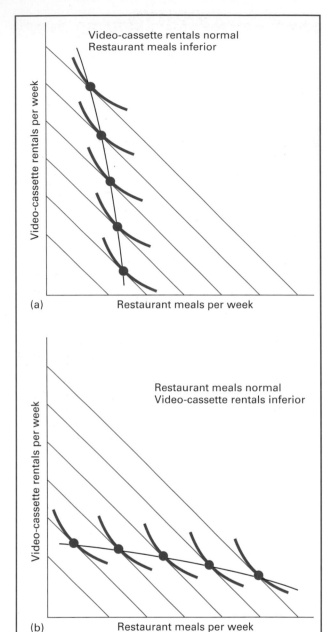

(a)

Video-cassette rentals normal
Restaurant meals inferior

Restaurant meals per week

Restaurant meals normal
Video-cassette rentals inferior

(b)

Restaurant meals per week

Figure 19.12
Inferior and normal goods
We define an inferior good as one for which the quantity demanded decreases as income increases. We define a normal good as one for which the quantity demanded increases as income increases. In (a) we show that, as income increases, the quantity of video-cassettes rented increases, while the quantity of restaurant meals consumed decreases. In (a) video-cassette rentals are a normal good and restaurant meals are an inferior good. In (b) the quantity of video-cassettes rented decreases as the quantity of restaurant meals consumed increases. In (b) video-cassette rentals are an inferior good and restaurant meals are a normal good.

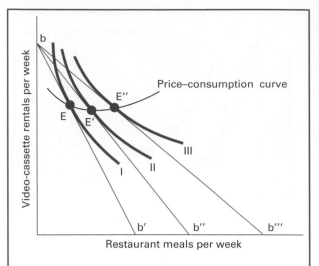

Figure 19.13
Price–consumption curve
In this experiment we hold the price of video-cassette rentals constant, as well as money income. We keep lowering the price of restaurant meals. As we lower the price of restaurant meals, income measured in terms of restaurant meals per week increases. We show this by rotating the budget constraint from bb' to bb" and finally to bb"'. We then find the highest indifference curve that is attainable for each successive budget constraint (which is drawn with a lower and lower price of restaurant meals). For budget constraint bb', the highest indifference curve is I, which is tangent to bb' at point E. We do this for the next two budget constraints. When we connect the optimum points E, E' and E", we derive the price–consumption curve, which shows the combinations of the two commodities that a consumer will purchase when money income and the price of one commodity remain constant while the other commodity's price changes.

constant and income constant. If the price of restaurant meals decreases, the budget line rotates from bb' to bb". The two optimum points are given by the tangency at the highest indifference curve that just touches those two budget lines. This is at E and E'. But those two points give us two price–quantity pairs. At point E the price of restaurant meals is £20; the quantity demanded is two. Thus we have one point that we can transfer to Figure 19.14(b). At point E' we have another price–quantity pair. The price has fallen to £10; the quantity demanded has increased to five. We therefore transfer this other point to 19.14(b). When we connect these two points (and all the others in between), we derive the demand curve for restaurant meals; it is downward sloping.

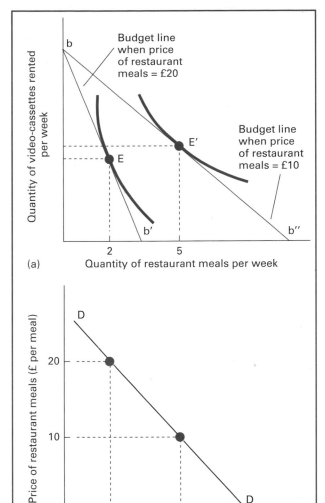

(a)

(b)

Figure 19.14

Deriving the demand curve

In (a) we show the effects of a decrease in the price of restaurant meals from £20 to £10. At a price of £20 the highest indifference curve touches the budget line bb' at point E. The quantity of restaurant meals consumed is two. We transfer this combination – the price of £20, quantity demanded two – down to part (b). Next, we decrease the price of restaurant meals to £10. This generates a new budget line, or constraint, which is bb". Consumer optimum is now at E'. The optimum quantity demanded of restaurant meals at a price of £10 is five. We transfer this point – the price of £10, quantity demanded five – down to part (b). When we connect these two points, we have a demand curve, DD, for restaurant meals.

KEY POINTS

19.3

■ An indifference curve is a set of consumption alternatives, each yielding the same total amount of satisfaction.

■ By definition, an indifference curve cannot intersect with another and each curve is usually convex with respect to the origin.

■ Convex-shaped indifference curves reflect diminishing marginal rates of substitution between the relevant two items.

■ Purchasers of goods and services face a budget constraint and the optimum point of consumption is reached where the slopes of the budget line and of the highest indifference curve possible are the same.

■ If income changes while prices remain fixed, the new series of optimum consumption points is termed 'an income–consumption curve'. When consumers buy more of a good as income rises, it is a normal good; if they buy less, it is an inferior good.

■ If relative prices alter but income remains unchanged, the new series of optimum consumption points is termed 'a price–consumption curve'. The demand curve can be derived from the price–consumption curve.

The snob effect

In 1899 Veblen, an American economist and social critic, published the first proper study of consumerism, a book called *The Theory of the Leisure Class*. Its central concept, and his lasting contribution to economics, was 'conspicuous consumption'.

Veblen's argument was that, as wealth spreads, what drives consumers' behaviour is increasingly neither subsistence nor comfort but the attainment of 'the esteem and envy of fellow men'. At the time, academics thought this mildly convincing. By the 1980s it was commonplace. As economies boomed, the *nouveaux riches* joined the *vieux riches* in the Veblenian binge. Designer labels filled an increasing number of wardrobes; Rolexes were worn loose on bronzed wrists. In the City of London, people watered their plants with Perrier and watered themselves with Dom Perignon ...

Veblen turned on its head the idea that acquisition was always for consumption. Acquisition, he argued, confers honour; it suggests prowess, and achievement. 'In order to gain and to hold the esteem of men,' he wrote, 'wealth must be put in evidence, for esteem is awarded only on evidence.'

Hence the theory of conspicuous consumption. In what Veblen called 'barbarian culture', trophies such as property or slaves were signs of successful aggression. But in modern societies booty is a sign of status and class. Certain sorts of goods convey education and taste. So consumers seek them for two reasons: to show they are members of the classes above and to distinguish themselves from those below ...

For evidence that he was right about the relationship between the price and the perceived value of snobby goods, look at the table below, which reviews the situation over the last century for a range of selected items.

Clearly, the real cost of many classic luxury items has soared. As wealth has spread, so rich consumers have been prepared to pay ever-larger sums to demonstrate status. This has not been lost on luxury-good firms. As the marketing manager at one such company puts it: 'Our customers do not want to pay less. If we halved the prices of all our products, we would double our sales for six months and then we would sell nothing.'

1 Give an example of conspicuous consumption that:
   (a) you are involved in today;
   (b) another member of your family is presently involved in.
2 Why did the demand for snob goods take off in the 1980s?
3 With snob effect goods, what happens to utility when price rises?
4 When income increases, what happens to demand for
   (a) snob goods;
   (b) normal goods;
   (c) inferior goods?
5 (a) Using indifference curve analysis, derive a demand curve to illustrate the Veblen effect.
   (b) Using the diagram, explain the income effect and the substitution effect which happens when the price increases for a good that has snob appeal.

The spiralling cost of luxury-good prices

	Price (£) (year)	1992 price (£)	Percentage increase		Average annual percentage increase
			Nominal	Real terms	Real terms
Russian caviar (2 oz)	0.29 (1912)	85	29 210	645	2.5
Jaguar: most expensive two-seater	310.00 (1932)	48 385	15 510	275	2.2
Parker Duofold fountain pen	1.50 (1927)	155	10 230	278	2.1
Purdey shotgun: top of the line	89.00 (1901)	25 250	28 270	494	2.0
Dunhill lighter 'Rollagas', silver plate	6.75 (1958)	135	1 900	78	1.7
Louis Vuitton suitcase	1.50 (1912)	9 000	5 900	299	1.7
Cartier Tank watch	40.50 (1921)	2 750	6 690	217	1.6
Champagne: non-vintage bottle	0.38 (1912)	22	5 770	49	0.5

Source: Adapted from *The Economist*, 26 December 1992–8 January 1993

Exam Preparation

Multiple choice questions

1 A downward-sloping demand curve
  A has constant price elasticity throughout its length
  B shows the effects of increasing income of consumers
  C can be derived from the theory of diminishing marginal utility
  D shows the effects of changes in the price of substitutes
  E indicates the response of demand to changes in price expectations

2 Assume that a person with a fixed income spends it on only two goods, X and Y. Total utility will be maximized when the total income is distributed so that
  A the average utility of the last unit of X purchased equals the average utility of the last unit of Y purchased
  B the marginal utility of the last unit of X purchased equals the marginal utility of the last unit of Y purchased
  C the marginal utility of the last unit of X purchased divided by the price of X equals the marginal utility of the last unit of Y purchased divided by the price of Y
  D the marginal utility of the last unit of each good purchased is equal to zero
  E the total utility of good X is equal to the total utility of good Y

3 A consumer's marginal utility for an economic good is greater than the price he has to pay for it. This defines
  A complementary goods
  B consumer's surplus
  C a Veblen effect
  D the Giffen concept
  E opportunity cost

4 Assume that a consumer can only purchase three commodities. Satisfaction will be maximized if he purchases
  A equal quantities of each commodity
  B the commodity with the lowest price
  C the commodity which gives the highest total utility
  D the commodity which has the highest marginal utility
  E sufficient quantities of each to make the ratio of price to marginal utility equal for all three commodities

5 Consumers' surplus is
  A the difference between the quantity demanded and the quantity supplied
  B unsatisfied consumer demand
  C unspent disposable income
  D excess demand
  E the difference between the aggregate amount consumers are prepared to pay and the amount they do pay

6 In the diagram below, at output OQ consumer surplus is represented by the area
  A RSQO
  B PSTO
  C PSQO
  D RSP
  E STQ

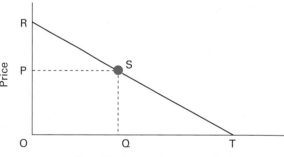

7 The market demand curve for a good slopes down from left to right primarily because
  A marginal utility diminishes as consumption rises
  B substitutes for the good are not available
  C consumers' incomes are finite
  D complementary goods are available
  E price falls as supply increases

8 The diagram below represents the market demand schedule for a product. The increase in consumer surplus enjoyed as a result of a price reduction from OQ to OP is shown by the area
   A PQXY
   B PRZ
   C PQXZ
   D YXZ
   E SXZT

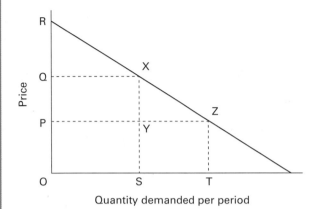

9 If the marginal utility of a good to a consumer is zero it must follow that
   A total utility is also zero
   B total utility for that good is at a maximum
   C the good has no utility (that is, gives no satisfaction)
   D the consumer is in equilibrium with respect to purchases of the good

Essay questions

1 Discuss and illustrate the relevance of total and marginal utility for the determination of consumer demand in the cases of water and gold.

2 Why are demand curves normally thought to be downward sloping? Why is this not always the case?

3 Distinguish between the income and substitution effects of a price change for
   (a) a normal good and
   (b) a Giffen good.

4 Using any economic theory with which you are familiar, explain how consumers allocate their expenditure between different products. Discuss how persuasive advertising and marketing of products affect, if at all, the value of this theory.

5 (a) What assumptions about the nature of consumer tastes underlie the concept of an indifference curve?
   (b) Consider whether the proposition that a decrease in the price of a good will increase the quantity demanded invariably follows from the theory of consumer choice.

6 Given the superiority of indifference analysis as a technique, what use is there for the concept of marginal utility?

7 Do you agree that the theory of consumers' behaviour rests on assumptions which are undermined by the imperfections which exist in the real world?

8 (a) How does economic theory explain the optimum pattern of consumption for an individual consumer?
   (b) Do you agree that in the market-place 'the consumer is king'?

20

Businesses and their costs

LEARNING OUTCOMES

On completing this chapter you should understand:

- The meaning of business, profit maximization and competitive behaviour

- How the economist's definition of profit differs from the accountant's

- The relationship between inputs and output

- The law of diminishing marginal returns

- The meaning of short-run costs to the firm

- The meaning of long-run costs and the benefits arising from economies of scale

The last chapter dealt with a theory of the behaviour of consumers. We were looking at the behind-the-scenes elements that affected the demand side of microeconomics. But, as highlighted previously, knowing about the demand side is not sufficient to understand how the world works; we also have to know about the supply side. Therefore, we now develop a theory of how suppliers behave. We look at what is known in economics as the **theory of the firm**. How do owners of businesses react to changing taxes, changing input prices and changing government regulations? In order to answer these questions, we have to understand the nature of production costs and revenues for each firm owner. In this chapter, we examine the nature of productivity and costs, and in the following chapters we look at the revenue side of the picture.

Defining a business

What is a business? Everybody knows the answer. It is the supermarket down the street, the dress shop around the corner, British Petroleum, the market stall, Marks & Spencer, etc. The list will get very large indeed if we attempt to name every business in the United Kingdom. Everybody also knows that there is a difference between a corporate giant like Coca Cola and the local dress shop. In terms of our analysis, however, we shall not usually make a distinction between these types of firms, except with regard to the market power they have, that is, the extent to which they control the prices of commodities they sell.

There are legal differences, of course, between the various types of businesses, and these are briefly summarized in Table 20.1.

The firm

In general terms we can define a business, or firm, as follows:

> A firm is an organization that brings together different factors of production, such as labour, land and capital, to produce a product or service which it is hoped can be sold for a profit.

The actual size of a firm will affect its precise structure, but a common set-up involves entrepreneur, managers and workers. The entrepreneur is the person who takes the chances. Because of this, the entrepreneur is the one who will get any profits that are made. The entrepreneur also decides who to hire to run the firm. Some economists maintain that the true quality of an entrepreneur becomes evident when he or she can pick good managers. Managers, in turn, are the ones who decide who should be hired and fired and how the business should generally be set up. The workers are the ones who ultimately use the machines to produce the products or services that are being sold by the firm. Workers and managers are paid

Table 20.1

Types of business ownership

Type of business	No. involved in ownership	Examples	Sources of finance	Liability for debts	Profit distribution	Authority and control
Sole proprietor	1	Newsagent, corner shop, butcher, baker	Bank loans and/or personal savings, HP finance, credit etc.	Owner is fully liable for all debts incurred	Owner keeps all profits	Full control by proprietor
Partnership	2 to 20	Doctors, solicitors, dentists, builders	Bank loans and/or personal savings, HP finance, mortgages etc.	At least one partner is fully liable for all debts	Profits shared according to deed of partnership	All partners have equal power (except sleeping-partners)
Private joint-stock company	2 to ∞	Small local breweries[a]	All the above plus the issue of shares to agreed members	Limited liability for debts; each shareholder only risks the amount put in to buy shares	Distributed between all shareholders – dividends being paid per share	Normally directed by shareholders (in proportion to the number of shares held)
Public joint-stock company	2 to ∞	ICI, Shell, banks, Sainsbury[a]	All the above, but the ownership of shares is open to all via the Stock Exchange	As for private joint-stock company, but annual general report must be available to the public and accounts publicized in the national press (a minimum amount of share capital is another prerequisite)		Shareholders appoint a board of directors to act on their behalf (these directors are voted in/out at the AGM)

Note: All the above types of business organization are owned and controlled by private individuals, that is, they form part of the private sector. In contrast government-funded and -organized firms (not detailed above) constitute the public sector.

[a] Since the 1980 Companies Act, a private joint-stock company must include the word 'limited' in its title, and a public joint-stock company must have the words 'public limited company' at the end of its name (this is commonly abbreviated to PLC).

contractual wages. They receive a specified amount for the specified time period. Entrepreneurs are not paid contractual wages. They receive no specified 'reward'. Rather, they receive what is left over, if anything, after all expenses are paid. Profits are therefore the reward paid to the entrepreneur for taking risks.

Profit

The costs of production must include an element of profit to pay for the entrepreneur's services. If the level of profits falls in one area of activity, entrepreneurs may move their resources to an industry where the returns are higher. To illustrate this behaviour economists employ a concept of **normal profit**. Normal profit may be defined as

the minimum level of reward required to ensure that existing entrepreneurs are prepared to remain in their present area of production.

Normal profit is included in the cost of production, as it is an essential minimum reward necessary to attract the entrepreneur into economic activity. Normal profit also highlights that all resources can be employed in several ways (that is, all resources have alternative uses). Consequently, what is meant by 'profit' in economics differs from its general meaning.

To portray the general meaning of profit the following formula could be used:

profits = total revenues − total costs

For economists an alternative formula is required:

economic profits = total revenues − total opportunity cost of all inputs used

What the economic profits formula actually involves will become clearer by looking at two areas of resource allocation and the related cost accounting calculations. The first resource is capital and the second is labour.

Opportunity cost of capital

Firms enter or remain in an industry if they earn, at a minimum, *a normal rate of return*, that is, normal profit. By this term, we mean that people will not invest their wealth in a business unless they obtain a positive competitive rate of return, that is, unless their invested wealth pays off. Any business wishing to attract capital must expect to pay at least the same rate of return on the capital as all other businesses of similar risk are willing to pay. For example, if individuals can invest their wealth in almost any publishing firm and get a rate of return of 10 per cent per year, then each firm in the publishing industry must *expect* to pay 10 per cent as the normal rate of return to present and future investors. This 10 per cent is a *cost to the firm*. This cost is called the **opportunity cost of capital**. The opportunity cost of capital is the amount of income, or yield, forgone by giving up an investment in another firm. Capital will therefore not stay in firms or industries where the expected rate of return falls below its opportunity cost.

Opportunity cost of labour

Sole traders often grossly exaggerate their profit rates because they forget about the opportunity cost of the time that they personally spend in the business. For example, you may know people who run small grocery stores. These people, at the end of the year, will sit down and figure out what their 'profits' are. They will add up all their sales and subtract what they had to pay to other workers, what they had to pay to their suppliers, what they had to pay in taxes and so on. The end result they will call 'profit'. However, they will not have figured into their costs the salary that they could have made if they had worked for somebody else in a similar type of job. For somebody operating a grocery store, that salary might be equal to £6 an hour. If so, then £6 an hour is the opportunity cost of the grocery-store owner's time. In many cases, people who run their own businesses lose money in an economic sense. That is, their profits, as they calculate them, may be less than the amount of labour income they could have earned had they spent the same amount of time working for someone else. Take a numerical example. If an entrepreneur can earn £6 per hour, it follows that the opportunity cost of his or her time is £6 × 40 hours × 52 weeks, or £12 480 per year. If this entrepreneur is making less than £12 480 per year in accounting profits, he or she is actually losing money. (This does not mean that such entrepreneurs are 'stupid'. They may be willing to pay for the non-pecuniary benefits of 'being the boss'.)

We have spoken only of the opportunity cost of capital and the opportunity cost of labour, but we could have spoken in general of the opportunity cost of all inputs. Whatever the input may be, its opportunity cost must be taken into account in order to figure out true economic profits.

Another way of looking at the opportunity cost of running a business is that opportunity cost consists of all explicit (direct) and implicit (indirect) costs. Accountants are only able to take account of explicit costs, though. Therefore, accounting profit ends up being the residual after only explicit costs are subtracted from total revenues.

Accounting profits are not equal to economic profits

You should have a good idea by now of the meaning of profits in economics.

The term *profits* in economics means the income that entrepreneurs earn, over and above their own opportunity cost of time and the opportunity cost of the capital they have invested in their business. Profits can be regarded as total revenues minus total costs – which is how the accountants think of them – but we must now include *all* costs.

We indicate this relationship in Figure 20.1. We are assuming that the accountants' bookkeeping costs for all factors of production except capital are correct.

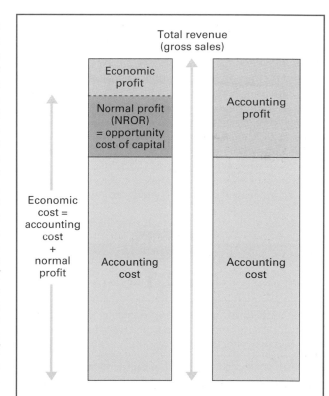

Figure 20.1
Simplified view of economic and accounting profit
Here we see that on the right-hand side total revenues are equal to accounting costs plus accounting profit. That is, accounting profit is the difference between total revenues and total accounting costs. However, we see on the left-hand side that economic costs are equal to accounting costs plus a normal rate of return or normal profit on invested capital, which is the opportunity cost of capital.

Did the university graduate make the right decision?

A university graduate, looking for her first job, turns down a £20 000 per year job offer in order to open her own business. She borrows £150 000 to purchase equipment. Total sales during her first year were £250 000. Total labour costs for the first year were £160 000 and raw material costs were equal to £50 000. She pays £15 000 interest on the loan per year.

1 Estimate the economic profit of this business for the first year.

2 How does this differ from the accounting profit?

3 Why do economists and accountants use different concepts of profit?

The goal of the firm

In most instances we shall use a model that is based on maximization of profits. In other words, the firm's goal is to maximize profit; it is expected to attempt to make the positive difference between total revenues and total cost as large as it can. We use a profit-maximizing model because it allows us to analyse a firm's behaviour with respect to quantity supplied and the relationship between cost and output. Whenever this profit-maximizing model produces poor predictions, we shall examine our initial assumption about profit maximization. We might have to conclude that the primary goal of some firms is not to maximize profits but rather to maximize sales, the number of workers, the prestige of the owners and so on. However, we are primarily concerned with generalizations. Therefore, provided the assumption of profit maximization is correct for most firms, then the model will suffice as a good starting point.

KEY POINTS

20.1

■ The basic forms of private enterprise in the United Kingdom are sole trader, partnerships, private and public joint-stock companies.

■ A firm is an organization that brings together production inputs in order to produce a good or service that can be sold for a profit.

■ Accounting profits differ from economic profits.

■ Economic profits are defined as total revenues minus total costs, where costs include the full opportunity cost of all the factors of production.

■ Single-owner proprietorships often fail to consider the opportunity cost of the labour services provided by the owner.

■ The full opportunity cost of capital invested in a business is generally not included as a cost when accounting profits are calculated. Thus, accounting profits overstate economic profits.

■ Profit maximization is regarded as the main objective when considering a firm's behaviour.

The relationship between inputs and output

A firm takes numerous inputs, combines them using a technological production process, and ends up with an output. There are, of course, many, many factors of production, or inputs. We classify production inputs into two broad categories (ignoring land) – labour and capital. The relationship between output and these two inputs is as follows:

$$\frac{\text{output per unit}}{\text{time period}} = \begin{array}{c}\text{some function of capital}\\\text{and labour inputs}\end{array}$$

Short run versus long run

The time period here is important. Throughout the rest of this chapter we consider a 'short' time period as opposed to a 'long' time period. In other words, we are looking at *short-run* production relationships and *short-run* costs associated with production.

Any definition of the short run will necessarily be arbitrary. We cannot talk in terms of the short run being a specific time period such as a month, or even a year. Rather, we must deal in terms of the short run having to do with the ability of the firm to alter the quantity of its inputs. For ease of understanding, we shall simply define the **short run** as any time period when there is at least one factor of production that has a fixed cost. In the **long run**, therefore, all costs are variable. That is, all factors are variable.

How long is the long run? That depends on each individual industry. For McDonald's (hamburgers), the long run may be four or five months – because that is the time period during which it can add new franchises. For British Steel the long run may be several years – because that is how long it takes to plan and build a new plant.

In most short-run analyses, the factor that has a fixed cost, or is fixed in quantity, is capital. We therefore state that in our short-run model capital is fixed and invariable. This is not unreasonable: in a typical firm, the number of machines *in place* will not change over several months, or even over a year. After all, the input that changes the most is labour. The production relationship that we use, therefore, holds capital constant, or given; labour is variable.

The production function – a numerical example

The relationship between physical output and the quantity of capital and labour used in the production process is sometimes called a **production function**. The term 'production function' in economics owes its origin to production engineers for it is used to describe the technological relationship between inputs and outputs. It therefore depends on the available technology.

Look at Table 20.2. Here we show a production function relating total output in column 2 to the quantity of labour measured in worker-weeks in column 1. When there are no worker-weeks of input, there is no output. When there are five worker-weeks of input (given the capital stock), there is a total output of 50 bushels per week. (Ignore for the moment the rest of that table.) In Figure 20.2 we show this particular hypothetical production function graphically. Note, again, that it relates to the short run and that it is for an individual firm.

Figure 20.2 shows a total physical product curve, or the amount of physical output that is possible when we add successive units of labour while holding all other inputs constant. The graph of the production function in Figure 20.2 is not a straight line. In fact, it peaks at seven worker-weeks and starts to go down. To understand why such a phenomenon occurs with an individual firm in the short run, we have to analyse in detail the **law of diminishing (marginal) returns**.*

Diminishing marginal returns

The concept of diminishing marginal returns applies to many different situations. If you put one seat-belt over your lap, a certain amount of additional safety is obtained. If you add another seat-belt, some more safety is obtained but less than when the first belt was secured. When you add a third seat-belt, again the amount of *additional* safety obtained must be even smaller. In a similar way, Winston Churchill apparently believed that there were diminishing returns to dropping more and more bombs on German steel mills during the Second World War; extra bombs, he felt, merely moved about the wreckage from prior bombs.

The same analysis holds for firms in their use of productive inputs. When the returns from hiring more workers are diminishing, it does not necessarily mean that more workers will not be hired. In fact, workers will be hired until the returns, in terms of the value of the extra output produced, are equal to the additional wages that have to be paid for those workers to produce the extra output. Before we get into the decision-making process, let us demonstrate that diminishing returns can be represented graphically and can be used in our analysis of the firm.

* Other names for this law are diminishing marginal productivity, diminishing marginal returns, diminishing marginal physical productivity, and the law of variable proportions.

Table 20.2

Diminishing returns: a hypothetical case in agriculture
In the first column, we measure the number of workers employed per week on a given amount of land with a given amount of machinery and fertilizer and seed. In the second column, we give their total product, that is, the output that each specified number of workers can produce in terms of bushels of wheat. The last column gives the marginal product. The marginal product is the difference between the output possible with a given number of workers minus the output made possible with one less worker. For example, the marginal product of a fourth worker is 8 bushels of wheat. With four workers, 44 bushels are produced, but with three workers only 36 are produced; the difference is 8.

Input of labour (no. of worker-weeks)	Total product (output in bushels of wheat per week)	Marginal physical product (in bushels of wheat per week)
0	0	
		10
1	10	
		16
2	26	
		10
3	36	
		8
4	44	
		6
5	50	
		4
6	54	
		2
7	56	
		–1
8	55	

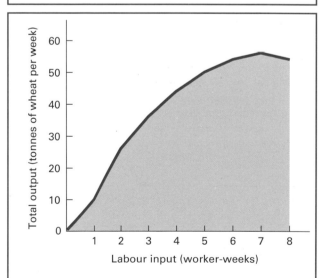

Figure 20.2
A production function
A production function relates outputs to inputs. We have merely taken the numbers from columns 1 and 2 of Table 20.2 and presented them here.

Measuring diminishing returns

How do we measure diminishing returns? First, we limit the analysis to only one variable factor of production (or input). Let us say that that factor is labour. Every other factor of production, such as machines, must be held constant. Only in this way can we calculate the marginal returns from using more workers and know when we reach the point of diminishing marginal returns.

Marginal returns for productive inputs are sometimes specifically referred to as the **marginal physical product**. The marginal physical product of a worker, for example, is the change in total product that occurs when that worker joins an already existing production process. It is also the change in total product that occurs when that worker resigns or is laid off an already existing production process. The marginal productivity of labour therefore refers to the change in output caused by a one-unit change in the labour input.

The marginal productivity of labour may increase initially. That is, a firm starts with no workers, only machines. The firm then hires one worker, who finds it difficult to get the work started. When the firm hires more workers, however, each is able to specialize, and the marginal productivity of the additional workers may actually be greater than it was with the previous few workers. Therefore, at the outset increasing marginal returns are likely to be experienced. Beyond some point, however, diminishing returns must set in; each worker has (on average) fewer machines with which to work (remember, all other inputs are fixed). Eventually, the firm will become so crowded that workers will start running into one another and will become less productive. Managers will have to be hired to organize the workers.

Using these ideas, we can define the law of diminishing returns. For example, consider the two following possible definitions:

> As successive equal increases in a variable factor of production, such as labour, are added to other fixed factors of production, such as capital, there will be a point beyond which the extra or marginal product that can be attributed to each additional unit of the variable factor of production will decline.

or more formally

> As the proportion of one factor in a combination of factors is increased, after a point, the marginal product of that factor will diminish.

Put simply, diminishing returns merely refer to a situation in which output rises less than in proportion to an increase in, say, the number of workers employed.

An example

An example of the law of diminishing returns is found in agriculture. With a fixed amount of land, fertilizer and tractors, the addition of more people eventually yields

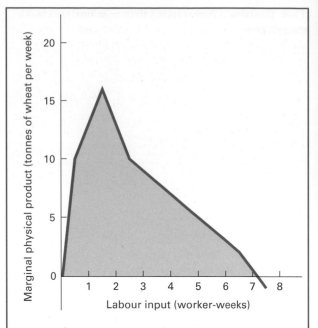

Figure 20.3
Marginal product – diminishing marginal return
On the horizontal axis, we plot the number of workers; and on the vertical axis, we plot the marginal physical product in bushels of wheat (in each case we have taken the data from Table 20.2). Hence, when we go from no workers to one worker, marginal product is 10. We show this at a point between 0 and 1 worker-weeks to indicate that marginal product relates to the change in the total product as we add additional workers. When we go from one to two workers, the marginal product increases to 16. After two workers, marginal product declines. Therefore, after two workers we are in the area of diminishing marginal physical returns. Since total product, or output, reaches its peak at seven workers, we know that after seven workers marginal physical product is negative. In fact when we move from seven to eight workers, marginal product becomes negative.

decreasing increases in output. A hypothetical set of numbers illustrating the law of diminishing marginal returns is presented in Table 20.2. The numbers are presented graphically in Figure 20.3. Marginal productivity (returns from adding more workers) first increases, then decreases, and finally becomes negative. When one worker is hired, total output goes from 0 to 10. Thus, marginal physical product is equal to 10. When another worker is added, marginal physical product increases to 16. Then it begins to decrease. The point of diminishing marginal returns occurs after two workers are hired.

Diminishing marginal returns and the theory of the firm

If we now introduce business costs we can begin to sense the central importance of the law of diminishing returns.

For example, consider the relationship between marginal cost, that is, the cost of an extra unit of output, and the incidence of diminishing marginal physical returns. Let us assume that each unit of labour can be purchased at a constant price. Further assume that labour is the only variable input. We see that, as more workers are hired, marginal physical product first rises and then falls after the point where diminishing returns are encountered. Thus, the marginal cost of each extra unit of output will first fall as long as marginal physical product is rising, and then it will rise as long as marginal physical product is falling. Consider, for example, the data in Table 20.2 (page 347). Assume that a worker is paid £100 a week. When we go from zero labour input to one unit, output increases by 10 bushels of wheat. Thus, each of those 10 bushels of wheat has a marginal cost of £10. Now the second unit of labour is hired, and it, too, costs £100. Output increases by 16. Thus, the marginal cost is £100/16 = £6.25. We continue the experiment. We see that the next unit of labour yields only 10 additional bushels of wheat, so that marginal cost starts to rise again back to £10. The following unit of labour increases marginal physical product by only 8, so that marginal cost becomes £100/8 = £12.50.

All the action lies at the margin

Units of labour (per eight-hour day)	Marginal product of labour (per eight-hour day)
1	2
3	6
5	10
7	14
9	18
11	22
12	20
13	10
14	5
15	3
16	2

Examine the table, which gives the record of marginal physical product for an imaginary firm, and answer the following questions relating to output.

4 Suppose that this firm wants to increase output over the short run.
   (a) How much labour time is required to produce the first unit?
   (b) Do the fourth, fifth and sixth units of output require more or less labour time than the first unit? How does this differ from the accounting profit?
5 (a) Suppose that we have hired eleven labourers and now want to increase short-run output in batches of 20. To produce the first batch of 20 (beyond the eleventh labourer), how many extra labour hours are required?
   (b) What will the next consecutive batch of 20 cost, in labour hours?

For questions 6 to 9, assume that wage rates are equal to £100 per eight-hour day.

6 By hiring the twelfth unit of labour, what was the extra cost to the firm of this first batch of 20?
7 What was the marginal cost of output in that range? (Hint: If 20 units cost £100, what did one unit cost?)
8 What will the next batch of 10 cost the firm?
9 What is the marginal cost of output per unit over that range?
10 What is happening to the marginal cost of output?
11 How are the marginal product of labour and the marginal cost of output related?

Marginal costs in turn affect the pattern of other costs, for example, average variable costs and average total costs. Once these other costs have been discussed, the importance of marginal cost analysis (and the above section) will become clearer.

KEY POINTS

20.2

- The technological relationship between output and input is called the production function. It relates output per unit time period to the several inputs, such as capital and labour.
- After some rate of output, the firm generally experiences diminishing marginal returns.
- The law of diminishing returns states that, if all factors of production are held constant except one, equal increments in that one variable factor will eventually yield decreasing increments in output.
- A firm's short-run costs are a reflection of the law of diminishing marginal returns. Given any constant price of the variable input, marginal costs decline as long as marginal product of the variable resource goes up. At the point of diminishing marginal returns, the reverse occurs. Marginal costs will rise as the marginal product of the variable input declines.

Short-run costs to the firm

In the short run, a firm incurs certain types of costs. Economists label all costs incurred as **total costs**. Then we divide total costs into total fixed costs and total variable costs, which we explain below. The relationship, or identity, is therefore

total costs ≡ total fixed costs + total variable costs

After we have looked at the elements of total costs, we shall find out how to compute average and marginal costs.

Total fixed costs

Let us look at a business such as the Ford Motor Company. The decision-makers in that corporate giant can look around and see big machines, thousands of parts, huge buildings, and a multitude of other pieces of plant and equipment that are in place, that have already been bought. Ford has to take account of the wear and tear of this equipment, no matter how many cars it produces. The payments on the loans taken out to buy the equipment and the rates on the land have to be paid regardless of output. All these costs are unaffected by variations in the amount of output. That is, they are mainly the overhead costs. This leads us to a very straightforward definition of fixed costs:

> All costs that do not vary, that is, costs that do not depend on the rate of production, are called fixed costs, or *sunk* costs.

Let us take as an example the fixed costs incurred by a manufacturer of pocket calculators. This firm's total fixed costs will equal the cost of the rent on its equipment and

the insurance it has to pay. We see in Table 20.3 that total fixed costs per day are £10. In Figure 20.4, these total fixed costs are represented by the horizontal line at £10 per day. They are invariant to changes in the output of calculators per day: no matter how many are produced, fixed costs will remain at £10 per day.

The difference between total costs and total fixed costs is total variable costs (total costs − total fixed costs = total variable costs).

Total variable costs

Total **variable costs** are those costs whose magnitude varies with the rate of production. They are sometimes referred to as *operating costs*. One obvious variable cost is wages paid. The more the firm produces, the more labour it has to hire, the more it has to pay. There are other variable costs, though. One is parts. In the production of calculators, for example, microchips must be bought. The more calculators that are made, the more chips must be bought. Part of the rate of depreciation (the rate of wear and tear) on machines that are used in the production process can also be considered a variable cost, if depreciation depends partly on how long and how intensively the machines are used. Total variable costs are given in column 3 of Table 20.3. These are translated into the total variable cost curve in Figure 20.4. Notice that the variable cost curve lies below the total cost curve by the vertical distance of £10. This vertical distance represents, of course, total fixed costs.

Table 20.3

An example of the costs of production

1 Total output (Q/day)	2 Total fixed costs TFC	3 Total variable costs TVC	4 Total costs TC = (2) + (3)	5 Average fixed costs AFC = (2)/(1)	6 Average variable costs AVC = (3)/(1)	7 Average total costs ATC = (4)/(1)	8 Total costs TC (4)	9 Marginal cost MC = change in (4)/change in (1)
0	£10.00	0	£10.00	–	–	–	£10.00	
								£5.00
1	10.00	£5.00	15.00	£10.00	£5.00	£15.00	15.00	
								3.00
2	10.00	8.00	18.00	5.00	4.00	9.00	18.00	
								2.00
3	10.00	10.00	20.00	3.33	3.33	6.67	20.00	
								1.00
4	10.00	11.00	21.00	2.50	2.75	5.25	21.00	
								2.00
5	10.00	13.00	23.00	2.00	2.60	4.60	23.00	
								3.00
6	10.00	16.00	26.00	1.67	2.67	4.33	26.00	
								4.00
7	10.00	20.00	30.00	1.43	2.86	4.28	30.00	
								5.00
8	10.00	25.00	35.00	1.25	3.13	4.38	35.00	
								6.00
9	10.00	31.00	41.00	1.11	3.44	4.56	41.00	
								7.00
10	10.00	38.00	48.00	1.00	3.80	4.80	48.00	
								8.00
11	10.00	46.00	56.00	0.91	4.18	5.09	56.00	

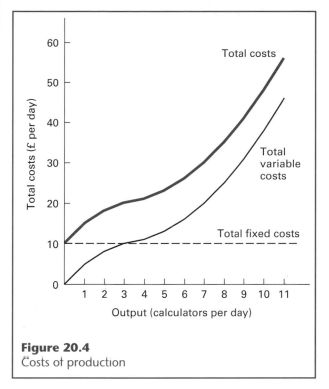

Figure 20.4
Costs of production

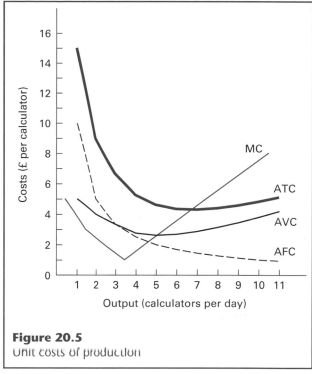

Figure 20.5
Unit costs of production

Short-run average cost curves

In Figure 20.4 we see total costs, total variable costs and total fixed costs. Now we want to look at average cost. The average cost concept is simply one in which we are measuring cost per unit of output. It is a matter of simple arithmetic to figure the averages of these three cost concepts. We can define them simply as follows:

$$\text{average total costs} = \frac{\text{total cost}}{\text{output}}$$

$$\text{average variable costs} = \frac{\text{total variable cost}}{\text{output}}$$

$$\text{average fixed costs} = \frac{\text{total fixed cost}}{\text{output}}$$

The arithmetic is done in columns 5, 6 and 7 of Table 20.3, while the numerical results are translated into graphical format in Figure 20.5. Let us see what we can observe about the three average cost curves in that figure.

Average fixed costs

Average fixed costs (**AFC**) continue to fall throughout the output range. In fact, if we were to continue the diagram further to the right, we would find that average fixed costs would get closer and closer to the horizontal axis. This is because total fixed costs remain constant. As we divide this fixed number by a larger and larger number of units of output, the result, AFC, has to become smaller and smaller. In business this is called 'spreading the overhead'.

Average variable costs

We assume a particular form of the **average variable cost** (**AVC**) curve. The form that it takes is U-shaped: first it falls; then it starts to rise. It is certainly possible to have other shapes of the average variable cost curve.

Average total costs

This curve has a shape similar to the average variable cost curve. However, it falls even more dramatically in the beginning and rises more slowly after it has reached a minimum point. It falls and then rises because **average total costs** (**ATC**) is the summation of the average fixed cost curve and the average variable cost curve. Thus, when AFC plus AVC are both falling, it is only logical that ATC would fall too. At some point, however, AVC starts to increase while AFC continues to fall. Once the increase in the AVC curve outweighs the decrease in the AFC curve, the ATC curve will start to increase and will develop its familiar U-shape.

Marginal cost

We have stated repeatedly in this text that the action is always on the margin – movement in economics is always determined at the margin. This dictum holds true within the firm also. Firms, according to the analysis we use to predict their behaviour, are very interested in their **marginal cost**. Since the term *marginal* means additional or incremental, marginal costs refer to those costs that result from a one-unit change in the production rate. For example, if the production of ten calculators per day costs a firm £48 and the production of eleven calculators costs it £56 per day, then the marginal cost of producing the eleventh calculator per day is £8.

National Health Service costs

National Health Service trusts are required to publish the costs of all major medical activity; they are then ranked in league tables of efficiency. This became necessary as large variations in the costs of treatment became apparent. For example, a hip replacement on the National Health can cost as little as £2000 in some areas and more than £8000 in other areas.

12 For the purposes of publishing efficiency tables, which category of short-term costs would be most useful?

13 Using the marginal cost of hip replacements, explain the importance of identifying a normal rate of return for the National Health Service.

14 Explain why costs differ in a national-based service such as health.

We find marginal cost by subtracting the total cost of producing all but the last unit from the total cost of producing all units, including the last one. Marginal costs can therefore be measured by using the formula

$$\text{marginal cost} = \frac{\text{change in total cost}}{\text{change in output}}$$

We show the marginal costs of calculator production per day in column 9 of Table 20.3, where marginal cost is defined as the change in total cost divided by the change in output. In our particular example, we have changed output by one unit every time, so we can ignore the denominator in that particular formula.

This marginal cost schedule is shown graphically in Figure 20.5. Like average variable costs and average total costs, marginal costs first fall and then rise. It is interesting to look at the relationship between marginal costs and average costs.

The relationship between average and marginal costs

There is always a definite relationship between averages and marginals. Consider the example of ten football players with an average weight of 200 lb. An eleventh player is added. His weight is 250 lb. This represents the marginal weight. What happens now to the average weight of the team? It must increase. Thus, when the marginal player weighs more than the average, the average must increase. Likewise, if the marginal player weighs less than 200 lb, the average weight will decrease.

There is a similar relationship between average variable costs and marginal costs. When marginal costs are less than average costs, the latter are falling. Conversely, when marginal costs are greater than average costs, the latter are rising. When you think about it, the relationship is obvious. The only way for average variable costs to fall is for the extra cost of the marginal unit produced to be less than the average variable cost of all the preceding units. For example, if the average variable cost for two units of production is £4 a unit, the only way for the average variable cost of three units to fall is for the variable costs attributable to the last unit –the marginal cost –to be less than the average of the past units. In this particular case, if average variable cost falls to £3.33 a unit, then total variable cost for the three units would be three multiplied by £3.33, or (to round it off) £10. Total variable cost for two units is two multiplied by £4, or £8. The marginal cost is therefore £10 minus £8, or £2, which is less than the average variable cost of £3.33.

A similar type of computation can be carried out for rising average variable costs. The only way for average variable costs to rise is for the average variable cost of additional units to be more than that for units already produced. This incremental cost is the marginal cost. Therefore, in this particular case, the marginal costs have to be higher than the average variable costs.

There is also a relationship between marginal costs and average total costs. Remember that average total cost is equal to total cost divided by the number of units produced. Remember also that marginal cost does not include any fixed costs. Fixed costs, by definition, are

A quiz: find the missing numbers

Output (units)	Fixed cost (FC) (£)	Average fixed cost (AFC) (£)	Variable cost (VC) (£)	Average variable cost (AVC) (£)	Total cost (TC) (£)	Average total cost (ATC) (£)	Marginal cost (MC) (£)
1	100	___	40	___	___	___	___
2	100	___	70	___	___	___	___
3	100	___	120	___	___	___	___
4	100	___	180	___	___	___	___
5	100	___	250	___	___	___	___
6	100	___	330	___	___	___	___

15 In the accompanying table we list some cost figures for a hypothetical firm. You should be able to complete all the columns that are left blank. Try to complete this exercise, then check your answer with that shown at the back of the book. **A✓**

fixed and cannot influence marginal costs. Our example can therefore be repeated substituting the term *average total cost* for the term *average variable cost*.

In other words, when marginal costs are less than either average total costs or average variable costs, the last two are falling. Conversely, when marginal costs are greater than either average total costs or average variable costs, the last two are rising. Finally, marginal costs will equal both average total costs and average variable costs at their respective minimum points. These rising and falling relationships can be seen in Figure 20.5. You can also see there that MC intersects AVC and ATC at their respective minimum points.

A taxing exercise on cost curves

It might be useful at this point to consider how to represent the effects of tax on a firm. Let us talk about VAT. Such a tax will affect the cost of each unit produced. It is based on the value of the output, and will affect each unit at a rate of 17.5 per cent.

Let us ask ourselves what happens to fixed costs. The tax is incurred only if the firm produces something. If it produces nothing, it does not have to pay the tax. This means that fixed costs do not change; average fixed costs will remain the same also, so the AFC curve does not change. When it comes to average variable costs, things do change. Each time a new unit is produced, the tax has to be paid. This means that the average variable cost curve will move up vertically by the amount of the tax. Since the average total cost moves up, so does the average total cost curve, and by the same amount.

What about marginal costs? Marginal costs will have to move up also. The marginal cost curve, MC, will move up vertically by the amount of the tax on each unit of production. After all, marginal cost is defined as the increment in costs. If the firm must pay a tax when it produces one more calculator, or whatever, this means that the marginal cost will go up by that tax also.

16 Show what happens to costs as a result of a unit tax such as VAT by copying Figure 20.5 and indicating how the curves will shift after the imposition of VAT. **A✓**

17 What would a lump-sum tax, such as a levy for production, do to each firm's marginal cost curves?

18 Show on a diagram similar to Figure 20.5 how a lump-sum tax affects the average fixed cost curve. **A✓**

Finding minimum costs

At what rate of output of calculators per day does our representative firm experience the minimum average total costs? Column 7 in Table 20.3 shows that the minimum average total cost is £4.28, which occurs at an output rate of seven calculators per day. We can find this minimum cost also by finding the point in Figure 20.5 at which the marginal cost curve intersects the average total cost curve. This should not be surprising. When marginal cost is below average

total cost, average total cost falls. When marginal cost is above average total cost, average total cost rises. At the point where average total costs are neither falling nor rising, marginal cost must be equal to average total cost. When we represent this graphically, the marginal cost curve will intersect the average total cost curve at its minimum.

The same analysis applies to the intersection of the marginal cost curve and the average variable cost curve. When are average variable costs at a minimum? According to Table 20.3, average variable costs are at a minimum of £2.60 at an output rate of five calculators per day. This is exactly where the marginal cost curve intersects the average variable cost curve in Figure 20.5.

KEY POINTS

20.3

- The short run is that period of time during which the firm cannot alter its existing plant size.

- Total costs equal total fixed costs plus total variable costs.

- Fixed costs are those that do not vary with the rate of production; variable costs are those that do vary with the rate of production.

- Average total costs equal total costs divided by output, or ATC = TC/Q.

- Average variable costs equal total variable costs divided by output, or AVC = TVC/Q.

- Average fixed costs equal total fixed costs divided by output, or AFC = TFC/Q.

- Marginal cost equals the change in total cost divided by the change in output.

- The marginal cost curve intersects the minimum point of the average total cost curve and the minimum point of the average variable cost curve.

Long-run cost curves

The long run, as you will remember, is defined as a time period during which *full* adjustment can be made to any change in the economic environment. That is, *in the long run, all factors of production are variable*. For example, in the long run the firm can alter its plant size. Consequently, there may be many short-run curves as a firm develops over the years but only one long-run curve. Long-run curves are sometimes called planning curves, and the long run may be regarded as the **planning horizon**.

We start our analysis of long-run cost curves by considering a single firm contemplating the construction of a single plant. The firm has, let us say, three alternative plant sizes from which to choose on the planning horizon. Each particular plant size generates its own short-run average total cost curve. Now that we are talking about the difference between long- and short-run cost curves, we shall label all short-run curves with an S; short-run average (total) costs will be labelled SAC, and all long-run average cost curves will be labelled LAC.

Look at Figure 20.6(a). Here we have shown three short-run average cost curves for three plant sizes that are successively larger. Which is the optimal plant size to build? That depends on the anticipated rate of output per unit time period. Assume for a moment that the anticipated rate is Q_1. If plant size 1 is built, the average costs will be C_1. If plant size 2 is built, we see on SAC_2 that the average costs will be C_2, which is greater than C_1. Thus, if the anticipated rate of output is Q_1, the appropriate plant size is the one from which SAC_1 was derived.

Note, however, that if the anticipated permanent rate of output per unit time period goes from Q_1 to Q_2, and plant size 1 had been decided upon, average costs would be C_4. However, if plant size 2 had been decided upon, average costs would be C_3, which is clearly less than C_4.

Long-run average cost curve

If we make the further assumption that during the development of a firm the entrepreneur is faced with an infinite number of choices regarding plant size, then we can conceive of an infinite number of SAC curves similar to the three in Figure 20.6(a). We are not able, of course, to draw an infinite number; we have drawn quite a few, however, in Figure 20.6(b).

By drawing the envelope of these various SAC curves we find the **long-run average cost curve** (**LAC**). To be academically precise, the LAC curve should be described as 'wavy' or 'scalloped', since it follows the path of the SAC curves enclosed. By tradition, however, it is portrayed as being tangent to the minimum point of the SAC curves from which it is derived. Either way, the long-run average cost curve represents the cheapest way to produce various levels of output – provided the entrepreneur is prepared to change the size and design of his or her plant. Consequently, long-run average cost curves are sometimes referred to as **planning curves**.

Why the long-run average cost curve is U-shaped

Notice that the long-run average cost curve, LAC in Figure 20.6(b), could be described as U-shaped, similar to the U-shape of the short-run average cost curve developed earlier in this chapter. The reason for the U-shape of the long-run average cost curve is not the same as that for the short-run U-shaped average cost curve. The short-run average cost curve is U-shaped because of the law of diminishing marginal returns. However, that law cannot apply to the long run, because in the long run all

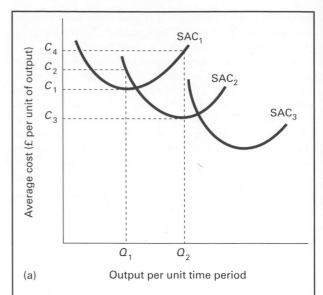

(a) Output per unit time period

Figure 20.6

(a) A preferable plant size

If the anticipated permanent rate of output per unit time period is Q_1, the optimal plant to build would be the one corresponding to SAC_1 because average costs are lower. However, if the rate of output increases to Q_2, it will be more profitable to have a plant size corresponding to SAC_2. Unit costs fall to C_3.

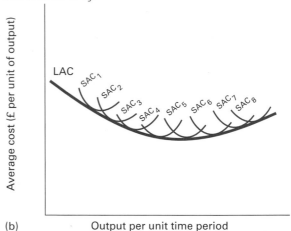

(b) Output per unit time period

(b) Deriving the long-run average cost curve

If we draw all the possible short-run average cost curves that correspond to different plant sizes and then draw the envelope to these various curves, $SAC_1, ..., SAC_8$, we obtain the long-run average cost curve, or the planning curve.

factors of production are variable, so there is no point of diminishing marginal returns since there is no fixed factor of production. Why, then, do we see the U-shape in the long-run average cost curve? The reasoning has to do with changes in the scale of operations. When the long-run average cost curve slopes downwards, it means that average costs decrease as output increases. Whenever this happens the firm is experiencing

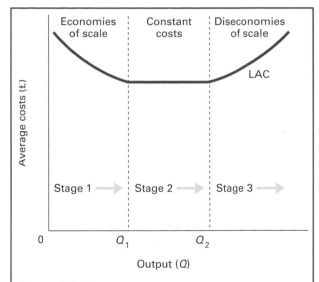

Figure 20.7
Economies of scale, constant returns to scale and diseconomies of scale
Long-run average cost curves will fall when there are economies of scale, as shown in stage 1 until Q_1. There will be constant returns to scale when the firm is experiencing output Q_1 to Q_2, as shown in stage 2. And finally, long-run average costs will rise when the firm is experiencing diseconomies of scale, beyond Q_2 in stage 3.

economies of scale. If, however, the long-run average cost curve is sloping upwards, the firm is incurring increases in average costs as output increases. The firm is said to be experiencing **diseconomies of scale**. Finally, if long-run average costs are invariant to changes in output, the firm is experiencing **constant returns to scale**. In Figure 20.7, we show these three stages. The first stage is for a firm experiencing economies of scale, the second stage for constant returns to scale and the third stage for diseconomies of scale.

Reasons why we see economies of scale

Here we list some of the reasons why a firm might be expected to experience economies of scale. Following Professor E.A.G. Robinson's approach, we shall consider five possible categories.

Technical economies

Large firms can take advantage of machinery of increased capacity. For example, a double-decker bus can carry twice as many passengers as a single-decker bus. But the purchase costs and the running costs are not doubled. Similarly with boats and planes, the larger the carrier the greater the saving. This economy is often linked to the principle of increased dimensions, because the volume of a sphere increases more than proportionately with its circumference. Consequently, as oil tankers and storage containers increase in size they become relatively cheaper to maintain and run.

In fact, a management consultancy agency once estimated that the day-to-day running costs of a 90 000-tonne oil tanker were £1870 compared with £996 for a 30 000-tonne oil tanker. In short, the costs were barely doubled, while the capacity was trebled.

Managerial economies

In a small firm the manager may perform the role of cost accountant, foreman, salesperson, personnel officer, stock controller etc. However, as a firm increases in size it can take advantage of specialization of labour. Each managerial role can be allocated to a specialist in that field. Furthermore, bigger firms can buy in management services and afford large in-house salaries to entice and retain the best management.

Commercial economies

The large firm can buy its raw materials in bulk at favourable rates. Similarly, the products of the firm can be sold in bulk with reduced costs. It is only necessary to pay a salesperson marginally more wages for taking an order of 5 million units compared with 5000; packaging and administration costs are also reduced.

Large firms can afford to advertise in the national press and on television. This can lead to some kind of brand loyalty for larger organizations, where one product of the firm leads to sales of other products with that brand name. Much of Marks & Spencer's success, for example, is owed to this type of customer loyalty.

Financial economies

The larger the firm is, the greater the number of financial advantages. The larger firm can negotiate loans from banks and related institutions easily and at favourable rates. Shares may be sold on the new issue market.

Risk-bearing economies

All firms are subject to risk at some time or other. However, the larger firm has distinct advantages in this area. First, changes in supply and/or demand can often ruin the smaller firm. The larger firm, however, can cover these by producing a variety of products for a variety of markets. These tactics are known as 'diversification of output' and 'diversification of markets'. For illustration, list the products made by Heinz, Wall's and/or ICI and identify as many of their market outlets as possible – an exercise which should help you to appreciate what is meant by the concept of 'diversification'. Similarly, one section of a large conglomerate can lean on other parts of the company when developing or going through some irregular phase. For example, one bank branch may gain funds from another in the group. Larger firms can also afford to spend money on research and development. This type of expenditure can yield particularly high returns by securing footholds in tomorrow's market, whereas small firms face the risk of going out of business. Using modern terminology, some of these risk-bearing economies can be classified as **economies of scope**.

These arise where there are common costs in producing two (or more) products, for example wool and mutton or optic fibres for telephone and computer technology. This diversification of output gives a firm that competes in all of these markets an advantage over a firm operating in only one market.

Minimum efficient scale

When economies of scale are exhausted, constant returns to scale begin. Economists often regard the commencement of this stage as the **minimum efficient scale**, since it signals the first point of output at which long-run average costs are lowest. In short, no further economies of scale can be achieved in the present time period. The point is represented by Q_1 in Figure 20.7 and the concept will be developed further in Chapter 23, when we discuss why oligopoly occurs.

How big is beautiful?

According to a government White Paper published in 1999, small sixth forms offer poor value for money. The statistics that formed the crux of the report are displayed in the table below.

Are small sixth forms on the way out?

Costs per 'A' level student	
Schools	£7380
Further education colleges	£6250
Sixth form colleges	£5910

Results: Average 'A' level point scores	
School sixth forms (200+ students)	18.6
Sixth form colleges	17.2
Tertiary colleges	14.2
School sixth form (50 or fewer students)	10.8
General further education colleges	9
(A-level point scores where 10 = A and 2 = E)	

19 Select appropriate figures to support an argument that larger 'A' level centres give better value for money due to economies of scale.

20 Can you suggest any arguments for or against large sixth forms that are not to do with economies of scale?

21 In your opinion, what is the minimum efficient scale for a sixth form?

22 How might a small sixth form overcome the problems suggested by the report?

Why a firm might experience diseconomies of scale

After a certain stage in output average unit costs may start to rise. One of the basic reasons that the firm can expect to experience such diseconomies of scale is that there are limits to the efficient functioning of management.

Moreover, as more workers are hired, a more-than-proportionate increase in managers may be needed, and this could cause increased costs per unit. For example, it might be possible to hire from one to ten workers and give them each a shovel to dig ditches; however, as soon as ten workers are hired, it may also be necessary to hire an overseer to co-ordinate their ditch-digging efforts. Thus, perhaps constant returns to scale will remain until ten workers and ten shovels are employed; then decreasing returns to scale set in. As the layers of supervision grow, the costs of information and communication grow more than proportionately. Hence, the average per unit cost will start to increase.

A final note on technical terms

The economies (listed above) are all *internal* to the firm. That is, they do not depend on what other firms are doing or what is happening in the economy. They are formally referred to as **internal economies** (or **diseconomies**) of **scale**. This phrase is necessary to distinguish them from **external economies** that arise through the growth of the whole industry.

External economies of scale

When expansion of a *whole industry* occurs all the component firms benefit. Firms can buy in services more easily; firms can collude to fund research and/or training; firms often become more specialized; and a trade association and/or journal may be started. These developments normally lead to savings for all the firms involved.

It is therefore possible to envisage a firm benefiting from internal and external economies of scale, the former being the direct result of internal company policy and the latter the by-product of being a firm involved in an expanding industrial sector.

KEY POINTS

20.4

- The long run is often called the planning horizon.

- The long-run average cost is the planning curve. This is established by drawing a line tangential to the lowest point on a series of short-run average cost curves, each corresponding to a different plant size.

- The firm can experience economies of scale, diseconomies of scale and constant returns to scale, all according to whether the long-run average cost curve slopes downwards, upwards or is horizontal (flat). Economies of scale refer to what happens when all factors of production are increased.

- We can classify internal economies of scale into five sections: (1) managerial, (2) commercial, (3) financial, (4) technical and (5) risk-bearing.

- The minimum efficient scale occurs at the lowest rate of output at which long-run average costs are minimized.

- The firm may experience diseconomies of scale because of limits to the efficient functioning of management.

- Internal economies of scale arise from the growth of one firm, regardless of what is happening to other firms.

- External economies of scale relate to the whole industry.

Case Study

Models of competitive behaviour

Having identified the various costs that a firm must cover, we need to consider the various competitive frameworks in which this may be achieved. The starting point, as in our next chapter, is perfect competition, which is a model based on a large number of competing firms. In many instances, however, economies of scale make **perfect competition** a non-starter. As explained above, the minimum efficient scale may simply be too large to permit competing firms to exist. An extreme example would be where it is only economically viable for one firm to supply the whole market. This theoretical extreme is a **monopoly**, the topic of Chapter 22. The subsequent chapter (23) deals with the most commonly encountered market structure – oligopoly – where a few firms dominate. The traditional argument is that firms operating within an oligopoly or monopoly 'administer' their prices, whereas firms operating in a crowded competitive situation have to accept a fair price dictated by the market.

This type of economic theory has supported government moves towards deregulation. The textbook argument is that deregulation should lead to competition and fairer prices. The classic examples seem to discuss the various attempts since the 1970s to deregulate the highly concentrated airline markets of America and Europe. Nevertheless, monopolies on specific routes still exist. Prices, however, remain reasonably competitive, as firms operating these routes cannot afford the risk of administering their prices to secure higher profits.

This strange phenomenon can be explained by a modern model of competitive behaviour, titled **the theory of contestable markets**. The main proposition is that markets do not have to contain many firms for profits to be held near the competitive level. The threat of a potential new entrant into a specific market sector – such as a particular air route – is quite sufficient to constrain prices. In other words, those firms that are actually in the industry (known as the 'incumbents')

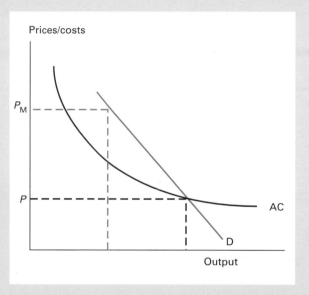

Figure 20.8
Models of competitive behaviour

avoid encouraging potential entrants. This recent theory can be explained with the aid of a diagram that shows business costs alongside demand. The idea of analysing costs and revenue (demand) simultaneously is a technique used in the subsequent chapters, so this exercise should prove a useful introduction.

In Figure 20.8, demand is denoted by D and the average cost by AC. We assume that presently only one firm makes up the entire industry and there are many potential rivals. The astute firm should select a price that enables it to break even, i.e., where all its costs are being met and demand is being satisfied – the appropriate point in this instance is P. If the firm selected (i.e., administered) a higher return, such as P_M, to reflect its monopoly position, it could end up cutting its own throat as a competitor may be enticed to enter the market and undercut the incumbent's price. Although the first firm in the market would then probably retaliate, it causes unnecessary competition. The most ethical and stable decision, therefore, is to aim for a normal profit. In other words, a threat that other firms will enter should be sufficient to deter the single firm from raising its price above the average cost, i.e., beyond its breakeven point.

The theory of contestable markets therefore makes the case for selecting a competitive price to avoid the threat of entry. Clearly, this is radically different from most of the subsequent presentations of how markets work, but it has been presented here to promote some critical awareness as we proceed. Moreover, it is a theory that has earned its place in introductory texts since the mid-1980s. In fact, we shall review it more fully in Chapter 26.

1 (a) In your own words, define the theory of contestable markets.
  (b) For a market to be contestable in nature, which costs need to be low?
  (c) Name some other industries that could be regarded as having a contestable market.
2 Explain in economic terms what constitutes a competitive price.
3 How could you explain the shape of the AC curve?
4 Explain how the demand curve represents revenue.
5 (a) Describe (as fully as possible) one other form of competition that you understand.
  (b) Discuss how prices are determined in that market structure.
  (c) Describe the type of profits that one may expect.
  (d) Discuss the significance of economies of scale to the chosen market structure.

Exam Preparation

Multiple choice questions

1 In the table below, a firm producing 'widgets' displays its short-run total costs for differing levels of output.

Quantity of widgets	Short-run total costs (£)
0	1000
10	1200
20	1400
30	1600
40	1800

The variable cost per unit at an output of 20 is
A £1000
B £70
C £400
D £20
E none of the above

2 The following table relates the total output and the total costs of a firm:

Output (units)	Costs (£)
100	125
200	200
300	250
400	275
500	290

The firm's production shows
A increasing returns throughout
B decreasing returns throughout
C increasing returns for output between 100 and 300 units and decreasing returns for output larger than 300 units
D decreasing returns for output between 100 and 300 units and increasing returns for output larger than 300 units
E constant returns throughout

3 Each curve in the diagram below describes the different combinations of capital and labour capable of producing the level of output indicated.

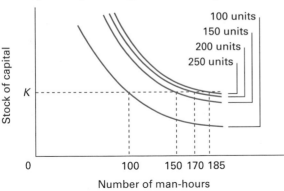

It may be deduced from the diagram that, with a fixed stock of capital K, as output increases
A the average product of capital diminishes
B short-run average costs fall faster than long-run average costs
C there are diseconomies of scale
D the marginal product of labour is constant
E the marginal product of labour increases

4 The diagram shows the relationship between the total output of a firm and the number of units of labour employed.

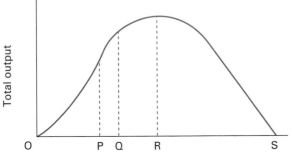

Diminishing marginal productivity of labour sets in
A from the very first unit of labour employed
B after OP units of labour are employed
C after OQ units of labour are employed
D after OR units of labour are employed
E after OS units of labour are employed

5 Which of the following conditions is necessary for the law of diminishing returns to apply?
A at least one factor must be in fixed supply
B demand must be falling
C total production must be falling
D all factors are variable

6 If marginal cost is lower than average total cost then it is necessarily the case that
A marginal cost is falling
B average total cost is falling
C marginal revenue is less than marginal cost
D total fixed cost is falling

7 From the data below it can be concluded that one of the statements A–D is wrong. Which one?

Output (units)	Total cost (£)
0	100
1	150
2	180
3	280
4	460

A average fixed cost at 2 units of output is £50
B average variable cost at 4 units of output equals £90
C the marginal cost of the third unit of output is £180
D average total cost at 4 units of output is £115

Essay questions

1 Distinguish between internal and external economies of scale. How do economies of scale affect the number of firms in an industry?

2 Explain clearly the law of variable proportions. How does the working of this law influence a firm's cost of production?

3 What is an entrepreneur? Can governments encourage entrepreneurship?

4 Explain the distinction between diminishing returns to a variable factor and diseconomies of scale. With reference to examples, explain how diseconomies of scale might arise.

5 (a) Explain the terms 'diminishing returns' and 'economies of scale' and distinguish between the two.
  (b) To what extent do economies influence the size of firms?

6 Why are many theories of economic decisions, such as to buy, to produce and to save, expressed in marginal rather than total or average values? Explain whether or not you think that this is realistic and whether realism is important in formulating economic theories.

21

Pricing and output decisions in perfect competition

Firms have to know not only about costs, discussed in the last chapter, but also about revenues when they make pricing and output decisions. In order to understand, for example, the relationship between output, revenues and price, a firm has to know the structure of the market or industry in which it is selling its product. There are various **market structures**, all dependent upon the extent to which buyers and sellers can assume that their own buying and selling decisions do not affect market price. At one extreme, when buyers and sellers correctly assume that they cannot affect market price, the market structure is one of **perfect competition** – the subject of this chapter. Whenever buyers and sellers must take into account how their individual actions affect market price, we are not in a market structure of perfect competition and have entered an *imperfectly competitive market*. We examine such markets in the subsequent chapters relating to monopoly and oligopoly.

The characteristics of perfect competition

In this chapter we are interested in studying how a firm acting within a perfectly competitive market structure makes decisions about how much to produce. Before we go ahead with this analysis, we want to give the characteristics of the market structure called perfect competition. These characteristics are as follows.

1 The product that is sold by the firms in the industry is *homogeneous*. This means that the product sold by each firm in the industry is a perfect substitute for the product sold by every other firm. In other words, buyers are able to choose from a large number of sellers of a product that the buyers believe to be the same. The product is thus not in any sense differentiated as a result of whoever is the source of supply.
2 *Any firm can enter or exit the industry without serious impediments.* Resources must be able to move in and out of the industry without, for example, government legislation that prevents such resource mobility.
3 *There must be a large number of buyers and sellers.* When this is the case, no one buyer or one seller has any influence on price, and also when there are large numbers of buyers and sellers they will be acting independently.
4 *There must be complete information.* Both buyers and sellers must clearly know about market prices, product quality and cost conditions.

Now that we have defined the characteristics of a perfectly competitive *market* structure, we can consider the position of an individual constituent unit. We define a **perfectly competitive firm** as follows:

> it is one that is such a small part of the total industry in which it operates that it cannot significantly affect the price of the product in question.

LEARNING OUTCOMES

On completing this chapter you should understand:

■ The characteristics of perfect competition

■ Whether perfect competition is possible and/or desirable

■ How to use marginal analysis

■ The meaning of profits in the short run from the point of view of the firm and the industry

■ Ways to determine entry and exit points for business opportunities

Since the perfectly competitive firm is a small part of the industry, that firm has no control over the price of the product. This means that each firm in the industry is a **price-taker** – the firm takes price as given, as something that is determined outside the individual firm.

The price that is given to the firm is determined by the forces of market supply and market demand. That is, when all individual consumers' demands are added together into a market demand curve, and all the supply schedules of individual firms are added together into a market supply curve, the intersection of those two curves will give the market price, which the purely competitive or price-taking firm must accept.

This definition of a competitive firm is obviously idealized, for in one sense the individual firm has to set prices. How can we ever have a situation where firms regard prices as set by forces outside their control? The answer is that, even though every firm, by definition, sets its own prices, a firm in a perfectly competitive situation will find that it will eventually have no customers at all if it sets its price above the competitive price. Let us now see what the demand curve of an individual firm in a competitive industry looks like graphically.

Demand curve of the perfect competitor

In Chapter 5 we talked about the characteristics of demand schedules. We pointed out that, for completely elastic demand curves, if the individual firm raises the price by 1p, it will lose all its business. Well, this is how we characterize the demand schedule for a perfectly competitive firm – it is a horizontal line at the going market price. That is, it is completely elastic (see Chapter 5). And that going market price is determined by the market forces of supply and demand. Figure 21.1 is the hypothetical market demand schedule faced by an individual pocket calculator manufacturer who sells a very, very small part of the total pocket calculator production in the industry. At the market price, this firm can sell all the output it wants. At the market price of £5 each, which is where the horizontal demand curve for the individual producer lies, people's demand for the pocket calculator of that one producer is perfectly elastic. If the firm raises its price, they will buy from some other producer. We label the individual producer's demand curve dd, whereas the market demand curve is always labelled DD.

How much should the perfect competitor produce?

As we have shown, a perfect competitor has to accept the given price of the product. If the firm raises its price, it sells nothing. If it lowers its price, it makes less money per unit sold than it otherwise could. The firm has only one decision variable left: how much should it produce? We shall apply our model of the firm to this question to come up with an answer. We shall use the profit maximization model and assume that firms, whether competitive or monopolistic,

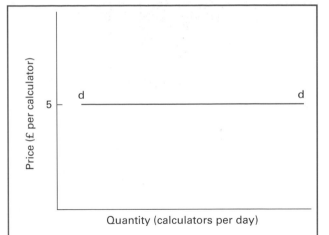

Figure 21.1
The demand curve for an individual pocket calculator producer
We assume that the individual pocket calculator producer is such a small part of the total market that he or she cannot influence the price. The firm accepts the price as given. At the going market price it faces a horizontal demand curve, dd. If it raises its price by even 1p, it will sell no calculators. The firm would be foolish to lower its price below £5 because it can sell all that it can produce at a price of £5. The firm's demand curve is completely, or perfectly, elastic.

will attempt to maximize their total profits, that is, the positive difference between total revenues and total costs.

Total revenues
Every firm has to consider its **total revenues**. Total revenues are defined as the quantity sold multiplied by the price. (They are also the same as total receipts from the sale of output.) The perfect competitor must take the price as given.

Look at Table 21.1. Much of the information comes from Table 20.3, but we have added some essential columns for our analysis. Column 3 is the market price of £5 per calculator, which is also equal to average revenue (AR), since

$$AR = \frac{TR}{Q} = \frac{P \times Q}{Q} = P$$

Column 4 shows the total revenues TR as equal to the market price P multiplied by the total output in sales per day, Q. Thus, TR = $P \times Q$. We are assuming that the market supply and demand schedules intersect at a price of £5 and that this price holds for all the firm's production. We are also assuming that, since our calculator maker is a small part of the market, it can sell all it produces at that price. Thus, Figure 21.2(a) shows the total revenue curve as a straight line. For every unit of sales, total revenue is increased by £5.

The housing market far from perfect

To understand the housing market, it is necessary to take account of its four main idiosyncrasies. First, there are large transaction costs involved in buying and selling houses. Second, information asymmetries abound between buyers and sellers, both about individual properties and about the state of the market. Third, expectations about future house prices and future interest rates can be more important than their current levels. And fourth, markets are highly localized, which can result in severe excess demand and supply in different areas (and different price brackets) at the same time.

Source: *Economic Bulletin*, Lloyds TSB, 27, July 1999

1 Take any one of the four idiosyncrasies listed in the extract and explain fully why competition in the housing market is far from perfect.
2 Would a specific local market for three-bedroom semi-detached houses be a better example of a perfectly competitive market? Explain your answer fully.
3 Think of four further examples of real-life markets, ranging from one that is near perfect to three others that progress further and further away from the perfect competition model.

Total costs

Revenues are only one side of the picture. Costs must also be considered. **Total costs** are given in column 2 in Table 21.1. Notice that when we plot total costs in Figure 21.2(a) the curve is not straight but a wavy line, which is first above the total revenue curve then below it, and then above it again. When the total cost curve is above the total revenue curve, the firm is experiencing losses. When it is below the total revenue curve, the firm is making profits. (When we refer to profits, we shall always mean economic profits.)

Comparing total costs with total revenues

By comparing total costs with total revenues, we can work out the number of pocket calculators that the individual competitive firm should produce per day. Our analysis rests on the assumption that the firm will attempt to maximize total profits. In Table 21.1 we see that total profits reach a maximum at a production rate of between seven and eight pocket calculators per day. We can see this graphically in Figure 21.2(a). The firm will maximize profits at that place on the graph where the total revenue curve exceeds the total cost curve by the greatest amount. This occurs at a rate of output and sales of either seven or eight calculators per day; this rate is called the **profit-maximizing rate of production**.

We can also find this profit-maximizing rate of production for the individual competitive firm by looking at marginal revenues and marginal costs.

Table 21.1

The costs of production and the revenues from the sale of output
Profit maximization occurs at a rate of sales of either seven or eight calculators per day.

1 Total output and sales per day	2 Total cost TC	3 Market price P	4 Total revenue TR = (3) × (1)	5 Total profit = TR − TC = (4) − (2)	6 Average total cost ATC = (2) ÷ (1)	7 Average variable cost AVC[a]	8 Marginal cost MC = change in (2) change in (1)	9 Marginal revenue MR = change in (4) change in (1)
0	£10.00	£5.00	0	−£10.00	–	–		
							£5.00	£5.00
1	15.00	5.00	£5.00	−10.00	£15.00	£5.00		
							3.00	5.00
2	18.00	5.00	10.00	−8.00	9.00	4.00		
							2.00	5.00
3	20.00	5.00	15.00	−5.00	6.67	3.33		
							1.00	5.00
4	21.00	5.00	20.00	−1.00	5.25	2.75		
							2.00	5.00
5	23.00	5.00	25.00	2.00	4.60	2.60		
							3.00	5.00
6	26.00	5.00	30.00	4.00	4.33	2.67		
							4.00	5.00
7	30.00	5.00	35.00	5.00	4.28	2.86		
							5.00	5.00
8	35.00	5.00	40.00	5.00	4.38	3.13		
							6.00	5.00
9	41.00	5.00	45.00	4.00	4.56	3.44		
							7.00	5.00
10	48.00	5.00	50.00	2.00	4.80	3.80		
							8.00	5.00
11	56.00	5.00	55.00	−1.00	5.09	4.18		

[a] Taken from Table 20.3.

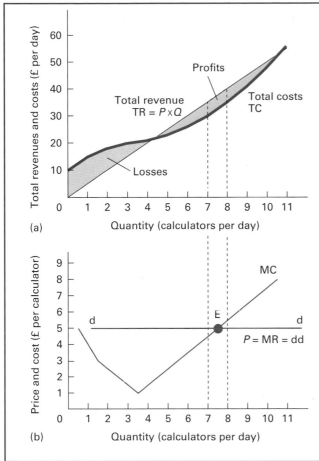

Figure 21.2
(a) Finding maximum total profits
Total revenues are represented by the straight line, showing that each calculator sells at £5. Total costs first exceed total revenues, then are less than total revenues, and then exceed them again. We find maximum profits where total revenues exceed total costs by the largest amount. This occurs at a rate of production and sales per day of seven or eight calculators.

(b) Profit maximization using marginal analysis
Profit maximization occurs where marginal revenue equals marginal cost. Marginal revenue is represented by the individual firm demand curve dd, which is a horizontal line at £5. The marginal cost curve is represented by MC. It intersects the marginal revenue curve at a rate of output and sales of somewhere between seven and eight calculators per day.

Using marginal analysis

Marginal cost was introduced in Chapter 20. It was defined as the change in total cost due to a one-unit change in production. This leaves only **marginal revenue** to be defined.

Marginal revenue

What amount can our individual calculator manufacturer hope to receive each time it sells an additional (marginal) pocket calculator? Since the firm is such a small part of the market and cannot influence the price, it must accept the price determined by the market forces of supply and demand. Therefore, the firm knows it will receive £5 for every calculator it sells in the market. So the additional revenue the firm will receive from selling one more calculator is equal to the market price of £5; marginal revenue, in this case, equals price.

Marginal revenue is the increment in total revenues attributable to producing one additional unit of the product in question. Marginal revenue is also defined as the change in total revenue resulting from a one-unit change in output. Hence, a more formal definition of marginal revenue is

$$\text{marginal revenue} = \frac{\text{change in total revenue}}{\text{change in output}}$$

In a perfectly competitive market, the marginal revenue curve is exactly equivalent to the price line or, in other words, to the individual firm's demand curve, since the firm can sell all of its output (production) at the market price.

Thus, in Figure 21.1 the demand curve dd for the individual producer is at a price of £5 – the price line is coincident with the demand curve. But so, too, is the marginal revenue curve, for marginal revenue in this case also equals £5.

The marginal revenue curve for our competitive pocket calculator producer is shown as a horizontal line at £5 in Figure 21.2(b). Notice again that the marginal revenue curve is equal to the price line, which is equal to the individual firm's demand curve dd.

When profits are maximized

Now we add the marginal cost curve MC taken from column 8 in Table 21.1. As shown in Figure 21.2(b), the marginal cost curve first falls and then starts to rise, eventually intersecting the marginal revenue curve and then rising above it. Notice that the numbers for both the marginal cost schedule and the marginal revenue schedule in Table 21.1 are printed between the figures that determine them. This indicates that we are looking at a change between one rate of output and the next.

In Figure 21.2(b), the marginal cost curve intersects the marginal revenue (or dd) curve somewhere between seven and eight calculators per day. Consider a rate of production that is less than that. At a production rate of, say, six calculators per day, marginal cost is clearly below marginal revenue. That is, the marginal cost curve at an output of six is below the marginal revenue curve at that output. Since it can receive £5 per calculator and since marginal cost is less than this marginal revenue, the firm has an incentive to increase production. In fact, it has an incentive to produce and sell until the amount of the additional revenue received from selling one more calculator just equals the additional costs incurred from producing that calculator. This is how it maximizes profit. Whenever marginal cost is less than marginal revenue, the firm will always make more profit by increasing production.

Now consider the possibility of producing at an output rate in excess of eight – say, at ten calculators per day. The marginal cost curve at that output rate is higher than the marginal revenue (or dd) curve. The individual producer would be spending more to produce that additional output than it would be receiving in revenues. The firm would be foolish to continue producing at this rate.

Where, then, should it produce? It should produce where the marginal cost curve intersects the marginal revenue curve (at point E in Figure 21.2(b)). Since the firm knows it can sell all the calculators it wants at the going market price, marginal revenue from selling an additional calculator will always equal the market price. Consequently, the firm should continue production until the cost of increasing output by one more unit is just equal to the revenues obtainable from that extra unit. Profit maximization is always at the rate of output at which marginal revenue equals marginal cost. (To be strictly correct, we should add 'and the MC curve cuts the MR curve from below'.*)

In our particular example, our profit-maximizing, perfectly competitive pocket calculator producer will produce at a rate of between seven and eight units a day. Notice that this same profit-maximizing rate of output is shown in both Figure 21.2(a), where the total revenue and total cost curves are drawn, and Figure 21.2(b), where the marginal revenue and marginal cost curves are drawn. We can find the profit-maximizing output solution for the perfectly competitive firm by looking at either diagram.

---

* The marginal cost curve MC also cuts the marginal revenue curve dd from above at an output rate of less than one.

KEY POINTS

21.1

- A perfectly competitive firm is a price-taker. It takes price as given. It can sell all that it wants at the existing market price.

- The demand curve facing a perfect competitor is a horizontal line at the going market price. The demand curve is also the perfect competitor's marginal revenue curve, since marginal revenue is defined as a change in total revenue due to a one-unit change in output.

- Profit is maximized at the rate of output where the positive difference between total revenues and total costs is the greatest. Using a marginal analysis, the perfectly competitive firm will produce at a rate of output where marginal revenue equals marginal cost. Marginal revenue, however, is equal to price. Therefore, the perfectly competitive firm produces at an output rate where marginal cost equals the price of the output.

Profits in the short run

To find what our individual, competitive pocket calculator producer is making in terms of profits in the short run, we have to add the average total cost curve to Figure 21.2(b). We take the information from column 6 in Table 21.1 and add it to Figure 21.2(b) to get Figure 21.3. Again, the profit-maximizing rate of output is between seven and eight calculators per day. If we have production and sales of seven calculators per day, total revenues will be £35 a day. Total costs will be £30 a day, leaving a profit of £5 a day. If the rate of output in sales is eight calculators per day, total revenues will be £40 and total costs will be £35, again leaving a profit of £5 a day.

It is certainly possible, also, for the competitive firm to make short-run losses. We give an example in Figure 21.4. Here we show the firm's demand curve shifting from dd to d′d′. The going market price has fallen from £5 to £3 per calculator because of changes in market supply and/or demand conditions. The firm will always do the best it can by producing where marginal revenue equals marginal cost. We see in Figure 21.4 that the marginal revenue (or d′d′) curve intersects the marginal cost curve at an output rate of about 5.5 calculators per day. The firm is clearly not making profits, because average total costs at that output rate are greater than the price of £3 per calculator. The losses are shown in the shaded area. By producing where marginal revenue equals marginal cost, however, the firm is minimizing its losses; that is, losses would be greater at any other output.

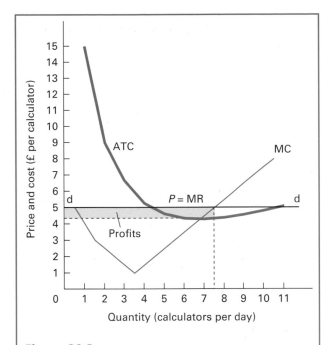

Figure 21.3
Measuring total profits
The profit-maximizing rate of output and sales is where marginal revenue equals marginal cost. Profits are the difference between total revenues and total cost. Total revenues will equal the rate of output and sales multiplied by the market price of £5. Total costs will equal the quantity produced and sold multiplied by average total cost (ATC). Profits are represented by the shaded area.

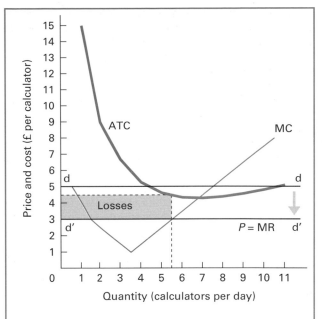

Figure 21.4
Minimizing short-run losses
In cases where average total costs exceed the average revenue or price, profit maximization is equivalent to loss minimization. This again occurs where marginal cost equals marginal revenue. Losses are shown in the shaded area.

Closing down in the short run

In Figure 21.4, the firm is making economic losses. Will it go out of business? Certainly in the long run it will, for the owners of the firm will not incur economic losses forever. But in the short run, the firm may not go out of business. As long as the loss from staying in business is less than the loss from going out of business, the firm will continue to produce. Now how can we tell when that is the case, that is, when sustaining economic losses in the short run is still worthwhile? We must compare the cost of staying in business (with losses) with the cost of closing down. The cost of staying in business in the short run is given by the total variable cost. Looking at the problem on a unit basis, as long as average variable costs are covered by average revenues (price), the firm is better off staying in business. In other words, if average variable costs are exceeded even a little by the price of the product, then staying in business produces some revenues in excess of variable costs that can be applied towards covering fixed costs.

A simple example will demonstrate this situation. Let the price of a product be £8. Let average total costs equal £9 at an output of 100. In this hypothetical example, average total costs are broken up into average variable costs of £7 and average fixed costs of £2. Total revenues, then, equal £8 × 100, that is, £800, and total costs equal £9 × 100, or £900. Total losses therefore equal £100. However, this does not mean that the firm will shut down. After all, if it does shut down, it still has fixed costs to pay. And in this case, since average fixed costs equal £2 at an output of 100, the fixed costs are £200. Thus the firm has losses of £100 if it continues to produce, but it has losses of £200 (the fixed costs) if it shuts down. The logic is fairly straightforward: as long as the price per unit sold exceeds the average variable cost per unit produced, the firm will be paying for at least part of the opportunity cost of capital invested in the business. Although the price is below average total cost and the firm is not making a normal or competitive rate of return on its investment, at least it is making some return. A small rate of return on an investment is better than no rate of return at all.

The short-run breakeven point

Let us look at demand curve dd in Figure 21.5. It just touches the minimum point of the average total cost curve, which, as you will remember, is exactly where the marginal cost curve intersects the average total cost curve. At that price, which is about £4.30, the firm will be making exactly zero short-run economic profits. Thus, that particular price is called the short-run breakeven price. And point E is therefore called the **short-run breakeven point** for a competitive firm. It is the point at which marginal revenue equals marginal cost equals average total cost. The breakeven price is the one that yields zero short-run profits or losses.

Calculating the closing-down point

In order to calculate the firm's shut-down point, we must add the average variable cost (AVC) to our graph. In Figure 21.5 we have plotted the AVC values from column 7 in Table 21.1. For the moment, consider two possible demand curves, dd and d'd', which are also the firm's respective marginal revenue curves. Then, if demand is dd, the firm will produce at E, where the curve intersects the marginal cost curve. If demand falls to d'd', the firm will produce at E'. The special feature about the hypothetical demand curve d'd' is that it just touches the average variable cost curve at the latter's minimum point, which is where the marginal cost curve intersects it also. This price is labelled the short-run close-down price. Why? Below this price the firm is paying out more in variable costs than it is receiving in revenues from the sale of its product. With each unit it sells, it is adding to its losses. Clearly, the way to avoid incurring these additional losses, if price falls below the closing-down point, is in fact to shut down operations. (Of course, if price falls below the short-run close-down price, a firm may still continue in business in the short run if it decides it can afford to wait until the price moves up again and it can profitably re-enter production.)

The intersection of the price line, the marginal cost curve and the average variable cost curve is labelled E'. We called it the **short-run close-down point** (or **price**). This point is labelled short run because, of course, in the long run the firm will not produce below a price that yields a normal rate of return and hence zero economic profits.

The meaning of zero economic profits

Perhaps the fact that we labelled point E in Figure 21.5 the breakeven point may have puzzled you. At point E, price is just equal to average total cost. If this is the case, why would a firm continue to produce if it were making no profits whatsoever? If we again make the distinction between accounting profits and economic profits, then at that price the firm has zero economic profits but positive accounting profits.

Accounting versus economic profits revisited
Think back to the last chapter when we discussed how an accountant must total up costs. The accountant adds up all the expenses, subtracts them from all the revenues and calls the result profit. What is ignored is the reward offered to investors. Those who invest in the firm, whether they be proprietors or shareholders, must antic-

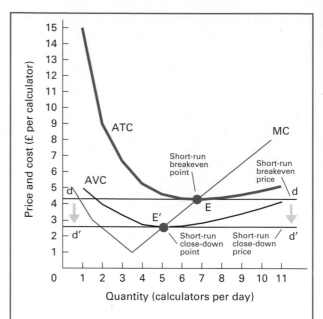

Figure 21.5
Short-run close-down and breakeven prices
We can find the short-run breakeven price and the short-run close-down price by comparing the price with average total costs and average variable costs. If the demand curve is dd, then profit maximization occurs at output E, where MC is equal to marginal revenue (the dd curve). Since the ATC curve includes all relevant opportunity costs, point E is the short-run breakeven point, and zero economic profits are being made. The firm is earning a normal rate of return. If the demand curve falls to d'd', then profit maximization (loss minimization) occurs at the intersection E' of MC and MR (the d'd' curve). Below this price, it does not pay the firm to continue in operation, because its average variable costs are not covered by the price of the product.

ipate a rate of return that is at least as great as could be earned in similar investments of equal risk. Looking at capital alone, we know that the cost of capital is its opportunity cost. Accountants, in conforming with tax laws, do not enter the opportunity cost of most of the capital involved as a cost of doing business. (Moreover, accountants do not have an exact figure on the opportunity cost of capital; therefore, it is appropriate for them to talk in terms of profits without making the distinction that we make here.)

In our analysis, the average total cost curve includes the full opportunity cost of capital. Indeed, the average total cost curve includes the opportunity cost of all factors of production used in the production process.

We have defined economic profits as those profits over and above what is required to keep capital in the firm. At the short-run breakeven price, economic profits, by definition, are zero. However, accounting profits at that price are not equal to zero; they are positive. Let us consider an example different from the one used in Figure 21.5. A squash-racket manufacturer sells rackets at a particular price. The owners of the firm have invested only their own capital in the business: they have borrowed no money from anyone else. Moreover, assume that they explicitly pay the full opportunity cost to all factors of production, including any managerial labour that they themselves contribute to the business. In other words, they pay themselves salaries that show up as a cost in the books, and those salaries are equal to what they could have earned in the next-best alternative occupation. At the end of the year, the owners find that, after they subtract all explicit costs from total revenues, they have earned £100 000. Let us say that their investment was £1 million. Thus, the rate of return on that investment is 10 per cent per year. We assume that this turns out to be equal to the rate of return that, on average, all other squash-racket manufacturers make in the industry.

This £100 000, or 10 per cent rate of return, is actually, then, a competitive, or normal, rate of return on invested capital in that industry or in other industries with similar risks. If the owners had only made, say, £50 000, or 5 per cent on their investment, they would have been able to make higher profits by leaving the industry. Thus, we say that the 10 per cent rate of return is the opportunity cost of capital. The accountant shows it as a profit; we call it a cost. We also include the cost in the average total cost curve similar to that shown in Figure 21.5. Thus, at the short-run breakeven price, average total cost, including this opportunity cost of capital, will just equal that price. The firm will be making zero economic profits but a 10 per cent accounting rate of return.

Now we are ready to derive the firm's supply curve.

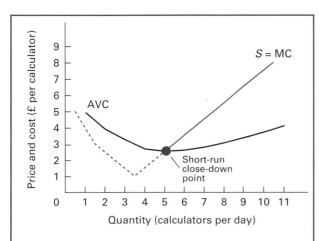

Figure 21.6
The individual firm's short-run supply curve
The individual firm's supply curve is that portion of its marginal cost curve above the average variable cost curve. It is shown as the solid part of the MC curve.

The firm's short-run supply curve

What does the supply curve for the individual firm look like? Actually, we have been looking at it all along. We know that when the price of calculators is £5 the firm will supply seven or eight units per day. If the price falls to £3, the firm will supply five or six units per day. And if the price falls below £3, the firm will shut down in the short run. Hence, in Figure 21.6 the firm's supply curve is the marginal cost curve above the short-run close-down point. The definition, then, of the individual firm's supply curve in a competitive industry is its marginal cost curve equal to and above the point of intersection with the average variable cost curve.

Opening up or closing down

The accompanying table shows *short-run costs* and average revenue for five hypothetical firms. Complete the missing information and then answer the questions below.

Firm	AFC	AVC	AR	Open/Close
A	100	200	250	_____
B	100	200	300	_____
C	100	200	200	_____
D	100	200	150	_____
E	100	200	450	_____

4 Which of the five firms should stay open and which would you advise to shut?

5 Explain in detail the decisions that you have made for firms A and C.

6 Are there any criteria other than profits or loss that could justify a firm continuing in business?

7 As you no doubt realize, this type of data can also be displayed graphically. With this in mind, we suggest that you attempt the multiple choice questions numbered 1–4 on page 376.

The industry short-run supply curve

An industry is merely a collection of firms producing a particular product. Therefore, to work out the total supply curve of, for example, pocket calculators, we merely add, for every possible price, the quantities that each firm will supply. In other words, we horizontally sum the individual supply curves of all the competitive firms. But the individual supply curves, as we just saw, are simply the marginal cost curves of each firm. Consider doing this for a hypothetical world in which there are only two calculator producers in the industry,

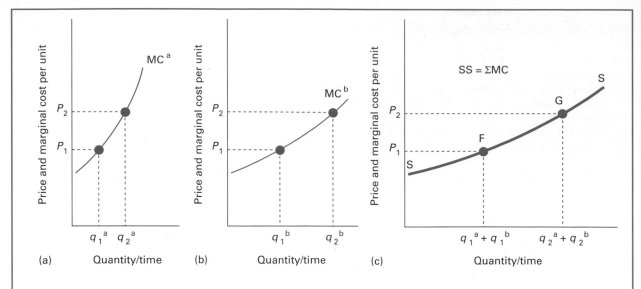

Figure 21.7
Deriving the industry supply curve

Marginal cost curves above average minimum variable cost are presented in (a) and (b) for firms A and B. We horizontally sum the two quantities supplied, q_1^a and q_1^b, at price P_1. This gives us point F in (c). We do the same thing for the quantities at price P_2. This gives us point G. When we connect these points, we have the industry supply curve SS.

firm A and firm B. These two firms' marginal cost curves are given in Figures 21.7(a) and 21.7(b). The marginal cost curves for the two separate firms are presented as MC^a in (a) and MC^b in (b). These two marginal cost curves are drawn only for prices above the minimum average variable cost for each respective firm. Hence, we are not including any of the section of the marginal cost curves below minimum average variable cost. In (a) for firm A at price P_1, the quantity supplied would be q_1^a. At price P_2, the quantity supplied would be q_2^a. In (b), we see the two different quantities corresponding to those two prices that would be supplied by firm B. Now we horizontally add for price P_1 the quantities q_1^a and q_1^b. This gives us one point, F, for our **industry supply curve** SS. We obtain the other point, G, by doing the same horizontal adding of quantities at P_2. When we connect points F and G, we obtain industry supply curve SS, which is also marked as ΣMC,* indicating that it is the horizontal summation of the marginal cost curves (above the respective minimum average variable cost of each firm).

Factors that influence the supply curve

As you have just seen, the industry supply curve is the horizontal summation of all the individual firms' supply curves above their respective minimum average variable cost points. This means that anything that affects the

marginal cost curves of the firm will influence the industry supply curve. Therefore, the individual factors that will influence the supply function in a competitive industry can be summarized as those factors that affect the individual marginal cost curves, such as changes in factor costs – the wages paid to employees and the prices of raw materials. Changes in productivity on the part of the individual firm, taxes and anything else that would influence the individual firm's marginal cost curves also determine the industry supply curve.

All these are non-price determinants of supply. Since they affect the position of the marginal cost curve for the individual firm, they indeed affect the position of the industry supply curve. A change in any of the above-mentioned non-price determinants of supply will shift the market supply curve. Thus, once we are given the market demand curve in the perfectly competitive industry, if we know there has been a shift in a non-price determinant of the market supply curve, we can predict what will happen to the equilibrium price and quantity of the product being produced by the perfectly competitive industry.

---

* The Greek sigma Σ is the symbol for summation.

KEY POINTS

21.2

■ Short-run profits and losses are determined by comparing average total costs with price at the profit-maximizing rate of output. In the short run, the perfectly competitive firm can make economic profits or economic losses.

■ The competitive firm's short-run breakeven output occurs at the minimum point on its average total cost curve, which is where the marginal cost curve intersects the average total cost curve.

■ The competitive firm's short-run shut-down output is at the minimum point on its average variable cost curve, which is also where the marginal cost curve intersects the average variable cost curve. Close-down will occur if price falls below average variable cost.

■ The firm will continue production at a price that exceeds average variable costs even though the full opportunity cost of capital is not being met; at least some revenues are going towards paying some rate of return to capital.

■ At the short-run breakeven price, the firm is making zero economic profits, which means that it is just making a normal rate of return in that industry.

■ The firm's short-run supply curve is that section of its marginal cost curve equal to or above minimum average variable costs.

■ The industry short-run supply curve is a horizontal summation of the individual firms' marginal cost curves above their respective minimum average variable costs.

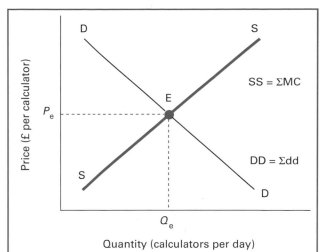

Figure 21.8
The industry demand and supply curves
The industry demand curve is a representation of the demand curve for all potential consumers. It is represented by DD. The industry supply curve is the horizontal summation of all those sections of the marginal cost curves of the individual firms above their respective minimum average variable cost points. We show it as SS and mark it as equal to ΣMC. The intersection of the demand and supply curves at E determines the equilibrium or market price P_e.

Price determination in a perfectly competitive market

How is the market price, or 'going' price, established in a competitive market? This price is established by the interaction of all the firms and all the demanders. The market demand schedule DD in Figure 21.8 represents the demand schedule for the entire industry, and the supply schedule SS represents the supply schedule for the entire industry. Price P_e is established by the forces of supply and demand at the intersection of SS and DD. Even though *each individual firm* faces a horizontal demand curve and hence has no control or effect on the price of its product in a competitive industry, the interaction of all the producers determines the price at which the product will be sold. We say that the price P_e and the quantity Q_e in Figure 21.8 constitute the competitive solution to the pricing–quantity problem in that particular industry. It is the equilibrium where suppliers and demanders are both maximizing.

The long-run industry situation – exit and entry

In the long run, we surmise that firms in perfect competition will tend to have average total cost curves that just touch the price (marginal revenue) or individual demand curve dd. That is, in the long run in a competitive situation, firms will be making zero economic profits. How does this occur? It is through an adjustment process that depends on economic profits and losses. In Chapter 6 we referred to changes in demand and technological progress having the effect of changing prices and profits, signalling resource owners about where their resources should flow. Now we can be more precise about this process.

Exit and entry of firms

Go back and look at Figures 21.3 and 21.4. The existence of either profits or losses is a signal to owners of capital within and outside the industry. If the industry is characterized by firms showing profits as represented in Figure 21.3, this will signal to owners of capital elsewhere in the economy that they, too, should enter this industry. If, however, there are firms in the industry that are like those suffering economic losses represented in Figure 21.4, this signals resource owners outside the industry to stay out. It also signals resource owners within the industry not to reinvest and, if possible, to leave the industry. It is in this sense that we say that profits direct resources to their highest-valued use. Capital and labour will flow into industries where profitability is highest, and will flow out of industries where profitability is lowest.

The price system therefore allocates capital according to the relative expected rates of return on alternative investments. Entry restrictions will thereby hinder economic efficiency by not allowing resources to flow to their highest-valued use. Similarly, exit restrictions will act to trap resources in sectors in which their value is below that in alternative uses.

In addition, when we say that in a competitive long-run equilibrium firms will be making zero economic profits, we must realize that at a particular point in time it would be pure coincidence for a firm to be making *exactly* zero economic profits. Real-world information is not as exact as the curves we use to simplify our analysis. Things change all the time in a dynamic world, and even in a very competitive situation firms may not, for many reasons, be making exactly zero economic profits. Remember, in any event, that the concept of long-run zero economic profits in a competitive industry is a long-run concept. We say that there is a *tendency* towards that equilibrium position, but firms are adjusting all the time to changes in their cost curves and in their (horizontal) dd curves.

Long-run supply curves

In Figure 21.8, we drew the summation of all the portions of the individual firms' marginal cost curves above each firm's respective minimum average variable costs as the upward-sloping supply curve of the entire industry. We should be aware, however, that a relatively steep upward-sloping curve may only be appropriate in the short run. After all, one of the prerequisites of a competitive industry is free entry.

Remember that our definition of the long run is a period of time in which adjustments can be made. The **long-run industry supply curve** is a supply curve showing the relationship between quantity supplied by the entire industry at different prices after firms have been allowed either to enter or to exit from the industry, depending on whether there have been positive or negative economic profits. The long-run industry supply curve is drawn under the assumption that entry and exit have been completed.

There are three possible types of long-run industry supply curves, depending on whether input costs stay constant, increase or decrease. What is at issue here is the effect on input prices of a change in the number of firms in the industry. In the last chapter, we assumed that input prices remained constant to the firm, no matter what the firm's rate of output was. When looking at the entire industry, that assumption may not be correct: for example, when all firms are expanding and new firms are entering, they may simultaneously bid up input prices.

Constant-cost industries

In principle, there are small industries that utilize such a low percentage of the total supply of inputs necessary for their production that firms can enter the industry without bidding up input prices. In such a situation we are dealing with a **constant-cost industry**. Its long-run industry supply curve is therefore horizontal and is represented by $S_L S_L$ in Figure 21.9(a).

We can work through the case in which constant costs prevail. We start out in 21.9(a) with demand curve DD and supply curve SS. The equilibrium price is P_e. There is an increased demand for the product in question, which is shown by a rightward shift in market demand to D'D'. In the short run, the supply curve remains stable. The equilibrium price rises to P'_e. This generates positive economic profits for existing firms in the industry. Such economic profits induce capital to flow into the industry. The existing firms expand and/or new firms enter. The supply curve shifts out to S'S'. The new intersection with the new demand curve is at E''. The new equilibrium price is again P_e. The long-run supply curve is obtained by connecting the intersections of the corresponding pairs of demand and supply curves, E and E''. It is labelled $S_L S_L$ and is horizontal. Its slope is zero. In a constant-cost industry, long-run supply is perfectly elastic. Any shift in demand is eventually met by an equal shift in supply, so that the long-run price is constant at P_e.

Increasing-cost industries

In an **increasing-cost industry**, expansion by existing firms and the addition of new firms causes the price of inputs within the industry to be bid up. As costs of production rise, short-run supply curves (each firm's marginal cost curve) shift inwards to the left. The result is a long-run industry supply curve that is upward sloping and is represented by $S_L S_L$ in Figure 21.9(b).

Decreasing-cost industries

It is possible that an expansion in the number of firms in an industry leads to a reduction in input costs. When this occurs, the long-run industry supply curve will be downward sloping. An example is given in Figure 21.9(c). This is a **decreasing-cost industry**.

Industry-wide economies and diseconomies of scale

An industry can be other than constant cost if there are industry-wide economies or diseconomies of scale. If there are industry-wide economies of scale, the long-run supply curve shown in Figure 21.9(c) will result. If there are industry-wide diseconomies of scale, the upward-sloping long-run industry supply curve presented in Figure 21.9(b) will result. The concept of economies and diseconomies of scale at the *firm* level was introduced in Chapter 20. Economies and diseconomies of scale at the firm level resulted from factors *internal* to each separate firm.

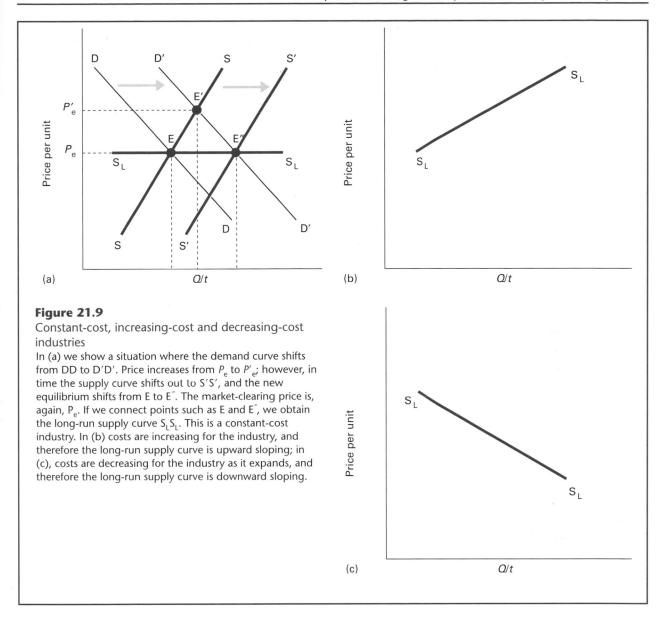

Figure 21.9
Constant-cost, increasing-cost and decreasing-cost industries

In (a) we show a situation where the demand curve shifts from DD to D'D'. Price increases from P_e to P'_e; however, in time the supply curve shifts out to S'S', and the new equilibrium shifts from E to E". The market-clearing price is, again, P_e. If we connect points such as E and E", we obtain the long-run supply curve $S_L S_L$. This is a constant-cost industry. In (b) costs are increasing for the industry, and therefore the long-run supply curve is upward sloping; in (c), costs are decreasing for the industry as it expands, and therefore the long-run supply curve is downward sloping.

External economies of scale occur when an increase in the output of the entire industry (not just one firm) allows suppliers to the industry to engage in increased specialization or innovative activities, which help to lower the unit costs of inputs to that industry. Take an example. One firm starts a business in a small residential area that has been set aside for offices and light industrial activity. This firm has photocopying needs but not enough to justify the purchase of its own equipment. The firm must take its originals to be photocopied some distance away. If many firms move into the same area, however, it may become profitable for a specialist photocopying firm to start business. There will at least be a reduction for the original firm in the time cost of having its photocopying done because it will not have to go so far. Additionally, the new photocopying firm may be able to use large machines with a lower cost per unit, which will also lower the monetary outlay involved in getting photocopies. The result will be a downward-sloping long-run industry supply curve, as represented in Figure 21.9(c).

External diseconomies of scale occur when input prices rise because the expansion in the industry puts pressure on all the suppliers to the industry. No individual firm has control over this phenomenon. It is all firms taken together that cause the input prices to rise. In such a situation, industry-wide diseconomies of scale will cause an upward-sloping long-run industry supply curve, similar to that depicted in Figure 21.9(b).

Long-run industry response to increasing or decreasing demand

One of the reasons we attempt to develop a model of a market structure is to predict what will happen when there are changes in the economy. Figure 21.9 can be used to predict what will happen when there are changes in a perfectly competitive industry.

In the case of increasing demand, we first need to determine whether we are dealing with a constant-cost, increasing-cost or decreasing-cost industry. Once we have determined that, we can then tell what will happen to price as industry demand increases. The simplest case is when we are dealing with a constant-cost perfectly competitive industry. This situation is, in fact, depicted in Figure 21.9(a). An increase in industry demand leads to a larger output being sold in the long run at a constant price P_e. However, if we are dealing with an increasing-cost industry, increasing demand in the long run will lead to increased production and also an increased price. Finally, if we are dealing with a decreasing-cost industry, in the long run an increase in demand will lead to an increase in output and a decrease in price.

Our predictions can be made in a similar fashion if we are dealing with a declining, perfectly competitive industry – one in which market demand is falling. If we are dealing with a constant-cost perfectly competitive industry, then in the long run output will be reduced but price will remain constant at P_e, as in Figure 21.9(a). If we are dealing with an increasing-cost industry, a decline in industry demand will eventually lead to a reduction in output and a *reduction* in price. And, finally, if we are dealing with a decreasing-cost industry, a reduction in market demand will lead to a long-run reduction in output and an *increase* in price.

Long-run equilibrium

In the long run, the firm can change the scale of its plant. In the long run, the firm will adjust plant size in such a way that it has no further incentive to change. It will do so until profits are maximized. Figure 21.10 shows the long-run equilibrium of the perfectly competitive firm. Long-run average costs are at a minimum, and so too are short-run average costs. Price is set equal to both marginal costs and minimum average costs. In other words, the long-run equilibrium position is where 'everything is equal', which is at point E in Figure 21.10. There, *price* equals *marginal revenue* equals *marginal cost* equals *average cost* (minimum, short run and long run).

Perfect competition and minimum average total cost

Look again at Figure 21.10. In the long-run equilibrium, the perfectly competitive firm finds itself producing at output rate Q_e. At that rate of output, the price is just equal to the minimum long-run average cost as well as the minimum short-run average cost. In this sense, perfect competition results in no 'waste' in the production system. Goods and services are produced using the least costly combination of resources. This is an important attribute of a perfectly competitive long-run equilibrium, particularly when we wish to compare the market structure of perfect competition with other market structures that are less than perfectly competitive. We examine these other market structures in Chapters 22 and 23.

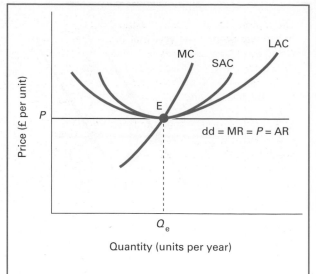

Figure 21.10
Long-run firm competitive equilibrium
In the long run, the firm operates where price equals marginal revenue equals marginal cost equals short-run minimum average cost equals long-run minimum average cost. This is point E.

Perfect competition and marginal cost pricing

In a perfectly competitive industry, each firm produces where its marginal cost curve intersects its marginal revenue (or dd) curve from below. Thus, perfectly competitive firms always sell their goods at a price that just equals marginal cost. For many economists, this represents a 'desirable' pricing situation because the price that consumers pay just reflects the opportunity cost to society of producing the good. In order to understand this, consider what marginal cost represents. It represents the cost of changing production by one incremental unit. Suppose a marginal cost curve shows that an increase in production from 10 000 pocket calculators to 10 001 pocket calculators will cost £1.50. That £1.50 represents the opportunity cost to society of producing one more pocket calculator. Thus, the marginal cost curve gives a graphic representation of the opportunity cost of production.

The competitive firm produces up to the point where the market price just equals the marginal cost. Herein lies the element of the 'desirability' of a competitive solution. It is called **marginal cost pricing**. The competitive firm sells its product at a price that just equals the cost to society – that is, the opportunity cost – for that is what the marginal cost curve represents.

Perfect competition and efficiency

When an individual pays a price equal to the marginal cost of production, then the cost to the user of that product is equal to the sacrifice or cost to society of producing that quantity of that good as opposed to more of some other

The Italian social scientist Vilfredo Pareto was born in the year that the Communist Manifesto was first published. By the time he had died in 1923, his work had contributed to the downfall of central planning, which we associated with communism in Chapter 2. The significant concept that he left students of economics was the idea of efficiency. In Pareto's terms, efficiency is related to concern with well-being of those in the economy. Those studying for degrees in the subject will undoubtedly have encountered the related meanings of producer, consumer and exchange efficiency. At the very least, all students will have heard the phrase 'Pareto optimality'.

It was Pareto's work that initiated the discussion by highlighting that an economy characterized by perfect competition in all markets, and with no externalities, would allocate resources in an efficient way in all sectors, the basic argument being that in a competitive equilibrium, no one wishes to produce more or less or to demand more or less; all the exchanges that members of the economy are willing to make have been agreed at fair prices. No one desires to change, so no one can benefit unless they take advantage of

Vilfredo Pareto

(1848–1923)

someone else. There is a general equilibrium. In Pareto's terms, this would be an ideal or optimum allocation of resources as it would become impossible to make somebody better off without making somebody else worse off.

This was a rather unique application of markets, especially as most of Pareto's contemporaries argued that welfare was best catered for by governments. Using a similar logic, he made a case for free trade, arguing

that tariffs and quotas only granted special benefits to some, while others would lose out.

As an economist, Pareto was intellectually at odds with the mainstream. Having graduated in engineering in 1869, he was involved for the next twenty years in business and politics, eventually reaching the position of director of an iron works. Finally, in his forties, he entered academic life, gaining the Chair of Economics at the University of Lausanne in Switzerland and publishing his first paper on economics in 1896. Most of his academic writing was used as an excuse to attack the government, and most of his works were from a political or sociological perspective.

Consequently, where his ideas are relevant to economics they often have an ethical edge, and they are normally expressed in a mathematical manner. These two qualities alone make Pareto's work more relevant to the specialist, especially welfare economists, where his ideas on evaluating efficiency form an important starting point. Indeed, Pareto's influences can be traced to modern theories on compensation, equity, second-best theory and cost–benefit analysis. His short career as an economist has certainly left its mark.

good. (We are assuming that *all marginal social* costs are accounted for.) The competitive solution, then, is called *efficient*. It is efficient in the economic sense of the word. Economic efficiency means that it is impossible to increase the output of any good without lowering the total *value* of the output produced in the economy. No juggling of resources, such as labour and capital, will result in an output that is higher in value than the value of the goods and services already being produced. In an efficient situation, when all markets are perfectly competitive, it is impossible to make one person better off without making someone else worse off. All resources are used in the most advantageous way possible. Everything is perfect. All goods and services are sold at their opportunity cost, and marginal cost pricing prevails throughout. A free-market economy full of perfectly competing firms can be regarded as 'optimal'. Vilfredo Pareto defined the idea in the early twentieth century (see box).

Is perfect competition possible?

The analytical model presented here represents a situation that, by definition, can never be seen in reality. For example, perfect competition can exist only if information is freely available. After all, the only way for a price to be uniform at every moment in time (corrected for quality changes and transportation costs) is for everybody to know what is happening everywhere at every moment in time. Obviously, information is never perfect. In fact, the cost of trying to achieve perfect information would be prohibitive and therefore undesirable.

A profit-maximizing firm will produce at the point where the additional revenues obtained from producing more goods exactly cover the additional costs incurred (where marginal revenue equals marginal cost). Similarly, if we are concerned to maximize the state of market information we would never spend more than we get in return for improving information flows. We would improve information in the market-place only up to the point where the value of doing so is equal to the marginal cost. That is certainly at a point well below *perfect* information. The case study at the end of this chapter will develop this point further as the problems that occur as a result of the absence of symmetric information are discussed via a so-called market for lemons – not the fruit, but used cars.

A purely competitive industry has been defined as one with many sellers. To satisfy the criterion of perfect competition where each seller has no control whatsoever over the price of his or her product, we would have to have a tremendous number of firms. Free entry into an industry would have to be possible and firms would be operating with constant-returns-to-scale production functions. However, in the real world we quickly observe that the number of firms is not large and therefore individually each firm has – at least in the short run – some control over its price. But analysing the industry in the long run, we might say that it was *tending* towards a competitive solution all the time because there were a sufficient number of firms *on the margin* attempting to increase their total sales by undercutting the other firms. Notice we said that the industry might *tend* towards a competitive solution at all times. That is a dynamic process – which is to say that it operates through time and never ends. At any time, an investigation of the particular industry would reveal that the industry was tending towards a competitive solution, but the industry would probably never reach that point.

How pure is the water market?

Not content with making clothes or selling perfumes, the likes of Chanel, Donna Karan and the Gap are now launching their own designer brands of bottled water. Long the staple drink of health-conscious supermodels, for whom a bottle of Evian or Volvic is a compulsory accessory, the fashion industry says it is only natural that it should now put its own label on water. Think of it as Haute H_2O – still or sparkling.

'It just seems so right,' said Patti Cohen, an executive at Donna Karan, which will market water next month. 'Water is international. It's real. Pure, refreshing – all those adjectives that go with it describe both us and the water.'

Ralph Lauren may also launch its own line soon.

The inspiration for fashion's wading into water appears to have been the London show for Bella Freud's collection late in 1993, in which Kate Moss sashayed down the catwalk guzzling from a bottle of Vittel.

Now the elite Maxfield boutique in Los Angeles serves customers its own-brand H_2O for free, having had a chic launch party for it in June 1994. Restaurants in Los Angeles sell it for about £1 a glass, and it has been the beverage of choice at several Hollywood parties.

'It's somewhat like me trying to get into the dress business,' sniffed Ron Davis, the head of Perrier in the United States. Frances Perroud of Nestlé, which owns the Vittel brand, said: 'It will come and go – like fashion.'

The designers insist that their products have extra taste, sharpness and smoothness compared with the waters of their rivals.

But most observers see it as a perfect example of people paying only for the label. For instance, most of the designer label water comes from a Californian bottler who sells the same water to a supermarket chain – where it retails for 65p a quart.

Source: Adapted from *The Guardian*, 25 October 1994

8 State three characteristics that make the bottled water market imperfect.

9 (a) Taking the characteristics of perfect competition as the measurement criteria, arrange the following six markets in sequence from those that come closest to the perfectly competitive extreme to those that are highly imperfect in their market structure:
  bottled water
  pick-your-own strawberries
  sewage disposal
  tap water
  letter delivery
  parcel delivery

(b) Briefly justify the six positions you have chosen.

(c) Select two other products/services to add to the spectrum started in 9(a) and justify their positions.

(d) Which of the conditions of perfect competition seem to occur most often within these markets?

10 Using examples from the bottled water market, what advantages and disadvantages do imperfect markets create for
(a) producers and
(b) consumers?

11 Could government regulation of the bottled water market make it more perfect? Explain your answer and decide whether it would be worth the effort.

Even if an industry is not perfectly competitive, it does not necessarily follow that steps should be taken to make it more competitive so as to ensure efficiency. After all, it is not possible to change an industry's structure from non-competitive to competitive without using resources. We shall discuss some of the ways of doing this, such as legislation against restrictive business practices and regulation of non-competitive industries, in Chapter 27.

The fact that we use the model of perfect competition in economic analysis does not mean that perfect competition is accepted as the only type of industry structure to be tolerated. As you should have recognized through this chapter, it is a theoretical abstraction. Remember that the purpose of a theory or model is not to provide an accurate description of the world but rather to create a reference point that may help to explain and predict reality.

KEY POINTS

21.3

- The competitive price is determined by the intersection of the market demand curve with the market supply curve; the market supply curve is equal to the horizontal summation of those sections of the individual marginal cost curves above their respective minimum average variable costs.

- In the long run, competitive firms make zero economic profits because of the entry and exit of firms into and out of the industry whenever there are industry-wide economic profits or economic losses.

- Economic profits and losses are signals to resource owners.

- A constant-cost industry will have a horizontal long-run supply curve. An increasing-cost industry will have a rising long-run supply curve. A decreasing-cost industry will have a falling long-run supply curve.

- In the long run, a competitive firm produces where price equals marginal revenue equals marginal cost equals short-run minimum average cost equals long-run minimum average cost.

- Competitive pricing is essentially marginal cost pricing, and therefore the competitive solution is efficient because marginal cost represents the social opportunity cost of producing one more unit of a good.

- If consumers in all markets faced a price equal to the full opportunity cost of the products they were buying, their purchasing decisions would lead to Pareto optimality; the economy would be at its most efficient.

Case Study

No friction, no problems

The first year student of economics learns how a perfect economy ought to behave, how the interaction between many buyers and many suppliers in markets produces the optimum outcome for society as a whole. Bill Gates, chairman of Microsoft, has called it a 'friction-free capitalism'.

After the sweet-sounding introduction, the study of economics, however, becomes a study of imperfection, an analysis of how the real world diverges from the ideal. To take just one well-documented example, if the information in a market is incomplete low-quality products can quite easily dominate. This situation is referred to as **asymmetric information**, as buyers and sellers are not privy to the same level of product knowledge. A common example occurs with used cars, to the extent that cars of doubtful quality in America are sometimes referred to as lemons.

Professor George Akerlof was the first to discuss the market for lemons in a paper on asymmetric information. His argument was that the potential buyer of a used car has relatively little information about the true quality of the car – its motor, transmission, brakes and so on. The only way the buyer can find out is to purchase the car and use it for a time. In contrast, sellers usually have much greater information about the quality of the car; for instance, they may have been using it for some time. In Akerlof's American terminology, the owner of a used car knows whether or not it is a lemon. In situations like this, with asymmetric information between buyer and seller, buyers typically tend to want to pay only a price that reflects the average quality of the used car in the market, not a price that reflects the higher value of a truly good used car.

From the car seller's point of view, given that the price of used cars will tend to reflect average qualities, all the owners of known lemons will want to put their cars up for sale. The owners of high-quality used cars will be more reluctant to do so. The logical result of this adverse selection is a disproportionate number of 'lemons' on the used car market and consequently relatively fewer sales than would exist if information were symmetric.

1 There are a large number of used car sellers and buyers. Does this fact mean that the used car market is perfectly competitive? (Explain your answer.)
2 Describe some of the techniques used in the marketplace to overcome the lemons problem.
3 The lemons problem occurs in other markets. Describe at least one other example.
4 (a) Do you think that information is distributed symmetrically in the health-care market?
   (b) What does your answer to (a) suggest about this market?

5 Consider one of the following actions designed to promote consumer welfare, and explain how it relates to the lemons problem:
  ● health warnings on cigarette packets
  ● nutritional labelling on food products
  ● advertising standards and legislation
  ● octane rating displayed on petrol pumps
  ● kitemarks for design
  ● British Standards Institute recognition
6 Apart from asymmetric information, what other problems exist in imperfect markets?
7 Would a sophisticated Internet with interactive electronic sites for all high street markets create what we refer to as a perfect retailing market? (Fully explain your answer.)
8 Why is perfect competition such an important reference point in economics?

Exam Preparation

Multiple choice questions

Consider the accompanying graph showing four hypothetical positions of firms operating in a perfect market. The points labelled **A**, **B**, **C**, **D** designate differing price–cost relationships. Use these letters to answer questions 1–4.

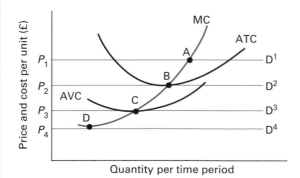

1 Which point indicates that the firm is earning normal profits?

2 Which point indicates that the firm is earning abnormal profits?

3 Which point indicates that the firm is indifferent between shutting down and producing?

4 At which point should the firm definitely shut down?

5 The demand curve for the product of a firm operating under conditions of perfect competition
  A is identical to the marginal revenue curve
  B intersects the marginal revenue curve at the point where its marginal costs are equal to marginal revenue
  C intersects the average variable cost curve at its lowest point
  D is of varying elasticities in different price ranges
  E is perfectly inelastic

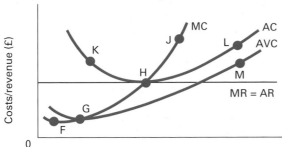

Costs/revenue (£)

Output per period

MC

AC

AVC

MR = AR

J

K

L

H

M

G

F

0

6 The diagram illustrates a firm operating under conditions of perfect competition. In the *short run*, the quantity of output which the firm will supply to the market at various prices is shown by
   A the marginal cost curve between points H and J
   B the marginal cost curve between points G and J
   C the marginal cost curve between points F and J
   D the average cost curve between points K and L
   E the average variable cost curve between points G and M

For questions 7–9 the following information applies.

A firm which operates in a perfectly competitive market has fixed costs of £120. When the firm sells 5 units of output its total revenue is £275. Other information about the firm is as follows:

	Units of output	Average cost (£)
A	1	145
B	2	75
C	3	55
D	4	50
E	5	54

From the options A–E above, select that level of output at which:

7 average variable cost is £30

8 the firm would maximize its profit

9 the firm earns normal profit

10 The figures below relate to a firm's sales and revenue:

Unit sales per week	Total revenue (£)
10	200
20	360
30	480
40	560
50	600
60	600
70	560
80	510

If fixed cost is £20 and average variable cost is £5, at what output will profits be maximized?
   A 30 units per week
   B 40 units per week
   C 50 units per week
   D 60 units per week

Essay questions

1 Why is competition in an industry thought to be desirable? Discuss the likely economic effects of policies to introduce competition into the supply of public sector services such as education and health.

2 Construct and explain the supply curve for a perfectly competitive industry in both the short run and the long run.

3 Define, concisely, total, average and marginal costs. Explain the relationships between the three types of cost. Should a firm cease production if it cannot cover its average costs?

4 (a) Distinguish between the short run and the long run in the theory of the firm.
   (b) Explain how
      (i) the law of diminishing returns and
      (ii) diseconomies of scale
      affect the production costs of a firm in these two time periods.

5 (a) Explain the meaning of the terms 'short run' and 'long run' in the theory of supply.
   (b) Consider how a perfectly competitive industry might react to an increase in demand in the short run and the long run.
   (c) Why is it argued that in certain circumstances an increase in demand may result in a lower long-run price in a perfectly competitive industry?

22

Pricing and output decisions in monopoly

LEARNING OUTCOMES

On completing this chapter you should understand:

- The meaning of monopoly and the related barriers to entry
- The typical demand curves facing a monopolist
- Monopoly profits and price discrimination
- The costs and benefits of monopoly
- Predatory pricing and dealing arrangements

The world, of course, does not consist of *perfectly competitive* industries. In this chapter, we present a model of a monopoly business and discuss how a monopolist decides what prices to charge and how much to produce. Most of the analytical tools needed have already been introduced, in Chapters 19 to 21.

Definition of a monopoly

The word *monopoly* or *monopolist* probably brings to mind a business that takes undue advantage of the consumer, sells faulty products, gets rich quick and any other bad thoughts that one can have about big business. If we are to succeed in analysing and predicting the behaviour of non-competitive firms, however, we shall have to be somewhat more objective in our definition. A pure **monopolist** is defined as a *single supplier* of a good or service for which there is no close substitute. In short, one firm constitutes the entire industry. Such a definition of monopoly could be applicable to a small business or a company selling on a nationwide basis.

As we have suggested, in a monopoly market structure, the firm (the monopolist) and the industry are one and the same. Care is needed, therefore, when identifying a monopoly, for the more narrowly we define a product, the more easily we come up with a monopoly situation. For example, consider a small town with a single newspaper. By our definition of monopoly, the owner of the newspaper is a monopolist. He or she sells the only newspaper printed in the locality. What if we consider this product – the only local newspaper – as part of the news media industry? Do the owners of this newspaper have a monopoly in all news media? Certainly not, for they are in competition with radio, television, magazines, newspapers from nearby towns, as well as national newspapers. Thus the uniqueness about the monopolist is indeed one of degree and few monopolists are likely to face no competition at all.

As we shall see in this chapter, a seller prefers to have a monopoly than to face competition. In general, we think of monopoly prices as being somewhat higher than competitive prices, and of monopoly profits as being higher than competitive profits (which are in the long run merely equivalent to a normal rate of return). How does a firm obtain a monopoly in an industry? Basically, there must be **barriers to entry** that enable firms to receive monopoly profits in the long run. We define barriers to entry as the difficulties facing potential new competitors in an industry. The sorts of difficulties that we have in mind are discussed below.

Barriers to entry

For monopoly power to continue to exist in the long run, there has to be some way in which the market is closed to entry. Either legal means or certain aspects of the industry's technical or cost structure must somehow prevent entry. Below, we discuss several of the barriers to entry that have allowed firms to reap monopoly profits in the long run.

Lack of availability of inputs

Preventing a newcomer from entering an industry is often difficult. Indeed, there are some economists who contend that no monopoly acting without government support has been able to prevent entry into the industry unless that monopoly has had the control of some 'essential' natural resource. Consider the possibility of one firm owning the entire supply of a raw material input that is essential to the production of a particular commodity. The exclusive ownership of such a vital resource serves as a barrier to entry until an alternative source of the raw material is found or an alternative technology not requiring the raw material in question is developed. A good example of control over a vital input is the Aluminum Company of America (Alcoa), a firm that prior to the Second World War controlled the world's bauxite, the essential raw material in the production of aluminium. (Such a situation is rare, though.)

Government regulations and exclusivity agreements

In many industries it is illegal to enter without a licence provided by the government. For example, in the United Kingdom you could not operate an unlicensed postal service or radio service. Similarly, it is necessary to obtain a licence from the Independent Broadcasting Authority before you can manage a regional independent television service. Successful applicants will receive monopoly rights to the sale of TV advertising space in their areas for eight years. Since these licences are not granted very often, long-run monopoly profits can be earned by those firms already in the industry. Historically, TV franchises have been very profitable to own. One franchise-holder described it as 'a licence to print money'!

An equivalent type of situation was found (in 1989) to exist in the supply of beer. Many brewers, especially the largest, were involved in brewing, wholesaling and retailing. In fact, it was estimated that 75 per cent of public houses were owned by brewers. A managed house is a pub run by an employee of the brewer; a tied house is operated by a tenant who pays a rent to the brewer and earns a living from the profit generated by the pub. In both types of pub the brewer-owner is able to restrict the range of beers offered for sale. In other words, competitors are faced with barriers to entry.

Patents

A patent is issued to an inventor to protect him or her from having the invention copied for a period of years. At the end of the patent period the patented invention is no longer private property but public property which anyone can copy or reproduce. Patents were first enacted in the United Kingdom as long ago as 1623 to encourage the process of invention by giving short-term reward for promoting scientific discovery. As one would expect, patent owners jealously guard their interests and try to enforce their exclusive rights. If, in fact, the costs of enforcing a particular patent are greater than the benefits, the patent may not bestow any monopoly profits on its owner – the policing costs are then too high.

Brand image

The development of strong brand names is a common feature of many markets. In the minds of consumers, the dominant brand name is often synonymous with a specific firm's product, for example Hoover, Calor Gas, Tampax and Durex. The brand image is taken to represent high quality. Hence it is often difficult or costly for entrants to attract consumers away from the well-known brand, especially as the dominant firm may employ price cuts to deter potential entrants to the industry.

Problem in raising adequate capital

Certain industries require a large initial capital investment. The firms already in the industry, according to some economists, can obtain monopoly profits in the long run because no competitors can raise the large amount of capital needed to enter the industry. This is the 'imperfect' capital market argument employed to explain long-run, relatively high rates of return in certain industries. These industries generally are ones in which large fixed costs must be incurred in order merely to start production. Their fixed costs generally are for expensive machines necessary in the production process.

Economies of scale

Sometimes it is not profitable for more than one firm to exist in an industry. Such a situation may arise because of a phenomenon we have already discussed – economies of scale. When economies of scale exist, costs increase less than proportionately to the increase in output. If the long-run average cost curve continues to fall as output increases, then a situation of **natural monopoly** might arise.

Within a natural monopoly the *first* firm that is established is able to enjoy very low average costs per unit. If it charges a price that reflects this favourable cost situation then no rival firm can threaten its position. It is sure not to be undercut and thus is assured of being a monopolist. The natural monopoly case originally provided a justification for utilities such as water, electricity, gas and telecommunications to be managed by the government: to avoid the problems of unfair pricing.

Privatization, however, has recently altered this perspective. Nowadays, governments structure the public–private sector divide in ways that encourage natural monopolies to behave as if supply were being provided competitively. This modern phenomenon is justified to some extent by a relatively new model of competition. This model is called the **theory of contestable markets**. The hypothesis suggests that when there are a few firms in an industry they are forced to price their products competitively because there are fewer barriers to entry. We have already introduced this new theory in the case study at the close of Chapter 20 and will examine it further when reviewing competition policy in Chapter 26.

Did Railtrack miss the point?

25 Franchised train operators	
Passenger fares	2802
Government subsidy	1817
Other income	382
Total revenues	5001
Costs:	
Rolling-stock companies	-797
Staff	-907
Railtrack charges	-2149
Other	-1024
Profit*	124

Railtrack Group PLC	
Access charges	2149
Freight access charges	164
Property and other income	172
Total revenues	2485
Costs:	
Staff	-275
Other	-471
Infrastructure maintenance:	
Subcontracted costs	-650
Other costs	-53
Depreciation	-137
Asset maintenance charge	-501
Profit*	398

3 Rolling-stock companies	
Revenues	797
Costs:	
Heavy maintenance	-248
Own costs	-40
Depreciation	-122
Profit*	387

19 Maintenance companies	
Revenue from Railtrack	900
Revenue from rolling-stock co's	124

*Before interest and tax

Source: Adapted from *The Economist*, 3 July 1999

In July 1992 the government published its plans to privatize the railways. The stated objective was to 'improve the quality of railway services by creating many new opportunities for private sector involvement'. Subsequently, British Rail was broken into 100 pieces comprising four main sectors: track, rolling stock, maintenance and train operators. The related companies were sold off during the years 1995–7. The flow chart shows an approximation of how these companies interrelate and an estimate of their financial position at the end of 1998. This complex arrangement has been described by a former director of British Rail as 'an orchestra where 100 odd musicians have individual contracts with the conductor, and with each other'.

1 What types of market structure represent the rail industry in its new privatized format? (Answer with reference to the four main sectors: operators, track, rolling stock and maintenance.)
2 Using facts and figures from the chart, describe two major barriers to entry that continue to benefit the privatized rail system.
3 Ultimately, costs must be considered alongside revenue. Which sector is showing the best rate of returns?
4 Make an economic case for British Rail being a natural monopoly.
5 What has happened to the railways in Britain since the year 2000?

KEY POINTS

22.1

- A monopolist is defined as a single seller of a product or a good for which there are no close substitutes.

- In order to maintain a monopoly there must be barriers to entry. Barriers to entry include ownership of resources without close substitutes, large capital requirements in order to enter the industry, legally required licences, franchises and certificates of convenience, patents, and economies of scale.

- In the extreme, economies of scale may create natural monopolies.

The demand curve facing a monopolist

How does a monopolist determine how much to produce? To answer this question, let us briefly recap on the situation for the firm in perfect competition. You will recall that a competitive firm has a horizontal demand curve. That is, the competitive firm is such a small part of the market that it cannot influence the price of its product. It is a **price-taker**. Each time production is changed by one unit, total revenue changes by the going price, and price is always the same. Marginal revenue never changes: it always equals price, or average revenue. Average revenue is total revenue divided by quantity demanded:

$$\text{average revenue} = \frac{\text{TR}}{Q} = \frac{P \times Q}{Q} = P$$

Monopolists' marginal revenue

What about a monopoly firm? Since a monopoly is the entire industry, the monopoly firm faces the entire market demand curve. The market demand curve is downward sloping, just like the others that we have seen. Therefore, in order to sell more of a particular product given the industry demand curve, the monopoly firm must lower the price. Thus, the monopoly firm moves *down* the demand curve. If all buyers are to be charged the same price, the monopoly must lower the price on all units sold in order to sell more.

Imagine that you are a monopoly ferry-boat owner. Assume that you have a government-granted legal franchise, and no one else can compete with you in operating a service ferry between two islands. If you are charging, say, £1 per crossing, there will be a certain quantity demanded of your services. Suppose that you are ferrying 100 people per day each way at that price. If you decide that you would like to ferry more individuals, you must lower your price to all individuals – you must move *down* the existing demand curve for ferrying services. In order to calculate the marginal revenue of your change in price, you must first calculate the total revenues you received at £1 per passenger per crossing, and then calculate the total revenues you would receive at, say, 90p per passenger per crossing.

The only way the monopolist can increase sales is by getting consumers to spend more of their incomes on the monopolist's product and less on all other products combined. Thus, the monopolist is constrained by the entire market demand curve for its product. We see this in Figure 22.1, which compares the perfect competitor's and monopolist's demand curves.

Here we see the fundamental difference between the monopolist and the firm in perfect competition. The latter does not have to worry about lowering prices to sell more. In a purely competitive situation, the competitive firm sells such a small part of the market that it can sell its entire output, whatever that may be, at the same price. The monopolist cannot. The more the monopolist wants to sell, the lower the price it has to charge on the last unit (and on all units put on the market for sale). Obviously, the extra revenues the monopolist receives from selling one more unit are going to be smaller than the extra revenues received from selling the next-to-last unit. The monopolist has to lower the price on the last unit to sell it because it is facing a downward-sloping demand curve. The only way to move down the demand curve is to lower the price.

The monopolist's marginal revenue is therefore going to be falling. But it falls even more than one might think,

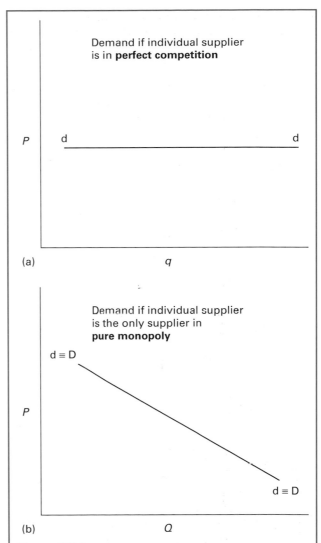

Figure 22.1

Comparison of the perfect competitor's and the monopolist's demand curves
The perfect competitor faces a horizontal demand curve dd in (a). The monopolist faces the entire industry demand curve in (b), and it is downward sloping.

because to sell one more unit the monopolist has to lower the price on *all* previous units, not just on the last unit produced and sold. This is because information flows freely; the monopolist will not usually be able to charge one consumer £2 and another consumer £3 on the same item. The consumer who could buy the product for £2 would buy lots of it and resell it for a price of, say, £2.50 to the one who was willing to pay £3. Unless the monopolist is successful in somehow *discriminating* between the different markets to prevent secondary transactions among the consumers in those markets, it will have to sell all goods at a uniform price. (We examine this possibility of discriminatory pricing later in the chapter, but for the moment we assume that a common price is charged to all buyers.) Therefore, when a monopolist increases production, he must charge a lower price on the last unit *and on all previous units.*

The monopolist's marginal revenue is less than price

An essential point in the above discussion is that for the monopolist marginal revenue is always less than price. To understand why, look at Figure 22.2. Here we show a unit increase in sales due to a reduction in price of one pocket calculator from P_1 to P_2. After all, the only way that sales can increase, given a downward-sloping demand curve, is for price to fall. The price P_2 is the price received for the last unit. Thus, that price P_2 multiplied by the last unit sold represents what is received from the last unit sold. This is equal to the horizontally shaded column (that is, a one-unit increase in sales) multiplied by P_2.

But the price multiplied by the last unit sold is not the addition of total revenues received from selling that last unit. Why? Because price was reduced on all previous units sold (Q) in order to sell the larger quantity $Q + 1$. The reduction in price is represented by the distance from P_1 to P_2 on the vertical axis. We must therefore subtract the vertically shaded section from the horizontally shaded column in order to find the change in total revenues due to a one-unit increase in sales. Clearly, the change in total revenues, that is, marginal revenue, must be less than price, because marginal revenue is always the difference between the two shaded areas in Figure 22.2.

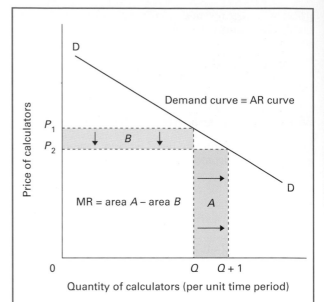

Figure 22.2
Marginal revenue is always less than price
The only way to sell one more unit when facing a downward-sloping demand curve is to lower the price. The price received for the last unit is equal to P_2. The revenues received from selling this last unit are equal to P_2 multiplied by 1 unit. However, if a single price is being charged for all units, total revenues do not go up. The price has to be reduced on all the previous units that were being sold at price P_1. Thus, we must subtract the vertical rectangle P_1–P_2 from the horizontal rectangle $Q - (Q + 1)$ in order to derive marginal revenue. Marginal revenue is therefore always less than price.

Elasticity and monopoly

The monopolist faces a downward-sloping demand curve. This means that it cannot charge just *any* price (a common misconception) because, depending on the price charged, a different quantity will be demanded. In other words, there is a unique relationship between the price the monopolist charges and total revenues, which equal price multiplied by quantity. Thus, there is a relationship between the total revenues and the price elasticity of the demand curve. We have already discussed this relationship, but it is worth going over again briefly. The demand curve of a monopolist has varying elasticities, depending on where we are on the demand curve. Remember that a straight-line demand curve has a price elasticity of demand that goes from infinity to zero as we move down the demand curve. (Thus, it is *not* true that a monopolist faces an inelastic demand curve.)

We earlier defined a monopolist as the single seller of a specific good or service with no *close* substitutes. That does not mean, however, that the demand curve facing a monopoly is vertical, or exhibits zero-price elasticity of demand. After all, consumers have limited incomes and alternative wants. The downward slope of a monopolist's

demand curve occurs because individuals compare the marginal satisfaction they will receive with the cost of the commodity to be purchased. Take the example of the telephone service. Even if miraculously there were absolutely no substitute whatsoever for telephone service, the market demand curve will still slope downwards. At lower prices, people will add more phones and separate lines for different family members.

Additionally, the demand curve for telephone service slopes downwards because there are several *imperfect* substitutes available, such as letters, telexes, faxes and CB radios. Thus, even though we defined a monopolist as a single seller of a commodity with no *close* substitutes, we can talk about the range of *imperfect* substitutes. The larger the number of imperfect substitutes, the more elastic will be the demand curve facing the monopolist, all other things held constant.

We can see the relationship now between the price elasticity of demand for a monopolist, marginal revenue and total revenues. This relationship is presented in Figures 22.3(a) and 22.3(b). At point A' on the demand schedule, the point corresponding to zero marginal revenues, we

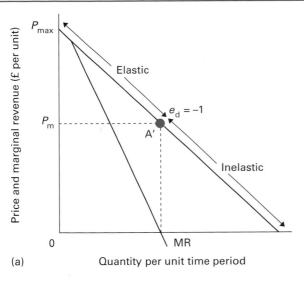

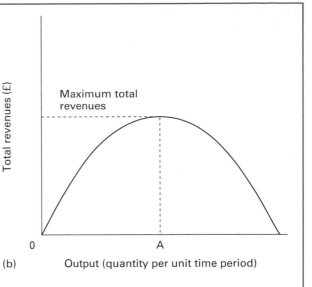

Figure 22.3

(a) Elasticity of demand and total revenues
Here we show the relationship between marginal revenue, the demand curve and the elasticity of demand. From the point where marginal revenue equals zero – that is, point A' – demand is inelastic to the right and below, and elastic to the left and above. At point A', demand has unitary elasticity, or equals –1. To the right, the monopolist would find that, if it lowered price, the quantity demanded would increase less than proportionally. To the left of A', as it raised price, the quantity demanded would fall more than proportionally.

(b) Total revenues and the demand curve
Here we show the relationship between the demand curve, the elasticity of demand and total revenue. When the price is set at P_{max} in (a), the total revenues are, of course, zero. When the price is set at zero, total revenues are also zero. In between these two ends of the price possibilities scale, we will find some price that maximizes total revenues. That price happens to be where marginal revenue equals zero, or at point A' in (a).

have marked $e_d = -1$. That is, the elasticity of demand is such that a change in price elicits a proportional and opposite change in quantity demanded. That portion of the demand schedule to the right of point A' we have labelled inelastic. That is, to the right of point A', a change in price elicits a proportionately smaller change in quantity demanded. That portion of the demand curve to the left and above point A' (above price P_m) we have labelled elastic. This means that to the left of A' a change in price will cause a proportionately larger change in quantity demanded.

We show the relationship between elasticity and total revenue graphically in Figure 22.3(b). Obviously, total revenues are zero at a zero price and at P_{max} where no units are sold. Between these points, total revenues rise and then fall. The maximum revenue is where the elasticity of demand is unity, as shown in Figure 22.3(b).

KEY POINTS

22.2

■ The demand curve facing a monopolist is downward sloping by definition.

■ The monopolist must consider the marginal revenue curve, where marginal revenue is defined as the change in total revenues due to a one-unit change in quantity sold.

■ For the perfect competitor, price equals marginal revenue equals average revenue. For the monopolist, price is always greater than marginal revenue. Otherwise stated, for the monopolist, marginal revenue is always less than price because of the downward slope of the demand curve.

■ The price elasticity of demand facing the monopolist depends on the number and closeness of substitutes. The more numerous and the closer the substitutes, the greater the price elasticity of demand for the monopolist's demand curve.

■ The monopolist will never produce in the inelastic portion of its demand curve.

Table 22.1

Monopoly costs, revenues and profits

1 Rate of output	2 Price per unit (£)	3 Total revenue (£)	4 Total costs (£)	5 Total profit (£)	6 Marginal cost (£)	7 Marginal revenue (£)
0	31.50	0	10	–10		
1	29.00	29.00	29	0	19	29
2	26.00	52.00	42	10.00	13	23
3	22.90	68.70	53	15.70	11	16.70
4	20.25	81.00	65	16.00	12	12.30
5	17.30	86.50	79	7.50	14	5.50
6	14.60	87.60	96	–8.40	17	1.10
7	11.50	80.50	116	–35.50	20	–7.10
8	8.60	68.80	138	–69.20	22	–11.70
9	5.80	52.20	162	–109.80	24	–16.60

Costs and monopoly profit maximization

In order to find at what rate of output the perfect competitor would be maximizing profits, we had to add cost data. We shall do the same now for the monopolist. We assume profit maximization is the goal of the pure monopolist, just as we assumed it was the goal of the perfect competitor. With the perfect competitor, however, we had only to decide on the profit-maximizing rate of output, because price was given. The competitor is a price-taker. For the pure monopolist, we must seek a profit-maximizing price–output combination. The monopolist is a *price-maker*. We can determine the profit-maximizing price–output combination in either of two ways: by looking at total revenues and total costs, or by looking at marginal revenues and marginal costs. Both approaches are given here.

Total revenue and total costs approach

We show hypothetical demand (rate of output and price per unit), revenues, costs and so on in Table 22.1. In column 3 we see total revenues for our hypothetical monopolist, and in column 4 we see total costs. We can transfer these two columns to Figure 22.4(a). The only difference between this total revenue and total cost diagram and the one we showed for a perfect competitor in the last chapter is that the total revenue line is no longer straight. Rather, it curves. For any given demand curve, in order to sell more, the monopolist must lower price. The basic difference, therefore, between a monopolist and a perfect competitor has to do with the demand curve facing the two different types of firm. Fundamentally, the costs faced by the perfect competitor and the pure monopolist are the same. Monopoly market power is derived from facing a downward-sloping demand curve.

Profit maximization involves maximizing the positive difference between total revenues and total costs. This occurs at an output rate of about 4 units. We can also find this profit-maximizing rate of output by using the marginal revenue and marginal cost approach.

Marginal revenue and marginal cost approach

Profit maximization will also occur where marginal revenue equals marginal cost. This is as true for a monopolist as it is for a perfect competitor (but the monopolist will charge a higher price). When we transfer marginal cost and marginal revenue information from columns 6 and 7 in Table 22.1 to Figure 22.4(b), we see that marginal revenue equals marginal cost at an output rate of about 4 units. Profit maximization occurs at the same output in Figure 22.4(b).

If the monopolist goes past the point where marginal revenue equals marginal cost (4 units of output), marginal cost will exceed marginal revenue. That is, the incremental cost of producing any more units will exceed the incremental revenue. It would not be worthwhile, as was true also in perfect competition. However, if the monopolist produces less than that, then it is not making maximum profits. Look at output rate Q_1 in Figure 22.5. Here the monopolist's marginal revenue is at A, but marginal cost is at B. Marginal revenue exceeds marginal cost on the last unit sold; the profit for that *particular* unit Q_1 is equal to the vertical difference between A and B, or the difference between marginal revenue and marginal cost. The monopolist would be foolish to stop at output rate Q_1 because, if output is expanded, the marginal revenue will still exceed marginal cost and therefore total profits will rise. In fact, the profit-maximizing monopolist will continue to expand output and sales until marginal revenue equals marginal cost, which is at output rate Q_m. The monopolist will not produce at rate Q_2 because here we see that marginal costs are at C and marginal revenues are at D. The distance between C and D represents the reduction in total profits from producing the additional unit. Total profits will rise as the monopolist reduces its rate of output back towards Q_m.

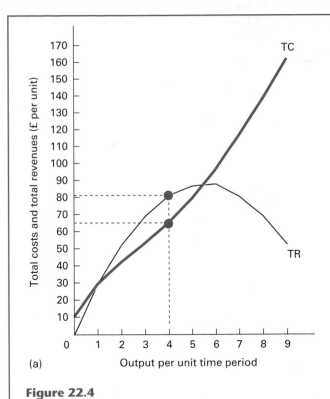

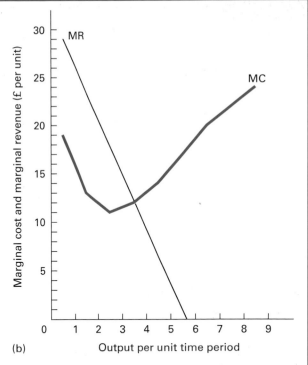

Figure 22.4

(a) Profit maximization: the TR–TC approach
The monopolist maximizes profits where the positive
difference between TR and TC is greatest. This is at an
output rate of 4 units. Notice the difference between the TR
curve here and the one shown in the last chapter for a
perfect competitor. This one is curved to reflect a
downward-sloping linear demand curve.

(b) Profit maximization: the MR–MC approach
Profit maximization occurs where marginal revenue equals
marginal cost. This is at an output rate of 4 units. (Also, the
MC curve must cut the MR curve from below.)

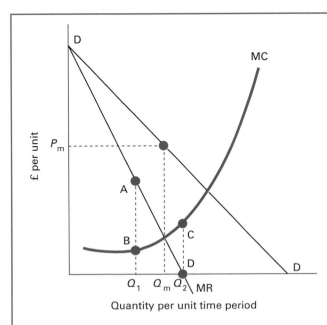

Figure 22.5

Maximizing profits
The monopolist will maximize profits where marginal
revenue equals marginal cost; it will produce up to the point
where MC equals MR and then will find the highest price at
which it can sell that quantity. The profit-maximizing
production rate is Q_m, and the profit-maximizing price is P_m.
The monopolist would be unwise to produce at the rate Q_1
or at the rate Q_2. You should satisfy yourself why this is so
with reference to points A, B, C and D.

What price to charge for output?

How does the monopolist set prices? We know the quantity is set at the point where marginal revenue equals marginal cost. The monopolist then finds out how much can be charged, that is, how much the market will bear for that particular quantity, Q_m in Figure 22.5. We know that the demand curve is defined as showing the maximum price for which a given quantity can be sold. This means that our monopolist knows that in order to sell Q_m it can only charge P_m, because that is the price at which that specific quantity, Q_m, is demanded. This price is found by drawing a vertical line from the quantity Q_m to the market demand curve. The price is determined where the line hits the market demand curve. We find that price by drawing a horizontal line from the demand curve to the price axis; this gives us the profit-maximizing price P_m.

In our detailed numerical example, at a profit-maximizing rate of output of 4 in Table 22.1, the firm can charge a maximum price of £21.50 and still sell all the goods produced.

The basic procedure for finding the profit-maximizing short-run price–quantity combination for the monopolist is first to determine the profit-maximizing rate of output, either by the total revenue and total cost method or the marginal revenue and marginal cost method, and then to determine by use of the demand curve DD the maximum price that can be charged to sell that output.

The decision-making that a monopolist must engage in to maximize profit is summarized in Table 22.2.

Calculating monopoly profit

We have talked about the monopolist making profit, but we have yet to indicate how much profit the monopolist makes. We have actually shown total profits in column 5 of Table 22.1. We can also find total profits by adding an average total cost curve to Figure 22.4(b). We do that in Figure 22.6. When we add the average total cost curve, we find that the profit that a monopolist makes is equal to the shaded area. Given the demand curve and a uniform pricing system, there is no way for a monopolist to make greater profits than those shown by the shaded area. The monopolist is maximizing profits where marginal cost equals marginal revenue. If the monopolist produces less than that, it will be forfeiting some profits. If the monopolist produces more than that, it will be forfeiting profits.

The same is true of a perfect competitor which produces where marginal revenues equal marginal costs because it produces at the point where the marginal cost schedule intercepts the horizontal dd curve. The horizontal dd curve represents the marginal revenue curve for the pure competitor, for the same average revenues are obtained on all the units sold. Perfect competitors maximize profits at MR = MC, as do pure monopolists. But the perfect competitor makes no true economic profits in the long run. Rather, all it makes is a normal competitive rate of return.

Table 22.2

	Production decision		
Situation	MR = MC	MR < MC	MR > MC
Decision	Stay put = profit-maximization rate of output	Increase production	Decrease production

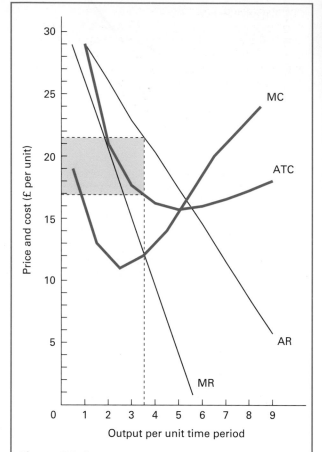

Figure 22.6
Monopoly profit
We find monopoly profit by subtracting total costs from total revenues at an output rate of 4 units, which is the profit-maximizing rate of output for this monopolist. Monopoly profit is given by the shaded area. This diagram is similar to Figure 22.4(b) except that we have added the short-run average total cost curve (ATC).

Microsoft versus NOISE
(**N**etscape, **O**racle, **I**BM, **S**un and **E**verybody else)

Bill Gates of Microsoft finds himself in a very powerful position in the worldwide computer market, as his Windows operating system is used for over 90 per cent of all personal computers sold.

The American Justice department, which regulates monopolistic behaviour, claims that Microsoft has the power to set prices and foreclose competition. Consequently, in October 1998 the United States Justice department and nineteen states began a landmark battle to break up Microsoft. At the time of writing, this legal battle continues.

In his defence, Bill Gates is quick to point out that over the twenty-three-year period in which his company has operated, computing costs have markedly been reduced; in terms of price to power, 10 million-fold! If other industries had maintained the same pace of improvement, a new car would now cost about £1.50 and you would be able to travel 600 miles on a thimble of petrol. A Boeing 747 would sell for the price of a pizza.

6 Traditionally, monopoly prices tend to creep upwards, yet Bill Gates claims that Microsoft has enabled the cost of computing to fall. So what can be the argument against Microsoft?

7 Does Microsoft benefit from any barriers to entry?

8 If the computer industry became more competitive and average and marginal costs increased by 10 per cent, would the increase in market price show up more in a competitive or monopolistic market?

9 An equivalent monopoly investigation of IBM in 1969 dragged on for thirteen years. Are the costs of monopoly investigation worth the benefits they secure?

Monopoly does not guarantee profits

The term *monopoly* conjures up the notion of a greedy firm ripping off the public and making exorbitant profits. However, the mere existence of a monopoly does not guarantee high profits. Numerous monopolies have gone bankrupt. Look at Figure 22.7. Here we show the demand curve facing the monopolist as DD and the resultant marginal revenue curve as MR. It does not matter at what rate of output this particular monopolist operates; total costs cannot be covered. Look at the position of the average total cost curve. It lies everywhere above DD (the average revenue curve). Thus, there is no price–output combination that will allow the monopolist to earn profits. This situation is typical of millions of monopolies that exist because, although owners of patented inventions have a legal monopoly, often the demand and cost curves that they face mean that production is not profitable. Indeed, many inventions have not been put into production as to do so would be uneconomic.

KEY POINTS

22.3

■ We assume the monopolist will maximize profits.

■ The profit-maximizing price–output combination is found by choosing that output where marginal revenue equals marginal cost and then charging the highest price possible as given by the demand curve for that particular output.

■ The basic difference between a monopolist and a perfect competitor is that a monopolist faces a downward-sloping demand curve and therefore marginal revenue is less than price.

■ Monopoly short-run profits are found by looking at average total costs compared with the price per unit. When this difference is multiplied by quantity, monopoly profit is determined.

■ A monopoly does not necessarily mean profit. One could have a monopoly, but if the average total cost curve lies everywhere above the monopoly demand curve, it will not pay to produce because there will be losses.

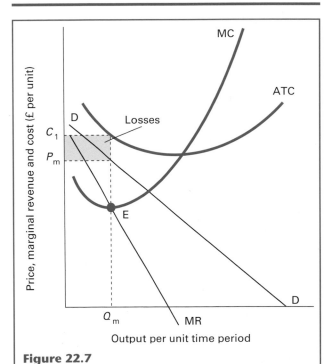

Figure 22.7
Monopolies are not always profitable
The diagram depicts the situation confronting some monopolists. The average total cost curve ATC is everywhere above the average revenue or demand curve DD. In the short run, the monopolist will produce where MC = MR at point E. Output Q_m will be sold at price P_m, but cost per unit is C_1. Losses are the shaded rectangle.

Price discrimination

In a perfectly competitive market, each buyer is charged the same price for every unit of the particular commodity. Since the product is homogeneous, and since we also assume full knowledge on the part of the buyers, a difference in price cannot exist. Any seller of the product who tried to charge a price higher than the going market price would find that no one would purchase from that seller. In this chapter, we have assumed up to now that the monopolist charged all consumers the same price for all units. A monopolist, however, may be able to charge different people different prices and/or different unit prices for successive units sought by a given buyer. Either one or a combination of these is called **price discrimination**. The reason a firm wishes to engage in price discrimination is that, where feasible, such a practice will lead to increased profits.

It must be made clear at the outset that charging different prices to different people that reflect differences in the cost does not amount to price discrimination. This is **price differentiation**: differences in prices that reflect differences in marginal cost.

We can turn this around to say that a uniform price does not necessarily indicate an absence of price discrimination. Charging all customers the same price when production costs vary by customer is actually a case of price discrimination.

Necessary conditions for price discrimination

There are four necessary conditions for the existence of price discrimination.

1 The firm must have some market power (that is, it is not a price-taker).
2 The firm must be able to separate markets.
3 The buyers in the different markets must have different price elasticities of demand. (And these should be identifiable at a reasonable cost.)
4 The firm must be able to prevent resale of the product or service.

For example, charging students a lower admission price to see a film at a cinema than the price charged to non-students can be done relatively easily: the cost of checking out student IDs is not significant. Also, it is fairly easy to make sure that students do not resell their tickets to non-students.

Graphic analysis

We can see how a price-discriminating monopolist will act if there are two classes of buyers with identifiable differences in their demand curves. In Figure 22.8 group I buyers are presented in part (a), group II buyers in part (b). To simplify matters, marginal cost for the monopolist is assumed to be constant. For profit to be at a maximum,

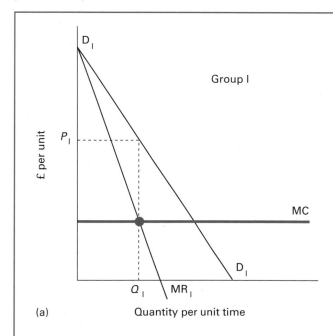

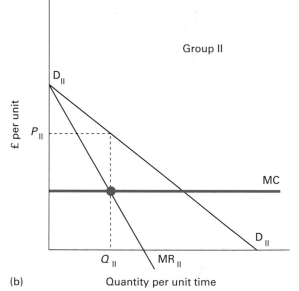

Figure 22.8
Price discrimination
Here the monopolist has separated buyers into those with relatively less elastic demand curves (group I) and those with relatively more elastic demand curves (group II). Profit maximization occurs when marginal revenue equals marginal cost. Therefore, our monopolist sets marginal revenue equal to marginal cost in each individual category. Hence, those with the relatively less elastic demand end up paying more than do those with the relatively more elastic demand for the same service.

we know that marginal revenue must equal marginal cost. We have a common marginal cost here, MC. We have two sets of marginal revenue curves, MR_I and MR_{II}. Thus, for profit maximization, $MR_I = MR_{II} = MC$. It is as if the goods sold to groups I and II were two different goods having exactly the same marginal cost of production.

We assume for simplicity that the marginal costs for servicing both groups of consumers are both equal and constant. Marginal cost equals marginal revenue for group I at quantity Q_I. The price at which the quantity can be sold is P_I. However, for buyers in group II who have a more elastic demand curve (at any given P) than buyers in group I, the intersection of marginal cost with MR_{II} is a quantity Q_{II}. The price at which this quantity is sold is P_{II}, which is lower than P_I. In other words, the price-discriminating monopolist will sell the same product to the group of buyers having a relatively less elastic demand curve at a higher price than the price charged to the other group of buyers with a relatively higher elasticity of demand. In such a situation, the monopolist earns a greater income than it would by charging a single price to all customers.

Examples of price discrimination?

Consider the conditions necessary for price discrimination and discuss how they might apply in the following markets. In each case, state specific examples to illustrate your answer.

1 The services of a heart surgeon.
2 Remedies for cold and flu.
3 Admission charges to a nightclub (disco).
4 Car hire.
5 Premier league football players.
6 An economics textbook published by Collins Educational.

The costs of monopoly

We now consider the desirability of a monopolistic market structure compared with a perfectly competitive industry. In Figure 22.9 we show an industry where long-run marginal costs are constant. From our analysis in Chapter 21 we know that in a perfectly competitive industry the equilibrium price would be P_c – price equals marginal cost. Now let us assume that the industry is suddenly transformed into a monopoly and there is no change in the cost situation facing the monopolist. The monopolist would charge a price P_m: output would be reduced from Q_c to Q_m. A monopolist therefore produces a smaller quantity and sells it at a higher price. This is the reason usually given when one attacks monopolists. Monopolists raise the price and restrict production compared with a competitive situation. For a monopolist's product, consumers are forced to pay a price that exceeds the marginal cost of

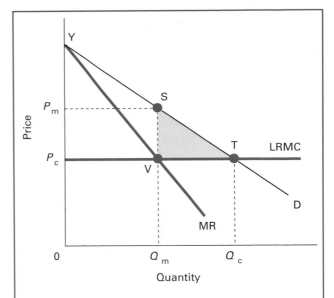

Figure 22.9
The effects of monopolizing an industry
If there are constant long-run marginal costs in a perfectly competitive industry then the equilibrium price will be P_c and the equilibrium quantity supplied and demanded will be Q_c. Now we assume that the industry is suddenly monopolized. We assume that the costs stay the same; the only thing that changes is that the monopolist now faces the entire downward-sloping demand curve. The monopolist will produce at the point where marginal revenue equals marginal cost. The monopolist therefore produces at Q_m and charges a price P_m. We see, then, that a monopolist charges a higher price and produces less than an industry in a competitive situation.

production. Resources are misallocated in such a situation – too few resources are being used in the monopolist's industry and too many are used elsewhere. As we have pointed out before, this difference between monopoly and competition arises not because of differences in costs but rather because of differences in the demand curves facing the individual firms. The monopolist has monopoly because it faces a downward-sloping demand curve. The individual perfect competitor does not have any market power.

Consumer surplus and producer surplus

We can examine the adverse impact of monopoly on resource allocation still further using the concept of consumer surplus that was defined in Chapter 19. In Figure 22.9 the area of consumer surplus is YTP_c in the case of the perfectly competitive industry. If the industry is suddenly monopolized and there is no change in the cost situation facing the monopolist, then the area under the demand curve shrinks to YSP_m. The monopolist has gained the area P_mSVP_c at the expense of consumers: this area is defined as producer surplus. The remaining part of the former area of consumer surplus is, of course, the triangular area STV. Neither consumers nor the monopolist now obtain this as a surplus: it is lost to both parties. Because of this it is called the **deadweight welfare loss** arising from monopolization of the competitive industry. This very term highlights how we can build up a strong case against monopoly and a presumption in favour of competition. However, there are several other aspects that still need to be considered.

Some other costs of monopoly

There are at least two additional costs in terms of resource misallocation that may occur when monopolies exist. One involves the resources used by individuals in order to obtain and maintain monopoly, and the other involves possible inefficiencies within the monopoly firm.

The resource cost of obtaining and maintaining a monopoly firm

As we recognized earlier in this chapter, some monopolies can be obtained by using the help of government in the form of restrictive licences, certificates of convenience and the like. Individuals, in their quest for higher-than-normal rates of return, will expend resources to obtain government-bestowed monopolies. These resources (from society's point of view) can be considered wasted. For example, the UK government announced that it would allow only one agent to organize the state lottery that commenced in November 1994. The *full* procedure by which an individual or a firm would obtain the licence was never explicitly stated in any government documents, but it certainly involved lobbying and offering hospitality to important civil servants, agreeing to distribute some of the profits to charity, and the like. These activities of course use scarce resources. If, however, the licence had been simply sold to the highest bidder, virtually no resources would have been spent wining and dining officials.

Economist Gordon Tullock has drawn an analogy between this type of activity and theft. A thief may steal £10 000 a year. This is a transfer from the victims to the thief. There are costs involved in theft, however. Thieves invest effort, time and other resources. In addition, victims must invest resources to protect themselves from theft. From the viewpoint of society as a whole, both these costs are wasted. Tullock argues that monopoly can be analysed similarly. From a social point of view, monopolists waste various resources attempting to establish and maintain monopoly profits. Society ends up expending resources in preventing monopolies or trying to break them up.

In the economics profession, this additional cost of monopoly has been inelegantly labelled **monopoly rent-seeking**, which is defined as the resources used in the attempt to establish and maintain monopolies in order to earn monopoly profits.

Efficiency loss in monopoly

We have assumed that all firms – whether they be perfect competitors or monopolists – will seek to minimize their costs of production. Implicit in our discussion of perfect competition was the necessity of each perfectly competitive firm to minimize costs. Because of the competitive process, if it does not minimize costs – given the large number of competitors minimizing their costs – then it will go out of business in the long run. This same argument cannot be applied directly to a monopolist. In principle, a monopolist cannot be completely minimizing the costs of production and that monopolist will not necessarily go out of business in the long run. To be sure, such non-cost-minimization will reduce monopoly profits, but bankruptcy is not the consequence as it is in a perfectly competitive firm.

The notion that costs are not minimized by effective management or that *organizational slack* occurs in monopoly has been called **X-inefficiency**. This term was used by Professor Harvey Leibenstein,[*] who ascribed X-inefficiency to a lack of motivational efficiency and to an inefficient market for knowledge. According to Leibenstein, X-inefficiency arises largely from losses of output due to motivational deficiency of resource owners.

> (With a given) … set of human inputs purchased and … knowledge of production techniques available to the firm, a variety of outputs are possible. If individuals can choose, to some degree the APQT bundles (Activity, Pace, Quality of work, Time spent) they like, they are unlikely to choose a set of bundles that will maximize the value of output.[†]

One of Leibenstein's favourite examples from the field of economic development involves two identical inefficient petroleum refineries in Egypt. The introduction of a new manager at one of the refineries (the one that produced less output) apparently brought about an immediate improvement in output. After some time passed, there was a further spectacular improvement in output. The increase in output was attributed to the new manager. In the United Kingdom the dramatic improvement in efficiency in those firms which have experienced major changes in senior management, for example some of the state monopolies that have now been privatized, is evidence that X-inefficiency exists.

---

[*] Harvey Leibenstein, 'Allocative efficiency versus X-inefficiency', *American Economic Review*, 56 (June 1966), pp. 393–415.
[†] Harvey Leibenstein, 'Competition and X-inefficiency: reply', *Journal of Political Economy*, 81 (May–June 1973), pp. 765–77.

KEY POINTS

22.4

- A monopolist can make higher profits if it can price discriminate.

- Price discrimination should not be confused with price differentiation. The latter occurs when there are differences in prices which reflect differences in marginal cost.

- The four necessary conditions for price discrimination are (1) the firm has some market power; (2) the firm must be able to separate markets; (3) buyers in different markets have different price elasticities of demand; and (4) resale of the product or service must be preventable.

- By price discrimination, a monopolist can divert part of consumer surplus to himself and enjoy producer surplus.

- Deadweight welfare loss refers to the loss of welfare arising from the monopolization of a competitive industry. It is a measure of society's loss of welfare due to the misallocation of resources arising from the presence of monopoly.

- Besides raising price and restricting output, monopoly creates a situation in which resources are spent to obtain and to maintain monopoly status. Additionally, there may be organizational slack within a monopoly; this has been called X-inefficiency.

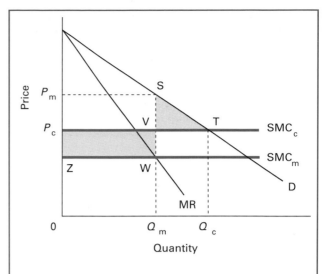

Figure 22.10
Deadweight welfare loss reconsidered
If the monopolist is able to reduce costs from SMC_c to SMC_m then resource savings can offset the deadweight welfare loss STV. (P_cVWZ is the area representing cost savings due to the lower SMC of the monopolist not available to the perfectly competitive firm.)

The benefits of monopoly

Our analysis has indeed built up a critical picture of monopoly. Both from a consumer viewpoint and in general terms of resource allocation, we do not end up with a favourable view of the single seller. But if you recall our analysis of the monopolization of a perfectly competitive industry, we must repeat that our analysis was based on a heroic assumption. That assumption was that the monopolization of the perfectly competitive industry does not change the cost structure. Of course, if monopolization results in higher marginal cost, then the cost to society is even greater. However, if monopolization results in cost savings, then the cost to society of monopolies is less than we infer from the above analysis. Indeed, we can present a hypothetical example in which monopolization leads to such a dramatic reduction in cost that society actually benefits.

Figure 22.10 shows such a possibility. If the monopolist can enjoy scale economies and thus operate on a lower short-run marginal cost curve, it can produce cost savings to set against the deadweight welfare loss. The perfectly competitive price is P_c and the monopolist charges a profit-maximizing price P_m. The deadweight welfare loss is now STV – a smaller area than in Figure 22.9. The rectangle P_cVWZ represents the saving in resource costs achieved by the monopolist. If this area exceeds the area STV then our antipathy to the monopolist looks less well founded.

A further point is that the monopolist may not actually charge the profit-maximizing price P_m but a price nearer P_c. Why might it do so? Simply because it will be drawing less attention from government and its customers if its price does not appear 'excessive'. If it charges a price resulting in high profits it may attract the concern of government, which may investigate its business with ensuing possible adverse publicity. A rival may be encouraged to compete with it with explicit government financial support. Better therefore not to charge too much above the competitive price and enjoy the benefit of continued security of at least some monopoly profits. Thus if P_m is nearer to P_c the magnitude of consumer surplus that is diverted and enjoyed by the monopolist is diminished and our case against the single seller is thereby weakened.

The process of innovation

Our discussion of the monopolist has so far concerned the costs and prices of existing products. What about development of new products? Joseph Schumpeter, the distinguished Austrian economist, argued strongly that the process of innovation is best encouraged by monopolists who can afford to take a long-term view and finance expensive – and uncertain – research and development programmes. The security offered to the monopolist thus benefits society through the appearance of new products. The monopolist enjoys profits in the short term, but sooner or later competition forces down prices and the monopolist finds its dominant position eroded away. Consider the ball-point pen. In October 1945, Milton Reynolds patented a new writing instrument tipped with a ball-bearing instead of a nib. It cost about 80 cents to make but sold at Gimbels, the New York department store, for $12.50. On the first day the pen was on sale, Gimbels sold 10 000. By March 1946, the Reynolds International Pen Company had been making profits of $500 000 a month. However, by Christmas 1946, there were roughly a hundred makers of ball-point pens in production, some of them selling models for as little as $2.98. Production costs had fallen below 30 cents a pen. By mid-1948, pens were selling for 39 cents and costing 10 cents to make.

Thus the monopolist creates a new market ultimately only to see its dominance destroyed. Society can gain from the appearance of the new product and expect competitive forces to limit the monopolist from continually charging a price well above the costs of production.

What can we offer as a comment on this dynamic case for monopoly? First, it has to be said that there is no certainty that the monopolist will innovate. As the Nobel Laureate Lord Hicks once put it, the greatest benefit of a monopoly can be 'the quiet life'. The security of very limited competition means that there are no immediate market pressures on the monopolist to reduce costs and innovate at all: it can sit back and enjoy at least some monopoly profits. Second, the Schumpeterian case needs to be supported by empirical evidence. If the process of innovation is not strongly related to the sheer size of a firm, then the basis for arguing that only very large firms are innovators looks suspect. Current evidence indeed hardly provides one with a confident basis for viewing small firms as unwilling agents seeking technical change. Schumpeter's argument is thus relevant in considering a government policy towards monopoly and size of firm, but in itself is not a conclusive one that justifies a monopolistic structure.

Patents, monopoly and competition

Patents create a legal monopoly. Consequently, when a company like Glaxo discovers an anti-ulcer drug such as Zantac, it can establish property rights in the design of that drug and become the sole seller for a number of years. As it is currently the top-selling drug in the world, this means securing annual sales in the region of £2 billion. Similarly Pfizer, the manufacturers of Viagra, the controversial treatment for impotence, is set to earn over £1 billion per year once the drug's use becomes an accepted part of national health services.

Standard textbook analysis suggests that monopolies are bad things since they can use their market position as sole sellers to maintain a higher price, by limiting supply, than would occur through competition. This means that there will be potential customers of the drug who are not supplied (because to supply them would lead to prices lower than the profit-maximizing level for the monopolist). The customers who are not supplied are ill and, given the nature of the illnesses that the top-selling drugs treat – ulcers, heart conditions, cancer – probably very seriously ill. This might lead us to believe that the ending of patents is no bad thing.

Source: Adapted and updated from *Economic Review*, September 1994

10 (a) What are the arguments supporting patents for drug companies?
   (b) What are the arguments against patents continuing?
   (c) Assuming a cure for AIDS is discovered, which argument would be strongest?
11 When the patent for a drug expires, any firm can produce it. The drug that is produced as a result is called a generic, which means that it is sold according to its chemical composition rather than its brand name.
   (a) What advantages does this have for the public?
   (b) What advantages does this have for the competing firms?
12 In general terms, do you think monopolies should be supported by governments when they are producing a specialized good or service? Explain your answer carefully, using relevant examples from any sector.

Predatory pricing and dealing arrangements

Our discussion of what constitutes a monopoly began with reference to various difficulties facing potential new competitors. We identified several aspects and discussed them under the heading 'Barriers to entry'. We now need to add to this list pricing policies and trading arrangements, which can also deter entry.

A monopolist can make life difficult for a potential competitor by setting price at such a low level that a would-be entrant feels disinclined to persist with plans to enter this market. Where a monopoly attempts to protect its dominant position by temporarily pricing its product such that losses are incurred not only by itself but for any competitor, it is said to be practising **predatory pricing**.

How else could a monopolist protect its position? It could also make life difficult for a potential competitor by trying to deny it wholesalers who might consider distributing the product of a rival firm. Exclusive dealing arrangements with wholesalers such that only the monopolist's goods are handled can limit the sources of custom for a new firm. Alternatively, those wholesalers and importers who wish to handle the goods of a new entrant may find they do not enjoy such favourable trading terms as other merchants who only stock the monopolist's goods.

These short-term defences in the form of pricing and trading deals could be contemplated by the monopoly as literally a price well worth paying in order to protect its secure position. Whether society as a whole should view this anti-competitive practice with enthusiasm is quite another matter. It should not surprise you, therefore, that in developed economies like the United Kingdom the abuse of a dominant market position is typically frowned upon by the authorities concerned with competition policy. We shall consider this policy in detail in Chapter 26.

KEY POINTS

22.5

- A monopolist may not charge the profit-maximizing price in order to avoid the disadvantages of government scrutiny and of stimulating competition from rivals.

- Monopoly has been held to be desirable in order to foster innovation, but so far the empirical evidence does not appear to be convincing.

- A monopolist may practise predatory pricing to deter new entry. Exclusive dealing arrangements with wholesalers can also limit the force of new competition.

Case Study

How natural is a monopoly?

In the UK the Office of Telecommunications (Oftel) has closely monitored the performance of the fixed telephone industry since it was privatized in 1984. For example, during the period 1996–2001 price controls were imposed on BT to allow competition to develop.

A consultative paper published by Oftel in July 1999, however, implied that subsequent five-year plans would require far less intervention. Ever since the early 1990s when competing companies were allowed access to the BT 'local loop', which is the last section of cable between a telephone exchange and a customer's premises, charges have fallen. BT now faces such fierce competition from the mobile and cable industries that market forces do the regulators' job for them. In fact, in the fast-moving telecommunications industry, many of the controls, in the regulated parts of the market, had become irrelevant before they expired.

Oftel's proposed plans, therefore, are largely confined to safeguarding some basic social obligations, such as the interests of low users and that of providing a universal service. The upshot is that probably less than 10 per cent of revenues are going to end up price regulated. Given that this is likely to be the 10 per cent of sales nobody wants, a separate issue may arise as to whether competitors should be forced to contribute to the costs of servicing them.

Nevertheless, Oftel will have a continued important role in policing the market and ensuring fair competition. That in itself requires price regulation, but at the wholesale rather than the retail end of the market. Someone has to set the prices competitors pay for using BT's network. That someone is Oftel.

Furthermore, as voice telephony moves progressively over to mobile phones, leaving the fixed-line market to broadband services, there may be a case for Oftel regulating the at present untouched mobile market.

Source: Adapted from *The Independent*, 8 July 1999

1 (a) Describe the type of market BT is now in. For instance, is it operating nearer to the perfect competition or pure monopoly model?
  (b) Using a cost and revenue diagram, explain and discuss the types of profits it should be earning.
  (c) Choose one of the following four concepts to describe BT's most probable pricing policy in the years 1990–2000: price discrimination, price differentiation, predatory pricing or price-making.
2 In 1998, BT had to pay a one-off windfall tax to allow the government to share in the large profits it made during the first four years in the private sector. Use this tax development to form an argument for or against BT being privatized in the first place.
3 Is there an economic case for Oftel to intervene in the mobile telephone market and/or the Internet market? (You may want to refer to recent developments to make your argument clear.)
4 In the second edition of *Economics Explained* (published in 1991), BT was discussed as a natural monopoly. Is there any relevance to this concept in the competitive telecommunications industry today?

Exam Preparation

Multiple choice questions

1 A profit-maximizing monopolist will seek to produce at a level of output where
   A average costs are lowest
   B there is the greatest difference between marginal revenue and marginal cost
   C the highest price can be obtained
   D price equals marginal cost
   E marginal cost equals marginal revenue

2 Which of the points labelled A to E on the diagram below indicates the equilibrium position of a profit-maximizing monopolist?

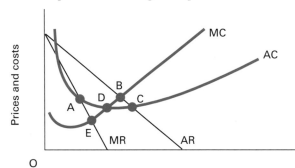

3 The diagram below shows the cost and revenue functions of a monopolist. It has been labelled with five possible output positions. Select the output level where the price elasticity of demand would be unity.
   A 1
   B 2
   C 3
   D 4
   E 5

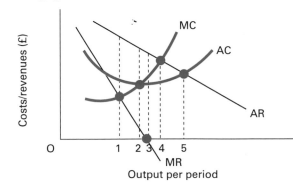

4 The diagrams below represent the operations of a price-discriminating monopolist who is able to separate the market for his product between domestic and industrial consumers. His marginal cost (MC) curve is the same in both markets.

How much will be supplied in each market in order to maximize profits?

	Domestic consumers	*Industrial consumers*
A	OA	OD
B	OA	OC
C	OB	OD
D	OB	OC

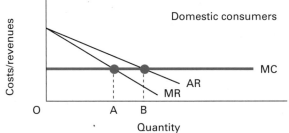

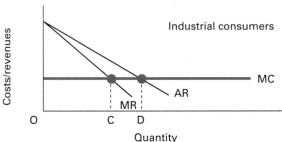

5 The data given below refer to a single-firm monopoly aiming to maximize short-run profits.

Output	Price per unit (£)	Total cost (£)
1	12	8
2	11	12
3	10	14
4	9	20
5	8	30
6	7	48
7	6	70

Given these conditions, at the equilibrium level of output the total profits of the firm will be
   A £9
   B £10
   C £12
   D £16

Essay questions

1 (a) What is a monopoly?
   (b) How do the price charged by a monopolist and the output produced differ from the price and output of a competitive firm? Explain your reasoning.

2 'Too much attention is paid to the theoretical disadvantages of monopoly.' Discuss.

3 'The uncritical acceptance of profit maximization in the theory of the firm has distorted our understanding of monopoly.' Discuss.

4 Examine the factors which might give rise to a firm being dominant in a market. Discuss two pricing policies which such a firm might adopt.

5 Is it (a) profitable and (b) desirable for a monopoly supplier to practise price discrimination?

6 'Under conditions of perfect competition there will be only one price charged by firms, but in the case of a single supplier there may be more than one price.' Explain this statement.

7 (a) Explain why a monopolist may be able to earn abnormal profits.
   (b) Why have economists argued that monopoly leads to economic inefficiency? What qualifications would you make to this argument?

8 (a) Briefly explain the meaning of the terms 'barriers to entry' and 'barriers to exit'.
   (b) How might barriers to entry be expected to affect the way in which markets operate in the real world? Illustrate your answer with relevant examples.

23

Pricing and output decisions in monopolistic competition and oligopoly

Up to this point, we have discussed the two extremes in market structure – perfect competition and pure monopoly. In the perfectly competitive model, we assume that there are numerous firms that produce the same product and that have no influence over price: they are *price-takers*. In the pure monopoly model, we assume that the firm is a single seller of a good to the entire market: the firm is a *price-maker*. There are obviously market situations that fall between these two extremes. Indeed, almost all the UK economy is characterized by firms that are neither perfectly competitive nor purely monopolistic. After all, most firms have some control over price, that is, individually they do not face a perfectly elastic (horizontal) demand curve, but they are not really pure monopolists. In this chapter, we look at the two market structures that lie between perfect competition and monopoly. There is monopolistic competition, where each seller has a small amount of market power but is in competition with a large number of others selling *almost* identical products, and oligopoly, with a small number of competitors and considerable market power.

LEARNING OUTCOMES

On completing this chapter you should understand:

■ Price and output determination in monopolistic competition

■ How perfect competition differs from monopolistic competition

■ Theories of oligopolistic competition

■ The meaning of industry concentration

■ Non-price competition

Monopolistic competition

Back in the 1920s and 1930s, economists became increasingly dissatisfied with the polar extremes of market structure mentioned above. There seemed to be many industries for which neither the perfectly competitive model nor the pure monopoly model applied; neither seemed to yield very accurate predictions.

Theoretical and empirical research got under way to develop some sort of middle ground. Two separately developed models of **monopolistic competition** resulted. In the United States Edward Chamberlin published *The Theory of Monopolistic Competition* in 1933. In the same year, Britain's Joan Robinson published *The Economics of Imperfect Competition*. The following account is based on their important contributions to the theory of the firm.

The characteristics of monopolistic competition

We define monopolistic competition as a market structure in which there is a relatively large number of firms offering similar but differentiated products. Monopolistic competition therefore has the following characteristics:

1 a significant number of firms in a highly competitive market due to the freedom of entry into the industry;
2 differentiated products;
3 the existence of advertising.

We now analyse these three characteristics in turn.

Joan Robinson (1903–83)

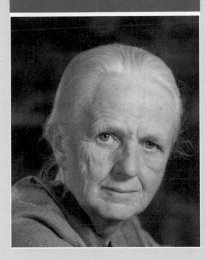

Joan Robinson taught at Cambridge University, England, for more than forty years. She wrote and lectured widely on economic theory, and made original contributions to the theories of imperfect competition and the accumulation of capital.

Robinson is best known for developing a theory of 'imperfect competition', a way of making sense of the market in an age when many industries are dominated by relatively few large firms. Through brand names Robinson argued that firms can differentiate their products slightly from those of other firms producing in the same markets. Thus competition amongst these firms is partial.

Later, in the early 1970s, Robinson showed how monopolistic corporations grow by 'continuously expanding capacity, conquering new markets, producing new commodi-ties, and exploiting new techniques'. Though the growth of monopolies has tended to reduce competition within individual countries, she said, competition among the industries of different countries has increased. Now, 'modern industry is a system not so much of monopolistic competition as of competitive monopolies'. She criticized orthodox economists in the West for ignoring the social and moral issues inherent in her theories. The central assumption behind most economic thought since Adam Smith is that individuals pursuing their own self-interests will yield public good, and morality will therefore take care of itself. Although Keynes showed that the market does not necessarily provide a means for a harmonious reconciliation of conflicting interests, and the Great Depression gave ample evidence of the fallacy of this assumption, she contended, it still pervades much contemporary thought.

Number of firms

In a perfectly competitive situation, there is an extremely large number of firms; in pure monopoly there is only one. In monopolistic competition there are quite a large number of firms but not as many as in perfect competition.

Several important implications for monopolistically competitive industry follow. We list these as further characteristics of this form of market structure.

4 *Small market shares* With so many firms, each firm has a relatively small share of the total market. Thus, each firm has only a very small amount of control over the market-clearing price.

5 *Collusion is difficult* With so many firms, it is very difficult for all of them to get together to collude, that is, to set a pure monopoly price (and output!). Thus collusion in a monopolistically competitive industry is virtually impossible.

6 *Independence* Since there are so many firms, each one acts independently of the others. That is, no firm attempts to take into account the reaction of all its rival firms – that would be impossible with so many rivals. Rivals' reactions to output and price changes are largely ignored.

Product differentiation

The most important feature of the monopolistically competitive market is **product differentiation**. Each individual manufacturer of a product has an absolute monopoly over its own product, which is slightly differentiated from other similar products. Consider the abundance of brand names for such things as toothpaste, soap and shampoo.

Indeed, it appears that product differentiation characterizes most markets for consumer goods. Consumers are not obliged to buy just one make of television set, toothpaste, sweatshirt or motor car. There are usually a number of similar but differentiated products from which to choose. Each separate differentiated product has numerous close substitutes. This clearly has an impact on the price elasticity of demand facing the individual firm. One determinant of demand elasticity is the availability of substitutes. The greater the number of substitutes available – other things being equal – the greater the price elasticity of demand. In other words, if the consumer has a vast array of alternatives that are just about as good as the product under study, a relatively small increase in the price of that product will lead consumers to switch to one of the many close substitutes. Thus, the ability of a firm to raise price above the price of close substitutes is very small.

Advertising and sales promotion

Monopolistic competition differs from perfect competition in that in the latter there is no sales promotion. By definition, the perfect competitor is selling a product that is identical to the product that all other firms in the industry are selling.

But such is not the case for the monopolistic competitor. Since the monopolistic competitor has at least some monopoly power, advertising may result in increased profits. How much advertising should be undertaken? Spending should be carried on to the point where the additional revenue from one more pound of advertising just equals the marginal cost of supply.

Shifting the demand curve

The goal of advertising is to shift the demand curve to the right. Advertising, it is hoped, will lead to a larger volume of business that more than covers the cost of the advertising. This is shown in Figure 23.1. At price P_1, with demand curve dd, the quantity sold will be q_1. If advertising shifts the demand curve over to d'd', then at that same price the quantity q_2 will be sold.

It is possible, however, that advertising is necessary just to keep the demand curve at dd. Without advertising, the demand curve might shift inwards to the left. This presumably is the case with competitive advertising. For example, cigarette manufacturers may have to expend large outlays on advertising merely to keep the share of the market they now have. If they discontinue advertising, they would lose ground to all the other companies that are engaged in heavy advertising.

Advertising and economies of scale

An alleged reason for advertising is that the subsequent increased sales can lead to economies of scale. This is possible only if the economies of scale outweigh the advertising costs. Look at Figure 23.2. Here we find that the hypothetical average total cost curve without advertising is ATC. With advertising, it is ATC'. If production is at q_1, then without advertising average total costs will be ATC_1. If advertising campaigns shift demand and increase the profit-maximizing output to q_2, then average total costs will fall to ATC_2. The reduction in average total costs will more than outweigh the increased expenses due to advertising. If the advertising campaign were not successful and demand and production remained where they were, then the firm would stop advertising. It would not be profitable to continue.

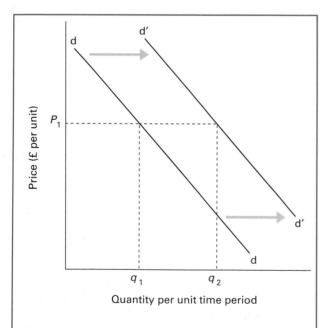

Figure 23.1
Advertising's desired effect
The firm that advertises hopes that the advertising will shift the demand schedule for its product to the right.

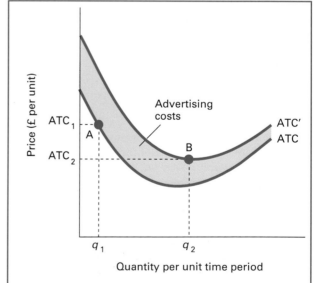

Figure 23.2
Another desired effect of advertising
We start out on the average total cost curve ATC at point A with production of q_1. Here average total costs are ATC_1. Advertising is added, and the average total cost curve shifts up to ATC'. However, if we move out to point B, the quantity produced will be q_2 with an average total cost of only ATC_2, which is lower than ATC_1.

KEY POINTS

23.1

- Monopolistic competition is a market structure that lies between pure monopoly and perfect competition.

- A monopolistically competitive market structure has a large number of firms because there is freedom of entry into the industry.

- There is product differentiation created by advertising and sales promotion.

- Because of the large number of firms, each has a small share of the market and collusion is difficult; firms ignore the reactions of rivals to changes in prices.

- The goal of advertising is to shift the demand curve outwards to the right and at the very least maintain existing market share.

- Proponents of advertising argue that it leads to increased sales, which allow firms to take advantage of economies of scale.

Price and output for the monopolistic competitor

Now that we have presented the assumptions underlying the monopolistic competition model, we can analyse the price and output behaviour of each firm in a monopolistically competitive industry. We assume in the analysis that follows that the desired product type and quality have been chosen. Further, we assume that the budget and the type of promotional activity have already been chosen and do not change.

The individual firm's demand and cost curves

Since the individual firm is not a perfect competitor, its demand curve is downward sloping, as is shown in Figure 23.3. Thus, it faces a marginal revenue curve that is also downward sloping and below the demand curve. To find the profit-maximizing rate of output and the profit-maximizing price, we go to the output where the marginal cost curve intersects the marginal revenue curve from below. This gives us the profit-maximizing output rate. Then we draw a vertical line up to the demand schedule. This gives us the price that can be charged to sell exactly the quantity produced. This is what we have done in Figure 23.3. A marginal cost curve has been drawn in each part of the figure. It intersects the marginal revenue curve at E. The profit-maximizing rate of output is q_e and the profit-maximizing price is P.

The short-run equilibrium

In the short run, it is possible for a monopolistic competitor to make economic profits, that is, profits over and above the normal rate of return, or profits over and above what is necessary to keep that firm in that industry. In Figure 23.3(a) we show such a situation. The average total cost curve is drawn below the demand curve dd at the profit-maximizing rate of output q_e. Economic profits are shown by the shaded rectangle in 23.3(*a*).

Losses in the short run are clearly also possible. They are presented in Figure 23.3(b). Here the average total cost curve lies everywhere above the individual firm's demand curve dd. The losses are marked as the shaded rectangle.

As with any market structure or any firm, in the short run it is possible to observe either economic profits or economic losses. In the long run, however, such is not the case with monopolistic competition.

The long run – economic profits are competed away

The long run is where the similarity between perfect competition and monopolistic competition becomes more obvious. In the long run, since there are so many firms making substitutes for the product in question, any economic profits will be competed away. They will be competed away either through entry by new firms seeing a chance to make a higher rate of return than elsewhere, or by changes in product quality and advertising outlays by existing firms in the industry. (Profitable products will be imitated by other firms.) As for economic losses in the short run, they will disappear in the long run because those firms that suffer them will leave the industry. They will go into another business where the expected rate of return is at least normal. Thus, Figures 23.3(a) and 23.3(b) represent only short-run situations for a monopolistically competitive firm. In the long run, the average total cost curve will just touch the individual firm's demand curve dd at the particular price that is profit maximizing for that particular firm. This is shown in Figure 23.3(c).

A word of warning. This is an idealized, long-run equilibrium situation for each firm in the industry. That does not mean that even in the long run we shall observe every single firm in a monopolistically competitive industry making *exactly* zero economic profits or *just* a normal rate of return. We live in a dynamic world. All we are saying is that, if this model is correct, the rate of return will *tend* towards normal, that is, economic profits will tend towards zero.

Comparing perfect competition with monopolistic competition

If both the monopolistic competitor and the perfect competitor make zero economic profits in the long run, then how are they different? The answer lies in the fact that the demand curve facing the individual perfect competitor is horizontal, that is, the price elasticity of demand is infinity. Such is not the case for the individual

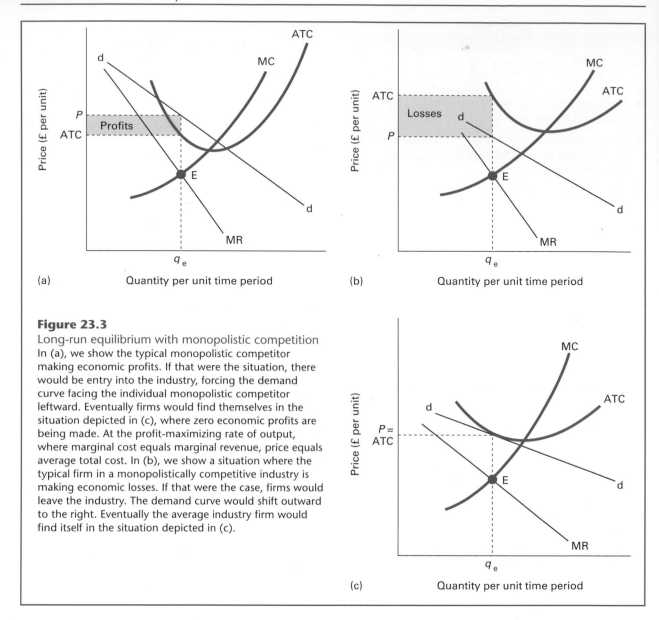

Figure 23.3

Long-run equilibrium with monopolistic competition
In (a), we show the typical monopolistic competitor making economic profits. If that were the situation, there would be entry into the industry, forcing the demand curve facing the individual monopolistic competitor leftward. Eventually firms would find themselves in the situation depicted in (c), where zero economic profits are being made. At the profit-maximizing rate of output, where marginal cost equals marginal revenue, price equals average total cost. In (b), we show a situation where the typical firm in a monopolistically competitive industry is making economic losses. If that were the case, firms would leave the industry. The demand curve would shift outward to the right. Eventually the average industry firm would find itself in the situation depicted in (c).

monopolistic competitor. The demand curve has *some* slope to it. This firm has some control over price; it has some market power. Price elasticity of demand is not infinite. We see the two situations in Figures 23.4(a) and 23.4(b). Both show average total costs just touching the respective demand curves at the particular price at which the firm is selling the product. Notice, however, that the perfect competitor's average total costs are at a minimum. This is not the case with the monopolistic competitor. The equilibrium rate of output is to the left of the minimum point on the average total cost curve where price is greater than marginal cost. (The monopolistic competitor cannot expand output to the point of minimum costs without lowering price; and then marginal cost would exceed marginal revenue.)

It has been argued, therefore, that monopolistic competition involves waste because minimum average total costs

are not achieved and price exceeds marginal cost. There are too many firms producing too little output. This situation is described as one of 'excess capacity'. According to critics of monopolistic competition, society's resources are being wasted.

In his book *The Theory of Monopolistic Competition*, Chamberlin had an answer to this criticism. He contended that the difference between the average cost of production for a monopolistically competitive firm in an open market and the minimum average total cost represented what he called the cost of producing 'differentness'. In other words, Chamberlin did not label this difference in cost between perfect competition and monopolistic competition necessarily a waste. In fact, he argued that it is rational for consumers to have a taste for differentiation; consumers willingly accept the resultant increased production costs in return for choice and variety of output.

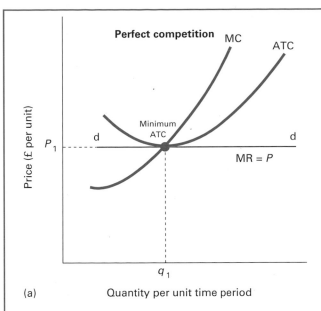

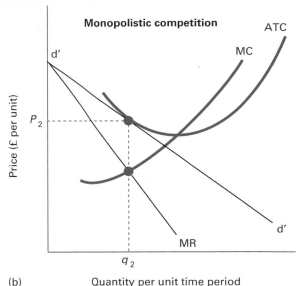

(a) Quantity per unit time period

(b) Quantity per unit time period

Figure 23.4
Comparison of the perfect competitor with the
monopolistic competitor
In (a), the perfectly competitive firm has zero economic
profits in the long run. Its long-run average total cost curve
is tangent to the demand curve dd just at the point of
intersection with the marginal cost curve. The price is set
equal to marginal cost, and that price is P_1. There are zero
economic profits. Also, its demand curve is just tangent to
the minimum point on its average total cost curve, which
means that the firm is operating at its optimum rate of
production. With the monopolistically

competitive firm in (b), there are also zero economic profits
in the long run, because the average total cost curve is
tangent to the individual monopolistic competitor's demand
curve, d'd', at the output where production occurs. The
price, however, is greater than marginal cost; the
monopolistically competitive firm does not find itself at the
minimum point on its average total cost curve.

KEY POINTS

23.2

■ In the short run, it is possible for monopolistically
competitive firms to make economic profits or
economic losses.

■ In the long run, monopolistically competitive firms
will make zero economic (or super-normal) profits,
that is, they will make a normal rate of return.

■ Because the monopolistic competitor faces a
downward-sloping demand curve, it does not
produce at the minimum point on its average total
cost curve. Thus, a monopolistic competitor has
higher average total costs per unit than a perfect
competitor would have. The term for this is 'excess
capacity'.

Which industries exhibit monopolistic competition?

There is no particular number of firms in a market which
defines the existence of monopolistic competition. Nor is
there an absolutely clear-cut example of a market that
meets all our six characteristics. Estate agents, hair-
dressers, restaurants, clothing manufacturers or hotels are
all possible examples. Note that these examples include
some in the service sector. Easy entry to the market-place
is a crucial characteristic. This means that competition
tends to be keen and the individual business will have to
price carefully, and in so doing consider the nature of the
competition.

We must reflect again on our six characteristics of the
market structure of monopolistic competition. They
describe markets where entry is easy and, as a result, the
number of firms is sufficiently large for any one of them in
producing slightly differentiated products or services to
act independently of its many rivals. The discerning
student will see that there is obviously tension between
assuming the existence of product differentiation and at
the same time ease of entry. In practice it is apparent in

many real-world markets that one or more of the six characteristics we have identified is not satisfied. Whilst there is differentiation of products and advertising, the number of competitors in many markets is not large. Entry into some markets is difficult to achieve, and it is very certain that where there is a handful of firms they are *interdependent* in the sense that the actions of one firm can affect the behaviour of its rivals. Arguably, the models developed by Joan Robinson and Edward Chamberlin need to be seen as less relevant in our contemporary world where in many markets there are few competitors.

Hunting the snark?

1 We have suggested that hairdressing is a possible example of a monopolistically competitive market. Explain how this industry can satisfy the characteristics listed above.
2 The retail trades have been frequently cited as offering possible examples of monopolistic competition. Why might the retail grocery market in the UK at the present time seem a much more dubious example than, say, twenty years ago? **A⁄**
3 How could you account for the comparative absence of examples of monopolistic competition in the manufacturing sector of the UK economy? **A⁄**

Oligopoly

The second form of market structure that we have yet to discuss is an important one indeed. It involves a situation where there are several large firms that dominate an entire industry. They are clearly not competitive in the sense that we used the term in Chapter 21; they are clearly not even monopolistically competitive. In an oligopoly there are just a few firms that are interdependent. There are several characteristics of oligopoly that we now comment on.

Small number of firms

If under oligopoly there are few firms, does that mean more than two but fewer than ten, twenty or thirty? The question is not easy to answer, but there must be several firms dominating the industry so that they really are able to set the price. Domination is measured by the percentage of total industry output accounted for by the few top firms.

You can probably think of quite a few examples of an oligopolistic market structure. The confectionery industry in the United Kingdom is dominated by three large firms: Nestlé, Mars and Cadbury Schweppes. In the case of the clearing banks, we have already noted in Chapter 18 that the National Westminster, Barclays, HSBC and Lloyds together have the largest number of domestic current accounts. Pie charts are often used to show the leading firms in oligopolistic markets. Figure 23.5 shows that when there are relatively few suppliers of heavy building materials, the leading companies account for significant market shares. Blue Circle Industries accounted for just under one-half of supplies of cement to building firms in

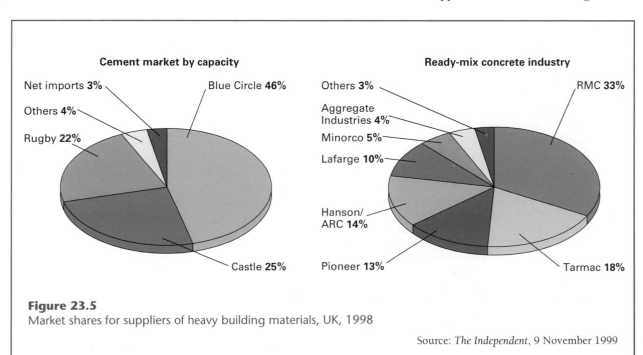

Figure 23.5
Market shares for suppliers of heavy building materials, UK, 1998

Source: *The Independent*, 9 November 1999

the UK in 1999. Two other firms each supplied about one-quarter of the market for cement. In the ready-mix concrete industry the largest supplier, RMC Group, accounted for one-third of industry output. Four other suppliers had a market share of 10 per cent or more.

Interdependence

When there are only a few large firms dominating the industry, they cannot act independently of one another. In other words, they recognize that there is mutual *interdependence*. Each firm will react to what the other firms do in terms of output and price, as well as to changes in quality and product differentiation. To specify a complete model of oligopoly, we would somehow have to specify the manner in which an oligopolist expects his or her rivals to react. You will recall that in a perfectly competitive model each firm ignores the reactions of other firms because each firm can sell all that it wants at the going market price. In the pure monopoly model, the monopolist does not have to worry about the reaction of rivals since, by definition, there are none.

We must stress here that the mutual interdependence results from the small number of firms in the industry that produce the largest share of total industry output. In fact, we might state that in an oligopoly market structure the firms must try to predict the reaction of rival firms. Otherwise, poor business decisions could be made that would spell lower profits.

Why oligopoly occurs

Why is it that some industries are dominated by a few large firms? What are the reasons that will cause an industry that might otherwise be competitive to tend towards oligopoly?

Economies of scale

Perhaps the strongest reason that has been offered for the existence of oligopoly is economies of scale. Remember that economies of scale are defined as a production situation in which a doubling of output results in less than a doubling of the total costs. When economies of scale exist, the firm's average total cost curve will be downward sloping as it produces more and more output. That is, average total cost can be reduced by continuing to expand the scale of operation. Smaller firms will have a tendency in such a situation to be inefficient; their average total costs will be greater than those incurred by a large firm. They will tend to go out of business (or be absorbed into the larger firm, which we discuss below). Historically, in many of the industries that have become oligopolistic, it has been technical progress that has made economies of scale obtainable.

Minimum efficient scale

The number of firms must be examined in the light of the **minimum efficient scale** for a firm in the industry. We introduced this concept in Chapter 20. The minimum efficient scale is the lowest rate of output per unit time period at which average costs reach a minimum point for a particular firm. The long-run average cost curve is determined by the nature of the returns to scale. In Figure 23.6 we show how economies of scale initially determine a declining long-run average cost curve before such economies become exhausted. When scale economies are exhausted and constant returns to scale begin, the minimum efficient scale for the firm is encountered.

Minimum efficient scale is thus concerned with that rate of output where the long-run average cost of the firm flattens out. Empirical evidence suggests that scale economies explain why the number of efficient competitors will be relatively few in industries such as motor vehicles and chemicals.

Barriers to entry

It is possible that certain barriers to entry have prevented more competition in oligopolistic industries. We defined barriers to entry in Chapter 22. They include legal barriers, such as patents, control and ownership over critical supplies, all of which can result in the existence of a pure monopoly situation. But there may be entry barriers of a less overwhelming kind which may result in the presence of some competitors but not as many as would create a market structure of monopolistic competition. The sort of difficulties that we have in mind in becoming a new entrant into an industry are the large sums of finance that

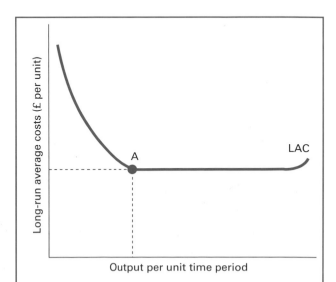

Figure 23.6
Minimum efficient scale
This long-run average cost curve reaches a minimum point at A.

may be required in order to set up in production, advertise heavily and create a new brand awareness – to product differentiate – and also to build up a national distribution system.

In recent years barriers to entry seem to have changed their nature. New technologies can make smaller scales feasible, for example in printing and publishing. So technical economies of scale will not always be so important. In fact it is often now the case that, where industries are very concentrated and strongly oligopolistic, the crucial factor is the marketing economies of scale which make it possible for large firms to advertise extensively. We will return to the issue of barriers again later in this chapter.

Oligopoly by merger

Another reason that explains the development of oligopolistic market structures is that a number of firms have merged. A merger is the joining of two or more firms under single ownership or control. There are three types of merger – horizontal, vertical and conglomerate.

Horizontal mergers involve firms selling a similar product. If two shoe manufacturing firms merge, that is a horizontal merger or *horizontal integration*. If a group of firms all producing, say, cars merge into one, that is also a horizontal merger.

Vertical mergers occur when one firm merges with either a firm from which it purchases an input or a firm to which it sells its output. Vertical mergers occur, for example, when a shoe manufacturer purchases retail shoe outlets. Another way of describing such a merger would be *vertical integration* or, more precisely, *forward vertical integration*. If a footwear retail firm purchased a shoe supplier this would be an example of *backward vertical integration*.

Conglomerate mergers involve the joining together of two firms which have unrelated activities. For example, a tobacco firm might seek to acquire firms producing beer and foodstuffs in order to ensure that its future growth is not restricted by a decline in cigarette-smoking. This is sometimes referred to as an example of one company diversifying its product base.

The rationale for mergers

We must presume that the decision by, say, the boards of directors of two firms to merge is not taken lightly. There must be some rationale for the firms involved to wish to give up their independence. One would assume that the directors perceive benefits from the merger which outweigh any of the disadvantages involved. The wish to take advantage of scale economies by combining outputs

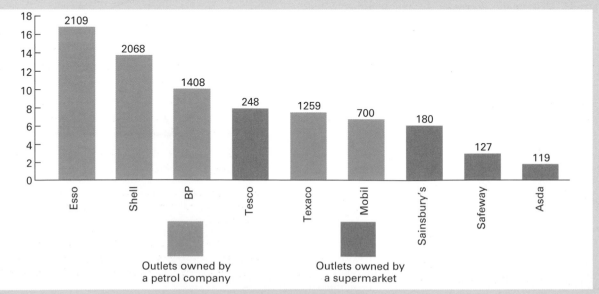

Major petrol retailers

4 Why does it seem appropriate to describe the petrol retail market in the UK as being oligopolistic? **A✓**

5 Given that the leading firms in the petrol retailing market are owned by oil companies, what type of integration does this market illustrate? **A✓**

6 What benefits arise for oil companies owning petrol outlets? **A✓**

7 What possible benefits might arise if two petrol firms decide to merge? For example, when in 1996 BP and Mobil announced their intention to merge their petrol retailing operations, what factors may have led to this decision? **A✓**

Esso 2109 | Shell 2068 | BP 1408 | Tesco 248 | Texaco 1259 | Mobil 700 | Sainsbury's 180 | Safeway 127 | Asda 119

Outlets owned by a petrol company

Outlets owned by a supermarket

The figures above each bar indicate the number of retail outlets

Source: *The Observer*, 3 March 1996

is clearly one such potential gain from merger activity. Mergers allow companies to grow and, indeed, to expand in size overnight. An alternative method of company growth is for a firm to win some of the market held by its rivals. Compared with a merger, this method of growth is typically slow since it takes time to win new customers. Mergers permit a quick and more certain expansion. However, sometimes a firm is reluctant to lose its independence and is faced not with a merger option but with a take-over bid from a rival. It is then a matter of persuading the shareholders of the desirability of staying independent rather than accepting an attractive offer for their shares. In this case we are referring to a take-over bid that may be contested by an unwilling recipient and the desirability of a merger keenly disputed by the two parties.

In such situations the bidding firm will be much involved in winning support from the major shareholders of its intended victim. In most companies these large shareholders are financial institutions rather than individuals. These large shareholders – pension funds, insurance companies, unit and investment trusts – thus effectively have the determination of take-over bids in their hands. In this sense they provide the **market for corporate control** of companies.

Sometimes the enthusiasm for mergers and take-overs appears to be based less on the quest to realize scale economies and more on a jockeying for position by the senior management of large firms to build ever larger companies. 'Empire-building' for its own sake and the attempt by senior managers to keep competition restricted by eliminating awkward competitors are motives for mergers that are indeed well documented. We must therefore not assume that the merger process is necessarily always in the interests of consumers. This point will be a major matter for us to consider in Chapter 26 in our review of what policies government might wish to adopt in seeking the promotion of competitive markets.

We have so far been considering the creation of oligopolies in a theoretical manner and we must now look at the actual picture of oligopolies in the United Kingdom.

Industry concentration

Oligopoly is a situation in which a very few interdependent firms control a large part of total output in an industry. Output of the industry is *concentrated* in a few hands. How do we measure this concentration of industry output?

Concentration ratio

The most frequent way to compute industry concentration is to determine the percentage of total sales or production accounted for by, say, the top four or top eight firms in an industry. This then gives the four- or eight-firm concentration ratio. An example of an industry with twenty-five firms is given in Table 23.1. We account for 90 per cent of total output in the hypothetical industry, which certainly describes an oligopoly situation.

UK concentration ratios over time

The case study shows the five-firm concentration ratios for various industries in 1992. But is there any way we can show or determine which industries we classify as oligopolistic? There is no definite answer. The concept of an 'industry' is necessarily arbitrary. As a consequence, concentration ratios rise as we narrow the definition of an industry and fall as we broaden it. Thus, we must be certain that we are satisfied with the definition of the industry under study before we jump to conclusions about whether the 'industry' is truly 'too' concentrated, as evidenced by a high measured concentration ratio.

KEY POINTS

23.3

- Oligopoly means a market structure where there are just a few firms which are highly interdependent.

- An oligopolistic market structure can come about because of (1) returns to scale, (2) barriers to entry, and (3) horizontal mergers.

- Horizontal mergers involve two or more firms, selling a similar product, becoming one integrated concern.

- Vertical mergers involve the merging of one firm with either the supplier of an input or a firm to which it sells its output.

- Industry concentration can be measured by the percentage of total sales, output or employment accounted for by the leading specified number of firms.

Table 23.1

Computing the four-firm concentration ratio

	Annual sales (£m)	
Firm 1	150	
Firm 2	100	
Firm 3	85	= 405
Firm 4	70	
Firms 5–25	45	
	450	
Four-firm concentration ratio =	405/450	= 90 per cent

Exercises in concentration

8 Referring back to the figure on page 404, what proportion of the total petrol market did the three leading retailers together account for in 1996? **A✓**

9 What is significant about the shares of the petrol market accounted for by the leading retail supermarket chains given the number of retail outlets where they sell petrol? **A✓**

Industry	Size group	Number of enterprises	Employment ('000s)	Gross output (£ million)
Non-ferrous metals	1–99	610	8.5	833.7
	100–199	23	3.4	278.6
	200–499	18	5.8	638.7
	500–999	8	6.2	796.0
	1000 and over	5	12.5	1893.5
		664	36.5	4440.5

Source: *Census of Production*, 1992, Table 13, Business Monitor, PA 1002, 1995

10 What was the five-firm concentration ratio in terms of (a) employment and (b) gross output? **A✓**

11 How would you explain why these two ratios are not similar? **A✓**

Industry (in order of the standard industrial classification)	Number of enterprises	Five-firm concentration ratio (expressed as a %)	
		Employment	Gross output
Iron and steel	27	90.9	95.3
Cement, lime and plaster	181	79.6	77.7
Glass and glassware	850	44.5	49.9
Pharmaceutical products	340	31.5	43.5
Soap and toilet preparations	415	44.8	58.8
Production of man-made fibres	21	88.6	92.7
Foundries	759	17.8	22.0
Agricultural machinery and tractors	943	51.5	71.6
Motor vehicle parts	1 259	26.2	22.7
Aerospace equipment, manufacture and repairs	470	67.9	80.5
Wines, cider and perry	60	88.4	91.1
Tobacco	22	97.7	99.5
Clothing, hats and gloves (including fur goods)	7 173	19.9	20.7
Builders' carpentry and joinery	2 327	17.1	17.3
Printing and publishing	18 828	12.8	14.5

Source: *Census of Production*, 1992, Table 13, Business Monitor, PA 1002, 1995

12 In terms of output, which industry had (a) the lowest five-firm concentration ratio and (b) the highest five-firm concentration ratio? **A✓**

13 How might you account for the high and low concentration ratios in your answers to question 8? **A✓**

14 With reference to examples in the table, what relationship might you expect to find between concentration ratios and the degree of competition within industries? **A✓**

15 Apart from concentration, examine one factor which might affect the degree of competition in any *one* of the industries in the table. **A✓**

Oligopoly price and output determination

When we analysed perfect competition, pure monopoly and monopolistic competition, we were able to present the profit-maximizing rate of output and price combination explicitly. In each case, we were able to draw a demand curve, a marginal revenue curve and a marginal cost curve. (For all three cases, profit maximization occurred when marginal revenue equalled marginal cost.) We cannot so easily do the same thing for oligopoly. Indeed, it is impossible for us to draw any one specific demand curve facing the oligopolist. Each oligopolist has to take account of the reaction of other oligopolists. How can a demand curve be known or even guessed without specifying the way that the other oligopolists will react? The answer is, it cannot. Under oligopoly, we must take account explicitly of rivals' reactions.

In a perfectly competitive model, each firm ignores the reactions of other firms because each firm can sell all that it wants at the going market price. In the pure monopoly model, the monopolist does not have to worry about the reaction of rivals, since by definition there are none.

Being able to ignore what other firms are doing in an industry – whether it is perfectly competitive or purely monopolistic – is therefore the key distinction to be made between those two forms of market structure and the one under study, oligopoly. We are referring again here to **interdependence**. This interdependence lies at the heart of every oligopoly model. We can characterize it by saying

Each firm expects that any change in price will be matched by all other firms in the industry.

Other, non-price, aspects of competition will also be subject to this interdependence. Any action by any oligopolist will be likely to produce some kind of reaction from competing firms.

Price rigidity and the kinked demand curve

Suppose now that the decision-makers in an oligopolistic firm assume that rivals will react in the following way: they will match all price *decreases* (in order not to be 'undersold'), but not price *increases* (because they want to capture more business). This outcome will involve rigid prices and a **kinked demand curve**, which we explain now.

In Figure 23.7 we draw a kinked demand curve, which is implicit in the assumption that oligopolists follow price decreases but not price increases. We start off at a given price P_0 and assume that the quantity demanded at that price for this individual oligopolist is q_0. The oligopoly firm assumes that, if it lowers its price, rivals will react by matching that reduction to avoid losing their respective shares of the market.

Thus, the oligopolist that lowers its price will not increase its quantity demanded greatly. The portion of its

demand curve to the right of and below point E in Figure 23.7 is much less elastic. However, if the oligopolist increases price, no rivals will follow suit. Thus, the quantity demanded at the higher price for this oligopolist will fall off dramatically. The demand schedule to the left of and above point E will be relatively elastic. This is the flatter part of the curve to the left of point E. Consequently, the demand curve facing the oligopolist is dd, which has a kink at E.

But one of the criticisms waged against the kinked demand curve is that we have no idea how the existing price, P_0, came into being. Seemingly, if every oligopolistic firm faced a kinked demand curve, it would not pay for it to change prices. The problem is that the kinked demand curve does not show us how supply and demand originally determine the going price of an oligopolist's product. Moreover, empirical evidence for the existence of kinked demand curves has been conspicuously thin.

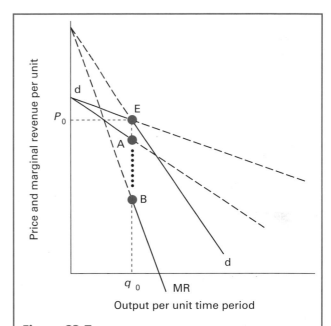

Figure 23.7

The kinked demand curve

At price P_0, the quantity demanded will be q_0. If the firm raises the price above P_0, few if any firms will follow suit. So at price P_0 the individual oligopolist's demand curve is relatively elastic – it will lose large amounts of business if it raises price. If we were to extend it, the demand curve would follow the broken line after point E. Now consider a reduction in price by the individual oligopolist. The rest of the firms will follow suit, so that a drop in price will result in very little increase in business. Demand will be relatively inelastic below price P_0, as shown by the steeper demand-curve portion from E to d. That demand curve, if it continued, would go up the broken line past point E towards the vertical axis. We can now draw marginal revenue curves for these two separately sloped demand curves. Only those portions of the two marginal revenue curves that are relevant are shown in solid black (A and BMR). The kink occurs at point E.

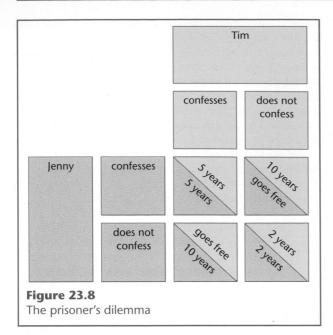

Figure 23.8
The prisoner's dilemma

Game theory

Game theory (or the theory of games) has been developed to try to see how decisions are made by those who have to take other people's responses into account. Game theory is not of course restricted to oligopolists, but firms are an appropriate example of where decision-making is indeed strategic, in the sense that one firm cannot wholly determine its own destiny. What a given firm in oligopoly does will affect its rivals just as much as their decisions on price and output levels will affect itself. Game theory began back in 1944 with the key ideas spelt out by John van Neumann and Oskar Morgenstern in their book, *Theory of Games and Economic Behaviour*. Fifty years later in 1994, three games theorists – John Nash, John Harsanyi and Rheinhard Selton – shared the Nobel Prize for Economics, a reflection of the esteem in which their work was viewed. However, we owe the best-known game – the prisoner's dilemma – to someone else – Albert Tucker – who in 1950 demonstrated how decisions by two persons may not achieve a joint outcome that is in their own interest.

The prisoner's dilemma

Figure 23.8 shows the *pay-off matrix* for Tim and Jenny, who have each been arrested as suspects who have committed a major robbery. After being taken to separate cells, the police explain to them that they can each confess to having committed the robbery and receive a five-year jail sentence. Alternatively, if neither confesses then each will be certain of being convicted of a minor offence such as driving without a taxed and insured motor vehicle and face a two-year jail sentence. A third possibility is that just Tim or Jenny feels willing to confess. Their dilemma here is that if, say, Tim confesses, he is promised that he can 'go free', but this means his accomplice gets a severe sentence

of ten years. This poses a real dilemma for Tim and Jenny. Their problem in separate cells is working out whether the other one will feel it is best in their own individual interest to confess. In the terminology of John Nash, the *dominant strategy* for both Tim and Jenny is indeed to confess. It is in the interest of Tim and Jenny individually to confess, but it is easy to see from the matrix in Figure 23.8 that they would be *as a pair* better off if neither confesses. Game theory may not resolve the problem facing Tim and Jenny, but it does highlight the problems of co-operative behaviour. In the context of firms, we can extend the logic of game theory to the situation showing conflicts of interest arising when it is possible for firms to agree on prices to be charged. We are now going to consider the world of collusion and cartels.

Collusion

The basic problem of the oligopolist is to try to estimate how rivals will react. The world of oligopoly is one of *uncertainty*. This is in contrast to the situation under perfect competition, where the number of firms is large and the decisions made by an insignificant single producer are trivial to the outcome of the whole industry. Interdependence means that oligopolists, in a freely competing market, are always unsure what will be the impact of one firm's change in market behaviour. One firm's decisions have consequences for all.

The presence of uncertainty provides managers of firms with an incentive to reduce the risks inherent in business life. How can managers in an oligopolistic market structure try to minimize the uncertainties they all face? They can try to agree on restraints on their independent decision-making. If they *collude* they limit their ability to use the crucial variable of price to try to gain sales from rivals.

Study of the business environment in the United Kingdom in the nineteenth century shows a 'natural' tendency for firms in concentrated industries to try to act in concert. Indeed, the operation of capitalism seems to prompt efforts by businessmen to reach either implicit or explicit agreement on prices that should be charged. This raises the very relevant issue of government policy towards such restraints on price competition and is discussed in Chapter 26. For the moment we need to consider what are the possible advantages for oligopolists of engaging in **collusion**.

First we need to define what we mean by collusion. Collusion that takes place in a **cartel** is an agreement made by a number of independent entities to co-ordinate decisions. The purpose of the cartel is to earn monopoly profits. Thus the operation of a cartel that fixes prices takes us back to our discussion of the behaviour of a monopolist who attempts to increase total revenue by restricting output. The analysis of a profit-maximizing monopolist is the same as that of a cartel which seeks to maximize the joint profits of its member firms. In effect, the cartel combines its member firms into a single monopoly decision-maker.

Duopoly

The simplest way to approach the operation of cartel pricing is to consider the case of just two firms in an industry. This situation is called a **duopoly**. Suppose the two firms, Smith PLC and Jones PLC, each account for half of an industry's output which is not differentiated by product and produce under identical cost conditions. These two assumptions mean that the costs and revenue functions for both Smith PLC and Jones PLC are as in Figure 23.9. Profits are maximized for both firms at the level of output Q and the shaded area PRST indicates the short-run economic profits accruing to both Smith PLC and Jones PLC. Neither firm has any incentive to charge a price other than P. A cut in price by, say, Smith PLC would result in both firms suffering reduced profits. The interests of Smith PLC square with those of Jones PLC if the price is P.

But what happens if in the duopoly there is one higher-cost producer, perhaps because its production facilities are older and less productive or even because of managerial inefficiency? The two firms cannot then sell at a price that will equate their individual interests with that of the industry as a whole. The two firms' interests conflict and neither firm would wish to see the price determined by its rival. By colluding – if it is legally allowed – the two firms can try to resolve their differing outlooks on the matter of price and output determination. But their collusion is likely

to be unstable because the firm with lower costs will want to cut the price.

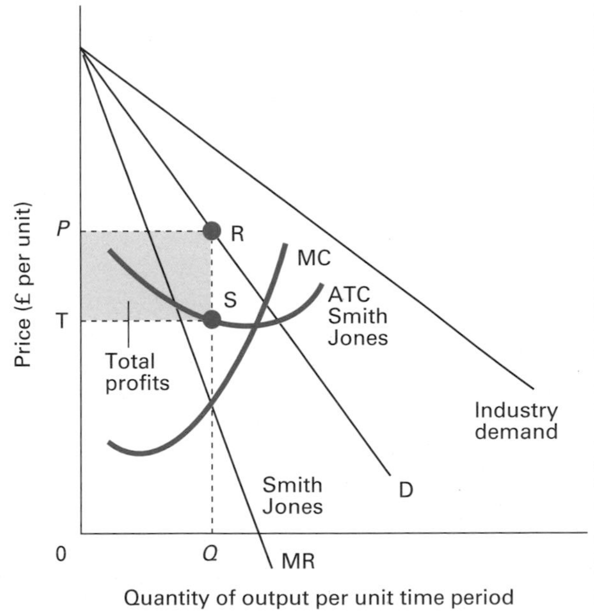

The outcome is not at all predictable. Collusion can produce a fragile and uncertain-lasting interlude between periods of active price competition. Once price cuts become apparent and all parties engage in price concessions, the effectiveness of the cartel is eroded until common cause is again established. Thus cartels are beset by the problem of their members being prompted to cheat on what they promise to uphold in common cause: self-interest clashes with the wider interest of the industry as a whole. This was the point we noted in the prisoner's dilemma earlier in the chapter.

Price leadership and tacit agreement

The term *price leadership* refers to the possibility of one firm within an oligopolistic market acting as the leader in effecting changes in prices. One firm may wish to raise its prices because its costs have risen and its profitability has therefore fallen. Its rivals, facing common cost pressures, such as higher wages, could thus be in a similar position and content to follow suit. Then the lead given by the first firm is one the rest of the industry is more willing to accept. As long as the leader has carefully judged the magnitude of the price rise, the problem of the kinked demand curve would not arise. The price leadership model thus describes how in an oligopolistic market virtually simultaneous changes in prices (so-called **parallel pricing**) can occur. The result appears to point to collusive behaviour but may well simply reflect how all firms await a suitable lead by one firm which acts as a *barometer* for the rest of the industry. The **barometric leader** need not be the same firm on every occasion of a change in price. However, it could be the case that the largest firm in the industry is accepted as the price leader. In this case as the **dominant firm** it might be recognized as the appropriate guide for the rest of the industry. Much smaller firms may hesitate to challenge the determination of market price by the most powerful firm within the industry for fear of starting a challenge from which they may ultimately be the losers.

Sometimes it appears that firms must be colluding because they all seem to charge about the same price for similar items. There is no obvious price leader, yet they do not seem to be competing on price. This is referred to as **tacit agreement**. No consultation has taken place and no formal agreement has been made. The competing firms simply choose not to charge prices which are much different from each other's.

Limit pricing

Our discussion has emphasized the interdependence of firms in oligopolistic markets. With this point in mind we can now reconsider one aspect of pricing that we introduced in Chapter 22. It will be recalled that there we considered the possibility of a monopolist trying to deter

Figure 23.9
Duopoly with identical costs and market shares
The two firms, Jones and Smith, are assumed to have similar costs in producing the same product, and equally share the output of the industry. They each maximize profits at output Q and each gains the short-run profits PRST. Neither firm has any reason to undercut the other: they would both charge the common price of P.

new entry by predatory pricing. But now we have more than one existing firm currently in the market. Thus we need to broaden the issue of pricing to refer to several competitors, all of whom share the goal of seeking to prevent yet more new competitors appearing on the scene. The concept of **limit pricing** is just such a concept. It refers to the possibility that oligopolists jointly seek to agree on a price which is the highest they can charge without prompting a new entrant to appear.

As you would expect, the precise level of the limit price cannot be determined without knowledge of the difficulties that a new firm actually faces. But the higher the barriers to entry are, then the higher is the possible level of the limit price.

Price wars

Although in general oligopoly tends to be characterized by price stability, the unstable nature of collusive or tacit agreements means that price wars do break out from time to time. The markets for petrol, package holidays and newspapers have all witnessed price wars in the United Kingdom at some point in recent years. Sometimes a price war will drive one or more of the weakest firms in the industry out of the market. A strong contender in the market may initiate the price war with this in mind. Once the number of competing firms has shrunk in this way, those remaining will return to a situation of price stability. Because there will be fewer competitors, they may then be able to achieve a larger market share and make more profit.

However, a price war may have the effect of reducing profits for all. If overall demand for the product is inelastic, all firms in the industry will face a fall in total revenue. It does not follow that the biggest firm in a market where there is a price war is the one that comes off best. In November 1999 British Airways (BA) reported a sharp fall of 77 per cent in its pre-tax profits for the first half of its financial year. In contrast Ryanair, which is only one-tenth the size of BA, reported that its profits for the same half-year were up by 17 per cent, thus maintaining almost a decade of spectacular growth. For BA the price war on North Atlantic routes in a market characterized by excess capacity proved to be one in which its sheer size made it more vulnerable than its much smaller competitor.

Being a market leader can sometimes prompt such a firm to feel it must defend its position in perpetuity. In the market for package holidays in the UK the leading firm has been Thomson, with a market share of 25 per cent. In 1999 one of its main rivals, Airtours, made a hostile bid for First Choice which, if successful, would have given the combined company a one-third market share of the package holiday market. The chairman of Thomson announced that it would 'defend' its market leadership that it had enjoyed for 25 years and was unwilling to surrender this position. Thomson proposed to increase its capacity to offer package holidays and offer new discounts in an effort to frustrate the threat perceived

Up and away far from peanuts

BA is now changing its strategy. By trimming capacity, switching to smaller aircraft with fewer economy seats sold at marginal cost, and dropping 20 European routes, BA is hoping to restore its profits. Michael O'Leary, managing director of Ryanair, is delighted with BA's strategy because he thinks that it opens the door to higher growth for him. 'We're going after BA traffic,' he says. 'We are courting the back-packers they are dropping off their flights.' Indeed, Ryanair's profits have been growing by about 33 per cent a year since 1995; it has become Europe's largest low-fare carrier. This year it will carry 6 million passengers. Its operating margin beats even America's legendary Southwest Airlines, making it the world's most profitable airline. Until 1991 Ryanair had been a struggling private airline, shuttling tourists and expatriate Irish folk between London and Dublin. From its humble beginnings, Ryanair has added about six routes a year, so that it now has 35 routes covering 11 countries. Passengers starting from Ireland now account for only a fifth of the total, and the main hub has shifted from Dublin to Stansted. Mr O'Leary likes to fly to and from secondary airports around Europe. From London Stansted a Frankfurt-bound flight lands at Frankfurt Hahn, 70 km (43 miles) outside the city centre; Paris means Beauvais, 70 km north in Normandy. This means both lower landing charges and fewer costly hold-ups because of air-traffic congestion. BA can claim to be the most punctual mainstream carrier, but Ryanair is the most punctual overall, thanks to landing in the middle of nowhere. Buses or train services meet each flight; and fares are one-fifth the levels charged by most carriers.

A basic service allows Ryanair to have only two flight attendants in its 130-seater aircraft, whereas big carriers have five. Ryanair does sell cheap sandwiches but, unlike Southwest, no peanuts. 'They mess up the cabin and slow things down,' says Mr O'Leary. Passengers are asked to take their crumpled newspapers and other rubbish with them before a cabin attendant tidies up. Ryanair owns only one kind of aircraft, the Boeing 737, which minimizes service costs. Big airlines in big airports are lucky to turn aircraft round inside an hour. Partly because Ryanair's airports are empty, Mr O'Leary can get an airliner back into the sky only 20–25 minutes after it has landed. Ryanair thus gains three hours from six turn-arounds, letting each aircraft make two more flights a day than it otherwise would.

Source: *The Economist*, 13 November 1999

16 Identify the bases of Ryanair's successful growth in the market for European air travel.

17 How does the passage suggest that demand for air travel is one that is price-sensitive?

18 What factors could threaten Ryanair's continued growth in the twenty-first century?

John Kenneth Galbraith has consistently warned of the power of big business. In his long career as professor of economics, journalist, public servant, and through his books which include *The Affluent Society* (1958), *The New Industrial State* (1967), *The Age of Uncertainty* (1977) and *The Culture of Contentment* (1992), the witty and urbane Galbraith has attempted to demonstrate how the growth of monopoly and the power of advertising have irrevocably transformed the nature of both economics and society.

Ever since Galbraith investigated the decline of farm prices during the 1930s Depression, the overriding theme of his writings has been the

J.K. Galbraith

(1908–)

break-up of the free-market economy into a competitive sector and a relatively monopolistic one. Giant corporations, he contends, now dominate large segments of the market, deciding what is to be produced and channelling the needs of consumers to feed corporate interests. Only by asserting its larger interests can the community put the industrial system in its proper place, subordinate to human needs instead of dominant over them.

from a merger of two of its smaller rivals. Critics pointed out that the management of Thomson seemed over-concerned about its market share and too little concerned about its profitability. Not surprisingly, the share price of Thomson Travel fell sharply when it seemed the company was prepared to enter a price war to preserve its market leadership.

Potential entry

In our discussion of monopolistic competition we stressed the relevance of free entry by those who feel they wish to compete with existing firms in a market. When we turned to a world of fewer existing firms we emphasized how in the real world some may have significant market shares. For many economists high market concentration ratios have been a source of concern. Can a few firms, well entrenched in a particular market, be virtually guaranteed to remain unchallenged simply because no new rival seems likely to emerge? The challenge to those concerned about market concentration came in 1982 from William J. Baumol, who in a paper in the *American Economic Review* and subsequently in a co-authored text emphasized the role of entry and exit. Baumol pointed to the irrelevance of high concentration if a firm can enter a market with a 'hit and run' competitive strategy and compete away existing high levels of profits. Such new entrants can more readily enter markets where profits are above normal if they can exit the industry without difficulty. Baumol thus pointed to the relevance of the absence of **sunk costs**, i.e. those costs which cannot be recouped following a decision to leave the industry. In Baumol's view, in a market where sunk costs are low, existing firms have a continual concern that new entry is always possible. In these circumstances, abnormal profits cannot prevail. Hence such a situation

describes a **contestable market**, a term we introduced in Chapter 20. The presence of just a handful of existing suppliers is thus in his view not a point of concern. Baumol's approach has not won over the whole economics profession, but the contestable markets theory has pointed up the relevance of how governments should address the matter of whether competition policies stimulate potential new competition. We reconsider this aspect in Chapter 26. Meanwhile, we can note that if governments restrict entry in a particular market then contestability is much reduced. Thus if, for example, competition on some air services is restricted on a given route by government regulation or take-off/landing slots, then a potential new entrant cannot easily bid down the fares charged. However, any potential entrant has little worry over investing in aircraft since they can be used on alternative routes or, *in extremis*, sold on the second-hand market. In these circumstances sunk costs are minimal. The risks of entry now are minimized if it ever came to it, leaving the market as not something where particular assets cannot be realized. It would, of course, make a difference if heavy expenditure on non-recoverable items like advertising was involved. In the case of promotional and marketing expenditures, no second-hand market exists to allow an entrant to exit and cut losses without too much pain.

KEY POINTS

23.4

- The kinked demand curve model predicts that oligopolists may not change prices once these are determined, but the existing price is not satisfactorily explained.

- Oligopolies may experience long periods of price stability, but price wars may occur in between periods of relatively stable prices.

- Because the world of oligopoly is one of uncertainty, there is an incentive for oligopolists to try to collude such that competition in price is at least partly eliminated. There may be tacit agreement.

- Price leadership may be one method by which oligopolists avoid the uncertainties in price determination when they do not collude. The leader may be the largest firm in the industry, or simply one firm that hopes its rivals will accept its proposed change in price.

- A market is perfectly contestable if there are no barriers to entry or exit. The absence of barriers means any new entrant can compete with existing firms without being handicapped.

- Baumol and others argue that under conditions of free entry and exit, existing firms, even a monopolist, will not raise prices above the competitive level.

Non-price competition

By their very nature, oligopolistic firms do not usually exhibit active price competition. The benefits from cutting prices tend to be small given the reactions of rivals. Hence a situation where rivals keep trying to undercut one another in the battle for supremacy in the market in a so-called *price war* is unlikely to persist. The likelihood of becoming a victor is slim if cost conditions are similar. Thus price wars do erupt occasionally, but these are only temporary. Therefore, competition for an increased percentage of total sales in the market must take some other form. The alternative form is what is generally called **non-price competition**. Non-price competition cannot be neatly subdivided into categories because it takes on a large number of aspects. The only thing that we can say about non-price competition is that it is an attempt by one oligopolistic firm to attract customers by some means other than a price differential. Here we consider advertising, quality variations and branding, but in addition to these aspects of non-price competition there are many

other strategies which firms use. Free gifts and other inducements, quality of service, and changes in packaging are just a few examples.

Nothing illustrates the aspect of non-price competition better than the detergent market. In 1994 Unilever announced it was launching Persil Power, a 'revolutionary' new detergent, throughout Europe. This was a new soap powder that had involved ten years of research, incorporating a patented manganese 'accelerator' or catalyst to enhance stain removal. However, Unilever's rival, Procter & Gamble (P&G), alleged that the new detergent was too powerful as it weakened the fabrics. Unilever replied, issuing writs for product defamation, but later dropped its lawsuit, saying it was to reformulate the new detergent. As a result of consumer reaction, Unilever lost its brand leadership to P&G's Ariel. However, in May 1998 Unilever launched Persil tablets, a new detergent in a nylon mesh bag designed to ensure they fully dissolved in the wash, and found households were enthusiastic. The innovation helped restore brand leadership to Persil, and, predictably, early in 1999, P&G launched its own version of the solid detergent tablet that had quickly proved successful for Unilever.

Unilever's discomfort in 1994 related to product innovation. A more obvious example of how non-price competition can prove to be counterproductive is that of Hoover's promotion in 1993.

On a magic carpet?

Hoover's recent promotional campaign in Britain and Ireland will go down as one of the great marketing gaffes of all time. For some reason not entirely clear, the company offered consumers two free return flights to Europe or America if they purchased any of its vacuum cleaners, washing machines or other household appliances worth more than £100 ($150). If Hoover's aim was to draw

attention to its name, which is one of Britain's best-known brands, then the campaign was perfect. Too perfect. Every national newspaper has run articles about the offer. On 30 March Maytag, one of America's biggest domestic appliance manufacturers and Hoover's American parent, stepped in and sacked the company's top three executives, including its managing director. Having dispatched a team of managers from America, Maytag now admits the free-flights promotion was a disaster.

Hoover's mistake was to expect most people to be attracted by the promise of free flights, but to be deterred from collecting their air tickets by the offer's small print, which lays down conditions about when its flights can be taken and which hotels may be visited. To make matters worse, a lot of Hoover's recent sales seem to have been to people more interested in free flights than household appliances. Although Hoover put aside some money to pay for air tickets, it was nothing like enough. Maytag said this week that it will take a $30 million charge against after-tax profits in the first quarter of 1993 to pay for the mess created by its British-based subsidiary. That is equivalent to nearly half of Maytag's net income last year. The subsidiary had lost money since Maytag acquired Hoover's American parent, also called Hoover, for nearly $1 billion in 1989.

Last year the British Hoover, which also covers Europe, made an operating loss of $12 million on sales of $495.5 million. Hoover's ill-fated promotional campaign was a ploy dreamed up to tempt people back into last year's depressed market. Britain's Consumer Association has been flooded with complaints from angry customers still waiting for their tickets.

Source: *The Economist*, 3 April 1993

19 Why was the purchase of a new Hoover vacuum cleaner in 1993 worthwhile? **AV**
20 The author of the passage commented that for Hoover, 'at the time it seemed to have the advantage of raising cash on extra sales now, with costs that did not have to be paid until later, in the form of heavily discounted air tickets, after the appliance market had improved. The error was as unbelievable as the offer.' Why should the author conclude the logic of the promotion was an error?
21 Retailers of second-hand vacuum cleaners claimed that following the Hoover promotion, this market collapsed. Explain why you would predict such an outcome. **AV**
22 Most promotions try to persuade people contemplating a purchase to favour one brand rather than another. Why was Hoover's promotion a problem because of its generous nature?
23 Why do companies offering promotions typically use computer models to forecast the likely take-up by eligible applicants?
24 How can insurance help companies contemplating attractive promotional campaigns?

Advertising

As we pointed out previously, the primary purpose of advertising is to shift the demand curve to the right. This allows the seller, whether it be an oligopolist, a monopolistic competitor or a monopolist, to sell more at each and every price. Advertising may also have the effect of differentiating the product and of making the product's availability better known. A firm will advertise as a way of gaining a non-price competitive advantage over other firms. Whatever can be said about advertising, its effect on the oligopolistic firm is certainly not completely predictable.

Quality variations

Quality differentiation results in a division of one market into a number of sub-markets. We talked earlier about differentiating product through quality variation when we discussed monopolistic competition. Now we can apply the same discussion to oligopoly. The prime example of product differentiation is the motor vehicle industry. There are specific physically definable differences between different automobile models within one single firm. A Fiesta and a Mondeo are certainly not the same product. If we examine cars, we see that competition among oligopolistic firms creates a continuous expansion and redefinition of the different models that are sold by any one company. There is competition to create new quality classes and thereby gain a competitive edge. Being the first in the market in a new quality class has often meant higher profits. Thus oligopolists are always looking for best-selling new models. New product development can promise higher sales and profits in a way that avoids the alternative risk of engaging in price competition with rivals.

Branding

The use of **brand names** can be a powerful form of product differentiation, and highly effective in raising sales. Often a business will seek to develop and advertise a brand in such a way that the brand name becomes synonymous with quality or style. In some cases, the brand name has come to be used in place of the name of the product, as in Thermos flask or Hoover. The price premium which a brand can command may make the brand name a significant asset for the firm.

In recent years, the importance of branding has been somewhat undermined by the growth of own-brands bearing the name of particular retail outlets, e.g. Tesco, B&Q and House of Fraser. Own-label products have become an important element in the markets for many foodstuffs and household products. Nevertheless, you have only to think of Coca-Cola, Heinz beans, Black Magic and numerous other examples to see that branding is still an important aspect of non-price competition. Branding can be particularly important when new products are being developed.

Table 23.2

Comparing market structures

Market structure	Number of sellers	Unrestricted entry and exit	Ability to set price	Long-run economic profits possible	Product differentiation
Perfect competition	Numerous	Yes	None	No	None
Monopolistic competition	Many	Yes	Some	No	Considerable
Oligopoly	Few	Partial	Some	Yes	Typical
Pure monopoly	One	No	Considerable	Yes	The product is unique

Comparing market structures

Now that we have looked at perfect competition, pure monopoly, monopolistic competition and oligopoly, we are in a position to compare the attributes of these four different market structures. We do this in summary form in Table 23.2, where we compare the number of sellers, their ability to set price and whether product differentiation exists.

KEY POINTS

23.5

■ Non-price competition is typical of oligopolistic market structures since if one firm tries to expand sales through price competition, it is unlikely to be successful without damage to its profit situation.

■ Advertising campaigns are one means by which oligopolists try to differentiate their products. Such expenditures often highlight the new products that oligopolists strive to develop in order to win consumer support.

■ Branding is still an important aspect of non-price competition, even though own-label brands have become more significant.

Case Study

Fiery chocolate

Per capita confectionery consumption in the UK is among the highest in the world, exceeded only by Ireland and Denmark. Chocolate confectionery accounts for around 70 per cent of sales value in the UK market, with sales of sweets (sugar confectionery) at around 30 per cent. Historically, the chocolate confectionery market has been characterized by the dominance of a number of well-established brands, such as Cadbury's Dairy Milk, Mars Bar and Kit Kat. Brand-led innovation is a vital component in the growth of this market as it enables organizations to build competitive advantage. Over recent years, competitors in the chocolate market have made significant investments in new product development. Indeed, over 15 per cent of volume sales in the last ten years have been generated by new products. This case study focuses on the launch of Cadbury's Fuse. In the face of strong competition from well-known brands in an already busy market

sector, the launch of Fuse represented a significant investment in a new brand.

The 'Fuse' concept was developed after market research identified the growth of snacking and a definite gap in the market for a more chocolatey snack. A number of ingredients were devised and tested following a survey which questioned consumers about their snacking habits and preferences. A research and development team was then asked to develop a number of product recipes that addressed the needs expressed by consumers. Considerable development time was spent on Fuse, carefully engineering the ingredients in order to deliver the right balance of chocolate, food elements and texture. More than 250 ingredients were tried and tested in various combinations before the recipe was finalized.

Whereas other confectionery snacking products focus primarily upon ingredients, with chocolate used only to coat the bar, the product developers decided to use Cadbury's chocolate to 'fuse' together a number of popular snacking ingredients such as raisins, peanuts, crisp cereal and fudge pieces. The design brief for Fuse had two clear requirements:

1 To communicate the dynamic and slightly wacky 'personality' of the new product and create interest at point-of-purchase (i.e. in store).
2 To bring the brand name to life by communicating the fusion of Cadbury's chocolate with the snacking ingredients.

The packaging achieved impact by using bright, fiery colours for the product name and contrasting them against the deep, instantly recognizable 'Cadbury purple', which communicated the manufacturer's heritage and suggested an explosive taste. The new product aimed to have broad appeal to 16–34-year-olds, although it was primarily targeted at 16–24-year-olds. The name Fuse was chosen to communicate the fusion of snacking ingredients. The logo was vivid with a mock fuse – alight in several places – which aimed to give the new bar the quirky and humorous style that Cadbury's sought to appeal to this younger target market.

In research, Fuse scored higher for texture, 'interesting eat' and combination of ingredients than its competitors and achieved the highest rating ever for a new Cadbury product – 82 per cent of consumers rated Fuse as excellent or very good, and 83 per cent said they would buy it regularly.

Traditionally, new confectionery products are initially launched in one region of the country, in order to gauge the product's success, before moving on to other regions over a period of time. Time Out and Wispa Gold, for example, were launched in this way. The commitment to the success of Fuse was so great, however, that it was Cadbury's first completely national launch for twenty years.

Secrecy had to be paramount!

Having a catchy 'hook' for a new launch helps to make consumers notice the product. Cadbury and its trade customers managed the first availability of Fuse around one day, Tuesday 24 September 1996, aptly christened 'Fuseday'. This involved tight management of stock distribution, with more than 40 million bars being moved from Cadbury depots into the trade only a few days prior to the launch date. Within just one week of the launch, a record 40 million Fuse bars were sold into the trade and within eight weeks of sale, Cadbury's Fuse was the UK's favourite confectionery line, outselling both Mars Bar and Kit Kat by 20 per cent and capturing an astonishing 6.5 per cent of hand-held confectionery product sales. It had also contributed significantly to Cadbury's growth in 1996. The launch had exceeded expectations, with consumers buying 70 million Fuse bars within the first three months of its launch.

Source: Cadbury's website, 30 October 1999

1 Chocolate confectionery forms part of the market for snack foods. In 1998 total sales of snack foods were £2.25 billion, having grown since 1994 much faster than spending on many other types of food. Explain why the market for snack foods has grown rapidly.
2 Explain why the case study states that 'secrecy had to be paramount'.
3 What are the respective merits of either launching a new product in one region of the UK and then moving to national coverage, or launching such a product nationally?
4 Cadbury's claim that the launch of Fuse was based on three clear aspects of innovation in the chocolate confectionery market. In the light of the case study, identify these three aspects.
5 Discuss which was more important in the successful launch of Fuse – its taste or its appearance?
6 Fuse turned out to be successfully launched. What decisions face Cadbury's in maintaining its position in the chocolate confectionery market?

Exam Preparation

Multiple choice questions

1 The combination of branding, non-price competition and barriers to entry is characteristic of which of the following market structures?
   A perfect competition
   B monopoly
   C monopolistic competition
   D oligopoly
   E public goods markets

2 Monopolistic competition differs from perfect competition in that only in the former
   A can profit be above normal in the short run
   B can profit be above normal in the long run
   C is there no freedom of entry
   D will the demand curve for a firm be downward sloping
   E will the most profitable level of output be achieved while marginal cost is below marginal revenue

3

Output (units)	Total cost (£)	Total revenue (£)
1	8	30
2	18	50
3	30	66
4	46	80
5	65	90
6	90	96

The data in the above table relate to a firm operating under conditions of
   A perfect competition and constant marginal costs
   B imperfect competition and falling marginal costs
   C perfect competition and rising marginal costs
   D imperfect competition and rising marginal costs
   E perfect competition and falling marginal costs

4 Non-price competition is common in oligopolistic markets because an oligopolist's
   A demand curve slopes down from left to right
   B demand curve is likely to be inelastic in relation to a price rise
   C pricing decisions have no effect on other firms in the market
   D demand curve is likely to be inelastic in relation to a fall in price
   E marginal revenue is less than the market price

5 In industry X the four largest firms produce 50 per cent of the industry's output.

In industry Y the four largest firms produce 70 per cent of the industry's output.

It can be concluded from the information that
   A firms are larger in industry Y than in industry X
   B there are more economies of scale in industry Y than in industry X
   C the concentration ratio is higher in industry Y than in industry X
   D small firms have more chance of survival in industry X than in industry Y

6 In a perfectly contestable market
   A firms are likely to earn normal profit in the long run
   B producers have monopoly power which enables them to fix prices
   C the minimum efficient scale of production is likely to be high
   D there are likely to be significant barriers to entry

7 An important characteristic of a contestable market is that
   A the fixed capital employed in the industry can be transferred to an alternative use
   B there is more than one firm in the industry
   C homogeneous products are produced
   D firms spend large sums on advertising and product promotion

8 Which of the following defines the minimum efficient scale of output?
   A where a plant of a given size is used to full capacity
   B where the firm can avoid making a loss
   C where the firm's operating profits are maximized
   D where the long-run average costs of a firm stop falling

9 The diagram shows a firm's cost curves. The firm enters a collusive agreement with other firms in the industry in which it is agreed that all firms will charge a common price, OP, and each firm agrees to restrict the level of its output to a production quota set by the industry cartel. The firm is allocated a production quota, Oq.

What is the maximum short-run increase in

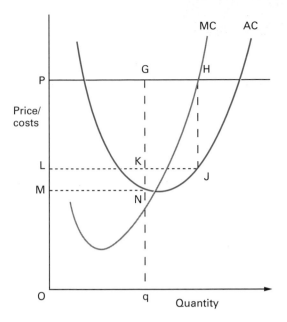

profits the firm could achieve by cheating on the agreement?

A GHJK
B GHJK – LKNM
C GHJK + LKNM
D LKNM

10 It is reported that there is a potential new entrant into an oligopolistic market. Which of the following measures seems likely to increase the possibility of the new firm entering the industry?

A the existing firms advertise their products more heavily
B existing firms lower their prices
C patent rights on a process vital to the industry continue to exist for ten years
D existing firms raise their prices
E the government imposes tight environmental regulations on the industry

11 Firm X sells its product in a perfectly competitive market, Firm Y operates in an oligopolistic market in which there are many competing brands, and Firm Z is a pure monopoly. Which of the following descriptions of these products is correct?

Products supplied by:

	Firm X	Firm Y	Firm Z
A	Differentiated	Differentiated	Unique
B	Unique	Differentiated	Differentiated
C	Identical	Differentiated	Unique
D	Unique	Unique	Differentiated
E	Identical	Unique	Differentiated

Questions 12 and 13 are based on the following information:

Holiday capacity by tour operator, 1998–9

	(millions of passengers)
1 Thomson	4.4
2 Airtours	3.4
3 Thomas Cook/Carlson	3.3
4 First Choice	3.1
5 Cosmos	1.0
Others	5.8
Total	**21.0**

12 From the above information, the three-firm concentration ratio is approximately

A 11.1 per cent
B 15.2 per cent
C 21.0 per cent
D 52.9 per cent
E 72.4 per cent

13 This market corresponds most closely to that of

A monopoly
B perfect competition
C monopolistic competition
D duopoly
E oligopoly

14 According to the chart, which of the following statements relating to the UK home shopping market is correct?

Home shopping (mail order) market shares (%)

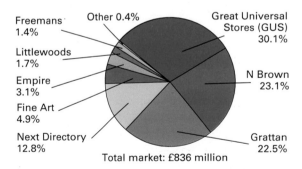

Source: Business in Focus 1995/96, Causeway Press

A the three-firm concentration ratio is 70 per cent
B all firms in the market will have perfectly elastic demand curves
C the cross-elasticity of demand between the products of Grattan and GUS is likely to be negative
D the share of the market held by GUS exceeds £300 million in value
E the market structure is likely to be oligopolistic

15 Which of the following would threaten the long-run success of a producer cartel?
  A non-members of the cartel produce insignificant levels of output
  B the cartel produces a homogeneous product
  C legislation against anti-competitive practices is ineffective
  D barriers to entry are relatively low
  E the demand for the cartel's product is price inelastic and rising

Essay questions

1 (a) Explain and discuss the following statements:
  (i) 'Competition is always beneficial.'
  (ii) 'Competitive actions include price changes, advertising, and product differentiation.'
  (iii) 'Only firms in imperfect competition, broadly defined, indulge in these kinds of competition.'

  (b) Would it therefore be true to say that only imperfect competition benefits consumers?

2 'Supernormal profit can exist only in the absence of competition.' Discuss this assertion.

3 (a) Briefly explain the meaning of the terms 'barriers to entry' and 'barriers to exit'.

  (b) How might barriers to entry be expected to affect the way in which markets operate in the real world? Illustrate your answer with relevant examples.

4 (a) Explain what is meant by each of the following:
  (i) price discrimination
  (ii) non-price competition
  (iii) marginal cost pricing
  (iv) limit pricing

  (b) Evaluate the economic implications of one of these pricing strategies from the points of view of both firms and consumers.

5 'Soap powder manufacturers operate in an oligopolistic market.'

  (a) Explain what is meant by this statement.

  (b) What evidence could an economist use to determine the validity of this statement?

  (c) How might firms in such a market be expected to compete?

6 'Advertising is the means by which most firms compete with each other.'

'Advertising is a wasteful use of economic resources and just helps protect established firms from newcomers.'

Using examples, critically evaluate these statements.

7 'The market for hairdressing in London is monopolistically competitive, the market for soap powder is an oligopoly, and the market for water supply is a monopoly.'

  (a) Distinguish the features of these three markets.

  (b) Contrast the way in which suppliers in each of these markets might market their products or services.

24

Demand and supply in the labour market

LEARNING OUTCOMES

On completing this chapter you should understand:

- Marginal productivity
- The supply of labour and wage determination
- Factor and product markets
- The imperfect nature of the labour market
- How economic theory compares with the real world

How much people are paid, and the extent to which their labour resources are used, are crucial issues in economics because they determine who is rich and who is poor, who is employed and who is unemployed.

In this chapter, we shall try to predict the amount of a particular input that firms will demand and the price they will pay for it. We assume that there is only one variable factor of production – labour – and that all other factors of production are fixed; in other words, the firm has a fixed number of machines but can hire or fire workers.

A firm's demand for inputs can be studied in much the same manner as we studied the demand for output in different types of market situations. Our analysis will always end with the conclusion: a firm will hire employees up to the point where it is not profitable to hire any more. It will hire employees to the point where the marginal benefit of hiring a worker will just equal the marginal cost. We start our analysis under the assumption that the market for input factors is perfectly competitive and that the output market is perfectly competitive also. This provides a benchmark against which to compare other situations where labour markets and/or product markets are not perfectly competitive.

We take as our main example a prerecorded-tape-manufacturing firm that is in competition with many companies selling the same kind of product. Assume that the labour hired by our tape-manufacturing firm needs no special skills. The firm sells its product in a perfectly competitive market and also buys its variable input – labour – in a perfectly competitive market. The firm can influence neither the price of its product nor the price that it must pay for its variable input; it can purchase all the labour it wants at the going market wage without affecting that wage. The 'going' wage is established by the forces of supply and demand in the labour market. The total labour demand is the sum of all the individual firms' demands.

Marginal productivity

Look at Table 24.1. In column 1 we show the number of worker-weeks that the firm can hire. In column 2 we show total physical product (TPP) per week. In other words, column 2 shows the units of total physical production or real output that different quantities of the labour input will generate in a week's time. In column 3 we show the additional output gained when a tape-manufacturing company adds additional workers to its existing capital capacity. You will notice that the third column, **marginal physical product** (MPP), represents the extra (additional) output attributed to employing additional units of the variable input factor, which in this case is labour. Thus, if this firm adds a seventh worker, the marginal physical product is 118. You will recall that the law of diminishing marginal returns predicts that additional units of a variable factor, after some point, will cause the marginal physical product to decline, other things being equal.

Table 24.1

1 Labour input (worker-weeks)	2 Total physical product (per week) (TPP)	3 Marginal physical product (MPP)	4 Price of tape (P = £2.50) × MPP ≡ marginal revenue product (MRP) (£ per additional worker)	5 Wage rate (£ per week) Marginal factor cost (MFC) ≡ change in total costs / change in labour
6	882			
		118	295	£200
7	1000			
		111	277.50	£200
8	1111			
		104	260	£200
9	1215			
		97	242.50	£200
10	1312			
		90	225	£200
11	1402			
		83	207.50	£200
12	1485			
		76	190	£200
13	1561			

Why does marginal physical product decline?

If our tape-manufacturing firm wants to add one more worker to an assembly line, it has to crowd all the existing workers a little closer together because it does not increase its capital stock (the assembly line equipment) at the same time that it increases the workforce. Therefore, as we add more workers, each one has a smaller and smaller fraction of the available capital stock with which to work. If one worker uses one machine, adding another worker will not normally double the output, because the machine can run only so fast for so many hours per day.

What additional information do we need to determine the number of workers to be employed? Since we have assumed that labour is employed in a competitive market, then every worker we employ is paid the same wage rate. Figure 24.1 assumes that this wage rate is £200 per week.

In addition, we need to know the price of the product. Since we have assumed perfect competition, the hypothetical market equilibrium price established in Table 24.1 is £2.50. Our firm will employ workers up to the point where the marginal revenue, or benefit, of hiring a worker will equal the additional (marginal) cost.

The marginal cost of workers is the extra cost we incur in employing that factor of production. We recall that

$$\text{marginal cost} = \frac{\text{change in total cost}}{\text{change in amount of resource used}}$$

In our example, one additional worker can be hired at a constant cost of £200 per week.

Marginal revenue product

We now need to translate the physical product into a money value. This is done by multiplying the MPP by the

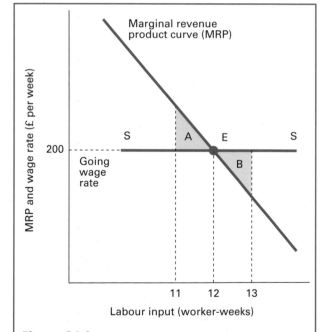

Figure 24.1
Marginal revenue product curve
The employer hires 12 worker-weeks. If the employer hired only 11 worker-weeks, potential profit represented by triangle A would be lost. If 13 worker-weeks are hired, profit is reduced by the amount shown in triangle B. E is the equilibrium at the intersection of demand and supply, or the point where the marginal revenue product (MRP) equals the going wage.

market price of tapes. If the seventh worker's MPP is 118 and the market price is £2.50 per tape, then the **marginal revenue product** is £295 (118 × £2.50). The marginal revenue product is shown in column 4 of Table 24.1. We call the individual worker's contribution to total revenues the *marginal revenue product (MRP)*.

Now in column 5 of Table 24.1 we show the wage rate or marginal cost of each worker. Since each worker is paid the same competitively determined wage of £200 per week, the marginal cost is the same for all workers.

In a perfectly competitive labour market, the wage rate of £200 per week really represents the supply curve of labour. The firm faces this horizontal supply curve because it can purchase all the labour it requires at that going wage rate, being a small employer in relation to the total labour market.

How many employees?

A general rule for the hiring decision of a firm is as follows: the firm hires workers up to the point where the additional cost associated with hiring the last worker is equal to the additional revenue generated by that worker.

In a perfectly competitive situation, this is the point where the wage rate just equals the marginal revenue product. If the firm hired more workers, the additional wages would not be sufficiently covered by additional increases in total revenue. If the firm hired fewer workers, it would be forfeiting the contributions that extra workers could make to total profits.

Therefore, referring to columns 4 and 5 of Table 24.1, we see that this firm would certainly employ the seventh worker, because the MRP is £295 while the MFC (marginal factor cost) is only £200. The firm would continue to employ workers up to the point where MFC = MRP because, as workers are added, they contribute more to revenue than to cost.

We can also use Figure 24.1 to find how many workers our firm should hire. The horizontal supply curve, SS, intersects the marginal revenue product curve at 12 worker-weeks. At the intersection E, the wage rate is equal to the marginal revenue product. This MRP curve is also a *factor demand curve*, assuming only one variable factor of production and perfect competition in both the factor and product markets, because it shows how much labour employers want at each level of wages. The firm in our example would not hire the thirteenth worker, who will only add £190 to revenue but £200 to cost. If the firm were to hire the thirteenth worker, its net income would be reduced by £10 (shown by triangle B). If the firm hired only eleven workers it would be forgoing £7.50 of revenue over and above the cost of a twelfth worker (shown by triangle A).

Derived demand

This demand curve is *derived*, that is, it shows a **derived demand**, because the tape firm does not want to purchase the services of workers simply for the services themselves. Factors of production are rented or purchased, not because they give satisfaction, but because they can be

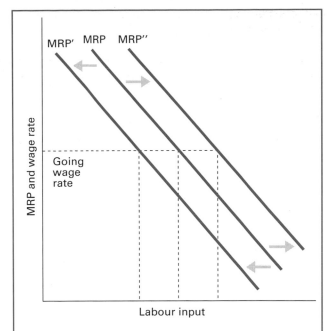

Figure 24.2
Demand for labour, a derived demand
The demand for labour is a derived demand – derived from the demand for the final product being produced. The marginal revenue product curve will shift whenever the price of the product changes.

used to produce things that can be sold at a profit. This is different from a consumer's desire to buy a product.

The MRP curve, because it is derived, will shift whenever there is a change in the demand for and price of the final product. If, for example, the demand for tapes goes down, the price will go down, and the marginal revenue product curve will shift inwards to the left, to MRP' in Figure 24.2. If the demand for and price of tapes go up, the MRP curve will shift outwards to the right, since MRP = MPP × price of product. If output and price fall, so, too, does the demand for labour; at the same going wage rate, the firm will require fewer workers. Conversely, if output and price rise, the demand for labour will also rise, and the firm will want to hire more workers at each and every possible wage rate. Hence wages will generally be higher in industries with growing demand than in industries with declining demand. Growing demand may be associated with a rise in the relative price of a substitute, with rising incomes, with shifts in tastes and fashions or with a fall in the price of a complement. Changing technology may be an integral part of the picture.

Equally, a change in productivity (output per worker) can change MRP. If marginal physical product rises, for example because of more efficient management or better technology, MPP × price, or MRP, will be higher for any given quantity of labour. In other words, the MRP curve will have shifted to the right.

A marginal test

Quantity of labour	Total product per week	MPP	MRP
1	250	——	——
2	450	——	——
3	600	——	——
4	700	——	——
5	750	——	——
6	750	——	——

Assume the product sells for £2 per unit.

1 Use the information above to derive a demand schedule for labour. **A🗸**

2 What is the most that this firm would be willing to pay each worker if five workers were hired? **A🗸**

3 If the going salary for the quality of labour is £200 per week, how many workers would be hired? **A🗸**

KEY POINTS

24.1

■ The change in total output due to a one-unit change in one variable input, holding all other inputs constant, is called the marginal physical product, or MPP.

■ When we multiply marginal physical product by the price per unit of output, we obtain the marginal revenue product (MRP). MRP, defined as $P \times$ MPP, applies only to perfect competition where a firm sells all output at a constant price per unit.

■ A (perfectly) competitive firm will hire workers up to the point where the additional cost of hiring one more worker is equal to the additional revenues generated. For the individual firm, therefore, its MRP curve is also its demand for labour curve.

■ The demand for labour is a derived demand, derived from the demand for final output. Therefore, if the price of final output changes, this will cause a shift in the MRP curve.

■ If demand for the product is growing, it will sell at a relatively high price, and the wages of those producing it will tend to be above average. This will be evident in a growing industry.

■ If demand for the product is declining, its price may be falling relatively, MRP will fall and wages in that industry will tend to be low.

Determinants of demand elasticity for inputs

Just as we were able to discuss the price elasticity of demand for different commodities in Chapter 5, we can discuss the price elasticity of demand for labour. The price elasticity of demand for labour is the percentage change in quantity demanded divided by the percentage change in the price of labour (the wage rate). When this ratio is less than 1, it is considered inelastic; when it is 1, unitary; and when it is greater than 1, elastic.

There are four principal determinants of the price elasticity of demand for an input.

1 The easier it is for a particular input to be substituted for by other inputs, the more price elastic the demand for that variable input will be.
2 The greater the price elasticity of demand for the final product, the greater the price elasticity of demand for the variable input.
3 The smaller the proportion of total costs accounted for by a particular variable input, the lower its price elasticity of demand.
4 The price elasticity of demand for a variable input will be greater in the long run than in the short run.

Substitute factors

If it is technically possible to substitute capital for labour, an increase in real wages will probably lead to an increase in labour-saving capital investment; more capital-intensive methods of production will be adopted. So an increase in wages may lead to a more than proportional decrease in quantity demanded: the demand for labour is price elastic. Equally, if the price of capital falls, wage costs rise relatively and the outcome will be similar. In some situations no substitution of capital is possible and demand for labour will be inelastic.

Final product price elasticity

The second determinant of factor demand elasticity is the price elasticity of demand for the final product. We have already seen that the demand for an input is a *derived* demand. So we would expect the elasticity of the derived demand to mirror the elasticity of the demand for the final product, other things being equal.

Assume the elasticity of demand for electricity is very low. If the wages of skilled workers in the electricity industry are forced up by a strong union, the companies will pass on part of the increase in costs to customers in the form of higher prices. But since the elasticity of demand for electricity is relatively low, customers will not reduce by very much the quantity of electricity demanded. The electricity companies will lay off very few workers. The low elasticity of demand for the final product leads to a low elasticity of demand for the factors of production. The converse is also true. If firms cannot pass on increased costs to the consumer, because quantity demanded would fall sharply if they did, they will be unable to pay higher wages without a substantial cut in employment.

Proportion of total input costs

The third elasticity determinant is the proportion of total costs accounted for by the input under study. This determinant merely points out that if a factor of production accounts for only a very small part of the total cost of the product, any given price change will not affect total costs by much. Take the example of electricity as an input of manufacturing. If electricity accounts for exactly 1 per cent of total costs and prices double, only 1 per cent more would be added to total costs. Hence, demand for electricity will not fall by very much. If the labour input constitutes a very small percentage of the total cost of producing a commodity, then an increase in wages will not add very much to total cost. In such situations, trade unions will be able to get their members higher wage rates than they would when labour input constitutes a significantly greater percentage of total production costs.

Length of time allowed for adjustment

The fourth determinant concerns the difference between the short run and the long run. The long run is usually defined as the time period during which people adjust easily to a change in their business environment. The more time there is for adjustment, the more elastic both the supply and the demand curves will be. This assertion holds for input demand curves as well. The longer the time allowed for adjustment to take place, the more responsive firms will be to a change in the price of a factor of production. Particularly in the long run, firms can reorganize their production process to minimize the use of a factor of production that has become more expensive relative to other factors of production.

KEY POINT

24.2

- The price elasticity of demand for labour is determined by several factors:
- The easier it is to substitute other inputs for the input under study, the more price elastic will be that input's demand.
- The greater the price elasticity of demand for the final product, the greater the price elasticity of demand for the variable input.
- The smaller the proportion of total costs accounted for by the variable input under study, the lower its price elasticity of demand.
- The greater the time allowed for adjustment, the greater the price elasticity of demand for an input.

The supply of labour

Having developed the demand curve for labour in a particular industry, let us turn to the labour supply curve for the labour market as a whole. By adding supply to the analysis, we can come up with the equilibrium wage rate that workers earn in an industry. We can think in terms of a supply curve for labour that is upward sloping in a particular industry. At higher wage rates, more workers will want to enter that particular industry – in our example, tape manufacturing. The individual firm, however, does not face the entire market supply curve. Rather, in a perfectly competitive case, the individual firm is such a small part of the market that it can hire all the workers that it wants at the going wage rate. We therefore say that the industry faces an upward-sloping supply curve but that the individual firm faces a horizontal supply curve for labour. Figure 24.3 shows the difference.

The market supply curve of labour is simply the sum of the individual supply curves of labour. We do assume, however, that the individual supply curve of labour is upward sloping.

The labour–leisure choice and the individual labour supply curve

All work involves an opportunity cost – the highest-valued alternative non-work choice. As such, analysing the individual decision about how much to work is similar to analysing the consumer's decision about what to buy in the product market. In essence, the individual is choosing between leisure (not working) and the consumption of commodities that can be bought in the market-place (because that is what one can do with the income earned from working). A decision to increase the consumption of purchased commodities is, by necessity, a decision to reduce the consumption of leisure.

In order for an individual to make a decision, that individual must know the opportunity cost of leisure. That opportunity cost is best represented by the wages that could have been earned (after taxes). Assume that the worker can make, after taxes, £4 an hour. A decision to work four hours less therefore represents a decision not to be able to consume £16 worth of purchased commodities.

Consider, then, the effect of an increase in wages. The worker is given an incentive to work more because leisure has become more expensive. Therefore, the worker substitutes in favour of work and against leisure. This is called the substitution effect of an increase in wages. Looking only at the substitution effect, any increase in wages will cause the worker to want to work longer hours.

But there is also an *income effect*, and it works in the opposite direction. A higher wage rate means that, for any given number of hours worked, the worker has a greater income. With a greater income, the worker will tend to purchase more of everything, including leisure. Thus, a

Labour supply in a small country town

Mr Cartwright has a shop in the high street of a small country town and sells ready-made and made-to-measure curtains. He employs women who are skilled seamstresses to make up high-quality material into curtains. Recently he has found that he cannot get as many women as he needs to complete the jobs he has undertaken on time. Several of the women he relied on in the past have found other jobs and are no longer available.

4 Why might the women have found other jobs? **A✓**
5 Is there anything Mr Cartwright can do about this? **A✓**
6 If he is unable to find replacements, what might the reason be? **A✓**
7 Can a skill shortage of this sort persist? **A✓**

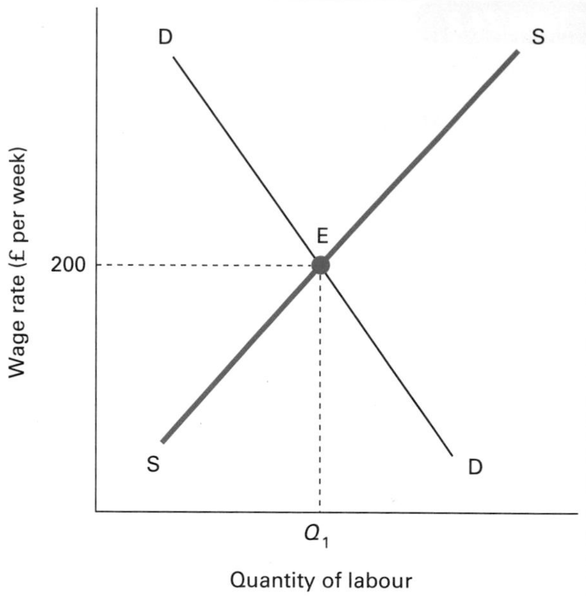

Figure 24.6
The equilibrium wage rate and the tape industry
The intersection of demand and supply curves is at point E, giving an equilibrium wage rate of £200 per week and an equilibrium quantity of labour demanded of Q_1. At a price above £200 per week there will be an excess quantity of workers supplied. At a price below £200 per week there will be an excess quantity of workers demanded.

Wage rate determination

Going back to the tape industry, and assuming again that all markets are perfectly competitive, we put the demand curve for labour in that industry as DD in Figure 24.6, and the supply curve of labour is shown as SS. When we put supply and demand of labour in the tape industry together on one graph, we find that the equilibrium wage rate of £200 a week is established at the intersection of the two curves. The quantity of workers both supplied and demanded at that rate is Q_1. If for some reason the wage rate fell to £150 a week, we would find in our hypothetical example that there was an excess quantity of workers demanded at that wage rate. Conversely, if the wage rate rose to £250 a week, there would be an excess quantity of workers supplied at that wage rate.

Shifts in the supply of and demand for labour

Just as we discussed shifts in the supply curve and the demand curve for various products in Chapter 3, we can discuss the effects of a shift in supply and/or demand in labour markets.

Reasons for shifts in the labour demand curve include the following:

1 the demand for final products shifts;
2 the price of a related factor of production changes (a substitute or a complement);
3 labour becomes more or less productive.

Determinants of the supply curve of labour

There are several reasons why the supply curve of labour in a particular industry will shift. For example:

1 the alternative wage rate offered in other industries changes;
2 non-monetary aspects of the particular occupation change.

Consider the first reason for a shift in the supply curve of labour. If wage rates for factory workers in the prerecorded-tape industry remain constant but wage rates for factory workers in the laser compact disc industry go up by 50 per cent, the supply curve of factory workers in the prerecorded-tape industry will shift inwards to the left.

If working conditions in the prerecorded-tape industry improve markedly because of some new production technique, then the supply curve of labour in the prerecorded-tape industry will shift outwards to the right. The converse will be true if working conditions deteriorate.

Shifts in demand and the problem of labour market shortages

Labour markets do not adjust instantaneously. When there is an increase in demand, wage rates do not change immediately. Consider Figure 24.7. Here we show the supply

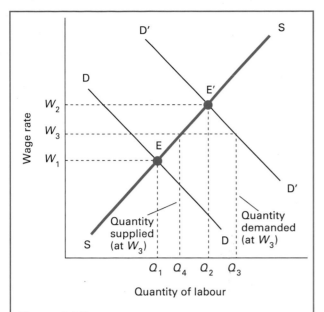

Figure 24.7
Adjustments to increases in demand for computer programmers
At point E the wage rate is W_1 and the quantity of employment of computer programmers is Q_1. Assume demand increases to D'D'. The new market-clearing equilibrium occurs at point E'. The wage rate would be W_2, and the amount of employment of computer programmers would be Q_2. However, because of lags in adjustment, the wage rate at first only rises to W_3. At that wage rate, firms will experience a 'shortage' of computer programmers.

curve of computer programmers as SS. The demand curve is DD. The wage rate is W_1, and the equilibrium quantity of programmers is Q_1.

Consider that a big breakthrough has occurred in the computer industry so that businesses want 50 per cent more computers and therefore more computer programmers. The demand curve shifts outward to D'D'. There would be no shortage if the wage rate increased to W_2, because at W_2 the new demand curve intercepts the stable supply curve at E'. The equilibrium quantity of computer programmers would be Q_2.

But the wage rate does not rise instantaneously to its equilibrium rate. It moves gradually and, during this period of transition, shortages do indeed exist at the lower-than-equilibrium wage rates. For example, consider the wage rate W_3. The organizations desiring to hire computer programmers during this period will experience what they call a 'shortage'. They will not be able to hire all the computer programmers they want at the going wage rate. A shortage of this sort can take many years to be eliminated when the demand curve continues to shift to the right faster than the wage rate and people adjust.

The equilibrium wage rate

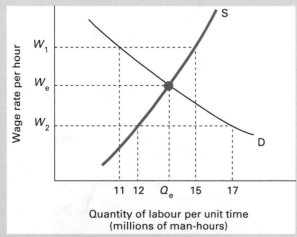

The graph indicates the supply and demand for labour in the construction industry.

8 (a) When wage rates are W_1 per hour, how much do labourers intend to offer per unit?

(b) How much do businesses intend to buy at this wage rate?

(c) Which group is able to realize its intentions and which cannot?

(d) What forces will be set in motion at wage rate W_1, given a free market for labour? **A✓**

9 Using the graph left, answer the following questions.

(a) At wage rate W_2, how many labour hours do labourers intend to offer?

(b) At W_2, how many labour hours do businesses intend to purchase?

(c) Which group can realize its intentions and which cannot?

(d) What forces will be set in motion at W_2 if a free market for labour exists in this industry?

(e) What will the equilibrium wage rate be? **A✓**

10 Some people argue that the extraordinary earnings of entertainment and sports 'superstars' are not pure economic rents at all but merely the cost of ensuring that a steady stream of would-be stars and starlets continues to flow into the sports and entertainment fields. Outline the argument. **A✓**

KEY POINTS

24.3

- The individual competitive firm faces a horizontal supply curve – it can buy all the labour it wants at the going market wage rate.

- The industry labour supply curve is upward sloping.

- Each individual faces a labour–leisure choice. The individual may have a backward-bending labour supply curve.

- When we put on the same diagram an industry-wide supply curve for labour and an industry-wide demand curve for labour, we obtain the equilibrium wage rate in that industry.

- The supply of labour is affected by the population and the age of entering and leaving the labour force.

- When the supply of labour is inelastic, a part of earnings is termed economic rent, being that part which is in excess of transfer earnings (the opportunity cost of earnings in an alternative occupation).

- The labour demand curve can shift because (1) the demand for final product shifts, (2) the price of a related (substitute or complementary) factor of production changes or (3) labour changes in its productivity.

- The supply curve of labour will shift if the alternative wage rate offered in other industries changes and if the non-monetary aspects of the job change.

- Abrupt changes in demand in a particular industry may lead to temporary 'shortages' as wage rates move gradually to their long-run equilibrium level.

Factor and product markets

So far, we have kept factor and product markets separate. We examined supply of and demand for products in Part A. To some extent, as we have seen, supply and demand analysis is applicable to labour markets. We call this approach **partial equilibrium analysis**. The meaning of partial equilibrium analysis can best be expressed by a particular qualifying statement that we have tacked onto most of our 'laws' and theories. That particular statement is: 'other things being equal'. In partial equilibrium analysis, it is assumed that, aside from whatever else we are analysing, almost everything else is held constant. In essence, partial equilibrium analysis allows us to focus on a single market and view it in isolation. For analytical purposes, the market is viewed as independent and self-contained. That is, it is

independent of all other markets. However, it is useful sometimes to look at how changes in the market-place affect both product and labour markets.

General equilibrium analysis

General equilibrium analysis regards all sectors as important. General equilibrium analysis recognizes the fact that everything depends on everything else. It takes account of the interrelationships between prices and quantities of various goods and services. It is a more precise analysis than partial equilibrium analysis, but also a more difficult one to undertake. Just as partial equilibrium analysis does not require that all other things be held constant, general equilibrium analysis does not permit *all* other things to vary. There is a limit to how many markets can be taken into account in any analysis. That limit is reached either by the cerebral limits of the economist doing the analysis or by the capacity of the computer that he or she is utilizing. When economists talk of general equilibrium analysis in dealing with practical problems, they are taking account of *several markets* and the relationships between them. One would want to use general equilibrium analysis when analysing the effects of, say, a new law requiring the producers of steel to pay a 300 per cent tax on the value of all steel produced. There would be important interrelationships between the steel industry, the car industry and the labour markets involved in both industries, as well as effects on and from a multitude of other industries in the economy. Let us now look at the simplest general equilibrium model. We shall use the traditional example of guns and butter.

The circular flow in a two-good world

Assume that there are only two goods available – guns and butter. Nothing else is produced, nothing else is consumed. All income is spent on either guns or butter. Thus, there are two industries. We show the circular flow of income and product in Figure 24.8. We have broken the factor markets and the product markets into two industries – guns and butter. We have also assumed that there is only one factor of production – labour. (Of course, there have to be others, but we want to make the model simple to show the interrelationships involved.) Let us start off in equilibrium in both labour markets and both product markets. The equilibrium prices and quantities of guns and butter are P_G, P_B, Q_G and Q_B, respectively. The equilibrium wage rates and quantities of labour are W_G, W_B, L_G and L_B, respectively.

Now, to show how the interrelationships work, we assume an increase in the demand for guns. This is shown by a shift in the demand schedule in the product market from $D_G D_G$ to $D'_G D'_G$. The short-run equilibrium price, given the supply curve $S_G S_G$, will rise from P_G to P'_G. This means that firms in this industry will be making higher than normal profits. (We assume they were in equilibrium before; thus, they were making normal profits, or a competitive rate of return.) That is why output expands to Q'_G.

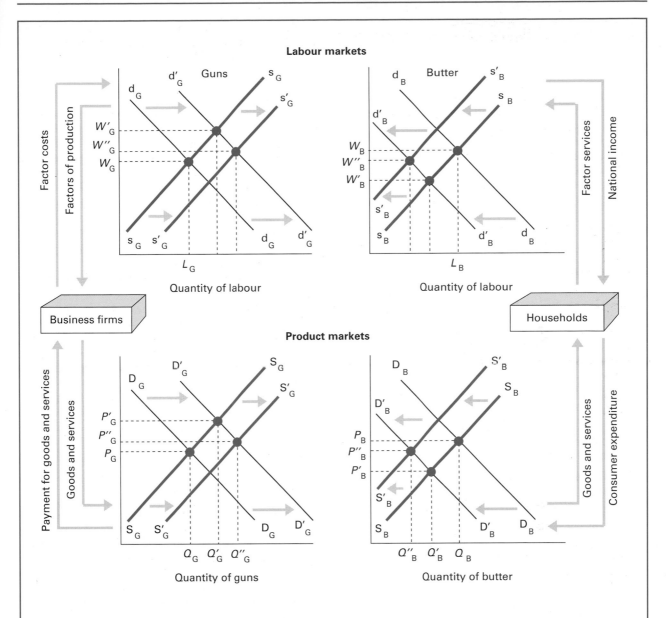

Figure 24.8
A simplified general equilibrium model: guns and butter
In this world we have just two products, guns and butter. We have a simplified circular flow diagram in which firms purchase resources in the labour market and sell goods and services in the product market. Households sell factor services to the labour market and receive national income as factor payments. Households purchase goods and services in the product market and make consumer expenditures. We assume that there is a shift in tastes in favour of guns. In the diagrams we use lower-case d and s for the demand and supply curves in the labour markets and upper-case D and S for the demand and supply curves in the product markets. The demand curve for guns shifts out to $D'_G D'_G$. The price

increases to P'_G. This causes the derived demand curve for labour in the gun industry to shift outwards to $d'_G d'_G$. Wage rates in the gun industry increase to W'_G. Concurrently, the demand curve for butter shifts inwards to $D'_B D'_B$. The price of butter falls to P'_B. The derived demand for labour in the butter industry decreases to $d'_B d'_B$. Wage rates fall in the butter industry to W'_B. In the long run, further shifts occur. Labour and resources flow into the gun industry so that the supply curve shifts outwards. The supply curve in the butter industry shifts inwards. Prices move to P''_G in the gun industry and to P''_B in the butter industry. Workers move into the gun industry and so its supply curve of labour shifts outwards. The supply curve of labour shifts inwards in the butter industry. The equilibrium wage rate in the gun industry goes to W''_G, and in the butter industry goes to W''_B.

The labour market

There is one way for firms in the guns industry to expand, however. More resources must be obtained. Considering labour alone, the demand curve for labour in the gun industry must shift from $d_G d_G$ to $d'_G d'_G$. It will shift outwards to the right because, as you will remember, the demand for labour is a derived demand. Now that output (guns) can be sold at a higher price (P'_G), the marginal revenue product curve shifts outwards to the right, and so too does the demand curve for labour in the gun industry. The only way the industry can attract more workers is for the wage rate to increase. This is why we show an upward-sloping labour supply curve $s_G s_G$. The wage rate rises to W'_G.

What about the butter industry?

The opposite short-run adjustments will occur in the butter industry. The product demand curve will shift leftwards from $D_B D_B$ to $D'_B D'_B$. This is because we are living in a two-good, full-employment world. The only way for the population to demand and consume more guns is to reduce its demand for and consume less butter. Given the supply curve $S_B S_B$, the short-run equilibrium price will fall in the butter industry to P'_B. Looking at the labour market, since the demand for labour is a derived demand, the demand curve will shift leftwards from $d_B d_B$ to $d'_B d'_B$. The market-clearing wage rate will fall to W'_B, and labour will leave the butter industry and enter the gun industry.

General equilibrium in the long run

What we have done is trace the short-run adjustments to a shift in demand in favour of guns and away from butter. This is only a short-run situation because, at the new equilibrium, economic profits are being made in the gun industry while economic losses are being made in the butter industry. Resources will flow out of the butter industry into the gun industry. That is, firms may go out of business in the butter industry; they or others will quickly see a place to make higher profits and move into the gun industry even before bankruptcy threatens. Thus, the supply curve in the gun industry will shift outwards from $S_G S_G$ to $S'_G S'_G$. Simultaneously, the supply curve will shift inwards in the butter industry. A new long-run equilibrium price will prevail in both industries. It will fall in the long run from P'_G to P''_G in the gun industry. In the butter industry, it will rise from P'_B to P''_B.

There will be long-run adjustments also taking place in the resource markets. Workers will shift out of the butter industry and into the gun industry. The supply curve in the former will shift leftwards while simultaneously the supply curve in the latter will shift rightwards. The new equilibrium wage rate in the long run will fall slightly in the gun labour market from W'_G to W''_G. It will simultaneously rise in the butter labour market to W''_B.

Further adjustments

The process does not end there, for the demand curve for labour in both markets will have to shift again. Remember, the demand for labour is a derived demand. When the price of guns and the price of butter change again to P''_G and P''_B, this will cause the marginal revenue product to change also. We do not show these further changes, but they will continue with the demand and supply curves shifting until the long-run equilibrium is established in both the labour markets and the product markets. If we were to consider the possibility of other markets existing, that is, a world in which there were more than two goods, we would also take into account shifts in the demand for other goods due to a change in the price of guns and of butter. We would then have to find out what would happen to the resources used in other industries. A true general equilibrium analysis would take account of every relevant market.

Looking at wages and productivity

An increase in productivity will imply that marginal revenue product rises. Economic theory predicts that the demand curve for labour will shift to the right and wages will rise. In recent years, productivity in manufacturing has risen sharply, making it possible for higher wages to be paid.

Productivity rises more slowly in the service sector. It is not so easy to substitute bigger and better machines for the services provided by people. More efficient time management increases productivity, but not to the same extent that automated and electronically controlled machines have in manufacturing. On this basis, we might expect wages to rise more slowly in the service sector.

Meantime, as incomes have risen, demand has grown for goods with high income elasticity of demand. Which do you want more, a second washing machine or a second foreign holiday? More food or a meal in a restaurant? Demand for services tends to rise more than demand for manufactures.

Other things are happening, too. As productivity has risen in manufacturing, it has become possible for firms to satisfy demand with fewer employees. Table 24.3 shows how earnings in different sectors can change over time.

11 In the data given, what can you observe about (a) the level of wages in different sectors and (b) the rate of change of wages?

12 Applying the analysis described, what would you expect to be happening to wages in different sectors?

13 Hourly wage rates are higher in manufacturing than in services. How might this be explained?

14 What other factors not so far mentioned do you think might help to explain the level of wage rates and the changes?

Table 24.3

Average earnings of manual employees
Full-time hourly earnings, at adult rates (£)

	Energy/water supply	Manufacturing	Construction	Services
Men				
1990	6.83	5.55	5.31	4.85
1994	8.82	6.72	6.13	5.81
Women				
1990	–	3.77	–	3.64
1994	–	4.59	–	4.46

Source: ONS, *Annual Abstract*, 1999

Economic efficiency revisited

Underlying this description is a perfectly competitive economy. It turns out that the perfectly competitive price system has a very special quality. There is a correspondence between an efficient allocation of resources and the results of the allocation from a perfectly competitive price system. Indeed, this correspondence is exact. Every perfectly competitive allocation in long-run equilibrium yields an economically efficient allocation of resources. The definition of economic efficiency is a situation in which the economy is deriving maximum economic value from the economy's given resources. Once we have attained a position of economic efficiency, it is impossible to make any person better off without making another person worse off. Costs are kept to a minimum and each pound spent on inputs yields output of equal value.

The meaning of a perfectly competitive price system
Let us be specific about what we mean by a perfectly competitive price system. In such a system, each good has an equilibrium price that is established by the interaction of supply and demand. The equilibrium price clears each market; the quantities demanded and supplied of each good are equal.

Consumers take the price of the goods and services they buy as given. Subject to their budget constraints, they adjust their behaviour to maximize satisfaction, or utility. Firms, of which there are a large number, each operate to maximize profits. Under these conditions, three things happen:

1 Profit-maximizing competitive firms produce at an output rate at which

   price equals marginal cost

   Price reflects the worth to consumers, because they are willing to pay the price of a product. Marginal cost reflects the social opportunity cost of the resources needed in production. Thus, when price is set equal to marginal cost, the extra value placed on goods and services by consumers is just equal to the extra social opportunity cost of producing those goods and services. We say, then, that the optimal output of each commodity gets produced.

2 Perfect competition results in each good or service being produced at

   minimum long-run average total cost

   Thus, there is no 'waste' in the system. Goods and services are produced using the least costly combinations of resources. Specifically, for each industry, the last pound spent on each factor input generates the same marginal physical product.

3 Consumers will choose in competitive markets so that the distribution of output will

   maximize consumer satisfaction, or utility

   That is, each consumer will buy goods and services in such amounts that the last pound spent on each good or service yields the same amount of extra satisfaction, or marginal utility.

When patterns of demand change, the composition of output will change in response (that is, there will be structural change). It will be characterized by changing patterns of wage differentials, as demand for some kinds of labour rises and that for other kinds falls. Because structural change is sometimes slow and difficult, it is sometimes accompanied by considerable unemployment.

KEY POINTS

24.4

■ Partial equilibrium analysis does not take account of interrelationships between markets.

■ General equilibrium analysis attempts to take into account the interrelationships between different markets.

■ A change in the demand for one good will elicit changes in the demand for another good and also cause changes in the corresponding factor markets.

■ It is possible to show that there is a correspondence between perfect competition and economic efficiency.

An imperfect labour market

So far, we have assumed that employers compete to hire workers. We have also assumed that workers are actively competing in the sale of their labour services to employers. In reality there are many imperfections in the labour market. In particular, there are two situations in which these assumptions must be altered. The first involves restraints on the competition among workers arising from trade union activities. Then we look at restraint among employers in their bidding for workers.

Trade union power and the labour movement

The concept of **trade unions** goes back at least as far as the Middle Ages when guilds were formed. By the twelfth century, Western European guilds were of two broad types: merchant and craft. The medieval craft guilds were the original occupational associations, formed by the artisans in a particular field.

Modern trade unions use their bargaining power to influence wage rates, working conditions and, often, the actual production arrangements. The majority of unions are relatively small: only nine are larger than 250 000, although they account for 66 per cent of all union members. The largest is Unison, with 1 400 000 members. Craft unions include workers with similar skills. General unions attract a wide range of occupations, mainly from the semi-skilled and unskilled groups. The Transport and General Workers' Union (TGWU) is one of these, with 850 000 members. Industrial unions cover all or most of the employees in one industry, as in the case of the Union of Communication Workers. White-collar unions restrict membership to professional, administrative and clerical occupations. MSF (Manufacturing, Science and Finance) exists for supervisory and managerial staff in industry. This type of union membership has tended to grow in recent years; most other unions face falling membership except where they have amalgamated. Increasing unemployment caused union membership to fall during the 1980s and early 1990s.

Unions and collective bargaining

Unions can be looked at as setters of minimum wages. Through collective bargaining, unions establish minimum wages below which no individual worker can offer his or her services. Collective bargaining is collective in the sense that the union leaders bargain for all workers in the bargaining unit. Typically, collective bargaining contracts between management and the union apply also to non-union members who are employed by the firm or the industry.

While it is still true to say that the strike is an important source of union power, its use has greatly diminished since the early 1980s. Figure 24.9 shows the days lost through strike action in recent years. The reasons for this change

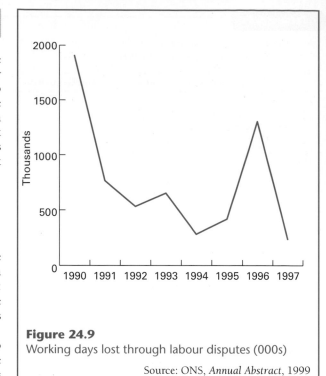

Figure 24.9
Working days lost through labour disputes (000s)

Source: ONS, *Annual Abstract*, 1999

include legislation which reduced union power, increased unemployment (which makes jobs vulnerable generally), falling union membership and changing patterns in the workplace. To some extent these changes are interconnected.

Closed shops

Quite a few management–labour contracts contain a provision requiring all workers to join the same union. This is a **closed shop**. It gives the union greater bargaining power but it may also suit the employer, who is saved the necessity of negotiating with a number of unions.

Negotiated wage rates

We have already pointed out that unions can be looked at as setters of minimum wages. In many situations, any wage rate set higher than a competitive market-clearing wage rate will reduce total employment in that market. This can be seen in Figure 24.10. We have a competitive market for labour. The market demand curve is DD and the market supply curve is SS. The market-clearing wage rate will be W_1; the equilibrium quantity of labour will be Q_e. If the union establishes by collective bargaining a minimum wage rate that exceeds W_1, there will be an excess quantity of labour supplied (assuming no change in the demand schedule). For example, if the minimum wage established by collective bargaining is W_2, the quantity supplied will be Q'_e; the quantity demanded will be Q_d. The difference is the excess quantity supplied, or 'surplus'. The union which establishes a wage rate above the market-clearing price may try to ration available jobs

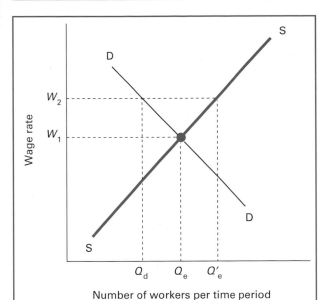

Figure 24.10
Union wage rates
If demand for labour is DD and supply is SS, the equilibrium wage rate is W_1 and the number employed Q_e. If the union negotiates higher wages, W_2, demand for labour will be Q_d and supply will be Q'_e. There will be an excess supply of labour equal to $Q'_e - Q_d$.

curve for union labour outwards by having staffing arrangements which result in overmanning. Also, unions have been accused of trying to prevent capital from being used in the place of labour. In addition, any time there is a strike, there is a reduction in productivity, and this reduction in productivity in one sector of the economy can spill over into other sectors.

Recently, this traditional view against unions has been countered by a view that unions can actually increase productivity. Some economists contend that unions act as a collective voice for their members. In the absence of a collective voice, any dissatisfied worker simply remains at his or her job and works in a disgruntled manner. But unions, as a collective voice, can listen to worker grievances on an individual basis and then apply pressure on the employer to change working conditions. The individual worker does not run the risk of being singled out by the employer and harassed. Also, the individual worker does not have to spend his or her time in trying to convince the employer that some change in the working arrangements should be made. Given that unions provide this collective voice, worker turnover in unionized industries should be less, and this should contribute to productivity. Indeed, there is strong evidence that worker turnover is reduced when unions are in place. Of course, this evidence may also be consistent with the fact that wage rates are so attractive to those in unions that they will not change jobs unless working conditions become unbearable. It has been found that output losses during strikes are quickly made up after the return to work.

among the excessive number of workers who wish to work in unionized industries. There is a trade-off here that must be faced by any union.

This is what the theory predicts. However, since the advent of the minimum wage, the evidence has been rather mixed. Some surveys suggest that raising wages does not make an appreciable difference to the numbers employed. This mixed evidence would call into question the idea that if unions succeed in raising wages, employment will fall.

Have unions raised wages?

Unions are able to raise the wages of their members if they are successful in limiting the supply of labour in a particular industry. However, very few unions are now able to do this. The existence of competition from people who are unemployed has reduced unions' bargaining power.

In the past, on average, unions appear to have been able to raise the wage rates of their members relative to non-union members by between 10 and 20 per cent. Now that unions are so much less powerful in most situations, any effect they may have is likely to be much smaller in most, though perhaps not all, sectors of the economy.

Can unions increase productivity?

The traditional view of union behaviour is that it decreases productivity through attempts at shifting the demand

Do unions still unite?

Forty thousand electrical contract workers are to receive a 30 per cent earnings increase over the next two years in a national deal agreed between employers and the moderate AEEU manufacturing union.

The size of the deal will irritate the government and the Bank of England's Monetary Policy Committee at a time when the inflation trend is running at less than 2 per cent a year.

There are fears that other skilled workers will be encouraged to press for similar increases over the next two years, raising expectations that could trigger a return of wage-push inflation.

Despite the national deal, hundreds of contract electricians staged another unofficial 24-hour stoppage on London's prestige sites in pursuit of more substantial increases.

Workers in the provinces are already averaging £350 a week. But London earnings are as high as £1200 a week for working on prestige projects such as the Millennium dome, the Jubilee line extension and the Royal Opera House.

The Electrical Contractors Association is satisfied with the outcome after threatening at one point to walk out of the talks because of the unofficial and illegal stoppages on large London sites.

The agreement will be put to a secret ballot of workers across the UK over the next two weeks. Both sides are confident of overwhelming support.

Source: *Financial Times*, 30 September 1999

15 Why was it possible for the electricians to secure such a large pay increase?

16 Why were the employers prepared to pay so much more?

17 How would you expect the pay increase to affect (a) the employers and (b) the economy as a whole?

18 Have there been recent examples of large pay increases? Explain the circumstances.

Other market imperfections

Sometimes there will be only one employer of significance within a given area. This employer will be a monopoly buyer of labour, known as a monopsonist. In these circumstances the employer may well be able to get the required amount of labour for lower wages, because employees have no alternative. This would be most likely if geographical immobility was a serious problem.

Exploitation may be defined as paying a resource less than its value. By one definition, labour exploitation would be equal to the difference between the wage rate and the marginal revenue product of labour.

It will be possible for exploitation to occur if employers have more market power than employees, that is, where employers have a degree of monopsony while employees are competing to obtain work. Exploitation allows a larger proportion of total revenue to accrue as profit while a smaller proportion of revenue accrues to labour.

Sometimes a monopsony can be created by an **employers' association**. While there may be many employers, they can agree to negotiate as a unified association, all paying the same wage rate. **Bilateral monopoly** exists in the labour market when a single employer or employers' association negotiates with a single union that covers all the employees in the industry. An example of this is when the London Underground negotiates with RMT, the drivers' union.

Some large retail chains are big enough to have some power in the labour market. The alternative jobs available can be rather few in number for some employees. This means there is competition for the jobs and employers can drive quite a hard bargain. They may insist on employing people when they need them rather than full-time, and wages are often low.

KEY POINTS

24.5

■ Unions negotiate minimum wage rates and working conditions.

■ Union activity can lead to higher wages but may lead also to fewer jobs being available.

■ Some economists believe that unions can increase productivity by acting as a collective voice for their members, thereby freeing members from the task of spending their time trying to convince their employers that some change in their working arrangements should be made.

■ Trade unions have become less significant in the labour market as their powers have been reduced and membership has fallen.

■ Unions may reduce employee turnover, thus adding to productivity.

■ Exploitation may occur if there is a monopsony, or a single employer (buyer of labour).

■ Bilateral monopoly exists when a single employer deals with a single union, so that there is one buyer and one seller.

Economic theory and the real world

We now attempt to sum up the findings of this chapter. When trying to determine how many workers a firm would hire, we had to construct an MRP curve. We found that, as more workers were hired, the MRP fell due to diminishing marginal returns. If the forces of supply and demand established a certain wage rate, workers would be hired until marginal revenue product was equal to the going wage rate. Then the hiring would stop. This analysis suggests what *all* workers can expect to be paid in the labour market. They can each expect to be paid the *value of their marginal product* or MRP, assuming, of course, that there are low-cost information flows and that the labour and product markets are competitive.

We have already seen that rising demand for a product will result in higher prices, and therefore increasing MRP. Other things being equal, wages will rise as MRP rises. Rising demand may occur for a number of reasons. Improved competitiveness with substitutes, whether for price or non-price factors, will increase demand. Rising incomes will be important for products with high income elasticity of demand. Falling demand will be associated with the development of efficient production of a substitute abroad, or of new substitutes. Shifting tastes and fashions can work both ways.

Competition

In a competitive situation, with mobility of labour resources (at least on the margin), workers who are being paid less than their MRP will be bid away to better employment opportunities. This process will continue until each worker is paid his or her MRP. In general, employers will not want to keep workers if their wage rates are greater than their MRPs. In such a situation, it would pay an entrepreneur to fire or lay off those workers who are being paid more than the worth of their contribution to total output.

Full adjustment is never obtained

Individuals are not always paid their MRPs. This can be because we do not live in a world of perfect information, or in a world with perfectly competitive input and output markets. Employers cannot always seek out the most productive employees available. It takes resources to research the past records of potential employees, their training, their education and their abilities. You may know musicians, artists, photographers, singers and other talented people who are being paid much less than well-known publicized 'stars'. But this does not mean that marginal productivity theory is invalid. It merely indicates that information is costly. Furthermore, we must distinguish carefully between the market evaluations of an individual worker's worth and subjective evaluations. You may subjectively believe that the output of a particular artist is extremely valuable. Unfortunately for the artist, and perhaps for your sense of fairness, few other people may share your subjective evaluation. Therefore, the artist is unable to sell his or her work very easily or at very high prices. Finally, the marginal productivity theory of wages applies in the large, that is, on average. It will not necessarily explain every single case.

Bearing in mind that it is sometimes very difficult to determine what an employee's contribution to production actually is, we would expect to find many cases where the connection between pay and product is not obvious.

If we accept marginal productivity theory, then we have a way to find out how people can, in fact, earn higher incomes. If they can manage to increase their marginal physical product, they can expect to be paid more. Some of the determinants of marginal product are innate intelligence, education, experience and training. Most of these are means by which marginal product can be increased. Ways of doing this are explored in the next chapter.

Problems with marginal productivity theory

Marginal productivity theory can help us to understand why some differentials in wages exist and persist. It does not imply that people should be paid any particular wage. It may, in fact, lead to some people being paid very poorly indeed. But this is not all. A weakness of the theory is that, for many people, it is very difficult to determine what their marginal physical product is. How would we evaluate the productivity of a railway signalman, a restaurant cleaner or a primary school teacher?

Another weakness of marginal productivity theory as we have described it is that it assumes perfect competition in the product market. A business with a monopoly in the supply of its product will be in a different position relative to its employees than one which does not have a monopoly. Conclusions drawn on the basis of marginal productivity theory will need to be modified to allow for this.

In conclusion, it is vitally important to consider whatever marginal productivity theory can tell us about the demand for labour. But there are many other relevant factors at play in the labour market, including the market imperfections which exist. Some of these affect the demand for labour, such as the existence of monopoly buyers of labour. Others affect supply: immobilities, restrictions on supply and monopoly sellers of labour. In addition there are often special conditions relating to individual occupations and localities. All these are important in determining the returns to labour.

KEY POINTS

24.6

- There are numerous determinants of income differences.

- If we accept the marginal productivity theory of wages, workers can expect to be paid their marginal revenue product. Note, however, that full adjustment is never obtained, so that some workers may be paid more or less than their marginal revenue product. The marginal productivity theory does not necessarily explain every single individual case.

- Marginal revenue product rises when the price of the product rises.

- Marginal productivity depends on (1) innate abilities and attributes, (2) education, (3) experience and training and (4) capital invested per employee.

- Wages and salaries may be greatly affected by factors other than marginal productivity, such as labour market imperfections, including trade unions.

Case Study

£90 million for Beecham boss

Jan Leschly, the chief executive of drugs producer SmithKline Beecham, now has a pay, perks and shares package worth more than £90 million.

The record-breaking pay package, which has risen in value by more than £20 million in 12 months, is the biggest ever awarded by a public company in the UK. It dwarfs all previous fat-cat rewards and is bound to provoke fury among shareholders and workers.

The 30 per cent increase in his vast wealth compares to the 10 per cent increase in profits SmithKline chalked up last year. Details of Mr Leschly's mega-pay package come just weeks after the company announced 3000 manufacturing job cuts, some of which are expected to fall in the UK.

Part of the increase in the value of his package is due

to an increase in SmithKline's share price, which automatically makes his contract worth more. But it is also partly due to the award of more free and cheap shares last year.

In the report and accounts the company says 'SB needs a global approach to directors' remuneration, one which recognises the competition for top talent in an international market'.

Source: *The Guardian*, 25 March 1999

1 How can you decide what the marginal revenue product of an individual may be?
2 Analyse directors' pay in terms of economic rent and transfer earnings.
3 What is the justification for performance-related pay?
4 What effect are high levels of executive pay likely to have on consumers, employees and shareholders?

Exam Preparation

Multiple choice questions

1 An increase in wage rates for a factor of production will leave demand unaffected when
   A the product has many substitutes
   B capital can easily be substituted for labour
   C the elasticity of demand for the product is high
   D the elasticity of demand for the factor of production is close to zero

2 A firm in an initial profit-maximizing position employs two factors, X and Y, to produce a good which is sold for £3.

Factor prices and productivities change. The new values are given in the table.

Factor	Marginal physical product	Price (£)
X	2	4
Y	5	20

What should the firm employ to achieve equilibrium?
   A less of both X and Y
   B more of X and less of Y

   C more of Y and less of X
   D more of both X and Y

3 A factor of production is most likely to earn economic rent if
   A the factor of production is very scarce
   B transfer earnings are high
   C the demand for the product is inelastic
   D the supply of the product is highly elastic

4 The following diagram illustrates the effect on the wage rate of an increase in the demand for engineers from KD_1 to HD_2. The economic rent received by the engineers will increase by
   A FTVG
   B ONVG
   C NLV
   D MHVT
   E MLVT

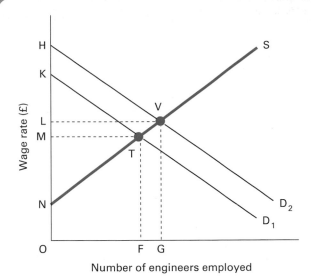

Number of engineers employed

5 The elasticity of supply of a specific type of labour will be partly determined by
  A the marginal revenue productivity of that labour
  B the elasticity of supply for the final product
  C the ease with which labour can be substituted for capital
  D the ease with which the skills used by that labour can be acquired

Essay questions

1 Explain the income differentials between hospital cleaning staff and accountants.

2 How are factor earnings related to productivity?

3 Distinguish between economic rent and transfer earnings. With reference to examples, explain what determines the economic rent earned by factors of production.

4 (a) Why do shop assistants earn less than television newsreaders?
  (b) What problems may arise if the government tries to ensure that all public sector employees have the same percentage annual pay increase?

5 Examine the economic causes of the changing number of trade union members in Great Britain.

6 Outline the theory of relative pay determination in a freely competitive market. How far is it possible to explain salary differentials within the teaching profession and between teaching and other professions in terms of labour supply and demand analysis?

7 (a) Why are there differences in the wage rates paid to people in different occupations?
  (b) Discuss the view that high wages will inevitably result in lower levels of employment.

8 (a) How does economic theory explain why some groups of workers are paid more than others?
  (b) Discuss whether this theory fully explains why women are often paid less than men.

9 How can the UK labour market be said to be imperfect? What measures could the government employ to make the labour market less imperfect?

10 Explain what is meant by the elasticity of supply of labour. What impact would you expect a successful programme of UK government-funded training schemes to have on labour supply and wages in the economy?

11 (a) Explain why there has been an increase in the proportion of the working population employed in the service sector in the UK.
  (b) Discuss the economic significance of this change in the pattern of employment.

Rent, interest and profits

We have talked about four factors of production – labour, land, capital and entrepreneurship. So far in Part D, we have discussed only the demand and supply of labour and the factor payments to labour – wages and salaries. The other three factors of production and their respective factor payments – rent, interest and profits – are also important. In this chapter, we shall look at the determination of each of these factor payments. And we examine the relationship between factor and product markets. We then examine the idea of human capital. People invest in themselves by improving their qualifications and skills. In so doing they increase their earning capacity, which provides a return on their investment. They are creating income-earning assets.

The returns to labour and capital

Income accrues to factors of production in return for their services. Table 25.1 shows the share of total income arising from labour and capital, that is, wages and profit. 1993 illustrates an exceptionally bad year for profits. Worldwide recession and government counter-inflation policies combined to reduce company profits.

The shares of income going to wages and profit do vary over time. Low levels of profit suggest that incentives to invest may be depressed. High levels of profit might suggest that the distribution of income is veering away from earned income and towards unearned income.

KEY POINTS TO REVIEW

Table 25.1

Factor incomes, £ billion, current prices

	1983	1988	1993	1998
Income from employment	170	257	356	463
% of GDP	56	55	56	55
Operating surplus of corporations	73	110	140	194
% of GDP	24	24	22	23
GDP at market prices	302	467	638	844

Source: ONS, *Economic Trends*, 1999

LEARNING OUTCOMES

On completing this chapter you should understand:

- The nature of rent, interest and profit
- The function of economic profit
- Investment in human capital
- How capital may be substituted for labour

Rent

The term rent has been associated with payments for the use of land, for land seems to be the best example of a resource that is in fixed supply. If at all prices the quantity supplied and the quality of a resource will remain fixed, then we say there is **pure economic rent**. (Chapter 24 examined this in relation to labour.) We define pure economic rent as that price paid to any factor of production that is in completely inelastic supply. The term rent is generally used to mean the return on investment in property. In Table 25.1, the operating surplus of corporations includes both profit and rent.

Does economic rent have an allocative function?

In a price system, changes in prices usually cause people to change their behaviour. If the price of petroleum products goes up relative to other prices, suppliers are induced to supply more, and consumers are induced to consume less. Does economic rent have a similar allocative function? Some economists would answer yes, and others would answer no. Those who do not believe that economic rent serves an allocative function point out that, by definition, it is associated with unique properties of a resource that cannot be changed. If an exceptionally productive tract of land exists, does this property's high economic rent mean that somehow additional tracts with the same high productivity will come into being? The answer is no. After all, if economic rent exists, it means that it is attributed to a factor's qualities that cannot be altered in the long run. Therefore, by definition, if economic rent is being earned, it cannot serve an allocative function.

Those who believe that economic rent does serve an allocative function indicate that it serves the purpose of regulating the use of society's resources, particularly its natural resources that are fixed in supply. In a competitive market-place, economic rent serves as a guide by rationing the available supply to the most efficient use.

Property values

If you are thinking about economic rents in the property market, try looking at the prices of an average house in all the regions of the UK.

	Price in 1999 (£)	% increase on one year ago
London	131 353	20.6
South-east	112 550	13.3
South-west	84 719	12.6
West Midlands	73 469	4.1
East Midlands	65 679	9.1
East Anglia	74 215	10.1
North-west	59 868	5.6
Yorks and Humberside	54 839	2.7
North	56 462	4.0
Scotland	60 347	-1.3
Wales	61 230	6.5
Northern Ireland	66 000	6.0
UK average	78 881	8.8

Source: www.halifaxplc.com/hpi/index.html

1 What determines the level of demand for housing? Explain your reasoning.

2 Using diagrams to illustrate your answer, explain what is happening in Scotland and south-east England.

3 In which areas would you expect commercial properties to earn economic rent?

4 How would a change in the demand for financial services affect the prices of houses in London?

5 'All revenues obtained by the Italian government from Renaissance art museums are pure economic rent.' Is this statement true or false, and why?

Quasi-rent

A **quasi-rent** is defined as a payment over and above what is necessary to keep a factor of production in existence *in the short run* in its current quantity and quality. In the long run, if the quasi-rent is inadequate, the factor of production will be allowed to depreciate and not be replaced. Consider a factory that has a fixed amount of plant and machinery. Assume that nothing can be done with the capital equipment; it can be used only to continue producing the same product. In the short run, it is possible for the owners of that fixed capital not to be paid very much at all. In the long run, however, if those owners of fixed capital are not paid at least a normal rate of return for their investment, they will keep the equipment running until it wears out, but will not then replace it.

Economic rents to other factors of production

This analysis is equally applicable to any other factor of production that is fixed in supply. Economic rents accrue to individuals possessing scarce natural talents. It is defined as any payment over and above what is necessary to maintain a factor of production in its current activity. Natural talents that human beings possess will be more significant in some occupations than in others. They seem to be particularly important in athletics, acting, music and other entertainment endeavours. In some cases, pure economic rents can explain a great part of the difference between the extraordinary earnings of highly successful musicians, for example, and the earnings of the average musician.

KEY POINTS

25.1

- The share of income from employment and profits in total GDP can give an idea of the returns to labour and capital.

- Pure economic rent is defined as any payment to a factor of production that is completely inelastic in supply.

- Pure economic rent is a payment to a resource over and above what is necessary to keep that resource in existence at its current level in the long run.

- Economic rent serves an allocative function by guiding available supply to the most efficient use.

- A quasi-rent is that payment over and above what is necessary to keep a resource in its current quality and quantity in the short run, but not sufficient to do so in the long run.

- Factors of production other than land can earn pure economic rents if their supply is completely price inelastic.

Interest

Interest is the price paid for the use of capital. Capital is the factor of production that is typically considered man-made. Capital exists because individuals, as a group, have been willing in the past to forgo consumption – to save. Those resources not consumed were usually used by firms for investment purposes, which added to our stock of capital. The production of capital goods occurs in our society because of the existence of credit markets, where borrowing and lending take place.

Owners of capital, whether directly or indirectly, obtain income in the form of interest. They receive a specific interest rate. Thus, we can look at the interest rate as either the rate earned on capital invested or the cost of borrowing – the two sides of the credit market. For the moment, we shall look only at the cost of borrowing.

Interest is different from profit. People receive profit because they have risked their capital. When people lend in return for interest, the risk is much less because the borrower is legally obliged to pay interest and make the repayment.

Interest and credit

When you obtain credit, you actually obtain money in order to have command over resources today. We can say,

then, that interest is the payment for current rather than future command over resources. Thus, interest is the payment for obtaining credit. If you borrow £100 from me, you have command over £100 worth of goods and services today. I no longer have that command. You promise to pay me back £100 plus interest at some future date. The interest that you pay is usually expressed as a percentage of the total loan calculated on an annual basis. Thus, if at the end of one year, you pay me back £110, the annual interest is £10/£100, or 10 per cent.

When you go out into the market-place to obtain credit, you will find that the interest rate charged differs greatly. A loan to buy a house (a mortgage) may cost you 6–10 per cent annual interest. An instalment loan to buy a car may cost you 10–15 per cent annual interest. The government, when it wishes to obtain credit (by selling bonds), might pay 5–7 per cent annual interest. Variations in the rate of annual interest that must be paid for credit depend on the following factors.

Length of loan

In some (but not all) cases, the longer the loan will be outstanding, other things being equal, the greater will be the interest rate charged.

Risk

The greater the risk of non-repayment of the loan, other things being equal, the greater the interest rate charged. Risk is assessed on the basis of the creditworthiness of the borrower. It is also assessed on the basis of whether the borrower provides collateral for the loan. Collateral consists of any asset that will automatically become the property of the lender should the borrower fail to comply with the loan agreement. Typically, when you borrow to purchase a car, the car itself is collateral for the loan. Should you default on payments to the lending institution, it can, in most cases, repossess the car, sell it and pay off the loan that way. The more and the better the collateral offered for a loan, the lower the rate of interest charged, other things being equal.

Administrative charges

It takes resources to set up a loan. Papers have to be filled out and filed, credit references have to be checked and so on. It turns out that the larger the amount of the loan, the smaller will be the administrative charges as a percentage of the total loan. Therefore, we would predict that, other things being equal, the larger the loan, the lower the interest rate.

Loans are taken out both by consumers and by firms. It is useful for us to separate the motives underlying the demand for loans by these two groups of individuals. We shall therefore treat consumption loans and investment loans separately. But before we do that, we examine the relationship between interest rates and present value – or how to relate the value of future sums of money to the present by a process known as **discounting**.

In the discussion that follows, it will be assumed that

there is no inflation; that is, there is no consistent increase in general prices. Interest rates usually rise when inflation is expected, and vice versa.

The interest rate; future and present values

Interest rates may be used to link the present with the future. After all, if you have to pay £110 at the end of the year when you borrow £100, that 10 per cent interest rate gives you a measure of the value of the loan one year from now compared with the value of the loan today. If you want to have things today, you have to pay the 10 per cent interest rate in order to have purchasing power.

Turned around somewhat, the question could be put this way: what is the present value (the value today) of £110 that you could receive one year from now? That depends on the market rate of interest, or the rate of interest you could earn in a bank account. To make the arithmetic simple, let us assume that the rate of interest (also called the **rate of discount**) is 10 per cent. Now you can figure out the **present value**, as it were, of £110 to be received one year from now. You figure it out by asking the question, 'How much money must I put aside today at the market rate of interest of 10 per cent to receive £110 one year from now?' Mathematically, we represent this question by the following:

$$(1 + 0.10)P_1 = £110$$

where P_1 is the sum that you must set aside now.

Let us solve this simple equation to obtain P_1:

$$P_1 = £110 \div 1.10 = £100$$

That is, £100 will accumulate to £110 at the end of one year with a market rate of interest of 10 per cent. Thus, the present value of £110 one year from now, using a rate of interest of 10 per cent, is £100. The formula for present value of any sums to be received one year from now thus becomes

$$P_1 = A_1/(1 + i)$$

where P_1 is the present value of a sum one year hence, A_1 is the future sum of money paid or received one year hence, and i is the market rate of interest.

The same method can be used to calculate the present value of income expected in the more distant future. We call this **discounting**. It enables firms to assess the present value of the income they are likely to receive from an investment project. This helps them in deciding whether a given capital expenditure is likely to be worthwhile.

What determines interest rates?

The overall level of interest rates in the economy is generally determined by the supply of loanable funds and the demand for loanable funds. Let us first look at the supply and then the demand.

The supply of loanable funds

The supply of loanable funds depends on individuals' willingness to save. To induce people to save more, one must offer a higher rate of interest. Thus, we expect that the supply curve of loanable funds will be upward sloping. At higher rates of interest, savers will be willing to offer more current consumption to borrowers, other things being equal. For example, in Japan there is a high savings ratio by Western standards and this tends to keep interest rates low.

The demand for loanable funds

There are three major sources of the demand for loanable funds:

1 households that want funds for the purchase of services, non-durable goods and consumer durables, such as cars and houses;
2 firms that want funds for investments;
3 governments that want to cover their deficits – the excess of government spending over tax revenues, or PSNCR.

In general the quantity of loans demanded will be influenced by the price of the loan – the interest rate. So changes in monetary policy will have an impact on the demand for loans. Other things being equal, the three influences mentioned will be important.

The consumer demand for loanable funds

On average, consumers prefer earlier consumption to later consumption. By borrowing, consumers can spread out purchases more evenly during their lifetimes. Consider that sometimes individual household income falls below the average income level expected over, say, the next few years. Individuals will go to the credit market to borrow whenever they perceive a temporary dip in their current income – assuming they expect their income to go back to normal later on. (The permanent income hypothesis described in Chapter 15 showed how consumption is related to long-term income.)

The demand by consumers for loanable funds will be inversely related to the cost of borrowing – the rate of interest. Why? For the same reason that all demand curves slope down: a higher rate of interest means a higher cost of borrowing, and a higher cost of borrowing must be weighed against alternative uses of limited income. At higher costs of borrowing, consumers will forgo current consumption.

Firms' demand for loanable funds

Firms demand loanable funds to make investments in new plant and machinery, new production techniques, research and development, new types of organizations, and any other type of investment that they believe will increase productivity. Any time a business believes that, by making an investment in its production process, it can increase revenues (net of other costs) by more than the cost of capital (the rate of interest on loanable funds), it will borrow and invest. Firms compare the interest rate that they must pay in the loanable funds market with the rate of return or profit that they think they can earn by investing. This comparison helps them to decide whether to invest.

At higher interest rates, fewer investment projects will make economic sense to firms – the cost of capital will exceed the rate of return on the capital investment. Conversely, at lower rates of interest, more investment projects will be undertaken because the cost of capital will be less than the expected rate of return to the capital investment. (We can relate this to the planned investment function in Chapter 15. J.M. Keynes called the rate of return on capital the 'marginal efficiency of capital'.)

The demand for loanable funds by households, firms and the government, and the supply of loanable funds, interact to produce an equilibrium interest rate. (In practice there are, as we have seen, a number of interest rates for loans of different duration and for different purposes.) Funds are traded, that is, lenders lend and borrowers borrow, on the capital or money markets. This consists of a wide range of financial intermediaries, including banks, building societies, insurance companies and pension funds, discount houses, merchant banks and finance houses. These institutions aim to provide a very wide range of loans for borrowers with different needs, and similarly varied ways of saving for potential lenders. They will compete to offer their customers the most favourable terms and interest rates. This is one market which will clear all the time. Interest rates are flexible and the institutions can lend to one another on a short-term basis should there be excess supply of or demand for their funds. The theory relating to the supply of and demand for money is examined in Chapter 27.

Real versus nominal interest rates

Up to now, we have assumed that there is no inflation. In a world of inflation – a consistent rise in all prices – **nominal**, or market, **interest rates** will be higher than they would be in a world with no inflation. Basically, market rates of interest eventually rise to take account of the anticipated rate of inflation. If, for example, there is no actual or expected inflation, the market rate of interest might be, say, 5 per cent for mortgages. If the rate of inflation goes to 10 per cent a year and stays there, then everybody will anticipate that inflation rate. The market, or nominal, rate of interest will rise to 15 per cent to take account of the anticipated rate of inflation. We generally say that the real rate of interest is equal to the nominal rate of interest minus the rate of inflation.

When loans are made in terms of a fixed sum of money, the purchasing power of that money declines if there is inflation so that the lender is repaid a smaller amount of real purchasing power. The higher nominal interest payments compensate for this. In short, you can expect to see high nominal rates of interest in periods of high and/or rising inflation rates. **Real rates of interest** may not necessarily be high, though. We must correct the nominal rates of interest for inflation before determining whether real interest rates are, in fact, higher than normal. In practice,

expectations of inflation can lag behind events, as people take time to get used to new situations.

Loans and interest rates

An individual who wants to borrow from the bank, using an overdraft facility, might have to pay 10–12 per cent per annum interest. Borrowing on a credit card will usually cost about 18 per cent. A business borrower, well known to the bank and in a position to offer some collateral, might be offered a loan at 9.0 per cent. (Collateral means security: the borrower may agree that, if the loan is not repaid, the bank may recover its debt by liquidating the borrower's shares or property or other assets.)

Bear in mind that these are approximate rates at the time of writing, with an inflation rate of 2 per cent. They will change.

6 Why is borrowing on a credit card so expensive?

7 At the time of writing, interest paid by banks on deposit accounts is usually in the range 2.5–3.5 per cent. Why is the interest rate so much higher for the borrower than it is for the lender?

8 Why would the bank be prepared to lend at a much lower rate to a business with which it has a long-standing relationship?

9 To what extent do interest rates ration borrowing, allocating funds to the most efficient users?

10 How have interest rates changed since 1999? For what reasons?

The allocative role of interest

Interest is a price that allocates funds (credit) to consumers and to firms. Within the business sector, interest allocates funds to different firms and therefore to different investment projects. Those investment, or capital, projects whose rates of return are higher than the market rate of interest in the credit market will be undertaken, given an unrestricted market for loanable funds. For example, if the expected rate of return on the purchase of a new factory in some industry is 20 per cent and loanable funds can be acquired for 15 per cent, then the investment project may take place. If, however, that same project had only an expected rate of return of 9 per cent, it would not be undertaken. In sum, the interest rate allocates loanable funds to those industries where resources will be the most productive.

It is important to realize that the interest rate performs the function of allocating money capital – loanable funds – but that what this ultimately does is allocate real physical capital to various firms for investment projects. Often, non-economists view the movement of loanable funds (credit) simply as something that has to do with 'money' and not with the 'real' world of machines and factories.

25.2

■ Interest is the price paid for the use of capital. It is also the cost of obtaining credit.

■ In the credit market, the rate of interest paid depends on, among other things, the length of the loan, the risk and the administrative charges.

■ In order to express a future sum of money (or income stream) in terms of today's pounds, we must discount the future sum back to the present by using the appropriate discount rate. The result is the present value.

■ The interest rate is determined by the interaction of the supply of credit, or loanable funds, and the demand for credit, or loanable funds.

■ The demand for loanable funds comes from households, firms and governments.

■ Nominal, or market, interest rates adjust to take account of inflation. Therefore, during periods of high anticipated inflation, nominal or market interest rates will be historically high. Real interest rates, however, may not, because they are defined as the nominal interest rate minus the anticipated rate of inflation.

Profit

In Chapter 1, we called entrepreneurship, or entrepreneurial talent, the fourth factor of production. Profit is the reward that this factor earns. You may recall that entrepreneurship involves engagement in the risk of starting new businesses. In a sense, then, nothing can be produced without an input of entrepreneurial skills.

We cannot easily talk about the demand and supply of entrepreneurship. For one thing, we have no way to quantify entrepreneurship. What measure should we use? First, we point out what profit is not. Then we examine the sources of true, or economic, profit. Finally, we look at the functions of profits in a market system.

Distinguishing yet again between economic profits and business or accounting profits

In Chapter 20 we saw a distinction between economic and accounting profit. The accountant calculates profit for a business as the difference between total explicit revenues and total explicit costs. Consider an extreme example. You are given a large farm as part of your inheritance. All the land, fertilizer, seed, machinery and tools are fully paid for. You take over the farm and work on it diligently with half a dozen labourers. At the end of the year you sell the output for, say, £200 000. Your accountant then subtracts your *explicit* expenses.

The difference is called profit, but it is not economic profit because no account was taken of the implicit (as opposed to the explicit) costs of using the land, seed, tools and machinery. The only explicit cost that was considered was the labourers' wages. As long as the land could be rented out, the seed could be sold and the tools and machinery could be leased, there was an opportunity cost of using them. To derive the economic profits that you might have earned last year from the farm, you must subtract from total revenues the full opportunity cost of all factors of production used (which will include both implicit and explicit costs).

As a summary, then, accounting profits' main use is for the definition of taxable income and, as such, includes returns to both owner's labour and capital. Economic profit, on the other hand, represents a return over and above the opportunity cost of all resources (including a normal profit to the owner's entrepreneurial abilities and labour).

When viewed in this light, it is possible for economic profit to be negative, even if accounting profits are positive. Using the farming case again, what if the opportunity cost of using all the resources turned out to be £220 000? Then you would have suffered economic losses.

In sum, the accountant's definition and the economist's definition of profits usually do not coincide. Economic profits are a residual. They are whatever remains after all economic, or opportunity, costs are taken into account.

Is economic profit a payment for managerial skill?

It is often argued that profit is a payment for 'managing' a business venture well. Clearly, better managed firms will earn higher rewards than poorly managed ones, but *profit* cannot be called the reward for good management, because managerial skill is a *service* available on the market. Any entrepreneur can hire a manager, in other words. Better managers, typically, earn higher salaries than poorer ones. The good entrepreneur who apparently earns high profits because of his or her good management is only earning an *imputed salary*, in effect what he or she could have earned *elsewhere* by managing *someone else's* business.

Economic profit, strictly speaking, cannot be called the reward for managerial skill. For the firm that prospers owing to good management, payment for management is a cost of production rather than profit.

Is economic profit a payment for taking risk?

Unlike a manager who might be employed by the owner, the person owning the enterprise takes the risk that the enterprise may fail. It is often argued, therefore, that profits are the reward for bearing such risks. After all, if the business fails, it is the owner who suffers a reduction in net worth. However, many risks can be reduced by purchasing an *insurance policy*. Small and big businesses alike may purchase strike insurance, crop failure insurance and so on.

So what is profit?

Profit is a residual. But it does not arise accidentally; it is a consequence of the unique capabilities of the firm's owner. It rewards the taking of risks which cannot be spread by insurance. It can be explained in other ways, too.

The marginal product of capital can have a substantial effect on profit. We can analyse the returns to capital in much the same way as we analyse the returns to labour. The more efficiently capital is used, the larger its marginal product will be, and the greater the likely demand for its services. Those who are prepared to pay most for capital will be those who can use it most effectively and productively to generate a profit.

Analysing the marginal product of capital

11 Below are some production function data for a firm in which the only variable input is capital; the labour input is fixed. First fill in the other columns. What quantity of capital will the firm use if the price of capital is £90 per machine-week? If the price of capital is £300 per machine-week, what quantity of capital will the firm use?

Quantity of capital (machine-weeks)	Total product (units/week)	Marginal product of capital (units/week)	Product price (£/unit)	MRP (£/week)
0	0	—	£10	—
1	25	—	10	—
2	45	—	10	—
3	60	—	10	—
4	70	—	10	—
5	75	—	10	—

Exploitation

The classical economists' view of profit was indistinguishable from what we would now call interest. This is because their concern was not for individual markets and individual factor prices, but rather for the share of *national income* earned by various *social classes*.

Karl Marx, whose ideas were introduced in Chapter 2, argued that the source of profits was **exploitation**. His definition of exploitation was phrased quite carefully, and was different from our normal use of the word. As he used the word, firms actually 'exploited' workers by paying them precisely what their labour was *worth*.

Marx based his entire argument upon the **labour theory of value** – a theory accepted by all the classical economists – which stated that the force underlying the value of all goods was the amount of labour needed to produce them. This amount included 'direct' labour – the actual amount of work expended by a labourer of average skill – and 'indirect' labour – the labour-value of the portion of the *tools* used in producing the commodity.

Marx put forward his exploitation thesis by asking: if the value of any commodity is measured by the direct and indirect labour-time needed to produce it, what can the value of *labour-time* itself be? He answered that it must be *subsistence*, the amount of goods and services needed to enable a worker and his or her family to keep body and soul together. This is what it cost, in other words, for society itself to 'produce' one worker. Therefore, when the worker earned subsistence, he or she was earning a 'fair wage', because the labour power provided by the worker was priced in a fashion similar to that of all other commodities.

Marx was restating (albeit in a highly potent, political fashion) what all the classical economists believed: owners of firms earned profit because they could legitimately claim anything 'left over' after all costs of production had been paid. But Marx went further. Even though the source of profit was 'exploitation', in that workers produce goods of much higher value than the price of their subsistence, by the rules of the game of capitalism itself, 'exploitation' was a perfectly fair wage. When workers 'sold their labour power', as Marx put it, if they earned subsistence they received the full value of the service they provided. This argument led to Marx's conclusion that a complete revolutionary change in, rather than reform of, the capitalist system was in the best interest of the working class.

Restrictions on entry

We pointed out in Chapter 22 that monopoly profits – a special form of economic profits – are possible when there are barriers to entry. Monopoly profits due to entry restrictions are often called monopoly rents by economists. Entry restrictions exist in many industries, including taxis, cable television franchises, prescription drugs and spectacles, and numerous others. Basically, monopoly profits are capitalized into the value of the business that owns the particular right to have the monopoly.

Innovation

A number of economists have maintained that economic profits are created by innovation, which is defined as the creation of a new organizational strategy, a new marketing strategy or a new product. The innovator creates new economic profit opportunities by his or her innovations. The successful innovator obtains a temporary monopoly position, allowing him or her to have temporary economic profits. When other firms catch up, those temporary economic profits disappear. In order to encourage innovation, this temporary advantage may be extended by granting patents, which prevent copying of the innovation for a certain length of time.

The function of economic profit

In a market economy, the expectation of profits induces firms to discover new products, new production techniques and new marketing techniques – literally all the new ways to make higher profits. Profits in this sense spur innovation and investment.

As we pointed out in Chapter 4, profits cause resources to move from lower-valued to higher-valued uses. Prices and sales are dictated by the consumer. If the demand curve is close to the origin, then there will be few sales and few, if any, profits. The lack of profits therefore means that there is insufficient demand to cover the opportunity cost of production. In the quest for higher profits, firms will take resources out of areas where either accounting losses or lower-than-normal rates of return are being made and put them into areas where there is an expectation of higher profits. The profit incentive is an inducement for an industry to expand when demand and supply conditions warrant it. The existence of economic losses, however, indicates that resources in the particular industry are not as valued as they might be elsewhere. These resources therefore move out of that industry, or, at a minimum, no further resources are invested in it. Therefore, resources follow the firm's quest for higher profits. They allocate resources, guiding them towards production of the goods and services which consumers most want.

Harvey Goldsmith Entertainments

Harvey Goldsmith is the great showman of British pop who tried to change with the times and did not quite manage it.

Yesterday, the business empire he has built since the 1960s was in trouble after administrative receivers were brought in to his main operation, Harvey Goldsmith Entertainments.

Its most recent blow was a £1 million loss on the Total Eclipse Festival in August, when far fewer revellers than expected made the trek to Cornwall.

The real problems began a year ago when three of his executives left to form Triple A, a rival organization. They took with them important artists, including Eric Clapton, Boyzone and Michael Flatley, although others such as Sting and the Pet Shop Boys remained loyal.

Mr Goldsmith's career began at Brighton University, where he was a student. From booking bands to play at Saturday night hops, he went on to become the biggest impresario of the age. He handled UK tours by the great American names of the 1960s, 1970s and 1980s, from Bob Dylan to Madonna, as well as presenting British stars such as the Rolling Stones, Elton John and Sting. He also put on many great open-air festivals, culminating in Live Aid at Wembley in 1985.

Mr Goldsmith discovered early on the financial gain from booking the biggest stars – the money for tickets flowed in months before the bills had to be paid.

Recent diversification into classical music has brought more prestige than profit. He brought Pavarotti to Hyde Park and had a critical success with a lavish production of Carmen at Earl's Court. But some of his operatic ventures lost money. For all his big plans, Mr Goldsmith has always operated in a low-profit-margin business. The stars take most of the money from touring, leaving the promoter with a sliver. There is no margin for failure.

Source: *Financial Times*, 30 September 1999

12 Explain how profit and loss influence the entry to and exit from the market of an entrepreneur.

13 Show how resources have been reallocated in the process.

14 Why did Harvey Goldsmith move away from his traditional line of business and promote opera?

KEY POINTS

25.3

- Profit is the reward to entrepreneurial talent, the fourth factor of production.

- It is necessary to distinguish between accounting profits and economic profits.

- Accounting profits are measured by the difference between total revenues and all explicit costs.

- Economic profits are measured by the difference between total revenues and the total of all opportunity costs of all factors of production.

- There are numerous theories of why profits exist. These include the notions that profits are (1) a reward to risk-taking, (2) a result of disequilibrium in the market-place and (3) a result of imperfect competition.

- The function of profits in a market economy is to allocate scarce resources. Resources can be expected to flow to where profits are highest.

Investment in human capital

Investment in human capital is just like investment in any other thing. If you invest in a building, you expect to receive a rate of return on your investment. You expect to receive some reward for not consuming all your income today. The same is true for investment in human capital. If you invest in yourself by going to college rather than going to work after school and earning more money, you presumably will be rewarded in the future by a higher income and/or a more interesting job.

On average, the rate of return to investment in human capital is similar to the rate of return to investment in other areas. The main cost of education is the income forgone, or the opportunity cost, through not working. The extra income earned over a lifetime is almost always more than enough to compensate for this. (Chapter 11 shows this in Figure 11.7.)

Individuals' earning capacity can have to do with innate abilities and attributes, which can be strong determinants of their potential productivity. Strength, good looks, co-ordination, mental alertness and so on are all facets of non-acquired human capital and thus have some bearing on a person's ability to earn income. But the additions to human capital which take place as people acquire education and training are usually even more important. Each time a person acquires more human capital, their marginal productivity will increase. Their attractiveness to an employer is enhanced and their choice of employment is less restricted. Experience or on-the-job training can be just as important as formal education. Both can give the individual firm- and industry-specific skills which can be used to make more efficient use of resources. This in turn will lead to lower costs and perhaps to higher wages or profits.

Substituting capital for labour

As countries develop, the relative prices of labour and capital change. Rising productivity makes it possible to pay higher wages. This makes capital relatively cheaper. At the same time, technological change makes machines more efficient and therefore, again, relatively cheaper. This makes labour relatively dearer. The two trends reinforce each other.

As labour becomes more expensive, employers have an incentive to substitute capital for labour. This increase in the capital stock will increase productivity. The process is circular. The higher the level of wages, the more capital-intensive production is likely to be. The more capital people have to work with, the higher their productivity.

In conclusion, therefore, labour and capital are often substitutable and a change in the price of one will lead to a change in the demand for the other.

KEY POINTS

25.4

- Human capital is increased when people acquire more education or training.

- If wages (the price of labour) rise, there will be an increase in the demand for capital investment, other things being equal.

Finding finance for investment

When a firm wants to invest, it can seek funds internally or externally, or both. Internal finance is generated from the firm's own savings. This is known as corporate saving, or retained profit, or sometimes depreciation allowances. Its purpose is to provide for the replacement of productive capacity. Typically, a profitable firm saves for several years, during which it will seek to obtain the best interest rate it can on its surplus funds. (It may obtain a certificate of deposit or some other high-interest-yielding asset.) When it has accumulated assets, it will try to identify the most profitable investment project open to it. This may be a replacement of existing productive capacity, perhaps with more technically advanced machinery. Or it may add to existing capacity: this would be expansion, or net investment. The more profitable the firm is, the more profit it can retain for future investment, and the more likely it is to have dynamic plans for the future. In general, firms may often be more willing to take risks if they have substantial retained profits. They do not have to justify the use of internal funds to their bankers and so may undertake riskier projects.

In addition to internal finance, the firm may seek external finance. This may come from a number of sources, all of which are part of the capital or money markets. Debt finance involves borrowing fixed amounts on which a predetermined rate of interest is paid. Equity finance involves issuing shares in the company; the returns will be not interest but dividends, a share of the profit which will vary from year to year depending on the performance of the company.

Debt finance

Companies can borrow either short or long term. Much the most important source of short-term finance or working capital is the bank overdraft. The advantage of this is that interest is payable only on the amount outstanding; the disadvantage is that the company must regularly review its position with the bank, and may have to pay more for the loan when interest rates rise.

Long-term loan finance may involve the issue of corporate bonds or debentures. These allow the firm to borrow at a fixed rate of interest; repayment at maturity may be twenty years hence. The company then has an assured source of finance which may be linked to the life of its capital equipment. However, it must be able to offer reasonable security to lenders, and of course the interest must be paid irrespective of whether the firm is making profits. The other sources of long-term loans are banks and finance houses. Such loans would normally be tied to the life of a particular investment project, so that both interest and repayments are paid from the income gener-

ated by the investment. Such loans may extend over five to ten years.

Equity finance

When people buy equities, or shares in a company, they buy, literally, an entitlement to a share of the future profits of the company. When a firm needs more capital, it will make a new issue of shares through a merchant bank acting as an issuing house. The latter will advertise the new issue; alternatively, the company may offer a rights issue to existing shareholders. This gives each shareholder the right to buy a certain number of the new shares usually in proportion to his or her existing holdings. A rights issue is cheaper than a new issue; the latter is likely to be used only if large amounts of capital are being sought.

From the company's viewpoint, the attraction of equity finance is that the buyer shares the risks. In a bad year little or no dividend need be paid. From the shareholders' viewpoint, precisely because they have carried the risk, they can expect to get a higher rate of return over the long run than they would from a fixed-interest loan. Also they may make capital gains. Inflation erodes the value of assets denominated in money terms, so that the lender loses some of the real value of the loan and the interest paid. Meanwhile, profits will tend to be at least stable in the long term, or perhaps will grow. In money terms the value of the share will grow, provided the firm is healthy. If the firm is very profitable then, of course, the share price will rise further. So inflation may increase the attractions of equities as assets, provided business confidence does not suffer.

At the same time, inflation can lead to high nominal interest rates and this can cause firms with extensive loan finance to have difficulty in meeting interest payments. They will have a cash-flow problem. This can further enhance the attractiveness of using equity finance for investment.

Markets

When we speak of the capital market, we refer to the market in funds for investment, that is, for loans and new issues, both of which provide long-term finance. When we speak of the money market, we refer to the market in short-term funds, lent by selling bills or lending money for short periods. The Stock Exchange is separate and has particular functions: it allows the exchange of stocks (bonds and equities), that is, the transfer of ownership of stocks from one body to another. It does not lead to the creation of new loans or equities. Just to confuse you, though, the Stock Exchange does handle new issues of government bonds; they are issued through the primary dealers on the Stock Exchange who have been accepted as such by the Bank of England.

These very many ways of lending and borrowing money, of putting money productively to work, mean that there are many different rates of return to be had, depending on the circumstances. Blue chip companies can be relied upon to pay dividends. Firms seeking venture capital are going to be adventurous with your capital, probably in an area of high technology. They will pay little in dividends, but may provide substantial capital growth (that is, the share price will go up) if the companies themselves grow rapidly. The government will pay relatively low rates of interest but is very safe – hence, gilts. Other sorts of loans will have interest rates falling between the extremes, but higher for longer loans, and vice versa.

Banks which have bought shares in the stockbroking firms that trade on the Stock Exchange are financial conglomerates. They offer many different kinds of financial products through their different departments.

1 Why do interest rates vary at any given time?
2 In what circumstances will firms seek external finance?
3 (a) Compare and contrast debt finance and equity finance.
   (b) What factors will determine the choice?
4 What factors will savers take into account when deciding how to invest their funds?

Case Study

Investing in students

Student life in Britain was never quite as cushy as its caricature, in which hours not spent in bed were whiled away in the pub, and lectures were never attended before noon, if at all. And all this sloth was financed by the taxpayer, who not only paid tuition fees but also forked out a grant to keep students in beer. These days, the caricature is a long way from the truth. When they are not poring over their books, students are likely to be working in Tesco. Even during term, most students have part-time jobs to make ends meet.

Money looks set to get tighter still. The crop of students that began their university courses this month will enjoy less state support than any since governments undertook to subsidize the expansion of higher education in the early 1960s. During the 1990s, this support has gradually been removed. Maintenance grants (for living costs) have been reduced since the introduction of student loans in 1990. Last year, means-tested tuition fees (linked to inflation and currently £1025 a year at most)

were introduced. And this October saw the abolition of the maintenance grant.

The latest evidence suggests that the changes in student funding are discouraging precisely the people the Labour government most wants to see at university – adults, the poor and non-whites – from entering higher education. Tuition fees seem to have put students off, even though a degree or higher national diploma (HND) would boost their earning power.

1 Why does it make sense to continue in education as long as possible?
2 Why do graduates earn more than non-graduates?
3 Why might it make sense for the government to subsidize higher education?
4 Many people thought that support for students was mainly helping the better-off students, whose future looked rosy anyway because they already had many educational advantages. What is your view? Give reasons.

Home applicants for degrees and HNDs, by age

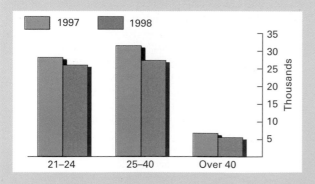

Home applicants for degrees and HNDs, by social class of family

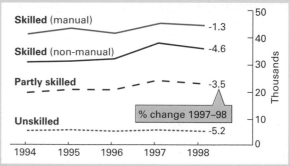

Source: *The Economist*, 30 October 1999

Exam Preparation

Multiple choice questions

1 Which of the following activities is investment in the economic sense?
   A The purchase of shares using personal savings.
   B The purchase of mobile phones by households.
   C Receipt of interest, profits and dividends by a multinational company.
   D The payment of state pensions by the government.
   E The installation of equipment to increase the output of synthetic fibres.

2 If the demand for a factor in absolutely inelastic supply were to increase, then
   A the transfer earnings would fall
   B the transfer earnings would rise
   C the economic rent would fall
   D the economic rent would rise
   E the quasi-rent would fall

3 A factor of production will *not* earn economic rent if
   A demand is perfectly elastic
   B demand is perfectly inelastic
   C supply and demand both have unit elasticity
   D supply is perfectly elastic
   E supply is perfectly inelastic

4 In a given production process, labour and capital are substitutable. What will be the effect on the quantities of labour and capital employed if the government introduces a subsidy on capital investment?

	Quantity of labour	*Quantity of capital*
A	less	less
B	less	uncertain
C	uncertain	more
D	more	less
E	more	more

5 Which of the following diagrams represents a situation where a factor's earnings are all economic rent?

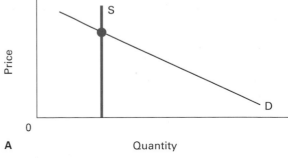

A

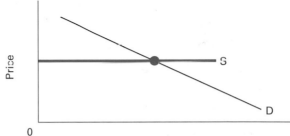

B

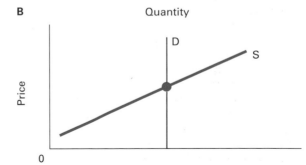

C

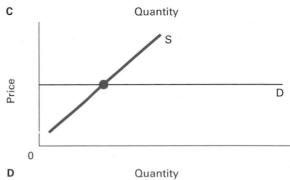

D

6 'Income for which no good or service has been provided in exchange.' Which of the following does this statement define?

A consumers' surplus
B quasi-rent
C transfer earnings
D transfer payments.

Essay questions

1 (a) What are the returns to the various factors of production?

(b) How and why do the levels of economic rent received by factors of production differ?

(c) Consider critically what role the government should play in increasing the quantity and quality of the workforce.

2 Distinguish between transfer earnings and economic rent. Discuss the contention that economic rent may be earned by any factor of production.

3 What is the role of profit in a free enterprise system? To what extent does profit perform this role in a mixed economy?

4 How might knowledge of the average and marginal productivities of a factor of production be useful to an entrepreneur?

5 'Economic rent can be earned by all factors of production. The elasticity of supply of a factor is critical in this respect.' Discuss.

PART

E ECONOMIC ISSUES AND POLICIES

On completing PART E
you should find the
following websites
useful and interesting.

■ **www.ifs.org.uk**

The Institute of Fiscal Studies (IFS) was established in 1969 following a general dissatisfaction that far reaching tax reforms could be introduced without prior public debate. In fact, the present government's annual pre-budget reports (published around November) were inspired by the IFS, as they provide the opportunity for public debate before the finalised budget is announced in March. Since 1995 the institute's publications, conferences and current research have been available via the web.

Of particular interest for this section on economic issues and policies is a recently developed economic model to experiment with – namely the 'Virtual Economy'. This is an associated website where students can try out their own policies to see if they can run the economy better than the Chancellor. At the heart of the Virtual Economy are sophisticated computer models similar to those used to prepare the budget. If you participate you will get feedback on how your plans would perform over the subsequent ten years. The virtual economy can also be accessed via www.bized. ac.uk the first site listed in part A.

■ **www.competition-commission.gov.uk**

The Competition Act 1998, replaced the Monopolies and Mergers Commission with the Competition Commission. Accordingly, the Internet site was revamped. However, it still includes the usual range of background information such as summaries of reports, 'press releases' and 'annual reviews'. A list of answers to 'frequently asked questions' opens with two useful items regarding the role of the Competition Commission and a list detailing what is currently under investigation. Unfortunately it does not respond to the joke question 'why is there only one Competition Commission?' But Chapter 26 should help you appreciate the answer to that question.

■ **www.euro-emu.co.uk**

The primary function of this site is to encourage an in-depth discussion and provision of information on international issues via the Internet, in particular Europe's economic and monetary union. Visitors to the site will find a comprehensive coverage of European matters, which could be used in conjunction with the case study in Chapter 29 and wherever else an up-to-date European angle is required.

■ **www.worldbank.org**
■ **www.oecd.org**

The resources provided by international organisations via the Internet are phenomenal. We reference here just two good examples.

The World Bank which is an institution dating back to the post-war Bretton Woods conference, seeks to help developing countries to reduce poverty. Via their website you can read about its work, resources and partners. The World Bank's annual report can be downloaded in full the day after its publication, and this itself provides a wealth of up-to-date economic ideas and data. For example, the statistics contained in Tables 30.1 & 31.1 can be updated from this site each September.

The Organisation for Economic Co-operation and Development (OECD) is briefly described in an exercise box on page 539. Some of the subsequent questions can be answered using this site. Sets of statistics relating to most high-income countries and specific profiles of member states are both easy to search from the homepage.

Finally, language students have the opportunity to view these sites in French and/or Spanish.

■ **www.amosweb.com/tst**
■ **www.tutor2u.com**

Clearly, the internet offers many opportunities for revision. For instance several of the sites already referenced should enable you to catch up on latest events and data relating to the economy. Here we list two further possibilities.

The amos website is an American treat that 'can be used to practice up for the real thing'. The site provides a bank of multiple-choice questions for you to try, and provides feedback on how you have done. Each test comprises ten questions and there are many topics to choose from, covering most syllabus areas. Try it and see what grade you get.

Finally the tutor2u.site provides the resources of a dedicated and experienced Economics teacher. The site has been established since July 1999 and it is relevant to all the parts of our text. To follow just one possibility: look up any of our emboldened technical terms in the glossary provided by tutor.2u and you will find links to several related pages. The site also offers a quiz on Economics, advice on exam technique, essay plans, regularly updated information on the UK economy, web reviews and more. Indeed tutor2u has one main objective – to maximize students' examination performance by providing a high quality learning resource and an online community of students.

Competition and industrial policies

In Chapter 2 we considered the provision of goods and services by the government. We saw that in the case of the United Kingdom the post-war Labour government effected the transformation of several private monopolies into public monopolies. From 1979 the Thatcher government began to return these nationalized industries to the private sector through its privatization policies. We consider these policies in this chapter and also measures aimed at enhancing the economic performance of firms in industry and commerce as part of industry policy. However, we begin the chapter by reviewing policies which represent the attempt by government to prevent the creation of monopolies and also to foster keen competition between firms. We shall see that the British approach to devising competition policies has been essentially cautious in espousing any of the virtues associated with the competition ethic. We showed in Chapter 4 that competition is the driving force in a capitalist economy. But while competition may be 'a good thing', governments in the United Kingdom have not exhibited a consistent and enthusiastic acceptance of such a viewpoint.

LEARNING OUTCOMES

On completing this chapter you should understand:

- How policies towards competition have evolved in the UK
- Why policies have been the subject of keen debate
- The rationale for privatizing state-owned undertakings
- How governments have been concerned about the UK's international competitiveness

The legislation and institutions of competition policy

When we look at the state of competition in the UK economy in the early years of the twentieth century we find that most sections of manufacturing industry were characterized by explicit arrangements to restrict competition and control prices. Firms in an industry would often seek to fix prices by discussion in national organizations called **trade associations**. Domestic firms found their common cause a matter of increasing relevance as they faced growing competition in the UK market from imports. The Lloyd George coalition government in 1920 began the cautious approach that has characterized the spirit of British competition policy. Price-fixing arrangements were recognized as having the *potential* for firms to charge excessive prices to the detriment of consumers. But the situation was not sufficiently clear-cut for it to be considered appropriate that such practices restricting competition between firms should be *prohibited* by legislation. What was required was a review of the particular situation in individual industries. Thirty industries were investigated by the Board of Trade in 1920 and 1921 as the basis for establishing whether the interests of consumers were *in practice* being adversely affected. But this concern for consumers quickly evaporated during the 1920s and 1930s as the three major political parties showed increased disenchantment with the desirability of stimulating greater competition. Competition was now seen as a hindrance to the development of strong national concerns capable of meeting foreign competition. Mergers were thus encouraged so that 'wasteful competition' could be eliminated and firms could achieve economies of scale while the macroenvironment was so depressing.

Thus by 1939 very little emphasis in government policy towards industry was placed on the desirability of competitive rivalry. This muted enthusiasm for competitive free enterprise contrasted strongly with the explicit presumption in favour of competition that characterized policy in the United States. Let us now see how the UK's post-war legislation concerning competition has continued to reflect an uncertain commitment to the cause of the competitive economy. There have been seven pieces of legislation in the past half century and we note the main provisions of the following Acts:

- The 1948 Monopolies and Restrictive Practices (Inquiry and Control) Act
- The 1956 Restrictive Practices Act
- The 1964 Resale Prices Act
- The 1965 Monopolies and Mergers Act
- The 1973 Fair Trading Act
- The 1980 Competition Act
- The 1998 Competition Act

We shall firstly review how the legislation passed in 1948, 1956, 1964, 1965, 1973 and 1980 constituted one approach to competition policy which was subsequently found to be unsatisfactory. As a result, the tenth decade of the twentieth century saw yet another piece of legislation which shifted the thrust of policy in another direction. We need to understand why this was the case by outlining how the existing policy stance was the subject of considerable criticism. We thus begin with the legislation by a Labour government in 1948 and then show how its proposed new approach fifty years later was thought an appropriate response to the shortcomings in the interim period.

The 1948 Monopolies and Restrictive Practices (Inquiry and Control) Act

This Act did not condemn monopoly outright. Instead a case-by-case approach was adopted such that each situation could be judged on its merits. A monopoly situation was presumed neither good nor bad and it was up to the newly created Monopolies and Restrictive Practices Commission to investigate particular situations and make a judgement in accordance with some vague expression of 'the public interest'. The Commission was not able to begin an investigation unless at least *one-third* of the supply of goods was supplied by one person or by two or more persons who restricted competition by agreement (thus including the restrictive activity of trade associations). The Commission consisted mainly of part-time lay persons and they could consider only situations referred to them by the Board of Trade. Action on a report by the Monopolies Commission was left in the hands of the government.

The Act was thus a modest statement on the desirability of a competitive economy. Members of the Commission found the terms of 'the public interest' capable of uncertain interpretation and even a cursory examination of section 14 of the 1948 Act shows why this was so. The public interest was defined as the need to achieve

1 the production, treatment and distribution by the most efficient and economical means of goods of such types and qualities, in such volume and at such prices, as will best meet the requirements of home and overseas markets;

2 the organization of industry and trade in such a way that their efficiency is progressively increased and new enterprises are encouraged;

3 the fullest use and best distribution of men, materials and industrial capacity in the United Kingdom; and

4 the development of technical improvements, the expansion of existing markets and the opening up of new markets.

As one member of the Commission, the late Professor G. C. Allen, put it:

> The guidance given by the Act consisted of a string of platitudes which the Commission found valueless and it was left for the members themselves to reach their own conclusions by reference to the assumptions, principles or prejudices which their training and experience caused them to apply to economic affairs.

(G.C. Allen, *Monopoly and Restrictive Practices*, Longman, 1968, p. 66)

The Commission worked slowly and between 1948 and 1956 produced just seventeen reports. But these reports nonetheless presented a clear picture of how widespread were **restrictive practices** throughout British industry. Firms typically agreed common prices for goods sold, whether to wholesalers, retailers or in contracts supposedly subject to secret tendering. Private 'courts' punished individual members of agreements who infringed the rules of the trade. Manufacturers were able to prevent competition between wholesalers or retailers as a result of laying down rigid trading terms for the sale of goods. This was the practice of **resale price maintenance**.

In a general report on collective discrimination published in 1955 the Commission assembled evidence on a variety of restrictive practices and declared itself satisfied that all of them adversely affected the public interest. The Conservative government responded with its 1956 Restrictive Trade Practices Act.

The 1956 Restrictive Trade Practices Act

This Act had three elements to it. On restrictive practices the Act obliged firms to register their agreements with a Registrar of Restrictive Trading Agreements. These registered agreements were to be open to public inspection and presumed contrary to the public interest unless the parties involved could satisfy otherwise before the Restrictive Practices Court. Thus the legislation represented a much clearer statement in favour of competition than the 1948 Act. The Act affected the whole industry and not merely those parts selected for inquiry. There was a precise government commitment against the desirability of price-fixing. The unwillingness by government to take action on Monopolies Commission reports now contrasted with the precise requirement of the Registrar to refer every price agreement to the Court. The judgement of the Court was binding on the respondents if contempt proceedings were to be avoided.

A second aspect of the 1956 Act was its prohibition of the *collective* enforcement of resale price maintenance by the withholding of supplies by a group of manufacturers. This made it no longer possible for a uniform stance to be taken by several manufacturers against a retailer who wished to trade on terms other than those laid down by his suppliers. But the 1956 Act did not have a dramatic impact on the manufacturer–retailer relationship since *individual* suppliers were able to take action in the courts against traders not maintaining their specified trading terms. The ending of individual resale price maintenance was not brought about until 1964 (see below).

In respect of restrictive practices, the Restrictive Practices Court was given the task of hearing applications by manufacturers to continue a form of competitive behaviour now generally deemed unacceptable. The Court began to set a precedent in its early cases concerning price-fixing cartels which left very few manufacturers expecting to make a successful defence. Thus by the end of the 1960s there was little doubt that competition policy had become effective by virtue of the fact that legislation expressed a clear presumption in favour of free competition. Price-fixing and collusion were no longer seen as desirable practices.

Few trade associations chose to defend these restrictive practices before the Court when the evidence was clear that the chances of a successful defence were slim. Thus although over 4000 agreements were registered under the Act, the vast majority have been voluntarily abandoned and not the subject of a Court case.

The 1956 Act had yet a third element: the restricting of the Monopolies and Restrictive Practices Commission. Given the creation of the Restrictive Practices Court, the Commission was now confined to investigation of monopoly situations and thus appropriately lost two words in its title. But the hesitant nature of UK policy towards large firms continued to manifest itself. The new Commission was reduced to a maximum membership of ten persons and it was no longer able to function in separate panels on particular investigations, as it had done since 1953. In 1956 the Commission was viewed critically in some quarters as simultaneously 'prosecutor, judge and jury', but at least it was not so actively at work that it troubled many of Britain's major firms. Any revival in the significance of the Commission had to await the development of UK policy towards the acquisition of one firm by another as expressed by the legislation in 1965. But before discussing this, we need briefly to reconsider resale price maintenance.

The 1964 Resale Prices Act

The Resale Prices Act adopted the same approach as the 1956 Act, with the practice of minimum resale prices being prohibited subject to exemptions on specific grounds. There have been very few cases before the Court and only books and medicines have provided the supporters of fixed trading terms the satisfaction of a costly legal appraisal that survived a Court hearing.

The 1965 Monopolies and Mergers Act

Policy on mergers effectively began in 1965 in the wake of a take-over bid by Imperial Chemical Industries for Courtaulds. The Labour government found itself with no explicit means to declare its position on such a merger. Its solution was to make use of an existing body, the Monopolies Commission, as the appropriate forum where the desirability of a change in the structure of an industry could be examined. The Board of Trade was now able under the Monopolies and Mergers Act to refer a merger proposal to the Commission if the market share of the two firms satisfied the one third share of the market or if the value of assets taken over exceeded £5 million. The Labour government had equipped itself with this new power but intended neither automatic referral to the Commission nor any presumption of hostility to a proposed merger. A Mergers Panel consisting of civil servants was created to advise the appropriate government minister. The Commission, when a merger case was referred to it, had to operate with some speed and normally report back within six months. Its remit was simply whether the proposed merger was against 'the public interest'. Inevitably, this same vague principle which had given the Commission such an uncertain orientation back in 1948 was to prove the basis of growing criticism in its handling of merger cases after 1965. Before examining these criticisms, we first appraise the legislation introduced in 1973.

The 1973 Fair Trading Act

This Act brought about changes not only in the administration of competition policy but also in its substance. The newly created office of Director-General of Fair Trading assumed the functions of the Registrar of Restrictive Trading Agreements, but with much wider responsibilities. It was charged with keeping under review commercial activities relating to monopoly situations or uncompetitive practices and also trade practices which might adversely affect the interests of consumers. The Director-General was thus now formally given the task of advising the Secretary of State about all these matters as a continuing brief. Of particular significance was the new legal definition of monopoly – the criterion reduced to *one-quarter* market share – and the broader interpretation of the market compared with the 1948 Act. The Fair Trading Act made it now possible to refer monopolies of a local character to the Monopolies and Mergers Commission

(MMC) rather than just those relating to the United Kingdom as a whole. Furthermore, the monopoly situations of the nationalized industries and other statutory trading bodies were brought within the scope of the Act. But apart from these extensions of the work of the Monopoly and Mergers Commission, the Act spelt out a much clearer orientation for the members of that body. Section 84 made the promotion of competition a key aspect of its approach to particular investigations. If you compare the following criteria with section 14 of the 1948 Act (see above), you will note the new emphasis on the process of competition as a means of securing economic efficiency.

> the Commission shall take into account all matters which appear to them in the particular circumstances to be relevant and, among other things, shall have regard to the desirability
> (a) of maintaining and promoting effective competition between persons supplying goods and services in the United Kingdom;
> (b) of promoting the interests of consumers, purchasers and other users of goods and services in the United Kingdom in respect of the prices charged for them and in respect of their quality and the variety of goods and services supplied;
> (c) of promoting, through competition, the reduction of costs and the development and use of new techniques and new products, and of facilitating the entry of new competitors into existing markets;
> (d) of maintaining and promoting the balanced distribution of industry and employment in the United Kingdom; and
> (e) of maintaining and promoting competitive activity in markets outside the United Kingdom on the part of producers of goods, and of suppliers of goods and services, in the United Kingdom.

The 1973 Act thus represented a more confident belief in the virtues of competition than had been the case in the immediate post-war years. Legislation seven years later actually included the word in its title – the 1980 Competition Act. Before considering this Act, we need to stress that competition policy does not exist in a vacuum. The macroeconomic situation is very relevant to concerns over the competitiveness of British industry.

The 1980 Competition Act

This Act tried to deal with business behaviour which might amount to an *anti-competitive practice*. Responsibility for supervising the investigation of such practices was given to the Director-General of Fair Trading. Procedures were laid down in the Act for investigating the course of business conduct pursued by a person which, of itself or when taken together with a course of conduct pursued by persons associated with him, has or is intended or is likely to have the effect of restricting, distorting or preventing competition in connection with the production, supply or acquisition of goods in the United Kingdom or any part of it or the supply or securing of services in the United Kingdom or any part of it.

When the Office of Fair Trading (OFT) gets a complaint it makes inquiries and investigates whether a particular course of conduct amounts to an anti-competitive practice; it then informs the Secretary of State for Trade, the Company and the public. If such a practice is identified in the OFT investigation in a study lasting three months, the OFT then seeks negotiation of voluntary undertakings. If these are not negotiated, then the OFT refers the matter to the MMC for its investigation (lasting up to nine months). If then the MMC reports that the practice is against the public interest, the firm must either voluntarily abandon the practice or anticipate an Order from the Trade Secretary prohibiting the practice.

But *what* practices might in specific instances constitute an anti-competitive practice? In 1980 the OFT identified three possible instances of an anti-competitive practice concerning the pricing of goods. It also specified six practices relating to distribution which might distort competition. These are briefly explained in Table 26.1.

Read all about it

In September 1993 the price of *The Times* was reduced from 45p to 30p. On 23 June 1994 the price of the *Daily Telegraph* was reduced from 48p to 30p (other than on a Saturday). On the following day, the price of *The Times* was cut from 30p to 20p.

1 Is this healthy price competition, a price war or predatory pricing?
2 What difficulties can you think of that arise in trying to establish the existence of predatory pricing?

The provisions of the 1980 Act were not to apply in the case of small firms (those with an annual turnover of less than £5 million and which have less than a 25 per cent share of a relevant market). Also specifically exempted from the Act were sectors such as international shipping and civil aviation (where governments have long agreed to regulation of prices and services).

Two further aspects of the 1980 Act illustrate how the public sector was now seen as appropriate for inclusion within legislation concerned with the promotion of competition and efficiency. The Act empowered the Secretary of State for Trade to refer to the MMC questions about the efficiency and costs of, the service provided by, and the possible abuse of a monopoly situation by nationalized industries. It also empowered the Secretary of State to direct the Director-General of Fair Trading to investigate questions, about prices, of major public concern, either because they are of general economic importance or because consumers are significantly affected.

Table 26.1

Forms of competitive conduct that might constitute an anti-competitive practice

(a) Pricing policy

Price discrimination	The practice of selling goods or services, where there are no cost differences, to distinct and separate groups of customers, these groups being charged varying prices according to their degree of sensitivity to price levels. Some variants of price discrimination take the form of differential rates of discount or rebate from list prices, perhaps in return for loyalty or exclusive supply arrangements. An important variant arises where a purchaser's buying power enables him to insist that suppliers grant him advantageous terms, so artificially enhancing his ability to compete on price in the market in which he sells
Predatory pricing	Usually defined as the practice of temporarily selling at prices below cost with the intention of driving a competitor from the market, so that in the future prices may be raised and enhanced profits extracted
Vertical price squeezing	Can arise when a vertically integrated firm controls the total supply of an input which is essential to the production requirements of its subsidiary and also its competitors. The input price can be raised and the downstream output price reduced so that the profits of competitors are squeezed, possibly with a view to driving them from the market

(b) Distribution policy

There are a number of practices which might serve to restrict, distort or prevent competition, at either manufacturing or distribution level. These include the following:

Tie-in sales	A stipulation that a buyer must purchase part or all of his requirements of a second (tied) product from the supplier of a first (tying) product
Full-line forcing	Requires a buyer to purchase quantities of each item in a product range in order to be able to buy any of them
Rental-only contracts	Restrict customers to rental or lease terms only, which can be anti-competitive where there are no alternative methods of acquiring those goods
Exclusive supply	A seller supplies only one buyer in a certain geographical area, which limits competition between that buyer and his or her competitors
Selective distribution	The practice of choosing as sales outlets only those which satisfy specific qualitative or quantitative criteria
Exclusive purchase	When a distributor contracts to stock only the products of one manufacturer, possibly in return for an exclusive supply arrangement

Source: Office of Fair Trading, 1980

Counting types of anti-competitive practices

Table 26.1 identifies nine types of competitive conduct that might constitute an anti-competitive practice. Six of these nine have not been mentioned in previous chapters. The remaining three were introduced in Chapter 22.

3 Identify these three forms of competitive conduct.

KEY POINTS

26.1

■ UK competition policy has developed from a concern with monopoly (the 1948 Act) to restraints on price competition (the 1956 Act) and only in the late 1960s to take-over bids (the 1965 Act).

■ UK policy has been pragmatic rather than doctrinaire. The approach has essentially been to consider individual cases on their merits.

Competition policies: an assessment

Our review of the development of competition policy until 1980 has attempted to show that Labour and Conservative governments in the post-war period have each introduced legislation concerned with the structure of markets and forms of business behaviour. The whole subject has been continually debated to establish whether the nature of policy is appropriate to current conditions. A key underlying issue is whether all the legislation since 1948 really amounted to a clear statement by the government on the desirability and benefits of competition. Several observers felt that the stance of competition policy suffered from an ambivalent view of the benefits of competitive markets. The 'every case to be judged on its merits' meant that no clear picture was offered of those forms of business behaviour that are regarded as unacceptable. In short, was there explicit policy *for* competitive markets?

Some have argued that, rather than rely on the OFT for redress for those persons who feel aggrieved by forms of anti-competitive conduct, we should adopt a more judicial approach. Rather than OFT official action, there should be encouragement for *private* actions to deter the business community from participating in behaviour such as predatory pricing. The US approach incorporates criminal penalties and payment of damages amounting to three times the alleged loss (the so-called 'triple damages concept'). However, given the way in which the legislative system evolved, how effective has UK competition policy been? Let us consider in turn monopolies, mergers, restrictive practices and resale price maintenance. But before doing so, we consider the European dimension to competition policy.

Competition policy in the European Union

Competition policy is clearly very relevant to the creation of an internal market. It is obvious that an integrated market is only meaningful if in all countries the rules relating to competitive behaviour and state support for industry are reasonably similar. How did those seeking European unification in the 1950s approach policies to promote competition and prevent the distortion of competition in member states? The 1957 Treaty of Rome included two Articles – 85 and 86 – to give expression to a common approach to competition policy in the then six members of the EC.

Article 85 prohibits, and declares automatically void, agreements between member states that have as their object or effect the prevention, restriction or distortion of competition within the EU. These agreements include market-sharing, price-fixing and quota allocation arrangements, restrictions of supplies and discriminatory distribution arrangements. If the European Commission finds that Article 85 is being infringed, the agreement is automatically banned and fines of up to 10 per cent of the turnover of each company can be levied. Article 86 of the Rome Treaty prohibits any abuse of a dominant firm within the EU, or within a substantial part of it, insofar as it may affect trade between member states. The Treaty of Rome contained no provision for a European approach to mergers and it was not until 1990 that the European Commission assumed responsibility for vetting mergers amongst the very largest companies in Europe.

The cost of cartels

It is not hard to show the impact of this stance of European competition policy. In 1988 BPB, the largest plasterboard firm in the United Kingdom, was fined over £2 million for alleged abuse of its market power to stop imported plasterboard from Spain being sold in the United Kingdom. In 1989, twenty-three chemical companies were fined £92 million for operating a price-fixing cartel in the European market for PVC and low-density polyethylene. In 1994, sixteen European steelmakers were fined a total of £79 million for operating a cartel in the supply of steel beams used by the construction industry. The largest individual fine was £24 million imposed on British Steel. In July 1994, nineteen manufacturers of carton board were fined a record total of £180 million for operating a price-fixing cartel. In December 1994 thirty-three cement producers were fined £193 million for operating an illegal cartel. Action in such cases shows that competition policy can be made effective in order to realize the aims of a genuinely competitive single market.

4 How does the stance of EU competition policy contrast with that adopted since 1948 in the UK? **AV**

5 What is the significance of the examples of companies that have been affected by Article 85 of the Treaty of Rome for the working of European competition policy? **AV**

Monopolies

Until 1994 the reports of the MMC attracted relatively little critical attention compared with its judgements on take-over bids. One exception was its recommendation in March 1989 that two-thirds of the retail outlets of the big six national brewing firms should be sold, and all subsidized loans to secure exclusive dealing arrangements should be ended. These strong recommendations proved too radical for the government to accept, and compulsory divestment by the brewers was absent from the government's modified plans to increase competition in the industry. Nonetheless, the government's response – the Beer Orders – has had a profound effect on the structure of the brewing industry. The largest six brewing groups were required to sell one-half of their public houses over the limit of 2000 each. As a result, over 11 000 pubs had to be sold. The free-trade share of the public house market has risen as a result of these structural changes.

The MMC was the subject of much criticism concerning its reports featuring various aspects of vertical restraints that appeared to concern the OFT. In its reports on the supply of new motor cars (1992), fine fragrances and perfumes (1993), national newspapers and impulse ice-cream (1994), the MMC did not recommend any radical changes concerning retail distribution systems in any of the markets. In addition, the MMC was criticized, notably by the Consumers' Association, for allegedly timid reports on other references, including the price of contact lens solutions (1993), the cost of mortgage valuations (1994), and the price of compact discs and music cassettes (1994). A theme underlying the criticism of these reports was that the MMC was placing the interest of firms under investigation ahead of those of consumers: it was held that the public interest was being interpreted too narrowly in favour of producers rather than the public at large. The MMC had recommended in 1994 that the British Medical Association should stop issuing guideline prices for operations performed by its members. In 1993 it had recommended that British Gas should separate its trading arm from its transportation interests. But neither of these 'radical' recommendations was seen as any compensation for an alleged pro-business stance in the other reports cited above. One critic said that the MMC should be a fearless guardian of the consumer interest, but that it was diminishing into a 'toothless watchdog'.

Mergers

In its work on *take-overs* after 1965 the MMC typically entered a politically charged atmosphere. Mere referral to the MMC prompted some bidders to abandon plans to continue with an acquisition. During the recession in the UK economy between 1989 and 1991, the number of merger bids fell sharply, and this reduced the number of potential references to the MMC. The bus industry has featured strongly in those references that have been made (see page 465 below).

It has been argued for several years by some that mergers policy is misdirected. These critics hold that rather than establish whether a merger between two firms would not be against the public interest, the MMC should explicitly seek for *benefits* that might follow from a change in market structure. In other words, it should apply an explicit weighing-up of the benefits and costs arising from a change in the status quo. The Labour Party said in 1994 that it favoured such an approach but declined to adopt it when elected into government in 1997. Our discussion of consumer surplus in Chapter 22 appraising the desirability of monopoly is a formal expression of such a shift in approach to mergers.

Of course the MMC can in the meantime become involved only in those merger situations referred to it by the government. These are mergers in which the assets taken over exceed £70 million. The Secretary of State for Trade and Industry receives advice from the OFT on whether to refer a merger to the MMC, but the ultimate decision rests with the minister. Inevitably, acceptance or rejection of the OFT's advice exposes a minister to keen political debate. The bid by Nestlé for Rowntrees in 1988 was not referred to the MMC and provoked a major debate on the desirability of such a large British firm passing into foreign ownership without any scrutiny of the implications arising from the take-over. Many business people have argued that mergers policy is unclear and there has been no predictability in ministerial decisions to refer mergers to the MMC.

Neither has the OFT been immune from the political process. Several bids were recommended by the OFT for scrutiny by the MMC, for example the hostile bid by Airtours for Owners Abroad in February 1993. The unwillingness of Mr Heseltine, the then Secretary of State for Trade and Industry, to accept the impartial advice of the OFT provides some evidence of tension between the OFT and the Department of Trade and Industry (DTI) concerning the emphasis to be placed on various aspects of competition policy.

The effect of a merger

In a guidance note issued in March 1994 the OFT outlined its informational requirements to establish whether or not a merger qualifies for reference to the MMC.

We particularly ask for information on three matters. First, 'demand side substitutability' – whether there are products which are close substitutes for those made or sold by both the merging businesses. Secondly, 'supply side substitutability' – whether other companies may be considered to be in the same market as the merging enterprises, even if they do not currently supply the same goods and services. Thirdly, the geographic market – generally the geographic boundaries of a market will be the area within which current buyers of the product (and close substitutes) could readily buy from other suppliers.

Source: Office of Fair Trading, Mergers: The Content of Submissions

6 Why is both demand-side and supply-side substitutability relevant in defining markets when the OFT assesses the likely effects of a merger?

7 What factors affect the ability of buyers of a product to turn to alternative suppliers within the geographic boundaries of a market?

8 What justification is there for the OFT being concerned only where the value of assets being taken over at the time of a take-over exceeds £70 million?

Restrictive practices

As regards *restrictive practices*, critics feel the ostensible success of the 1956 Act flattered the true position on the enforcement of competitive markets. When firms have defied rulings in the Restrictive Practices Court they have not been heavily fined. This inevitably puts doubt on what deterrence there is when the penalties are far from being penal. Extensive price-fixing and collusive tendering arrangements have come to light in industries as varied as bread-making, photocopying equipment, concrete pipes, road black-top materials and telephone cables. Not surprisingly, both Sir Gordon Borrie and his successor as Director-General of Fair Trading, Sir Bryan Carsberg, sought tougher sanctions and favoured the EU approach which prohibits anti-competitive practices. At present only trade between the United Kingdom and the rest of the EU is governed by the Common Market's rules.

In a White Paper published in July 1989, the government proposed to strengthen current legislation by making price-fixing cartels illegal and applying the sanction of fines up to 10 per cent of turnover for large firms found in contempt of the new law. This proposal, had it been implemented, would effectively have brought UK anti-competitive legislation more into line with the rest of the EU. The new legislation would also have included a wide range of professions – barristers, solicitors, doctors, nurses, opticians, accountants, architects and teachers – within its scope. However, the government did not proceed with its proposals. This was despite publication of a Green Paper in November 1992, *Abuses of Market Power*, which made clear that existing policies had little deterrent effect on anti-competitive practices.

Whilst some of the successful defences before the Restrictive Practices Court in its early years allowed restrictive agreements to continue, these have not been immune from broader influences on the competitive situation. For example, price-fixing arrangements of the Cement Makers' Federation were abandoned mainly as a result of growing competition from foreign suppliers at a time of sluggish demand from the construction industry. As indicated above, it is now the professions that are facing keen scrutiny of their regulations on competitive pricing. The demise of the trading arrangements between brokers and jobbers on the Stock Exchange illustrates this particularly well. In 1979 the OFT referred the rules of the Stock Exchange to the Restrictive Practices Court. An agreement was reached between the government and the Stock Exchange in July 1983 whereby special legislation was introduced to exempt the Stock Exchange from the 1956 Act and end the impending court case. As part of the 'deal' the Stock Exchange agreed to give up its minimum commission scales. It was soon realized that increased competition would undermine the traditional separation of functions by brokers and jobbers (single-capacity trading), and plans were made to allow dual-capacity trading from 27 October 1986. Without doubt the pending court case set in train the opening up of more competitive

financial markets. So ultimately, one might argue that the thrust of the 1956 Act prevailed.

Resale prices

There were just two cases where suppliers were successful in the Restrictive Practices Court in defending resale price maintenance. One was the Net Book Agreement (NBA). In August 1994 the OFT referred the NBA to the Court for a second time, and in 1997 the Court withdrew its exemption under the Resale Prices Act. The other successful defence of retail price maintenance concerned over-the-counter drugs and medicines in 1971.

The 1998 Competition Act

Our discussion of the evolving history of competition policy in the UK has emphasized the discretionary and administrative nature of the broad policy stance. It has been flexible in the support it has given to encouraging competition between those engaged in business activity. The critic of such an approach can easily point to the fact that it has amounted to being essentially weak when measured by an alternative policy stance that explicitly lays down what are regarded as unacceptable forms of competition behaviour. The alternative **legal prohibition approach** envisages heavy fines on firms shown to have been a party to price-fixing arrangements. It can also include prison sentences for senior management held responsible for business behaviour that constitutes a criminal offence. This approach is thus explicit and rigid in nature in promoting competition, and contrasts with the case-by-case manner in which UK governments have more tentatively applied a pro-competition policy.

However, by the time of the 1997 general election, the Conservative, Labour and Liberal Democrat parties judged that the ad hoc approach that had characterized competition policy since 1920 was no longer satisfactory. All three political parties saw grounds for a move towards a more legalistic policy stance. We have noted already how several of the MMC's reports were considered to have upheld the interests of firms rather than of consumers. In 1995 a House of Commons Trade and Industry Select Committee (TISC) urged the creation of a new Competition Authority to replace both the OFT and MMC. The TISC also recommended a prohibition approach in dealing with restrictive trade practices.

Once elected into office, the new Labour government quickly moved in the direction proposed by the TISC. A draft Competition Bill was published within three months of Labour being returned to power. Margaret Beckett, President of the Board of Trade, proposed two prohibitions

● a prohibition on anti-competitive agreements, cartels and concerted practices, based on Article 85 of the EC Treaty

and, secondly

- a prohibition covering abuse of a dominant market position, based on Article 86 of the EC Treaty.

The Bill proposed that the Director-General of Fair Trading (DGFT) should be the instrument to enforce this new policy stance. The DGFT would have strong investigatory powers to detect cartels and have the power to set fines on companies found to be in breach of the proposed policy on anti-competitive agreements. Margaret Beckett's Bill proposed that companies could appeal against decisions of the DGFT by seeking the views of a new body, the Competition Commission. This latter body was a renamed Monopolies and Mergers Commission, whose former role in reviewing merger cases would still continue. The Bill became law in the 1998 Competition Act and the prohibitions modelled on EU competition law took effect on 1 March 2000. As with EU law, the DGFT is able, if he or she finds that a company has breached the prohibition, to require it to pay a penalty of up to 10 per cent of its turnover in the UK. At the time of writing, no case involving any breach of the new competition law had arisen.

One can only speculate on how far the potential for the 1998 Competition Act to give new substance to combating restraints on competition will be realized in the coming decade. However, one can be rather more decisive in commenting on other aspects of competition policy – monopolies and mergers – and judge here that the Labour government has, like its predecessors, found it difficult to accept the advice it receives from the DGFT and Competition Commission. Critics argue that rejection of advice from these specialist bodies not only raises concern over the rationale of political interference, but also adds an element of unpredictability on how competition policy is being conducted.

Meddle or muddle?

Since succeeding Peter Mandelson as Secretary of State for Industry and Trade, Stephen Byers has rejected the advice of both the DGFT and the Competition Commission. Mr Byers referred the merger of Cable & Wireless Communications cable television interests with that of NTL to the Competition Commission, despite the OFT's advising that the merger raised no competition issues. More controversial was his rejection of the Competition Commission's recommendations on milk distribution, and that Birds Eye Wall's should be prohibited from selling ice-cream directly to retail outlets. In the latter case, the Commission and its predecessor as the MMC had reported on the ice-cream industry three times since 1994. On the other hand, Mr Byers, the Monopolies Commission (as it then was) and the OFT did share a common view that BSkyB should not be allowed to take over Manchester United Football Club.

9 Does it matter whether there is intervention by ministers in take-over-bid cases?

10 In Chapter 18, we discussed the determination of interest rates. There was an important change in policy in 1997 immediately following Labour's general election win. How does that new policy contrast with competition policy?

In 1999 the Labour government launched a campaign to curb excessive prices for groceries, clothes and services in the wake of a number of international price comparisons suggesting that UK consumers pay more than in other countries. For its part, the DGFT referred the £60 billion groceries market to the newly named Competition Commission after concluding that there was evidence that the leading retail multiple chains were making excessive profits. It also referred the sale of new motor cars to the Competition Commission. It will be late in 2000 before it is apparent what action the government proposes to take in the light of recommendations from the Competition Commission in these two studies, both of which prompted considerable media attention.

Raids at dawn

Businesses operating price-fixing or market-share agreements should beware – from 1 March, the Office of Fair Trading (OFT) takes on hugely extended powers to investigate anti-competitive abuses and hand out large fines. One senior lawyer says: 'If I were the OFT, I would have a hit-list of companies to target as soon as the Competition Act comes into force.'

James Flynn, a barrister and co-author of *Competition: Understanding the 1998 Act*, says the Act is a revolution in UK competition law. 'Previous legislation was essentially administrative, without much in the way of pro-active powers or penalties. What we will have after 1 March is a replica of the EC system, with very strong investigatory and coercive powers and impressive-looking fines. It will be much more worthwhile for people to complain or sue about anti-competitive behaviour – firms will really get hit if they are found out.'

The Act gives the OFT and sectoral regulators, such as Oftel and Ofwat, extensive new powers to launch dawn raids, search offices, demand documents and answers to questions if they have reasonable grounds for suspecting that the Act is being infringed. The OFT's Competition Policy Division has taken on fifty-five new staff and has a budget of £7 million. Most investigations will be triggered by complaints and 'whistleblowers', who are being encouraged to come forward by a leniency policy – the first member of a cartel to provide evidence of its activities will receive immunity from financial penalties. Other members can reduce their fines by up to 50 per cent if they co-operate with the OFT. Kate Rees, the head of competition law at Pinsent Curtis, says big companies trading internationally would not be affected much because they are covered by European competition law. Small businesses with less than 25 per cent of market share are largely exempt. 'Where the Act will really bite is with large domestic enterprises, such as transport companies, banks and insurers', she says.

You are as liable for an agreement based on a nod and a wink as for a written agreement. Companies concerned that an agreement might fall foul of the Act can submit it to the OFT for notification. However, the OFT charges £5,000 for guidance and £13,000 for a decision. Chris Bright, the head of European Competition at Clifford Chance, reckons the Act fits in with the focus on 'rip-off Britain', and says: 'It is likely to seem a bit of a whimper at first, because the OFT cannot just go off on fishing expeditions.'

Source: *The Times*, 22 February 2000

11 Explain why the new Act is seen as a significant development in UK competition policy.

12 What is the rationale of the OFT launching raids on company offices out of normal office hours? **A✓**

13 Why is the OFT likely to find 'whistleblowers' a more productive source of information than 'going off on fishing expeditions'? **A✓**

14 Why is it relevant to identify the potential impact of the Act on (a) big companies trading internationally, (b) large domestic enterprises and (c) small businesses?

15 Explain what is meant by the statement: 'You are as liable for an agreement based on a nod and a wink as for a written agreement.'

16 Why might it be expected that the OFT would have a list of companies to target early in 2000?

KEY POINTS

26.2

■ The pragmatic style of UK competition policy has given rise to criticism that it is too uncertain in operation and has lacked a positive commitment to the virtues of competition.

■ The 1998 Competition Act represents a shift to the prohibition-based approach of Articles 85 and 86 of the EU Treaty.

Privatization

In Chapter 2 we discussed the debate on the desirability of public ownership or nationalization of the energy and transport sectors of the UK economy based on both political and economic grounds. Since 1979 there has been a major change in the importance of the public sector in the United Kingdom as a result of about fifty state-owned businesses being transferred to the private sector. This process is known as **privatization**. In 1979 the then nationalized industries employed 1.5 million people. In 1988 the proportion of the total workforce in employment within the public sector was just under a quarter. However, privatization was a major factor in reducing this proportion to 18 per cent by 1998. The sale of former state-owned undertakings has yielded about £50 billion of proceeds to the government and thus has had implications for taxpayers. Many citizens became shareholders for the first time as a result of the attractive terms on which state-owned undertakings were sold off to individuals who wished to apply to become partial owners of now privately run companies.

The case for privatization in the United Kingdom

Privatization became a central theme of the Conservative government that took office in 1979. In general terms, it involves the transfer of assets and opportunities from the public sector to the private sector. This can take many forms, for example **contracting-out** or **deregulation**. An example of the former is the contracting-out of previous 'in-house' activities in hospitals and schools, such as cleaning and laundry services. Examples of deregulation are the removal of restrictions on new entry into the supply of local bus services and the measures taken to end monopoly situations in house conveyancing by solicitors and in the supply of spectacles by opticians. We briefly discuss these two forms of privatization later in the chapter but focus here on the high-profile meaning which involves the formation of a public joint-stock company from a nationalized industry (or similar public sector corporation) and the subsequent acquisition by private shareholders of at least 50 per cent of the newly formed company. The industries that were privatized first were not particularly controversial. The transfer of British Aerospace, Cable & Wireless and the National Freight Corporation involved transferring state-owned firms to the discipline of a competitive private marketplace. There was no pressing need on political grounds for continued state ownership of these undertakings. However, in the mid-1980s the process of privatization became more radical, involving the sale of **natural monopolies** and other key industries that are recognized as being at the 'commanding heights' of an economy, exemplified by British Telecom, British Gas, water and electricity. In these cases the newly privatized companies enjoyed considerable monopoly power. As a result, regulatory regimes were created for these companies which vary according to their individual technical and economic characteristics. We discuss these below. The privatization process has not yet run its full course, although the sale of Railtrack can be seen as almost the end of this policy. There are now few undertakings within the public sector that can be sold off! The Post Office is one where the concern over social obligations makes even some Conservative MPs reluctant to contemplate the postal system wholly in private ownership. The privatization of the coal industry was achieved in 1994 via bids from interested parties – mainly private mining companies; RJB Mining purchased the pits operated by British Coal in England in late 1994.

Obviously such a large transfer of activities from the public to the private sector has had several consequences. Out of this privatization process developed a host of related commercial activities for the merchant bankers that administer the flotations and for the advertising agents that promote it. Indeed, the United Kingdom has established a significant element of invisible earnings, as governments across the world have taken advantage of the City's expertise – and paid the London institutions handsomely for their services in advising on the sale of state-owned undertakings. Privatization is therefore no longer solely a British phenomenon. It has been adopted by many countries of different political persuasions and in varying stages of economic development.

The market forces argument

To a large extent *unsuccessful* public sector organizations can continue to operate regardless of their finances, whereas private firms which perform poorly cease to trade. This is because in the private sector firms are subject to market forces; they seek maximum profit for their owners and if they fail their resources are directed elsewhere. In the public sector efficiency is interpreted differently, goals are altered through government intervention and state backing disturbs the incentives to maximize profit.

Once privatized, firms become subject to direct market forces in both the capital and the product markets. Within the product market suppliers have to become sensitive to price to gain consumers' preferences; this may entail altering quality, lowering costs, adapting quickly to changes in taste, and so on. Within the capital market firms become accountable to shareholders. If these shareholders become disappointed with their returns on investment, they will be hesitant to purchase any further shares when the firm attempts to raise capital for new projects. Shareholders clearly have alternative investment opportunities. Indeed, to a large extent the commercial world of finance is far more concerned with profits and repayments than the open purse of the government Treasury, which in the final resort will always honour any debts generated. As some reviewers on this topic have neatly put it: 'the government as banker is a softer touch than a commercial bank'.

The important objective is to expose the public sector to market forces on the basis that competition increases efficiency. To use our terminology from earlier chapters, it is argued that the development of competitive markets in privatized industries will be more efficient in terms both of allocative efficiency (where prices charged relate to marginal cost) (Chapter 21) and of X-efficiency (the lowest possible cost of producing any level of output) (Chapter 22).

The share-ownership argument

Phrases such as 'popular capitalism' and 'a share-owning democracy' have become important tags associated with the privatization process in the United Kingdom. These ideological aspects of wider share ownership are of importance to the government; sponsored surveys by the Treasury on a regular basis to investigate the distribution of share ownership epitomize this importance. Based on the findings of these surveys, privatization could be deemed a success. The 1988 survey showed that 9 million people in the United Kingdom (that is, 20.5 per cent of the adult population) owned shares. This compares with an estimated 3 million people in 1979 (that is, 7 per cent of the adult population). Of this threefold increase, a significant number held shares in privatized companies (13 per cent of all adults – approximately 6 million people), and more than half of this number owned the shares of privatized companies only. Interestingly, 1.5 million shareholders owned shares in the company for which they worked.

The economic significance of these statistics, in quantitative terms, can be made to look impressive. The total number of UK shareholders is now similar to the number of trade union members. Moreover, the former may be increasing whilst the latter has certainly been declining. Workers owning shares of the company for which they work can be seen potentially to improve industrial relations. The 'enterprise culture' can be characterized as thriving. In qualitative terms, however, it is worth recognizing that approximately half of the UK shareholders own shares in only one company, and many of these holdings are small.

Privatization: an appraisal

When British Telecom was privatized in 1984, an independent regulator was created, the Office of Telecommunications (Oftel), with Bryan Carsberg as its Director-General. (The OFT felt that it had more than enough work to do and could not take on this additional responsibility.) Thereafter, as other state-owned public utilities were privatized, specialist regulators were set up – the Office of Gas Supply (Ofgas) in 1986, the Office of Water Services (Ofwat) in 1989, and the Office of Electricity Regulation (Offer) in 1990. A rail regulator has been appointed to oversee the privatization of British Rail. These regulators ensure that the privatized companies operate according to the terms of their licences as determined by the government. But it was intended that the regulators would exercise minimal intervention in order to allow the benefits of privatization to be realized. However, given their status as key sectors of the economy and reflecting certain natural monopoly characteristics, the government introduced price and profit controls which aim to protect customers from the abuse of monopoly power. These controls took the form of **price caps**, which restricted the permitted change in the average charge for a bundle of services to movements in a general price index, normally the retail price index (RPI). In their most basic form, price caps are expressed as RPI – X, where X denotes expected efficiency gains. The RPI – X formula differs from US-style rate-of-return regulation and aims to provide the privatized companies with profit incentives and the encouragement of efficiency not present in rate-of-return regulation. At first this approach was thus widely regarded as superior to the US approach, but during 1994 there was growing criticism of the regulators in the press. This concerned their alleged lax treatment of relevant companies which, it was held, made it possible both for shareholders to receive 'unduly' large dividends and for senior executives to receive 'unduly' high salary increases. In particular, Ofwat and Offer were the subject of keen attention for decisions made concerning the 1994 review of the determination of price caps. Others have criticized the fact that about 20 per cent of GDP in the United Kingdom is in the hands of what are seen as unaccountable and unelected regulators. However, it should be pointed out that the present system has detached ministers and politicians from day-to-day matters in privatized companies, which may well be a relevant offsetting benefit.

Privatizing utilities

Of the policies introduced by the Conservatives between 1979 and 1997, none has proved as significant as privatization – above all, the privatization of utilities. This revolution has been followed, with greater or lesser success, worldwide. The British innovation consisted of three elements: the move to private ownership; transparent price-cap regulation, under the RPI-X formula (retail price inflation, less a given percentage fixed for some years ahead); and the promotion of competition. Except with water utilities, it is the combination of all these components that has driven the extraordinary upheavals in these industries. Littleshild, progenitor of RPI-X regulation and, until 1998, the electricity regulator, detailed some of the changes in his industry. Employment has fallen by roughly one-third in electricity transmission, and one-half in distribution. Similarly, operating costs fell by nearly 40 per cent in transmission between the average of the first three years (1990–1 to 1992–3) and 1997–8. Better still, as regulation tightened, these improvements in efficiency produced correspondingly big reductions in prices. The fall in the real prices of electricity to business was between 25 per cent and 34 per cent, from 1990 to the start of 1999. For domestic consumers, the reduction was about 26 per cent.

Competition has also increased. In 1989–90, National Power and PowerGen were still responsible for 78 per cent of generation. But their share is now below 30 per cent. The largest 5000 consumers were already allowed to choose suppliers from the time of privatization, while the next largest 50 000 were freed from 1994; 80 per cent of the former and 60 per cent of the latter now buy from new suppliers. Since May 1999, domestic consumers have also been able to choose among suppliers. The best price reductions on offer have been between 8 and 15 per cent. In response, 3.3 million domestic customers had already switched by the end of September.

All this amounts to a huge success. The question is: what now? The answer must be, 'more competition'. Much industry-specific regulation could, quite soon, be withdrawn. The exception would be for the inherently monopolistic common carrier element: the pipes (in gas) and the wires (in fixed-line telecommunications and electricity). The regulator's chief job would then be to determine charges and conditions for access to these facilities.

How far does the government see things this way? Not far enough, is the answer. It has come a long way towards accepting the principal features of the regulatory regime, including the price caps and the impulse toward enhanced competition. But there are reasons for concern. First, there was the decision to halve further investment in gas-fired generating capacity. Second, the government intends 'to issue guidance to regulators on social and environmental matters, including energy efficiency, and to place the regulators under a duty to have regard to that guidance'. This raises the third concern: the prime objective of regulation. The government intends to replace the duty of promoting competition with a single primary duty to protect the interests of consumers. Companies will always argue that a particular proposal to increase competition will hurt all, or at least some, consumers, in one way or another. Regulators who are working under the new objective may find it more difficult to resist such arguments than hitherto.

Privatization of the utilities has been an enormous success. It has led to better regulation and far more competition, except in water, than ever expected. Now it is possible to envisage the withdrawal of regulation from large areas of previously regulated activity. The objectives of regulation should remain simple and transparent.

Source: *Financial Times*, 18 October 1999

17 How do the data suggest that the old nationalized industries must have been characterized by considerable inefficiency?

18 How has competition been promoted for the benefit of consumers in the case of electricity?

19 Why has competition not been a feature of the market for water? ▲✓

20 Why could the government have decided to halt the building of more gas-fired generating capacity in the electricity industry? ▲✓

21 Suggest an alternative policy to that of issuing guidance to utility regulators on encouraging energy efficiency. What are the advantages and disadvantages of such an alternative approach?

22 What is the merit of the proposition that regulation should be 'simple and transparent'?

23 Is it the case that the regulators will be ultimately successful when they have no need to regulate prices on behalf of consumers?

As regards the other strands of privatization defined earlier in this chapter – contracting-out and deregulation – there is a similar story of debate and criticism concerning their experience in practice. After 1980, a number of local authorities organized competitive tenders for the provision of refuse collection rather than relying on 'in-house' provision by direct labour. The 1988 Local Government Act required that a wide range of local authority services should be open to competitive tender at regular intervals. These services included refuse collection, street cleaning, school catering and a wide range of cleaning and maintenance work. This Act thus moved tendering from a voluntary option to a compulsory basis. Most contracts since 1988 have been won by in-house organizations. Thus the degree to which there is widespread bidding for tenders would disappoint some of those enthusiastic about the benefit of competition for local authority management. It is still relatively early days to appraise how these new markets are actually operating. However, certain 'white-collar' local authority construction services are now subject to private sector competition. Architecture, engineering, surveying and valuation are now areas of local authority purchasing that are '**market tested**'. Authorities are free not to take the lowest bid and are able to judge the trade-off between cost and quality. However, each local authority must publish accounts, and this will enable comparisons to be made with others.

Deregulation has become almost synonymous with the bus industry given that in that market keenly competitive conditions have arisen in many parts of the United Kingdom since the 1985 Transport Act was passed. This Act abolished road service licensing by Traffic Commissioners for local bus services outside London and thus allowed new entry by private operators on routes previously dominated by local authority bus operators and the National Bus Company (NBC). The NBC was privatized and local authorities were required to operate their bus interests at arm's length. Since 1985 there have been price wars between competing bus operators in several parts of the United Kingdom and one operator – Stagecoach, based in Perth – has been the subject of many OFT investigations and several MMC reports. Small operators have claimed that Stagecoach engages in predatory pricing in several parts of the United Kingdom. They fear that take-overs by Stagecoach may end up with the former public monopoly being replaced by a private monopoly. Studies show that despite keen price competition there has not been any recovery in the demand for bus travel since 1985. Where available, people much prefer to use car transport for reasons of convenience. Critics of the 1985 legislation regard some form of **franchising** as being a better way of incorporating competition into the bus market.*

KEY POINTS

26.3

■ Privatization was a policy of the Conservative government which involved the transfer of assets from the public sector to the private sector.

■ A case for privatization can be made out based on the use of market forces. Once privatized, firms are directly affected by market forces in both the capital and the product markets, and consequently it is argued that they should become more efficient.

■ The share-ownership argument relies on the idea of an 'enterprise culture' where managers and employers have greater freedom and better motivation as shareholders.

■ In the former public utilities price caps (RPI − X) have tried to counter any abuse of market power by dominant private monopolies.

■ Privatization includes both contracting-out (market testing) and deregulation.

■ Privatization has helped to stimulate competition and eliminate inefficiency in former nationalized industries.

* This was suggested in the penultimate paragraph of the MMC's report on the supply of bus services in mid- and west Kent in 1993.

Industrial policies

The United Kingdom does not have an industrial policy in the sense of government policies explicitly seeking the achievement of particular production targets or favouring certain industries at the expense of others. This contrasts with policies taken in Japan in the early 1950s, which had the aim of channelling resources into a number of industries as the basis of post-war recovery. There was a clear strategy with long-term aims. Policy in the United Kingdom has been essentially pragmatic and amounts to a series of piecemeal measures lacking a clear coherent strategy. Many of the measures that one could envisage as part of industrial policy during the past decade have related to improving market performance by removing various barriers to entry. These barriers may formally be referred to as **structural rigidities**.

Structural rigidities are obstacles that hinder the efficiency of many markets. Examples of such rigidities include excessive taxes, an insufficient supply of trained labour, subsidies, wages that are above the equilibrium level as a result of union activity, minimum wage legislation and excessive social security payments. We shall consider fiscal policy in Chapter 28, having already discussed various aspects of the labour market in Chapters 12 and 24.

In very broad terms, industrial policy measures during the 1980s aimed at shifting the emphasis on intervention and a related 'culture of dependence' to the freeing of market forces and policies promoting an **enterprise culture**. An enterprise culture is one dependent on profit, freedom, competitiveness, liberalization, deregulation, incentives, ownership and decentralization. We now consider some separate strands of industrial policy and try to pull these together with reference to a series of government White Papers on competitiveness. We consider briefly regional policy, small-firms policy, technology policy, and finally the Public Finance Initiative.

Regional policy

Regional policy dates back to 1934 when the Special Areas Act was passed, which identified certain depressed areas as being in need of incentives to promote industrial diversification. Consequently, certain areas today can offer firms financial assistance to entice them to develop within their locality. These areas, designated **assisted areas**, were last revised in 1984. The 1960s and 1970s were very much the heyday of regional policies. The decline in emphasis since then is epitomized by the 1988 legislation, which involved the abolition of the automatic (mandatory) Regional Development Grant and the creation of a discretionary system. Regional Selective Assistance (RSA) grants are available to firms in assisted areas. They are provided for projects that maintain or create employment. The monies paid out in grants relate mainly to capital expenditure.

Alongside RSA payments are Regional Enterprise Grants (REGs), which are payable to small firms (that is, those with fewer than twenty-five employees) that wish to invest in those regions designated as development areas. Regional assistance clearly represents a small and declining percentage of industrial expenditure. One feature of the 1989–91 recession was the relatively steep increase in unemployment in south-east England. This contrasted with the small increase in unemployment in Scotland, Wales and the north and north-west of England, which hitherto had compared unfavourably with the rest of the country. However, until June 1993 no part of London or the south-east was accorded assisted-area status. As from that date, Lea Valley, Park Royal and the London end of the Thames corridor received assistance, as did some towns in the south-east (Dover, Hastings) and the south-west (Torbay).

It is important to note that assistance from the EU, including the European Regional Development Fund and the European Social Fund, is now a very significant part of regional policy in the United Kingdom. Assistance from the EU has risen, whereas domestic regional spending has fallen.

Small-firms policy

The current emphasis on policy for small firms is not confined to Britain. A whole range of policies to encourage and support the development of small firms is in force throughout Europe, America and Canada. In the United Kingdom the expression of this emphasis is given by the fact that within the DTI there is a minister responsible for small firms and consumer affairs.

The Conservative government took over a hundred specific measures during the 1980s to influence the development of the small-firm sector. Much of the small-firms policy introduced since 1979 has involved tax benefits and incentives aimed at rewarding enterprise and encouraging the development of small businesses. Another group of measures has been aimed at removing the administrative 'red tape' that seems to complicate the life of so many small firms, for example the *exemption* of small firms from requirements relating to industrial tribunals, maternity reinstatement and unfair dismissal procedures. These have been extended since the mid-1980s to include simple planning procedures, building regulations and auditing requirements.

In June 1994 the government announced measures that would help small firms by relieving them from potential investigation under the Competition Act. In future, businesses will be excluded if their annual relevant turnover is less than £10 million (previously £5 million) or if they have less than 25 per cent of the relevant market.

Three specific financial schemes have also been created directly to encourage small businesses. The Enterprise Allowance Scheme aimed to encourage the budding but as yet unemployed entrepreneur to run his or her own business. The Loan Guarantee Scheme has involved the government since 1981 acting as guarantor for bank loans to small firms. The Business Expansion Scheme provided tax relief to individuals investing in qualifying unquoted companies with which they were not connected. However, this scheme, introduced in 1983, was abolished in 1993 on the grounds that it had become a tax-avoidance measure for the wealthy interested in non-productive investments such as art and fine wines.

Whilst there has been much activity by government concerning small firms, it is pertinent to question whether there is a clear direction for this strand of industrial policy. An assessment based on a programme of research based at the University of Warwick has raised the need for a White Paper that could identify the objectives of small-firms policy together with specified targets to enable progress to be monitored. Given the continued absence of such a White Paper, it is hard to take stock of the many shifts of direction that have appeared in the past decade. It is therefore difficult not to agree with critics who see small-firms policy as being unduly dominated by political considerations – a concern by government to be seen to be doing something.*

Technology policy

For many years governments have assisted industry in the financing of research and development (R&D) and industrial innovation. The DTI has sponsored an annual 'scoreboard' since 1991 which gives particulars of R&D spending by over 360 companies listed on the London Stock Exchange. Critics of the state of UK technology tend to be less concerned about total spending on R&D than about its distribution. They say that defence-related projects account for a large proportion of R&D spending, which appears to be falling behind that of some other developed countries. One indicator of technical progress in the United Kingdom is the share of registered patents in the United States held by British-owned companies; critics feel there are grounds for concern given that this share is declining.

The Private Finance Initiative

Since 1992 there has been, arguably, a new dimension to industrial policy in the UK. The **Private Finance Initiative** (PFI) was begun by the Conservative government as a means of enhancing investment in the UK's infrastructure without adding further strain on the government's management of public finance. In short, it amounted to a means whereby the social fabric of schools, hospitals and prisons could be maintained and replaced through a partnership of the private and public sectors. We showed in Chapter 2 how the process of privatization pursued by the Thatcher government after 1979 rolled back the frontier of the state and diminished the role of the public sector. The PFI represented an extension of this philosophy once major state assets had been sold off. Health and education offered possibilities of introducing the discipline of the private sector whilst allowing the government to claim it was maintaining public sector service within these more sensitive sectors of the economy. How was a PFI deal supposed to operate? In essence a consortium within the private sector (a contractor and finance source) would sign a contract to construct a public building for which a public sector client would agree to pay annual charges during the life of the contract – usually lasting twenty years or more. In opposition the Labour Party opposed the PFI, but following the 1997 election and a review of the state of progress moved from opposition to embrace the concept with great enthusiasm through a Treasury Task Force. The number of PFI deals rose sharply to exceed £11 billion by the end of 1998.

The change of heart is not hard to explain. As indicated above, PFI offered the prospects of more schools, hospitals and transport projects like the Channel Tunnel Rail Link without disturbing the size of the PSNCR and the implied concerns for eligibility for participation in European monetary union. Critics have, however, pointed to doubts whether the discipline of the private sector can help offset the lower cost of funding projects, which would have been the case if they had been government funded. Moreover, if a hospital trust signs up for a PFI-funded new hospital, will it necessarily be one of the trusts with land to sell or funds raised elsewhere which may be able to maintain the annual sums required to adhere to the terms agreed with the private contractor? Does it follow that hospital provision can be satisfied by hospital trusts, in relevant geographical areas, being able to fund new capacity by PFI deals? What is certain is that more PFI deals are now becoming operational, for example the rebuilding of the government's Communication Headquarters (GCHQ), the development of Luton Airport and new facilities at London Underground. As a result, the debate whether these private sector–public sector contracts do help citizens and taxpayers in the UK in the long term will no doubt become more lively.

---

* D.J. Storey, *Understanding the Small Business Sector*, Routledge, 1994.

KEY POINTS

26.4

- Industrial policy is concerned with affecting the structure and performance of industry and includes regional assistance, help for small firms and also R&D policy.

- Much industrial policy of the 1980s and 1990s related to improving market performance by reducing structural rigidities.

- Regional policy dates back to 1934, and since then a range of incentives to encourage firms to develop in certain areas has been on offer. The range of incentives available depends upon geographical location.

- Regional assistance from the EU is now more significant than that provided by the UK government.

- In the United Kingdom small-firms policy has taken three main forms: changes to the tax system; changes to the administrative 'red-tape' requirements; and several financial incentives made available through various schemes.

- The government has shown concern about the level of R&D spending in the United Kingdom relative to other countries.

- The Private Finance Initiative involves partnerships of the public and private sectors concerning infrastructure investment.

Competition and competitiveness

In May 1994 the government published a White Paper called *Competitiveness: Helping Business to Win*. Mr Heseltine, then President of the Board of Trade, stated that

> The purpose of the paper was to provide an assessment of the strengths and weaknesses of UK industry relative to its competitors, a snapshot of Government initiatives in progress and some pointers as to where the Government was going to focus its efforts in the future.

The White Paper charted almost a century of relative decline by the United Kingdom. It stated that

> We are back in touch with the leaders but there remains a lot of ground to make up. Although we have many world-beating companies, average productivity levels in manufacturing have not risen to those of our main competitors. To prosper in this rapidly changing world we have to improve our economic performance across the board. We must raise our performance and adapt our

skills, the way we work, and our products to new circumstances and opportunities.

The White Paper identified ten key factors underlying the UK's relatively weak economic performance. These were the macroeconomy; education and training; employment; management; innovation; trade; finance for business, communications and infrastructure; regulation; law; and tax and purchasing.

The then Conservative government followed up the 1994 White Paper with further annual commentaries of progress perceived by the government as improving the 'competitiveness' of the UK economy. The Conservative government's stance on competitiveness was to 'benchmark' the UK's performance, both overall and in terms of a number of factors of competitiveness, against that of other countries. On its return to power, the new Labour government has maintained the previous administration's enthusiasm to issue Competitiveness White Papers to benchmark UK performance on a sectoral and national level. Like the Conservative government before 1997, the Labour White Papers claim that the UK has made progress but that incomes (a key measure of competitiveness) are lower in the UK than in most developed countries, even though many Britons work longer hours than average elsewhere. Reasons for the relatively poor performance of the UK economy are held to be insufficient investment in both research and development and training, and labour skill shortages. However, a much-quoted study by the McKinsey Institute in October 1998 asserted that in most cases, such problems were consequential or secondary effects rather than root causes. The McKinsey study said that UK labour productivity was 37 per cent lower than in the US, and 26 per cent lower than in France and Germany. The study identified two main causes of 'the productivity gap'. The first cause was seen as tight planning regulations that prevent businesses such as food retailers from expanding. The second factor for low productivity in the UK was held to be regulations and agreements affecting specific product markets, such as building controls on hotels. Another example cited was the voluntary restraints on Japanese car imports. This example illustrates how the McKinsey study was underlining the relevance of insufficient competition and overregulation. The Labour government's move in 1999 to support efforts to establish whether UK consumers were indeed being 'ripped off' – a theme popularized by *The Sunday Times* – might be seen as one of the repercussions of the McKinsey study.

In the December 1998 White Paper, the then Trade and Industry Secretary Peter Mandelson committed the Labour government to facilitating the transfer of knowledge. Unlike previous Labour governments, Mr Mandelson proposed to steer the emphasis away from interventionism to one that viewed knowledge as a key factor in economic growth. This new approach thus saw IT and scientific and technical advances as crucial to enhancing competitiveness. 'The knowledge economy' was seen as one where international success depends on entrepreneurs exploiting science and technology and where employees are highly skilled. Entrepreneurs can only exploit the opportunities presented by rapid change if their workforce is highly productive. Here, like the McKinsey study, the government noted the labour productivity gap between the UK and the US, France and Germany. In tune with this thinking, the DTI has unveiled several 'enterprise schemes' aimed at helping growing 'high-tech' businesses. These measures have been reinforced by announcements in 1999 from the Chancellor of the Exchequer to encourage and reward executives who join high-risk companies through special tax reliefs.

However, for some observers, fundamental doubts have remained about what really constitutes the role of the Department of Trade and Industry in achieving tangible results to improve competitiveness. Such critics have not been slow to highlight the fact that the DTI has been something of a graveyard for ministers appointed to it. During eighteen years of office, there have been no fewer than thirteen Secretaries of State for Trade and Industry. By December 1998, the new Labour government had already appointed three persons to hold office at the DTI

(Margaret Beckett, Peter Mandelson and Stephen Byers). So, by continuing in office into 2000, Mr Byers was proving a more durable occupant of the DTI than most of his predecessors. However, as we saw earlier in this chapter, his handling of take-over bids has generated criticism, which is something that has characterized most Secretaries of State for Trade and Industry.

KEY POINTS

26.5

- ■ Since 1994 governments in the UK have issued White Papers aimed at enhancing the competitiveness of the UK economy.

- ■ The 1998 Paper rejected the role of interventionist policies and planning and argued in favour of promoting entrepreneurship, developing the skills base and collaborative business activity.

Case Study

Do we need the DTI?

What does the Department of Trade and Industry do? The question has taxed the DTI's many ministerial incumbents over the past twenty years. The Trade and Industry Minister must face up to a seemingly intractable problem. In a non-interventionist economy, there appears little the DTI can or should do apart from keeping an eye on competition policy. The last few governments have been keen on their supply-side reforms, but the majority of these, and particularly tax and training, belong in the hands of other departments. Not surprisingly, the post has developed a reputation for a fast turnover as ministers move in search of a more fulfilling job or disappear into obscurity. There have been some big names in charge – Lord Young, Norman Tebbit and, most energetically, 'President Heseltine' – but you would be hard pressed to draw up a list of departmental achievements beyond deregulation task forces that have cut very little red tape and expensive trade missions to countries with dubious human rights records.

Business itself stops short of following this argument to its logical extent and calling for the abolition of the DTI. It feels that the DTI does have a role to play as a kind of mediator between business and the government. The DTI should act as a listening post for business views and make sure the Cabinet and the Treasury are made fully aware of when their policies are likely to prove damaging to busi-

ness. At the same time, the department can act as a support service for business, providing advice and encouragement on trade and best practice issues.

Source: *The Times*, 31 July 1998

1 When appointed to the DTI, Nicholas Ridley was widely quoted in 1989 on his arrival at the DTI offices in Victoria Street, London, as asking: 'What is this place for?' Does the passage above suggest that it is inevitable that the DTI has no clear role?

2 What do you understand by the word 'competitiveness'? Does competitiveness matter?

3 To what extent do you think competition policy helps to determine competitiveness?

4 Is it the responsibility of the government to determine competitiveness?

5 It has been said that healthy firms do not need government support, whereas unhealthy ones do not deserve it. Is this, in your view, an appropriate basis on which to determine interventionist policies in respect of industry?

6 Suppose you hold the view that the UK should expand the number of highly skilled people. Should responsibility for this lie with the DTI or another government department?

Exam Preparation

Multiple choice questions

1 The establishment of agencies such as the Office of Water Regulation (Ofwat) to regulate privatized utility industries has been justified for all the following reasons **except** one. Which is the **exception**?
   A to reduce barriers to market entry
   B to promote market contestability
   C to prevent the abuse of monopoly power
   D to enable shareholders to exercise more power over the companies they own

2 When the UK government privatized industries such as water and telecommunications, regulatory organizations (e.g. Ofwat and Oftel) were established. Regulation of these industries in the United Kingdom has included
   A setting a limit upon the amount of profit which can be earned
   B preventing overseas companies competing with domestic suppliers
   C imposing restrictions upon the extent to which prices can be increased
   D preventing all the regulated industries from engaging in any form of price discrimination

3 A policy of banning all monopolies and mergers may be preferred to one which considers each on its merits because
   A a competitive industry must produce a higher output and charge a lower price than a monopolist
   B a monopolist will be inefficient because it does not have any competitors
   C barriers to entry will always lead to excessive profits for the monopolist
   D the costs of investigating monopolies and mergers may outweigh the benefits

Essay questions

1 Offer an economic appraisal of government policies concerned with the maintenance of competition between firms in industry and commerce.

2 'The central purpose of competition policy is to promote industrial efficiency through the identification and control of monopolies, cartels, and other potential abuses of market power' (C.J.M. Hardie). Discuss.

3 What have been the results thus far of privatizing nationalized industries?

4 (a) Why did the government create regulatory agencies such as Oftel (for the telecommunications industry) and Ofgas (for the gas industry) when it privatized previously nationalized industries?
   (b) Discuss the various ways in which such regulatory agencies can influence the performance of these industries.

5 In 1995 some European cement firms were fined by the European court for maintaining a price-fixing cartel.
   (a) Explain the conditions under which a cartel can be established and maintained.
   (b) Analyse the economic effects of the cartel on (i) the producers and (ii) the consumers of cement.

27

Money, monetary policy and inflation

LEARNING OUTCOMES

On completing this chapter you should understand:

- The demand for and supply of money
- The transmission mechanism
- The quantity theory of money
- How monetary policy actually works
- The relationship between inflation and unemployment

A major factor in the determination of monetary policy is the need to control inflation. Under successive Conservative governments, from 1979 until 1997, control of inflation was the dominant objective: the party made it the highest priority. From 1997, the Labour government set out to follow similar policies. At the time of writing, inflation is low at 1 per cent and some economists have said that it is, perhaps, dead. Yet many believe that signs of overheating in the UK economy make the threat of inflation very much a live issue.

The economic theory relating money and inflation is awash with old debates. The problem is that events often require the theory to be adapted, or at least viewed in a different way. Then, later, it turns out that an old theoretical idea has become relevant again. The relevant theories are outlined here, indicating where they may have some insight to offer in relation to recent situations.

Before we investigate the effect of money on the economy, we should consider why inflation has become so important. Why is it so unpopular? Part of the answer is that people dislike uncertainty, and inflation leads to uncertainty about price levels in the future. Further, uncertainty may make it difficult for firms to estimate future profits; they may be deterred from investing if they are not sure what the returns will be. If this does happen, then economic growth will be less than it might have been.

Inflation reduces the real incomes of people whose incomes are fixed in money terms. Perhaps more significantly, it reduces the purchasing power of all assets which are denominated in money terms. So people who lend will receive a repayment which is of less real value than the original loan. Bank balances will lose value. Meantime, borrowers will find their debts shrinking in real terms. They will tend to gain from inflation.

Expectations of inflation have in the past led to very high rates of interest. Lenders have to be compensated for the loss of the real value of their loans. Furthermore, interest rates are often very variable when governments are trying to control inflation. A steady diet of lower inflation, and lower expectations of inflation, might allow interest rates to fall in the long run.

We will start by exploring the Keynesian theory of money and the way money affects prices. We will then look briefly at the quantity theory of money, which is older than the Keynesian theory but was revamped to help explain the events of the late 1960s and 1970s. With the modern quantity theory came a new view of the relationship between inflation and unemployment. Finally, we will consider how we can explain the events of the late 1980s and the 1990s, and what the future prospects may be.

The demand for money

There is a market for money just as there is a market for goods and services. There is a demand for money – for a number of different purposes. There is a supply of money.

The Bank of England's monetary policy seeks to control aggregate monetary demand in the economy. The objectives of policy are to achieve a high level of employment without undue inflation, and to maintain external balance.

Since banking systems were deregulated worldwide during the 1980s, controlling the *supply* of money (that is, banks' willingness to lend it) has become more difficult. So the Bank of England has used interest rates to control the *demand* for money.

Why do people want to hold money instead of alternative assets such as bonds, stocks and durable goods? J.M. Keynes distinguished three different reasons why we hold money.

1 *Transactions demand* Households and firms hold a certain amount of money because of its usefulness as a generally acceptable medium of exchange. Holding money facilitates economic exchanges. With money we can buy products and financial assets quickly when and where we want. The transactions demand for money relates to the fact that our receipts of money income do not match our expenditures. For example, throughout a year you may get paid on the first of each month but spend your income at a relatively even rate throughout the entire month. The transactions demand for money increases when incomes rise or prices rise.

2 *Precautionary demand* A certain amount of money holdings are desired by households and firms in order to meet unplanned emergencies. The transactions demand for money relates to planned expenditures. Precautionary demand relates to unplanned expenditures, such as unexpected illness, unemployment and so on. People like to hold a certain amount of their wealth in the form of very liquid assets, that is, assets denominated in money terms, such as bank balances and building society deposits. The precautionary demand for money will rise with incomes.

3 *Speculative demand* The nominal value (in money terms) of money is fixed. This is not true for a share in a company or for a bond, a house or a painting. A household could own any or all of these, or it could choose to hold some or all of its assets in the form of money. People particularly wish to hold money as an alternative to other assets when the market prices of other assets are falling or when they anticipate that the value of non-money assets such as shares will fall in the future.

The price of holding money

Money has an opportunity cost: the income which could have accrued had it been held in the form of other assets. So the decision to hold money will to some extent reflect the rate of interest obtainable on those other assets. This will be traded off against the convenience of money, which stems from its **liquidity**.

Thus we would expect to find an inverse relationship between the quantity of money demanded and the cost of holding it, which is the interest rate. Money provides the services of liquidity. The higher the opportunity cost of liquidity, the less you will buy. In other words, the higher the alternative interest rate you could earn on money, the less money you will want to hold. In the framework of the Keynesian model which we studied in Chapter 16, the demand for money is sometimes referred to as liquidity preference.

The alternative to holding money

For a given demand for money, if the interest rate rises, a smaller quantity of money will be demanded but a larger quantity of other financial assets will be desired. This means that, as the interest rate rises, individuals attempt to purchase bonds with some of their money holdings. In other words, they substitute income-earning (or higher-income-earning) financial assets for part of the money that they are holding. Alternatively, if the interest rate in the economy falls, a larger quantity of money will be demanded because the lower interest rate does not make it worthwhile to forgo the convenience of money. Individuals will attempt to sell off some of the income-earning financial assets that they own in order to have more cash. It is sometimes said, they go liquid.

The price of bonds and the interest rate

If individuals, for whatever reason, feel that they have more money (cash holdings) than they need, there is an excess supply of money. People will attempt to replace some of their money holdings with, say, bonds. What will this increasing demand for bonds do to the price of *already existing* bonds? It will cause their price to rise. But this price rise for already existing bonds can only mean one thing – the interest yield on those old bonds will *fall*. The value of interest payments on a bond is fixed, but the actual *yield* (or rate of return) on a bond is not. Consider a simple example. You have just purchased a £1000 bond that promises to pay you £100 a year for twenty years. This means that your interest yield is £100 ÷ £1000, which is equal to 10 per cent per year. Now let us say that everyone suddenly demands more bonds, so that the price of all bonds goes up. You find that you can now sell the old bond that you have for £2000. It still pays £100 a year as before, but what has happened to the effective interest yield on that bond received by the buyer of the bond? It has fallen, for it is now £100 per year divided by £2000, which equals 5 per cent per year. The important point to be understood is:

> The market price of existing bonds (and all fixed-income assets) is inversely related to the rate of interest prevailing in the economy.

This analysis shows us that as interest rates (the price of money) fall, the quantity of money demanded will rise. In other words, the demand curve for money will be downward sloping, as in Figure 27.1.

Calculating bond prices and interest rates

1 Assume that a bond promises to the holder £1000 per year for ever.
   (a) If the interest rate is 10 per cent, what is the bond worth now?
   (b) What happens to the value of the bond if interest rates (i) rise to 20 per cent or (ii) fall to 5 per cent?

2 Suppose there were an indestructible machine expected to generate £2000 per year in revenues but costing £1000 per year to maintain – for ever. How would that machine be priced relative to the bond described above in 1(a)?

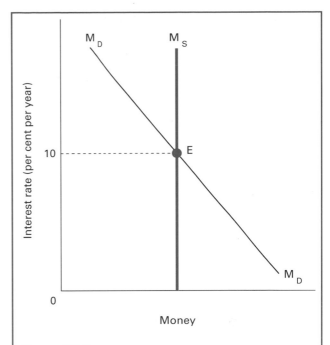

Figure 27.1
Putting together the demand and supply of money
The demand schedule M_DM_D is downward sloping; the supply schedule is not only upward sloping, it is vertical at some given quantity of money supplied by the monetary authorities. The equilibrium rate of interest is at 10 per cent.

KEY POINTS

27.1

- Inflation can cause problems because it increases uncertainty and reduces the real value of assets denominated in money terms.

- Money is an asset that is desired because of the services of liquidity that it provides.

- The opportunity cost of holding money is the interest forgone.

- The demand for money is therefore inversely related to the rate of interest.

- The alternative to money as an asset is assumed in the Keynesian approach to be other financial assets only, such as bonds.

- There is an inverse relationship between the rate of interest in the economy and the market price of bonds.

The supply of money

We saw in Chapter 18 that money can be measured in different ways. When we speak of the supply of money we are using the term loosely to mean the amount of money in circulation. The best estimate of this might be M4.

The theory

We continue with the Keynesian approach to the supply of money. At any given time there is a specific stock of money in the economy. Figure 27.1 shows the quantity of money fixed at the level M_S. This assumes that the supply of money is determined solely by the banking system and the Bank of England. With this supply schedule and a demand schedule, we should be able to find an equilibrium point. It is at the intersection of the supply schedule and the demand schedule, or point E. At point E, the equilibrium interest rate happens to be 10 per cent per year. This is the interest rate that equates the quantity of money demanded with the quantity of money supplied.

Monetary expansion

In theory, the interaction of the demand for money with the supply of money determines the interest rate. The rate of interest will determine the rate of planned investment. In Chapter 15, we drew the planned investment schedule as a downward-sloping curve, with the interest rate on the vertical axis and planned investment on the horizontal axis. Figure 27.2(b) shows a similar planned investment schedule. The lower the rate of interest is, the greater is the quantity of planned investment.

Figure 27.2(a) shows the demand and supply of money. Assume that the equilibrium rate of interest r_1 is established by the intersection of the money supply schedule M_S and the money demand schedule M_DM_D. At interest rate r_1, we can see in 27.2(b) that the quantity of planned investment

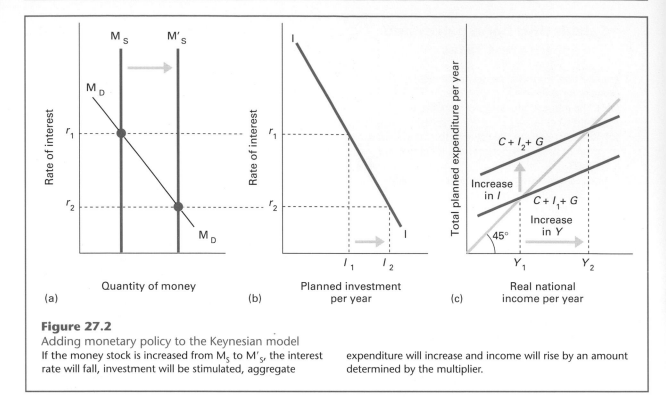

Figure 27.2
Adding monetary policy to the Keynesian model
If the money stock is increased from M_S to M'_S, the interest rate will fall, investment will be stimulated, aggregate expenditure will increase and income will rise by an amount determined by the multiplier.

per year will be I_1. This quantity of investment will yield – given the consumption function and government expenditures – the total planned expenditures curve labelled $C + I_1 + G$ in 27.2(c). It intersects the 45° line where total planned expenditures are identically equal to real national income (why?) at a real national income per year of Y_1.

We have observed that the Bank of England controls the money supply by influencing the rate of interest. Higher interest rates make loans more expensive, and vice versa. Both consumers and firms will borrow less. Now, supposing the Bank of England wants to encourage investment and cuts interest rates. What happens next? If banks increase their lending, there is a rightward movement in the money supply curve from M_S to M'_S in 27.2(a). The equilibrium rate of interest will fall to r_2, as shown in 27.2(a), for at this interest rate the quantity of money demanded and the quantity of money supplied are now equal again. But at interest rate r_2 in 27.2(b), we see that there is an increase in the quantity of planned investment per year. That increase is shown by the horizontal arrow from I_1 to I_2.

The investment component of the total planned expenditures curve, $C + I_1 + G$ in 27.2(c), will now have to move upwards by the full amount of the increase in planned investment. This upward movement is shown by the vertical arrow. The new total planned expenditure curve becomes $C + I_2 + G$. The equilibrium level of real national income per year will increase from Y_1 to Y_2. Note, as always, that this change in the equilibrium level of real national income per year is greater than the change in planned investment. This is because there is a multiplier at work – the investment multiplier.

The effects of a contractionary monetary policy with high interest rates can be shown in a similar way. The money supply schedule will shift to the left, causing the equilibrium rate of interest to rise. This will cause a decrease in total planned expenditures and a decrease in the equilibrium level of real national income per year.

The transmission mechanism

We are assuming that there is a specific transmission mechanism by which changes in interest rates bring about changes in the equilibrium level of real national income. The change in the interest rate causes a change in investment, which causes a change in income and employment. This transmission mechanism is shown in Figure 27.3.

The overall effect of a change in monetary policy will be somewhat offset by feedback effects. Rising incomes increase the transactions demand for money, shifting the demand-for-money function rightwards. This will tend to raise interest rates, reversing the original trend but only by a limited amount, not sufficient to alter our initial conclusions about the direction of the changes.

A Keynesian theory of inflation

In practice we have seen that the outcome of a change in monetary policy depends crucially on whether *real* income *can* increase. In Chapter 14 we examined the effect of changes in aggregate demand on the price level. We saw

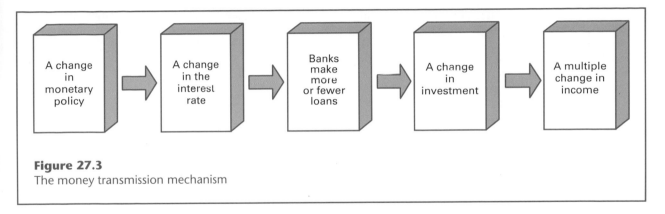

Figure 27.3
The money transmission mechanism

that if there were spare capacity in the economy – under-utilized labour and capital – then output could increase with little or no increase in the price level. (The unemployment would have to be caused by demand deficiency and there would have to be unemployed people with the skills needed by employers.) But if the economy is already producing at or near its full capacity output, then increasing demand will lead to rising prices rather than rising output. Supply constraints will cause wages to be bid up, and competition for scarce resources generally will allow prices to be raised so that inflation will accelerate.

In Chapter 16 we examined the Keynesian approach to expansion in the economy. It was pointed out that the simple Keynesian model assumes that output can be expanded, that is, that the economy is on the horizontal section of the aggregate supply curve. So, given some unemployed resources, increased spending can lead to increased output and employment provided that the unemployed people have skills which are appropriate to employers' needs.

The concern here is the *nature* of unemployment. If people are made unemployed by demand deficiency, then monetary expansion and increased spending will create jobs they can fill. But if they are unemployed for structural reasons and if there are occupational and geographical immobilities, then increased spending will not help unless at least some of it is geared to measures which will be effective in overcoming immobilities. If there is no under-utilized capacity in the economy, monetary expansion will lead to excess aggregate monetary demand and accelerating inflation.

Applying the theory: stage 1

In 1985–8 there was strong growth in the UK economy. Money supply expanded, partly because of bank deregulation, which made banks very keen to lend. Also, savings were falling and there were several cuts in tax rates, the last in 1988.

3 Describe the effect of the expansion of aggregate demand on output, employment and inflation.

4 Draw aggregate supply and aggregate demand (AS–AD) diagrams to show what happens if aggregate monetary demand is growing (a) when there is under-utilized capacity in the economy and (b) when supply constraints are developing.

5 What would you expect to see happening in 1988–90, on the basis of your analysis? Is this what did happen? Look at the data for the case study at the end of Chapter 15.

6 What happened when strong growth was again in evidence in the period 1994–7? Was the situation similar to that of 1988? What conclusions can you draw?

KEY POINTS

27.2

- The intersection of the demand-for-money function and the supply-of-money function generates the equilibrium rate of interest.

- A decrease in interest rates increases the quantity of investment spending, leading to a multiple expansion in output, income and employment.

- Increased demand may lead to increased output, but only if suitable unemployed resources are available. Otherwise it will lead to accelerating inflation.

The quantity theory of money

At this point it will be useful to examine an older theory of money and the price level. The view that money *does* matter in influencing the equilibrium level of real national income and the rate of inflation has its origins in the theories which preceded Keynes's work. The idea that changes in the money supply result in changes in the price level was a fundamental tenet of classical economic reasoning. In fact, this relationship is one of the oldest known in the history of economic thought. We can look at the link between money and prices by means of the **equation of exchange** formally developed by an American economist, Irving Fisher, at Yale University in the early 1900s (also known as the Fisher equation).

The equation of exchange

Banknotes that you have in your wallet, purse or bank account are eventually spent and in the process change hands. It is difficult to see how fast each individual five-pound note is spent, but we can compute an average velocity of the number of times five-pound notes generally change hands to purchase final goods or services during the year. We call this the **velocity of circulation**, which is designated V. The velocity of circulation is defined as the average number of times per year that the nation's stock of money is spent on purchasing the economy's annual flow of output (or its gross national product (GNP)). If we let M stand for the total money supply, then our formula for the velocity of circulation is

$$V = \frac{GNP}{M}$$

Let us take an example. If GNP were £260 billion and the money supply were approximately £100 billion, the velocity of circulation V would equal £260 billion divided by £100 billion, or 2.6. In other words, each pound would change hands an average of 2.6 times that year.

Transposing the equation
Let us multiply both sides of the equation by M. This gives us

$$MV \equiv GNP$$

Now let us break down GNP into its separate components – quantities and prices. We let P stand for the average price of final products produced during the year in question. We let Q stand for the physical, or real, quantities of final outputs. Thus, the value of final output is price multiplied by quantity, or GNP = $P \times Q$. Now the equation can be rewritten as*

$$MV \equiv PQ$$

In fact, this is the standard notation and form in which the equation of exchange is presented.

Consider a simple numerical example in which we consider a one-commodity economy. In this economy, the total money supply M is £100. The quantity of output Q is

50 units of a good. The average price of this output is £10 per unit. Thus, using the equation of exchange we have

$$MV = PQ$$

$$£100V = £10 \times 50$$

$$£100V = £500$$

$$V = 5$$

Therefore, each pound is spent an average of five times a year.

The equation of exchange is an identity
The equation of exchange is an identity. It is true by definition. It is what we call an *accounting identity*, which tells us that the total amount of money spent on final output, MV, is equal to the total amount of money received for final product, PQ. Thus, we can look at a given flow of money from either the buyers' or the producers' side of the picture. The value of goods purchased is equal to the value of goods sold. This is true by definition.

Quantity theory of money and prices

If we make some assumptions about certain components of the equation of exchange, we can actually come up with one of the oldest theories about inflation – the **quantity theory of money and prices**. This theory states that the level of prices in the economy is directly proportional to the quantity of money in circulation per unit of output. To state the theory in symbols, we divide both sides of the equation of exchange by Q. Thus $MV = PQ$ becomes

$$P = M \times \frac{V}{Q}$$

To derive the quantity theory of money and prices, we now have to make an assumption. If we assume that both V and Q are fairly constant, then, as M increases or decreases, so too does P, and at the same rate. In fact, classical economists believed that V was constant because it was determined by the long-run money-holding habits of firms and households, which seemed to them to be fairly stable. Q was also assumed fairly constant because of their prediction that the economy tended towards full employment. Given that V and Q are constant, one could therefore predict that a 10 per cent increase in M would cause a 10 per cent increase in P.

The empirical evidence

Evidence for the quantity theory of money and prices seems relatively favourable if we look at fairly long periods of time. For example, the inflation that occurred in England during 1750–1800 was probably due to the rapid expansion of banks and the resultant increase in money supply during that period. The inflation of the 1970s is similarly explained as a possible by-product of the money supply expansions caused by deficit financing by governments striving to maintain full employment. Thus it may be said that M and P

---

* Sometimes Q for quantity is represented by T for transactions.

The iconoclast as institution

Milton Friedman is a controversial figure. He has seen his views embraced by the libertarian right and dismissed as nonsense by Keynesian liberals; by the left, he has been damned for his opposition to social welfare programmes and for his advisory role to the Chilean authorities during the years of military dictatorship in Chile. For many years an outsider to the Keynesian orthodoxy, Friedman, who won the Nobel Prize in 1976 for his monetary theories, gained so much influence among economists during the 1970s and early 1980s that he threatened to become a prominent part of the status quo himself.

Friedman's standing among contemporary economists derives primarily from his advocacy of the modern quantity theory of money and prices, of what has come to be known as monetarism – the doctrine that the one crucial ingredient shaping short-run economic fluctuations is change in the amount of money in circulation.

Milton Friedman
Economist, formerly of the University of Chicago

The key to a healthy and non-inflationary economy, Friedman argued persistently for three decades, is a constant rate of growth in the money supply. Monetary authorities, Friedman said, instead of tightening money during booms and loosening money during recessions (which is ineffective because of the time lags), should simply increase the supply of money at a steady rate of between 3 and 5 per cent or less per year.

Friedman's work showed quite impressively that, rather than being ineffective, monetary policy *caused* the Great Depression. He pointed out that the money supply was reduced dramatically at the hands of the Fed (the US Central Bank) during that period; that, and that alone, caused a serious recession to descend into the greatest depression the United States has ever had. Friedman, like most monetarists, believed that the macroeconomy is intrinsically stable – if left alone by the prying hand of government.

His philosophy carried over into all areas of government intervention. He pointed out time and again the unintended negative effects of government intervention in the economy. His solution to many of society's ills was a more competitive private market-place, rather than increased government regulation, intervention and spending. This message had enormous impact.

---

are correlated – but they are certainly not proportional to the extent that if *M* is doubled *P* will rise twofold. However, there is no compelling evidence to show that the quantity theory applies in the short run. There are many possible changes which can obscure the connection between money and prices over a period of a year or two.

Modern monetarism

For a time during the 1950s and 1960s it was thought that money was not very important in determining price levels. The view was that spending was not very sensitive to changes in interest rates. (At the time this was largely true.) Changes in fiscal policy (government spending and taxes) were felt to be more significant influences upon aggregate demand. This view was associated with the work of Keynes and the Keynesians.

But during the 1960s some economists began again to believe that the quantity of money has a major part to play in the determination of price levels. Professor Milton Friedman at the University of Chicago and others at that time started research on the relationship between changes in the rate of growth of the money supply and changes in macroeconomic variables such as national income and the price level. Not surprisingly, Friedman and his followers

took on the name of monetarists. The monetarists have stressed the need for strict control of the money supply and, in times of inflation, very high real interest rates. (The real interest rate is the difference between the nominal rate, that is, the rate actually charged, and the rate of inflation.)

For a time, Keynesian and monetarist approaches to macroeconomic management were very much in opposition to each other. Keynesians emphasized the importance of fiscal policy while monetarists emphasized monetary policy. The monetarist approach was in the ascendancy all through the early 1980s, all over the world. It blamed the high inflation of the 1970s on Keynesian policy and promised sound management on the basis of tight money, which would restore low expectations of inflation and buoyant growth.

There turned out to be some difficulties in implementing the monetarist approach. Central banks found it harder than anticipated to control the money supply, especially after they had deregulated the banking system to make it freer and more competitive. This meant that they had to have recourse to very high nominal rates of interest. Further, the recessions which resulted from tight monetary policies turned out to be long and severe. Out of this experience there emerged a more eclectic or integrated view of monetary policy – in very broad terms, like the one outlined earlier in the chapter. However, while neither strict monetarism nor strict Keynesianism is much in vogue, current thinking owes much to both influences.

We must now turn from this brief overview of policy issues to examine the theory underlying tight monetary policy.

KEY POINTS

27.3

- The equation of exchange, in its simplest form, states that the money supply multiplied by velocity (MV) is equal to national income (GNP).

- Viewed as an accounting identity the equation of exchange is always correct, since the amount of money spent on final output must be equal to the total amount of money received for final output.

- If we can assume that V (the velocity of circulation) and Q (output) are fairly constant, then any change in the money supply (M) will change the price level (P) by the same proportion.

- Monetarists believe that changes in the rate of growth of the money supply determine, to a large extent, changes in numerous macroeconomic variables such as the equilibrium level of national income and the price level.

- Keynesians see a role for fiscal as well as monetary policy in macroeconomic management.

Tight monetary policy today

So far we have been concerned with the theoretical effect of an increase in the money stock. What happens in practice if the government imposes a monetary squeeze?

Let us suppose that there is inflation (the usual reason for tightening monetary policy). Rising prices are increasing the demand for money. In Figure 27.4(a), the demand-for-money function shifts to the right. The government seeks to hold the money stock constant and, as a result, interest rates rise. Loans become more costly and investment is discouraged (27.4(b)). There is a downward multiplier effect on real income and employment (27.4(c)). Firms will experience decreased demand for their output, stocks will pile up and unemployment will rise.

Other things will happen too. Consumers will reduce spending. If they have mortgages, more of their income will be needed to pay the extra interest. And the exchange rate will rise in response to higher interest rates. This means that exports will be dearer and imports cheaper; so demand will fall for both exports and products which compete with imports.

In this way the tight monetary policy will reduce aggregate demand in the economy. But exactly how is the resulting fall in output and employment going to reduce the rate at which prices are increasing?

In the simple, aggregate demand versus aggregate supply approach developed in Chapter 14, monetary policy shifts the aggregate demand function to the left, reducing overheating and relieving supply constraints in the economy. But the policy goes beyond this. A component part of inflation is a continuing series of pay increases

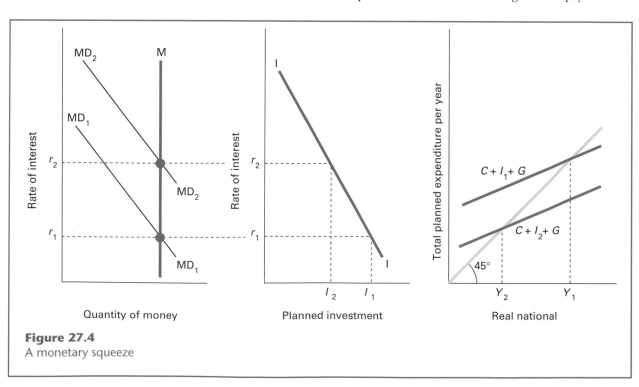

Figure 27.4
A monetary squeeze

throughout the economy. As unemployment increases, trade unions and individuals become much more wary of negotiating large pay increases. They will do so only if they feel confident that they will not lose their jobs. In 1981–2 and 1991–3 inflation fell sharply, partly because many firms were close to bankruptcy. Further pay increases would have brought even more job losses.

Contractionary policy operates through this effect on output and employment. But how much unemployment is needed to reduce inflation by a given amount?

Many economists believe that labour markets are not very flexible. Wages seldom fall in real terms. Many people are able to negotiate wage increases, even in hard times, because their jobs are not seriously threatened. So output and employment might fall far before expectations of future inflation were much reduced. The experience of 1990–2 should be considered. Unemployment rose from 5.9 per cent to 9.9 per cent during that time, as high interest rates discouraged spending.

Alternatively, if labour markets are, or were to become, more flexible, then employers will be able to obtain the employees they need without difficulty. Equally, if demand falls they can easily dismiss people they do not need. As unemployment rises, people will be prepared to work for less. Pay increases will become quickly smaller and the contractionary policy will produce lower rates of inflation. Competition for jobs will then tend to keep wage claims from going much above the growth of productivity.

One possible explanation for the subdued inflation rates of the late 1990s is that the UK labour market has indeed become more flexible. The important thing to remember is that the control of inflation works through the effect of monetary policy on borrowing and the effect which reduced demand has on employment, unemployment and pay deals.

The importance of the labour market

Clearly, our view of the way macroeconomic policies work is very dependent on our assumptions about the way the labour market works. If wages cannot fall even in real terms because people expect their pay always to keep pace with inflation, then tight monetary policy and weak demand can lead to substantial and lasting unemployment as employers seek to cut their labour costs in difficult times. We may find the prospect of falling real wages unpalatable if we are concerned about income distribution issues. But the alternative may be higher unemployment.

Union-negotiated minimum wage rates and closed shops can mean that wages are very inflexible in some occupations. Quite often, existing employees can both retain their jobs and obtain higher wages, especially if the employer is investing in additional capital equipment and productivity is rising. The employer cuts the workforce by natural wastage – the departure over time of employees who retire or move to other jobs. The unemployment then falls upon the young and those made redundant from declining industries who cannot find jobs. Unemployment

is much lower among those in their middle years than among the young and the old.

Applying the theory: stage 2

In the third quarter of 1996, base rate stood at 5.75 per cent. At that time, signs of skill shortages were beginning to appear in the UK economy and the demand for loans was rising. It looked as though the economy could possibly be headed for a period of unsustainable growth. The Bank of England raised base rate by degrees, a quarter per cent at a time. By quarter 3, 1998 it stood at 7.5 per cent as fears of inflation continued. The table shows what happened to inflation.

Inflation, 1996–9

1996 III	2.1
1996 IV	2.6
1997 I	2.7
1997 II	2.7
1997 III	3.5
1997 IV	3.7
1998 I	3.4
1998 II	4.0
1998 III	3.4
1998 IV	3.0
1999 I	2.2
1999 II	1.4
1999 III	1.0

Source: *National Institute Economic Review*, 4, 1999

7 Explain how you would expect the rise in interest rates to affect aggregate demand, output, employment and inflation.
8 Which borrowers would be most strongly affected by the rise in interest rates?
9 Draw aggregate supply and aggregate demand (AS–AD) diagrams to show what happens if interest rates are raised.
10 What do you think happened to the important variables in 2000?

Time lags

So far we have suggested that a tight monetary policy will take time to work, without being specific about the time lags. As we review recent UK experience it will become clear that there are lags at every stage. People do not immediately cut their planned spending when interest rates rise; it takes a little time for them to adjust. When they do, firms may quickly cut output but will take time to cut employment. They will hope the fall in demand is temporary, and then hope that natural wastage will reduce the labour force painlessly, before they face dismissing people. Thus the lag between a fall in output and a fall in employment is likely to be in the range of one to two years.

Only when unemployment leads to increased competition for jobs will the threat of redundancy cause people to settle for lower wage increases, and only then can the process of adjusting expectations of inflation really begin. So the raised interest rates beginning in 1988 finally bore fruit in the shape of an inflation rate of 3.7 per cent in 1992 and an inflation rate of 1.6 per cent in 1993. Meantime, unemployment rose from 5.9 per cent in 1990 to 10.4 per cent in 1993.

KEY POINTS

27.4

- A contractionary monetary policy will lead to a fall in aggregate demand and in output and employment.

- Only when expectations of inflation have been reduced will the rate of inflation actually fall.

- Monetary policy works with long time lags.

- The nature of the labour market is crucial in determining the response to monetary policy.

Monetary policy in practice

It is clear that monetary control can be an important tool of macroeconomic policy. We must now look in more detail at the way in which the Bank of England has operated over the years.

Slump followed by boom, 1980–1988

When the Conservatives came to power in 1979, they were determined to solve the problem of inflation. They had followed Friedman's arguments and they set about raising base rates to cure the disease. By 1981, the economy was very depressed. Unemployment rose to 3 million. It was some time before recovery got under way, though by the time it did, inflation was very much lower.

Helped by low oil prices, output and standards of living rose from 1983 onwards. By 1986, GDP was growing at 3.5 per cent and getting faster. Unemployment fell. The Chancellor was confident that aggregate supply would grow fast enough to meet the fast-growing aggregate demand. Interest rates were mostly below 10 per cent.

By spring 1988 it was clear that the UK economy was overheating. Skill shortages were developing. Inflation was accelerating. House prices were rising sharply. Consumers were turning to imports to obtain the extra goods which the United Kingdom could not produce fast enough. The Chancellor raised interest rates sharply.

Contraction and slump, 1988–1992

Base rate rose from 8.5 per cent at the beginning of 1988 to 13.5 per cent at the beginning of 1991. At first higher interest rates had little effect. Unemployment went on falling and output went on rising until 1990. But in time, a long and painful slump developed, hitting the service sector as well as manufacturing. House prices dropped, leaving many people with an asset of less value than the loan outstanding on it – known as negative equity. Distress was great. By early 1994 interest rates were down to 5.25 per cent in an attempt to encourage investment and activity generally. Meantime, the government had increased spending as well as cutting interest rates. It looked remarkably like an old-fashioned Keynesian policy designed to pull the economy out of depression.

Figure 27.5 shows inflation rates and interest rates over a long period. It tells us something about how interest rates have affected economic growth rates in the period under discussion.

Recovery and growth from 1992

Although output began to rise in early 1992, unemployment did not start to fall from its peak of 10.6 per cent until early 1993. Slow at first, the recovery gradually gathered pace. Yet in mid-1994 the Bank of England began again to raise interest rates, saying that the rapid growth of output (3.8 per cent) signalled a need to keep the economy growing at a rate sustainable in the long run. Otherwise accelerating inflation could become a problem. Yet unemployment was still 8.5 per cent, 2.5 million.

Despite this early remedial action, growth continued all the way to 1997, and with little sign of a resurgence of inflation until that year. Then evidence of skill shortages mounted up. The newly created Monetary Policy Committee (MPC) flexed its muscles and raised interest rates. (The creation of the MPC was dealt with on page 316 in Chapter 18.) Yet within a few months, the Asian financial crisis began to bite. Manufacturers who depended on Asian markets experienced a significant fall in orders. They were not helped by the high pound. By 1998, the MPC was backtracking again and cutting interest rates to bring relief to the manufacturing sector. The service sector was never in any serious difficulty.

The interesting thing about this mini-recession was the way unemployment kept on falling. Plenty of job losses occurred in manufacturing. The service sector just went on soaking up labour. Yet inflation stayed low and fell further in 1999. Admittedly, there were big regional variations. While there was an acute shortage of many kinds of labour in the south-east, the traditional manufacturing areas still had some unemployment. Overall, though, unemployment was lower at 4.5 per cent than it had been since 1980.

The experience of the late 1990s suggests that the MPC provides a very flexible way to review and adjust monetary policy. The committee looks at likely future trends, allowing for possible time lags. It may have been lucky, of course: the concluding case study will address this question.

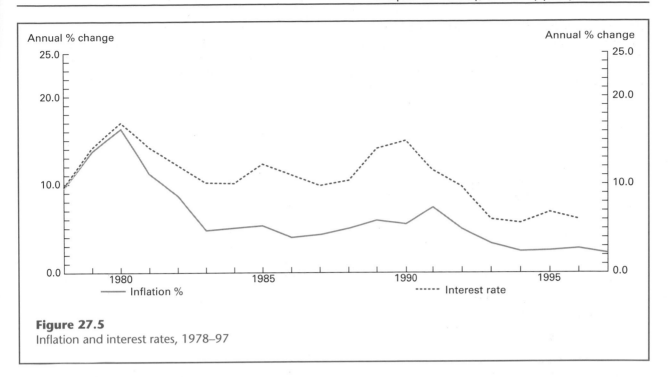

Figure 27.5
Inflation and interest rates, 1978–97

Inflation and unemployment revisited

In Chapter 17, we considered the Phillips curve, which suggests an inverse relationship between inflation and unemployment. It fits with the predictions of the Keynesian model, which show inflation accelerating when the economy is booming and decelerating when it is in recession. For many years, this relationship looked broadly accurate.

Then in the 1970s something very different happened. Inflation accelerated in an unprecedented way. Partly, this change grew out of a sharp increase in oil prices. But it was well under way before that. It reflected increased pressure for pay increases. At the same time, unemployment rose dramatically. The Phillips curve looked quite dead. Meantime, Milton Friedman had been at work on the relationship between inflation and unemployment. The important insight which he contributed lay in his view that expectations were of paramount importance in determining inflation rates.

Friedman believed very strongly that unemployment is almost never caused by demand deficiency. The real causes are structural, created by rigidities in the labour market. It follows from this that increased spending will not cure unemployment. He went on to define what is sometimes called the **natural rate of unemployment**, or NAIRU, which stands for the non-accelerating inflation unemployment rate. This is the amount of unemployment that would prevail when inflation is stable and correctly anticipated. Consequently, the natural rate of unemployment can be regarded as the rate of unemployment that would

exist in the absence of cyclical fluctuations in the economy.

Each economy will have its own natural rate of unemployment and it may change with time. The level will depend upon the amount of frictional unemployment, a topic that we discussed in Chapter 8. If the labour market is functioning smoothly, with workers able to find out quickly about the availability of job vacancies, then, other things being equal, the natural rate of unemployment might be relatively low. If there are a large number of effective impediments to a smoothly functioning labour market, then the natural rate of unemployment might be high. We surmise, for example, that the more restrictions there are in the labour market, the higher the natural rate of unemployment. These restrictions might be minimum wage legislation, occupational training requirements, strict union membership requirements and so on. In addition, geographical and occupational immobilities, visible when structural change has altered employers' requirements, are major factors in the NAIRU.

The expectations-augmented Phillips curve

Friedman went on to adapt the traditional Phillips curve. He showed that experience of inflation creates expectations of inflation. People seek to protect their real incomes by negotiating pay increases sufficient to compensate (and usually to provide some real increase as well).

In Figure 27.6, we see two curves similar in appearance to the standard Phillips curve (hence the alternative name). On the horizontal axis, we measure unemployment; on the vertical axis, we measure the *actual* rate of inflation. The

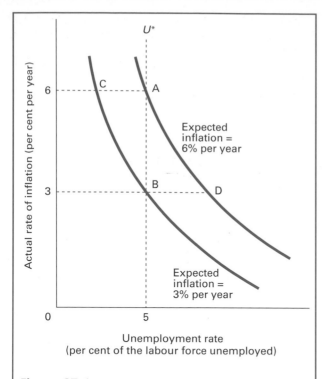

Figure 27.6

An expectations-augmented Phillips curve
If expectations of inflation increase, the trade-off between
inflation and unemployment shifts to a higher curve.

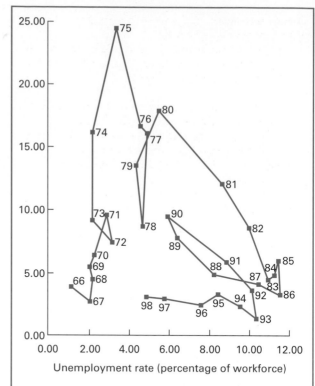

Figure 27.7

Inflation and unemployment rates, 1966–98

Source: Adapted from *Labour Market Trends*,
September 1998

Phillips curves, however, are drawn for two different levels
of expected rates of inflation. The left one is drawn for an
expected rate of inflation of 3 per cent; the right one is
drawn for an expected rate of inflation of 6 per cent. The
vertical line labelled U^* represents the so-called natural rate
of unemployment, which we will assume to be 5 per cent.

If inflation is stable at 6 per cent, then the long-run
equilibrium unemployment level will be maintained at
point A. However, if the *actual* rate of inflation then falls to
only 3 per cent per year, the economy will be at point D,
where there is excess unemployment – that is, unemployment over and above the normal long-run U^* of 5 per
cent. Inflation is falling and unemployment is rising.

If the rate of inflation remains at 3 per cent, expectations of inflation will adjust and in time unemployment
will return to its 'normal' long-run level of 5 per cent. We
will be at point B. But if then the rate of inflation rises
again to 6 per cent, we shall find ourselves at point C.
There will be over full employment – that is, unemployment will be less than its long-run or normal level of 5 per
cent. At this point, inflation may stabilize with a return to
A, or it may continue to accelerate so that the economy
moves onto an even higher curve.

If we look at Figure 27.7, which shows inflation and
unemployment rates from 1966 to 1998, we can see that
there have been times when both inflation and unemployment have been rising: this is known as stagflation. It
occurred in the mid-1970s and in the mid-1980s. This

theory emphasizes the importance of expectations in determining the level of wage bargains, and so of inflation itself.
The fact is that when expectations are rising, it is possible
for inflation to accelerate even when unemployment is
growing. The effect is to take the unemployment–inflation
trade-off onto a higher curve.

A reduction in inflationary expectations has been
achieved by rising unemployment, thus increasing competition for jobs. This forces people to accept lower wage
bargains through fear of redundancy. The economy can
then shift onto a lower curve and achieve lower levels of
inflation. You can see how this happened in the early
1980s and in the early 1990s recessions.

The data suggest that during the mid- to late 1990s,
expectations of inflation diminished further.

Watching what happens

Thinking about both kinds of Phillips curve, 1999 seems a
bit odd. On the one hand, economic growth slowed to 1
per cent, so it does not seem odd that inflation slowed
too, also to 1 per cent. (These were early estimates. The
statisticians generally adjust the figures for a year or two
after the event, as better data come in.) The puzzling factor in the situation was unemployment, which carried on

falling. This was at least consistent with the evidence of skill shortages developing.

By the time you read this you should be able to work out what was happening. To be specific, why were both inflation and unemployment *falling*?

11 In late 1999, the MPC thought there was evidence of inflationary pressures building up. In order to head off *future* inflation, it raised interest rates. What effect did this have on output and employment?

12 Has a trade-off between inflation and unemployment reappeared?

13 Have there been unforeseen events which have altered our view of the economy in a different way?

An independent central bank?

Around 1992, people began to suggest that monetary policy might be best entrusted to an independent central bank. It was observed that the Bundesbank in Germany was independent and appeared to be effective in keeping the rate of inflation low. The objective would be to remove monetary policy from political control, thus making it impossible for politicians to manipulate policy for electoral reasons, for example by creating a boom shortly before an election. It might be hoped that this would

reduce instability. By degrees, the then Chancellor, Kenneth Clarke, began to give the Bank a bigger role in interest rate decisions.

In 1997 there came the big change to an independent Monetary Policy Committee. However, the biggest issue relating to the role of the Bank of England in the future is likely to be the decision about the euro. This will be taken up in Chapter 30.

KEY POINTS

27.5

- The emphasis of UK monetary policy is upon the control of interest rates.

- The Bank of England's Monetary Policy Committee can announce a higher rate of discount (or base rate) if it wants interest rates to rise.

- The government responded to the overheating of the economy in 1988 with sharp increases in interest rates, which led to a prolonged recession.

- The relationship between inflation and unemployment is complex and depends greatly on people's expectations of inflation.

Case Study

A view from the Monetary Policy Committee

When the government handed over control of interest rates to the Bank of England's Monetary Policy Committee (MPC) in 1997, some commentators were not impressed. Now after two years of consistently low inflation, most critics have eaten their hats. But at a recent conference, one distinguished economist said that the MPC had largely been lucky. Sour grapes? Not at all. The accuser, Charles Goodhart, is himself a member of the committee.

What accounts for Mr Goodhart's surprising modesty? First of all, he does not think that the MPC can properly take all the credit for the low inflation of the past two years. The MPC's remit is to keep inflation as close as possible to the government's target of 2.5 per cent a year. It tries to achieve this by raising or lowering the interest rate at which the Bank of England lends money to commercial banks. Higher interest rates, at least in theory, make people more reluctant to borrow and spend, and so should cut inflation.

The problem is that inflation does not respond to interest rate changes straight away. It takes time for rate changes to feed through to the real economy, and even longer for them to have their full effect on the rate of inflation. How long? Around two years, thinks Mr Goodhart. But the MPC has been in operation for only two years. In other words, much of the credit for Britain's recent spell of low inflation does not belong to the MPC at all, but can be attributed to the interest rate decisions taken before it was set up, by the then Chancellor, Kenneth Clarke. Mr Clarke, much criticized for 'taking risks' with inflation, may enjoy the vindication.

So what? Mr Goodhart's modesty is commendable. But if interest rates do affect inflation with a two-year delay, then future inflation will indeed affect the MPC's decisions. And although academics quibble about individual interest rate decisions, most applaud the MPC's overall record. Interest rates were raised progressively until last summer, when people feared an inflationary boom, and have been cut sharply since then, to head off a recession. Such a swift about turn would have been more difficult if interest rate decisions had remained in the hands of a politician, sensitive to the opinion polls.

Yet there is a problem, for inflation is not influenced only by interest rates. A strong pound, for example, lowers the sterling price of imported goods, and can reduce inflation. So can a recession in a country with which Britain trades. On the other hand, an expansionary British budget can push it up, and quickly. The pound, the Chancellor, and overseas economies may affect inflation faster than the MPC's interest rate decisions. Trying to control short-term inflation with interest rates alone is like trying to eat Chinese food with only one chopstick.

For these reasons, even if the MPC's actions succeed in keeping inflation on average at its 2.5 per cent target, you would expect significant fluctuations around that target in the measured inflation figures. When the Chancellor obliged the MPC to write to him to explain whenever measured inflation differed from the target by more than one percentage point, Mervyn King, now one of the Bank's deputy governors, joked that this edict would restore the lost art of letter-writing. In fact, the MPC has not had to write the Chancellor a single letter. It is not just the rate of inflation that has stayed low. But the fluctuations in inflation have been lower than ever before.

Can this continue? Up to a point. When the rate of inflation is low, the fluctuations in the rate of inflation also tend to be smaller. But the almost bull's-eye precision of the inflation figures in the past two years has been due to a lot of different factors cancelling each other out. Hints of

domestic inflation – such as rising labour costs – have been balanced by the strong pound and the financial crisis in Asia.

The MPC, whose only weapon is interest rate changes, cannot ensure this balancing act continues. But Mr Goodhart worries that people do not understand this. If the inflation figures suddenly, say, go up, people will not see it as an expectable fluctuation, but as a sign that the MPC has lost its touch. So he thinks it vital to educate people about the limits of what the MPC can reasonably be expected to achieve. Either that, or just pray that its luck continues to hold.

Source: *The Economist*, 5 June 1999

1 Why is it important to understand the nature of the time lags with which monetary policy operates?
2 What are the significant factors which kept inflation low in the period 1997–9?
3 What are the advantages of interest rate decisions being taken by experts in the field, rather than by the Chancellor in consultation with the Bank of England?
4 Study the record of the years 1999–2001, i.e. the years in which the actions of the MPC during its first two years had their effect. Evaluate the record. How much luck has the MPC had?

Exam Preparation

Multiple choice questions

1 If undated government bonds originally sold for £1000 with a nominal interest rate of 3 per cent, and their price has since fallen to £200, their yield is now
   A 3 per cent
   B 9 per cent
   C 15 per cent
   D 18 per cent
   E 25 per cent

2 The diagram illustrates an aggregate supply (AS) schedule and aggregate demand schedules for an economy. Which of the following statements is correct?
   A The full employment level of real national income is OY.
   B An increase in aggregate demand from AD3 to AD4 could have been caused by an increase in savings.

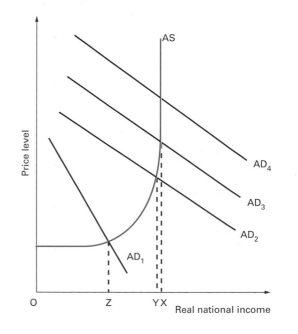

C An increase in aggregate demand from AD2 to AD3 could have been caused by a fall in investment.

D The non-accelerating inflation rate of unemployment is OZ.

E An increase in aggregate demand from AD1 to AD2 would be associated with rises in output and in the price level.

3 An increase in aggregate monetary demand is **least** likely to result in inflation when

A aggregate supply is elastic

B the government allows the exchange rate to fall

C factors of production are immobile

D real wages are rising more slowly than money wage rates

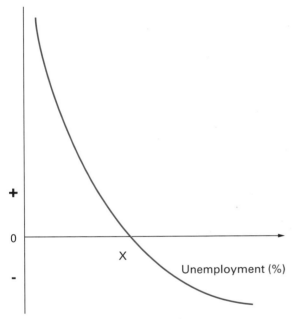

4 If point X in the above diagram represents the natural rate of unemployment, the scale on the vertical axis measures the

A level of aggregate demand

B change in aggregate demand

C rate of interest

D percentage rate of inflation

E money supply

Essay questions

1 (a) Why might a country wish to restrain inflationary pressures?

(b) Examine the policies which a member country of the European Union might use in an attempt to prevent an increase in the domestic rate of inflation.

2 (a) Which *two* objectives of macroeconomic policy do you consider to be the most important for the UK government to pursue at the present time? Justify your answer.

(b) Explain how these objectives might conflict with each other and with other macroeconomic goals.

3 In the UK, the growth in retail sales in the year ending June 1996 was higher than expected. As a result, it was suggested that the Chancellor should consider raising interest rates to prevent inflation.

(a) Would you support the implication of this statement that inflation is caused by consumer spending?

(b) Discuss whether interest rates alone are likely to be an effective method of controlling inflation.

4 (a) Explain what is meant by 'the natural rate of unemployment' (also known as NAIRU).

(b) Evaluate the effects of demand-side and supply-side policies on the natural rate of unemployment.

5 Explain why inflation is regarded as a major problem for macroeconomic management. Discuss whether or not, in your view, zero inflation is a feasible or desirable objective for economic policy.

6 Examine the relative importance of the various factors that determine the level of interest rates in the UK economy.

7 Outline what constitutes monetary policy. Explain how and why monetary policy has changed in the United Kingdom.

28

Fiscal policy

Fiscal policy means the use of taxation and expenditure to achieve political ends. These ends are many and varied. A range of them was identified in Chapter 7. They were discussed under the general headings of efficiency and equity. Here we divide them into three categories: macroeconomic control of the economy, redistributing income and wealth, and influencing the allocation of resources.

In seeking to *control the economy*, the government will try to promote economic growth, stable prices and low levels of unemployment and will try to avoid balance-of-trade deficits. It will usually be difficult to achieve all these at once, but governments act according to their priorities at any given time.

Expansionary fiscal policies will promote economic growth and high levels of employment. They may lead to acceleration of inflation. They may well lead to increases in imports. Further, the buoyant home market may deter firms from exporting, which demands more effort than home sales. So expansion may produce an external deficit. Contractionary policies reduce inflation, but also growth and employment. However, imports will fall, and firms will turn to export markets to maintain sales. So the balance of trade will improve, and a current account surplus may develop.

Fiscal policy can be used to *redistribute income and wealth*. Progressive income taxes raise funds which can provide benefits for those who are badly off. Capital gains tax and inheritance tax reduce somewhat the value of individuals' holdings of wealth.

The government has a substantial effect on the *allocation of resources* towards consumption, investment and exports. It achieves this partly through the operation of the tax system: taxes reduce disposable income and therefore personal consumption. Discriminatory taxes on firms affect the profitability and therefore the level of investment. Also, because fiscal policy affects aggregate demand, it influences the levels of imports and, indirectly, of exports.

In a quite different way, the government influences the microeconomic allocation of resources too. By taxing some products and subsidizing others, a particular consumption pattern is promoted. In the UK economy, pension contributions are subsidized whilst alcohol, tobacco and petrol are taxed.

Tax structures and government expenditure create a pattern of *incentives* which may be very important in determining how resources are allocated. While the incentive effects of very large incomes are uncertain, the disincentive effects of some benefits are much less so.

Different governments have different approaches to fiscal policy. During the 1980s fiscal policy became steadily less and less important as a macroeconomic policy tool. Also, rather less redistribution of income took place. This had an effect on the overall distribution of income and wealth. In the 1990s the need to reduce government borrowing led to tax increases, despite the government's overall commitment to tax cuts in the long term.

LEARNING OUTCOMES

On completing this chapter you should understand:

- How taxation is used to raise revenue
- How a deficit may be financed
- How fiscal policy can be used to create incentives
- The impact of fiscal policy on the UK economy

Significant changes took place in the way resources were allocated. Privatization, changes in the composition of public spending, and tax changes all contributed.

Raising revenue – taxation

Tax revenues are needed for a range of purposes. They must, first, raise revenue simply to finance expenditure. But they may also be used to redistribute income and wealth, to affect consumption patterns and to influence the level of aggregate demand. Obviously, taxes which raise substantial revenue will also be effective in reducing aggregate demand.

Each tax has its own role to play in meeting government objectives. The composition of tax revenue has important effects on the economy. Table 28.1 shows the relative contributions of each kind of tax to total tax revenue, as well as the main categories of expenditure.

Table 28.1

The government's income and expenditure, 1999–2000, £ billion

Income		Expenditure	
Income tax	94	Social security	97
National insurance	56	Health and social services	40
VAT	56	Education	41
Excise duties	41	Debt interest	26
Corporation tax	34	Defence	21
Business rates	16	Law and order	11
Council tax	13	Environment and transport	38
Other	42	Trade and industry	3
		Other	72
Total	352	Total	349

Source: *Daily Telegraph*, 10 November 1999

Direct taxes

These are levied directly on incomes and profits. Income tax is progressive in two respects. The personal allowance (£4335 in 2000) is tax free. Then there is the 10 per cent band, which takes in the first £1500 of taxable income. Subsequent income is taxed at the standard rate of 22 per cent, up to £28 500 of taxable income. Beyond that, additional tax is payable at a marginal rate of 40 per cent. So tax as a proportion of income rises as income rises.

Income tax applies not only to wages and salaries but also to unearned income from interest, profits and rent. It is therefore important as a revenue raiser, as a means of redistributing income and sometimes as a means of increasing or reducing aggregate demand. It is the progressive nature of income tax which makes it effective as an automatic stabilizer, reducing demand when incomes are high and may exceed output, and increasing demand when incomes are low and unemployment is an increasing problem.

Corporation tax is levied on firms' profits at a rate of 30 per cent; generally it contributes only a small amount to total tax revenue. Small companies pay a reduced rate of 20 per cent.

National Insurance charges (NICs) include both the employers' and employees' contributions. Up to an income level of £28 000 (in 2000), contributions rise with income. (Very low incomes, those below £87 a week, are exempt.) Above that level, contributions are constant. The employees' contributions are not unlike an income tax, although they are less progressive. It should be remembered that an increase in income will be subject to both increased tax and increased NIC. So the marginal rate of taxation, including both income tax and NICs, is generally just over 30 per cent. The employer's contribution, by contrast, is in effect a pay-roll tax. It raises the cost of employing labour. Changes in the rates at which it is levied have been made in an attempt to modify its impact so that employers are encouraged to take on more low-paid labour and reduce unemployment. The main function of NICs is to raise revenue for the payment of benefits.

Property taxes

Council taxes have contributed substantially to local authority revenue. The other major components are the Uniform Business Rate and the Rate Support Grant paid by central government. Council tax is levied on property, so its impact varies according to the size and value of the property.

Inheritance tax will continue to be levied on the estates of the richer deceased. It is aimed at redistributing wealth by reducing the amount of wealth concentrated in the hands of a few individuals.

Capital gains tax is levied on the increase in the value of property. This means that owners of shares which show substantial capital growth must pay tax on the capital gain when they come to sell the shares.

Expenditure taxes

Excise taxes are generally levied at a flat rate – so many pence per item. **Value-added tax** (VAT), in contrast, takes 17.5 per cent of value added at each stage of production. The value added is the revenue from sales minus the cost of inputs other than land, labour and capital. It is the value added *by* the factors of production.

In principle, expenditure taxes tend to be more regressive than income taxes. They are seen mainly as revenue raisers. They also serve to reduce consumption of harmful goods, such as tobacco and alcohol, and of goods which are potentially scarce in the long run or have an effect on the environment, such as petrol. In practice, because VAT is not levied on food for home preparation, housing, public transport and printed matter, it is not very regressive in its impact.

The composition of tax revenue

The balance between direct and indirect taxation can be varied to suit circumstances. While income tax must always be the most effective tax for redistributive purposes, it is evaded (illegally) and avoided (legally) in a number of ways, thus losing some of its usefulness. Expenditure taxes tend to be more regressive because poorer individuals spend a higher proportion of their incomes than do richer individuals. They can be expensive to collect, but are harder to avoid than direct taxes.

During the 1970s, with VAT at 8 per cent, the United Kingdom was deriving more revenue than now from direct taxes. Other European countries relied more heavily on indirect taxes. The Conservative government shifted the balance markedly in 1979, reducing income taxes and raising VAT. It had many reasons, giving as the primary reason improving the incentive to work. The reduced income redistribution which resulted from the change was in line with the Conservative political philosophy of encouraging people to take care of themselves.

If tax evasion and avoidance become more of a problem, a further shift towards expenditure taxes might be considered advisable. Another possible reason for shifting further towards expenditure taxes reflects the political popularity of income tax cuts.

KEY POINTS

28.1

- Taxation is used to raise revenue, to redistribute income and wealth, to control the level of aggregate demand and to influence the allocation of resources.

- Taxes may be levied by indirect and direct methods, and the balance between the two can be varied according to circumstances.

Are taxes too high?

Taxation in Europe, 1997, % of GDP at market prices

	Direct taxes	Indirect taxes	Social security
France	10.5	15.4	20.7
Germany	10.3	12.6	20.1
Italy	15.4	12.3	15.4
Sweden	22.0	15.8	15.0
UK	12.8	16.8	6.2

Source: *Eurostat*, via Secos 4

1 Is the UK population heavily taxed? **AV**
2 How are tax rates affected by high rates of unemployment? **AV**

3 A substantial part of most social security taxes (NICs in the UK) is paid by employers. How will this affect businesses? **AV**
4 Do high rates of taxation create an incentive or a disincentive to work? Explain your reasoning. **AV**

Revenue and expenditure

To the extent that government expenditure exceeds revenue, there must be borrowing. The annual amount needed to cover the difference between spending and tax revenue (the deficit) is the **Public Sector Net Cash Requirement** (PSNCR). The accumulated past debt – the sum total of all government debt outstanding – is the **National Debt**. Borrowing may be financed by selling Treasury bills (for short-term borrowing) or bonds (for long-term borrowing).

When revenues exceed expenditure, there is a surplus known as the **Public Sector Debt Repayment** (PSDR). The surplus funds can be used to buy back bonds, reducing the size of the National Debt.

Whether the government is in surplus or deficit depends upon a number of factors. One is the state of the trade cycle; another, interest rates. Over time, however, demands for government spending do rise, so there is a tendency for borrowing to rise also. The conflicting political demands for low tax rates together with good health care and pensions for an ageing population can create difficulties for governments, which can be relieved in the short run by borrowing. However, a growing economy automatically generates growing tax revenues. In the later 1990s these growing revenues, together with tight control over spending, meant that the budget was close to being in balance, as Figure 28.1 shows. Figure 28.2 shows some comparisons.

The trade cycle

During the boom phase of the trade cycle, high incomes generate large tax revenues. Unemployment is low and so benefits are less costly. Automatically, the government's finances move towards surplus. Conversely, in a slump, benefits rise, tax revenues fall and a deficit is likely to develop (or get larger). Discretionary fiscal policy can be used similarly: taxes can be reduced and government expenditure increased if there are resources in the economy which are unemployed because of a deficiency of demand. Other things being equal, the PSNCR would grow if incomes were falling or stagnating and would diminish if incomes were rising. If there is a PSDR, it will shrink when incomes fall and grow if they rise.

Interest rates

To finance a PSNCR, the Bank of England will want to sell government bonds. To induce the public to buy them, attractive interest rates must be paid. The government can obtain finance relatively cheaply because it can guarantee repayment, based on its right to tax. (Bonds are often known as gilts – they are as good as gold.) But the more finance the government needs, the higher the rate of interest on bonds must be.

If there is a substantial deficit, the government may need to borrow on a large scale. It will compete for funds in the money markets with private borrowers contemplating investment projects. If high interest rates are available on government bonds, the returns to private investment will need to compare favourably or few people will be prepared to invest. So it is possible for government borrowing to make private investment more expensive. Governments never want to discourage investment. An urge to keep interest rates down for this reason can cause governments to cut the PSNCR.

A surplus, which can be used to buy back government bonds, should in theory help to keep interest rates down. It will reduce the burden of future interest payments and should lead to taxes being lower than would otherwise have been possible.

Financing a deficit: the options

We have seen that the size of a deficit may have some effect on interest rates. Financing it affects monetary growth in other ways also. To see this we must examine the ways in which a PSNCR can be funded.

We have identified two ways of financing a PSNCR: the sale of bonds and bills. **Treasury bills** raise finance for three months. They can be used to make good the weekly shortfall between spending and revenue. They are very liquid reserve assets to the banks, which are the main providers of bill finance. **Bonds** raise long-term funds from a wide range of sources such as individuals and from financial institutions such as pension funds. There are two other sources of finance. A major source is **National Savings** (non-marketable debt). For the government, this is very favourable because it pays relatively low interest

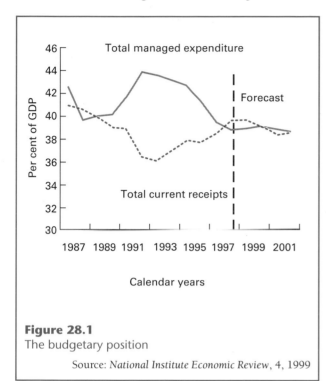

Figure 28.1
The budgetary position

Source: *National Institute Economic Review*, 4, 1999

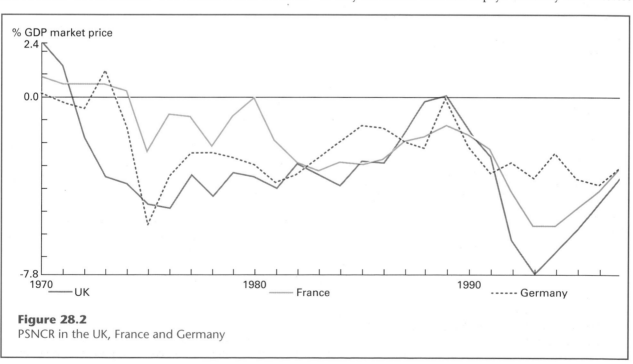

Figure 28.2
PSNCR in the UK, France and Germany

rates and the funds are cheap and reliable. For savers, funds kept in National Savings are very liquid and convenient. A fourth source of finance is the Bank of England. By itself holding bonds, the Bank can create credit, making a loan to the government which is then spent. The recipients of the government spending place the funds in their bank accounts, and banks' balances with the Bank of England rise. This is base, or high-powered, money and will allow banks to create extra credit by a multiple of the original increase in their liquid reserves (in the way described in Chapter 18).

In sum, if the PSNCR is funded through the issue of bonds or bills which are held within the banking system, then monetary expansion will follow. If monetary growth is supposed to be carefully controlled, then it is important that the Bank of England funds the government's debts by selling bonds to the non-bank public or encouraging National Savings. These tend to grow slowly over time, so any increase in PSNCR means that more bonds must be sold. If this means raising interest rates, the government may prefer to avoid increasing its deficit.

Table 28.2

Deficit and surplus as a percentage of money GDP

Year	Government receipts	Government expenditure	PSNCR/PSDR
1985	41.3	44.1	−2.8
1986	40.1	42.9	−2.9
1987	39.5	40.8	−1.6
1988	39.1	38.9	−0.2
1989	38.6	38.7	0
1990	38.8	40.3	−1.5
1991	38.2	40.9	−2.6
1992	36.9	43.2	−6.3
1993	35.9	43.7	−7.8
1994	36.5	43.3	−6.8
1995	37.8	43.6	−5.8
1996	37.7	42.1	−4.6
1997	37.9	40.7	−3.5

Source: *Eurostat*, via Secos 4

KEY POINTS

28.2

- The PSNCR covers the government's deficit. It is the amount which the government must borrow in any given year to cover the difference between expenditure and tax revenue.

- The PSNCR will tend to rise in a recession and fall in a boom because of automatic stabilizers; discretionary policy may also be used in the same way.

- A large PSNCR may require higher interest rates.

- Unless it is financed by bond sales to the general public or National Savings, government borrowing may increase monetary expansion.

- If tax revenue exceeds government expenditure, there will be a surplus or PSDR.

From deficit to surplus and back again

Traditionally, fiscal policy was used to control aggregate demand, in the way outlined in Chapter 17. Expansionary policies with lower taxes and more government spending would be pursued in times of stagnation and high unemployment. The response to inflation would be contractionary, with tax increases and expenditure cuts.

With the advent of monetarism in the 1980s, however, fiscal policy (in the macroeconomic sense) became subordinate to monetary policy. The argument was that fiscal expansion could do little to create employment but would lead to inflation. This inflation should be controlled by a tight monetary policy, supported by fiscal contraction, and in particular by minimizing government borrowing. In time, the deficit did fall, and by 1989, the budget was in balance. The recession of the early 1990s put a spanner in the works and inevitably led to sizeable deficits returning. All this can be seen in Table 28.2.

A change in the 1990s

The recession which began in earnest in 1990 coincided with the arrival of John Major in Downing Street. The approach to fiscal policy was more pragmatic after that.

In the early 1990s, the PSNCR rose again. Recession reduced income, and therefore the revenue obtained from both direct and indirect taxes. Rising unemployment meant more expenditure on benefits. The government once more suggested that increased borrowing in a recession was to be expected. Also in 1992 the recession had become so serious that the government actually went against its long-held principles and increased spending on health and transport and other infrastructure items. But by 1993 borrowing was growing so fast that the government was worried and proceeded to implement tax increases, mostly by increasing indirect taxes and reducing income tax allowances (such as mortgage interest relief). There was also a fresh round of expenditure cuts.

After 1995, economic growth brought a steady increase in tax revenues and a reduction in unemployment, which gradually reduced the deficit.

Tax and the British public

Throughout the 1980s and 1990s, the electorate consistently showed a preference for tax reductions. Few politicians felt able to offer higher taxes in return for better public services. Mostly, the electorate seems to want lower taxes *and* better services. Successive Chancellors have tried to square this circle in a variety of ways. In 1993, tax increases were presented as 'responsible government'. There were some attempts to introduce new taxes and to disguise changes. These are sometimes referred to in the press as 'stealth taxes'. Early in 2000, Gordon Brown abolished mortgage tax relief and the married man's allowance, while cutting taxes in other ways.

This predilection for tax cuts means that it is much harder to use fiscal policy as a means of influencing aggregate demand. This has reinforced the tendency to rely on monetary policy as a means of controlling the economy.

Taxes remained important both as a means of raising revenue and as a means of influencing the allocation of resources. Examples of the latter include taxes on petrol and the reduction of National Insurance charges on low-paid workers (designed to encourage the creation of more jobs by making labour cheaper to employ).

Deficits and surpluses

Deficits and surpluses are not easy to predict, and there can be surprises. They are the difference between two very large numbers. Revenue depends on income levels and will change as do incomes. Spending depends on changes in the economy: if unemployment changes, social security payments change. Neither can always be predicted precisely. Table 28.2 shows just how sharply the difference between taxation and spending can fluctuate.

The Maastricht criteria for entry to EMU require that the government's total net debt (the National Debt) be no more than 60 per cent of GDP, while the budget deficit for the year must be no more than 3 per cent. The graph shows that the UK government debt was 40.6 per cent in 1999. The bar chart provides some international comparisons of budget deficits for 1999.

Public sector net debt, UK

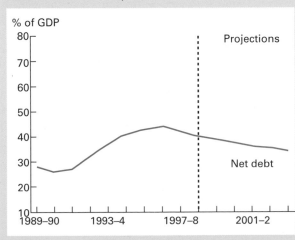

Source: *Financial Times*, 10 March 1999

Government debt: comparisons

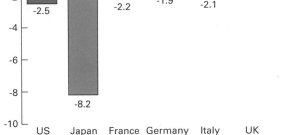

Source: *National Institute Economic Review*, 4, 1999

5 Using Figure 28.1 and Table 28.2, show how the PSNCR in the UK has been affected by the trade cycle.

6 Which kinds of spending are hardest to control?

7 Under what circumstances might it make sense to borrow more?

8 Why does Japan have the highest budget deficit in 1999?

KEY POINTS

28.3

- Fiscal policy in the 1980s was used mainly as a complement to monetary policy.

- Fiscal policies can be used to achieve microeconomic objectives.

- Fiscal policy has been used more actively in the 1990s than it was in the 1980s.

Redistribution issues

When it is politically desirable to cut taxes, there are inevitably implications for the process of redistributing income. Cutting marginal tax rates makes them less progressive. On the other hand, there is some evidence that past reductions in the higher rate of tax have reduced both avoidance and evasion. There is less incentive to do either if the marginal rate is lower. Tax revenues did not shrink as much as expected when the rate was cut in the early 1980s.

The redistribution process has also been affected by the way the level of benefits has been set. For the most part, they have kept pace with the rate of inflation, so their real value has been preserved. But meantime, most people in work have had rising real incomes most of the time. So the gap between those in work and those who are unemployed or retired has grown.

Increasing benefits brings with it the problem of incentives to work. Currently, the standard example is of a married man with two children who earns £150 a week and would receive 87 per cent of his income in work if he were unemployed. (This percentage is known as the replacement ratio.) This gives him only a very limited incentive to work, because the difference is barely enough to cover the extra costs of working.

The Working Families Tax Credit has been brought in to address this issue. It uses the tax system to supplement the incomes of low-paid working parents in order to create a bigger incentive to work. The evidence suggests that it will be of some value in reducing the poverty and unemployment traps.

The creation of a 10 per cent tax band has done something to help the lower paid. However, the help will be limited so long as the 10 per cent band covers only £1500 of taxable income or thereabouts.

Creating incentives

The well-known examples of taxes that affect the allocation of resources include alcohol, tobacco and petrol. Tobacco and alcohol taxes have created a particular bone of contention because they are traditionally higher in the UK than they are in the rest of Europe. This creates an incentive to smuggle, and there is plenty of evidence that it takes place on a grand scale. The Chancellor said in late 1999 that smuggling was costing the Exchequer £2.5 billion.

Smuggling reduces the usefulness of alcohol taxes as revenue raisers and hardly contributes to reduced consumption. Tax rates are not always raised fully in line with inflation. Quite a large group of people oppose increasing these taxes, besides the heavy drinkers. Off-licences along the south coast of England are said to be suffering.

Meantime, tobacco has been given an escalator. Taxes are being raised by 5 per cent above the rate of inflation each year. For the first time in 2000, all the additional proceeds from this tax will be given to the NHS. The cigarette manufacturers and the tobacconists, again, especially those along the Channel coast, are unhappy.

Perhaps the biggest fuss has involved fuel taxes. In order to meet its international obligations to reduce the emission of greenhouse gases, petrol and diesel taxes were raised significantly by the use of an escalator: taxes were raised by inflation plus 6 per cent each year during the late 1990s. This brought petrol prices to a level above those of other EU countries.

New Deal for the over-50s

In 2000, an Employment Credit was introduced which guarantees the over-50s a minimum income of £175 if they move back into full-time work. Nearly a third of men between 55 and 65 were out of work in the late 1990s, mostly after being made redundant or forced to retire early.

9 Why would the government be keen to see more people over the age of 50 working?

10 How will this incentive help the people concerned?

11 How might such a measure help the economy generally?

Some fiscal policy issues

Attitudes to fiscal policy are affected by a person's political stance. Parties on the left of the political spectrum will favour more taxation and more provision of public services, and those on the right will favour less. But things are not always as they seem. Table 28.2 gave a rough measure of the 'scale' of government activity in the figures showing government expenditure and receipts as a percentage of gross domestic product (GDP).

Within this broad debate, there is a series of questions about fiscal policy, some of which have been debated for a long time. There are also many myths for which there is very little hard evidence.

An old debate: is the National Debt a burden?

It is true that the National Debt grew continuously until 1987, and continues to grow whenever the government runs a deficit. However, the total National Debt is not what we should look at to analyse the burden of the debt. In relation to GDP the National Debt has been falling steadily. One reason for this is that the government borrows in money terms. If it sells a bond, it borrows, say, £100. If the bond matures twenty years later the holder is still repaid £100. But by then inflation will usually have reduced the real value of the repayment to rather less. As a borrower the government gains from inflation. The lenders lose. So the National Debt as a proportion of GDP fell from 116 per cent in 1960 to 40 per cent in 1999.

It is possible that more borrowing in the future could increase the interest burden. It should be remembered that this would not be a *national* burden, however. It involves transfer payments from one group of people (taxpayers) to another (holders of government bonds). If, however, bonds are sold abroad, then interest payments are made to foreigners and are an outflow of funds on the invisibles account of the balance of payments. Whether or not increased borrowing makes sense therefore depends partly on what sort of spending it will finance.

Is it alright to borrow more in order to finance investment?

Government capital expenditures should yield an income in the future which will cover the interest and repayment of the debt. The investment could be in plant and machinery, or in infrastructure – roads, say – or in education, which is investment in human capital and makes people more productive. All these things can be expected to generate income, upon which taxes will be paid. These will fund both interest on the debt and eventual repayment.

Some people hold that the PSNCR should not be allowed to rise above the level of government investment. This is the so-called 'Golden Rule', sometimes propagated by Chancellor Gordon Brown and other politicians. However, governments do find it easier to cut capital-spending projects because the effects are not felt immediately, as they are with current spending cuts. This has probably led to under-investment in some areas.

Fiscal policy and the City

All Chancellors show some concern about the attitude of 'the markets' to their policies. If financiers lose confidence in the government's economic policies, difficulties ensue. Suppose a very generous government came to power, promising the electorate greatly increased spending on public services without a tax increase. The view from the City would be that this would entail a large increase in government borrowing, and the Bank of England would need to sell quantities of bonds. Buyers of bonds would expect these bonds to carry a high rate of interest. Raising interest rates would in turn imply loss of confidence as investment would be made more costly. Alternatively, if the authorities financed the deficit by allowing monetary expansion, expectations of inflation would probably increase, again reducing confidence in the government.

If confidence becomes shaky in the foreign exchange markets, the result may be a run on the currency. This can create uncertainties for importers and exporters.

Conservative governments tend to enjoy the confidence of many in the City, most of the time. Labour governments have found it more difficult to maintain confidence without disappointing some of their supporters. However, the Blair government that was returned to power in 1997 made a particular effort to secure the hearts and minds of people in business, and appears to have gained the confidence of the City, at least for the time being.

Why is government spending so hard to control?

All governments find it hard to control spending. In particular, many developed countries now have ageing populations. At the same time, the possibilities for medical care are improving and this means that there are more treatments available, and therefore greater demand for curative treatment. The need to provide pensions and health care, on the level typical in European countries, can be expensive.

As trade increases, the need for competitiveness becomes greater. In order to retain some advantage in trade, governments need to consider infrastructure and education. Without adequate investment in both, it is likely that costs will turn out to be higher than those in competing countries. Both require commitment from governments. Electorates do not often warm to proposals to increase taxes. This means that governments have harsh choices to make.

KEY POINTS

28.4

- The National Debt is the accumulated total debt of the government.
- Borrowing to finance investment generates income in the future.
- Fiscal policy may be affected by attitudes in the financial markets.
- Ageing populations lead to increased demands on social security and health spending.

Has government borrowing been inflationary?

Chapter 17 showed how Keynesian fiscal policies developed. Until the late 1960s, counter-cyclical fiscal policies were quite successful in stabilizing economies. Then unemployment began to rise. The standard Keynesian response would have been to increase aggregate demand by increasing government spending, reducing taxes and perhaps using expansionary monetary policies as well.

But from the start of the 1970s inflation began to accelerate and remained a major threat. In these circumstances expansionary fiscal policy can lead to accelerating inflation rather than increased output and employment. The crucial question is whether there is under-utilized capacity in the economy or whether supply constraints will prevent output from growing further. If there is spare capacity then the unemployment is at least partly due to demand deficiency, and expansionary policies may be effective. The implication is that the economy is operating on the horizontal section of the aggregate supply curve. If there is no spare capacity, then the unemployment is rooted in structural problems and immobilities and will not be reduced by increased aggregate demand: the economy is on the upward-sloping or vertical section of the aggregate supply curve.

Unemployment of this sort must be dealt with by microeconomic measures rather than by expanding aggregate demand. These policies seek to make labour more mobile, to improve information and to increase generally the efficiency with which the labour market functions.

Clearly, if the economy is close to full capacity output, increased government spending or tax cuts can lead to excess demand, overheating, supply constraints and accelerating inflation. The experience of 1988, when income taxes were cut at a time when there was a fall in savings and increased borrowing made possible by house price appreciation, is instructive in this respect. The resulting increase in aggregate demand led to increased consumption and substantial overheating, which ended in accelerating inflation from 1988 to 1990.

Can expansionary policy ever create jobs?

As we have seen, the Keynesian view would be that, if there are unemployed labour and capital in the economy, fiscal expansion could lead to increasing output without accelerating inflation. Here again, recent experience is relevant. If there is real competition in the labour market, and there are people available to fill vacancies, then output can expand without creating excess aggregate demand. The rising output and employment which followed the recession of the early 1990s provide evidence for the benefits of cautious expansion.

Do taxes act as a disincentive to work?

It has been strongly felt by politicians that tax cuts create an incentive to work harder. The evidence for this is rather sketchy. A study in the United States some time ago found that there was some evidence of a rise in incentives when top tax rates were cut from 60 to 45 per cent.

Cutting the top UK income tax rate to 40 per cent may not have reduced tax revenue by much. When marginal rates are lower people have less incentive to avoid tax (legally) or evade tax (illegally). So a larger share of higher incomes has been taxed at a lower rate.

At the other end of the scale, there is strong evidence that low-paid workers and unemployed people face disincentives. A low-paid worker who gets an increase in income may find that tax payments together with lost benefits (which are usually means-tested) take most or all of their increased income. Unemployed people with families may be little better off in work. The long-term unemployed are especially vulnerable. Recent changes in the way benefits are calculated have reduced this disincentive, but have not eliminated it. Perhaps a million or more families are affected to some degree by very high effective marginal tax rates.

How have contractionary policies worked?

When fiscal and monetary policies reduce aggregate monetary demand they cut the demand for many firms' products. These firms will begin to make losses. They may contract, making some of their workforce redundant, or they may close, reducing employment still further. If they face rising costs of production they will be unable to pass them on in the form of higher prices, because if they did sales would fall further.

In this situation, with unemployment rising, demands for higher wages will be somewhat reduced. Trade unions will know that higher wages will create more losses and thus contract the number of jobs further. Wage settlements will be gradually reduced. In theory, the knowledge that tight fiscal and monetary policies will be introduced and adhered to could induce unions to accept lower wage settlements. In practice, unions must advance the interests of their working members, and unemployment may rise substantially before they are pressured into accepting less. So while contractionary policy does reduce inflation, it may do so at quite a high cost in terms of lost output and employment.

How will fiscal policy be used in the future?

With monetary policy in the hands of the Monetary Policy Committee of the Bank of England, the Chancellor controls only fiscal policy. Of course, macroeconomic policy should be co-ordinated, and the frequent meetings between the Chancellor and the Governor of the Bank of England make this possible. The fact remains that fiscal policy could become more important as a policy tool in the future, because for the Chancellor it is the weapon that is to hand. Certainly, we know that Chancellor Gordon Brown has used microeconomic policy tools in a very active way.

However, this could change again. There are pressures within the EU for fiscal harmonization. This would mean that many tax rates would be the same right across the EU. It would greatly facilitate the working of the single market. At the moment, the 'level playing field' which the single market is supposed to provide, within which producers are all competing freely on an equal basis, is only level in some places. We have already seen that variations in taxes on alcohol and tobacco are making it very difficult for some sellers to compete.

Harmonization may be hard to achieve. It involves substantial loss of sovereignty for national governments, so we can expect further big battles. Germany has supported harmonization strongly in the past and may take a dim view of UK reluctance to hand over responsibility to Brussels.

KEY POINTS

28.5

- If the economy is close to full capacity output, fiscal expansion can cause excess demand and accelerating inflation.

- Fiscal expansion can create jobs if there is demand-deficiency unemployment.

- In practice, government deficits have mostly been financed in non-inflationary ways.

- Taxes can sometimes act as a disincentive, especially for people on low incomes or benefits.

- Tight fiscal and monetary policies can reduce inflation, but the loss of output and employment may be substantial.

Case Study

Brown looks less green after easing environment taxes

The Chancellor's environmental credentials were questioned last night after he watered down two of the government's most contentious green taxes and signalled his desire to see high-technology industry expand in open countryside.

Gordon Brown told the Commons that the government would honour its environmental commitments, but his retreat on the energy tax and scaling back of fuel duty rises dismayed many in the green lobby.

The energy tax, or climate change levy, will still be applied to large industrial users of gas and coal, but Mr Brown said the total levy could be cut from £1.7 billion to £1 billion. The retreat, which followed intensive lobbying by industry, is accompanied by an 80 per cent discount to energy-intensive sectors which sign efficiency agreements.

Mr Brown said he would encourage environment-friendly fuel by exempting renewable energy and combined heat and power from the proposed tax.

All the revenues from the tax would be recycled to business, with every company enjoying a cut in National Insurance Contributions.

There would be a 100 per cent investment allowance to companies which moved from environmentally unfriendly industries to environmentally friendly ones, with cash to support energy efficiency.

The vocal motoring lobby won its own success when Mr Brown announced the ending of the fuel duty escalator, currently set to increase fuel prices by an automatic 6 per cent above inflation each year until 2002. Future duty rises would be decided on an annual basis and set at a lower rate.

Revenue from any real increases in duty will go straight to a ring-fenced fund for the modernization of roads and public transport.

The announcement marked an extension of the role of hypothecation – ring-fencing revenues for a particular purpose – in public finance. The Treasury has resisted hypothecation in the past, but yesterday's pre-Budget Report extended its use to the fuel duty escalator and to tobacco duties which will be applied to the health budget.

Environmental groups expressed disappointment at what they saw as the Chancellor's climbdown. Charles Secrett, director of Friends of the Earth, said: 'The Chancellor's green promises look a little brown today'. But industry gave a cautious welcome to the proposed tax changes.

Adair Turner, CBI director general, said modifications to the climate change levy would 'lessen the impact of the tax on competitiveness, without sacrificing the aim of improving the environment and increasing energy efficiency'.

Industry also gave a muted response to the proposed changes in the fuel duty escalator. The Road Haulage Association said its members planned to continue with a traffic-disrupting protest over diesel fuel duties in Birmingham on 20 November. A spokesman for the Freight Transport Association said 'The Chancellor has

29

Economic policy in an open economy

LEARNING OUTCOMES

On completing this chapter you should understand:

■ How changing trade patterns affect the domestic economy

■ The relationship between trade, capital movements, exchange rates and the balance of payments

■ The influence of the exchange rate on trade

■ The role of the international institutions

■ The development of the European Union

■ The dilemmas of exchange rate policy

■ The controversies surrounding trade policy

Over the years, almost all economies have become more open. They export and import more. Small countries tend to be the most open of all, larger countries less so, since it is rather easier for them to be more self-sufficient.

Increasing openness has resulted from increasing exploitation of comparative advantage. As countries develop, they discover new and competitive ways of exploiting their resources. Exports expand. The income they earn can be spent on more imports. The developed countries which already produce many and diverse products will innovate, produce new products and trade more manufactures with each other, as individual firms develop a comparative advantage in the design or the attractiveness of their products.

About one-third of UK economic activity is devoted to exporting, and about the same proportion of total expenditure is on imports (depending on which measure of gross domestic product is used). We saw in Chapter 6 how important trade can be in contributing to economic growth and rising standards of living.

Throughout this chapter we shall be very much concerned with the process of **globalization**. This term was first mentioned at the end of Chapter 2. Fast-growing trade is beginning to integrate economies as never before. However, it is not just the trade in goods and services that does this. The free movement of capital across much of the world has had an equally dramatic effect. Increasingly, capital moves wherever it may be most profitably invested. This means that banking systems and financial markets are becoming very much more integrated. So economies are experiencing growing interdependence. This makes it vital to co-operate in policy matters. Figure 29.1 shows how trade and growth have expanded.

Table 29.1 shows some of the trends for the UK. Visible imports and exports have grown much faster than inflation. The current balance includes visible trade, trade in

Table 29.1

UK visible exports and imports and the trade balance
£ billion, current prices

Year	Visible exports	Visible imports	Current balance	Current balance as % of GDP
1987	79.2	90.7	−5.0	−1.1
1988	80.3	101.8	−16.6	−3.5
1989	92.2	116.8	−22.5	−4.4
1990	101.7	120.5	−19.0	−3.4
1991	103.4	113.7	−8.2	−1.4
1992	107.3	120.4	−9.7	−1.6
1993	122.0	135.4	−10.3	−1.6
1994	135.3	146.4	−1.4	−0.2
1995	153.7	165.4	−3.2	−0.4
1996	167.4	180.5	0.1	0.0
1997	171.8	183.7	7.4	0.9
1998	164.1	184.9	0.5	0.1

Source: *National Institute Economic Review*, 4, 1999

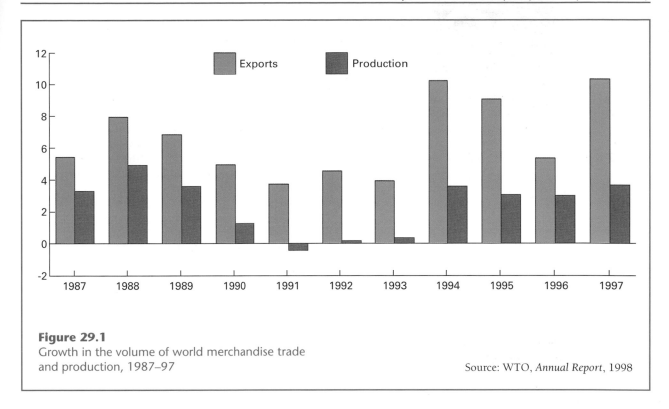

Figure 29.1
Growth in the volume of world merchandise trade
and production, 1987–97

Source: WTO, *Annual Report*, 1998

services and net interest, dividends and profits on overseas investments (i.e. all the invisibles). It is clear that from 1994 onwards there were few problems with the balance of payments in the UK.

Changing trade: the effect on the domestic economy

Changing patterns of demand and supply imply changes in the structure of output. When competitive sources of imports are newly available, competing domestic industries face falling demand. Two kinds of adjustment are possible. As the domestic industry declines, its revenues fall (relatively if not absolutely) and wages and profits in the industry will be less attractive. The resources employed in the industry (both labour and capital) will have an incentive to move to more lucrative uses.

Meantime, somewhere in the economy, alternative opportunities will be opening up: there may be growing demands for a new product, or a product being produced with a new, cheaper technology, or a product which can be exported to meet growing demand abroad, or (if incomes are rising) for a product with high income elasticity of demand. So structural change takes place and resources are reallocated.

An alternative adjustment route may take place through exchange rate changes. Rising imports will increase the supply of sterling. This will depress the exchange rate. The price of imports will rise; the price of

exports will fall (or they will become more profitable). New opportunities to make competitive exports will open up and unemployed resources will be attracted into exporting industries.

The increase in trade which takes place in this way leads to lower production costs, worldwide, and is a potent source of economic growth. The globalization process is driven by the identification of new and profitable markets.

More trade means more structural change, which is not costless. In the short run both labour and capital are often immobile. There may be a long transition period when industries decline in painful ways. Governments may wish to protect industries threatened by competition by implementing import controls. The ways in which this may be done are examined later in the chapter, as is the World Trade Organization, which creates rules to minimize the extent to which protection can reduce trade.

Trade, capital movements, the exchange rate and the balance of payments

If trade patterns shift, a change in the exchange rate acts to restore equilibrium in the balance of payments. Take the case of the UK and North Sea oil. As oil became available from 1978 onwards, less imported oil was needed. The amount of sterling supplied to the foreign exchange market (in order to buy foreign currency) fell. The supply curve of sterling shifted leftwards. The exchange rate appreciated. Figure 29.2 shows this. (This may seem to be rather a long time ago, but it is still the simplest example of a shift in the pattern of trade.)

What was happening meanwhile to the balance of payments? When less oil was imported, the balance of trade swung into surplus. The subsequent rise in the exchange rate made imports cheaper and exports dearer. Exports (other than of oil and especially of manufactures) fell. Imports rose. The short-term balance of trade surplus (disequilibrium), resulting from the reduced oil imports, was eliminated and equilibrium was restored.

From time to time a much longer-run trend also is discernible. During the past thirty years, the countries that compete with the United Kingdom in manufacturing production have grown in numbers and efficiency. For some products – cars and televisions, for example – they have reduced (though not eliminated) the UK's comparative advantage. Over the years, therefore, UK imports have often risen faster than exports. There has been a tendency towards a balance of trade deficit.

Figure 29.3 shows that there are shifts in both the supply of and demand for sterling. Fewer exports mean reduced demand for sterling to pay for them. More imports mean an increased supply of sterling needed to pay for the foreign currencies to buy the imports. Figure 29.3 shows how the exchange rate depreciates. This depreciation now makes imports dearer and exports cheaper. (Try it: If £1 = $1.50, a £10 000 car sells for $15 000 in the United States. If £1 = $1, the car now sells for $10 000: it has become a much better bargain and is more competitive in relation to other countries' cars.) Exports will sell better. There will be fewer imports: the domestic product will be better able to compete on the home market. The balance of trade will improve: the deficit will be gradually eliminated over a period of one to two years.

These kinds of exchange rate changes are a response to changes in trade patterns and help to prevent long-run balance of payments disequilibrium (surplus or deficit). Note that, if the exchange rate is to be fixed at a certain parity, market forces will operate but will be countered by central bank action.

During the late 1990s, UK exporters managed to stay competitive despite the high pound. This suggests that productivity gains have been sufficient to counter the effects of cheaper imports.

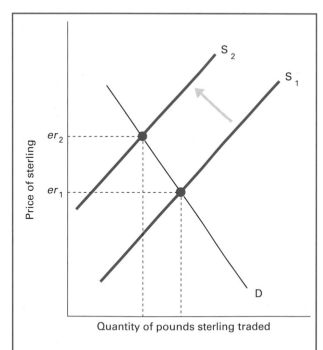

Figure 29.2
Appreciation
As less oil was imported, fewer pounds were supplied to the foreign exchange market as less foreign currency was needed. The supply curve of the pound shifted leftwards and the new equilibrium exchange rate was higher.

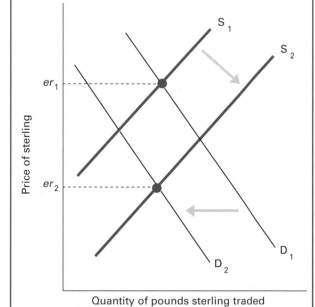

Figure 29.3
Depreciation
As more imports are demanded the supply of sterling shifts rightwards: at any given exchange rate more sterling will be supplied to pay for foreign currency. As fewer exports are demanded the demand for sterling shifts leftwards. The new equilibrium exchange rate will have depreciated.

Comparative advantage and the exchange rate

China has a comparative advantage in the manufacture of telephones. The United Kingdom has a comparative advantage in the manufacture of certain speciality chemicals.
Draw diagrams to show the following.

1 What will happen to the pound if China increases its purchases of UK chemicals?

2 What will happen to the pound if people in the United Kingdom buy more Chinese telephones?

3 What will happen if UK people buy more Chinese telephones while China buys its chemicals from Germany?

The effect of capital movements

In Chapter 6, we found that international **capital movements** have an important influence on exchange rates. Capital movements may happen for two reasons. There may be profitable opportunities to invest in productive capacity, for example by setting up a factory abroad. This is direct investment. Ford Dagenham is an overseas investment of the US Ford parent company. Such investments are long term in nature. The other reason for capital movements is interest rate differentials. Funds available for a short time will be placed in bank accounts in the currency which earns the highest interest rate. So if one country raises its interest rate it can expect a capital inflow of what are sometimes called footloose funds, or **hot money**. These flows may be speculative in nature.

How will capital movements affect exchange rates? If a UK bank decides to buy dollars, the supply of sterling rises. This will depress the price of sterling. Other things being equal, sterling will depreciate. The effect will be reversed if there is a capital inflow. The dramatic short-run changes in exchange rates that we hear about on the news are the result of capital movements rather than underlying trade patterns. The latter have an influence over the long run.

Exchange rates, inflation and the rate of interest

There is a complex relationship between the exchange rate, the rate of inflation and the interest rate. Inflation means that the currency is losing its purchasing power. Inevitably, if one country is inflating faster than its trading partners, its currency will depreciate. If the exchange rate remains stable for a while, export prices will rise and demand will fall. This will reduce demand for the currency and depress its value. Similarly, import prices will rise (if at all) more slowly than prices of domestic products; imports will be more competitive and demand for them will rise. The supply of the currency will rise as people buy more foreign currency to pay for the imports. Again, the exchange rate will be pushed downwards.

High inflation rates may lead to higher interest rates as governments try to control monetary expansion. Higher interest rates are likely to attract a capital inflow. This increases demand for the currency, pushing it upwards. The way in which inflation affects exchange rates is often an important reason why governments regard the control of inflation as a high priority.

Market convulsions

For some time up to 1997, the Asian Tigers had been famous for their high rates of economic growth. The four most successful, Singapore, Taiwan, Hong Kong and the Republic of Korea, took off and prospered enough to be considered as developed economies. Thailand and Malaysia did well, too. Then, during the summer of 1997, Thailand got into difficulties. A number of its firms were in situations of falling profitability. Some banks were implicated: it seemed possible that they might have made large loans to some businesses with poor prospects of repaying. Share prices were falling and there was a general loss of confidence in the economy. Foreign investors responded by withdrawing funds, quite rapidly, and that started a run on the foreign exchange markets.

Before very long, Korea ran into similar difficulties. The IMF came along to help with loans that would help prop up the currencies. It prescribed an increase in interest rates to try to stabilize the exchange rate. It insisted that the new exchange rates should be lower than before – to help exporters to become profitable again – but not as low as they had already sunk. The trouble was that these policies brought with them serious recessions.

Some people blamed the international financial system for what happened. Many thought that the crisis would spread and bring about a worldwide recession. Malaysia refused the IMF advice and introduced stringent controls on the movement of capital. In time, the affected economies recovered. By 1999 most observers thought the worst was over and it was clear that the effects on the rest of the world would not be lasting.

The free movement of capital is very beneficial to emerging economies, which need investment funds in order to develop. But if the banks then lend to firms that are not performing very well, and if their failures rub off on the banks, the international capital gets frightened and tries to get out. The results can be chaotic. Hindsight suggests that banks and other financial institutions need to be tightly regulated by carefully considered systems of commercial law.

4 Why did holders of currency in the countries affected by the Asian financial crisis sell?

5 What effect did their flight from those currencies have?

6 What makes people want to hold and trade particular currencies?

7 Why are global financial markets sometimes unstable?

The role of the Bank of England

In Chapter 18 we saw how the Bank of England uses the exchange equalization account to intervene in the foreign exchange market. It irons out day-to-day fluctuations in exchange rates and keeps the rates within a target range. It cannot resist a major market movement, perhaps with a panic leading to a run on the pound. But it can defend the exchange rate against market forces to a considerable extent, provided it has sufficient foreign currency reserves.

How will domestic monetary policy affect all this? If interest rates are being kept high in order to constrain the growth of expenditure, a capital inflow will be attracted. Demand for the currency, and the exchange rate, will tend to rise. Imports will become cheaper. Exports will lose competitiveness. Spending on domestically produced goods and services will be further reduced. Excess demand will be prevented, but the trade balance (exports minus imports) will probably worsen. In fact, this is an important aspect of the way in which high interest rates work to reduce aggregate demand.

Alternatively, the logic may be quite different. Interest rates might be kept high to ensure that the exchange rate is kept stable. A consequence of that would be a contraction of the domestic economy. In an open economy, domestic, trade and exchange rate policy are very closely linked. To the extent that the UK government intends to try to keep the exchange rate stable, adjustment must take place via interest rate and other domestic policies.

KEY POINTS

29.1

- Economies have tended to become more open with time.

- Changing patterns of trade lead to changes in the structure of output.

- Changing patterns of trade lead to exchange rate changes, as do capital movements.

- Trade and exchange rate changes affect the domestic economy and interact with interest rate changes.

The exchange rate and trade

We have looked at how trade affects the exchange rate. But the links are two-way. Supposing there are exchange rate changes, in response not so much to shifting trade patterns as to large capital movements.

A major banking and financial centre such as the United Kingdom can experience very large capital inflows

and outflows, and in recent years capital movements have been the major influence on the sterling exchange rate. A large capital inflow shifts the demand for sterling to the right. Other things being equal, the exchange rate will appreciate. Domestic producers will lose competitiveness; imports will increase and exports decrease. A balance of trade deficit will develop. Capital movements can produce an exchange rate at which firms have difficulty in competing. Connect this up with a conclusion we drew just now about monetary policy: a high interest rate, a capital inflow (or less outflow perhaps), a high exchange rate. Tight monetary policy dampens growth of the economy through its influence on the exchange rate. Higher imports mean more leakages. Lower exports mean less injections. The economy will contract.

Price elasticities

When working out the likely effect of an exchange rate change, remember that the exchange rate determines prices of traded goods, and the response to price changes is determined by elasticities. The demand for most UK exports (other than oil) is fairly elastic. Foreigners can go somewhere else on holiday and buy their aircraft engines from Pratt and Whitney instead of Rolls Royce. UK exports often have good substitutes. Appreciation causes competitiveness to deteriorate and exports fall. Depreciation and improved competitiveness can lead to substantially increased exports of manufactures.

Looking at imports, the picture is rather different. Where there are good domestic substitutes, that is, demand is elastic, as with cars, depreciation will encourage falling imports. For products such as iron ore or coffee, demand is rather inelastic because there is no close domestic substitute. (Also, for raw materials, they form only a small part of total production costs.) Depreciation will make little difference to the level of imports of raw materials and food products. It will have more effect on imports of manufactures if these compete with UK products.

Elasticities in the short run

What will happen *immediately* after an exchange rate depreciation? Initially, many importers and exporters will have contracts to fulfil. It will take time for foreigners to discover that UK exports are now more competitive. So the elasticity of demand for exports will be much lower in the short run than in the long run. Similarly, it may take time to find alternative domestic supplies to replace imports. Demand for imports will be inelastic in the short run.

Even if the demand for more exports exists, supply may not. Depreciation will make exports increasingly profitable but, if producers actually do not increase output, more cannot be sold. In other words, supply constraints would prevent depreciation from leading to increased production for export and for home consumption. The chances of output for export increasing are much greater in the long run than in the short run, because supply will become more elastic as adjustments take place over time.

This phenomenon is known as the **J-curve effect**. Figure 29.4 shows why.

Because the United Kingdom now exports some oil, the oil price affects the exchange rate. Rising oil prices strengthen the pound in the same way as the initial growth of oil output did. Falling oil prices lead to a lower exchange rate for the pound against most other currencies, and therefore to improved competitiveness for other products.

The UK experience

In 1990, the UK joined the European exchange rate mechanism (ERM). This was a forerunner of Economic and Monetary Union (EMU). The arrangement kept member currencies floating within a very narrow band. The objective was to give businesses within the member countries a degree of confidence in the exchange rates of other member countries. This reduced uncertainty and made business planning easier.

Unfortunately, the UK joined the ERM at an exchange rate which was quite high. This made it difficult for UK exporters to compete within the ERM member countries, which by this time had become a very significant market for UK exports. Meantime, Germany had begun a huge reconstruction programme as a result of the unification of East and West Germany in 1989. Capital was flowing steadily out of sterling and into the deutschmark. These two factors brought intense pressure from the financial markets, pushing sterling through its ERM floor. At first the government tried to maintain the ERM rate and borrowed heavily to support it.

Eventually, on what became known as 'Black Wednesday', it gave in to market forces and took the

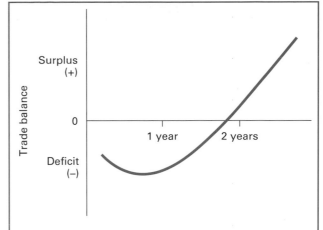

Figure 29.4
The J-curve
A depreciation will lead at first to a worsening of the trade balance. In time (twelve to twenty-four months) it will usually improve. After an appreciation a reverse (upside down) J-curve may be observed.

pound out of the ERM. This turned out to be highly beneficial for UK exporters. Effectively, the pound had depreciated against the ERM currencies by about 15 per cent. There was a J-curve effect but then exports surged. The increased demand brought the recession to an end and manufacturing industry enjoyed several years of very pleasing growth.

During the life of this book, the UK may join EMU. The theoretical analysis used here applies to the euro as well as to the pound: the euro floats against the dollar and most other currencies. Influences on trade in the eurozone can be analysed in the same way.

Trade, inflation rates, interest rates and the exchange rate

Trade by volume, inflation, interest rates and the exchange rate, 1992–8

	Exports, 1995 = 100	Imports, 1995 = 100	Base rate, %	Inflation rate, %	Exchange rate, 1994 = 100
1992	79.9	87.3	9.6	3.7	108.7
1993	82.9	90.6	6.0	1.6	99.7
1994	91.3	94.6	5.5	2.5	100
1995	100	100	6.7	3.4	95.1
1996	107.7	109.1	6.0	2.4	96.7
1997	116.5	118.9	6.6	3.1	112.7
1998	118.0	129.1	7.2	3.5	116.5

Source: *National Institute Economic Review*, 4, 1999

8 How did imports and exports change over the period 1992–8? **AV**

9 Is there a connection between the exchange rate and the levels of imports and exports? **AV**

10 What has happened to real rates of interest? **AV**

11 Do interest rates have an influence upon the effective exchange rate? **AV**

12 Have you allowed for time lags in your answers?

KEY POINTS

29.2

- The effect of exchange rate changes on the trade balance will depend upon price elasticities of demand and supply.

- A depreciation may initially cause the trade balance to worsen, but eventually it will usually improve.

International institutions

So far we have been looking at the background to policy: the links between trade, the domestic economy and the exchange rate. We cannot discuss policies without being aware of the international institutions, too.

The International Monetary Fund

We saw in Chapter 6 how the IMF was set up to preside over the system of fixed exchange rates which lasted from 1945 to 1971. The IMF has its head office in Washington, DC, United States. Its original brief was to provide international finance to maintain exchange rate stability. Primarily, it was intended to assist member countries by lending to them in times of deficit from its holdings of gold and currencies. These are accumulated from subscriptions by members in relation to their quotas. Each member's quota was set according to a formula that took into account its importance in the world economy.

This arrangement, set up after the Second World War, was known as the Bretton Woods system. (J.M. Keynes played an important part in the conference that laid the foundations of the system.) Eventually, however, it gave way to a system of floating exchange rates, and this changed the IMF's role somewhat. In time it became clear that floating exchange rates would not eliminate payments' surpluses and deficits. So IMF loans have continued to be needed to help with short-term deficits. An IMF loan can prevent destabilizing lurches in exchange rates, allowing countries time to make necessary adjustments.

Nowadays all IMF loans are made to developing or East European countries. The developed countries generally survive deficits by means of loans between their own central banks.

IMF loans are not freely given. They are lent on condition that certain policies are followed. Sometimes these policies are very unpopular in borrowing countries. They may be required to devalue their currencies, raise taxes and cut government spending. The borrower government may need to blame the IMF for the tough policies.

The IMF has an important role as a co-ordinator. It provides a framework for international discussion. It undertakes surveillance: it observes member governments' policies and tries to ensure that they are not inconsistent with other member countries' policies. All countries cannot have trade surpluses and surplus countries can be encouraged to help deficit countries by reducing the surplus.

During the Asian financial crisis, the IMF was strongly criticized for its policies. The problem was that the policies that stabilized the currencies also caused very problematic recessions. In relatively poor countries, recession creates serious suffering and, sometimes, political instability.

The World Bank

The other international organization set up at Bretton Woods in 1945 was the **International Bank for Reconstruction and Development**, informally referred to as the World Bank. As its official title suggests, its funds were meant to promote the development of countries' economies, especially those in the developing world (see Chapter 30). Projects such as dams, roads and power stations have been undertaken, and monies have been provided for certain kinds of private enterprise. In addition, the World Bank provides extensive technical assistance. It gives advice on all aspects of economic and development policy. Increasingly, the work of the World Bank and the IMF is integrated.

In general, the World Bank's funds are borrowed on commercial terms on the world's major capital markets (London, New York, Tokyo etc.). They are lent at market rates of interest to the borrowers. They are not really aid, since the projects they finance must pay their way. What the World Bank can do is make finance available to bodies that would not have access to ordinary bank loans – they may lack contacts or be considered too risky.

For purposes where commercial borrowing is impossible (for example, for health-care facilities for poor people), the World Bank has its soft loan agency, the International Development Association (IDA). This is financed by member countries' subscriptions (similar to the IMF's quota system). Money can be given in grant form or lent at concessional rates of interest (that is, lower than commercial rates). This is known as multilateral aid: it comes from many countries via an international body.

The World Trade Organization

After the Second World War, when the IMF and the World Bank were set up, the intention was to set up a World Trade Organization. In the event the necessary agreements did not materialize. In its place, the General Agreement on Tariffs and Trade (GATT) was set up. It was a comparatively modest organization with limited funds and a very small secretariat in Geneva.

Despite its small stature, the GATT presided over a series of trade negotiations which had a profound impact on the world. The Kennedy and Tokyo Rounds led to cuts in the general level of tariffs and encouraged massive increases in world trade, to the benefit of all concerned. However, there were still major restrictions on trade in agricultural products and services, and many developing countries still suffered from trade barriers. The Uruguay Round of trade negotiations (1986–94) set out to address needs in these areas. It also provided for the transformation of the GATT into the WTO, a much larger organization with greater research potential and a higher profile.

The WTO does not just mastermind trade negotiations. One of its most important functions is to provide a disputes-settlement procedure. This helps to resolve trade disputes between member countries and provides a forum for the airing of complaints about unfair trade restrictions.

In late 1999, there was an attempt to launch a 'Millennium Round', a fresh attempt to address outstanding trade issues. There were still worries about restrictions on trade in agricultural products; developing countries still felt marginalized from the progress made to date; many people were worried about working conditions in developing countries, and there were many other live issues. Unfortunately, the negotiating teams had not agreed an agenda in advance and the initial discussions in Seattle broke up as the talks became more and more acrimonious. Nevertheless, this may have been the beginning of a further important round of negotiations.

The Group of Seven

The seven countries involved are the United States, Germany, Japan, the United Kingdom, France, Italy and Canada – collectively known as G7. They meet, sometimes at the same time as the IMF, to discuss regularly matters of mutual economic interest. The Group of Five (G5) does not include Italy and Canada. If Russia is invited, then the group becomes G8. There have been proposals to invite China, too.

These meetings have come about because it is now recognized that nations are interdependent. Economic policies in any one major country will have repercussions in its trading partner countries. Different countries' economic policies may conflict with one another.

These groupings provide an opportunity for collaborative discussion when economic issues affect a number of countries and co-operative action is needed.

The European Union

The European Communities consisted initially of France, West Germany, Italy, Belgium, The Netherlands and Luxembourg. They combined in the 1950s with the objective of creating freer trade between themselves. The Treaty of Rome, which defined the relationship between the member countries, came into force in 1958.

The Common External Tariff (CET) gave EU members a unified trade policy with respect to the rest of the world.

The United Kingdom, Denmark and Ireland joined in 1973. Greece joined in 1981 and Spain and Portugal joined in 1986. Sweden, Austria and Finland joined in 1995.

The objective is to promote trade within the community by reducing trade barriers and harmonizing regulations. Potentially this process can cut costs through increased specialization and increased competition. The possible gains over the long run are large.

Over the past thirty years there has been a steady shift in the direction of UK trade towards the rest of the EU. As trading partners the United States and the Commonwealth countries have diminished in relative importance for the United Kingdom.

Other trading blocs

There have been other attempts to set up trading blocs. The most recent is the North American Free Trade Area (NAFTA). A free trade area eliminates tariffs on trade between its own members but does not attempt to create a common trade policy with the rest of the world. NAFTA dates from the beginning of 1994. It has involved considerable structural change in the member countries, Canada, the United States and Mexico. So far it would appear to be increasing trade and economic activity for all its members. It is too soon to say what its long-run effect may be.

A number of European countries outside the EU in 1959 set up EFTA, the European Free Trade Area. During the early 1990s EFTA negotiated with the EU to form the European Economic Area (EEA), a free trade area covering much of Europe. This allows unrestricted trade but does not attempt to harmonize policy in the way that the EU does. Since most of the original EFTA members have now joined the EU, it is not now of great significance.

Does the world need more rules?

The Asian financial crisis spawned a rash of proposals to improve the regulation of banking systems on a worldwide basis. At the time of writing, nothing conclusive has come of this, but this too may change. It is possible that the Bank for International Settlements in Basle will have a stronger role. This is an organization which exists to co-ordinate the activities of central banks. Possible areas for action include encouraging individual central banks to regulate their national banking systems more tightly. This would involve requiring them to keep adequate reserves to cover possible bad loans. Perhaps also some system will be developed to monitor the functioning of international capital markets and make them more stable.

The development of the European Union

The EU is a customs union: it fosters free trade between members and deals as a single entity with its trading partners beyond its borders. The common external tariff creates a unified trade policy for all members. A customs union increases economic activity within its borders in two ways. **Trade creation** results from there being a larger market within which countries can specialize. They are encouraged to exploit their comparative advantage relative to each other, increase the international division of labour and so generate economic growth. The same resources are used more efficiently than before to create a larger output.

Trade diversion works differently. Member countries have an advantage in trade with each other because they can trade freely. Other countries have to pay import duties which will raise the cost of their goods to buyers. So they are at a disadvantage. Member countries will tend to buy from each other rather than from countries outside the union.

Since its inception, the members of the EU have become steadily more economically integrated. The rest of the world does sometimes perceive the EU as tending to exclude imports when possible. EU agricultural policy is particularly unpopular with the United States, Australia and other exporters of agricultural products.

EU revenue and expenditure

The original intention within the EU was that richer countries would seek to make transfers of real resources to poorer ones. As we have already observed, trade brings about structural change, which in turn creates losers: people who have been working in or investing in industries which do not have a comparative advantage. The losers from structural change were to be compensated through the EU's regional and social funds. Agricultural policy was intended to protect farmers from the natural tendency of farm incomes to fall.

EU revenue comes from agricultural levies and tariffs on imports, from a share paid by governments according to ability to pay, and from VAT. Currently VAT is levied at the rate of 1 per cent. (This is included in the UK total VAT of 17.5 per cent.)

Just under half of EU expenditure goes to support farm prices. The Structural Funds, which are to redress economic and social disparities throughout the union, take another 30 per cent. The rest is spent on social policy, energy, the environment, industry, consumer protection and research.

The European Single Market

In 1992 EU members entered a new phase in which the objective was to remove all barriers to trade. This was embodied in the Maastricht Treaty. So internal border controls ceased to exist and the free movement of people, capital and goods became a reality. That was the theory, anyway. There has been some reduction in the bureaucracy associated with trade, and this has speeded up the transport of goods somewhat.

The practical impact of the Single Market is rather uncertain. However, it had a substantial psychological effect: many firms were encouraged to look at EU markets with more vigour and energy. In this respect it may have been quite important.

The free movement of people has been encouraged by mutual recognition of other member countries' qualifications. Capital controls have been removed. EMU makes an integrated capital market much more of a reality: until 1999, capital movements were always subject to exchange rate risk.

The European Union and UK policy

The EU has had major effects on UK economic policy. One is that, as a member, the United Kingdom no longer decides its trade policy alone but is a party to collective decisions made in Brussels. For example, the United Kingdom participates in the trade negotiations of the WTO as a member country of the EU delegation.

The other major area of impact has been through the Common Agricultural Policy (CAP). This sets agreed prices on agricultural products and protects farmers from cheap imports by means of a variable levy, equal to the difference between the world price and the CAP price. Prices have usually been quite high, and agricultural output within the EU has grown steadily, helped by technological change. The result has been that imports of agricultural products are now much reduced. (Chapter 9 looked at this issue.)

If the United Kingdom decides to join the Economic and Monetary Union, this will have a major impact on exchange rate policy, which is considered later in the chapter.

EU competition and employment policy can have potentially very significant effects on UK regulations. However, these areas often give rise to disputes.

The principle of **subsidiarity** is sometimes advanced as a guide that can be used to decide where decisions should be taken. The principle is that political decisions should be taken as close as possible to the location of the people they affect. So health and safety regulations, employment regulations and so on are determined by Brussels: after all, they are very much part of the 'level playing field' of the single market, by which it is intended that all EU businesses are competing on the same terms. Criminal law is determined by national governments, each of which has a rather different system. Health policy is determined by a combination of national governments and regional health authorities. You can see at once that there are many anomalies and, although the principle of subsidiarity may be useful, it can hardly be said to be applied consistently.

The UK has from time to time opposed some of the collective agreements negotiated within the EU. The Conservative government opted out of the Social Chapter of the Maastricht Treaty, but the Labour government opted in again in 1997. So far it is not obvious that the measures involved – principally improved working conditions, opportunities for employee involvement in business decisions and a minimum wage – are going to have a disastrous effect on British industry.

Expanding the EU

Many countries want to join the EU. The so-called 'fast-track' applicants include Estonia, Poland, the Czech Republic, Hungary and Slovenia. Behind them in the queue there are Latvia, Lithuania, Slovakia, Romania and Bulgaria. The earliest date for new entrants might be 2002. Many outstanding problems have to be solved, such as how new members might be accommodated within the CAP.

KEY POINTS

29.3

- The IMF exists primarily to help countries deal with balance of payments deficits. It provides a forum for international discussion.

- The World Bank lends on commercial terms for major projects in developing countries.

- G5, G7 and G8 allow for possible co-operation in economic policy matters for interdependent countries.

- The EU exists to increase specialization and competition within member countries and by so doing to promote economic growth.

- The WTO works to encourage the reduction of all trade restrictions and to resolve disputes between member countries.

- UK economic policy-making has been substantially affected by EU regulations.

Exchange rate policy

A vital issue concerns the nature of the exchange rate regime. Broadly, we need to consider three alternatives – although there are all kinds of fine gradations possible between them. Fixed exchange rates imply stable parities: that is, exchange rates will be maintained over time by means of central bank intervention. Floating rates respond to market forces, without any intervention (other than that required to iron out day-to-day fluctuations). A managed exchange rate implies that there will be considerable central bank influence but also a strong element of market forces in the determination of the exchange rate.

The exact balance between the two will depend on exchange rate policy at any given time.

Fixed exchange rates

The Bretton Woods system which served well until 1971 was based on the dollar, which was in turn based on a fixed value in terms of gold. It was stable in that the dollar provided a fixed point, and other currencies' values were defined in terms of the dollar. Central bank intervention ensured that the rate stayed fixed. It was also flexible. If a fundamental balance of payments deficit developed, devaluations (or, for a surplus, revaluations) could be negotiated within the IMF framework for all countries other than the United States.

Why did fixed exchange rates break down?

Up to the late 1960s, most developed countries had similar, fairly low inflation rates. After that time, inflation rates started to diverge. A country with inflation which is faster than that of its trading partners will lose competitiveness. To maintain it, it will need a lower exchange rate. Its currency loses value both externally and internally. It cannot very well keep its exchange rates fixed. If inflation is fast and variable, frequent devaluations are needed and the point of fixed exchange rates, stability, is lost.

During the course of 1972 most major currencies were floated with only a minimum of management from their central banks. Shifting trade patterns brought more pressure for flexibility in exchange rates. If these forces in combination had not finished off fixed exchange rates, then the massive oil price rises of 1974 certainly would have.

This is not just ancient history. It is important to remember *why* fixed exchange rates ceased to work well. As the world shifts gradually away from floating rates in the search for greater stability, we should remember what problems fixed rates can bring.

Floating exchange rates

The great advantage which floating rates have (in theory) is that they allow the balance of payments to adjust automatically to change. If imports grow faster than exports, the supply of currency grows, there is exchange rate **depreciation**, imports become dearer and exports become cheaper. The country becomes more competitive. After a time lag, imports will fall and exports will rise. The current account deficit will be automatically eliminated. The reverse process occurs if there is a current account surplus.

The big problem with floating rates is, of course, instability. Traders cannot predict the price at which they will be doing business in the future. Risks are greater and some deals may, as a result, not take place. Economic activity is inhibited. Forward markets develop, in which currency can be bought forward (as opposed to spot), that is, a contract is made to exchange currencies at a fixed, agreed price on a certain future date. These reduce the risks somewhat.

Managed exchange rates

A managed exchange rate allows the government to have an exchange rate policy without having to defend its currency if market forces build up strongly. It means that exchange rate policy can be linked to domestic monetary policy. It is possible to keep the exchange rate strong in order to prevent rising import prices. Cheap imports can be used to force domestic producers to cut costs. Equally, if depreciation is judged to be beneficial, it can just be allowed to happen.

Floating exchange rates have not, in fact, eliminated current account surpluses and deficits. This weakens the case for a floating exchange rate policy and makes management of the exchange rate more likely.

Fixing exchange rates in Europe

The exchange rate mechanism (ERM) of the European Monetary System was set up by the EU in 1979 in order to provide greater stability for member currencies. The hope was that predictable exchange rates would make it easier to trade and would reduce uncertainty for businesses. In time, the ERM was transformed into the Economic and Monetary Union. Starting at the beginning of 1999, exchange rates were permanently fixed. The euro becomes the only currency in use from 2002. All EU members have joined except for the UK, Denmark, Greece and Sweden.

In order to be a part of EMU, member countries had to satisfy the convergence criteria. These include the requirement that total government debt be no more than 60 per cent of GDP, and that public borrowing be no more than 3 per cent of GDP in a year. Inflation rates must be within 1.5 per cent of the three member countries with the lowest inflation rates. Long-term interest rates must be no more than 2 per cent above those of the three member countries with the lowest inflation rates. Convergence is needed because otherwise the monetary policy of the eurozone as a whole would cause problems in the country concerned. A high inflation rate would cause the country to become very uncompetitive, quickly reducing aggregate demand and bringing depressed trading conditions.

The European Central Bank (ECB) was set up in Frankfurt. Its governing council takes all decisions relating to interest rates and monetary policy. There is a base rate which operates in a similar way to that of the UK. The governing council includes a representative from each of the eleven members. The ECB has a target ceiling rate for inflation of 2 per cent. Wim Duisenberg, the ECB President, has worked hard to establish the credibility of the ECB, believing that there must be great confidence that it will preserve and enhance financial stability.

For most of 1999, the euro fell against the dollar and there were some fears that it would prove to be a weak currency. Nevertheless it is clear that in terms of world trade, the euro will be a very important currency.

EMU should cement the single market. It had become clear that the 'level playing field' could not be completely level unless member countries were part of a fully unified economy. The euro will probably bring that into being.

A change of interest rates at the ECB

The European Central Bank yesterday raised interest rates by 0.5 per cent in a move to contain inflation and lay to rest uncertainty over the course of monetary policy.

The increase, the first since the euro's launch, took the ECB's refinancing rate to 3 per cent.

Financial markets had anticipated the ECB's move, which reversed a reduction by 0.5 per cent made in April in response to fears of recession and deflation in the eurozone.

Wim Duisenberg, the ECB's President, said the rate rise was intended to counter accelerating private credit and money supply growth, rising industrial producer prices and the possibility of high wage settlements in next year's pay negotiations. 'All indicators point in the direction that the risks on the upside are increasing,' he said.

The ECB signalled in July that it was moving to a tightening bias in its monetary policy, but Ernst Welteke, the new Bundesbank head, was reluctant to support an early rate rise because Germany's economic recovery was less strong than in other eurozone countries, notably France.

Source: *Financial Times*, 5 November 1999

13 What effect would the rate rise have on the eurozone economies?
14 At the time the rate of inflation in the eurozone was 1.2 per cent. Why then did the ECB raise interest rates?
15 Why did Germany not support an interest rate increase the previous July?

KEY POINTS

29.4

■ Fixed exchange rates worked well until 1971, under the Bretton Woods system.

■ Changing inflation rates brought a shift to floating exchange rates.

■ Floating exchange rates are less stable than fixed rates but allow easier adjustment to balance of payments problems.

■ Exchange rates are usually managed by central banks.

■ Exchange rate policy and monetary policy are closely linked.

■ The Economic and Monetary Union (EMU) came into being in 1999. The euro is the second-largest trading currency, after the dollar.

Trade policies

Governments can implement a wide range of policies which affect trade. Exchange rate policy is of course one of these. What else may be important?

Governments may decide that domestic producers require **protectionist policies**: that is, they need to be protected from competition from firms abroad. Quite often there is a debate between those who want to pursue free trade policies, which will encourage more trade and specialization, and those who want to see domestic producers given more protection through import controls. The arguments for and against free trade were dealt with in Chapter 6.

If free trade is the policy of the day, then governments will want to find other ways of helping firms to compete effectively, and they will pursue policies which enhance competitiveness.

Import controls

Protection of domestic markets can be achieved in all sorts of ways: tariffs, quotas, export subsidies, quality regulations and so on. The most important of these are **tariffs** and **quotas**. Tariffs work by imposing a tax on imports, quotas by setting a physical limit on imports.

Figure 29.5 shows how a tariff may affect price and quantity imported. If demand is inelastic, as in 29.5(a), people will carry on importing the item and most of the cost of the tariff will be passed on to the consumer. (The principle is the same as that of tax incidence, which is described in Chapter 9.) The quantity of imports will not fall much, but the government will receive some revenue from the tariff.

If, however, demand is elastic, as in 29.5(b), the tariff will be effective in reducing imports. This is more likely to happen if there is a good domestically produced substitute, that is, precisely the circumstances in which protection is likely to be favoured by the government.

Tariffs have been applied since time immemorial to a wide range of goods.

Quotas work quite differently (Figure 29.6). The physical limit on imports creates a perfectly inelastic supply above the limit. The more inelastic the demand, the more the price will rise. The government gets nothing from this, but the exporter will benefit from it. Sometimes quotas have been introduced under the name of voluntary export restraints (VERs). Governments negotiate with the exporting government, agreeing a limit. Cars, video recorders and textiles have all had VERs at one time or another.

All import controls reduce the level of trade. They raise prices to consumers, reducing the purchasing power of their incomes. They will reduce welfare in the long run, because they inhibit the growth that could ensue from increased specialization, efficiency and trade. They can be used to buy time when structural change is proving painful.

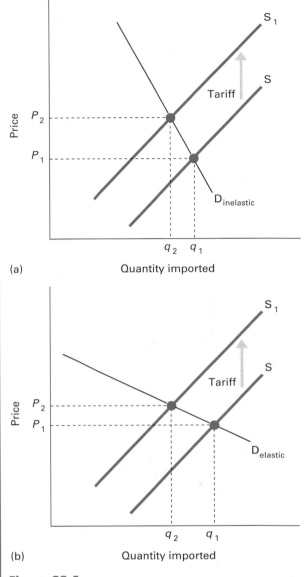

(a)

(b)

Figure 29.5
Tariffs

A tariff shifts the supply curve upwards by the amount of the tax. If it is placed upon a good with inelastic demand, most of the extra cost will be passed on to the consumer, as in (a). If demand is elastic, this will not be possible and the price will rise by much less than the amount of the tariff. The quantity imported will fall significantly.

Controlling import controls

The GATT and the WTO have always opposed quotas altogether. They have always tried to get tariffs reduced by international agreement. Certain kinds of trade restriction are illegal under WTO rules. This is why VERs have become more widespread: because they are voluntary, they are permitted. The exporting country may accept the

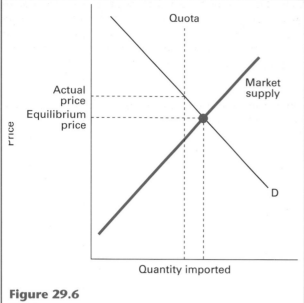

Figure 29.6
Quotas
A quota will raise the price for the consumer and the exporter.

has brought real benefits to developing countries. Their economies have been growing at an average rate of nearly 4 per cent per annum – faster than the developed world. Their exports have risen 6 per cent a year and they need faster growth. The gains have been possible thanks to improved access to the markets of the industrialized world. But that access is limited. That is why we need a new round of negotiations. Measures such as further market opening, reduction of agricultural subsidies, harmonization of rules of origin and the simplification of customs procedures would make it easier and more profitable for developing countries to export.

Source: Clare Short, Secretary of State for International Development, writing in *The Guardian*, 22 November 1999

16 What do developing countries stand to gain from better access to industrialized markets?
17 How might workers in industrialized countries benefit from improved access?
18 All developed countries protect their farmers. Why?
19 What other measures might be required, in addition to trade liberalization, to reduce poverty in developing countries?
20 It has been estimated that restrictions on imports of textiles and clothing have in the past cost a typical UK family £83 per year. How could this have been justified?

necessity for them because it is afraid of more damaging restrictions if it does not.

On the whole, WTO has been highly successful in promoting trade, especially in manufactures. However, many developing countries feel that they have been left out of the benefits that have resulted.

The Minister's view

The developing world cannot escape from poverty unless its economic growth increases year-on-year. Attracting foreign investment is crucial, and so is the ability to gain access to world trade markets.

Some feel better trade access for developing countries will damage jobs at home. Others want to protect poor countries from exposure to multinational capital. Both fears are wrong. It is possible to support jobs at home and promote development for the world's poor through better trading arrangements. More economic growth for them means more trade for all.

Many argue that globalization represents the worst aspects of materialism – a lack of respect for people and the environment – and growing inequality and instability. Some argue that developing countries have not gained from the process so far.

But globalization is unstoppable and some poor countries are benefiting. Our challenge is to manage the process so that the wealth being generated is shared more equally.

The last thirty years has shown that liberalizing trade

Competitiveness

Trade has the potential to raise real incomes. But what happens if a country cannot compete? Then it will suffer from unemployment, and something will have to be done to enhance competitiveness.

One way round this is to allow the currency to depreciate. This will automatically raise import prices and reduce export prices. However, if one objective of government policies is exchange rate stability, it will not be seen as helpful. Within the eurozone, it will be impossible.

How else can competitiveness be increased? All the policies that have been considered elsewhere in this book, which increase productivity, will be useful. Education and training increase human capital. Investment can cut costs. Research and development can lead to new products and new processes, both of which can give producers a competitive edge. Improved management strategies can also be helpful, although it is not always possible for the government to influence them.

The DTI view

Competition has been facilitated in part by reduced communication costs, which have opened up markets to consumers by reducing search costs. International transport costs have fallen for many businesses, while other businesses can deliver their products or services down a phone line. The size of the market available to these companies has correspondingly increased. The ease with which information can be transferred also means that products and processes can be quickly imitated. Knowledge spreads more quickly, making us all better off, but in order to compete a firm needs to innovate more quickly and make use of its distinctive know-how.

Source: *Our Competitive Future: Building the Knowledge-Driven Economy*, White Paper from the Department of Trade and Industry, 1999

21 Explain how new technologies create changing competitive pressures.

22 What are the implications of the above statement for individual firms?

23 What practical measures might currently be useful in increasing competitiveness in the UK?

Balance of payments policies

Dealing with a payments deficit

A current account deficit may be purely short term. Imports and exports fluctuate month by month, and imports could exceed exports for some months or even years before it came to be seen as a serious problem. But a persistent deficit, sometimes known as a fundamental balance of payments disequilibrium, reflects a real imbalance somewhere in the system. There must be some serious difficulty in maintaining competitiveness. A number of policy responses are possible.

A short-run deficit

Quite often, a current account deficit can be balanced by a surplus on capital account. This could mean that foreign investment in the United Kingdom is larger than usual and the inflow of currency can be offset against the outflow of payments for imports. Provided interest rates are high enough to attract lending on the scale required, this kind of short-run finance will plug the gap. So initially, raising interest rates may be an appropriate policy response.

A long-run deficit

Foreign creditors will lend for quite a while to a country with a current account deficit and an attractive interest rate. But eventually they will begin to suspect that the debtor country does not have the ability to repay. At this point they may panic and sell currency before it is too late. If many people panic there will be a currency crisis, and a very sharp depreciation will take place over the space of just a few days.

Of course, this may be exactly what is needed to restore competitiveness. Depending on the exchange rate regime, we use different language to describe the situation. Under fixed rates, market forces may be such that the central bank can no longer defend the currency and the fixed exchange rate will be devalued. Alternatively, the exchange rate may be maintained by the central bank at its high level, but reserves will fall sharply. Loans may be arranged through official financing, usually from friendly central banks in other countries. These loans, it is hoped, will restore confidence in the currency and allow time for other measures to work.

Under a floating exchange rate, there will be a depreciation.

Expenditure-switching policies

Expenditure-switching policies work by shifting expenditure away from foreign-produced goods towards domestically produced goods. This could happen by means of a devaluation (under fixed exchange rates), or under floating rates the government and central bank may simply allow the exchange rate to fall. Then imports will be dearer, so demand will fall and spending on foreign goods will decrease. There will be increased demand for domestically produced substitutes. Export prices will fall and demand and sales will rise. Expenditure switching takes place.

There is another way of bringing about expenditure switching. Tariffs, quotas and other import controls make imports dearer. They protect domestic producers. To the extent that imports are reduced and demand turns towards domestic products, there is expenditure switching.

Expenditure-reducing policies

Imports generally depend on the level of income, and they tend to have a high income elasticity of demand. **Expenditure-reducing policies** (tax increases, government expenditure cuts, high interest rates) reduce income and aggregate demand. They lead to falling imports. They also lead to falling demand for domestic output. Faced with falling sales, firms which can export will pursue export markets with increased vigour. Contractionary policies reduce spending and in so doing lead to an improvement in a current account deficit.

The only problem is that expenditure-reducing policies are not popular. They reduce incomes. They tend to inhibit economic growth. Unemployment may rise.

Policy packages

Single policies usually work less well than combinations. Supposing a depreciation takes place. There is increased aggregate demand and expansion follows. What happens if the economy is close to full capacity output? There will be excess demand, overheating and accelerating inflation. The recently gained competitiveness will be lost.

Conclusion: If depreciation or devaluation are accompanied by expenditure-reducing policies, the increase in foreign demand will be offset by a decrease in domestic demand. Excess demand can be avoided. The UK was lucky in 1992 when the pound was taken out of the ERM and promptly fell: the economy was still stuck in recession and there was plenty of spare capacity.

If depreciation is felt to be impossible, high interest rates will attract capital and then slow the economy down so as to remove inflationary pressure. The most important aspect of policy will then be measures which improve productivity and therefore competitiveness.

Current trends

Current account imbalances have caused less trouble in recent years than in the past. The increased integration of world capital markets has meant that deficits can be financed more easily with foreign loans.

Furthermore, the growth of multinational enterprises has meant that production may often be integrated across national boundaries. You may be importing a Volvo, but perhaps 40 per cent of it will be UK made. This will increase trade figures as some parts of the product will have crossed a national border several times.

At the time of writing, it is hard to say how EMU will work out. It is even harder to decide whether the UK will join within the foreseeable future. If so, UK exporters and importers will probably appreciate the stability and convenience. But the necessary political consensus may not emerge. The debate may run and run.

KEY POINTS

29.5

- Import controls can be used to protect domestic producers from foreign competition.

- Tariffs are a tax on imports and raise the price of imported goods to consumers.

- Quotas impose a physical limit on the quantity of certain imported goods, and usually lead to higher prices.

- The World Trade Organization (WTO) exists to keep trade restrictions to a minimum.

- Governments may try to improve competitiveness with a range of policies designed to increase efficiency.

- A short-run current account deficit may be financed by borrowing foreign currency, usually from banks.

- A persistent deficit may require expenditure-switching policies, or expenditure-reducing policies, or a combination of the two.

- Expenditure switching can be achieved by exchange rate depreciation or by import controls.

- Expenditure-reducing policies reduce income by increasing taxes or interest rates, or cutting government expenditure, or all of these.

Case Study

The promise behind the euro threat

For the small and medium-sized businesses that have sprung up and flourished since the mid-1980s, the arrival of the single currency presents the greatest threat and the greatest opportunity. Which of these two options it will turn out to be is in the hands of each of them. Their future will rest on the extent to which they anticipate and prepare for the changes that are coming. Those changes will come whether we adopt the single currency or not. And that is why it is right for managers now to prepare for probably the greatest overnight change in our trading conditions that we have ever faced.

You can see the dawning of what it all means in industry. No, I'm not talking about the clearly expounded warnings from Jack Nasser, the head of Ford, that investment planning, with all the job implications that means, could be diverted from the UK to the mainland if Britain distances itself from Europe. That is dangerous enough – but alongside that, and adding to it, is the threat to our smaller companies. Just one example: one euro, one sta-

ble currency. One pound, different value euro. Every day a new VAT calculation to reflect the fluctuating exchange rate to keep Customs and Excise rules. Wait till the small companies take that on board.

We have heard incessantly about high-cost Europe, unemployed Europe, over-regulated Europe, and there is much in those arguments. What we are only now beginning to hear is about cheaper Europe. For all their high social costs, regulations and protective instincts, they manage to provide for their consumers products at least the equal of ours in quality but at cheaper prices. They do so, of course, because they have invested more and achieved higher productivity. They have a better long-term inflation record than we do and consequently interest rates are close to half ours, making investment easier to justify. And most of their economies are faster-growing than ours.

Put all that on one side. The single currency is going to open the floodgates of choice. Hidden today behind the familiar currencies of their own countries, consumers buy where they understand. But when, in a couple of years' time, these national currencies disappear, and one single currency replaces them, a tide of transparency will sweep the continent. British companies will have to compete in euros. That means pricing in euros and being paid in euros. The market will demand it. Companies that resist will swiftly lose business.

Source: Michael Heseltine, writing in *Management Today*, November 1999

1 What likely benefits could membership of EMU bring to the UK?
2 How can we be sure that the euro will be a stable currency?
3 What are the drawbacks to UK membership?
4 What is the current business view of this controversy?
5 What has happened since this was written?

Exam Preparation

Multiple choice questions

1 If there were an excessive outflow of sterling from the UK, which of the following would you expect to occur?
   A a rise in the exchange value of the £
   B a fall in the exchange value of the £
   C an upward revaluation of sterling

   D an improvement in the UK's terms of trade
   E a fall in interest rates

2 A rise in the market price of imported goods may be the result of
   A the introduction of import quotas
   B a rise in UK interest rates
   C a rise in the sterling exchange rate
   D overseas suppliers increasing productivity

3 A substantial rise in UK interest rates is likely to result in
   A a permanent increase in the money supply
   B a fall in the rate of growth of gross domestic product
   C an increase in the level of investment
   D a fall in the foreign exchange value of the pound sterling

4 The establishment of a monetary union between countries, such as the Economic and Monetary Union, requires
   A convergence of their macroeconomic policies
   B increased flexibility in their monetary policy
   C increased reliance on devaluation to deal with short-term economic difficulties
   D the imposition of a national minimum wage

5 Two countries, X and Y, use interest rate policy to maintain their exchange rates within set margins. Country X's currency is expected to depreciate in relation to country Y's.

   What will be the relationship between the two countries' interest rates?
   A Country X's interest rate will be higher to compensate for the added risk of holding its currency.
   B Country X's interest rate will be higher to increase the supply of its currency on foreign exchange markets.
   C Country X's interest rate will be lower to avoid an outflow of capital.
   D Country X's interest rate will be lower to reduce the growth of its domestic money supply.

Essay questions

1 (a) Examine the benefits to a country of being a member of a monetary union.
  (b) Outline two ways in which joining a monetary union imposes constraints on the government's macroeconomic policy options.

2 Will a depreciation of the exchange rate necessarily improve the balance of trade of an economy?

3 (a) What may cause a rise in the external value of a country's currency?
  (b) What may be the likely economic consequences of such a rise for your country?

4 (a) Explain why one would expect the Uruguay Round of trade negotiations to have had an impact on specialization and on international trade.

   (b) (i) Why might there be gainers and losers from such a reduction in protectionism?
       (ii) Identify the likely gainers and losers.

5 Evaluate the extent to which the EU encourages free trade:
   (a) between member countries, and
   (b) between member countries and the rest of the world.

6 (a) Explain how changes in the external value of the pound (the exchange rate) affect the volume and value of UK exports.
  (b) Discuss other factors which influence the sales of UK products in overseas markets.

7 (a) Examine the costs and benefits for firms and consumers of a country being part of a free trade area.
  (b) What might be the economic advantages and disadvantages for a member of the EU which does not join the Economic and Monetary Union?

8 (a) What are the benefits of international trade?
  (b) Discuss whether or not the formation of trading blocs such as the EU contributes to an increase in economic welfare.

9 Between 1990 and 1996 the value of the UK's exports of goods rose by about 63 per cent and the value of its imports rose by about 48 per cent.
   (a) Analyse the factors which might have contributed to these increases in (i) the value of the UK's exports and (ii) the value of its imports.
   (b) How might this increase in the value of the UK's exports have affected the level of economic activity?

30

Economic development

In our final chapter we discuss economic growth with particular reference to countries such as the United Kingdom. In the present chapter we examine the same topic in relation to those countries in the world that are not yet developed. Here we enter the study of economic development. It is hard for us to realize that what we consider a low level of income in the United Kingdom exceeds the average income in a good part of the world. In fact, many of the world's people live at or close to subsistence: just enough to eat for survival. Developed nations encounter problems associated with being relatively rich such as obesity, urban sprawl and pollution. The **less-developed countries** (LDCs) or developing countries are grappling with abject poverty and squalor; in short, with mere existence. Can governments do more to assist such countries? Before considering this we must first examine the nature of developing countries and consider why some countries are more developed than others.

LEARNING OUTCOMES

On completing this chapter you should understand:

■ How to define a developing country

■ Non-monetary indicators of human development

■ The development process

■ The development goals and strategies facing developing countries

■ The role of international trade to developing countries

■ The role of private capital and official aid flows

Defining a developing country

There have been a number of ways of classifying nations by level of economic development. The 'three worlds' classification scheme was once much quoted but, for reasons that will become clear, has now lost much of its relevance. The **First World** referred to the highly industrialized, non-communist Western European nations, plus the United States, Australia, Canada, New Zealand and Japan. The **Second World** included the nations of Eastern Europe and the Soviet Union. The **Third World** was the term given to identify most remaining countries, that is, in Africa, Asia and Latin America. But this classification of the globe has as much a political dimension to it as economic. Given the changes in Eastern Europe and the collapse of communism that we noted in Chapter 2, the distinctive identity of the Second World has almost disappeared. A more basic distinction can be made between mainly developed countries situated in the northern hemisphere – 'the North' – and those countries which are less developed and are located below the Equator – 'the South'. The rich North–poor South distinction is necessarily a crude one but still begs the question: what is the definition by which a country is deemed developed rather than developing?

Economists have traditionally used a cut-off point in gross national product (GNP) data to make this distinction. The precise figure used is of course quite an arbitrary one. In 1999 the World Bank defined sixty-three low-income developing countries as those with a per capita income of less than $760 in 1998. Ninety-four economies were distinguished as middle-income economies with GNP per head between $761 and $9360. (Fifty-four further economies were defined as high-income economies with GNP of $9361 or more.)

Table 30.1 identifies those countries where the World Bank calculated that in 1998 the gross national product per capita data were the lowest of 210 countries. The so-called

'Atlas' method of calculating GNP per capita converts national currency data into dollars at prevailing exchange rates adjusted for inflation and averaged over three years. With reference to India, we can thus compare India's GNP with that of the United States. How?

We need a common unit of measurement. Translating all the GNP data into one country's currency seems to solve this problem. As we have just seen, the World Bank uses dollars as this common currency. Thus India's GNP in terms of dollars is measured as follows:

$$\frac{\text{India's GNP per capita in rupees}}{\text{India's exchange rate between rupees and dollars}} = \frac{\text{India's GNP per capita in dollars}}{}$$

The calculation implies that the foreign exchange rate is an international barometer of the cost of living. But a few moments' reflection should make you realize that the exchange rate is determined by the supply of and demand for international currency. Some items of consumer spending do not enter into world trade, for example going to a disco, getting a haircut. Thus our GNP data expressed in dollars (or pounds sterling) present an imperfect picture of the actual cost of living throughout the world. You can see this with respect to just one product if you turn back to the exercise on the price of a McDonald's Big Mac in a number of countries (Chapter 6, page 97). The data for 1994 showed that a dollar did not buy the same amount of hamburgers in each of the ten countries. This exercise is an approach to what economists call **purchasing power parity** (PPP). It involves establishing the cost of a common basket of goods and services purchased in various countries. Using the PPP basis of determining gross domestic product (GDP) results in lowering the share of world output produced by the developed economies compared with converting each country's GDP using market exchange rates.

The world's poorest countries

Table 30.1 depicts those economies which are at one end of a spectrum of just over 200 in the world.

1 What is apparent about the location of most of these economies?

2 What is depressing about their recent economic growth record?

3 Does the calculation of GNP by the PPP method significantly alter their world ranking as compared with the Atlas method?

Table 30.1 focuses on GNP in particular countries. An alternative approach is to ask the question: 'Where do most of the world's poorest peoples live?'. Figure 30.1 provides the answer based on estimates by the World Bank.

Table 30.1

The low-income economies

Countries in descending rank order (according to GNP per capita in 1998 – column 4)	Population millions in 1998	GNP billions of dollars	GNP per capita			GNP per capita measured at PPP	
			Dollars	Rank	% average annual real growth 1990–7	billions of dollars	Rank
Ethiopia	61	6.1	100	210	2.2	500	208
Congo, Dem. Rep. of	48	5.3	110	209	–9.6	750	200
Burundi	7	0.9	140	206	–5.9	620	207
Sierra Leone	5	0.7	140	206	–5.7	390	210
Niger	10	1.9	190	204	–1.9	830	198
Eritrea	4	0.8	200	202	–2.9	950	193
Malawi	11	2.1	200	202	–0.8	730	203
Nepal	23	4.8	210	199	–2.2	1090	189
Mozambique	17	3.6	210	199	–2.6	850	196
Tanzania	32	6.7	210	199		490	209
Rwanda	8	1.9	230	197	–5.7	690	206
Chad	7	1.7	230	197	–1.0	na	na
Burkina Faso	11	2.6	240	196	–0.8	1020	191
Mali	11	2.6	250	194	–0.3	720	204
Madagascar	15	3.8	260	193	–1.6	900	194
Cambodia	11	3.0	280	191	–2.7	1240	184

Note: The rankings are based on 210 economies. For some economies there is incomplete data. Small countries with a population below 1.5 million are separately classified by the World Bank.

Source: World Bank, *World Development Report*, 1999–2000 and *World Bank Atlas*, 1999

Twelve countries accounted for 80 per cent of the world's poor in 1993

Cumulative % in poverty

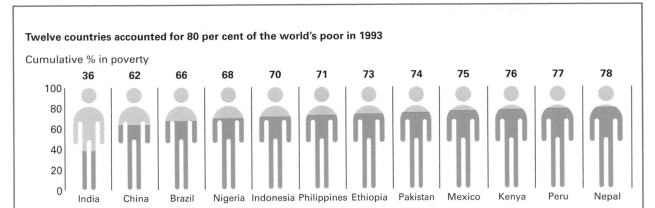

Note: The figure shows countries with more than 10 million people in poverty and for which comparable data are available. Data for Bangladesh and the Democratic Republic of Congo are not available, but they are included in world estimates.

International comparisons of extreme poverty are based on a common international poverty line of $1 a person a day, expressed in 1985 international prices and adjusted to local currencies using purchasing power parity exchange rates. Most countries have their own poverty lines based on local views of minimum socially acceptable living standards.

Figure 30.1
Locating the world's poor

Source: World Bank

---

4 How does study of the countries in Figure 30.1 give a different view on the world's poorest countries as compared with that posed in question 1?

But whatever measure we use, it is now evident that, taken as a group, developing countries account for a growing proportion of world output. In 1984 their share was 34 per cent compared to 57 per cent for all industrial countries. By 1994 the LDC share had risen to 40 per cent and is expected to rise further to 48 per cent by 2004. The forecast share of industrial countries for 2004 is 47 per cent, eight percentage points lower than in 1994: the tiny 5 per cent proportion accounted for by the Eastern European countries in transition that we identified in Chapter 2 is not expected to alter between 1994 and 2004, a reflection of their economic difficulties we noted in Figure 2.5 on page 36.

Figure 30.2 shows the World Bank's forecasts of economic growth for six different parts of the world. The forecasts indicate that the **emerging economies** of East Asia are expected to form the world's fastest-growing regional group of developing countries in the next decade.

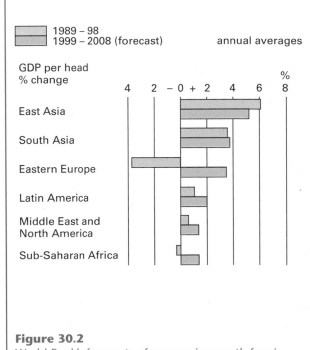

Figure 30.2
World Bank's forecasts of economic growth for six different parts of the world

Source: World Bank

KEY POINTS

30.1

■ Any definition of a less-developed country (LDC) is arbitrary. There were sixty countries where GNP per capita was less than $760 in 1998.

■ LDCs can also be defined in terms of so-called non-monetary indicators such as their levels of literacy, education, infant mortality and life expectancy.

Measuring human development

GDP data do not provide a precise picture of the welfare of the people of the world, however, as we indicated in Chapter 13. For some years now economists have tried to establish the extent to which so-called **non-monetary indicators** correlate with GDP data in portraying relative living standards. In 1990 the United Nations Development Programme (UNDP) introduced a Human Development Index (HDI) which combined indicators of the PPP measurement of GNP, health (life expectancy) and education (years of schooling, adult literacy) as a more comprehensive measurement of development than GNP data alone. Since 1990 *Human Development Reports* have been published on an annual basis, just like the World Bank's *World Development Reports*.

The HDI in all developing countries is about half that in the industrial countries but varies considerably between continents. Of the 174 countries for which the HDI was constructed for 1997, 45 were in the high human development category (HDI of 0.8 or greater); 94 in the medium human development category (0.5 to 0.79) and 35 in the low human development category (below 0.5). Figure 30.3 shows the spread of HDI values across the globe. Canada, Norway and the United States were at the top of the HDI rankings; Sierra Leone, Niger and Ethiopia at the bottom. Canada's HDI value of 0.932 was more than three times that of Sierra Leone's 0.254. On the basis of the HDI, Canada's shortfall in human development was thus about 7 per cent, whereas it was one of 75 per cent in the case of Sierra Leone. On the basis of the 1997 values of HDI, 92 countries ranked higher on the HDI than on GDP per capita measured at PPP. But for 77 countries the HDI rank was lower than the GDP per capita ranking. The UNDP regard the 92 countries as having been effective in converting their national income position into a more satisfactory state of human development. However, for the 77 countries the lower ranking of HDI relative to GDP per capita implies that the monetary measure of development has not effectively been translated into a better living standard for the average citizen in those countries.

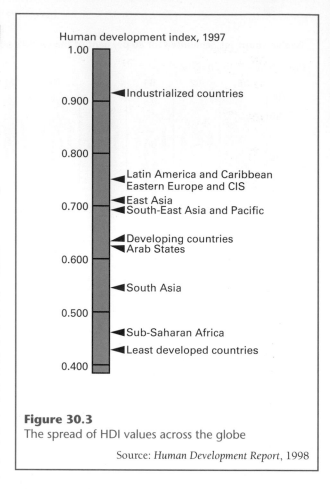

Figure 30.3
The spread of HDI values across the globe

Source: *Human Development Report*, 1998

Figure 30.4 shows a comparison between Sri Lanka and the Ivory Coast (Côte d'Ivoire).

Two countries compared

5 How do these data illustrate the UNDP's conclusion that 'the link between economic prosperity and human development is neither automatic nor obvious'?

6 How might the data suggest that a country's HDI value is crucially determined by policy measures taken by government rather than by something outside a government's control?

7 The UNDP view the HDI as a more comprehensive index than per capita income. With reference to the data, explain its conclusion that 'income is only a means to human development, not an end'.

Between 1975 and 1997 most countries achieved a higher HDI value. Indonesia, Egypt and Swaziland were the developing countries with the fastest rise in the HDI after 1975. Only one country had a lower HDI in 1997 than in 1975: this was Zambia, largely as a result of the impact of HIV/AIDS on life expectancy.

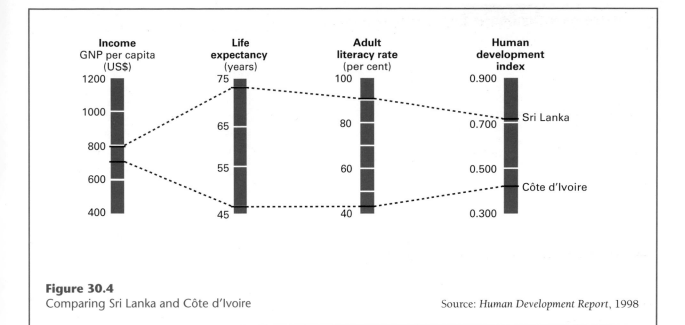

Figure 30.4
Comparing Sri Lanka and Côte d'Ivoire

Source: *Human Development Report*, 1998

The HDI is a national average just like one of its components, real income per head. As with any national statistic, there will be a range of values depending on the distribution of income, the locality and any disparity in income between males and females. Since 1997 the UNDP has also calculated a Human Poverty Index (HPI) as a more ambitious measure of poverty. It is a composite index of deprivation in several dimensions of human life – a long and healthy life, knowledge and economic provisioning. The first of these four aspects in developing countries is measured by the percentage of people not expected to survive to age 40. The second measure of deprivation is measured by illiteracy. Economic provision is calculated by the percentage of people lacking access to health services and safe water, together with the percentage of children under five who are moderately or severely under-weight. The UNDP has also adjusted the HDI values for gender inequality to produce a gender development index (GDI). This gender index focuses on women's opportunities as reflected in the number of seats in national parliaments held by women and also the proportion of female administrators. Predictably, the HPI and GDI reveal that there are both disparities between and within countries, and in particular a marked urban–rural divide in many developing countries.

Table 30.2

Human welfare in 15 countries

Nation	GNP per capita ($), 1997	Life expectancy of males at birth (years), 1996	Infant mortality rate per 1000, 1996	Access to health care (% population), 1990–5
Ethiopia	110	48	177	46
Malawi	220	43	217	35
Burkina Faso	240	45	158	90
Bangladesh	270	57	112	45
Haiti	330	54	130	60
Kenya	330	57	90	77
Ghana	370	57	110	60
India	390	62	85	85
Nicaragua	410	65	57	83
Lesotho	670	57	113	80
Côte d'Ivoire	690	53	150	30
Sri Lanka	800	71	19	93
China	860	68	39	88
Ecuador	1590	67	40	88
Mexico	3680	69	36	93

Sources: *World Development Report*, 1998/99; *Human Development Report*, 1998

Human welfare in developing countries

8 To what extent could one conclude that the standard of living for the average citizen in, say, Nicaragua was twice that of his or her counterpart in Malawi? Is the average Chinese citizen four times better off than the average person in Malawi?

9 Explain why a relationship between per capita income (column 1) and life expectancy (column 2) might be expected.

10 Examine factors that might account for the differences in life expectancy and infant mortality rates.

11 Why might expenditure on health care in developing countries be justified as one form of investment spending?

The development process

How does economic development happen? This seemingly innocently put question is in practice a difficult one to answer quite so briefly! At the outset of this book we stressed the relevance of capital accumulation. In Chapter 1 we noted the trade-off between current consumption and capital goods. We showed how in Figure 1.5 spending on capital goods can lead to greater production of consumer goods in the future. Economic development can be seen as a pushing-out of the production possibilities curve. In Chapter 2 we noted how Adam Smith saw how private enterprise could promote the growth of an economy. In Chapter 4 we again referred to Adam Smith and the way in which he saw the division of labour as leading to enhanced efficiency in production. Adam Smith may indeed be seen as 'the father of economic development' in bringing together the roles of capital accumulation, the division of labour and technical progress as sources of economic development. Smith's optimism about the prospects of cumulative economic development was not shared by later classical economists such as David Ricardo and Thomas Malthus, who were also referred to earlier in this book. We also noted briefly how Karl Marx expected the capitalist system eventually to collapse. What Marx shared with other theorists is a recognition of the relevance of technical progress. However, in Marx's case he saw this as a key factor in the way the capitalist class would ultimately bring about its own downfall.

In Part C of this book we saw how Keynes pointed out how the neo-classical economists assumed full employment as the norm. He was able to underline the role of private investment in accounting for the instability of a private enterprise economy around the potential role of counter-cyclical government policies. Economists after Keynes thus saw the need to work out how the Keynesian concepts of the multiplier and the accelerator could be modelled to achieve full employment such that aggregate expenditure equated with the growth of output brought about by net new investment. Prominent among these theorists were Evsey Domar and Roy Harrod, whose separate work is frequently referred to as the **Harrod–Domar growth model**. The Harrod–Domar model views an economy growing with reference to a (stable) capital–output ratio and the propensity to save. The capital–output ratio relates to the amount of capital required to raise output by one unit. Thus if there are 4 units of capital needed to increase the level of output by 1 unit, then the capital–output ratio is 4:1. The Harrod–Domar approach led to economists seeing growth of an economy as being therefore crucially determined by how much the stock of physical capital – machinery, equipment – could be enhanced by the savings available. However, in the last half of the twentieth century evidence emerged that economic development was frequently greater than was explainable by extra physical capital investment. Economists thus developed an interest in human capital, as we noted in Chapter 11. Nevertheless, it appears that even with the addition of human capital the record of economic development cannot easily be accounted for, as Figure 30.5 shows with regard to South Korea's recent growth relative to Ghana. What, therefore, is missing in explaining 'the residual' part of economic growth not due to physical and human capital?

It appears that technical progress remains a key factor, itself promoted by knowledge and scientific discovery. What this all means is that economists still do not have a general theory of economic development that can enable governments and international bodies such as the World Bank to programme faster development with reference to a clear, predetermined model that will guarantee an intended outcome. This is rather disappointing, but a brief look at the world makes the idea of treating every country as the same obviously suspect.

We indicated at the start of this chapter that the term 'three worlds' was now rather questionable. In part this is because, as we noted, the 'Second World' countries in Eastern Europe have now abandoned a command economy and are in transition to developing the characteristics of a market economy. But there is a further objection in using the term 'Third World'. The concept of the Third World is rather vague, because it masks a marked variation. It lumps together countries that are very different, not only in economic terms but also in cultural, political, racial and ethnic terms. A number of geographic regions and social classes within the Third World have living standards that are closer to those of Western Europe than to those of other Third World countries. Consider the oil states, for example. Those countries are normally classified as Third World countries, yet the total output per person in the United Arab Emirates in 1998 was $18 220. These figures can be compared with $21 400 for the United Kingdom, $29 340 for the United States and $40 080 for Switzerland!

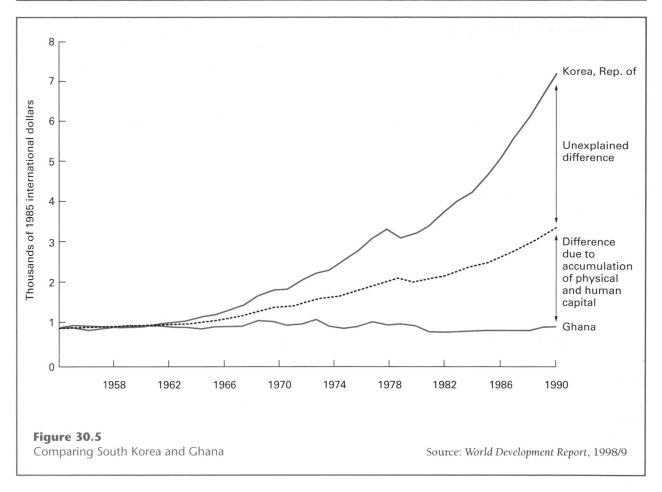

Figure 30.5
Comparing South Korea and Ghana

Source: *World Development Report*, 1998/9

Some LDCs have developed so rapidly that they have come to be termed **newly industrializing economies**. Such countries as Mexico, Brazil, South Korea and Malaysia now provide increasingly stiff competition for firms in the manufacturing sectors of the older industrialized countries of Western Europe and the United States.

One can identify rather different problems in each of the three continents of Latin America, Africa and South Asia. In Latin America many economists see the unequal distribution of land as a significant problem. It is held that this indicates that incentives to develop agriculture are weak, thus frustrating the growth of agriculture. While many African countries face major pressing problems in feeding their populations, a longer-established constraint on their development has been the relative inefficiency of many institutions within the public sector. It is also unhappily the case that civil wars in several African countries have hampered their economic advance. When one turns finally to South Asia it is, arguably, less easy to generalize about which has been the key constraint on its economic development. Mentioning Sri Lanka, Cambodia, Laos and Vietnam illustrates that wars have, sadly, also been present as in several countries in Africa. However, the sheer pressure of population on available land supplies is one issue facing several Asian countries such as India and Bangladesh. On the other hand, the spectacular economic development of the so-called **Asian tigers** like Singapore and Hong Kong highlights the diversity of economic development in South Asia.

KEY POINTS

30.2

■ The Human Development Index is a composite measure of living standards and shows some marked differences in ranking compared with per capita income rankings.

■ The standards of living within LDCs differ almost as much as the differences between them and the developed countries.

■ Economists recognize the role of physical and human capital but have no general theory of how to promote economic development readily applicable to all countries.

Policy objectives

Economists are now aware of the relevance of objectives of policy other than maximization of the growth rate. Until quite recently, most economists took the view that in a rapidly growing economy the benefits of faster growth would ultimately 'trickle down' throughout all sections of society. Thus economic growth would in due course provide a solution to any problems of unemployment and disparities in income distribution. This optimistic view is now much less popular than it once was. For example, Brazil grew impressively in the twenty-one years of military rule, becoming the eighth largest economy in the Western world. But its rapid economic development left many sections gaining little or no benefit from this very creditable achievement.

Economists have given increased attention to the real meaning of economic development. As the late Dudley Seers once put it, the critical questions in an LDC are as follows.

> What has been happening to poverty? What has been happening to unemployment? What has been happening to inequality? If all three of these have declined from high levels then beyond doubt this has been a period of development for the country concerned. If one or two of these central problems have been growing worse, and especially if all three have, it would be strange to call the result 'development' even if per capita income doubled.

> (D. Seers, 'The meaning of development', Eleventh World Conference of the Society for International Development, New Delhi, 1969, p. 3)

Another economist, the late Mahbub ul Haq (who in 1990 played a key role in developing the Human Development Index), argued that:

> Development goals must be defined in terms of progressive reduction and eventual elimination of malnutrition, disease, illiteracy, squalor, unemployment and inequalities. We were taught to take care of our GNP as this will take care of poverty. Let us now reverse this and take care of poverty as this will take care of the GNP.

> (Mahbub ul Haq, quoted in *New Internationalist*, August 1976)

These views thus challenged the orthodox view that economic development would ultimately achieve its intended objectives of improving living standards. But those concerned with the growing problem of urban unemployment emphasized the pressing need for new job creation. More recently, some economists have argued that those economies with a more equal distribution of income than others can achieve a faster rate of economic growth than those countries where incomes are more unequal. The research evidence is as yet still a matter of debate. However, Dani Rodrik is one economist who claims that the combination of greater income equality and very high

school enrolment ratios has been the crucial factor in accounting for the rapid development of the East Asian countries – the so-called 'Asian tigers'.

Whatever the policy objectives – rapid growth per se, employment creation or a more equal pattern of income distribution – any particular country has to consider priorities relating to different sectors of the economy. Is agriculture to be given the main emphasis so that foreign exchange can be earned from exporting primary products? Or is it thought that there are better prospects in developing a manufacturing sector? Is tourism a relevant candidate for development if neither the primary nor secondary sectors of the economy is considered a promising means of enhanced development? We now briefly consider each of these sectors as possible strategies for development.

Exporting primary products

In Chapter 6 we noted the gains from international trade if countries specialize in the production of goods in which they enjoy a comparative advantage. Given their relative abundance of land, this would point to LDCs being exporters of primary products exchanged for manufactures and capital equipment. Indeed, many of today's independent countries were sources of raw materials and foodstuffs in former colonial days. But these countries are now able to determine their own economic policy and have expressed reservations about the wisdom of specializing in primary production. They have grounds for their hesitation in relying on international exchange based on primary products to spur economic development. Why is this? Several LDCs rely on a single commodity for more than half their export earnings. This marked dependence requires broadly stable market conditions for such reliance on one commodity not to cause problems. If for whatever reason export earnings fluctuate, then the whole economy is affected. Why should there be fluctuations in these earnings? A key problem is that, because both supply and demand are insensitive with respect to price, commodity prices fluctuate much more than in the case of manufactured goods. In Chapter 9 we saw that this prompted efforts by governments to try to stabilize agricultural prices in developed economies. Thus, later in this chapter, we shall need to reconsider how LDCs can try to stabilize the prices of tea, coffee and copper on the world's commodity markets.

A further problem facing some commodity producers is that scientific advance has promoted the development of synthetic substitutes for natural products. Rising prices for products like rubber and copper prompt a search in the West for more stable sources of raw materials which is not abandoned with any subsequent decline in price of the natural product. Sisal is another example of a natural product that has faced the problem of a synthetic substitute. Furthermore, technological progress in the broadest sense is reducing the volume of metals used. Goods such as radios and computers have become smaller and use fewer materials per unit weight than before. Foodstuffs are now packed in lighter and thinner cans than a decade or so ago, resulting in a reduction in the demand for tin.

In Chapter 9 we pointed out that the income elasticity of demand for foodstuffs is typically below unity. This means that the demand for foodstuffs shows very little significant growth as time goes by. Indeed, in a country like the United States, it has reached virtual saturation. The concern over obesity in Western Europe is encouraging the demand for 'healthy' foods which may be based on synthetic sources. This situation is hardly encouraging for the sugar-cane producers in the Third World! Furthermore, the growth in the market due to population increases in the developed economies does not provide any sales expansion in commodity markets in terms of volume.

In Chapter 6 we defined the relationship between a country's average export prices and its average import prices as the terms of trade. Falling commodity prices have left many LDCs with a worsening terms of trade situation in recent years.

Given these depressing factors at work it should not surprise you that LDCs have for many years sought to stabilize world commodity prices. They have seen international commodity agreements (ICAs) as a means of effecting this objective. While these are simple in concept they have proved difficult to implement. ICAs are in essence the buffer stock schemes that we examined in Chapter 9 on a world scale. ICAs require agreement between producing countries and importers: the interests of the producers and importers conflict in determining what price the buffer stock should try to maintain by support buying. If it is decided that the buffer stock should try to set a price which proves to be above the long-run free-market price level, it needs unlimited funds to keep up the regulated price (as was found with the Tin Agreement in 1985). In 1989 the International Coffee Agreement collapsed because of the differing interests of producing and consuming countries. The International Cocoa Agreement had previously failed. Was the aim of such agreements to stabilize prices around the long-term market trend or to raise returns to growers as a form of aid to producing countries? When commodity prices rise sharply, consuming countries have a keen interest in 'stability', but when they are declining such countries have little incentive to accept regulated market prices. Ambitious plans in the mid-1970s for an integrated programme of buffer stocks for a wide range of commodities financed from a common fund failed to get beyond the discussion stage. They have thus not achieved the goal of what LDCs see as being needed – a new international economic order, that is, a recasting of the whole basis of international exchange between rich and poor countries.

The African problem

The decline in African agriculture is partly self-induced but can also partly be blamed on the rich industrialized countries. North America, Western Europe and Japan practise relatively free trade in the manufactured goods and services in which they have a comparative advantage but remain determinedly protectionist about food, a sector in which African countries offer competitive products at attractive prices. Their tariff and non-tariff barriers to agricultural trade include duties, quotas, subsidies to domestic producers and complex health and safety regulations.

The United States protects its sugar, tobacco and groundnut growers, its ranchers and dairy farmers. The European Union will not allow free trade in agricultural products that compete with those of its member states, notably wine, citrus fruits, tobacco, vegetable oils and tomatoes. Japan so protects its beef farmers and rice growers that Japanese shoppers have to pay a multiple of the world price for their products. The periodic dumping of milk powder, wheat, beef and other European and American food surpluses on African markets ruins prices for local farmers. The agencies and consultancies that advise African governments too often make things worse by arrogantly assuming that traditional African ways are useless and Western methods are invariably superior. Africa's capacity to feed itself has been further damaged by an intellectual bias in the industrialized countries against subsistence agriculture.

Malawi made it hard for its smallholders to profit from growing the most lucrative crops. It required them to sell their tobacco to a state-owned agricultural marketing board. Such state-owned marketing companies have long been a major problem for African agriculture. Inefficiencies in agriculture are not tolerable given Africa's desperate food supply situation. Neither are over-valued exchange rates, export taxes on agricultural commodities or price controls on food, which keep urban consumers' grocery bills artificially low. Governments can no longer count on a world food surplus to shield them from the consequences of policy mistakes and bureaucratic bungles.

12 To what extent are sub-Saharan African countries more adversely affected by policies in the industrialized countries than by inappropriate policies that they themselves have pursued?

13 How do over-valued exchange rates have an adverse effect on food supplies?

14 Why do African governments impose taxes on exports of agricultural commodities?

15 What is the rationale of controls on domestic food prices?

Industrialization through import substitution

The worries of today's LDCs concerning world trade as an engine of growth are not new. Latin American countries found that the 1930s Depression had a devastating impact on their export earnings. When Brazil experienced a fall in revenues by one-half, it is not surprising that it did not wish to contemplate this experience for a second time. Thus countries such as Brazil, Chile and Argentina resolved to become less dependent on external demand for their coffee, copper and beef. They decided to build up manufacturing industries behind high tariff walls. Imported consumer goods were thus made uncompetitive and domestic manufacture was given encouragement through the process of **import substitution**. The rationale was not only understandable given the situation of the 1930s but could draw support from the **infant industry** case for temporary protection that we noted in Chapter 6. The problem in practice has come to be that the growth of the infants has not always been healthy. Behind high tariffs and import quotas the pressures to become efficient are weak. The opportunity costs incurred in terms of resource use have in some cases been enormous. Thus, on the one hand, we can appreciate that the Ricardian theory of comparative advantage that we saw in Chapter 6 is set in a static context. It follows that LDCs may reject its message on the grounds that they wish to *develop* a comparative advantage and not just accept that they are forever condemned just to be purveyors of fuels and foodstuffs and never participants in manufacturing or services. But, on the other hand, grossly inefficient production of manufactured goods involves a misallocation of *today's* resources which cannot be easily discounted.

The import substitution policies in Latin American countries like Brazil in the 1930s have come to be called an **inward-looking development strategy**. By this is meant that countries looked to greater self-sufficiency and self-reliance rather than relying on growth impulses based on export demand. In contrast, an **outward-looking development strategy** is one which seeks to gain the full benefits of international exchange whether in trade, capital or technology. It welcomes foreign investment rather than being hostile to it. Those economists who favour an outward-looking development strategy are in sharp contrast with other economists who doubt the beneficial effects of international trade.

The **trade pessimists** point to the factors appearing to limit the extent to which LDCs can expect to gain from specializing in primary products, which we noted on page 522. The **trade optimists**, however, argue that export promotion policies can help propel the rate of economic growth. These economists believe that international trade can still be a powerful beneficial force in LDCs rather than a drag on economic progress. The trade optimists see a policy of trade liberalization as allowing competition to perform the role we outlined in Chapter 4. It should improve the process of resource allocation and stimulate

the pressure to achieve efficiency, thus leading to an acceleration in the rate of economic growth.

Inward-looking import substitution is no longer fashionable as it was in the early post-war years. The evidence points to gains being reaped by LDCs who positively seek out markets for manufactured goods in which they can enjoy the benefit of relatively low labour costs. During the last two decades the structure of LDC export trade has been changing, with the importance of primary products falling. Manufactures now provide the dynamic element in LDC exports.

During the 1980s the share of manufactured goods in total exports of all LDCs rose sharply from about 15 per cent to about 50 per cent. For some countries in South and East Asia this proportion of manufactures rose to over three-quarters of the total. The strategy of export-oriented industrialization led to rapid growth of the whole economy in the case of South Korea, Hong Kong, Taiwan and Singapore. Whilst these Asian 'tigers' were exceptional cases, it is nonetheless remarkable how many other LDCs showed an ability to increase markedly the proportion of total exports accounted for by manufactures. Examples are Indonesia, Morocco, Tunisia and Thailand. Furthermore, by increasing the proportion of exports of manufacture which were semi-processed or processed, these countries were able to gain the benefit of higher value-added export earnings. There is room for debate whether all LDCs can emulate the dramatic export experience of countries like Singapore and Malaysia in exporting sophisticated electronic and other technically advanced products. Nonetheless, the truly remarkable change in the composition of exports of LDCs within the past two decades provides a much more cheerful outlook for the economic prospects of LDCs based on international exchange. LDCs are no longer mainly dependent on exports of primary commodities. They can now attract investment from multinational corporations if host country governments appear enthusiastic to welcome foreign capital inflows in order to provide jobs and spur economic growth.

Table 30.3 shows the changing map of world manufacturing production.

16 Discuss possible reasons for the rise in the regional share of global manufacturing shown in Table 30.3 accounted for by East Asia.

17 UNIDO suggested that sub-Saharan Africa's static share was due to a combination of inappropriate policies, high transport costs and a huge technology gap compared with 'best practice' manufacturing in East Asia. Why would each of these factors be relevant to frustrate export-led growth of manufactures in Africa?

18 'Labour costs now matter less than its quality.' Discuss this proposition in the context of the global economy.

Table 30.3

World manufacturing production

	1970 (%)	1980 (%)	1990 (%)	1995 (%)	2000 (projection) (%)
Industrialized countries	88.0	82.8	84.2	80.3	71.0
Developing countries	12.0	17.2	15.8	19.7	29.0
of which:					
Latin America	4.7	6.5	4.6	4.6	4.4
North Africa and West Asia	0.9	1.6	1.8	1.9	2.4
South Asia	1.2	1.3	1.3	1.5	1.7
East Asia, including China	4.2	6.8	7.4	11.1	20.0
Sub-Saharan Africa	0.6	0.5	0.3	0.3	0.3

Note: the totals for developing countries have been rounded.
Data source is the United Nations Industrial Development Organization (UNIDO).

Source: *Financial Times*, 27 September 1996

Tourism

For some small island economies tourism seems a self-evident source of earning foreign exchange. The alternatives of being an efficient source of exports of either primary products or manufactures may not be as credible as harnessing their attractions of sandy beaches and a reliable climate. However, tourism may require heavy importation of food and drink to ensure that Western tourists continue to enjoy the lifestyle to which they are accustomed. Moreover, employment in hotels and beach resorts tends to be highly seasonal in a sector which itself tends to suffer from fickle fluctuations in popularity. Hence net foreign exchange earnings and new employment creation may turn out to be much less than suggested by a superficial consideration of tourism's potential. So, like the export of primary commodities or developing a manufacturing sector, there are no easy solutions for a developing country in determining a development strategy.

The benefits of tourism

There is some consensus that crude numbers are not a good indicator of the contribution of tourism to a local economy. The more tourists you have, the more expensive infrastructure you have to provide for them, and the quicker your environment will be degraded past a point of diminishing returns. The Caribbean offers the best testing ground for the effect of tourism on the developing world, since within a small region there are some territories that have encouraged tourism and some that have not. Over the past ten years, whether measured in terms of either economic growth or income per head, the evidence is clear: those that have encouraged tourism have done better. For many Third World countries, natural beauty and exotic culture are the only commodities in which they have a comparative advantage. That does not, however, conclude the matter, for if some countries allow tourism to get out of hand, then environmental degradation will destroy the very prosperity it has created.

Source: *The Economist*, 23 March 1991

19 For which countries do you think it is true that natural beauty and exotic culture are their sources of comparative advantage?
20 What demand-side factors seem to promise a buoyant market for tourism?
21 Why is environmental degradation a key problem in the development of tourism?

KEY POINTS

30.3

- As a broad generalization, there are some discouraging aspects relating to the demand for and supply of primary commodities which make international trade appear an uncertain influence on LDCs.

- The terms of trade have fallen in recent years for many LDCs.

- International commodity agreements have been neither easy to arrange nor free from trouble where they have been introduced.

- The export of manufactures has been a dramatic growth point for many LDCs within the past decade, offsetting the pessimism over the export of primary products.

- Tourism may offer potential for development, but it is not the easy strategy it appears at first sight.

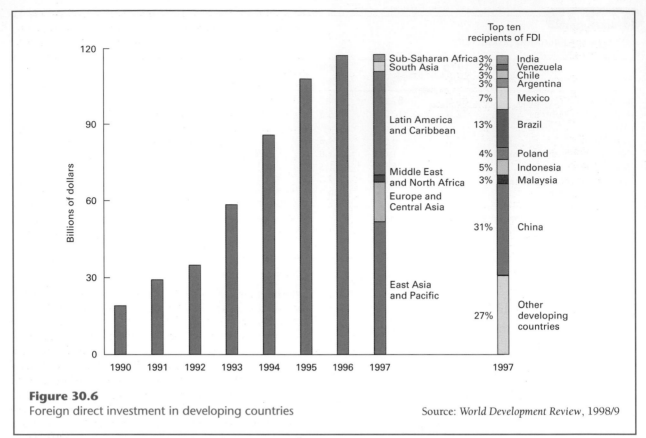

Figure 30.6
Foreign direct investment in developing countries

Source: *World Development Review*, 1998/9

Foreign capital flows

Whatever the choice of strategy a developing country makes, it is highly likely that it will find that investment needs exceed domestic sources for funding those capital requirements. Where can external funds be raised to fill the gap between domestic savings and investment needs? Two possibilities exist. Firstly, to seek profit-seeking capital from multinational firms, and secondly, to seek capital from Western governments on concessionary terms in the form of aid. We now consider both of these potential sources.

Private capital

Figure 30.6 shows how flows of foreign direct investment rose rapidly during the 1990s, but not all developing countries attracted such capital.

Capital inflows

22 Why should China have attracted more foreign direct investment than, say, India?

23 Why has sub-Saharan Africa attracted very little foreign capital inflows?

24 What benefits do multinational corporations (MNCs) enjoy from having interests in different parts of the world?

25 What non-economic factors may deter MNCs from investing in some developing countries?

26 To what extent would you expect that investment by multinationals in developing countries might have an impact on employment in the industrialized countries where MNCs are based?

Capital from governments: official aid

The developed economies can assist LDCs through funds from their government, that is, aid or (to use its proper name) official development assistance. This, as its name implies, is help that rich countries can bring to poor countries so as to augment their sparse sources of domestic finance. However, despite the call from LDCs for rich nations to make contributions equal to 0.7 per cent of their gross national product, few countries have consistently met this target, as Figure 30.7 shows. They have felt able to plead various reasons as justifying an inability to contribute more generously. In truth, Western governments have seen aid programmes as an easy area in which to effect

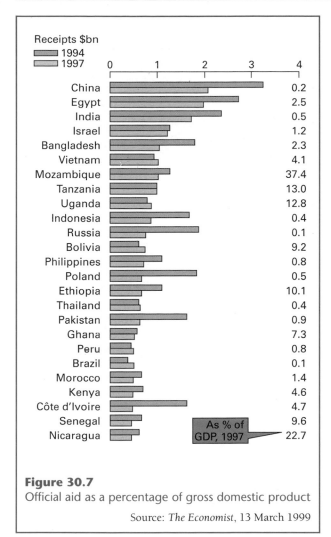

Receipts $bn
■ 1994
■ 1997

	As % of GDP, 1997
China	0.2
Egypt	2.5
India	0.5
Israel	1.2
Bangladesh	2.3
Vietnam	4.1
Mozambique	37.4
Tanzania	13.0
Uganda	12.8
Indonesia	0.4
Russia	0.1
Bolivia	9.2
Philippines	0.8
Poland	0.5
Ethiopia	10.1
Thailand	0.4
Pakistan	0.9
Ghana	7.3
Peru	0.8
Brazil	0.1
Morocco	1.4
Kenya	4.6
Côte d'Ivoire	4.7
Senegal	9.6
Nicaragua	22.7

Figure 30.7
Official aid as a percentage of gross domestic product
Source: *The Economist*, 13 March 1999

economies when they have sought cuts in public expenditure programmes. If we try to examine the rationale of official development assistance, we find that the case for it is not everywhere taken for granted merely because it is called aid. Critics, notably Peter Bauer, have argued that aid cannot really promote development because it is *given to governments*. Because the flow of funds is put too much into a political arena, they see aid as strengthening the position of governments whose policies in the past have rarely been directed towards easing the lot of the poorest peoples in LDCs. Furthermore, they argue that aid weakens the need for self-reliance and the need to tackle internal problems without relying on the easy option of external help. Even those who feel that the critics overstate their case concede that in LDCs there have been pressures for aid to be directed towards *urban-biased* projects, which arguably have been of marginal significance in many LDCs. Michael Lipton has argued that the possibility of rural-based projects has been relatively ignored by Western donors. As a result the supporters of aid have not had the opportunity of pointing to as many success stories as they would have wished to

underpin their case. The fact is that, within LDCs, there has been bias towards large, urban-based prestige investments.

Both the IMF and the World Bank have favoured policies which required LDCs to lower domestic government spending and liberalize their trade and exchange rate strategies. Whilst these policies are in line with the outlook of the trade optimists mentioned earlier, they have not been lacking criticism from other quarters. Critics of the World Bank's **structural adjustment programmes** have argued that cuts in government spending lead to hardship for the poorest sections of society. It is held, for example, that the elimination of food subsidies and a smaller-sized role of government leads to rising unemployment, infant mortality and malnutrition. In so far as this is the outcome, the terms on which the World Bank gives adjustment loans are held to be perverse – the opposite of what development is about.

Indebtedness

Since the early 1970s the topic of the debt burden of developing countries has become a pressing issue and has received much media attention. What is this issue, and how did it arise? In brief, the subject arose because of the 1973 hike in oil prices by OPEC. As a result of their enhanced export earnings, OPEC countries deposited large sums in Western banks, which found a ready demand for these funds in many of the developing countries lacking oil reserves. For oil-dependent countries the servicing of these debts later in the 1970s was not a problem at this time, but it was in the 1980s. Why? There were two reasons. Interest rates rose sharply following the 1979 oil price rise and the dollar appreciated relative to many other currencies. Interest rates rose because Western industrialized countries adopted measures to curb inflationary pressures. The rising value of the dollar was also a crucial factor in the charged circumstances because most of the loans to developing countries were denominated in dollars. The measures adopted by the rich countries had the predictable effect of slowing down the rate of export earnings of developing countries. Together with rising interest rates, the capacity of developing countries to service loans diminished sharply. Several initiatives have been announced to attempt to ease the debt burden for many developing countries which, as Figure 30.8 shows, is now so large that it is no longer credible to expect repayment ever to be possible. In 1996 the IMF and World Bank announced another initiative for the Heavily Indebted Poor Countries (HIPC) to help reduce the debt burden. However, the conditions surrounding the initiative have proved too restrictive to be an effective means of solving the problem. 'Debt forgiveness' has been a theme of much media coverage, most notably by Jubilee 2000, a combination of interest groups including non-governmental organizations (NGOs), charities and voluntary groups. The case for such debt forgiveness is opposed by critics who maintain that some countries led by corrupt rulers do not merit relief from debt servicing because they have mismanaged funds in the past. Moreover, they claim, might such rulers be inclined to borrow even more irresponsibly in the future if the slate of debts is wiped out now? Nonetheless, there is now virtually no debate that many of the countries in Figure 30.8 have no chance of fully servicing their debts and some form of major debt cancellation seems inevitable very soon.

KEY POINTS

30.4

- LDCs can turn both to governments in the developed world and to commercial banks for external funds in order to assist their development efforts. Both forms of finance have given rise to difficulties.

- Official development assistance or aid is a form of external finance from donor governments to recipient governments. Critics argue that this means that certain types of project are favoured and that these are not always the best choice that could be made using overseas finance.

- Borrowing from banks in the 1970s gave rise to a sudden indebtedness in some upper-middle-income developing countries.

- The terms on which both the IMF and the World Bank have assisted LDCs have been criticized for their adverse impact on the poor.

- Efforts to relieve developing countries of debt repayment have been protracted and as yet are far from being agreed by all relevant lending sources in developed economies.

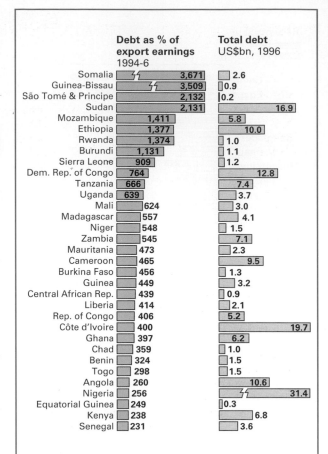

Figure 30.8

The debt burden of developing countries: Africa

Source: *The Guardian*, 15 May 1998

Case Study

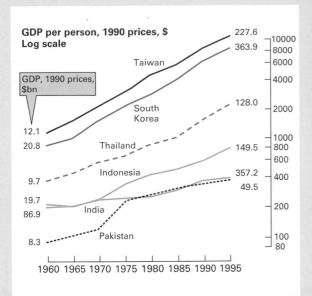

**GDP per person, 1990 prices, $
Log scale**

GDP, 1990 prices, $bn

Taiwan	227.6 — 10000
	363.9 — 8000
	— 6000
	— 4000
South Korea	128.0 — 2000
12.1	— 1000
20.8	— 800
Thailand	149.5 — 600
9.7	— 400
Indonesia	357.2
19.7	49.5 — 200
86.9	
India	— 100
8.3	Pakistan — 80

1960 1965 1970 1975 1980 1985 1990 1995

Modern India was born on 15 August 1947 when British rule on the subcontinent of Asia came to an end. Later this year, as the country celebrates its first half-century of independence, it will be praised far and wide for what it has achieved since then. Much of this praise will be deserved. However, the number of comparably poor countries is now much smaller than it was in 1947. And although foreign statesmen, financiers and academics, joining in the celebrations, will once more pay tribute to India's growing industrial strength, to its fine achievements in agriculture and social development, and to its steady material progress against the odds, they will be telling less than the truth. The plain fact is that in all these respects India has failed. Much of the developing world, especially in Asia, has left India far behind. Between 1960 and 1990 India's GDP grew by an average of a little under 4 per cent a year – the 'Hindu rate of growth', as it came to be known. However, over the same period Pakistan's GDP grew by 5 per cent a year, Indonesia's by 6 per cent, Thailand's by 7 per cent, Taiwan's by 8 per cent and South Korea's by 9 per cent.

In a country of nearly a billion people, the World Bank reckons 328 million fall below the poverty line. That means they have an income of less than $25 a month. Education, except at university level, is a disgrace. More than half of India's adults are illiterate. (In China the corresponding figure is less than 20 per cent; in Thailand less than 10 per cent.) In a World Bank study of the performance of ten comparable developing countries in reducing poverty and infant mortality during the 1970s and 1980s, India came seventh on reducing poverty and tenth on reducing infant mortality. The view that India's record on growth, conventionally measured, may be explained by its far-sighted development priorities, is unsustainable.

For decades India has been an all but closed economy. Its currency was inconvertible and over-valued, its industries isolated behind huge tariff walls and an exceptionally severe import licensing regime. In 1991 bold steps were taken to begin opening the economy to the outside world. Many tariffs were cut, the import licensing system was liberalized, the rupee was devalued and made convertible for trade, and inward foreign investment was encouraged.

To be cut off from the world economy had been bad enough. Making matters worse was a repressive system of domestic planning and regulation. India's capacity licensing regime obliged companies to seek government planners' permission to invest or make new products. Its avowed aim was to prevent growing (i.e. successful) enterprises from claiming an unduly large share of the economy's resources. It worked: failure, by any non-Indian yardstick, was assured.

In 1991 this system was virtually dismantled and domestic economic policy was given a thorough shake-up. The government curbed its borrowing, simplified the tax system, and partially liberalized the domestic financial system. The main instruments of a regime that had tried to combine a large measure of private ownership with a Soviet-inspired system of industrial micro-planning began to be set aside.

Source: *The Economist*, 22 February 1997

1 On what basis could you argue that the record of economic development in India has not been one of failure?
2 On what criteria would you find it hard to defend India's record of economic development?
3 Why would the reforms be expected to contribute to a faster rate of economic development?
4 In what way can you see the 1991 liberalization measures in India as being similar to the changes in the Soviet Union at the same time?
5 How would you judge whether India was successful in becoming an open economy in 1991?
6 Who loses out when there is a major change in development strategy, as in the case of India in 1991?

Exam Preparation

Multiple choice question

Growth rates
Average annual growth 1986-95, %

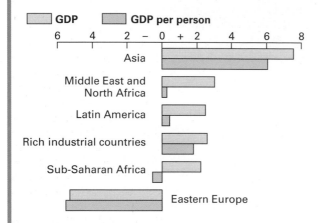

Source: *The Economist*, 9 March 1996

1   The chart shows growth rates for six different
    groups of countries. In the light of these data, it
    can be concluded that, between 1986 and 1995,
    A GDP and GDP per person rose in all regions
       including the developing countries
    B the greatest difference between the growth
       rate of GDP and GDP per head was in Asia
    C the average rate of growth of GDP fell in
       Africa, Latin America and Eastern Europe
    D in Sub-Saharan Africa, population growth was
       faster than that of GDP
    E the growth rate of rich industrial countries
       was slower than in any of the other five
       regions

Essay questions

1   What role do international economic
    organizations play in improving the economies of
    developing countries?

2   Describe the problems, both in their domestic
    economies and in international trade, that may
    hinder the economic progress of less-developed
    countries.

3   'Economic growth in less-developed countries
    may be assisted by receiving aid from more-
    developed countries and by increasing
    opportunities for trade.'
    (a) Describe the ways in which aid can be given
         and trade encouraged.
    (b) What problems may arise from the various
         countries concerned as a result of this
         assistance?

4   (a) What are the main economic problems
         facing less-developed countries?
    (b) Why have some less-developed countries
         experienced a faster rate of economic growth
         than others over the last twenty years?

5   (a) Explain the causes of the current problem of
         international debt.
    (b) Discuss the implications of this problem for
         the stability of the world economy.

6   What are the fundamental characteristics of the
    world's less-developed economies? Evaluate debt
    relief, international loans, and stabilizing the
    demand for, and the price of, primary
    commodities as a means of stimulating the
    economic development of these economies.

7   (a) What needs to be developed in a developing
         country?
    (b) Once an economy has achieved developed
         status, does this mean that the economy's
         difficulties cease?

8   It has been reported that 'in the last 30 years
    Indonesia has struggled out of poverty into the
    ranks of the world's middle-income countries.
    The average Indonesian is better off than five
    years ago'.
    (a) If you were asked as an economist to show
         that 'the average Indonesian is better off
         than five years ago', explain what
         information you would need.
    (b) Comment on the difficulties of making
         comparisons of living standards between
         countries and over time.

31

Economic growth

LEARNING OUTCOMES

On completing this chapter you should understand:

- The meaning of economic growth and the importance of its size
- Growth and its relationship to the production possibilities curve
- Growth and its analysis via aggregate supply and aggregate demand curves
- The factors that determine economic growth
- The possible policies to employ in order to promote growth
- The arguments put forward by the anti-growth lobby

The world today is more prosperous than at any time during the twentieth century. Global GDP has increased more than tenfold in the last fifty years and now exceeds $30 trillion per year. Regardless of this phenomenal rate of increase in prosperity, economic growth remains a controversial topic.

Many politicians see economic growth as the only way that the poor and disadvantaged will ever attain higher standards of living. In direct contrast, other sectors of society want economic growth to stop. They contend that it increases pollution, and that crowded urban environments lower the quality of life. These arguments mask a great unevenness across the world where the so-called high-income countries benefit from everyone's resources. For instance, consider the figures relating to the richest countries displayed in Table 31.1 and contrast the data with the equivalent for low incomes displayed in Table 00.0 on page 00. Clearly, a very small proportion of the world's population benefits from the world's resources. In fact, in 1999 the UN estimated that one-fifth of the world's population had 86 per cent of the world's GDP, whilst the poorest fifth shared only 1 per cent of the world's GDP. This disparity and associated problems were the topic of the preceding chapter. Here our intention is to focus on developed nations such as the UK and to discuss what might be done to improve the prospects for still higher growth rates in the future. As it is the closing chapter, we shall also revisit many of the topics dealt with so far in this book.

Defining economic growth

By this point in the text, most of you should have a general idea of what the term *economic growth* means. When a nation grows, its citizens are in some ways better off, at least in terms of material well-being. A general definition of economic growth might read as follows:

> Economic growth is the increase in an economy's level of real output over time.

Generally, economic growth is measured by the *rate of change* of some measure of output. In the UK, and in most other countries today, the most commonly used measure of economic output is gross domestic product (GDP).

Correcting for inflation
In discussing the rate of change of actual output, we have to correct nominal (money) GDP for changes in prices through the use of a price index. When we do, we get what is called *real* GDP, as discussed and illustrated in Chapter 13. Hence a more formal measure of economic growth may be defined as the rate of change in real GDP over time. For example, between 1992 and 1993 the UK rate of growth in nominal terms (that is, uncorrected for price changes) was 5.4 per cent. During that year the rate of inflation, as measured by the GDP deflator, was 3.5 per

Table 31.1

The richest economies

Countries in rank order (According to GNP per capita in 1998)	Population Millions	Gross National Product (GNP)			GNP per capita		
		Billions of dollars	% Average annual real growth rate	% Average annual growth rate	Dollars	Rank	% Average annual real growth rate
	1998	1998	1997–8	1988–98	1998	1998	1997–8
Switzerland	7	284.8	2.1	1.1	40 080	3	1.8
Norway	4	152.1	2.4	3.2	34 330	4	1.8
Denmark	5	176.4	3.0	2.3	33 260	6	2.6
Japan	126	4089.9	–2.6	1.9	32 380	7	–2.8
Singapore	3	95.1	1.5	1.9	30 060	9	–0.4
United States	270	7921.3	3.7	2.8	29 340	10	2.8
Austria	8	217.2	3.4	2.6	26 850	12	3.2
Germany	82	2122.7	–0.4	2.1	25 850	13	–0.4
Sweden	9	226.9	3.5	1.2	25 620	14	3.5
Belgium	10	259.0	2.9	2.0	25 380	15	2.7
France	59	1466.2	3.2	1.8	24 940	17	2.9
Netherlands	16	388.7	3.3	3.0	24 760	18	2.7
Finland	5	124.3	5.2	1.7	24 110	19	4.8
Hong Kong, China	7	153.3	–5.1	3.3	23 670	21	–7.8
United Kingdom	59	1263.8	2.0	1.7	21 400	22	1.9

Source: Adapted from World Bank, *World Development Report*, 1999/2000 and *OECD in Figures*, 1999 edition

Note: The rankings are based on 210 economies – the main table, however, only displays economies where the populations exceed 1.5 million and the data sets are complete. For example, Liechtenstein and Luxembourg rank first and second respectively, but are not included above, as their populations are too small.

cent. Therefore the annual increase in *real* GDP was 5.4 per cent minus 3.5 per cent, or 1.9 per cent.

Correcting for population

The above measure might be misleading if, for example, the population is growing rapidly at the same time that real gross national product (GNP) is growing. An alternative and perhaps more appropriate definition of economic growth is in terms of per capita output: the total production of goods and services in a one-year period divided by the population. The self-explanatory mathematical formula for this calculation has already been presented and discussed in Chapter 13 on page 254. We can therefore move to yet another definition, the fullest and official measure, namely:

Economic growth is the increase in per capita real output.

This is officially measured as the percentage rate of change in *real* GDP *per head* of the population from one time period to another – normally a year.

Measuring growth accurately

Consider the following table, which describes the growth-rate data for four *hypothetical* countries between 1990 and 2000.

Annual growth rate (%)

Country	J	K	L	M
Nominal GDP	20	15	10	5
Price level	5	3	6	2
Population	5	8	2	1

1 Which country has the highest rate of real growth?

2 Which country has the lowest rate of real growth?

3 Which country has the highest rate of real growth per capita?

4 Which country has the lowest rate of real growth per capita?
Now consider the data shown for *actual* countries in Table 31.1 and answer questions 5 to 7.

5 During 1997–8 four countries experienced a decrease in per capita income. Using the data, give one or two general reasons to explain why in each case.

6 Stating examples from Table 31.1, try to identify a pattern between population size, economic activity and its rate of change.

7 In Table 31.1, countries are ranked according to their GNP per capita. Countries may also be ranked according to their total GNP. State one advantage and one disadvantage of ranking countries in this other way.

Problems of definition

Nothing is stated in the above definitions about the *distribution* of output and income. A nation might grow very rapidly in terms of increases in total or even per capita real output, while at the same time the nation's poor people remain poor or become even poorer.

Nothing has been said about changes in the leisure time available to the nation. In one sense, 'real' standards of living can improve without there being any positive economic growth as measured by increases in real per capita output, since individuals may be enjoying more leisure by working fewer hours but producing as much as they did before.

Similarly, nothing in the above definitions of economic growth relates to the spiritual, cultural and environmental quality aspects of the 'good' life. These themes have already been reviewed in Chapter 13, under the heading 'Limitations of national accounts' and in the case study entitled 'Can GDP stand for green domestic product?' (pages 253 and 256). These ideas are worth reviewing as they underpin the arguments of the anti-growth school. Students of economics therefore recognize that no measure of economic growth is perfect. Yet, the measures that we do have allow us to make comparisons across countries and through time and, if used judiciously, can provide important insights. In sum, GDP may be a defective measure of well-being, but it is a serviceable measure of economic activity.

Is economic growth desirable?

Some commentators on our current economic situation believe that the definition of economic growth ignores its negative effects. Some psychologists even contend that we are made worse off because of economic growth. They say the more we grow, the more 'needs' are created, so that we feel worse off as we become richer. Our expectations are rising faster than reality, so we presumably always suffer from a sense of disappointment. Clearly, the measurement of economic growth cannot take into account the spiritual and cultural aspects of the good life. As with all activities, there are costs and benefits. Some of them are listed in the following table.

Benefits	Costs
Reduction in illiteracy	Environmental pollution
Reduction in poverty	Breakdown of the family
Improved health	Stress
Longer lives	Urban congestion

8 Define in your own words the meaning of economic growth.
9 (a) Describe with examples one of the costs of economic growth.
  (b) Describe using examples one of the benefits of economic growth.
10 Add one more cost and one more benefit to the list in the table.

11 Does the rate of growth affect the types of cost and benefit that occur?
12 Make an argument either to support the policy of economic growth, or to support the anti-growth lobby.

The growth record

Economic growth in a country's total and per capita output has become the expected norm of all developed nations. In fact, economists often arrange the countries of the world in a kind of 'league table', showing their comparative progress over the years. As an example, the average annual figures for the OECD economies from 1990 to 1998 are presented in Figure 31.1. On average, most of these economies managed to record growth rates of just over 2 per cent, and the forecasts implied that this would be sustained into the twenty-first century. Indeed, the average OECD growth rate was estimated to be 2.8 per cent in 1999 and was expected to continue at a similar pace, slowing slightly to 2.4 per cent by 2002. Specifically for the United Kingdom, the economy grew by 1.8 per cent in 1999 and was forecasted to accelerate to 2.5 per cent by 2002. Clearly, the OECD anticipates average growth rates to continue on an upward path indefinitely, and the United Kingdom is well positioned to stay in the race.

The importance of growth rates

The question therefore arises: how important are these percentage point differences? The answer is twofold.

First, you must always ask the question, 'percentage of what?' Any developed country's growth rate in percentage terms will tend to be lower than that of a developing country. In the developed country one is thinking along the lines of a 2 or 3 per cent increase on £800 billion, whereas in a developing nation one is considering a percentage increase of a far smaller total. It is like comparing a 5 per cent increase of £100 with a 5 per cent increase of £1 billion – the latter is clearly far larger.

The second problem is slightly more complex since it relates to compounded rates of growth. If a nation consistently has a low or high rate of growth, the time it will take to double its present economic size will vary immensely. The principle is the same as putting a £1 coin in the building society and getting 5 per cent interest a year. If the dividend is added annually and you leave the amount untouched for fifteen years, you will recoup £2.08. If you left another £1 coin in a building society offering only 3 per cent interest per year, it would take twenty-four years to double. Therefore, just 2 percentage points result in a nine-year difference in 'doubling-time'. These concepts are illustrated in a more international setting in Table 31.2. France has been chosen because it is similar in population size to Britain.

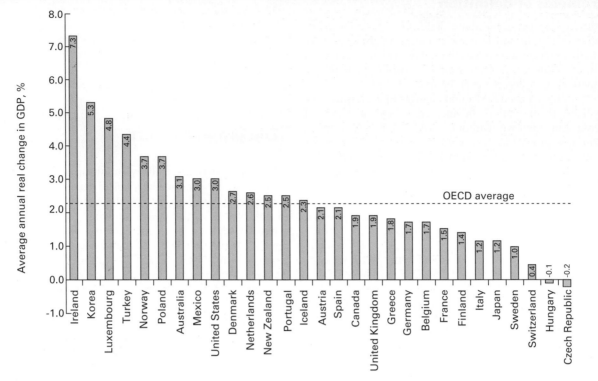

Figure 31.1

The OECD growth league, 1990–8

The chart shows approximate growth rates in the twenty-nine OECD countries based on their national accounts. The figures should be regarded as broad approximations only, since they are the official statistics of governments and omit the varying rates of growth of unrecorded sectors of economies, which are substantial in some countries. Nevertheless, they do indicate marked differences. The average figure for the OECD as a whole was approximately 2 per cent.

Source: *OECD in Figures*, 1999 edition

Table 31.2

Comparing growth in France and the UK

The line showing income per head suggests that France was more developed as an economy in 1998. More importantly, if the 1997/8 growth trends continue the development gap will broaden – this is suggested by the shorter doubling-time in the final line.

	United Kingdom	**France**
Population (mid-1992)	59 million	59 million
Income per head in 1998 ($)	21 400	24 940
Average yearly growth rate 1997–8 (%)	2.0	3.2
Doubling-time (if existing growth rate is maintained)	36 years	22.5 years

Source: World Bank, *World Development Report*, 1999

KEY POINTS

31.1

■ Economic growth is the increase in an economy's real level of output over time. It is measured by the annual rate of change of real output.

■ Economic growth can also be defined as the increase in real per capita output measured by its annual rate of change.

■ The benefits of rapid economic growth include reductions in illiteracy, poverty and illness. The costs of economic growth include pollution, stress and urban congestion.

■ A nation's percentage growth rate will always be relative to the size of its total GNP.

■ Small percentage point differences in growth rates lead to large differences in GNP over time.

Growth and the production possibilities curve

We can show economic growth graphically by using the production possibilities curve presented in Chapter 1. Figure 31.2 shows the production possibilities curve for 1995. The output of agricultural goods is measured on the horizontal axis and that of manufactured goods on the vertical axis. If there is economic growth between 1995 and 2005, then the production possibilities curve will shift to the right (or outwards). The distance that it shifts represents the amount of economic growth, that is, the increase in the productive capacity of the nation.

Potential and actual output

Remember that the production possibilities curve represents the maximum rate of output that *can* be achieved with the nation's available resources. It is possible for resources to be under-utilized. The production possibilities curve could shift outwards, but the actual utilization of resources might be less than the maximum use represented by the curve. Look at Figure 31.3. Here we show the production possibilities curve for 1995 shifting out as it did in Figure 31.2. We start at point A but find that by the year 2005 we have ended up at point B because of under-utilization of actual resources. It is even possible for the economy to have a decrease in actual output and move inwards to point C. Thus, in a sense, the production possibilities curve for 2005

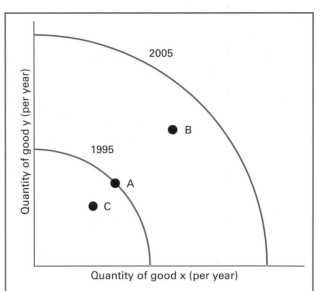

Figure 31.3
Potential versus actual output
The production possibilities curve may shift out from 1995 without necessarily ending up on the new potential production possibilities curve for 2005. For example, if we start out at position A, we may only progress to point B. The 'actual' output rate symbolized by B represents an under-utilization of resources. We are not producing at our maximum potential rate.

is a representation of maximum potential output, which is defined as the level of output that a nation could attain if it were operating on the production possibilities curve. Actual output will therefore never exceed potential output but it may be smaller. In the long run, it may be changes in potential output that determine government and business planning, but in the short run it is changes in actual output that are important.

Let us develop this concept of potential output. Enlarging productive capacity, which is a long-run process, can increase potential output. In contrast, therefore, economic growth achieved by simply utilizing existing spare capacity should be recognized as qualitatively and quantitatively different – and certainly short term in nature. The latter type of growth can be regarded as a kind of recovery phase. Economic growth built on a recovery basis only will ultimately lead to full-capacity use of *existing* resources. A distinction therefore needs to be drawn between a shorter-term recovery phase (based on *existing* resources) and a long-term shift in a nation's potential output.

How do we increase long-term potential?

Long-term potential grows by people making the decision not to consume all their income today. The more saving by

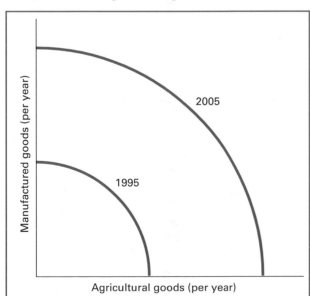

Figure 31.2
Economic growth
If there is growth between 1995 and 2005 then the production possibilities curve for the entire economy will shift outwards from the line labelled 1995 to the outer curve labelled 2005. The distance that it shifts represents an increase in the productive capacity of the nation.

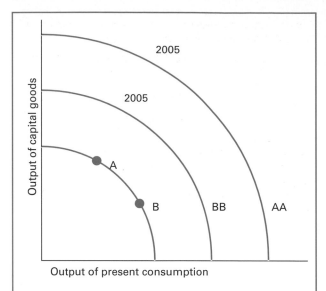

Figure 31.4

The importance of capital for growth

Here we show a production possibilities curve with two points on it, A and B. At point A we are consuming less today and providing more consumption for tomorrow in the form of capital goods. At point B, we are consuming more today and providing less for future consumption. If we operate at point A, we may end up on production possibilities curve AA in year 2005. However, if we are at point B, we may end up at a production possibilities curve of only BB in year 2005.

Finding the point

The graph shows the production possibilities frontier for an economy.

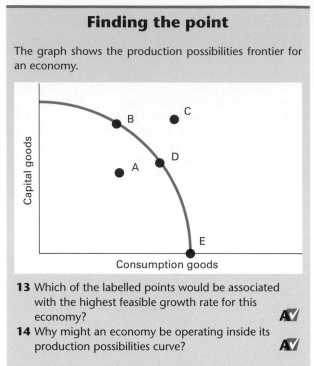

13 Which of the labelled points would be associated with the highest feasible growth rate for this economy?

14 Why might an economy be operating inside its production possibilities curve?

Growth: aggregate supply and aggregate demand curves

households and the more investment by firms there is, as a percentage of total income, the larger will be the capital stock, and therefore the higher will be possible future income. We can perhaps demonstrate this decision by again using a production possibilities curve.

In Figure 31.4 we show two potential production possibilities curves for the year 2005. The horizontal axis is labelled present consumption and the vertical axis output of capital goods. We would expect that, if our economy is at present operating at A where relatively more capital goods are being produced than at B, the potential production possibilities curve in 2005 would be further to the right than if we were producing at B. We have labelled the outside curve AA and the middle curve BB. The rate of growth from point A is greater than the rate of growth at point B. Therefore the pie gets potentially larger the more people are willing to save today.

A way of exemplifying this issue is to examine the sacrifice of current income (and thus current consumption) by students in order to acquire human capital. By not consuming as much now and acquiring education and skills instead, society should become more productive.

To put economic growth into the context of macroeconomic analysis, the concepts of aggregate supply and aggregate demand introduced in Chapter 14 can be used. Look at Figure 31.5. We start in equilibrium with AD and SRAS intersecting the long-run aggregate supply curve LRAS at a price level of 100. Real GDP per year is £8 billion. Economic growth occurs as a result of labour force expansion, capital investments and other factors. The result is a rightward shift in the long-run aggregate supply curve to LRAS'. As the long-run productive capacity of the nation grows, the economy does not stay on its short-run aggregate supply curve SRAS. Rather, SRAS shifts along with shifts in aggregate demand. It is thus possible for us to achieve a real GDP of £9 billion without any increase in the price level. The short-run aggregate supply curve moves outwards to SRAS' and intersects AD' at E', where the new long-run aggregate supply curve LRAS' has moved.

In the world just described, aggregate demand shifts outwards so that, at the same price level (100), it intersects the new short-run aggregate supply curve SRAS' at the rate of real GDP that is consistent with the natural rate of unemployment (on LRAS'). Firms sell all the output produced at the new level without changing prices. If, however, aggregate demand increased and there was not a

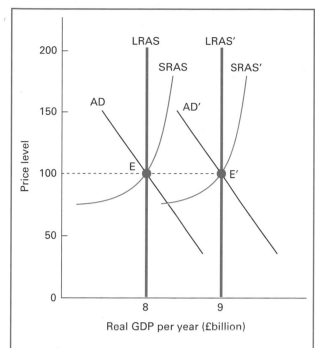

Figure 31.5
Economic growth, aggregate supply and aggregate demand

Economic growth can be shown using short-run and long-run aggregate demand and supply curves. Aggregate demand AD intersects short-run aggregate supply SRAS at E, £8 billion of real GDP per year at a price level of 100. This GDP is consistent with the natural rate of unemployment. The long-run aggregate supply curve is vertical at £8 billion and is labelled LRAS. With economic growth, LRAS moves outward to £9 billion per year. Short-run aggregate supply shifts to SRAS', and aggregate demand increases to AD'. The new equilibrium is at E', still at a price level of 100. In this scenario there is no inflation.

New technology and growth

There is a growing dichotomy in developed economies between fast-growing sectors and slow-growing sectors. Fast-growth industries are associated with new technology and slow-growth industries with old technology. That has sparked debate about whether new technology has increased the pace economies can grow without generating inflation. Nowhere is the debate more intense than in the United States, where economic growth has been running at 4 per cent for the last four years but inflation has stayed low. The so-called 'new paradigm' theory argues that information technology – the Internet, increasing usage of computer software, the growth in communications, etc. – has pushed productivity growth up to higher, and more sustainable, levels than previously. This in turn means that a given level of economic expansion is less

inflationary and hence growth can be sustained at higher rates and for longer periods than in the past.

Source: Lloyds TSB Economic Bulletin, December 1999

15 Using an AS and AD diagram, explain the new paradigm theory.
16 Why would information technology improve productivity?
17 What economic problems could information technology create that are not alluded to in the extract?
18 What other factors may encourage a high level of growth?

related increase in capacity, that is, there was not a shift from LRAS to LRAS', inflation would accompany growth.

KEY POINTS

31.2

■ Growth is shown by an outward movement in the production possibilities curve for the entire economy.

■ Economists make a distinction between potential and actual growth rates. The former represents maximum efficiency with resources and provides a target; the latter represents resource utilization in practice and illustrates the outcome.

■ Growth can be achieved in two forms: (1) through increased productive capacity and (2) by utilizing existing capital equipment more fully. The former should lead to long-term growth; the latter simply represents short-term recovery.

■ Growth can be shown by an outward movement in the LRAS, which is a vertical line at the rate of real GDP consistent with the natural rate of unemployment.

Factors determining economic growth

Potential economic growth is largely determined by the factors of production that a nation has at its command. Actual growth, however, is determined by how effectively these factors are developed and combined.

Natural resources

A large amount of natural resources is not sufficient to guarantee economic growth. A number of less-developed countries are fantastically rich in natural resources, although for various reasons they have not been overly successful in exploiting them. Natural resources must be converted to useful forms, which requires people equipped with appropriate skills. Countries endowed with similar natural resources vary in their ability to devise methods to develop resources into usable things.

Capital accumulation

It is often asserted that a necessary prerequisite for economic development is a large capital stock, such as machines and other durable goods; and it is true that developed countries do spend a significant amount on fixed capital formation. For example, in 1998 and 1999 the United Kingdom spent over 12 per cent of its annual GDP on fixed capital. These figures give us some indication of production potential during subsequent years; however, they say nothing about how wisely the capital investment is chosen or how effectively it is used. We shall leave these problems relating to the quality and application of capital until the next section.

Capital, regardless of the problems outlined, is still seen as a major factor affecting economic growth. The logic is: the larger the capital stock for any given population, the higher the possible level of productivity and real income. Obviously, if very few machines are available, a nation will be able to make fewer goods and services and therefore income will be lower. Conversely, more machines will mean that more income can be generated. Therefore, the larger the capital stock, the larger is the potential income. To sum up, other things being equal, investment in capital should increase the productive potential of an economy.

Rate of saving

You may recall from Chapter 16 the model that relates measured savings to measured investment, the basic proposition being that if you want more tomorrow, you have to take less today. Resources released from producing goods for current consumption allow more investment to occur. Or, from another angle, you have to save to have a future. Without saving we cannot have investment, and without investment into capital stock there can be little hope of much economic growth. On a national basis, this implies that higher saving rates eventually mean higher living standards, all other things held constant. To state the extreme case, if all income is consumed each year, there is nothing left over for saving, and thus no funds for businesses to invest. Empirical data from various nations support the theory, for in those economies where savings run at a high level, so too does economic growth.

Technological and academic progress

It is generally accepted that the single most important reason for an economy to grow is linked to its pace of technological progress. This is because technology makes it possible to obtain more output from the same amount of inputs as before. Economies therefore must invest in knowledge just as they must invest in fixed capital. In fact, we have already seen some discussion of the considerable returns to investment in education in Chapter 11.

Indeed, the ability of a nation to initiate and sustain technological change depends on

1 the scientific capabilities of the population;
2 the quality and size of the nation's educational and training system; and
3 the percentage of income that goes into basic research and development each year.

Technological progress does not occur only in the industrial sector of developed nations. In the less-developed countries, technological change has involved the use of improved pesticides, higher-yielding hybrid seeds and improved irrigation techniques. Much of the technological change that first occurred in the developed countries has been transferred to the less-developed countries, thereby allowing them to increase their rate of growth. Consider the example of the invention and widespread use of 'miracle' rice, which has caused a 'green' revolution in less-developed countries. Miracle rice, although requiring more fertilizer, has much greater yields per acre planted than any other previously existing strain of rice. The innovation and use of miracle rice has increased the actual output for the limited capital and skilled labour available to less-developed countries.

Computers have had a similar 'miracle' effect on the productivity of manufacturing and office workers throughout the world.

A logical conclusion, therefore, is that technological progress, along with the associated accumulations of human and material capital, is most important in determining a nation's rate of economic growth.

Globalization

Increasing importance is being attributed to the opening up of the world economy. Detailed studies suggest that there is a positive correlation between the lowering of tariffs and an increase in per capita income. In other words, the more open an economy, the higher its rate of growth.

Developments in Eastern Europe and the World Trade Organization (discussed in Chapters 2 and 29) highlight that during the last twenty years, more and more areas of the world economy have been brought into the competitive market-place. Such openness to trade, investment and competition are clearly important determinants to productivity growth.

As the *OECD Observer* (an academic journal produced six times a year) remarked when reviewing the future of the global economy in the summer of 1999, 'The creation

The Organization for Economic Co-operation and Development

According to the Convention signed in Paris on 14 December 1960, which came into force on 30 September 1961, the Organization for Economic Co-operation and Development (OECD) promotes policies designed:

- to achieve the highest sustainable economic growth and employment and a rising standard of living in member countries, while maintaining financial stability, and thus to contribute to the development of the world economy;
- to contribute to sound economic expansion in member as well as non-member countries in the process of economic development; and
- to contribute to the expansion of world trade on a multilateral, non-discriminatory basis in accordance with international obligations.

The 20 original member countries of the OECD are Austria, Belgium, Canada, Denmark, France, Germany, Greece, Iceland, Ireland, Italy, Luxembourg, the Netherlands, Norway, Portugal, Spain, Sweden, Switzerland, Turkey, the United Kingdom and the United States. The following nine countries became members subsequently: Japan (1964), Finland (1969), Australia (1971), New Zealand (1973), Mexico (1994), the Czech Republic (1995), Hungary (1996), Poland (1996) and Korea (1996).

Source: Adapted from Preface, *OECD in Figures*, 1999 edition

19 (a) Using the data displayed in Figure 31.1, identify the country with the highest and lowest growth rate of the OECD group.
(b) Attempt to explain why these two nations have achieved the rates of growth shown.
(c) Using the OECD website, identify the countries with the highest and lowest growth rates at the start of this millennium.

20 In the publication *OECD in Figures*, there are statistics for demography, employment, health, investment, economic growth, agriculture, industry, services, transport, public sector, taxation, energy, education, research and development, science and technology, environment, trade and aid.
(a) Rank in order of significance which of these you regard as the most important factors contributing to the growth of member countries.
(b) State two sets of data that are important but not in the list.
(c) Make some assumptions to account for why these two items are not listed.

21 In one sentence, state the main aim of the OECD.

22 Try to explain why maintaining financial stability is an important policy objective of the OECD.

of national or regional spaces for the free flow of goods, services, finance and technology has had telling effects on long-term growth. Extended world-wide, such integration offers huge scope to improve both the efficient allocation of resources and the competition of ideas'.

KEY POINTS

31.3

- Natural resources are not sufficient to guarantee economic growth; many countries without a large natural resource base have had relatively high growth rates.

- Physical capital accumulation is a major determinant of growth. The more capital goods we produce today, the higher our potential growth, other things being equal.

- There is a trade-off between present goods and future (capital) goods.

- Growth will not occur without saving.

- Technological progress allows a nation to produce greater output with a given amount of labour and capital.

- Worldwide competition opens up opportunities for economic growth.

Can we tell which factor is most important?

Is it possible to find out which factor is most important in determining a nation's economic growth rate? This is difficult to answer. One way to simplify the problem, though, is to talk in terms of two determinants of economic growth that can be measured – at least in theory:

1 growth of capital stock and
2 growth of the labour force.

If we assume that these two determinants alone will account for all the economic growth that is achieved, it should be relatively straightforward to find the numerical importance of the factors. The researcher simply estimates the average annual rate of growth in capital and labour.

But the task is not really so easy. Certainly we can measure the value of the number of machines that are put in place and the number of workers that have entered the labour force. But what about the *quality* of the capital we use? And the *quality* of the labour force? Part of the growth in our capital stock and labour force has to do with quality improvement. 'One unit' of a machine today is certainly of a higher quality than the 'same' machine of a hundred years ago. Similarly, the average worker today has much better training and a higher educational attainment level than the worker of a hundred years ago. Thus we can say that to a large extent the measurement of the growth in capital and in labour does not take into account the growth in the *quality* of these two factors.

Is there a growth theory?

Because of the quality–quantity dilemma outlined above, it is most difficult to identify which factor – labour or capital – is the more important contributor to the growth process.

Furthermore, other factors – such as natural resources and technological progress – need to be brought into the formula. But these two factors also have inherent problems of measurement.

Consequently, until recently economists could not agree on the relative importance of the factors that contribute to economic growth. Indeed, an article on the growth theme published in *The Economist* in January 1992 began as follows: 'Until recently, economics had little of interest to say about economic growth. Now this is changing … '. What economists are now saying is that growth is closely associated with the application of science and technology to economic activity. For instance, mechanization raised blue-collar and farm labour productivity, and now computers and their related products and services are transforming the nature of white-collar work.

As yet, however, there is no clear view on how a government can direct or stimulate the innovation that drives technological advancement. According to modern economic growth theory, *innovation* is the key as this is the element that transforms an invention into something that benefits the community by lowering production costs or providing new goods and services. For example, when the Internet was first conceived during the late 1960s as a network for the American defence department to exchange scientific information and intelligence in order to forestall nuclear attack, no one had envisaged public access. But within thirty years innovative ideas had transformed the Internet into a market-place of its own. The commercial potential of this global network is still to be fully exploited. There is no guarantee that economic growth will occur, but with the right innovation it could be truly phenomenal.

KEY POINTS

31.4

- Capital, labour, natural resources and technological progress all contribute to economic growth.

- When considering changes in capital and labour, there is a problem distinguishing between quantity and quality aspects. (The same is true of measuring technological progress and natural resources.)

- Modern economic growth theorists place an emphasis on harnessing scientific and technological development to economic activity – but they are not sure how this can be positively promoted.

Policies to promote growth

It follows from what has been discussed above that when governments wish to promote economic growth their advisers have no unanimous policy package to follow. All that exists are possibilities, some of which are outlined below.

Promote savings

The logic is straightforward: capital is recognized as a key determinant of growth, and capital accumulation can depend on the level of savings. If resources are fully utilized, increased investment may require reduced consumption. Therefore, increased investment, or capital accumulation, would require increased savings. Why? Quite simply because savings can be defined as *non-consumption*, in the short term, and investment can be defined as the creation of future productive capacity in the long term. Only if individuals are willing not to consume

Japan's slump

Under Japan's historical calendar, 1999 was the year of the Rabbit. In economic terms, it was the year of the frightened rabbit caught in the headlights of the world's disapproval. Japan dragged down the world's markets in 1998 and 1999 with negative rates of growth.

What made this decline particularly noticeable was the fact that during the period 1965 to 1995, Japan's average annual rate of growth was particularly impressive – indeed, it had been more than double that of the United Kingdom.

Many had attributed the phenomenal growth record to Japan's high rate of saving. But even during the 1990s the Japanese saved more than most industrialized countries. For example, in 1998 the UK saved approximately 15 per cent of its GDP, whereas in Japan the savings rate was still over 30 per cent.

23 During the 1990s, was the average Japanese person richer or poorer than their UK equivalent?

24 (a) Try to suggest what may have caused Japan's slump. (It may be helpful to visit the OECD website referred to on page 452.)
   (b) What is the economic position of Japan today? (Again, it may be useful to gain up-to-date information from the Web.)

25 'Savings alone are not sufficient to ensure economic growth.' Discuss.

everything will businesses be able to obtain resources for their investment activities. The theory behind these propositions was introduced in Chapter 15, and the case study to that chapter traced the links between the level of investment and the savings ratio.

Consequently, it should be apparent that potentially we could drastically increase the rate of growth in the United Kingdom if somehow we increased the saving rate of the population and if this additional saving led to the additional production of capital goods.

Consequently, throughout Europe changes have been made to legislation, tax and stamp duty to encourage a wider ownership of shares and the habit of saving. Specifically in the UK, there have been experiments to increase Save As You Earn (SAYE) schemes, using tax benefits as the incentive. For example, during the tax year 1999–2000 savers in the UK could invest up to £7000 tax free in an Individual Savings Account (ISA), without having the disadvantage of tying funds up for any specified period.

Promote mobility

Economic growth implies change and development. Therefore, factors of production will need to be reallocated from industrial sectors that are declining into those that are expanding. However, restrictive practices, such as union-enforced staffing levels, have prevented some reallocation taking place in the United Kingdom. Added to this are the

Definition of immobility of labour

Labour may be occupationally or industrially immobile because of a lack of the skills and abilities required by those firms with job vacancies, or because workers do not have the qualifications or experience demanded by the government, employers, professional associations or trade unions. Labour may be geographically immobile because of a lack of suitable housing in areas of labour shortage, or because of family ties or responsibilities. Other factors contributing to labour immobility are the existence of unemployment benefit and other social security benefits, and ignorance about job vacancies.

Source: F. Livesey, *Dictionary of Economics*, Pitman, 1993

26 Identify some government policies aimed to encourage labour to become more occupationally mobile. **A**✓

27 Identify some government policies aimed to encourage labour to become geographically more mobile. **A**✓

28 Do other factors of production suffer from immobility? **A**✓

universal problems that people are hesitant to uproot themselves or change jobs mid-career. Consequently, immobility, as outlined in Chapter 12, may cause growth to slow down.

Equally, measures designed to improve mobility may encourage faster growth. Such measures may involve legislation against unions. Alternatively, incentives may be offered to make labour and capital more mobile; some of these are discussed in the next chapter.

Promote education and training

Spending on education and training is regarded by economists as investment in human capital, and through this term it can be seen as complementary to, and just as important as, investment in physical capital. Investment in physical capital involves putting time and money into machinery; investment in human capital involves putting time and money into labour. We need specialized labour to operate and develop specialized machinery for we live in a capital-intensive society. In other words, economies must invest in knowledge just as they invest in machines. In fact, the two are closely associated to the extent that one can envisage an investment–knowledge cycle in which investment spurs knowledge and knowledge spurs investment.

Levels of investment in human capital must therefore be maintained and/or increased for economic growth to continue. Consequently, we could tabulate the expenditure on education and training from one country to another and assess its importance in the growth process. However, such figures are complicated by the fact that expenditure on education and training is carried out by both the public and private sectors. Furthermore, as with physical capital, how does one measure its effectiveness, especially as the benefits of education and training are often only realized in the long run?

At present the UK government is trying to make the educational process more vocational. It is shifting funds to science and technology subjects and placing an increased emphasis on business training – in this way, it is hoped that the quality of our human capital will improve. But only time will tell.

Promote research and development

So far in this section we have recognized that investment can be put into human capital or physical capital. We can now complete this by introducing **R&D capital**. R&D capital is the money used for research and development or, to use other words, for invention and innovation. Clearly, such breakthroughs would play an important part in the growth process. Consequently, governments engage in funding and undertaking R&D through research grants and joint projects with business. However, the UK government is niggardly in this regard, with two possible exceptions: R&D spending is allowable against tax, and R&D related to defence is generally state funded.

As with all investments in capital, the returns can only

be measured in the future. Any analysis of R&D investment expenditure is complicated by the fact that some of it results in no commercial developments, whilst the benefits

---

An academic perspective on R&D

Historically, the UK has adopted a *laissez-faire* approach to R&D with relatively little government intervention in funding (with the exception of defence). However, the United States, Japan, France and Canada have all utilized some form of R&D tax credit, which might explain why over the last twenty years the UK's R&D investment growth has lagged behind the OECD average. Now the Labour government is rightly placing greater emphasis on its support of R&D investment. Indeed, the White Paper *Our Competitive Future*, published in December 1998, set out a range of measures aimed at enabling UK business to close the productivity gap with other OECD countries.

Source: Adapted from *Economic Review*, April 1999

29 Explain why the *laissez-faire* approach does not lead to R&D.

30 State one argument against R&D tax credits.

31 Would tax credits solve the problems in Britain?

32 What is the UK position on R&D tax credits since the year 2000?

33 What other forms of fiscal or monetary policy may help growth?

34 It is acknowledged that the UK produces less per person than other major economies. How may this productivity gap be closed by fiscal or monetary policy?

---

of successful R&D frequently spill over to parties who were not involved in the research in the first place. For example, one country's R&D expenditures may benefit third parties abroad who import goods from the technologically developed country and then use the imports to make their own industries more efficient, or simply imitate the new product. Consequently, economists are uncertain about the precise importance of R&D policies to the growth process, and this is a question that academics are currently studying.

Promote the supply side

Supply-side ideas have been at the centre of government thinking since 1979, the aim being to increase the incentives for businesses and labour to supply their goods and services. Theoretically, the outcome should be to shift the LRAS curve to the right, as discussed with regard to Figure 31.5. The position of the aggregate supply curve can be shifted to the right by changes in factors such as

● the stock of capital

● the state of technology
● the level of state benefits relative to wages
● peoples' preference for leisure

The ways to achieve these changes are seen to lie within markets, by removing as many structural rigidities and barriers to entry as possible. For example, regulations relating to minimum wages, union practices and Sunday trading can be abolished. Taxes may be reduced and training possibilities increased. Such changes encourage markets, especially the labour market, to become more flexible. In fact, they are part of the whole process of deregulation that has occurred in many sectors since 1979. These competition-oriented policies were discussed in Chapter 26.

Promote sustainable development

As suggested in Chapter 10, controlling the environmental impact of increasing economic activity has become an important economic objective of governments at home and abroad. In fact, the world leaders of more than 175 countries met in Rio de Janeiro in 1992, at the world's first Earth Summit, to discuss global environmental problems. Since then policies of sustainable development have become an important cornerstone of many governments.

As we discussed on page 194, the most often-quoted definition of sustainable development originates from a report by the World Commission on Environment and Development as: 'development that meets the needs of the present without compromising the ability of future generations to meet their own needs'. Even though this concept was introduced over twenty years ago, it has not put an end to the view that continued economic growth is essential. Indeed, the main purpose of the definition has been interpreted to highlight that there needs to be some balancing of resource use between current and future generations.

Many mainstream economists view this as an opportunity for still more growth. The challenge to lighten the ecological footprint of tomorrow's society is seen as an incentive to spur the rapid development of a new and environmentally benign economy. In short, improve the efficiency of the more traditional forms of consumption and production. Policies such as the climate change levy and the reduction on vehicle excise duty for small cars that were introduced, via the 1999 Budget, into the UK could accelerate the development of new technologies: leaner, more efficient engines, hydrogen fuel cells that could generate electricity, renewable energy sources using the sun and wind, computers that are so fast and cheap that office productivity could increase with minimal impact on physical resources, etc.

Environmental economists, on the other hand, emphasize that policies concerned with sustainable development place a serious constraint on the level and nature of future growth. Their concern is that material growth is often associated with environmental costs. The point they make is that production and consumption rely upon the ecological system. As suggested by the first exercise of Chapter 10, the environment enables the process of production to begin by providing the source of our raw materials, and it also provides the sink that finally carries away our wastes. These 'sources' and 'sinks' are what environmental economists refer to as natural capital, and as far as they are concerned this cannot be easily substituted by technology. Some of their arguments will be considered in the next section.

KEY POINT

31.5

- Several government policies can be envisaged to promote economic growth. There is no agreed optimal mix of policies for countries to pursue. The recognized possibilities include (1) promoting savings, (2) promoting mobility, (3) promoting education and training (human capital), (4) promoting research and development, (5) promoting the supply side of the economy and (6) promoting the importance of technology and change via policies concerning sustainable development.

The anti-growth lobby

The anti-growth lobby was mainly supported by academics in the 1960s and 1970s. During the 1980s and 1990s, however, support broadened from the university corridors to the House of Commons. At the centre of this lobby's argument are issues relating to pollution and resource depletion. These are both by-products of economic growth. Pollution is the overuse of the environment as a sink, and the term is used quite loosely to refer to a variety of problems relating to waste. For example, industrial emissions into the air and water are classed as pollutants. Resource depletion is caused by harvesting resources at a rate that exceeds their generation. This is easiest to envisage with non-renewable resources such as fossil fuels, but it also occurs with renewable resources (such as timber or fish) when they are harvested in excess.

When asked how much pollution or resource depletion there should be in the economy, many people will respond, 'None'. But if we ask those same people how much starvation or deprivation of consumer products should exist in the economy, many will again say, 'None'. Harvesting and distributing food or producing consumer products creates pollution and depletes resources. In effect, therefore, there is no correct answer to how much pollution or resource depletion there should be in an economy because we are asking people to express values.

To some extent the price system does allow us to express our concerns regarding short-term resource depletion, but pollution is more problematic, since these externalities are not controlled by market forces. Much of the anti-growth argument therefore derives from the fact that market-oriented economies do not effectively consider the long-term resource implications and pollution damage.

As we saw in Chapter 21, a perfect market would enable us to arrive at a Pareto solution where it is impossible to make one person better off without making someone else worse off. Consequently, in conceptual terms we could begin to approach a discussion of the 'correct' amount of pollution or resource depletion by using marginal analysis – similar to the process we used in our discussion for optimizing a firm's employment and output decisions. In marginal analysis terms, we should only pursue measures to reduce environmental problems up to the point at which the marginal benefit from further reduction equals the marginal cost of further reduction.

To consider a more specific example, look at Figure 31.6. On the horizontal axis we show the degree of cleanliness of the air. A vertical line is drawn at 100 per cent cleanliness – the air cannot become any cleaner. Consider

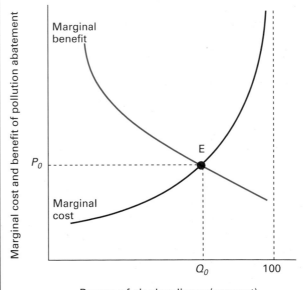

Figure 31.6

The optimal quality of air pollution

As we attempt to get a greater degree of air cleanliness, the marginal cost rises until even the slightest attempt at increasing air cleanliness leads to a very high marginal cost, as can be seen at the upper right of the graph. Conversely, the marginal benefit curve slopes downward: the more pure air we have, the less we value an additional unit of pure air. Marginal cost and marginal benefit intersect at point E. The optimal degree of air cleanliness is something less than 100 per cent at Q_0. The price that we should pay for the last unit of air clean-up is no greater than P_0, for that is where marginal cost equals marginal benefit.

the benefits of obtaining a greater degree of air cleanliness. These benefits are represented by the marginal benefit curve, which slopes downward because of the law of diminishing marginal utility.

When the air is very dirty, the marginal benefit from air that is a little cleaner appears to be relatively high, as shown on the vertical axis. As the air becomes cleaner and cleaner, however, the marginal benefit of a little bit more air cleanliness falls.

For example, consider the marginal cost of pollution abatement related to motor transport – that is, the marginal cost of obtaining cleaner air through the use of catalytic exhausts and lead-free fuels. In the 1960s automobiles had no pollution-abatement devices. Eliminating only 20 per cent of the pollutants emitted by internal-combustion engines entailed a relatively small cost per unit of pollution removed. The cost of eliminating the next 20 per cent certainly rose, though. Finally, as we now get to the upper limits of removal of pollutants from the emissions of internal-combustion engines, we find that the elimination of one more percentage point of the amount of pollutants becomes astronomically expensive. To go from 97 per cent cleanliness to 98 per cent cleanliness involves a marginal cost that is many times greater than that of going from 10 per cent cleanliness to 11 per cent cleanliness.

It is therefore realistic to draw the marginal cost of pollution abatement as an upward-sloping curve, as shown in Figure 31.6. (The marginal cost curve slopes up because of the law of diminishing returns.)

Issues such as these are highlighted by the work of NGOs (non-governmental organizations) such as Greenpeace and Friends of the Earth. The anti-growth lobby is consequently growing in size and there is some possibility that in the future we may see the whole process of economic growth being challenged.

KEY POINTS

31.6

- The problems of pollution and resource depletion are by-products of growth, and their solutions form a central concern of the anti-growth lobby.

- The marginal cost of cleaning up the environment rises as we get closer to 100 per cent cleanliness. Indeed, it rises at an increasing rate.

- The marginal benefit of environmental cleanliness falls as we have more of it.

- Pollution abatement is a trade-off, the trade-off being goods and services for cleaner air and water, and vice versa.

- There are non-governmental organizations that would argue that there are *limits* to economic growth.

Mesmerized by the myth of growth?

I can remember vividly sitting at the dinner table arguing with my father about progress, using upon him all the experience and wisdom I had gathered at the age of fifteen. 'Of course we live in an era of progress,' I said. 'Just look at cars – how clumsy and unreliable and slow they were in the old days, how sleek and efficient and speedy they are now.'

He raised an eyebrow, just a little. 'And what has been the result of having all these wonderful, new, sleek, and efficient cars?' he asked. I was taken aback. I searched for a way to answer. He went on.

'How many people die each year as a result of these speedy cars? How many are maimed and crippled? What is life like for the people who produce them, on those famous assembly lines, the same routine job hour after hour, day after day, like Chaplin's film, *Modern Times*? How many fields and forests and even towns and villages have been paved over so that these cars can get to all the places they want to get to – and park there? Where does all the petrol come from, and at what cost, and what happens when we burn it and exhaust it?'

Before I could stammer out a response, he went on – thankfully – to tell me about an article written on the subject of progress …

Source: *Resurgence*, January/February 1999

35 (a) In economic terms, define progress.
   (b) In economic terms, define pollution.
   (c) Use some form of graphic analysis to explain and account for the trade-offs that may exist between economic growth and pollution.
36 (a) What are the benefits of growth?
   (b) Using the tables in Chapter 13, put monetary value to some of the benefits.
37 Think up your own example to illustrate the problematic nature of progress. In one or two paragraphs, make a case against future economic growth.

Case Study

Can economic growth go on and on?

The classical economists of the eighteenth and nineteenth centuries were pessimistic about the prospects for economic growth. For example, Thomas Malthus, in 1798, expressed concern that rapid increases in population size would quickly outstrip the agricultural capacity to feed all the mouths. In his terms: the geometric increases in population (that is, 2, 4, 8, 16, 32, 64, 128) would outstrip the arithmetic increases that were potentially available to agricultural production. Geometric increases are rapid since they involve 'doubling'; arithmetic increases are straightforward numeric increases (that is, 1, 2, 3, 4, 5, 6, 7). He predicted doom as the eventual outcome unless natural disasters or population control could hold things in check.

David Ricardo (possibly the most famous of all the classical economists) wrote in 1817: 'The natural tendency of profit is to fall; for, in the progress of society and wealth, the additional quantity of food required is obtained by the sacrifice of more and more labour … '

In the opinion of economists such as Malthus and Ricardo, long-run economic growth would cease. Economies would either self-destruct or settle at a stationary state. Not surprisingly, in its early days economics began by being nicknamed 'The dismal science'.

Regardless of these dismal forecasts, the period from 1750 to the year 2000 represented a time of fantastic growth. This surge of economic activity was no doubt due to industrialization (see Figure 31.7 for the portrait across Western Europe). Nowadays, people living in these high-income economies have come to expect their standard of living to improve as a matter of course year by year.

Whether this continuous upward pattern can prevail for the next 250 years is again being called into doubt by economists of the twenty-first century. They either point to the constraints that resources and the environment may present, or suggest that the frontier of technology has moved much closer to the frontier of science. Or, as *The Economist* magazine neatly expressed it in its millennium special edition (January 1000 to December 1999): 'there are fewer wheelbarrows waiting to be invented'.

1 (a) In your own words, identify the basis of the argument that some pessimistic economists use to suggest that economic growth cannot go on for ever.

  (b) Use a diagram such as a production possibilities curve or aggregate supply curve to elaborate on your idea further.

2 In order of importance, state at least three factors that have enabled economies to achieve continual growth during the last 250 years.

3 State three factors that would enable the phenomenal rate of growth to continue for a further 250 years.

4 Using supply and demand curves, show how it is possible for a nation to consume more of a resource over time, even though the resource is becoming relatively scarcer.

5 Make a case for or against continued economic growth.

6 'Economics remains a "dismal science".' Explain and discuss.

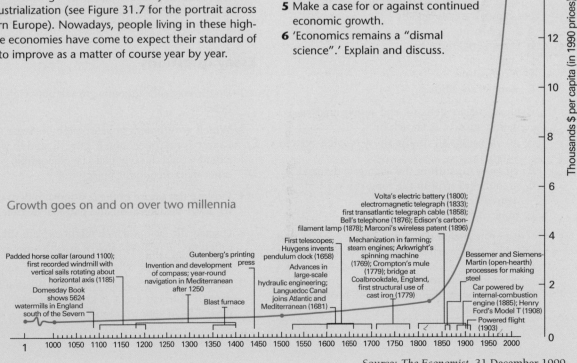

Growth goes on and on over two millennia

Source: *The Economist*, 31 December 1999

Exam Preparation

Multiple choice questions

1 Economic growth is usually defined as
   A the rate of increase in output divided by the increase in labour
   B the increase in output over time
   C the increase in input availability
   D the reduction in the real cost of necessities

2 Which of the following would reduce the average standard of living in a country?
   A A rise in population and the same percentage rise in GNP.
   B A rise in population and a proportionately smaller rise in GNP.
   C No change in population and a rise in GNP.
   D A fall in population and no change in GNP.
   E A fall in population and a smaller proportionate fall in GNP.

3 Each of the following should always lead to economic growth, **except**
   A a discovery of additional natural resources
   B increased investment and capital equipment
   C a higher price level
   D immigration of skilled labour

4 If there has been a 6 per cent increase in nominal GDP, a 4 per cent increase in the price level and a 2 per cent increase in the population, real GDP per capita has changed by
   A −2 per cent
   B 0 per cent
   C 2 per cent
   D 6 per cent
   E none of the above

5 Using aggregate demand and supply analysis, economic growth is shown by
   A an outward shift in the short-run aggregate supply
   B an outward shift in the aggregate demand
   C an outward shift in the long-run vertical aggregate supply
   D none of these

6 If aggregate demand shifts out more rapidly than the shift in the vertical aggregate supply, there will be
   A a reduction in real income
   B an increase in real income with no change in the price level
   C an increase in real income with an increase in the price level

D an increase in the price level but no change in real income

7 The diagram below shows two production possibilities curves.

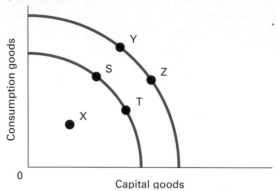

Which of the following movements represents a decrease in actual output?
   A T to X
   B S to T
   C Z to Y
   D S to Z
   E T to Y

8 Economic growth is most effectively defined as
   A an increase in money GDP
   B an increase in real GDP
   C an increase in both material and social welfare
   D an increase in real GNP per head

Essay questions

1 Do the costs of economic growth outweigh the benefits?

2 Which government policies might increase a country's rate of economic growth, and to what extent would these policies be compatible with other macroeconomic objectives?

3 Explore the nature of the relationship between the level of investment and national income.

4 Discuss the factors which might explain the difference in relative rates of growth among the industrialized nations.

5 Discuss the main causes of Britain's economic growth in recent years. Is growth necessary, or desirable, in your opinion?

6 (a) What is a country's gross national product?
  (b) Analyse and comment on the factors which may cause an increase in a country's real gross national product.

7 'Increase in people's welfare can be measured by increases in the economic growth rate.' Discuss this statement with reference to one country only.

8 What factors are likely to increase the level of 'labour productivity' in an economy? Would rapid growth in labour productivity solve the UK's economic and social problems?

9 A newspaper reported that after two years of high economic growth in a country, domestic cost pressures unfortunately have started to increase.
  (a) Consider why the newspaper suggests that domestic cost increases are unfortunate.
  (b) Is economic growth beneficial?

10 Explain whether or not you regard a high growth rate as a desirable economic objective. Discuss the implications of growth for (a) Britain and Europe and (b) the less-developed world.

Glossary

absolute advantage The ability to produce a good or service at an 'absolutely' lower cost, usually (but not necessarily) measured in hours of work required to produce the good.

absolute or nominal prices The prices that we observe today in terms of today's pounds. Also called nominal or current prices.

accelerator The level of investment depends upon the rate of growth of demand. A given percentage change in demand may require a larger percentage change in investment. The accelerator shows by how much the rate of growth of investment exceeds the rate of growth of demand (and of output).

accounting profit The difference between total revenues and total explicit costs.

ad valorem **tax** A duty on a good that is a percentage of the price charged by producers.

age–earnings cycle The way in which over a lifetime earnings tend to vary in a predictable way. They will usually rise early on in life, until the extra benefits of training and experience have been reaped, and fall towards the end of the working life as productivity may then diminish.

aggregate demand All planned expenditures for the entire economy summed together.

aggregate demand curve Planned purchase rates for all goods and services in the economy at various price levels.

aggregate demand shock Any shock that causes the aggregate demand curve to shift inwards or outwards.

aggregates Total amounts or quantities: aggregate demand, for example, relates to the total quantity demanded within a nation.

aggregate supply All planned production for the entire economy summed together.

aggregate supply curve The relationship between planned rates of total production for the entire economy and the price level.

aggregate supply shock Any shock that causes the aggregate supply curve to shift inwards or outwards.

annually managed expenditure An accounting device associated with public finance. *See* total managed expenditure.

anticipated inflation That inflation rate which individuals believe will occur; when it does, we are in a situation of fully anticipated inflation.

appreciation The increasing of the value of a domestic currency in terms of other currencies. This occurs in a freely floating exchange market when the quantity demanded for the domestic currency exceeds the quantity supplied at the current price. In a fixed exchange rate market, appreciation cannot occur spontaneously; it must be done officially. Then it is called revaluation.

asset Anything of value that is owned. Customers' deposits create assets in that the bank holds sums of money which it can use until customers withdraw them.

assisted areas Geographical areas that have been designated by government as needing special encouragement of industrial development – hence they are assisted by having government incentives available to locate firms there.

asymmetric information A situation where two parties to a transaction involving a good or service have unequal knowledge of the properties or risks involved in making that transaction.

automatic, or built-in, stabilizers Built-in stabilizers do not require initiation and action on the part of the government. Examples are the progressive income tax system and unemployment benefits, both of which have built into the system the ability to modify changes in disposable income caused by the change in overall business activity.

autonomous consumption That part of consumption that is independent of, or does not depend on, the level of disposable income. Changes in autonomous consumption shift the consumption function.

average fixed costs Total fixed costs divided by the number of units produced.

average propensity to consume (APC) Consumption divided by disposable income for any given level of income. The proportion of total disposable income that is consumed.

average propensity to save (APS) Saving divided by disposable income. The proportion of total disposable income that is saved.

average tax rate The total tax payment divided by the total income upon which the tax was based. In other words, the proportion of tax paid on income – after allowances have been deducted.

average total costs Total costs divided by the number of units produced.

average variable costs Total variable costs divided by the number of units produced.

B

balance of payments A summary of transactions concerning visible goods and invisibles (services, investment earnings and transfers) (the current account) and financial assets.

balance on current account A summary of transactions concerning visible goods and invisibles (services, investment income and transfers).

bank bills Bills which will be honoured at a stated date in the future (usually ninety-one days). This helps with cash flow as the seller (often an exporter) is effectively giving a period of 'grace' before payment. A distinguishing feature of these bills is that they may be passed on for cash to another party (at a rate slightly below face value) before the pay due date. The final holder of the bill will then present it for payment on maturity. Similar bills may be drawn up by commercial organizations, local authorities and the Treasury to help with cash-flow problems. It may be simpler to regard all these 'bills' as post-dated cheques which may be redeemed for cash at a slight loss before the pay date if necessary. Bank bills may be known as commercial bills or acceptance credits.

bankers' balances The balances, or deposits, that commercial banks keep with the central bank (that is, the Bank of England).

bankruptcy The situation when a business entity is unable to meet its debts.

barometric price leader A price increase announced by one firm is quickly followed by rivals. The leader may or may not be the same firm on each occasion of a price increase.

barriers to entry Barriers that make it either impossible or difficult for firms to enter an existing industry and offer competition to existing producers or suppliers. Some barriers include government restrictions and legislation.

barter A system of exchange in which goods or services are exchanged for goods or services without the use of money.

base year The year that is chosen as the point of reference for a comparison of prices in other years.

benefits in kind The government provides certain goods and services, such as housing, medical care and education. To be contrasted with benefits in cash, which is simply income that can be used to buy *any* goods and services.

bilateral monopoly A situation in which the market consists of a single buyer and a single seller.

black economy The unofficial economic activity that cannot be precisely measured because it fails to go through official accounts.

black market A situation where the official 'white' market price is controlled but buyers are prepared to pay a price that reflects the relative scarcity of the good. Black markets usually exist only in a war-time economy when the availability of civilian goods is curtailed.

bonds The government issues bonds in order to raise long-term finance (typically for twenty years). (Private companies may issue corporate bonds.) Government bonds are known as gilts because they are 'as good as gold' – there is no risk of default.

boom A period of time during which overall business activity is rising at a more rapid rate than its long-term trend.

brand names These are used to differentiate a particular product in the mind of the consumer. They may come to be associated with specific product qualities and may become a substantial asset to the firm if consumer awareness of the product is very strong.

broad money In the UK broad money is measured by M4, the main measure of money supply. It includes notes and coin, banks' balances with the Bank of England, and most deposits with banks and building societies. It provides an important indicator of spending power in the economy.

budget constraint The resource constraint imposed on households and firms at any point in time. It represents the set of opportunities facing each decision-maker.

buffer stock An organization, whether owned and run by a group of producers or financed by the government, that attempts to smooth out fluctuations in prices by the purchase and sale of stocks.

building societies A group of financial institutions that specialize in providing long-term loans for house purchase (that is, mortgages).

business fluctuations The ups and downs in overall business activity, as evidenced by changes in national income, employment and prices.

C

capital All manufactured resources, including buildings, equipment, machines and improvements to land.

capital adequacy ratios Rules concerning the ratio of liquid reserve assets which banks must keep to balance their lending activities. Without adequate reserve assets, banks are in danger of becoming short of liquidity and therefore unable to make good depositors' requests for cash.

capital consumption *See* depreciation, which is another name for the same concept.

capital gains The positive difference between the purchase price and the sale price of an asset.

capital goods Goods that are used in the production of other goods. Examples include cranes, factories and foundries. Consumers do not directly consume capital goods.

capital intensive Describes the situation where large amounts of capital are used in the production process, and relatively little labour or other resources.

capitalism An economic system in which individuals privately own productive resources; these individuals can use the resources in whatever manner they choose, subject to common protective legal restrictions.

capital movements The flow of funds across international boundaries for investment in plant and machinery, or in response to interest rate changes or expectations of interest rate changes.

cartel The most explicit means by which oligopolists effect collusion. A cartel is an association of independent entities that attempts to determine output, sales and prices such that cartel members can secure monopoly profits. Members of a cartel invariably face a conflict between self-interest and the common cause of all producers.

cash-flow problem Some firms develop a cash-flow problem because the money coming into the business on a monthly basis is insufficient sometimes to cover all the outgoings. This can happen even if the business is fundamentally profitable.

central bank A banker's bank, usually an official institution that also serves as each country's Treasury's bank. Central banks supervise commercial banks.

certificate of deposit (CD) A time deposit with a fixed maturity date offered by banks and other financial institutions.

***ceteris paribus* assumption** The assumption that all other things are held equal, or constant, except those under study.

circular flow A model of the flows of resources, goods and services, as well as money, receipts and payments for them, in the economy.

claimant unemployment This is a record of the number of people claiming unemployment-related benefits on one particular day each month.

clearing system A mutually agreed system shared by commercial banks in the United Kingdom. It refers to the process by which the debts between these banks, generated by their customers' cheques, are settled each day.

closed economy An economic system that has no transactions with any other economy.

closed shop A business enterprise in which an employee must belong to the union before he or she can be employed. That employee must remain in the union after he or she becomes employed.

cobweb A dynamic model which tries to explain why cyclical fluctuations in output and prices, for example in the agricultural sector, can occur.

coincident indicators Economic statistics that act as reference points for the general business cycle. For example, changes in output and stocks of raw material confirm that an economy is changing.

collective bargaining Bargaining between management of a company or of a group of companies and management of a union or a group of unions for the purpose of setting a mutually agreeable contract on wages, fringe benefits and working conditions for all employees in the union(s). Different from individual bargaining, where each employee strikes a bargain with his or her employer individually.

collective decision-making How voters, politicians and other interested parties act and how these actions influence non-market decisions.

collusion Price determination by oligopolists which is co-ordinated and aims to avoid the danger of price wars.

command and control A government approach to regulation that is executed by bureaucrats rather than markets.

command economic system A system in which the government controls the factors of production and makes all decisions about their use and about the distribution of income. The political character of such a government is indeterminate.

commercial bank This is a privately owned profit-seeking institution, sometimes referred to as a joint-stock bank to highlight the fact that it has shareholders. Most high street banks, such as HSBC and Barclays etc., are commercial banks.

commercial bills *See* bank bills.

common property Property that is owned by everyone and therefore by no one. Air and water are examples of common property resources.

communism In its purest form, an economic system in which the state has disappeared and in which individuals contribute to the economy according to their productivity and are given income according to their need.

comparative advantage An advantage arising out of relative efficiency, which follows from scarcity of resources. Comparative advantage is the advantage measured in terms of other goods that could be produced, not in terms of factor inputs. If a country has a comparative advantage in one good, it must have a comparative disadvantage in another. As long as the opportunity cost of doing the same job differs for different people or different countries, each will have a comparative advantage in something.

competition Rivalry among buyers and sellers of outputs or among buyers and sellers of inputs (that is, factors of production).

complement Two goods are considered complements if a change in the price of one causes an opposite shift in the demand for the other. For example, if the price of tennis rackets goes up, the demand for tennis balls will fall; if the price of tennis rackets goes down, the demand for tennis balls will increase.

concentration ratio The percentage of all sales contributed by the leading four or leading eight firms in an industry; sometimes called the industry-concentration ratio.

conglomerate A firm which has interests in several very different markets.

conglomerate merger A merger between firms which are not in a related business.

constant capital approach This approach to sustainable development regards natural capital as substitutable with man-made capital. Hence the claim that as long as aggregate capital stock remains constant, there will be a future.

constant-cost industry An industry whose total output can be increased without an increase in per-unit costs; an industry whose long-run supply curve is horizontal.

constant prices An expenditure aggregate or a measure of expenditure expressed in terms of real purchasing power, using a particular year as the base or standard of comparison.

constant returns to scale A situation in which the long-run average cost curve of a firm remains flat, or horizontal, as output increases.

consumer goods Goods that are used directly by consumers to generate satisfaction. To be contrasted with capital goods.

consumer optimum A choice of a basket of goods and services that maximizes the level of satisfaction for each consumer.

consumers The buyers of goods and services whose spending in a free-market economy directs what is produced.

consumer sovereignty The concept of the consumer as the one who, by his or her spending, ultimately determines which goods and services will be produced in the economy. In principle, competition among producers causes them to adjust their production to the changing desires of consumers.

consumer surplus The difference between the amount that a consumer is willing to pay for a commodity and the amount that is actually paid. This surplus utility which is not paid for is measured by the area above the price charged and below the demand schedule.

consumption That which is spent on new goods and services out of a household's current income. Whatever is not consumed is saved. Consumption includes buying food, going to the cinema, going to a concert and so on.

consumption function The relationship between the amount consumed and disposable income. A consumption function tells us how much people plan to consume out of various disposable income levels.

consumption goods *See* consumer goods.

contingent valuation method This is a technique used to identify the price of an externality. It involves a survey of the interested parties in an attempt to elicit a hypothetical (monetary) value attributed to some environmental gain or loss.

contracting-out When this term is used in the context of privatization it refers to the transference of publicly provided activities to private contractors, usually through competitive tendering.

contractionary policy (or deflation) The use of tax increases and expenditure cuts to reduce inflationary pressure, or overheating, in the economy, or to reduce a balance of trade deficit.

cost–benefit analysis (CBA) This is a way of appraising an investment proposal. It is normally undertaken by government departments, since it involves adding the indirect (external) costs and benefits to the conventional direct costs and benefits (revenue). This is done by estimating monetary values for aspects such as health, time, leisure and pollution.

cost-push inflation Rising prices caused by rising production costs, union wage negotiations or bosses seeking more profits.

counter-cyclical policy The use of fiscal and monetary policy to offset booms and slumps by contractionary and expansionary policy, respectively.

cross-price elasticity of demand The percentage change in the demand for one good divided by the percentage change in the price of a related good. Cross-price elasticity of demand is a measure of the responsiveness of one good's quantity demanded to changes in a related good's price.

cross-section data Empirical observations about one or more variables gathered at a particular point in time.

crowding out The expansion of public sector expenditure which reduces private sector spending.

currency Notes and coin – often simply referred to as 'cash'.

currency crisis A situation in the international money market that occurs when a country no longer has the foreign exchange resources to support the price of its currency. A currency crisis brings forced devaluation under a fixed exchange rate system.

current prices *See* nominal values.

cyclical unemployment Unemployment resulting from business recessions that occur when total demand is insufficient to create full employment.

D

deadweight welfare loss A measure of the reduction in consumer surplus arising from monopolization of a competitive industry which may be partially or even wholly offset by resource savings accruing to the monopolist.

debt finance Loans which can be used to invest in new productive capacity.

decreasing-cost industry An industry in which an increase in output leads to a reduction in per-unit costs, such that the long-run industry supply curve is downward sloping.

deficiency payment A payment made to farmers for any difference between the target price for their product and the market price that they actually received; a direct subsidy paid to farmers.

deficit spending Government spending that is in excess of government tax revenues.

deflation The situation in which the average of all prices of goods and services in an economy is falling.

demand curve A graphic representation of the demand schedule. A negatively sloped line showing the inverse relationship between the price and the quantity demanded.

demand-deficiency unemployment *See* cyclical unemployment.

demand-pull inflation Inflation caused by total demand exceeding the current supply. This is a particular problem when the economy is at full capacity output.

demand schedule A set of pairs of numbers showing various possible prices and the quantities demanded at each price. This is a schedule showing the rate of planned purchase per time period at different prices of the good.

demerit good The opposite of a merit good; one which the political process has decided is socially undesirable.

departmental expenditure limit *See* total managed expenditure.

depreciation (capital) The reduction in the value of capital goods over a one-year period due to physical wear and tear and also to obsolescence.

depreciation (currency) A lessening of the value of a domestic currency in terms of foreign currencies. Depreciation occurs in a freely floating foreign exchange market when there is an excess supply of the domestic currency. In a fixed exchange rate market, depreciation can occur if the government allows it.

depression *See* recession.

deregulation Often used in the context of privatization to describe the opening up of state monopolies to competition from other suppliers.

derived demand Input factor demand derived from demand for the final product being produced.

devaluation The same as depreciation except that it occurs officially under a regime of fixed exchange rates.

diminishing marginal utility The smaller increase in total utility from the consumption of a good or service as more is consumed.

direct taxation Tax liability targeted at one person on the basis of income.

discount houses A small group (seven in 1994) of specialized institutions which borrow for very short periods of time from the banks (*see* money at call) and invest in 'bills' (*see* commercial bills) and other short-term assets. The discount houses are therefore specialists in the movement of short-term funds between financial institutions. Indeed, they often act as a middle-man between the Bank of England and commercial banks.

discounting The method by which the present value of a future sum or a future stream of sums is obtained.

discount rate (intervention rate) The interest rate at which the Bank of England discounts bills (intervenes in the discount market).

discretionary fiscal policy Government policy with respect to taxes or spending, or both, that involves a deliberate change legislated by Parliament for the purpose of altering the equilibrium level of real national income.

diseconomies of scale When increases in output lead to increases in long-run average costs.

disinflation A term coined in the early 1980s to describe the process whereby high rates of inflation begin to reduce as a result of counter-inflationary policies.

distribution of income The way income is distributed among the population. This may be equal or unequal. An unequal distribution of income might involve, for example, the top 20 per cent of income-earners receiving 35 per cent of total income while the bottom 20 per cent received only 5 per cent.

division of labour The segregation of a resource into different specific tasks; for example, one car worker puts on bumpers, another doors and so on.

dominant firm In a situation of oligopoly there may be one firm which is able to dominate the market. It may set the price, have a substantial market share and face only limited competition from other firms.

dominant price leader The leading firm in an industry which is the first to change prices. A smaller firm may be content to let the larger firm judge when prices need to be adjusted or feel that the kinked demand curve situation could apply if it led an increase in prices.

double-count An accounting problem that occurs when measuring output. The problem is that final output is made up of many stages. Hence, you must take care either to include the extra value added at each stage of production or only to record the final values of output.

dumping The export of products at a price below their cost of production.

duopoly A market structure in which there are only two sellers of a commodity and thus the matter of interdependence is critical for price determination.

durable consumer goods Goods used by consumers which have a lifespan of more than one year; that is, goods that endure and can give utility over a longer period of time.

E

economic efficiency The use of resources that generate the highest possible value of output as determined in the market economy by consumers.

economic good Any good or service that is scarce.

economic growth Defined either as the increase in an economy's real level of output over time or as the increase in the economy's real per capita level of output over time. Economic growth is therefore measured by the rate of change of real output or real per capita output.

economic indicators Statistics relating to the main economic variables. For examples *see* retail price index, money supply, balance of payments, economic growth.

economic profit The difference between total revenues and the opportunity cost of all factors of production.

economic rent That part of earnings which is in excess of transfer earnings. Economic rent will be earned when the supply of a particular skill or personality is restricted, that is, inelastic.

economics A social science studying human behaviour, and, in particular, the way in which individuals and societies choose among the alternative uses of scarce resources to satisfy wants.

economic system The institutional means through which resources are used to satisfy human wants.

economies of scale When increases in output lead to decreases in long-run average costs.

economies of scope These occur if it is cheaper to produce two or more goods together than it is to produce each separately.

emerging economies A term used to describe the rapidly growing developing economies and principally referring to the 'second wave' East Asian 'Tiger' economies such as Indonesia, Malaysia and Thailand.

employers' association A group of employers who negotiate wages jointly with trade unions.

endogenous variables Economic factors which affect other aspects of a theory or model from within. For example, the level of unemployment will determine the amount of income tax collected.

enterprise culture A relatively new idea used to describe a hard-working, efficient society driven forward by the profit motive, in freely competitive markets, towards greater amounts of wealth.

entrepreneurship The fourth factor of production involving human resources that perform the functions of raising capital, organizing, managing, assembling other factors of production, and making basic business policy decisions. The entrepreneur is a risk-taker.

equation of exchange The number of monetary units multiplied by the number of times each unit is spent on final goods and services is identical to the price multiplied by output (or national income). Formally written as $M \times V = P \times Q$.

equilibrium A situation in which the plans of buyers and sellers exactly coincide so that there is neither excess supply nor excess demand.

equilibrium price *See* market-clearing price.

equity finance The proceeds of a share issue which allow the firm to invest in capital equipment.

Eurodollar deposits Deposits denominated in US dollars but held in banks outside the United States, usually (but not always) in overseas branches of US banks.

eurozone The area which is covered by the Economic and Monetary Union (EMU). At the time of writing, this includes eleven EU countries: all except Denmark, Greece, Sweden and the UK.

exchange The act of trading, usually done on a voluntary basis, in which both parties to the trade are subjectively better off.

exchange equalization account An account held and managed by the Bank of England on behalf of the government. It is used to prevent undesirable fluctuations in the sterling exchange rate.

exchange rate target The Bank of England may set a target range for the exchange rate. Maintaining this may promote stability in the economy more effectively than adherence to a monetary target, which may be subject to change for other reasons than the growth of the money supply.

excise duties on alcohol *See* taxation.

excise tax A tax placed on specific products, such as alcohol, petrol and tobacco. The tax will be a specific sum rather than a proportion of the value and will be changed from time to time.

exclusive purchase A distributor contracts to stock only the products of one manufacturer, possibly in return for an exclusive supply arrangement.

exclusive supply A seller supplies only one buyer in a certain geographical area, which limits competition between that buyer and his or her competitors.

exit Firms exit from the market-place when there is no longer sufficient demand for their product to make it worthwhile staying in business.

exogenous variables Economic factors, for example the weather, which impinge upon a theory or model from the outside. They are sometimes referred to as autonomous variables and they contrast with endogenous variables.

expansion A business fluctuation in which overall business activity is rising at a more rapid rate than previously, or at a more rapid rate than the overall historical trend for the nation. This is sometimes referred to as a 'boom'.

expansionary gap Exists whenever the equilibrium level of real national income exceeds the full-employment level of real national income; the positive difference between total desired spending and the full-employment level of real national income.

expansionary policy (or reflation) The use of tax cuts and increased government spending (perhaps along with an easy monetary policy) to increase aggregate demand and promote increased economic growth and employment.

expenditure approach A way of computing national income by adding up the values of all spending at current market prices on final goods and services.

expenditure-reducing policies Contractionary macroeconomic policies designed to reduce incomes and so reduce spending on imports and on goods which could be exported.

expenditure-switching policies Policies which lead to a fall in spending on imports and a rise in spending on domestically produced goods for both the export and the domestic markets.

exploitation Paying a resource less than its value (marginal revenue product).

external economies of scale These are the savings a firm can achieve, per unit of output, due to increases in the size of the whole industry in which it is based; for example, state-funded training.

external finance Firms that are expanding can use external finance, which they may borrow from banks or individuals. Other possible external sources of finance include share issues.

externality A cost or benefit external to an exchange. In other words, the external benefits or costs accrue to parties other than the immediate seller and buyer in a transaction.

F

factor markets In the factor market, households are the sellers; they sell resources such as labour, land, capital and entrepreneurial ability. Businesses are the buyers in factor markets; business expenditures represent receipts or, more simply, income for households (see Figure 13.1).

fiduciary monetary system A system in which currency is issued by the government, and its value is based uniquely on the public's faith that the currency represents command over goods and services.

finance houses A group of financial institutions that specialize in providing funds for hire-purchase agreements.

financial conglomerates Large financial institutions which do not specialize in particular types of business but offer their customers a wide range of financial products, including bank accounts, mortgages, insurance and so on.

financial intermediaries Those financial institutions that take money from depositors and make loans to borrowers, for example commercial banks.

financial markets Those markets through which saving passes before it goes either to governments or to business firms for investment purposes. Included are insurance companies, commercial banks and pension plans.

firm An organization that brings together different factors of production, such as labour, land and capital, to produce a product or service that can be sold for a profit. A firm is usually made up of an entrepreneur, managers and workers.

First World The industrialized non-communist countries of Western Europe plus the United States, Australia, New Zealand, Canada and Japan.

five-year plans Economic plans set up by the central government in a country that plots the future course of its economic development. The first five-year plan was devised in Russia by Stalin after Lenin's death.

fixed costs The costs that do not vary with output. Fixed costs include such things as rent on a building and the price of machinery. These costs are fixed for a certain period of time; in the long run they are variable.

fixed exchange rates A system of exchange rates that requires government intervention to fix the value of each nation's currency in terms of every other nation's currency.

fixed investment Purchases, made by business, of newly produced producer durables, or capital goods, such as production machinery and office equipment.

fixed throttle Controlled growth of aggregate monetary demand at a constant rate, equal to the long-run growth of productive capacity.

flow A term used to describe activities that occur over time. For example, income is a flow that occurs per week, per month or per year. Consumption is also a flow, as are production and unemployment.

foreign banks The name given to banks whose country of origin is overseas. Many have branches located in London.

foreign exchange market The market for buying and selling foreign currencies.

foreign exchange rate The price of foreign currency in terms of domestic currency, or vice versa. For example, if the foreign exchange rate for francs is 25p, this means that it takes 25p to buy 1 franc. An alternative way of stating the exchange rate is that the value of the pound is 4 francs. It takes 4 francs to buy £1.

45° line The line along which planned expenditures equal real national income or output per year; a line that bisects the total planned expenditures–real national income quadrant.

fractional reserve banking system A system of banking whereby banks keep only a fraction of their deposits on reserve.

franchising In the context of competition policy the process of the government seeking bids from interested parties to win the right to provide a service for a specified period of time and enjoy certain monopoly rights, for example to be a regional television service provider.

free enterprise A system in which private business firms are able to obtain resources, to organize those resources and to sell the finished product in any way they choose.

free good Any good or service that is available in quantities larger than are desired at a zero price.

freely floating (or flexible) exchange rates Exchange rates that are allowed to fluctuate in the open market in response to changes in supply and demand. Sometimes called free exchange rates or floating exchange rates.

free-rider problem A problem associated with public goods in which individuals presume that others will pay for the public goods, so that individually they can escape paying for their production without a reduction in production occurring.

frictional unemployment Unemployment associated with frictions in the system that may occur because of the imperfect job market information that exists.

full-line forcing This requires a buyer to purchase quantities of each item in a product range in order to be able to buy any of them.

G

GDP deflator A price index measuring the changes in prices of *all* new goods and services produced in the economy. Hence a more comprehensive index than the retail price index.

general equilibrium analysis Economic analysis that takes account of the interrelationships among markets; to be contrasted with partial equilibrium analysis, which does not.

geographically immobile *See* mobility of labour.

Gini coefficient of inequality A numerical representation of the degree of income inequality in a nation; defined as the ratio of the area between the diagonal line and the actual Lorenz curve to the triangular area under that diagonal line.

globalization The term used to refer to the growing interdependence of the world's economies due to the growth of international trade and also flows of capital and technology.

government failure This term has developed, along with the emphasis on microeconomics, to highlight how government policy may not necessarily improve economic efficiency.

government, or political, goods Goods and services provided by the public sector; they can be either private or public goods.

gross domestic investment The creation of capital goods, such as factories and machines, that can yield production and hence consumption in the future. Also included in this definition are changes in business stocks and repairs made to machines or buildings. In sum, it is investment before depreciation.

gross domestic product (GDP) The most common measurement of a nation's income generated from resources within its own boundaries: the value of its output of goods and services.

gross national product (GNP) Another measurement of the wealth of a country. It represents the total output of goods and services produced by the country in a year, plus the value of net property income from abroad.

guaranteed (or target) price A price set by the government for specific agricultural products. If market-clearing prices fall below target prices, a 'deficiency' payment equal to the difference between the market price and the target price is given to each farmer who qualifies.

H

harmonized indices of consumer prices (HICP) A measure of consumer price inflation that allows comparison between European Union countries. The series of figures commenced in January 1996.

Harrod–Domar growth model A model where economic growth is determined by a stable capital–output ratio and the propensity to save.

headline rate The change in the retail price index that is announced by the ONS and widely quoted in the press. It contrasts with the underlying rate of inflation, which is adjusted to exclude mortgage interest payments.

hedonic price method This is a technique used to identify the price of an externality. It involves attempting a calculated estimate of the implicit price of an environmental attribute, by comparing the value of two identical goods, one with the environmental element and the other without.

hidden unemployment Official unemployment statistics are not 100 per cent accurate since people may be incorrectly included or excluded.

horizontal merger The joining of firms that are producing or selling a similar product.

hot money When capital flows quickly from one currency to another for largely speculative reasons, it is known as hot money.

human capital Investment which has taken place in education and training which enhances the productivity of the individual.

I

ILO unemployment rate A measure of unemployment administered by the International Labour Organization. It defines unemployment as persons who are without work, yet actively seeking employment. Data are gathered through labour force surveys.

import levy A tax imposed on a good when it is landed at a port or other point of entry into a country.

import substitution The process by which many less-developed countries have begun to industrialize, that is, they attempt to manufacture consumer goods rather than resort to foreign supplies to meet domestic demand.

income approach A way of measuring national income by adding up all factor rewards, namely wages, interest, rent and profits.

income–consumption curve The set of optimum consumption points that would occur if income were successfully increased, nominal and relative prices remaining constant.

income differentials The differences in incomes which create an incentive to move from one occupation or job to another.

income effect The change in people's purchasing power that occurs when, other things held constant, a change in the price of one product causes a change in real income. When the price goes up, real income, or purchasing power, falls; and when the price goes down, real income, or purchasing power, increases.

income-elastic demand A given change in income will result in a larger percentage change in quantity demanded in the same direction.

income elasticity of demand The percentage change in the quantity demanded divided by the percentage change in money income; the responsiveness of the quantity demanded to changes in income.

income-inelastic demand A given change in income will result in a less than proportionate change in demand in the same direction.

increasing-cost industry An industry in which an increase in industry output is accompanied by an increase in per-unit costs, such that the long-run industry supply curve is upward sloping.

independent variable A variable whose value can change freely.

indexing Linking a specific nominal sum to the rate of inflation; for example, under some schemes pensions can be indexed so that they increase at the rate of inflation.

indicative planning A system which involves the government setting up general targets for the major sectors of the economy to assist the private sector in their decision-making.

indifference curve A curve composed of the set of consumption alternatives each yielding the same total amount of satisfaction.

indifference curve analysis A theoretical process used for studying consumer behaviour. The method employed involves ranking combinations of products in terms of more or less satisfaction.

indirect taxation The taxes imposed on spending. In this case the seller has ultimate responsibility to pay.

induced spending A variable which depends on the level of income is said to be induced.

industrial unions Labour unions that consist of workers from a particular industry, such as car manufacturing or steel manufacturing.

industry supply curve The locus of points showing the minimum prices at which given quantities will be forthcoming; also called the market supply curve.

infant industry argument An argument in support of tariffs: tariffs should be imposed to protect (from import competition) an industry that is trying to get started. The presumption is that, after the industry becomes established and technologically efficient, the tariff can be removed.

inferior good A good of which the consumer purchases less as income increases.

inflation A sustained rise in prices, formally measured by the retail price index.

inflow A measure used to record the number joining the monthly unemployment statistics.

inheritance tax *See* taxation.

injections Supplementary expenditures not originating in the household sector; can include investment, government purchases and exports.

institutions The laws of the nation as well as the habits, ethics, mores, folkways and customs of the citizens of that nation.

interdependence The situation where a small number of firms are each affected by the others' actions in the market-place. This leads to their watching each other's decisions very closely and revising their own in consequence. Alternatively, interdependence may refer to the situation of a number of nations which are so closely linked by trade and financial relationships that they depend on each other economically.

interest The payment for current rather than future command over resources; the cost of obtaining credit. Also, the return paid to owners of capital.

internal finance Firms that are expanding can use internal finance to do so; this means they use retained profits from the past to invest in capital equipment or property.

International Bank for Reconstruction and Development (IBRD) More commonly referred to as the World Bank. Founded following the Bretton Woods conference in 1944, it is an institution based in Washington which provides funds for developing countries.

international commodity agreement An arrangement between buyers and sellers of a primary product such as coffee that attempts to reduce price fluctuations in that product for the mutual benefit of both consumers and producers.

International Monetary Fund (IMF) An institution set up to manage the international monetary system. It came out of the Bretton Woods conference in 1944, which established more or less fixed exchange rates in the world.

intra-industry trade The export and import between two countries of goods in an industry, for example cars, which means that firms in both countries enjoy a reputation for particular products or models.

inverse relationship A relationship such that an increase in one variable is associated with a decrease in the other, and a decrease in one variable is associated with an increase in the other.

investment The spending by businesses on items such as machines and buildings, which can be used to produce goods and services in the future. The investment part of total income is that portion which will be used in the process of producing goods in the future. Sometimes the term is used simply to mean any spending which generates future income.

inward-looking development strategy An outlook where a developing country looks to greater self-sufficiency and self-reliance rather than promoting its export potential.

J

J-curve effect This refers to the way in which the trade balance may initially worsen after an exchange rate depreciation.

joint-stock company A legal entity owned by stockholders. The stockholders are liable only for the amount of money they have invested in the company. These firms are sometimes referred to as corporations.

K

kinked demand curve A model of pricing in an oligopolistic market structure in which rivals follow one firm's decision to make a price decrease but not a price increase. The demand curve is thus bent or kinked and the associated marginal revenue curve has a discontinuous part in it.

L

labour The human resource involving productive contributions of persons who work, which involve both thinking and doing.

labour intensive A term used to describe the production process when relatively large amounts of labour are employed and relatively little of other resources.

labour theory of value A theory that the value of all commodities is equal to the value of the labour used in producing them.

lagging indicators Economic statistics (such as unemployment and investment) that change approximately six months after a change in overall activity (gross domestic product).

laissez-faire The viewpoint that government should not intervene in a detailed way in the business life of a country other than to remove legal restraints on trade. Adam Smith's *Wealth of Nations* represents this doctrine.

land The natural resources that are available without alteration or effort on the part of labour. Land as a resource includes only original fertility and mineral deposits, topography, climate, water and natural vegetation.

law of diminishing (marginal) returns After some point, successive increases in a variable factor of production, such as labour, added to fixed factors of production will result in less than a proportional increase in output.

law of increasing relative costs An economic principle that states that the opportunity cost of additional units of a good generally increases as society attempts to produce more of that good.

leading indicators Economic statistics (such as retail sales and consumer credit) that change approximately three to six months in advance of gross domestic product and are used to predict changes in the economic cycle.

leakages Those parts of national income not used for consumption, for example net taxes, saving and imports.

legal prohibition approach A stance towards competition policy that prohibits agreements having the effect of restraining competition. This explicit pro-competition policy position adopted by the EU in 1957 contrasts with the more muted, discretionary approach adopted by the UK until 1998.

lemons problem The situation in which consumers, who do not know details about the quality of a product, are willing to pay no more than the price of a low-quality product, even if a higher-quality product at a higher price exists.

less-developed countries (LDCs) Those countries that are in the process of development and that have not yet reached an arbitrary per capita living standard. Countries whose per capita income in 1998 was less than $760 are defined as low-income economies, and those where GNP per head was between $761 and $9360 are middle-income economies. The developed countries are defined as high-income economies where GNP per head in 1998 was $9361 or more.

liability May be thought of as an amount that is owed. Customers' deposits create a liability in that the bank must be prepared to repay the customer at any time.

licensed deposit-takers (LDTs) Institutions permitted (licensed) by the Bank of England to take deposits from the public.

limit pricing The determination of prices by existing firms in an industry lower than a profit-maximizing price which seeks to deter the entry of new firms. Also known as the entry-forestalling price.

liquidity A characteristic of any asset; it describes the degree to which the asset can be acquired or disposed of without much danger of any intervening loss in nominal value and with small transaction costs. Money is the most liquid asset.

local authority bills *See* commercial bills.

localized industry This is when one industry dominates a whole geographical area, that is, it is dominant in one locality.

long run That time period in which all factors of production can be varied.

long-run average cost curve This represents the cheapest way to produce various levels of output given existing technology and current resource prices. It is derived by joining the minimum point of various short-run average cost curves.

long-run industry supply curve A market supply curve showing the relationship between price and quantities forthcoming after firms have been allowed the time to enter or exit from an industry, depending on whether there have been positive or negative economic profits.

Lorenz curve A geometric representation of the distribution of income. A Lorenz curve that is perfectly straight represents perfect income equality. The more bowed a Lorenz curve, the more unequally income is distributed.

M

macroeconomics The study of economy-wide phenomena, such as unemployment and inflation.

managed floating A freely floating exchange system that involves governments stepping in to stabilize the value of their currencies. To be contrasted with a 'clean' float, where there is no government intervention in the foreign exchange market.

marginal cost (MC) The change in total costs due to a one-unit increase in the variable input. The cost of using more of a factor of production.

marginal cost pricing A system of pricing in which the price charged is equal to the opportunity cost to society of producing one more unit of the good or service in question. The opportunity cost is the marginal cost to society.

marginal physical product (MPP) The output that the addition of one more worker produces. The marginal physical product of the worker is equal to the change in total output that can be accounted for by hiring the worker, holding all other factors of production constant.

marginal private benefit The marginal gain to an individual resulting from the provision of an additional unit of supply of a public good.

marginal propensity to consume (MPC) The ratio of the change in consumption to the change in disposable income. A 0.8 marginal propensity to consume tells us that an additional £100 earned will lead to an additional £80 consumed.

marginal propensity to import The proportion of an increase in income which is spent on imports.

marginal propensity to save (MPS) The ratio of the change in saving to the change in disposable income. A 0.2 marginal propensity to save indicates that out of an additional £100 earned £20 will be saved. Whatever is not saved is consumed. The marginal propensity to save plus the marginal propensity to consume must always equal 1, by definition (if taxes are ignored).

marginal rate of taxation *See* marginal tax rate.

marginal revenue (MR) The change in total revenues resulting from a change in output and sale of one unit of the product in question.

marginal revenue product (MRP) The marginal physical product multiplied by the price at which the product can be sold in a competitive market.

marginal social benefits The value of the benefits from one additional unit of consumption, both the benefit to the direct buyer and the indirect benefits to all others in society.

marginal social cost The cost of producing one additional unit of output reflecting both a producer's marginal costs and the marginal external costs imposed on others in society.

marginal tax rate The change in the tax payment divided by the change in income, or the percentage of additional pounds that must be paid in taxes. The marginal tax rate is applied to the last tax bracket of taxable income reached.

marginal utility The change in total utility due to a one-unit change in the quantity of a good consumed.

market An abstract concept concerning all the arrangements that individuals have for exchanging with one another. Thus, we can speak of the labour market, the car market and the credit market.

market-based instruments These are incentive systems, such as taxes and emission charges, that operate by establishing prices for environmental services.

market-clearing price The price that clears the market when there is no excess quantity demanded or supplied. The price at which the demand curve intersects the supply curve.

market economic system A system in which individuals own the factors of production and decide individually how to use them; a system with completely decentralized economic decision-making.

market economy An economy in which prices are used to signal firms and households about the value of individual resources. It is also called the price system, or a system using the price mechanism.

market failure A situation in which an unfettered market leads to either an under-allocation or an over-allocation of resources to a specific economic activity. Externalities are cases of market failure.

market for corporate control The situation that arises in a contested take-over bid when one company, in seeking to acquire another, is involved in the crucial task of winning the support of a majority of the shareholders of the take-over target.

market structures The characteristics of a market which determine the interrelationships between participants in that market. Decision-making in any given market will depend on whether buyers and sellers can assume that they can or cannot affect market price. Thus the type of market structure is determined by the number of buyers and sellers and the ease of entry (and exit) into the market.

market tested The process whereby certain government-provided activities are made subject to competitive tendering.

medium of exchange Money is anything that is generally accepted for the buying and selling of goods and services. Money therefore acts as a means (medium) of payment (exchange).

merchant banks The name given to a small group of banks whose specialisms involve raising money for companies and advising on portfolio management.

merit good A good that has been deemed socially desirable via the political process.

microeconomics The study of the economic behaviour of households and firms and of how prices of goods and services are determined.

minimum efficient scale The lowest rate of output per unit time period at which average costs reach a minimum point.

minimum wage rate The hourly wage rate that must be paid to workers in a given industry.

mixed economy An economic system in which the decision about how resources should be used is made partly by the private sector and partly by the government.

mobility of labour The ease with which labour can be transferred from one type of employment to another. Mobility of labour can thus be considered in terms of geographical or occupational mobility. The converse concept – immobility of labour – is often employed by economists.

models, or theories Simplified representations of the real world used to make predictions or to understand the real world better.

monetarists Individuals who believe that changes in the money supply are important in the determination of the equilibrium level of nominal national income. Monetarists place money in a more important role in their national income determination model than do Keynesians.

monetary base The notes and coin in circulation and banks' balances with the Bank of England. Also known as M0 or high-powered money.

money at call Very-short-term lending by commercial banks, ranging from an overnight loan to one that lasts for fourteen days. The discount houses are the principal borrowers of these funds.

money multiplier The reciprocal of the reserve asset ratio, assuming no leakages into currency and no excess reserves. It gives the amount by which credit expands as a result of a given increase in the monetary base.

money supply A generic term used to denote the amount of 'money' in circulation. In the United Kingdom today there are just two versions of money supply published on a regular basis, M0 and M4.

monopolist The single supplier that comprises the entire industry.

monopolistic competition A market situation where a large number of firms produce similar but not identical products. There is relatively easy entry into the industry.

monopoly A simple market structure where a single supplier dominates the market. In theory the market only has one seller; in legislative terms a monopoly exists when one supplier accounts for more than 25 per cent of the market.

monopoly rent-seeking The resources used in an attempt to create and maintain monopolies in order to earn monopoly profits.

monopsonist A single buyer.

multiplier The ratio of the change in the equilibrium level of real national income to the change in expenditures which brought it about; that number by which a change in investment or autonomous consumption, for example, is multiplied to get the change in the equilibrium level of real national income.

N

NAIRU The non-accelerating inflation rate of unemployment. Often used to mean the same as the natural rate of unemployment.

narrow money A measure of money known as M0 in the UK. M0 includes only notes and coin and banks' balances with the Bank of England.

National Debt The accumulated government debt, the total outstanding.

national income The value of the flow of goods and services becoming available to a nation during a given period of time (usually one year).

national income accounting A measurement system used to estimate national income and its components.

nationalization The taking into public ownership of part or all of economic activity in a key sector of the economy.

National Savings Bank A public sector institution that offers banking-type facilities over post-office counters.

natural capital approach This approach to sustainable development regards the environment as critically important. It stands in stark contrast to the constant capital approach.

natural monopoly A monopoly that arises from the peculiar production characteristics in the industry. Usually a natural monopoly arises when production of the service or product requires extremely large capital investments such that only one firm can profitably be supported by consumers. A natural monopoly arises when there are large economies of scale relative to the industry demand, and one firm can produce at a lower cost than can be achieved by multiple firms.

natural rate of unemployment That rate of unemployment which remains even when the labour market clears. Often used synonymously with NAIRU to refer to that level of unemployment where there is a stable rate of inflation. Any government attempts to reduce unemployment below NAIRU will result in accelerating inflation.

negative equity A situation where the value of a house is less than the sum owed as a loan from a building society or a bank.

negative income elasticity A given rise in income will result in a fall in the quantity demanded.

net investment Gross investment minus an estimate of the wear and tear on the existing capital stock. Net investment therefore measures the change in our capital stock over a one-year period.

net national product (NNP) Gross national product minus depreciation.

new international economic order A proposed international institution to be sponsored by the United Nations that would basically attempt to stabilize raw material prices and increase the amount of foreign aid given by industrialized nations to less-developed countries.

new issue A firm may make a new issue of shares when it wishes to raise finance for investment from sources external to the firm.

newly industrializing economies Those upper-middle-income developing countries such as Mexico and South Korea that have developed rapidly over the past decade and are now increasingly significant exporters of consumer goods.

nominal national income *See* nominal values.

nominal rate of interest The market rate of interest that is expressed in terms of today's pounds.

nominal values The values of variables such as gross national product and investment expressed in current pounds. Also called money values. Otherwise stated, the actual market prices at which goods are sold.

non-durable consumer goods Goods used by consumers that are used up within a year.

non-monetary indicators Measures of the state of development such as the number of persons who are literate and average life expectancy. Such measures avoid the problems of using gross national product data in making international comparisons.

non-oil balance Imports minus exports excluding oil.

non-price competition The means by which firms strive to increase sales and increase market share other than by undercutting rivals. Instead of lowering prices and competing by price, firms resort to advertising campaigns, encourage new product development and regard sales as being sensitive to effective marketing.

non-tariff barriers Restraints on international trade other than import duties.

normal goods Goods for which demand increases as income increases. Most goods that we deal with are normal.

normal profit The normal rate of return to investment; otherwise known as the opportunity cost of capital.

normative economics Analysis involving value-judgements about economic policies; relates to whether things are good or bad. A statement of what ought to be.

O

occupationally immobile *See* mobility of labour.

OECD The Organization for Economic Co-operation and Development. This could be regarded as a club comprising all the capitalist countries as members, who discuss together economic issues of mutual interest. The OECD includes Australia, Austria, Belgium, Canada, the Czech Republic, Denmark, Finland, France, Germany, Greece, Hungary, Iceland, Ireland, Italy, Japan, Korea, Luxembourg, Mexico, the Netherlands, New Zealand, Norway, Poland, Portugal, Spain, Sweden, Switzerland, Turkey, the United Kingdom and the United States. The organization's offices are based in Paris and it produces various economic publications each year.

Office for National Statistics (ONS) The government department formed by the amalgamation of the Central Statistical Office (CSO) and the Office of Population Censuses and Surveys (OPCS) in April 1996 which is responsible for the government's statistical services.

oligopoly A market situation where there are very few sellers. Each seller knows that the other sellers will react to its changes in prices and quantities.

open economy An economy that is in some way dependent on one or more other economies. Goods are traded and international exchange takes place.

open-market operations The buying and selling of government securities (for example bonds) in the open market by the Bank of England.

opportunity cost The highest-valued alternative that must be sacrificed to attain something or satisfy a want.

opportunity cost of capital The normal rate of return or the amount that must be paid to an investor to induce him or her to invest in a business. Economists consider this a cost of production.

organization The co-ordination of individuals each doing different things in the furtherance of a common end.

outflow A term associated with the number leaving the official unemployment statistics each month.

output approach A way of measuring national income by adding up the value of the output produced by each specific sector of the economy. (The emphasis is on 'value added'. See Table 13.1.)

output gap Exists whenever the equilibrium level of real national output is less than the full-employment level; the negative difference between total desired expenditures and the full-employment level of real national income.

outward-looking development strategy An outlook where a developing country favours exploiting any means of enhancing economic growth by access to world trade, capital or technology.

P

paradox of thrift An increased desire to save (an increase in the marginal propensity to save) will lead to a reduction in the equilibrium level of saving.

parallel pricing The simultaneous changes in prices in an oligopolistic market situation which are explained by collusion or barometric price leadership.

partial equilibrium analysis A way of analysing a market in isolation without taking account of the interrelationships among markets.

partnership A business entity involving two or more individuals who join together for business purposes. In most instances, each partner is liable for the debts of the business to such an extent that he or she can lose his or her personal wealth if the business becomes bankrupt.

per capita A Latin phrase used to convey 'per head of the population'.

perfect competition A market structure in which the decisions of buyers and sellers have no effect on market price.

perfectly competitive firm A firm that is such a small part of the total industry picture that it cannot affect the price of the product it sells.

perfectly elastic demand A demand curve characterized by a horizontal line at the prevailing price indicating that there is unlimited demand at that price.

perfectly elastic supply The same as perfectly elastic demand but referring to supply.

perfectly inelastic demand A demand curve that exhibits zero responsiveness to changes in price; that is, no matter what the price is, the quantity demanded remains the same.

perfectly inelastic supply The characteristic of a supply curve for which quantity supplied remains constant, no matter what happens to price.

permanent-income hypothesis A theory of the consumption function that states that people's desire to spend is a function of their permanent or long-run expected income rather than of their current disposable income.

Phillips curve A curve showing the relationship between unemployment and changes in wages or prices. The Phillips curve gives the trade-off between unemployment and inflation.

planning curve Another name for the long-run average cost curve.

planning horizon Another name for long-run cost curves. All inputs are variable during the planning period.

positive economics Analysis that is strictly limited to making either purely descriptive statements or scientific predictions; for example, if A, then B. A statement of what is. Positive statements can be checked against the evidence.

potential output The maximum level of output achievable if the economy were operating on its production possibilities curve.

poverty trap A situation in which people experience a fall in disposable income if they cease to be unemployed and start a job, or if their earnings rise, because benefits are withdrawn and they reach a tax threshold. The combined effect of these is to create a very high marginal tax rate.

precycling A word introduced in the 1990s to convey the idea that recycling problems can be reduced or eliminated by considering resources devoted to packaging beforehand.

predatory pricing The practice of temporarily selling at prices below cost with the intention of driving a competitor from the market, so that in the future prices may be raised and enhanced profits extracted.

present value The value of the future amount expressed in today's pounds; the most that someone would pay today to receive a certain sum at some point in the future.

price cap The regulation of prices in privatized companies by reference to movements in a general price index. If in the form RPI – X, the latter denotes assumed efficiency gains.

price–consumption curve The set of consumer optimum combinations of two goods that the consumer would choose as the relative price of the goods changes while money income remains constant.

price control Government regulation of free-market prices such that a legal maximum price is specified.

price differentiation A situation in which price differences for similar products reflect only differences in marginal cost in providing those commodities to different groups of buyers.

price discrimination This is a system of pricing often employed by nationalized industries and other monopolists; it involves charging different prices to different customers who have different elasticities of demand for the product.

price-elastic demand A characteristic of a demand curve in which a given percentage change in price will result in a larger percentage change in quantity demanded, in the opposite direction. Total revenues and price are inversely related in the elastic portion of the demand curve.

price elasticity of demand The responsiveness of the quantity demanded for a commodity to changes in its price per unit. The price elasticity of demand is defined as the percentage change in quantity demanded divided by the percentage change in price.

price elasticity of supply The responsiveness of quantity supplied of a commodity to a change in its price. Price elasticity of supply is defined as the percentage change in quantity supplied divided by the percentage change in price.

price index The cost of today's basket of goods expressed as a percentage of the cost of the same basket during a base year.

price-inelastic demand A characteristic of a demand curve in which a given change in price will result in a less than proportionate change in the quantity demanded, in the opposite direction. Total revenue and price are directly related in the inelastic region of the demand curve.

price mechanism Prices are used as a signalling system between firms and households concerning the use of resources. Where the price mechanism operates there is a market economy.

price supports Minimum prices set by the government. To be effective, price supports must be coupled with a mechanism to rid the market of 'surplus' production that arises whenever the supported price is greater than the market-clearing price.

price system An economic system in which (relative) prices are constantly changing to reflect changes in supply and demand for different commodities. The prices of those commodities are signals to everyone within the system about what is relatively expensive and what is relatively cheap.

price-taker Another definition of a competitive firm. A price-taker is a firm that must take the price of its product as given. The firm cannot influence its price.

principle of exclusion This simply means that anyone who does not pay will not be allowed to benefit from consuming a particular good or service – they will be left out.

principle of rivalry Stated briefly, when I use a private good, my use prevents the possibility of your use. You and I cannot eat the same apple simultaneously.

private costs Those costs incurred by individuals when they engage in using scarce resources. For example, the private cost of running a car is equal to the petrol, oil, insurance, maintenance and depreciation costs. Also called explicit costs.

Private Finance Initiative A consortium whereby the private sector signs a contract to build something for a public sector client for which the latter pays annual charges over the life of the contract.

private goods Goods that can only be consumed by one individual at a time. Private goods are subject to the principles of exclusion and rivalry.

private property rights The legal entitlement of an owner to use, transfer and exchange property.

privatization In very general terms, this involves the transfer of assets from the public sector to the private sector.

producer price index A statistical measure of a weighted average of prices of commodities that retail outlets in the UK purchase from manufacturers in the UK.

producer surplus The difference between the amount that a producer is willing to be paid for a commodity and the amount that is actually paid. This surplus is measured by the area above the supply curve and below the line indicating the market price. This area is the difference between producers' receipts and total variable costs.

product differentiation When consumers perceive that there are differences in the characteristics of products which are alternatives to each other. Product differentiation thus gives producers some freedom in price determination.

production function The relationship between inputs and output. A production function is a technological, not an economic, relationship.

production possibilities curve A curve representing all possible combinations of total output that could be produced assuming (a) a fixed amount of productive resources and (b) efficient use of those resources.

product markets Transactions where households buy goods occur in the product markets, that is, where households are the buyers and businesses are the sellers of consumer goods (see Figure 13.1).

profit The income generated by selling something for a higher price than was paid for it. In production, the income generated is the difference between total revenues received from consumers who purchase the goods and the total cost of producing those goods.

profit-maximizing rate of production That rate of production which maximizes total profits, or the difference between total revenues and total costs; also, that rate of production at which marginal revenue equals marginal cost.

progressive taxation A tax system in which, as one earns more income, a higher percentage of the additional pounds is taxed. Put formally, the marginal tax rate exceeds the average tax rate as income rises.

proportional taxation A tax system in which, as the individual's income goes up, the tax bill goes up in exactly the same proportion. Also called a flat rate tax.

protectionist policies These involve import controls, which may be tariffs, quotas or any other trade restriction, which benefit domestic producers of similar products by enabling them to charge a higher price or be substituted for imports.

public goods Goods for which the principles of exclusion and rivalry do not apply; they can be jointly consumed by many individuals simultaneously, at no additional cost, and with no reduction in the quality or quantity of the provision concerned.

public sector The simplest (but rather misleading) definition is all forms of public expenditure by all types of government.

Public Sector Debt Repayment The amount by which government revenue, from tax and other sources, exceeds government expenditure in any one year.

Public Sector Net Cash Requirement The difference between government expenditure and tax revenue, which must be financed by borrowing.

purchasing power parity A theory that exchange rates are in equilibrium when the domestic purchasing power of currencies is the same at those exchange rates.

pure economic rent The payment to any resource that is in completely inelastic supply. The payment to any resource over and above transfer earnings.

pure monopoly A market structure where a single firm supplies the whole market.

Q

quangos Quasi-autonomous non-government organizations which have been set up by the government. They are not staffed by elected persons but by ministerial patronage. There is a concern whether quangos operate without effective parliamentary and democratic control.

quantity theory of money and prices The theory that changes in the price level are directly related to changes in the money supply. The quantity theory is based on the equation of exchange.

quasi-rent A payment over and above what is necessary to keep a factor of production in existence in its same quality in the short run, but not in the long run.

queuing *See* waiting list.

quotas A quota is a form of import control which places a fixed ceiling on imports of a product.

R

R&D capital The monies invested into research and development with the aim of inventing and exploring new products/areas.

rate of discount The rate of interest used to discount future income streams back to present value.

rationing A distribution of restricted supplies by the government which is based on some objective criterion (such as numbers per household) at a time when quantity demanded exceeds quantity supplied. Rationing tries to effect a fair distribution of the limited supplies of basic necessities such as foodstuffs in a war-time economy.

real gross domestic product *See* constant prices, real terms.

real rate of interest The rate of interest obtained by subtracting the rate of inflation from the nominal rate of interest.

real terms Measurement of economic values after adjustments have been made for changes in prices between years.

recession A period of time during which the rate of growth of business activity is consistently less than its long-term trend, or is negative for two consecutive quarters. This state of the economy is referred to as an economic depression if it is unduly prolonged, as in the 1930s.

recognized banks The generic title given to those institutions recognized as banks by the Bank of England.

recycling The reuse of raw materials derived from manufactured products.

regional policy Government grants and incentives made available to firms moving into certain designated areas. Previously these designated areas were referred to as 'areas for expansion'; now they are referred to as 'assisted areas'.

regional unemployment A type of structural unemployment that occurs in specific areas of the country.

regressive taxation A tax system in which, as more pounds are earned, the percentage of tax paid on them falls. The marginal tax rate is less than the average tax rate as income rises.

relative price The price of a commodity expressed in terms of the price of another commodity or the average price of all other commodities.

rental-only contracts Restrict customers to rental or lease terms only and can be anti-competitive where there are no alternative methods of acquiring those goods.

resale price maintenance The practice whereby manufacturers specify trading terms for wholesalers and retailers, thus preventing competition.

reserve asset ratio The percentage of total assets that banks must hold in liquid form.

reserve assets Liquid assets and cash which can be used to make good customers' requests for withdrawals from the bank.

reserves Foreign exchange reserves are held by the central bank in order that it can manage the foreign exchange rate. It may use them to buy currency if market forces are causing it to depreciate, thus defending the exchange rate. If the exchange rate is rising, it may buy currency and accumulate reserves.

resource allocation The assignment of resources to specific uses. More specifically, it means determining what will be produced, how it will be produced, who will produce it and for whom it will be produced.

resources Inputs used in the production of the goods and services that we desire. Also called factors of production.

restrictive practices Agreements between firms to charge common prices and preclude price competition between them.

retail price index (RPI) A statistical measure of a weighted average of prices of a specified set of goods and services purchased by representative families.

revaluation The opposite of devaluation.

rights issue The issue of new shares to existing shareholders who are given the chance to buy more and expand their holding of the shares.

rivalry A basic definition of competition in which individual economic agents attempt to improve their relative position in a market by advertising, marketing, developing new products, seeking improved deals and so on.

RPIX This is the retail price index excluding mortgage interest payments. It indicates the underlying rate of inflation without interest rate distortions. RPIX is now used as the official target in the United Kingdom.

S

saving The act of not consuming all one's current income. Whatever is not consumed out of spendable income is, by definition, saved. Saving is an action measured over time, whereas savings are an existing accumulation resulting from the act of saving in the past.

scarcity A reference to the fact that at any point in time there exists only a finite amount of resources – human and non-human. Scarcity of resources therefore means that nature does not freely provide as much of everything as people want.

seasonally adjusted Official statistics are often corrected to take account of seasonal variations that distort the overall annual trend.

seasonal unemployment Unemployment due to seasonality in the demand or the supply of a particular good or service.

Second World A now dated term referring to the former communist nations of Eastern Europe plus the Soviet Union and the People's Republic of China.

selective distribution The practice of choosing as sales outlets only those which satisfy specific qualitative or quantitative criteria.

services Things purchased by consumers that do not have physical characteristics. Examples of services are those obtained from doctors, lawyers, dentists, repair personnel, house-cleaners, educators, retailers and wholesalers.

shortage Another term for an excess quantity demanded or insufficient quantity supplied. The difference between the quantity demanded and the quantity supplied at a specific price below the market-clearing price.

short run That time period in which a firm cannot alter its current size of plant.

short-run breakeven point The price at which a firm's total revenues equal its total costs. In economics the breakeven price is where the firm is just making a normal rate of return.

short-run close-down price The price where the profit-maximizing price just covers average variable costs. This occurs just below the intersection of the marginal cost curve and the average variable cost curve.

sight deposits Those bank accounts that allow the customer immediate access to his or her funds. Often called 'current accounts'.

social costs The full cost that society bears when a resource-using action occurs. For example, the social cost of driving a car is equal to all the private costs plus any additional cost that society bears, including air pollution and traffic congestion. (Some authors use this term to imply simply external costs.)

socialism An economic system in which the state owns the major share of productive resources except for labour. Also, socialism usually involves a greater redistribution of income than would be the case with a purely capitalist system.

sole proprietorship A business owned by only one person.

special deposits Interest-earning accounts that are not active; held at the Bank of England on behalf of the commercial banks. The Bank of England can request these funds if they wish to curb liquidity. No commercial bank makes a special deposit unless requested to do so as it would involve losing free access to some of its funds. The facility has not been used since 1981.

Special Drawing Rights (SDRs) A reserve asset created by the International Monetary Fund that countries can use to settle international payments.

specialization The division of productive activities among persons and regions so that no one individual or one area is totally self-sufficient. An individual may specialize, for example, in law, medicine or car production. A nation may specialize in the production of coffee, computers or cameras.

stable equilibrium A situation in which, if there is a shock that disturbs the prevailing equilibrium between the forces of supply and demand, there will normally be self-corrective forces that automatically cause the disequilibrium eventually to return to equilibrium.

stagflation A period of simultaneous high unemployment and rising prices. In other words, a period of both economic stagnation and inflation.

standard of deferred payment A quality of an asset that makes it desirable for use as a means of settling debts maturing in the future; an essential prerequisite of money.

stock The quantity of something at a point in time. A bank account at a point in time is a stock. Stocks are defined independently of time, although they are assessed at a point in time; different from a flow. Savings are a stock, as are wealth and unemployment.

stock appreciation This represents the increased value of stock due to inflation.

Stock Exchange The market in which existing shares are sold by one shareholder to another.

stocks (inventories) Inasmuch as stocks of goods can be sold in the future, they too are classed as investment. They may consist of unused inputs, kept by the firm for use in future production, or unsold products.

store of value The ability of an item to hold value over time; a necessary quality of money.

structural adjustment programmes Loans from the International Bank for Reconstruction and Development to some developing countries in the 1980s which aimed to assist them overcome development problems but at the cost of sometimes painful domestic policies which adversely affect the poorer members of society.

structural change A change in the composition of output which necessitates reallocation of resources.

structural rigidities These are obstacles within markets which prevent a swift response to changing forces of supply and demand. They are more prevalent in some markets than others; for example, trade union activity affects the dynamics of the labour market.

structural unemployment Unemployment resulting from fundamental changes in the structure of the economy.

subsidiarity A principle by which political decisions are taken by a representative body which is as close as possible to the people who will be directly affected by the decision. On this principle, the European Union is the appropriate forum only for those decisions which need to apply across member states.

subsidies Negative taxes; payments to producers or consumers of a good or service, for example farmers.

substitute Two goods are considered substitutes when a change in the price of one causes a shift in demand for the other in the same direction as the price changes. For example, if the price of butter goes up, the demand for margarine will rise; if the price of butter goes down, the demand for margarine will decrease.

substitution effect The tendency of people to substitute in favour of cheaper commodities and away from more expensive commodities.

sunk costs Costs which cannot be recouped by a firm that decides to leave an industry.

supply The relationship between the price and the quantity supplied (other things being equal) which is usually a direct one.

supply constraints If it is not possible, or if it is very costly, to increase quantity supplied, supply constraints are said to exist.

supply curve The graphic representation of the supply schedule; a line showing the supply schedule, which slopes upwards (has a positive slope).

supply schedule A set of numbers showing prices and the quantity supplied at those various prices; a schedule showing the rate of planned production at each relative price for a specified time period, usually one year.

supply-side economics This generally applies to attempts at creating incentives for individuals and firms to increase productivity; it relates to discussions of what causes the aggregate supply curve to shift.

surplus Another name for an excess quantity supplied or insufficient quantity demanded. The difference between the quantity supplied and the quantity demanded at a price above the market-clearing price.

sustainable development Economic progress that meets the needs of the present without compromising the ability of future generations to meet their own needs.

T

tacit agreement An agreement by which firms will not reduce prices or compete in some other way, and which exists without any meeting or discussion, even on an informal basis, by the firms concerned.

tariffs Indirect taxes on specific imports.

taxation The compulsory transfer of funds from individuals and businesses to the government. These transfers may be levied on, for example, tobacco, alcohol or petroleum – to name just a few of the specific taxes that exist.

tax and price index (TPI) A measure of inflation that combines changes in direct taxation and changes in retail prices.

tax bracket A specified interval of income to which a specific and unique marginal tax rate is applied.

tax expenditures Allowances made so that certain sorts of spending (for example mortgage interest) are deducted from taxable income.

tax incidence The distribution of tax burdens among various groups in society.

technical efficiency The utilization of the cheapest production technique for any given output rate; no inputs are wilfully wasted.

technological unemployment Unemployment caused by technological changes that reduce the demand for labour in some specific tasks.

terms of exchange The terms under which trading takes place. Usually the terms of exchange are given by the price at which a good is traded.

terms of trade The relationship between the weighted average price of exports and the weighted average price of imports. Expressed as an index based on 100 in the base year, the terms of trade have become more favourable if the index rises and have worsened if the index falls.

theory of contestable markets A hypothesis concerning pricing behaviour that holds that, even though there are only a few firms in the industry, they are forced to price their products more or less competitively because of the ease of entry by outsiders. The key aspect of a contestable market is relatively costless entry into and exit from the industry.

theory of demand Quantity demanded and price are inversely related – more is bought at a lower price, less at a higher price (other things being equal).

theory of public choice The study of collective decision-making.

theory of the firm A theory of how suppliers of commodities behave – how they make choices – in the face of changing constraints.

third parties Parties who are external to negotiations and activities between buyers and sellers. If you agree to buy a car with no brakes and then run me over, I am a third party to the deal struck between you and the seller of the car, and my suffering is the negative externality.

Third World The less-developed countries (LDCs).

tie-in sales A stipulation that a buyer must purchase part or all of his or her requirements of a second (tied) product from the supplier of a first (tying) product.

time deposits Savings account balances and certificates of deposit held in commercial banks and building societies. The bank or building society can require, say, thirty days' notice of your intent to withdraw from your deposit account, but often this time requirement is waived.

time lags The length of time which elapses between an economic event which acts as a cause and its consequential effects. For example, a rise in interest rates will cut aggregate demand, but only after a time lag.

time series data Empirical observations about the value of one or more economic variables taken at different periods over time.

total costs All the costs of a firm combined, including rent, payments to workers, interest on borrowed money and so on.

total expenditure The total monetary value of all the final goods and services bought in an economy during the year.

total income The total amount earned by the nation's resources (factors). National income therefore includes wages, rent, interest payments and profits that are received, respectively, by workers, landowners, capital owners and entrepreneurs.

total managed expenditure This represents all public sector spending. It is made up of two components: department expenditure limits, which set the amount allocated to each government department, and an annually managed expenditure, which deals with monies that cannot be set, over a multi-year period.

total output The total value of all the final goods and services produced in the economy during the year.

total revenues The price per unit multiplied by the total quantity sold.

tradeable permits Licences that can be bought or sold between producers involved in an economic activity that causes environmental damage.

trade association An organization of firms within an industry that undertakes activities on behalf of its members. In the United Kingdom trade associations developed in the nineteenth century to reduce the intensity of competition between members, but since 1956 they are involved in public relations activities and the dissemination of statistics concerning the relevant trade.

trade creation Takes place when countries are able to trade more freely, so that increased specialization occurs, with more international division of labour and increased efficiency.

trade cycle The sequence of boom, recession, depression and recovery which characterizes short-term changes in national income and output. The duration of the cycle varies, but the standard view is that it is about nine years on average. Policies and external events can affect the cycle and its duration.

trade deficit When imports exceed exports there is a trade deficit; in the alternative situation, a surplus.

trade diversion Takes place when the reduction in import controls occurring in a free trade area makes it profitable to trade within the area rather than outside it.

trade-off A term relating to opportunity cost. In order to obtain a desired economic good, it is necessary to trade off some other desired economic good whenever we are in a world of scarcity. A trade-off involves a sacrifice, then, that must be made in order to obtain something.

trade optimists Those economists who feel that, given an appropriate effort, a developing country can enjoy the benefits of faster economic growth arising from being a competitive international supplier of goods and services.

trade pessimists Those economists who tend to doubt the potential benefits of international trade to developing countries.

trade surplus The situation in which earnings from visible exports exceed the earnings from visible imports.

trade unions Organizations of workers that usually seek to secure economic improvements for their members.

transaction costs All the costs associated with exchanging, including the informational costs of finding the price and quality, service record, durability etc. of a product, plus the cost of contracting and enforcing that contract.

transfer earnings The amount which an employee could earn in an alternative occupation.

transfer payments Money payments made by governments to individuals for which no services or goods are concurrently rendered. Examples are social security payments and student grants.

transitional unemployment *See* frictional unemployment.

transmission mechanism The way in which changes in the money stock affect income, output and prices.

travel cost method This is a method used to identify the price of an externality. The central premise involves estimating how much people are willing to pay to travel in order to experience an environmental asset.

Treasury bill A means of borrowing by the government for a short period of time (usually ninety-one days).

trickle down The process where it is held that the benefits of economic growth reach the rest of the population having first been enjoyed by just a few of the population.

U

unanticipated inflation Inflation whose rate comes as a surprise to an individual. Unanticipated inflation can be either at a higher or a lower rate than anticipated.

unitary price elasticity of demand A property of the demand curve where the quantity demanded changes exactly in proportion to the change in price. Total revenue is invariant to price changes in the unit-elastic portion of the demand curve.

unit of account A measure by which prices and values are expressed; the common denominator of the price system, and a central quality of money.

util An artificial unit by which utility is measured.

utility The want-satisfying power that a good or service possesses.

utility analysis The analysis of consumer decision-making based on utility maximization.

V

value added The value of an industry's sales minus the value of intermediate goods (for example raw materials and parts) purchased for use in production.

value-added tax (VAT) A tax assessed on the value added by each producing unit. In other words, it is the total sale price of output minus the cost of raw materials and intermediate goods purchased from other firms.

variable costs Those costs that vary with the rate of production. They include wages paid to workers, the costs of materials and so on.

velocity of circulation The average number of times per year each pound is spent on final goods and services. It is equal to net national product divided by the money stock.

vertical merger The joining of a firm with another that either sells an input or buys an output.

vertical price squeezing When a vertically integrated firm controls the total supply of an input which is essential to the production requirements of its subsidiary and also its competitors, the input price can be raised and the downstream output price reduced, so that the profits of competitors are squeezed, possibly with a view to driving them from the market.

vicious circle The opposite of a virtuous circle, that is, a self-reinforcing set of interrelationships that make any progress difficult, if not impossible, and this is an unwelcome situation.

virtuous circle A series of self-supporting interrelationships that all have the effect of enhancing an outcome that is regarded as desirable.

W

waiting list A situation where, as in health care, a person's name is added to a number of other names of people who are expecting further medical attention or an operation.

wealth That which has value; usually, the difference between what a person owns (assets) and what a person owes (liabilities).

wealth effect When a fall in the money value of assets leads to a lower level of personal wealth, consumer spending may fall.

welfare state A nation that provides minimum standards in respect of certain social expenditures such as health, education, housing and social benefits to ensure that all its citizens enjoy adequate access to a minimum standard of provision as a result of free or subsidized government action.

workforce Those who are employed, self-employed, claiming benefit or in the Forces.

working capital Investment into working capital involves changes in the stocks of finished goods and goods in process, as well as changes in the raw materials that businesses keep on hand. Whenever stocks are decreasing, investment is negative; whenever they are increasing, investment is positive.

World Bank *See* International Bank for Reconstruction and Development.

X

X-inefficiency Organizational slack within a firm that results in costs per unit being higher than would be the case if strong competitive pressures existed. Since a monopolist faces weak competition X-inefficiency is held to be associated with this form of market structure.

Answers

Chapter 1

5 (a) AltaVista and Yahoo! search engines can be considered as 'prime real estate' because so many people see them every day. But there is such limited space on the screen that they face an opportunity cost, since any space that is used to promote their own services and products cannot be sold to other advertisers.

(b) The owners of commercial television want to broadcast as many adverts as they can in order to generate income. However, the more they broadcast, the less airtime can be given to programmes that are the incentive that attracts the viewers in the first place. The owners of any commercial channels that carry advertisements faces an opportunity cost, and need to decide carefully about their programme mix.

6 (a) The price of coffee would be part of the cost incurred by going to the Internet café.

(b) The mobile phone call would increase the cost of visiting the café since it would not have been incurred had you stayed at home.

9 (a) The curve would shift to the right representing greater growth in the economy. Hence more NHS Viagra could be provided, alongside the alternative you have chosen.

(b) The curve would shift to the right representing a greater amount of output from existing resources due to improved technology.

(c) The diagram would not change – but there would be a change in the pattern of demand. A redistribution of resources may follow and the economy may move to a new point on the production possibilities frontier.

13 See the figure.

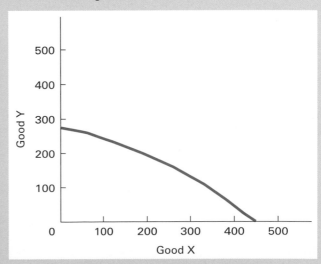

14 In the case of both good X and good Y additions of 100 extra workers to an initial workforce of 100 workers at first lead to a rise in total production, but later additions lead to a modest increase in total output.
The changes in output per 100 extra workers once 100 are employed are as follows:

X	Y
60	40
70	45
70	50
70	40
50	35
40	25
30	15

15 The production possibilities curve would move outwards to the right. Thus a new set of combinations of output of X and Y would now be possible.

16 In the second year there is a reduction in the output of consumer goods. This would be regarded as a fall in the living standards of this economy but there is every prospect of the economy growing more rapidly in the future as a result of the enhanced productive potential arising from the greater use of resources for investment. Thus living standards in the longer term might be higher than if present consumption levels are maintained at the expense of investment.

Chapter 2

1 NHS Trusts and the NHS employed 1.616 million, whereas education employed 1.204 million.

2 The fall of 1.94 million employees represented a 36 per cent reduction in 1998 compared with 1988.

3 Numbers employed in construction fell by 47 per cent between 1988 and 1998.

4 Police numbers rose between 1988 and 1998.

5 Education.

6 In 1988 the public sector proportion of those in education was 83 per cent, but in 1998 this figure was 64 per cent.

7 A rise of 42 per cent.

8 In one word – privatization.

Chapter 3

2 An increase of 64 per cent.

Chapter 4

4 Neither Mr Jones nor Mrs Jones has an absolute advantage; therefore neither has a comparative advantage. As a consequence, total output would not change if specialization occurred.

5 Mrs Jones has an absolute advantage in jacket production as she can produce twice as many as can Mr Jones. Mr Jones does not have an absolute advantage in anything; he is less productive than Mrs Jones at jacket production and equally productive at tie production. Mrs Jones has a comparative advantage in the production of jackets; she is twice as productive as Mr Jones in jacket production and equally productive in the production of ties. Mr Jones has a comparative advantage in the production of ties; he is just as productive in tie production and only half as productive in jacket production. If Mrs Jones specializes in jackets and Mr Jones specializes in ties, total production equals 16 jackets and 24 ties; tie output remains the same but jacket production increases from 12 to 16.

6 The relative price of whisky in relation to beer has fallen from 10 beers per bottle to 8 beers per bottle.

7 Although the absolute prices of beer and whisky rose, the relative prices of both commodities fell in relation to all other goods and services, because neither rose by as much as 150 per cent.

8 The firm will choose technique C because it incurs the lowest cost of the three methods at the prices given – £107, as opposed to £120 for A and £168 for B.

9 The firm's maximum profit will be £65.

10 If labour increases to £4 per unit, technique A becomes the most profitable, because its cost increases to only £132, less than the £143 that C now costs. Therefore A would be chosen. Profits would drop to £40.

Chapter 5

2 A rectangular hyperbola, which means the area under the demand curve is unchanging, moving between any two points on the demand curve.

5 No, because demand for cakes and pastries in 1989 was in general very price inelastic.

6 The price elasticity of demand using the arc elasticity formula is –3.77.

$$\frac{2}{13} \div \frac{200}{4900}$$

7 If the price elasticity of demand is assumed to be –0.5 then the increase in sales will be much less than that assumed by the Vehicle and General Workers' Union. In this case the arc elasticity measure of the change in price (£200) is 4.0 per cent. This means that sales will increase by just 240 000 cars, much less than the situation in question 6. The car firms will thus receive lower revenues and, unless costs fall significantly, lower profits.

8 The income elasticity figures for foodstuffs tend to become lower as one compares the lowest one-fifth of households with the higher-income groups. This is what one would expect to find.

9 The income elasticities typically fall between the two dates, again as one would expect.

10 There is, in terms of income, a fall in consumption of these items.

11 Fruit is one item of foodstuff where consumption is more income sensitive than for the other items shown in Table 5.7.

Chapter 6

1 Measured in dollars the Big Mac was cheapest in China and dearest in Switzerland.

2 The Big Mac is a universal commodity available throughout the world. This justifies it being used as a measure of the purchasing power of many of the world's currencies.

3 and 4

	Column 4	Differences between column 4 and column 3 (%)
Great Britain	0.78	+25.8
Spain	154.32	0
Switzerland	2.42	+63.5
Taiwan	28.80	–15.2
France	3.49	–42.7
Mexico	8.18	–14.2
Russia	13.78	–44.5
Australia	1.09	–31.4
China	4.07	–50.8

5 Spain.

6 (a) China.
   (b) Switzerland.

7 (i) If beef production is subsidized in some countries more than in others, then this could be expected to affect local prices of a Big Mac. There could also be differences in the tariffs on beef imports in different countries.
   (ii) Beef may not be a suitable commodity to compare relative prices where, for religious reasons say, it is not regarded as an appropriate main item of diet.

8 The prospect of currency changes would be expected to have a decisive influence on the scale and direction of capital flows.

9 See the figure. The equilibrium exchange rate is £1 = $1.50.

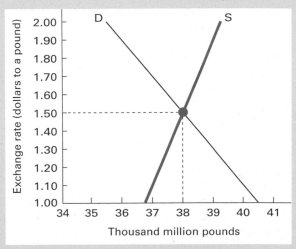

10 (a) The new equilibrium exchange rate will now be $1.565 as the supply of pounds curve shifts to the left.
   (b) Demand for sterling rises by £100 million. The new equilibrium exchange rate is £1 = $1.635.
   (c) As in (b).
   (d) The new equilibrium exchange rate is $1.435.

11 The value of sterling appreciated from one year to the next against the dollar in twelve years of the twenty-four during the period shown. Sterling appreciated against the deutschmark in eight years between 1973 and 1998.

12 A visitor from the United States would ideally want to offer as few dollars as possible to obtain pounds sterling. In nineteen of the twenty-four years the exchange rate was two dollars per pound or less, and it was never above two dollars after 1980. So, relative to the years 1973–80, the decade thereafter was one where someone from the United States would have found the United Kingdom a relatively attractive place to visit on a regular basis.

13 The trend in the deutschmark–pound sterling exchange rate would have made visits to the Munich Beer Festival increasingly expensive in terms of currency, let alone any rise in the price of the beer! In only one year after 1985 has the number of deutschmarks per pound exceeded three – that is, in 1988.

14 The exchange rate of the pound fell by 55 per cent against the deutschmark and 39 per cent against the dollar during the period 1973–98.

15 With concern! The stronger value of the pound sterling would not help the competitive position of UK exports of manufactured goods.

18 Oil and other fuels due to the North Sea oilfields.

19 Financial services.

20 Net credit on investment income.

21 Net debt on transfers.

22 Net contributor to the EU.

23 One would expect the UK to be a net contributor of aid to developing countries.

26 The cost of sending cargo by sea in 1990 was about half that in 1930.

27 Passenger transport costs fell even faster than costs for cargo and hence became relatively cheaper.

28 The cost of a telephone call in 1990 was but a tiny fraction of what it cost to make a telephone call to London from New York sixty years earlier.

29 Falling real costs of communication spur the growth of trade and financial markets. Transactions costs have fallen rapidly, thus widening the benefits for interchange between buyers and sellers on a global basis.

Chapter 7

1 (a) At the end of 1990/beginning of 1991.
 (b) At the end of 1992.

9 (a) France.
 (b) United Kingdom.

10 France.

18 The rich got richer and the poor got poorer. The change was most marked in the top fifth, where the share of disposable income had increased by 6 per cent.

21 It had become less progressive.

22 (a) The average rate of tax was less than 23 per cent. Technically speaking, there was a tax-free allowance of £4335, and the first £1500 was taxed at 10 per cent. The precise average rate of tax was nearer 19 per cent.
 (b) The marginal rate of tax was 23 per cent – since a gross income of £30 000 did not reach the 40 per cent band of taxable income.

Chapter 8

1 For the answers to each part of this question see the data presented in Table 8.1

3 In a strong economy the GDP figures will increase (showing economic growth); the inflation figures will be low (suggesting stable prices) and unemployment will be falling (as more people find employment).

11 (a) C; (b) S; (c) F; (d) S; (e) C; (f) F; (g) F; (h) C.

17 RPIX: Inflation measured by the retail price index *excluding* mortgage interest payments.
 RPIY: Inflation measured by the retail price index *excluding* mortgage interest payments and indirect taxes.
 TPI: Inflation measured by the retail price index *combined* with changes in direct tax (including national insurance contributions).
 PPI: Inflation measured by the factory-gate prices of manufactured goods.
 RPI: Inflation measured by the retail price index (a basket of 600 goods and services).

Chapter 9

1 19.5 per cent.

2 The average wheat yield rose each year between 1992 and 1996 but it fell in 1997. The inconsistent rise in yield could be explained by variable growing and harvesting seasons.

3 Yes, because rising wheat yields would lead to rising production unless the area devoted to wheat growing falls and more than offsets the extra output from a given acreage devoted to wheat production.

5 Fluctuations in crop and livestock production which result in price and income instability. Reference could be made to the inelastic nature of supply and demand and the plausibility of 'cobweb' movements. In terms of real specific factors, students could refer to the adverse impact of BSE on livestock production and the strong pound, which has affected exports.

6 Real farm income in 1997 was down sharply compared with that in 1993. Thus many farmers were worse off in 1997 compared with four years previously. The index is based on 1990=100 and in 1997 the index was at this level. Hence real incomes rose after 1990 but fell as sharply as they had risen early in that decade.

7 Joseph had the benefit of perfect foresight – knowing precisely when years of plenty would change to the reverse situation. Hence he took action on the basis of certainty, which is not the case of a buffer stock operating in the twenty-first century.

8 Joseph aimed to store excess stocks without reference to support buying at determined prices. Hence the need for funding stocks was not a pressing issue. There was not the complication of negotiating with consumers and producers over the terms of interventionist support buying and selling.

11 Just under 80 per cent.

12 No, in most countries the cost of agricultural support policies has tended to fall. Turkey and Poland are the two exceptions shown in Figure 9.11.

13 It was the lowest of all the thirteen countries shown and was much less than in many of the countries in the Northern hemisphere.

14 Generally falling in most countries, although for the EU as a whole there was no change comparing 1998 with 1991–3.

15 Switzerland.

16 The sheer size of the US economy made the cost of agricultural support, although large in absolute terms, lower than typically the case in other OECD countries.

17 Six countries are net beneficiaries in Figure 9.13. These are Spain, Belgium, Denmark, Greece, Portugal and Ireland.

18 Yes, in part because their agricultural sectors are unlikely to be highly efficient and also because there may be transitional arrangements that are likely to result in new members of the EU being net beneficiaries of the CAP.

19 £4.

20 Total tax revenue is 20 units × £10 = £200. Consumers pay £80, suppliers £120.

21 £6.

22 60 per cent.

Chapter 10

9 Subsidize or take over production.

10 See the figure.

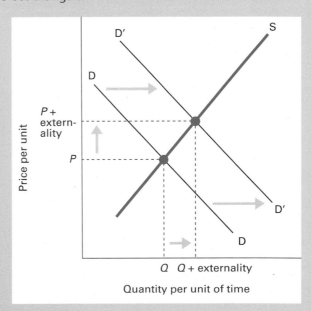

11 Under-allocated.

26 Taking each of the categories in consecutive order, possible examples are: toll-gate money, road-building cost, reduced travelling time, noise and air pollution. (These are just examples – other possibilities exist.) The 'polluter pays principle' attempts to internalize the negative externalities.

27 Route A.

28 Route B.

43 The diagram shows two functions of the environment very clearly, namely: it provides material inputs and carries away waste. A third function is that the environment provides an amenity for recreation.

Chapter 11

5 In most countries the proportion of health expenditure spent by governments typically accounts for three-quarters or more of all expenditure on health. The United States is a notable exception compared to the other eleven countries.

6 Health care appears to be an area of spending that is income elastic.

7 Spending on health care denotes all the activity to help people recover from illness. Increased productivity in health-care spending would be illustrated by increases in the number of operations performed per operating theatre and in the throughput of persons seeking out-patient care. How does health-care spending relate to changing staff numbers? Use of hospital beds?

8 Whilst much more is spent in the United States than in the United Kingdom, this is essentially by individuals. Health care in the United States leaves large sections of the US population (the old and the poor) without effective means of meeting the cost of operations should they require them.

9 The advantages to society of a growing number of children capable of reading and writing and competent in simple quantitative skills should be self-evident. Such children can in due course become effective entrants to the labour force as well as receptive to appropriate advice on issues such as a good diet, clean water and health care. However, ever larger numbers of graduates in a low-income economy may not find suitable jobs for their skills. They are likely to be a less pressing priority for a government with a limited budget for educational spending.

10 As the number of graduates increases as the level of income per head rises, graduates no longer enjoy a situation of relative scarcity. The benefit to society at the margin of another 1000 graduates can be expected to diminish.

11 If more women could enjoy the same educational opportunity as typically is the case for men, then it is argued that this would be the most cost-effective way of tackling the key problem of population control, let alone the concerns about the poor diet and state of health of many in less-developed countries. If education can influence the decisions of a mother within a family on these matters, it may well have a high rate of return as far as society is concerned.

12 The availability of long-term loans for house purchase from specialist institutions – building societies – has been a feature of the UK economy. In more recent years, the commercial banks have competed with the building societies in offering housing finance. The latter have historically not been motivated by profit, unlike the banks.

13 Tax relief on the interest element of loans for house purchase and the provision of publicly rented accommodation at rents below market levels.

Chapter 12

1 Two years.

2 Although the economy was growing more slowly, it was still growing. This would imply that demand for labour was still increasing.

3 The price elasticity of demand for soap, cat food and refrigerators is low. Demand will not grow much when prices fall and labour-saving investment will tend to take place. With computers and fax machines, demand is probably more price elastic. If prices fall, demand will grow more than proportionately and labour-using investment will take place.

4 See the figure.

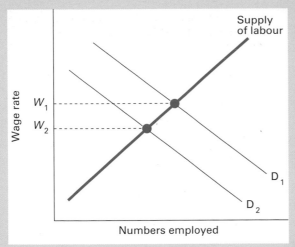

As demand for the product shifts to the left, so will the demand for labour (from D_1 to D_2). Wages will fall.

5 Often people will not be able to move easily because of geographical and occupational immobilities. Newly created jobs often require skilled people and those made redundant may not have the right skills or access to retraining. High house prices may prevent owner occupiers from moving to where the jobs are.

6 Jobs will be created as a result of new product development, in labour-intensive services for which there is a high income elasticity of demand, and in areas where the economy is buoyant.

Chapter 13

1 Incomes: wages, rents, interest and profits.

2 The factor services provided by land, labour, capital and entrepreneurs.

3 See glossary for guidance.

4 The total expenditure on goods and services.

5 The total output that businesses produce.

6 See glossary for guidance.

10, 11 See diagram.

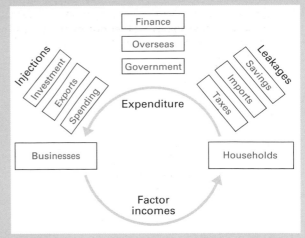

13 Vegetables grown for own consumption.

14 The national accounts will show less activity.

15 Nothing; illegal activities are not counted anyway.

16 These goods represent economic activity within the nation.

17 Value added equals total sales minus the cost of raw materials. £18 000.

19 Using the figures as given in the table, GDP for 1996 was £754 billion and 1997 £803 billion.

22 Gross domestic product equals £19 000 million.

23 The GDP at market prices was £844 billion (rounded to the nearest billion).

24 GDP (at market prices) = C + I + G + NX (net exports)

25 GDP at basic prices = C + I + G + NX – indirect taxes + subsidies

26 GNI = GDP + net property and entrepreneurial income from abroad

27

	Net measures in £ million		
	1996	1997	1998
Net domestic product at current market prices	670 632	718 055	754 954
Net domestic income at current market prices	674 855	726 627	766 691

31 4.39 per cent in the period 1993/4.

32 (a) 1991, –2.33 per cent.

Chapter 14

1 1994.

2 9.4 and falling.

3 It accelerated.

4 Yes, if some of the unemployed have been affected by structural change. If they have been made redundant from declining industries but lack the skills needed to fill existing vacancies, or if they cannot move to another area, they are not in a position to relieve the skill shortage even though they are unemployed.

5 1991–3 inclusive.

6 See the figure.

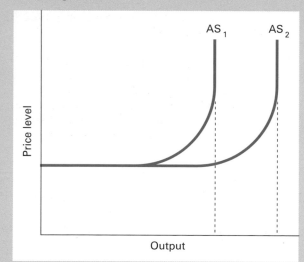

7 See the figure.

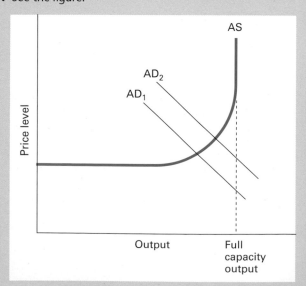

Chapter 15

1

Year	Percentage of GDP consumed
1950	69.4
1960	68.1
1970	64.3
1980	67.1
1990	72.6
1998	83.0

2 It varies over time. It will depend on the saving ratio, and probably also in practice on the level of taxation.

3

Disposable income (£)	Consumption (£)	Saving (£)
500	510	–10
600	600	0
700	690	10
800	780	20
900	870	30
1000	960	40

(a) See the figure of disposable income, consumption and saving.

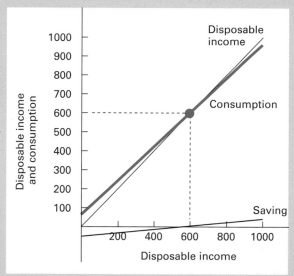

(b) The marginal propensity to consume is 0.9; the marginal propensity to save is 0.1.

(c)

Disposable income	Average propensity to consume	Average propensity to save
500	1.0200	–0.0200
600	1.0000	0
700	0.9857	0.0143
800	0.9750	0.0250
900	0.9667	0.0333
1000	0.9600	0.0400

4 (a) $80 \div 100 = 0.8$; $155 \div 200 = 0.775$
(b) It falls.
(c) $(80 - 5) \div (100 - 0) = 0.75$;
$(155 - 80) \div (200 - 100) = 75 \div 100 = 0.75$
(d) It remains constant.
(e) The APC is always falling and approaches the MPC, or 0.75.
(f) $C = 5 + 0.75Y$

5 (a) $80 \div 100 = 0.8$; $160 \div 200 = 0.8$
(b) It remains constant at 0.8.
(c) $(80 - 0) \div (100 - 0) = 0.8$;
$(160 - 80) \div (200 - 100) = 0.8$
(d) It remains constant at 0.8.
(e) $C = 0 + 0.8Y$
(f) There is no autonomous element in consumption, that is, there is no dissaving at low levels of income.

6 Both. There was a movement up the consumption function because incomes were rising in real terms. Also the consumption function shifted upwards because the saving ratio was falling and people were borrowing more.

7 See the figure.

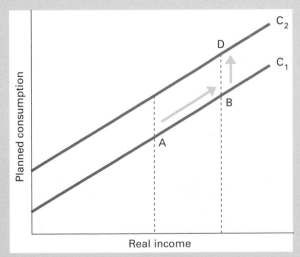

If A is the starting point, there is a movement along the consumption function to point B. There is also a shift upwards in the consumption function from C_1 to C_2 so that the level of consumption is eventually at D.

Case study: Tracing the links, p. 279

1 Investment. Consumption tends to rise steadily most of the time, whereas investment can fall sharply in times of recession.

2 Income fell in 1991 by 2.2 per cent. Consumption fell by 2.1 per cent. In 1992, income fell by 0.4 per cent while consumption fell infinitesimally by 0.03 per cent. Consumption does tend to change less than income. People find ways of maintaining consumption even when incomes are falling, sometimes by saving less, though that was clearly not what happened in 1991–2.

3 Over the long run income is clearly a very important determinant of consumption.

4 Investment is affected by interest rates. The low interest rate in 1987 may have contributed to the fast-growing investment in 1987 and 1988. The rate at which income is growing is important, too. Rapid growth in 1986–8 is associated with growing investment.

5 The saving ratio does not appear to be linked to changes in interest rates. There is some connection with the rate of inflation. Saving seems to be higher for a while after periods of higher inflation. This fits with the theory that people try to rebuild the value of their stock of savings after inflation has eroded their value.

Chapter 16

1 One year.

2 1990, 0.35 per cent.
1991, 4.0 per cent.
1992, 0.40 per cent.

3 The data do not show this clearly, but it appears to be a year.

4 Aggregate demand is clearly a component part of the unemployment problem. However, unemployment which persisted through 1989 is likely to have had at least some structural causes; so the 1990 unemployment figure of 5.9 per cent gives us a rough guide as to what unemployment might have been at that time if aggregate demand could absorb all the conveniently located labour with appropriate skills.

6

Real national income	Consumption expenditures	Saving (£)	Investment (£)
1000	1100	−100	100
2000	2000	0	100
3000	2900	100	100
4000	3800	200	100
5000	4700	300	100
6000	5600	400	100

APC	APS	MPC	MPS
1.1	0.1	0.9	0.1
1.0	0	0.9	0.1
0.967	0.033	0.9	0.1
0.950	0.050	0.9	0.1
0.940	0.060	0.9	0.1
0.933	0.067	0.9	0.1

(a) See the figure.

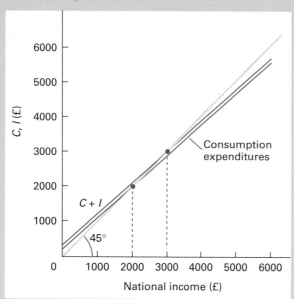

(b) See the figure.

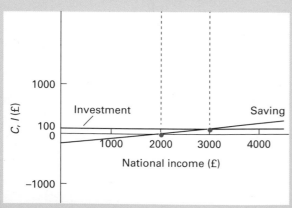

(c) The value of the multiplier is 10.

(d) Equilibrium income will rise by £1000.

(e) Equilibrium income will again rise by £1000 to £4000.

7 (a) 2, 4, 10, infinity: an increase in aggregate demand would lead to an infinite expansion in income.
  (b) It rises.
  (c) Zero to infinity.

8 Aggregate supply $\equiv Y = C + I =$ aggregate demand.

$$Y\left(30 + \frac{3}{4}\,Y\right) + 25 = 55 + \frac{3}{4}\,Y$$

$$\frac{1}{4}\,Y = 55$$

$$Y = £220$$

9 (a) Since MPC = 3 ÷ 4 (the slope of the consumption function), the multiplier is 4.
  (b) Aggregate supply $\equiv Y = C + I =$ aggregate demand.
  $Y = 30 + (3/4)Y + 30.\ Y = £240.$

10 Aggregate supply $Y = C + I$ in equilibrium; therefore, $Y = 35 + (3/4)Y + 25.\ Y = 240.$

11 See the figures.

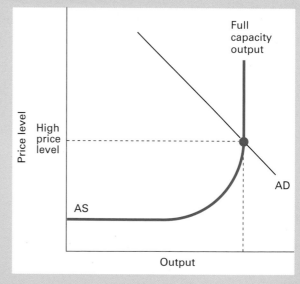

12

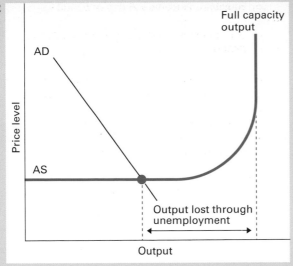

As aggregate demand rises, the economy approaches full capacity output. Supply constraints develop as firms try to attract the scarce skills they require to expand output. Wages are bid up, which raises costs, and firms will try to raise prices to match in order to maintain profits. There will be pressure on any resources which are fixed in supply, so land and property prices may be bid up too.

Unemployment develops when aggregate demand is low because firms are reducing employment as sales fall.

Chapter 17

4 See the figure.

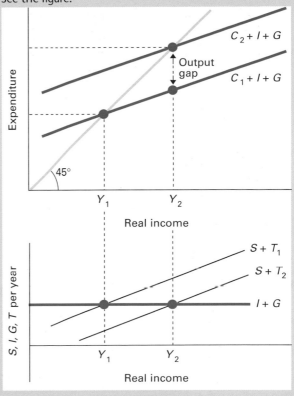

5 See the figure.

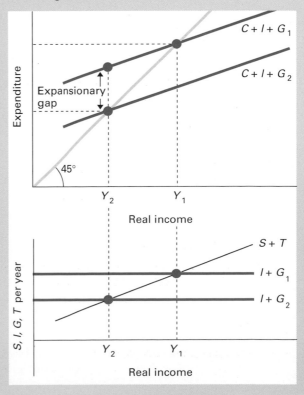

6 (a) C = 6100, S = 1400, T = 2500.
   (b) MPC = 0.8. APC will be higher than MPC but, as disposable income rises, it will fall until it is almost equal to MPC.
   (c) Y falls by £1000 million.
   (d) The budget deficit is £250 million.
   (e) This means raising G by an amount equivalent to the fall in I. However, it is unlikely that the consumption function will remain unchanged if the benefits are paid mainly to people with relatively low incomes.

7 In early 1992 the UK economy was only just beginning to recover after a long period of recession.

8 As output and income were low, tax revenue from income-related taxes was low too. This reduced leakages from the circular flow. As large numbers of people were unemployed, benefits were running at a high level, thus increasing injections.

9 The PSNCR was therefore rising.

10 The PSDR is the difference between government expenditure and tax revenues when the former is less than the latter. It occurs when the economy is booming so that tax revenue is high and the level of unemployment is low.

Chapter 18

1 M4 is broad money: it includes notes and coin and balances held by the banks with the Bank of England (M0) and all sterling bank deposits. During the early 1990s recession, monetary growth was slow. It peaked in 1997 and grew more slowly thereafter.

2 Increased bank lending can mean more spending. However, it can also mean that more money is being held in deposits rather than being spent. If spending does rise, then the consequences will be the same as those of any other increase in aggregate demand.

3

Liabilities	Assets
(a) demand deposits	(b) notes and coin
(c) time deposits	(d) deposits with the Bank of England
(h) borrowing from other banks	(e) advances to customers
	(f) holdings of bonds
	(g) buildings and fixtures

Notes and coin are perfectly liquid because they are cash. So are deposits with the Bank of England. Bonds are less liquid because the price at which they may be sold does vary. Bank buildings and fixtures are not very liquid because the price at which they can be sold is uncertain and a sale may take time. Advances to customers are very illiquid because most borrowers will not be able to make repayments immediately. Some may not be able to repay at all.

Chapter 19

1 20.

2 10.

3 With the consumption of the third unit of X.

5 Total utility is maximized when three pints of beer and four sandwiches are bought.

6 Total utility would be optimized at one pint of beer and four sandwiches.

Chapter 20

1 Economic profit = £250 000 (sales) minus £160 000 (labour) minus £50 000 (raw materials) minus £15 000 (interest) minus £20 000 (opportunity cost of turning down the job) = £5000.

2 It differs by £20 000. Accounting profit would be £25 000.

3 To highlight the opportunity cost involved in choosing one business venture instead of another.

4 (a) Approximately four hours.
   (b) They will have less work hours embodied in them.

5 (a) Eight hours.
   (b) Thirty-two hours.

6 £100.

7 £5.

8 £100.

9 10.

10 It is rising.

11 When the marginal product of labour is rising, the marginal cost of output falls; when the marginal product

of labour is falling the marginal cost of output rises.

15

Output (units)	AFC (£)	AVC (£)	TC (£)	ATC (£)	MC (£)
1	100	40	140	140	40
2	50	35	170	85	30
3	33.3	40	220	73.3	50
4	25	45	280	70	60
5	20	50	350	70	70
6	16.67	55	430	71.67	80

16

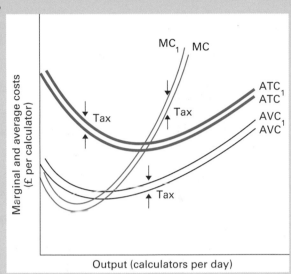

18

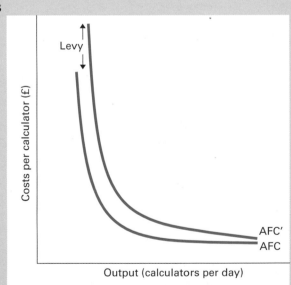

Chapter 21

4

Firm	AFC	AVC	AR	Open/Close
A	100	200	250	Open
B	100	200	300	Open
C	100	200	200	Indifferent
D	100	200	150	Close
E	100	200	450	Open

5 The important key to these answers is that in the short term the variable costs are the costs of being open for business, whereas fixed costs have to be paid regardless of whether the business is open or shut (e.g., the rent will have to be paid for six months, or whatever). Hence firm A would stay open, despite making a loss, because its average revenue is more than sufficient to cover the AVC. In the case of firm C, however, the situation is not so clear-cut since the AR and the AVC are equal; once this is acknowledged, the answer could be argued either way.

Chapter 23

2 The retail grocery market is one where the leading multiple chains such as Tesco and Sainsbury now account for an increasingly significant proportion of total sales. This market is thus now one illustrating an oligopolistic market structure.

3 The characteristics of a large number of firms, free entry, small market shares and independence (in terms of taking account of rival firms) are not easy to satisfy in many manufacturing industries in the UK.

4 There is a high concentration of output in a few firms and interdependence clearly exists because it is difficult to differentiate petrol as a product.

5 Forward vertical integration by oil companies.

6 A greater assurance of sales compared with the situation where the product is supplied to several competing customers. There is the prospect of greater control of retail prices if one owns the retail outlet rather than negotiate with independent retail outlets. If an oil firm has retail outlets it has direct contact with customers: it may gain from early awareness of changes in consumer spending patterns.

7 BP and Mobil may have thought that by merging they could compete more effectively with Esso, the market leader, and other leading firms. Some economies may be achieved by shutting overlapping outlets. The newly merged concern may derive economies in production, distribution and marketing, as the scale of operations is now larger than before.

8 Just over 40 per cent of the petrol market.

9 Some of the retail supermarket chains have relatively few outlets selling petrol but have a high throughput. Tesco's market share exceeds that of Texaco, but the latter has over 1000 more petrol outlets. The same contrast can be made between Mobil and Sainsbury's.

10 (a) 34 per cent.
(b) 42 per cent.

11 It would appear that the largest enterprises in the non-ferrous metal industry are characterized by more capital-intensive forms of production than smaller enterprises. The combined gross output of the leading five enterprises was more than double that of those enterprises (eight in total) that employed more than 500 employees but fewer than 1000 employees.

12 (a) Printing and publishing.
(b) Tobacco.

13 Printing is not an industry where one would expect significant economies of large-scale production. Hence in most large towns several independent printing firms will be found. In contrast, in the tobacco industry scale economies could be expected to exist in the production, distribution and marketing of cigarettes.

14 A tentative expectation is that where concentration ratios are low, then competition between firms will focus on price. Thus printing companies would be expected to find sales sensitive to how competitive they are when potential customers for printed work seek price quotations. In this market non-price competition is unlikely to be a key aspect of competition. In contrast, in the soap and toilet preparations industry, where the five-firm concentration ratio is much higher, competition seems to feature the relevance of branding, sales marketing and new product development.

15 In man-made fibres, patents may be a factor affecting the availability of close substitutes. In the motor vehicle parts industry, firms may perceive that their customers – motor vehicle manufacturers – could integrate backwards into their own industry. In the wines, cider and perry industry, competition seems to focus on spending in support of well-known branded drinks. However, in the iron and steel industry, output is not characterized by branding, as it is an industry essentially in the producer goods sector.

16 Ryanair has favoured using 'secondary' airports that offer lower landing charges and rapid turn-around of aircraft. These factors have helped it keep down air fares, which in turn has prompted growing custom from those seeking low-cost air travel.

19 A modest purchase of just over £100 entitled one to two free return flights to Europe or America – worth much more than a new vacuum cleaner.

21 The popularity of the promotion meant many householders bought a new vacuum cleaner that they did not really need at the time (to replace an older cleaner). Efforts to sell the new cleaners meant that older models were now virtually worthless. The supplies of new cleaners meant the stocks of any older models had little appeal to anyone wanting a vacuum cleaner. One could acquire an unused new model (sometimes still in its original packaging!) without paying much given the plentiful supplies of householders keen to realize on what was a means to an end – free air tickets to go abroad.

Chapter 24

A marginal test, p. 422

Quantity of labour	Total product per week	MPP	MRP (£)
1	250	250	500
2	450	200	400
3	600	150	300
4	700	100	200
5	750	50	100
6	750	0	0

1 Demand schedule for labour:

Weekly wage	Labourers demanded per week
500	1
400	2
300	3
200	4
100	5

2 If five workers were hired, the firm would be willing to pay no more than £100 for each one.

3 At £200 per week, four labourers would be hired.

4 Because of their skills, these women may have had a range of opportunities. These might not use their sewing skills, but the fact of their having acquired one lot of skills may have made it easier for them to acquire others. Sewing is not well paid, so these other opportunities may have been more lucrative.

5 He could pay more to retain his valued employees.

6 There may not be much incentive to train as a seamstress, because the pay is low.

7 There can be rigidities in the system which make it likely that skill shortages will persist. Also, paying seamstresses more would mean that the curtains would cost more. The demand for hand-made curtains may drop if the price rises. There may therefore be excess demand for curtains at lower prices but not at higher prices.

8 (a) 15 million man-hours per unit of time;
(b) 11 million man-hours per unit of time;
(c) buyers can get all the labour they want at W_1; labourers cannot sell all they want to sell at W_1;
(d) since a surplus of labour exists, the unemployed will offer to work for less and industry wage rates will fall toward W_e.

9 (a) 12 million man-hours per unit of time;
(b) 17 million man-hours per unit of time;
(c) sellers of labour are working as much as they care to at W_2, but buyers of labour cannot get all they want at that rate;
(d) since a shortage of labourers exists, buyers of labour will compete for labour and drive wage rates up towards W_e;
(e) W_e, since neither a surplus nor a shortage exists at that wage rate.

10 We already know that any payment above that which is required to keep a resource in its current use is an economic rent. It must follow, then, that there is some economic rent going to the superstars if they are receiving more than their next best opportunity would provide. To make the argument in this question, it is necessary to draw on the distinction between short-run and long-run supply and demand. Human beings are not eternally durable. They grow old and step aside for more popular and more productive younger talent. It is possible that younger talent in the entertainment field is not attracted by 'scale' wages that are paid to the majority who never reach stardom. Rather, it is the chance of making the astronomical salary that draws great talent. Without this possibility, potential actors and athletes would seek other employment. Even as they continue to work at mediocre wages, young performers may be deriving non-money income because they are building and investing in their own talent and they are buying the opportunity to be available when stardom calls. Thus, although the high salaries may be more than is necessary to keep current talent performing (their short-run supply curve is inelastic), such prizes may be needed to attract future talent (their long-run supply curve is elastic).

Chapter 25

6 From the lender's point of view, the loan is very risky. Many people borrow more than they can repay on credit cards so the rate of interest is higher to compensate lenders for the number of bad debts.

7 Partly because of the costs of administering the loan and partly because the bank is carrying the risks associated with lending. Despite these factors many people feel that banks make excessive profits some of the time.

8 Because the risks are much lower. This reflects the amount of information the bank has about the borrower.

9 Interest rates ration funds among those with the highest demand. A firm may be very inefficient but still face strong demand in the short run. This will cause it to demand a loan in order to expand.

11

Quantity of capital (machine-weeks)	Marginal product of capital (units per week)	MRP (£ per week)
0		
1	25	250
2	20	200
3	15	150
4	10	100
5	5	50

The firm will use 4 units of capital if the price is £90 per machine-week. At £300 per machine-week the firm will cease to operate: it cannot cover fixed costs at any level of output.

Chapter 26

3 The three forms of competitive conduct referred to in Chapter 22 that might constitute an anti-competitive practice were price discrimination, predatory pricing and exclusive dealing.

4 The examples given in fines on companies found guilty of operating in a cartel indicate that EU competition policy has been explicitly in favour of open competition. This contrasts with the more tentative stance of UK policy until the 1998 Competition Act.

Chapter 30

1 Fourteen of the sixteen countries are in Africa.

2 Six countries had a negative growth rate in the period 1990–7 and four others had a growth rate of 1 per cent or less.

3 For nine of the fifteen countries for which both world rankings are available, the GNP by the PPP method leads to a somewhat lower ranking than that by the Atlas method. However, in many cases, the ranking change is a marginal one.

4 It highlights the extent of poverty in terms of number of people in Asia, whereas Table 30.1 identifies low income per head in many relatively small African countries measured in terms of their population.

5 Sri Lanka's GNP per capita at $800 in 1997 was about 12 per cent higher than that of the Côte d'Ivoire at $170, but the constituent items of the HDI indicate that it has a higher level of human development. Life expectancy is far higher in Sri Lanka than in the Côte d'Ivoire, and the adult literacy rate double that in the Côte d'Ivoire.

6 Adult literacy is something that is fundamentally determined by government policy measures that extend access to education to a country's citizens.

9 One would expect that, as a country's GNP per capita rises, the quantity and quality of health care increase. As a result, the incidence of infant mortality decreases, as does that of life-threatening illnesses.

10 Access to health care appears to have a marked negative impact on infant mortality rates. However, access is likely to vary considerably even within a country. Access to clean drinking water and adequate sanitation are also factors in accounting for the differences between countries in life expectancy and infant mortality rates.

11 Health-care spending can be seen as adding to the productivity of a country's labour force; hence it adds to a country's stock of human capital.

13 Over-valued exchange rates have the effect of penalizing earnings of agricultural exports whilst reducing the cost of imported goods.

14 Taxes on exports are an easily identifiable tax source given that goods leave a country at an airport, seaport or land-border crossing point. Given the difficulties of generating other tax revenues, taxing goods that leave a country is superficially a promising source of tax revenue; the danger is that a country may, however, penalize the competitiveness of its exporters by raising the cost to final customers.

15 Controls on domestic food prices aim to contain inflationary pressures – see the final section in Chapter 9. In a developing country, food prices are even more politically significant than in more developed countries.

16 East Asia's rising share of global manufacturing reflects the interest of its countries pursuing aggressive export promotion policies and welcoming inward investment. MNCs were attracted by countries with low rates of inflation and labour forces having high skills relative to other developing countries.

19 Tropical countries which are small islands, as in the Caribbean, typically have attractive beaches to appeal to potential tourists. Do such countries have little chance to be a source of manufactured goods? Do they have a comparative advantage in producing agricultural commodities? One needs such information in order to answer this question.

20 Rising real incomes and the falling real cost of air travel are both promising bases for the growth in world tourism. In addition, increased leisure time and early retirement from working help reinforce interest in world travel.

21 The popularity of some places for tourists to visit means that they can lose their appeal through sheer congestion, noise and pollution. As a result, a successful tourist industry has the problem of maintaining the original reasons why particular places have an appeal on 'becoming discovered', and thereafter may lose this appeal through sheer pressure of the number of tourists.

22 As a large market with much apparent future growth potential, China has been a powerful magnet for the world's multinational firms. It has seemed to offer a much more attractive investment opportunity as it left its communist past behind (see the second case study in Chapter 2). In contrast, India has been independent for over half a century but has struggled to achieve rapid economic growth.

23 Small and slowly growing markets offer little to profit-seeking MNCs.

24 They diversify their risks so that, if countries vary in their economic growth performance, MNCs are not exposed to any downturns in a particular country.

25 Political concerns can be expected to loom large in the decision-making by MNCs. Are foreign investments safe from being taken over by a newly elected government?

26 Is an investment abroad by an MNC at the expense of investment at home? Does an investment abroad lead to the MNC importing from its foreign subsidiary? If so, will this mean that the level of employment in its home country base becomes threatened because labour costs are much higher than abroad?

Chapter 31

For questions 1 and 2, divide the growth in nominal GDP by the growth in the price level, to find the following.

1 The country with the highest rate of real growth is K.

2 The country with the lowest rate of real growth is L.

For questions 3 and 4, divide the real growth by the growth in population, to find the following.

3 The country with the highest rate of real growth per capita is M.

4 The country with the lowest rate of real growth per capita is K.

For question 5, examine the columns headed '% Average annual real growth rate (1997–8)' for GNP and GNP per capita, and it is possible to draw the following conclusions.

5 In Japan and Germany there was a decrease in economic activity. In Singapore there must have been an increase in the size of the population. In Hong Kong the figures suggest a decrease in economic activity and an increase in the size of the population.

13 Point B is associated with the highest feasible growth rate (since this conveys the highest feasible ratio of capital goods to current consumption).

14 If the resources of an economy are under-utilized.

23 Using the data in Table 31.1, it can be asserted that the average person in Japan was richer than his or her UK counterpart – throughout the 1990s. In fact, the data show that the respective incomes per head in 1998 were $32 380 for Japan compared to $21 400 for the UK.

26 For example, policies oriented towards training and education.

27 For example, policies oriented towards regional development and housing.

28 Yes. To take the two extremes: land is the most immobile factor and capital is the most mobile factor of production.

Answers to multiple choice questions

The answers that have been provided for multiple choice questions set by examination boards are entirely the responsibility of the authors of this book; answers have been neither provided nor approved by the boards concerned.

Chapter	Question number: 1	2	3	4	5	6	7	8	9	10	11	12	13	14	15
1	B	C	A	B	D	B	B	C							
2	C	D													
3	E	C	A	B	E										
4	C	C	D												
5	C	A	D	C	B	E	C	D	B						
6	D	B	C	D	B	A	B	C	D						
7	D	C	A	D	C	C	A	D							
8	D	E	E	C	D	B									
9	B	A	C	C	A	D	E	E							
10	A	C	C	A	C	B	C	B							
11	D	C	A	C	C	A									
12	D	A													
13	B	D	A	A	D	E	E	B							
14	C	C	B												
15	B	C	C												
16	D	A	A	D	D	D									
17	D	D	B	B	B										
18	D	B	D	B	A										
19	C	C	B	E	E	D	A	C	B						
20	D	A	E	B	A	B	C								
21	B	A	C	D	A	B	B	D	C	B					
22	E	E	C	B	D										
23	D	A	D	D	C	A	A	D	B	D	C	D	E	E	D
24	D	B	A	E	D										
25	E	D	D	C	A	D									
26	D	C	D												
27	C	A	E	D											
28	A	D	D	D	B	D	B	C							
29	B	A	B	A	B										
30	D														
31	B	B	C	B	C	C	A	D							

Index